Evan Fleischer

GLOBAL INTERNET LAW

by

Michael L. Rustad

Thomas F. Lambert Jr. Professor of Law &
Co-Director Intellectual Property Law Concentration
Suffolk University Law School

HORNBOOK SERIES®

Mat #41508709

Hornbook Series is a trademark registered in the U.S. Patent and Trademark Office.

© 2014 LEG, Inc. d/b/a West Academic
    444 Cedar Street, Suite 700
    St. Paul, MN 55101
    1-877-888-1330

West, West Academic Publishing, and West Academic are trademarks of West Publishing Corporation, used under license.

Printed in the United States of America

ISBN: 978-0-314-28962-9

Dedicated to

Janice Marilyn Knowles, R.N. (1924–2013)

Acknowledgments

Many people contributed to this book including Suffolk University Law Students, legal academics and business lawyers from around the world. My research assistants included J.D. and LL.M. students who are lawyers in their own country as well as U.S. law students. Camila Rocio Valenzuela Araya, Marty Cachapero, Andrew Clark, Nicola Condella, Salvatore Cultrano, Kristina Foreman, Ibrahim Kaylan, Wenzhoo Liu, and Manuel Ignacia Miranda all served with distinction. Wenzhoo Liu, who has experience as a Chinese lawyer working with Johnson and Johnson, conducted research and edited every chapter. I appreciated her technical expertise as well as her considerable analytical abilities. Manuel Miranda, who is a LL.M. graduate and lawyer from Venezuela, edited and researched Internet law developments in Latin America. Vit Svejkovsky, a business and intellectual property lawyer, from the Czech Republic, provided extensive editorial suggestions and examples from Eurozone. Hyeonieong Woo, Suffolk Law Student, and Yina Kim, a South Korean lawyer and graduate of Suffolk University Law School, accomplished superb research as well as giving helpful editorial comments. Thanks to Kara Ryan my administrative assistant at Suffolk for her assistance on drafts. I also appreciate the assistance of Shannon Edgar at Stetson University College of Law for administrative support during the summer of 2013.

Diane D'Angelo and Rick Buckingham, Suffolk University Law School reference librarians, provided me with useful suggestions. I greatly benefitted from teaching international business lawyers from around the world in Suffolk's LL.M. program. I gained an understanding about European licensing law from Professors Patrik Lindskoug and Ulf Maunschbach, who taught with me five summers at the University of Lund.

My family has been supportive and encouraging. My daughter the attorney, Erica Rustad Ferreira, and my son the doctor, James Knowles Rustad, contributed a great deal by researching, editing, and offering suggestions along the way. Finally, my wife, Chryss J. Knowles, deserves special thanks for her editorial assistance.

I would like to acknowledge the recent loss of my beloved mother-in-law, Janice Marilyn Knowles, R.N., of St. Johnsbury, Vermont, a very distinguished member of the "greatest generation." This book is dedicated to Janice's life so full of joy and loving contributions to society and her family.

Summary of Contents

Table of Contents

GLOBAL INTERNET LAW

Chapter 1

OVERVIEW OF THE GLOBAL INTERNET

You must imagine at the eventual heart of things to come, linked or integrated systems or networks of computers capable of storing faithful simulacra of the entire treasure of the accumulated knowledge and artistic production of past ages and of taking into the store new intelligence of all sorts as produced. Lasers [and] satellites [among others] will operate as ganglions to extend the reach of the systems to the ultimate users.[1]

§ 1.1   WHAT IS GLOBAL INTERNET LAW?

Where to begin in explaining a topic as vast as global Internet law? The global perspective is important because the Internet is, by definition, not just a U.S. information technology. There is an inherent problem in writing about the omnipresent Internet, which is continuously in the process of becoming—a moving stream, not a stagnant pond. The Internet is relentlessly transforming all aspects of law. The Second Circuit explained the unique issues of Internet-related trademark law as "attempting to apply established trademark law in the fast–developing world of the Internet is somewhat like trying to board a moving bus."[2] It is not just U.S. lawyers that need to keep up with Internet developments and understand the technologies. Internet Law can no longer be U.S. centric. A U.S. company with 24/7 e-commerce business must understand and comply with consumer, competition, and regulations where they do business. Internet law is rapidly evolving in mature markets and is just beginning to evolve in less developed countries. The global perspective for Internet is important because the problems created by this disruptive technology frequently cross national borders. A cybercriminal located in Eastern Europe may masquerade as a customer to intercept a wire transfer originating in the U.S. or credit cards of unsuspecting European consumers. The .su domain for the former USSR accounts for nearly half of all cybercrime.[3] Cybercrime is cross-border and difficult to detect because the criminal does not leave a traditional crime scene.

Internet and information technology companies are hegemonic as the economy shifts from making durable goods to the transfer of software, databases, or digital information. Apple, Google, Facebook, and IBM, leading Global Internet players, are in the top ten of innovative companies.[4] KPMG's global study of general counsel confirms that new technologies present a changing risk environment for companies.[5] The KPMG study interviewed more than three hundred general counsel in large global

---

[1] BENJAMIN KAPLAN, AN UNHURRIED VIEW OF COPYRIGHT LAW (1967).

[2] Bensusan Restaurant Corp. v. King, 126 F.3d 25 (2d Cir. 1997).

[3] Associated Press, USSR's Old Domain Name Attracts Cybercriminals (June 1, 2013) (quoting Oren David manager at RSA's anti-fraud unit).

[4] Andrew Taylor, et. al, The Most Innovative 2012 Companies: The State of the Art in Leading Industries.

[5] KPGM, Beyond the Law: KPMG's Global Study of How General Counsel Are Turning Risk to Advantage (2012).

organizations in thirty-two different countries across Europe, North America, Latin America, Asia Pacific, and Australasia. Forty percent of the respondents rated data security and protection a "strong risk." This same percentage rated ensuring compliance with differing regulatory risks around the world as a "strong risk."[6] The KPMG intensive interviews with general counsel found compliance with the "variety of regulatory models around the world" as a "key difficulty."[7] The general counsel rated North America and Europe as the strictest regulatory systems, but these mature systems were more stable than less mature market economies.[8]

EBay Inc. connects millions of buyers and sellers around the world through online platforms including eBay, PayPal, and GSI. EBay's online auction website is subject to U.S. law but also the law of many foreign countries. EBay continually audits foreign as well as U.S. laws and regulations within the geographic scope of its products and services, which is worldwide. EBay's SEC 10Q filing highlights the enhanced risks of their international operations:

> EBay Inc., headquartered in San Jose, California, is a global commerce platform. Our Payments business is subject to a number of laws and regulations, including those governing banking, money transmission, and payment services that vary in the markets where we operate and any violations of such laws and regulations could subject us to liability, licensure and regulatory approval, and may force us to change our business practices.[9]

For example, eBay has a significant cross-border payments system subject to radically different anti-money laundering, counter-terrorist financing laws, or trade regulations.[10] EBay, like every other Global Internet enterprise is subject to the:

> Trans–Pacific Partnership Agreement ("TPP"), the European Consumer Rights Directive and the proposed revisions to the European Data Protection Directive) and interpretations of existing laws or regulations, including national court interpretations of the European Court of Justice's decisions.[11] EBay's ability to understand and manage the costs of compliance with existing and new laws in countries around the world is an example of transnational Internet law.

It is no longer sufficient to focus solely on U.S. Internet law, as there are many intriguing developments from around the world. Increasingly, litigants in Internet law cases are located in different regions of the world. In *Pair Networks v. Lim Cheng Soon*,[12] Soon was a resident of Malaysia, a co-defendant resided in Toronto, and the plaintiff company was headquartered in Pennsylvania but had thousands of Web servers located in Pennsylvania, Ohio, and Nevada. Pair Networks, a web hosting company, had clients in over 100 countries.

---

[6] Id. at 19.

[7] Id. at 20.

[8] Id.

[9] eBay SEC 10Q Filing (July 19, 2013).

[10] Id.

[11] Id.

[12] 2013 WL 452565 (W.D. Pa., Feb. 6, 2013).

In another transnational Internet case,[13] the plaintiff, was a California corporation that created copyrighted adult entertainment products. One of the defendants was Yandex N.V., a Dutch holding company headquartered in the Netherlands that owned a family of companies under the "Yandex" brand. Subsidiary Yandex LLC is a Russian technology company, which operated yandex.ru, Russia's most popular search engine. Subsidiary Yandex Inc., a Delaware corporation located in Palo Alto, provides software-development services to Yandex LLC. Yandex owned servers in Nevada, which hosted the search index for Yandex LLC's international version of its search engine. This Internet-related case raises issues such as the extraterritorial application of copyright law, transnational jurisdiction, and the legal significance that servers are physically located outside the United States.

The court rejected Perfect 10's argument that display of a copyrighted image anywhere in the world creates direct copyright liability in the United States merely because the image could be downloaded from a server abroad by someone in the United States. Perfect 10 objected to Yandex.com's image search that linked the thumbnail directly to a larger version of the image, a form of in-line linking. The court ruled that Yandex.com's thumbnails stored on U.S. servers for a short period were protected by fair use, while servers located in Russia were outside the jurisdiction of U.S. copyright law because of the doctrine of extraterritoriality. Fifteen years ago, few courts addressed any of these issues arising out of disruptive Internet technologies. Today Internet law must extend its boundaries to a study of developing countries as well as U.S., European, or other mature market economies.

Courts and legislatures around the world must continually update the law as the Internet creates new legal dilemmas. The empirical reality is that all law has an Internet dimension that even reaches wills and estates. In a Massachusetts case, the co-administrators of their brother's estate brought action against e-mail service for declaratory judgment that e-mail messages in brother's e-mail account were the property of the estate.[14] A growing number of companies are conducting e-commerce transactions involving mass-market software on their websites. Consumers, as well as business customers, place orders from hundreds of countries with radically different legal cultures. The Internet, by its very nature, is international, yet there is no uniform legal infrastructure for determining whether a given court has competence to decide disputes. Inequality in Internet access within and between countries is an emergent policy issue. Thirty nine percent of the 7.1 billion world population is using the Internet.[15] In Norway, ninety-five percent of citizens have Internet access versus eighty-one percent of U.S. citizens.[16] The majority of the world's citizens still lack Internet access. In many African countries, less than one in ten have Internet access. Nevertheless, the Internet is creating a global marketplace, which Anupam Chandler dubbed, *The Electronic Silk Road*:

---

[13] Perfect 10 Inc. v. Yandex N.V., 2013 WL 3668818 (N.D. Cal. July 12, 2013) (granting partial summary judgment in favor of Russian search engine and other defendants).

[14] Ajemian v. Yahoo, Inc., 83 Mass.App.Ct. 565, 987 N.E.2d 604 (Mass. Appeals Ct., May 7, 2013) (remand was required for full briefing and further proceedings regarding ultimate question of whether Stored Communications Act prohibited disclosure by service of the contents of brother's e-mail account.

[15] International Communications Union, Worldwide Internet Users (2013).

[16] Id.

The modern Silk Road winds its way through undersea fiber-optic cables and satellite links, ferrying electrons brimming with information. This electronic Silk Road makes possible trade in services heretofore impossible in human history. Radiologists, accountants, engineers, lawyers, musicians, filmmakers, and reporters now offer their services to the world without passing a customs checkpoint or boarding a plane. Like the ancient Silk Road, which transformed the lands that it connected, this new trade route promises to remake the world.[17]

Microsoft Corp. announced quarterly revenue of $19.90 billion for the quarter ending June 30, 2013. Operating income, net income, and diluted earnings per share for the quarter were $6.07 billion, $4.97 billion, and $0.59 per share respectively. These financial results are in large part due to Microsoft's global customers. Microsoft's Electronic Silk Road creates new legal dilemmas for protecting privacy, financial integrity, intellectual property and consumer rights in cyberspace. Companies traveling on the transnational Internet confront new jurisdictional, choice of law, and choice of forum dilemmas.

The unique legal issues arising from an ocean of data on an international computer network of interoperable packet switched data networks is the subject of Internet law. Internet law is more than applying traditional principles of procedural and substantive law to the web or old wine in new bottles. Internet law was predominately U.S. law during the first fifteen years of the World Wide Web. U.S. courts and legislatures led the way in developing specialized statutes and cases to accommodate traditional principles of law to the Internet.

The majority of corporations in *Business Week's* Top 25 are registered and headquartered outside the United States. EBay reported that 52% of its revenue for the first half of 2013 originated outside the United States.[18] EBay's expansion in Germany, the U.K. and Korea was the source of the greatest revenue.[19] The online auction website also expanded into Turkey in 2011 by purchasing shares in a Turkish company.[20] EBay's global business plan requires it to comply with foreign statutes and regulations. EBay requires a comprehensive legal audit to comply with the laws of:

> numerous and sometimes conflicting laws and regulations include internal control and disclosure rules, data privacy and filtering requirements, anti-corruption laws, such as the Foreign Corrupt Practices Act and U.K. Bribery Act, and other local laws prohibiting corrupt payments to governmental officials, and antitrust and competition regulations, among others.[21]

In many foreign countries, Internet law is beginning to evolve at a fast pace because of transnational licensing of software, the Internet, and the removal of international trade barriers.[22] Non–U.S. sales now represent more than 50% of

---

[17] ANUPAN CHANDER, THE ELECTRONIC SILK ROAD 1 (2013).

[18] eBay SEC Q-1 Filing (July 25, 2013).

[19] Id.

[20] Id.

[21] Id.

[22] "No law specifically regulates Internet services in Mexico. Online services are generally contracted for and supplied in accordance with a services agreement that is regulated by the contractual principles of law referred to in the Federal Civil Code and the Code of Commerce. Article 75 of the Code of Commerce establishes which acts are considered to be acts of commerce and are therefore regulated by such law." María José Carrillo Gallástegui and Eduardo Corzo Ramos of Holland + Knight–Gallástegui y Lozano, S.C., 2

revenues for most of publicly traded software companies.[23] Private ordering among global Internet companies is evolving into a transnational Internet law. Social media sites like Google and Facebook have created what Rebecca MacKinnon refers to as a globally networked public sphere.[24] In this sphere, more than a billion users are subject to one-sided terms of use, which increasingly requires users to submit to predispute mandatory arbitration in distant forums.

Maria Pallantas, the Register of the U.S. Copyright Office, calls for Congress to update copyright law to accommodate to the Internet. The Register's list of hot button issues for the next great copyright law includes:

> clarifying the scope of exclusive rights, revising exceptions and limitations for libraries and archives, addressing orphan works, accommodating persons who have print disabilities, providing guidance to educational institutions, exempting incidental copies in appropriate instances, updating enforcement provisions, providing guidance on statutory damages, reviewing the efficacy of the DMCA, assisting with small copyright claims, reforming the music marketplace, updating the framework for cable and satellite transmissions, encouraging new licensing regimes, and improving the systems of copyright registration and recordation.[25]

The United States Register of Copyrights noted that Congress updated copyright law to account for Internet developments in the past fifteen years by enacting the Digital Millennium Copyright Act.[26] In October 2011, the U.S. Copyright Office released its strategic plan that prioritized its activities for the next two years. Among the U.S. Copyright Office's call for legislative action is to find new ways to deter "rogue websites" that enable widespread copyright infringement of copyrighted works, particularly motion pictures, television programs, books, and software.

Another legislative priority for many developed countries is to ramp up criminal penalties for unauthorized online streaming of content. Congress and other national legislatures need to ensure that the criminal law remains relevant and functional given that many crimes are now committed on the Internet. At present, there is no international treaty creating uniform penalties for Internet crimes and their

---

MEDIA, ADVERTISING, & ENTERTAINMENT LAW THROUGHOUT THE WORLD § 25:7 (March 2013). (Andrew B. Ulmer, Editor-in-Chief, and MULTILAW International Contributors).

[23] Business Software Alliance, Software Industry Facts and Figures (2008) at 2 (In 2008, the US share of the packaged software market was $136.6 billion, or 45.9% of the world market. Although the US is the single largest software market in the world, more than half of the world's software market lies outside the U.S.).

[24] REBECCA MACKINNON, CONSENT OF THE NETWORKED: THE WORLDWIDE STRUGGLE FOR INTERNET FREEDOM 8 (2012).

[25] Statement of Maria Pallante, Register of Copyrights, U.S. Copyright Office, before the Subcommittee on Courts, Intellectual Property and the Internet Committee on the Judiciary (March 20, 2013) (The Register's Call for Updates to U.S. Copyright Law).

[26] "It has been fifteen years since Congress acted expansively in the copyright space. During that period, Congress was able to leave a very visible and far-reaching imprint on the development of both law and commerce. It enacted the Digital Millennium Copyright Act ('DMCA'), which created rules of the road for online intermediaries (e.g., Internet service providers) and a general prohibition on the circumvention of technological protection measures (so-called 'TPMs') employed by copyright owners to protect their content. The DMCA also created a rulemaking mechanism by which proponents could make the case for temporary exemptions to the TPM provisions in order to facilitate fair use or other noninfringing uses (the "section 1201 rulemaking"). Id.

enforcement.[27] Nevertheless, James Boyle warns against the creation of overly futuristic concepts inspired by the vastness of the Internet. He attempts to transcend the style of legal writing that he describes, "As Jetson's Jurisprudence[28]—a listing of technological marvels in the hope they will make a related set of legal rules alluringly futuristic by association."[29] Cliff Stoll's *Silicon Snake Oil*, as its name suggests, contends that the Internet is not all that it is cracked up to be.[30] His sardonic critique of the Internet is as scathing as Mark Twain's critique of organized religion in *Letters from the Earth*. Stoll argues that the Internet is being sold with the same techniques used by snake oil sales representatives of the nineteenth century. Specifically, he finds that the Internet is a poor substitute for human interactions, and that net-citizens should "get a life," demonstrated by his argument in the following passage:

> Me, an Internet addict? Hey—I'm leading a full life, with family, friends, and a job. Computers are a sideline, not my life. . . . Tonight, twenty letters want replies . . . How can I keep up? I see my reflection in the screen and a chill runs down my spine. Even on vacation, I can't escape the computer networks. I take a deep breath and pull the plug.[31]

Courts as well as academics need to temper their boundless admiration of the Internet and avoid cyberbile. Tort injuries such as defamation are far more injurious to reputation than a libelous story in a print publication. A defamatory tweet to your followers will have a cascading effect, as "they'll tweet to all of their followers and so on and so on."[32] The Internet is the nexus for issues such as when intermediaries such as Google or Facebook turn over metadata to the National Security Agency ("NSA"). President Obama has identified cybercrime as an endemic threat to national security. PRISM, a NSA surveillance project, has systematically collected metadata from the Internet and mobile phones with the cooperation of leading Internet companies. The *Washington Post* described this panoptical surveillance as having both a public and private dimension:

> We know that PRISM is a system the NSA uses to gain access to the private communications of users of nine popular Internet services. We know that Section

---

[27] The Convention on Cybercrime (also known as the Budapest Convention) is the first international treaty addressing Internet and computer crime. However, the Convention is aspirational in that signatories agreed to enact national cybercrime or computer crime legislation and cooperate with investigating cybercrime. The Convention was not a treaty creating a cross-border cybercrime statute nor giving law enforcement a means to enforce computer or Internet crimes committed across borders. See Council of Europe, Convention on Cybercrime CETS: 1985 (Nov. 23, 2001)(place: Budapest).

[28] "The Jetsons TV show was an animated kids TV series about the lives of the Jetson family who live with their dog Astro and housekeeper robot Rosie in a high rise home of the future . . . complete with a parking garage for their space car. Mom, dad, and the kids have it made in some ways with instant food preparation, ionic showers, and workdays where all one needs do is push one button . . . then go home, but the future is not all "Rosie" either! The Jetsons get into their share of jams (especially George, Elroy, and Astro), but they typically find some "way of the future" to get out of trouble!" The Jetson's TV Show, CrazyaboutTV.com (2012).

[29] JAMES BOYLE, SHAMANS, SOFTWARE, AND SPLEENS: LAW AND THE CONSTRUCTION OF THE INFORMATION IX (1996); See also, CLIFFORD STOLL, SILICON SNAKE OIL: SECOND THOUGHTS ON THE INFORMATION HIGHWAY (1995).

[30] CLIFFORD STOLL, SILICON SNAKE OIL: SECOND THOUGHTS ON THE INFORMATION HIGHWAY (1995).

[31] Id. at 1.

[32] Rich Steeves, Risk Monitoring a Key Component of Social Media Strategies: Chobani Greek Yogurt Learns Firsthand the Power and Pitfalls of Social Media, INSIDE COUNSEL (Sept. 18, 2013)(describing how negative social media posts about Chobani's yogurt caused the company to "become inundated with social media comments and phone calls" resulted in a voluntary withdrawal of its products from the marketplace)

702 of the Foreign Intelligence Surveillance Act, which was enacted in 2008, governs access.[33]

The Internet is not just about the "enemy within," but is a vast cesspool for hate speech, Nigerian scams, computer viruses, economic espionage, child pornography, and cybercrime. The Internet has had a dramatic impact upon global politics and there is no insurgency driven by Facebook, Twitter, YouTube and other social media. In Tunisia and around the Middle East, activists deployed social media to spread the word and organize anti-government demonstrations.[34] Mobile phones are also the enablers of social movements such as the Arab Spring; for example, in 2013, Turkish protestors against President Recep Tayyip Erdoğ mobilized social media to communicate with each other in organizing demonstrations. Additionally, Turkish student protestors use Twitter, Facebook, Upstream, and Vine to cover protests that Turkish print media or television do not cover. Turkish protests have been a boon for Silicon Valley-based Anchor Free that sells the application 'Hotspot Shield,' allowing anonymous Internet surfing through a virtual private network."[35] The Internet is ideological as well as utopian. Rebecca MacKinnon notes that the Internet is 'contested political space.'[36] The question of who controls or has access to the Internet is an unobtrusive measure of whether a society is open or closed.

The same technologies used for interconnecting friends and families can be deployed to create a 1984–like state. Unlocking iPhones using thumbprints creates new legal issues such as whether law enforcement can compel defendants to self-incriminate by forcing them to place their thumb on the iPhone to conduct searches.[37] Illinois has recently amended its "Right to Privacy in the Workplace Act to allow employers to screen, monitor, and retain communications of employees' and applicants' professional accounts to comply with state insurance laws, federal laws, or rules of a self-regulatory organization as defined under the Securities Exchange Act of 1934."[38] Totalitarian states such as China are able to choke off and control the Internet locally by annexing or commandeering access points, an example being when the regime shut down the Net in the Xinjiang region after riots. Nevertheless, today's Internet is a cross-border entity, beyond the control of any one country. China may cause the Internet to go dark in a given city or region, but it is unable to shut down the entire World Wide Web. "Authoritarian governments," Rebecca MacKinnon writes, with "unaccountable relationships with telecommunications companies, enables authoritarian governments to control and manipulate citizens."[39] Daily headlines confirm the transnational nature of Internet law. The Federal Trade Commission as well as European authorities investigated Google's billion-dollar buyout of Israeli online navigation and traffic app Waze. When Google released its Glass, data protection authorities "from Australia,

---

[33] Timothy B. Lee, Here's Everything We Know About Prism to Date, WASHINGTON POST (June 13, 2013).

[34] REBECCA MACKINNON, CONSENT OF THE NETWORKED: THE WORLDWIDE STRUGGLE FOR INTERNET FREEDOM XIII (2012).

[35] Steve Dorsey, Turkey's Social Media and Smartphones Key to 'Occupy Gezi' Protests, THE MEDIA LINE, June 9, 2013.

[36] MacKinnon, Consent of the Networked, Id. at xxiii.

[37] Danny Yadron, Canyou're your IPhone Thumbprint Be Used Against You? DIGITS: TECH NEWS & ANALYSIS FROM THE WSJ (Sept. 12, 2013).

[38] Steptoe & Johnson LLC, Illinois Allows Employer Snooping on Professional Social Media, E-COMMERCE LAW WEEK (Aug. 13, 2013).

[39] Id. at xxiv.

Canada, Israel, Mexico, New Zealand, and Switzerland" asked the Internet giant how it intends to comply with privacy laws.[40] The European Union acknowledged the necessity of surveillance but question whether PRISM complies with privacy regulations.[41]

Internet law interconnects with all other substantive and procedural legal disciplines. Trademark infringement, copyright infringement, patent law, privacy issues, Internet fraud, cybertorts and crimes are increasingly cross-border and transnational.[42] The Internet shapes the law of contracts, torts, civil procedure, intellectual property, administrative law, and consumer rights. Hardly a week goes by without Congress introducing a new bill regulating Internet conduct. H.R. 2487, introduced in June 2013, would require online retailers that track and use consumer's personally identifiable information to calibrate or change prices to disclose this practice. The Deter Cyber Theft Act of 2013, for example, would require the Director of National Intelligence with creating a list identifying foreign countries that engage in the cyber theft of trade secrets from U.S. companies. A May 2013 U.S. Senate Report, "expressed serious concerns about China's misappropriation of U.S. trade secrets."[43] Cyberwarfare is a routinized part of military policy for many countries.

Trade wars, too, increasingly have an Internet nexus. An example of a global Internet dispute is the trade war between Antigua and the United States. Congress enacted the Unlawful Internet Gambling Enforcement Act ("UIGEA") of 2013 that ratcheted up criminal penalties for online gambling businesses that accept payment through credit cards, checks, or fund transfers.[44] Antigua and Barbuda demanded that the U.S. open its marketplace to online gaming. Antigua's response to UIGEA was to apply to the World Trade Organization to "lift intellectual property protection on [U.S.] goods and services."[45] "The WTO ruled in 2005 that the United States had scheduled market access commitments for gambling services under the GATS despite U.S. protests that it never intended to do so."[46]

In 2013, an Australian consumer protection agency charged Google with deception in its search engine keyword practices. The High Court of Australia ruled in favor of Google "that it did not create the sponsored links that it published or displayed. Google uncovered a massive spying campaign by the Iranian government on its citizens. Google "said that thousands of its users inside Iran had been the targets of a sophisticated e-mail phishing campaign in which attackers send users a link that, when clicked, sent them to a fake Google sign-in page where the attackers could steal

---

[40] Article 29 Party, Canada, Other DPAs Question CEO on Google Glasses, Bloomberg BNA, Electronic Commerce and the Law (June 21, 2013).

[41] Stephen Gardner, EU Officials Accept Need for U.S. PRISM But Concerned About Data Subject Redress, BLOOMBERGBNA ELECTRONIC COMMERCE AND THE LAW (June 14, 2013).

[42] See e.g., Alexandra Frean, Mail–Order Degree Scam Closed Down, THE AUSTRALIAN, March 12, 2003, at 19 ("[shutting] down a series of websites selling invalid degrees from bogus universities which used an address in Palmers Green, North London, to give their operation a cloak of respectability and defrauded hundreds of thousands of mostly American customers).

[43] Senate Bill Seeks to Establish Special 301–Style List for Cyber Theft, BLOOMBERG BNA, ELECTRONIC COMMERCE LAW & POLICY (May 7, 2013).

[44] Daniel Pruzin, WTO Clears Antigua to Impose Sanctions on U.S. Imports, IPR in Gambling Disputes, BLOOMBERG BNA, ELECTRONIC COMMERCE LAW & POLICY (Jan. 28, 2013).

[45] Id.
[46] Id.

login credentials."[47] The globalized Internet is a new realm governed by many nations but without a transnational sovereign, international treaty, specialized court system, or virtual alternative dispute system.[48] While once exclusively the U.S. government's province, today other countries are pressing for a more transparent, codetermined, and democratically governed cyberspace. Transnational Internet law is undeveloped and Internet users do not have minimum adequate remedies for the invasion of privacy, consumer fraud, identity theft, and secret surveillance.

The Internet has created new legal issues such as anonymous and pseudonymous speech online, as well as new demands for open government and calls for greater transparency. Disillusionment runs deep when it comes to Internet privacy. The information superhighway has devolved into a road to suspicion because it creates the potential for a 1984-like state. These questions grew more insistent when a whistleblower revealed widespread surveillance of cell phone and Internet communications. Under the National Security's PRISM program, the federal agency had access to "over one hundred millions phone records on a daily basis. The information would also include a list of all the people that Verizon customers call and who called them; how long they spoke; and perhaps, where they were on a given day."[49]

In May of 2013, privacy regulators in Australia, Canada, Estonia, Finland, France, Germany, Hong Kong, Ireland, Macao, Macedonia, New Zealand, Norway, United Kingdom, and the United States conducted an Internet Privacy Sweep of private sector websites to identify compliance issues such as whether the websites had "clear and understandable" privacy policies or protected the online privacy of children age 13 or under.[50] U.S. mobile app developers, for example, will need to comply with data protection regulations in the twenty-eight countries of the European Union. Under a proposed U.S. statute, foreign Internet providers will need to provide users with notice about a specific app's collection and use of personal information and obtain the user's consent to those terms and conditions.

The Internet has spawned shocking, far-reaching, and often anonymous crimes originating in foreign jurisdictions. Nearly every company is a potential cybercrime target and no one is immune. One of the most spectacular examples of Internet lawlessness occurred in May of 2013 when cybercriminals orchestrated an ATM heist that netted them more than $45 billion in twenty-seven countries. Hackers were able to break into credit card processing companies and "raise the limit on prepaid debit

---

[47] Eric Grosse, Iranian Phishing on the Rise as Elections Approach, Google Blog (June 12, 2013).

[48] The World Intellectual Property Organization devised the Uniform Dispute Resolution Policy ("UDRP"), which establishes panels to decide domain name disputes. All domain name registrants agree to submit to jurisdiction of the UDRP panels as a condition of registration. The UDRP was adopted by the Internet Corporation for Assigned Names and Numbers ("ICANN") and is incorporated by reference into every domain name Registration Agreement beginning in 1999. One of the terms and conditions applies to a dispute between the registrant and third parties over the registration and use of an Internet domain name. UDRP panels are conducted according to the Rules for Uniform Domain Name Dispute Resolution Policy (the "Rules of Procedure"), which are available at http://www.icann.org/en/dndr/udrp/uni form-rules. The UDRP panels are, in effect, a de facto global Internet law for trademark disputes. Plaintiffs have the option of filing trademark disputes in national courts or pursuing remedies under the UDRP.

[49] Former U.S. Prosecutor Sues Obama and NSA Over PRISM Scandal, TORRENTFREAK (June 10, 2013).

[50] Group of 19 Data Protection Authorities Launches Internet Enforcement Sweep, BNA, ELECTRONIC COMMERCE LAW & POLICY (May 8, 2013).

cards kept in reserves at two large banks."[51] The Internet has created the need for all companies to invest in a culture of compliance to manage cyber risks.

In a digital age, trade secrets may be lost at the click of a mouse because a disaffected employee, ex-employee, or hacker decides to misappropriate a company's crown jewels such as customer lists or business plans. The Internet is a gargantuan copying machine allowing seamless, costless, and widespread infringement. Websites are also an instrumentality for counterfeit goods that violate patents and trademarks. Some of these websites sell pharmaceutical products that endanger the health of consumers around the world. In October of 2012, Operation Bitter Pill seized 686 websites selling counterfeit prescription medicines. Increasingly, criminal counterfeiting law enforcement is focused on the global Internet. In November 2012, U.S. Immigration and Customs Enforcement ("ICE") and Department of Homeland Security, in cooperation with law enforcement officials in Belgium, Denmark, France, Romania the United Kingdom, and the European Police Office ("Europol") seized 132 domain names used in selling "counterfeit merchandise online."[52]   EBay's PayPal operates in 190 countries and must comply with all legal systems where it does business:

> While PayPal currently allows its customers with credit cards to send payments from approximately 190 markets, PayPal only allows customers in 110 of those markets (including the U.S.) to receive payments, in some cases with significant restrictions on the manner in which customers can withdraw funds. These limitations may affect PayPal's ability to grow in these markets. Of the markets whose residents can use the PayPal service, 32 (28 countries plus four French overseas departments) are members of the European Union, or EU. Since 2007, PayPal has provided localized versions of its service to customers in the EU through PayPal (Europe).[53]

Counsel advising a buyer or seller in a cross-border transaction will need to comply with foreign as well as domestic law to protect its rights and to avoid infringing upon the rights of others. For example, the European authorities charged Microsoft with anticompetitive conduct in its licensing practices in Europe. EU competition law does not permit the restriction of passive sales. The European Commission has imposed a fine of €1.06 billion euros on Intel Corporation for violating EC Treaty antitrust rules on the abuse of a dominant market position (article 82) by engaging in illegal anticompetitive practices to exclude competitors from the market for computer chips called x86 central processing units ("CPUs").

The Commission has also ordered Intel to cease the illegal practices immediately to the extent that they are still ongoing. Throughout the period of October 2002–December 2007, Intel had a dominant position in the worldwide x86 CPU market.[54] One of the difficult issues in assessing competition law is to extend the concept of

---

[51] Cybercrime Experts Impressed with a Bloodless Bank Heist, ENTERPRISE SECURITY (May 14, 2013).

[52] Homeland Security, HCI Seizes 686 Websites Selling Counterfeit Medicines to Unsuspecting Consumers (Oct. 4, 2012). http://www.ice.gov/news/releases/1210/121004washingtondc.htm (last visited June 29, 2013).

[53] eBay SEC 10–Q Filing (July 19, 2013).

[54] Press Release, Europa, Antitrust: Commission Imposes Fine of ·1.06 bn on Intel for Abuse of Dominant Position; Orders Intel to Cease Illegal Practices (May 13, 2005), available at http://europa.eu/rapid/pressReleasesAction.do? reference=IP/09/745.

vertical guidelines to the Internet. This EU enforcement action illustrates why a U.S. counsel needs a culture of compliance that includes foreign legal systems where it sells goods or renders services. The greatest challenge for counsel representing Internet companies is to manage an uncertain risk environment that is cross-border and transnational.

Most law school courses on Internet law are U.S. centric with almost no coverage of foreign or international developments. To update Benjamin Franklin, our cause is not the cause of all countries connected to the Internet.[55] These examples illustrate the necessity for cross-border solutions versus regulation by any one country. The rapid expansion of the global consumer marketplace creates inevitable clashes between diverse legal traditions about legal norms[56] E-commerce companies, which are highly dependent on proprietary software, have gone global and therefore need a sophisticated familiarity with the legal regimes of multiple nations.[57] As social media sites increasingly target consumers in Europe and beyond, corporate counsel and outside lawyers need to keep abreast of worldwide trends in consumer law to avoid costly cross-border litigation, fines, and regulatory actions.[58]

How might law and society be different if the U.S. government never invented the Internet? It is difficult to overestimate the impact of the Internet on every essential aspect of society. In less than two decades, we have come to take the Web for granted when we book flights, communicate with each other, contribute to social media sites, purchase e-books, shop in virtual bookstores, listen to music, and explore trending videos. Netflix, an on-line entertainment service providing movies and television programming to subscribers by streaming content through the Internet, has driven Blockbuster and other brick and mortar video stores out of business. In addition, the bookstores that have survived the Internet's disruption of their business model need to adapt to changing consumer behavior.

Dick Tracy, the classic comic book character, used revolutionary technologies such as the two-way wrist radio and later the two-way wrist television. At the time, these devices were futuristic, but now seem almost quaint with the ceaseless innovation and technological advances in smartphones and iPads. There are now 6.7 billion smartphone subscriptions. Mobile phones are displacing personal computers just as this technology displaced mini-computers and mainframe systems. Today a world without text messages, mobile phones, and social media is difficult to imagine but these inventions have been part of mass culture for less than two decades. This introductory chapter focuses on the technology, history, and the distributed geography of

---

[55] Benjamin Franklin critiqued U.S. exceptionalism when he said: "Our cause is the cause of all mankind."

[56] The nation of Georgia was ranked first in the Business Software Alliance's global survey of intellectual property violations with a 95% of software pirated followed by Bangladesh and Armenia with a 92% piracy rate. In 2008, worldwide software piracy broke the $50 billion mark. The highest aggregate piracy losses outside the U.S. were found in China, Russia, and India.

[57] Peter Thomas Luce, Hiding Behind Borders in a Borderless World: Extraterritorial Doctrine and the Inadequate of U.S. Patent Protection in a Networked Economy, 10 TULANE J. OF TECH. & I.P. 259, 260 (2007).

[58] Michael L. Rustad, Circles of E–Commerce Trust: Old America v. New Europe, Symposium Issue on Electronic Commerce: Challenges to Privacy, Integrity and Security in a Borderless World, 16 MICH. ST. J. INT'L LAW 577 (2007).

the Internet to provide context for understanding the cases and statutory developments in the following chapters of this hornbook.

Designing legal solutions for the global networked information society requires a clear conception of what is technologically possible as well as an understanding of the practical and business context for Internet law disputes. In May of 2012, NBC launched a television program, *Revolution,* which begins with the basic premise that some unknown force disables all electrical technology on the planet. What would happen if the Internet suddenly collapsed and shut down worldwide? In a real-life incident, the American public learned about the consequences of software failure when a programming error caused the shutdown of the New York Mercantile Exchange and interrupted telephone service in several East Coast cities in February 1998. The failure of the Internet would prevent companies from taking customer orders, shipping products, billing customers, handling support calls, or communicating among their offices around the world. Many companies' support centers depend entirely upon telephone and data services provided by third party telecommunications service vendors and our IT and telecommunications system. President Barack Obama described the ways that the infrastructure and national security are dependent upon the functioning of the Internet:

> Digital infrastructure is increasingly the backbone of prosperous economies, vigorous research communities, strong militaries, transparent governments, and free societies. As never before, information technology is fostering transnational dialogue and facilitating the global flow of goods and services. These social and trade links have become indispensable to our critical life-sustaining infrastructures that deliver electricity and water, control air traffic, and support our financial system, and all depend on networked information systems. Governments are now able to streamline the provision of essential services through Government initiatives. Social and political movements rely on the Internet to enable new and more expansive forms of organization and action. The reach of networked technology is pervasive and global for all nations, and the underlying digital infrastructure is or will soon become a national asset.[59]

Businesses already suffer interruptions in supply chains and operations from malicious code and defective software design, but attacks on Internet hubs could create a breakdown of critical information infrastructure, which would cost hundreds of billions of dollars.[60] An outage would affect cell phones that would stop working as well as desktop computers, laptops, and GPS devices. Financial institutions would face a demand for cash if Internet or electronic payments systems went off-line.[61] Businesses employing cloud computing would be interrupted as they would have no access to accounting or other operational software.[62] This chapter only scratches the surface

---

[59] WHITE HOUSE, INTERNATIONAL STRATEGY FOR CYBERSPACE: PROSPERITY, SECURITY AND OPENNESS IN A NETWORKED WORLD (May 2011) at 3.

[60] BUSINESS ROUNDTABLE, GROWING BUSINESS DEPENDENCE ON THE INTERNET: NEW RISKS REQUIRE C.E.O. ACTION at 1 (2007) (estimating that a shutdown of the Internet would result in $250 billion in losses not counting down the economic ripples throughout the economy).

[61] Id. at 17.

[62] "Cloud computing is a model for enabling ubiquitous, convenient, on-demand network access to a shared pool of configurable computing resources (e.g. networks, servers, storage, applications and services) that can be rapidly provisioned and released with minimal management effort or service provider

about how the Internet works under the hood. Lawyers need to have a solid understanding of the software and hardware comprising the Internet in order to frame arguments about such topics as cross-border jurisdiction, deep linking, framing, metatags, or domain names.

§ 1.2   A BRIEF HISTORY OF THE INTERNET

The word, "cyberspace," was coined by William Gibson in his 1984 science fiction classic, *Neuromancer*, which was the story of a computer hacker for hire planning the ultimate computer intrusion.[63] Warren Agin notes that cyberspace is a term that is a misnomer:

> The term cyberspace is a bit of a misnomer (much like the term "virtual reality," which describes three-dimensional, computer-controlled interactive environments). Contrary to the impression provided by movies such as *The Lawnmower Man* or television episodes of *The X–Files*, where a computer hacker merges her identity with that of a computer and takes up existence in cyberspace, no actual world exists in the computer realm. Cyberspace refers to the network of computers that can be accessed over the Internet and the information available on that network.[64]

The Internet as a network of networks was conceived as an academic and military project, but emerged as a commercial enterprise in the mid-1990s with the development of the World Wide Web. The Internet is a network that connects millions of computers together around the world. This disruptive information technology disregards national borders and has no regard for place or geographic location.[65] The Internet has forever changed how the world does business. It is a reality, taken for granted, that companies market their products and services in a virtual space—twenty-four hours a day, seven days a week—targeting customers around the world.

Tim Berniers–Lee's development of the first graphical user interface ("GUI") browser in 1990, which he called the "Worldwide Web, "jumpstarted the Internet. The definition of the "Internet" is an interconnected worldwide web network of networks employing the TCP/IP. The Internet evolved as a product of a joint private and public partnership that networked university and government computers, enabling computer-to-computer communications. One pundit said, "Describing the Internet as the Network of Networks is like calling the Space Shuttle, a thing that flies."[66]

Until the mid-1990s, relatively few Americans outside of the military or university research centers accessed the Internet.[67] A turning point occurred when computer

---

interaction." European Parliament, Directorate General for Internal Policies: Policy Department A: Economic and Scientific Policy, Cloud Computing Study (May 2012) at 3.

[63] A science fiction writer, William Gibson in his novel Neuromancer, coined the term, 'Cyberspace'". WILLIAM GIBSON, NEUROMANCER 51 (1984). Gibson's novel describes a virtual reality in which the information technologies are the crown jewels horded and sought after by mega-corporations.

[64] WARREN AGIN, BANKRUPTCY AND SECURED LENDING IN CYBERSPACE § 1:5 (updated 2012).

[65] BARRY M. LEINER, ET. AL., A BRIEF HISTORY OF THE INTERNET, INTERNET SOCIETY (2000).

[66] IMP'S INTERNET GUIDE, THE INTERNET (quoting John Lester) (Oct. 1, 2012) visited August 1, 2013).

[67] A brief in an Electronic Privacy Communications Act case about "electronic storage" gives context and perspective to the rise of e-mail as a routinized activity:

From 1981 to 1995, a search of the keyword 'email' in the New York Times article archive generates 268 articles, and a search isolated between 1995–1998 generates 1,564 results. Finally, a search that isolates 1998 to 2013 yields 87,042 articles. Obtained by a search of the word 'email' on

scientists at the University of Minnesota created Gopher, the first user-friendly interface in 1991. The Gopher search engine enabled users to search, distribute, and retrieve documents from the Internet, prefiguring the World Wide Web's friendly user interfaces. The National Center for Supercomputing Applications at the University of Illinois launched "Mosaic," the first graphical web browser in 1993. Carl Sagan famously said, "We live in a society exquisitely dependent on science and technology, in which hardly anyone knows anything about science and technology."[68] This seems particularly true about the Internet.

Historians of the Internet will agree that the technology for a global system of interconnected computer networks reached its takeoff point in the 1990s. The NSF describes the 1990s as the decade when the world went online. Cooperative efforts and the vision of creative minds in both the U.S. government and private corporations shaped the evolution of the Internet as a technology accessible to all Americans. The Internet was not assimilated into the mass culture until the mid-1990s when the World Wide Web went online. For the past fifteen years, cyberspace law has been undergoing extraordinary development and challenging core assumptions in every branch of global law. "Change and flux are the law of life; they are also the life of the law. We live in a dynamic world; it would be strange, indeed, if the law—a reflection of life itself—were static and unchanging."[69]

Courts and legislatures have generated a continually developing body of law to accommodate private and public international disputes, e-mail searches, social media disputes, cybertorts, cybercrimes, media content, constitutional law, consumer protection, and intellectual property dilemmas causally connected to the rise of the Internet. The late Alaskan Senator Ted Stevens once described the Internet as "a series of tubes." In an episode of *The Daily Show*, Jon Stewart made fun of Senator Stevens by diagramming how a tube-based Internet might work. To appreciate the tremendous impact of the World Wide Web on both procedural and substantive law, one must first have a rudimentary understanding of how the Internet works. Nevertheless, even the answer to the question, "What is the Internet?" The answer depends upon whom you ask. Thus, there is no single answer to question of defining the Internet. The Federal Network Council agreed to the following language:

> Internet refers to the global information system that—(i) is logically linked together by a globally unique address space based on the Internet Protocol ("IP") or its subsequent extensions/follow-ons; (ii) is able to support communications using the Transmission Control Protocol/Internet Protocol ("TCP/IP") suite or its subsequent extensions/follow-ons, and/or other IP-compatible protocols; and (iii)

---

http://www.nytimes.com/ref/membercenter/nytarchive.html on January 15, 2013. By 1989, the New York Times—which had published the two earlier articles doubting email's future—recognized that email had become increasingly prevalent in society: 'The number of installed publicly accessible electronic mailboxes in the United States grew to 1.8 million from 210,000 between 1980 and 1989, while the number of in-house computer mail systems jumped to 6.8 million from 220,000.' John Markoff, Computer Mail Gaining a Market, N.Y. TIMES, Dec. 26, 1989, http://www.nytimes.com/1989/12/26/business/computer-mail-gaining-a-market.html?scp=9&sq=email&st=nyt (last visited Aug. 1, 2013).

Brief of Amici Curiae Nineteen National Privacy, Civil Liberties, and Consumer Organizations in Support of Petition for a Writ of Certiorari, Jennings v. Broome, 2013 WL 494174 (S.C. Sup. Ct., Feb. 7, 2013).

[68] Thomas Goetz, Life Hacker, WIRED (June 2012) at 110.

[69] Robert Kratovil, Book Review 54 CHICAGO BAR RECORD 144, of MODERN MORTGAGE LAW AND PRACTICE (1972).

provides, uses or makes accessible, either publicly or privately, high level services layered on the communications and related infrastructure described herein.[70]

Understanding the Internet and information technologies is essential to the practice of law. "To maintain the requisite knowledge and skill, a lawyer should keep abreast of changes in the law and its practice, including the benefits and risks associated with relevant technology, engage in continuing study and education and comply with all continuing legal education requirements to which the lawyer is subject."[71] The Internet is composed of hardware and software that creates an interconnected network of millions of computers that has worldwide broadcasting capability. It is a network of networks linking computer networks all over the world enabling e-mail, surfing and interaction between individuals and entities in hundreds of countries around the world. How many computers are connected to the Internet? The answer to that question depends upon what is meant by being connected to the Internet. Servers are connected to the computers 24/7 but mobile phones or other devices may be connected only for a short time. The development of user-friendly browsers and the rise of commercial networks such as America Online, Prodigy, and CompuServe in the mid-1990s were the key factors in increasing the number of Internet users.

In 1995, there were fewer than 40 million users but by 2000, this number skyrocketed to 361 million persons. Today, there are over 2 billion Internet users.[72] The current "Internet Protocol version 4" ("IPv4") has the capacity to support 4.2 billion addresses. Each computer assigned to the Internet has a unique IPv4 address and thus it is a critically important element of Internet infrastructure. By the end of 2011, consumers used six billion mobile phones to answer email, to instant message, and to surf the Internet. Still only one in three persons in the world has Internet access: there are 2.4 billion Internet users out of an estimated 7.1 billion in the world population. Mobile payments and commerce are the leading edge of the global Internet marketplace.

"In order for these software-driven protocols to work there must be a way of identifying each machine connected to the Internet. Each machine connected to the Internet has an address known as an Internet Protocol address ("IP address"). The IP address takes the form of a series of four numbers separated by dots, for example: 123.45.67.890."[73] The DNS "is a protocol within the set of standards for how computers exchange data on the Internet and on many private networks, known as the TCP/IP protocol suite."[74] The DNS's role is to turn a user-friendly domain name into an IP address.[75] "It's like your computer's GPS system for the Internet."[76] Warren Agin argues that the Internet is the physical network as compared to the information-based Internet writing that:

---

[70] BARRY M. LEINER, ET AL., BRIEF HISTORY OF THE INTERNET, Internet Society.org, (last visited Aug. 1, 2013).

[71] American Bar Association, Model Rules of Professional Conduct § 1.1, comt. 8.

[72] Pingdom.com, The Rather Petite Internet of 1995: Worldwide Users in 1995, http://royal.pingdom.com/2011/03/31/Internet-1995/.

[73] Id.

[74] Marshall Brain and Stephanie Crawford, How Domain Name Servers Work, http://computer.howstuffworks.com/dns.htm (last visited Jun. 18, 2012).

[75] Id.

[76] Id.

The nature of that space, how we use it, how we access it, and how it appears on a computer, depends on a variety of protocols. A protocol is essentially a formalized method of transmitting or communicating information over the Internet. The basic protocol used to transmit information, TCP/IP, dictates the basic structures used to arrange and transmit information. Overlying protocols such as FTP (file transfer protocol) and HTTP (hypertext transmission protocol), are designed to support different functionality over the Internet. In other words, they allow us to use the Internet in different, constructive ways. For example, FTP is used for copying a file from one computer to another. HTTP is used to transfer information in HTML coded web pages. The protocol makes the World Wide Web possible. Standardized protocols enable companies to design server software and client software that can communicate with each other universally, creating the communication networks, including e-mail, web pages, and other functions, that comprise cyberspace.[77]

(A) DARPA & ARPANET

E-mail was not well established prior to the 1980s, nor were Internet protocols and distributed computing. The Internet evolved as a product of a joint private and public partnership that configured university and government computers, and enabled computer-to-computer communications. The rapid evolution of the cyberspace has given rise to many new legal concepts and forced an overhauling of many traditional legal principles. Nearly every branch of substantive and procedural law in the United States and around the globe is currently being transformed. The Advanced Research Projects Agency Network ("ARPANET"), a project of the U.S., prefigured the World Wide Web. Department of Defense's Advanced Research Projects Agency ("DARPA") in 1969.[78] ARPANET's exceptional computer scientists developed the testing ground for "long distance packet switching" technology, enabling host-to-host computer communications.[79] Packet switching, a technology developed by Paul Baran, was based upon redundancy:

---

[77] WARREN AGIN, BANKRUPTCY AND SECURED LENDING IN CYBERSPACE § 1:5 (updated 2012).

[78] "The Internet traces its origins to concepts developed in the United States of America more than 40 years ago, which made significant investments—financial, intellectual and human—in the development of early and later iterations of the Internet. Various technologies underpin the Internet (such as computing, digital communications and semiconductors). For example, in 1973, TCP/IP was first proposed and experimentally deployed a few years later to link packet-based networks. Thus was born the set of interconnected networks, computers and applications known as the Internet. In 1983, the Domain Name System (DNS) was introduced to allow the use of semantic names for host computers, which could be resolved to IP addresses, thus simplifying use of the Internet." International Communication Union, FOURTH DRAFT OF THE SECRETARY-GENERAL'S REPORT FOR THE FIFTH WORLD TELECOMMUNICATION/INFORMATION AND COMMUNICATION TECHNOLOGY POLICY FORUM (Jan. 10, 2013).

[79] "The structure and decentralized management environment of the Internet is the product of its history of explosive and somewhat haphazard growth. In 1969, the United States Department of Defense Advanced Research Projects Agency ("DARPA") founded an experimental prototype network, the Advanced Research Projects Agency Network ("ARPANET"), which became the basis for the Internet. ARPANET was created to facilitate real-time access to remote research resources such as supercomputers, radio telescopes, and specialized databases. During the 1970s, DARPA promulgated the set of computer communication standards known as the "Internet protocols," which were quickly adopted by independent networks attached to the ARPANET backbone. By the early 1980s, ARPANET became so heavily used that the Department of Defense moved operational military traffic onto a separate network known as Milnet. By the late 1980s, ARPANET traffic had entirely outstripped its technology; ARPANET users were moved to a new Defense Research Internet ("DRI") and ARPANET was 'honorably retired.'" Dan L. Burke, Patents in Cyberspace: Territoriality and Infringement on Global Internet Networks, 68 TUL. L. REV. 1, 16 (1993) (discussing history of Internet).

This design, which included a high level of redundancy, would make the network more robust in the case of a nuclear attack. This is probably where the myth that the Internet was created as a communications network for the event of a nuclear war comes from. As a distributed network, the ARPANET definitely was robust, and possibly could have withstood a nuclear attack, but the chief goal of its creators was to facilitate normal communications between researchers.[80]

ARPANET evolved during an age when computers were largely in the hands of government agencies and educational institutions. In 1953, IBM introduced its first electronic computer, the model 701. The term software had not yet been invented (it came into use around 1960) and the programs that IBM supplied for the 701 consisted of only a few hundred lines of code—a tiny fraction of the amount one would get with a domestic PC today. "The ARPANET connected large mainframe computers together via smaller gateway computers, or routers, known as Interface Message Processors ("IMPs"). On September 1, 1969, the first IMP arrived at UCLA. A month later, the second one was installed at Stanford. The University of California, Santa Barbara and then the University of Utah."[81] The Internet Society's history of the Internet notes that the first description of a galactic network was in 1962 when a M.I.T. researcher described networked computers.[82]

In 1970, ARPANET machines operated "at locations around the country, including those at a Network Control Center at the technology corporation Bolt Beranek & Newman, at Harvard, the RAND Corporation and the Massachusetts Institute of Technology."[83] File–Transfer Protocol ("FTP")—the method for allowing computers to exchange files was posted as RFC 354 in July 1972.[84] The ARPANET went on public display for the first time at the International Conference on Computer Communication in October 1972. The first electronic mail delivery engaging two machines was accomplished in 1972 by Ray Tomlinson—also the originator of the use of the @ to indicate an e-mail address. By 1973, three-quarters of all traffic on the network was e-mail—still mostly researchers sharing information. An e-mail list group at the time named MsgGroup is believed to have been the first "virtual community," where the scientists had been using Network Control Protocol (NCP) to transfer data from one computer to another running on the same network." [85]

By 1977, ARPANET's network of interconnected computers spanned the continent but not yet the world. IBM held a press conference in August of 1981 to introduce a new concept, the IBM Personal Computer. Eleven years later, the software industry had revenues that equaled to the sale of hardware. Since then, software and software-services expanded at a rate many times that of hardware. In 1981, the Internet consisted of only 300 computers, and by 1985, the Internet grew to 2,000 connected computers.[86] "Before NASDAQ and millionaire making IPO's, the computer industry

---

[80] Internet Pioneers, http://www.ibiblio.org/pioneers/index.html (last visited June 13, 2013).

[81] Id.

[82] BARRY M. LEINER, A BRIEF HISTORY OF THE INTERNET, INTERNET SOCIETY (2003).

[83] Elon University School of Communications: Imagining the Internet: Quick Look at the Early History of the Internet (2013).

[84] Id.

[85] Elon University School of Communications, Imagining the Internet, Quick Look at the Early History of the Internet, http://www.elon.edu/e-web/predictions/early90s/internethistory.xhtml (last visited June 13, 2013).

[86] JANET ABBATE, INVENTING THE INTERNET 186 (1999).

occupied a reclusive corner of mainstream America. Before the 1980s, computers were large and expensive, thus restricting ownership to the government, universities and a few major corporations."[87] "The Internet protocols that characterized ARPANET allowed it to unite with other networks and eventually assimilated it into the conglomerate Internet. Consequently, the networks' growth has been phenomenal; the Internet comprised about fifty networks in 1983 and over five hundred by 1988."[88]

As late as 1989, the number of computers connected to the Internet was fewer than 90,000. ARPANET and U.S. Department of Defense contractors developed the Tier One ("T1") backbone for the Internet, which were the principal data routes in the Internet's formative period. Prior to the 1990s, the Internet was obscure and an information technology inaccessible for consumers. Prior to the early 1980s, no one even used the term, "Internet." The rapid evolution of the cyberspace has given rise to many new legal concepts and forced an overhauling of many traditional legal principles. Nearly every branch of substantive and procedural law in the United States and around the globe is being transformed by the Internet.

(B) Internet Pioneers

Who invented the Internet? It is difficult, if not impossible to acknowledge all of those who contributed to the development of the Internet. Paul Baran, Donald Davies and Leonard Kleinrock were the mathematicians who "designed packet switching, which is how computers send information over the Internet.[89] Rather than send data as a giant file, computers divide files up into packets.[90] Elon University's School of Communication's history of the Internet acknowledges that today's Internet is the product of thousands of contributors:

> Thanks to the work of thousands of collaborators over the final four decades of the 20th century, today's Internet is a continually expanding worldwide network of computer networks for the transport of myriad types of data. In addition to the names above, there were direct contributions from Ivan Sutherland, Robert Taylor, Alex McKenzie, Frank Heart, Jon Postel, Eric Bina, Robert Cailliau, Tom Jennings, Mark Horton, Bill Joy, Douglas Engelbart, Bill Atkinson, Ted Nelson, Linus Torvalds, Richard Stallman, Dave Clark and so many others—some of them anonymous hackers or users—it is impossible to include them all.[91]

In the late 1960s and 1970s, there were a large number of firsts that led to development of the Internet. In 1969, the first network switch was operative. The first distributed message was sent from Professor Kleinrock's computer at UCLA, but the

---

[87] Daniel B. Ravicher, Facilitating Collaborative Software Development: The Enforceability of Mass–Market Public Software Licenses, 5 VA. J.L. & TECH. 11, P. 9 (2000).

[88] Dan L. Burke, Patents in Cyberspace: Territoriality and Infringement on Global Internet Networks, 68 TUL. L. REV. 1, 16 (1993).

[89] The initial idea is credited as being Leonard Kleinrock's after he published his first paper entitled "Information Flow in Large Communication Nets" on May 31, 1961. Computer Hope, Who Invented the Internet (2013) (explaining that the Internet developed in the late 1960s and there were multiple inventors).

[90] Jonathan Strickland, Who Invented the Internet, How StuffWorks, http://science.howstuffworks.com/innovation/inventions/who-invented-the-internet1.htm (last visited June 30, 2013).

[91] Elon University School of Communications, Imagining the Internet, Quick Look at the Early History of the Internet, http://www.elon.edu/e-web/predictions/early90s/internethistory.xhtml (last visited June 13, 2013).

message could not completed, because the computer system crashed.[92] Researchers introduced e-mail as a messaging system in 1972.[93] Telenet, the first commercial network was launched in 1974.[94]

(1) Vint Cerf & Bob Kahn

Vinton Cerf, a Stanford University researcher, together with Bob Kahn, developed a number of important protocols including the TCP/IP, packet switching, the development of email, and data infrastructure.[95] The Transmission Control Protocol/Internet Protocol (TCP/IP) was the key to the Internet infrastructure. These protocols allow the sending and receiving of e-mails, viewing of Web pages, the transfer of files between one computer and instant messaging with other users.[96] The ACM citation described Vint Cerf and Bob Kahn's contribution to the development of the Internet:

In the spring of 1973, Kahn approached Cerf with the idea of developing a system for interconnecting networks—what would eventually be called an "internet." Kahn felt that his own knowledge of the problem of connecting dissimilar networks, combined with Cerf's expertise in writing host software, would create a strong partnership. Additionally, Kahn and Cerf demonstrated farsighted leadership by inviting networking experts from around the world to weigh in on the Internet design at a seminar in June 1973. This move not only led to more robust protocols, but also laid the groundwork for the global adoption of the Internet. Cerf and Kahn outlined the resulting Internet architecture in a seminal 1974 paper, *A Protocol for Packet Network Intercommunication.*[97]

This remarkable invention made interoperability possible that is essential to networked communications. Without interoperability and common protocol, networked communications is not possible. "The implementation of TCP allowed the various networks to connect into a true 'Internet.'"[98] While Cerf and Kahn were given credit for the "fundamental design principles of networking, specified TCP/IP to meet these requirements, prototyped TCP/IP, and coordinated several early TCP/IP implementations."[99] Vint Cert acknowledges that the Internet was created by the contributions of many including his work with Bob Kahn developing the TCP/IP protocol:

The Internet was prefigured by the ARPANET project, which the federal government funded as a national defense project to ensure continued communications in the event of a nuclear attack. In addition, Xerox deserves credit for great work, Cerf wrote, including creation of the Ethernet protocol, the ALTO personal computer, the Xerox Network System and PARC Universal

---

[92] Who Invented the Internet (2013) (explaining that the Internet developed in the late 1960s and there were multiple inventors).

[93] Id.

[94] Id.

[95] Thomas Goetz, How to Spot the Future, WIRED (May 2012) at 159.

[96] Biz/Ed, Explanation of the Internet and the WWW: How Does It Work? (Feb. 5, 2005), business/marketing/lesson/Internet1.htm (last visited June 29, 2013).

[97] Id.

[98] Internet Pioneers, http://www.ibiblio.org/pioneers/index.html (last visited June 13, 2013).

[99] A.C.M. A.M. Turing Award, United States (2004), http://awards.acm.org/award_winners/kahn_4598637.cfm (last visited June 13, 2013).

Packet. "XEROX did link homogenous Ethernets together but the internetworking method did not scale particularly well.[100]

Nevertheless, Cerf and Kahn deserve much of the credit for creating basic Internet infrastructure. The TCP/IP protocol enabled computers to communicate with each of two critically important elements:

> First was a host protocol called the Transmission Control Protocol ("TCP"), which was intended to provide reliable, ordered, flow-controlled transmission of packets over the interlinked networks. Second was a set of gateways or routers that would sit between networks, passing traffic between them and handling inter-network addressing and routing. There was also a hierarchical address system, whereby packets were first sent by the gateways to a network address and then directed internally to a host address within that network. The Internet architecture was designed to make minimal demands on participating networks, to provide a seamless user experience, and to scale up gracefully, key features that would facilitate the Internet's rapid expansion in the 1990s.[101]

Hal Roberts explains that these two core protocols "that define the Internet—TCP and IP—are both designed to allow separate networks to connect to each other easily."[102] As Roberts notes, "Interoperability is a feature of the Internet not a bug, which China—with its extensive explicit censorship infrastructure—can interact with the rest of the Internet."[103]

(2) Tim Berners–Lee

Tim Berners–Lee is the George Washington of the World Wide Web as well as the Internet's Thomas Jefferson and Benjamin Franklin. He conceptualized the World Wide Web, developing its inimitable URL structure, hyperlinks, and invented the first web browser in 1992. URLs and user-friendly browsers are inimitable features of the accessible World Wide Web.[104]. He developed the first "Graphic User Interface" ("GUI") browser, named the "World Wide Web," and launched the first web page on August 6, 1991. The birth of the commercialized World Wide Web was made possible by Tim Berners–Lee's development of GUI, which he called the "Worldwide Web."

These information technology developments led to the creation of web pages and websites. Berners-Lee launched the first web page on August 6, 1991. "A web page consists of computer programming that is decoded by an Internet browser to show the 'graphic user interface' that ranges from a simple combination of graphics and text to interactive applications."[105] As a researcher at the European Organization for Nuclear Research ("CERN"), he developed a new tool for sharing information on the Internet

---

[100] Colin Wood, Who Really, Really Invented the Internet, GOVERNMENT TECHNOLOGY: E–GOVERNMENT (July 27, 2012).

[101] Id.

[102] Hal Roberts, Internet Censorship and Control, Berkman Center: Harvard University (2013) (last visited June 21, 2013).

[103] Id.

[104] Tim Berners–Lee developed the World Wide Web at CERN in Switzerland in 1991. It was not until the mid-1990s that the World Wide Web reached its takeoff point. See BEN SEGAL, A SHORT HISTORY OF INTERNET PROTOCOLS AT CERN, at http://wwwinfo.cern.ch/pdp/ns/ben

/TCPHIST.html (April 1995).

[105] Conwell v. Gray Loon Outdoor Marketing Group, Inc., 906 N.E.2d 805, 810 (Ind. App. 2009).

using hypertext that he called the World Wide Web in 1990.[106] Berners–Lee invented the "hypertext protocol" ("HTTP") while employed at the European Particle Physics Laboratory in Switzerland. This was the first software code used for real time communications graphics and text processing.[107] Berners–Lee's invention of HTTP did more than any other information technology invention to create the World Wide Web. His work on Internet protocol is emblematic of the quote: "The best way to predict the future is to invent it."[108]

(3) Jon Postel

Jon Postel, another Internet founding father, developed the "User Data Protocol" ("UDP"), providing a "procedure for application programs to transmit messages to other programs with a minimum of protocol mechanism."[109] With UDP, computer applications can send messages or datagrams to other hosts on an Internet Protocol network. "The UDP offers only a minimal transport service—non-guaranteed datagram delivery—and gives applications direct access to the datagram service of the IP layer."[110] In contrast to UDP, TCP performs the sole function of connection to the Internet.[111]

(4) Marc Andreessen

Wired is an American magazine that reports on new and developing technologies on the World Wide Web as well as other emergent technologies. In January 2013, *Wired*'s editors featured a series of in-depth interviews with the Internet pioneers. *Wired's* first interview was with Marc Andreessen, a cofounder of Netscape. Wired described how Andreessen, "backed an astonishing array of Web 2.0 companies from Twitter to Skype from Groupon to Instagram and Airbnb."[112] In 1993, Andreessen and Eric Bina co-created Mosaic, the first graphical web browser, which made the Internet accessible for mass culture. Mosaic was a user-friendly browser for locating information on the Internet and "the first freely available Web browser to enable Web pages to incorporate both graphics and text."[113]

(C) National Science Foundation's NSFNET

The U.S. government initially governed the Internet but Internet governance became decentralized with its commercialization. The National Science Foundation ("NSF") received a grant from the federal government and assumed control of the T1 backbone from ARPA in the mid-1980s. NSFNET originally limited the Internet to education, military, and other governmental purposes, prohibiting commercial uses. By the mid-1980s, the NSF employed packet switching to develop the major backbone

---

[106] "Tim Berners–Lee invented the World Wide Web at CERN, The European Organization for Nuclear Research, in Geneva, Switzerland. He made the first successful hypertext communication on December 25, 1990." HUBPAGES, QUOTES ABOUT THE INTERNET (2012). http://writerfox.hubpages.com/hub/quotes-about-Internet.

[107] Thomas Goetz, How to Spot the Future, WIRED (May 2012) at 159.

[108] W3C, Who's Who at the World Wide Consortium (2008).

[109] Jon Postel, User Datagram Protocol (1980).

[110] RFC, RFC SOURCE BOOK (2012).

[111] WINDOWSNETWORKING.COM, UNDERSTANDING THE UDP PROTOCOL (2012).

[112] The Man Who Knows What's Next, WIRED (May 2012) at 162.

[113] NATIONAL SCIENCE FOUNDATION, A BRIEF HISTORY (2012).

communications service for the Internet. Scientists at ARPANET further developed TCP/IP to enable computers to communicate with each other across the United States.

NSF worked with several voluntary organizations in developing the infrastructure for the NSFNET, which governed the nascent Internet:

> The National Science Foundation started the Computer Science Research Network (CSNET) and had more than 70 sites online by 1983. In the mid-'80s, a coordinating group called the Internet Activities Board centralized networking efforts; late in the decade its membership numbered in the hundreds, and it was split into two groups, the Internet Engineering Task Force ("IETF") and the Internet Research Task Force ("IRTF"). By 1986, most U.S. computer science departments were connected through NSFNET paying the NSF annual operation fees in order to use the network. In 1985, NSFNET, a 'backbone' to connect five supercomputer centers located all over the United States, allowed the establishment of regional networks around the country, making a brighter, more-connected future possible for more people.[114]

The NSF Network ("NSFNET") surfaced as a program of coordinated, evolving projects sponsored by the NSF that replaced ARPANET in the mid-1980s.[115] "In 1988, the NSF began work on the NSFNET to interconnect a small number of supercomputer centers and to sponsor the creation of intermediate-level or regional networks to provide access to the NSFNET."[116] The second stage in the development of the Internet occurred in the late-1980s through the early 1990s when the NSF still controlled the Internet.

More networks emerged, including BITNET, USENET and UUCP. In cooperation with NSF, U.S. companies developed a T3 backbone, connecting the networks of major companies. The NSF "took over the T1 backbone and private industry developed a T3 backbone connecting the networks of major companies. Several other governmental agencies also developed computer networks so their researchers could communicate and share data."[117] ARPANET created the TCP/IP communications standard that enabled computers to communicate with each other. The TCP is the data packeting protocol whereas IP is the protocol for routine packets. "Internet Protocol Numbers" ("IP") encompass four groups of digits separated by periods, such as "192.215.247.50," pinpointing the location of a specific computer connected to the Internet. The domain name system ("DNS") protocol replaces strings of numbers with easier to remember words. The TCP/IP protocol is the most widely used communication system within the Internet, evolving as a necessary infrastructure to enable file transfers, e-mail, remote terminal access, and other vital essential tools of the World Wide Web. Service providers collect IP addresses for administrative purposes to improve system performance.

In 1986, the Internet Engineering Task Force ("IETF"), a voluntary organization, took "responsibility for short-to-medium term Internet engineering issues, which had

[114] Elon University School of Communications, Imagining the Internet, Quick Look at the Early History of the Internet, (last visited June 13, 2013).

[115] STEVEN KARRIS, NETWORKS DESIGN AND MANAGEMENT 1–205 (2009).

[116] CONSTANCE M. PECHURA, INSTITUTE OF MEDICINE (U.S.). COMMITTEE ON A NATIONAL NEURAL CIRCUITRY DATABASE, MAPPING THE BRAIN AND ITS FUNCTIONS 85 (1991).

[117] NATIONAL SCIENCE FOUNDATION, A BRIEF HISTORY OF THE NSF AND THE INTERNET (2003).

previously been handled by the Internet Activities Board."[118] IETF was the developer of IPV6 protocol for IP addresses, which serve as the communications protocol identifying and locating computers and routing Internet traffic. While ARPANET prefigured the Internet with its implementation of the TCP/IP protocol, the IETF developed the protocol that enabled interoperability for Internet users, irrespective of the type of computer. The privatization of the Internet began in the early 1990s when NSF opened the Internet up for business.[119] In 1990, the NSF held the first workshop on "The Commercialization of the Internet" at Harvard University. In 1991, the NSF lifted the ban on commercial traffic, launching the 24/7 virtual marketplaces we know today.[120] The first banner ads appeared in 1994 for Zima, an alcoholic beverage. That same year, the White House launched its website, and the word "spam" became part of the popular lexicon. In 1994, relatively few companies, law firms and professional associations had a homepage, let alone a cyberspace presence. That same year, the first known domain name hijacking took place when a Sprint employee registered MCI.net. The year 1994 marked the first time a major company began to take orders online with Pizza Hut's initiative. In 1994, an anonymous hacker launched the "Good Times Virus" that is credited in being the first of many virus hoaxes. That same year, America Online linked to the Internet for the first time. In 1994, Amazon.com, the Earth's largest bookstore, incorporated and Yahoo! was launched. Microsoft released its Windows 95 operating system, incorporating Internet Explorer. The first Internet gambling casinos were organized in 1995 the same year as the World Wide Web became part of the popular lexicon. By September 1995, the demand for Internet registration became largely commercial (97 percent) expanding exponentially. By September 1995, the demand for Internet domain name registration had become largely commercial (97%) and expanded exponentially. User-friendly browsers such as Mosaic enabled the commercialized Internet.

The path of Internet law shifted dramatically when millions of ordinary Americans went online in the mid-1990s. From January 1, 1992 to January 1, 1995, the word "Internet" appeared in state and federal court opinions only seven times. Nevertheless, by 1995, there was a dramatic turning point for the law of intellectual property in cyberspace. The commercialized Internet created new legal conflicts between domain names and trademarks. As businesses went online, new questions arose as to the enforceability of online contracts such as terms of use or service. E-Commerce law began to evolve as Congress, state legislatures, the courts, and the nascent e-business industry began to forge new rules and standards for doing business online.

During this era, the federal government appointed the NSF to supervise domain name registration. Previously, NSF had subsidized the cost of registering all domain names. Network Solutions, Inc., ("NSI") operated the domain name registry under a sub-contract with the U.S. Defense Information Systems Agency ("DISA") beginning in

---

[118] FEDERAL COMMUNICATIONS COMMISSION, COMMON STANDARDS (2008).

[119] Id.

[120] In less than a decade after the commercial use ban was lifted on the Internet, the 24/7 virtual marketplace was well institutionalized: "Cyberselling is here to stay. The Internet makes it possible for persons worldwide to buy, sell and ship goods to or from anywhere in the world from their own living room using a computer and an Internet hook-up. Courts and legislatures must keep pace with the ever-changing world of cyberspace." Euromarket Designs, Inc. v. Crate & Barrel Ltd., 96 F. Supp.2d 824, 824 (N.D. Ill. 2000).

1981. From 1981 to 1992, NSI registered domain names in .com, .org, .mil, .gov, .edu and .net for no charge. The Internet Corporation for Assigned Names and Numbers ("ICANN") assumed control of the "domain name system" ("DNS") in 1998.[121] ICANN has a board of directors and a contractual obligation with the U.S. government to manage the domain name system.[122] Thus, ICANN is a non-state actor, a not-for-profit corporation:

> ICANN is a non-profit organization formed by a broad coalition of the Internet's business, technical, academic, and user communities to assume responsibility for the IP address space allocation, protocol parameter assignment, DNS management and root server management functions.[123]

ICANN agreed to the following DNS management functions:

> a. Establishment of policy for and direction of the allocation of IP number locks;
>
> b. Oversight of the operation of the authoritative root server system;
>
> c. Oversight of the policy for determining the circumstances under which new top level domains would be added to the root system;
>
> d. Coordination of the assignment of other Internet technical parameters as needed to maintain universal connectivity on the Internet; and
>
> e. Other activities necessary to coordinate the specified DNS management functions, as agreed by the Parties.[124]

By 1998, one in four businesses with ten or more employees had a domain name and a website. In September 1998, when NSF's agreement with NSI expired, the number of registered domain names had passed two million. The U.S. Government decommissioned NSF's role in Internet governance in 1998. Since that time, Internet governance has been in a constant stage of evolution, struggling over whether a multistakeholder model should be adopted as opposed to national control. As Laura DeNardis notes: "Internet governance is not fixed any more than Internet architecture is fixed."[125]

(D) The Internet's Unfathomable Dimensions

> Thirty years ago, few understood that something called the Internet would lead to a revolution in how we work and live in that short time, millions now owe their livelihoods—and even their lives—to advances in networked technology. A billion more rely on it for everyday forms of social interaction. This technology propels

---

[121] Memorandum of Understanding ("MOU") Between ICANN and U.S. Department of Commerce (25 November 1998) (last visited July 12, 2013).

[122] Peter K. Yu, Intellectual Property Training and Education for Development, 28 AM. UNIV. INT'L L. REV. 311, 343 (2012). See generally, Milton L. Mueller, RULING THE ROOT: INTERNET GOVERNANCE AND THE TAMING OF CYBERSPACE (2002).

[123] SUBRATA GOSWAMI, INTERNET PROTOCOLS: ADVANCES, TECHNOLOGIES AND APPLICATIONS at 23 (2003).

[124] Memorandum of Understanding (MOU) Between ICANN and U.S. Department of Commerce, Id.

[125] David McAuley, Former Envoy Say Internet Governance Should Not be Ceded to Multinational Control, Bloomberg BNA: Electronic Commerce & the Law (May 23, 2013) (quoting Laura DiNardis author of the Global War for Internet Governance (Yale University Press 2014)).

society forward, accomplishing things previous generations scarcely thought possible.[126]

Barack Obama

How vast is the Internet? Due to its decentralized architecture, it is very difficult, if not impossible, to determine the Internet's precise dimensions at a specific point in time. The Internet is an ocean of data with billions of pages of text. A single multinational company, for example, may store documents that comprise hundreds of petabytes in the clouds. The task for corporate counsel is to manage this ocean of data. How can a plaintiff's counsel conduct e-discovery and locate a given document stored in a private cloud? For defense counsel, the task is to manage e-mail, which courts consider to be discoverable. Companies are drowning in an ocean of data. Each hour the amount of information sent on the Internet could fill seven million DVDs.[127] Google's CEO estimated that, "all human knowledge created from the dawn of man to 2003 totaled 5 exabytes."[128] A "yottabyte" ("YB") equals one million exabytes and constitutes "a septillion bytes—so large that no one has ever coined at term for the next highest magnitude."[129] The U.S. Department of Defense seeks to build a Global Information Grid with yottabytes or 10^{24} bytes.

YouTube claims more than a billion views daily "with more than 24 hours of new video uploaded to the site every minute."[130] The actual number of web pages is unknown and unknowable. The vastness of the Internet makes it difficult to enforce intellectual property rights. Consider that YouTube visitors upload approximately "10 hours—or 600 minutes—of new content every minute."[131] It would take 600 persons watching YouTube 24/7 just to classify the content as infringing or not.[132]

A repressive regime would have to hire an army of censors to determine which vulgar or subversive websites to block. Today, employing human censors to screen out website content would be akin to attempting to hold back the ocean with a broom. By late 2011, Google Book contained over fifteen million books, not counting forward contracts to digitalize numerous other library collections.[133] The Internet of the mid-1990s seems small as compared to today's gargantuan dimensions.[134] In 2005, The

---

[126] WHITE HOUSE, INTERNATIONAL STRATEGY FOR CYBERSPACE: PROSPERITY, SECURITY AND OPENNESS IN A NETWORKED WORLD (May 2011) at 27.

[127] Graeme McMillan, How Big is the Internet? (Spoiler Not as Big as It Will Be in 2015, TIME TECH (June 6, 2011).

[128] Id.

[129] Id.

[130] Viacom Intern. Inc. v. YouTube, Inc., 2013 WL 1689071 *2 (S.D. N.Y. 2013).

[131] John Ozimek, UK.gov Says: Regulate the Internet, THE REGISTER (Oct. 20, 2008). www.theregister.co.uk/2008/10/20/govern ment_Internet_regulation/.

[132] Id.

[133] Stephanie Latimer & Anandashankar Mazumdar, Google Books Roundtable Participants Clash Over Lawsuit's Path Forward, 16 BLOOMBERG BNA ELEC. COMM. L. REV. 1103, 1103 (2011).

[134] In 1996, I wrote: "Since the Clinton Administration endorsed the establishment of a National Information Infrastructure (NII), Internet use has risen dramatically. As of July 1995, the Internet links an estimated twenty-four million individuals, and the number of users continues to grow an astonishing twenty percent per month. A 1994 estimate indicated that the Internet connects computers in approximately 135 countries, and the number of electronic users is 'expected to double each year for the foreseeable future.' Michael L. Rustad, Legal Resources for Lawyers Lost in Cyberspace, 30 SUFFOLK U. L. REV. 317, 317 (1996). See also, Arthur Middleton Hughes, Internet DB Marketing with CD–ROMS, DM News, Aug. 21, 1995, at 22 (stating network consists of approximately five million server computers and millions of users); April Streeter, Don't Get Burned by the Internet, LAN TIMES, Feb. 13, 1995, at 58 (quoting 20 percent growth

Authors Guild, an association of authors, filed a copyright infringement lawsuit through the Library Project of its "Google Books" search tool by scanning and indexing more than 20 million books and making available for public display "snippets" of most books upon a user's search."[135] In November of 2013, a federal judge held that Google was protected by the doctrine of fair use in digitally reproducing millions of copyrighted books, making them available for its library project partners to download, and display "snippets" from the books to the public.[136] The court found that the Google Book project was transformative by turning books into data.[137] In addition, the court concluded that Google Books increases sales of books for copyright holders.[138]

"In 2011, a study sponsored by EMC estimated that the total amount of data in existence will surpass 1.8 zettabytes (1.8 trillion gigabytes), a figure reflecting a growth factor of nine in just five years and representing enough data to fill a stack of DVDs reaching halfway from Earth to Mars."[139] Ben Kaplan's prediction of a vast computer network storing all accumulated knowledge is close to fruition in less than two decades. The growth of the Internet is spectacular. How much content is on the Internet? The boom of the Internet showered genuine benefits by creating a storehouse of knowledge. The scale of information on the Internet is difficult to fathom. Wikipedia is the largest encyclopedia in the world, consisting of sixteen million articles in over 260 languages, created and maintained by more than 100,000 contributors from around the world.

Each month, contributors add four million entries to Wikipedia and edit a vast amount of its existing text. Jimmy Wales, Wikipedia's founder, asks us to imagine a world where everyone has free access to the treasure trove of human knowledge. Jack Dorsey, Evan Williams, Biz Stone and Noah Glass created Twitter in March of 2006. In the past seven years, users tweeted nearly two billion times. Flickr users contribute five million images each day or sixty photographs a second.[140] Google estimates that there are fifteen billion web pages and, by the time you are reading this, it will be even greater as 60,000 new websites go online each day. With 250 million domain name registrations, there is the potential for innumerable disputes with trademark owners.

Google's storage, taken as a whole, is five petabytes, five thousand terabytes, or quadrillion bytes of data; and is still expanding at an exponential rate.[141] Barnes and Noble claims that its e-reader Nook is: "The world's largest bookstore in your

---

figure); see also Rex S. Heinke & Heather D. Rafter, Rough Justice in Cyberspace: Liability on the Electronic Frontier, THE COMPUTER LAW, July 1994, at 1 (reporting Internet carried approximately 45 billion packets of information a month at end of 1993).

[135] Authors Guild Inc. v. Google, Inc., 2013 WL 3286232 *1 (2d Cir., July 1, 2013) (vacating certification of class action because of the necessity to take fair use into account).

[136] Authors Guild, Inc. v. Google Inc., 2013 WL 6017130 (S.,D. N.Y., Nov. 14, 2013)

[137] Id. at *7.

[138] Id. at *10 (observing, "Google Books provides significant public benefits. It advances the progress of the arts and sciences, while maintaining respectful consideration for the rights of authors and other creative individuals, and without adversely impacting the rights of copyright holders").

[139] Jeffrey S. Follett, MCLE MASSACHUSETTS DISCOVERY PRACTICE § 20.1 (2012).

[140]Shane Snow, How Much Content is on the Web? THE CONTENT STRATEGIST (2012). http://contently.com/blog/how-much-content-is-on-the-web/.

[141] Thomas Goetz, How to Spot the Future, WIRED (May 2012) at 156 (describing the exponential progress in technologies such as networks, sensors and data storage).

pocket."[142] Nook gives users over two million books, newspapers and magazines, and access to them through Wi–Fi. Kindle 2 developed by Amazon.com allows a consumer to download thousands of books and periodicals from "long tail" digital stores. By early March 2012, consumers downloaded 25 billion applications from Apple's App Store. Kindle incorporates firmware-enabling automatic upgrades that download automatically when the device goes into sleep mode.[143] The first iPod in 2001 had a capacity of only 5 gigabytes. The iPods of 2012 store 160 gigabytes.[144] In December of 2011, an estimated 370 million websites were active on the Internet. By October 1, 2013, there were 4.32 billion pages.[145] By January 2014, there will be a billion websites online.[146]

More than two billion computers are connected to the Internet but the actual number is unknown and unknowable.[147] Global Internet traffic, made possible by "interchange exchange points," ("IXPs"), will increase four times from "2010 to 2015, reaching 966 exabytes per year."[148] The surface web is the portion of the World Wide Web indexed by search engines, which alone consist of between 25 and 64 billion Web pages.[149]

§ 1.3   DEFINING THE INTERNET & THE WORLD WIDE WEB

Strictly speaking, the Internet is a network of smaller computer networks that use a specific protocol to communicate, but the range of policies and behaviors that influence and are influenced by the Internet is much broader. These include physical infrastructure and broadband policies, content creation and distribution mechanisms, copyright regimes, international law, social and professional communication, citizen-government interactions, and much more.

Robert Farris & Rebekah Heacock

Berkman Center for Internet & Society[150]

The Internet is enabled by shared protocol making it possible for millions of interconnected computers to communicate with each other. Internet hardware includes routers, hubs, servers, cell phone towers, satellites, radios, smartphones and countless other devices. Yochai Benkler in his *Wealth of Networks* describes the Internet as three layers: (1) the physical layer; (2) the logical layer, and the (3) content layer.[151] This

---

[142] Barnes & Noble Introduces the All–New NOOK, The Simple Touch Reader (May 24, 2011). http://www.barnesandnobleinc.com/press_releases/2011_may_24_all-new_nook_press_release.html.

[143] Geoffrey A. Fowler, Amazon Upgrades Users' Kindles Automatically, WALL ST. J. BLOG (Nov. 24, 2009).

[144] Thomas Goetz, How to Spot the Future, WIRED (May 2012) at 156 (describing the exponential progress in technologies such as networks, sensors and data storage).

[145] The Size of the Worldwide Web (The Internet) (Oct. 2, 2013).

[146] Toni Schneider, 1 Billion Websites in 2013 (May 3, 2012).

[147] INTERNET WORLDSTATS, WORLD INTERNET USAGE STATISTICS (Dec. 31, 2011), http://www.Internetwoldstats.com/stats.htm (last visited June 29, 2013).

[148] James Bamford, Inside the Matrix, WIRED (April 2012) at 78, 83.

[149] Id.

[150] Robert Farris & Rebekah Heacock, Measuring Internet Activity: A (Selective) Review of Methods and Metrics, Internet Monitor Special Report Series No.2: Mesasuring Internet Activity: a (Selective) Review of Methods and Metrics (Nov. 2013) at 1.

[151] Id. at 1-2 (discussing Benkler's conceptualization of the Internet).

part of the chapter focuses on the physical infrastructure and the logical layers. The remainder chapters will focus on the content layer.

Internet architects created the physical layer of the Internet. The physical layer is built on an analogous backbone called the Tier 1 ("T–1") network, "which is a huge system of underground and even under-ocean cables that span the entire globe. Just as different U.S. states and foreign countries manage the U.S. interstate highway system, the Tier 1 network is owned and managed by private companies such as MCI, AT&T, Qwest, and Sprint."[152] These private companies sell access to their backbones, which have the capacity to carry vast amounts of Internet traffic. Software is the brick and mortar that connects the computers in the network of networks known as the Internet.

Many people conflate the World Wide Web with the Internet. The Web is a means of accessing information using HTTP protocol. "The Web also utilizes browsers, such as Internet Explorer or Firefox, to access Web documents called Web pages that are linked to each other via hyperlinks. Web documents also contain graphics, sounds, text and video."[153] The World Wide Web with its hyperlinks linking web pages did not evolve until the mid-1990s whereas the Internet was prefigured by the ARPANET in the 1940s. Alfredo Lopez explains the difference between the often confused terms, the Internet and the World Wide Web, in the following passage:

> As ubiquitous and popular as social networking is, it represents a contradiction to the Internet that created it and to the World Wide Web on which it lives. You may think the World Wide Web and the Internet are synonyms. They're not. The Web is to the Internet what a city is to human existence. The first can't live without the second; the second is extended by the first. The Internet is a system of communications comprised of billions of computers that connect to each other through telecommunications lines. It allows people to interact in different ways like email, file upload, chat and, of course, the good old Web. The Web is a function of the Internet, a kind of subset through which data files stored on a computer (called a server) can be accessed and viewed by people using a special piece of software called a browser.[154]

The Internet's hardware, routers and bridges, transmit information from one network area to another. A gateway is the network point that acts as an entrance to another network. A switch is a "network device" that selects how data gets to the next destination. Systems administrators use routers to transmit data from the Internet to LAN destinations and vice versa. Companies may connect their personal computers to a Wide Area Network ("WAN"). The WAN utilizes routers to transmit data between LANs. Gateway nodes are traffic cops for a company's computer network and the Internet.

A gateway may also be used if the LAN does not recognize Internet protocols such as the Transmission Control Protocol/Internet Protocol ("TCP/IP"). The five types of hardware comprising key Internet technology infrastructure are: (1) hubs, (2) bridges,

---

[152] METAMORPHOSITE.COM, WHO OWNS THE INTERNET AND HOW DOES IT WORK? (Jun. 19, 2012). http://www.metamorphosite.com/who-owns-Internet-how-it-works-domain-registration.

[153] Vangie Beal, The Difference Between the Internet and the World Wide Web, Webopedia (last updated May 14, 2013).

[154] Alfred Lopez, Social Networking and the Death of the Internet, RADIO: VOICE OF RUSSIA (July 21, 2013).

(3) gateways, (4) repeaters, and (5) routers.[155] Routers and bridges transmit information from one network area to another. A switch is a network device that selects how data gets to its next destination. These devices may be used to transmit data from the Internet to LAN destinations and vice versa. Companies may connect their personal computers to a Wide Area Network ("WAN"), which utilizes routers to transmit data between LANs.

(A) Hubs or IXPs

Hubs or Internet exchange points ("IXPs") are network access points that enable Internet Service Providers ("ISPs") to exchange traffic. Internet Exchange ("IX") acts as a junction between multiple points of Internet presence. Here, peers are able to connect to each other to exchange local Internet traffic. An Internet exchange point ("IX or IXP") is a network switch through which Internet service providers ("ISPs") exchange Internet traffic between their networks (autonomous systems). "The primary purpose of an IXP is to allow networks to interconnect directly, via the exchange, rather than through one or more 3rd party networks. The advantages of the direct interconnection are numerous, but the primary reasons are cost, latency, and bandwidth."[156] IXPs require Internet Service Providers to provide three things to join: "(1) ASN (Autonomous System Number)—this number is used in both the exchange of exterior routing information (between neighboring ASNs), and as an identifier of the AS itself; (2) BGP-4 (Border Gateway Protocol Version 4) — Peering between Members' routers across the IXP will be via BGP-4; and (3) a willingness to sign a connection agreement."[157] IXPs will also require ISPs to agree to supplemental terms and conditions.[158]

Initially, the IXs were part of the Defense Advanced Research Projects Agency ("DARPA") and later the NSF Tier 1 backbone ("NSFNET"). Today, Internet hubs "focus not only on exchange functions, but also on the hosting of bandwidth intensive content."[159] Traffic at these facilities typically grows at a compound level doubling each year. The experience of the past few decades demonstrates that hubs can fail, leaving "Internet nodes unable to communicate with other nodes."[160] The architecture of control permits repressive countries to remove one or more nodes or completely take the Internet off line in a given country without affecting the global communications system as a whole. The Syrian government, for example, controls hubs to interfere with communications in areas controlled by the rebels. In November of 2012, the Bashar al-Assad regime blocked ISP addresses shutting down the Internet for all of Syria. Five ISP addresses, controlled by the regime, were deployed to deliver malware to anti-

---

[155] PRESTON GRALLA, HOW THE INTERNET WORKS 9 (4th ed. 1998).

[156] BGP: the Border Gateway Protocol Advanced Internet Routing Resources, GLOBAL INTERNET EXCHANGE POINTS, (last visited June 17, 2013).

[157] European Internet Exchange Association, Joining an IXP, (last visited June 17, 2013).

[158] Id.

[159] Joseph Y. Hui, The Economics and Competitive Pricing at Internet Exchanges, in DANNY H. K. TSANG, PAUL J. KÜHN, BROADBAND COMMUNICATIONS: CONVERGE OF NETWORK TECHNOLOGIES (2000) at 155.

[160] Edward Skoudis, Evolutionary Trends in Cyberspace, Chapter 6 in FRANKLIN D. KRAMER, STUART H. STARR, LARRY K. WENTZ, CYBERPOWER AND NATIONAL SECURITY 119 (2009).

activists.[161] Officials "shut down Internet and mobile phone access to opposition-held areas" to interrupt communications as a strategic tactic.[162]

China, too, creates temporary blackouts of its Internet to stifle political opposition, a policy sarcastically referred to as "The Great Firewall of China." "China's Green Dam, a client side application that filters pornography and political content, was installed on all computers manufactured in China starting July 1, 2009. One way the application blocks access to sites is to kill the browser window when it tries to visit an offending site."[163] The more limited the connections, the more likely countrywide Internet shutdowns will occur. In 2011, an elderly woman in the Republic of Georgia shut down the Internet in Armenia when she sliced through a cable while scavenging for copper.

The United States Congress continues to evaluate proposals to install a kill switch that could shut down the Internet in the event of a national emergency. Critics who note that Hoshni Mubarak, Egypt's then president, caused the Internet to go dark in order to quell massive demonstrations against his regime during the Arab Spring in 2012 oppose the proposed "kill switch." "Today you can run an approximation of *1984* out of a couple of rooms filled with server racks."[164] The supporters of the kill switch contend that the U.S. President or other official will deploy it only in a true emergency against cybercriminals or terrorists that threaten national security. Hubs also have a seamy side aspect in that they enable repressive regimes to censor content by controlling these communication centers. John Gilmore explains how Internet architecture was originally antithetical to censorship but today has morphed into today's architecture of control:

> In its original form, it meant that the Usenet software (which moves messages around in discussion newsgroups) was resistant to censorship because, if a node drops certain messages because it doesn't like their subject, the messages find their way past that node anyway by some other route. This is also a reference to the packet-routing protocols that the Internet uses to direct packets around any broken wires or fiber connections or routers. (They don't redirect around selective censorship, but they do recover if an entire node is shut down to censor it).[165]

The Open Initiative Project conducted by Harvard University's Berkman Center established that twenty-five out of forty-one countries in Asia, the Middle East, and North Africa blocked access to information on the Internet.[166] The Berkman Center

---

[161] Martin Chulov, *Syris Shuts Off Internet Access Across the Country: Shutting Down of Communications Seen as Bid to Stymie Rebel Moves as Militias Attempt Assault on the Regime's Power Base*, THE GUARDIAN (Nov. 29, 2012), http://www.theguardian.com/world/2012/nov/29/syria-blocks-internet.

[162] Id.

[163] Hal Roberts, *Watching Technology: China Bans the Letter 'F'*, The Berkman Center for Internet & Society Berkman Center (2009) ("What's happening in the video is GD fails to block falundafa.org the first time it is loaded, so 'falundafa.org' gets into the history of the browser. Eventually GD recognizes the offensive content on the sites and kills the whole browser after briefly flashing a 'you have been filtered' image. Any time GD flags a site as politically offensive, that url gets entered into a list of urls to trigger a kill-block whenever it is entered into the location bar or window. But that auto-kill-block applies to text brought up in the auto-complete list as well as text in the entry box proper").

[164] Matthieu Aikins, *Jamming Tripoli*, WIRED, (June 2012), at 146, 176 (comparing server capacity with George Orwell's novel 1984).

[165] John Gilmore, *Homepage, Things I've Said*, http://.com/gnu/.

[166] Berkman Center for Internet & Society, *Survey of Government Internet Filtering Practices Indicates Increasing Internet Censorship: First Year of Global Survey Examines 41 Countries by Political,*

study concluded that: Saudi Arabia, Iran, Tunisia, and Yemen engage in substantial social content filtering. "These countries block Internet materials they classify as obscene or political content. In contrast, the study found no evidence of filtering in a sample of fourteen countries that included Egypt, Iraq, Israel, West Bank and Gaza."[167] Saudi Arabia, Iran, and Yemen censor content using similar repressive methods to block information as in China.[168] "In Saudi Arabia, for example, the government has closed a number of Internet cafes, especially those established for women who have been specifically targeted as being used for 'immoral purposes.'"[169] The Syrian government blocks access to free email services and disrupt "the lines were used to access Internet providers outside the country."[170] In the June 2009, elections in Iran, the government blocked instant messaging as well as Internet content.

(B) Bridges

A bridge is an intelligent connectivity device connecting computers on a Local Area Network ("LAN") and World Area Network ("WANS").[171] "Any time you connect two networks, you must use a tool that translates the address and control data used by each network into values that the other network can understand. When a device simply examines the address on a packet and decides which packets to forward, it is a bridge."[172] "The bridge acts as an address filter which picks up one LAN that is intended for a destination on another LAN and passes this packet on the network."[173]

(C) Gateways

Gateways are network points that act as an entrance into another network. They are a combination of software and hardware that enable two different network segments to exchange data; a gateway facilitates communication between different networks or subnets; in other words, a gateway is simply a network point that controls traffic. A gateway typically includes a firewall that serves a proxy between local applications and foreign or remote systems,[174] which permits only verified electronic data packets to be passed on by the packet filter. A company or individual will typically

---

Social, and National Security Filtering, Berkman Center (May 18, 2007). http://cyber.law.harvard.edu/newsroom/first_global_filtering_survey_released (last visited July 10, 2013).

[167] Berkman Center for Internet & Society, Survey of Government Internet Filtering Practices Indicates Increasing Internet Censorship: First Year of Global Survey Examines 41 Countries by Political, Social, and National Security Filtering, Berkman Center (May 18, 2007). http://cyber.law.harvard.edu/newsroom/first_global_filtering_survey_released (last visited July 10, 2013).

[168] Philip J. Oliveri, Technological Software That Counters Internet Jamming: Its Role in the U.S. and in Non–Democratic Countries, 2003 SYRACUSE L. & TECH. J. 2 (2003).

[169] Id.

[170] Id.

[171] Dan L. Burk describes the role of bridges in connecting networks: "All the computers on these networks, as well as those on other national and international networks that have adopted the Internet protocols, have the capability of communicating together. Consequently, the Internet is not a single integrated entity; rather, it is a loosely connected web of local, regional, and national computer networks that share certain procedures for addressing and routing computer data. Indeed, two or more networks may be connected together by computers called gateways or bridges, which translate dissimilar messages. The virtue of the Internet protocols, however, is that they obviate the need for such expensive bridges by allowing ready linkage of disparate networks." Dan L. Burke, Patents in Cyberspace: Territoriality and Infringement on Global Internet Networks, 68 TUL. L. REV. 1, 4 (1993).

[172] JOHN ROSS, NETWORK KNOW–HOW: AN ESSENTIAL GUIDE FOR THE ACCIDENTAL ADMIN. 32 (2009).

[173] Ramesh Bangia, INTERNET & WEB DESIGN 20 (2005).

[174] ALAN MAYER, AVISHAI WOOL & ELISHA ZISKIND, FANG: A FIREWALL ANALYSIS ENGINE (2000).

install anti-virus software at its gateway.[175] Firewalls authenticate data and identify users, preventing intruders from intercepting data or planting viruses. The proxy server, or application gateway, runs on the firewall.

Application gateways employ authentication and logging tailored for high security businesses or the military. The tort of negligent enablement of cybercrime is just beginning to evolve as courts determine whether financial institutions, like credit card processors or commercial websites, owe a duty to protect date of third parties by implementing security that thwarts hacker attacks. Chapter 6 examines the issue of whether websites have a duty to implement reasonable security such as firewalls to block unwanted traffic and secure data on gateways. In the law of torts, courts determine duty on the probability of risk: the greater the risk, the greater the duty of care. Cyber-attacks on U.S. computer networks skyrocketing increasing seventeen times in a two-year period, from 2009 to 2011.[176] One of the most recent cyberlaw duty-risk developments is the duty of companies to disclose computer intrusions because they have defectively configured firewalls. Congress has yet to enact Cybersecurity legislation, as The Cybersecurity Act of 2012 did not gain traction in the U.S. Senate.

(D) Routers

The Internet is principally a collection of communication networks interconnected by bridges and/or routers. A router is a piece of hardware that essentially routes, or guides, computer traffic along a network. "Some communication may be meant strictly for the inside, or home, network while other traffic is meant for the outside (the Internet)."[177] Routing is the process of finding a path from a source to every destination in the network.[178] Cisco Systems is a leading producer of routers, which are intelligent devices conjoining routed data over many networks.[179] Users exchange information in the form of "packets," which do not travel along predestined routes. Software engineers and Internet architects conceptualize the packet switching system as enabling routing options for efficient traffic control. Routers are devices that enable data to move on the Internet.[180] Historians credit Robert E. Kahn and Vinton G. Cerf as Internet founding fathers because of their role in introducing routers as part of Internet communications:

> In order to work properly, the architecture required a global addressing mechanism (or Internet address) to enable computers on any network to reference and communicate with computers on any other network in the federation. Internet addresses fill essentially the same role as telephone numbers do in telephone networks. The Internet architects assumed first that the individual networks could not be changed to accommodate new architectural requirements; but this was

---

[175] TAMARA DEAN, NETWORK+GUIDE TO NETWORKS 496 (5th ed. 2009).

[176] Linda Sandler, SEC Guidance on Cyber–Disclosure Becomes Rule for Google, BLOOMBERG (Aug. 29, 2012) (citing study of National Security Agency and U.S. Cyber Command).

[177] JOHN BENNETT JR., THE DIGITAL UMBRELLA: TECHNOLOGY'S ATTACK ON PERSONAL PRIVACY IN AMERICA (2004) at 183.

[178] A. Lyman Chapin Communication Systems: The State of the Art: IFIP 17th World Computer Congress, TC6 STREAM ON COMMUNICATION SYSTEMS, THE STATE OF THE ART, August 25–30, 2002 (2002) at 38.

[179] Cisco Systems, Inc. is in the business of selling Internet Protocol based networking and other products related to the communications and IT sectors and provides services associated with their product.

[180] Vinton G. Cerf & Robert E. Kahn, A Protocol for Packet Network Intercommunication, 22 IEEE TRANS. ON COMMS. 1 (1974), available at http://www. cs. princeton. edu/courses/archive /fall06/cos561/papers/ cerf74.pdf (last visited June 29, 2013).

largely a pragmatic assumption to facilitate progress. A key architectural construct was the introduction of gateways (now called routers) between the networks to handle the disparities such as different data rates, packet sizes, error conditions, and interface specifications.

The gateways would also check the destination Internet addresses of each packet to determine the gateway to which it should be forwarded. These functions would be combined with certain end-end functions to produce the reliable communication from source to destination. The TCP/IP protocol suite was developed and refined over a period of four more years and, in 1980, the U.S. Department of Defense adopted it as a standard. On January 1, 1983, the ARPANET converted to TCP/IP as its standard host protocol. Software engineers used routers or gateways to pass packets to and from host computers on "local area networks. Refinement and extension of these protocols and many others associated with them continues to this day by way of the Internet Engineering Task Force.[181]

(E) Repeaters

The strength of wireless networks ranges from poor to excellent depending upon the distance between transmitter antennas. Wireless repeaters amplify a signal once it loses strength or is otherwise attenuated as it is transmitted along a cable network. This repeater takes a signal from a router or access point and rebroadcasts it, creating what is, in effect, a second network. Installers place wireless repeaters in "hot spots" to improve signal range and strength. In a home wireless network, repeaters help extend a signal across a wider area. They both remove noise and solve the problem of attenuation caused by cable loss. A network repeater is a device used to expand the boundaries of a wired or wireless network.[182] "In the past, wired network repeaters were used to join segments of Ethernet cable.[183] The repeaters amplify the data signals before sending them on to the uplinked segment, thereby countering signal decay that occurs over extended lengths of wire."[184]

(F) Cable Modems

In the formative period of the Internet, the telephone was the chief way to connect to the Internet. Cliff Stoll once made fun of the Internet "as a telephone system that's gotten uppity."[185] By the early 1990s, DSL and broadband displaced telephone access to the Internet. A computer user's dialup access begins with the computer modem attached to the customer's computer. A modem modulates the digital data of computers into analog signals, transmittable over telephone lines. It then demodulates or transforms the data back into digital signals ("modulator/demodulator"). Today

---

[181] MICHAEL L. RUSTAD & CYRUS DAFTARY, E-BUSINESS LEGAL HANDBOOK 24 (1st ed. 2000).

[182] "Wireless repeaters extend your wireless network range without requiring you to add any wiring. Just place the wireless repeater halfway between your wireless router, modem router, or access point and your computer, and you can get an instant boost to your wireless signal strength." Microsoft, 10 Tips to Help Improve Your Wireless Network, http://www.microsoft.com/athome/setup/wirelesstips.aspx#fbid= 8YKJOgAoWs7 (last visited June 10, 2013).

[183] "Ethernet now supports high-bandwidth, carrier-grade environments with enhanced granularity at a significantly lower price per bit than traditional technologies. As a result, network operators are expected to shift more of their capital budgets towards purchasing Ethernet-based solutions." CYAN Inc. SEC 424B4 Filing (May 9, 2013).

[184] WiseGeek, What is a Network Repeater? (2013).

[185] Cliff Stoll Quotes, (2013).

Internet users access the Internet using three methods: (1) by smartphones, (2) Wi–Fi, and (3) a broadband connection. Smartphones enable consumers to make phone calls, send text and e-mail messages, surf the Internet, navigate using GPS, and play media files. In 1999, the Internet was able to transmit at a speed of 2.5 Gbps; less than a decade later, software engineers beta tested transmission speeds of more than 10 billion bits (10 Gbps). Comparatively, wireless microwave links, or WiFi, operate at up to 540 million bits per second, while cable modems and digital subscriber lines transmit data at "broadband" speeds of 5 million bits per second (5 Mbps).

(G) Bandwidth

Broadband is a much-expanded pipeline for the transmission of digital data. Today's video, social media, gaming "and enterprise software-as-a-service, are increasingly bandwidth intensive and latency sensitive. For example, according to a June 2012 IDC report, global video captured by device users grew by approximately 15% in 2011 to 9.1 billion gigabytes, to which "3.2 billion gigabytes were recorded on mobile phones, representing a 68% year-over-year increase."[186] "Gartner estimates that revenue from enterprise Ethernet data services is expected to be $20 billion in 2012 and grow to $26 billion in 2016."[187] Thus, high bandwidth is the predicate of fast transmission on the Internet. The basic measurement unit for bandwidth is bits per second ("bps"). To place bandwidth in perspective, the first modems developed in 1958 had a capacity of only 300 bps. Modern modems, using standard telephone lines, have the capacity to transmit data at up to 56 thousand bits per second, or 56 Kbps. In contrast, the Federal Communication Commission ("FCC") classifies broadband speeds as ranging from 200 Kbps, or 200,000 bits per second, to six Mbps, or 6,000,000 bits per second.

(H) DSL

Digital Subscriber Line ("DSL") includes high-speed data transmission of digital data over regular copper telephone wire. DSL features an uninterrupted, high-speed connection directly to an Internet Service Provider ("ISP"). Asymmetrical Digital Subscriber Line ("ADSL") is broadband for principally residential users. ADSL allows faster downstream data transmission over the same line used to provide voice service without disrupting regular telephone calls using that line. Symmetrical Digital Subscriber Line ("SDSL") is a broadband application with equal downstream and upstream traffic speed used by many businesses. "Downstream" refers to data sent from the ISP "down" to the PC; conversely, "upstream" means data transmission from the PC to the ISP

(I) Mobile Devices

Smartphones, such as Google's Android, Apple's iOS, and Blackberry OS to name a few, enable consumers to surf the Internet, answer e-mail, take photographs, and run hundreds of thousands of software applications ("apps").[188] Clearwire, an affiliate of

---

[186] CYAN Inc., SEC 424B4 Filing (May 9, 2013).

[187] Id.

[188] An amicus brief describes the interrelationship of technologies built into smartphone technologies:

The original equipment manufacturer ("OEM") provides the hardware (the mobile phone or tablet); the carrier provides the data connection; and multiple software companies provide the platform and the specific software applications enjoyed by the consumer. Each of the suppliers provides a piece of the process without controlling the whole.

Sprint Nextel, provides a "wireless broadband Internet access service" that is known as the "fourth generation" or "4G," which "merges voice, video and other information into a single wireless platform available to Sprint's end users via their mobile devices such as telephone and smartphones."[189] The fourth generation of cell phones, 4G, features applications such as mobile web access and high-definition mobile television.

Verizon's 4G LTE states that its speed is up to ten times faster than the prior generation, 3G. Smartphones and other devices are rapidly displacing the personal computer as an instrumentality for accessing the Internet. Apple's iPad3 has far more pixels than high definition television. Samsung will be releasing a 4.6–inch smartphone that has a "resolution of 1280x720 pixels with 319 ppi pixel density."[190] This smartphone features an "Android 4.0 operating system" also known as the Ice Cream Sandwich.[191] Android owners downloaded over 10 billion Apps from Google's Android Market, which featured 400,000 Apps by January 2012. Samsung and Apple are the leading contenders in the smartphone market and are currently embroiled in patent litigation, which Chapter 13 covers. Apple's iPad features a 9.7–inch screen and claims to have a million more pixels than HDTV.[192] The iPad enables laptops and other devices to be Internet-enabled. Smartphones typically feature an operating system that gives the device the potential to connect to the Internet, computational power, and location information through its Global Positioning System ("GPS").[193]

Smartphones enable owners to be able to use devices to access the Internet while traveling or outside their homes or offices. Akin to miniature personal computers, mobile devices have operating systems that come with application software that the manufacturers preloads and installs. Application software is a type of software that, at the most basic level is task-oriented. The Barnacle app from the Android market permits a user to tether or share a mobile phone's connection with a laptop.

(J) Mobile Applications

An estimated thirty-five percent of adults in the United States owned smartphones by 2011 exceeding sales of personal computers.[194] These mobile devices can connect to the Internet through wireless connections on fixed networks and through satellite mobile broadband services.[195] The first mobile phones with Internet connectivity arrived in 1999 and by 2008, there were more devices connected to the Internet than there were people on Earth. Mobile phones are displacing browsers to access the Internet in Generation "C" ("Connected"). In 2009, the United Arab Emirates have 232.1 mobile phone subscribers per 100 people, while Russia had 164

Brief of Google, Inc.; Cisco Systems, Inc.; Oracle Corp.; Red Hat Inc.; SAP America Inc.; Symantec Corp.; Xilinx, Inc. as Amici Curiae in Support of Petitioner, Limelight Networks, Inc. v. Akamai Technologies, Inc., Limelight Networks, Inc. v. Akamai Technologies, Inc., 2013 WL 417686 (U.S. Feb. 1, 2013).

[189] Clear Wireless LLC v. Building Dept. of Village of Lynbrook, 2012 WL 826749 (E.D.N.Y. March 8, 2012).

[190] Samsung Galaxy S3 vs. LG Optimus 4X HD: Battle of the Titans, INT'L BUS. TIMES (March 16, 2012).

[191] Id.

[192] Walter S. Mossberg, The iPad: Millions More Pixels than HDTV, WALL ST.J. (March 15, 2012) at D1.

[193] Andrew Charlesworth, The Ascent of Smartphone, ENGINEERING & TECH (Feb. 2009) at 32–33.

[194] Scott R. Peppet, Freedom of Contract in an Augmented Reality: The Case of Consumer Contracts, 59 UCLA L. REV. 676, 678–79 (2012).

[195] Daniel Wagner et al., Pose Tracking From Natural Features on Mobile Phones, PROC. OF THE SEVENTH IEEE INT'L SYMP. ON MIXED & AUGMENTED REALITY 125 (2008).

mobile phones per 100 people in its population.[196] In contrast, Canada ranks first in the world with 108.6 computers per 100 of its population followed by the Netherlands with 103 and Sweden with 102.[197] These hundreds of millions of computers with a connection to the Internet communicate with each other through a set of common software standards known as protocols.

Web devices that access the Internet directly through web devices are displacing browsers for the Generation "C" signifying the connected generation. Eighty-five percent of all American adults own a cell phone and over half of them use their phones to access the Internet. The mobile application marketplace is robust "with more than 1,600 new mobile apps being introduced every day."[198] Applications ("Apps") are computer programs designed to assist users in performing certain tasks. Facebook's $1 billion purchase of Instagram evidences the growing impact of mobile applications as the gateway for Internet access.[199] Instagram, which was designed specifically for mobile Apps, enables Facebook to capture a larger segment of the ever-increasing population of Internet users accessing the Internet via smartphones or other mobile devices. [200] The market value of startup mobile app providers such as Pandora, Millennial Media, and Instagram are valued in billions of dollars. Without being physically connected to a network, the users of mobile applications have the ability to send e-mails, update their calendars, check the weather forecast, access databases, play games, get directions, and make financial transactions, among other productivity functions. Approximately four hundred thousand mobile apps are available to smartphone owners with hundreds more being released daily.[201] Micro social networking services have launched mobile-only private social networking services such as a parents' interest site.[202]

(K) Jailbreaking

Smartphone users downloaded more than six billion apps from Apple's app Store by mid-2010.[203] The iPhone locks in users to the Apple's app Store.[204] Manufacturers will often restrict a user's ability to install new apps from outside of their market place. Some users disable the protection measures in order to be able to use apps from outside of the manufacturer's marketplace. This act of disabling protections, known as "jail breaking," violates Section 1201 of the Digital Millennium Copyright Act ("DMCA") and its anti-circumvention provisions. To deter jail breaking, many manufacturers threaten that a phone, which has been unlocked, voids the warranty.[205] Federal regulators are updating regulations to address mobile phones. The Federal Trade

---

[196] Pocket World in Figures, THE ECONOMIST 92 (2012 ed.).

[197] Id.

[198] Kamala D. Harris, Attorney General, California Justice Department, Privacy on the Go: Recommendations for the Mobile Ecosystem (Jan. 2013) (Message from the Attorney General).

[199] Facebook to Acquire Instagram, FACEBOOK.COM (April 9, 2012).

[200] Spencer E. Ante, Riches in Mobile Ads, Just No Profits, WALL ST. J. (April 17, 2012) at B1.

[201] Remarks of Comm'r Robert M. McDowell, 2010 WL 4154040 (F.C.C., Oct. 21, 2010).

[202] Kidfolio. Sarah Perez, Kidfolio, TECHCRUNCH (April 15, 2012).

[203] Charles Cooper, Apple Revamps iPod Line, UpgradesiTunes, Apple TV, CBSNEWS.COM (Sept. 1, 2010).

[204] Michael K. Cheng, IPhone Jailbreaking Under the DMCA: Towards A Functionalist Approach in Anti-Circumvention, 25 BERKELEY TECH. L. J. 215, 216 (2010).

[205] Timothy J. Maun, Comment, iHack, Therefore iBrick: Cellular Contract Law, The Apple IPhone, and Apple's Extraordinary Remedy for Breach, 2008 WIS. L. REV. 747, 752 (2008).

Commission ("FTC") is proposing that mobile service providers develop improved privacy protection including short, meaningful disclosures.

§ 1.4   SOFTWARE PROTOCOLS THAT POWER THE INTERNET

(A) TCP/IP

The TCP/IP protocol is the most widely used communication system within the Internet, and functions to enable file transfers, e-mail, remote terminal access, and other vital tools of the World Wide Web. The TCP is the data packeting protocol whereas IP is the protocol for routine packets. Each packet has a header containing its source and destination, a block of data content, and an error checking code. A packet is a basic unit of data formatted for transmission on a packet switching computer network. Each TCP/IP packet is comprised of three parts: (1) a header containing its source and destination enabling Internet routers to transport the packet, (2) a body, which contains the payload, or application data, and (3) the tail, with its error checking code. CYAN, Inc. describes modern routing on an Ethernet-based network, which has evolved as the dominant network protocol:

> Ethernet services edge routing, which routes traffic on the edge of the network without accessing routers at the network's core; access aggregation, which aggregates traffic on the edge of the network; metro WDM, or wave-division multiplexing, which allows a single optical fiber to carry multiple optical signals on separate wavelengths; multi-service provisioning platforms, which interconnects with legacy optical equipment and Ethernet local area networks; and packet-optical equipment, which enables the transport of packets on optical network infrastructure. According to ACG Research, markets for these products were forecasted to collectively represent approximately $15.7 billion in worldwide revenue in 2012.[206]

TCP/IP is a two-layer program with the TCP and IP serving different functions. Every computer needs some way to communicate on the Internet and it is usually built into the computer's operating system (e.g. Windows, UNIX, etc.). "The protocol stack used on the Internet is referred to as the TCP/IP protocol stack because of the two major communication protocols used."[207] The TCP's positive acknowledgment system ensures that the Internet functions properly. If the packet does not arrive within a timeout interval, the data is simply retransmitted or rerouted. The receiver employs a sequence of numbers to organize segments in the correct order. "This process not only sequences the packets, but also prevents duplicates. The TCP identifies broken packets by adding extra data, called a checksum, to each segment transmitted, checking it at the receiver, and disposing of damaged segments."[208] The IP component of TCP/IP provides routing from the department to the enterprise network, then to regional networks, and finally to the global Internet. "TCP is responsible for detecting errors or lost data, triggering retransmission until the data is correctly and completely received. TCP/IP is broken down into layers just like all other communications protocols."[209] The higher

---

[206] CYAN, Inc., SEC 424B4 Filing (May 9, 2013).

[207] Rohan Chakraborty, How Does the Internet Work, ROHANGRR (May 6, 2012). 2012/ 05/how-does-Internet-work.html#!/2012/05/how-does-Internet-work.html.

[208] Information Sciences Institute, Transmission Control Protocol (2012).

[209] TCP/IP Tutorial How Does TCP/IP Work? (2012).

packets are transmitted over the Internet, received by a TCP layer, and then reassembled into the original message. The lower layer, Internet Protocol, handles the address part of each packet so that it gets to the correct destination.[210]

(B) FTP & HTTP

(1) FTP

The Internet user accesses web pages through browsers such as Google Chrome, Firefox or Internet Explorer. Proxies consist of communications protocols or sets of rules or standards so computers can exchange information with a minimum of errors. Proxy servers retrieve data from foreign servers and save a copy of it, so repeated requests from different users for the same data do not require accessing the foreign server each time. In this manner, large numbers of users can access a website (that otherwise could not handle the volume of traffic) with only a nominal delay. Such requests are sent using the File Transfer Protocol ("FTP") a standard enabling permits data, and images to be copied and transmitted on the Internet from one machine to another over TCP/IP networks. The downside to FTP is that it sends files as they are, without any extra security or encryption.[211]

(2) HTTP

The Hypertext Transfer Protocol ("HTTP"), developed in 1990, remains an important protocol for transferring application level protocol for distributed, collaborative, and hypermedia information systems. HTTP is a high-level protocol, like FTP, that enables the user to transfer files from one machine to another over TCP/IP networks. In 2008, the W3C released HTTP-1.1, which resolved problems in the original protocol. HTTP interprets and classifies metadata in files, which in turn, enables browsers to exhibit hypertext files as web pages in HTML. HTML5 is a format often employed in mobile game apps. HTML5 WebSockets, for example, will "upgrade the Web architecture to one that works like a telephone with fast, direct connections, rather than a walkie-talkie system that operates on a request and response model."[212]

(3) SFTP

Since 9/11, the federal government is requiring companies to support Simple File Transfer Protocol ("SFTP"), which is a secure FTP implementation incorporating secure shell encryption.[213] The federal government requires contractors and other companies to send data or information using SFTP. The secure FTP or SFTP is a network protocol providing secure file management functionalities over any data stream. In addition to the federal government, a growing number of states are

---

[210] Id.

[211] Encryption raises a host of legal issues. See generally, A. Michael Froomkin, The Metaphor is the Key: Cryptography, the Clipper Chip and the Constitution, 143 U. PA. L. REV. 709 (1995) (discussing legal implications of Clipper Chip and encryption software); Michael Rustad & Lori E. Eisenschmidt, The Commercial Law of Internet Security, 10 HIGH TECH. L.J. 213 (1995) (surveying legal issues surrounding Internet security); Charles L. Evans, Comment, U.S. Export Control of Encryption Software: Efforts to Protect National Security Threaten the U.S. Software Industry's Ability to Compete in Foreign Markets, 19 N.C. J. INT'L L. & COM. REG. 469 (1994) (examining export control of encryption).

[212] TAVANT TECHNOLOGIES AND KAAZING FORM TECHNOLOGY PARTNERSHIP, PROFESSIONAL SERVICES CLOSE–UP (Feb. 26, 2012).

[213] Id.

requiring vendors to use secure FTP or Virtual Private Networks. IBM and other companies have adopted the secure FTP as a condition of doing business with the government.

(C) Microformats & XML

Extensible Markup Language ("XML"), like HTML, is a micro format to transport and store data. XML "is a simple text-based format for representing structured information: documents, data, configuration, books, transactions, invoices, and much more. It was derived from an older standard format called SGML ("ISO 8879"), in order to be more suitable for Web use."[214] The HTML is the visual web format enabling authors to create web pages using a very simple and intuitive programming language. The creator places hypertext links between objects and documents. XML, unlike HTML, allows users to create their own formatting tags and converts data into indexed data. XML is used in "Universal Plug and Play ("UPnP") for home electronics, word processing formats such as ODF and OOXML, graphics formats such as SVG; it is suitable for communication with XMLRPC and Web Services, it is supported directly by computer programming languages and databases, from giant servers all the way down to mobile telephones."[215]

(D) MPEG & MP3

The Motion Picture Expert Group ("MPEG") sets standards for compressing and storing video, audio, and animation in digital form. MPEG developed the MP3 and MP4 highly compressed formats. MPEG–1 is a standard for CD–ROM video whereas MPEG–2 is a standard for full screen, broadcast quality video whereas MPEG–4 is the standard for video telephony. MPEG–1 Audio Layer 3 ("MP3") is a digital audio encoding format. MP3 does not signify the borderland between MPEG–2 and MPEG–4, but is short for MPEG–1, Layer 3 Audio. MP3 is able to compress WAV audio making audio files easily downloadable. CD burners convert MP3s into customized CD tracks.

(E) XML's Metalanguage

XML is a metalanguage for documents enabling users to create custom made tags organizing and delivering content more efficiently. The World Wide Web Consortium conceptualized the three layers as: (1) application rules, (2) Document Type Definition ("DTD"), and (3) XML syntax. "Extensible means that the language is a shell, or skeleton that can be extended by anyone who wants to create additional ways to use XML. Markup means that XML's primary task is to give definition to text and symbols. Language means that XML is a method of presenting information that has accepted rules and formats."[216] One example of how this metalanguage works is explained in an e-tutorial:

> Why bother with a markup metalanguage? Because, as the familiar proverb goes, the W3C wants to teach us how to fish so we can feed ourselves for a lifetime. With XML, there is a standardized way to define markup languages that are customized for different needs, rather than having to rely upon HTML extensions.

---

[214] W3C, Semantic Web (2012).

[215] W3C, What is XML Used For? (2012).

[216] Bryant University, XBRL Educational Resource Center at Bryant University, (last visited June 13, 2013).

Mathematicians need a way to express mathematical notations; composers need a way to present musical scores; businesses want their websites to take sales orders from customers; physicians look to exchange medical records; plant managers want to run their factories from web-based documents. All these groups need an acceptable, resilient way to express these different kinds of information, so that the software industry can develop the programs that process and display these diverse documents.[217]

(F) Application Program Interfaces

Application Program Interfaces ("APIs") are programming instructions that are interface protocols enabling software to access and use other software.[218] A proprietary API is a software library interface "specific to one device or, more likely to a number of devices within a particular manufacturer's product range."[219] APIs can be conceptualized on several levels including operating systems (API for Apple Macs), programming languages (Java), application services (API for SAP), web infrastructure (Amazon Web API), or web services (Twitter's API).[220] Microsoft's operating system has an API that enables application developers to ensure that their apps interact with this computer system. During the formative era of the software industry, developers were able to work with Microsoft's APIs:

Microsoft was one of the most successful companies to exploit their APIs for business advantage. They made massive investments to attract the largest base of application developers to write apps for MS Windows and the Windows API. Once they achieved critical mass, it became a self-reinforcing cycle of customers choosing Windows because of the large selection of apps, which led more developers to write apps on this platform in order to reach the largest possible customer base.[221]

Microsoft's strategic use of its APIs was a central issue in antitrust lawsuits on both sides of the Atlantic. During the EU and U.S. Microsoft antitrust trials, the software mogul's strategic use of APIs was the key smoking gun evidence of anticompetitive conduct. Microsoft freely exposed their APIs to third-party software developers "so they could seamlessly integrate this functionality in their own programs without having to devote time and resources to developing and testing alternative functionality."[222] In the U.S. side of the Microsoft antitrust case, the U.S. Justice Department charged Microsoft with being a monopoly arising out of the way it bundled its Explorer web browser with operating system software.[223] The government's Sherman Act antitrust case was that was that competing web browsers (such as Netscape Navigator) interacted slower and did not work as well with the Microsoft operating system.[224] In

---

[217] OneTutorial.org, Section 15.1: Languages and Metalanguages, (last visited May 13, 2013).

[218] 3Scale Infrastructure for the Web: Your Guide to the Internet, [B]usiness Revolution 4 (2011).

[219] Wikimedia Foundation, Free and Open Software 157 (2013).

[220] 3Scale Infrastructure for the Web, Id. at 5.

[221] Id.

[222] LUCA RUBINI, MICROSOFT ON TRIAL LEGAL AND ECONOMIC ANALYSIS OF A TRANSATLANTIC ANTITRUST CASE 156 n. 51 (2010).

[223] United States v. Microsoft Corporation, 253 F.3d 34 (Fed. Cir. 2001).

[224] In the ensuing DOJ antitrust case against Microsoft, the defendant was accused of abuse of a dominant, near-monopoly position in microcomputer operating systems. Although it is not illegal per se for Microsoft to possess a dominant market share, it is illegal to abuse one's position in . . . The challenge to

addition, prosecutors contended that Microsoft distributed a polluted Java that did not interface well with competing browsers.[225]

The U.S. Justice Department's contention was that Microsoft corrupted its APIs so Internet Explorer worked better than third party web browsers.[226] The federal district court ruled that Microsoft had committed monopolization, attempted monopolization and tying in violation of Sections 1 and 2 of the U.S. Sherman Antitrust Act. The emblem of illegality in tying agreements is the wielding of monopolistic advantage such as when a computer software maker exploits their dominant position in one market to expand into another. Microsoft entered into a consent decree with the U.S. Justice Department in 2001 to settle a claim that their browser and personal computers constituted illegal tying. The consent decree that took effect in 2002 required Microsoft to split its operating system and browser into separate units. As part of the settlement, Microsoft agreed to publish hundreds of APIs that they had previously kept as trade secrets.[227] After the U.S. Justice Department settlement, Microsoft was charged for failing to share APIs, which it agreed to do in the 2001 consent decree.[228]

Today Web servers freely distribute their APIs in order for software developers to customize the way they interact with the service. Thus, APIs enable a level of customization greater than a Common Gateway Interface ("CGI"), which is an older interface.[229] Apache's API is custom designed to enable open source designers to design products that interact with it.[230] APIs serve as a software-to-software interface, not a user interface:

> With APIs, applications talk to each other without any user knowledge or intervention. When you buy movie tickets online and enter your credit card information, the movie ticket Web site uses an API to send your credit card information to a remote application that verifies whether your information is correct. Once payment is confirmed, the remote application sends a response back to the movie ticket Web site saying it's OK to issue the tickets.[231]

Microsoft Windows as a dominant application programming interface (API). LARRY L. DUETSCH, INDUSTRY STUDIES 344 (2002).

[225] Id.

[226] "Microsoft corrupted applications programming interfaces (APIs) to . . . competing providers of work group server operating systems to 'viably stay on the market.'" KATARZNA CZAPRACKA, INTELLECTUAL PROPERTY AND THE LIMITS OF ANTITRUST: A COMPARATIVE STUDY OF U.S. AN E.U. APPROACHES 56 (2010).·

[227] Microsoft published "hundreds of new, previously secret Windows 2000 and Windows XP APIs later this month, royalty free. About 100 proprietary communication protocols will also be disclosed but available to competitors and others for a licensing fee." Paula Rooney, Microsoft To Publish 385 Windows APIs, Protocols To Make Antitrust Case Go Away, CRN, (Aug. 25, 2002) (Microsoft released last week Windows 2000 Service Pack 3 and plans to release Windows XP Service Pack 1 in late August or mid-September. Both service packs offer compliance with the decree by making changes to the Windows user interface that makes it easier for users to remove Microsoft middleware and add and use competitive middleware from AOL, RealNetworks and others").

[228] In 2007, the European Commission fined Microsoft 3 million euros per day for failure to provide proper documentation for its APIs. Similarly, a class action of Microsoft users and developers in Iowa charged that the software giant failed to disclose APIs to them. Associated Press, Microsoft Antitrust Plaintiffs Allege Misconduct Over Lack of API Sharing (Jan. 19, 2007) (discussing EU and Iowa cases).

[229] MARK DOWD, JOHN MCDONALD, JUSTIN SCHUH, THE ART OF SOFTWARE SECURITY ASSESSMENT: IDENTIFYING AND PREVENTING SOFTWARE VULNERABILITIES 24 (2006) (discussing European commission's case charging Microsoft with abusing its dominant position).

[230] Id.

[231] Dave Ross, How Things Works, How to Leverage an API for Conferencing (2013).

Software developers use APIs so that their computer programs can interact with Google's AdWords server.[232] Cloud providers have APIs that permit their customers to access software applications, store data, or process it.[233] Mashups, too, depend upon APIs so developers can interact with web services.[234] The Internet of things such as automobiles, refrigerators, and thermostats also depends upon APIs, which "revolution the way humans and machines interact. . ."[235]

(G) Web 1.0 & 2.0

(1) Web 1.0: The Asynchronous Internet

Web 1.0 corresponds to the "passive" Internet, where forums and bulletin boards were the exclusive way to post information. Dave Barry, writing about Web 1.0, asked, "What, exactly, is the Internet? Basically it is a global network exchanging digitized data in such a way that any computer, anywhere, that is equipped with a device called a "modem", can make a noise like a duck choking on a kazoo."[236] Web 1.0 had little by way of interactivity other than users sharing files, writing in guest books, and posting comment forms. Under Web 1.0, the owner of the website was the one and only publisher and communications were asynchronous, that is independent of time and place.

(2) Web 2.0: The Synchronous Internet

Web 2.0 describes the contemporary WWW as interactive, individuated, and user generated. Web 2.0 launched a "social revolution," transforming the Internet from a content based forum to one based upon social interactivity. Web 2.0 users connect through blogs, social networks; Wikis are an example of a Web 2.0 project that allows users to work collaboratively. User generated content continues to be the watchword of the Web 2.0 with the rise of social media and micro blogging. Web 2.0 increases the scope of synchronous communications, such as online chats, audio, or video.

(H) Web 3.0's Ontology Language

The Internet is no longer primarily about listservs or non-interactive bulletin board for posting information. RDF is a standardized language of the web, which enables computer systems to infer or extrapolate relationships between databases and computer users. The Web 3.0 language fashions the multi-tier representation behind a web page using Universal Resource Identifiers. Web 3.0 will continue to evolve but it will not entirely displace Web 2.0. Web 3.0 designers fashion the multi-tier representation behind a web page using Universal Resource Identifiers. The semantic web is beginning to advance out of Web 2.0 formats of XML tagging, folksonomies, and

---

[232] HENRY H. LIU, SOFTWARE PERFORMANCE AND SCALABILITY: A QUANTITATIVE APPROACH 1–43 (2011).

[233] "Cloud and mobile computing APIs are used to build applications and *software* that operate in the cloud or on mobile devices. These APIs expose the functionality provided by the service provider and provisioning, management, orchestration." MANO PAUL, SEVEN QUALITIES OF HIGHLY SECURE SOFTWARE 115 (2012).

[234] "The development of mashups is supported by the gradually growing number of web *APIs* offered by a variety of companies. An API provides an easy way for a programmer to create new *programs*, which use services or data provided by web companies. LEV MANOVICH, SOFTWARE TAKES COMMAND 190 (2013).

[235] Sara Reiner, The Internet of Things: How Humans and Machines Interact Thanks to APIs, mashery.com (Jan. 10, 2013).

[236] Dave Barry Quotes, search@quotes (2012).

microformats to the computer readable format of RDF and OWL. The RDF is layered on top of the HTML and other WWW protocols:

> RDF gives meaning to data through sets of "triples." Each triple resembles the subject, verb, and object of a sentence. For example, a triple can assert, "person X" [subject] "is a sister of" [verb] "person Y" [object]. A series of triples can determine that [car X] [is brand] [Toyota]; that [car X] [condition is] [used]; that [car X] [costs] [$7,500]; that [car X] [is located in] [Lenox]; and that [Lenox] [is located in] [Western Massachusetts].[237]

This triple structure enables Internet users to yield far more focused searches. The W3C describes the semantic web as the use of common formats for integration and combinations of data. Web 1.0 was about the exchange of documents whereas Web 3.0 or the semantic web enables a person to "move through an unending set of databases, which are connected not by wires but by being about the same thing."[238] Wright State University owns a patent on Twitris a "semantic web application designed to draw collective meaning about major events from huge numbers of public messages as they are posted on the Internet via Twitter."[239]

The website dishtip.com uses Web 3.0 technologies "to aggregate and analyze unstructured web content to provide over 1 million specific restaurant dish recommendations."[240] Crowdsourcing is a Web 3.0 term "used for a service that allows users to pool their collective knowledge."[241] The evolving Web 3.0 consists of three primary components: IDs, New Web Standards, and Ontology:

> *IDs.* Machines need a unique, consistent way to identify a thing or concept. For example, if I mention "Bill Clinton," how does a machine know that this is the same person as President William Jefferson Clinton? People can usually tell by context, but a machine needs that unique identifier.

> *New web standards.* Web 1.0 and 2.0 were built on standards like HTML, XML, and CSS. Some new standards have been developed specifically for expressing metadata and metadata relationships. Standards such as RDF, OWL, SKOS and Dublin Core are used to define metadata in a machine readable way.

> *Ontology.* These shared classifications, relationships and logic will allow machines to integrate distinct data sets and extrapolate new, unexpected information from stated information. Think of it as a hyper-glossary.[242]

Web 3.0 creates a need to accommodate personal jurisdiction tests and the meaning of purposeful availment to cyberspace, a topic addressed in Chapter 3.[243]

---

[237] Nigel Shadbolt & Tim Berners–Lee, Web Science Emerges, SCIENTIFIC AMERICAN (Oct. 2008) at 79.

[238] W3C, Semantic Web Activity (2008).

[239] Dave Larson, Wright State Wins Patent for Computing Project, DAYTON DAILY NEWS (March 7, 2012).

[240] Destination.news, Food AirGuideOnline.com (Jan. 16, 2012).

[241] Id.

[242] Rachel Lovinger, Web 3.0 is on its Way: Why Should You Care? MASS HIGH TECH (Sept. 26, 2008) at 1.

[243] See e.g., Williams v. Adver. Sex, No. 1:05CV51, 2007 WL 2570182, at *6 (N.D. W. Va. 2007) (applying purposeful availment test to cyberspace); See generally, A. Benjamin Spencer, Jurisdiction and the Internet: Returning to Traditional Principles to Analyze Network–Mediated Contacts, 2006 U. ILL. L. REV. 71, 96.

Courts will need to rethink the meaning of interactivity of a website, which has long been a test for determining personal jurisdiction.

§ 1.5   WORLD WIDE WEB APPLICATIONS

(A) Search Engines

Google also provides diverse products and services including e-mail through its Gmail service, online video through YouTube.com, and a blogging tool through Blogger Google, Bing, Yahoo!, Ask, America Online, and MyWebSearch are among the most popular search engines in the United States according to an eBiz/MBA survey assessing Alexa Global Traffic rankings. Google is by far the leading U.S. Internet search engine with an estimated 900 million monthly users.[244] Google's search engine retrieves websites relevant to a search term as well as sponsored links. Microsoft's search engine, Bing, which changed its name from MSN search in 2009, is in second place. The World Wide Web hit popular culture like a tidal wave just at the time search engines gave ordinary Americans easy access to the Internet. "Search engines commonly compete for users by expanding the database that they search in response to requests or, at least, optimizing the database that their target user audience wants to search."[245] "In this regard, the critical objective is not just to give searchers the most complete results, but, even more important, to enable searchers to find information they seek most quickly, by placing it near the top of the list of search results."[246] Search engines have three parts:

> a database of copied web pages, a system for identifying additional web pages to add to the database, and software that determines what pages from its database should be identified in response to a given search request by an Internet user, in what order, and how those pages should be displayed. Each search engine uses a proprietary formula, or algorithm, to rank the "relevance" of web pages to the search terms selected by the search engine's users.[247]

When I wish to listen to my son's music, I can access it by typing the keywords, "James Rustad," and "music" into my browser. The web browser uses a search engine to locate all web pages on the Internet containing these keywords. Users can download and listen to performances by James Rustad and learn about his latest gigs at www.jamesrustad.com. Search engines such as Google create lists of websites corresponding to the searched phrase, "James Rustad." "These lists allow the search engine to provide faster searches, because the sites are all cataloged in the search engine's memory which negates the need to access the web to compile search results."[248]

---

[244] Perfect 10, Inc. v. Amazon.com, Inc., 487 F.3d 701, 711 (9th Cir. 2007) ("Google operates a search engine, a software program that automatically accesses thousands of websites (collections of webpages) and indexes them within a database stored on Google's computers. When a Google user accesses the Google website and types in a search query, Google's software searches its database for websites responsive to that search query. Google then sends relevant information from its index of websites to the user's computer. Google's search engines can provide results in the form of text, images, or videos.").

[245] Public Citizen Amicus Brief in Rosetta Stone Ltd. v. Google, Inc., 2010 U.S. 4th Cir. Briefs (2011).

[246] Id.

[247] Id.

[248] Healthcare Advocates, Inc. v. Harding, Earley, Follmer & Frailey, 497 F. Supp. 2d 627, 631 (E.D. Pa. 2007).

(1) Google's Global Search Engine

In 1996, Stanford University graduate students Larry Page and Sergey Brin developed BackRub, a new search engine that morphed into Google, the operator of the most popular Internet search engine.[249] Google launched Google Groups in 2001, and in that same year, Google made its services available in twenty-six different languages.[250] "Using Google's website, a person searching for the website of a particular entity in trade (or simply for information about it) can enter that entity's name or trademark into Google's search engine and launch a search."[251] Google's links are presented in descending relevance based on its proprietary algorithms. In 2000, Google released its Google Toolbar and its new AdWords program. AdWords enabled keyword targeting and a feature that tracked its online performance.

Google released the Google Toolbar in 2000. By 2002, Google launched Google News with 4,000 news services. That year Google's AdWords program was still in its infancy, with only 350 customers. The next year, Google developed Google Print—a service that later became Google Books. In 1994, Google developed Google Local that later became Google Maps. In 1995, Google's index of websites reached the milestone of 8 billion smites, and Google Image indexed 1.1 billion images. Google is making plans in 2013 to become the leading web television provider.

(2) Browser Wars

For much of the 1990s, Netscape Navigator and Internet Explorer dominated the browser marketplace. During the past decade, the browser has lost ground to smartphones and other intelligent devices. Web devices that access the Internet directly through web devices are displacing browsers for the Generation "C" signifying the connected generation. Today the browser wars are largely between Microsoft's Internet Explorer, Google's Chrome, Mozilla's Firefox5, Apple's Safari, and Opera. Marc Andreessen, the developer of the first browser, predicted that "computers would dispense with feature-heavy operating systems . . . [and] would use a browser to run programs over the network," which is what has happened with Google Chrome OS.[252] Firefox5's Full Zoom capacity gives users the ability to view web pages up close. Mozilla Corporation administers Firefox, which is a multi-user collaborative community of software coders and users.

Mozilla administers Firefox, which is an open source browser, improved by a multi-user collaborative community of software coders and users. "The most important feature in Firefox 4 and 5 is Sync. Sync now smoothly syncs a user's Bookmarks, Passwords, Preferences, History, and Tabs not only with other computers, but also with your Android version of Firefox."[253] A new generation of browsers integrates Facebook, Twitter, and other social media. The RockMelt Web browser, for example,

---

[249] Google, Company History, 1995–1997 About Google (2012), http://www. google.com/about/company/history/#1995–1997.

[250] Google, Company History, 2001 About Google (2012), http://www.google.com/about/company/history/#1995–1997.

[251] Rescuecom Corp. v. Google, Inc., 562 F.3d 123, 125 (2d Cir. 2009).

[252] The Man Who Knows What's Next, WIRED (May 2012) at 165.

[253] Seth Rosenblatt, Mozilla Firefox: A Newer Version of Mozilla Firefox is Available, CNET.COM (June 20, 2011).

makes it possible to be connected to Facebook and other social media while surfing.[254] Mozilla claims 450,000,000 Firefox users.

(B) Voice Over Internet Protocol

The term "IP telephony" includes Voice Over Internet Protocol ("VoIP") VoIP and Fax over IP services, including transmission on private IP-based networks as well as the Internet. IP telephony connects PCs and Internet-based telephones through remote voice gateways. VoIP has advantages in cost and flexibility for long distance services.[255] VoIP uses the Internet and its TCP/IP network to transmit telephone signals rather than using public switched telephone networks. Millions of users around the world use Skype, which offers VoIP service to Android and Java-enabled phones, and Intel-based Mobile Internet Devices.[256] VoIP communicates "voice" encoded as data packets and data streams simultaneously.

The Federal Communications Commission's ("FCC") rules define interconnected VoIP as "a service that: (1) enables real-time, two-way voice communications; (2) requires a broadband connection from the user's location; (3) requires Internet protocol-compatible customer premises equipment ("CPE"); and (4) permits users generally to receive calls that originate on the public switched telephone network and to terminate calls to the public switched telephone network."[257] Traditional networks, in contrast, communicate a single signal at a time. In 2012, the FCC widened its outage reporting requirements from traditional telephone services to VoIP service providers. The FCC reasoned this was necessary because consumers would rely upon emergency 911 services while using VoIP.[258] The FCC is considering further regulation of VoIP as noted in the following SEC filing:

> The use of the public Internet and private Internet protocol networks to provide voice communications services, including VoIP, has been largely unregulated within the United States. To date, the FCC has not imposed regulatory surcharges or most forms of traditional common carrier regulation upon providers of Internet communications services, although it has ruled that VoIP providers must contribute to the USF. The FCC has also imposed obligations on providers of two-way interconnected VoIP services to provide E911 service, and it has extended CALEA obligations to such VoIP providers. The FCC has also imposed on VoIP providers the obligation to "port" customers' telephone numbers when customers switch carriers and desire to retain their numbers. As a provider of interconnected VoIP services, we will bear costs because of these various mandates. The FCC may determine that certain types of Internet telephony should be regulated like basic interstate communications services. The FCC's pending review of intercarrier

---

[254] RockMelt Boosts Facebook, Twitter Integration, COMMWEB (May 7, 2011).

[255] Clark v. Time Warner Cable, 523 F.3d 1110, 1112 (9th Cir. 2008).

[256] See Oracle Am., Inc. v. Google Inc., 2012 U.S. Dist. LEXIS 75896 *11 (N.D. Ca., May 30, 2012) ("Java was developed by Sun, first released in 1996, and has become one of the world's most popular programming languages and platforms. The Java platform, through the use of a virtual machine, enables software developers to write programs that are able to run on different types of computer hardware without having to rewrite them for each different type. Programs that run on the Java platform are written in the Java language. Java was developed to run on desktop computers and enterprise servers.").

[257] 47 C.F.R. § 9.3.

[258] K.C. Halm and James W. (Jim) Tomlinson, FCC Extends Outage Reporting Requirements to Interconnected VoIP Providers, REPORT BY DAVIS, WRIGHT, TREMAINE, LLP (Feb. 28, 2012).

compensation policies (discussed above) also may have an adverse impact on enhanced service providers. In a series of decisions issued in 2004, the FCC clarified that the FCC, not the state public utility commissions, has jurisdiction to decide the regulatory status of IP-enabled services, including VoIP.[259]

In 2004, the FCC issued an order preempting traditional telephone company regulation of VoIP service by the Minnesota Public Utility Commission.[260] The FCC reasoned that the VOIP service is not conductive to a bright-line between interstate and intrastate communications without negating federal rules and policies.[261] The FCC acknowledged that other aspects of VoIP and Internet telephony services, "such as regulations relating to the confidentiality of data and communications, copyright issues, taxation of services, and licensing, may be subject to federal or state regulation."[262] In November 2011, the FCC adopted intercarrier compensation rules under which all traffic, including VoIP–PSTN traffic, ultimately will be subject to a bill-and-keep framework.[263]

(C) Web Portals

The term "web portal" signifies the entry point for web browsers. A portal is the initial page that loads when a user starts up their web browser. Web portal was first used to describe the homepage of ISPs such as Yahoo!, Excite, MSN, Netscape NetCenter, and AOL where users begin their web surfing. Portals such as iGoogle typically provide e-mail, news, shopping, finance, sports, music, television, weather, and countless other sources of information. Google is a portal on steroids with its websites tailored to particular audiences such as enterprises or non-profit organizations. Hardly a week goes by when Google does not announce some new application or service. In 2002, Google launched Google News with initially a treasure trove of 4,000 news services. The next year Google developed Google Print, a service that prefigured into Google Books. In December of 2010, Google released Google eBooks, its "digital bookselling platform."[264]

In May of 2008, Google unveiled Google Health, enabling users to upload and store medical records. With Google Health, consumers have password protection and can access medical records from anywhere. Google has more than 450,000 applications available and by early 2012, registered 10 billion downloads. In February 2012, Google launched *Google Chrome Beta* for Android 4.0 devices. A month later, Google launched a new controversial privacy policy, which aggregates personally identifiable information stored on its applications.[265] Today, Google has evolved as an Internet portal preferred by two out of three Internet users worldwide.

Google's Glass is an optical head-mounted display ("OHMD") that allows the user to take photographs or videos and conduct searches on the Internet hands-free through

---

[259] A.R.C. Networks, SEC S-1/A Filing (June 5, 2013).

[260] Id.

[261] Id.

[262] Id.

[263] Id.

[264] Jason Kincaid, Good Acquires eBook Technologies, TECHCRUNCH (Jan. 12, 2011), 2011/01/12/ google-acquires-ebook-technologies/.

[265] Kang Ye-won, Google's New Privacy Policy Rekindles Privacy Debate, KOREAN TIMES (March 4, 2012).

natural language commands.[266] Glass is a wearable computer with an optical format that can communicate with the Internet by natural language voice commands. The speech recognition software in the OHMD is sophisticated much like having a smartphone sitting on the user's face that responds to voice commands. For example, when the user says, "take a picture" or "make a video," Glass obeys the voice command. Users of Glass can speak to send messages and its software will translate what they say into different languages. An OHMD enables a traveler to purchase a kilo of pickled herring by interacting with the Swedish clerk in their native language. A Glass user might ask for directions to Boston's Museum of Fine Arts and they will receive turn-by-turn directions as they walk to destination. The user might ask a question such as how do you say pasta in Swahili and Glass translates it. A Suffolk University Law Professor uses the OHMD in the classroom, enabling students to text questions to him while he is lecturing.[267] A filmmaker wearing an OHMD recorded "footage of two men in a fight, with some shouts of "get him!" and a shirtless man being led off in handcuffs. He later posted the video to YouTube, writing in the post that the "video is proof that Google Glass will change citizen journalism forever!"—and causing many to speculate about the video's privacy implications."[268] Glass raises unique questions of privacy because it is a technology that can be worn 24/7 recording everything in its path. Legislatures will need to update distracted driving laws to encompass Glass devices. Tort lawyers will undoubtedly form practice groups to address the liability issues arising out of accident committed by distracted Glass users.

(D) E–Mail

E-mail is one-to-one messaging from computer to computer. E-mail relies on an address scheme specific to computer networks relying on packet switching and just-in-time reassembling at delivery. Sending an e-mail to Michael Rustad at Suffolk University Law School requires the sender to type mrustad@suffolk.edu in the address line. "Mrustad" isolates the specific user, Michael Rustad. The "at" symbol or @, first proposed in 1971 as a protocol, continues to be used in e-mail addresses. The @ symbol is the connector of the specific e-mail recipient with the latter part of the address. This part of the e-mail address represents the computer network on which Michael Rustad is a member. "Suffolk" in mrustad@suffolk.edu signifies Michael Rustad has an affiliation with Suffolk University; the .edu suffix identifies Suffolk as an educational institution. Similarly, the most popular endings of e-mail addresses in the United States are .com, .edu, .mil, .net, .org, and .gov, but domain name registrants may also register names ending with .aero, .biz, .com, .coop, .info, .museum, .name, .net, or .pro. ICANN launched new generic top-level domains ("gTLDS") in 2013. Although social media sites, such as Facebook, have centralized and integrated various communicative avenues, according to a recent study e-mail is still the more popular means of Internet communication.[269]

---

[266] Google Glass, What It is? (2013) (last visited July 9, 2013).

[267] Jordan Graham, Suffolk Prof Relishes Role as 'Explorer' in Visual Frontier, Boston Herald (July 19, 2013).

[268] Google Glass Captures Arrest on Camera, Sparks Controversy, HUFFINGTON POST (July 8, 2013).

[269] Todd Wasserman, E–Mail Is More Popular Than Social Media, MASHABLE SOCIAL MEDIA (March 27, 2012).

§ 1.6   SOCIAL NETWORKS

Social network sites ("SNS") enable users to create profiles, upload photos and videos, and connect with others. Social media creates an entirely new paradigm in the history of the World Wide Web. "E-mail led to instant messaging, which has led to social networks such as Facebook . . . and the emergence of user generated portals."[270] Digital natives coming to age in the new millennium are conversant in the digital language of computers, video games, and the Internet. LinkedIn has evolved into a multi-purpose site: "Social network, news aggregator, personal branding platform, networkers' paradise."[271] LinkedIn, for example, builds employment or prospective employment networks among law students, faculty, graduates, and other contacts. LinkedIn, Facebook, Twitter, and other social media are displacing "business cards for keeping track of important contacts."[272] Digital natives use SNS to form new connections melding real space and digital in a 24/7 social environment.[273] Klout is a social media site that computes a social media's Klout score, or online influence on a scale from "1 to 100" based on their social media connections.[274] Just as Google ranks web page relevance, Klout "is on a mission to rank the influence of every person online."[275]

Nearly one in two of the most popular SNSs launched after 2005. SNS, sometimes-called social media, typically enable users to create unique personal profiles online in order to interact with friends or business associates. Two-thirds of the world's online population regularly uses social networking sites. SNSs began to evolve in the mid-1990s but reached their takeoff point in the second decade of the twenty-first century. Social media sites are enrolling hundreds of millions of new users around the world. YouTube, a video-sharing service, was created in 2005 and allowed users to upload, share, and watch videos. In addition to YouTube, Facebook, Twitter, Flickr, Second Life, and delicious, hundreds of other social media sites enabled persons of diverse interests to share their interests with others around the world. Facebook is available in seventy languages; it qualifies as a global multilingual business.[276] By 2009, Facebook built an online community of 350 million members around the world. Facebook claims 1.06 billion users and is by far the largest social network.[277]

"Social media has toppled governments, changed the way people interact, and altered our modes of communication. Facebook is the undisputed social networking giant only eight years after it was launched in 2004."[278] In May of 2013, Yahoo!

---

[270] Nigel Shadbolt and Tim Berners–Lee, Web Science Emerges, SCIENTIFIC AMERICAN 76 (Oct. 2008).

[271] Haydn Shaughnessy, How to Power Your Professional Networking Through LinkedIn, FORBES (March 29, 2012).

[272] Social Networks, Nimble Contact Integrates Connections Across Mail, COMMWEB (May 20, 2011).

[273] John Palfrey & Urs Gasser, BORN DIGITAL: UNDERSTANDING THE FIRST GENERATION OF DIGITAL NATIVES (2008) (coining the term digital natives to refer to those who have grown up with the Internet versus older persons who have had to learn how to adapt to online culture).

[274] Seth Stevenson, Popularity Counts, WIRED (May 2012) at 120.

[275] Id.

[276] Statistics, FACEBOOK, de fault.aspx?NewsAreaId=22 (last visited Aug. 10, 2012).

[277] Pingdom, Pinterest Beats Facebook in Number of Users in Minutes, PINGDOM.COM (Feb. 26, 2013). http://royal.pingdom.com/2013/02/26/pinterest-users-per-employee/ (last visited May 25, 2013).

[278] Steven Johnson, The Facebook Juggernaut, WIRED (June 2012) at 116.

purchased Tumblr, a social media site with more than 100 million users.[279] By 2012, Pinterest, a virtual bulletin board where users "pin" images from the Internet, claimed "over 10.4 million registered users, 9 million monthly Facebook-connected users, and 2 million daily Facebook users."[280] By March of 2013, the number of Pinterest users skyrocketed to 40 million users.[281] Pinterest is a growing number of criminal prosecutions find "smoking gun" evidence on social networking sites. In *United States v. Kettle*,[282] the defendant placed a link on his Facebook page to a YouTube video of himself in which he is seen throwing large amounts of money on the floor. "The video itself was not admitted, but a private chat between [the defendant] and one of his friends after he posted the video link was admitted. In the chat, the friend states: "Dat money fake on dem videos." Kettles responds: "I know that."[283]

In *United States v. Williams*,[284] the police uncovered three syringes and a spoon in the defendant's motel room enabled by his girlfriend's posting "a picture to Facebook with the caption 'up partying all night long.'"[285] The evidence in the Facebook posting was the "smoking gun" that sustained a finding that the defendant manufactured methamphetamine at the motel. The photograph depicted all of the materials necessary to manufacture methamphetamine and these illegal materials were found in the defendant's motel room after a police search. The police and prosecutors routinely search Facebook and other social media to investigate crimes in the twenty-first century. Social media is evidence and increasingly the venue for smoking gun photographs or postings.[286] Hundreds of social network sites with hundreds of millions of users have evolved in less than a decade. Social media lawsuits are skyrocketing in diverse substantive fields.[287]

---

[279] Joann S. Lublin, Amir Efrati, & Spencer E. Ante, Yahoo! Deal Shows Power Shift: Tumblr Commands $1.1 Billion Price as Web Giants Circle Fast–Growing Startups, THE WALL STREET J (May 20, 2013) at 1.

[280] Josh Constine, Where the Ladies Are, TECH CRUNCH (Feb. 11, 2012).

[281] Pingdom, Pinterest Beats Facebook in Number of Users in Minutes (Feb. 26, 2013). http://royal.pingdom. com/2013/02/26/pinterest-users-per-employee/ (last visited May 25, 2013).

[282] 2013 Fed. App. 0287N (6th Cir. 2013).

[283] Id. at *1.

[284] 2013 U.S. App. LEXIS 5890 (4th Cir. March 25, 2013).

[285] Id. at *20.

[286] See e.g., Wright v. City of Los Angeles, 2013 WL 1385703 (Cal. Super. March 26, 2013)(noting that Facebook postings of police office supervisors were introduced by African–American police officer in lawsuit against the City of Los Angeles for a hostile work environment based on racial harassment, in violation of the California Fair Employment and Housing Act, where jury awarded the plaintiff $1,200,000); Williams vs. Leading Edge Aviation Services Inc., 2013 WL 1898804 (Cal. Super. Feb. 11, 2013) (defending against racial discrimination with evidence that the plaintiff made derogatory comments about Hispanics on Facebook); Big Cat Rescue Corp. v. Big Cat Rescue Entm't Group, 2013 WL 3339369 (M.D. Fla. Feb. 11, 2013) (defending against trademark infringement case by asserting that plaintiff made defamatory postings on postings and tortious interfered with its contracts); Lewis v Rapp, 2013 WL 940220 (N.C. Super. Jan. 1, 2013)(stating that defendant "posted a blog entry on Carolina Talk Network and on Facebook, which was entitled 'Dirty Politics by the Good Ol Boys. The post not only criticized Rabon, but also stated that plaintiff's endorsement violated the state's judicial conduct code."); FLIR Sys. v. Sierra Media, 2012 WL 7964335 (D. Or. Dec. 19, 2012)(contending that plaintiff's video was aired on YouTube, Facebook and other social media sites and that Fluke had threatened it with litigation for trademark infringement regarding its use of the phrase 'IR Fusion').

[287] Armstrong v. Shirvell, 2012 WL 4059306 (E.D. Mich. Aug. 16, 2012) (stating that defendant in stalking and defamation case started a Facebook blog defaming University of Michigan student body president); Ebersole v. Kline-Perry, 2012 WL 6839462 (E.D. Va., July 25, 2012) (stating, "defendant Bridget Kline-Perry, a Virginia horse breeder, began posting statements about plaintiff on Facebook and other social media outlets. Defendant also reportedly sent emails to numerous individuals, including German Shepherd

Trademark wars are increasingly fought in social media site trenches. A Vermont folk artist used social media extensively to gain popular support after Chik-fil-A sued him claiming his "T-shirt business built around the phrase 'Eat more kale' allegedly infringed on the restaurant chain's 'Eat more chikin' slogan.'"[288] Smaller companies sued by large trademark owners use social network sites to enlist popular support, sometimes shaming the more established company into dropping their demands.[289] By portraying a trademark dispute as David v. Goliath on social media, the smaller trademark company gains leverage not possible in print media. Social media websites are also the venue for protracted cybertort cases such as the lawsuit filed by a former Cincinnati Bengals cheerleader against the gossip website, TheDirty.com. In that case, a poster allegedly defamed Sarah Jones, the cheerleader, claiming that she had sex with all of the members of the NFL team. One of the postings on TheDirty.com stated:

> Nik, here we have Sarah J, captain cheerleader of the playoff bound cinci Bengals. Most ppl see Sarah has [sic] a gorgeous cheerleader AND high school teacher. Yes she's also a teacher . . . but what most of you don't know is. . . . Her ex Nate . . . cheated on her with over 50 girls in 4 yrs. In that time he tested positive for Chlamydia Infection and Gonorrhea. . . so im sure Sarah also has both . . . what's worse is he brags about doing sarah in the gym . . . football field . . . her classroom at the school where she teaches at DIXIE Heights.[290]

Jones filed a Second Amended Complaint alleging claims for defamation, libel per se, false light publicity, and intentional infliction of emotional distress against the website and its operator.[291] In a retrial, a Kentucky jury held the website operator liable for $338,000 in damages for malicious posting anonymous defamatory statements.[292] The Kentucky lower court decision is a rare victory for plaintiffs against third party intermediaries as websites, generally shielded by Section 230 of the Communications Decency Act, a topic that Chapter 6 covers in depth.

(A) YouTube: Broadcast Yourself

YouTube is the largest music video sharing site allowing anyone with Internet access to sign up for an account. A family, for instance, might post a video of a child's soccer game in California so grandparents may view it in Illinois. Similarly, "young writers might write film, produce their own television show, and broadcast the episodes in serial form online, as in the case of the show lonelygirll5," which drew millions of viewers on YouTube[293] A video posted on YouTube about Joseph Kony, a ruthless Ugandan resistance leader who abducts children to serve as soldiers and sex slaves, was viewed more than 26 million times on YouTube and 12 million more times on Vimeo.[294]

---

owners who were longtime customers of plaintiff's kennel."). Evans vs. The Millard Group Inc., 2011 WL 7006556 (Cal. Superior, Sept 16, 2011) (use of Facebook evidence to impeach plaintiff in negligence case).

[288] Social Media Puts West Sixth, Magic Hat in the Court of Public Opinion, Kentucky.com, May 25, 2013) (discussing role of social media in trademark case pitting Vermont's Magic Hat brewery versus West Sixth).

[289] Id.

[290] Jones v. Dirty World Entertainment Recordings, LLC, 766 F.Supp.2d 828, 830–31 (E.D. Ky. 2011).

[291] Id. at 831.

[292] WLWT.com, Jury Reaches Verdict in Sarah Jones Case (July 11, 2013), (last visited Aug. 1, 2013).

[293] Doe v. Geller, 533 F. Supp. 2d 996, 1001 (N.D. Cal. 2008).

[294] Ethan Zuckerman UnPacks "Kony 2012." The Berkman Center for Internet and Society, Harvard University (March 9, 2012).

Internet visitors viewed Kony video more than 100 million times in a single week in August 2012. YouTube videos are increasingly evidence and sometimes smoking guns in court cases. Courts mentioned YouTube in thirty-two state and federal cases as of September 22, 2008. By March 16, 2012, federal and state courts referenced YouTube in more than 400 cases. Law enforcement officials routinely search YouTube and other social media in their criminal investigations. In March 2010, for example, law enforcement officials began an investigation of an individual using a YouTube.com account to share sexually explicit materials involving underage girls.[295] YouTube is an example of a social media website that disrupts extant law as to content regulation, intellectual property, cybertorts, and other substantive areas of the law.

(B) Second Life & Virtual Worlds

An avatar is a computer user's representation of himself/herself or an alter ego. Courts have yet to decide whether avatars Second Life, a virtual world created by Linden Research, enables "users to create three-dimensional environments, animated avatars and other creatures" enabled by Linden Scripting Language" software. Second Life has millions of users and many create avatars or virtual personalities, interacting in three-dimensional cities. Judge Richard A. Posner even made an appearance in Second Life as a "balding, bespectacled cartoon" who taught copyright law, the law of terrorism, and other topics to fellow animated characters including humanoid animals, supermodels, and intermittent fireballs.[296] Courts have yet to decide whether avatars in Second Life or other virtual worlds can defame a living person, commit trade libel, or infringe intellectual property rights of famous companies. Avatars representing celebrities such NBA stars may appropriate their identity thus infringing their right of publicity. Millions of users produced copyrightable Second Life creations. Second Life attempts to replicate many interactions users have in real life. Virtual worlds are "sophisticated pieces of software that enable their users to project an identity into a generated three-dimensional reality through the use of advanced computer graphics and—through the eyes of this digital persona or avatar—interact with other players and wander through this computer-generated reality."[297]

The DMCA's notice and takedown policies extended to Second Life in *Amaretto Ranch Breedables v. Ozimals, Inc.*[298] The lawsuit between the creators of the virtual bunnies and virtual horses has its origins in the three-dimensional world of cyberspace. Amaretto Ranch Breedables opened its virtual horse business in Second Life in September 2010. The Amaretto team created and sold these "animated, virtual digital animal and associated products in its virtual store in Second Life."[299] Prior to opening the Amaretto Ranch in Second Life, the creators consulted with Ozimals who already had a thriving virtual bunnies business in Second Life.[300] Ozimals' creators

---

[295] United States v. Doe (In re Grand Jury Subpoena), 2012 U.S. App. LEXIS 3894 (11th Cir. Feb. 22, 2012).

[296] See Bragg v. Linden Research, Inc., 487 F. Supp. 2d 593, 595 n.4 (E.D. Pa. 2007) (portraying Judge Posner's avatar in Second Life as promoting property rights in virtual reality).

[297] Albert C. Lin, Virtual Consumption: A Second Life for Earth?, 2008 B.Y.U.L. Rev. 47, 49 (2008).

[298] No. C 10–05696 CRB, 2010 WL 5387774 (N.D. Cal. Dec. 21, 2010).

[299] See Josie Cooperstone, Making Strides Against Breast Cancer . . ., AMARETTO BREEDABLES, April 18, 2011, archived at http:// www.webcitation.org/6213hvFHd (pinpointing when the site launched).

[300] See Candy Cerveau, Regarding the Lawsuit Against Ozimals by Amaretto, Ozimals Blog, Dec. 16, 2010, archived at http://www.webcitation.org/6216VcOzF (recounting the June 2010 conversation between Ozimals and Amaretto Breedables).

advised Amaretto's development team that the team's "breedable" horses were "virtually identical" to Ozimal's "breedable" bunnies and in violation of Ozimals' copyrights in these three dimensional images.

Ozimals next sent Amaretto a "cease and desist" order threatening to file a lawsuit under Section to file a lawsuit under Section 512 of the Digital Millennium Copyright Act (DMCA). Title II of the DMCA, "The Online Copyright Infringement Liability Limitation Act ("OCILLA")," limits the liability of service providers for the infringing acts of others on their listserv.[301] Service providers that comply with the DMCA §512(c)(1) and (2) notice-and-takedown procedure are immunized from secondary liability for copyright infringement.[302] Section 512 of the DMCA shielded Linden Labs, the service provider and creator of Second Life from secondary copyright infringement claims. Websites have no liability for secondary copyright infringement under DMCA Section 512(c) so long as they comply with the DMCA's procedure for taking down infringing content and are properly registered with the U.S. Copyright Office.[303] On April 22, 2011, the court dismissed many of Amaretto's claims.

Ozimals moved to dismiss Amaretto's claims for: (1) DMCA misrepresentation, (2) tortious interference with prospective business advantage, (3) unfair competition under California law, and (4) copyright misuse. The court dismissed the DMCA misrepresentation claim with prejudice and the tortious interference claim without prejudice upholding the preliminary injunction. The court dismissed the DMCA claim because Second Life did not actually take down Amaretto's virtual horses because an actual takedown notice was never filed and the claim was premature.[304] In the future, virtual land and person property disputes will become increasingly common.[305] In July of 2013, the federal district claim dismissed all remaining claims based upon defamation, unfair competition, intentional interference with prospective advantage and other business torts claims. Chapter 6 examines business torts and Chapter 10 analyzes the Digital Millennium Copyright Act and other Internet-related copyright law issues.

The courts have not resolved the question of who owns user-generated content and that issue is challenging in the context of social media cases.[306] Many social media or other websites require users to grant the provider a non-exclusive, royalty-free license

---

[301] See 17 U.S.C. § 512 (providing protections for Internet Service Providers).

[302] See id. § 512(c)(1) (setting forth the requirements under which a service provider's safe harbor can take effect).

[303] Service providers such as Linden Labs are eligible for a DMCA safe harbor if they implement and adopt a policy to terminate the account of recidivist copyright infringers. See 17 U.S.C. § 512(a)(d). Service providers must also remove or block access to allegedly infringing material upon receiving notice of legal infringement from the copyright owner or their assignee. See id. § 512(c)(iii).

[304] See Amaretto Ranch Breedables, LLC v. Ozimals, Inc., No. C 10 05695 CRB, 2011 WL 2690437, at *1 (N.D. Cal. July 8, 2011).

[305] See also, Virtual Vendors in Second Life File Real–World Lawsuit in NYC, (Oct. 28, 2007), http://www.siliconvalley.com/news/ci_7306539?nclick_check=1 (product trademark and copyright claims).

[306] "Disputes over virtual world items, such as virtual money, Second Life islands, and even "sex beds," can inform property law generally. Rights in these virtual world items, such as rights in software and many other intangible assets, are transferred by standard form agreements that are often designated as licenses. Other intangible assets, such as internet domain names, are likewise transferred by standard form agreements that convey ambiguous property rights. In this Article, I suggest that a study of virtual world assets and the agreements used in their transfer can help us to better understand property law as applied to intangible assets." Juliet M. Moringiello, What Virtual Worlds Can Do for Property Law, 62 FLA. L. REV. 159, 159–60 (2010).

to distribute content made with social media tools. The borderland between contract law and intellectual property is illustrated in terms of use and other license agreements, which is a topic examined in Chapter 6.

(C) Twitter

Twitter, created in 2006, is a real life communications platform that enables users to communicate with short messages. The social media service enables users to post messages (up to 140 characters) to their accounts from their phones, tablets, and personal computers, which can be viewed by all of their followers, in real time. Twitter claims 140 million users who tweet 340 million times per day. By May 25, 2013, 318 state and federal courts mentioned Twitter in judicial opinions. One of the hot button items is when jurors tweet during an ongoing trial.[307] In Saudi Arabia, the government recently enacted a blanket prohibition on judges using Twitter. Twitter has become ubiquitous for millions of Americans. Creators of these frequent, short messages, or "tweets," post them to their profiles, blogs or send them to followers. By 2011, Twitter had 100 million users.[308] Twitter users send out over 340 million of these messages (or, tweets) per day.[309] Hillary Clinton and Barack Obama famously tweeted to their followers in the Democratic Party's 2008 Presidential primaries. Twitter is now so institutionalized that a *New York Times* profile for the late blogger Andrew Breitbart mentioned how he "jacked into the Web early and never unplugged."[310] Another commentator noted that Breitbart "was a magnet for hatred, and he used Twitter for a full frontal assault, a tool of combat."[311] Twitter postings are often important exhibits in recent lawsuits. The U.S. government filed a *subpoena duces tecum* in order to obtain access to WikiLeaks accounts. Another court required Twitter to hand over deleted postings material to a disorderly conduct lawsuit. "On June 30, 2012, a Manhattan criminal court judge ruled that Twitter must provide to police the records of Malcolm Harris, a Twitter user charged with disorderly conduct during an Occupy Wall Street protest in October 2011."[312] Courts are deciding what rights plaintiffs have in the authentication of social media postings.

A California jury awarded Dawn Simorangkir, a fashion designer, $430,000 against Courtney Love, lead singer of the internationally known band Hole.[313] Simorangkir alleged Love flew her out to Los Angeles and gave her garments to make custom clothes. Simorangkir alleged that Love, presumably angry over the most recent bills, "began posting defamatory statements on her personal Twitter feed, MySpace blog, and the feedback section on Simorangkir's page on etsy.com, an online

---

[307] See e.g., United States v. Fumo, 655 F.3d 288 (3d Cir. 2011) (stating that a "television station reported that one of the jurors, hereinafter referred to as "Juror 1," had made postings on both his Facebook and Twitter pages related to the trial" of a former Pennsylvania state senator).

[308] United States v. Fumo, 655 F.3d 288, 331 (3d Cir. 2011).

[309] Twitter Turns Six, (last visited September 14, 2012).

[310] David Carr, The Provocateur, N.Y. TIMES (April 13, 2012), http://www.nytimes. com/2012/04/15/business/media/the-life-and-death-of-andrew-breitbart.html?pagewanted=all.

[311] Id.

[312] Marianna Mao, Current Data Privacy Laws Undermine Expressive Freedoms, HERDICTBLOG (July 26, 2012) ("As Judge Sciarrino himself acknowledges, the Internet's central role in civic and private life has created a new privacy interest that is not yet explicitly protected by existing statutes. Adapting the law to safeguard these interests may be essential if the Internet is to remain a vibrant forum for free expression.").

[313] Dawn Simorangkir v. Courtney Michelle Love, 2011 WL 1193794 (Cal. Super. Ct. March 3, 2011).

marketplace for independent designers."[314] The plaintiff's claim against Love was for libel, false light, invasion of privacy, tortious interference with economic advantage and breach of contract. The gist of her complaint was that Love's rants on Twitter were part of a "malicious campaign" to ruin and destroy the plaintiff's "reputation and livelihood."[315]

Torts and infringement on Twitter and on social media sites raise difficult legal dilemmas especially when the litigants are from radically different legal cultures. The Union of Jewish French Students filed suit against Twitter who refused to turn over the "names of anti-Semitic tweet authors, despite a French court ruling commanding their identification."[316] In the United States, these tweets, though objectionable by many, are not illegal because of the First Amendment of the U.S. Constitution. Even if the tweets were not protected expression, Twitter could not be held liable because of Section 230 of the Communications Decency Act shielding service providers from liability for third party postings. Neither the Digital Millennium Copyright Act nor CDA Section 230's takedown policy apply to trademark infringement. Nevertheless, Twitter adopted its private takedown and put back policy in its Trademark Policy. User names that violate a trademark holder's rights through unauthorized use will be suspended by Twitter or released to the trademark holder. Courts have only recently decided cases involving the misuse or abuse of trademarks on Twitter.[317]

---

[314] Id.

[315] Id.

[316] Twitter Sued for $50 Million After Refusing to Reveal Anti-Semitic Tweeter Identities, RT.COM (March 24, 2013).

[317] Pair Networks, Inc. v. Lim Cheng Soon, 2013 WL 452565 (W.D. Pa. Feb. 6, 2013) (providing copy of court court to twitter so so that Twitter can release the @pairmixer user account to pair Networks, Inc. in compliance with twitter's Trademark Policy).

Chapter 2

PERSPECTIVES ON GLOBAL INTERNET LAW

§ 2.1 OVERVIEW OF GLOBAL INTERNET LAW

Modern philosophers such as Martin Heidegger describe society as a moving stream rather than a stagnant pond. The Internet is not a timeless essence but rather the fastest growing information technology in world history and therefore the laws and regulations are constantly in the process of becoming. This chapter explores contemporary debates about Internet law and its nature. Covering competing models of Internet governance, this chapter begins with the arguments for and against the study of the Internet. This chapter summarizes the leading theories of governance and helps the reader recognize when courts and legislatures have adopted these perspectives. After providing a theoretical overview, the chapter concludes with the leading theories for Global Internet governance.

The daily headlines of *The Wall Street Journal* confirm that transnational pressure points are ubiquitous in the networked world. The paucity of transnational solutions for cyberspace transactions illustrates legal lag. In the field of civil procedure, courts have mechanically stretched the due process model of jurisdiction to the global electronic marketplace. The problem of adapting the American minimum contacts doctrine to the Internet is that no other country follows a due process model for personal jurisdiction.[1] Much of Internet law is stretching extant principles of procedural and substantive law. Nevertheless, courts and legislatures must update Internet governance as it limps along in the rear lagging behind technological developments. In the field of civil procedure, for example, courts have stretched the due process model of jurisdiction to cyberspace. The U.S. has led the world in the number of specialized statutes dealing with e-commerce and Internet conduct. The problem of adapting the American minimum contacts doctrine to the Internet is that no other country follows a due process model for personal jurisdiction and the Internet is, by its very nature, a global phenomenon. Enormous conflict of law issues arise since the user seamlessly crosses national borders, without tollgates or even user awareness.

The advent of the Internet has forced every branch of the law to adapt and those ongoing changes are examined in each chapter of the *Global Internet Law* hornbook. A world without e-mail (1971), text-messages (1992), Twitter (2006), Skype (2003), or Facebook (2004) is difficult to imagine, but these Internet-based inventions have only been a part of mass culture for the past decade. Today, children learn the ABCs: Apple, Bluetooth, and Chat followed by Download, E–Mail, Facebook, Hewlett–Packard, i-Phone, and Java. The online world is affecting every aspect of social existence, thus it is not surprising that all law has been reshaped and crafted by disruptive digital technologies. Internet law, or cyberlaw, is the study of how online activity affects long-

---

[1] Douglas D. McFarland, Dictum Run Wild: How Long–Arm Statutes Extended To The Limits of Due Process, 84 B.U.L. Rev. 491, 499 (2004) (stating that "Sections 16 and 17 of the Civil Practice Act reflect a conscious purpose to assert jurisdiction over nonresident defendants to the extent permitted by the due-process clause.").

established doctrines of jurisdiction, choice of law, contracts, torts, criminal law, intellectual property, privacy, regulation, constitutional law, and cross-border transactions.

The emergence of a global network of interconnected computers able to access, store, process, and transmit vast amounts of information in digital form has already altered our cultural landscape and in the decades to come, may help to transform many of our assumptions about communication, knowledge, invention, information, sovereignty, identity, and community.[2] Cyberspace is a new realm without a transnational sovereign, international treaty, specialized court system, or virtual dispute resolution system. National differences among the regimes of different countries connected to the Internet will inevitably lead to conflicts of law. President Obama's 2013 Executive Order requires Homeland Security and the U.S. Commerce Department to develop a cybersecurity framework by the end of 2013.

In 1897, Nikola Tesla invented telegraphing without wires, which made it possible to transmit electrical signals the unfathomable distance of twenty miles. That same year, Justice Oliver Wendell Holmes, Jr. wrote an essay on the common law; sketching more than six hundred years of Anglo–American cases. "The law embodies the story of a nation's development through many centuries," he wrote, "In order to know what it is, we must know what it has been, and what it tends to become."[3] Justice Holmes wrote during a period of rapid advances in transportation and communication technologies. Centuries of tort law confirm how this branch of law accommodates to sociological and technological changes.[4] The automobile, for example played an important role in important subfields of torts such as products liability, comparative negligence, and accident law.

Prior to the late nineteenth century, the law of torts was fundamentally concerned with defending community tranquility and mediating conflicts between neighbors. Torts, such as seduction or the alienation of affections, reflected the importance of protecting the family as a social unit. In the late nineteenth century, the law of negligence progressed to provide remedies for mass accidents caused by broken-down rail trestles, slipshod maintenance of streetcars, or the reckless operation of steamboats. By the beginning of the twentieth century, torts were beginning to address auto accidents and the novel technology of instantaneous photography.[5] Currently, the

---

[2] PATRICIA L. BELLIA, ET AL., CYBERLAW: PROBLEMS OF POLICY AND JURISPRUDENCE IN THE INFORMATION AGE (3rd ed. 2007).

[3] Oliver Wendell Holmes Jr., The Path of the Law, 10 HARV. L. REV. 457 (1897).

[4] 1 FOWLER V. HARPER ET AL., THE LAW OF TORTS xxvi (3d ed. 1996) (describing how common law of torts, property, and contract has historically been adaptable).

[5] At the time Justice Holmes gave his "Path of the Law" talk in 1897, tort law was evolving in response to changes in transportation and communication technology:

> Privacy-based torts, along with remedies for misuse of novel technologies such as "instantaneous photographs," were being born. In the new millennium, American society is once again undergoing a technological conversion of great consequence. This time, America is evolving from a durable commodities-based economy to one based on the licensing of software, intellectual property, and other intangibles.

Michael L. Rustad & Thomas H. Koenig, Rebooting Cybertort Law, 80 WASH. L. REV. 335, 364 (2005). "Judge Cardozo's ground-breaking opinion in MacPherson v. Buick Motor Co., 111 N.E. 1050 (N.Y. 1916), opened the door to development of products liability. The tort of invasion of privacy had its genesis in a law review article by Samuel Warren and Louis Brandeis. See generally, Samuel Warren & Louis Brandeis, The Right to Privacy, 4 HARV. L. REV. 193 (1890). See also MADELEINE SCHACHTER, INFORMATIONAL AND DECISIONAL

Internet is enabling a remarkable variety of digital crimes and civil wrongs beyond the reach of traditional criminal law and tort categories. Global Internet Law is a massive subject although it consists of less than two decades of cases, statutes, international agreements, and cross-border jurisdictional rules. As a result, American society is once again undergoing a technological transformation of great consequence. In the 1990s, America began to evolve from a durable, commodities-based economy, to one based on the licensing of intangible information such as software, databases, and intellectual property.[6] However, because the United States has become more competitive during the recent recession, some manufacturers are beginning to return.[7] For the immediate future, the United States economy will be based, in part, on manufacturing and not evolve solely into an information-based service economy. This mixed economy creates new complexities because Internet Law must continue to evolve to address tangible products as well as intangible assets. Sociologist William F. Ogburn defined "cultural lag" as what happens when a culture that regulates society, limps behind technological and social changes.[8] Related parts of a culture, Ogburn noted, "react to some change to strikingly different degrees, or with different speeds."[9] The Senate Judiciary Committee is in the process of reworking "the Electronic Communications Privacy Act ("ECPA") in light of the growth of 'cloud computing' and other technological changes" since Congress enacted this act three decades ago.[10] Gmail, for example, is predicated upon "cloud-based" computing service. The data and applications of the user reside on remote computer servers, operated by Google. The proposed ECPA amendments would prohibit electronic service providers "from voluntarily disclosing the contents of customer email or other electronic communications to the government."[11] Paul Goldstein contends that cloud computing raises new questions for copyright law as to the meaning of a public performance:

> Just think of an Internet-based music storage system or cyberlocker. Whether a "dumb" locker or a "smart" locker, he said, "basically the question is whether streaming from the cloud to an individual, one at a time, on demand, constitutes a public performance or not.[12]

Under a theory of legal lag, not all societal institutions change at the same pace. For example, in the area of substantive and procedural law, courts and legislatures

---

PRIVACY 3 (2003) (attributing conceptualization of privacy as right to be left alone to THOMAS M. COOLEY, A TREATISE ON THE LAW OF TORTS 29 (1879)).

[6] Id. at 363.

[7] Once Made in China: Jobs Trickle Back to U.S. Plants, WALL ST. J. (May 21, 2012) (reporting study that 39% of U.S. companies were "considering moving some manufacturing back to the U.S.").

[8] Professor Ogburn's argument was that "the various parts of modern culture are not changing at the same rate, some parts are changing much more rapidly than others; and that since there is a correlation and interdependence of parts, a rapid change in one part of our culture requires readjustments through other changes in the various correlated parts of culture." SOCIAL SCIENCE QUOTATIONS: WHO SAID WHAT, WHEN & WHERE 175 (David L. Sills & Robert K. Merton eds., 2000) [hereinafter Social Science Quotations] (reporting survey of American life commissioned by President Herbert Hoover and published during Franklin Roosevelt's presidency).

[9] See generally, WILLIAM F. OGBURN, SOCIAL CHANGE (1923).

[10] Alexei Alexis, Senate Judiciary Committee to Take Up Bill Proposing New Protections for 'Cloud Data, BLOOMBERG ELECTRONIC COMMERCE & LAW REPORT (April 24, 2013).

[11] Id.

[12] Joyce E. Cutler, Developers and Content Owners Debate Permission for Performance Retransmission, Bloomberg BNA: Electronic Commerce & the Law (July 5, 2013) (quoting Paul Goldstein).

must update the law because it lags behind technological developments.[13] The failure of tort law remedies to keep pace with new cyberwrongs is a form of legal lag.[14] EBay explains how the Internet raises new business as well as legal dilemmas:

> governing issues such as property ownership, copyrights, trademarks and other intellectual property issues, parallel imports and distribution controls, consumer protection, taxation, libel and defamation, obscenity and personal privacy apply to online businesses such as ours. Many of these laws were adopted prior to the advent of the Internet and related technologies and, as a result, do not contemplate or address the unique issues of the Internet and related technologies.[15]

The rise of the Internet and the World Wide Web created new legal dilemmas and that highlighted the need to modernize every branchy of procedural and substantive law.

> The law of Cyberspace has become interesting, as the emerging technologies have become institutionalized. Legal academics and practitioners have focused their attentions on such questions as: How do plaintiffs establish minimum contacts as to a defamatory statement made on an online discussion group? Can the practice of using obscene and pointed e-mails ever constitute an intentional infliction of emotional distress? In addition, is an increase in stalking and child pornography prevalent on the electronic frontier? There are, however, no well-accepted statistics about such problems in Cyberspace. We know next to nothing about the extent of injuries on the Internet, let alone how legally protectable interests should be vindicated in respect to the forum. Doing business on the Internet raises a host of challenging issues, such as how to deal with electronic cash, online banking, commercial transactions in digital information, and digital signatures. The rise of Intellectual property on the Internet poses new legal dilemmas for preserving a firm's crown jewels, its information assets.[16]

In the early years of the World Wide Web, intellectual property law limped in the rear, unable to keep pace with technological changes.[17] Courts have yet to develop cybertort remedies for negligent computer security, spam, or failing to prevent unauthorized computer intrusions, the foul cellar dives of the Internet. The United States has not yet experienced an "electronic Pearl Harbor" but high profile cyberattacks on key infrastructure are increasingly common. Judges have yet to confront the question of whether they will impose a duty of care for companies to implement measures to protect against hacking, virus attacks, or even terrorism. Chinese hackers broke into *The New York Times'* computer system over a four-month

---

[13] Michael L. Rustad, et al, Copyrights in Cyberspace: A Roundup of Recent Cases, 12 J HIGH TECH L 106, 137–40 (2011) (explaining how copyright law has accommodated to cyberspace).

[14] Ezra Dodd Church, Note, Technological Conservatism: How Information Technology Prevents the Law from Changing, 83 TEX. L. REV. 561, 581–86 (2004) (explaining how software code and nature of information technologies creates legal lag).

[15] eBay SEC 10Q Filing (July 19, 2013).

[16] Michael L. Rustad, Legal Resources for Lawyers Lost in Cyberspace, 30 SUFFOLK U. L. REV. 317, 317–18 (1996).

[17] The earliest commentator about legal lag in copyright law wrote prior to the development of the Worldwide Web. See June M. Besek, Future Copyright Protection, N.Y. L.J., Dec. 5, 1994, at 1 (discussing modification to copyright law necessary to meet challenges inherent in Internet).

period.[18] The hackers used a "spear-phishing" attack, sending e-mails with malicious code that installs remote access tools when the recipient clicks on a link in the e-mail or downloads an attachment.[19] Courts and legislatures are struggling with whether to create a duty of reasonable security but they are limping behind rapidly evolving cybercrimes. The tort of privacy, for example, was forged to address the telephone and photography. In the new millennium, the Internet is reshaping the law of privacy. The National Security Agency collects metadata from major social media sites and the CIA acknowledges that it monitors Facebook and other social media, all of which creates new privacy law dilemmas. Never before has a federal agency had the means to monitor countless conversations without a warrant. During the Vietnam War, the NSA "tapped the overseas communications of Martin Luther King Jr., Muhammad Ali, Sen. Frank Church (D. Idaho)" as well as humorist Art Buchwald.[20] Edward Snowden's disclosures about the NSA's PRISM project have unleashed a firestorm in many countries connected to the Internet. What is clear from the WikiLeaks disclosures about NSA spying is that Internet privacy is a transnational problem. Anupam Chander argues that the global Internet creates pressures in the law as evidenced by high profile transnational touch points:

> The pressure on law from both kinds of network is clear. Consider some transnational flashpoints from the first decade of the twenty-first century: Antigua's WTO challenge to US rules barring online gambling; the outsourcing of radiology to India; Brazil's demands to Google to identify perpetrators of hate speech; an Alien Torts Statute suit in the United States charging Yahoo! with abetting torture in China; a WTO complaint brought by the United States against Chinese state media controls on foreign movies, financial information, and music such as iTunes. These cases reveal the unsettled legal issues at stake in cybertrade, from jurisdiction to protectionism, from consumer protection to human rights.[21]

Internet transnational pressure points are evidenced in the enormous conflict of law issues where users cross national borders at the click of a mouse without tollgates or even user awareness that they are operating in a cross-border environment. Privacy-based torts, along with remedies for misuse of novel technologies such as "instantaneous photographs," were born in the first decades of the twentieth century. In the new millennium, the law of privacy is being reshaped as American society is once again undergoing a technological conversion of great consequence because of the Internet. Courts, legislatures, and industry standards need to be in a state of continual evolution to keep pace with developments such as Twitter, Facebook, and GPS tracking.

In the 1990's, it was not yet clear how existing intellectual property law would be modified to accommodate the unique features of the Internet and online commerce. In the case of software law, there has been a forty-year "legal lag" between the rises of software as a separate industry and the development of specialized contracting

---

[18] Nicole Perlroth, *Hackers in China Attacked The Times for Last 4 Months*, N.Y. Times, Jan. 30, 2013, at A1.

[19] Id.

[20] Richard Leiby, Declassified Documents Show NSA Listened in on MLK, Muhammed Ali, and Art Buchwald, THE WASHINGTON POST (Sept. 25, 2013).

[21] ANUPAM CHANDER, THE ELECTRONIC SILK ROAD 7 (2013).

principles that govern software.[22] The drafters of the Uniform Commercial Code ("UCC"), for example, realized that the Code would be revised often to accommodate to new social changes and ways of doing business. Article 2 of the U.C.C. governing the sales of goods was authored fifty years ago, decades before the development of the software industry and the Internet. Accordingly, the U.C.C. and the software industry have both suffered from legal as well as cultural lag because software is an intangible not covered by any Article.

The U.S. Copyright Act recognizes a broad variety of forms by which ownership of copyright interests may be transferred: "an assignment, mortgage, exclusive license, or any other conveyance, alienation, or hypothecation of a copyright or of any of the exclusive rights comprised in a copyright, whether or not it is limited in time or place of effect, but not including a nonexclusive license."[23] Transfer of ownership requires a writing signed by the copyright owner or his agent, which memorializes the rights conveyed.[24] The ease of copying software has made licensing a flexible contracting practice that helps commodify software and other information products. In the age of the Internet, creators of digital data can reproduce code infinitely for no cost at the click of a download button. Unlike toasters, rental cars, or plasma televisions, the number of software users can be increased without whittling away or diminishing the product. Today, courts and software lawyers have had little recourse but to adapt the principles of sales law to software licensing because the law of licensing exists in a "legislative void."[25] Through licensing, the developer can protect his intellectual property while granting access under restricted terms and conditions. The Uniform Computer Information Transactions Act defines license to mean:

> a contract that authorizes access to, or use, distribution, performance, modification, or reproduction of, information or informational rights, but expressly limits the access or uses authorized or expressly grants fewer than all rights in the information, whether or not the transferee has title to a licensed copy. The term includes an access contract, a lease of a computer program, and a consignment of a copy. The term does not include a reservation or creation of a security interest to the extent the interest is governed by [Article 9 of the Uniform Commercial Code].[26]

A licensor of software, digital data, or other information gives the licensee permission to use content but subject to limitations. With a sale of goods, the seller conveys the buyer all rights as well as title. A seller of hardware such as an iPod, high definition television, or snowmobile cannot specify that the consumer may only use the device for six months or in certain locations, but a licensor of digital information may control the permitted locations, duration of use, number of users, geographic scope, and

---

[22] Michael L. Rustad & Maria Vittoria Onufrio, The Exportability of the Principles of Software: Lost in Translation, 2 Hastings Sci. & Tech. L.J. 25, 29 (2010); i.Lan Sys., Inc. v. Netscout Serv. Level Corp., 183 F.Supp.2d 328, 332 (D. Mass. 2002) ("[A]cross most of the nation, software licenses exist in a legislative void. Legal scholars . . . have tried to fill that void, but their efforts have not kept pace with the world of business.").

[23] 17 U.S.C. § 101.

[24] 17 U.S.C. § 204(a).

[25] i.Lan Sys. Inc. v. Netscout Servs. Level Corp., 183 F. Supp. 2d 328, 332 (D. Mass. 2002).

[26] UCITA § 102(a) (41).

allowable uses of the software.[27] The software licensing industry has evolved since the mid-1980's to enable arbitrage on a great number of dimensions. Licensing conveys a lower-order property interest from the licensor to the licensee. Under a license, the licensee receives a right to use software or digital information for a designated period of time or under specified conditions and covenants.

Although software is an intangible and title does not pass from the licensor to licensees, courts nevertheless continue to treat software as goods.[28] The licensing of software always involves federal intellectual property rights, which is seldom an issue for the sale of goods. The commercial law for licensing information lags far behind social and technological developments as evidenced by treating software as a good. Without a specialized law governing the licensing of intangibles, courts have no practical alternative but to stretch sale of goods law to include the law of licensing. However, the courts' attempt to apply a fifty-year-old law of sales to the licensing of intangibles is like applying horse and buggy laws to cyberspace commercial transactions. Courts are just beginning to recognize that financial institutions have to implement reasonable computer security to protect customers from Internet crime, for example, and to inform customers in the event of a security breach. The Internet's new technologies have created a continuous legal lag in criminal law and procedure. In *United States v. Cotterman*,[29] the Ninth Circuit U.S. Court of Appeals describes the challenges to the meaning of a border search when data is located in the ethereal cloud:

> In the "cloud" a user's data, including the same kind of highly sensitive data one would have in "papers" at home, is held on remote servers rather than on the device itself. The digital device is a conduit to retrieving information from the cloud, akin to the key to a safe deposit box. Notably, although the virtual 'safe deposit box' does not itself cross the border, it may appear as a seamless part of the digital device when presented at the border. With access to the cloud through forensic examination, a traveler's cache is just a click away from the government.[30]

Courts are reconceptualizing the meaning of a border search where the data is stored in the "clouds." Criminal law is continuously being updated to accommodate a networked world where territoriality is indeterminate. Beginning in the early 1980's, state and federal legislatures updated criminal codes to account for the rise of computer crimes. Additionally, traffic laws are being updated in many states to address the problem of drivers using mobile technologies for text messaging, blogging, or e-mail, which causes accidents. As an example, a Los Angeles commuter train engineer was text

---

[27] Michael L. Rustad, Making UCITA More Consumer–Friendly, 18 J. MARSHALL J. COMPUTER & INFO. L. 547, 551–52 (1999) (arguing the software licensing law is less developed than the law for durable goods).

[28] Gross v. Symantec Corp., No. C 12–00154 CRB (N.D. Cal. July 31, 2012) (ruling that the licensing of software constituted goods subject to U.C.C. Article 2 governing sales in a class action against Symantec over the claim that a free trial was fraudulent); see also, RRX Indus., Inc. v. Lab-Con, Inc., 772 F.2d 543, 546 (9th Cir. 1985); "The paradigm contractual model for a transaction in intangible goods is a license agreement. Under the license, the creators of the product authorize the use of their work, but, because of its intangible nature, restrict its use." Sean F. Crotty, The How and Why of Shrinkwrap License Validation Under the Uniform Computer Information Transactions Act.

[29] 709 F.3d 952 (9th Cir. 2013).

[30] Id. at 965.

messaging shortly before he collided with another train, an accident that killed twenty-five people.[31]

Debate about Internet law has revolved around a question that is simple to ask but difficult to answer: Should there be a specialized Internet Law? In 1996, Judge Frank Easterbrook, a Seventh Circuit U.S. Court of Appeals judge, spoke at a University of Chicago academic conference on cyberspace law. Likewise, he argued that cyberspace law deserved no more standing in a law school than an elective on the law of horses. The thrust of Judge Easterbrook's thesis is that it is a disservice to students to study Internet law. He saw no urgency in harmonizing either the procedural or substantive Internet law, arguing that Internet law is nothing more than everyday cases whose only common element is the incidental use of a new technology. Judge Easterbrook thought it was better for law students interested in horse law to study subjects such as property, torts, contract law, and intellectual property and stretch these principles to cases that involved horses:

> When asked to talk about "Property in Cyberspace," my immediate reaction was, "Isn't this just the law of the horse?" I don't know much about cyberspace; what I do know will be outdated in five years (if not five months!); and my predictions about the direction of change are worthless, making any effort to tailor the law to the subject futile. And if I did know something about computer networks, all I could do in discussing "Property in Cyberspace" would be to isolate the subject from the rest of the law of intellectual property, making the assessment weaker.[32]

Judge Easterbrook's broader observation is that the law of cyberspace requires no reworking of basic property law and there is no need to develop a specialized Internet law. Internet Jurisdiction, discussed further in Chapter 3, illustrates how courts have stretched the minimum contacts framework to cyberspace without creating special rules. Similarly, in Chapter 6, discussing torts, also confirms Judge Easterbrook's point because cybertorts are simply "new wine in old bottles." His prescription for Internet Law was to follow three basic principles: "Make things clear; create property rights where now there are none; and facilitate the formation of bargaining institutions" and let "cyberspace evolve as it will."[33]

He acknowledged that the World Wide Web was "mutating faster than the virus in The Andromeda Strain."[34] What would be different about the trajectory of IP law if the Internet had never been created? In the fifteen years since Judge Easterbrook's talk on "The Law of the Horse," the Internet has recalibrated IP rights, as well as liabilities. Further, in less than two decades, the Internet has generated an exponential number of innovations, due in large part to collaborations such as that which led to the free and open software movement. Each substantive branch of Internet Law has accommodated the World Wide Web. Federal and state legislatures have formulated specialized rules for Internet-related crime, torts, intellectual property, taxation, and regulation.

---

[31] Michael L. Rustad & Thomas H. Koenig, Cybertorts and Legal Lag: An Empirical Analysis, 13 S. CAL. INTERDISC. L.J. 77, 80 (2003) ("[T]ort law continues to lag behind the technological dilemmas created by an increasingly networked society.").

[32] Frank H. Easterbrook, Cyberspace and the Law of the Horse, 1996 U. CHI. LEGAL F. 207 (arguing that there is no such field as Internet law).

[33] Id.

[34] Id.

The Internet has skyrocketed in the past fifteen years in large part because of its architecture of open standards.[35] Like Judge Easterbrook, Joseph Sommer also contends that cyberspace law is not a distinct body of law and technologies normally do not define law. He also argues that most legal issues posed by the Internet are not new and that extant law will accommodate to these emergent issues.[36] Sommer contends that "not only is *cyberlaw* nonexistent, it is dangerous to pretend that it exists."[37] In the decades since the debate over cyberlaw, every branch of substantive and procedural law has been shaped by this new information technology. All lawyers need an understanding of how the Internet law shapes their practice.

Contrary to those agnostics who oppose the study of cyberlaw as a distinct subject, the experience of the past two decades illustrates the emergence of many unique issues causally connected to the Internet. For example, the dynamic development of cyberlaw led to a complete reworking of intellectual property law. The Internet's gravitational pull on the law of every country is undeniable. To update the philosopher, Seneca: "Our plans miscarry because they have no aim. Having no Internet governance models is like the man who does not know what harbor he is making for, no wind is the right wind."[38] Thus, general principles need to be formulated that explain the impact of the Internet's protean qualities and impact on daily life.

Lawrence Lessig, a founding father of the Berkman Center at Harvard University, is the Roy L. Furman Professor of Law and Leadership at Harvard Law School, and director of the Edmond J. Safra Center for Ethics, contends that Internet law illuminates the entire legal landscape, offering new perspectives on topics such as intellectual property, globalization, private regulation, and Internet governance. His response to Judge Easterbrook was that Internet law represents an entirely new paradigm and way of thinking about intellectual property, privacy, and private regulation.[39] Lessig explains how cyberspace raises new challenges in regulating pornography not found in the bricks-and-mortar world.[40] He notes how difficult it is for websites to distinguish adults from children—not an issue outside of cyberspace.[41] The Internet is a unique legal space because its "anonymity and multi-jurisdictionality . . . makes control by government in cyberspace impossible. The nature of the space makes behavior there *unregulable*."[42] Cyberlaw is not just about statutes or cases but also encompasses the architecture of the Internet, informal norms, as well as industry standards. In his book *Code and Other Laws of Cyberspace*, Lessig took issue with libertarians and others who argued that the Internet was not regulable. Lessig identified four modalities of Internet regulation: law, norms, markets, and software architecture.[43] The functions of architecture or real-space code are not a matter of technological necessity but rather a human-created mechanism for controlling the

---

[35] The Web's New Walls, THE ECONOMIST (Sept. 4, 2010) at 11.

[36] Joseph H. Sommer, Against Cyberlaw, 15 BERKELEY TECHN. L.J. 1145 (2000).

[37] Id. at 1147.

[38] The Epistles to Lucilius, N.Y. TIMES BOOK REVIEW (Aug. 30, 1970) at 39 (quoting Seneca).

[39] See Lawrence Lessig, The Law of the Horse, What Cyberlaw Might Teach, 113 HARV. L. REV. 501 (1999); See also PATRICIA BELLIA ET. AL., CYBERLAW: PROBLEMS OF POLICY AND JURISPRUDENCE IN THE INFORMATION AGE (3d ed. 2007) (contending that the Internet transforms basic assumptions about the nature of communication, knowledge, invention, information, sovereignty, identity, and community).

[40] Id. at 504.

[41] Id.

[42] Id. at 505.

[43] LAWRENCE LESSIG, CODE AND OTHER LAWS OF CYBERSPACE (1999).

Internet. In Lessig's view, the software code infrastructure is a form of law, "[W]e can build, or architect, or code cyberspace to protect values that we believe are fundamental." The Internet, for example, creates new copyright wars that influence the future of the public domain of ideas because of conscious decisions to encrypt or protect code.

In 1998, Lessig taught a path-breaking course at Harvard Law School entitled, *The Law of Cyberspace: Protocols*, which examined the interrelationship between law, policy, and technology. The course explored how the various architectures of cyberspace affected free speech, privacy, copyright, and encryption. Protocols are electronic communications "rules" which allow for the orderly, reliable transfer of data. FTP permits transfers of files between computers with unique software and hardware configurations. Other examples of protocols are the International Standards Organization and the standard ASCII character set. Lessig contends that the functions of architecture or real-space code are expanding control of the Internet.[44] He suggests that we "think about the '*bot man*' theory of regulation—one focused on the regulation of code. We will learn . . . [w]e can build, or *architect,* or code cyberspace to protect values that we believe are fundamental."[45] In his 2004 book, *Free Culture*, Lessig explained how new technology created new copyright law wars that influence the future of the public domain of ideas.[46] Lessig contends that we must not lose our freedom to create, our freedom to build, and, ultimately, our freedom to imagine. He also argues that cyberlaw illuminates the entire legal landscape versus being a myopic perspective about specific topics like torts in cyberspace, cybercrimes, or Internet security. Lessig sees much value in closely examining the intersections of law and cyberspace. Similarly, Patricia Bellia and her co-editors, also begin their Internet law casebook emphasizing how cyberlaw uses the ". . . rise of the Internet to encourage [students] to reconsider various assumptions in traditional legal doctrine. The value of this subject is to provide broad based and sophisticated training in Internet-related legal issues while also helping to shape cyberlaw as a coherent and useful field of study."[47]

§ 2.2   VOLUNTARY ORGANIZATIONS SETTING STANDARDS

Who controls the Internet? Who runs the Internet? No sovereign or international convention has hegemony in today's Internet.[48] Yochai Benkler conceptualized three layers of Internet governance: the "physical infrastructure" layer, the "content" layer,

---

[44] LAWRENCE LESSIG, CODE VERSION 2.0 273 (2008) (stating "you cannot ignore the constraint (of software code) and suffer the consequences later").

[45] Id. at 11.

[46] LAWRENCE LESSIG, FREE CULTURE: HOW BIG MEDIA USES TECHNOLOGY AND THE LAW TO LOCK DOWN CULTURE (2004).

[47] PATRICIA L. BELLIA, ET AL., CYBERLAW: PROBLEMS OF POLICY AND JURISPRUDENCE IN THE INFORMATION AGE 2 (3rd ed. 2007).

[48] "No single entity—academic, corporate, governmental, or non-profit—administers the Internet. It exists and functions as a result of the fact that hundreds of thousands of separate operators of computers and computer networks independently decided to use common data transfer protocols to exchange communications and information with other computers (which in turn exchange communications and information with still other computers). There is no centralized storage location, control point, or communications channel for the Internet, and it would not be technically feasible for a single entity to control all of the information conveyed on the Internet." American Civil Liberties Union v. Reno, 929 F. Supp. 824, 830–32 (E.D. Pa. 1996).

and the "logical" layer.[49] No one country has sovereignty over the three layers of Internet governance especially for conduct occurring outside their territory. For example, Germany's Justice Minister called "for Internet service providers in the U.S. and elsewhere to remove neo-Nazi images, text and other content that can be viewed inside the country in violation of laws forbidding any Nazi symbols."[50] It is a myth that the Internet is a separate realm beyond the regulatory reach of countries connected to the Internet.[51] Mueller contends that voluntary organizations, service providers, and network operators should also be considered as a form of Internet governance.[52]

The romantic idealism of Barlow, Johnson and Post and cyber-libertarians gave way to a pragmatic realism that reflected more faithfully how governments have exercised control of the Internet enacting countless civil and criminal statutes backed by fortified sanctions. This chapter examines themes in Jack Goldsmith and Tim Wu's 2008 book, *Who Controls the Internet?: Illusions of a Borderless World*. Goldsmith and Wu argue that individual countries have imposed regulations on the Internet contrary to the assertions of libertarians who believe that the Internet is a separate sovereign free of national regulations. Twitter, for example, obeyed a French court order to unveil anonymous speakers with Anti–Semitic on its service.[53] The International Federation of Human Rights ("FIDH") and the French League of Human Rights ("LDH") filed suit on the U.S National Security Agency for its PRISM data collection program as well as Internet companies such as Facebook and Skype for violating the privacy rights of French citizens.[54]

An Italian court issued a court order to Google to modify their search engine in order to "suspend the association between the first name and second name of a businessman and words such as 'truffa'"(fraud) and 'truffatore' (swindler) which would automatically appear when typing the businessman's first name and second name

---

[49] "We are making regulatory choices at all layers of the information environment—the physical infrastructure, logical infrastructure, and content layers—that threaten to concentrate the digital environment as it becomes more central to our social conversation. These include decisions about intellectual property law, which can make ownership of content a point of reconcentration, decisions about the design of software and its standards, and the regulation of physical infrastructure available to Internet communications, like cable broadband services. At all these layers, the wrong decisions could enable a reproduction of the mass media model, with all its shortcomings, in the digitally networked environment. Avoiding making these mistakes should be the focus of the efforts we have traditionally focused on structural media regulation." Yochai Benkler, From Consumers to Users: Shifting Deeper Structures of Regulation: Toward Sustainable Commons and User Access, 52 FED. COMM. L.J. 561, 562 (2000).

[50] Patrick McGroarty, Germany Calls for Ban of Neo–Nazi Sites Abroad, SYDNEY MORNING HERALD (July 10, 2009).

[51] "A distinctive global politics is developing around the Internet. Like global trade and environmental policy, Internet governance has become a point of international conflict among states and a target of transnational policy advocates from business and civil society." MILTON MUELLER, NETWORKS AND STATES: THE GLOBAL POLITICS OF INTERNET GOVERNANCE 2 (2010).

[52] MILTON MUELLER, NETWORKS AND STATES: THE GLOBAL POLITICS OF INTERNET GOVERNANCE 5 (2010) (calling for a broadening of Internet governance to encompass tens of thousands of network operators and service providers).

[53] Twitter Releases User Data to France After Lawsuit Over Anti-Semitic Tweets (July 12, 2013), http://www.jns.org/news-briefs/2013/7/12/twitter-releases-user-data-to-france-after-anti-semitic-tweets-lawsuit (last visited July 13, 2013).

[54] The French attorney representing the French human rights organizations contend: "We have never seen such an infringement on individual freedoms, to such a large scale, from a foreign nation and it potentially affects all French citizens and all French internet users when they use Google, Microsoft, Apple, Skype and other companies." France to Sue NSA? Rights Groups Urge Court to Open Lawsuit Over U.S. Spying, RT.com (July 11, 2013), http://rt.com/news/french-sue-us-nsa-947/.

followed by the letter 't'on the search engine."[55] Google complied with the Italian court order even though its defense was that the search queries were based upon previous searches of users, not Google's strategic decisions.[56]

These decided cases demonstrate that Internet-related conduct is subject to jurisdiction by foreign governments and plaintiffs. The growing number of foreign plaintiffs filing suit about U.S. Internet company practices evidences that the Internet is not a liability-free zone beyond the reach of national authorities. Lothar Detterman's survey of media privacy issues raises this issue for social networking sites:

> Thus, the usual games begin: innovators, early adopters, libertarians, and businesses assert that social media is not, should not, and cannot be regulated, as previously with cyberspace and virtual worlds. Concerned politicians, on the other hand, claim that social media is new, dangerous, and in dire need of regulation.[57]

They cast doubt on the utopian view that the Internet has transcended governments, borders, and our physicality. Voluntary organizations also play a significant role in setting standards and creating protocols, which make an interconnected system of computer possible. Today, the question is not whether the Internet is governable, but what role transnational institutions should play.[58]

(A) Open Systems Initiative

The International Standards Organization's Open Systems Initiative Model ("OSI") conceptualized networking as an assembly line composed of seven different layers or stages for implementing protocols to enable worldwide communications. OSI's aim is to create an open networking environment in which all systems can interconnect and are interoperable worldwide so that computer systems made by different vendors can communicate with each other. The seven-layer model processes the data after the web browsers or other applications make requests. Each of the seven generalized layers performs precise functions to ensure that data travels seamlessly across the network. The OSI converts data into packets that consist of zeroes and ones, and are transferable over the network. When a computer receives one of these packets, it runs through the assembly line backwards. After this "disassembly," the OSI reassembles the data into the order sent.

(B) World Wide Web Consortium

The World Wide Web Consortium ("W3C"), an international voluntary organization, develops open standards to ensure the long-term growth of the Web through standard protocols, ensuring interoperability. The W3C is working on standards for a more interactive Web 3.0. "This "semantic web" enables people to create data stores on the Web, build vocabularies, and write rules for handling data."[59] The

---

[55] Giusella Finocchiaro, Towards Provider Responsibility for Content, Law and the Internet, Finocchiaro (April 15, 2011), http://www.blogstudiolegalefinocchiaro.com/wordpress/tag/google-italian-lawsuit/ (last visited July 12, 2013).

[56] Id.

[57] Lothar Determann: Social Media Privacy: A Dozen Myths and Facts, STANFORD TECHNOLOGY LAW. REVIEW. ¶ 1 (2012).

[58] Milton Mueller, Networks and States, Id. at 1 (reframing the question of Internet governance as whether new global institutions are required).

[59] W3C, Semantic Web (2012).

W3C led "semantic web" employs groundbreaking languages such as the Resource Description Framework ("RDF") and the Web Ontology Language ("OWL"). The originators of the Internet worked collaboratively as the W3C developing specifications for writing eXtensible Markup Language ("XML") code, as well as the template for Web 3.0 languages.[60] The W3C released proposed "do not track" ("DNT") specifications and sets out best practices for websites to comply with this preference. The W3C specification states:

> The specification applies to compliance with requests through user agents that (1) can access the general browsable Web; (2) have a user interface that satisfies the requirements in Determining User Preference in the [*TRACKING–DNT*] specification; (3) and can implement all of the [*TRACKING–DNT*] specification, including the mechanisms for communicating a tracking status, and the user-granted exception mechanism.[61]

(C) Internet Engineering Task Force

The Internet Society ("ISOC") supports the two standards-setting organizations, The Internet Engineering Task Force ("IETF") and the Internet Architecture Board ("IAB"). The IETF aims "to make the Internet work better."[62] The IETF developed the IPv4 protocol for Internet addresses in 1983 and the IPv6 protocol "in the 1990s that uses unique numerical IP addresses."[63] Standards or protocol controls the Internet and how it works. The IETF's mission includes the following:

- Identifying, and proposing solutions to, pressing operational and technical problems on the Internet.

- Specifying the development or usage of protocols and the near-term architecture to solve such technical problems for the Internet.

- Making recommendations to the Internet Engineering Steering Group ("IESG") regarding the standardization of protocols and protocol usage on the Internet

- Facilitating technology transfer from the Internet Research Task Force ("IRTF") to the wider Internet community.

- Providing a forum for the exchange of information within the Internet community between vendors, users, researchers, agency contractors, and network managers.[64]

The IETF seeks ways to make the engineering of the Internet better and is an example of the generativity of collaborative community described by Jonathan Zittrain in his 2009 book, *The Future of the Internet and How to Stop It*. The IETF and the Internet Architecture Board ("IAB") are two of the most important global standards-

---

[60] Nigel Shadbold, Wendy Hall, and Tim Berners–Lee, The Semantic Web Revisited. IEEE COMPUTER SOCIETY (2006).

[61] World Wide Web Consortium, Tracking Compliance and Scope—June Draft (Unofficial Draft 14 June 2013).

[62] The Internet Engineering Task Force (IETF), http://www.ietf.org/ (last visited June 30, 2013).

[63] David McAuley, User Resistance to IP 'Dual Stack May Allow Telco to Assert Web Influence, BNA BLOOMBERG: ELECTRONIC COMMERCE & LAW REPORT, (May 28, 2013).

[64] Id.

setters for the Internet.[65] The IETF identifies and proposes solutions for technical problems facing the Internet such as policy, governance, and open development of standards or protocol. The IAB is engaged in developing Internet protocols to protect user privacy. The IAB released a statement in 2013 opposing "dotless domains in the root zone, observing that some existing top-level domains (TLDs) are already operating in such a mode."[66] The public Internet is a generative technology because it allows individuals and voluntary organizations to improve it. In contrast, digital rights management ("DRM") to prevent unauthorized use of copyrighted works is emblematic of the closed, walled Internet. The IETF, like Zittrain, favors an open, generative Internet as opposed to a "walled garden" without significant user input.[67]

(D) ISOC

The Internet Society ("ISOC") is a "cause-driven voluntary organization that supports the IETF and the IAB to ensure that the Internet remains open and transparent."[68] "ISOC is the organizational home of the Internet Engineering Task Force ("IETF"), the Internet standards body responsible for developing the Internet's technical foundations through its open global forum."[69] The Internet evolved rapidly in large part because of the role of nonhierarchical, open standards-setting organizations such as ISOC. "ISOC was founded in 1992 by a small group of Internet pioneers who came together to promote principals of Internet design openness. ISOC's focus is on connecting the world, collaborating with others, and advocating for equal access to the Internet."[70] ISOC works on issues such as access, privacy, Internet exchange points or hubs, children and the Internet, net neutrality, spam, domain names, and open network standards. The organization provides insurance coverage for those involved in the IETF standards-setting groups. ISOC is also a hub for other voluntary organizations:

> One of the ways that ISOC does this is through financial and legal support of the other "I" groups described here, particularly the IETF. ISOC provides insurance coverage for many of the people in the IETF process and acts as a public relations channel for the times that one of the "I" groups wants to say something to the press.[71]

(E) International Telecommunication Union

The International Telecommunication Union ("ITU") is an intergovernmental agency of the United Nations. Today, the ITU has 191 Member States and more than

---

[65] The Internet Architecture Board (IAB) is the committee charged with oversight of the technical and engineering development of the Internet by the Internet Society (ISOC). "The IETF is an open international community of network designers, operators, vendors and researchers concerned with the evolution of the Internet architecture and the smooth operation of the Internet." Internet Engineering Task Force, Ripe Network Coordinating Centre (2013) The IETF, established in 1996, also coorindates the work of the IAB. Id.

[66] Internet Architecture Board, IAB Statement: Dotless Domains Considered Harmful (July 10, 2013).

[67] JONATHAN ZITTRAIN, THE FUTURE OF THE INTERNET (AND HOW TO STOP IT) (2009).

[68] Internet Society (ISOC), https://www.arin.net/participate/governance/isoc.html (last visited June 3, 2013).

[69] Id.

[70] Id.

[71] Paul Hoffman, The Tao of IETF: A Novice's Guide to the Internet Engineering Task Force (2012) at 3.2.1.

700 Sector Members and Associates, which includes private entities and non-government organizations. The ITU works on international public policy issues pertaining to the Internet and the management of Internet resources, including domain names and addresses. The ITU favors greater Internet access for less developed countries as well as multi-stakeholder Internet governance. The U.S. government has consistently opposed the ITU's role in governance. The 193 countries of the ITU oppose designating the United Nations as the "new international regulator of the Internet."[72] In May of 2013, the ITU adopted six non-binding opinions on a range of topics that included "the role of Internet Exchange Points ("IXPs") in increasing connectivity in developing countries, the IPv6 transition, and supporting multistakeholder participation in Internet governance."[73]

Currently, the ITU treaty does not address "technical standards, infrastructure, or content. Some governments are advocating expansion of the ITU's authority to include Internet regulation."[74] The ITU is seeking to incorporate Internet regulation into its international treaties. China and Russia are two treaty signatories interested in expanding the ITU treaties to include Internet regulation. ITU seeks to incorporate principles of net neutrality, openness, and decentralization in its global mission.[75] The ITU's focus continues to be on telecommunications policy as opposed to broader Internet governance regulation.[76] In December 2012, the World Conference for International Telecommunications Union ("WCIT") met in Dubai.[77]

The U.S. Government position on WCIT is to "oppose changes to revisions to international telecommunications that would restrict the free flow of content, impede the natural growth, and evolution of the Internet, or impose uneconomic pricing or transfer-payment obligations on Internet content providers or backbone operators."[78] The Council of the International Telecommunication Union ("ITU") in its June 2013 meetings led discussions on International Internet-related public policy issues such as protecting children online, worldwide standardization, and stakeholder participation.[79] In early 2013, ITU representatives from Russia, China and a number of Latin American nations backed a proposal for greater multi-stakeholder Internet governance.[80] Russia's ITU "representative said that Internet governance 'is really

---

[72] Paul Barbagallo, State Department Official: Countries Unlikely to Vote on Making U.N. Internet Regulator, ELEC. COMM. L. REPORT (May 31, 2012).

[73] Id.

[74] ITU Resource Center, https://www.cdt.org/issue/ITU (last visited May 17, 2013).

[75] Cynthia Wong, As ITU Eyes the Internet, Center for Democracy and Technology (March 16, 2012).

[76] Id.

[77] Amy E. Bivins, Internet Governance Bono Mack Urges Senate to Take Up House Internet Governance Bill After August Recess, ELEC. COMM. L. REPORT (Aug. 15, 2012).

[78] Id.

[79] Brazil calls for a greater participation of governments and an enhanced role for the United Nations' International Telecommunication Union (ITU). Daniel Pruzin, U.S. Satisfied With Internet Forum Has Concern on Brazil Proposal, BLOOMBERG BNA, ELECTRONIC COMMERCE & LAW REPORT (May 21, 2013); Internet Governance: Brazil Gains Support for Enhancing Government Role in Internet Policymaking, BNA, ELECTRONIC COMMERCE LAW & POLICY (May 15, 2013).

[80] "A working definition" of Internet governance was developed by the Working Group on Internet Governance (WGIG, a group comprising all stakeholders) and later adopted by Summit and included in para. 34 of the Tunis Agenda, which states that Internet Governance is "the development and application by governments, the private sector and civil society, in their respective roles, of shared principles, norms, rules, decision-making procedures, and programmes that shape the evolution and use of the Internet". Para. 58 of the Tunis Agenda notes that Internet governance includes more than Internet naming and addressing;

going astray. We're starting to see each country adopting their own domestic laws on managing the Internet. We have to define the international rules, top to bottom.'"[81]

§ 2.3   MODELS OF GLOBAL INTERNET GOVERNANCE

The International Monetary Fund ("IMF") defines civil society to include diverse voluntary organizations such as business forums, labor organizations, local community groups, as well as nongovernmental organizations ("NGOs"). The World Summit on the Information Society ("WSIS") formed a large number of civil society caucuses including those representing youth, gender, scientific information, media, and cities. ICANN, the quasi-governmental authority, responsible for domain names, receives policy suggestions from such civil society groups. Most Internet theories of governance fall into five camps: (1) self-governance or libertarian, (2) global transnational, (3) code and Internet Architecture, (4) national governments and law, and (5) market-based or economic-based regulation. Lawrence Solum developed a typology of five theories based upon values and interests of Internet Governance.[82] The chart below provides the basic attributes of the five models of Internet Governance. Courts and legislatures may use one or more of these models in their decision-making. At present, there is no agreement as to which model best fits global Internet governance.

Five Models of Internet Governance	Domain Assumptions
(1) Self–Governance or Libertarian	The Internet is beyond governmental control.
(2) Global Transnational	Transnational legal institutions need to govern the Internet since it transcends national borders.
(3) Code and Internet Architecture	Voluntary organizations make regulator decisions when they construct protocols and develop software dictating how it operates.
(4) National Governments and Law	National governments impose their laws and regulations on the

therefore it also includes other significant public policy issues such as, inter alia, critical Internet resources, the security and safety of the Internet, and developmental aspects and issues pertaining to the use of the Internet." INTERNATIONAL COMMUNICATION UNION, FOURTH DRAFT OF THE SECRETARY GENERAL'S REPORT FOR THE FIFTH WORLD TELECOMMUNICATION/INFORMATION AND COMMUNICATION TECHNOLOGY POLICY FORUM (Jan. 10, 2013).

[81] Id.

[82] Lawrence Solum, Models of Internet Governance, Chapter 2 in MODELS OF INTERNET GOVERNANCE INFRASTRUCTURE AND INSTITUTIONS 48–55 (Lee A. Bygrave et al. 2009).

	Internet.
(5) Market–Based or Economic–Based Regulation	Clinton Administration approach let market forces and industry practices shape Internet governance.

The foremost theories of Internet governance fall broadly into one of these five rival camps conceptualized by Lawrence Solum. Judges deciding Internet law cases often incorporate one or more Internet governance theories into their legal opinions. Solum's first model of Internet governance, self-governing cyberspace, evolved during the formative period of the Internet. Lawrence Solum's first model of Internet governance, self-governing cyberspace, evolved during the formative period of the Internet. Idealistic libertarian theorists conceptualized cyberspace as a separate sphere beyond the reach of governments.[83] A second theoretical perspective required the creation of new transnational institutions premised on the idea that cyberspace "transcends national borders." This multi-stakeholder approach assumes that no one government should control the Internet.[84] Multi-stakeholders contend that transnational legal institutions that are transparent and broadly representative must govern cyberspace. Solum's third model is governance determined in large part by software code or Internet-related architecture. A fourth model assumes cyberspace regulation is not essentially different from brick and mortar regulation. The experience of the past two decades confirms that national, state, and local governments are able to enforce their statutes and regulations, although there are unique features of cyberspace that create gaps in the law. Lawrence Solum's fifth model views forward market regulation and economics as central levers. Internet governance is not restricted to the activities of governments but also encompasses civil society."[85]

§ 2.4   SELF–GOVERNING OR LIBERTARIAN GOVERNANCE

(A) Libertarian Manifesto

John Perry Barlow, an Internet visionary, libertarian, and former lyricist for The Grateful Dead, adopts a libertarian view of Internet governance arguing that governments have no business censoring content in the flattened world of cyberspace: "In our world, all the sentiments and expressions of humanity, from the debasing to the angelic, are parts of a seamless whole, the global conversation of bits."[86] Barlow thundered, "On behalf of the future, I ask you of the past to leave us alone."[87] His utopian vision was an Internet free from government censorship: "Governments of the Industrial World, you weary giants of flesh and steel, I come from Cyberspace, the new home of

---

[83] A number of other academics recognized that law adopted for bricks and mortar needed to be revised, retrofitted or reformed for cyberspace. See e.g., I. Trotter Hardy, The Proper Legal Regime for 'Cyberspace', 55 U. PITT. L. REV. 993, 994 (1994) (asserting old legal concepts inappropriate for Cyberspace).

[84] Solum, Five Models of Internet Governance, Id.

[85] ISOC, INTERNET GOVERNANCE (2008).

[86] John Perry Barlow, A Declaration of Independence for Cyberspace (1996).

[87] Id.

Mind."[88] He famously stated, "The First Amendment is a local ordinance, where is the consent from Netizens for any country imposing its laws on the Internet?"[89] By what authority does the U.S. impose its First Amendment on the rest of the world? Barlow additionally proclaimed that governments must take a "hands-off" approach to cyberspace governance:

> We have no elected government, nor are we likely to have one, so I address you with no greater authority than that with which liberty itself always speaks. I declare the global social space we are building to be naturally independent of the tyrannies you seek to impose on us. You have no moral right to rule us nor do you possess any methods of enforcement we have true reason to fear.[90]

The thrust of Barlow's libertarian-based argument brings to mind a *Seinfeld* episode, "The Pothole," which featured Kramer complaining about a poorly maintained highway outside of New York City after he ran over an abandoned sewing machine. Kramer proceeded to repaint the four-lane highway creating two extra-wide lanes with the intent to transform it into a "two lane comfort cruise." By what authority did Cosmo Kramer have the right to repaint the lines on the highway converting it to a two-lane comfort zone? When can a given nation-state legitimately impose its sovereignty on the borderless Internet? There is a similar legitimacy problem when a given nation state imposes its sovereignty on the borderless Internet.

John Perry Barlow's insight is that legitimacy must ultimately come from the consent of Internet users in hundreds of countries. Barlow wrote his famous Manifesto in response to the German government's prosecution of a Bavarian Internet service provider ("ISP"). The Bavarian ISP was prosecuted for permitting Internet users to access objectionable content such as Nazi memorabilia or hateful commentary posted by third parties. By what authority can a Bavarian court order a U.S. service provider to block content to German citizens? Under this same argument, what gives the European Union the right to demand that U.S. companies get the consent of users before dropping cookies that capture consumer information?

By what authority do fundamentalist Islamic governments demand that the degrading portrayal of Mohammed in the film trailer, *Innocence of Muslims,* be stricken from the cyberspace landscape? Authoritarian regimes view the Internet as an "existential threat and are quick to erect roadblocks and access controls to censor subversive content.[91] The legitimation crisis for cyberspace governance is the byproduct of an Internet binding countries with radically different cultural and legal traditions. Barlow is also critical of governmental content regulations such as the Communications Decency Act ("CDA"), which enables restraints of political expression as well as

---

[88] Id.

[89] Id.; see also, James Boyle, Foucault in Cyberspace: Surveillance, Sovereignty and Hardwired Censors, 66 U. CIN L. REV. 177, 179 (1997) (quoting John Perry Barlow that "In Cyberspace, the First Amendment is a local ordinance."); See generally, David R Johnson and David Post, Law and Borders–The Rise of Law in Cyberspace 48 STAN. L. REV. (1996).

[90] Id.

[91] Phil Verveer, Remarks at the Geopolitics of Internet Governance. Center for Strategic and International Studies (May 23, 2013), http://csis.org/event/geopolitics-internet-governance (last visited June 3, 2013).

pornography. Utopian theorists like John Perry Barlow believe that the Internet will be generative of the democratization of the world system.[92]

Privacy advocates such as the Electronic Freedom Foundation worry about the potential for widespread surveillance and the emergence of a new form of Jeremy Bentham's Panopticon, where anyone and everyone can be seen without being able to tell when they are being watched. As Lawrence Lessig notes, libertarians appear somewhat naive: "Cyberspace, it is said, cannot be regulated. It 'cannot be governed;' its 'innate ability' is to resist regulation. In its essence, cyberspace is a space of no control."[93] In fact, a change in the architecture of the Internet can radically restrict the freedoms of users. ISPs and broadband providers historically only examined the header section of packets for routing purposes but message content can also be scanned to increase social control or to target potential customers.

Internet protocols permit the easy identification of individual users and their preferences by their IP address but changing the architecture of the Internet could increase anonymity. For example, the World Wide Web Consortium's P3P protocol enables individuals to control their preferences about the exchange of private information. Currently, ISPs use deep packet inspection to examine the underlying data, enabling total surveillance of Internet users including websites visited and surfing preferences. Software freedom activist Richard Stallman, the founding father of the Open Source software movement, also has a utopian view of Internet governance:

> The Internet cannot function if crowds frequently block websites, just as a city cannot function if its streets are constantly full by protesters. Nevertheless, before you advocate a crackdown on Internet protests, consider what they are protesting: on the Internet, users have no rights. As the WikiLeaks case has demonstrated, what we do online, we do on sufferance.[94] The term "open source" gets its name from the distribution model in which source code accompanies the software module. Free software is a matter of the users' freedom to run, copy, distribute, study, change, and improve the software. The history of the free software movement begins in the 1970s with Richard Stallman's work in MIT's Artificial Intelligence Lab:

> Stallman decided to solve a problem with the lab's centralized printer: paper jams. With access to the printer's software source code, Stallman modified the printer software so that it would notify all lab members when the printer jammed. When the lab received a new Xerox printer, Stallman tried to improve it in the same manner. However, Xerox would not release the printer's source code. Stallman's encounter with this proprietary software model marked the beginning of his vision of the free software movement. He believed proprietary software was fundamentally incompatible with his conception of the 'golden rule.' For Stallman, sharing source code was, and is, a moral obligation.[95]

---

[92] Jonathan Zittrain, Law in A Networked World: Privacy 2.0+, 2008 U. CHI. LEGAL F. 65, 65 ("The [I]nternet is generative: it allows contributions from all corners. . . . This simple feature has allowed a blossoming of users."). See also Jonathan Zittrain, THE FUTURE OF THE INTERNET AND HOW TO STOP IT (2008).

[93] LAWRENCE LESSIG, CODE AND OTHER LAWS OF CYBERSPACE 24 (1999).

[94] Richard Stallman, DEMOCRATIC UNDERGROUND.COM (Feb. 17, 2010).

[95] John Tsai, Review 2008: For Better or Worse: Introducing the GNU General Public License Version 3, Annual Review 2008, 23 BERKELEY TECH. L. J. 547, 549 (2008).

More precisely, open source refers to four kinds of freedom, for the users of the software:

- The freedom to run the program, for any purpose (freedom 0);

- The freedom to study how the program works, and adapt it to your needs (freedom 1), access to the source code is a precondition for this;

- The freedom to redistribute copies so you can help your neighbor (freedom 2); and

- The freedom to improve the program, and release your improvements (and modified versions in general) to the public, so that the whole community benefits (freedom 3) access to the source code is a precondition for this.[96]

The Electronic Freedom Foundation described the proprietary model as similar to a consumer purchasing an automobile but being prohibited from looking under the hood to see how the engine works. Microsoft Vista, iTunes, Adobe Photoshop, and RealPlayer are examples of the closed proprietary software model because they do not permit their licensees to access source code to improve or modify computer software programs. In contrast, the FOSS software-licensing paradigm requires the licensor to give the licensee an opportunity to look under the hood so they "can easily understand and change those instructions." [97] The open source movement has also shaped and been shaped by Internet-related software developments. The term "Open Source" was coined in 1998 by computer programmers responding to Netscape's release of source code to users through its Mozilla Public License for its Internet browser.[98] That same year the Open Source Initiative (OSI) launched to enable the business community to share their source code, permitting "users to copy, modify, and redistribute the source, whether modified or unmodified, and object code derived from it."[99]

Free and Libre Open Source Software ("FLOSS") power a growing number of Internet applications. The Firefox browser, for example, is built entirely upon open-source code. FLOSS software is gaining new disciples in the business world because of its time-to-market advantage, reliability, and lower cost. Apache License Version 2.0 grants the licensee a "perpetual, worldwide, non-exclusive, no-charge, royalty-free, irrevocable copyright license to reproduce, prepare Derivative Works of, publicly display, publicly perform, sublicense, and distribute the Work and Derivative Works in Source or Object form." When programmers write code, they write in "source code"; a programming language that humans can understand.

This "source code" is then compiled into "object code," essentially a translation of source code into something the computer can understand and execute. Generally, when profit-making software is distributed, only the compiled "object code" is distributed and the programmer retains the source code as a trade secret. Regardless of whether the computer program is in object code or source code form, it is copyrightable and protectable. A number of major software licensors have devised open source license

---

[96] Free Software Foundation, What is Free Software and Why It Is So Important For Society?, http://www.fsf.org/about/what-is-free-software (last visited July 10, 2013).

[97] Brief of Amicus Curiae Electronic Freedom Foundation, KSR Int'l Co. v. Teleflex Inc., 2004 U.S. Briefs 1350 (Aug. 22, 2006).

[98] Adam Cohn, Open Source Business Models, OPEN SOURCE SOFTWARE 2007: RISKS, REWARDS AND PRACTICAL REALITIES IN THE CORPORATE ENVIRONMENT, 916 PLI/PAT 83 (Nov/Dec. 2007).

[99] Id.

agreements including: Apple Corporation's Public License; Intel's Open Source License, The University of California's BSD License; Sun Microsystems' Common Development and Distribution License, and IBM's Common Public License and the General Public License ("GPL"). Software licensors "copyleft" software by first stating that it is copyrighted and then adding "distribution terms, which are a legal instrument that gives everyone the rights to use, modify, and redistribute the program's code or any program derived from it but only if the distribution terms are unchanged. Thus, the code and the freedoms become legally inseparable."[100]

Open source software is distributed with a mandatory term that requires the licensee or any other downstream user to distribute derivative products under the same terms. The GNU/GPL Version 3, like its predecessors, requires the licensor to distribute the software's source code ("human readable code") to encourage collaboration and sharing by future users. Conversely, "field of use" is a restriction placed on how software may be used. A software program, for example, may be restricted to non-commercial or educational purposes. The GPL does not permit field of use restrictions. One of the foundational principles of open source software is the freedom to use software for any purpose.[101]

The free flow of content of any kind, shielded from governmental control, is a central assumption behind cyberspace libertarianism. Furthermore, the free and open Internet remains an important core value for transnational governance. The Council of Europe, in its Internet Governance Report (2012–2015) advocated for an Internet that is "at all times accessible and uninterrupted (i.e. not "switched off") by fostering inter-state and international cooperation."[102] According to Internet libertarians, the seamy side of the Internet is one where the Internet is a technology of control, best illustrated by repressive governmental control and censorship. The dystopian Internet resembles Jeremy Bentham's idea of a panoptic prison, where citizens are always under scrutiny by the state.[103] Lawrence Lessig summarized the Internet libertarian position well: "There is an idea that defines first generation thought about the [Internet]. Cyberspace, it is said, cannot be regulated. It "cannot be governed"; its "innate ability" is to resist regulation. In its essence, cyberspace is a space of no control."[104]

(B) Decentralized Internet Governance

Cyberspace as a separate legal space was a theory proposed in the mid-1990s focusing on the limits of national government attempting to impose its legal regime on a borderless technology. David Johnson and David Post's classic article on the sovereign Internet also illustrates "a romantic conception of cyberspace as a separate realm."[105] They argue that cyberspace resists governance as applied to physically, geographically define territories. Cyberspace challenges the law's central assumption of reliance on territorial borders. "It is a "space" bounded by screens and passwords rather than

---

[100] GNU Operating System, What is Copyleft? (2008).

[101] Brett Smith, A Quick Guide to GPLV3, http://www.gnu.org/licenses/quick-guide-gplv3.html (last visited June 18, 2013).

[102] COUNCIL OF EUROPE, INTERNET GOVERNANCE 5 (2012–2015) (Sept. 20, 2011).

[103] JAMAIS CASCIO, THE RISE OF THE PARTICIPATORY PANOPTICON (2005).

[104] LAWRENCE LESSIG, CODE AND OTHER LAWS OF CYBERSPACE 24 (1999).

[105] David R. Johnson & David Post, Law and Borders—The Rise of Law in Cyberspace, 48 STAN. L. REV. 1367, 1367–75 (1996).

physical markers."[106] Their approach to Internet law is to displace territorially based law with customary law tailored to cross-border transactions and the protection of rights. They contend:

> New rules will emerge to govern a wide range of new phenomena that have no clear parallel in the nonvirtual world. These new rules will play the role of law by defining legal personhood and property, resolving disputes, and crystallizing a collective conversation about online participants' core values.[107]

By way of example, Johnson and Post explained that there is no global trademark registration. Therefore, owners of famous trademarks must register their marks in every country and be vigilant to avoid "territorially based claims of abandonment, and to dilution arising from uses of confusingly similar marks." To protect their intellectual property, they must master each country's different registration requirements "as well as procedural and jurisdictional laws."[108] The Johnson and Post theory of governance illustrates how "taking Cyberspace seriously" as a sovereign place can lead to the development of both clear rules for online transactions and effective legal institutions.[109] They describe how cyberspace actors can disregard government regulators sidestepping territorial-based law enforcement. E-mail, for example, does not indicate the geographical location of the server processing the communication:

> Many of the jurisdictional and substantive quandaries raised by border-crossing electronic communications could be resolved by one simple principle: conceiving of Cyberspace as a distinct "place" for purposes of legal analysis by recognizing a legally significant border between Cyberspace and the "real world." Using this new approach, we would no longer ask the unanswerable question "where" in the geographical world a Net-based transaction occurred. Instead, the more salient questions become: What procedures are best suited to the often unique characteristics of this new place and the expectations of those who are engaged in various activities there? What mechanisms exist or need to be developed to determine the content of those rules and the mechanisms by which they can be enforced? Answers to these questions will permit the development of rules better suited to the new phenomena in question, more likely to be made by those who understand and participate in those phenomena, and more likely to be enforced by means that the new global communications media make available and effective.[110]

Johnson and Post posit a hypothetical explaining the complexities of Internet jurisdiction:

> A, in Austria, posts a file to the World Wide Web using a service provider in the Netherlands. The file is transported from the host machine in the Netherlands to C's service provider, located in Virginia, by way of intermediate machines located in Great Britain and Mexico. C retrieves the file and displays it on her screen in California. The file contains something that may be unlawful (either criminally or civilly) in California, Austria, the Netherlands, Great Britain, and Mexico, or in some of them but not others, a threat, perhaps, or an offer to sell securities, or a

---

[106] Id. at 1367.

[107] Id.

[108] Id.

[109] David G. Post, Governing Cyberspace, 43 WAYNE L. REV. 155, 159–161 (1996).

[110] David R. Johnson & David G. Post, Law and Borders, Id. at 1378–9.

hard-core pornographic image, or the complete text of a poem that has fallen out of copyright in some countries but not others. Whose law applies here? Which country can rightfully assert "jurisdiction" over this communication and these parties? Can California prosecute or punish A, under California law? Can Mexico, under its law? Austria? If C has suffered harm because of this communication, where can C bring suit against A?[111]

Johnson and Post predicted a new stateless sovereign will emerge without a clear parallel to law, based upon geographic boundaries. Geography is traditionally the decisive test for determining personal jurisdiction. However, geography is a "virtually meaningless construct on the Internet."[112] In contrast, Neil Netanel finds cyberpopulistic governance models unrealistic and argues they would be dystopian if implemented,[113] he writes:

> An untrammeled cyberspace would ultimately be inimical to liberal democratic principles. It would free majorities to trample upon minorities and would serve as a breeding ground for invidious status discrimination, narrowcasting and mainstreaming content selection, systematic invasions of privacy, and gross inequalities in the distribution of basic requisites for netizenship [net citizen] and citizenship in the information age.[114]

In the early years of Internet law, idealistic academic commentators described the Internet as a liability-free zone. The Internet law-in-action has demonstrated that the question should be not whether the Internet is regulable, but rather who shall regulate it? The experience of the past fifteen years is that no separate Internet sovereign has emerged to displace territorial governance. The argument that cyberspace is beyond the rule of territorial sovereigns is factually implausible given the experience of the past two decades. Nevertheless, as Milton Mueller reminds us, it was this radical liberal vision that was the first critique of nation-state based governance. The utopians opened up the possibility for the global Internet.[115]

Post and Johnson's clarion call for transnational Internet legal institutions have made some headway. WIPO's Uniform Dispute Resolution Policy has largely displaced national cybersquatting litigation.[116] Cybersquatting involves the registration as domain names of well-known trademarks by non-trademark holders who then try to sell the names back to the trademark owners.[117] Today the battle over cyberspace as a

---

[111] David G. Post, Symposium Issue: Governing Cyberspace: Law, 24 SANTA CLARA J. & HIGH TECH L. J. 883, 885–86 (2008).

[112] American Libraries Ass'n v. Pataki, 969 F. Supp. 160, 169 (S.D. N.Y. 1997).

[113] Neil Weinstock Netanel, Cyberspace Self–Governance: A Skeptical View from Liberal Democratic Theory, 88 CALIF. L. REV. 395, 406 (2000).

[114] Id.

[115] MILTON MUELLER, NETWORKS AND STATES: THE GLOBAL POLITICS OF INTERNET GOVERNANCE 5 (2010).

[116] "The Uniform Domain Name Dispute Resolution Process ("UDRP") was adopted by ICANN in 1999 on the basis of recommendations made by WIPO in the First WIPO Internet Domain Name Process. The UDRP is limited to clear cases of bad-faith, abusive registration and use of domain names and has proven highly popular among trademark owners. To date, some 35,000 UDRP cases have been processed. Looked at holistically, the results speak for themselves in terms of overall numbers of cybersquatting disputes kept out of the courts. World Intellectual Property Organization, The Uniform Domain Name Resolution Policy and WIPO (Aug. 2011).

[117] Sporty's Farm L.L.C. v. Sportsman's Mkt., Inc., 202 F.3d 489, 493 (2d Cir.2000).

special place apart from national statutes and case law is so 1995. In the twenty-first century, the buglers for cyberspace as a unique legal space are largely silent. Many policymakers outside the United States overestimate the degree to which Internet governance is U.S. centric. The quiet revolution of the past fifteen years is a gradual acceptance of the need for multistakeholder approved global legal institutions based upon transparency.

§ 2.5   GLOBAL TRANSNATIONAL GOVERNANCE

The Internet is reshaping every aspect of human social existence, creating legal dilemmas in every procedural and substantive field of law. Radically different legal cultures encounter each other on a 24/7 basis for the first time in history." Courts and legislatures are increasingly scrambling to update the law to account for the global Internet. The Internet is the functional equivalent of a global village, first anticipated by Canadian philosopher Marshall McLuhan, who coined the phrase, "The media is the message."[118] Every human being born since the mid-1990s belongs to a historical moment when the Internet's cultural heritage is truly heterogeneous. Other questions clamor for answers in the second decade of the new millennium. What should be done about the endemic epidemic of cybercrime, economic espionage, and Internet insecurity? President Barack Obama explains how cyberspace is increasingly cross-national and critical to national security:

> These challenges come in a variety of forms. Natural disasters, accidents, or sabotage can disrupt cables, servers, and wireless networks on U.S. soil and beyond.
>
> Technical challenges can be equally disruptive, as one country's method for blocking a website can cascade into a much larger, international network disruption.
>
> Extortion, fraud, identity theft, and child exploitation can threaten users' confidence in online commerce, social networks and even their personal safety. The theft of intellectual property threatens national competitiveness and the innovation that drives it. These challenges transcend national borders; low costs of entry to cyberspace and the ability to establish an anonymous virtual presence can also lead to "safe havens" for criminals, with or without a state's knowledge cybersecurity threats can even endanger international peace and security more broadly, as traditional forms of conflict are extended into cyberspace.[119]

The number of Internet users worldwide surpassed 530 million in 2001, increasing from fewer than 200 million users at the end of 1998. By 2012, there were 2.3 billion Internet users. United States Supreme Court Justice Benjamin Cardozo's 1921 description of judicial process applies equally well to the Internet: "Nothing is stable. Nothing absolute. All is fluid and changeable. There is an endless "becoming."[120] Internet law too is a moving stream not a stagnant pond and prone to transformative mutations.

---

[118] The Guardian, Why McLuhan's Chilling Vision Still Matters Today, THE GUARDIAN (July 20, 2011), http://www.guardian.co.uk/commentisfree/2011/jul/20/marshall-mcluhan-chilling-vision (last visited June 27, 2013).

[119] WHITE HOUSE, INTERNATIONAL STRATEGY FOR CYBERSPACE: PROSPERITY, SECURITY AND OPENNESS IN A NETWORKED WORLD (May 2011) at 4.

[120] BENJAMIN N. CARDOZO, THE NATURE OF JUDICIAL PROCESS 28 (1921).

To paraphrase Danish theologian and philosopher Søren Kierkegaard, Internet law ". . . can only be understood backwards; but it must be lived forwards."[121] The endemic problem with Internet governance is that many countries have not found the correct balance between regulating this technology too little or too much. In June 2013, France announced that it was reversing course and revoking its three-strike policy for illicit file sharers. This reversal of copyright law policy is emblematic of the unsettled nature of many branches of Internet law. *The New York Times* reported that the 2009 French law was enacted as the "toughest anti-piracy law in the world. Repeat offenders who ignored two warnings to quit downloading movies or music illegally were confronted with the prospect of a suspension of their Internet connection."[122] The impossibility of cutting off Internet access as well as limited evidence of the effectiveness of such a draconian law were factors that led to its revocation.[123] Many of the major stakeholders such as website content providers, and Internet content providers are openly hostile to developing international solutions, preferring market-based solutions. The Clinton Administration's White Papers on Internet governance endorsed market-based regulation as opposed to top down command models.[124] Internet law is not settled, until it is settled right. It is unclear which governance model is best-suited for the Internet of the new millennium.

(A) Co–Regulation of the Internet

Envision a future in which reliable access to the Internet is available from nearly any point on the globe, at a price that businesses and families can afford. Computers can communicate with one another across a seamless landscape of global networks permitting trusted, instantaneous communication with friends and colleagues down the block or around the world. Content is offered in local languages and flows freely beyond national borders, as improvements in digital translation open to millions a wealth of knowledge, new ideas, and rich debates. New technologies improving agriculture or promoting public health are shared with those in greatest need, and difficult problems benefit from global collaboration among experts and innovators. This, in part, is the future of cyberspace that the United States seeks—and the future we will work to realize.[125]

President Barack Obama

Co-regulation of the Internet is a utopian and pluralistic ideal, visualizing multiple countries involved and participation by civil society. Confusion abounds about the exact meaning of civil society for Internet governance. Georg Hegel's *Philosophy of Right* conceptualized civil society to encompass civic organization, churches, social organizations, and other voluntary institutions in the borderland between the family and the state. Hegel's thesis was that civil society is the emblem of modern society. The

---

[121] Encyclopedia Britannica, Søren Kierkegaard (2012).

[122] Eric Pfanner, French Appear Ready to Soften Law on Media Piracy, N.Y. Times (June 2, 2013).

[123] Id.(quoting a French Minister: "Today, it's not possible to cut off Internet access," she said. "It's something like cutting off water.").

[124] See U.S. Department of Commerce, NTIA, Management of Internet Names and Addresses, Action: Statement of Policy, 63 Federal Register No 111, 10 June 1998; See also, Steven Hetcher, The FTC as Internet Privacy Norm Entrepreneur, 53 VAND. L. REV. 2041 (2000) (arguing that the FTC has attempted to guide self-regulatory efforts through regulation).

[125] White House, International Strategy for Cyberspace: Prosperity, Security and Openness in a Networked World (May 2011) at 7.

European Union uses the term civil society to refer to private organizations outside of government thus:

> Internet governance is the development and application by Governments, the private sector and civil society, in their respective roles, of shared principles, norms, rules, decision-making procedures, and programmes that shape the evolution and use of the Internet.[126]

The role of civil society in Internet governance, largely UN-driven, has expanded unevenly. The United Nations Secretariat established the Working Group on Internet Governance ("WGIG") to study and make proposals for Global Internet Governance. The WGIG convened the World Summit on the Information Society ("WSIS") held in Geneva in 2003 and in Tunis in 2005.[127] The WGIG illustrates Lawrence Solum's second model of Internet governance, Transactional Internet Governance. Transnational Internet Governance is a counter-hegemonic alternative to top-down governance. In its Final Report, the WSIS concluded that the international management of the Internet should be multilateral, transparent and democratic with the full involvement of stakeholders. The WSIS recognized the roles of the various stakeholders.[128] In its report to the United Nations, the WGIG indicated that a vacuum exists within the context of existing Internet governance structures, since there is no global multi-stakeholder forum to address Internet-related public policy issues. It concluded that there would be merit in creating such a space for dialogue among all stakeholders.[129]

The Internet Governance Forum's ("IGF") Secretariat administers the IGF, which supports the United Nations Secretary General in carrying out the mandate from the WSIS to enable an information society. The UN established a working group defining Internet governance as including governments, the private sector, and civil society. The WSIS discussions focused on broad themes such as security, safety, cybercrime, intellectual property, international trade, and problems of access for less developed countries. The WGIG ultimately agreed upon two overarching requirements for Internet governance legitimacy; both related to developing countries: the "effective and meaningful participation of all stakeholders, especially from developing countries."[130]

The WGIG report examined current Internet infrastructure and institutions within the Global Internet. The WGIG defines Internet Governance as "the development and application by governments, the private sector and civil society, in their respective roles, of shared principles, norms, rules, decision-making procedures and programmes that shape the evolution and use of the Internet."[131] The WGIG conferees agreed that the Internet's stability and security was a key issue. The WGIG's ideal type of Internet governance included the Government, private society, and civil society. Shared governance and meaningful participation by diverse stakeholders is the ideal, where no

---

[126] EUROPE'S INFORMATION SOCIETY: INTERNET GOVERNANCE (2008).

[127] CHATEAU DE BOSSEY, REPORT OF THE WORKING GROUP ON INTERNET GOVERNANCE (2005).

[128] Abdullah A. Al–Darrab, The Need for International Internet Governance Oversight (2005).

[129] Id.

[130] LAURA DENARDIS, Protocol Politics: The Globalization of Internet Governance 171 (2009) (explaining further that the European Community's Treaty of Lisbon, too, embodied principles, rules, and decision-making procedures comprising civil society).

[131] European Commission, What is Internet Governance?, http://ec.europa.eu/information_society/policy/Internet_gov/index_en.htm (2012) (last visited May 25, 2013).

single country controls the Internet. The preferred organizational form is multilateral, transparent, and democratic. Table One below identifies WGIG's highest priority governance issues for cyberspace.

WGIG Priorities

(1) The United States Government's unilateral control of root servers without a formal relationship with any authority is a concern. Root servers are pointers for all Top–Level Domains (TLD) [i.e. .com, .org, .edu] currently managed by the Internet Assigned Numbers Authority's (IANA) root zone file.
(2) The problem of ISPs at long distance or remote from Internet backbones paying the full cost of international circuits.
(3) No multilateral mechanism implements network security to all Internet-related services, and applications. This failure to develop multinational tools to prevent cybercrimes poses problems for E–Commerce transactions.
(4) The need to develop a global definition of spam and to address or enforce anti-spam laws and practices is critical.
(5) The development of a "multi-stakeholder" civil society approach to global policy development requires transparency, openness, and wide participation from all stakeholders including those civil society organizations in developing countries.
(6) More resources are necessary to enable Internet management at the national level, especially in developing countries.
(7) The need for developing policies and procedures for gTLDs is a priority. Internet governance needs to address issues such as domain name space, multilingualism, and access issues.
(8) The allocation policies for IP addresses need to address the unequal distribution of IPv4 addresses.
(9) The problem of protecting intellectual property rights in cyberspace requires balancing the rights of IP owners against the rights of users. The governance issue is to cope with digital piracy without solidifying market oligopolies and "the impediments to access and use of

digital content."
(10) Measures to fight cybercrime or enhance Internet security must not chill expression.
(11) The Internet must secure user's privacy giving users control over the use of the personal data.
(12) Internet governance requires global standards for consumer rights in cyberspace. Global Internet consumer rights are necessary for the trustworthy cross-border purchases of goods and services.

Since the Tunis Meetings of WSIS in 2005, there have been continual calls to create new multi-stakeholder bodies to replace the Internet Corporation for Assigned Names and Numbers ("ICANN") for managing the assignment of domain names and IP addresses. ICANN has become the focus of protests since its formation. The agreement between the U.S. Commerce Department and ICANN called for top-down governance. "ICANN's monopoly of Internet governance was challenged by a number of governments worldwide, including Brazil, China, South Africa, the EC and the UK Presidency of the EU."[132] Nevertheless, ICANN affirmed its commitment to top-down governance:

> DOC affirms its commitment to a multi-stakeholder, private sector led, bottom-up policy development model for DNS technical coordination that acts for the benefit of global Internet users. A private coordinating process, the outcomes of which reflect the public interest, is best able to meet the changing needs of the Internet and of Internet users. ICANN and DOC recognize that there is a group of participants that engage in ICANN's processes to a greater extent than Internet users generally. To ensure that its decisions are in the public interest, and not just the interests of a particular set of stakeholders, ICANN commits to perform and publish analyses of the positive and negative effects of its decisions on the public, including any financial impact on the public, and the positive or negative impact (if any) on the systemic security, stability and resiliency of the DNS.

ICANN[133] is here to stay and the only issue is whether this quasi-governmental agency will institute greater transparency and participation by civil society to improve its legitimacy.

(B) UN–Anchored WGIG Models

(1) Global Internet Council

WGIG posited four alternatives for international Internet governance that illustrate Solum's second model of transnational institutions. Each model transnational entity performs functions such as audit, arbitration, policy setting, regulation, and day-to-day

---

[132] The Global Battle to Rule the Internet, POST-EUROPE (Oct. 3, 2010).

[133] Affirmation of Commitments by the United States Government and Internet Corporation for Assigned Names and Numbers (Sept. 20, 2009), http://www.icann.org/en/about/agreements/aoc/affirmation-of-commitments-30sep09–en.htm (last visited July12, 2013).

operational management and has a different organizational structure. The UN-anchored Global Internet Council ("GIC") consists of national governments with appropriate representation that would displace ICANN's Government Advisory Committee. The GIC first identifies public policy issues relevant to Internet governance and work with existing organizations much like the civil society process overseen by the WGIG. The GIC synchronizes Internet public policies and oversees Internet resource management for intellectual property, domain names, and Internet security, and cybercrime as well as development issues.

The GIC, for example, would supervise IP addresses, introduce new TLDs, and delegate country code top-level domains ("ccTLDs"). Examples of ccTLDs include .us (United States) and .de (Germany). The GIC would also set public polices as to spam, privacy, cybersecurity, and cybercrime currently not addressed by other intergovernmental organizations. Most significantly, this new transnational entity would oversee all Internet public policy issues including trade and intellectual property protection. Why eliminate ICANN's Government Advisory Committee? The concern is that ICANN is a private, nonprofit corporation under contract with the U.S. Government. While under continual criticism, ICANN continues to manage technical aspects of the Domain Name System ("DNS"). In July of 2012, ICANN began selling new top-level domains for $185,000. This new initiative is the equivalent to a license to print money and will likely lead to further calls to reform or replace ICANN.

(2) No Specific Oversight

The "no specific oversight" alternative is a second UN-anchored governance model that would create a more democratic oversight of ICANN to resolve current domain name management issues in a more inclusive way. This minimalist model posits participation of a wider spectrum of stakeholders to counter governmental control. The reformulated multinational forum would create a transparent space to resolve current issues. The forum would seek full participation of stakeholders that includes the private sector and civil society, not just the government. "The model posited that there is no need for a specific oversight organization, whether operated by one government or many. Instead, the model merely suggests that it may be necessary to enhance the role of GAC in order to meet the concerns of some governments on specific issues."[134]

(3) International Internet Council

WGIG's third alternative is a multilateral International Internet Council ("IIC") that displaces ICANN's Government Advisory Committee ("GAC"). The IIC will spearhead public policy issues such as Internet resource management and universal access. The IIC will resolve Internet resource management issues and institute transparent and democratic decision-making in a coordinated way. Eurozone governance, for example, stresses the need to have an open, transparent and regular dialogue between the European Union and diverse sectors of civil society. The European Community ("EC") has adopted these values as critically important to implementing cross-border rules within the European continent.

Europe's harmonized system of procedural and substantive law has its roots in the unifying principles of the 1957 Rome Treaty. The European Union ("EU") formed new

---

[134] William J. Drake, Why the WGIG Process Mattered (2005).

legal institutions to carry out its objective of transcending national borders.[135] The European Council represents twenty-seven member states and drafts legislation for Europe as a whole.[136] This unified approach has allowed Europe to take the lead in formulating a harmonized legal regime for the information age.

The European Union's harmonization of rules for twenty-seven countries serves as a possible model for multilateral Internet governance. For example, the EC has formulated the legal framework to advance free competition in a Single Market. The Council would have powers of initiative, implementation, management, and control; allowing it to formulate harmonized regulations. In the past two decades, the European Commission has approved Internet regulations such as the E–Commerce Directive, the Data Protection Regulation, and the Copyright Directive. The European Union recognizes that E–Commerce cannot flourish without revamping the legal infrastructure. Eurozone governance stressed the need to have an open, transparent and regular dialogue between the Union and civil society.

(4) Mixed Model

The mixed or hybrid model conceptualizes government as leading public policy development with oversight by a Global Internet Policy Council ("GIPC"). The hypothetical GIPC calls widespread participation of civil society and the private sector not just top-down governance. The World Internet Corporation for Assigned Names and Numbers ("WICANN") would theoretically displace ICANN as well as the preeminent role performed by the U.S. Department of Commerce. WICANN has not gained traction as a mechanism to displace today's piecemeal and decentralized Internet governance.

(5) International Communication Union ("ITU")

While the current ITU treaty does not address Internet governance, the ITU began a debate over how to bring about a transparent, multi-stakeholder governance model. At its May 2013 Geneva meeting, the ITU proposed a multistakeholder model of the governance of the Internet:

- Global Principles for the governance and use of the Internet;

---

[135] Article 2 of the Treaty of Rome states the following principle:

The Community shall have as its task, by establishing a common market and an economic and monetary union and by implementing the common policies or activities referred to in Articles 3 and 3a, to promote throughout the Community a harmonious and balanced development of economic activities, sustainable and non inflationary growth respecting the environment, a high degree of convergence of economic performance, a high level of employment and of social protection, the raising of the standard of living and quality of life, and economic and social cohesion and solidarity among Member States.

Treaty of Rome, art. 2, March 25, 1957, 298 U.N.T.S. 11 available at http://www.hri.org/docs/Rome57/ (last visited June 17, 2013).

[136] The Council of European Union is a key decision-making institution that is responsible for foreign affairs, farming, industry, transport, and other emergent issues. See Gateway to the European Union, http://europa.eu/index_en.htm (last visited June 17, 2013). The Council, known even as the Council of Ministers, is the principal legislative and decision-making body in the EU. The Council includes ministers of the governments of each of the Member States and is divided into different functional areas called formations. European citizens directly elect the European Parliament every five years. The Parliament consists of 785 Members of the European Parliament ("MEP"), representing nearly 500 million European citizens. The European Council and the Parliament are principally responsible for the legislative functions of the single EU market. The MEP is divided into political groups rather than representing national blocs. Each political group reflects its parties' political ideology as opposed to national political ideologies. Some MEPs are not attached to any political group. Id.

- Development and diffusion of ICTs and strategies for developing Internet connectivity globally;

- How to develop an enabling environment for encouraging growth, interoperability and development of the Internet;

- How can the Internet contribute to developing an enabling environment for encouraging growth?

- Strategies for increasing affordable global connectivity: the critical role of IXPs.

- On the basis of reciprocity, to explore ways and means for greater collaboration and coordination between ITU and relevant organizations—including, but not limited to, the Internet Corporation for Assigned Names and Numbers ("ICANN"), the Regional Internet Registries ("RIRs"), the Internet Engineering Task Force ("IETF"), the Internet Society ("ISOC") and the World Wide Web Consortium ("W3C")—involved in the development of IP-based networks and the future internet, through cooperation agreements, as appropriate, in order to increase the role of ITU in Internet governance so as to ensure maximum benefits to the global community.[137]

(C) Council of Europe's Internet Governance

The Council of Europe's ("COE") Secretariat released a report identifying priorities for 2012–2015 to advance the rule-of-law and democracy on the Internet, while respecting human rights. The COE's principal objectives for Internet governance were proposed as the following six priorities: (1) protecting the Internet's universality, integrity and openness; (2) maximizing rights and freedoms for Internet users; (3) advancing data protection and privacy; (4) enhancing the rule of law and effective co-operation against cybercrime; (5) maximizing the Internet's potential to promote democracy and culture; and (6) protecting and empowering children.[138] The COE adopted recommendations urging member States to focus on search engines and social media sites.[139] The COE's Committee of Ministers seeks to "promote coherent strategies to protect freedom of expression, access to information and other human rights and fundamental freedoms in relation to search engines."[140]

The COE is concerned that search engines' role as gatekeepers that cooperate with repressive regimes, thus blocking, biasing, and chilling expression. Another risk is that unprecedented power of the search engine is that they can now assemble private information "never intended for mass distribution."[141] Finally, COE is concerned that social media sites do not have adequate protection for children.[142] The European leaders call for greater scrutiny of social media sites by civil society.

---

[137] Fourth Draft of the Secretary–General's Report for the Fifth World Telecommunication/Information and Communication Technology Policy Forum (Jan. 10, 2013).

[138] COUNCIL OF EUROPE, INTERNET GOVERNANCE 2 (2012–2015).

[139] Search engines are "on-line tools used for finding Websites. . . . There are two types of search engines, namely, 'automated' search engines and search engines that rely upon people to review and catalogue Websites." Pablo Asbo Baistrocchi, Liability of Intermediary Service Providers in the EU Directive on Electronic Commerce, 19 SANTA CLARA COMPUTER & HIGH TECH. L.J. 111, 116 (2002).

[140] European Leaders Weigh Search Engine Regulation, BLOOMBERG BNA ELECT. COMM. L. REV. (May 21, 2012).

[141] Id.

[142] Id.

§ 2.6   INTERNET LAW & CODE; MARKETS & NORMS

Lawrence Lessig released *Code and Other Laws of Cyberspace* in 1999 and updated this work in *Code: Version 2.0* in 2006. From Lessig's perspective, Internet law is about the intersection of laws, norms, architecture, and market forces. From my perspective, Internet law scholars need to know plumbing as well as architecture. Internet "plumbers" tend to map Internet law topics to traditional doctrinal fields such as jurisdiction, contract law, torts, antitrust, or intellectual property, whereas Internet law architects map out telescopic theories about the place of Internet law in governance, culture, technological change, or historical development. Internet architects construct theories of governance whereas plumbers adapt traditional doctrinal principles to cyberspace in individual cases. Lawrence Lessig's work is emblematic of Solum's third model of Internet governance as he identified four interrelated constraints on cyberspace: (1) laws or legal sanctions, (2) social norms, (3) the market, and (4) code or architecture.

Four Modalities of Internet Law

Law: "Norms constrain through the stigma that a community imposes; markets constrain through the price that they exact; architectures constrain through the physical burdens they impose; and law constrains through the punishment it threatens."[143]	*Architecture (computer software and hardware):* "The code or software or architecture or protocols set these features, which are selected by code writers. They constrain some behavior by making other behavior possible or impossible. The code embeds certain values or makes certain values impossible. In this sense, it too is regulation, just as the architectures of real-space codes are regulations."[144]
Market Forces: "Market forces encourage architectures of identity to facilitate online commerce. Government needs to do very little—indeed, nothing at all—to	*Norms (collectively determined social norms):* "Talk about Democratic politics in the alt.discuss. knitting newsgroup, and you open yourself to flaming; "spoof" someone's identity in a MUD, and

---

[143] LAWRENCE LESSIG, CODE: VERSION 2.0 124 (2006).

[144] Id. at 125.

induce just this sort of development. The market forces are too powerful; the potential here is too great."[145]	you may find yourself "toaded" filter."[146]

Lawrence Lessig's theory is that "architecture, law, norms and markets together regulate behavior. Together, they set the terms on which one is free to act or not; together, they set the constraints that affect what is and is not possible. They are four modalities of regulation."[147] Law interacts with the other three modalities in ordering conduct in cyberspace: software code, social norms, and architecture. The law shapes and is shaped by norms, architecture, and the market. Lessig states, "Every time AOL decides that it wants to regulate a certain kind of behavior, it must select from among at least four modalities—rules, norms, prices, or architecture. And when selecting one of these four modalities, selecting architecture as a regulator will often make the most sense."[148] Lawrence Lessig conceptualizes software code as the architecture of control in cyberspace. His concern is with private and public architecture that infringes privacy, restrains speech, and hamstrings collaborative culture.

In December of 2011, The Electronic Privacy Information Center ("EPIC") filed suit against the Department of Homeland Security to require it to disclose how it is utilizing social networking, networks for secret surveillance. Homeland Security's omniscient eye is an example of Lessig's architecture of control. Anti-circumvention software, for example, constrains fair use and has the potential to chill speech.[149] Open source architecture, on the other hand, enables a culture of collaboration and sharing. Architecture determines the shape of cyberspace and is always in the process of evolution. The architecture of Internet law began to reshape every branch of law beginning in the 1990s. In 1991, a federal court convicted a computer hacker for gaining unauthorized access to BellSouth's 911 computer files and publishing this confidential information in a hackers' newsletter.

(A) Statutes and Cases as Internet Law

Internet law, like other fields of law, consists of federal and state cases, administrative rulings, statutes, regulations, and local ordinances. Nevertheless, cyberlaw also consists of social norms, industry standards, international conventions, European Union ("EU") regulations, directives, and conventions as well as foreign law from hundreds of countries. Internet law is not a unified body of law; it lacks comprehensive international conventions, codes, or directives covering diverse topics

---

[145] Id. at 177.

[146] Id. at 124.

[147] Lawrence Lessig, Architecting for Control: Version 1.0, Keynote given at the Internet Political Economy Forum Cambridge Review of International Affairs, Cambridge, UK (May 11, 2000) at 4.

[148] LAWRENCE LESSIG, CODE VERSION 2.0 94 (2006).

[149] 17 U.S.C. § 1201(a)(2)(A)–(C) (highlighting conduct which DMCA's anti-circumvention provisions seek to prevent). The anti-circumvention provision of the Digital Millennium Copyright Act states: "No person shall circumvent a technological measure that effectively controls access to a work protected under this title." Id. at § 1201(a)(10)(A); "[T]o circumvent a technological measure" means to descramble a scrambled work, to decrypt an encrypted work, or otherwise to avoid, bypass, remove, deactivate, or impair a technological measure, without the authority of the copyright owner." Id. at § 1201(a)(3)(A).

such as computer security, e-commerce law, cybertorts, cybercrimes, Internet privacy, intellectual property, content regulation and cross-border jurisdictional rules. Cyberspace raises inevitable jurisdictional issues because, by its very definition, the Internet involves transborder communications across hundreds of countries. Internet presence automatically creates a transnational presence, triggering the potential for cross-border litigation.

Lawrence Lessig urges policymakers to look beyond statutes or common law decisions and consider how Internet architecture, norms, and markets influence governance. He acknowledges that case law and statutes matter. Nevertheless, he contends that local government control of gambling, obscenity, and other online content matter. At the federal government level, the classification of cryptographic protected software as munitions by the U.S. Department of Commerce illustrates code as law.[150] Lessig is concerned that ever-expanding copyright law and the law of patents chill expression in cyberspace. Private fences, not law, play a greater role in regulating cyberspace.[151] To Lessig, private ordering, software architecture and code as well as community norms are also sources of cyberspace law.

(B) Code as Internet Law

The architecture of the Internet refers to the constraints imposed by technical standards or protocols.[152] The basic Internet constraints that are standards or protocols permit the identification of a user by their IP address. Lessig cites the role of the World Wide Web Consortium's P3P protocol that enables individuals to tailor their preferences about the exchange of private information. The evolving architecture of the Internet codetermines laws, norms, and markets. Lessig conceptualizes architecture as the physical world "as we find it." He describes how the architecture of Paris and its large boulevards limited the ability of revolutionaries to protest.[153] Another architectural example Lessig uses is the geographical separation of the German Constitutional Court in Karlsruhe and its capital city of Berlin.[154] He describes how this geographic separation limits the influence of each branch on each other; or, in the words of Winston Churchill: "We shape our buildings, and afterwards our buildings shape us."[155] The architecture of the Internet shapes the path of the law. The Internet is "layered architecture" which enables "specialized efficiency, organizational coherency, and future flexibility."[156] The Berkman Center for Internet and Society at Harvard University monitors how totalitarian countries are erecting virtual guard posts that censor websites that are perceived to threaten the regime. By way of example, China is requiring microbloggers to

---

[150] See generally, LAWRENCE LESSIG, THE FUTURE OF IDEAS (2001). See also Lawrence Lessig, The Law of the Horse: What Cyberlaw Might Teach, 113 HARV. L. REV. 501, 505 (1999) (explaining how the anonymity of the Internet makes it difficult to enforce Internet law).

[151] LAWRENCE LESSIG, CODE: AND OTHER LAWS OF CYBERSPACE 127 (1999).

[152] See Mark A. Lemley & Lawrence Lessig, The End of End-to-End: Preserving the Architecture of the Internet in the Broadband Era, 48 U.C.L.A. L. REV. 925, 940 (2001) (discussing the increasing importance of the software "level" of the architecture of the Internet and other networks).

[153] LAWRENCE LESSIG, ARCHITECTING FOR CONTROL: VERSION 1.0, Id. at 3 (noting how Napoleon III had Parisian boulevards widened to make it more difficult for revolutionaries to erect blockades).

[154] The geographic dispersion principle means that the legislative and executive branches will be less likely to exert undue influence. LAWRENCE LESSIG, CODE: AND OTHER LAWS OF CYBERSPACE 92 (1999).

[155] Winston S. Churchill quoted in THE ELOQUENCE OF WINSTON CHURCHILL 40 (F.B. Czarnomski ed. 1957).

[156] Timothy Wu, Application-Centered Internet Analysis, 85 VA. L. REV. 1163, 1189 (1999).

register with their real names as a mechanism of legal control to censor "online troublemakers."[157] . John Perry Barlow's fears of censorship on the Internet have been realized in China, Syria, Saudi Arabia and countries, which have no traditional value on expression.

A 2012 Carnegie–Mellon study confirmed that the Chinese Government is monitoring, censoring, and deleting postings on popular social media sites and Twitter. In this first empirical study of how the Chinese Government is censoring content on social media, the research team from Carnegie–Mellon University concluded that a certain set of terms such as the Tibetan Independence Movement or 89 (referring to 1989, the year of the Tiananmen Square Protest) ". . . in a posting or blog . . . leads to a higher likelihood for that message's deletion."[158] Journalists report that China is tightening its iron grip on the Internet routinely censoring microblogs and posts of dissidents.[159]

The Chinese government is employing software as well as human monitors to locate and remove anti-regime or other objectionable postings on microblogs. Totalitarian governments employing filtering software use architectures of control. The Open Net Initiative ("ONI") found 42 out of 74 countries engaged "in some form of filtering of content that ONI tests for, while 21 have been found to be engaging in 'substantial' or 'pervasive' filtering based on the breadth and/or depth of content filtered."[160] "In 2011, both Egypt and Libya severed all Internet access for brief periods during the "Arab Spring." Similar tactics have been employed in Nepal (2005), Burma (2007), and China (2009)."[161] Chander argues that only less developed countries can shut down the Internet:

> Governments can ultimately control the Internet, at least through this blunt instrument. But turning off the Internet is the desperate measure of a government that is willing to wreak enormous economic damage. When the Mubarak regime was under siege, the Egyptian government initially spared the Internet access provider to the country's stock exchange, until it realized that dissidents were turning to this provider. Turning off the Internet can only be sustained in a largely undeveloped country whose government is willing to sacrifice the economic progress and knowledge advances that the Internet offers. North Korea, for one, bans its civilian population from accessing the Internet.[162]

Nevertheless, nearly a billion Internet users are subject to some content filtering. The Internet architecture of its code is what enables content filtering. IP addresses are a technology of control enabling law enforcement to trace users that surf to illegal sites.

Code not only constrains but it can give consumers greater control over their personal information. The Platform for Privacy Preference ("P3P"), for example, is a protocol proposed by the WC3 enabling persons to select their preferences about the exchange of private information. This in turn enables computer agents to negotiate the

---

[157] The Power of Microblogs: Zombie Followers and Fake Re–Tweets, THE ECONOMIST (March 17, 2012) at 56.

[158] Id.

[159] Id.

[160] Open Net Initiative, Global Internet Filtering in 2012 at a Glance (April 3, 2012).

[161] Id.

[162] ANUPAM CHANDER, THE ELECTRONIC SILK ROAD 112 (2013).

trading of data each time an individual user connects to a site. The P3P's architecture implemented on a website gives visitors more control over their personal information than they would have visiting a brick and mortar store. The technical specifications of the P3P strictly control the data flow of personally identifiable information of consumers. Consumers can control their private information by their choice of browser preferences. The Internet allows end users "to access the content and applications of their choice, without requiring permission from broadband providers."[163]

"This architecture enables innovators to create and offer new applications and services without needing approval from any controlling entity, be it a network provider, equipment manufacturer, industry body, or government agency."[164] The Internet's openness assumes an "end-to-end" network architecture developed by standard-setting organizations not the government.[165] Software and hardware define the architecture of cyberspace and may either constrain freedom or enhance it. "Cisco decides how data packets are routed on the Internet. Microsoft determines how the majority of us browse the Web, and Google gets to choose the results of most of our searches."[166]

Encryption or digital locks also illustrate the role of software code constraining Internet behavior. Digital locks prevent unauthorized users from accessing materials and are thus an instrumentality for cabining conduct. It is arguable, for example, an online company's failure to encrypt data constitutes a breach of the duty to protect trade secrets of third parties. The architecture of the Internet enables government officials around the world to monitor and filter out content created by dissidents. The term "screening software" means software programmed to limit access to material on the Internet. By way of example, I tried to download a draft of my Congressional Testimony from my TWEN site on Westlaw while in a community library. I was unable to download the file because of the library's crude software filter that blocked my file because of the salacious word, "hornbook." The library software blocked my searches on breast implants verdicts, which was relevant to my testimony about products liability reform proposals.

Community libraries' use of content filtering programs is an example of what Lessig calls, code as law. Similarly, content providers use anti-circumvention software to protect copyrighted content.[167] When hackers circumvent digital locks, a content creator has recourse under the Digital Millennium Copyright Act's anti-circumvention provisions. Lessig describes the Internet as one of the most regulable spaces ever devised because of its architecture and code. IXPs or hubs, for example, make it possible for totalitarian countries to block content and even shut down access to the Internet.

Face recognition technologies are the newest tool for social control in the People's Republic of China. The Chinese government installed 3,000,000 cameras for video surveillance of political dissidents.[168] Software publishers have already received patents for software that uses wireless sensors permitting the government or employers to

---

[163] Federal Communications Commission, Report and Order 6 (Dec. 23, 2010).

[164] Id.

[165] Vinton G. Cerf & Robert E. Kahn, A Protocol for Packet Network Interconnection, COM-22, IEEE TRANSACTION OF COMMUNICATIONS TECH. 637 (1974).

[166] Viktor Mayer-Schonberger, Demystifying Lessig, 2008 WISC. L. REV. 713, 720.

[167] See LAWRENCE LESSIG, CODE VERSION 2.0 (2006).

[168] I Spy, With My Big Eye, THE ECONOMIST (April 28, 2012) at 68.

monitor heart rates, stress levels, and whether the person is smiling or frowning. In George Orwell's novel 1984, he described how posters of leaders bore the caption "BIG BROTHER IS WATCHING YOU" and a telescreen monitored the private and public lives of all citizens. The secret surveillance depicted in Orwell's novel is now possible through use of Internet applications and software. Google's countermeasure against state spying is to release a warning when government agencies attempt to gain access to Gmail accounts.[169] Google recommends two-step identification verification coupled with high-security passwords to thwart state spying.[170]

(C) Norms as Internet Law

Law, norms, markets, and architecture according to Lessig's theory of "Code as Law" interrelate to accomplish social control in cyberspace. Network architecture illustrates code as law because it determines who has access to what digital data. Sociologists distinguish between mores (important social norms) and folkways (customary ways of doing things. Cyberspace, too, is governed by mores and folkways. The proper function of law," Benjamin Cardozo stated, "is to articulate and enforce at least some of the obligations recognized in and by the community."[171] Lawrence Lessig adopts a sociological insight because he conceptualizes norms as a form of social control or law. Sexting, the texting of sexually explicit pictures, is the modern form of a risqué love letter popular with teenagers. Overzealous prosecutors abuse their discretion by filing child pornography charges against teenage girls who sext their boyfriends. In Pennsylvania, one overzealous prosecutor filed child pornography charges against three teenage girls who sent photographs of themselves in bras and panties to teenage boys. Two of the girls prosecuted were photographed wearing training bras while the third bared her breasts sending these risqué pictures to a teenage boy hoping to make him jealous.[172]

Overzealous prosecutors abuse their discretion by filing child pornography charges against teenage girls who sext their boyfriends. The Internet gives users the ability to join and impose informal sanctions by posting pictures taken by mobile phones. Daniel Solove tells the story of how customers in a San Francisco Apple computer retail store "noticed a vaguely androgynous person spending a lot of time there with a computer" using the store's free wireless.[173] "Some people became annoyed at the person, and they blogged and posted pictures online."[174] The YouTube video of the annoying Apple user illustrates the Internet unprecedented power to name, blame, and shame.[175]

Whenever the legal sanctions are out of pace with norms, it creates a legitimation crisis.[176] The Sociology of Law Department at Lund University is conducting long-range studies of the gap between legal statutes and social norms arising on the Internet;

---

[169] Paul Mozur & Loretta Chao, Google Flags Government Monitoring, WALL S. J. (June 7, 2012) at B4.

[170] Id.

[171] John C.P. Goldberg, Note, Community and the Common Law Judge: Reconstructing Cardozo's Theoretical Writings, 65 N.Y.U. L. REV. 1324, 1335 (1990).

[172] Radley Balko, Ruining Kids in Order to Save Them, REASON.COM, Jan. 25, 2010).

[173] DANIEL J. SOLOVE, THE FUTURE OF REPUTATION: GOSSIP, RUMOR, AND PRIVACY ON THE INTERNET 83 (2007).

[174] Id.

[175] Id.

[176] Robert C. Post, The Social Foundations of Privacy: Community and Self in the Common Law Tort, 77 CAL. L. REV. 957, 974–78 (1989) (arguing that law of torts reflects community norms).

beginning with a study of peer-to-peer sharing of files that infringe the law of copyright.[177] The Lund University researchers employed a new Legal Realism perspective by distinguishing between European copyright law-in-the books and norms evolving in e-communities. They identified a mismatch between copyright law and norms in the age 15–25 group in Sweden in their new report.[178] Seventy-five percent of their sample "did not regard the file sharing of copyright protected material to be illegal," or as a reason strong enough to stop downloading illegal content.[179] "Almost as many [respondents] state that more stringent legislation will not stop them."[180] The Lund University law school researchers concluded:

> As the establishment tries to maintain copyright laws with methods that worked during the analogical era, younger generation's respect for society's norms are hollowed out in a manner that in the end will not benefit anyone. It is striking, that the respondents feel no social pressure to follow the law, whether from parents, friends, teachers, neighbors, etc. Quite simply, there are no social norms to back up the judicial norms in this field.[181]

The Lund University study confirms that the younger generation does not perceive copyright law to be fair. "Copyright law must be perceived as being fair to the many copyright constituents (creators, publishers, remixers, consumers, fair users, corporations, universities, and many more)."[182]

(1) International Mores for Cyberspace

Sociologists divide norms into mores (norms reflecting fundamental values) and folkways (customary ways of doing things). Communities, rather than the government, determine which norms constitute mores.[183] In the early years of the Internet, users would stigmatize conduct that violated social mores such as spamming, online ads, or other commercial conduct on professional forums. Internet folkways and mores are more accountable to Darwin than to Newton, responsive to felt needs, shaped by the pressures of life and always in the process of being. A 2011 White House Report highlighted the role of norms in Internet governance at the nation-state level:

> In other spheres of international relations, shared understandings about acceptable behavior have enhanced stability and provided a basis for international action when corrective measures are required. Adherence to such norms brings predictability to state conduct, helping prevent the misunderstandings that could lead to conflict. The development of norms for state conduct in cyberspace does not require a reinvention of customary international law, nor does it render existing international norms obsolete. Long-standing international norms guiding state behavior—in times of peace and conflict—also apply in cyberspace. Nonetheless,

---

[177] The University of Lund project is entitled, "The Normative Anatomy of Society–Relations Between Norms and Law in the 21st Century."

[178] MÅNS SVENSSON AND STEFAN LARSSON, SOCIAL NORMS AND INTELLECTUAL PROPERTY (Lund University Law School 2009) (reporting results of study of 1,047 respondents on emergent norms supporting peer-to-peer sharing of infringing copyrighted materials).

[179] Id.

[180] Id.

[181] Id.

[182] Mark Fischer, The Next Great Copyright Act, DUANE MORRIS COPYRIGHT BLOG (July 8, 2013).

[183] LAWRENCE LESSIG, CODE: 2.0 341 (2006).

unique attributes of networked technology require additional work to clarify how these norms apply and what additional understandings might be necessary to supplement them. We will continue to work internationally to forge consensus regarding how norms of behavior apply to cyberspace, with the understanding that an important first step in such efforts is applying the broad expectations of peaceful and just interstate conduct to cyberspace.[184]

The White House proposed a framework of mores for cyberspace that all nation states should endorse:

Rules that promote order and peace, advance basic human dignity, and promote freedom in economic competition are essential to any international environment.

These principles provide a basic roadmap for how states can meet their traditional international obligations in cyberspace and, in many cases, reflect duties of states that apply regardless of context. The existing principles that should support cyberspace norms include:

*Upholding Fundamental Free*doms:

States must respect fundamental freedoms of expression and association, online as well as off.

Respect for Property:

States should in their undertakings and through domestic laws respect intellectual property rights, including patents, trade secrets, trademarks, and copyrights.

Valuing Privacy:

Individuals should be protected from arbitrary or unlawful state interference with their privacy when they use the Internet.

Protection from Crime:

States must identify and prosecute cybercriminals, to ensure laws and practices deny criminals safe havens, and cooperate with international criminal investigations in a timely manner.

Right of Self–Defense:

Consistent with the United Nations Charter, states have an inherent right to self-defense that may be triggered by certain aggressive acts in cyberspace.[185]

The White House normative framework for cyberspace is significant for what it omits. The framework, for example, made no mention about cross-border consumer protection or consumer rights. In contrast, the European Commission emphasizes the need for seamless consumer protection in cyberspace.

(2) Norms by Non–State Actors

Community norms have legitimated the practice of sharing infringing copies of music and video on peer-to-peer networks. Hollywood and other media moguls have been

---

[184] White House, International Strategy for Cyberspace: Prosperity, Security and Openness in a Networked World (May 2011) at 9.

[185] Id. at 10.

unable to convince communities of users that exchanging copyrighted materials constitutes infringement.[186] In 1997, two Arizona attorneys placed an advertisement captioned, "Green Card Lottery Final One?" on thousands of UseNets, contrary to newly minted mores opposing commercial postings. Exasperated Internet users responded with a wave of cancel bots that shut down the spammer's mail server. The vigilantes' actions to drive a spammer off-line exemplify the power of norms as Internet law. Bar associations are educating their members about these "social engineering" hoaxes, which have victimized a large number of lawyers. In these "spear-phishing" attacks, cyber criminals target attorneys who have websites or have posted information about their being a member of the bar. "Often, the e-mails contain accurate information about victims obtained via a previous intrusion, or from data posted on social networking sites, blogs, or other websites. This information adds a veneer of legitimacy to the message, increasing the chances the victims will open the e-mail and respond as directed."[187]

Spear phishing attackers convinced victims that software or credentials they use to access specific websites needs to be updated. The e-mail contains a link for completing the update. If victims click the link, they are taken to a fraudulent website through which malicious software (malware) harvests details such as the victim's usernames and passwords, bank account details, credit card numbers, and other personal information. The criminals can also gain access to private networks and cause disruptions, or steal intellectual property and trade secrets. Internet users that deliberately plant malware or steal digital assets are violating social mores in cyberspace. Increasingly, these violations are punishable by criminal law or punitive damages in a cybertort lawsuit.

In the early years of the Internet, the Internet community was smaller and more cohesive than today's Internet. Still, informal social control plays a role on social media sites and the blogosphere where posting can escalate from snarky to vicious at the click of a mouse. Online chats or social media exchanges may seem relaxed, but a conversation in a chat room, newsgroup, or website may become the basis of a defamation lawsuit. A company may be liable for defamation for repeating false rumors about individuals or entities. Messages on the Internet may be retransmitted and posted to social media or other websites by anonymous individuals, leading to costly lawsuits.

Lawrence Lessig observed how Internet users "flame" those who violate social norms such as advertising products or services. He also noted how users employ "bozo filters" to block messages from too garrulous participants in discussion groups. Finally, he explained how user communities employ informal sanctions to enforce norms against users who "spoof" another's identity in virtual reality. In Second Life or other virtual

---

[186] LAWRENCE LESSIG, HOW BIG MEDIA USES TECHNOLOGY AND THE LAW TO LOCK CREATIVITY 1255 (2006).

[187] Internet Crime Complaint Center (IC3), Cybercriminals Continue to Use Spear Phishing Attacks to Compromise Computer Networks (June 25, 2013), http://www.ic3.gov/media/2013/130625.aspx (last visited July 13, 2013) ("Recent attacks have convinced victims that software or credentials they use to access specific websites needs to be updated. The e-mail contains a link for completing the update. If victims click the link, they are taken to a fraudulent website through which malicious software (malware) harvests details such as the victim's usernames and passwords, bank account details, credit card numbers, and other personal information. The criminals can also gain access to private networks and cause disruptions, or steal intellectual property and trade secrets.").

reality sites, the deviant user is "toaded" or fellow users remove his characters. Social ostracism augments acceptable use policies, which also tend to be norms based. Moderators, too, play a role in enforcing norms against purposeful harassment or distasteful Internet postings even though such expression is legal. On Cyberprof, a forum for cyberspace law teachers, the moderator periodically sends messages to remind users about inappropriate and off-topic postings.[188] At some point, moderators employ the equivalent of capital punishment for those who violate norms and are labeled as persistently noxious users of listservs.

Lawrence Lessig illustrates how norms control obnoxious behavior on interactive websites. Social Networking site administrators suspend subscribers for spamming, profanity, harassment, or other breaches of Internet-related etiquette. The sociology of Internet governance continues to be an important source of evolving e-commerce law, as well as in virtual worlds. There is currently a chasm between norms of privacy and the commoditization of personally identifiable information by social networking sites and other websites. U.S. online advertisers drop cookies with impunity to track user's preferences and collect personally identifiable information. The cultural ethos and customs of any culture constrain conduct. The European Commission has approved a cookies directive that gives consumers a right to control their personal information.[189]

(D) Markets as Internet Law

Lawrence Lessig also views the market as a significant instrumentality controlling cyberspace conduct. Markets regulate by placing a price on Internet activities. "Markets can be structured in many different ways. The structure of any given market will affect the supply, demand, and price in that market and, in turn the conduct of buyers and sellers."[190] A monopoly market like electricity, "characterized by extremely high fixed costs and dedicated immovable fixed assets" will create inefficiencies with more than a single supplier.[191] Technological changes such as the Internet will have an impact on the structure of the market.[192] Lessig favors a regime of net neutrality guaranteeing a free market for Internet content. He maintains that telecommunication companies such as AT&T, Verizon, and Comcast should not be permitted to create different tiers of online service. Internet architecture is the software and hardware determining interoperability, services, and access. He observed that software control determines access:[193] Professor Mayer–Schonberger argues that:

---

[188] "The purpose of this list is to provide a forum where actual and potential teachers of "Cyberspace Law" or a similar course can discuss issues of mutual concern. It is my hope that subjects to be discussed will include syllabi, course coverage, mechanisms for electronic courses, cooperation between different law schools in offering courses, and other issues or problems that arise in this context. In addition, we regularly have substantive discussions of Internet law issues." Cyberprof, Info, Page, https://mailman.stanford.edu/mailman/listinfo/cyberprof.

[189] "Article 5.3 of Directive 2002/58/EC as amended by Directive 2009/136/EC has reinforced the protection of users of electronic communication networks and services by requiring informed consent before information is stored or accessed in the user's (or subscriber's) terminal device." European Commission, The Working Party on the Protection of Individuals With Regard to the Processing of Personal Data,hhttp://ec.europa.eu/justice/data-protection/article-29/documentation/opinion-recommendation/files/2012/wp194_en.pdf (last visited May 25, 2013).

[190] THEODORE M. HAGELIN, TECHNOLOGY INNOVATION LAW AND PRACTICE: CASES AND MATERIALS 31 (2011).

[191] Id. at 32.

[192] Id. at 33.

[193] LAWRENCE LESSIG, CODE: VERSION 2.0 (2006).

Lessig conceives of the market as a mechanism that can and should be facilitated through government regulation to ensure competition, symmetry of information, and an equitable initial allocation of rights. For Lessig, however, the market is more than a mechanism of allocating scarce goods. For him it becomes an overarching metaphor, as much of cyberspace can be conceptualized in terms of choice and transparency.[194]

(E) Generative Internet Architecture

Jonathan Zittrain, the Jack N. and Lillian R. Berkman Professor for Entrepreneurial Legal Studies at Harvard University Law School, is an Internet law icon for his influential work on governance. Zittrain's work, like that of his Berkman Center colleague Lawrence Lessig, reflects Solum's third model because of his emphasis on how software code and architecture affects Internet governance. Code architecture is Janus-faced in that it can either advance or constrain creative expression and innovation on the Internet.[195] Telecommunications equipment as well as software may serve as instrumentalities of control by foreign governments.[196] His clarion call is to consider the way that open Internet architecture advances "generativity." To Zittrain, the Apple II Computer was the "quintessentially generative technology."[197] "It was a platform. It invited people to tinker with it. Hobbyists wrote programs."[198] He compares the open architecture of Apple II to the appliance-like platform incorporated in the tethered i-Phone or i-Pad, which is under the total control of Apple without the possibility of improvements by communities of users.

In Professor Zittrain's testimony before the United Kingdom's House of Lords Science and Technology Committee, he stated: "I see the iPhone as essentially the poster child, the canonical example, of an utterly non-generative device . . . it does not, and then some merchant can distill it into a pure appliance size form like Vonage."[199] In contrast, the generative Internet is comprised of tens of millions of Internet users collaborating to produce code and content. Internet security is critical to businesses that must protect themselves from economic espionage from China and other foreign countries. President Barack Obama contends that cybercrime is challenging the open and interoperative Internet, which is also a recurrent theme in Jonathan Zittrain's work:

> The world must collectively recognize the challenges posed by malevolent actors' entry into cyberspace, and update and strengthen our national and international policies accordingly. Activities undertaken in cyberspace have consequences for our lives in physical space, and we must work towards building the rule of law, to prevent the risks of logging on from outweighing its benefits. The future of an open, interoperable, secure and reliable cyberspace depends on nations

---

[194] Viktor Mayer-Schonberger, Demystifying Lessig, 2008 WISC. L. REV. 713, 720.

[195] JONATHAN ZITTRAIN, THE FUTURE OF THE INTERNET—AND HOW TO STOP IT 2 (2008).

[196] Id.

[197] Id. at 2.

[198] Id.

[199] Great Britain, House of Lord, Science and Technology Committee, Personal Internet Security 303 (5th Report of Session 2006–07).

recognizing and safeguarding that, which should endure, while confronting those who would destabilize or undermine our increasingly networked world.[200]

Apple counters widespread security threats through digital certificates, passwords, secure socket layer protocols, and other security devices. Apple's iPhones and iPods are reliable and easy to use but have chilling effects on user innovation. DRM systems that control access to copyrighted works discourage innovation in the user community. Zittrain contends that Internet governance is based in large part upon social and technological control, which is an argument closely akin to Lessig's code as law:

> Control over software—and the ability of PC users to run it—rather than control over the network, will be a future battleground for Internet regulation, a battleground primed by an independently motivated movement by consumers away from open, *generative* PCs and . . . the PC environment is arguably becoming more open, with *open source* and free programs and applications, and peer-to-peer (P2P) distribution and royalty-free licensing, the mobile and games environment remain subject to vertically integrated network operators.[201]

Zittrain's generative Internet requires interoperability enabled by reverse engineering and participation by the user community. The idea underlying Gray Hat Hacking is to develop constructive uses for reverse engineering such as hacking malware or spotting problems in software before they become full-blown disasters.[202] Reverse engineering is a process by which a computer or software engineer works backward by taking apart the underlying code of software to determine how the software works. In the context of software, a customer may reverse engineer software to extract non-copyrightable elements in the software. "Reverse engineering is the process of "starting with [a] known product and working backwards to divine the process which aided in its development or manufacture."[203]

The Electronic Freedom Foundation describes reverse engineering as a distinctive practice prefigured by industrious persons tinkering with inventions such as crystal radios or automobiles in order to make improvements.[204] "Open software projects invite computer programmers from around the world to view software code and make changes and improvements to it."[205] The Free Software Foundation ("FSF"), founded in 1985, developed the "copyleft" software licensing that defends software freedom, and fostered the creation of the GNU operating system. "Software licensors copyleft software by first stating that it is copyrighted and then adding "distribution terms," which are a legal instrument that gives everyone the rights to use, modify, and redistribute the program's code . . . Thus, the code and the freedoms become legally inseparable."[206]

---

[200] White House, International Strategy for Cyberspace: Prosperity, Security and Openness in a Networked World (May 2011) at 3.

[201] Christopher T. Marsden, Internet Co–Regulation, European Governance and Legitimacy 72 (2007) (discussing Zittrain's generative Internet theory).

[202] Shon Harris, Allen Harper, Chris Eagle & Jonathan Ness, Gray Hat Hacking: The Ethical Hacker's Handbook 6 (2007).

[203] Kewanee Oil Co. v. Bicron Corp., 470 U.S. 470, 476 (1974).

[204] Electronic Freedom Foundation, Coder's Rights Project Reverse Engineering FAQ, http://www.eff.org/issues/coders/reverse-engineering-faq#footnote1_hp63zrh.

[205] Jacobsen v. Katzer, 535 F.3d 1378, 1378–79 (9th Cir. 2008).

[206] GNU Operating System, What is Copyleft? (2008).

What forms of Internet governance threaten to chill content or creativity on the Internet? Zittrain contends "walled gardens" created by Apple and scores of other information-based companies are the greatest threat to the generative Internet. He sees the explosion of malware as impelling the increased "appliancing in networks of control." The lockdown of the Internet is a backlash to the security problem developing rapidly in cybercafés in less developed countries. Zittrain contrasts the generative Apple II with its collaborative community of users with the applianced iPhone; closed and tethered to a closed network of control. He compares the PC revolution with innovation by users of Microsoft's Windows operating system to the closed Microsoft's Xbox 360 video game console. By March of 2012, "the average amount of time Xbox 360 users spend on Microsoft's online service, "Xbox Live," is 84 hours a month, up 30% from 2011."[207]

Jonathan Zittrain contends that Apple has adopted a network of control gradually displacing the generative Internet. He argues that Apple adopted this paradigm of control in part, as a backlash against cybercriminals exploiting the openness of the generative Internet. Cybersecurity creates generative dilemmas as Internet users cede autonomy and creativity to greater network control in order to feel safe in cyberspace. The *zeitgeist* of Internet generativity accounts for much of its creative breakthroughs but it is prone to security intrusions. Information appliances and their manufacturers threaten the innovative capabilities of the Internet and personal computers. The appliancing of the Internet and the creation of "walled gardens" is an attempt by companies to cope with security threats. The Internet is not Cole Porter's Paris but is beginning to resemble an urban decay film such as *Taxi Driver*, or *Blade Runner*.

§ 2.7 WHY TERRITORY MATTERS IN GLOBAL INTERNET GOVERNANCE

(A) Local Governance of the Global Internet

Lawrence Solum's fourth model of Internet governance is local regulation by individual governments. Absent a body of law that establishes international standards for Internet law, every country imposes their national or domestic laws on the Internet. The lesson of the last fifteen years is that online companies such as Google, Microsoft, and eBay have all capitulated to domestic regulations of the United States, the European Union, and other countries where they target consumers or do business. These companies have a Hobson's choice.[208] They must either accommodate to the wishes of repressive regimes or forfeit the market. In the flattened global economy, software companies have a double-edged dilemma about how to best work with repressive regimes. Members of Congress chastised Google, Yahoo!, Microsoft, and Cisco for their software licensing agreements with repressive regimes. Representative Smith, a New Jersey Republican, charged Google with enabling evil by cooperation with the Chinese regime:

> China's policy of cutting off the free flow of information is prohibitive for the growth of democracy and the rule of law. Many Chinese have suffered imprisonment and torture in the service of truth—and now Google is collaborating with their persecutors. . . Internet companies like Google, Yahoo!, and Microsoft

---

[207] Xbox Now Used More for Online Entertainment Than Online Gaming, L.A. TIMES (March 6 2012).

[208] A Hobson's choice is presented as a free choice, when there is really one choice.

attract some of the best and brightest minds to develop cutting edge technology that can be used for good throughout the world," said Smith. "The ability to communicate openly is the key to unlock the door to freedom for those who cannot feel its touch, and these companies can help to provide that.[209]

In May 2008, a leaked presentation from Cisco engineers touted the opportunity of supplying software as that country upgrades its "security network infrastructure."[210] The Chinese government required Yahoo! to filter materials critical of the Communist Party regime as a condition of access to Chinese markets. A Congressman charged Yahoo! with collaborating with the Chinese government in the imprisonment of a dissident:

> In 2005, Yahoo!'s cooperation with Chinese secret police led to the imprisonment of the cyber-dissident Shi Tao. And this was not the first time. According to Reporters Without Borders, Yahoo! also handed over data to Chinese authorities on another of its users, Li Zhi. A Chinese court sentenced Li Zhi to eight years in prison for "inciting subversion." His "crime" was to criticize in online discussion groups and articles the well-known corruption of local officials.[211]

The Chinese government blocks Internet users from accessing Taiwanese websites and other websites critical of the government. The government requires Yahoo! to block access to Chinese users from anti-government chat rooms and other dissident forums. In 2006, a member of Congress criticized companies for bringing free speech to China instead of working with the "Chinese censorship brigade."[212] The response of these companies is that they object to Chinese censorship, but believe that working with the country will broaden the political debate.[213] Google's response to Congressional criticism is that it has a duty, as a good corporate citizen, to obey local laws. Eric Smith, Google's chief executive, defended the company by stating that Google has also restricted Internet links to neo-Nazi materials and memorabilia:

> We've made a decision that we have to respect the local law and culture. So it's not an option for us to broadly make information available that is illegal or inappropriate or immoral or what have you.[214]

U.S. companies will increasingly face a difficult choice of doing business or refusing to work with repressive regimes around the world.[215] A software company will need to anticipate criticism to avoid a public relations crisis and possible loss of trust by its customer base. Like the customer who visited Hobson's stable; they can either

---

[209] U.S. Fed. News, Rep. Smith Criticizes Google for Caving to China's Demand for Internet Censorship, U.S. FEDERAL NEWS SERVICE (Jan. 25, 2006).

[210] Cory Doctorow, Cisco Internal Memo: Chinese Censorship and Surveillance Are 'Opportunities,' BOINGBOING.NET, May 22, 2008) http://www.boingboing.net/2008/05/22/cisco-internal-memo.html.

[211] Testimony of Christopher H. Smith (R. N.J.), Proccedings of the 109th Congress, 2d Sess., The Internet in China, 152 CONG. REC. E205–04 (Feb. 28, 2006).

[212] Grant Gross, U.S. Lawmakers Scold Tech Companies for China Censorship, INFOWORLD.COM (Feb. 15, 2006) (quoting the late California Congressman Tom Lantos).

[213] Id.

[214] Tim Johnson, Internet Giant Google Defends Its Expansion into China, Saying It Made the Right Decision, Despite Trade–Offs Over Free Speech, MIAMI HERALD (April 13, 2006) at 1C.

[215] Jack L. Goldsmith, Against Cyberanarchy, 65 U. Chi. L. Rev. 1199, 1217–22 (1998) (noting "a nation can regulate people and equipment in its territory to control the local effects of the extraterritorial activity," by constraining, "the local means through which foreign content is transferred.").

take the horse nearest the barn door or take none at all.[216] They must either accommodate to the wishes of repressive regimes or forfeit the market. The hope is that even despite compromises, the Internet will be a modernizing force in the end.

The United States Constitution requires courts to give full faith and credit to judgments of sister states. However, "U.S. courts are not required to give full faith and credit to foreign judgments."[217] Nevertheless, U.S. courts do recognize foreign judgments because of comity. International comity, too, is a doctrine mandating the broad enforceability of foreign judgments and decrees unless enforcement is prejudicial or contrary to U.S. public policy.[218] However, the practical reality is that U.S. companies are increasingly complying with extraterritorial laws. The EU Cookie Directive, for example, addresses the problem of privacy on the Internet.[219] "In 2009, the European Parliament and European Union Council passed the EU Cookie Directive which amended Article 5(3) of the 2002 Directive and requires member countries to modify their laws to require entities that access information from subscribers or users' computers or other electronic devices to (1) give a user advanced written notice that a cookie is being placed on his or her device and describes what the cookie is doing; and (2) obtains the user's consent to the placement of the cookie before placing the cookie on the user's device."[220] The EU Cookie Directive is forward-looking in the sense that it applies to all future technologies that allow companies to track users' preferences.[221]

Much of the Internet economy is based upon online advertising and dropping cookies to capture consumer information. The 2009 Cookie Directive requires non-European Union-based companies using cookies to document user consent before they can use tracking cookies.[222] European consumer authorities in Norway and Sweden have investigated Google, America Online and iTunes for one-sided terms of use. U.S. companies must either comply with the European Community's Cookies Directive or face investigations by consumer agencies that will lead to injunctions or fines. The Anti–Spam Act, recently enacted by Canada, "prohibits sending commercial electronic messages without a recipient's prior consent. It provides rules governing the sending of

---

[216] The phrase is said to originate with Thomas Hobson (1544–1631), a livery stable owner in Cambridge, England. To rotate the use of his horses, he offered customers the choice of either taking the horse in the stall nearest the door or taking none at all. Wikipedia, Hobson's Choice (2013).

[217] RALPH H. FOLSOM, ET AL., INTERNATIONAL BUSINESS TRANSACTIONS: CONTRACTING ACROSS BORDERS 455 (12th ed. 2012).

[218] International comity (the mutual respect of sovereigns) requires the courts of one nation to avoid, where possible, interfering with the courts of another. See Allendale Mutual Ins. Co. v. Bull Data Systems, Inc., 10 F.3d 425, 431–33 (7th Cir. 1993).

[219] Directive 2009/136/EC of the European Parliament and of the Council of 25 November 2009 amending Directive 2002/22/EC on universal service and users' rights relating to electronic communications networks and services, Directive 2002/58/EC concerning the processing of personal data and the protection of privacy in the electronic communications sector and Regulation (EC) No 2006/2004 on cooperation between national authorities responsible for the enforcement of consumer protection laws Text with EEA relevance

[220] Carr McClellan, Impact of the EU Cookie Directive on U.S. Companies, CARR MCCLELLAN LAW BLOG, http://www.carrmcclellan.com/impact-of-the-eu-cookie-directive-on-us-companies/ (last visited May 25, 2013).

[221] "A cookie' is a data string downloaded by a website onto a visitor's computer. It allows the website to track that visitor's activity with regard to the website and recall that information for use during future visits." WARREN E. AGIN, BANKR. AND SECURED LENDING IN CYBERSPACE § 2:15 (updated 2012).-

[222] The E-Privacy Directive, 2002/58/EC, went into effect on May 26, 2012. Internet users must be informed that cookies are dropped and have a right to opt-out of the use of cookies. See art. 2(5) (requiring consumer consent to cookies).

those types of messages, including a mechanism for the withdrawal of consent."[223] U.S. companies, too, must follow Europe's rules about cookies when they target consumers in the European Union. The EC is, in effect, able to regulate Internet conduct beyond its borders.

(B) EU Regulations of the Net

Jack Goldsmith and Tim Wu argue that national governmental authorities often impose their extraterritorial will on cyberspace activities through directives such as the European Community's Data Protection Directive.[224] EU regulations apply automatically to all twenty-eight countries and need not be ratified by a convention or treaty.[225] After the European Commission, European Council, and European Parliament approved a Data Protection Directive, the Member States approved national legislation implementing the directive. Directive 95/46/EC3, adopted in 1995, had two objectives: (1) to protect the fundamental right to data protection; and (2) to guarantee the free flow of personal data between Member States. With the European Commission's approval of the Data Protection Directive, the European Community achieved greater harmonization of data protection. The Data Protection Directive requires each of the twenty-eight Member States to enact national legislation that protects "the fundamental rights and freedoms of natural persons, and in particular their right to privacy with respect to the processing of personal data."[226] This legislation must fulfill the six legal grounds defined in the Directive, which are: consent, contract, legal obligation, vital interest of the data subject or the balance between the legitimate interests of the people controlling the data, and the people on whom data is held (i.e., data subjects). The Data Protection Directive of October 1995 requires any E.U. based company to comply with specific rules for processing and transferring European consumer data.[227]

The European Union's Data Protection Directive gives data subjects control over the collection, transmission, or use of personal information. The data subject has the right to be notified of all uses and disclosures about data collection and processing. A software vendor or data base developer must obtain explicit consent as to the collection of data on race, ethnicity, or political opinions. The Data Protection Directive requires

---

[223] Jeremy Hainsworth, *E–Mail Marketing Companies Risk Fines, Class Actions Under Canadian Anti-Spam Law*, 17 ELEC. COM. & L. REP. (BNA) 929 (May 23, 2012).

[224] The protection of individuals with regard to the processing of personal data is solely governed by Directive 95/46/EC of the European Parliament and of the Council of 24 October 1995 on the protection of individuals with regard to the processing of personal data and on the free movement of such data; Directive 97/66/EC of the European Parliament and of the Council of 15 December 1997 concerning the processing of personal data and the protection of privacy in the telecommunications sector.

[225] A European regulation is a legal instrument binding in all of its part and, more important it is self-executing, which means that it is immediately enforceable as law in all Member States. By contrast an European directive is not self-executing and it is binding on the Member States as to the result to be achieved but leaves to individual countries the choice of the form and method they adopt to realize the Community objectives within the framework of their internal legal order. Regulations are legal instruments whose purpose is to the unify or harmonize European law. By contrast, directives are more flexible because they require Member States to meet just a certain minimum standard, but Member States can improve that minimum with more stringent provisions. The purpose of the Directive is the harmonization of European law because they are meant just to align the legislation of Member States.

[226] Council Directive 95/46/EC of the European Parliament and of the Council of 24 October 1995 on the protection of individuals with regard to the processing of personal data and on the free movement of such data.

[227] Id.

that all companies' personal information be protected by adequate security. Data subjects have the right to obtain copies of information collected as well as the right to correct or delete personal data. Software makers need to be mindful that consent be obtained from the data subject prior to entering in to the contract.[228] Article 23 creates liability for companies that misuse or unlawfully process of personal data.

A company may not transfer data to other countries without an "adequate level of protection."[229] Damages may be assessed for collection or transmitting information without data subject consent. This is what occurred in *Union Fédérale des Consommateurs (UFC) v. AOL France*.[230] AOL France's standard contracts contained a clause to the effect that the subscriber's personal data would be transferred outside the EU and that this data would be communicated to third party direct marketers. The Court pointed out that consent needs to be specified and communicated by a "positive act" and that in this respect; the opt-out approach urged by AOL was too complex in terms of steps to be taken by consumers.[231] The UFC case also illustrates the folly of U.S. companies exporting one-sided terms of use that violate French (and European Union) mandatory consumer law. U.S. businesses targeting European consumers need to comply with mandatory rules governing disclaimers and the elimination of remedies as well as contract formation and payment terms.[232] This lesson of UFC is that an e-commerce company must tailor its contracting practices to comply with local law.

U.S. software companies must also consider privacy regulations of individual nations in Europe and around the world. The Swedish Data Protection Act, for example, prohibits U.S. companies from harvesting names, addresses, and other personal information from its website without prior consent. U.S. companies will need to examine the data protection laws and practices of many countries to ensure that they will not be sued in a distant forum. American based companies doing business online are subject to E.U. privacy regulations. Google, for example, negotiated an agreement with the European Commission in 2008 agreeing to reduce the period in which it retains personally identifiable data to eighteen months.[233] U.S. companies must determine what personally identifiable information it is collected and how long to retain it. It must also determine what personal data is transferred to its subsidiaries or other third parties.

---

[228] Id. at art. 7.

[229] Id. at art. 25.

[230] Morrison & Foster, B2C in Europe and Avoiding Contractual Liability: Why Businesses with European Operations Should Review their Customer Contracts Now (Sept. 5, 2004) (discussing Union Fédérale des Consommateurs v. America Online, The Court of First Instance of Nanterre, June 2004).

[231] David Naylor & Cyril Ritter, B2C in Europe and Avoiding Contractual Liability: Why Businesses with European Operations Should Review Their Customer Contracts Now, LEGAL UPDATES & NEWS (Morrison & Foerster LLP), (last visited July 10, 2013), http://www.mofo.com/news/updates/files/update1297.html. (last visited August 1, 2013).

[232] The UFC court struck down AOL's browsewrap contract that purported to base contract formation or acceptance by the user on performance. Id. In addition the UFC court found the following terms to be problematic: "Cross-border transfer and disclosure of personal data, Modifications to / discontinuance of service, Modifications to payment terms, Late payments, Billing disputes, Connection fees, Per-minute billing, Disclaimers of liability for AOL content, third party content, service interruptions, service performance, results from the use of the service and negligence, AOL rights of termination, Customer rights of termination, Limitation of customer remedies and AOL liability, Customer indemnities,and License of customer content to AOL." Id.

[233] Drake Bennett, Does Google Know Too Much? BOSTON GLOBE (June 30, 2008).

The U.S. did not satisfy the European Commission's ("EC") standard for adequate privacy precautions. In 1998, the EC threatened to enjoin the transfer of European personally identifiable data to the United States. If a U.S. company processes information in the marketing of its software products or services, The European Union Directive on Data Protection will classify it as a service provider. Under the EU Data Protection Directive, a company is required to get explicit consent from data subjects as to the collection of data on race, ethnicity, political opinions, union membership, physical health, mental health, sexual preferences, and criminal records. Further, the company must implement adequate security to protect personal information.[234] Member States prohibit the transfer of personal information across national borders unless the receiving country has implemented an adequate level of protection. The United States' sectorial privacy protection did not comply with the European standard of adequately protecting consumer privacy.

If the Europeans enjoined data flow between the continents, the result would trigger a worldwide depression. To avert this financial disaster, the United States' Department of Commerce and the European Commission successfully negotiated a privacy safe harbor enforced by the Federal Trade Commission. For example, a software provider will qualify for the FTC's safe harbor if it implements consumer awareness, choice, data security, data integrity, and consumer control over personally identifiable data on its website, which are norms inconsistent with the Data Protection Directive. The software provider's software licensing activities are subject to European privacy regulations in the interconnected world of the Internet.

U.S. companies receiving consumer data from Europe must certify that they comply with Data Protection Directive principles.[235] "The U.S.–EU Safe Harbor Framework

---

[234] Directive 95/46/EC of the European Parliament and of the Council of 24 October 1995 on the Protection of Individuals With Regard to the Processing of Personal Data and on the Free Movement of such Data, OJ L 281, 23.11.1995.

[235] The Safe Harbor Principles are:

(1) An organization must provide notice to data subjects about the purposes for their information's collection and use, contact information for any inquiries or complaints, types of third parties to which the organization discloses the data, and the choices and means the organization offers for limiting use and disclosure.

(2) The organization must offer a choice to opt out from a disclosure of personal data to a third party or use of such data for a purpose incompatible with the purpose for which it was originally collected or subsequently authorized. (Opt-in requirements may apply to certain information deemed especially sensitive).

(3) Subject to (1) and (2), while transferring personal data to a third-party agent, an organization must ensure such agent subscribes to the Safe Harbor principles or is subject to the E.U. Directive or another adequacy finding. Alternatively, the organization may enter into a written agreement with such agent requiring the agent to provide at least the same level of privacy protection required by the relevant principles.

(4) Data subjects must have access to their personal information and be able to correct, amend, or delete that information where it is inaccurate (though certain exceptions may apply).

(5) Organizations must take "reasonable precautions" to protect personal information from loss, misuse, and unauthorized access, disclosure, alteration, and destruction.

(6) In accordance with item (1), organizations must use the personal information only for the intended purposes and "should take reasonable steps" to ensure that data are reliable for the intended use, accurate, complete, and current.

(7) Finally, organizations' policies must include: (i) readily available and affordable independent recourse mechanisms to investigate complaints by data subjects, resolve disputes, and award damages, where applicable; (ii) procedures for verifying that the Safe Harbor principles have been implemented

provides a safe harbor for U.S. companies to transfer personal data outside of Europe that is consistent with the requirements of the European Union Directive on Data Protection."[236] The safe harbor relies almost completely on self-policing and almost no empirical evidence exists on whether U.S. companies comply with the safe harbor principles.[237] The United States historically prefers that the business community develop its own voluntary industry standards to protect online privacy. The Data Protection Regulation, effective in 2012, requires companies to prove that they have the data subject's consent prior to collecting and distributing their personal information. The proposed Regulation will require companies to expunge personally identifiable data where the data subject withdraws consent. In other words, European consumers have a right to change their minds about whether they give permission to collect personally identifiable information, even where that data has been sold to third parties. U.S. companies that collect data from European consumers will need to conduct legal audits to comply with European law. Privacy advocates call for the EU Commission to revoke its safe harbor agreement with the United States given the revelation that the National Security Agency ("NSA") was analyzing 'meta data' of all calls sent and received on the Verizon telecommunications network via a secret order issued by the Foreign Intelligence Surveillance Act ("FISA") Court under "Business Data" provisions of the PATRIOT Act—domestic and foreign."[238] European e-commerce firms targeting Massachusetts consumers must comply with that state's privacy regulations. Massachusetts, for example, has restrictions on the distribution of the first name, last name, social security number, drivers' license number, and state identification numbers, classifiable as personally identifiable information.

Under Goldsmith's model of governance as national sovereignty, customary international law enables individual national states to impose legal sanctions on cross-border conduct that creates local detrimental effects.[239] Milton Mueller describes this inevitable acceptance of nation state control as "cyberconservatism."[240] Mueller argues that the Internet has placed pressure on individual national control as a disruptive technology by globalizing the scope of communications, making it more difficult to impose social control.[241] When borderless communication is the default, it is difficult to impose an effective regime of censorship and thought control. Secondly, the Internet

---

at the organization; and (iii) obligations to remedy problems arising out of a failure to comply with the principles.
Vadim Schick, Data Privacy Concerns for U.S. Healthcare Enterprises' Overseas Ventures, 4 J. HEALTH & LIFE SCI. L. 173 (2011) (presenting safe harbor principles).

[236] Catherine Schmierer, Better Late Than Never: How the Online Advertising Industry's Response to Proposed Privacy Legislation Eliminates the Need for Regulation, 17 RICH. J.L. & TECH. 13 (2011).

[237] "This program relies heavily on the self-policing practices of participating entities and has a limited deterrent effect because the Federal Trade Commission (FTC), charged with Safe Harbor enforcement, has limited jurisdictional reach. The basic punishment for violating the Safe Harbor principles is being de-listed from the Safe Harbor program's participant list. However, the FTC still may bring a claim against a violator of the Safe Harbor provisions under the FTC Act. Furthermore, failure of a repeated violator to notify the Department of Commerce of such violations is actionable under the False Statements Act." Id.

[238] Alexander Hauff, European Commission Should Revoke U.S. Safe Harbor Immediately (June 7, 2013), http://www.alexanderhanff.com/Revoke-Safe-Harbour-Status (last visited June 7, 2013).

[239] Jack L. Goldsmith, Against Cyberanarchy, 65 U. CHI. L. REV. 1199, 1208 (1998).

[240] MILTON MUELLER, NETWORKS AND STATES: THE GLOBAL POLITICS OF INTERNET GOVERNANCE 4 (2010).

[241] Id.

"overwhelms" government's capacities to respond to" counter-hegemonic thought.[242] Thirdly, Mueller argues that the Internet, by definition, involves distributed control. The Internet's chief protocol is not owned or even controlled by any one nation-state.[243] Fourth, the Internet spawned new institutions such as the Internet Engineering Task Force ("IETF") that forged standards and rules. He cited ICANN as an emblematic example of a "new locus of authority."[244] The Internet's lowering of the cost for joint political action[245] is also a feature integral to Yochai Benkler's theory of governance.

§ 2.8   THE WEALTH OF NETWORKS

(A) Benkler's Economics–Based Governance

Lawrence Solum's fifth model of Internet governance focuses on the role of markets and the economy. The U.S. and much of the rest of the world are transitioning to an information-based economy.[246] The Intellectual Property Alliance's 2006 report concluded that the U.S. "core" copyright industries accounted for $819.06 billion or 6.56% of the U.S. gross domestic product ("GDP").[247] Core copyright industries include the production and distribution of copyright materials. The core copyright industries accounted for nearly 13% of the total growth of the U.S. economy in 2006 leading all major industry sectors.[248] "The first move, in the making for more than a century, is to an economy centered on information (financial services, accounting, software, science) and cultural (films, music) production, and the manipulation of symbols (from making sneakers to branding them and manufacturing the cultural significance of the Swoosh)."[249]

Yochai Benkler describes a networked information economy where Karl Marx's sharp division between workers and bourgeoisie is increasingly becoming a false dichotomy. Marx predicted class conflict between the bourgeoisie who controlled the means of production and the proletariat who were wage slaves. Benkler sees the rise of the Internet as democratizing the means of production because it lowers the cost of the means of production.[250] Law is also both a means of oppression and a means of resistance in Benkler's theory of networked society. His argument is that copyright law has the potential to either liberate or oppress information-based workers. Free and

---

[242] Id.

[243] Id.

[244] Id.

[245] Id. at 5.

[246] SOFTWARE & INFORMATION INDUSTRY ASSOCIATION, SOFTWARE AND INFORMATION: DRIVING THE GLOBAL KNOWLEDGE ECONOMY 7 (2008), available at http://www.siia.net/estore/ globecon-08.pdf (stating that the U.S. software and information industries "grew more than three times faster than the overall U.S. economy in 2005, with growth of 10.8 percent compared with 3.2 percent for U.S. Gross Domestic Product (GDP). And in 2004, these industries grew 11.1 percent compared with 3.9 percent for GDP.").

[247] International Intellectual Property Alliance, Investigation No. TA–2104–024, U.S.–Korea Free Trade Agreement, www. iipa.com (June 25, 2007).

[248] STEPHEN SIWEK, COPYRIGHT INDUSTRIES IN THE U.S. ECONOMY: 2006 Report (2007).

[249] YOCHAI BENKLER, THE WEALTH OF NETWORKS: HOW SOCIAL PRODUCTION TRANSFORMS MARKETS AND FREEDOM 3 (2006).

[250] Yochai Benkler and Helen Nissenbaum write, "We suggest that the emergence of peer production offers an opportunity for more people to engage in practices that permit them to exhibit and experience virtuous behavior. We posit: (A) that a society that provides opportunities for virtuous behavior is one that is more conductive to virtuous individuals; and (B) that the practice of effective virtuous behavior may lead to more people adopting virtues as their own, or as attributes of what they see as their self-definition.") Yochai Benkler & Hellen Nissenbaum, Commons-Based Peer Production and Virtue, 14 J. POLIT. PHIL. 394, 394 (2006).

open source software, for example, is generative, controlled by those who produce it, whereas proprietary software reflects an older model, where the software publishers own the code, and control the means of production. With free and open source software, there is a complete freedom to tweak and change it and make those modifications available for other users.

Yochai Benkler's concept of Networked Information Economics ("NIE") considered commons-generated content as decoupling physical constraints on production. One Internet feature that is central to the de-differentiation of workers from capitalists is the cheap computational capabilities.[251] To Benkler, information technologies begin to break down the distinction between the proletariat and capitalists owning the means of production. Benkler's thesis about shared infrastructure of the Internet brings to mind Sly and the Family Stone's *Everybody is a Star*. Where there were once walls preventing ordinary persons from access to mass media distribution, now the free-flowing information superhighway is available to anyone with an Internet connection. YouTube videos of stupid cat tricks go viral and get millions of views. Another example of how social production of content has been extended to a larger population by the Internet is the open source software movement. The production and improvement of open software by a decentralized community of users illustrates what Benkler calls "commons-based peer production."[252]

(B) Open Source & Democratic Production

The General Public License version 3 ("GPL/V3") requires licensees to return modifications to the public under the same terms. To qualify as a GPL, the license permits users to redistribute software that enables licensees to have access to source code. The GPL license also prohibits licensors from including restrictions on other included software. Contrary to public opinion, free software is not free in the same sense as free beer or free Wi–Fi. Linus Torvalds, the developer of the "Linux kernel," famously stated, "Software is like sex; it's better when it is free." The Linux kernel is an open source operating system kernel.[253] Free software does not mean this distribution method is noncommercial. Red Hat/Linux charges users for its software products. In addition, open source licensors sometimes distribute their products at no charge but do charge for consulting services. The Internet presents the possibility of a more diffuse ownership of the means of production and thus a more collaborative culture. Benkler and Nissenbaum view open source as successful peer-to-peer production predicated upon the commons:

> Free or open source software development is an approach to developing software that resembles nothing so much as an idealized barn raising—a collective effort of individuals contributing towards a common goal in a more-or-less informal and loosely structured way. No single entity "owns" the product or manages its direction. Instead, it emerges from the collaboration of groups of developers, ranging from a few individuals up to many thousands. Many of the participants

---

[251] Yochai Benkler, Wealth of Networks, Id. at 3 ("The second is the move to a communications environment built on cheap processors with high computation capabilities, interconnected in a pervasive network—the phenomenon we associate with the Internet.").

[252] Yochai Benkler & Helen Nissenbaum, Common-Based Peer Production and Virtue, 14 J. POLIT. PHIL. 394 (2006).

[253] See generally, GREG KROAH–HARTMAN, LINUX KERNEL IN A NUTSHELL (2006) (explaining kernel configuration and building).

are volunteers working in their spare time. Corporations that do not themselves claim ownership in the product, but benefit from its development by selling services or equipment associated with the software pay some royalties.[254]

Benkler's concept of peer production in creating open software illustrates how a greater segment of the population has access and control to the means of production. Under industrial capitalism, the means of production were solidly in the hands of the bourgeoisie according to classical Marxist theory. In a durable goods-based economy, there is a constant push for investment in physical capital. In contrast, the information age economy allows larger proportions of the population to control the means of intellectual capital production.[255] Individuals can communicate with millions around the world, which was not possible in an earlier stage of capitalism.

Yochai Benkler cites the triumph of user driven innovation, such as GNU/Linux, as an alternative human centric economy. He declares the networked information economy enhances autonomy and a reflective culture outside the market sphere. The battle over the Internet pits a pro-capitalist proprietary paradigm against a collaborative community of users. Benkler views most Internet-related intervention, such as copyright as reflecting outmoded assumptions of a durable goods economy antithetical to the collaborative social economy. The larger battle is over the opportunity to build an "open, diverse, liberal equilibrium."[256]

(C) Copyright Commons

A spacious intellectual commons is a core component of a free-networked society. However, Hollywood and the recording industry are systematically undermining the innovation of the collaborative-networked economy. Yochai Benkler concludes that we should not let "yesterday's winners dictate the terms of tomorrow's economic competition."[257] Urs Gasser, Benkler's Berkman Center colleague, describes the Internet as an information ecosystem that enables anyone with access to create messages, dramatically reducing the cost of production. Glasser argues that anyone with a computer has access to the means of production:

> First, anyone with a computer and Internet access can create a message, while the costs of production have dramatically decreased in the digital age. Second, the message network of the Internet enables global and real-time transmission of information at marginal costs close to zero. Third, the Internet leads to an unprecedented level of access both to information infrastructure and to content. Fourth, the Internet has shaped what users do with information. These four shifts have in turn permitted the emergence of new businesses and business models: Wikipedia and MySpace illustrate the power of user-created content. Grokster and iTunes are two examples of distribution.[258]

---

[254] Id. at 395.

[255] James Boyle noted that for the "past twenty years we have been told that we are shifting from the industrial to the information society." JAMES, BOYLE, SHAMANS, SOFTWARE, AND SPLEENS: LAW AND THE CONSTRUCTION OF THE INFORMATION IX (1996).

[256] "No benevolent historical force will inexorably lead this technological-economic moment to develop toward an open, diverse, liberal equilibrium." Id. at 22.

[257] Yochai Benkler, Wealth of Networks, Id. at 28.

[258] Urs Gasser, Berkman Center for Internet & Society, Online Law and Business in a Globalized Economy: Seminar-Spring 2012.

Greater control of the means of production can potentially lead to a more participatory and egalitarian society with a broader governing class. Nevertheless, Benkler concedes that there is no inexorable logic driving us toward a more open, diverse, liberal equilibrium.

§ 2.9   CIVIL SOCIETY & NET NEUTRALITY

Net neutrality is the core principle that Internet service providers and governments should treat all data on the Internet equally and not engage in price discrimination or arbitrage. In the United States, the Federal Communications Commission ("FCC") has jurisdiction over interstate and foreign communications by wire and radio. The FCC's role in net neutrality arises out of "specific statutory mandates in the Communications Act and the Telecommunications Act of 1996 including provisions that direct the Commission to promote Internet investment and to protect and promote voice, video and audio communications services."[259] The FCC adopted three basic principles to promote net neutrality:

Transparency. Fixed and mobile broadband providers must disclose the network management practices, performance characteristics, and terms and conditions of their broadband services;

No blocking. Fixed broadband providers may not block lawful content, applications, services, or non-harmful devices; mobile broadband providers may not block lawful websites, or block applications that compete with their voice or video telephone services; and

No Unreasonable Discrimination. Fixed broadband providers may not unreasonably discriminate in transmitting lawful network traffic.

Neutrality is threatened when broadband providers block or slow down Internet traffic based upon the customer's wealth or financial condition. The FCC noted that as early as 2005, a broadband provider that was a subsidiary of a telephone company paid $15,000 to settle a Commission investigation into whether it had blocked Internet ports used for competitive VoIP applications. In 2008, the Commission found that Comcast disrupted certain peer-to-peer ("P2P") uploads of its subscribers, without a reasonable network management justification and without disclosing its actions.[260] Yochai Benkler views communication policies as key to the future of the Internet:

The emergence of the digitally networked environment makes possible the development of a robust, open social conversation in which all can participate as peers. This technological and economic possibility is not, however, preordained. Decisions about the organization and regulation of the content, logical, and physical layers of the Internet will determine whether the digital environment will eventually in large measure, replicate the mass media model, or whether it will indeed change the deep structure of our information environment.[261]

Network neutrality or "net neutering" raises issues about Internet users' access and expression in addition to regulatory issues. Comcast, for example, prohibited its

---

[259] Federal Communications Commission, Report and Order (Dec. 23, 2010).

[260] Id.

[261] Yochai Benkler, From Consumers to Users: Shifting Deeper Structures of Regulation: Toward Sustainable Commons and User Access, 52 FED. COMM. L.J. 561, 579 (2000).

users from using legal file-sharing programs. AT&T, a major DSL provider, blocked Pearl Jam after its lead singer Eddie Vedder criticized President George W. Bush's foreign policy.[262] In early 2012, the D.C. Circuit agreed to hear Verizon and MetroPCS lawsuit challenging the FCC's neutrality rules that "forbid ISPs from discriminating against packets on their networks."[263] "Advocates of network neutrality regulations have long worried that incumbent broadband providers would create a 'fast lane' open only to content providers that paid a premium for access."[264]

§ 2.10   THE PROBLEM OF LEGAL LAG

(A) Legal Lag & Evolving Internet Technologies

In 1922, sociologist William Ogburn wrote that the various institutions of American society do not change at the same rate, thereby creating a "cultural lag" when one element has not yet accommodated to developments in another.[265] Ogburn observed that any disruptive technology created "grave maladjustments."[266] The rise of the World Wide Web has disrupted every branch of substantive and procedural law. Rigid tort rules, forged in the "horse and buggy" era, need to evolve to address problem such as online stalking, the negligent enablement of cybercrime, and spam email. Similarly, the rapid assimilation of the Internet in today's era creates maladjustments between technology and consumer law. Recent technological advances in cyberspace that affect society rapidly outpace the courts' ability to adjust. United States Supreme Court Justice Joseph Story wrote how the law "must forever be in a state of progress, or change, to adapt itself to the exigencies and changes of society."[267] In less than twenty-five years, Internet law has created new challenges in accommodating the law limps along lagging behind new information technologies. The Internet is the world's largest marketplace, copy machine, and instrumentality for committing crimes and torts, and invading privacy, all achieved with the click of a mouse. In the early 1990s, owners of trademarks had no efficient method to delete or transfer domain names containing their trademarks.

During the mid-1990s when the World Wide Web was in its infancy, "cybersquatters" created a land office business in registered domain names of famous companies or public figures in order to sell them back for a handsome price. Domain names such as sex.com were traded, hijacked, or even converted in a Wild West style virtual land boom. In 2009, talk show host Jay Leno won a cybersquatting case against a defendant who used the domain name, "thejaylenoshow.com to direct Internet users to

---

[262] See generally, DAWN NUNZIATO, VIRTUAL FREEDOM: NEUTRALITY AND FREE SPEECH IN THE INTERNET AGE (2009).

[263] 20 No. 2 MULTICHANNEL VIDEO COMPLIANCE GUIDE NEWSL. 4 (April 2012).

[264] Timothy B. Lee, Net Neutrality Concerns Raised by Comcast's Xbox on Demand Services, ARS TECHNICA (March 26, 2012).

[265] Professor Ogburn's argument was that "the various parts of modern culture are not changing at the same rate, some parts are changing much more rapidly than others; and that since there is a correlation and interdependence of parts, a rapid change in one part of our culture requires readjustments through other changes in the various correlated parts of culture." SOCIAL SCIENCE QUOTATIONS: WHO SAID WHAT, WHEN & WHERE 175 (David L. Sills & Robert K. Merton eds., 2000) [hereinafter Social Science Quotations] (reporting survey of American life commissioned by President Herbert Hoover and published during Franklin Roosevelt's presidency).

[266] Id.

[267] JOSEPH STORY, THE MISCELLANEOUS WRITINGS OF JOSEPH STORY 508 (1852).

a real estate website."[268] The Uniform Domain Name Dispute Resolution Policy ("UDRP") developed an online procedure for resolving complaints made by trademark owners about domain names a decade ago. Today, the UDRP has largely displaced court actions to resolve disputes between trademark owners and domain name registrants.

Lawmakers have yet to sort out how digital assets such as Facebook or e-mail accounts should be treated for purposes of trusts and estates. After a user's death, does the decedent's representative have rights to control the deceased's Facebook account? Attorneys are beginning to deal with digital assets in wills that include "photos, projects, hobbies, personal records, career information, entertainment and e-mail."[269] The Hamburg, Germany Data Protection Commissioner noted that "collecting increasing amounts of personal data from users is growing even more important to Facebook, [which is] striving to live up to its impressive market value with real profits."[270] What does the reasonable expectation of privacy mean if Facebook's software can recognize uploaded photos and smartphones can recognize users?[271] Courts and legislatures must bring privacy law up to date to take into account the revolution in mobile telephones and countless applications that raise new issues.

(B) Legal Lag in Substantive Internet Law

"The globally-networked world has created new civil wrongs such as cyberpiracy, online gambling, pop-up advertising, cybersquatting, spamming, cybersmearing, and dot.org hate websites for which effective legal remedies are only beginning to evolve."[272] Chapter 6 examines the full range of cybertorts evolving to address problems such as revenge porn, computer security and the invasion of privacy. Internet torts are different from bricks and mortar torts largely because of the nature of damages suffered by plaintiffs. The predominant injury in a cybertort case is a business tort causing financial loss, reputation injury, or emotional injury rather than personal injury or physical damage to property.[273] For individual consumers, the injury is more likely to be reputational or an emotional injury rather than physical injury or death.

Torts in cyberspace arose out of e-mail, website, or software distribution, rather than traditional categories of injury such as automobile accidents, slip and fall mishaps, premises liability, medical liability, and injuries due to dangerously defective products. The growing impact of information technologies "is already creating a tremendous cultural lag, making nonsense of existing laws."[274] As of yet, the progressive principles of tort law have played relatively little role in cyberspace. Tort

---

[268] Stephanie Nebehay, Jay Leno Wins Cybersquatting Case, REUTERS (July 2, 2009) (reporting WIPO UDRP decision that real estate agent registered the domain name in bad faith and that Jay Leno had common law rights in his name).

[269] Kelly Green, Passing Down Digital Assets, WALL ST. J. (Sept. 1–2, 2012) at B8.

[270] Id. (quoting Hamburg Data Protection Commissioner Johannes Caspar).

[271] I Spy With My Big Eye, THE ECONOMIST (April 28, 2012) at 68.

[272] See Michael L. Rustad & Thomas H. Koenig, Cybertorts and Legal Lag: An Empirical Analysis, 13 S. CAL. INTERDISC. L.J. 77, 79–80 (2003).

[273] Chapter 11 covers trademark infringement in cyberspace. Trademark infringement was originally conceptualized as a commercial tort. THOMAS MCCARTHY, 1 MCCARTHY ON TRADEMARKS AND UNFAIR COMPETITION § 2:7 (4TH ED. 2009) ("Since trademark infringement is a type of unfair competition and unfair competition is a tort, it follows that trademark infringement is a commercial tort.").

[274] N.D. Batra, Space, Cyberspace, and Inner Space, THE STATESMAN (Dec. 26, 1999) (arguing that the digital technologies are creating lags in law and ethical standards).

law continues to lag behind the technological dilemmas created by an increasingly networked society. In the absence of Internet contract law, courts have no practical alternative but to stretch sales law to e-contracts. However, the courts' attempt to stretch a fifty-year-old law of sales to the licensing of intangibles is like applying horse and buggy laws in the industrial age. The licensing of software, the subject of Chapter 4, validates the legal concept of the right to use property without the passage of title. To date, the law of contracts has yet to evolve to address software licensing comprehensively. Internet law can "never be completely charted and as long as change is one of the great facts of life, it never will be."[275]

(C) Legal Lag & Telecomms

Telecommunication regulations were originally devised for landlines, wireless telephone providers, cable television providers, land-based Internet service providers, and wireless Internet providers separately. In the age of the Internet, telecommunication regulations must be updated to account for companies offering converging technologies that is phone and Internet "bundling."[276] The Internet has also created the need for a different regulatory framework to take into account mobile service not in existence in 1996 when the Telecommunications Act of 1996 was passed. Telecommunications law needs to be continually updated because of developments like VoIP, DSL service, and mobile telephone applications.

(D) Legal Lag & Tax Law

Courts do not agree about how software should be taxed.[277] The rise of the Internet has challenged the ability of government to promulgate responsive tax regulations. Sales and use taxes, first enacted by Congress in the 1930s, need to be revised to accommodate Internet developments. The New Jersey Division of Taxation ruled, "The sale of software accessed as part of a service, without transfer or delivery of the software to the consumer, is not subject to sales and use tax."[278] "In New Jersey, web-hosted services where software is accessed, but not delivered or transferred to the user, are not subject to sales and use tax" because they are a service, not a sale.[279] Commentators identify nine basic dilemmas for Internet-related tax law: (1) Who is the taxpayer? (2) Where does the transaction occur or its situs? (3) What is the nature of the transaction? (4) Where does the customer reside? (5) Is a given transaction a sale, a service, or a hybrid transaction? (6) Which jurisdiction has the authority to tax, if the transaction is a sale? (7) When may local entities impose taxes for online activities? (8) Can states compel

---

[275] Arthur T. Vanderbilt, A Report on Prelegal Education 25 N.Y.U. L. REV. 264, 264 (1950) ("Life has never been completely charted and as long as change is one of the great facts of life, it never will be; and law, we must always remember, is but one aspect of life.").

[276] Sandra A. Jeski, Leading Lawyers on Examining Privacy Issues, Addressing Security Concerns and Responding to Recent IT Trends, ASPATORE, 2011 WL 3020561 (2011) ("The lack of concern for intellectual property in software may seem surprising, but as late as 1970 manufacturer-supplied programs accounted for only about 3 percent of the cost of a computer. There was little economic incentive to press for an appropriate IP regime for software protection"). Martin Campbell–Kelly, Not All Bad: An Historical Perspective on Software Patents, 11 MICH. TELECOMM. & TECH. L. REV. 191, 210 (2005).

[277] Graham Packaging Co., LP v. Com., 882 A.2d 1076 (Pa. Commw. Ct. 2005) (summarizing jurisdictional differences in the taxability of software).

[278] New Jersey Advises Sale of Software As Service Not Subject to Sales and Use Tax, BLOOMBERG BNA ELECTRONIC COMMERCE & LAW REPORT (July 28, 2012) (quoting N.J. Div. of Taxn., Letter Ruling LR: 2012–4–SUT, 6/22/12).

[279] Id.

buyers to pay self-assessed "use" taxes? and (9) What kind of record retention requirements apply to Internet transactions?[280]

Tax rules based upon place of delivery were forged decades before the rise of electronic commerce. Robert Desiderio explains how the traditional rule for taxing sales of tangible personal property "was attributed to the place-of-delivery of the property—the destination state or market state. For sourcing sales of services and intangible property, however, the Uniform Division of Income for Tax Purposes Act ("UDITPA") has a different sourcing rule. The UDITPA principle on which the sourcing of sales of services or intangible property is based is the place-of-performance—the origin or production state."[281] Neither federal nor state tax law authorities have creatively found a method of determining nexus in cyberspace, preferring to stretch bricks and mortar rules to the virtual marketplace. Internet transactions continue to "challenge tax rules that have not been updated for a world where borders and tangible goods are not the focal points."[282] Sales taxes, first originating in the Great Depression, illustrate legal lag in tax law. "We are now in the information-age where borders are not very important, and intangibles and services are a bigger part of GDP than they were years ago."[283]

(1) Nexus in Cyberspace

Whether sales or use taxes may be imposed depends upon whether there is a nexus to the individual state seeking to collect these taxes. "Nexus has traditionally meant a degree of business activity that must be present before a taxing jurisdiction has the right to impose a tax."[284] Even in the case of Amazon.com, it is unclear whether the nexus is substantial enough with a given state for collecting state and local taxes. "The diversity of tax systems creates an administrative nightmare for multinational businesses."[285] The prospect of an Internet tax collector concerns businesses as well as libertarians.[286] State and local taxes were predicated upon physical presence within territorial boundaries. The Internet involves virtual presence and with the click of a mouse, a user can access content in hundreds of jurisdictions.

(2) Patchwork of Diverse Tax Rules

In the U.S., tax systems impose different rules for the sale of tangible property, intangibles, and services. Alabama, for example, defines the sale of goods over the Internet, but Alaska imposes no sales tax. Access to the Internet is taxable in Alabama, but not in Alaska. Alabama taxes downloadable information and software, whereas Alaska does not tax this transaction. The substantial presence and taxable nexus tests determine state tax liability, in part. However, it is unclear when an Internet retailer has a sufficient physical presence to create a taxable nexus. Many countries connected to the Internet, impose a "value added tax" ("VAT"). In the European Union, VAT

---

[280] MICHAEL L. RUSTAD & CYRUS DAFTARY, E-BUSINESS LEGAL HANDBOOK 6–104, 6–110 (3rd ed. 2003).

[281] Robert Desiderio, State Taxation: Sourcing Rules for Sales of Services and Intangible Property, 2013 EMERGING ISSUES 7006 (June 3, 2013).

[282] Annette Nellen, Overview of Internet Taxation Issues, BNA: INTERNET LAW RESOURCE CENTER (2012) at 1.

[283] Id. at 11.

[284] Karl A. Frieden and Michael E. Porter, State Taxation of Cyberspace, THE TAX ADVISER (Nov. 1, 1996).

[285] Id.

[286] Id.

legislation distinguishes between the supply of goods and the supply of services. In addition, the VAT distinguishes between different kinds of goods and different kinds of services. The U.S. approach is in the form of "sales and use taxes" ("SUT") that are indirect taxes. The Commerce Clause of the U.S. Constitution provides that Congress has the power to "regulate Commerce . . . among the several States."[287] The Commerce Clause of the U.S. Constitution prohibits states from imposing taxes that unduly burden interstate commerce.

(3) Cross–Border Internet Tax Issues

In general, foreign countries levy international taxes if a company maintains a permanent establishment within the foreign jurisdiction and profits from it. The U.S. will not tax a website business so long as it has no physical presence in the country. It is unclear whether having a server in a country can ever qualify as a permanent establishment for purpose of tax law. Permanent establishments such as Microsoft are subject to sales, use, franchise, income, customs, corporation and VATs. Unresolved issues include: (1) Which jurisdiction has the authority to tax the sale? (2) When may a country impose a tax on an E–Commerce transaction? (3) What kind of record retention requirements is necessary? and (4) Can a business strategically reduce their international tax liabilities by claiming to have permanent establishments in tax havens?

With cloud computing, there are questions of where the sites for taxable presence should be determined. Other tax issues include "the nature of the transaction (services, purchase or license of software, access to intangibles), and where income should be sourced."[288] Tax issues for cloud computing "can arise over character and source of income, permanent establishment, transfer pricing and indirect taxes."[289] One of the key issues for counsel is to determine how income should be classified:

> The characterization of income from transactions that occur in the Cloud, as a first question, then determines much of the subsequent analysis regarding source, taxable presence, applicability of transfer pricing and anti-deferral rules, the incidence of indirect taxes (e.g., VAT, GST and sales taxes), and many other tax issues. Once income from the Cloud is characterized, applying the source rules alone can be challenging. Consider, for example, the sale of a tangible good where the source rule is the place where title and risk of loss pass from seller to buyer, which is usually specified in each contract or purchase order. The source rule for services income in the US income tax world is the place of performance of the services. Depending on the facts, this place of performance could be the end-user's laptop, the server from which the user accessed the service, or the place where the code was created to be loaded onto the server (especially if the server viewed as is a mere means of delivery).[290]

---

[287] U.S. Const. art. I, § 8, cl. 3 (stating, "The Congress shall have Power . . . To regulate commerce . . . among the several State.").

[288] Id.

[289] Kent Wisner, Steve Labrum, Richard Baxter and Leigh Clark, Alvarez & Marsal, Ascending Into 'The Cloud': What Changes in the Tax Environment?, BLOOMBERG BNA ELECTRONIC COMMERCE & LAW REPORT (June 6, 2013).

[290] Id.

KPMG, one of the four largest auditors and one of the largest service companies in the world, contends that cloud computing presents a basic issue of transaction. In many, if not most cloud transactions, "there will be no such transfer and the rules governing the taxation of services income" would likely apply.[291] Cloud computing frequently is a cross-border legal environment. The U.S. government's arrest of Kim Dotcom, founder of the cloud computing storage site, Megaupload, raises new issues as to future of digital copyright issues.[292] Megaupload was a seven-year-old cloud computing storage site with tens of millions of users.[293] The U.S government charged Megaupload with violating "the Racketeer Influenced and Corrupt Organizations ("RICO") Act branding the website as a criminal enterprise that had the sole purpose of enabling copyright infringement.[294] The prosecutors based the criminal RICO action on the predicate offense of secondary copyright infringement, which is a civil action.[295]

(E) Legal Lag in Stages of Litigation

(1) Digital Smoking Guns

In the past two decades, the Internet has grown from an infant technology to occupy a central place in the American economy. The seamy side of the Internet is that this exciting new forum for informal communication and commercial interchange is also an instrumentality for many new civil wrongs. Legislatures and courts will need to rework laws of evidence and procedure for criminal as well as civil law to accommodate to the development of the Internet and related information technologies. Discovery requests for e-mail communications, social networking site postings and tweets[296] are the latest discovery frontiers.[297] Jeffrey Follett's laundry list for e-discovery includes the following platforms, which may (or may not) be in the custody or control of third parties. Litigators must take into account: databases, networks, computer systems, software servers, archives, PDAs, handheld wireless devices, mobile telephones Back up or Disaster Recovery Systems, Internet data, Tapes, discs, drives, cartridges and other storage media, paging devices, and audio devices.[298] Litigators must also determine the extent

---

[291] KPMG International, Tax in the Clouds: A Briefing for Tax Directors (2013), http://www.kpmginstitutes.com/taxwatch/insights/2012/pdf/tax-cloud-briefing.pdf (last visited June 14, 2013).

[292] Megaupload the Copyright Lobby and the Future of Digital Rights: The United States versus You (and Kim Dotcom) (White Paper by Robert R. Amsterdam & Ira P. Rothken (2013), http://kim.com/whitepaper.pdf (last visited June 20, 2013).

[293] Id. at 3.

[294] Id.

[295] Id.

[296] A "tweet" is a short message published on Twitter, a social-networking service, that allows users to post pithy messages and read the tweets of others.

[297] "Today it is black letter law that computerized data is discoverable if relevant." Anti–Monopoly, Inc. v. Hasbro, Inc., No. 94 Civ. 2120, 1995 WL 649934, at *2 (S.D.N.Y. Nov. 3, 1995). The Federal Rules of Civil Procedure were revised to include a new rule requiring litigants to turn over electronic data. See FED. R. CIV. P. 26(a)(1) advisory committee's note (1993 Amendments). Electronic smoking guns are the star witnesses in a growing number of cases. See e.g., Knox v. Indiana, 93 F.3d 1327, 1330 (7th Cir. 1996) (citing e-mail messages from one employee to another asking plaintiff whether she wished "horizontal good time"); Comiskey v. Automotive Indus. Action Group, 40 F. Supp. 2d 877, 888 (E.D. Mich. 1999) (finding sexually charged e-mails served as part of harassment claim); Harley v. McCoach, 928 F. Supp. 533, 540 (E.D. Pa. 1996) (noting that e-mails documented racial discrimination); See generally, Lisa Thomas, Social Networking in the Workplace: Are Private Employers Prepared to Comply with Discovery Requests for Posts and Tweets?, 63 SMU L. REV. 1373, 1373 (2010).

[298] JEFFREY FOLLETT, ET. AL., MCLE MASSACHUSETTS DISCOVERY PRACTICE § 20.1 (2012 ed.).

to which parties must restore or reconstruct electronic data previously deleted.[299] A set of interrogatories in a Florida federal district court reveals the extent to which the Internet is affecting all aspects of discovery:

Interrogatory 10

Please identify every personal cell phone number and provider that you have had at any time from July 5, 2012–February 1, 2013. For each account, please provide the cell phone number, the cell phone provider, the type of cell phone (e.g.—iPhone 3, iPhone 4, Galaxy S, etc.), the dates of the account, and/or whether the account is still active.

Interrogatory 11

Please identify every personal e-mail address that you have had at any time from July 5, 2012–February 1, 2013. For each account, please provide the e-mail address, the service provider, the dates of the account, and/or whether the account is still active.

Interrogatory 12

Please identify whether you had any social media accounts and/or profiles including, but not limited to, Facebook, Twitter, MySpace, you have had at any time from July 5, 2012–February 1, 2013. For each account, please provide the name and/or username associated with the profile and/or social media account, the type of social media account (e.g.—Facebook, Twitter, etc.), the email address associated with the social media account, the dates you've maintained the account, and/or whether the account is still active.

Interrogatory 13

Please identify whether you are a member of any list-serves and/or message boards, and/or websites. For each membership, please provide the name and/or username associated with the account, the URL and/or name of the list-serve and/or message board and/or website, the e-mail address associated with the account, the dates you've maintained the account, and whether that account is still active.

Interrogatory 14

Have you commented on any Internet news article and/or any other internet article and/or blog, and/or website that relate in any way to the incident that is described in the Second Amended Complaint? If so, please provide the URL for each website page that contains your comments.

Request No. 1

Please produce a copy of your personal cell phone(s) records, including all text-messages that were sent from July 5, 2012—February 1, 2013, that relate in any way to the incident that is described in the Second Amended Complaint. Please exclude any text-messages that were sent and/or received exclusively between yourself and your attorney.

Request No. 2

---

[299] Id.

Please produce a copy of all e-mails sent and/or received by your personal e-mail address(es) between July 5, 2012–February 1, 2013 that relate in any way to the incident that is described in the Second Amended Complaint. Please exclude any e-mails that were sent and/or receive exclusively between yourself and your attorney.

Request No. 3

Please produce a copy of all electronic communication either sent or received by you through social networking sites, including, but not limited to, Facebook, Twitter, and/or MySpace, between July 5, 2012—February 1, 2013, that relate in any way to the incident that is described in the Second Amended Complaint. Please exclude any electronic communications that were sent and/or received exclusively between yourself and your attorney.

Request No. 4

Please produce a copy of any and all comments that were made by you on any website, news article, message board, social networking website, that relate in any way to the incident that is described in the Second Amended Complaint.[300]

The interrogatories are emblematic of the ubiquity of e-mail, social media, and blogs in the litigation landscape. Closing jury instructions need to be update to remind jurors not to consult Facebook, Twitter, or to blog up the case. Florida's jury instructions for closing argument were recently updated to control the juror's use of social media or use of the Internet:

Members of the jury, you have now heard all the evidence, my instructions on the law that you must apply in reaching your verdict and the closing arguments of the attorneys. You will shortly retire to the jury room to decide this case. [Before you do so, I have a few last instructions for you.]

During deliberations, jurors must communicate about the case only with one another and only when all jurors are present in the jury room. You will have in the jury room all of the evidence that was received during the trial. In reaching your decision, do not do any research on your own or as a group. Do not use dictionaries, the Internet, or any other reference materials. Do not investigate the case or conduct any experiments. Do not visit or view the scene of any event involved in this case or look at maps or pictures on the Internet. If you happen to pass by the scene, do not stop or investigate. All jurors must see or hear the same evidence at the same time. Do not read, listen to, or watch any news accounts of this trial.

You are not to communicate with any person outside the jury about this case. Until you have reached a verdict, you must not talk about this case in person or through the telephone, writing, or electronic communication, such as a blog, twitter, e-mail, text message, or any other means. Do not contact anyone to assist you, such as a family accountant, doctor, or lawyer. These communications rules apply until I discharge you at the end of the case. If you become aware of any

---

[300] Salvato v. Miley, 2013 WL 2712206 at *1–2 (M.D. Fla., June 11, 2013).

violation of these instructions or any other instruction I have given in this case, you must tell me by giving a note to the bailiff.[301]

This disruptive information technology of the Internet influences every stage of trials and is changing the office practices of litigators as well as business lawyers. Attorneys operating "virtual offices" must implement reasonable computer security and use due diligence to prevent third party hackers to capturing client information. E-mail and other electronic documents are no less subject to discovery requests than are paper-based records. Computer forensic experts have been retrained to prove perjury when an ex-employee of a company deletes a smoking gun portion of an e-mail message. E-mails served as electronic smoking guns in special prosecutor Kenneth Starr's investigation of President Clinton. Blog postings, pictures posted on Facebook and tweets, are the star exhibits in a growing number of cases. An e-mail, for example, may qualify as an excited utterance under the law of evidence. E-mail messages are classified as company records, subject to statutory or regulatory record keeping.[302] Rule 34 of the Federal Rules of Civil Procedure permits a party to request an inspection and copy of documents that includes electronic information.[303]

(2) Social Media & Evidence

The Internet has the potential to link lawyers across the world. In addition, lawyers can access the federal code, court decisions, and administrative rulings through the Internet. Today lawyers routinely access materials in law schools, law firms, federal agencies, and international agencies merely at the click of a mouse. The Internet is revolutionizing the way lawyers practice law and challenges the traditional contours of the lawyer/client relationship. Ethan Katsh contended that the electronic legal culture would change the practice of law.[304] He argued that the Internet removed spatial distance as a constraint in obtaining information and even in working with people. His vision of the digital lawyer is a practitioner who can form complex relationships and communicate online across states and countries. Katsh wrote a decade before the development of Twitter that the new information technologies will: "foster new interpersonal and institutional relationships."[305] Social networks are the latest information technology to create new legal ethics issues. "Social networking sites" ("SNS") evolved first in the 1990s enabling users to develop personal profiles and

---

[301] In re Standard Jury Instructions—Contract and Business Cases, 2013 WL 2435441 (Fla. June 6, 2013).

[302] Service of process by email is well-established. In Rio Properties, Inc. v. Rio International Interlink, the plaintiff casino operator sued a foreign Internet gambling business, claiming that the defendant infringed the plaintiff's trademark. Rio Props., Inc. v. Rio Int'l Interlink, 284 F.3d 1007, 1012 (9th Cir. 2002). The plaintiff served the gambling business by regular mail to its attorney and its international courier, and by e-mail to its Internet address. Id. at 1013. The gambling business contended that service was insufficient and that personal jurisdiction was lacking. Id. at 1014. The court held that the alternative service was proper because the defendant actively evaded the conventional means of service attempted by the plaintiff. Id. at 1017. E-mail service was an appropriate alternative as the method of communication preferred by the defendant. Id. The defendant's advertisements in the forum state and the injury to the plaintiff in the forum state were sufficient to provide personal jurisdiction over the gambling business. Id. at 1021.

[303] FED. R. CIV. P. 34.

[304] M. ETHAN KATSH, LAW IN A DIGITAL WORLD (1995).

[305] Id at 17.

communicate with each other based upon affinities such as family, friendship, interests, hobbies, and racial or cultural identities.[306]

As of May 23, 2013, courts mentioned Facebook in 2,095 state and federal court decisions. Social media sites such as LinkedIn, Facebook, and MyLife are a major source of information for all Americans[307] Civil procedure and codes of ethics need to be revised to address the multifaceted ways that the Internet has the potential of infecting trials. It is unclear, for example, whether litigants can search social media during the *voir dire* proceedings to select juries. Discovery requests must also consider social media postings and tweets. A federal district judge and her law clerk surveyed courts on how to respond to jurors' use of social media during trials.[308] "Judges have long confronted juror misconduct, but the widespread use of social networking sites, such as Twitter and Facebook, [has] exponentially increased the risk of prejudicial communication amongst jurors and opportunity to exercise persuasion and influence upon jurors."[309] Federal judges now need to instruct jurors not to use the Internet or social media during a trial as well auditing their own usage:

> I know that many of you use cell phones, Blackberries, the Internet and other tools of technology. You also must not talk to anyone about this case or use these tools to communicate electronically with anyone about the case. This includes your family and friends. You may not communicate with anyone about the case on your cell phone, through e-mail, Blackberry, iPhone, text messaging, or on Twitter, through any blog or website, through any Internet chat room, or by way of any other social networking sites, including Facebook, My Space, LinkedIn, and YouTube.[310]

Social media usage by jurors is already tainting trials. On January 26, 2012, a New York court ordered a *subpoena duces tecum* (under penalty bring with you) to Twitter seeking user information including the e-mail address and physical address, and tweets posted for the period of September 15, 2011 to December 31, 2011, for the Twitter account @destructuremal.[311] A New York court ruled that the Twitter account user had no expectation of privacy and ordered Twitter to comply with the subpoena. This was the first time a New York court specifically addressed whether a criminal defendant had standing to quash a subpoena issued to a third-party online social networking site.

The court ruled that the criminal defendant had no standing to challenge the subpoena since Twitter's terms of service make it clear that information tweeted is not secret. Vandals of foreclosed homes use Twitter, Facebook, and smartphone text

---

[306] Matthew Weber & Peter Monge, Network Evolution, in ENCYCLOPEDIA OF SOCIAL NETWORKS 600 (2011).

[307] Shannon Awsumb, Social Networking Sites: The Next E–Discovery Frontier, 66 BENCH & B. MINN. 22, 22–23 (2009) (describing how a distinguished New Orleans, Louisiana prosecutor resigned after it was revealed that he posted provocative comments on the website NOLA.com under the pseudonym, Henry L. Mencken 1951). Cindy Chang, Social Media Are a Potential Mine Field on the Job, THE TIMES PICAYNE (March 25, 2012).

[308] Hon. Amy J. St. Eve & Michael A. Zuckerman, Ensuring an Impartial Jury in the Age of Social Media, 11 DUKE J. & L. TECH. 2 (2011).

[309] Id.

[310] Id.

[311] A *subpoena duces tecum* compels a person to appear in court and bring property in their possession including electronically stored documents.

messages to send social media invitations to parties to trash foreclosed homes.[312] In a California case, the prosecutor obtained search warrants for Facebook account and arrested several young persons for the vandalism.[313] In *Youkers v. State*,[314] found that a judge who was Facebook friends with the victim's father in a criminal case did not have to recuse himself. Youkers, the defendant was on parole for a previous felony conviction of tampering with evidence when prosecutors indicted him for assaulting his girlfriend, who was pregnant with his child. The defendant "describes two sources evidencing bias—(1) the judge's Facebook friendship with the father of Youkers's girlfriend, which continued during the pendency of the revocation hearing, and (2) emails to the judge from Youkers's community supervision officer."[315] The judge "testified they were designated as 'friends' on Facebook and were 'running at the same time,' but that was 'the extent of [their] relationship.' The two were not related, and, other than the private Facebook messages, they had had no other contacts through Facebook. At the time of the hearing, they were still Facebook 'friends.'"[316]

The appeals court ruled that the trial judge's Facebook communications, initiated by the victim's father, did not constitute an *ex parte* communication demonstrating partiality and bias. Key to the court's finding were the judge's actual relationship with the victim's father was limited and his prompt measures to minimize the appearance of impropriety. "The judge responded online formally advising the father the communication was in violation of rules precluding *ex parte* communications, stating the judge ceased reading the message once he realized the message was improper, and cautioning that any further communications from the father about the case or any other pending legal matter would result in the father being removed as one of the judge's Facebook 'friends.'"[317] The failure of courts to address the court's use of social media sites and rule, canon of ethics, or judicial ethics opinions addressing the issue illustrates legal lag.[318]

(3) Social Media Postings as Evidence

Incriminating Facebook postings are often "smoking guns" in online defamation, business tort, or criminal causes of action. Just as e-mail has played a crucial role in litigation, incriminating Facebook postings can also result in criminal prosecutions. A defendant's arrogant Facebook posting of an invitation to an underage keg party was the

---

[312] Tim Reid 'Sharpie Parties' Havoc on Foreclosed Home, REUTERS (Aug. 17, 2012).

[313] Id.

[314] 2013 WL 2077196 (Tex. App., May 15, 2013).

[315] Id. at 2.

[316] Id. at 3.

[317] Id. at 4.

[318] Id. (citing ABA Standing Comm. on Ethics & Prof'l Responsibility, Formal Op. 462 (2013) (concluding judge may participate in electronic social networking); Judge Susan Criss, The Use of Social Media by Judges, 60 THE ADVOC. (TEX.) 18 (2012); Judge Gena Slaughter & John G. Browning, Social Networking Dos and Don'ts for Lawyers and Judges, 73 TEX. B. J. 192 (2010)). Allowing judges to use Facebook and other social media is also consistent with the premise that judges do not "forfeit [their] right to associate with [their] friends and acquaintances nor [are they] condemned to live the life of a hermit. In fact, such a regime would . . . lessen the effectiveness of the judicial officer." Comm. on Jud. Ethics, State Bar of Tex., Op. 39 (1978). Social websites are one way judges can remain active in the community. For example, the ABA has stated, "[s]ocial interactions of all kinds, including [the use of social media websites], can . . . prevent [judges] from being thought of as isolated or out of touch." ABA Op. 462. Texas also differs from many states because judges in Texas are elected officials, and the internet and social media websites have become campaign tools to raise funds and to provide information about candidates. Id.

smoking gun leading to the criminal conviction in a recent case. Criminal prosecutors examine Facebook pages to discover evidence of illegal activities such as posted photographs of defendants making gang hand signs. Trayvon Martin's attorneys uncovered Zimmerman's MySpace postings that tend to show racist and sexist tendencies. "George Zimmerman's MySpace pages had postings that included insulting remarks about Mexicans. He referred to an ex-girlfriend as a "hoe," talked about beating a felony rap, and complained that every Mexican he ran into pulled a knife on him."[319] The defense attorney for George Zimmerman in Trayvon Martin murder case created a Facebook page for impression-management purposes to counter rumors and reframe perceptions. A few courts have resisted enforcing subpoenas against Facebook requiring it to reveal postings or personally identifiable information.[320]

"Users' tweets are what make Twitter an information network that has the ability to reach out to people in nearly every country in the world."[321] Litigants before family court are increasing the use of Facebook, Twitter and other social media postings as evidence in proceedings. For example, photographs posted on an opposing party's Facebook page might be useful in proving a client's allegations of adultery.[322] In *United States v. Landry*,[323] Landry was charged with brandishing a firearm and robbing a Wal–Mart in Fremont California along with a co-conspirator. His Facebook posting was a key "smoking gun" in determining whether he should obtain a pretrial release. The Facebook posting and cell phone photographs depict the defendant:

> flaunting large wads of cash, in excess of what appears to be several thousand dollars, as well as a photograph of Defendant next to a semiautomatic pistol. In addition, Defendant's Facebook page contains the following message in the "about" me section: "How many licks is it gone take for a young nig[XXX] to hit and get rich?" (expletive omitted). "Licks" is slang for committing a robbery.[324]

The court determined that the defendant posted a risk of flight or nonappearance in part because of his flaunting large amounts of cash in his Facebook posting and ordered him held without bail in a maximum-security unit.[325] This case confirms how law enforcement and courts use social media in their decisions. The Internet has created precedents for nearly every stage of the litigation process. Social media, in particular, is a disruptive technology for civil as well as criminal law. Courts and legislatures are just beginning to update civil and criminal procedures because of the potential of the Internet for infecting the institutional of the jury. The evolution and acceptance of the Internet has forever changed trial as well as appellate proceedings.

---

[319] Trayvon Martin's Social Media Posts May Come Up at Trial: George Zimmerman's Controversial MySpace Account Shows a Pattern of Profiling, Trayvon's Family's Lawyer Says, MIAMI HERALD (May 2, 2012).

[320] Crispin v. Christian Audigier Inc., 2010 WL 2293238 (C.D. Cal. May 26, 2010).

[321] Id. at *3.

[322] Shawn L. Reeves, Social Media Discovery in Family Court, THE SCITECHLAWYER 12 (Spring 2012).

[323] No.: CR-13–70716–MAG-1(KAW) (N.D. Ca. July 16, 2013).

[324] Id. at 4.

[325] Id. at 5.

§ 2.11 RESEARCH METHODS FOR GLOBAL INTERNET LAWYERS

(A) Need For Global Internet Lawyers

Businesses in the interconnected world information economy require a new kind of lawyer who is comfortable working in radically different legal traditions. By 2015, the number of Chinese speakers will outnumber those who predominately use the English language on the Internet. E–Businesses require lawyers to represent them who have sensitivity to foreign legal systems, customs, languages, and radically different cultural obligations. IBM's international licensing template has general terms and scores of country-specific terms. As Peter Yu writes, "Different countries have different historical traditions, political arrangements, social and economic priorities, cultural values, and legal philosophies."[326] Corporate counsel and outside lawyers need to keep up with regulatory and other legal developments around the globe. KPMG's global study of general counsel confirmed the need to manage risk in new frontiers, new markets and new technologies.[327] Counsel representing an Internet-based company cannot mechanically use the same terms of service template but must convert it to a cross-border legal milieu. Torts, contracts, and intellectual property rights need harmonized rules and standards in an increasingly heterogeneous legal environment for commercial transactions in cyberspace. Counsel advising E–Businesses must not only consider disparate legal traditions, but also the impact of local customs, currencies, codes, and export regulations in order to represent their client well.

The Internet's impact is so pervasive that in the twenty-first century all attorneys must become cyberspace lawyers or practitioners to some degree. As John Evans stated, "The Internet is like a large jellyfish. You cannot step on it. You cannot go around it. By the end of 2011, there were an estimated 2.3 billion Internet users. You have to go through it."[328] The number of Internet users worldwide passed 530 million in 2005.[329] Less than ten years later, Asia alone has over one billion Internet users accounting for 45% of the Internet users in the world. Europe has 501 million users accounting for 22% of the world Internet users. "Ten percent of the Internet users reside in Latin America. Together, Africa (6%), the Middle East (3%), and Oceana/Australia (1%) account for only 10% of the users."[330] North America accounts for only 12% of all Internet users in 2012.[331] Google is now the seventh largest company in the world with a market capitalization of 196.7 billion.[332] The Internet has created the necessity of courts rethinking what factors in addition to mere access to websites constitutes sufficient minimum contacts to satisfy due process.[333] The problem of adapting the American

---

[326] Peter K. Yu, Intellectual Property Training and Education for Development, 28 AM. UNIV. INT'L L. REV. 311, 332 (2012).

[327] KPMG, BEYOND THE LAW: KPMG'S GLOBAL STUDY OF HOW GENERAL COUNSEL ARE TURNING RISK TO ADVANTAGE (2012).

[328] John Evans, JOHN EVANS QUOTES (Oct. 1, 2012) http://thinkexist.com/quotes/john_evans/.

[329] Internet World Stats, Internet Users on Dec. 31, 2011 (2012).

[330] Id.

[331] Id.

[332] Pocket World in Figures 66 THE ECONOMIST, (2012 ed.) (reporting capitalization data on largest non-banks).

[333] "Procedural fairness, if not all that originally was meant by due process of law, is at least what it most uncompromisingly requires. Procedural due process is more elemental and less flexible than

minimum contacts doctrine to cyberspace is that no other country follows a due process model for personal jurisdiction.

For the first two decades of Internet law, academics, courts, and policymakers acted as if there was an invisible rope anchoring it to the United States. The thesis of each chapter of this Global Internet Law hornbook is that the Internet is a changing risk environment that requires lawyers to have an understanding of radically different legal cultures. In reality, countries connected to the Internet follow one of three basic traditions: civil law, the common law, and some form of theocracy. Lawyers of the twenty-first century will need an understanding of theocratic legal traditions if a company is doing business in countries where there is no separation of church and state. Counsel must also comply with civil law traditions, as most countries connected to the Internet do not follow a U.S. style common law. The civil-law system in Europe, for example, includes diverse legal systems derived from Scandinavian law, Germanic law, Roman law, as well as canon law. In other words, counsel for companies such as Google, eBay, and YouTube will need to ensure that websites are localized to take into account mandatory consumer rules and other different legal norms. Counsel will need to be aware of the different legal families and how they have radically different views of expression. For example the Koran, which is the foundation of Islamic law, classifies blasphemy, heresy and apostasy as crimes. In the U.S. and Europe, none of these capital offenses would even be crimes. The Internet has radically different approaches to nearly every substantive and procedural branch of law. Global Internet lawyers, are by definition, international lawyers because cyberspace is a cross-border legal environment.

(B) Electronic Internet Law Resources[334]

The evolution of the Internet has forever changed the legal landscape. Justice Holmes's classic essay on the path of the law drew upon six centuries of case reports and statutes. In less than twenty-five years, Internet law has created new legal dilemmas and challenges in accommodating new information technologies. More than a half century ago, a young lawyer adopted a practice tip from an experienced practitioner: "It is not so much in knowing the law as in knowing where to find the law."[335] Lawyers and legal academics have access to a treasure trove of civil codes, court decisions, statutes, and administrative rulings from around the world. Internet users can link to law schools, law firms, federal agencies, and international agencies.[336] Thanks to the creation of the Internet, both free and fee-based, legal resources have gained legitimacy in the world of legal research. When Westlaw and Lexis, two of the

---

substantive due process. It yields less to the times, varies less with conditions, and defers much less to legislative judgment." Shaugnessy v. Merzei, 345 U.S. 206, 224 (1953) (J. Jackson). To state claim for violation of procedural due process, a plaintiff must allege that (1) he was deprived of an individual interest that is encompassed within the Fourteenth Amendment's protection of life, liberty, or property, and (2) the procedures available to him did not provide due process of law

[334] This section is co-authored with Diane D'Angelo and is based in part upon our earlier article, Michael L. Rustad & Diane D'Angelo, The Path of Internet Law: An Annotated Guide to Legal Landmarks, DUKE LAW & TECH. 2012 at 012.

[335] Hon. Bernard Ryan, Presiding Judge, New York State Court of Claims in Foreward to the New York State Library Bibliography Bulletin by Ernest H. Breuer, THE NEW YORK STATE COURT OF CLAIMS: ITS HISTORY, JURISDICTION AND REPORTS (1959) at 5.

[336] Michael L. Rustad & Diane D'Angelo, The Path of Internet Law: An Annotated Guide to Legal Landmarks, 2011 DUKE L. & TECH REV. 12 (2011).

world's leading fee-based legal research databases, first switched to a web-based interface in the late 1990s, "they moved the search application to their servers and eliminated the need for software to be installed and updated on every computer used for research."[337]

Lawyers around the world may access all the resources on Westlaw and Lexis, 24/7, from any computer in the world by just entering a username and password. Lexis has customers in more than 100 countries and those customers can search over a billion records from more than 45,000 legal, news and business sources.[338] Westlaw also has more than 40,000 legal databases[339] and Thomson Reuters, Westlaw's parent company posted 2012 revenue of $3.3 billion for their legal collection.[340] Both of these legal research powerhouses, two of the largest law e-libraries in the world, are coming close to fulfilling Benjamin Kaplan's vision of networks of computers capable of storing simulacra of the entire treasure of the accumulated knowledge of courts, legislatures, and legal academics. The British Broadcasting Corporation has a web page that gives site visitors access to every program aired over the preceding eighty years. The Internet has done more than any technology to create a storehouse of human knowledge across cultures and legal landscapes.

(C) Blogosphere & Twitter as Sources of Internet Law

The blogosphere is a good resource for tracking global Internet law developments. Most blogs permit users to sign up for RSS feeds so they can automatically receive updates when something has been posted concerning a reader's area of interest. Feedly,[341] Digg Reader,[342] NewsBlur,[343] and the Microsoft Outlook RSS Feed Reader are excellent. Eric Goldman, a law professor and director of Santa Clara University School of Law's High Tech Law Institute, features Internet-related law and policy issues on his Technology and Marketing Law Blog.[344] His blog focuses on hot Internet law cases, statutory developments, and works-in-progress.

Under the supervision of University of Pittsburgh law professor Bernard Hibbitts, *Jurist* provides legal news and real-time legal research services, and is published by a mostly-volunteer team of part-time law student reporters, editors, and Web developers. *Jurist* includes state, federal, and international materials.[345] Other noteworthy blogs include the Berkman Center for Internet and Society at Harvard Law School,[346] the

---

[337] Diane Murley, Law Libraries in the Cloud, 101 LAW LIBR. J. 249, 254 (2009).

[338] LexisNexis, http://www.lexisnexis.com/en-us/about-us/about-us.page (last visited June 24, 2013).

[339] Thomson Reuters Launches WestlawNext—The Next Chapter in Legal Research, http://newsbreaks.infotoday.com/NewsBreaks/Thomson-Reuters-Launches-WestlawNextThe-Next-Chapter-in-Legal-Research-60975.asp (last visited June 24, 2013).

[340] Thomas Reuters, About Us, http://thomsonreuters.com/about-us/ (last visited June 24, 2013).

[341] Feedly, http://cloud.feedly.com/#welcome (last visited July 1, 2013)

[342] Digg Reader, http://digg.com/login?next=%2Freader (last visited July 1, 2013)

[343] NewsBlur, http://www.newsblur.com/ (last visited July 1, 2013)

[344] See generally, Technology & Marketing Law Blog, http://blog.ericgoldman.org/ (last visited July 8, 2013). Professor Goldman also comments on Internet-related symposiums such as the Stanford Technology Law Review symposium on Internet intermediary liability.

[345] See generally, Univerity of Pittsburgh School of Law, The Jurist, http://jurist.law.pitt.edu/ (last visited June 25, 2013).

[346] "Harvard University's Berkman Center blog has a remarkable collection of Internet law-related materials including blog entries, symposium proceedings, and podcasts. The Berkman Center conceives of itself as a center of public policy. It takes on the perspective of an architect rather than of a plumber, with its

Stanford Center for Internet & Society Blog[347] and the Info/Law blog that was created by former Berkman fellows who are now law professors.[348]

Twitter is another resource for learning about cutting-edge cyberspace issues, instantly, as news unfolds. Twitter is made up of tweets or brief bursts of information that can be no more than 140 characters long. According to Forbes, this real-time information network is "the fastest growing social platform in the world." According to Twitter's fourth quarter report for 2012, the number of active Twitter users grew 40% from the second to the fourth quarter in 2012, which is equivalent to 288 million monthly active users.[349] Twitter is used by people in nearly every country in the world, is available in more than 20 languages and users can use free Twitter apps for iPhone, iPad, Android, BlackBerry and Windows 7.[350] Leading Internet law scholars, like Eric Goldman, Ryan Calo, and Jonathan Zittrain regularly tweet about innovative Internet law developments.

(D) Researching Global Internet Law

The oracles of Internet law are drawn from two decades of court decisions, statutes, industry standards, and international organizations. The shrinking of national boundaries means that lawyers cannot properly represent their client if they are U.S.-centric and do not consider the impact of foreign law. Online companies are cross-national and must comply with mandatory foreign laws and regulations wherever they accept orders or render services. The Internet is, in effect, an international system of legal research. Lawyers representing e-businesses need to track foreign and international developments to protect clients' rights and avoid infringing the rights of others. Advances in online technology are transforming every aspect of U.S., international, and foreign law.

Google and other technological advances have allowed users to search the Internet and online databases with greater ease and efficiency. These advances led to a paradigmatic shift in legal research and the creation of WestlawNext and Lexis Advance. Launched on February 1, 2010, WestlawNext is being marketed as "simpler and more intuitive," and allows users to "search everything all at once" without having

---

focus on big policy, Internet trends, and how the present law restricts or fosters new Internet-related development. The Berkman Center offers a wide scope of information and resources, and the Berkman Buzz offers a weekly summary of online developments." Michael L. Rustad & Diane D'Angelo, The Path of Internet Law: An Annotated Guide to Legal Landmarks, DUKE LAW & TECH. 2012 at 012.(last visited June 24, 2013).

[347] Stanford University's Center for Internet and Society allows visitors to explore specific issues like cybercrime and Internet libel. For most Internet law categories, Stanford provides a list of up-to-date cases relevant to featured subject matter. Stanford University, Center for Internet and Society, http://cyberlaw.stanford.edu/blog (last visited June 24, 2013).

[348] Info/Law covers intellectual property doctrine, communications regulation, First Amendment norms, and new technology. It is edited by William McGeveran, Associate Professor of Law at the University of Minnesota Law School; Derek Bambauer, Associate Professor of Law at the University of Arizona James E. Rogers College of Law; Tim Armstrong, Professor of Law at the University of Cincinnati College of Law; and Jane Yakowitz Bambauer, Visiting Associate Professor of Law at the University of Arizona James E. Rogers College of Law, https://blogs.law.harvard.edu/infolaw/ (last visited June 24, 2013).

[349] T.J. McCue, Twitter Ranked Fastest Growing Social Platform In The World, http://www.forbes.com/sites/tjmccue/2013/01/29/twitter-ranked-fastest-growing-social-platform-in-the-world/ (last visited June 27, 2013).

[350] Id.

to choose specific databases or libraries.[351] Peter Warwick, CEO of Thomson Reuters Legal, explained that WestlawNext was created "to work the way our customers do . . ."[352] Lexis Advance allows users to search more than 40,000 legal, news and public records sources and makes legal research "faster and easier"[353]

Both WestlawNext & Lexis Advance are "radically different" from the older versions now known as Westlaw Classic and Lexis.com. Under the former legal research systems, "you had to know what you wanted to search. You had to drill down to find the right databases."[354] Now, both WestlawNext and Lexis Advance allow users to search all materials by running a search from just one main search field, very much like a Google search. They both also allow users to create and save their research in folders. What Westlaw and Lexis have both tapped into is that users want quick and easy research tools at their fingertips. These commercial services are accommodating to new norms where users often check Google first, before the fee-based services. Not surprisingly, the way academics, practitioners, and government officials conduct legal research is being transformed by the Internet.

This Google-ized research model adopted by WestlawNext & Lexis Advance is one of two main trends in global internet law research. The second is access to free or low cost resources and automatic alert services and tools that make it possible to keep abreast of global internet developments easily and instantly. Google Scholar, for example, has a free searchable library of state and federal cases. Over the course of the next several years, Google will continue to develop free user-friendly legal research tools that will increase accessibility for Internet users around the world and influence the way other sites allow users to access legal information.

The list of resources that specifically cater to foreign Internet case law and regulatory developments are extensive.[355] There are also a number of general international, computer, technology, and IP law reviews, journals and databases that now include comparative or foreign Internet-related articles. A few noteworthy specialized publications deal with international Internet legal developments on a regular basis. Among the best resources are: *Computer Law Review International; Computer & Telecommunications Law Review (UK); Computer, Computer Law &Security Review* (Netherlands); *Competition and Regulation in Network Industries* (Belgium); *Electronic Business & Technology Law* (New Zealand); *Global Review of Cyberlaw; International Review of Law, Computers & Technology,* and *World Internet Law Report.* Westlaw & Lexis are currently undergoing great changes, as they both transition from older, classic systems to new, more user-friendly systems. While these transitions take place, users will find that some resources, including global and international materials have not yet made the switch to the newer systems. Therefore, during this transition period, it might be necessary to search both old and new systems

---

[351] Robert Ambrogi, A Great Leap Forward: WestlawNext is a Complete Reworking of the Search Interface—and Engine, LAW TECH. NEWS (Feb. 28, 2010).

[352] Id.

[353] Lexis/Nexis, Lexis Advance http://www.lexisnexis.com/en-us/products/lexis-advance.page (last visited June 24, 2013).

[354] Inside the New Westlaw, Lexis & Bloomberg Platforms, http://www.abajournal.com/news/article/exclusive_inside_the_new_westlaw_lexis_bloomberg_platforms/ (last visited June 28, 2013).

[355] For a complete guide to researching global Internet law, See Michael L. Rustad & Diane D'Angelo, The Path of Internet Law: An Annotated Guide to Legal Landmarks, 2011 DUKE L. & TECH REV. 12 (2011).

when you are researching global issues. The following are some of the best sources for researching global Internet law.

(E) Fee–Based Resources[356]

(1) BNA's Electronic Commerce & Law Report[357]

BNA's daily service provides subscribers with national and global perspectives. It covers many areas of Internet law such as electronic contracting, web & software developments, privacy, online marketing, digital copyright, taxation of e-commerce, domain name disputes and telecommunications policies. The reports include current legal, legislative, and regulatory information, in-depth looks at the top news stories, and analysis of e-commerce legal trends. Subscribers can register to receive regular emails from BNA with summaries of recent developments.

(2) Westlaw

From the main Westlaw Classic page, select the directory link at the top of the page, and then select International/Worldwide materials for cases, regulations, treatises news & business materials as well as legal news highlights and current awareness for specific countries. On WestlawNext, on the main page, just below the main search field, under browse, select all content, international materials. Westlaw's All–RPTS database contains all judicial opinions from courts in the United Kingdom, other European countries, the European Union, EU member states, and other courts worldwide as selected by the editors. This commercial service includes decisions, judgments and orders as reported by the courts. "European Union Case Law" ("EU–CS") is another good Westlaw database to use to research Internet Law cases. In this database, the subscriber can perform a keyword field search for the word Internet, cyberlaw, or specific substantive topics.[358]

Westlaw Classic has a number of features that help its subscribers stay current with Internet developments. One of the best resources is Westlaw Topical Highlights: E–Commerce. This database contains documents prepared by the West editorial staff that summarize recent developments in the law, whether a court decision or other legal activity of interest.[359] The WestClip virtual clipping service on Westlaw enables subscribers to monitor thousands of news and business databases for legal, political, and business news. WestClip runs Terms and Connectors searches automatically at

---

[356] Public law libraries throughout the U.S. often provide some form of free access to Westlaw and/or Lexis and other subscription databases like HeinOnline, which is a treasure-trove of full-text law review articles and includes the Index to Foreign Legal Periodicals and other helpful global resources. For help finding a public law library in your state, take a look at these guides that were created by Suffolk University Law School's Office of Professional and Career Development and Moakley Law Library. Scroll down towards the bottom of the page to the "Getting Out of Dodge" section. Once you open the relevant city or state guide, go to the Public Law Libraries Section, http://www.law.suffolk.edu/offices/career/handouts/ (last visited July 8, 2013).

[357] BNA's Electronic-Commerce & Law Report is a subscription database. For more details go to http://www.bna.com/electronic-commerce-law-p6796/ (last visited July 8, 2013).

[358] Michael L. Rustad & Diane D'Angelo, The Path of Internet Law: An Annotated Guide to Legal Landmarks, 2011 DUKE L. & TECH. REV. 12 (2011).

[359] To access these topical highlights, go to the main Westlaw research page and in the Search for a Database field in the left margin type "topical highlights intellectual property" or "topical highlights e-commerce."

intervals selected by the user (e.g., daily or weekly) and deliver the results to the user's email address, fax machine, or printer.[360]

(3) Lexis

Lexis.com provides access to an extensive collection of foreign materials. To access these wide-ranging resources on Lexis.com, the subscriber goes to Area of Law—By Topic, Foreign Laws and Legal Sources. The user will then select a specific country or region to access cases, legislation and commentaries & treatises. International Law Emerging Issues is another noteworthy resource that global Internet law researchers will find helpful.

(4) Foreign Law Guide

This database includes descriptions of the legal systems of nearly two hundred countries and jurisdictions. It highlights mostly legislative resources but does include information about court decisions. It makes available foreign law resources, including complete bibliographic citations to legislation. This service often notes the existence of English translations. It also evaluates how current the materials are and lists secondary sources translated into English.[361]

(5) Bloomberg/BNA Internet Law Resource Center

BNA bills the Internet Law Resource Center as one of the most comprehensive resource for cyberlaw attorneys and scholars. This database includes an archive of full-text case law, pleadings, statutes, regulations, and analysis that address the internet's legal landscape. BNA's international materials include EU, WIPO, ICANN and UN documents.[362]

(6) Index to Foreign Legal Periodicals ("IFLP")

Produced by the American Association of Law Libraries ("AALL"), the IFLP offers a multilingual index to articles and book reviews from over 500 legal journals published around the world. Coverage includes public and private international law, comparative and foreign law, and the law of all jurisdictions.[363]

(F) Free Resources

One of the most recent trends in online legal research is "The Open Source/Free/Cost–Effective Movement."[364] In the last few years, economic strains and budget cuts have led to tremendous growth in the creation and use of complimentary or free online legal resources. As a result, "a majority of lawyers now use free online legal

---

[360] To save a search as an Alert, first run a search. When the user has the results they want, they need only click the "Save as Alert" link. They can then specify how frequently they want the Alert to run or how the results are to be delivered (email, print, etc.). The subscriber can specify the method by which they are notified of a current development.

[361] See generally, THOMAS REYNOLDS & ARTURO FLORES, FOREIGN LAW GUIDE, http://referenceworks.brillonline.com/browse/foreign-law-guide (last visited June 25, 2013).

[362] Bloomberg/BNA Internet Law Resource Center, http://www.bna.com/internet-law-resource-center-p6711/ (last visited June 26, 2013).

[363] Index to Foreign Legal Periodicals, http://www.law.berkeley.edu/library/iflp/index.html (last visited June 26, 2013).

[364] Deborah K. Hackerson, Access to Justice Starts in the Library: The Importance of Competent Research Skills and Free/Low-Cost Research Resources, 62 ME. L. REV. 473, 483 (2010).

resources in their research."[365] According to a 2012 ABA Technology Survey, Fifty-nine percent of lawyers use free online resources when they are doing legal research.[366] The "Open Source/Free/Cost–Effective Movement" is not just a U.S. phenomenon, but also a global one. There are a number of free resources that will allow lawyers to access global Internet law resources. Some contain documents written in the official language of a particular country or jurisdiction, but for many, either the English translations or the databases and their documents are available primarily in English.

(1) Curia

This caselaw database is part of the Europa site, which is the official website of the European Union.[367]   *Curia* publishes the full text of judgments, Opinions of the European Court of Justice, Advocates General's Opinions, and orders of the Courts of the European Union, from June 17, 1997 to the present. This website publishes the full text of selected unpublished decisions dating back to May 2004. The text of judgments is available on the day of delivery. The website publishes judicial opinions on the day they are issued, whereas the Advocate General publishes Advocates General's Opinions on the day of their delivery. Orders are only made public after the litigants have been notified. The texts are available in all EU official languages when they are published in the Reports of Cases before the Court of Justice and the Court of First Instance.[368]

(2) FLARE—Foreign Law Research

FLARE reflects collaboration between the major libraries collecting law in the United Kingdom: Institute of Advanced Legal Studies, Bodleian Law Library, Squire Law Library, British Library, and School of Oriental and African Studies. This site contains research guides that discuss case reporters for each jurisdiction.[369]

(3) GlobaLex

GlobaLex is a free product distributed by New York University Law School, which features research guides for many countries. The foreign legal system guides often highlight the preeminent resources for accessing international and foreign cases. GlobaLex publishes information used by many legal academics, practitioners and specialists including research and teaching resources. Scholars well known in their respective fields publish articles about foreign jurisdictions in these comprehensive GlobaLex resources. The shading of national boundaries means that Internet Law is no longer U.S.-centric. Online companies, by definition, are cross-border and thus they must be prepared to submit to mandatory foreign laws and regulations. The Internet is, in effect an international system for conducting legal research because of countless online databases. Lawyers representing e-businesses need to track foreign and

---

[365] David G. Badertscher & Deborah E. Melnick, Is Primary Legal Information on the Web Trustworthy? 49 JUDGE J. 13, 13 (2010).

[366] ABA Legal Technology Resource Center, 2012 AMERICAN BAR ASSOCIATION LEGAL TECHNOLOGY SURVEY REPORT V-xi (2012).

[367] See generally, Curia, Case–Law, http:// curia.europa.eu/jurisp/cgibin/form.pl?lang=en (last updated May 25, 2013).

[368] Id.

[369] FLARE, Foreign Law Research, http://ials.sas.ac.uk/flare/flare.htm (last visited May 25, 2013).

international developments to protect rights and avoid infringing the rights of others.[370]

(4) The Global Legal Information Network ("GLIN")

This public database contains official texts of laws, regulations, judicial decisions, and other complementary legal sources. GLIN membership and contributors, that include governmental agencies and international organizations, share original-language, officially published, full-text documents in electronic format.[371]

(5) World LII

The World Legal Information Institute ("World LII") is a comprehensive resource for searching international case law. It is a "free, independent and non-profit global legal research facility" and was developed collaboratively by the following legal information institutes: Australasian, British Irish, Canadian, Hong Kong, Cornell University, Pacific Islands, and the Wits University School of Law. This multi-jurisdictional website enables researchers to access all case law from national high courts or superior courts.[372]

(6) LegiFrance

This site includes all-inclusive French legislation and judicial decisions. Most resources are only available in French. LegiFrance does not publish English translations of the statutory materials. This service provides a user-friendly guide called "About Law" that discusses the organization of the French court system and judicial decisions.[373]

(7) German Law Archive

This German law website includes full-text decisions of judgments and other decisions by German courts. It also compiled a large bibliography that "aims to include everything published on German law in English language," and can be searched by author and title words. It is continuously updated and users can suggest new entries.[374]

(8) Legal Information Institute of India ("INDLII")

The goal of INDLII is to aggregate legal information about India and "publish it on the Internet with free and full public access." It is a comprehensive resource for Indian court decisions and tribunal judgments. It includes decisions of the Supreme Court, High Court, Central Administrative Tribunals, and District Courts.[375]

---

[370] New York University Law School, GlobaLex, Hauser Global Law School Program, http://www.nyulawglobal.org/Globalex/ (last visited June 26, 2013).

[371] Global Legal Information Network (GLIN), http://www.glin.gov/search.action (last visited May 25, 2013).

[372] World LII, http://www.worldlii.org/forms/search1.html (last visited May 25, 2013).

[373] See LegiFance, http://Legifrance.gouv.fr (last visited July, 8 , 2013). (Click on Traductions du droit français, in the left margin and select the English translation).

[374] German Law Archive, http://www.iuscomp.org/gla/ (last visited May 25, 2013).

[375] See generally, Legal Information Institute of India, http:// www.indlii.org/index.aspx (last visited May 25, 2013).

(9) The Incorporated Council of Law Reporting ("ICLP")

This database covers court decisions from England and Wales, as well as decisions from the Royal Courts of Justice and the European Court of Justice. Users can view daily case summaries by selecting the "Latest Cases" link at the top of the screen. Researchers can also perform a keyword search by selecting the "Subject Matter Search" link at the top of the screen. Readers can receive alerts and summaries of new decisions by selecting WLR (D) Alerts in the left margin. After registering, users receive email updates, at a frequency they choose, as soon as new case summaries are available online.[376]

(10) EUR–Lex

This site provides free access to European Union law and other documents. The database contains over 2,815,000 documents, dating back to 1951. EUR–Lex is updated daily, and the service adds approximately 12,000 documents every year. It has the Official Journal of the European Union online, simple and advanced searching, browsing options, and the ability to display and/or download documents in PDF, HTML, DOC, and TIFF formats.[377]

(11) Social Science Research Network ("SSRN")

The Social Science Research Network, unlike Westlaw and Lexis, is a free service where scholars disseminate working papers, law review articles, and excerpts from books and current research projects, often before they have even been accepted and published in law journals. SSRN is searchable and organized by field of law. This database features a network dedicated to working papers and publications on cyberspace law. It publishes abstracts of papers dealing with all aspects of the regulation of cyberspace through law, social norms, and the architecture of the network.[378]

(12) Research Guides

Law libraries throughout the U.S. compile research guides on a number of topics to help users do research faster and more efficiently. Many of the research guides are comprehensive and provide detailed soup to nuts lists highlighting resources and how to use them. A few noteworthy ones include Georgetown Law School's *International Cyberspace Law Research Guide,* Suffolk Law School's *Cyberlaw Research Guide*; or *The University of Washington's Foreign, Comparative & International Law Guide.*[379]

(13) WorldCat.org

WorldCat bills itself as "the world's largest network of library content" and lets you search the collections of libraries in your community and thousands more around

---

[376] The Incorporated Council of Law Reporting (ICLP), http://www.lawreports.co.uk/ (last visited May 25, 2013).

[377] EUR–Lex: Access to European Union Law, http://eur-lex.europa.eu/en/index.htm (law visited July 8, 2013).

[378] SSRN, Legal Scholarship Network, http://www.ssrn.com/lsn/ (last visited July 8, 2013).

[379] http://www.law.georgetown.edu/library/research/guides/cyberspace.cfm (last visited June 26, 2013); http://www.law.suffolk.edu/library/research/a-z/resguides/cyber.cfm (last visited June 24, 2013) and http://lib.law.washington.edu/ref/fcil.html (last visited June 26, 2013).

the world. [380] This database will come in particularly handy when you are searching for books, dissertations, treatises and loose-leaf sets. Often, researchers limit their research to only those resources owned by their specific library. WorldCat allows scholars to utilize a much wider world of information. If your library does not own a specific title, request that they borrow the material. For those of you not affiliated with a firm, academic or government library, be sure to take full advantage of local public libraries. Most offer robust interlibrary loan programs.

A few global Internet law books that one would discover by running a WorldCat search include: *Who Controls the Internet?: Illusions of a Borderless World*; *The Global Flow of Information: Legal, Social, and Cultural Perspectives*; and *Internet Jurisdiction and Choice of Law: Legal Practices in the EU, U.S. and China*.[381] There are a number of treatises and loose-leafs that address international Internet law issues. A few noteworthy ones include: Online Service Providers: International Law & Regulation; Internet Jurisdiction and Choice of Law: Legal Practices in the EU, U.S. and China; Cross-border Internet Dispute Resolution; International Computer Law: A Practical Guide to the International Distribution and Protection of Software and Integrated Circuits; and Global Perspectives in Information Security: Legal, Social and International.[382]

(G) Global Internet Law Websites

(1) World Intellectual Property Organization

The World Intellectual Property Organization ("WIPO") is a specialized agency of the United Nations. It is dedicated to "developing a balanced and accessible international intellectual property ("IP") system, which rewards creativity, stimulates innovation and contributes to economic development while safeguarding the public interest."[383]

(2) Council of Europe, Cybercrime

The Council of Europe "helps protect societies worldwide from the threat of cybercrime through the Convention on Cybercrime and its Protocol on Xenophobia and Racism, the Cybercrime Convention Committee ("T–CY") and the Project on Cybercrime. It serves as a guideline for any country developing comprehensive national legislation against Cybercrime."[384]

---

[380] WorldCat.org, What is WorldCat?, http://www.worldcat.org/whatis/default.jsp, (last visited June 26, 2013).

[381] JACK L GOLDSMITH AND TIM WU, WHO CONTROLS THE INTERNET?: ILLUSIONS OF A BORDERLESS WORLD, (2006); RAMESH SUBRAMANIAN & EDDAN KATZ, THE GLOBAL FLOW OF INFORMATION: LEGAL, SOCIAL, AND CULTURAL PERSPECTIVES (2011); FAYE FANGFEI WANG, INTERNET JURISDICTION AND CHOICE OF LAW: LEGAL PRACTICES IN THE EU, US AND CHINA, (2010).

[382] See generally, ONLINE SERVICE PROVIDERS: INTERNATIONAL LAW & REGULATION (Steven J. Barber & Christopher Gibson eds. 2003) FAYE FANGFEI WANG, INTERNET JURISDICTION AND CHOICE OF LAW: LEGAL PRACTICE IN THE EU, U.S. AND CHINA (2010); JULIA HORNLE, CROSS-BORDER INTERNET DISPUTE RESOLUTION (2009); J.A. KEUSTERMANS & I.M. ARCKENS, INTERNATIONAL COMPUTER LAW: A PRACTICAL GUIDE TO THE INTERNATIONAL DISTRIBUTION AND PROTECTION OF SOFTWARE AND INTEGRATED CIRCUITS (1988); HOSSEIN BIDGOLI, GLOBAL PERSPECTIVES IN INFORMATION SECURITY: LEGAL, SOCIAL AND INTERNATIONAL (2009).

[383] World Intellectual Property Organization, http:// www.wipo.int/ (last visited May 25, 2013).

[384] Cybercrime, Council of Europe, http://www.coe.int/t/DGHL/cooperation/economiccrime/cybercrime/default_en.asp (last visited May 25, 2013).

(3) Computer Crime Research Center

The Computer Crime Research Center was created in 2001 to research the legal, criminal, and criminological problems of cybercrime. It is a non-profit, non-government organization, and its mission is to "research and warn of unlawful acts involving computer and information technologies, including computer crimes, Internet fraud, and cyber terrorism.[385]

(4) Summaries of European Union Legislation

The Summaries of EU Legislation website provides approximately 3,000 summaries of European legislation, divided into thirty-two subject areas corresponding to the activities of the European Union. This site is unique because, unlike other EU databases like EUR–Lex and Europe Direct that often provide rather technical and lengthy pieces of legislation, it provides easy-to-read summaries.[386]

(5) Annual International Conference on Cyberlaw

This annual conference brings academics from all over the world and members of the judiciary together to exchange ideas and discuss recent cyberlaw topics. The conferences explore comparative approaches to intellectual property and discuss privacy, information technology and other late-breaking cyberlaw issues.[387]

(6) The Global Cyber Law Database ("GCLD")

The Global Cyber Law Database is a comprehensive source of cyber laws. This online resource has detailed cyber law profiles for forty-eight countries and aims to be the most comprehensive and authoritative source of cyber laws for all countries. The GCLD website is a public initiative of the Asian School of Cyber Laws. [388]

(7) ABA Cyberlaw Committee

The American Bar Association Business Law Section's Committee on Cyberspace Law posts frequent papers from ABA Business Law Section meetings as well as policy papers. One of the committee's areas of expertise is Ecommerce, online contracting and international trade.[389] It explores important policy issues in the crossroads between contract law and Internet law. The Section describes its mission as providing analysis of corporate, transactional and regulatory issues related to the Internet and digital technologies. The Committee works in a wide range of legal disciplines including electronic commerce and contracts, consumer protection, intellectual property, cybersecurity and privacy, jurisdiction, Internet governance, as well as online financial activities.[390]   The Cyberspace Committee is one of the best sources for locating and

---

[385] Computer Crime Research Center, http://www.crime-research.org/ (last visited May 25, 2013).

[386] Summaries of EU Legislation, EUROPA, http://europa.eu/legislation_summaries/index_en.htm (last visited July 8, 2013).

[387] See generally, Annual International Conference on Cyberlaw, Association Internationale de Lutte Contre la Cybercriminalite, http://www.cyberlaw-conference.org/ (last visited May 25, 2013).

[388] Global Cyber Law Database, http://www.cyberlawdb.com/main/ (last visited May 25, 2013).

[389] American Bar Association, Committee on Cyberspace Law Mission Statement, http://apps.americanbar.org/dch/committee.cfm?com=CL320000 (last visited June 25, 2013).

[390] Id.

evaluating Global E–Commerce regulations and cyberspace law cases and statutory developments.

(8) IP Mall, University of New Hampshire/Franklin Pierce

The University of Hampshire's Franklin Pierce Intellectual Property Mall ("IP Mall") provides comprehensive coverage of primary and secondary materials. Their goal is to offer unique content that is not available on Westlaw & Lexis and other Websites.[391] To access Franklin Pierce's IP Mall, users need only select the IP Links tab at the top of the main page. The IP Mall includes materials on e-commerce and technology and an IP in E–Commerce tutorial.[392]

---

[391] University of New Hampshire School of Law, Mission for IP Mall Hosted Resources Section, http://ipmall.info/about/fplchome.asp (last visited June 25, 2013).

[392] Id.

Chapter 3

CIVIL PROCEDURE IN CYBERSPACE

§ 3.1 INTRODUCTION

A growing number of U.S. courts routinely exercise jurisdiction over website activity occurring outside of the country's territorial boundaries. Conversely, U.S. companies are increasingly being sued in foreign jurisdictions for activities occurring on Web servers located in the United States. Clearly, civil procedure requires harmonization. Presently, almost no case law addresses international Internet jurisdiction, and no statutory solutions exist to answer the question of cross-border Internet jurisdiction. Traditional concepts of jurisdiction and enforcement of judgment need to be adapted to the Internet. In the United States, personal jurisdiction determines whether a court can decide a case involving this specific defendant. "Just as our traditional notions of personal jurisdiction have proven adaptable to other changes in the national economy, so too are they adaptable to the transformations wrought by the Internet."[1] Lawrence Lessig writes, "Here's the important point: given the architecture of the Internet (at least as it was circa 1999), it doesn't really matter where in real space the server is. Access doesn't depend on geography."[2] "Geographic indeterminacy is simply part of the network's normal operation."[3] This chapter asks whether *International Shoe* is fundamentally adaptable to cyberspace.[4] The borderless Internet challenges uniquely U.S. concepts such as the long-arm statute, due process, and minimum contacts. U.S. courts have mechanically stretched the parochial minimum contacts approach to personal jurisdiction into cyberspace, creating jurisdictional dilemmas. The localization of e-business requires companies to tailor their international business transactions to consider different consumer markets, business settings, linguistic differences, and cultural mores or folkways.

Adam D. Thierer and H. George Frederickson write, "What is perhaps most troubling about the current debate over Internet jurisdiction and governance is that little discussion has occurred about the principles of legitimacy and universality."[5] When radically different legal cultures come into contact in the free trade zone of cyberspace, jurisdictional choice of law and enforcement of judgment disputes are often intractable. The Internet's global legal environment makes it inevitable that "one country's laws will conflict with another's—particularly when a Web surfer in one country accesses content hosted or created in another country."[6] The European Union's Brussels Regulation creates very different jurisdictional rules in civil and commercial

---

[1] Gorman v. Ameritrade Holding Corp., 293 F.3d 506, 510–11 (D.C. Cir. 2002).

[2] LAWRENCE LESSIG, CODE 2.0 16 (2006).

[3] Dan L. Burk, Jurisdiction in a World Without Borders, 1 VA. J. L. & TECH. 3, 18 (1997).

[4] International Shoe Co. v. Washington, 326 U.S. 310, 316 (1945).

[5] ADAM D. THIERER & H. GEORGE FREDERICKSON, WHO RULES THE NET? NET GOVERNANCE AND JURISDICTION XXVII (2003).

[6] Peter Yu, Conflict of Laws Issues in International Copyright Cases, http://www.peteryu.com/gigalaw0401.pdf (last visited July 17, 2013).

disputes. Anupam Chander "hopping is a fundamental quality of global Internet trade" citing the following examples:

Consider two famous examples from the past decade. KaZaa, long the leading peer-to-peer file trading system, was founded in the Netherlands by a Swede and a Dane, programmed from Estonia, and then run from Australia while incorporated in the South Pacific island nation of Vanuatu. The online gambling site PartyGaming was founded by an American lawyer and an Indian expatriate programmer and run from headquarters in Gibraltar, using computer servers on a Mohawk Indian reserve in Canada, a London marketing office, and a workforce based mainly in Hyderabad, India.[7]Chander argues that "jurisdiction hopping" to avoid oppressive regulations will become more common in the global electronic marketplace.[8] The ability of Internet businesses to end-run jurisdictions is an example of why it is fool hardy to confine the study of Internet jurisdiction to the United States. This chapter begins with a close study of how U.S. courts approach cyberspace jurisdiction. Justice Oliver Wendell Holmes Jr. wrote, "The foundation of jurisdiction is physical power"—which is a territorial based concept.[9] The borderless Internet challenges the meaning of due process and minimum contacts. The parties' choices of law and forum clauses are contracts where the parties agree to jurisdiction and the applicable law in advance. Conflict of law refers to the principles courts use in determining what law applies in a cross-border transaction. At present, there is no multilateral convention to resolve conflicts of law or choice of law for Internet nor is there a treaty for the reciprocal enforcement of judgments. Internet lawyers representing companies doing business in Europe must consider the impact of European Union regimes such as the Brussels Regulation governing jurisdiction and the Rome I Regulation on choice of law if their client targets European consumer marketplaces.

In the European Union, the Brussels Regulation governs jurisdiction and enforcement of judgments in civil and commercial disputes between litigants and provides for the enforcement of judgments throughout the European Union, whereas the Rome I Regulation harmonizes rules for choice of law. Both Regulations enact mandatory consumer rules (non-waivable) that give consumers the right to litigate in their home court under their jurisdictions' consumer protection rules. What this means is that U.S. companies cannot require European consumers to agree to one-sided choice of forum and law clauses, as is the case in U.S. consumer transactions.[10] This chapter covers many areas of civil procedure influenced by the Internet including: (1) personal jurisdiction; (2) parties' choice of law and forum; (3) conflict of law, and (4) enforcement of cross-border judgments.

---

[7] ANUPAM CHANDER, THE ELECTRONIC SILK ROAD 5 (2013).

[8] Id. at 5.

[9] Ex parte Indiana Transport Co., 244 U.S. 456, 457 (1917).

[10] See e.g., Koch v. Am. Online, Inc., 139 F. Supp. 2d 690, 695–96 (D. Md. 2000) (upholding choice of forum clause requiring all claims against AOL to be adjudicated in Virginia); see also Forrest v. Verizon Comm., Inc., 805 A.2d 1007, 1012 (D.C. 2002) (similar holding); Am. Online, Inc. v. Booker, 781 So. 2d 423, 425 (Fla. Dist. Ct. App. 2001) (similar holding); Celmins v. Am. On Line, 748 So. 2d 1041, 1041–42 (Fla. Dist. Ct. App. 1999) (upholding AOL's forum selection clause); Groff v. Am. Online, Inc., No. PC 97–0331, 1998 R.I. Super. LEXIS 46, at 16 (Super. Ct. R.I. May 27, 1998).

§ 3.2   U.S. CENTRIC CYBERJURISDICTION

(A) U.S. Civil Procedure Generally

U.S. centric Internet law focuses on the procedural and substantive rules found in U.S. state and federal courts.[11] The rules of civil procedure govern civil law suits and dispute resolution in U.S. state and federal courts. Federal Courts in the U.S. use the Federal Rules of Civil Procedure ("FRCP"), while the state courts have their own rules of civil procedure. Many states model their state rules on the FRCP, with minor variation. Any system of civil procedure must have some basis for determining whether a particular court has jurisdiction over the parties as well as whether the parties have legal standing to file suit.[12] All countries must revise their rules of civil procedure to account for digital or e-discovery. Hundreds of countries are connected to the Internet and it is not surprising that U.S. civil procedure is not the point of reference for global Internet disputes. Rules determining personal jurisdiction, subject matter jurisdiction, and the enforcement of judgments vary significantly across different legal cultures.

(B) U.S. Subject Matter Jurisdiction

The majority of cyberlaw cases are decided in federal courts, where subject matter jurisdiction is based upon diversity of citizenship or federal question jurisdiction. To litigate a case in federal court, the plaintiff must establish constitutional standing, which requires a showing that the plaintiff has suffered an injury-in-fact that is traceable to the defendant's allegedly unlawful conduct and that the injury or damages suffered is likely to be redressed by the requested relief.[13] Diversity of citizenship gives federal courts original jurisdiction of all civil actions where the matter in controversy is greater than $75,000, exclusive of interest and costs. Diversity is between (1) citizens of different states; (2) citizens of a State and citizens or subjects of a foreign state; (3) citizens of different States and in which citizens or subjects of a foreign state are

---

[11] The U.S. centric approach to contract law was also documented in a recent empirical study entitled the "International Contracting Practices Survey Project." Professor Peter Fitzgerald, who was the principal investigator, observed: "In an era of globalization it is perplexing that so many U.S. practitioners, jurists, and legal academics continue to view contract issues as governed exclusively by state common law and the Uniform Commercial Code." Peter L. Fitzgerald, The International Contracting Practices Survey Project: An Empirical Study of the Value and Utility of the United Nations Convention on the International Sale of Goods (CISG) and the UNIDROIT Principles of International Commercial Contracts to Practitioners, Jurists, and Legal Academics in the United States, 27 J. L. & COM. 1, 1 (2008). Professor Fitzgerald found that 65% of his practitioner respondents do not address the UNIDROIT Principles at all in their commercial contracts. Id. at 16. Practitioners were more likely to be familiar with the CISG. However, practitioners either opt out of CISG or do not address it all in their commercial sales contracts. Id. at 14. His survey concluded that CISG and UNIDROIT Principles are "being ignored either out of outright ignorance or because these instruments are unfamiliar . . . ." Id. at 24.

[12] To file a lawsuit in a U.S. federal court, a plaintiff must have standing pursuant to Article III of the United States Constitution. To establish standing under Article III, a plaintiff must show: (1) injury in fact; (2) causation; and (3) redressability. Horvath v. Keystone Health Plan E., Inc., 333 F.3d 450, 455 (3d Cir. 2003); Lujan v. Defenders of Wildlife, 504 U.S. 555, 560–61 (1992). To establish an injury in fact, a plaintiff must demonstrate the "invasion of a legally protected interest which is (a) concrete and particularized; and (b) actual or imminent, not conjectural or hypothetical." Lujan, 504 U.S. at 560 (internal citations omitted). Whether in federal or state courts, plaintiffs must demonstrate "a causal connection between the injury and the conduct complained of-the injury has to be fairly . . . trace[able] to the challenged action of the defendant, and not . . . [the] result [of] the independent action of some third party not before the court." Id.

[13] U.S. Const. Art III § 2.

additional parties, and (4) a foreign state . . . as plaintiff and citizens of a State or of different States.[14]

Cross-border Internet disputes are becoming increasingly   common. For international diversity cases (litigants from different countries), "enforceability of judgments of courts of other countries is generally governed by the law of the state in which enforcement is sought."[15] Complete diversity is satisfied in any cyberspace case where a U.S. resident sues a foreign provider. It is important to keep in mind that diversity requires complete diversity from every party. Even if a single defendant and plaintiff are from the same state, diversity is destroyed and the action must be filed in state court. For class actions, diversity actions only require that named plaintiffs be from different jurisdictions than the defendant.[16] For corporations, citizenship is based upon two bases: the place of incorporation and the principal place of business.

Specific federal statutes will define whether federal courts have subject matter jurisdiction, like cases pertaining to patents and copyright.[17] The federal courts have jurisdiction over nearly every e-commerce patent, trademark/domain name dispute, or copyright case. For many Internet-related cases, the causes of action are within the exclusive jurisdiction of the federal courts.[18] Most cybercrime cases are brought under the Economic Espionage Act, the Computer Fraud and Abuse Act, and the Electronic Privacy Communications Act. If cyberlaw defendants are sued in state courts, they frequently assert removal jurisdiction that allows defendants to remove an action to federal court if that court would have had original jurisdiction. Federal courts use the doctrine of supplemental jurisdiction under 28 U.S.C. § 1367 to decide state claims under ancillary and pendent jurisdiction.

Supplemental jurisdiction, for example, would allow for Uniform Trade Secret Act claims (state law), in a federal Computer Fraud and Abuse Act or Electronic Communications Privacy Act civil claim, to be filed in federal court.[19] Similarly,

---

[14] 28 U.S.C. § 1332.

[15] Yahoo! Inc. v. La Ligue Contre le Racisme et L'Antisemitisme, 433 F.3d 1199, 1212 (9th Cir.2006) (en banc) (per curiam).

[16] FED. R. CIV. P. 23 governs class actions. Rule 23(a) requires plaintiffs to show that: (1) "the class is so numerous that joinder of all members is impracticable"; (2) "there are questions of law or fact common to the class"; (3) "the claims or defenses of the representative parties are typical of the claims or defenses of the class"; and (4) "the representative parties will fairly and adequately protect the interests of the class." FED. R. CIV. P. 23(a). If plaintiffs satisfy the threshold Rule 23(a) requirements, they must also show that the putative class satisfies one of the three forms provided in Rule 23(b). Rule 23(b)(1) permits certification of a class in situations where "prosecuting separate actions by or against individual class members would create a risk of" either "inconsistent or varying adjudications with respect to individual class members" or "would be dispositive of the interests of other members" or "would substantially impair or impede their ability to protect their interests." FED. R. CIV. P. 23(b)(2). Rule 23(b)(2) allows maintenance of a class action where "the party opposing the class has acted or refused to act on grounds that apply generally to the class, so that final injunctive relief or corresponding declaratory relief is appropriate respecting the class as a whole." Rule 23(b)(3) permits certification where "the court finds that the questions of law or fact common to class members predominate over any questions affecting only individual members, and that a class action is superior to other available methods for fairly and efficiently adjudicating the controversy." Unlike Rule 23(b)(1) and Rule 23(b)(2) classes, Rule 23(b)(3) actions require notice to members to provide an opportunity to opt out of the class. Complete diversity only requires that the named class representative is from a different jurisdiction than the named defendant(s).

[17] 28 U.S.C. § 1338 (conferring federal jurisdiction in patent and copyright cases).

[18] 15 U.S.C. § 78(a) (conferring federal jurisdiction in securities cases).

[19] Both the Computer Fraud and Abuse Act and Electronic Communications Privacy Act allow the victims of computer crime and wire tap offenses to file actions for monetary damages. This is a separate

supplemental jurisdiction could be invoked to decide a state right of publicity action in a federal trademark case. As Justice Stanley Reed stated, "A court does not have the power, by judicial fiat, to extend its jurisdiction over matters beyond the scope of the authority granted to it by its creators."[20] Federal district courts in the United States are courts of limited jurisdiction.

This means that a U.S. federal court only has competence to decide cases where there is a federal question i.e. federal statute or constitutional issue, or where there is diversity of citizenship i.e. the plaintiff and defendant are from different states or countries (complete diversity), and the amount at stake is $75,000 or greater.[21] The vast majority of U.S. Internet cases are decided in federal courts where plaintiffs must demonstrate both subject matter jurisdiction and personal jurisdiction. Federal subject matter jurisdiction depends upon whether the Internet-related case triggers a federal statute such as the Copyright Act, Computer Fraud and Abuse Act or the Electronic Signature Act, to name just a few statutes with an Internet nexus. Many intellectual property cases will involve a federal statute such as the U.S. Copyright Act, the Patent Act, or the Lanham Act of 1946. If there is a federal question, the plaintiff need not plead a minimum amount in controversy as in diversity cases.

(C) Venue in Cyberspace

A court, in its discretion, may to dismiss any action "where it is determined that the action, although jurisdictionally sound, would be better adjudicated elsewhere."[22] "For the convenience of parties and witnesses, in the interest of justice, a district court may transfer any civil matter to any other district or division where it might have been brought."[23] The statutory purpose of § 1404(a) is to "prevent the waste of time, energy, and money and to protect litigants, witnesses and the public against unnecessary inconvenience and expense."[24] "Venue refers to the location where an action is brought. Unlike subject matter and personal jurisdiction, however, venue relates to the convenience of the parties."[25] Essentially, venue means the location where an action may be filed assuming there is subject matter (and personal) jurisdiction. Venue rules in U.S. federal courts turn on whether the subject matter is based upon diversity of citizenship or a federal question.

The federal statute governing venue has special rules for federal question cases, which encompasses many Internet-related cases. The statute states that where jurisdiction is not based upon diversity, the action may be "brought [only] in (i) a judicial district where any defendant resides, if all defendants reside in the same State, (ii) a judicial district in which a substantial part of the events or omissions giving rise

---

action from the criminal action filed by federal prosecutors. Chapter 8 examines these federal statutes in depth.

[20] Stoll v. Gottlieb, 305 U.S. 165, 171 (1938).

[21] Federal courts have "original jurisdiction of all civil actions . . . between citizens of different States" when the amount in controversy exceeds $75,000. 28 U.S.C. § 1332(a)(1). "[C]omplete diversity between all plaintiffs and all defendants" is required; no plaintiff can be the citizen of the same State as any defendant." Lincoln Prop. Co. v. Roche, 546 U.S. 81, 89 (2005).

[22] M.B.S. Moda, Inc. v. Fuzzi S.P.A., 38 Misc.3d 1208(A), 967 N.Y.S.2d 867 (N.Y. Sup. 2013) (discussing New York's venue provision).

[23] 28 U.S.C. § 1404(a).

[24] Van Dusen v. Barrack, 376 U.S. 612, 616, 84 S.Ct. 805, 11 L.Ed.2d 945 (1964) (internal citations and quotation omitted).

[25] KENT D. STUCKEY, INTERNET AND ONLINE LAW 10–27 (1996).

to the claim occurred, or a substantial part of property that is the subject of the action is situated, or (iii) a judicial district in which any defendant may be found, if there is no district in which the action may otherwise be brought."[26] Venue accrues in a torts case:

> Where publication is made through electronic means, Florida Courts hold that publication occurs in the county where the acts first took effect. . . Even if the plaintiff suffers further damages in another county, the tort occurs where the action first took effect.[27]

Courts consider the following factors to determine which venue is more convenient to the parties and the witnesses: (1) plaintiff's choice of forum, (2) convenience of the parties, (3) convenience of the witnesses, (4) ease of access to the evidence, (5) familiarity of each forum with the applicable law, (6) feasibility of consolidation with other claims, (7) any local interest in the controversy, and (8) the relative court congestion and time of trial in each forum.[28] Venue for an in rem ACPA action, under 15 U.S.C. § 1125(d)(2)(C)(i), is in the judicial district in which the domain name's registrar, registry, or other domain name authority that registered or assigned the domain name is located.

(D) U.S. Personal Jurisdiction

Cyberspace places a new twist on the role that technological progress plays in transforming traditional rules of jurisdiction. The Internet is a disruptive technology that challenges traditional conceptions of jurisdiction. Personal jurisdiction means that a given court has power over a particular defendant. Traditionally, courts based jurisdiction upon territoriality or physical presence in the forum. These tests, which have ranged from "physical presence" to minimum contacts to "purposeful availment," rest upon each person's inherent right to choose the jurisdictions to which he will submit himself.[29] State courts may exercise personal jurisdiction over an out-of-state defendant who has "certain minimum contacts with [the state] such that the maintenance of the suit does not offend "traditional notions of fair play and substantial

---

[26] Id. (defining the contours of venue in federal question cases).

[27] Marc John Randazza, Suing for Internet Defamation in Florida, Make Sure You Pick the Right Venue (2013), http://www.avvo.com/legal-guides/ugc/suing-for-internet-defamation-in-florida—make-sure-you-pick-the-right-venue (last visited June 23, 2013).

[28] See Williams v. Bowman, 157 F.Supp.2d 1103, 1106 (N.D.Cal.2001); see also Jones v. GNC Franchising Inc., 211 F.3d 495, 498–99 (9th Cir.2000).

[29] The California Supreme Court held that merely posting a program for decrypting DVDs on the Internet did not subject a Texas resident to personal jurisdiction. Pavlovich v. Superior Court, 59 Cal. 4th 262, 277 (2002). The court in Pavlovich found that the fact that a Texas resident knew that his conduct was injuring the motion picture industry in California was an insufficient basis for personal jurisdiction. Id. The Ninth Circuit has adapted traditional jurisdictional tests for determining whether an out-of-state website operator's activities amount to purposeful availment of the forum state to render the exercise of personal jurisdiction over the out-of-state website operator constitutionally permissible: (1) the sliding scale approach, and (2) the effects test, endorsed by the U.S. Supreme Court in Calder v. Jones, 465 U.S. 783 (1984). See Northwest Healthcare Alliance, Inc. v. Healthgrades.com, Inc., 50 Fed. Appx. 339 (9th Cir. 2002). In Millennium Enterprises, Inc. v. Millennium Music, Inc., a court granted a website's motion to dismiss, finding that the court lacked general and specific jurisdiction over the defendant. 33 F. Supp. 2d 907 (D. Or. 1999). The South Carolina defendant sold music in its retail and Internet websites using the Millennium Music(R) trademark. The Millennium court ruled that there was no purposeful availment based upon sporadic sales in the forum. The defendants had sold only fifteen compact discs to nine customers in six states and one foreign country. The only sale within the forum state was made to a friend of the plaintiff's counsel upon his instruction. The court found no purposeful availment upon this "manufactured" contact, dismissing the action. Id.

justice."[30] The key issue as to Internet personal jurisdiction, as with the bricks and mortar world, is whether a court has jurisdiction over nonresident defendants.

Because plaintiffs file a case in a given court, he or she invokes or accedes to the court's jurisdiction. Personal jurisdiction may be based upon a defendant's presence in the forum where he or she can be served with process. In addition, states have jurisdiction over a nonresident where the defendant is a domiciliary. Nonresident defendants may choose to accede or consent to jurisdiction. The vast majority of terms of use require Internet users to consent, in advance, to jurisdiction by submitting to choice of forum clauses. Much of the Internet-related litigation about personal jurisdiction involves none of these factors. Personal jurisdiction cases often rest on the defendant doing something in the forum so that they are reachable by the state's long-arm statute. This is not infrequently a problem in Internet-related cases.

Personal jurisdiction cases turn on whether the non-resident defendant has sufficient "minimum contacts" with the forum where the case is filed. The minimum contacts test examines whether the defendant's forum-directed activities are sufficient, in light of the state's legitimate interests in subjecting the defendant to jurisdiction. Plaintiffs must demonstrate that defendants have sufficient "minimum contacts" with the forum such that finding personal jurisdiction will not offend "traditional notions of fair play and substantial justice."[31]

A U.S. plaintiff has the burden of demonstrating that the defendant has minimum contacts with the forum by either general jurisdiction (pervasive contacts) or specific jurisdiction (nexus between conduct and minimum contacts).[32] Once a court determines a defendant's conduct is subject to a forum's long-arm statute, it must next consider whether asserting personal jurisdiction over a nonresident defendant comports with the Due Process Clause of the Fourteenth Amendment.[33] The limits on the power of a state court to exercise personal jurisdiction over an out-of-state defendant are supplied by considerations of due process, under which a defendant must "have certain minimum contacts with [the forum State] such that the maintenance of the suit does not offend "traditional notions of fair play and substantial justice.[34]

(E) Res Judicata

Res judicata consists of two subissues, (1) issue preclusion and (2) claim preclusion. Issue preclusion, or collateral estoppel, refers to the effect of a court's

---

[30] International Shoe Co. v. Washington, 326 U.S. 310, 316 (1945) (quoting Milliken v. Meyer, 311 U.S. 457, 463 (1940)).

[31] Id.

[32] Personal jurisdiction over a non-resident defendant may exist if the defendant has either a continuous and systematic presence in the state (general jurisdiction), or minimum contacts with the forum state such that the exercise of jurisdiction "does not offend traditional notions of fair play and substantial justice" (specific jurisdiction). International Shoe Co. v. Washington, 326 U.S. 310, 316 (1945).

[33] "The Due Process Clause of the Fourteenth Amendment protects a corporation, as it does an individual, against being made subject to the binding judgments of a forum with which it has established no meaningful contacts, ties, or relations. Thus, the Due Process Clause sets the outer boundaries of a state tribunal's authority to proceed against a defendant. The canonical opinion in this area remains International Shoe, in which it was held that a State may authorize its courts to exercise personal jurisdiction over an out-of-state defendant if the defendant has certain minimum contacts with the State such that the maintenance of the suit does not offend traditional notions of fair play and substantial justice." Pervasive Software, Inc. v. Lexware GMBH & Co. KG, 688 F.3d 214, 220 (5th Cir. 2012).

[34] Id. at 316.

judgment foreclosing relitigation of an issue that has been litigated and decided. Claim preclusion refers to the effect of a court's judgment in foreclosing further litigation of a claim that has never been actually litigated by the parties and decided by a court, but which could have been advanced and litigated by the party in the earlier lawsuit. One unresolved issue is whether cyberspace is a separate jurisdiction or whether a cybertort lawsuit is precluded by a lawsuit in a national court.

§ 3.3   INTERNATIONAL SHOE IN CYBERSPACE: AN OVERVIEW

(A) Initiating & Responding to Complaints

Internet-related jurisdiction disputes began as companies created and established corporate identities online.[35] To date, there is no international convention that addresses cross-border Internet jurisdiction, transnational choice of law, or the enforcement of cyberspace judgments. Most Internet cases begin with the plaintiff filing a complaint claiming that they have civil recourse against a website or other Internet-related defendant. A complaint can arise under the law of torts, contract, or intellectual property-based causes of action or a statute, such as the Lanham Act or the U.S. Copyright Act. In the United States, many federal statutes recognize a private cause of action or a state's right to pursue criminal or civil penalties.

Defendants, who are located outside the forum where the action is filed, will typically answer the plaintiff's complaint with a motion to dismiss for lack of personal jurisdiction. With Internet-related cases, a defendant located in a distant foreign jurisdiction will frequently assert *forum non conveniens* because of the cost of appearing in a U.S. court.[36] It is unclear how the doctrine of forum shopping as a strategic concern applies to foreign defendants for torts arising in cyberspace. Nevertheless, forum shopping is of limited utility in countries that have mandatory consumer rules protecting consumers from being dragged into distant courts. In any *forum non convenience* determination, a U.S. court must consider: (1) the ease of access to sources of proof; (2) the availability of compulsory process for securing the attendance of unwilling witnesses; (3) the costs of obtaining the attendance of witnesses; (4) the ability to view premises; (5) the general facility and cost of trying the case in the selected forum; and (6) the public interest, including the local interest of having the controversy decided at home, and the interest of trying cases where the substantive law applies.[37]

---

[35] The Internet is "'a unique and wholly new medium of worldwide human communication.'" Reno v. Am. Civil Liberties Union, 521 U.S. 844, 850 (1997). As such, it "raises significant questions about the application of traditional personal jurisdiction doctrine." 4A CHARLES ALAN WRIGHT et al., FED. PRAC. & PROC. § 1073.1, at 322 (3d ed. 2002). "If the defendant is not physically present in or a resident of the forum state, and has not been physically served in the forum state, the federal court must undertake the traditional personal jurisdiction analysis." Pervasive Software, Inc. v. Lexware GMBH & Co. KG, 688 F.3d 214, 220, 226–27 (5th Cir. 2012) (discussing the need for courts to examine Internet jurisdiction on a case by case basis).

[36] The burden is on the defendant to establish that the assertion of jurisdiction in this forum will make litigation so gravely difficult that the defendant will be at a severe disadvantage in comparison to his opponent. Burger King v. Rudzewicz, 471 U.S. 462, 478 (1985).

[37] SAS Inst. Inc. v. World Programming Ltd., 2011 U.S. Dist. LEXIS 66748 (E.D. N.C. 2011).

(B) Defendant's Motion to Dismiss

Rule 12(b)(2) of the FRCP directs the court to dismiss a case when the court lacks personal jurisdiction over a defendant.[38] When opposing a defendant's motion to dismiss for lack of personal jurisdiction, the plaintiff bears the burden of establishing that jurisdiction is proper. *Forum non-conveniens* essentially means "forum not agreeing." The first step of a *forum non-conveniens* analysis asks whether another forum for resolving a plaintiff's complaints is, or would be, adequate. The second step of a *forum non conveniens* analysis requires consideration of the private interests of the parties, and the interests of the public in retaining the action for trial in the original forum. A *forum non conveniens* determination is committed to the sound discretion of a trial court, and may be reversed only when there has been a clear abuse of discretion. Assuming that the state's long-arm statute is satisfied, the question becomes whether there are sufficient minimum contacts with the forum to satisfy due process.

(C) Specific and General Jurisdiction

A federal court sitting in diversity must satisfy two requirements to exercise personal jurisdiction over a nonresident defendant. First, the forum state's long-arm statute must confer personal jurisdiction. Second, the exercise of jurisdiction must not exceed the boundaries of the Due Process of the Fourteenth Amendment. "*International Shoe* distinguished from cases that fit within the "specific jurisdiction" categories, instances in which the continuous corporate operations within a state are so substantial and of such a nature as to justify suit against it on causes of action arising from dealings entirely distinct from those activities."[39] Personal jurisdiction over a nonresident defendant may exist if the defendant has either a continuous and systematic presence in the state (general jurisdiction), or minimum contacts with the forum state such that the exercise of jurisdiction "does not offend traditional notions of fair play and substantial justice" (specific jurisdiction).

Specific jurisdiction depends on a relationship between the underlying controversy and the forum, the principal question being whether the specific activity or occurrence giving rise to the claim took place in the forum state and should, therefore, be subject to the state's regulation.[40] As the Supreme Court noted in *Goodyear,* specific jurisdiction involves an inquiry "whether there was 'some act by which the defendant purposefully avail[ed] itself of the privilege of conducting activities within the forum State, thus invoking the benefits and protections of its laws.'"[41]

A plaintiff has the burden of demonstrating that the defendant has minimum contacts with the forum by either general jurisdiction (pervasive contacts) or specific jurisdiction (nexus between conduct and minimum contacts). In order to establish specific personal jurisdiction, a plaintiff need to prove minimum contacts with the forum related to the claim or how it arises. A court can establish specific jurisdiction over a defendant only if he or she has "certain minimum contacts" which give rise to

---

[38] FED. R. CIV. P. 12(b)(2).

[39] Pervasive Software, Inc. v. Lexware GMBH & Co. KG, 688 F.3d 214, 221 (5th Cir. 2012).

[40] Goodyear Dunlop Tires Operations, S.A. v. Brown, 131 S.Ct. 2846, 2853 (2011).

[41] Id. at 2854 (quoting Hanson v. Denckla, 357 U.S. 235, 253 (1958).

the action in question in the forum such that the exercise of jurisdiction "does not offend traditional notions of fair play and substantial justice." [42]

(1) Long–Arm Statutes

"Statutes authorizing courts to reach beyond their own borders came to be known as 'long-arm' statutes: states were extending their jurisdictional 'arms.' The name has stuck."[43] "Personal jurisdiction over an out-of-state defendant is appropriate if the relevant state's long-arm statute permits the assertion of jurisdiction without violating federal due process."[44] Personal jurisdiction can be either general or specific, depending on the extent of a defendant's contacts with the forum state. A threshold question is, "Has the plaintiff demonstrated that the defendant's conduct falls within the long-arm statute of the state where the case is filed?" States have enacted one of two broad types of long-arm statutes: (1) statutes asserting jurisdiction over the person to the extent allowable by the Fourteenth Amendment in the U.S. Constitution (due process clause) or (2) statutes limited to specified activities such as transacting business or causing tortious injuries.

A growing number of state long-arm statutes assert control over the defendant's activities to the limit of due process. "Texas's long-arm statute has been interpreted to extend to the limits of due process."[45] In states with unlimited long-arm statutes, the state and federal due process limitations collapse and are therefore coextensive. For example, Illinois and federal due process limitations are the same as its statute extends to the limits of federal due process.[46] Assuming that a state's long-arm statute is satisfied, the next question is whether the plaintiff can prove that the defendant has sufficient minimum contacts with the forum to satisfy due process. If so, state courts may exercise personal jurisdiction over the defendant. A threshold question is, "Has the plaintiff demonstrated the compliance with the state's long-arm statute?" Pennsylvania's long-arm statute, for example, claims jurisdiction to the "fullest extent allowed under the Constitution of the United States."[47] California, too, enacted a long-arm statute co-extensive with federal due process requirements.[48] In contrast, the Massachusetts long-arm statute claims jurisdiction over defendants doing business in the state or deriving substantial revenues from goods or services. Personal jurisdiction can apply either specifically or generally from a defendant's contacts with the forum state. Florida's long-arm statute states that a person is subject to personal jurisdiction "for any cause of action arising from the doing of any of the following acts: operating, conducting, engaging in, or carrying on a business" or for "committing a tortious act within this state" of Florida.[49] Under New York's long-arm statute, a court may

---

[42] International Shoe Co. v. Washington, 326 U.S. 310, 316 (1945).

[43] STEVEN C. YEAZELL, CIVIL PROCEDURE 187 (4th ed. 1996).

[44] Schwarzenegger v. Fred Martin Motor Co., 374 F.3d 797, 800–01 (9th Cir. 2004).

[45] Pervasive Software, Inc. v. Lexware GMBH & Co. KG, 688 F.3d 214, 220 (5th Cir. 2012) (applying Texas law).

[46] be2 LLC v. Ivanov, 642 F.3d 555, 558 (7th Cir. 2011) (describing the state and federal due process inquiries as collapsing into whether the exercise of personal jurisdiction comports with due process).

[47] Zippo Manufacturing Co. v. Zippo Dot Com, Inc., 952 F.Supp. 1124 (W.D.Pa. 1997).

[48] Cal. Civ. Proc. § 410.10.

[49] Fla. Stat. § 48.193(1).

exercise personal jurisdiction over a non-domiciliary who, "transacts any business within the state or contracts anywhere to supply goods or services in the state."[50]

(2) General Personal Jurisdiction

"A court may assert general jurisdiction over foreign . . . corporations to hear any and all claims against them when their affiliations with the State are so 'continuous and systematic' as to render them essentially at home in the forum State."[51] "General jurisdiction over a website that has no intrinsic connection with a forum state requires commercial activity carried on with forum residents in such a sustained manner that it is tantamount to actual physical presence within the state."[52] General personal jurisdiction exists in cyberspace just as in the bricks and mortar world. When the defendant's contacts with the forum state are "substantial" and "continuous and systematic," the state may exercise personal jurisdiction over the defendant even if the action does not relate to the defendant's contacts with the state. If minimum contacts are sufficient to establish general jurisdiction, the out of state defendant may be sued in the forum state for any cause of action against them, regardless of whether the cause of action arose from in-state or out of state activity.

It should be emphasized that, as we are dealing with general jurisdiction, the commercial contacts here must be of a sort "that approximate physical presence" in the state—and "engaging in commerce with residents of the forum state is not in and of itself the kind of activity that approximates physical presence within the state's borders."[53] Courts are reluctant to find a defendant subject to general jurisdiction. Plaintiffs in all but a few Internet-related cases will attempt to satisfy specific jurisdiction because general jurisdiction is such a high barrier to clear. Specific jurisdiction turns on a nexus between the underlying controversy and the forum, the principal question being whether the specific activity or occurrence, giving rise to the claim took place in the forum state and should therefore, be subject to the state's jurisdiction.[54]

The jurisprudence underlying general jurisdiction is a defendant's contacts with the forum that are so extensive as to be the functional equivalent of a physical presence. "Systematic and continuous" activities in the forum state are required for a finding of general jurisdiction.[55] After seven decades of U.S. Supreme Court jurisprudence, the Court has found general jurisdiction in only one instance.[56] In *Goodyear Dunlop Tires Operations v. Brown*,[57] the Court strongly implies that general jurisdiction is more

---

[50] See CPLR § 302(a)(1).

[51] Goodyear, 131 S.Ct. at 2851.

[52] Shrader v. Beann, 2012 U.S. App. LEXIS 24587 (10th Cir., Nov. 29, 2012) at *6.

[53] Bancroft & Masters, Inc. v. Augusta Nat'l, Inc., 223 F.3d 1082, 1086 (9th Cir.2000).

[54] "A defendant whose contacts with a state are 'substantial' or 'continuous and systematic' can be haled into court in that state in any action, even if the action is unrelated to those contacts." Bancroft & Masters, Inc. v. Augusta Nat'l, Inc., 223 F.3d 1082, 1087 (9th Cir. 2000).

[55] Helicópteros Nacionales de Colombia. S.A. v. Hall, 466 U.S. 408 (1984) (ruling that U.S. citizens who died in a helicopter crash in Peru could not pursue a wrongful death lawsuit against the manufacturer in Texas because there was not sufficient general jurisdiction).

[56] Perkins v. Benguet Consol. Mining Co., 342 U.S. 437 (1952) (holding that general jurisdiction was appropriately exercised over Philippine corporation sued in Ohio, where the company's affairs were overseen during World War II).

[57] 131 S. Ct. 2846 (2011) (holding that Goodyear's foreign subsidiaries' connection not sufficiently continuous and systematic to satisfy general jurisdiction).

limited than what federal and state courts have treated it. The Court held that a corporation is subject to general jurisdiction in a "home" state (state of incorporation and principal place of business). The *Goodyear* Court implies that the exercise of general jurisdiction in states other than these paradigm forums will be limited. Justice Ginsburg's opinion in *Goodyear* does not provide further guidance on what is meant by the limited circumstances that constitute general jurisdiction, however, the Court's decision sends a signal to lower federal and state courts[58] that the threshold for a finding of general jurisdiction is extremely high. To date, the Supreme Court has not reviewed an Internet-related general jurisdiction case. "For a website to support a finding of general jurisdiction on its own, the defendant must systematically contact the forum state through the Internet over a significant period of time."[59]

To determine whether a non-resident defendant's contacts are sufficiently substantial or continuous and systematic, a court must consider their ". . . longevity, continuity, volume, economic impact, physical presence, and integration into the state's regulatory or economic markets."[60] "The standard for general jurisdiction is rigorous because the consequences can be severe: if a defendant is subject to general jurisdiction in a state, then it may be called into court there to answer for any alleged wrong, committed in any place, no matter how unrelated to the defendant's contacts with the forum."[61] Assuming the contacts with the forum are extensive enough to satisfy general jurisdiction, courts overlook the fact that the cause of action arose elsewhere. In contrast, specific jurisdiction requires a connection or nexus between the minimum contacts and the cause of action. With general jurisdiction, the defendant's contacts are so extensive in the foreign forum so that they are deemed to functionally or legally present, even though not physically present.

General jurisdiction is often asserted but rarely recognized by courts. The only U.S. court to find general jurisdiction in an Internet-related dispute was *Gator.Com Corp. v. L.L. Bean, Inc.*,[62] where the Ninth Circuit predicated general jurisdiction upon L.L. Bean's millions of dollars of sales with California consumers. The *L.L. Bean* court noted that this revenue stream was "driven by an extensive, ongoing, and sophisticated sales effort involving large numbers of direct e-mail solicitations and millions of catalog sales."[63] Gator.com Corp. filed suit against the outdoor outfitter in a California federal

---

[58] "A court may assert general jurisdiction over foreign (sister-state or foreign-country) corporations to hear any and all claims against them when their affiliations with the State are so 'continuous and systematic' as to render them essentially at home in the forum State." Goodyear Dunlop, 131 S. Ct. at 2851 (quoting Int'l Shoe, 326 U.S. at 317). In International Shoe, the Supreme Court explained that "continuous activity of some sorts within a state is not enough to support the demand that the corporation be amenable to suits unrelated to that activity . . . the continuous corporate operations within a state [must be] so substantial and of such a nature as to justify suit against it on causes of action arising from dealings entirely distinct from those activities." Int'l Shoe, 326 U.S. at 318; see also Goodyear Dunlop, 131 S. Ct. at 2856.

[59] 4A CHARLES ALAN WRIGHT & ARTHUR R. MILLER, FED. PRAC.& PROC. 1073.1 (3rd ed. 2007). See e.g., Lakin v. Prudential Sec, Inc., 348 F.3d 704, 712–13 (8th Cir. 2003) (noting determination of general jurisdiction over commercial website would require development of facts regarding quantity of transactions with forum residents).

[60] Mavrix Photo, Inc. v. Brand Techs., Inc., 647 F.3d 1218, 1224 (9th Cir. 2011).

[61] uBID, Inc. v. GoDaddy Group, Inc., 623 F.3d 421 (7th Cir. 2010)(finding no general jurisdiction but specific jurisdiction because the site had continuously and deliberately exploited the Illinois market for domain name registration and had profited from it, the site was subject to specific jurisdiction in Illinois under its long-arm statute).

[62] 341 F.3d 1072 (9th Cir. 2003).

[63] Id.

court, seeking a declaratory judgment that its pop-up ads did not infringe L.L. Bean's trademarks or constitute an unfair business practice. L.L. Bean is a Maine corporation with its principal place of business in Maine. L.L. Bean advertised in California, both by mail and over the Internet. The retailer sold significant quantities of retail merchandise to consumers in California. It did not have either property or employees in California. The district court granted L.L. Bean's motion to dismiss for lack of personal jurisdiction. However, the Ninth Circuit reversed the district court's decision holding there was a basis for general jurisdiction over the Maine outfitter.

The *L.L. Bean* court premised its finding of general jurisdiction in part upon L.L. Bean's extensive marketing and sales targeting California consumers and contacts with California vendors. In addition, the L.L. Bean website created a virtual California store satisfying general jurisdiction. Nevertheless, this sole general jurisdiction decision was vacated after the parties settled before the Ninth Circuit's rehearing *en banc*. Few Internet cases will satisfy the rigorous general jurisdiction test, which requires a showing of the website's physical presence in either the forum or "systematic and continuous contacts" to satisfy due process. In summary, websites "will subject a defendant to general personal jurisdiction only when the defendant has actually and deliberately used its website to conduct commercial transactions on a sustained basis with a substantial number of residents of the forum."[64] No court has ruled that general jurisdiction may be based solely upon the existence of a website that can be accessed by anyone in the state.

(3) Specific Jurisdiction

Assuming a court finds no general jurisdiction, the question becomes whether there is a basis for specific jurisdiction. "Specific jurisdiction requires a plaintiff to show that: "(1) there are sufficient (i.e., not 'random fortuitous or attenuated') pre-litigation connections between the non-resident defendant and the forum; (2) the connection has been purposefully established by the defendant; and (3) the plaintiff's cause of action arises out of or is related to the defendant's forum contacts. Once [the] plaintiff makes that showing, the defendant can then defeat the exercise of specific jurisdiction by showing (4) that it would fail the fairness test, i.e., that the balance of interest factors show that the exercise of jurisdiction would be unreasonable."[65]

Specific jurisdiction depends upon the plaintiff showing a relationship between the underlying controversy and the forum. Internet cases, like bricks and mortar lawsuits, always turn on whether the defendant targets the forum in some meaningful way. Beyond simply operating an interactive website that is accessible from the forum state, a defendant must expressly target the forum state's market to satisfy personal jurisdiction under "something more" tests discussed later in this chapter. Recent Internet cases turn on whether the defendant targets the forum in some way:

Beyond simply operating an interactive website that is accessible from the forum state, a defendant must in some way target the forum state's market. If the defendant merely operates a website, even a highly interactive website, that is accessible from,

---

[64] Smith v. Basin Park Hotel, Inc., 178 F. Supp. 2d 1225, 1235 (N.D. Okla. 2001).

[65] Pervasive Software, Inc. v. Lexware GMBH & Co. KG, 688 F.3d 214, 222 (5th Cir. 2012) (quoting 1 ROBERT C. CASAD & WILLIAM B. RICHMAN, JURISDICTION IN CIVIL ACTIONS § 2–5, at 144 (3d ed. 1998)).

but does not target the forum state, then the defendant may not be hauled into court in that state without offending the U.S. Constitution.[66]

(D) Personal Jurisdiction for Online Activities

U.S. courts' exercise of personal jurisdiction "based on the defendant's contacts with the forum through the Internet requires that the plaintiff satisfy the terms of the appropriate jurisdictional statute, and then show that the exercise of jurisdiction will not violate the Constitution.[67] The Fifth Circuit states that the test for online activities is a three-prong test just as with bricks and mortar cases: "(1) Did the plaintiff's cause of action arise out of or result from the defendant's forum-related contacts? (2) Did the defendant purposely direct its activities toward the forum state or purposely avail itself of the privilege of conducting activities therein? (3) Would the exercise of personal jurisdiction over the defendant be reasonable and fair?"[68] "A court without personal jurisdiction is powerless to take further action."[69]

In general, personal jurisdiction in cyberspace is positively correlated with commercial activity: the greater the interactivity of a website, the more likely a court will find the defendant subject to personal jurisdiction in an out-of-state forum. Courts frequently apply the "sliding-scale" analysis first articulated in 1997 by a federal district court in *Zippo Manufacturing Co. v. Zippo Dot Com, Inc.*[70] "Tortious acts committed through website postings, however, present a unique challenge: Unlike a phone call, chatroom conversation, or fax, images or words posted to a website are not electronic communications in the traditional sense. First, they are not generally directed at any particular person or even a particular state. Second, even when directed at a particular person or state, the website is still accessible from virtually any forum."[71]

(1) Zippo.com Sliding Scale

No Personal Jurisdiction	Gray Area	Personal Jurisdiction is found
Passive websites with little commercial activity	Middle Ground where there may or may not be minimum contacts	Interactive websites that permit online orders

---

[66] be2 LLC v. Ivanov, 642 F.3d 555, 558–559 (7th Cir. 2011).

[67] Pervasive Software, Inc. v. Lexware GMBH & Co. KG, 688 F.3d 214, 227 (5th Cir. 2012).

[68] Id. at 222.

[69] Carmel & Co. v. Silverfish, LLC, No. 1:12–cv21328–KMM, 2013 WL 1177857, at *1 (S.D.Fla. March21, 2013) (quoting Posner v. Essex Ins. Co., Ltd., 178 F.3d 1209, 1214 n. 6 (11th Cir.1999)).

[70] 952 F. Supp. 1119 (W.D. Pa. 1997) (formulating a "sliding scale" for measuring purposeful availment consisting of passive and active websites on each end and a broad middle ground).

[71] Roca Labs, Inc. v. Boogie Media, LLC, Slip Copy, 2013 WL 2025806 (M.D. Fla., May 14, 2003).

Zippo Mfg. Co. v. Zippo Dot Com, Inc.,[72] formulated an influential Internet jurisdiction test that turned on whether a website was interactive or passive. The *Zippo* court's interactive/passive website test continues to be used by courts to determine whether the defendant's website activities are sufficient to support personal jurisdiction. In Internet cases, courts classify a defendant's website into one of three separate categories: (1) interactive, (2) passive, and (3) a "gray area" in the borderland between the passive and active website. At one end of the continuum are passive websites that merely post information; a court is unlikely to find personal jurisdiction in such a scenario.[73] On the other end of the spectrum are interactive websites and under that scenario, a court will likely find personal jurisdiction.

Websites in the borderland, or "," are somewhat interactive websites that enable users to exchange information. In these "gray area" cases, the court will assess the level of interactivity and whether or not the exchanges are commercial.[74] Zippo.com was a corporation with its principal place of business in California whereas the plaintiff, Zippo Manufacturing ("Zippo Mfg."), was located in Pennsylvania. Zippo Mfg. filed suit against Zippo.com, a computer news service, alleging trademark dilution, trademark infringement, and false designation of origin under the Lanham Act. Zippo Mfg. also pleaded state law claims against Zippo.com in reference to the domain names "zippo.com," "zippo.net," and "zipponews.com" that the defendant website used to make its services available to its customers in Pennsylvania.

Zippo.com moved to dismiss Zippo Mfg.'s Pennsylvania trademark infringement complaint citing a lack of personal jurisdiction. The Pennsylvania federal court examined whether Zippo.com satisfied purposeful availment of doing business in Pennsylvania by conducting business through its website. In finding that jurisdiction was proper, the *Zippo* court posited a sliding scale test classifying Internet sites by the nature and quality of the online commercial activity. Under *Zippo*, the easy case for personal jurisdiction is when a defendant enters into contracts with residents of a foreign jurisdiction that involve the knowing and repeated transmission of computer files. For highly interactive websites, the exercise of personal jurisdiction in the foreign jurisdiction is clearly proper.

The federal district court found that Zippo.com's overall conduct constituted the purposeful availment of doing business in Pennsylvania because contacts with Pennsylvania were almost exclusively over the Internet. All of Zippo.com's employees, offices, and servers were located in California and the company had no offices, employees or agents in Pennsylvania. Lastly, Zippo.com's only advertising to Pennsylvania residents was through their web page. Personal jurisdiction is not proper

---

[72] 952 F. Supp. 1119 (W.D. Pa. 1997).

[73] On the opposite end of the spectrum are passive websites "that [do] . . . little more than make information available to those who are interested in it." Id. at 1121.

[74] "At one end of the spectrum are situations where a defendant clearly does business over the Internet. If the defendant enters into contracts with residents of a foreign jurisdiction that involve the knowing and repeated transmission of computer files over the Internet, personal jurisdiction is proper. . . . At the opposite end are situations where a defendant has simply posted information on an Internet Website, which is accessible to users in foreign jurisdictions. A passive Website that does little more than make information available to those who are interested in it is not grounds for the exercise [of] personal jurisdiction. . . . The middle ground is occupied by interactive Websites where a user can exchange information with the host computer. In these cases, the exercise of jurisdiction is determined by examining the level of interactivity and commercial nature of the exchange of information that occurs on the Website." Abdouch v. Lopez, 829 N.W.2d 662, 728 (Neb. 2013) (discussion Zippo.com sliding scale for determining personal jurisdiction).

where a defendant has simply posted information on an Internet website. Merely being accessible to foreign users does not confer jurisdiction if the site is classified as passive.

(2) Passive Jurisdiction

Bensusan Restaurant Corp. v. King,[75] a U.S. district court case from New York, is the emblematic example of the passive website where the court found no specific jurisdiction. The operator of "The Blue Note," a jazz club in New York City, filed a trademark infringement suit against "The Blue Note," a jazz club in Columbia, Missouri owned by Richard B. King ("King"). King created a web page for his club posting a calendar of events and ticket information, as well as a disclaimer reputing any affiliation with the New York-based club of the same name, but did not permit the online purchasing of tickets. The court reasoned that King did not purposefully avail himself of jurisdiction in New York by merely posting information on a website without interactivity or otherwise directing commercial activity in New York. The use of an identical mark by two different companies is sometimes allowed in trademark law under the concept of "concurrent use."[76] For example, the United States Patent and Trademark Office may register the exact same mark for two different users, if the use of the mark by both users is not likely to result in confusion, mistake, or deception.[77]

The *Bensusan* case also illustrates how the once geographically limited use of trademarks permitted by the doctrine of concurrent use is abridged by the Internet.[78] In *Cybersell Inc. v. Cybersell, Inc.*,[79] Cybersell Incorporated ("Cybersell AZ") registered its service mark with the U.S. Trademark Office in 1994. In 1995, a Florida father and son formed a family business to conduct website consulting services also under the trade name of Cybersell ("Cybersell FL"). The Cybersell AZ plaintiffs, Laurence Canter and Martha Siegel, were infamous spam e-mailers who then filed a lawsuit for trademark infringement against Cybersell FL.

The Arizona federal court dismissed the action finding that it had no personal jurisdiction over the Cybersell FL website because it was neither interactive nor conducting commercial transactions. Websites with online advertising are interactive so long as they have "something more," such as conducting commercial activity over the internet with forum residents, encouraging residents of the forum state to access the website, or earning income from residents in the forum state.[80] The court calibrated personal jurisdiction as "directly proportionate to the nature and quality of commercial activity that an entity conducts over the Internet."[81]

The court employed a three-part test to determine whether the defendant has such minimum contacts with a forum state. First, the "nonresident defendant must do some act or consummate some transaction with the forum or perform some act by which he

---

[75] 937 F. Supp. 295 (S.D. N.Y. 1996).

[76] See also, Robert Nupp, Concurrent Use of Trademarks on the Internet: Reconciling the Concept of Geographically Delimited Trademarks with the Reality of The Internet, 64 OHIO ST. L. J. 617, 619 n.11 (2003).

[77] 15 U.S.C. § 1052(d).

[78] David S. Barrett, The Future of the Concurrent Use of Trademarks Doctrine in the Information Age, 23 HASTINGS COMM. & ENT. L. J. 687, 688 (2001).

[79] 130 F.3d 414 (9th Cir. 1997).

[80] Id. at 419.

[81] Id.

purposefully avails himself of the privilege of conducting activities in the forum," thereby invoking the benefits and protections of the forum state.[82] The court found that Cybersell FL did not purposefully avail itself of the privilege of doing business in Arizona, ruling the defendant must do something akin to specifically targeting the forum, rather than merely posting a website accessible in the forum state. Under *Cybersell*, mere operation of a passive website is insufficient to establish personal jurisdiction over a defendant, while operation of an interactive, commercial website often is sufficient.[83]

To exercise specific jurisdiction, the trial court must first find that the defendant purposefully directed his conduct at California. In particular, the "nonresident defendant must do some act or consummate some transaction with the forum or perform some act by which he purposefully avails himself of the privilege of conducting activities in the forum," thereby invoking the benefits and protections of the forum state.[84] The greater the commercial activity, the more likely a court will exercise jurisdiction. In *Facebook, Inc. v. Teachbook.com, LLC*,[85] a federal court ruled that Teachbook's adoption of a confusingly similar trademark did not subject it to jurisdiction in California because it was a passive website. The court stated, "The fact that an essentially passive Internet advertisement may be accessible in the plaintiff's home state without 'something more' is not enough to support personal jurisdiction."[86]

(3) The Gray Zone: Maybe Interactivity

Courts closely inspect the gray region or the borderland between passive and interactive websites to determine whether a website targeted the forum with advertising, solicitation of orders, or other emblems of the defendant's presence in a forum.[87] The middle ground is the borderland between interactive and passive websites. In *Cambria Co., LLC v. Pental Granite & Marble, Inc.*,[88] a Washington company's website enabled Minnesota website visitors to pay bills online, which was a key factor in the court finding specific jurisdiction. Pental's website was in the middle ground having email and payment functions. In addition, visitors could "like" the website on Facebook and follow it on Twitter. In these cases, the exercise of jurisdiction is determined by examining the level of interactivity and commercial nature of the exchange of information that occurs on the website.

The court found the website to lie in the borderland between passive and active websites. A key factor in favor of jurisdiction was that the website advertised infringing products targeting Minnesota residents even though it had no agents,

---

[82] Id. at 418.

[83] Id. at 420 (holding that a nonresident defendant in a domain name dispute did not have sufficient "minimum contacts" with the forum state).

[84] Id.

[85] No. CV 10–03654 RMW, 2011 WL 1672464 (N.D. Cal. May 3, 2011).

[86] Id. at *7; Michelle R. Osinski, Personal Jurisdiction and Internet Torts: Michigan District Courts Require "Something More" Than Simply Registering Someone Else's Trademark as a Domain Name and Posting a Web Page on the Internet to Subject a Defendant to Personal Jurisdiction, 80 U. DET. MERCY L. REV. 249–268 (2003).

[87] See generally, Michael Geist, Relatively Recent Jurisdiction Decisions Said to be Falling Behind Web Technologies, INTERNET LAW & REG. (PIKE & FISHER) (June 5, 2001) (observing that "it is often difficult to determine whether a site is active or passive and that courts are moving away from the Zippo standard to a more target-based approach to jurisdiction").

[88] 2013 U.S. Dist. LEXIS 43323 (D. Minn., March 27, 2013).

operations, or facilities in Minnesota. The *Cambria* court's consideration of the defendant's presence on social media illustrates how *Zippo.com's* interactivity test has been overtaken by the evolving Internet. Today, all but a few websites are interactive by definition and, as such, courts need to consider factors beyond interactivity. In *GOFIT LLC v. GoFit LLC,*[89] the federal court held that a minimally interactive fitness website did not satisfy minimum contacts. The plaintiff, GOFIT LLC, an Oklahoma fitness equipment company, sued the defendant GoFit LLC, a Delaware company, for trademark infringement in an Oklahoma federal court. The court found that the only basis for minimum contacts in Oklahoma was the defendant's nationwide policy of giving free passes to its fitness centers. The federal appeals court reasoned that the defendant did not intend to do business in Oklahoma and found no personal jurisdiction.

(4) Zippo.com's Interactivity Test

An interactive website, where a visitor can order and pay for goods and services is sufficient to establish personal jurisdiction under the *Zippo.com's* interactivity test. A website's exceptionally interactive design is a key factor in favor of personal jurisdiction as noted by the court in *Stewart v. Hennessey.*[90] Defendants will not be able to challenge jurisdiction successfully where the website is open to residents in the forum and receives "hits" from the forum.[91] Sporadic sales are insufficient to confer jurisdiction. Nevertheless, Internet sites permitting users to download software are sufficiently interactive for personal jurisdiction. The *Zippo* interactivity test is an inadequate test for determining purposeful availment during the second wave of cases where all but a few commercial websites are interactive. Courts should not be tempted to continue stretching the well-worn grooves of *Zippo* to Internet jurisdiction cases because it does not fit the reality that nearly every website is interactive. "There is nothing more revolting if the grounds upon which it was laid down have vanished long since, and the rule simply persists from blind imitation of the past."[92] Courts, however, are mechanically extending traditional principles of personal jurisdiction rather than tailoring theories for the borderless Internet.

(E) The Effects Test for Cybertorts

In cybertort or IP infringement actions, the focus of minimum contacts is the "effects" or "brunt of the harm" test of *Calder v. Jones.*[93] Under the effects test, the defendant allegedly must have: (1) committed an intentional act, (2) expressly aimed at the forum state, and (3) causing harm that the defendant knows is likely to be suffered in the forum state. In *Calder*, the U.S. Supreme Court upheld a California state court's finding that it had personal jurisdiction over *The National Enquirer*, which had offices in Florida. In *Calder v. Jones*, a tabloid reporter wrote a libelous article about actress Shirley Jones, claiming that she was an alcoholic. The U.S. Supreme Court reasoned the tabloid knew the brunt of the harm would occur in California, a state where the tabloid had its largest circulation. The *Calder* Court reasoned that California was the

---

[89] 2013 U.S. Dist. LEXIS 5284 (N.D. Okla, April 12, 2013).

[90] 214 F. Supp. 2d 1198 (D. Utah 2002).

[91] See ComputerUser.com, Inc. v. Tech. Publ'ns., 2002 U.S. Dist. LEXIS 13453 (D. Minn. July 20, 2002).

[92] Oliver Wendell Holmes Jr., The Path of the Law, 10 HARV. L. REV. 457, 469 (1897).

[93] 465 U.S. 783 (1984).

focal point for the brunt of the harm because Ms. Jones worked and lived there and that the *National Enquirer* story about Jones's alcoholism would be felt the most there—the home of the movie and television industries.

An appellate court does not require that the brunt of the harm be suffered in the forum. Instead, the foreseeable-harm element is satisfied when defendant's intentional act has foreseeable effects in the forum. If a jurisdictionally sufficient amount of harm is suffered in the forum state, it does not matter that even more harm might have been suffered in another state.[94]

A federal court in *Kollective Co. v. Yang*[95] found that Asian-based websites hosting Korean pop songs copyrighted in the United States expressly were targeting California residents when they incorporated third party advertisements in their online messages. California's personal jurisdiction distinguishes between jurisdiction based upon purposeful direction in tort or infringement cases and purposeful availment, where the underlying cause of action arises out of contract. Courts have ruled that something more than email is necessary to pass the effects test. The court in *Johnson v. Mitchell*[96] stated that, "personal jurisdiction would be boundless" if sending an email was enough to satisfy due process.

Critics call for courts to abandon the *Calder* effects test for Internet jurisdiction because it generally preordains that the court finds sufficient minimum contacts. Court premise a finding of minimum contacts ". . . simply on the grounds that you have said nasty things—even defamatory things—about someone whom you happen to know lives in [that state] has always struck me as profoundly odd and misguided."[97] An appellate court typically does not require that the brunt of the harm be suffered in the forum. Instead, the foreseeable-harm element is satisfied when defendant's intentional act has foreseeable effects in the forum. If a jurisdictionally sufficient amount of harm is suffered in the forum state, it does not matter that even more harm might have been suffered in another state. The *Calder* effects test is ill suited for the Internet because it is overly inclusive.

In cybertort or IP infringement actions, the focus of minimum contacts is the "effects" or "brunt of the harm" test of *Calder v. Jones*.[98] Under the effects test, the defendant allegedly must have: (1) committed an intentional act, (2) expressly aimed at the forum state, and (3) caused harm that the defendant knows is likely to be suffered in the forum state. In *Calder*, the U.S. Supreme Court upheld a California state court's finding that it had personal jurisdiction over *The National Enquirer*, which had offices in Florida. In *Calder*, the U.S. Supreme Court upheld a California state court's finding that it had personal jurisdiction over *The National Enquirer*, which had offices in Florida. A tabloid reporter wrote a libelous article about Jones, claiming that she was an alcoholic. The U.S. Supreme Court reasoned the tabloid knew the brunt of the harm would occur in California, a state where the tabloid had its largest circulation. The *Calder* Court further reasoned that California was the focal point for the brunt of the harm because Ms. Jones worked and lived there and that the *National Enquirer* story

---

[94] Fiore v. Walden, 657 F.2d 838, 849 (9th Cir. 2011).

[95] No. 4:11–cv–01051–CW (E.D. Cal., March 28, 2013).

[96] Johnson v. Mitchell, No. 10–1968 (E.D. Cal., Feb. 15, 2013).

[97] David Post, Kill Calder v. Jones, THE VOLOKH CONSPIRACY (Nov. 19, 2010).

[98] 465 U.S. 783 (1984).

about Jones's alcoholism would be felt the most there—the home of the movie and television industries.

An appellate court does not require that the brunt of the harm be suffered in the forum. Instead, the foreseeable-harm element is satisfied when defendant's intentional act has foreseeable effects in the forum. If a jurisdictionally sufficient amount of harm is suffered in the forum state, it does not matter that even more harm might have been suffered in another state.[99]

The effects test for specific jurisdiction encompasses two distinct requirements: first that the out-of-state defendant must have purposefully directed its activities at residents of the forum state and second that the plaintiff's injuries must arise out of defendant's forum-related activities. Internet law disputes often present a highly charged context for jurisdictional disputes as was the case in *Bochan v. La Fontaine,*[100] In *Bochan*, the plaintiff, Steve Bochan of Virginia, filed a defamation lawsuit in the federal district of Virginia contending that defendants Ray and Mary La Fontaine of Texas, journalists and authors of *Oswald Talked: The New Evidence in the JFK Assassination*, defamed him. Bochan purchased the La Fontaines' book in Virginia and subsequently criticized it online through posts on an interactive newsgroup. Bochan quoted from the La Fontaines' acknowledgments to their book: "[W]e thank Charlotte and Eugenia for putting up with weird parents."[101] Bochan's caustic review of their book provoked the La Fontaines to post incendiary responses to the JFK assassination newsgroup, remarking, for example, that the Bochans should limit their prurient interest to "alt.sex.fetish.tinygirls" and leave the authors' children out of it.

The federal court concluded that the allegedly defamatory postings caused a tortious injury by an act or omission within the state, because the postings were made through the plaintiff's Virginia based America Online account. The postings were thus within the reach of the long-arm statute because Bochan's Virginia account enabled the La Fontaines' tortious postings. Bochan testified the La Fontaines' transmitted and stored his defamatory posting in Virginia. The *Bochan* court also noted that a Virginia based server transmitted the communications to servers around the world. These acts, according to the court, established a sufficient contact in Virginia. In addition, the court found Robert Harris, a New Mexico co-defendant and owner of a computer systems business, had sufficient advertising and solicitation of business in Virginia to support personal jurisdiction to try the defamation case.

The Virginia district court found the predominant "effects" of Harris and the LaFontaines' conduct to be in Virginia thereby enabling them to foresee being hauled into court in that state. "A judicial consensus has generally emerged that personal jurisdiction exists when Internet activities involve the conduct of business over the Internet, including on-line contracting with residents of the jurisdiction or other kinds of substantial commercial interactivity."[102] The problem with predicating jurisdiction on the location of servers is that it could make any Internet subscriber subject to personal jurisdiction.

---

[99] Fiore v. Walden, 657 F.2d 838, 849 (9th Cir. 2011).

[100] 68 F. Supp. 2d 692 (E.D. Va. 1999).

[101] Id. at 695.

[102] Id.

In *Daimler A.G. v. Shuanghuan Auto Co.*,[103] the court found that a website advertising cars similar to Daimler's automobiles did not satisfy the effects test for minimum contacts in Michigan. Des Moines Motors is a dealership that owns and operates a website under the domain names: www.shuanghuanusa.com and www.shuanghuanofdesmoines.com. The court found that Des Moines was not subject to the effects test since it had not targeted Michigan when it posted information about Chinese cars on its website.[104] To satisfy the effects test, the plaintiff must prove "something more" than the effects will be felt in the plaintiff's forum.[105] The plaintiff predicating specific jurisdiction on the effects must prove that the defendant was targeting the forum.

A federal court in *Kollective Co. v. Yang*[106] found that Asian-based websites hosting Korean pop songs copyrighted in the United States expressly targeted California residents when they incorporated third party advertisements in their online messages. California's personal jurisdiction distinguishes between jurisdiction based upon purposeful direction in tort or infringement cases and purposeful availment, where the underlying cause of action arises out of contract. Courts have ruled that something more than email is necessary to pass the effects test. Critics call for courts to abandon the *Calder* test for Internet jurisdiction because it generally preordains that the court finds sufficient minimum contacts. Courts premise a finding of minimum contacts ". . . simply on the grounds that you have said nasty things—even defamatory things—about someone whom you happen to know lives in [that state] has always struck me as profoundly odd and misguided."[107] An appellate court typically does not require that the brunt of the harm be suffered in the forum. Instead, the foreseeable-harm element is satisfied when a defendant's intentional act has foreseeable effects in the forum. If a jurisdictionally sufficient amount of harm is suffered in the forum state, it does not matter that even more harm might have been suffered in another state. Thus, the over-inclusiveness of the *Calder* effects test makes it ill-suited for Internet law cases. Recently, courts are examining factors beyond interactivity such as the nature and quality of online and offline contacts.[108]

(F) Purposeful Availment for Internet Contracts

Courts use a three-part test to determine whether a defendant purposefully availed itself of a particular forum: (1) the defendant must either purposefully direct its activities at the forum or purposefully avail itself of the privilege of doing business

---

[103] 2013 WL 2250213 (E.D. Mich. May 22, 2013).

[104] Id. at *6.

[105] Gregory v. Mihaylov, 2013 WL 75773 *6 (N.D. Ga., Jan. 4, 2013)(stating the connection between the tort claims and forum must not be too remote and that there must be something more than that the plaintiff feels the intentional conduct's effects in its forum)

[106] No. 4:11–cv–01051–CW (E.D. Cal., March 28, 2013).

[107] David Post, Kill Calder v. Jones, THE VOLOKH CONSPIRACY (Nov. 19, 2010).

[108] "As such, the Internet "raises significant questions about the application of traditional personal jurisdiction doctrine." 4A CHARLES ALAN WRIGHT ET AL., FED. PRAC. & PROC. § 1073.1, at 322 (3d ed. 2002); "'Although the Internet and the other new communications technologies do present some strikingly new factual patterns and do change the way personal jurisdiction is acquired over some defendants at the margins,'" id. at 322, "the analysis applicable to a case involving jurisdiction based on the Internet . . . should not be different at its most basic level from any other personal jurisdiction case. If the defendant is not physically present in or a resident of the forum state, and has not been physically served in the forum state, the federal court must undertake the traditional personal jurisdiction analysis." Id.

there, (2) the claim must arise from the defendant's forum-related activities, and (3) the exercise of jurisdiction must be reasonable. This test ensures that a defendant will not be subject to personal jurisdiction solely because of random, fortuitous, or attenuated contacts or of the unilateral activity of another party or a third person. Therefore, the issue becomes whether the specific activity or occurrence giving rise to the claim took place in the forum state and is subject to the state's regulation. A website's notice that it will not accept orders from a given forum is insufficient to shield it from a finding of purposeful availment; similarly, the fact that a defendant's postings were available over the Internet is not enough to establish purposeful direction toward a forum.

The "constitutional touchstone" of the minimum contacts analysis is embodied in the first prong "whether the defendant purposefully established" contacts with the forum state. Purposeful availment typically consists of action taking place in the forum that invokes the benefits and protections of the laws of the forum, such as executing or performing a contract within the forum. The defendant's contacts do not satisfy due process where they are merely fortuitous. The minimum requirements inherent in the concept of "fair play and substantial justice" may defeat the reasonableness of jurisdiction even if the defendant has the requisite minimum contacts with the forum. As a rule in these cases, this Court requires 'some act by which the defendant purposefully avail[ed] itself of the privilege of conducting activities within the forum state, thus invoking the benefits and protections of its laws.'[109] Specific jurisdiction depends upon the plaintiff showing a relationship between the underlying controversy and the forum. Purposeful availment requires some intentionality on the part of the defendant to target a foreign forum while specific jurisdiction requires a showing of a nexus between the claim and minimum contacts.[110] If a website simply gives notice that, it will not accept orders from a given forum, the notice alone will not shield it from personal jurisdiction. In *Illinois v. Hemi Group*,[111] the State of Illinois filed suit against Hemi Group ("Hemi"), a New Mexico company, for selling cigarettes online to Illinois residents in violation of state laws and for failing to report sales in violation of federal law.

Hemi sold discount cigarettes through its many websites and customers determined shipping costs by inputting their zip codes on the website. "The only specific sales to an Illinois resident that Illinois identified in its complaint were instigated by a special senior agent of the Illinois Department of Revenue, who purchased more than three hundred packs of cigarettes from Hemi-operated websites in 2005 and 2007."[112] The Seventh Circuit affirmed a lower court's decision refusing to dismiss for lack of personal jurisdiction. The court found that Hemi's contacts with Illinois were sufficient to satisfy minimum contacts because the commercial website "would ship to any state in the country except New York."[113] The court's reasoning assumed that Hemi elected to do business in Illinois and was thus subject to personal jurisdiction. The court's finding that Hemi's contact with Illinois satisfied due process was based in large part upon its interactive website where users could calculate

---

[109] Hanson v. Denckla, 357 U.S. 235, 253 (1958).

[110] Goodyear Dunlop Tires Operations, S.A. v. Brown, 131 S. Ct. 2846, 2853 (2011).

[111] 622 F.3d 754 (7th Cir. 2010).

[112] Id.

[113] Id. at 758.

shipping charges to their state. Hemi's website made it clear it was prepared to ship cigarettes to Illinois; therefore, it was electing to do business there. The court also found it significant that Illinois refused to ship to New York, which demonstrated its awareness that it could be dragged into court anywhere it shipped cigarettes.

Internet law disputes often presented a highly charged context for jurisdictional disputes. In *Bochan v. La Fontaine*,[114] the plaintiff, Steve Bochan of Virginia, filed a defamation lawsuit in the federal district of Virginia contending that defendants Ray and Mary La Fontaine of Texas, journalists and authors of *Oswald Talked: The New Evidence in the JFK Assassination*, defamed him. Bochan purchased the La Fontaines' book in Virginia and subsequently criticized it online through posts on an interactive newsgroup. Bochan quoted from the La Fontaines' acknowledgments to their book: "[W]e thank Charlotte and Eugenia for putting up with weird parents."[115] Bochan's caustic review of their book provoked the La Fontaines to post incendiary responses to the JFK assassination newsgroup remarking, for example, that the Bochan couple should limit their prurient interest to alt.sex.fetish.tinygirls and leave their children out of it.

The federal court concluded that the allegedly defamatory postings caused a tortious injury by an act or omission within state because the postings were made through the plaintiff's Virginia based America Online account. The postings were thus within the realm of the long arm statute because the Virginia Internet account enabled the La Fontaines' tortious act. Bochan testified the La Fontaines' transmitted and stored his defamatory posting in Virginia. The *Bochan* court also noted that a Virginia based server transmitted the communications to servers around the world. These acts, according to the court, established a sufficient contact in Virginia. In addition, the court found Robert Harris, a New Mexico co-defendant and owner of a computer systems business, had sufficient advertising and solicitation of business in Virginia to support personal jurisdiction to try the defamation case.

The Virginia district court found the predominant "effects" of Harris and the LaFontaines' conduct to be in Virginia thereby enabling them to foresee being hauled into court in that state. "A judicial consensus has generally emerged that personal jurisdiction exists when Internet activities involve the conduct of business over the Internet, including on-line contracting with residents of the jurisdiction or other kinds of substantial commercial interactivity."[116] The problem with predicating jurisdiction on where servers are located could make any Internet subscriber subject to personal jurisdiction.

(G) "Something More" Test

(1) GTE New Media Services

State and federal courts have adopted an effects test for torts or intellectual property infringement actions, but are beginning to demand "something more" in addition to website interactivity to support a finding of specific jurisdiction.[117]

---

[114] 68 F. Supp. 2d 692 (E.D. Va. 1999).

[115] Id. at 695.

[116] Id.

[117] A number of courts have found no personal jurisdiction despite highly interactive websites. Carefirst of Maryland v. Carefirst Pregnancy Ctrs., 334 F.3d 390 (4th Cir.2003); Rio Properties, Inc. v. Rio Intern.

Beginning in the new millennium, courts began to ask for more proof than effects to support personal jurisdiction. An emblematic case of this new Internet personal jurisdiction jurisprudence was *GTE New Media Services Inc. v. BellSouth Corp.*[118] GTE New Media ("GTE") filed a Sherman Antitrust Act complaint against Bell South ("Bell") alleging they were in a conspiracy to dominate the Internet directories market in the Washington, D.C. metropolitan area by diverting Internet users from the GTE website to the defendant's websites. The D.C. Circuit Court of Appeals found Bell lacked minimum contacts with the District of Columbia based solely upon the fact its residents could access its Internet Yellow Pages from locations within the city. The court ruled that GTE could conduct discovery in order to seek proof of whether Bell had sufficient contacts with the forum.

The district court followed the *Zippo.com* "sliding scale" approach, finding BellSouth's websites fell into the uncertain gray zone and that jurisdiction existed based on the highly interactive nature and commercial quality of the websites. The D.C. Circuit Court reversed, reasoning that jurisdiction based solely on the maintenance of a passive website would violate principles of personal jurisdiction.

The *GTE* court also reasoned that personal jurisdiction could not hinge solely on the ability of District of Columbia residents to access the defendant's websites, as this did not amount to persistent conduct in D.C. Additionally, the federal appeals court reasoned that a website is functionally equivalent to a telephone call and this did not qualify as persistent conduct under the D.C. long-arm statute. The *GTE* court found that consumers did not pay to use the search tool and any resulting commercial transactions were between the consumer and the businesses found in the Yellow Pages. The lack of any commercial relationship between the consumer and the provider of the Yellow Pages failed to meet the "something more" test. The *GTE* court brought common sense to the common law in updating personal jurisdictional rules for changes in Internet web technologies and practices.

(2) ALS Scan

The court in *ALS Scan v. Digital Services Consultants, Inc.*[119] held that an Internet service provider was not subject to personal jurisdiction based solely upon an interactive website that was an instrumentality for copyright infringement. The *ALS Scan* court defined the meaning of "something more" than interactivity by following well established principles. ALS Scan, a Maryland-based adult entertainment website, filed suit against Digital Service, a Georgia ISP, for enabling a third parties' misappropriation of its copyrighted photographs. The federal appeals court found no personal jurisdiction because the ISP did not engage in continuous and systematic activities within the forum. In *ALS Scan*, the plaintiff argued that Digital enabled Alternative Products' publication of the infringing photographs on the Internet caused ALS Scan injury in Maryland, thus supporting personal jurisdiction. The *ALS Scan* court stated that specific jurisdiction in the "Internet [sic] context may be based only on an out-of-state person's Internet activity directed at the forum and causing injury gives rise to a potential claim" in that forum. The court reasoned:

Interlink, 284 F.3d 1007 (9th Cir.2002); GTE New Media Services Inc. v. BellSouth Corp., 199 F.3d 1343 (D.C.Cir.2000); Minnesota Public Radio v. Virginia Beach Educ. Br., 519 F.Supp.2d 970 (D.Minn.2007).

[118] 199 F.3d 1343 (D.C. 2000).

[119] 293 F.3d 707 (4th Cir. 2002).

Applying the traditional due process principles governing a State's jurisdiction over persons outside of the State based on Internet activity requires some adaptation of those principles because the Internet is omnipresent—when a person places information on the Internet, he can communicate with persons in virtually every jurisdiction. If we were to conclude as a general principle that a person's act of placing information on the Internet subjects that person to personal jurisdiction in each State in which the information is accessed, then the defense of personal jurisdiction, in the sense that a State has geographically limited judicial power, would no longer exist. The person placing information on the Internet would be subject to personal jurisdiction in every State.[120]

The court's approach was that a state may exercise judicial power over a person outside of the state when a person: (1) directs electronic activity into the state; (2) with the manifested intent of engaging in business or other interactions within the state; and (3) the activity creates in a person within the state, a potential cause of action cognizable in the state's courts.[121] The Ninth Circuit found insufficient contacts to satisfy general jurisdiction stating that satisfying *Zippo*'s interactivity test was insufficient to support a finding of general jurisdiction. The court reasoned that it was possible for a website to be interactive, but to have no meaningful quantity of contacts. In other words, the contacts would be continuous, but could also not be meaningful or substantial.

(3) Euromarket Designs

Beyond interactivity, "something more" means proof that a defendant has some intentional interaction with the forum. Courts frequently turn to non-Internet contacts to determine whether there is "something more" than website interactivity. In *Euromarket Designs, Inc. v. Crate and Barrel Ltd.*,[122] a U.S. company operating a chain of housewares and furniture stores in the United States filed a trademark infringement lawsuit against Limited, a corporation organized under the law of Ireland with a principal place of business in Dublin where it operates a retail store with the name "CRATE & BARREL" prominently displayed on its facade.

"After the Crate & Barrel retail store was opened in Ireland, Limited also created and registered an Internet website at the domain name "www.crateandbarrelie.com."[123] Limited's website "identifies itself as Crate & Barrel, and allows website visitors worldwide to both view and purchase the same household goods and furniture sold in the retail store. The goods sold by Limited are similar to the types of goods offered for sale by plaintiff."[124] The court addressed the issue of whether an Irish retailer with an

---

[120] Id. at 712.

[121] "A State may, consistent with due process, exercise judicial power over a person outside of the State when that person (1) directs electronic activity into the State, (2) with the manifested intent of engaging in business or other interactions within the State, and (3) that activity creates, in a person within the State, a potential cause of action cognizable in the State's courts. Under this standard, a person who simply places information on the Internet does not subject himself to jurisdiction in each State into which the electronic signal is transmitted and received. Such passive Internet activity does not generally include directing electronic activity into the State with the manifested intent of engaging business or other interactions in the State thus creating in a person within the State a potential cause of action cognizable in courts located in the State." Id. at 714.

[122] 96 F.Supp.2d 824 (N.D.Ill. 2000).

[123] Id. at 828.

[124] Id. at 829.

interactive website allowing Illinois residents to order goods from Illinois shipped to Illinois could be sued in Illinois by an Illinois company for violation of the Lanham Act.

Limited filed motions to dismiss contending that the court lacked personal and subject matter jurisdiction. The *Euromarket* court singled out non-Internet contacts between the defendant and Illinois such as attendance at trade shows, ties with state suppliers, and advertisements in U.S. publications in finding sufficient minimum contacts to satisfy due process. The *Euromarket* court also relied on the fact that the defendant billed Illinois customers, collected revenues from Illinois customers, and recorded sales from goods ordered from Illinois, and that the website was designed to accommodate addresses in the United States.[125]

(4) Dudnikov

In *Dudnikov v. Chalk & Vermillion Fine Arts Inc.,*[126] the Tenth Circuit reversed a district court's dismissal of a complaint for lack of personal jurisdiction. In *Dudnikov,* a Connecticut-based company notified the online auction host eBay, based in California, that a line of prints featured in an eBay auction infringed its copyright. EBay responded by cancelling the auction for the prints. The online sellers of the prints lived and operated their business in Colorado. Dudnikov, a Colorado company, auctioned various products through eBay. In October 2005, Ms. Dudnikov and Mr. Meadors launched an auction on eBay offering fabric for sale with the imprint of the cartoon character Betty Boop wearing various gowns. One of these gowns closely resembled a famous Erte gown. Erte was a twentieth century Russian-born French artist and fashion designer famous for his iconic depiction of Parisian high fashion.

"In Erte's original works, *Symphony In Black* and *Ebony On White,* a tall, slender woman is pictured wearing a floor length form-fitting dress that trails her feet, and holding the leash of a thin, regal dog."[127] "The fabric offered for sale by Ms. Dudnikov and Mr. Meadors replaced the rather elegant woman in Erte's images with the rather less elegant Betty Boop, and substituted Erte's svelte canine with Betty Boop's pet, Pudgy."[128] EBay suspended Dudnikov's account when Chalk called eBay complaining that the contested Betty Boop image infringed its client's intellectual property rights.[129] Dudnikov filed suit in Colorado district court, and the court dismissed the case upon the defendant's motion claiming lack of personal jurisdiction.[130] The Tenth Circuit reversed finding that, although Chalk's enforcement activity occurred in California, the activity was directed at a Colorado resident and sufficient to subject Chalk to the specific personal jurisdiction of the Colorado courts.

(5) be2 LLC

A growing number of courts cite the *Zippo* interactivity test but also demand that plaintiffs produce "something more" than mere interactivity to support a finding of specific jurisdiction. In *be2 LLC v. Ivanov,*[131] a Delaware dating website sued a

---

[125] Euromarket Designs, Inc. v. Crate & Barrel Ltd., 96 F. Supp.2d 824 (N.D. Ill. 2000).

[126] 514 F.3d 1063 (10th Cir. 2008).

[127] Id. at 1068.

[128] Id.

[129] Id. at 1069.

[130] Id.

[131] 642 F.3d 555 (7th Cir. 2011).Burger King Corp. v. Rudzewicz, 471 U.S. 462 (1985).

Bulgarian resident of New Jersey who had a dating site in Illinois. Plaintiff be2 LLC is a Delaware limited liability with its parent company organized and headquartered in Germany. One online matchmaking service has sued another for trademark infringement. The issue on appeal is whether the defendant's Internet activity made him susceptible to personal jurisdiction in Illinois for claims arising from that activity. The court refused to find personal jurisdiction over the New Jersey defendant who operated a website accessible in Illinois, as there was no evidence that the defendant targeted the Illinois market. The court reversed and remanded with directions to dismiss for lack of personal jurisdiction.[132]

"Plaintiff be2 originally offered its dating service only to singles in Europe. Over the past few years, be2 Holding has extended its reach to 14 million users in 36 countries, including the United States."[133] The court found no jurisdiction in Illinois merely because twenty state residents registered with the defendant's website. If an Internet defendant simply operates a website, even a "highly interactive" one, which may be accessed in the forum, it is an insufficient basis for jurisdiction absent evidence that the website targeted the forum.[134] Courts consider *Zippo.com* factors such as the nature and quality of online and offline contacts to determine purposeful availment but are beginning to broaden their assessment on a case-by-case basis.[135] The *be2 LLC v. Ivanov*[136] case is emblematic of a recent trend of courts demanding a showing that the website directed its activities into forum in addition to interactivity to satisfy specific jurisdiction.

(6) Mavrix Photo

In *Mavrix Photo, Inc. v. Brand Techs., Inc.,*[137] the Ninth Circuit ruled that Brand Technologies was subject to jurisdiction because it attempted to exploit the California marketplace when it posted infringing copyrighted content on its website. Mavrix took "candid" photos of Stacy Ferguson, an American songwriter known by her stage name "Fergie," and her husband, actor Josh Duhamel while they were vacationing in California. Mavrix registered the copyrights for the Ferguson/Duhamel vacation photographs exclusively licensing them to celebrity news outlets. Mavrix filed a federal copyright infringement lawsuit against Brand Technologies, Inc. in a California federal court after it learned that the website posted the photographs without Mavrix's permission thus infringing its copyright. The federal district court granted Brand Technologies' motion to dismiss on the ground of lack of personal jurisdiction. The

---

[132] LLC v. Ivanov, Id. at 556.

[133] Id.

[134] The court noted that " "[c]ourts should be careful in resolving questions about personal jurisdiction involving online contacts to ensure that a defendant is not haled into court simply because the defendant owns or operates a website that is accessible in the forum state, even if that site is 'interactive.'" "Id. at 558.

[135] "As such, the Internet "raises significant questions about the application of traditional personal jurisdiction doctrine." 4A CHARLES ALAN WRIGHT ET AL., FED. PRAC. & PROC. § 1073.1, at 322 (3d ed. 2002); "Although the Internet and the other new communications technologies do present some strikingly new factual patterns and do change the way personal jurisdiction is acquired over some defendants at the margins,'" id. at 322, "the analysis applicable to a case involving jurisdiction based on the Internet . . . should not be different at its most basic level from any other personal jurisdiction case. If the defendant is not physically present in or a resident of the forum state, and has not been physically served in the forum state, the federal court must undertake the traditional personal jurisdiction analysis." Id.

[136] 642 F.3d 555 (7th Cir. 2011).

[137] 647 F.3d 1218 (9th Cir. 2011).

Ninth Circuit reversed finding specific jurisdiction to be satisfied. The *Mavrix* court predicated specific jurisdiction upon Brand Technologies' alleged copyright infringement on its website. The court pointed to "something more" factors, beyond a site's interactivity, such as Brand Technologies targeting California residents with a commercial purpose.[138]

The court found that Brand Technologies aimed its advertisements at California therefore satisfying the *Calder* effects test. "Brand anticipated, desired, and achieved a substantial California viewer base, because of the subject matter of the website and the "size and commercial value of the California market."[139] The "something more" factor was Brand Technologies' specific focus on the "California-centered celebrity and entertainment industries."[140] The court based its finding on the website's subject matter, as well as the size and commercial value of the California market. The court's "expressly aimed" requirement is a necessary, but not sufficient, condition for jurisdiction. In order to establish specific jurisdiction, a plaintiff must also show that jurisdictionally significant harm was suffered in the forum state.[141] A commentator on this case notes how the entire minimum contacts inquiry is marked by ". . . ambiguity and incoherence."[142] The *Mavrix* case reflects the "highly fact specific" and somewhat "disjointed" nature of any minimum contacts analysis extended to websites.[143]

(H) Posting of Defamatory Comments

In *Shrader v. Biddinger*,[144] Shrader, miffed by a negative review of his book, filed claims for defamation, false-light invasion of privacy, the intentional infliction of emotional distress, and civil conspiracy against Biddinger, a former business associate and the operators of Wave59, an online forum.[145] The court ruled that simply posting defamatory comments on an Internet website is an insufficient basis for personal jurisdiction in Oklahoma, where the author resided. The *Shrader* court reasoned that a geographically neutral message posted by the defendant gave no basis for a conclusion that he was targeting Oklahoma.[146] "On the contrary, every indication is that Mr. Biddinger targeted the post at a nation-wide or world-wide audience of market traders with no inherent interest in or ties to Oklahoma."[147] The *Shrader* court reflects a legal realism in calling for more rigorous principles to determine personal jurisdiction than the too malleable test that effects may be felt in a specific forum. The basic problem court face is to find a more nuanced test since the Internet operates everywhere thus making the territorial limits of personal jurisdiction meaningless.

---

[138] Id. at 1229.

[139] Id.

[140] Id. at 1230.

[141] 647 F.3d 1218, 1231.

[142] Comment, Ninth Circuit Holds That Exercise of Personal Jurisdiction Over Company Whose Website Cultivates Significant Forum State Users Base Comports With Due Process, Mavrix Photo, Inc. v. Brand Technologies, Inc., 647 F.3d 1218 (9th Cir. 2011).

[143] Id.

[144] 633 F.3d 1235 (10th Cir. 2011).

[145] A civil conspiracy requires: (a) an agreement between two or more parties; (b) to do an unlawful act or to do a lawful act by unlawful means; (c) the doing of some overt act in pursuance of the conspiracy; and (d) damage to the plaintiff as a result of the acts done under the conspiracy. Raimi v. Furlong, 702 So.2d 1273, 1284 (Fla. 3d D. Ct. App. 1997).

[146] Id. at 1245–46.

[147] Id. at 1242.

(I) Situs of the Cyberspace Injury

In *Penguin Group (USA) Inc. v. Am. Buddha*,[148] the Second Circuit considered the situs of injury under a New York state statute in a copyright infringement case where the operator of a website uploaded copyrighted literary works owned by the Penguin Group. Under New York's long-arm statute, the court must find the "situs of the injury" before finding jurisdiction. The federal district court ruled that the "situs of the injury" was where the books were electronically copied and the state where the computer servers were located was not in New York where Penguin was headquartered. The Second Circuit answered a certified question that in copyright infringement cases, the "situs of the injury" for purposes of determining long-arm jurisdiction under the New York statute, was the location of the copyright holder's principal place of business. The Second Circuit dismissed Penguin's copyright infringement claim remanding the case to the lower court.

(J) In Rem & Quasi In Rem Jurisdiction

Technically, *in rem* jurisdiction relates to the determination of title to, or the status of, property located within the court's territorial limits. *In rem* actions adjudicate the rights of all persons with respect to property within the state. In contrast, a *quasi in rem* judgment affects the interests of particular persons in designated property. The leading case governing *quasi in rem* jurisdiction is *Shaffer v. Heitner*.[149] The *Shaffer* Court applied the minimum contacts framework to *quasi in rem* cases. A court will therefore have no jurisdiction over property disputes in a cyberspace case where minimum contacts are absent. Neither *in rem* nor *quasi in rem* jurisdictions will typically apply to intangible Internet assets as these assets cannot be attached or garnished. Nevertheless, the Anticybersquatting Consumer Protection Act ("ACPA")[150] recognizes *in rem* jurisdiction over domain name where personal jurisdiction over cyberpirates is unavailing.[151] The plaintiff in an *in rem* action under ACPA is the trademark owner, while the defendant is the infringing domain name. A court has the power to adjudicate all rights with respect to a specific domain name.

Courts will not permit a trademark owner to proceed *in rem* absent proof that the identity and address of the registrant of defendant's domain name cannot be found and that *in personam* jurisdiction was not possible. In *Mattel, Inc. v. Barbie–Club*,[152] Mattel, the toy manufacturer responsible for creating Barbie dolls, filed an *in rem* action to enforce its Barbie trademarks against the registration and use of certain second-level Internet domain names. The parties agreed that "captainbarbie.com" was registered with Bulkregister.com in Baltimore, Maryland, and there was no *in rem* jurisdiction in New York. The *Barbie–Club* court ruled that *in rem* jurisdiction was only proper in Baltimore, Maryland, and dismissed the New York action. Chapter 11 explains the mechanics of how the ACPA *in rem* provisions operate in domain name/trademark lawsuits, and how *in rem* action is now rarely deployed to transfer or

---

[148] 640 F.3d 497 (2d Cir. 2011).

[149] 433 U.S. 186 (1977).

[150] 15 U.S.C. § 1125(d)(2)(A).

[151] Caesars World, Inc. v. Caesars-Palace.com, 112 F. Supp. 2d 502, 504 (E.D. Va. 2000) (holding that a domain name registration may serve as a res for purposes of in rem jurisdiction).

[152] 58 U.S.P.Q. 3d (BNA) (S.D. N.Y. 2011).

extinguish a domain name. In *Lucent Technologies, Inc. v. Lucentsuck.com*,[153] the federal court dismissed an *in rem* action because the trademark owner could ascertain the identity of the registrant of the domain name. Congress included an *in rem* remedy to assist trademark owners only where they could not locate the registrant of a domain name after best efforts. The *in rem* remedy allows the plaintiff to pursue an action against the domain name where the registrant has disappeared with the click of a mouse or used false registration information.

(K) Choice of Law & Forum

The licensor or dominant party in terms of the service agreement, clickwrap, or other mass-market license agreements will frequently include a choice of law and forum clause. U.S. courts broadly enforce choice of law and choice of forum clauses. Google's Adwords license agreement includes a typical choice of forum and law clause.

> MISCELLANEOUS. THE AGREEMENT MUST BE CONSTRUED AS IF BOTH PARTIES JOINTLY WROTE IT AND GOVERNED BY CALIFORNIA LAW EXCEPT FOR ITS CONFLICTS OF LAWS PRINCIPLES ALL CLAIMS ARISING OUT OF OR RELATING TO THIS AGREEMENT OR THE GOOGLE PROGRAM(S) SHALL BE LITIGATED EXCLUSIVELY IN THE FEDERAL OR STATE COURTS OF SANTA CLARA COUNTY, CALIFORNIA, USA, AND GOOGLE AND CUSTOMER CONSENT TO PERSONAL JURISDICTION IN THOSE COURTS.

If the parties do not include a choice of law and forum clause, the court will make that determination applying conflicts of law principles. In U.S. style mass-market license agreements, the dominant party specifies what forum and law applies, for which these provisions are seldom negotiated.

§ 3.4   GLOBAL INTERNET JURISDICTION

The Internet has no territorial boundaries. To paraphrase Gertrude Stein, as far as the Internet is concerned, not only is there perhaps 'no there,' the 'there' is everywhere there is Internet access.[154]

Judge Nancy Gertner

An Internet presence automatically creates an international presence, triggering the potential for cross-border litigation. Clearly, Global Internet Law requires harmonized jurisdictional rules.[155] U.S. courts "cannot assert extraterritorial jurisdiction over a foreign national simply on the basis that the foreign national's website contains images or data that violate the forum state's laws and that are accessible to users within the forum state."[156] The Internet is a new realm without a sovereign or international treaty establishing the ground rules governing Internet

---

[153] 95 F. Supp.2d 528 (E.D. Va. 2000).

[154] Digital Equip. Corp. v. AltaVista Tech., Inc., 960 F. Supp. 456, 462 (D. Mass. 1997) (J. Gertner).

[155] See also, Julia Lapis, The Internet Tort Dilemma, IT LAW TODAY 1 (Feb. 2002) (commenting that "many countries' legal systems have struggled with the issue of personal jurisdiction and the question of whether a court can legitimately exercise jurisdiction over an individual or company with no physical presence in the judicial forum, but whose website can be accessed from the forum state.").

[156] Walter C. Dauterman, Jr, Internet Regulation: Foreign Actors and Local Harms—at the Crossroads of Pornography, Hate Speech, and Freedom of Expression, 28 N.C. J. INT'L & COM. REG. 177, 201 (2002).

jurisdiction. Theoretically, it is possible for a U.S. business to be sued in hundreds of forums throughout foreign countries for the same course of online conduct; however, this has yet to happen due to the barriers in filing cross-border lawsuits—a topic explored throughout this Hornbook.

As businesses use the border-defying Internet, they will increasingly become subject to foreign procedural and substantive law. Accordingly, the U.S. business community needs legal audits for its websites sales and services whenever it targets European consumers. Further, websites that collect personally identifiable information need to comply with the Data Protection Directive even if they are not physically located in Europe.[157] Foreign websites that target U.S. users may be summoned into U.S. courts. The Internet is interconnected and transnational, challenging traditional sovereignty based upon geographic borders. No transnational sovereign devises uniform rules for Internet jurisdiction and the enforcement of online judgments. The uncertainty surrounding jurisdiction in cyberspace cases requires cross-border treaties or conventions. To date, the countries connected to the Internet have not agreed to cede their sovereignty in order to harmonize cyberjurisdictional rules. Instead, courts adapt their own national rules to determine jurisdiction.

Increasingly foreign companies are sued in U.S. courts arising out of Internet or software licensing transactions. Facebook, for example, filed a trademark infringement claim against www.Faceporn.com, a Norwegian website. Faceporn allows its users to create profiles, join groups, upload photos and video, and conduct live chats. Facebook's amended complaint asserted claims of trademark dilution, common law infringement, the Anticybersquatting Consumer Protection Act, unfair competition, and other trademark-related claims. In *Facebook, Inc. v. Pedersen*,[158] Faceporn filed a motion to dismiss on the grounds of lack of personal jurisdiction. Facebook's argument in the trademark suit was that Faceporn was likely to cause consumer confusion, but it did not offer proof that any of its users were confused by Faceporn's website.

The federal magistrate ruled that Faceporn acted intentionally in registering the Internet domains www.faceporn.com, www.faceporn.net, and www.faceporn.org and in operating the Faceporn website, which infringed the plaintiff's trademarks. However, the court ruled that the second prong of the *Calder* test was not met because the Norwegian online pornographers were not expressly aiming their illegal images at California residents. The *Faceporn* court reasoned that the Norwegian defendant's registering someone else's trademark as a domain name and posting a website did not constitute "something more" to satisfy the effects test. The court denied Facebook's default judgment because it could not prove specific or general jurisdiction over Faceporn.

The Third Circuit in *Toys "R" Us v. Step Two*[159] reversed a lower court and remanded for limited jurisdictional discovery about whether a Spanish website had sufficient contacts in New Jersey to satisfy due process. Toys "R" Us, Inc. ("Toys") filed

---

[157] "The six legal grounds defined in the Directive are consent, contract, legal obligation, vital interest of the data subject or the balance between the legitimate interests of the people controlling the data and the people on whom data is held (i.e. data subjects)." Press Release, European Commission, Council Definitively Adopts Directive on Protection of Personal Data, (July 25, 1995), http://www.ieee-security.org/Cipher/ConfReports/ECprivdirective.html (last visited July 17, 2013).

[158] 2012 WL 751922 (C.D. Cal., March 2, 2012).

[159] 318 F.3d 446 (2003).

a lawsuit in New Jersey federal court against Step Two, and Imaginarium Net, both headquartered in Spain. The toy retailer alleged that Step Two used its Internet websites to engage in trademark infringement, unfair competition, misuse of the trademark notice symbol, and unlawful "cybersquatting." Step Two owned franchised toy stores operating under the name "Imaginarium" in Spain and nine other countries. They registered the Imaginarium mark in Spain in 1991, and opened its first Imaginarium store in Zaragoza, Spain, in November 1992. Step 2 stores have the same look and feel as Toys "R" Us stores with similar facades. The conflict between the U.S. and Spanish toy retailers began when both parties sought an Internet presence. In 1995, Imaginarium Toy Centers, Inc., which Toys later acquired, registered the domain name and launched a website featuring merchandise sold at Imaginarium stores. In 1996, Step Two registered the domain name and began advertising merchandise that was available at its Imaginarium stores.

Imaginarium Toy Centers registered a domain name incorporating Imaginarium, and launched a website offering merchandise for sale. The Third Circuit framed the question as, "[w]hether the operation of a commercially interactive website accessible in the forum state is sufficient to support specific personal jurisdiction, or whether there must be additional evidence that the defendant has "purposefully availed" itself of the privilege of engaging in activity in that state."[160] The Third Circuit aligned itself with courts that require "something more" than mere interactivity to signal purposeful availment. The court found some evidence that Toys "R" Us had not shown, "Step Two maintained the type of contacts that supported jurisdiction in that the defendant intentionally and knowingly transacted business with residents of the forum state, and had significant other contacts with the forum besides those generated by its website."[161] The court remanded the case for further discovery because the limited record did not allow them to "spell out the exact mix of Internet and non-Internet contacts required to support an exercise of personal jurisdiction."[162] This case illustrates not only the "something more" requirement but also how U.S. courts apply this standard to foreign websites and businesses.

In *Pervasive Software, Inc. v. Lexware GMBH & Co. KG*,[163] a U.S. computer software manufacturer sued defendant, a German computer software developer, for breach of contract, *quantum meruit*, unjust enrichment, and conversion. The U.S. District Court for the Western District of Texas granted the developer's motion to dismiss for lack of personal jurisdiction over the company and the Fifth Circuit affirmed. The court found:

> Pervasive has not made a *prima facie* showing of any act by which Lexware purposefully availed itself of the privilege of conducting activities within the forum state of Texas, so as to invoke the benefits and protections of its laws. Accepting as true the facts alleged by Pervasive, all of Lexware's acts giving rise to Pervasive's claims against Lexware took place in Germany, not in Texas. Lexware purchased Pervasive's software product, Btrieve, in Germany from SOS, a third-party German software distributor. The DSLA, the license contract between Pervasive

---

[160] Id. at 451.
[161] Id. at 453.
[162] Id.
[163] 688 F.3d 214 (5th Cir. 2012).

and Lexware, was an off-the-shelf, out-of-the-box contract that was accepted and activated by Lexware's purchase of Btrieve from SOS in Germany. There were no prior negotiations between Pervasive and Lexware and SOS was not an agent of either company.

A growing number of U.S. courts routinely exercise jurisdiction over website activity occurring outside of the country's territorial boundaries. Conversely, U.S. companies are increasingly being sued in foreign jurisdictions for activities occurring on Web servers located in the United States. Clearly, civil procedure requires harmonization. Presently, almost no case law covers international Internet jurisdiction, and no statutory solutions exist to answer the question of cross-border Internet jurisdiction. Traditional concepts of jurisdiction and enforcement of judgment need to be adapted to the Internet. In the United States, personal jurisdiction is the issue of whether a court can decide a case involving this specific defendant. Adam D. Thierer and H. George Frederickson write, "What is perhaps most troubling about the current debate over Internet jurisdiction and governance is that little discussion has occurred about the principles of legitimacy and universality."[164] "Cyberspace is not some mystical incantation capable of warding off the jurisdiction of courts built from bricks and mortar.

Just as our traditional notions of personal jurisdiction have proven adaptable to other changes in the national economy, so too are they adaptable to the transformations wrought by the Internet."[165] "Geographic indeterminacy is simply part of the network's normal operation."[166]　Up to this point, this chapter asks the fundamental questions whether *International Shoe* is adaptable to cyberspace.[167] U.S. Courts have stretched minimum contacts test to websites without hesitation. The U.S. due process approach to jurisdiction and approach to the enforcement of judgments is not followed in other countries connected to the Internet. The borderless Internet challenges uniquely U.S. concepts such as the long-arm statute, due process, and minimum contacts. U.S. courts have mechanically stretched the parochial minimum contacts approach to personal jurisdiction into cyberspace, creating jurisdictional dilemmas. The countries of the European Community have adopted bright-line rules for jurisdiction. In 2000, the countries of the European Union adopted the Brussels Regulation governing jurisdiction and the recognition and enforcement of judgments in civil and commercial disputes.[168] The Internet has no overarching sovereignty to promulgate, let alone enforce rules for cross-border electronic commerce.

As a key piece of EU legislation, the Brussels Regulation governs cross-border jurisdiction for the twenty-eight Member States of the European Union. Uniformity in treatment of jurisdiction encourages the free movement of persons and judicial cooperation, thus advancing the internal market. Article 2 of the Brussels Regulation constitutes the most important default rule: persons domiciled in a Member State

---

[164] ADAM D. THIERER & H. GEORGE FREDERICKSON, WHO RULES THE NET? NET GOVERNANCE AND JURISDICTION XXVII (2003).

[165] Gorman v. Ameritrade Holding Corp., 293 F.3d 506, 510–11 (D.C. Cir. 2002).

[166] Dan L. Burk, Jurisdiction in a World Without Borders, 1 VA. J. L. & TECH. 3, 18 (1997).

[167] International Shoe Co. v. Washington, 326 U.S. 310, 316 (1945).

[168] Council Regulation (EC) No. 44/2001 of 22 Dec. 2000 on Jurisdiction and the Recognition and Enforcement of Judgments in Civil and Commercial Matters, 2003 O.J. (L 12), 16 Jan. 2001, art. 2.1 [hereinafter Brussels I Regulation].

shall, regardless of that person's nationality, be sued in the courts of that Member State.[169] Plaintiffs may sue individuals (including a sole proprietor or a partner in a business sued in his own capacity) in courts in the country where their principal residence was located. Additionally, Article 60 provides that the domicile of a company or other association (including a partnership) is where the company has its statutory seat (i.e., its registered office), its central administration or its principal place of business.[170] The Brussels Regulation governs jurisdiction in civil and commercial disputes between litigants and provides for the enforcement of judgments throughout the European Union. The Brussels Regulation, which replaced the Brussels Convention, governing jurisdiction and judgments applies to all Brussels Convention signatories except Denmark, which has opted out of the new regulations.

The Brussels Regulation generally endorses a freedom of contract in commercial contracts, but provides special protections for consumers.[171] American consumers would greatly benefit from the Brussels Regulation because it bases the rule for which court is competent to entertain a claim based upon the consumer's residence, which gives her a home court advantage. U.S. companies operating in any country of the European Union are already subject to the Brussels Regulation's consumer rule. An American company domiciled in a Member State can be sued in that state. American online providers have been steadfastly opposed to the Brussels Regulation because they favor mass-market licenses, which require consumers to litigate in their home court and according to their rules.

When radically different legal cultures clash in the free trade zone of cyberspace, jurisdictional, choice of law and enforcement of judgment disputes are not easy to resolve. The Internet's global legal environment makes it inevitable that "one country's laws will conflict with another's—particularly when a Web surfer in one country accesses content hosted or created in another country."[172] The European Union's Brussels Regulation creates very different jurisdictional rules in civil and commercial disputes. Anupam Chander argues "jurisdiction hopping is a fundamental quality of global Internet trade" citing examples:

Consider two famous examples from the past decade. KaZaa, long the leading peer-to-peer file trading system, was founded in the Netherlands by a Swede and a Dane, programmed from Estonia, and then run from Australia while incorporated in the South Pacific island nation of Vanuatu. The online gambling site PartyGaming was founded by an American lawyer and an Indian expatriate programmer and run from headquarters in Gibraltar, using computer servers on a Mohawk Indian reserve in

---

[169] Id. at art. 2.

[170] Id. at art. 60.

[171] Articles 15–17 of the Brussels Regulation confer additional jurisdiction over contractual disputes between consumers and businesses within the courts of the consumer's country of domicile. Article 15 defines "consumer" as someone who is acting "outside his trade or profession." Id. at art. 15. Additionally, Article 17 of the Brussels Regulation provides that a consumer cannot waive her right to sue a supplier in her local court. A supplier directing their activities to the consumer's home state is automatically subject to jurisdiction because he has directed activities to that state as defined in Article 15. Id. at art. 15 Finally, a consumer may enforce a judgment in any Member State upon completion of the formalities set forth in Article 53. Id. at arts. 15–17.

[172] Peter Yu, Conflict of Laws Issues in International Copyright Cases, http://www.peteryu.com/gigalaw0401.pdf (last visited July 17, 2013).

Canada, a London marketing office, and a workforce based mainly in Hyderabad, India.[173]

Professor Chander argues that "jurisdiction hopping" to avoid oppressive regulations will become more common in the global electronic marketplace.[174] The ability of Internet businesses to end-run jurisdictions is an example of why it is fool hardy to confine the study of Internet jurisdiction to the United States. This chapter begins with a close study of how U.S. courts approach cyberspace jurisdiction. This chapter covers many areas of civil procedure influenced by the Internet including: (1) personal jurisdiction; (2) parties' choice of law and forum; (3) conflict of law, and (4) enforcement of cross-border judgments. "Personal Jurisdiction" refers to the power of the court to preside over a defendant. Justice Oliver Wendell Holmes noted earlier, "The foundation of jurisdiction is physical power"—which is a territorial based concept.[175]

The borderless Internet challenges the meaning of due process and minimum contacts. The parties' choices of law and forum clauses are contracts where the parties agree to jurisdiction and the applicable law in advance. Conflict of law refers to the principles courts use in determining what law applies in a cross-border transaction. At present, there is no multilateral convention to resolve conflicts of law or choice of law for Internet nor is there a treaty for the reciprocal enforcement of judgments. Internet lawyers representing companies doing business in Europe must consider the impact of European Union regimes such as the Brussels Regulation governing jurisdiction and the Rome I Regulation on choice of law if their client targets European consumer marketplaces.

---

[173] ANUPAM CHANDER, THE ELECTRONIC SILK ROAD 5 (2013).

[174] Id. at 5.

[175] Ex parte Indiana Transport Co., 244 U.S. 456, 457 (1917).

Chapter 4

INTERNET–RELATED CONTRACT LAW

§ 4.1 OVERVIEW OF ONLINE CONTRACTS

Internet business is multi-hemispheric, as the sun never sets on a website that stands ready to communicate with customers 24 hours a day, seven days a week in all countries connected to the World Wide Web. During the past two decades, the Internet evolved as a business tool. Specialized Internet-related contracts emerged at a time of tremendous changes in the way business was conducted because of 24/7 e-commerce possibilities. Today social media websites are reshaping business and advertising.[1] Internet contract law is also rapidly evolving as industry groups, governments, and international organizations formulate new standards, usages of trade, regulatory initiatives, statutes, and court decisions. The rapid evolution of the Internet has created an endemic problem of "legal lag." The law of contracts is lagging behind the development of software law and the Internet. The timeworn doctrines of contract law are continually being eroded, fractured, and shattered by the Internet's rapid evolution. While Internet contracts take the form of contracts, they are really "unilaterally imposed rules to protect new business models."[2]

This chapter focuses on the concepts and methods of licensing which is the chief means of transferring value in an information-based economy.[3] Licensing software permits software publishers to commodify their intellectual property assets, while retaining control of its uses.[4] This chapter introduces the global contracting law covering topics such as licensing, shrinkwrap, clickwrap, terms of service agreements and service level agreements in wide currency. Unlike toasters, rental cars, or other tangible personal property, software can be reproduced at the click of a download button at almost no cost, which results in contracting practices being based primarily upon the licensing of information. Many Internet-related contracts are mass-market agreements such as terms of service agreements or software license agreements. As software companies go global, online contracts become subject to radically different legal

---

[1] "Social media has changed the way businesses communicate, enabling brands to directly engage with consumers. Companies are turning increasingly to social media platforms to structure innovative and edgy marketing and promotions that often include a mix of user-generated content, text messaging, Twitter messaging, Facebook applications, blogging, viral marketing, and other social elements." Alan L. Friel, Akash Sachdeva, Jesse Brody, and Jatinder Bahra, Safeguarding Brand Reputation in Social Media, CORPORATE COUNSEL (June 13, 2013).

[2] NANCY S. KIM, WRAP CONTRACTS: FOUNDATIONS AND RAMIFICATIONS 211 (2013).

[3] The paradigm contractual model for a transaction in intangible goods is a license agreement. Under the license, the creators of the product authorize the use of their work, but, because of its intangible nature, restrict its use." Sean F. Crotty, The How and Why of Shrinkwrap License Validation Under the Uniform Computer Information Transactions Act, 33 RUTGERS L.J. 745, 746 (2002).

[4] Adobe Sys., Inc. v. One Stop Micro, Inc., 84 F.Supp.2d 1086, 1092 (N.D. Cal. 2000)("[A] common method of distribution is through licensing agreements, which permit the copyright holder to place restrictions upon the distribution of its products."); Storm Impact, Inc. v. Software of Month Club, 13 F.Supp.2d 782, 791 (N.D. Ill. 1998) (reservation of right to distribute software made available to be downloaded over the Internet was valid and enforceable).

traditions. U.S. style terms of use widely enforced in the United States are unenforceable in the European Union. A new legal paradigm is necessary to facilitate E–Commerce, which may soon eclipse brick-and-mortar commerce. Paper-based signatures are rapidly giving way to digital signature in E–Commerce. Electronic agents with or without human review are increasingly forming contracts.[5] Trading partner agreements form rules in advance for protocols regarding the ordering of goods and payment through electronic messages. UCITA validates electronic data interchange ("EDI") trading agreements where the parties agree in advance to order goods by computer-to-computer interactions, without human review.

Since the 1980s, software publishers, as well as database and website developers have created a number of groundbreaking contracting forms that deviate markedly from the customary contract law "formation trilogy" of offer, acceptance, and consideration. Licenses are a specialized contractual form that protect intellectual property rights and enable vendors to realize their investments in developing code. The licensing of software, like leases, validates the legal concept of the right to use property without the passage of title. While the consumer's title to the tangible copy of the software (the purchased CD–ROM, for example) may be absolute, that does not confer property rights upon the intangible code that makes up the software.

The legal invention of licensing enables the software publishers to prohibit assignments or transfers of the product thus retaining control over the product after the licensee pays royalties. Licensing enable licensors to control the use of their digital products after delivery.[6] The licensor's retention of title enables them to slice and dice price (arbitrage) based upon a complex array of variables such as business-to-business or business-to-consumer or market segments within a given foreign country. A typical licensing provision specifies the following conditions of use:

> Licensee may not install, electronically transfer, or otherwise execute the FourGen Enterprise Software on any Computer other than the Designated Computer. Only one Computer can be specified as the Designated Computer in a network unless additional licenses are purchased.

Increasingly Internet contracts are being entered into a cross-border legal environment filled with pitfalls for the unwary. "The preparation of Internet contracts is difficult, since courts may apply laws and jurisdictional rules that are unknown to the drafters of the agreement."[7] So, how do people contract over the Internet? In the early 1990s, contracts were chiefly entered into by e-mail and there was uncertainty as to

---

[5] "This term refers to an automated means for making or performing contracts. The agent must act independently in a manner relevant to creating or performing a contract. Mere use of a telephone or e-mail system is not use of an electronic agent. The automated system must have been selected, programmed or otherwise intentionally used for that purpose by the person that is bound by its operations. The legal relationship between the person and the electronic agent is not equivalent to common law agency since the "agent" is not a human. However, parties that use electronic agents are ordinarily bound by the results of their operations." UCITA, Id. at § 102(23) (defining electronic agent).

[6] "Transferors use a licensing structure in part to restrict usage of the software. Enforcement of the restriction should not depend on whether the software transferor labels the transfer a license or a sale. Instead, enforcement should depend on (i) whether federal law renders the restriction unenforceable because it upsets the intellectual property balance between exclusionary rights and creating a rich public domain; (ii) whether the transferee had sufficient notice and opportunity to read the term restricting rights; and (iii) whether the restriction runs afoul of public policy or unconscionability norms." Principles of the Law of Software Contracts § 1.06 (2010).

[7] F. Lawrence Street & Mark P. Grant, The Law of the Internet 8 (1999).

whether the digital signature was valid. On June 30, 2000, Congress passed the Electronic Signatures in Global and National Commerce Act ("E–SIGN"), validating digital signatures as well as records, and making them equal to writing for interstate contracts.[8] "While new commerce on the Internet has exposed courts to many new situations, it has not fundamentally changed the principles of contract."[9] Nevertheless, the Internet has spawned new information-age contracting rules, which are the subject of this chapter.

§ 4.2   LICENSING AS THE CHIEF CONTRACTING FORM

A license is a form of contract where the licensor grants the licensee the right to use software or other information. A license is first a contract, generally between two parties —the licensor and the licensee—although licenses may also be assigned or sublicensed. Like a lease for personal property, a license agreement gives the licensee the right to use property under stated guidelines. For leases, it is the right to use personal property as opposed to intangible assets. Internet licenses may include computer software, website content, databases or other digital information. The licensor is the party that agrees to transfer software or to grant access to other computer information. The licensee's duty is to pay the licensing fee to the licensor in order to obtain access to or use of information under the terms and conditions specified in the agreement. Licensing is the principal contracting form used in E–Commerce and in the online world.[10]The licensing of software validates the licensee's rights to use intellectual property intangibles just as a lease of goods gives lessees the right to use durable goods such as equipment. A lessor leases equipment to a lessee for the term of the lease agreement. In contrast, a software license is a contractual arrangement where the licensor conveys the right to use software for the term of the agreement.

Licensors have an action for breach of contract if the licensee fails to pay royalties or exceeds the scope of the granting clause. The elements of a breach of a license agreement are: (1) the existence of a valid contract; (2) performance or tendered performance by the plaintiff; (3) breach of the contract by the defendant; and (4) resulting damages to the plaintiff. A software license is, in effect, a waiver of the copyright owner's right to sue for copyright or patent infringement. Nevertheless, a software license is not just a waiver to sue for infringement, but often involves conditions, covenants, and affirmative duties that sometimes survive beyond the term of the agreement. Licenses that address issues such as maintenance, data transmission, and use of data are ubiquitous in the Internet-based economy. Apple's iPhone User Agreement, for example, provides that:

> By using any location-based services on your IOS Device,[11] you agree and consent to Apple's and its partners', licensees' and third party developers' transmission, collection, maintenance and use of your location data and queries to provide such products and services.[12]

---

[8] Electronic Signatures in Global and National Commerce Act, 15 U.S.C. § 7001 (2000).

[9] Register.com, Inc. v. Verio, Inc., 356 F.3d 393, 403 (2d Cir. 2004).

[10] Michael L. Rustad, Making UCITA More Consumer–Friendly, 18 J. MARSHALL J. COMPUTER & INFO. L. 547, 551–52 (1999) (arguing the software licensing law is less developed than the law for durable goods).

[11] The IOS is the operating system for Apple's iPhone and iPod family of mobile devices.

[12] In re Smartphone Geolocation Data Application, 2013 U.S. Dist. LEXIS 62605 (E.D. N.Y. May 1, 2013) at 14.

Mass-market licenses are generally structured as non-exclusive and impose conditions such as prohibiting the product from being reverse engineered, assigned, or transferred to other users. Granting clauses for open source software give the licensee access to source code so they can modify or improve the product. The term "open source" means that source code is openly distributed and accompanies the software module.[13] Open source licensors make source code available and give users permission to make derivative works. Open source software is typically freely accessible, usable and modifiable. In addition, certain open source software licenses require the user of such software to make any derivative works of the open source code available to others on unfavorable terms or at no cost.

(A) The Concepts & Methods of Licensing Information

(1) Definition of Licensing

The greatest story never told about Internet-related copyright developments is how information age companies use license agreements to protect intangible assets such as software and website content. The software industry invented the shrinkwrap license agreement, the earliest form of mass-market license, in the 1970s, and vendors began using this contracting form by the early 1980s. Licensing is beginning to displace sales and leases as the chief means of transferring value in the information-based society already "ranked as the third largest segment of the U.S. economy, behind only the automotive industry and electronic manufacturing" and grew "five times faster than the economy as a whole between 1996 and 2006."[14] Mass-market software publishers employ licensing on a widespread scale accounting for over $500 billion in annual revenues.[15] Two of the world's largest companies, mass-market software producers Microsoft and Apple, with market caps of $270.6 billion and $188.6 billion respectively, rely heavily on revenues generated by software licensing.[16] Apple, whose revenues are driven in large part by its mobile phones, is the eighth largest company with a capitalization of $188.6 billion.[17] Software licensing has evolved as a leading means of transferring value in an increasingly information-based economy. With a license, the licensor gives the licensee the right to use software or other digital data for the term of the agreement.

A license is first a contract, generally between two parties, the licensor, and the licensee. The licensing of software and other intellectual property to transfer value is the emblematic feature of the information-based economy.[18] In the information-based

---

[13] SCO Group, Inc. v. Novell, Inc., 2008 WL 2783523 (D. Utah, July 16, 2008).

[14] Steve Lohr, Study Ranks Software as No. 3 Industry, N.Y. TIMES (June 3, 1997) at D2; Jon M. Garon, Media & Monopoly in the Information Age: Slowing the Convergence at the Marketplace of Ideas, 17 CARDOZO ARTS & ENT. L.J. 491, 574 (1999) (stating that by 1996 computer software was ranked as the "third largest segment of the U.S. economy, behind only the automotive industry and electronic manufacturing") (citing Ronald Rosenberg, Software Fastest Growing Industry, BOSTON GLOBE, June 5, 1997, at D2). The software industry has been "projected to grow five times faster than the economy as a whole between 1996 and 2006 . . ." One Million New Positions Seen by 2006—Software Sets Pace for Future Job Growth, ELEC. ENG'G TIMES, Jan. 5, 1998, at 1–2.

[15] Software & Information Industry Association, Software and Information: Driving the Knowledge Economy (January 24, 2008) at 7–8.

[16] THE ECONOMIST, POCKET WORLD IN FIGURES 66 (2012 ed.).

[17] Id.

[18] James Boyle, a visionary thinker, argues that the new economy includes a broad definition of information. "Consciously and unconsciously, we are already developing the language of entitlement for a

economy, software publishers market their products on the Internet or as a subscription service in the case of cloud computing. The makers of software games distribute its games on CD–ROMs, which are subject to an End User License Agreement ("EULA"). In a typical standard-form EULA license agreement, the end user agrees to the EULA terms prior to downloading the software.[19] For example, the game developer typically displays the EULA to the user during the initial installation of the game. If the user does not agree to the EULA by clicking on an "Agree" button, the game will not install on the user's computers.[20] In contrast to a sale or lease, a license grants the licensee contract rights that authorize "access to, or use, distribution, performance, modification, or reproduction of information or informational rights."[21] In a typical standard-form EULA license agreement, the end user agrees to the EULA terms prior to downloading the software.[22]

Licenses have evolved as advanced contracts that come in many flavors depending upon whether they are customized or for the mass-market.[23] A license agreement gives the licensee the right to access or use software or other computer information and typically consists of two parties: the licensor and the licensee. The licensor is the party that agrees to transfer software or to grant access to other computer information. The licensee pays the licensing fee to the licensor in order to obtain access to or use of information. The classic definition of a license is "a mere waiver of the right to sue" for infringement.[24] The concept of a license is explained as thus:

> A license is an agreement the terms of which entail a limited or conditional transfer of information or a grant of limited or restricted contractual rights or permissions to use information. A contract "right" is an affirmative commitment that a licensee may engage in a specific use, while contract "permission" means simply that the licensor will not object to the use. Either can be the basis of a license. No specific formality of language is required. For purposes of this Act, the term includes consignments of copies of information but does not otherwise alter the legal nature of a consignment.[25]

Box-top licenses were developed so that the license agreement or document would be placed under the plastic wrapping of the box containing the CD–ROM. Think of

---

world in which information—genetic, electronic, and proprietary—is one of the main sources and forms of wealth." JAMES BOYLE, SHAMANS, SOFTWARE AND SPLEENS: LAW AND CONSTRUCTION OF THE INFORMATION SOCIETY x (1996).

[19] Michael L. Rustad & Diane D'Angelo, The Path of Internet Law: An Annotated Guide, 2011 DUKE L. & TECH. REV. 12, 24 ("Courts generally will enforce EULAs so long as the "terms are clear and acceptance is unambiguous, regardless of whether [the user] actually reads them.'").

[20] Robert W. Gomulkiewicz, Getting Serious About User–Friendly Mass Market Licensing for Software, 12 GEO. MASON L. REV. 687, 687–88 (2004) (concluding that end user licenses ("EULAs") are here to stay for the foreseeable future despite hundreds of articles criticizing this form of contracting).

[21] UCITA § 102(41) (1999).

[22] Michael L. Rustad & Diane D'Angelo, The Path of Internet Law: An Annotated Guide, 2011 DUKE L. & TECH. REV. 12, 24 ("Courts generally will enforce EULAs so long as the "terms are clear and acceptance is unambiguous, regardless of whether [the user] actually reads them.'").

[23] See Raymond T. Nimmer et al., License Contracts Under Article 2 of the Uniform Commercial Code: A Proposal, 19 RUTGERS COMP. & TECH L.J. 281, 294 (1993) (defining a "software contract" as "an agreement that transfers or promises to transfer one or more rights in specific computer software, including the right to access, the right to use or to have used, the right to modify, the right to copy or the right to otherwise employ the computer software.").

[24] De Forest Radio Telephone Co. v. United States, 273 U.S. 236, 242 (1927).

[25] UCITA § 102(37).

licensing as an advanced form of contract law with a multiplicity of different conditions, covenants, and terms. Licensing is far more flexible than either sales or leases, because licensors can retain control over the licensee's use of the intangible information after delivery. In contrast, the seller of a snowmobile generally cannot specify that it may only be driven in state parks or farmland or within given state's boundaries. With the sale of goods, the buyer receives ownership and title and can do whatever they want with the product. With software and other information assets, the licensor retains control over the customer's uses. The license agreement determines who, what, when, why, and how software may be used. The unique aspect of licensing versus sales or leases is that it "enables a split of ownership and user rights in the information, but unlike hard goods, information can be both transferred and retained."[26] Licensing software permits software publishers to commodify their intellectual property assets. Unlike with sales or leases, it is possible to have an infinite supply of licensed software.

Software can be reproduced at the click of a download button for almost no cost to the licensor. As opposed to durable goods like plasma televisions, iPods, or dishwashers, there is an endless supply of intangible software. The inimitable feature of licensed content is that the number of users can be increased without whittling away or diminishing the product.[27] Licensing evolved as a contracting form that gives the licensee the right to use software or other digital code for a designated period in a bounded geographic area for specified purposes.

In contrast, a licensing agreement gives the licensor the ability to control users and uses. A clause in a license agreement may also limit use of software to a single Central Processing Unit ("CPU") on a computer workstation or server. A CPU license is the right to use software on a specific CPU or CPUs designated by make and serial number. Intersoft Solutions has devised a "multi-pack" license where the licensee may use a copy of the software "identified in the multi-pack on the number of computers associated with the multi-pack."[28] For example, a four-user multi-pack will give the licensee the right to use Intersoft software on four computers concurrently.[29] A software license is accurately described as an instrument in the borderland between the law of contracts and intellectual property law. Thus, the view that a license is a covenant not to sue is a myopic view of licensing.

Software publishers and content creators typically use licensing as the chief method of transferring value for mass-market software products. Comparable to the creation of the corporation or the limited liability company, the invention of the software license agreement is equally significant. Licensing allows the software developer to prohibit assignments or transfers of their product so the initial purchaser may not resell or reproduce the copy. The legal invention of licensing makes it possible for a software publisher to retain title to its information-based product and impose

---

[26] Id. at 4.

[27] "Dilution is grounded on the idea that a trademark can lose its ability to clearly and unmistakably distinguish one source through unauthorized use. It is a gradual whittling away of a distinctive trademark or name. In order to establish a dilution claim, two elements must be shown: (1) ownership of a distinctive mark, and (2) a likelihood of dilution. A likelihood of dilution can be established by a showing either of blurring or of tarnishment." Hormel Foods Corp. v. Jim Henson Prods., 73 F.3d 497, 506 (2d Cir. 2006).

[28] Clientui License Agreement, http://www.intersoftpt.com/ clientui/Licensing (2011) (last visited July 3, 2013).

[29] Id.

significant transfer restrictions. This enables the software publisher to slice and dice pricing based upon a complex array of variables. Software publishers have different fee schedules for databases depending upon whether the user is a large corporation, a community library, a small business, or a noncommercial user. Copyright publishers use copyright licenses to commodify their information-based assets:

Although the copyright model may, at first glance, seem to provide adequate protection for software, software providers frequently attempt to alter the relationship created by that model by contracting with parties who receive copies of the software, denominating such parties as copyright licensees rather than purchasers. This approach is in stark contrast to the general approach of publishers of hard copy materials. Such publishers usually simply place a copyright notice on works of authorship, using the U.S. Copyright Act's set of enumerated rights and limitations as, essentially, a boilerplate contract. The rationale behind these different approaches helps to illuminate the shortcomings of the copyright regime in dealing with software.[30]

A company's licensing fees reflect not only the product chosen and the identity of the user but the number of users for the chosen products. Software publishers and content creators can charge different prices for licenses and retain exclusive reproduction and other rights under copyright law. For enterprises, royalties are typically based upon such variables as the number of employees or the revenues of the licensee. The concept of a license gives the licensee permission to use software, information, or other content subject to conditions, permissions, and restrictions. Location and use restrictions are necessary tools for software developers to realize their investment in developing intangible information assets.[31] Licenses have long been used to protect intellectual property including patents, copyrights, and trademarks and trade secrets. While protecting the rights of the owner, licensing permits others to use the protected intellectual property subject to the terms of the license agreement. In addition, the granting of a license flows from the licensor to the licensee. In a license agreement, the licensor retains the title and the intellectual property rights. Just as with leases, there is no transfer of title or interest, only the right to use information.

In practice, software licensing typically includes affirmative obligations, conditions, and covenants in addition to the licensor waiving its right to file a copyright infringement lawsuit.[32] Software makers use license agreements to engage in wholesale price discrimination. This does not raise antitrust issues, but it does enable licensors to charge more for company-wide licenses. For example, a software publisher will charge Caterpillar or General Motors more for an enterprise-wide license than the price for a consumer license. Licenses may charge more for software used in North America than in Southeast Asia. Licensing enables the licensor to charge a university more for its product than for a consumer transaction. Licensing is the one advanced contracting form that makes arbitrage function well. EULAs give customers the right to use Microsoft software.[33] In a typical standard-form EULA license agreement, the

---

[30] Maureen O'Rourke, Drawing the Boundary Between Copyright and Contract: Copyright Preemption of Software License Terms, 405 DUKE L. J. 479, 486 (1995).

[31] A contract for the sale of goods is one in which a seller agrees to transfer goods that conform to the contract in exchange for valuable consideration. U.C.C. § 2–301 (2011).

[32] RAYMOND T. NIMMER & JEFF DODD, MODERN LICENSING LAW § 1:5 (Chapter One: Introduction and Overview (Sept. 2008).

[33] Microsoft.com, What Does the End User License Agreement (EULA) Say? http://www.microsoft.com/resources/documentation/windows/xp/all/proddocs/en-us/lic_what_eula_say.mspx?mfr=true (2012).

end user agrees to the EULA terms prior to downloading the software. A Single User License Agreement ("SULA") gives the licensee the right to use software on a single personal computer and to make a backup. Software publishers, such as Oracle, Adobe, and Microsoft, make it clear in their license agreement that they are only giving a right to use software not selling it. Symantec, a leading provider of anti-virus software, parcels out different bundles of rights with respect to its software; depending on whether it is licensing to a consumer or an enterprise. These rights bundled together as a "license," are the only "products" that Symantec conveys. Symantec retains the title and all rights to its software except for those rights that Microsoft expressly conveys through one of these licenses. When an end-user downloads an Adobe product, they are given a legal notice that the software is licensed not sold and that they are subject to the licensing agreement.

(2) Granting Clause

The granting clause determines what rights the licensor conveys to the licensee. A license will recite all rights granted to the licensee in the licensing agreement. The granting clause specifies whether a license is exclusive or non-exclusive to the licensee. An example of a broad granting clause in a license agreement is: "of all possible rights and media including all rights then existing or created by the law in the future."[34] Use restrictions determine what is not included in the software transfer. "Many non-exclusive licenses may be non-transferable without the licensor's consent. In some commercial licenses, the subject matter includes confidential information that is protected by enforceable contractual use restrictions."[35] Granting clauses will typically address the question of whether the licensee has a right to sub-license software or other information to a third party. Licensing agreements are either "Perpetual" or "Non–Perpetual." "Perpetual" license agreements last forever and maintain their validity as long as the "software is being used in accordance with the license-agreement requirements."[36] Conversely, "non-perpetual" license agreements specify "the right to use a particular licensed product until the end of the license-agreement term."[37]

A software licensor may place geographic restrictions on use and charge a different price for a license in a different country. Additionally, a Software License Agreement may grant a "non-exclusive and non-transferrable license" without specifying that the license is "personal" to the licensee. These software licenses define the scope and nature of the licensee's authorized use of the software. Software licenses may limit the customer's use to internal operations at a designated location or further restrict their use to a designated Central Processing Unit. Typically software licenses will state that the customers will not "lend, sell, give, lease, or otherwise disclose" the software systems without the licensor's approval. A licensor may also specify an event of default in a license agreement when the licensee merges or is reorganized.[38]

The granting clause is the action section of the license agreement, which determines how the licensed product may be used. The granting clause determines

---

[34] U.C.C. § 2B–307(1) (2011).

[35] UCITA § 503, cmt. 3(B).

[36] Microsoft.com, Licensing Basics, //partner.microsoft.com/ global/40067672 (2012).

[37] Id.

[38] Cincom Systems, Inc. v. Novelis Corp., 581 F.3d 431 (6th Cir. 2009) (software transaction was a license with a non-transfer provision, so subsequent acquiring entity infringed when it used the software).

what rights the licensor and licensees have in the right to use intellectual property under what terms and conditions. Software publishers typically classify their licensing transaction as exclusive, semi-exclusive, or nonexclusive. An exclusive software license, like a non-exclusive one, does not convey ownership, but does signify exclusive use of a product for the term of the agreement. Exclusive licenses are frequent in software development agreements where a company tailors a product to the specific needs of a single customer. With an exclusive license agreement, the royalties must pay not only the entire development costs of the software, projected profits as well. For example, CliniCon entered into a 2001 exclusive license agreement with a division of Bristol–Myers so that the pharmaceutical giant had the sole right to use software that determines clinically driven skin and wound care protocols.

Typically, the license grant will explain limitations on the number of users. The granting clause first determines who can use information. Software license agreements come in a mélange of affiliations ranging from the simple bipartite relationship between the licensor to licensee to complex development contracts.[39] Software licensing permits far greater control than either sales or leases of goods. Arbitrage, the practice of pricing licenses to software and other information based on the customer or its usage, is easily accomplished through licensing agreements because it entails the practice of calibrating the pricing of software to such factors as the nature of the customer or user.[40] For example, a software licensor may control the location, number of users, and even the permitted uses of the software.

(3) Definitions in Licensing Agreements

License agreements present key definitions in alphabetical order and define terms used more than once in the agreement. Courts will review the parties' definitions section as the best evidence of the parties' intent for the meaning of core provisions. Nevertheless, courts may interpret key terms in unintended ways if the parties do not define them precisely. Learned Hand famously stated, "Definitions are chameleons, which reflect the color of their environment."[41] Therefore, the parties to license agreements should define key terms with an eye to the possibility that a court will not understand either the commercial setting or the technology. As a result, the parties must consistently define and use key terms throughout the license agreement reflecting the operational environment where the software is being used.

(4) First Sale Doctrine & Licensing

Generally, if the software publisher grants only a license to the copy of software and imposes significant restrictions on the purchaser's ability to redistribute or transfer that copy, the purchaser is considered a licensee, not an owner, of the software. Software publishers are far more likely to license their products than they

---

[39] Id. at 316 ("As custom, therefore, software licensing has a historical pedigree that stretches to a maximum of thirty years. The structure and purpose of software "licenses" that developed at that time . . . in fairness cannot be compared to contemporary licensing practice, which developers rely on to limit competition.").

[40] CARL SHAPIRO AND HAL R. VARIAN INFORMATION RULES: A STRATEGIC GUIDE TO THE NETWORK ECONOMY (1998).

[41] Commissioner v. National Carbide Co., 167 F.2d 304, 306 (1948).

are to sell or lease them.[42] The first sale doctrine applies in all fields of intellectual property law.[43] Under the first sale doctrine, the patent owner cedes the right to file suit for patent infringement for the patented article that they have sold.[44] Similarly, the first sale doctrine of trademark law permits the purchaser of trademarked goods to resell the trademarked goods without infringing the owner's marks. The common result is that an intellectual property owner cannot place conditions on goods once they are sold—an undesirable result from the perspective of the intellectual property owner.

The U.S. Copyright Act confers several exclusive rights on copyright owners, including the exclusive rights to reproduce their works and to distribute their works by sale or rental.[45] The exclusive distribution right is limited by the first sale doctrine, an affirmative defense to copyright infringement that allows owners of copies of copyrighted works to resell those copies. What it means is that "once a copyright owner sells a copy of the copyrighted work, the owner has no continuing right to control either the use or distribution of a particular copy of a copyrighted work."[46] Under U.S. Copyright Law, the first sale doctrine gives the purchaser of a copyrighted works the right to "sell or otherwise dispose of the possession of that copy" without interference by the copyright owner.[47] The 1976 Act conceptualizes the public performance right to include the right "to transmit or otherwise communicate a performance . . . of the work . . . to the public, . . . whether the members of the public capable of receiving the performance . . . receive it in the same place or in separate places and at the same time or at different times."[48]

---

[42] As the Ninth Circuit stated, "the first sale doctrine rarely applies in the software world because software is rarely 'sold.'" Wall Data Inc. v. Los Angeles County Sheriff's Dep't, 447 F.3d 769, 786 n.9 (9th Cir. 2006).

[43] In patent law, the functional equivalent is the doctrine of exhaustion. Under 35 U.S.C. § 271, a defendant can only be liable for infringement if the allegedly infringing acts are carried out "without authority." 35 U.S.C. §§ 271(a), (f), (g). "The longstanding doctrine of patent exhaustion provides that the initial authorized sale of a patented item terminates all patent rights to that item." Quanta Computer, Inc. v. LG Elecs., Inc., 553 U.S. 617, 625 (2008). "The exhaustion doctrine prohibits patent holders from selling a patented article and then 'invoking patent law to control post-sale use of the article.'" Excelstor Tech., Inc. v. Papst Licensing GmbH & Co. KG, 541 F.3d 1373, 1376 (Fed. Cir. 2008). The rationale underlying the doctrine rests upon the theory that an unconditional sale of a patented device exhausts the patentee's right to control the purchaser's use of that item thereafter because the patentee has bargained for and received the full value of the goods. Princo Corp. v. ITC, 616 F.3d 1318, 1328 (Fed. Cir. 2010) (en banc). Trademark exhaustion principles provide trademark owners with certain rights to control the sale of a branded authentic product until it has been placed on the market and there is a first sale.

[44] The doctrine of patent exhaustion provides that the authorized sale of "an article that substantially embodies a patent" exhausts the patent holder's rights and prevents them from controlling post sale use of the article through the use of patent law. Quanta Computer, Inc. v. LG Elec., Inc., 553 U.S. 617 (2008); see also Jazz Photo Corp. v. Int'l Trade Comm'n, 264 F.3d 1094, 1105 (Fed. Cir. 2001) ("When a patented device has been lawfully sold in the United States, subsequent purchasers inherit the same immunity [as the seller possessed] under the doctrine of Patent exhaustion.").

[45] Vernor v. Autodesk, Inc., 621 F.3d 1102, 1107 n. 1 (10th Cir. 2010).

[46] MARK A. LEMLEY, ET AL., SOFTWARE AND INTERNET LAW 254–55 (4th ed. 2011) (explaining how licensing enables the software publisher to control price discrimination enabling arbitrage or selling the product at different prices in different markets (i.e. business-to-consumer vs. business-to-business pricing)).

[47] Bobbs–Merrill Co. v. Straus, 210 U.S. 339, 350–351 (1908) (recognizing first sale doctrine where copyright owner sold its book with a printed notice announcing that any retailer who sold the book for less than one dollar was responsible for copyright infringement; court held that the distribution right did not permit the plaintiff to dictate subsequent sales of the book.).

[48] 17 U.S.C. § 101.

The U.S. Supreme Court stretched the first sale doctrine to "copies of a copyrighted work lawfully made abroad."[49] In *Kirtsaeng v. John Wiley & Sons, Inc.,*[50] the U.S. Supreme Court considered a case of ongoing grey market infringement. Supap Kirtsaeng, a citizen of Thailand, asked his friends and family to buy copies of foreign edition English-language textbooks at Thai bookshops, where they sold at low prices, and mail them to him in the United States. Kirtsaeng would then sell them, reimburse his family and friends, and keep the profit. The U.S. Supreme Court held the "first sale" doctrine—which permits lawfully acquired copies of copyrighted works to be resold by their owners—also applies to works such as the books manufactured in Thailand.

In *Vernor v. Autodesk, Inc.,*[51] a first sale dispute arose out of Timothy Vernor's purchase of Autodesk software at a garage sale and other repurchases. Architects, engineers, and manufacturers used this high-priced software for design purposes. The issue for the court was to determine whether Vernor was the "owner of a particular copy"[52] and "owner of a copy"[53] for purposes of the "first sale" and "essential step" defenses created by those sections of the U.S. Copyright Act. In *Vernor*, Autodesk offered its software to customers subject to a license agreement that customers were required to accept before installing the software. The licensing agreement for the Autodesk software provided that Autodesk retained title to all copies and that the customer had a nonexclusive and non-transferable license to use it.[54]

EBay suspended Vernor's account when it received Digital Millennium Copyright Act takedown notices from Autodesk, protesting Vernor's eBay sales of used Autodesk software. In response to eBay's suspension of his account, Vernor filed suit against Autodesk, seeking a declaratory judgment to establish that he was a lawful owner of the software.[55] The Ninth Circuit ruled that Autodesk's customer, from whom Vernor acquired the used copies, was a licensee not an owner of the copies.[56]

The court reasoned that neither Autodesk's original customer nor Vernor could sell or resell copies of Autodesk's software under the first sale doctrine.[57] "The first sale doctrine does not apply to a person who possesses a copy of the copyrighted work without owning it, such as a licensee."[58] The court developed a three-part test to determine whether a software user was a licensee or owner of a copy where the copyright owner (1) specifies that the user is granted a license, (2) significantly

---

[49] Kirtsaeng v. John Wiley & Sons, Inc., 133 S.Ct. 1351, 1355–56 (2013).

[50] 2013 U.S. LEXIS 2371 (Sup. Ct., March 19, 2013).

[51] 621 F.3d 1102 (9th Cir. 2010) (holding that Vernor infringed Autodesk's copyright when he resold software products on eBay).

[52] 17 U.S.C. § 109(a).

[53] 17 U.S.C. § 117(a).

[54] Id. at 1104.

[55] To enforce its license agreement, Autodesk filed a number of DMCA takedown notices with eBay arising out of listings of the software. Id. at 1105–06. Eventually, eBay suspended Vernor's account. Id. at 1106. Chapter 10 explains the DMCA takedown procedures in detail.

[56] The court found that Autodesk reserved title to its software copies and imposed significant transfer and use restrictions. The court held that Autodesk's customer from whom Vernor acquired the used copies was a licensee not an owner of the copies. Id. at 1111–1112. The court thus concluded that neither Autodesk's original customer nor Timothy Vernor could sell or resell copies of the software under the first sale doctrine. Id. at 1116.

[57] Id. at 1116.

[58] Id. at 1107–1108.

restricts the user's ability to transfer the software, and (3) imposes notable use restrictions.[59] The court found that Autodesk was licensing its product and therefore the first sale doctrine was inapplicable.[60]

(B) Licensing Litigation

In *New-Crop LLC v. QED Clinical,*[61] a company failed to pay for an electronic prescribing system it contracted to use, and continued to use the system's data after the license agreement ended. In *NewCrop*, the licensor delivered an electronic medication prescribing system for CINA, the physicians and health care provider licensees. The software licensed to the health care defendants "allegedly allowed physicians to send prescriptions directly to pharmacies electronically via the Internet."[62] The defendant licensees gained access through NewCrop's website or through a software interface.[63] "NewCrop said it discussed entering into a formal licensing agreement with CINA during November 2007, but claimed it allowed CINA and its clients to access the system prior to execution of the contract."[64] Under the license agreement, the defendants agreed, "to pay monthly fees for the use of NewCrop's electronic prescribing system."[65] Because of CINA's clients' enrollment, CINA reportedly was obligated to submit a monthly report-detailing enrollment by its clients and the fees payable to NewCrop.

In its license agreement with NewCrop, INA agreed to discontinue or disable its links to NewCrop's websites, and destroy any copies of data from NewCrop's system upon termination of the license agreement. CINA failed to make licensing payments and the balance due was $44,117.[66] After declaring the license agreement to be in breach, the licensor "apparently blocked CINA from accessing its website, but CINA "continued to use NewCrop's data offline. NewCrop claimed it suffered damages totaling at least $37,351.80 for CINA's use of the data."[67] NewCrop filed a lawsuit against CINA bringing claims including *quantum meruit*, promissory estoppel, fraud and fraudulent inducement, money had and received unjust enrichment, and a violation of the Texas Theft Liability Act.[68] The parties settled for $118,000 plus costs and attorneys' fees and an injunction prohibiting CINA from further using NewCrop's software and data.[69]

In most software license litigation where the licensee files suit against the developer, it is because the software delivered does not conform to its specifications. In *Silicon Knights v. Epic Games,*[70] the video game developer licensed another company's

---

[59] Id. at 1111.

[60] Id. (holding that a software user is a licensee rather than an owner of a copy where the copyright owner specifies that the user is a licensee and noting that this arrangement significantly restricts the user's ability to transfer the software and imposes use restrictions).

[61] 2013 WL 1819926 (Tex. Dist., March 20, 2013).

[62] Id.

[63] Id

[64] Id.

[65] Id.

[66] Id.

[67] Id.

[68] Id.

[69] Id.

[70] 2012 WL 6919153 (E.D.N.C., May 30, 2012).

videogame engine software. Silicon Knights entered into a license agreement with Epic Games to license Unreal Engine 3 ("UE3"). Silicon Knights contended that it was licensing UE3 to use it in the development of videogames it was building for Xbox 360 and PlayStation 3. Silicon Knight contended that Epic misrepresented UE3's capabilities and filed to deliver updates or new releases in a timely manner. Silicon Knights also contended that UE3 did not work properly and developed its own game engine. Silicon Knights filed a lawsuit asserting claims of breach of warranty, breach of contract, unfair competition, and fraud. Epic filed a counterclaim that Silicon Knights breached their license agreement, misappropriated their trade secrets and infringed their copyright. A jury agreed with Epic finding that Silicon Knight breached the license agreement and awarded Epic $2,650,000 or damages. The jury also found Silicon Knights infringed Epic's trade secrets and awarded $1,800,000. This case illustrates the high stakes nature of many software development agreements. In many instances, there will claims, counterclaims, and judgments for many millions of dollars.

In most software licensing litigation where the developer is the plaintiff, the dispute is over the duty of the licensee to pay royalties. In *Educ. Logistics v. Laidlaw Transit*[71] a software developer was awarded $28.4 million after a licensee breached the licensing agreement by failing to remit royalty payments when due and by failing to use its 'best efforts' to promote the software to other users. Educational Logistics ("Edulog"), the software developer, licensed a proprietary computer software system that uses digitized maps and student databases to create bus routes for transporting students to and from school. Edulog represented that its software would help school districts save money by diminishing the number of school buses deployed for transportation services. Edulog formed Logistics Management to license their software to school systems. Logistics entered into a license agreement with Laidlaw Transit, one of the largest student transportation services in North America. Logistics entered into a five-year exclusive license agreement, but retained the right to directly market to other customers. At the end of the five-year exclusivity agreement, Laidlaw elected not to renew. Laidlaw though retained a non-exclusive right to continue using the transportation software.

Educlog and Logistics contended Laidlaw breached the perpetual, non-exclusive portion of their agreement by failing to use "best efforts" to promote the software. The plaintiffs also contended that Laidlaw failed to pay royalties as well as failed to promote the system. Laidlaw's defense was that it no longer had a duty of "best efforts" once the five-year exclusive agreement expired. Laidlaw also contended that Logistics (and Edulog) materially breached their side of the agreement. The jury awarded the plaintiffs $28,409,515, which included compensation for lost license fees, lost annual license maintenance fees, lost perpetual license fees, lost royalties and breach. The court remitted the judgment to $18,899,756. Each of these development or customized software license agreements were negotiated agreements and by their very nature, relational contracts. The lesson of these development software cases is the importance of drafting license or development agreements that limit liability. Contracts to develop Internet-related software will typically be business-to-business and will be negotiated.

---

[71] 2012 WL 8017634 (D. Mont., Nov. 15, 2012).

(C) Standard Form License Agreements

When most people think about software licensing, they think about standard form Terms of Use ("TOU"). They "come in a variety of forms with a variety of colorful names such as "shrink wrap," "boot screen," "click wrap," or "browse wrap" (or less charitably as "sneak wrap" or "autistic") licenses."[72] Standard form contracts are ubiquitous in twenty-first century contract law.[73] By the 1970s, more than ninety-percent of all contracts made were classified as "standard form" contracts.[74] Four decades before the rise of the World Wide Web, David Slawson contended that standard form contracts are not really contracts at all: "The conclusion to which all this leads is that practically no standard forms, at least as they are customarily used in consumer transactions, are contracts."[75]

In the 1980s, there was a swirl of uncertainty over the enforceability of shrinkwrap licenses as courts routinely struck them down on diverse contractual grounds.[76] Mass-market licenses are standard form contracts marketed to consumers with identical terms and no likelihood of individual negotiation. Typically, mass-market licenses are one-sided contracts that eliminate warranties and remedies.[77] They are presented to the customer on a "take-it or leave it" basis with identical, non-negotiable terms for all licensees. They are generally single-user licenses but may be bundled in multi-pack license, which delineates the number of users. Symantec, a leading anti-virus licensor, for example, parcels out different bundles of rights depending on whether the user is a business or a consumer entity. When an end-user of software downloads a digital product, they are given a legal notice that the software is licensed, not sold, and that they are subject to the terms of the licensing agreement, which is presented in the login screen. As mentioned above, a typical EULA requires the licensee to click "I

---

[72] The term "sneak wrap" refers to online TOU agreements. See Ed Foster, "Sneak Wrap" May Be a Good Way of Defining the Maze of Online Policies, INFOWORLD, July 26, 1999, at 73 (describing sneak wrap as "where the vendor reserves the right to change the terms of a deal at any time, and sneak notice of the change right past you if they possibly can"); See also, ROBERT W. GOMULKIEWICZ, XUAN–THAO NGUYEN & DANIELLE CONWAY–JONES, LICENSING INTELLECTUAL PROPERTY LAW AND APPLICATION 311 (2nd ed. 2012).

[73] The conventional explanation is that these mass market license agreements were invented to bypass the first sale but one commentator contends that it was invented as a competition law or antitrust reason. Steven A. Heath, Contracts, Copyright, and Confusion: Revisiting the Enforceability of "Shrinkwrap' Licenses, 5 CHI–KENT INTELL. PROP. 12, 13 (2005) (arguing that software licensing was invented to avoid "governmental scrutiny over anti-competitive practices at large in the computing industry.").

[74] W. David Slawson, Standard Form Contracts and Democratic Control of Lawmaking Power, 84 HARV. L. REV. 529, 544 (1971).

[75] Mass–market licenses are a classic example of adhesion contracts in which the weaker party adheres to the terms of the stronger party and there is no possibility of negotiations. The Edwin Patterson, The Delivery of A Life-Insurance Policy, 33 HARV. L. REV. 198, 222 (1919) (coining term in study of adhesionary contract in the life insurance industry).

[76] See e.g., Arizona Retail Sys., Inc. v. The Software Link, Inc., 831 F. Supp. 759, 766 (D. Ariz. 1993) (refusing to enforce terms of a shrinkwrap license because "whether the terms of the license agreement are treated as proposals for additional terms under U.C.C. § 2–207, or proposals for modification under U.C.C. § 2–209, the terms of the license agreement are not a part of the agreement between the parties."). See Step–Saver Data Sys. v. Wyse Technology, 939 F.2d 91 (3d Cir. 1991).

[77] Celeste M. Hammond, A Real Estate Focus: The (Pre) Assumed "Consent" of Commercial Binding Arbitration Contracts: An Empirical Study of Attitudes and Expectations of Transactional Lawyers, 36 J. MARSHALL L. REV. 589, 598–99 (2003) ("Most consumers and employees do not realize that they have waived these rights until they become necessary. Some of the rights most often waived in pre-employment or adhesion contracts are the aforementioned rights—trial, appeal, class action, and choice of the arbitrator."). See F. PAUL BLAND JR. ET. AL., CONSUMER ARBITRATION AGREEMENTS: ENFORCEABILITY AND OTHER TOPICS 6– 12 (2007) (surveying the reasons why predispute mandatory arbitration diminishes rights of consumers).

agree" to the terms of service or other license agreement before they are permitted to download and use the software.

Each mass-market form is an adhesive contract where the licensee adheres to the terms of the licensor and there is no semblance of balanced terms. The typical mass market license is characterized by (1) a vendor-oriented choice of law provision, (2) a warning that the intellectual property rights are not transferred to the consumer, (3) a restricted scope to a single user, (4) the consumer must de-install or destroy copies of the software if he terminates the license, (5) the vendor disclaims the implied warranty of merchantability and fitness for a particular purpose, (6) the licensor offers the consumer a limited rather than full warranty, (7) the consumer is not entitled to updates for free, and (8) the consumer submits in advance to jurisdiction in the vendor's home court.[78]

To paraphrase Woody Allen's character, Alvy Singer in Annie Hall, U.S.-style TOU agreements fall somewhere on the continuum between the horrible and the miserable.[79] TOU agreements, presented on a take it or leave it basis, are spreading faster than the 2011 New York City bed bug epidemic. Just as bed bugs hide in cracks and crevices of mattresses and box springs, sneakwrap documents, masquerading in the clothing of contracts, purport to bind consumers to oppressive and unfair terms. The vast majority of Internet contracts are standard form licenses defined in UCITA as transactions targeting a broad market.[80] Nancy Kim coined the term "wrap contract" to describe Internet-related contracting forms such as terms of use, browsewrap, clickwrap, or shrinkwrap. She uses the term "wrap contract" to mean "a blanket term to refer to a unilaterally imposed set of terms which the drafter purports to be legally binding and which are presented to the non-drafting party in a nontraditional form."[81] Professor Kim contends that "wrap contracts" take the form of a traditional contract but constitute a "coercive contracting environment."[82] The problem with "wrap contracts" is "their aggressive terms."[83]

Raymond T. Nimmer, Reporter for the Uniform Computer Information Transactions Act, is a defender of webwraps. UCITA validates webwrap contracts and provides a legal infrastructure of their enforcement. UCITA § 101(61) provides: "The

---

[78] The term "mass market license"is new and the definition must be applied in light of its intended and limited function. That function is to describe small dollar value, routine transactions involving information that is directed to the general public when the transaction occurs in a retail market available to and used by the general public. The term includes all consumer contracts and also some transactions between businesses if they are in a retail market.

[79] "I feel that life is divided into the horrible and the miserable. That's the two categories. The horrible are like, I don't know, terminal cases, you know, and blind people, crippled. I don't know how they get through life. It's amazing to me. And the miserable is everyone else. So you should be thankful that you're miserable, because that's very lucky, to be miserable." Annie Hall (Rollins–Joffe Productions 1977) (quoting the character Woody Allen); see also MICHAEL L. RUSTAD, SOFTWARE LICENSING: PRINCIPLES AND PRACTICAL STRATEGIES 292 (2010) (comparing this characterization of life by Woody Allen's character to quickwrap license agreements).

[80] "When most people think about software licensing, they think about standard form mass-market EULAs. These come in a variety of forms with a variety of colorful names such as "shrink wrap," "boot screen," "click-wrap," or "browse wrap" (or, less charitably, as "sneak wrap" or "autistic" licenses)." ROBERT W. GOMULKIEWICZ, XUAN–THAO NGUYEN, & DANIELLE CONWAY–JONES, LICENSING INTELLECTUAL PROPERTY: LAW AND APPLICATION 311 (2008); UCITA § 102(a)(44).

[81] NANCY S. KIM, WRAP CONTRACTS: FOUNDATIONS AND RAMIFICATIONS 2. (2013).

[82] Id. a 1-3.

[83] Id. at 4.

legal effect of online agreements may be "an emerging area of the law," but courts still "apply traditional principles of contract law and focus on whether the plaintiff had reasonable notice of and manifested assent to the online agreement."[84] Clickwrap agreements are increasingly common and "have routinely been upheld."[85] UCITA § 101(61) provides: "'Standard form' means a record or a group of related records containing terms prepared for repeated use in transactions and so used in a transaction in which there was no negotiated change of terms by individuals except to set the price, quantity, method of payment, selection among standard options, or time or method of delivery."[86] Wrap licenses are standard form contracts marketed to consumers with identical terms and no likelihood of individual negotiation. Typically, wrap licenses eliminate warranties and all meaningful remedies in order to spread allocate the risk of software failure to the user community.[87]

Increasingly, these agreements specify limited remedies and require the user to waive the right to jury or a court resolution in favor of predispute mandatory arbitration. Mandatory arbitration is sometimes coupled with its running partner, anti-class action waivers.[88] Consumer licensees must agree to forego the right to file actions in court or join class actions as a condition of using data or software. The chart below depicts the major form of mass license agreements in wide currency on the Internet.[89] In the 1980s, mass-market licensors began to use shrinkwrap license agreements to govern terms and conditions for their software products.[90] While the

---

[84] Burcham v. Expedia, Inc., 2009 WL 586513, at *2 (E.D.Mo. March 6, 2009)

[85] Clickwrap evolved out of shrinkwrap agreement "which are generally license agreements placed inside the cellophane 'shrinkwrap' of computer software boxes that, by their terms, become effective once the 'shrinkwrap' is opened." Stomp, Inc. v. NeatO, LLC, 61 F.Supp.2d 1074, 1080 n. 11 (C.D.Cal.1999) (upholding choice of venue clause); Zaltz v. JDATE, 2013 WL 3369073 *8 (E.D. N.Y. July 8, 2013) (upholding dating websites' clickstream agreement); Doe v. Project Fair Bid Inc., No. C11–809 MJP, 2011 WL 3516073, *4 (W.D. Wash. Aug. 11, 2011) (upholding clickwrap on Internet website.); TracFone Wireless, Inc. v. Anadisk LLC, 685 F. Supp. 2d 1304, 1315 (S.D. Fla. 2010) (upholding clickstream agreement); Burcham v. Expedia, Inc., 2009 U.S. Dist. LEXIS 17104 (E.D. Mo. 2009); Davis v. Dell, 2007 U.S. Dist. LEXIS 94767 (D.N.J. 2007) aff'd 2008 U.S. Dist. LEXIS 62490 (D.N.J. 2008); A.V. v. iParadigms, LLC, 544 F.Supp. 2d 473, 480 (E.D. Va. 2008) (upholding clickwrap agreement where a student had to register for a term paper service by creating a profile on defendant's website and clicking "I Agree" to the terms of the user agreement, which was displayed directly above the "I Agree" link that the student had to click);

[86] UCITA § 101(61).

[87] Michael L. Rustad, Commercial Law Infrastructure For The Age of Information, 16 J. MARSHALL J. COMPUTER & INFO L. 255, 300 (1997).

[88] These provisions will not be enforced in European consumer transactions. Companies including such provisions in terms of service, shrinkwrap, browsewrap, or clickwrap also face European enforcement actions by entities that enforce consumer rights. See Council Directive 93/13/EEC of April 1993 on Unfair Terms in Consumer Contracts, Annex, 1993 O.J. (L 95) 29, at letter (q) (excluding or hindering the consumer's right to take legal action or exercise any other legal remedy, particularly by requiring the consumer to take disputes exclusively to arbitration not covered by legal provisions, unduly restricting the evidence available to him or imposing on him a burden of proof which, according to the applicable law, should lie with another party to the contract).

[89] Robert A. Hillman & Jeffrey J. Rachlinski, Standard–Form Contracting in the Electronic Age, 77 N.Y.U.L. REV. 429, 464 (2002) ("Consumers enter into electronic contracts in two distinct ways: "browsewrap" and "clickwrap' contracts.").

[90] UCITA defines the Mass–market license as "a standard form that is prepared and used in a Mass-market transaction. UCITA, Id. at § 102(45). A Mass–market transaction, in turn, means "(A) A consumer transaction; or (B) any other transaction with an end user licensee if: (i) the transaction is for information or informational rights directed to the general public as a whole including consumers, under substantially the same terms for the same information; (ii) the licensee acquires the information or rights in a retail transaction under terms and in quantity consistent with an ordinary transaction in a retail market." § 102(46).

consumer's title to the tangible copy of the software (a purchased CD–ROM, for example) may be absolute, that does not confer property rights upon the intangible code that makes up the software.

Licensing enables the useful practice of arbitrage that is the common practice of strategically calibrating of software prices according to such factors as the amount of competition, the value added and the user's ability to pay.[91] During the formative period of mass-market licenses in the 1980s, licensors used the term "shrinkwrap" or box top license. In the new millennium, clickstream or clickwrap is the most popular type of contract. Software vendors include clickstream agreements in so-called installwrap agreements, where the customer agrees to the terms as a condition of downloading the software. The installwrap is an agreement, which "pops up on the screen when the software is actually being installed on the user's computer, requiring the user to click an "accept" button before the installation will conclude . . . if you decline to accept, the installation will abort."[92] VeriSign's installwrap for its Symbian export utility software license states:

> By clicking "I Accept" below, installing, or using this software, you are consenting to be bound by and are becoming a party to this agreement. If you do not agree to all of the terms of this agreement and any such third party license agreements, which are applicable, do not install or use the software, or click "I Do Not Accept," and, if applicable, return this product to VeriSign.[93]

The economic reality is that quickwrap licenses are an efficient form of contracting. Quickwrap licenses are seldom read before being entered into by millions of online consumers around the world. Nevertheless, consumers have a love/hate relationship with these mass-market license agreements, as Amy Schmitz characterizes it:

> On the one hand, consumers admit that they have no interest in reading form contracts, enjoy the convenience and efficiency of form contracting, and routinely accept forms "dressed up" as deals without stopping to read or question their content. On the other hand, consumers are often frustrated with the effectively nonnegotiable nature of these contracts and complain that they lack the requisite time or understanding to read or negotiate companies' impenetrable purchase terms.[94]

---

[91] CARL SHAPIRO AND HAL R. VARIAN INFORMATION RULES: A STRATEGIC GUIDE TO THE NETWORK ECONOMY (1998); ProCD, Inc. v. Zeidenberg, 86 F.3d 1447, 1449 (7th Cir. 1996) (noting that licensing enables software to be sold for a higher price for commercial users, while the same product may be priced lower if use restrictions are enforceable and the license is restricted to non-commercial use).

[92] Christain H. Nasdan, Open Source Licensing: Virus or Virtue? 10 TEX. INTELL. PROP. L.J. 349, 377 (2002).

[93] VeriSign, Symbian Key Export Software License Agreement, http://www.verisgn.com (last visited Feb. 10, 2009).

[94] Amy J. Schmitz, Pizza-Box Contracts: True Tales of Consumer Contracting Culture, 45 WAKE FOREST L. REV. 863, 864–65 (2010) (arguing that consumers bear some responsibility for acquiescing to the stronger party "run[ning] roughshod over their rights").

Types of Wrap Agreements

Mass–Market Forms	Formation Principle	Controversial Aspects
Shrinkwrap License	Licensee manifests assent when he or she tears open wrapping on software box.	Consumers may not be able to review or even learn of one-sided terms before being bound.
Clickwrap	By clicking on an icon or radio button, the user manifests assent to be bound by terms.[95]	Links to clickwrap agreements are sometimes below the fold of a web page, or presented inconspicuously.[96]
Browsewrap[97]	Binds consumers who merely browse or access a website without any act-manifesting assent. "Your use of the ___Website and/or the Services constitutes your agreement to be legally bound by these Terms of Use."[98]	Consumers may be bound even though they neither read the terms of use nor affirmatively manifested assent to its provisions.

---

[95] Specht v. Netscape Communications Corp., 150 F.Supp.2d 585, 593–94 (S.D. N.Y. 2001) ("A click-wrap license presents the user with a message on his or her computer screen, requiring that the user manifest his or her assent to the terms of the license agreement by clicking on an icon.") (citation omitted).

[96] "Whether a term is 'conspicuous' or not is a decision for the court and includes the following: (i) for a person: (A) a heading in capitals equal to or greater in size than the surrounding text, or in contrasting type, font, or color to the surrounding text of the same or lesser size; and (B) language in the body of a record or display in larger type than the surrounding text, or in contrasting type, font, or color to the surrounding text of the same size, or set off from surrounding text of the same size by symbols or other marks that call attention to the language; and (ii) for a person or an electronic agent, a term that is so placed in a record or display that the person or electronic agent may not proceed without taking action with respect to the particular term." U.C.C. § 2–103(1)(b) (2003).

[97] A number of courts have enforced browsewrap even though they do not require the user to click a specific box. Sw. Airlines Co. v. BoardFirst, L.L.C., 2007 WL 4823761, at 5 (N.D. Tex. Sept. 12, 2007); Molnar v. 1–800–Flowers.com, Inc., 2008 WL 4772125, at 7 (C.D. Cal. 2008) ("Courts have held that a party's use of a website may be sufficient to give rise to an inference of assent to the terms of use."). But see Hines, 668 F. Supp. 2d at 368 (holding that a forum-selection clause contained in browsewrap terms of use available through a link at the bottom of a website was not enforceable because it was not "reasonably communicated" to customer).

[98] Roller v. TV Guide Holdings, LLC, 2013 WL 3322348 (Ark. Sup. Ct., June 27, 2013) (refusing to enforcing browsewrap agreement absent evidence that the agreement was communicated to the user).

Terms of Use[99]	Binds consumers by either browsing or clicking agreement.	Terms of use include predispute mandatory arbitration,[100] class-action waivers, and eliminate meaningful warranties and remedies. One-sided terms of use often disclaim all warranties and meaningful remedies.[101]

(D) Types of Wrap Contracts

(1) Shrinkwrap Agreements

Software makers used shrinkwrap licenses in the early 1980s, prior to the development of the World Wide Web. Adobe, Inc., a leading software development and publishing company, claimed that all of its software products were subject to a shrinkwrap EULA that prohibited copying or commercial redistribution. Shrinkwrap contracts are license agreements or other terms and conditions of a putatively contractual nature, which can only be read and accepted by the consumer after they break open the plastic wrapping surrounding the boxed software. The first paragraph of a shrinkwrap license usually provides that the opening of the package signifies acceptance of the license's terms because a licensor needs to reference the fact that the

---

[99] Bradley E. Abruzzi, Copyright, Free Expression, and the Enforceability of "Personal Use–Only" and Other Use-Restrictive Online Terms of Use, 26 SANTA CLARA COMPUTER & HIGH TECH. L.J. 85, 105 (2010) (arguing that website terms of use or service evolved from shrinkwrap licensing practices).

[100] The Joint Commission of the American Arbitration Association, the American Bar Association, and the American Medical Association identified four different types of health care arbitration: (1) predispute, final and binding arbitration; (2) predispute, nonbinding arbitration; (3) post-dispute final and binding arbitration; and (4) post-dispute, nonbinding arbitration. Am. Arbitration Ass'n, Am. Bar Ass'n, & Am. Med. Ass'n, COMMISSION ON HEALTH CARE DISPUTE RESOLUTION: FINAL REPORT 10 (Jul. 27, 1998), http://www.ama-assn.org/ama1/pub/upload/mm/395/healthcare.pdf.

[101] Compulsory arbitration clauses in mass-market license agreements, computer contracts, or terms of service have been upheld by numerous U.S. courts. See e.g., Chandler v. AT&T Wireless Servs., Inc., 358 F. Supp. 2d 701, 706 (S.D. Ill. 2005) (ordering arbitration in case where a pre-dispute arbitration clause was added to the consumer's contract for wireless services); Lieschke v. RealNetworks, Inc., No. 99 C 7274, 99 C 7380, 2000 U.S. Dist. LEXIS 1683, at 7 (N.D. Ill. Feb. 10, 2000) (enforcing arbitration clauses in terms of service agreement); Westendorff v. Gateway 2000, Inc., 41 U.C.C. Rep. Serv. 2d (CBC) 1110, at 2–3 (Del. Ch. 2000) (holding that the plaintiff was bound to an arbitration clause because she kept her computer for thirty days, thereby accepting Gateway's terms and conditions for sale of the computer and related services); Caspi v. Microsoft Network, L.L.C., 732 A.2d 528, 530, 532–33 (N.J. Super. Ct. App. Div. 1999) (validating forum selection clause where subscribers to online software were required to review license terms in scrollable window and to click "I Agree" or "I Don't Agree"); Brower v. Gateway 2000, 246 A.D.2d 246, 256 (N.Y. App. Div. 1998) (ordering enforcement of arbitration clause in Gateway's standard computer contract); Barnett v. Network Solutions, Inc., 38 S.W.3d 200, 203–04 (Tex. App. 2001) (upholding forum selection clause in online contract for registering internet domain names that require users to scroll through terms before accepting or rejecting them); cf. Specht v. Netscape Commc'ns. Corp., 306 F.3d 17, 35 (2d Cir. 2002) (holding that user's downloading software where the terms were submerged did not manifest assent to arbitration clause); Klocek v. Gateway, Inc., 104 F. Supp. 2d 1332, 1341 (D. Kan. 2000) (declining to enforce arbitration clause on grounds that user did not agree to standard terms mailed inside the computer box).

software is licensed.[102] In general, it is advisable that the licensor include the terms of the license agreement in every copy of the software, manuals, and note that the software was licensed on the introductory screen display each time the software was used. The license conditions access to and use of its service on the subscriber's acceptance of its terms and conditions. Shrinkwrap license agreements were developed to side-step the U.S. Copyright Act's first sale doctrine."[103]

Shrinkwrap is cynically referred as "sneakwrap" as captured in a well-known *Dilbert* cartoon.[104] The cartoon begins with Dilbert stating: "I didn't read all of the shrinkwrap license agreement on my new software until after I opened it,"—and concludes with Dilbert lamenting: "Apparently, I agreed to spend the rest of my life as a towel boy in Bill Gates' new mansion."[105] Standard form agreements are adhesion contracts in which the licensee adheres to the terms of the stronger party.[106] The typical Internet related shrinkwrap or other mass-market license agreement does not provide warranties of any kind and foreclose any realistic remedy by requiring the consumer to litigate in a forum of the vendor's choice—often in a distant forum. Many shrinkwrap license agreements generally begin with a legal notice followed by a disclaimer, or terms of use, stating that breaking the shrinkwrap confirms the user's acceptance of the license terms.

(2) Click Stream Agreements

A clickwrap agreement is an "agreement [that] collects all of the terms of the agreement in a single dialog box and then requires the user to affirmatively accept the agreement before proceeding, makes every term equally visible."[107] "On the Internet, the primary means of forming a contract are the so-called 'clickwrap' (or 'click-through') agreements, in which website users typically click an 'I agree 'box after being presented with a list of terms and conditions of use, and the 'browsewrap' agreements, where website terms and conditions of use are posted on the website typically as a hyperlink at the bottom of the screen."[108]

---

[102] This example is drawn from Morgan Laboratories, Inc. v. Micro Data Base Systems, Inc., 1997 WL 258886 (N.D. Cal. 1997).

[103] The first sale doctrine of copyright law gives the owner of a lawfully made copy the power to ""sell or otherwise dispose of the possession of that copy" without the copyright holder's consent." Step-Saver Data Sys. v. Wyse Tech., 939 F.2d 91, 96 n.7 (3d Cir. 1991) (quoting Bobbs–Merrill Co. v. Straus, 210 U.S. 339, 350 (1908) (holding that a copyright owner's exclusive distribution right is exhausted after the owner's first sale of a particular copy of the copyrighted work)). The first sale doctrine is now codified as Section 109 of the U.S. Copyright Act. Section 109 of The U.S. Copyright Act states in relevant part: "the owner of a particular copy . . . lawfully made under this title . . . is entitled, without the authority of the copyright owner, to sell or otherwise dispose of the possession of that copy . . . ." U.S. Copyright Act, 17 U.S.C. § 109(a).

[104] The term "sneak wrap" refers to online TOU agreements. See Ed Foster, "Sneak Wrap" May Be a Good Way of Defining the Maze of Online Policies, InfoWorld, July 26, 1999, at 73 (describing sneak wrap as "where the vendor reserves the right to change the terms of a deal at any time, and sneak notice of the change right past you if they possibly can").

[105] Michael L. Rustad & Thomas H. Koenig, The Tort of Negligent Enablement of Cybercrime, 20 BERKELEY L.J. 1553, 1563 (2005).

[106] Southwest Airlines Co. v. BoardFirst L.L.C., No. 3:06–CV–00891–B, 2007 WL 4823761, at *5 (N.D. Tex. Sept. 12, 2007).

[107] Liberty Syndicates at Lloyd's v. Walnut Advisory Corp., Slip Copy, No. 09–1343, 2011 WL 5825777 (D. N.J. Nov. 16, 2011).

[108] Hines v. Overstock, Inc., 668 F. Supp.2d 362, 366 (E.D. N.Y. 2009); Hubbert v. Dell Corp., 359 Ill.App.Ct. 976, 984, 359 Ill.App.3d 976, 296 Ill.Dec. 258, 835 N.E.2d 113 (2005) (holding that within the "browsewrap" context a computer seller's use of a blue hyperlink to incorporate "Terms and Conditions of

The making of contracts over the internet "has not fundamentally changed the principles of contract."[109] Clickwrap evolved out of shrinkwrap agreements that are "generally license agreements placed inside the cellophane "shrinkwrap" of computer software boxes that, by their terms, become effective once the "shrinkwrap" is opened."[110] The typical "click through" website agreement requires end users to click on an "I agree" button that creates a contract where the user agrees to submit to all of the terms and conditions set forth by the licensor. Generally, the user must indicate acceptance of the clickwrap agreement to proceed with the installation.[111] Like shrinkwrap, the clickwrap spells out permitted and restricted uses by licensees. U.S. courts will enforce clickwrap agreements so long as the user has an opportunity to review the terms and manifest assent, even though most users fail to read the terms before clicking the "I agree" button.

Clickwrap agreements allow users to manifest assent to contractual terms presented to the user before installation of computer software programs. The clickwrap spells out permitted and restricted uses by visitors. In a clickstream agreement, the licensor conditions a licensee's use of a website on the user agreeing to the site's terms and conditions. The Tenth Circuit U.S. Court of Appeals observed:

> Clickwrap agreements are increasingly common and have routinely been upheld. Federal and state courts typically evaluate clickwrap agreements by applying state law contract principles. Courts evaluate whether a clickwrap agreement's terms were clearly presented to the consumer, the consumer had an opportunity to read the agreement, and the consumer manifested an unambiguous acceptance of the terms.[112]

A large number of courts have validated clickwrap agreements if they find users have an opportunity to review the terms and manifest assent.[113]

(3) Browsewrap

"A browsewrap agreement discloses terms on a website that offers a product or service to the user, and the user assents by visiting the website to purchase the product or enroll in the service."[114] The term "browsewrap" signifies a form of contracting that purports to bind website visitors even if they do no perform affirmative acts such as clicking "yes" to agree.[115] A defining feature of a browsewrap license is that

---

Sale" was conspicuous and provided notice to the buyer because the link was included on numerous pages which acted like a "multipage written paper contract").

[109] Register.com, Inc. v. Verio, Inc., 356 F.3d 393, 403 (2d Cir. 2004).

[110] See Stomp, Inc. v. NeatO, LLC, 61 F. Supp. 2d 1074, 1080 n.11 (C.D. Cal.1999) (upholding choice of venue clause).

[111] Realpage, Inc v. EPS, Inc., 560 F.Supp.2d 539 (2007) (quoting Specht v. Netscape Commc'ns. Corp., 306 F.3d 17, 22 n.4 (2d Cir. 2002)).

[112] Hancock v. AT&T Co., 701 F.3d 1248, 1256 (10th Cir. 2012).

[113] See e.g., Zaltz v. JDATE, 2013 WL 3369073 *8 (E.D. N.Y. July 8, 2013) (upholding dating websites's clickstream); Serrano v. Cablevision Sys. Corp., 863 F. Supp. 2d 157, 164 (E.D.N.Y. 2012) ("'[C]lick-wrap' contracts are enforced under New York law as long as the consumer is given a sufficient opportunity to read the end-user license agreement, and assents thereto after being provided with an unambiguous method of accepting or declining the offer."); Jallali v. Nat'l Bd. of Osteopathic Med. Examiners, Inc., 908 N.E.2d 1168, 1173 (Ind. Ct. App. 2009) (upholding clickwrap agreement under general contract principles).

[114] Schnabel v. Trilegiant Corp., 697 F.3d 110, 129 n. 18 (2d Cir.2012).

[115] Facebook, by far the largest social network site, structures its terms of use as a browsewrap with the following introductory clause: "By using or accessing Facebook, you agree to this Statement." Statement

it does not require the user to manifest assent to the terms and conditions expressly—the user need not sign a document or click on an "accept" or "I agree" button to be bound by the agreement. Courts usually uphold browsewraps if the user "has actual or constructive knowledge of a site's terms and conditions prior to using the site."[116]

"Unlike a clickwrap agreement, a browsewrap agreement "does not require the user to manifest assent to the terms and conditions expressly . . . [a] party instead gives his assent simply by using the website."[117] Bebo, for example, uses the browsewrap and does not require users to manifest assent after an opportunity to read terms. Bebo's browsewrap states: "by accessing or using the Bebo Service, you signify that you have read the following terms and conditions (the "Terms of Service") and accept and agree to be bound by them, whether or not you register with Bebo."[118] The contract formation of a "browse-wrap agreement" is that an agreement is formed simply by a website visitor's use of the website or browsing the website, without requiring the visitor to click on anything or indicate any other explicit manifestation of assent. Some U.S. courts are reluctant to enforce browsewrap because of the difficulty of proving that the terms of use were actually communicated to the user.[119]

The typical browsewrap provides that Internet users may not use a website unless they agree to the site's terms of service.[120] "So, for example, the term in its purest form includes an interface that presents a link at the bottom of the page to the terms and conditions. It also includes more ambiguous situations, such as where there is a statement that the purchase is governed by terms that are linked to the page," but requires no clicking of "a radio button acknowledging the terms."[121]

The agreement in *Major v. McAllister* illustrated a typical example of browsewrap.[122] In *Major*, the court found mutual assent when a website user of the ServiceMagic site assented to a forum selection clause contained in an Internet website browsewrap agreement, even though her assent did not require a "click."[123] In that browsewrap case, the website placed immediately visible notice of the existence of license terms on the site. The website stated: "By submitting you agree to the Terms of

---

of Rights and Responsibilities, Facebook, http://www.facebook.com/terms.php?ref=pf (last visited June 13, 2013).

[116] See Southwest Airlines Co. v. BoardFirst, LLC, 2007 WL 4823761, at *5 (N.D.Tex. Sept.12, 2007).

[117] Southwest Airlines Co. v. BoardFirst, L.L.C., No. 06–CV-0891–B, 2007 WL 4823761 at *4 (N.D.Tex. Sept. 12, 2007).

[118] Bebo.com, Terms of Use, http://www.bebo.com/TermsOfUse2.jsp (last updated June 19, 2013); see also Terms of Use, Caringbridge, (Mar. 28, 2012), http://www.Caringbridge.org/termsofuse ("By using this Service, you are bound by these Terms of Use.").

[119] Roller v. TV Guide Holdings, LLC, 2013 WL 3322348 *8 (Ark. Sup. Ct., June 27, 2013) (stating: "In this case, TV Guide has not demonstrated that the terms of the agreement were communicated to appellants. TV Guide's assertions that appellants had notice of the agreement stem from appellants' mention of the agreement in their complaint. However, this is insufficient as the dispositive issue in determining if an enforceable agreement existed is whether appellants had constructive or actual knowledge of the terms of the agreement and therefore agreed by their use of TV Guide's website to be bound by those terms.").

[120] "Most courts which have considered the issue, however, have held that in order to state a plausible claim for relief based upon a browsewrap agreement, the website user must have had actual or constructive knowledge of the site's terms and conditions, and have manifested assent to them[,]" Cvent, Inc. v. Eventbrite, Inc., 739 F. Supp.2d 927, 937 (E.D. Va. 2010).

[121] Ronald J. Mann & Travis Siebeneicher, Just One Click: The Reality of Internet Retail Contracting, 108 COLUM. L. REV. 984, 990 (2008).

[122] Major v. McCallister, 302 S.W.3d 227 (Mo App. 2009).

[123] Id. at 227.

Use" and placing a blue hyperlink next to the button that user pushed, second link to those terms was visible on the same page without scrolling, and similar links were on every other website page."[124] U.S. courts enforce forum selections in favor of the stronger party so long as they are not unreasonable. "A forum selection clause is unreasonable if: (1) its incorporation into the agreement was the result of fraud or overreaching; (2) the complaining party will be deprived of his day in court due to the grave inconvenience or unfairness of the selected forum; (3) the fundamental unfairness of the chosen law may deprive the plaintiff of a remedy; or (4) the clause contravenes a strong public policy of the forum state."[125]

Browsewrap binds the user when a user merely browses the website or social media site.[126] Facebook, for example, structures its terms of use as a browsewrap with the following introductory clause: "By using or accessing Facebook, you agree to this Statement." Browsewrap agreements dictate that additional browsing past the homepage constitutes the mutual assent.[127] Unlike shrinkwrap or clickwrap, browsewrap raises an issue of whether the user has manifested assent. Courts will strike down browsewrap where it is not clear whether users have notice. Browsewraps may take various forms but typically, they involve notice on a website that conditions use of the site upon compliance with certain terms or conditions. These terms may be included on the same page as the notice or accessible via a hyperlink. "A hyperlink electronically provides direct access from one internet location/file to another, typically by clicking a highlighted word or icon. An online reference work, for example, may hyperlink words or terms in its text to their respective definitions."[128]

In *Register.com, Inc. v. Verio, Inc.*,[129] the domain name database's terms of service ("TOS") were structured as a browsewrap. The TOS stated that the user was agreeing to the terms and conditions by merely submitting a query to the database. The court stated:

> [w]hile new commerce on the Internet has exposed courts to many new situations, it has not fundamentally changed the principles of contract, and holding that contract terms on website were enforceable when offeree who should have been aware of terms accepted services from offeror.[130]

The TOS provided that by submitting a query, they were bound by the terms and conditions.[131] The website visitor contended that it did not click agreement to Register.com's TOS and was thus not bound by its provisions. Nevertheless, the Second Circuit upheld the browsewrap finding that the defendant's submission of the WHOIS query manifested its consent to Register.com's TOS.[132] The court enjoined Verio from

---

[124] Id. at 228.

[125] Zaltz v. JDATE, 2013 WL 3369073 *8 (E.D. N.Y. July 8, 2013).

[126] Badoo, a U.K. based social network site popular in Europe and Latin America instructs users that their "Terms apply whenever you visit Badoo, whether or not you have chosen to register with us, so please read them carefully. By accessing, using, registering for or receiving services offered on Badoo (the "Services") you are accepting and agreeing to be bound by the Terms." Badoo, Terms and Conditions of Use, Badoo, http://www.badoo.com/terms (last visited June 13, 2013) (emphasis omitted).

[127] Woodrow Hartzog, Website Design as Contract, 60 AM. U. L. REV. 1635, 1642 (2011).

[128] Major v. McCallister, 302 S.W.3d 227, 228 (Mo App. 2009).

[129] 356 F.3d 393 (2d Cir. 2004).

[130] Id. at 403.

[131] Id.

[132] ICANN is considering a radical reform of its WHOIS system as noted in a recent report:

using a search robot to extract information from Register.com's WHOIS database of domain names. Register.com was entitled to injunctive relief because it demonstrated likelihood to succeed on the merits based upon a trespass to chattels claim as well as violation of the Computer Fraud Abuse Act and federal trademark claims.

Similarly, in *Hines v. Overstock*,[133] a consumer filed a class action against Overstock, an online retailer, alleging that retailer's imposition of "restocking fee" for returned goods amounted to breach of contract, fraud, and violation of New York statutes prohibiting deceptive business practices and false advertising. Overstock moved to dismiss or stay for arbitration, or for transfer of venue. The online retailer contended: "All retail purchases from Overstock are conducted through Overstock's Internet website. When an individual accesses the website, he or she accepts Overstock's terms, conditions and policies, which govern all of Overstock's customer purchases."[134] Overstock's "Terms and Conditions" purported to create a browsewrap agreement stating, "Entering this Site will constitute your acceptance of these Terms and Conditions" and include a provision that requires that "any dispute relating in any way to your visit to the Site . . . be submitted to confidential arbitration in Salt Lake City, Utah."[135] The plaintiff responded that she never had any notice that disputes with Overstock.com require mandatory arbitration in Salt Lake City, Utah."[136] Her argument was that:

> when she accessed Overstock's website to purchase the vacuum, she was never made aware of the Terms and Conditions; specifically, Plaintiff avers that: 'Because of this lawsuit, I later learned that if you scroll down to the end of the website page or pages, there is in smaller print placed between 'privacy policy' and Overstock.com's registered trademark, the words 'site user terms and conditions'. I did not scroll down to the end of the page(s) because it was not necessary to do so, as I was directed each step of the way to click on to a bar to take me to the next step to complete the purchase.[137] *I agree.*

The court found that the consumer representative "lacked notice of the Terms and Conditions because the website did not prompt her to review the Terms and Conditions and because the link to the Terms and Conditions was not prominently displayed so as to provide reasonable notice of the Terms and Conditions."[138] The court held that it would not enforce the Terms and Conditions unless the users "had an opportunity to see the Terms and Conditions prior to accepting them by accessing the website."[139] The

---

As the Expert Working Group on gTLD Directory Services (EWG), we have proposed a paradigm shift—a new system in which gTLD registration data is collected, validated and disclosed for permissible purposes only, with some data elements being accessible only to authenticated requestors that are then held accountable for appropriate use. Our objective is to reexamine and define the purpose of collecting and maintaining gTLD directory data, consider how to safeguard the data, and propose a next generation solution that will better serve the needs of the global Internet community.

Internet Corporation for Assigned Names and Numbers (ICANN), Explore the Draft Next Generation gTLD Directory Services Model (June 24, 2013), http://www.icann.org/en/news/announcements/announcement-3–24jun13–en.htm.

[133] 668 F. Supp.2d 362 (E.D. N.Y. 2009).

[134] Id. at 365.

[135] Id.

[136] Id.

[137] Id.

[138] Id. at 366.

[139] Id.

Overstock court held that there could be no binding manifestation of assent to, and acceptance of them, merely by doing so. The court reasoned: "Very little is required to form a contract nowadays-but this alone does not suffice."[140]

(4) Terms of Use or Service

Terms of use ("TOU"), sometimes called terms of service, take the form of clickwrap, browsewrap, or a combination of these contracting forms.[141] Terms of service must also be reasonably presented or risk that a court will not enforce them.[142] Common terms address user submissions, prohibited content (pornography, IP rights, rights of publicity, commercial content or endorsements, promotions, sweepstakes, software viruses, and other malicious or illegal content), community norms, responsibility for submissions posted on the service, ownership of the site, refusal to post or removal of postings, termination of accounts, ownership of content choice of law, choice of forum, privacy policies, warranty disclaimers, limitations of liability, intellectual property infringement, notice and takedown provisions, licenses to use submissions, third party websites and services (no endorsements), provisions for modifying the agreement, integration or merger clauses and provisions for the termination and modification of the agreement.[143] TOU may be deployed for all sorts of purposes. It may set the terms and conditions for online purchases; it may limit the site's liability for damage that its content and services cause to users.

A website may, through its TOU, obtain the rights to use and reproduce content users post to a website, such as comments to a blog. In addition, TOUs may condition or restrict the subsequent uses a website visitor may make of content that he or she previously accessed on the website. TOU are often structured as clickwrap, browsewrap, or a hybrid contracting form.[144] Courts considering browsewrap terms of service have held that "the validity of a browsewrap license turns on whether a website

---

[140] Id.

[141] For example, CafeMom's terms of service apply to all users of the site, and the provider reserves the right to change terms by simply posting them to the site. Terms of Service, CAFEMOM, http://www.cafemom.com/about/tos.php (last visited May 25, 2013) ("CafeMom reserves the right to update or change these TOS at any time by posting the most current version of the TOS on the Site. Your continued use of the Site after we post any changes to the TOS signifies your agreement to any such changes."); See also Terms and Conditions, AUDIMATED, http://www.audimated.com/legal.php (last visited May 25, 2013), 2012); Terms of Service, SECONDLIFE, http://secondlife.com/corporate/tos.php (last visited May 25, 2013)2); and Terms of Service, STUMBLEUPON, http://www.stumbleupon.com/terms (last visited May 25, 2013)).

[142] See e.g. Kwan v. Clearwire, No. 09–1392, 2012 WL 32380 at *9 (W.D. Wash., Jan. 24, 2012) ("this court finds that the breadcrumbs left by Clearwire to lead Ms. Brown to its [Terms of Service] did not constitute sufficient or reasonably conspicuous notice of the [Terms of Service].").

[143] See e.g., Terms of Use, Caringbridge (March 28, 2012), http://www.Caringbridge.org/termsofuse (specifying the conditions in which user-generated content may be used).

[144] "Sites condition access to their content on visitors' acceptance of these TOU, which generally assume an agreement between the website and user that is enforceable by state contract law. TOU may be deployed to all sorts of purposes. They may set the terms and conditions for online purchases; they may limit the site's liability for damage that its content and services cause to users. A site may, through its TOU, obtain the rights to use and reproduce content users post to a website, for example, comments to a blog. And TOU may condition or restrict the subsequent uses a site visitor may make of content that he or she accesses on the website." Bradley E. Abruzzi, Copyright, Free Expression, and the Enforceability of "Personal Use–Only" and Other Use-Restrictive Online Terms of Use, 26 SANTA CLARA COMPUTER & HIGH TECH. L.J. 85, 86 (2010). Some sites are a hybrid between a browsewrap and a clickwrap because they predicate the manifestation of assent upon either browsing a site or clicking agreement to the terms in a registration process. See e.g., User Agreement, LinkedIn, http://www.linkedin.com/static?key=user_agreement (providing an example of a hybrid user agreement).

user has actual or constructive knowledge of a site's terms and conditions prior to using the site."[145] The lesson from a decade of terms of service is that the terms of service must be presented to the plaintiff, rather than merely posted inconspicuously on a website.[146] Facebook, for example, calls its terms of use agreement, "Statement of Rights and Responsibilities."[147] In the Facebook agreement, users agree to a choice of law in Facebook's home court, Santa Clara County. Moreover, they agree to indemnify Facebook if the social media website is sued because of postings that infringe a third party's content or result in other lawsuits.[148]

Additionally, the U.S.-based social network website AsianAve requires users at signup to agree to the site's terms of service and privacy policy.[149] In *Kwan v. Clearwire Corp.*,[150] a U.S. federal court refused to enforce an Internet service provider's arbitral clause, finding it to be inconspicuous. The court ruled that mere access to a term of service agreement was insufficient to meet the conspicuousness test. The court ordered discovery to determine whether Clearwire's customers agreed to the TOS and to class action waivers.[151] The lesson of this case is that location and conspicuousness matter. Federal and state courts evaluate mass-market agreements by applying state law contract principles.

Courts evaluate whether a mass-market agreement's terms were clearly presented to the consumer, the consumer had opportunity to read the agreement, and the consumer manifested an unambiguous acceptance of the terms.[152] Social Network Websites ("SNSs) generally require users to enter into two kinds of contractual relationships, terms of service agreements and privacy policies, as a condition for accessing their websites. An SNS, website, or other brick-and-mortar company can reduce transaction costs by using a predispute mandatory arbitration clause because it need not defend lawsuits in state or federal court but in a forum where it can choose the arbitral provider and rules to govern the dispute.[153]

---

[145] Southwest Airlines Co. v. BoardFirst, L.L.C., 2007 WL 4823761, at *5 (N.D. Tex. Sept. 12, 2007). Molnar v. 1–800–Flowers.com, 2008 WL 4772125, at *7 (C.D. Cal. 2008); See also, Motise v. America Online, Inc., 346 F.Supp.2d 563, 564–65 (S.D.N.Y.2004) (finding the consumer had no notice where terms of use were available on website, but never presented).

[146] Most TOUs require the user to manifest assent to the TOU by clicking on the "I agree" icon or a hyperlink before they can proceed to download the software. See e.g., Moore v. Microsoft Corp., 741 N.Y.S.2d 91, 92–93 (N.Y. App. Div. 2002) (upholding TOU).

[147] Facebook, http://www.facebook.com/terms.php?ref=pf (last visited June 17, 2013).

[148] Id.

[149] AsianAveJobs Terms of Service, AsianAve, http://www.asianave.com/jobs/tac.html (last visited May 26, 2013).

[150] No. C09–1392JLR, 2012 WL 32380 (W.D. Wash. Jan. 3, 2012).

[151] Id. at 3.

[152] See e.g., Specht v. Netscape Commc'ns Corp., 306 F.3d 17, 28–32 (2d Cir. 2002) (applying California law); Serrano v. Cablevision Sys. Corp., 863 F. Supp. 2d 157, 164 (E.D.N.Y. 2012) ("'[C]lick-wrap' contracts are enforced under New York law as long as the consumer is given a sufficient opportunity to read the end-user license agreement, and assents thereto after being provided with an unambiguous method of accepting or declining the offer."); Jallali v. Nat'l Bd. of Osteopathic Med. Examiners, Inc., 908 N.E.2d 1168, 1173 (Ind. Ct. App. 2009) (upholding clickwrap agreement under general contract principles).

[153] See generally, Michael L. Rustad, Richard Buckingham, Diane D'Angelo, & Kate Durlacher, An Empirical Study of Predispute Mandatory Arbitration Clauses in Social Media Terms of Service, 34 U. ARK. LITTLE ROCK L. REV. 643 (2012).

§ 4.3   CONTRACT FORMATION ISSUES IN CYBERSPACE

this is not is easily to x rlice

(A) Formation Issues

Beginning in the 1990s, the law of contracts evolved to address the unique issues posed by e-commerce and the Internet.[154] In *Specht v. Netscape Communications Corp.*,[155] the Second Circuit refused to enforce a mass-market license agreement because it was unclear whether a consumer would have an opportunity to review the terms of the license agreement *prior* to manifesting assent. The consumer-plaintiff filed suit under the Computer Fraud & Abuse Act and ECPA charging Netscape with allegedly monitoring his activities over the Internet. Netscape moved to compel arbitration and to stay court proceedings, arguing that the plaintiffs agreed to submit to arbitration when it clicked agreement to a mass-market license agreement located on a submerged screen that the user would have needed to scroll through to read the full agreement.[156] The court concluded that, "Where consumers are urged to download free software at the immediate click of a button, a reference to the existence of license terms on a submerged screen is not sufficient to place consumers on inquiry or constructive notice of those terms."[157]

The Second Circuit refused to enforce Netscape's "Smart Download" software license agreement compelling arbitration, finding that Christopher Specht, the plaintiff, did not have reasonable notice of the license terms nor did he (and other users) manifest assent before downloading this plug-in program. Because Netscape's browsewrap "did not carry an immediately visible notice of the existence of license terms," the court refused to enforce them.[158] The key fact in screen was that link to the agreement was located on "a screen located below the download button."[159] The text of the license agreement "would have become visible to plaintiffs only if they had scrolled down to the next screen."[160] The court emphasized that an "unexplored portion" of text "remained below the download button.[161]

Netscape used a highlighted box that included a statement that read: "Please review and agree to the terms of the Netscape SmartDownload software license agreement before downloading and using the software."[162] While this statement was in

---

[154] "In the 1990s, however, things began to change. The rise in computer use by individuals coupled with the advent of the World Wide Web gave rise to two parallel developments, both of which challenged the law of contract formation. Increased computer use created a demand for software programs designed for the consumer market, and those programs were commonly transferred to users by way of standard-form licenses that were packaged with the software and thus unavailable before the consumer paid for the software. Also, parties in large numbers began to use electronic means—the computer—to enter into bargained-for relationships. The turn of the millennium brought two electronic contracting statutes, the Electronic Signatures in Global and National Commerce Act ("E-Sign") and the Uniform Electronic Transactions Act ("UETA"), which removed any doubts that contracts entered into electronically could satisfy the Statute of Frauds." Juliet M. Moringiello & William L. Reynolds, From Lord Coke to Internet Privacy: The Past, Present, and Future of the Law of Electronic Contracting, 72 MD. L. REV. 452, 454 (2013).

[155] 306 F.3d 17 (2d Cir. 2002) (Where the user was unaware that the license agreement appeared only on a submerged screen when downloading free software.).

[156] Id. at 14.

[157] Id. at 32.

[158] Id. at 31.

[159] Id. at 20.

[160] Id. at 23.

[161] Id. at 32

[162] Id.

the same typeface and size as most of the type on the page, it was specially emphasized by the use of a shaded box, and it was further highlighted by the use of a colored hyperlink.[163] Nevertheless, the court found that Netscape had not done enough to bring the terms of use to the attention of consumers and refused to enforce the arbitration clause. In addition, Netscape had not asked the consumer to click agreement to the DownLoad license, only for Netscape's Communicator.

The *Specht* court applied legal realism to cyberspace contracts by striking down Netscape's agreement as "stealthware."[164] The Second Circuit held that a consumer's clicking on a download button did not manifest assent to license terms if those terms were not conspicuous and it was not clear that clicking meant agreement with the terms of a license agreement containing a predispute mandatory arbitration clause. The consumer had no real opportunity to learn of the existence of an arbitration clause because it could not be seen prior to scrolling down the page to a screen located below the download button. The Second Circuit's ruling that location matters and that a reasonable Internet user should have an opportunity to review terms prior to being bound is a rare pro-consumer ruling.

Most U.S. courts are predisposed to enforce Internet license agreements, even when the consumer might not know of the existence of its one-sided terms.[165] In *Scherillo v. Dun & Bradstreet, Inc.*,[166] the federal court upheld a click-wrap forum selection clause finding it to be reasonably communicated to the plaintiff even though the user had to scroll down the page. The court gave no credence to the plaintiff's argument that he "checked" the terms and conditions box inadvertently and therefore had not consented to the agreement. The software licensor can create a "safe harbor" for proving manifestation of assent by using a "double assent procedure" that requires the user to reaffirm assent.[167] A licensor must give the licensee a right to a refund if the licensee has not had an opportunity to review the terms and manifest assent prior to payment.[168] Courts will generally validate contractual formation if it follows the Uniform Computer Information Transactions Act's ("UCITA") mandate of giving the user an opportunity to review the terms and a means to manifest assent. Manifestation of assent by the offeree is some decision based upon awareness of the terms of the license.[169]

---

[163] Id. at 23.

[164] Id.

[165] The limited empirical studies demonstrate beyond my examples that EULAs are tilted in favor of the seller. See Florencia Marotta–Wurgler, What's in a Standard Form Contract? An Empirical Analysis of Software License Agreements, 4 J. EMPIRICAL LEGAL STUD. 677, 703 (2007) (finding that end user license agreements were more pro-seller than the default rules of the UCC); See e.g., Cvent, Inc. v. Eventbrite, Inc., 739 F. Supp.2d 927, 937 (E.D. Va. 2010) (enforcing mass-market license and stating the UCITA was not useful for the plaintiffs); Burcham v. Expedia, Inc., 2009 WL 586512 (E.D. Mo. March 6, 2009) (rejecting plaintiff's argument that he was not bound to website's click-wrap agreement because others had access to his computer and could have created an account on his behalf without him seeing the terms.); See RESTATEMENT (SECOND) OF CONTRACTS § 208, cmt. d. ("gross inequality of bargaining power, together with terms unreasonably favorable to the stronger party, may confirm that the weaker party did not in fact assent or appear to assent to the unfair terms").

[166] 684 F. Supp. 2d 313 (E.D.N.Y. 2010).

[167] UCITA § 112, cmt. 5 (1999).

[168] Id. at § 209(b).

[169] Register.com, Inc. v. Verio, Inc., 356 F.3d 393, 403 (2d Cir. 2004)("It is standard contract doctrine that when a benefit is offered subject to stated conditions, and the offeree makes a decision to take the

(B) "Rolling Contracts"

Social media sites commonly use "rolling contracts," that give the provider the right to modify terms or add new ones after contract formation. Instagram users filed a class action because of the social media's rolling contract and unilateral changes to its terms of use regarding the ownership of copyrights of user generated content ("UGC").[170] Instagram's prior terms of use disclaimed ownership of UGC but the new terms claimed a royalty free license.[171] Travelocity's User Agreement is a rolling contract because it states, "Travelocity may at any time modify this User Agreement and your continued use of this site or Travelocity's services will be conditioned upon the terms and conditions *in force at the time of your use.*"[172] Courts have recognized a "layered" or "rolling" system of electronic contract formation, which is derived from the layered contract formation[173] that exists in the physical world for sophisticated products such as computer systems.[174] With a layered contract, agreement to a contract may not occur at a single point in time. Under webwrap contracts, a party will manifest assent to different terms at different points in time. Terms of service agreements, for example, reserve the right to later modify or add to the terms of use or service. The licensor or buyer requires payment first and provides terms later. The recent trend in judicial decisions is that courts enforce "cash now, terms later" licenses so long as the licensor gives reasonable notice to the user and an opportunity to decline the terms.

UCITA validates "rolling contracts" if the person had reason to know that terms would come later, had a right to refund if he declined the terms, and manifests assent after an opportunity to review them.[175] Online merchants typically offer consumers take it or leave it agreements. UCITA gives consumers a right to a refund if they have not had an opportunity to review the terms.[176] The predominant trend is for U.S. courts to legitimize software industry consumer licensing practices that disclaim warranties.[177] One commentator suggested the term 'sneak wrap' for online mass-market agreements.[178]

(1) ProCD, Inc. v. Zeidenberg: A Game–Changer

ProCD, Inc. v. Zeidenberg[179] nicely illustrates the trend in the law to enforce mass-market licenses even though they have an *avant-garde* form departing from classical

---

benefit with knowledge of the terms of the offer, the taking constitutes an acceptance of the terms, which accordingly become binding on the offeree.").

[170] (Rodriguez v. Instagram LLC, Cal. Super. Ct., No. CGC-13–532875 (Super. Ct. S.F. Cty., July 16, 2013) (stating that plaintiffs sought injunctive relief for unilateral changes in terms of use).

[171] Id.

[172] In re Online Travel Co., 2013 WL 2948086 *4 (N.D. Tex. June 14, 2013).

[173] CLAYTON P. GILLETTE & STEVEN D. WALT, SALES LAW: DOMESTIC & INTERNATIONAL 89 (rev. ed. 2002) (describing rolling contracts as layered).

[174] BRIAN W. SMITH, E–COMMERCE PRODUCTS & SERVICES 2.16 (2001); See also, Robert A. Hillman, Rolling Contracts, 71 FORDHAM L. REV. 743, 744 (2002).

[175] Raymond T. Nimmer, Licensing of Information Assets, 2 INFO. LAW § 11:147 (June 2009).

[176] Id. (explaining conditions of consumers' right to a refund).

[177] See Robert W. Gomulkiewicz, The Implied Warranty of Merchantability in Software Contracts: A Warranty No One Dares to Give and How to Change That, 16 J. MARSHALL J. COMPUTER & INFO. L. 393, 393 (1998) (describing trend in American courts).

[178] The term "sneak wrap" refers to online TOU agreements. See Ed Foster, "Sneak Wrap" May Be a Good Way of Defining the Maze of Online Products, INFOWORLD (July 26, 1999).

[179] 86 F.3d 1447 (7th Cir. 1996).

contract law. In *ProCD*, the Seventh Circuit upheld a shrinkwrap agreement in which the licensee, a computer science graduate student, paid first and was given the software licensing agreement only after he paid for the CD–ROM. ProCD compiled a computer database called "Select Phone" that consisted of more than 3,000 telephone directories and sought to protect its investment in the database by requiring licensees to enter into a licensing agreement limiting use and containing restrictions. Matthew Zeidenberg purchased a copy of ProCD's Select Phone in Madison, Wisconsin, but chose to ignore the terms of the agreement prohibiting transfers or assignments of rights. Zeidenberg then formed a company to resell the information provided in ProCD's database. He charged customers for access to the information in Select Phone and made the information available over the World Wide Web. ProCD filed a copyright infringement lawsuit seeking an injunction against Zeidenberg.[180] Peter Alces describes the factual setting for this "instant" classic of avant-garde contract formation:

> The transactional context is familiar: Zeidenberg went into a store that sold packaged computer software and purchased ProCD's product, essentially an electronic phone directory. Terms disclosed within the box and terms disclosed when Zeidenberg launched the software limited his rights to disseminate the information contained on the software. Zeidenberg ignored the term limiting his right of dissemination and ProCD brought an action to enjoin his (mis)use of the product. Zeidenberg responded that his contract with ProCD was formed when he paid for the software and left the store with it. Not anything proposed or imposed by ProCD in the box or on the computer screen thereafter could be part of the parties' 'agreement.'[181]

The injunction prevented Zeidenberg from further disseminating ProCD's software since such distribution exceeded the scope of the rights granted in his license. The federal district court held ProCD's license agreements were unenforceable since the terms did not appear on the outside of the package and a customer could not be "bound by terms that were secret at the time of purchase."[182] The Seventh Circuit disagreed, ruling that ProCD's license agreements were enforceable. The Seventh Circuit applied U.C.C. Article 2 to the license agreement, noting contract formation may be manifested in any manner sufficient to show agreement.[183] The court rejected the argument that license agreement was preempted: "Contracts . . . generally affect only their parties; strangers may do as they please, so contracts do not create 'exclusive rights.'"[184]

The *ProCD* court decided that Zeidenberg accepted the software "after having an opportunity to read the license at leisure."[185] The court held that terms inside a box of software bind consumers who use the software after an opportunity to read the terms and to reject them by returning the product. The court reasoned that ProCD "extended an opportunity to reject if a buyer should find the license terms unsatisfactory."[186] The court rejected Zeidenberg's assertion he had no choice but to adhere to ProCD's terms

---

[180] A plaintiff seeking a preliminary injunction must establish; (1) that he is likely to succeed on the merits; (2) that he is likely to suffer irreparable harm in the absence of preliminary relief; (3) that the balance of equities tips in his favor; and (4) that an injunction is in the public interest.

[181] Peter A. Alces, The Moral Impossibility of Contract, 48 WM. & MARY L. REV. 1647, 1653–54 (2007).

[182] 86 F.3d at 1450.

[183] Id. (citing U.C.C. § 2–204).

[184] Id. at 1454.

[185] 86 F.3d 1447 at 1452.

[186] Id.

once he opened the package. The court also gave short shrift to Zeidenberg's argument that shrinkwrap license agreements must be conspicuous to be enforced. Finally, the court rejected the argument that the U.S. Copyright Act preempts software licenses because the rights created by ProCD's license agreement were not found to be the functional equivalent of any of the exclusive rights of the U.S. Copyright Act.[187] "Notice on the outside, terms on the inside, and a right to return the software for a refund if the terms are unacceptable (a right that the license expressly extends), may be a means of doing business valuable to buyers and sellers alike."[188]

The *ProCD* decision is emblematic in that it validated contracts taking the form of "payment now, terms later." The Seventh Circuit adopted a law and economics perspective in validating "rolling contracts" because the court regarded this method as an efficient form of private ordering. The court observed that "notice on the outside, terms on the inside, and a right to return" was a useful business practice.[189] Nevertheless, this decision raises the question of how far the classical doctrine of master of an offer can be stretched. James J. White, co-author of a leading treatise on Commercial law, gives this hypothetical:

> "Suppose that your form asserts that my intentional tying my shoelaces tomorrow will be assent to all of your terms. Since I cannot tie my shoelaces unintentionally and since I have no valet, I'm stuck, not so?" How would you respond?[190]

Professor White notes that the path of Internet contract law is already legitimating functionally equivalent contracts. He notes how UCITA rules "that one has "manifested assent," (agreed to something) if he "intentionally engages in conduct . . . with reason to know that the other party . . . may infer from the conduct that the person assents to the . . . term."[191] One way to interpret *ProCD* is as an efficient evolution of the concept that a software licensor is the master of its offer.

(2) Hill v. Gateway 2000, Inc.

In the past two decades, the tide turned in U.S. courts in favor of the enforceability of mass-market licenses beginning with Judge Frank Easterbrook's decisions in *ProCD, Inc. v. Zeidenberg*[192] and *Hill v. Gateway 2000*.[193] In *Hill*, Judge Easterbrook cited his own opinion in *ProCD* validating the practice of pay now, terms later.[194] In *Hill*, a consumer picked up the telephone, spoke with a Gateway customer representative, ordered a Gateway personal computer, and gave his credit card number. The box arrived, containing the computer and a list of terms, said to govern

---

[187] Id. at 1454–55.

[188] Id. at 1453.

[189] Id. at 1451.

[190] James J. White, Contracting Under Amended 2–207, 2004 WIS. L. REV. 723, 736; See Roger C. Bern, "Terms Later" Contracting: Bad Economics, Bad Morals, and a Bad Idea for a Uniform Law, Judge Easterbrook Notwithstanding, 12 J.L. & Pol'y 641, 643 (2004) ("Judge Easterbrook's imposition of the 'terms later' contracting rule in ProCD and Hill was itself devoid of legal, economic, and moral sanction. Thus his opinions in those cases provide no legitimate support for other court decisions or for any uniform law that would validate 'terms later' contracting.").

[191] Id.

[192] 86 F.3d 1447 (7th Cir. 1996).

[193] 105 F.3d 1147 (7th Cir. 1997).

[194] Hill v. Gateway 2000, Inc., 105 F.3d 1147, 1149 (7th Cir. 1997) (applying ProCD to the sale of a boxed computer and noting that "[p]laintiffs ask us to limit ProCD to software, but where's the sense in that? ProCD is about the law of contract, not the law of software.").

unless the customer returns the computer within thirty days. Are these terms effective as the parties' contract, or is the contract term-free because the order-taker did not read any terms over the phone and elicit the customer's assent? This was the fact pattern in *Hill v. Gateway 2000, Inc.,*[195] where Rich and Enzo Hill challenged an arbitration clause in Gateway's software license agreement included in a standard form contract shipped with their home computer. Gateway's standard business practice was to mail the computer system—with a software license agreement included inside the box. Included in the software license agreement was a predispute mandatory arbitration clause. Under a predominant purpose test, the sale of a personal computer system with software installed falls under U.C.C. Article 2. Nevertheless, in this case, the court enforced the license agreement ruling against the consumers. Under classical contract law, silence or inaction by a party generally does not constitute assent, "where circumstances or the previous course of dealing between the parties places the offeree under a duty to act or be bound, his silence or inactivity will constitute his assent."[196] The court upheld the entire agreement, including the arbitration clause, finding that the inaction of Hill constituted a manifestation of assent. Writing for the Seventh Circuit, Judge Easterbrook validated delayed contract formation; the consumer pays for the product and receives the terms in the packaging of the product when the shipper sends it at a later point.[197]

The court found Hill to be the offeree and Gateway the offeror who had the power to dictate the manner of acceptance. The court enforced a shrinkwrap agreement even though it was included in a sealed software box giving the licensees no opportunity to review the terms prior to payment.[198] The Seventh Circuit said that the "terms inside Gateway's box stand or fall together."[199] The U.S. Court of Appeals held that Gateway's license agreement was enforceable because of the consumer's decision to keep the Gateway system beyond the 30–day period specified in the agreement. The *Hill* court determined there was acceptance by silence and the entire mass-market agreement was binding including the arbitration clause.[200]

Judge Easterbrook reasoned that U.C.C. § 2–207, the battle of the forms, was inapplicable, since there was not an exchange of forms at all, but rather a single form drafted by the licensor.[201] His contention that a battle of the forms requires both a buyer and a seller form conflicts with Official Comment #1 to U.C.C. § 2–207, which makes clear that the battle of the forms also applies to a written confirmation of an

---

[195] Id.

[196] See Circuit City Stores, Inc. v. Najd, 294 F.3d 1104, 1109 (9th Cir. 2002); see also Quevedo v. Macy's, Inc., 798 F.Supp.2d 1122, 1133–35 (C.D. Cal. 2011) (holding that when a Macy's employee admitted receiving the SIS handbook and signing the Acknowledgment Form, his failure to opt out constituted assent to the arbitration agreement.).

[197] Id.

[198] "A customer picks up the phone, orders a computer, and gives a credit card number. Presently a box arrives, containing the computer and a list of terms, said to govern unless the customer returns the computer within 30 days. Are these terms effective as the parties' contract, or is the contract term-free because the order-taker did not read any terms over the phone and elicit the customer's assent?" Id. at 1148.

[199] Id.

[200] See Hill v. Gateway 2000, Inc., 105 F.3d 1147, 1149 (7th Cir. 1998) (upholding rolling contract requiring consumers to submit to arbitration because they had entered into an enforceable contract only after retaining the personal computer beyond the thirty-day period specified in the agreement.).

[201] The court found that the UCC's battle of the forms provision was not relevant to a single form sent by the licensor. ProCD v. Zeidenberg, 86 F.3d at 1452.

earlier oral agreement and therefore does not require two forms. A battle of the forms may involve only the seller's form and a confirmation. U.C.C. § 2–207 would apply because Gateway's form could be construed as a written confirmation where the agreement had been reached by Mr. and Mrs. Hill and the Gateway representative on the telephone.[202] U.C.C. § 2–207(2) would construe the additional or different terms would be construed as "proposals for addition to the contract" since the transaction was not between merchants.[203] In other words, the Hills would need to agree to the arbitration term in order for it to be part of the contract.

Since *Hill*, many courts find these "pay now, terms later" agreements to be broadly enforceable. "Payment preceding the revelation of full terms is common for air transportation, insurance, and many other endeavors."[204] The Gateway style license agreement is now referred to as the "rolling contract" because the consumer pays now and the terms are conveyed later. "In a layered or 'rolling contract' setting, the opportunity to review can come after the initiation of the process of contracting and any preliminary agreement."[205] Consumer advocates charge that rolling contracts are comparable the bait and switch practices prohibited by the Federal Trade Commission.[206] Rolling contracts, once considered unenforceable, are commonplace in all standard form contracts, not just in terms of use or software licensing agreements.

(C) Policing Cyberspace Contracts

Internet content providers have created what is, in effect, a "liability-free" zone to insulate themselves from paying consequential damages or other significant remedies in the event for any cause of action.[207] By agreeing to pre-dispute mandatory arbitration, class action waivers,[208] and waivers of all meaningful remedies, Internet

---

[202] Peter Alces also criticized Judge Easterbrook's application of U.C.C. Article 2 in the ProCD case: "Judge Easterbrook's analysis misunderstood the meaning and application of three Uniform Commercial Code sections. And it is not clear that the U.C.C. was in the least pertinent to the issue presented. His analysis of the apposite Contract doctrine, though, is revealing, and demonstrates well the significance of doctrine to theory. You cannot explain (or even posit) the theoretical basis of Contract until you first determine what Contract is, and what Contract is what Contract doctrine determines it to be." Peter A. Alces, The Moral Impossibility of Contract, 48 WM. & MARY L. REV. 1647, 1653 (2007).

[203] U.C.C. § 2–207(2) (2011).

[204] Hill v. Gateway, Id. at 1149.

[205] Frederick H. Miller, Uniform Computer Information Transactions Act, 10 HAWKLAND U.C.C. SERIES UCITA § 113:1.

[206] Jean Bracer, Delayed Disclosure in Consumer E–Commerce as an Unfair and Deceptive Practice, 46 WAYNE L. REV. 1805, 1852–53 (2000) (stating that "[h]olding back terms can be seen either as involving a deceptive representation or a deceptive omission" and that the FTC policy presumes that this practice will mislead consumers.).

[207] "A social media company can dodge jury verdicts, punitive damages, class actions, consequential damages, and any other meaningful remedy by requiring their users to submit to arbitration. One-sided terms of use that, in effect, divest consumers of fundamental rights raise serious concerns of procedural and substantive unfairness. 'Users of ADR are entitled to a process that is fundamentally fair.' Social networking sites have designed arbitration agreements that operate as poison pills that eliminate minimum adequate rights and remedies for consumers, while preserving the full array of remedies for these virtual businesses." Michael L. Rustad, Richard Buckingham, Diane D'Angelo, & Kate Durlacher, An Empirical Study of Predispute Mandatory Arbitration Clauses in Social Media Terms of Service, 34 U. ARK. LITTLE ROCK L. REV. 643, 645 (2012).

[208] Absent a class action waiver, individuals with functionally equivalent complaints against a company may join in a class suit or representative action where a federal court consolidates the complaints into a single proceeding. Arbitration clauses did not typically address the distinction between class actions filed in federal and state courts and class action arbitrations. Class actions in court have radically different procedural and substantive rights than so-called class action arbitrations. For a discussion of the differences

users very often waive the right to discovery,[209] a jury trial, and an appeal in a court of law.[210] The supporters of these mass-market license agreements contend that they are efficient and beneficial to consumers.

(1) Unconscionability

The public policy underlying the doctrine of unconscionability is protection of the weaker contracting party. However, courts are seldom willing to strike down an Internet-related U.C.C. § 2–302 builds upon the theory of the late Arthur Neff by addressing the issue of unconscionable contracts.[211] Many courts adopted the requirement that plaintiffs must prove both procedural and substantive unconscionability in order for a court to strike down a contract or clause.[212] The use of hidden terms is procedural unconscionability, whereas an exorbitant price constitutes substantive unconscionability. In order to strike down a one-sided license agreement or a clause in an agreement, the court must find both an unfair bargaining process (procedural unconscionability), as well as unfair terms (substantive unconscionability).[213]

A court will not typically find an Internet-related contract or clause to be unconscionable unless it finds procedural and substantive unconscionability. In *Brower*

---

between court and arbitration class actions, see AT&T Mobility LLC v. Concepcion, 131 S. Ct. 1740, 1757 (2011) (citing empirical research that revealed that class arbitrations did not result in final award on the merits).

[209] Arbitral providers will sometimes permit general discovery but this requires an application to an arbitrator and is subject to the discretion of the arbitrator. See Paul Bennett Marrow, When Discovery Seems Unavailable, It's Probably Available, 80 N.Y. ST. B. ASS'N J. 44, 44–46 (October 2008), http://www.marrowlaw.com/articles/pdf/Journal-oct08–marrow.pdf. (last visited Aug. 1, 2013). JAMS, for example, permits depositions and discovery at the arbitrator's discretion, which is similar to the rule for the AAA. Id.

[210] "Over the past few years, a quiet revolution has begun as many social networking sites (SNSs) impose predispute mandatory arbitration on consumers. Senator Patrick Leahy (D. Vt.) stated, 'Mandatory arbitration makes a farce of the right to a jury trial and the due process guaranteed to all Americans.' [Social Network Sites] SNSs generally require users to enter into two kinds of contractual relationships, terms of service agreements and privacy policies, as a condition for accessing their websites. Hundreds of millions of consumers enter into mandatory arbitration clauses with SNSs through browsewrap, clickwrap, or registration forms. After a consumer has registered or accessed a site, SNSs reserve the right to modify substantive terms, sometimes without notifying users. An SNS, website, or other brick-and-mortar company can reduce transaction costs by using a predispute mandatory arbitration clause because it need not defend lawsuits in state or federal court but in a forum where it can choose the arbitral provider and rules to govern the dispute. Michael L. Rustad, Richard Buckingham, Diane D'Angelo, & Kate Durlacher, An Empirical Study of Predispute Mandatory Arbitration Clauses in Social Media Terms of Service, 34 U. ARK. LITTLE ROCK L. REV. 643, 644 (2012).

[211] See Arthur Neff, Unconscionability and the Code—The Emperor's New Clause, 115 U. PA. L. REV. 485, 487 (1967).

[212] Most courts require a finding of procedural unconscionability and substantive unconscionability. Procedural unconscionability concerns the formalities of making the contract, while substantive unconscionability concerns the terms of the contract itself. State ex rel. Vincent v. Schneider, 194 S.W.3d 853, 858 (Mo. en banc, 2006).

[213] See, e.g., Riensche v. Cingular Wireless, L.L.C., No. C06–1325Z, 2006 WL 3827477, at *9 (W.D. Wash. Dec. 27, 2006) (holding that the forum selection clause was substantively unconscionable); Comb v. PayPal, Inc., 218 F. Supp. 2d 1165, 1173, 1176 (N.D. Cal. 2002) (refusing to enforce pre-dispute mandatory arbitration clause in user agreement ruling that the forum selection clause was substantively and procedurally unconscionable). Additionally, the doctrine of unconscionability has been applied in a wide array of contexts. See, e.g., Scott v. Cingular Wireless, 161 P.3d 1000, 1006 (Wash. 2007) (holding a class action waiver unconscionable); Gatton v. T–Mobile USA, 61 Cal. Rptr. 3d 344, 358 (Cal. Ct. App. 2007) (holding a class action waiver unconscionable and unenforceable); Aral v. EarthLink, Inc., 36 Cal. Rptr. 3d 229, 238 (Cal. 2005) (holding a class action waiver unconscionable).

v. Gateway 2000, Inc., a New York state court modified an order that would have required a New York consumer to arbitrate a consumer claim in Chicago, Illinois.[214] In *Brower*, a consumer purchased a Gateway computer through the telephone or mail. The computer was shipped in a box, together with its "Standard Terms and Conditions Agreement," which provided, "By keeping your Gateway 2000 computer system beyond 30 days after the date of delivery, you accept these Terms and Conditions." The Agreement provided that any disputes would be exclusively settled by binding arbitration in Chicago, according to the rules of the International Chamber of Commerce. Gateway's arbitral provider charged an upfront $4,000 non-refundable registration fee to arbitrate personal computer claims generally valued at less than $1,000. Gateway's predispute mandatory arbitration clause reads as follows:

> Any dispute or controversy arising out of or relating to this Agreement or its interpretation shall be settled exclusively and finally by arbitration. The arbitration shall be conducted in accordance with the Rules of Conciliation and Arbitration of the International Chamber of Commerce. The arbitration shall be conducted in Chicago, Illinois, U.S.A. before a sole arbitrator. Any award rendered in any such arbitration proceeding shall be final and binding on each of the parties, and judgment may be entered thereon in a court of competent jurisdiction.[215]

Brower was the lead plaintiff in a class action alleging that Gateway's licensing practices constituted unfair and deceptive practices. Brower argued that it was unconscionable to be required to arbitrate in distant forum under rules promulgated by the International Chamber of Commerce ("ICC") and that the ICC's Rules of Conciliation and Arbitration imposed prohibitively expensive costs in relation to the size of their claim. "For example, a claim of less than $50,000 required advance fees of $4,000 (more than the cost of most Gateway products), of which the $2,000 registration fee was nonrefundable even if the consumer prevailed at the arbitration."[216] The ICC fees did not include the consumer's travel expenses that would be "$1,000 per customer in this action, as well as bear the cost of Gateway's legal fees if the consumer did not prevail at the arbitration" because the ICC adopted a loser pays rule.[217]

The *Brower* court upheld the license agreement reasoning that the consumer had the option of making an alternative purchase and was therefore not in a position of take it or leave it and could have returned the personal computer for a refund.[218] The court also found "a valid agreement to arbitrate between the parties," but ruled that the agreement "should be modified, on the law and the facts, to the extent of vacating that portion of the arbitration agreement as requires arbitration before the International Chamber of Commerce."[219] The court replaced the ICC with the American Arbitration Association ("AAA"), but could not determine on the record whether their charges were "so egregiously oppressive that they, too, would be unconscionable."[220] The United States Supreme Court acknowledges that high

---

[214] 676 N.Y.S.2d 569 (N.Y.A.D. 1st Dept. 1998).

[215] Id.

[216] Id. at 571.

[217] Id.

[218] Id. at 574.

[219] Id. at 575.

[220] Id.

arbitration costs can in and of themselves preclude a litigant from asserting her rights.[221]

The problem with unconscionability is that judges are reluctant to strike down substantive provisions because they adopt the legal fiction that a bargain was reached in a webwrap license. Courts are reticent to strike down one-sided and aggressive terms in webwraps.[222] One reform proposal for making fairer webwraps would be to presume that these standard forms are unconscionable except if validated by legislative decree or if there were meaningful alternatives in the marketplace.[223] Reconcepualizing unconscionability will lead to more balanced terms, less one-sided terms in webwraps.[224]

(2) Public Policy Limitations

The Uniform Computer Information Transactions Act ("UCITA") disfavors gag clauses that attempt to restrain public discussion about software or other digital content.[225] Courts will police Internet contracts violating "fundamental public policies."[226] UCITA § 105(c) forbids licensing terms that prohibit the discussion of the quality of performance of computer information. Courts will not invalidate choice of forum clauses except on strong public policy grounds that "enforcement of the clause deprives the plaintiff of his day in court."[227] UCITA seemingly gives the courts discretion to "avoid a result contrary to public policy, in each case to the extent that the interest in enforcement is clearly outweighed by a public policy against enforcement of the term" though there is no case law interpreting this provision.[228] The UCITA Standby Committee would go even further in prohibiting clauses restricting public comment:

> In a transaction in which a copy of computer information is offered in its final form to the public including consumers, a term of a contract is unenforceable to the extent that the term prohibits an end-user licensee from engaging in otherwise lawful public discussion of the quality of performance of the computer information. However, this section does not preclude enforcement of a contract term that establishes or enforces rights under trade secret, trademark, defamation, commercial disparagement, or other laws.[229]

Courts have rarely invalidated terms of service on public policy grounds. In *People v. Network Ass'n*,[230] New York Attorney General Elliot Spitzer challenged a "no public comment" rule in a license agreement. In that case, a New York trial court found a term in a license agreement that restrained reviews of the software in publications to be an invalid contractual restriction.[231] In *Network Ass'n*, Network Solutions, the

---

[221] Green Tree Fin. Corp. v. Randolph, 531 U.S. 79, 90 (2000).

[222] NANCY S. KIM, WRAP CONTRACTS: FOUNDATIONS AND RAMIFICATIONS 208 (2013),

[223] Id.

[224] Id.

[225] UCITA, Id. at § 105, cmt. 4.

[226] UCITA § 105(c).

[227] Misui & Co. (USA) v. Mira M/V, 111 F.3d 33, 35 (5th Cir. 1997).

[228] UCITA § 105(b).

[229]Report of UCITA Standby Committee, Recommendation 5 (Dec. 17, 2001) available at http://www.law.upenn.edu/bll /archives/ulc/ucita/UCITA_Dec01_Proposal.htm (last visited June 14, 2013).

[230] People v. Network Ass'n, 758 N.Y.S.2d 466 (2003).

[231] Id.

maker of McAfee anti-virus software, licensed its products over the Internet including a clickwrap agreement with the anti-publication term. The license agreement stated that the customer "shall not disclose the results of any benchmark test to any third party without Network Associates' prior written approval."[232] Network Associates prohibited its customers from publishing reviews of the software without their prior consent. The litigation stemmed from Network Associates' refusal to enjoin the publication of a negative review of their Gauntlet firewall program in comparison to six other software security programs. Network Associates protested the publication of the review quoting language from restrictive clauses of Gauntlet's clickwrap agreement. A U.S. court may theoretically strike the term or limit its application "so as to avoid a result contrary to public policy."[233] The software license agreement challenged by the state attorney general contained the following terms:

> Installing this software constitutes acceptance of the terms and conditions of the license agreement in the box. Please read the license agreement before installation. Other rules and regulations of installing the software are:
>
> (A) The product cannot be rented, loaned, or leased—you are the sole owner of this product.
>
> (B) The customer shall not disclose the result of any benchmark test to any third party without Network Associates' prior written approval.
>
> (C) The customer will not publish reviews of this product without prior consent from Network Associates, Inc.[234]

The New York trial court enjoined the enforcement of "language restricting the right to publish the results of testing and review."[235] In the past four decades since the advent of software licensing, few courts have addressed the enforceability of gag clauses. While there is no case law on point, it is likely that no court in the Eurozone would enforce these clauses. However, prohibitions against public comment clauses would likely be an unfair practice under the EU Directive on Unfair Contract Terms.

(3) Copyright Misuse

The intersection between copyright law and contract law is the province of licensing. Critics charged that UCITA created an imbalance by allowing software licensors to use contract law as the backdoor achieving purposes unwarranted by U.S. copyright law.[236] The Reporters of the Principles of Software Contracts describe copyright misuse as an equitable doctrine assertable as a defense to infringement. "When a court holds particular conduct misuse, the rightholder cannot enforce its

---

[232] Id. at 467.

[233] UCITA § 105(b).

[234] Id. at 467.

[235] Id. at 470.

[236] "Traditionally, contract and copyright co-existed peacefully, with contract law providing the legal framework for transactions in copyrighted works. UCITA threatens that relationship by empowering providers to impose unilaterally license terms that contravene foundational copyright policies and current user expectations. The act's overall framework and specific default rules support enforcement of mass-market adhesion contracts that restrict uses of information protected by current copyright law. In response to the threat of contractual foreclosure of user rights, some commentators have observed that copyright law may, in the future, serve as a "consumer protection" law, limiting the scope of restrictive contractual provisions through judicial application of doctrines such as preemption or copyright misuse." Deborah Tussey, UCITA, Copyright, and Capture, 21 CARDOZO ARTS & ENT. L.J. 319, 321 (2003).

licensing rights until it purges itself of the misuse. Copyright misuses is frequently a defense interposed in a breach of licensing agreement case.

"In subsection (c), the Principles take the position that, as a matter of intellectual property policy, when a claim in breach of contract is brought, courts should refuse to enforce any provision in the agreement that would have been considered misuse had the action been one for infringement."[237] The Reporters give the following illustration of copyright misuse in license agreements:

A's copyright on a spreadsheet program expires in 2090. A's standard form provides that its transferees agree not to implement the ideas contained in the program and/or develop a competing program independently for a period of 99 years from the date of the agreement. In 2009, A transfers its software to B using the standard form. The provision constitutes copyright misuse and is unenforceable. It would likely also be unenforceable under a preemption analysis.[238] The federal preemption doctrine has its roots in the Supremacy Clause of the Constitution, which provides that the Constitution and the laws of the United States "shall be the supreme Law of the Land."[239] In software licensing cases, the argument is that the federal copyright law preempts software licensing, which is state contract law.

Licensees in Internet-related licensing disputes may assert copyright misuse as an equitable defense when sued for copyright infringement.[240] Copyright misuse is a doctrine that licensees can sometimes deploy to challenge anticompetitive terms in software licenses that expand rights beyond the scope of the U.S. Copyright Act.[241] The first case to recognize the defense of copyright misuse was *Lasercomb Am., Inc. v. Reynolds*,[242] in which the Fourth Circuit imported the doctrine of patent misuse established in *Morton Salt Co. v. G.S. Suppinger*.[243] In *Lasercomb*, the Fourth Circuit stated, "Since copyright and patent law serve parallel interests, a 'misuse' defense should apply to infringement actions brought to vindicate either right."[244] Legal transplants can originate in other branches of law or in other legal cultures.[245]

Patent law represents a "carefully crafted bargain for encouraging the creation and disclosure of new, useful, and non-obvious advances in technology."[246] The *Lasercomb* court stretched the patent misuse doctrine to copyright law for the first time. Specifically, the misuse of copyright defense precludes a copyright holder from

---

[237] Principles of the Law of Software Contracts, Id. at § 1.09, cmt. d (2010).

[238] Principles of the Law of Software Contracts, Id. at § 1.09, illust. 8 (2010).

[239] Fid. Fed. Savings & Loan Ass'n v. de la Cuesta, 458 U.S. 141, 152 (1982) (interpreting U.S. Const., art. VI, cl. 2).

[240] Mark A. Lemley, Intellectual Property and Shrinkwrap Licenses, 68 S. CAL. L. REV. 1239 (1995) ("Software vendors are attempting en masse to "opt out" of intellectual property law by drafting license provisions that compel their customers to adhere to more restrictive provisions than copyright law would require.").

[241] Mark A. Lemley, Beyond Preemption: The Law and Policy of Intellectual Property Licensing, 87 CAL. L. REV. 111, 151–58 (1999).

[242] 911 F.2d 970, 977 (4th Cir. 1992).

[243] 314 U.S. 488 (1942).

[244] Lasercomb, 911 F.2d at 976.

[245] Julie Mertus, From Legal Transplants to Transformative Justice: Human Rights and the Promise of Transnational Civil Society, 14 AM U. INT'L L. REV. 1335, 1349 (1999).

[246] Bonito Boats, Inc. v. Thunder Craft Boats, Inc., 489 U.S. 141, 146 (1989).

recovering for copyright infringement "where the holder has attempt[ed] to suppress any attempt by the licensee to independently implement the idea which [the copyrighted material] expresses."[247]

(4) State Unfair and Deceptive Trade Practices Act

License agreements are also challengeable under state consumer law. Every state has enacted an unfair and deceptive trade practices act, which is the Swiss Army Knife for many state attorney generals and private attorneys general. Massachusetts' Chapter 93A, for example, allows private litigants as well as the attorney general to pursue actions. Chapter 93A permits plaintiffs to recover for up to three but not less than two times actual damages for willful or knowing violations of the act. Double or treble damages are awarded for "willful or knowing" violations of section 2 of Chapter 93A.[248] To date, few plaintiffs have challenged license agreements, where the rights and remedies are tilted in favor of the dominant party.

(D) Preemption of Licensing

In order to be preempted, a claim must involve a work "within the subject matter of copyright."[249] The Principles of the Law of Software Contracts makes it clear that federal intellectual property rights preempt licensing.[250] Plaintiffs have not been successful in persuading courts that the U.S. Copyright Act preempts licensing provisions. A large number of courts have ruled that licensing claims involving the subject matter of copyright do not constitute equivalent rights under the Federal Copyright Act.[251] "Intellectual property law usually does not preempt breach-of-contract actions or the enforcement of terms of private agreements because restrictive

---

[247] Id. at 371.

[248] M.G.L.A. ch. 93A, § 11.

[249] 17 U.S.C. § 301(a).

[250] Preemption may be either statutorily or constitutionally based and either express or implied. In its § 301, the U.S. Copyright Act contains an express preemption provision, stating that "all legal or equitable rights that are equivalent to any of the exclusive rights within the general scope of copyright . . . and come within the subject matter of copyright . . . are governed exclusively by this title." 17 U.S.C. § 301(a). Courts interpret this language to mean that a cause of action is preempted if the subject matter at issue is within the scope of the Act and the rights a party seeks to enforce or protect are not qualitatively different from rights under the Act. The Patent Act, in contrast, contains no such express language. The ultimate source of authority for implied preemption is the Supremacy Clause of the U.S. Constitution, which states, "Th[e] Constitution, and the Laws of the United States which shall be made in Pursuance thereof . . . shall be the supreme Law of the Land; and the Judges in every State shall be bound thereby, any Thing in the Constitution or Laws of any State to the Contrary notwithstanding." U.S. Const. art. VI, cl. 2. Whether the Intellectual Property Clause itself is an independent source of implied preemption is an open question. The Intellectual Property Clause states, "The Congress shall have Power . . . To promote the Progress of Science and useful Arts, by securing for limited Times to Authors and Inventors the exclusive Right to their respective Writings and Discoveries." Id., art. I, § 8, cl. 8. Because the intellectual property statutes are enacted pursuant to this power, the extent of Supremacy Clause preemption is necessarily related to the interpretation of the Intellectual Property Clause." Principles of the Law of Software Contracts, Id. at § 1.09 (2010), cmt.

[251] Utopia Provider Sys., Inc. v. Pro–Med Clinical Sys., L.L.C., 596 F.3d 1313, 1326–27 (11th Cir. 2010) (express contract); Bowers v. Baystate Techs., Inc., 320 F.3d 1317, 1324–26 (Fed. Cir. 2003) (applying First Circuit law to an express contract in a software license); Wrench, 256 F.3d at 456 (implied-in-fact contract); ProCD, 86 F.3d at 1454–55 (express contract in a software license); Nat'l Car Rental Sys., Inc. v. Computer Assocs. Int'l, Inc., 991 F.2d 426, 431 (8th Cir. 1993) (express licensing agreement); Taquino v. Teledyne Monarch Rubber, 893 F.2d 1488, 1490, 1501 (5th Cir. 1990) (express contract); Acorn Structures, Inc. v. Swantz, 846 F.2d 923, 926 (4th Cir. 1988) (per curiam) (express contract).

by operating against the world, compete directly with the federal system."[252] "Of course, preemption cannot be avoided simply by labeling a claim "breach of contract."[253] A plaintiff must actually allege the elements of an enforceable contract (whether express or implied-in-fact), including offer, acceptance, and consideration, in addition to adequately alleging the defendant's breach of the contract."[254]

§ 4.4   UNIFORM ELECTRONIC TRANSACTIONS ACT

(A) Provisions of UETA

The Uniform Electronic Transactions Act ("UETA") is a model state law act proposed by the National Conference of Commissioners on Uniform State Laws ("NCCUSL") to create more uniformity in state law for electronic transactions. UETA was enacted to respond to the "widespread use of the Internet for sale of goods and to provide uniformity."[255] UETA is solely concerned with the validity of records and digital signatures and is therefore not a statute concerned with substantive online contract law. The purpose of UETA is to remove barriers to E–Commerce, implement reasonable practices, and harmonize contracting procedural rules by enabling the electronic retention and transmission of digital information. UETA is strictly a procedural statute that modifies the meaning of writings and signatures. UETA substitutes the "record" for a paper-based writing and treats signatures in electronic form as signatures made by pen.

The UETA is law in forty-seven of the fifty states and the District of Columbia, as well as by the territories of Puerto Rico and the Virgin Islands. What this means is that an e-signature or e-record has the same validity as a paper and pen signature or writing. The UETA adopts a non-regulatory approach to electronic signatures and writings and validates electronic signatures and records in order to remove barriers to electronic commerce. A document bearing an electronic signature may be contested on the ground that an alleged signatory did not execute, adopt, or authorize the electronic signature. A digital signature is an electronic identifier created by computer with the same legal validity as a handwritten signature. The UETA "applies to any electronic record or electronic signature created, generated, sent, communicated, received, or stored on or after the effective date of the statute."[256]

> For example, when a person orders goods or services through a vendor's website, the person will be required to provide information as part of a process, which will result in receipt of the goods or services. When the customer ultimately gets to the last step and clicks "I agree," the person has adopted the process and has done so with the intent to associate the person with the record of that process. The actual effect of the electronic signature will be determined from all the surrounding circumstances, however, the person adopted a process which the circumstances indicate s/he intended to have the effect of getting the goods/services and being

---

[252] Principles of the Law of Software Contracts, Id. at § 1.09 (2010), cmt.

[253] "A breach of contract claim requires proof of actual damages. In order to recover for a breach of contract plaintiffs must prove by a preponderance of the evidence that the breaches are the cause of actual damages to the plaintiff." Pilar Servs. v. NCI Info. Sys., 569 F. Supp. 2d 563, 568 (E.D. Va. 2008).

[254] Forest Park Pictures v. Universal TV Network, Inc., 683 F.3d 424, 432 (2d Cir. 2012).

[255] JAMES J. WHITE & ROBERT S. SUMMERS, UNIFORM COMMERCIAL CODE, § 1–3 at 5 (6th ed. 2010).

[256] Section 4 states that the Act " . . . applies to any electronic record or electronic signature created, generated, sent, communicated, received, or stored." UETA, Id. at § 4.

bound to pay for them. The adoption of the process carried the intent to do a legally significant act, the hallmark of a signature.[257]

If there is a conflict between U.C.C. Article 2 governing sales, and the UETA, U.C.C. Article 2 holds the trump card. The UETA defines the "electronic signature" as an "electronic sound, symbol, or process attached to or logically associated with a record, and executed or adopted by a person with the intent to sign the record."[258] Section 5(a) of the UETA does not mandate that a consumer or other party use electronic signatures or records. However, if the parties agree to use electronic signatures or records, the courts will validate them.[259] UETA Section 5(b) applies "only to transactions between parties, each of which has agreed to conduct transactions by electronic means."[260]

Section 6 states that UETA's purpose is "to facilitate and promote commerce and governmental transactions by validating and authorizing the use of electronic records and electronic signatures."[261] Section 7 of the UETA provides "a record or signature may not be denied legal effect or enforceability solely because it is in electronic form."[262] Section 7(b) of the UETA legitimizes the concept of electronic contract, providing "a contract may not be denied legal effect or enforceability solely because an electronic record was used in its formation."[263] UETA is neither a general contracting statute nor a digital signatures statute. As of September 15, 2012, eighty U.S. courts weighed in on UETA-related issues in court decisions. UETA is the most influential state statute validating a wide range of e-contracts and e-transactions.

(B) UETA's Scope

UETA applies to electronic records and electronic signatures relating to a transaction.[264] The scope of UETA is "inherently limited by the fact that it only applies to transactions related to business, commercial (including consumer) and governmental matters."[265] Section 8(a) of UETA provides the ground rules for what constitutes an electronic record.[266] Electronic records must minimally be "capable of retention."[267] An online communication that prevents the recipient from either printing or storing the record does not qualify as a retained record.

For electronic contracts to be viable there must be some mechanism of attribution,[268] so the parties know each other's identity and authority to contract. For

---

[257] UETA, Id. at § 2, cmt. 7.

[258] Id. at § 2(8).

[259] Id. at § 5(a).

[260] Id.

[261] Id. at § 6.

[262] Id. at § 7.

[263] Id. at § 7(b).

[264] Id. at § 3.

[265] Id. at § 3, cmt. 1.

[266] Id. at § 8(a).

[267] Id. at § 8.

[268] An "attribution procedure" is a procedure used to identify the person who sent an electronic message or to verify the integrity of its content. In general, an attribution procedure has substantive effect only if it was agreed to or adopted by the parties or established by applicable law. Agreement to or adoption of a procedure may occur directly between the two parties or through a third party. For example, the operator of a system that includes information provided by third parties may arrange with database providers and customers for use of a particular attribution procedure. Those arrangements establish an attribution procedure between the customers and the database providers. An attribution procedure may also be established by two parties in the expectation that a third party may rely on it. For example, a digital

example, passwords are a well-established attribution method; a Westlaw user supplies a password authenticating the user's identity for each login. The attribution of messages between sender and receiver is a key feature of the infrastructure of online contracting. Attribution procedures also verify whether a message contains errors or alterations using algorithms or other codes, identifying words or numbers.

(C) UETA Requires Parties' Agreement

The parties must agree to contract electronically in order for digital signatures to be binding. Section 5 of UETA notes that the model act "does not require a record or signature to be created, generated, sent, communicated, received, stored, or otherwise processed or used by electronic means or in electronic form."[269] UETA only applies where the parties agree to enter into contracts electronically. Whether the parties agree to conduct a transaction by electronic means is determined from the context and surrounding circumstances, including the parties' conduct.[270] Section 5 makes it clear that UETA "is intended to facilitate the use of electronic means, but does not require the use of electronic records and signatures."[271] Comment 5 to Section 5 states:

> If Automaker, Inc. were to issue a recall of automobiles via its Internet website, it would not be able to rely on this Act to validate that notice in the case of a person who never logged on to the website, or indeed, had no ability to do so, notwithstanding a clause in a paper purchase contract by which the buyer agreed to receive such notices in such a manner.[272]

UETA states, "A record or signature may not be denied legal effect or enforceability solely because it is in electronic form."[273] Section 8 of UETA requires that electronic record be capable of retention or enforcement will be denied. "If a sender inhibits the ability of a recipient to store or print an electronic record," it is not enforceable against the recipient.[274]

(D) UETA's Risk Allocation for Errors

UETA's method for allocating the risk of errors in electronic records places the risk of loss of a transmission error on the party failing to employ an agreed upon security procedure. Thus, if both parties fail to use an agreed upon security procedure, the rule does not apply. The party following reasonable security procedures will avoid the effect of the changed or erroneous electronic record only if the other party deviates upon the agreed upon procedure. Persons entering into electronic contracts must be able to prevent and correct errors.

---

signature may be issued to an individual pursuant to an agreement between the issuer and the individual, but then accepted or relied on by another party in a separate transaction. Use of the signature is an attribution procedure in that transaction. Similarly, a group of member companies may establish attribution procedures intended to bind members in dealing with one another. Such arrangements are attribution procedures under this Act." UCITA, Id. at § 102(3).

[269] Id. at § 5(a).
[270] Id. at § 5(b).
[271] Id. at § 5, cmt. 1.
[272] Id. at § 5, cmt. 5.
[273] Id. at § 7.
[274] Id. at § 8.

§ 4.5   THE ELECTRONIC SIGNATURES IN GLOBAL AND NATIONAL COMMERCE ACT

The Electronic Signatures in Global and National Commerce Act (E–Sign Act), signed into law on June 30, 2000, provides a general rule of validity for electronic records and signatures for transactions in or affecting interstate or foreign commerce.[275] The federal E–Sign Act establishes that electronic signatures and records are functionally and legally equivalent to signatures or writings on paper.[276] Given that the vast majority of states had enacted UETA by 2000, the federal statute duplicated what was already well-established in the states. Together, UETA and E-Sign make it clear that courts recognize technologies for e-signatures that presently take the following forms:

Password or personal identification number (PIN)—a set of characters, numbers, or combination thereof, created by the system user and encrypted when transmitted over an open network;

Smart Card—a plastic card (like an ATM or credit card) containing a microprocessor or "chip" that can generate, store, and process data and that has programming capacity for activation when the user enters another identifier such as a PIN; Biometrics—technological method that measures and analyzes unique human characteristics, such as fingerprints, eye retinas and irises, voice and facial patterns, and hand measurements. The devices consist of a reader or sensor, and software that converts the received information into a digital form, and a database that stores the individual's known biometric data;

Digitized Signature—a type of biometric, consisting of a graphical image of a handwritten signature, entered using a special digitized pen and pad input device that is automatically compared with a stored copy of the digitized signature of the user and authenticated if the two signatures meet specifications for similarity; and

Digital Signature—a unique signature produced on a message that uses a key (a large, binary number) known only by the signer, and a signature algorithm (mathematical formula) that is publicly known.[277]

The federal statute treats electronic signatures the same as pen-and-ink signatures and records the same as legally required writings. The E–Sign Act allows the use of electronic records to satisfy any statute, regulation, or rule of law requiring that such information be provided in writing, if the consumer has affirmatively consented to such use and has not withdrawn such consent. The sphere E-Sign's application is less than what one would expect for a federal statute, because Congress included a provision explicitly stating that its provisions are superseded or modified by

---

[275] 15 U.S.C. §§ 7000 et seq.

[276] E-Sign provides that no contract, signature, or record shall be denied legal effect solely because it is in electronic form. Nor may a contract relating to a transaction be denied legal effect solely because an electronic signature or record was used in its formation. E-Sign, Id. at § 101(a).

[277] Kathy D. Smith, Chief Counsel & Milton Brown, Deputy General Counsel, Electronic Signatures: A Review of the Exceptions to the Electronic Signatures in Global and National Commerce Act (June 2003) at 6.

the UCC, which is a state statute.[278] Congress incorporated a saving clause, which defers to UETA where there is a conflict with E–SIGN.[279]

The vast majority of states already enacted UETA by the time Congress passed E–Sign in June of 2000. White and Summers describe the relationship between E–Sign and UETA: "E–Sign covers the same territory as UETA . . . Congress feared that UETA would not create uniformity in electronic contracting law because some states might not adopt it" and others threatened to adopt non-uniform amendments.[280] Section 102 of E–Sign provides an exemption to E-Signs's general preemption of state law:

> This section allows states to adopt statutes, regulations, and other rules of law to modify, limit, or supersede the provisions of section 101 with respect to state law. The state's law must be consistent with E–Sign *and* meet one of two conditions. The law must: (1) constitute an enactment or adoption of the Uniform Electronic Transactions Act (UETA) as approved by the National Conference of Commissioners on Uniform State Laws (NCCUSL) in 1999; or (2) specify alternative procedures or requirements for the use or acceptance of electronic records or electronic signatures, if the alternative requirements are technology neutral and do not accord greater legal status or significance to a specific technology.[281]

E–Sign carves out nine statutory exceptions outside its sphere: ((1) wills, codicils, and testamentary trusts; (2) laws governing domestic law matters; (3) state Uniform Commercial Code, except section 1–107 and 1–206, Articles 2 and 2A; (4) court orders or notices; (5) utility cancellation notices; (6) default, foreclosure, or eviction notices; (7) health or life insurance benefit cancellation notices; (8) product recall notices; and (9) hazardous, toxic, or dangerous materials notices.[282] Section 102(a)(2) gives the States the power to exempt certain further documents from E–Sign. Each of these exceptions reflects well-established law and the consumer expectation that a paper-based document memorialize the transaction. Transfers of land or dissolutions of marriage should not be executed by e-mail. Congress considered these carve-outs as documents where the consumer should receive a hard copy not just an electronic document.

E–Sign insures that courts may not deny the legal effect or the enforceability of contracts solely because the parties formed the contract through electronic signatures or electronic records. Internet-related contracts might take the form of sales, leases or the licensing of intellectual property. E–Sign validates electronic signatures to authenticate the identity of the sender of a message or the signer of a document, and ultimately to ensure the original content of the sent message or document is unchanged. Digital signatures can be automatically time stamped and are more transportable than physical

---

[278] Id. ("Apparently the drafters of revised Article 1 and Amended Article 2 feared that the revision might not get the protection of the 103 exemption [of E-Sign] because of the "in effect" language.").

[279] "At the date this report, 49 states, the District of Columbia, and the Virgin Islands, have adopted a version of an electronic transactions law. Although some state electronic transactions are modeled closely after E-Sign or UETA, others are incorporated into state commercial and business codes and contain language unique to the state and that refer to the underlying substantive law governing the transactions. Where a state has an electronic transactions law that complies with section 102 of E-Sign, the state law controls whether electronic signatures and documents relating to the nine E-Sign exceptions are to be given the same legal validity and effect as paper documents." Id. at 9.

[280] James J. White & Robert S. Summers, Uniform Commercial Code, § 1–3 at 5 (6th ed. 2010).

[281] Kathy Smith & Milton Brown, Electronic Signatures (June 2003), Id. at 8.

[282] E-Sign, Id. at § 103.

signatures. E-Sign § 101(c) is a rule of consent requiring that consumers affirmatively consent before receiving electronic communications in lieu of a writing.[283] Consumers must specifically opt-in to receive electronic communications.

The consent rule also gives consumers a prescribed method for withdrawing consent. Consumer disclosures are required if an electronic record is substituted for a paper based record. Consumers may not be compelled to use electronic contracting and must consent to this method of entering into contracts. Section 101(c)(1)(C)(ii) states that a consumer's consent to receive electronic records is valid only if the consumer consents electronically or confirms his or her consent electronically. The consumer's consent must demonstrate that the consumer can access the information that is the subject of the consent. Section 101(c) gives consumers the right to demand that sellers or services providers make a record available on paper or in another electronic form.

§ 4.6   REVISED U.C.C. ARTICLE 1

Article 1 of the Uniform Commercial Code ("U.C.C.") sets forth basic definitions and concepts that are utilized throughout the other articles of the U.C.C. In December 2001, the joint sponsors of the UCC, the National Conference of Commissioners on Uniform State Laws and the American Law Institute, revised Article 1. Section 1–108 is entitled, "Relation to Electronic Signatures in Global and National Commerce Act." This section makes it clear that U.C.C. Article 1:

> modifies, limits, and supersedes the federal Electronic Signatures in Global and National Commerce Act, 15 U.S.C. Section 7001 et seq., except that nothing in this article modifies, limits, or supersedes Section 7001(c) of that Act or authorizes electronic delivery of any of the notices described in Section 7003(b) of that Act.[284]

E–Sign "provides that the 'provisions of Section 7001 of this title shall not apply to a contract or other record to the extent it is governed by . . . the Uniform Commercial Code, as in effect in any State, other than sections 1–107 and 1–206 and Articles 2 and 2A."[285]

§ 4.7   UNIFORM COMPUTER INFORMATION TRANSACTIONS ACT

(A) History of U.C.C. Article 2B

In the early 1990s, lawyers representing the software industry began to press for a specialized law addressing software licensing. The empirical reality is that the licensing of downloadable software shares little common ground with the traditional attributes of a sale of goods. With the sale of goods, title passes when the buyer accepts and pays in accordance with the contract, and it is marked by physical delivery of tangible goods. No title passes with the licensing of software. A licensee is typically not permitted to resell licensed software. Software, unlike goods, may be delivered computer-to-computer without human intervention. The licensor retains title to software or other information and imposes restriction on use. No mass-market software

---

[283] Section 101(c)(1)(C)(ii) of E-Sign requires businesses to obtain from consumers electronic consent or confirmation to receive information electronically that a law requires to be in writing.

[284] U.C.C. § 1–108.

[285] KATHY SMITH & MILTON BROWN, ELECTRONIC SIGNATURES (June 2003), Id. at 24.

developer could stay in business if all rights were transferred to the software with the first sale. Licensing is a useful and necessary legal invention to permit software developers to realize their investment.

Industry, consumer and bar association groups hotly debated the innumerable drafts of Article 2B, which preceded UCITA. In March of 1995, the National Conference of Uniform State Laws (NCCUSL) approved a "hub and spoke" model that treated Article 2B as a separate spoke sharing hub provisions with Articles 2 and 2A. The hub and spoke model sought to harmonize Articles 2, 2A and 2B by forging general principles common to each article. The drafters of U.C.C. Article 2B envisioned a common hub and separate spokes for Articles 2, 2A and 2B (corresponding to sales, leases, and licenses). A wide variety of stakeholders such as The Software Publishers Association ("SPA") opposed the hub and spoke model. The SPA was critical of the model for being too anti-industry and too pro-consumer. A corporate counsel for a Fortune 500 company complained that the drafting committee included too many law professors with a pro-consumer bias. Other critics argued just the opposite, that Article 2B was a statute by and for the software industry against consumers. Consumer representatives argued that Article 2B was anti-consumer and that they were inadequately represented in the drafting process.

(B) UCITA: A Licensing Law for the Internet

In the late 1980s, the American Bar Association's Business Law Section considered revising commercial law to encompass software contracts. The impetus to create specialized legal infrastructure for software licensing gained speed in the early 1990s when NCCUSL[286] and the American Law Institute ("ALI") joined forces to develop a separate article of the Uniform Commercial Code called Article 2B.[287] The avowed purpose of U.C.C. Article 2B was to revise U.C.C. Article 2 concepts for the commercial realities of software licenses. The ABA's Business Law Section created a software licensing committee that explored the creation of separate software contracting law. The U.C.C. sponsoring organizations, ALI and NCCUSL, envisioned a common hub and separate spokes for Articles 2, 2A, and 2B that correspond to sales, leases, and licenses, respectively. The death knell for the hub and spoke model sounded in late July 1995, when NCCUSL abandoned the entire hub and spoke architecture in favor of making Article 2B a separate U.C.C. article.[288] NCCUSL eliminated the hub and spoke model but retained Professor Raymond Nimmer as the Article 2B Reporter. During the early to mid-1990s, NCCUSL and the American Law Institute developed a model software code to be included as U.C.C. Article 2B of the Uniform Commercial Code. UCITA customizes U.C.C. Article 2 concepts for the commercial realities of software licenses. In addition to Professor Nimmer, the key players for the Article 2B project were the American Bar Association, NCCUSL, and the ALI. The ALI withdrew from the Article 2B Drafting Project after the ALI Council surveyed its membership and

---

[286] The National Conference of Commissioners on Uniform State Law (NCCUSL is now the Uniform Law Commission: The National Conference of Commissioners on Uniform State Law ("ULC")). See Uniform Law Commission, http://www.nccusl.org/Update/ . (last visited June 15, 2013).

[287] I served on the ABA Business Law's Subcommittee on Software Licensing for a decade. He served as the task force leader for the scope of U.C.C. Article 2B and also worked on the sections on transfer and assignment of software.

[288] See Thom Weidlich, Commission Plans New U.C.C. Article, NAT'L L. J. (Aug. 28, 1995), at B1 (noting that NCCUSL appointed Houston law professor Raymond T. Nimmer as Technology Reporter for the new U.C.C. Article 2B).

determined that it would not approve the proposed software article. ALI's scuttling of the joint statutory project with NCCUSL to create a specialized U.C.C.

Article 2B preceded the Uniform Computer Information Transactions Act (UCITA) as a stand-alone statute. "The UCITA differs from U.C.C. Article 2 by recognizing that most transactions dealing with software and electronic data . . . As such, the UCITA attempts to tailor remedies and warranties to the transfer of information rather than the sale of goods."[289] NCCUSL approved UCITA as the comprehensive statute codifying software contracts.[290] In July of 1999, NCCUSL approved UCITA, which is the first statute to govern licensing:

> UCITA is the first uniform contract law designed to deal specifically with the new information economy. Transactions in computer information involve different expectations, different industry practices, and different policies from transactions in goods. For example, in a sale of goods, the buyer *owns* what it buys and has exclusive rights in that subject matter (e.g., the toaster that has been purchased). In contrast, someone that acquires a copy of computer information may or may not own that copy, but in any case rarely obtains all rights associated with the information.[291]

Raymond T. Nimmer stated: "The purpose of UCITA . . . is to develop contract law sensitive to computer information as subject matter. . . . Sales of goods are different from transactions in computer information. A sale of a chair or toaster (the grist of Article 2) is different from a license of a computer database or software (the focus of UCITA)."[292] UCITA harmonizes legal infrastructure for Web-site linking agreements, affiliate agreements, legal notices, license agreements, access contracts, clickwrap agreements, end-user agreements, online shopping, auction bidding agreements, terms of services agreements, and online licenses of all kinds. An "access contract" "means a contract to obtain by electronic means access to, or information from, an information processing system of another person, or the equivalent of such access."[293] The concepts and methods for attribution procedures, authentication, computer information, electronic agents, electronic events, electronic messages, and accommodating contracting law for advances created by the Internet. UCITA legitimates the widespread industry practice of licensing as a means of bypassing the first sale doctrine of the U.S. Copyright Act. Licensing is a useful legal invention, which permits the industry to realize value.

The final approved version of UCITA reflects the Reporter's compromise with various consumer and industry stakeholders. Nevertheless, the problem for the UCITA Drafting Committee was that each time a compromise was reached with one aggrieved stakeholder, another interest group stepped forward arguing that they were unrepresented in the drafting process. Wave after wave of UCITA critics have come forward in the ten-year war over its enactment. Critics claimed that UCITA legitimated oppressive choice of law and forum clauses in shrinkwrap, webwrap, or clickwrap agreements that effectively stripped consumers of any meaningful remedy.

---

[289] 2 George B. Delta & Jeffrey H. Matsuura, Law of the Internet 13–112 (2008).

[290] NCCUSL's commissioners, primarily appointed by state governors, serve for specific terms.

[291] Raymond T. Nimmer, Prefatory Note, UCITA Refs & Annos.

[292] Raymond T. Nimmer, UCITA: A Commercial Contract Code, Computer Lawyer (May 2000) at

[293] UCITA § 102(a)(1).

UCITA validated rolling contracts where a vendor provides new terms after the license is executed. Google, for example, claims the right to make unilateral modifications to its software license for developers in the following clause:

> Google may make changes to the License Agreement as it distributes new versions of the (Android Software Development Kit). When these changes are made, Google will make a new version of the License Agreement available on the website where the [Android] is made available.[294]

UCITA's endorsement of rolling contracts where the consumer pays now and gets its terms later was another issue of contention. UCITA "embraces the theory of 'layered contracting,' which acknowledges while 'some contracts are formed and their terms fully defined at a single point in time, many transactions involve a rolling or layered process. An agreement exists, but terms are clarified or created over time.'"[295] The business community other than large software vendors were generally opposed to the following UCITA provisions:

- Unconditional validation of "shrinkwrapped" or "clickthrough" licenses combined with onerous default provisions

- Restriction on number of permitted users as default provision

- Limitation on duration of license as default provision

- Limitation warranty of non-infringement

- Permitted disclaimer of implied warranty regarding defects—even those known to the software publisher at time of license

- Restriction on transferability—while prohibited under the recent proposed amendment to UCITA in the case of mergers or sales of business—are still allowed in other cases

- Permitted use of automatic or passive restraint—for a reason as vague as the "prevention of use inconsistent with the agreement"

- Waiver of remedy for breach of contract

- Deletion of the requirement to deliver a product conforming to the contract and the abandonment of perfect tender rule

- Electronic repossession or self-help[296]

NCCUSL initially approved UCITA in 1999, but the drafters amended the statute again in 2002 to respond to various drafting glitches.[297] The American Bar Association (ABA) Working Group on UCITA stated in a 2002 report that UCITA "is a very

---

[294]Android.com, Software License Agreement, http://developer.android.com/sdk/terms.html (last visited June 14, 2013).

[295] UCITA § 208, cmt. 3.

[296] Letter of April 2001 to Oklahoma Attorney General Drew Edmundson, http://www. ucita. com/pdf/ AG_letter.pdf+Stephen+Chow+Fair+Use+UCITA   &cd=2&hl=en&ct=clnk&gl=us&ie=UTF-8   (last   visited June 14, 2013).

[297] The National Conference of Commissioners on Uniform State Law (NCCUSL) is an "organization comprised of more than 300 lawyers, judges and law professors appointed by the states as well as the District of Columbia, Puerto Rico and the U.S. Virgin Islands to draft proposals for uniform and model laws on subjects where uniformity is desirable and practicable, and work toward their enactment in legislatures. See NCCUSL, About Us, http://www.nccusl.org. (last visited June 14, 2013).

complex statute that is daunting for even knowledgeable lawyers to understand."[298] The ABA Working Group was critical of UCITA's complexity, its scope, and its complicated structure:

> The text, which consists of black letter rules (or sections), together with the extended comments, is lengthy and filled with terminology that is largely unfamiliar to the average reader, necessitating lengthy definitions of those terms. These initial hurdles are then exacerbated by the general organizational structure of the statute and the manner of presentation. For example, in far too many instances it is impossible to understand a rule simply by reading the section that supposedly sets forth that rule. Instead, the reader must wend his or her way not only through some intricate prose, but also through a number of other sections that are cross-referenced in the rule. In addition, the text frequently suggests that there are other sections that may affect a particular rule (and which therefore should be considered), but which are not specifically referenced (e.g., pursuant to the applicable sections of this [Act], including Section 209, 211, and 102(a) (57)). Consequently, many of the black letter rules come across as convoluted and, at times, inscrutable.[299]

NCCUSL amended UCITA in 2002 after the model statute was stalled in state legislatures. The 2002 Amendments to UCITA implemented some of the ABA Report suggestions, but did not satisfy consumer groups and other critics. The 2002 Amendments prohibited "electronic self-help" but did not adopt a rule of pretransaction disclosures of terms or require licensors to disclose material defects or serious bugs.[300] UCITA's 2002 Amendments did not result in new states enacting the model software licensing statute. NCCUSL discharged its standby committee in August of 2003, stating that it was not expending further resources to engineer a consensus about UCITA's provisions.

Critics charged that UCITA would enable software publishers to shut down their customer's computer system without prior court approval. The Americans for Fair Electronic Commerce spearheaded an attack on self-help provisions in UCITA. They charged that remote repossession would give software publishers too much power "in a dispute over license rights, to remotely shut down an organization's mission-critical software."[301] UCITA opponents—large technology users and consumer rights groups who are strange bedfellows—contended UCITA would give software companies a virtual stranglehold on technology contracts.[302] The licensee community, too, joined the chorus against UCITA's self-help provisions.

---

[298] ABA Working Group on UCITA (Jan. 30, 2002).

[299] Id. at 9.

[300] Summary of AFFECT Response to 2002 UCITA Revisions.

[301] Americans for Fair Electronic Commerce Transactions, What is UCITA? http://www.ucita .com/what_problems.html (last visited June 14, 2013).

[302] "One of the reasons that the UCITA project did not succeed is that, although UCITA attempted to mask its real focus on mass market transactions with a purported paradigm of a negotiated transaction, it in fact explicitly addressed non-negotiated deals in a way that was inconsistent with U.C.C. Art. 2, which disfavors delayed disclosure of material terms. . . . UCITA seems to protect delayed disclosure of even significant terms in non-negotiated deals, thus revealing its real concern with validating an approach dubious under both commercial and consumer law. Most state attorneys-general in the United States —who enforce state consumer protection laws—and the Federal Trade Commission reacted negatively and pressed

Ultimately, UCITA's drafters limited electronic repossession, which did little to smother the firestorm.[303] The procedural rights and obligations for electronic repossession are not disclaimable and may not be waived by agreement. Just as with Article 9, no repossession can take place where a breach of the peace would result. UCITA does not want to grant licensors the unbridled right to use electronic self- help or disabling devices that will cause harm to computer systems. UCITA § 816 does not permit electronic repossession for consumer licenses. Nevertheless, critics contended that UCITA's electronic repossession provisions were imbalanced favoring large software licensors such as Microsoft and failing to protect licensee's rights.[304]

Critics of UCITA charge that it validated abusive practices such as requiring consumers to litigate in distant forums, depriving them of a meaningful remedy. Nevertheless, an empirical study of website licenses found that licensors did not abuse their market power by imposing harsh terms and conditions in standard-form license agreements.[305]

The firestorm over a few UCITA provisions deflects attention away from the empirical reality that many of its rules reflect best practices in the software industry developed over the past three decades.[306] The United States was the first post-industrial society to develop a specialized civil code covering the licensing of software. UCITA applies to computer information transactions; encompassing the vast majority of Internet-related terms of service or terms of use as well as software licensing.

(C) UCITA's Statutory Purposes

UCITA is a model state law that was approved by NCCUSL in 1999. Maryland and Virginia enacted UCITA and a number of states enacted "bomb shelter provisions" that prohibited the use of UCITA in parties' choice of law clauses.[307] UCITA "bomb

---

for changes." Jean Braucher, U.S. Influence with a Twist: Lesson About Unfair Contract Terms from U.S. Software Customers, 2007 COMPET. & CONSUMER L. J. 5, 12 (2007).

[303] Raymond Nimmer, the Reporter for UCITA (and U.C.C. Article 2B) was placed in an unenviable position of continually responding to stakeholders threatening to stymie the project. Article 2B, UCITA's predecessor, was continually drafted and revised to address a seemingly endless set of demands by stakeholders. Don Cohn, UCITA's ABA advisor noted how "[e]xtensive changes were made over the years to reflect the reasonable needs and requests of various interest groups and to accommodate the convergence of technologies that are within the scope of UCITA." UCITA ABA Advisor Report from Don Cohn to the ABA Staff and House of Delegates, (Jan. 16, 2003) available at http://www.nccusl.org/nccusl/UCITA /Cohn_Letter.pdf (last visited June 23, 2013). The incomprehensibility critique came largely from UCITA's ambitious scope as well as its tackling the complex borderland between contracting law and intellectual property. The undue complexity of UCITA is partially a testament to its aspirations. To update commercial law scholar and sociologist Max Weber, Ray Nimmer was "attempting the impossible, to achieve the possible."

[304] See e.g., Americans for Fair Electronic Commerce Transactions, What is UCITA?

[305] Florencia Marotta–Wurgler, Competition and the Quality of Standard-Form Contracts: An Empirical Analysis of Software Licenses (Aug. 22, 2005), http://papers.ssrn.com/sol3/papers.cfm?abstract_id= 799274 (last visited June 14, 2013) (summarizing results of a content analysis of 647 software license agreements, examining how competitive forces shape standard terms).

[306] K. King Burnett, NCCUSL President, UCITA Standby Committee is Discharged (Aug. 1, 2003), http://www.nccusl.org/nccusl/DesktopModules/NewsDisplay.aspx?ItemID=56 (last visited June 14, 2013).

[307] "One of the reasons that the UCITA project did not succeed is that, although UCITA attempted to mask its real focus on mass-market transactions with a purported paradigm of a negotiated transaction, it in fact explicitly addressed non-negotiated deals in a way that was inconsistent with U.C.C. Art 2, which disfavors delayed disclosure of material terms .... UCITA seems to protect delayed disclosure of even significant terms in non-negotiated deals, thus revealing its real concern with validating an approach dubious under both commercial and consumer law. Most state attorneys-general in the United States—who

shelter" statutes void choice of law clauses where UCITA is the choice of law. These "bomb shelter" statues shield users from the effect of UCITA in their choice of law clauses. Iowa, North Carolina, and West Virginia enacted "bomb shelter" statutes that prevent UCITA from being the operative law. Nevertheless, in Virginia and Maryland UCITA applies unless the parties' choice of law clause opts out of the model statute. UCITA gives the parties to a software license the right to opt out or alter the provisions of the statute.

It is also possible for software makers in other states to choose UCITA as the applicable law so long as that state has not adopted a measure prohibiting UCITA in choice of law agreements. UCITA § 104 allows for parties to a transaction not within the scope of UCITA to elect that their transaction be governed by UCITA, except for provisions that cannot be varied by contract under the law otherwise governing the transaction. The parties may elect that the UCITA contract formation rules apply in lieu of the common-law or U.C.C. Article 2, which would otherwise govern the transaction. Lawyers representing the software industry use UCITA provisions as default standard terms for their software licensing contracts.

(D) A UCITA Roadmap

The 2002 Version of UCITA: An Overview

Title of Parts & Subparts	*Section Numbers*
Part I: General Provisions: Short Title & Definitions, General Scope and Terms	§§ 101–118
Part II: Formation & Terms, Formation of Contract, Terms of Records & Electronic Contracts, Idea and Information Submissions	§§ 201–215
Part III: Construction: General Interpretation	§§ 301–308
Part IV: Warranties	§§ 401–410
Part V: Transfer of Interests and Rights: Ownership and Transfers, Financing Arrangements	§§ 501–511
Part VI: Performance: General Performance in Delivery of Products	§§ 601–618
Part VII: Breach of Contract: General, Defective	§§ 701–710

enforce state consumer protection laws—and the Federal Trade Commission reacted negatively and pressed for changes." Jean Braucher, U.S. Influence with a Twist: Lesson About Unfair Contract Terms from U.S. Software Customers, 2007 COMPET. & CONSUMER L. J. 5, 12 (2007).

Copies; Repudiation and Assurances	
Part VIII.: Remedies: General	§§ 801–816
Part IX. Miscellaneous Provisions	§§ 901–904

As the chart above depicts, UCITA is divided into nine parts: (1) General Provisions, (2) Formation and Terms, (3) Construction, (4) Warranties, (5) Transfer of Interests and Rights, (6) Performance, (7) Breach of Contract, (8) Remedies and (9) Miscellaneous Provisions. Lawyers frequently import UCITA provisions into their mass-market license agreement because of their flexibility. Even though UCITA has not been widely adopted, it is nevertheless a useful template for a wide array of software licensing transactions. Two leading scholars assert, "that UCITA maintains the contextual, balanced approach to standard terms that can be found in the paper world."[308] Douglas E. Phillips, vice president and general counsel of Promontory Interfinancial Systems, contends that counsel representing software licensors or licensees must master UCITA's provisions. For example, Phillips recommends that attorneys learn UCITA's provisions in deciding whether to opt in or out of the statute:

> [L]awyers who assist clients in computer information transactions must place their bets ... In negotiating software licenses and other computer information transactions, lawyers are being confronted with proposed contractual choice-of-law clauses that invoke UCITA.[309]

(E) UCITA's Sphere of Application

UCITA applies to "computer transactions"[310] which encompasses "contracts to create, modify, transfer or license computer information or informational rights in computer information."[311] A computer information transaction is defined as an agreement or the performance of it to create, modify, transfer, or license computer information or informational rights in computer information. The licensing of intangibles, like leases, validates the legal concept of the right to use property. The question of who has title to tangible copies of intangibles is not dispositive or even relevant to licensing rights. With software licensing, the medium is not the message, only the right to exploit information. The ease of copying software has made the invention of licensing the only efficient method of realizing value.

UCITA's scope is transactions in information, which is a broader concept than software licensing. A computer information transaction is defined as an agreement or the performance of it to create, modify, transfer, or license computer information or informational rights in computer information.[312]

---

[308] See Robert A. Hillman & Jeffrey J. Rachlinski, Standard–Form Contracting in the Electronic Age, 77 N.Y.U. L. Rev. 429, 491 (2002).

[309] Douglas E. Phillips, Consequential Damages Exclusions Under UCITA, 19 J. MARSHALL J. OF COMP & INFO. LAW 295, 295 (2001).

[310] UCITA, Id. at § 103(a).

[311] UCITA, Id. at § 112(12).

[312] See e.g., VA. CODE ANN. § 59.1–501.2(a)(11).

UCITA defines "computer information" as electronically based or capable of being processed by a computer. UCITA follows the NCCUSL text in defining information broadly to include data, text, images, sounds, mask works, or computer programs:

This term covers information that is in electronic form and that is obtained from, accessible with, or usable by, a computer; it includes the information, the copy of it (e.g., a diskette containing the information), and its documentation (including non-electronic documentation). As defined, "electronic" includes digital information or information in another form having similar capabilities. This covers analog and future computational technologies, eliminating the possibility that the Act might be limited to current technology. The term does not include information merely because it could be scanned or entered into a computer; it is limited to electronic information in a form capable of being directly processed in a computer. "Computer information" does not generally include printed information or information in other non-electronic formats.[313]

UCITA covers all transfers of computer information including licensing, assignments, or sales of copies of computer programs. UCITA also covers "multimedia products, software and multimedia development contracts, access contracts, and contracts to obtain information for use in a program, access contract, or multimedia product."[314] Nevertheless, the mere fact that parties agree to communicate in digital form does not bring a transaction within this definition. UCITA applies to transfers of computer information and informational rights in Maryland and Virginia. UCITA governs software licenses and other information-based transactions in Virginia or Maryland law unless the parties otherwise agree. A computer program is a set of statements or instructions to be used directly or indirectly in a computer to bring about a certain result. The statutory purposes of UCITA are: (1) to facilitate computer or information transactions in cyberspace; (2) to clarify the law governing computer information transactions; (3) to enable expanding commercial practice in computer information transactions by commercial usage and agreement of the parties; and (4) to make the law uniform among the various jurisdictions.

UCITA provides a legal infrastructure widely adopted for Web-site linking agreements, affiliate agreements, legal notices, license agreements, access contracts, clickwrap agreements, end-user agreements, online shopping, auction bidding agreements, terms of services agreements, and online licenses of all kinds. UCITA's concepts for attribution procedures,[315] authentication,[316] computer information,[317]

---

[313] UCITA § 102(a)(10), cmt. 8.

[314] UCITA § 102(a)(10), cmt. 9.

[315] "'Attribution procedure' means a procedure to verify that an electronic authentication, display, message, record, or performance is that of a particular person or to detect changes or errors in information. The term includes a procedure that requires the use of algorithms or other codes, identifying words or numbers, encryption, or callback or other acknowledgment." UCITA § 102(a)(5).

[316] UCITA defines authenticate to mean:

(A) to sign; or (B) with the intent to sign a record, otherwise to execute or adopt an electronic symbol, sound, message, or process referring to, attached to, included in, or logically associated or linked with, that record. UCITA § 102(a)(6).

[317] "'Computer information' means information in electronic form which is obtained from or through the use of a computer or which is in a form capable of being processed by a computer. The term includes a copy of the information and any documentation or packaging associated with the copy." UCITA § 102(a)(10).

electronic agents,[318] electronic messages,[319] and other legal infrastructure adaptable for diverse information age contracts. UCITA's statutory framework is flexible because parties may select which provisions to incorporate in their license agreements. UCITA customizes concepts imported from U.C.C. Article 2 such as the parol evidence rule, the statute of frauds, warranties, risk of loss rules, and remedies.

Similarly, UCITA continues to be a template useful in terms of use or service agreements. Lawyers charged with drafting a software licensing agreement incorporate many UCITA provisions in their contracts, and many of its provisions are not objectionable since they reflect the best practices of the software industry. UCITA has a continuing vitality in its daily impact on countless licensing agreements. The Reporters of the American Law Institute's "Principles of the Law of Software Contracts" acknowledge importing many UCITA concepts into its software contracting templates. UCITA's scope covers computer information transactions.[320] "Like Article 2, UCITA covers a variety of transactions, many of which take place solely between merchants. Article 2 governs sales of jet planes as well as toasters, not to mention the large-scale acquisition of jet and toaster parts."[321]

(F) Initial Provisions

UCITA § 102 defines key terms such as access contracts, attribution procedures, authentication, computer information, electronic agents, electronic events, electronic messages, mass-market licenses, receipt, and record. This section also defines electronic agents to mean "a computer program, or electronic or other automated means, used independently to initiate an action, or to respond to electronic messages or performances, on the person's behalf without review or action by an individual at the time of the action or response to the message or performance."[322] UCITA provides a legal infrastructure for standard form licenses, including access contracts, terms of service agreements, clickwrap agreements, shrinkwrap agreements, and website user agreements. UCITA gives licensees a statutory right to return mass-market products where they have had no opportunity to review terms.[323] If the licensee returns mass-market software, the licensor bears the shipping and related costs.[324]

---

[318] "'Electronic agent; means a computer program, or electronic or other automated means, used independently to initiate an action, or to respond to electronic messages or performances, on the person's behalf without review or action by an individual at the time of the action or response to the message or performance." UCITA § 102(a)(27).

[319] "'Electronic message' means a record or display that is stored, generated, or transmitted by electronic means for the purpose of communication to another person or electronic agent." UCITA § 102(28).

[320] "This term helps to define the scope of this Act. Section 103 requires an agreement involving computer information. The term includes transfers (e.g., licenses, assignments, or sales of copies) of computer programs or multimedia products, software and multimedia development contracts, access contracts, and contracts to obtain information for use in a program, access contract, or multimedia product. However, the mere fact that parties agree to communicate in digital form does not bring a transaction within this definition, nor does a decision by one party to use computer information when the contract does not require this." UCITA § 102(9).

[321] BRIAN W. SMITH, E–COMMERCE FINANCIAL PRODUCTS & SUCCESS, F-5 (2001).

[322] UCITA § 102(a)(27).

[323] Section 209(c) provides: "In a mass-market transaction, if the licensor does not have an opportunity to review a record containing proposed terms from the licensee before the licensor delivers or becomes obligated to deliver the information, and if the licensor does not agree, such as by manifesting assent, to those terms after having that opportunity, the licensor is entitled to a return." UCITA, Id. at § 209(c).

[324] UCITA §§ 112(e), 209(b).

UCITA adopts Article 2's concept of unconscionability, which give courts the power to strike down unconscionable contracts or terms, and this doctrine applies to all UCITA license agreements. Section 111 of UCITA gives courts the power to police contracts or any term.[325] A court may refuse to enforce the entire software license or the remainder of the contract without the unconscionable term. The court has broad equitable powers to limit the application of any unconscionable term to avoid any unconscionable result. The issue of unconscionability is always a matter of law and one for the trial judge rather than the jury. The basic test is whether the license agreement or term should be invalidated because it is "so one-sided as to be unconscionable under the circumstances existing at the time of the making of the contract."[326] Unconscionability is an amorphous doctrine designed to prevent "oppression and unfair surprise."[327]

Courts generally require procedural unconscionability, where there is a lack of a meaningful choice due to unfair bargaining and substantive unconscionability, which is the resultant unfair term. Procedural unconscionability means that the contract negotiation or bargaining was unfair and focuses on two factors, oppression and surprise.[328] Substantive unconscionability exists when the terms of the resultant contract are unfair or abusive. A substantively unconscionable bargain is "one that "no man in his senses and not under delusion would make on the one hand, and no honest and fair man would accept on the other."[329] In contrast, procedural unconscionability is often found when one of the parties has no reasonable opportunity to know what he is signing. A door-to-door sales representative, in a classic illustration, intentionally spills coffee on a prospective customer to divert his attention and then switches a promissory note for the sweepstakes entry form the consumer thought he was signing.

This creates a problem of procedural unconscionability. The use of hidden terms in software licenses will qualify as procedural unconscionability, whereas an exorbitant fee for arbitration could constitute substantive unconscionability. In order to strike

---

[325] Courts have refused to enforce clauses in a few Internet-related license agreements. See e.g., Riensche v. Cingular Wireless, L.L.C., No. C06–1325Z, 2006 WL 3827477, at 9 (W.D. Wash. Dec. 27, 2006) (holding that the forum selection clause was substantively unconscionable); Comb v. PayPal, Inc., 218 F. Supp. 2d 1165, 1173, 1176 (N.D. Cal. 2002) (refusing to enforce pre-dispute mandatory arbitration clause in user agreement ruling that the forum selection clause was substantively and procedurally unconscionable). Additionally, the doctrine of unconscionability has been applied in a wide array of contexts. See e.g., Scott v. Cingular Wireless, 161 P.3d 1000, 1006 (Wash. 2007) (holding a class action waiver unconscionable); Gatton v. T–Mobile USA, 61 Cal. Rptr. 3d 344, 358 (Cal. Ct. App. 2007) (holding a class action waiver unconscionable and unenforceable); Aral v. EarthLink, Inc., 36 Cal. Rptr. 3d 229, 238 (Cal. 2005) (holding a class action waiver unconscionable). See Brower v. Gateway 2000, Inc., 676 N.Y.S.2d 569, 575 (N.Y. App. Div. 1998) (explaining that New York requires "a showing that a contract is "both procedurally and substantively unconscionable when made"") (quoting Gillman v. Chase Manhattan Bank, 73 N.Y.2d 1, 10 (1988)). California's test for substantive unconscionability is whether the clause or contract "shocks the conscience." Am. Software, Inc. v. Ali, 54 Cal. Rptr. 2d 477, 480 (Cal. Ct. App. 1996). The test for procedural unconscionability is whether "the manner in which the contract was negotiated" was unfair. Id. at 479.

[326] U.C.C. § 2–302, cmt. 1 states this guidepost for unconscionability.

[327] This test was imported from U.C.C. § 2–302.

[328] Procedural unconscionability "concerns the manner in which the contract was negotiated and the circumstances of the parties at that time." Kinney v. United Healthcare Servs., Inc., 70 Cal.App.4th 1322, 83 Cal.Rptr.2d 348, 352–53 (Ct.App.1999). A determination of whether a contract is procedurally unconscionable focuses on two factors: oppression and surprise. See also, Stirlen v. Supercuts, Inc., 51 Cal.App.4th 1519, 60 Cal.Rptr.2d 138, 145 (Ct.App.1997) (discussing test for procedural unconscionability as being oppression from the inequality of bargaining power and surprise as hidden terms).

[329] Farrell v. Convergent Communications, Inc., No. C98–2613 MJJ, 1998 WL 774626, at *4 (N.D. Cal. Oct. 29, 1998).

down a license agreement or a clause in a license agreement, a court must find both an unfair bargaining process, which is procedural unconscionability, as well as unfair terms, which is substantive unconscionability. It takes a grossly unfair term such as a forum selection clause for a U.S. citizen in Oslo, Norway to constitute substantive unconscionability. Section 111(b) of UCITA follows U.C.C. § 2–302's methodology in requiring a court to hear evidence of the commercial setting and other circumstances before invalidating a license agreement on the grounds of unconscionability.

Unconscionability, however, has proved to be a toothless tiger when it comes to terms of service agreements.[330] There are few terms of service agreements where a court has struck down either a clause or an entire webwrap license agreement as unconscionable. A court will refuse to enforce a software contract or a single provision on unconscionability or public policy grounds. Courts will not strike down a contractual provision unless they believe it is so one-sided in favor of the dominant party to "shock the conscience." Courts will typically look at the contract's purpose and circumstances in play when the contract was executed in making a determination about unconscionability. A California court struck down EarthLink's arbitration agreement in a case where consumers filed suit for "improperly charging fees for a digital subscriber line, or DSL, prior to providing customers with the equipment necessary to utilize the service."[331] Typically, a court must find unfair bargaining (procedural unconscionability) as well as an unfair bargain in fact (substantive unconscionability). In *EarthLink*, the court found the provider's arbitration provision to be procedurally unconscionable because it was presented during installation or when the package was mailed with no right to opt out.[332] Hundreds of millions of consumers have entered into terms of service agreements with social networking sites. To date, however, a court has invalidated a terms of use or terms of service agreement on unconscionability grounds in only a single case.[333]

(G) Formation of Standard Form Licenses

UCITA's concept of a "record" enables the parties of an e-contract to satisfy the moth-eaten Statute of Frauds' requirement for a writing. Out of the hundreds of global nations conducting Internet commerce, the U.S. is the only country to require a Statute of Frauds for the sale of goods or the licensing of information. U.C.C. Article 2 continues to require a signed writing by the party against whom enforcement is sought unless there is an exception. UCITA updates the Statute of Frauds for online contracts by treating a "record" as a functional equivalent of "pen and paper" signatures. UCITA defines "records" to mean information inscribed on a tangible medium. Records may also be stored in an electronic library or other medium, permitting it to be retrievable in perceivable form.

---

[330] See Davidson & Associates, Inc. v. Internet Gateway, Inc., 334 F. Supp. 2d 1164 (E.D. Mo. 2004) (holding game maker's terms of service and end user license agreement to be enforceable and rejecting competing game maker's argument that these agreements was unconscionable even though these mass-market licenses prohibited reverse engineering, disassembling, and making derivative works).

[331] Mike McKee, Earthlink Chastised Over DSL Dispute, 129 THE RECORDER 1 (Nov. 30, 2005).

[332] Id.

[333] Bragg v. Linden Research, Inc., 487 F.Supp.2d 593 (E.D.P.A. May 30, 2007) (finding arbitration clause in Terms of Service for Second Life both procedurally and substantively unconscionable in case filed by attorney Second Life plaintiff).

Part 3 of UCITA covers topics such as the parol evidence rule, modification, changes in terms, and the interpretation of information-based contracts. UCITA's parol evidence rule substitutes the term "record" for a writing but is otherwise parallel to U.C.C. § 2–202. Like Article 2, UCITA permits integrated writings to be supplemented by course of performance and by course of dealing and usage of trade. UCITA § 301 permits a party to introduce evidence of consistent additional terms unless the record states that it is a "complete and exclusive" statement of the terms of the license. UCITA validates mass-market or standard form agreements "only if the party agrees to the license, such as by manifesting assent, before or during the party's initial performance or use of or access to the information."[334] Critics point to the hegemony of freedom of contract, but this principle was embodied in the U.C.C. as well:

> The general basis for UCITA's opposition is its application of freedom of contract to both traditional contracts issues, especially those involving product qualities, and to those associated with a licensor's desire to retain intellectual property rights in its software. UCITA's default rules, like those in the UCC, apply only if the parties have not otherwise agreed on a subject. If the law supports standard contracts based loosely on a freedom of contract principle, then the terms of that contract will tend to favor the drafter over the other side, unless a court adjudges the contract or provision unconscionable. Once again, UCITA is ostensibly doing what has previously been done and often endorsed.[335]

UCITA broadly enforces mass-market licenses.[336] UCITA also states, "A party adopts the terms of a record, including a standard form, as the terms of the contract if the party agrees to the record, such as by manifesting assent."[337] Mass-market contracts are enforced if three conditions are met: (1) the user has an opportunity to review the terms of the license, (2) the user manifests assent after having an opportunity to review the terms, and (3) the actions are "attributable in law" to the user. UCITA rejects the doctrine of acceptance by silence for standard form licenses, which is a criticism of browsewrap. Assent is not conditioned on whether the party has read or understood the terms of the agreement.[338] The concept of manifesting assent is based upon an objective standard rather than a subjective "meeting of the minds." A minimally adequate objective manifestation of assent is an opportunity to review the record coupled with an affirmative act that indicates assent.

However, one of the difficult policy issues to determine is to decide what affirmative conduct constitutes assent. In a paper-based contract, a signature establishes the manifestation of assent. UCITA permits the manifestation of assent to

---

[334] UCITA § 209(a).

[335] Nim Razook, The Politics and Promise of UCITA, 36 CREIGHTON L. REV. 643, 646 (2003).

[336] Professor Amy Schmitz describes the way in which American consumers have:

[a] love/hate relationship with form terms. On the one hand, consumers admit that they have no interest in reading form contracts, enjoy the convenience and efficiency of form contracting, and routinely accept forms "dressed up" as deals without stopping to read or question their content. On the other hand, consumers are often frustrated with the effectively nonnegotiable nature of these contracts and complain that they lack the requisite time or understanding to read or negotiate companies' impenetrable purchase terms.

Amy J. Schmitz, Pizza-Box Contracts: True Tales of Consumer Contracting Culture, 45 WAKE FOREST L. REV. 863, 864–65 (2010) (arguing that consumers bear some responsibility for acquiescing to the stronger party "running roughshod over their rights").

[337] Id. at § 208(1).

[338] Id. at § 208, cmt. 7.

be fulfilled by an affirmative act, such as clicking a display button reading: "I accept the terms of this agreement." A licensor must give the licensee a right to a refund if the licensee has not had an opportunity to review the terms and manifest assent prior to payment.[339] UCITA § 114 requires that the licensor of the terms of service give the potential customer an opportunity to review the terms of a standard-form license. UCITA § 114 is fulfilled so long as the licensor gives the customer an opportunity to review the terms of the license before the software maker delivers the software and the customer is bound to pay. Under Section 209(b), a licensor must give the licensee a right to a refund if the licensee has not had an opportunity to review the terms and manifests assent prior to payment.

As a result, mass-market licenses are a useful legal invention. The alternative to mass-market licensing would be retaining an attorney to negotiate the terms of each license, which would not be cost-efficient. One possible effect of increasing overall costs on the business may be that there would be fewer resources available for the development of new and improved products. In addition, negotiating mass-market agreements would limit the availability of the licensed products overall or sharply increase the price of licensed products in the market. For example, UCITA § 112 binds a licensee to the terms of a shrinkwrap, or clickwrap agreement as long as the party manifests assent to the terms of the agreement.

UCITA also validates "rolling contracts," permitting a content provider or software publisher to add, delete, or change terms after the licensee has paid royalties for access. The trend in recent judicial decisions is that courts enforce "cash now, terms later" software agreements so long as the licensor gives reasonable notice to the user and provides an opportunity to decline the terms. UCITA allows rolling contract terms to be adopted after performance if the licensee "had reason to know that their agreement would be represented by terms in a record that there would be no opportunity to review before performance or use began."[340] UCITA validates "rolling contracts" if the person had reason to know that terms would come later, had a right to a refund if he declined the terms, and manifests assent after an opportunity to review them.[341]

(1) Opportunity to Review Terms

As introduced above, mass-market or wrap contracts are enforced if three conditions are met: (1) the user has an opportunity to review the terms of the license, (2) the user manifests assent after having an opportunity to review the terms, and (3) the actions are "attributable in law" to the user. UCITA's mass-market licensing provisions are consistent with current judicial trends. Courts are inclined to validate mass-market license agreements so long as the licensee has an opportunity to review terms and a means of manifesting assent. UCITA § 114 requires that the licensor of the terms of service give the potential customer an opportunity to review the terms of a standard-form license.[342] In other words, UCITA § 114 is fulfilled so long as the licensor gives the customer an opportunity to review the terms of the license before the

---

[339] Id. at § 209(b).
[340] John E. Murray, Jr., The Definitive 'Battle of the Forms': Chaos Revisited, J. OF LAW & COMMERCE 1, 39 (2000).
[341] Raymond T. Nimmer, Licensing of Information Assets, 2 INFO. LAW § 11:147 (June 2009).
[342] UCITA § 114.

software maker delivers the software and the customer is bound to pay.[343] Under Section 209(b), a licensor must give the licensee a right to a refund if the licensee has not had an opportunity to review the terms and manifest assent prior to payment. If the licensee returns mass-market software, the licensor bears the shipping and related costs. UCITA's drafters are cognizant of the importance of proximity because the statute requires the terms must be either close to the description of the computer or available by clicking on a hyperlink to another site.

(2) Manifestation of Assent

Section 209(a) of UCITA validates mass-market or standard form agreements "only if the party agrees to the license, such as by manifesting assent, before or during the party's initial performance or use of or access to the information."[344] UCITA § 208(1) also states, "A party adopts the terms of a record, including a standard form, as the terms of the contract if the party agrees to the record, such as by manifesting assent."[345] Assent is not conditioned on whether a consumer read or understood the terms of the agreement. The concept of manifesting assent is based solely upon an objective standard rather than a subjective "meeting of the minds." UCITA validates mass-market licenses "only if the party agrees to the license, such as by manifesting assent, before or during the party's initial performance or use of or access to the information."[346] "A party adopts the terms of a record, including a standard form, as the terms of the contract if the party agrees to the record, such as by manifesting assent."[347] Simply clicking an "I accept" text or an icon evidences a user's manifestation of assent. A manifestation of assent to a record or term is not effective unless the licensee has an opportunity to review the record or term.[348] UCITA provides that individuals be deemed to have had an opportunity to review a term if the term is available in a manner that ought to call it to the attention of a reasonable person.

A party adopts the terms of a record, including a click-wrap or shrink-wrap agreement, only if there is a manifestation of assent. Section 112 binds a party to the terms of a shrink-wrap or click-wrap agreement if the party had reason to know his acts would be treated as assent to the terms. The manifestation of assent and opportunity to review the terms are mandatory terms and may not be varied by contract. UCITA critics point out that mass-market licenses are adhesive contracts that offer no possibility of negotiation. The contract formation process for mass-market licenses is flawed; the take it or leave it nature of the process is unfair; the "pay first, terms come later" sequence of events is flawed and unfair; it is too easy to hide terms; the method of contracting improperly extends intellectual property protection. Free market individualism is premised on the assumption that human beings are motivated primarily by economic self-interest and have a right to pursue self-interest "without interference from others or the imposition of alternative conceptions of the good by others."[349] It is in the self-interest of the software industry to disclaim all warranties

---

[343] Id. at § 114(1)(A)–(B).

[344] UCITA § 209(a).

[345] Id. at § 208(1).

[346] UCITA § 209(a).

[347] Id. at § 208(1).

[348] Id. at § 113, cmt. 2.

[349] MICHAEL J. TREBILCOCK, THE LIMITS OF FREEDOM OF CONTRACT 8 (1993).

and consequential damages, which may leave consumers without a minimum adequate remedy.

(3) Attributable to Licensee

UCITA spells out substantive rules needed for online transactions that provide safeguards and safe harbors against a user's inadvertent assent or attribution. Section 212(a) states that electronic events are attributable to either the person or their electronic agent. Under UCITA § 102(a)(5), for example, attribution procedure is defined as any electronic authentication or performance of a particular person that enables tracking of changes or the identification of errors in e-communications. Algorithms and other codes incorporating encryption, callback, or other acknowledgements are used to verify authenticity of messages. UCITA validates the use of electronic agents, automated means of initiating action, and responding to electronic records without review by human beings. Under UCITA § 206, the parties may closely track both E–Sign and UETA's concept of attribution. Under UCITA § 206, the parties may use electronic agents to enter into contracts (offer and acceptance) without the benefit of human review.[350] UCITA updates the concept of writing with a "record," which is the functional equivalent of a paper-based writing.

Section 107 of UCITA provides that "a record or authentication may not be denied legal effect or enforceability solely because it is in electronic form." [351] UCITA spells out substantive rules needed for online transactions that provide safeguards and safe harbors against a user's inadvertent assent or attribution. Section 212(a) states that electronic events are attributable to either the person or their electronic agent. Trading partner agreements often specify the protocols used in computer-to-computer transactions.

(H) Formation of Online Contracts

UCITA follows the U.C.C. definition of a contract that includes express terms plus supplemental terms. "An 'agreement' is the bargain of the parties in fact as found in their language or other circumstances, including course of performance, course of dealing, or usage of trade."[352] UCITA updates contract law substituting the concept of a record for a writing.[353] Mark Lemley criticizes UCITA's overly liberal formation rules:

> [S]ince [UCITA] makes it so easy to write and enforce the terms of a contract, a software vendor with a good lawyer can quite easily enforce *virtually whatever terms it likes* simply by putting them 'conspicuously' in a multi-page document that the user cannot even see (much less agree to) until after buying, installing, and beginning to run the software.[354]

---

[350] Id. at § 206.

[351] Id. at § 107.

[352] U.C.C. § 1–201(b)(3).

[353] "A 'record' is information that is inscribed on a tangible medium or that is stored in an electronic or other medium and is retrievable in perceivable form. UCITA § 102(a)(55).

[354] Mark A. Lemley, BEYOND PREEMPTION: THE LAW AND POLICY OF INTELLECTUAL PROPERTY LICENSING, 87 CAL. L. REV. 111, 122 (1999).

UCITA's broad enforceability of standard-form EULAs is aligned with software industry developments.[355] The second part of UCITA "supplies modified contract formation rules adapted to permit and to facilitate electronic contracting, and rules to determine the terms of contracts formed, including protections against "imposed" terms, unauthorized communications, and electronic error, and incentives for pre-transaction disclosure of all terms to be a part of the contract."[356]

UCITA provides Internet-related legal infrastructure that is an advance over U.C.C. Article 2. The concept of a "record" enables the parties of an e-contract to satisfy the moth-eaten Statute of Frauds that still is the law in every U.S. jurisdiction. England abolished its Statute of Fraud in sales in the early 1950s. UCITA allows computer-to-computer transactions by substituting the concept of an electronic record as the functional equivalent of writing. UCITA provides essential legal infrastructure for many different forms of electronic contracts. UCITA § 201 requires a writing for license agreements which are $5,000 or greater.

UCITA recognizes several exceptions to the Statute of Fraud's writing requirement. For example, a license agreement is enforceable after a completed performance, a court admission, or a merchant licensor's failure to answer a confirming record. "Part 3 of UCITA provides rules governing parol evidence, modification, changes in terms and for interpretation in the absence of explicit treatment by the parties."[357] UCITA's parol evidence rule substitutes the term "record" for a writing but is otherwise parallel to U.C.C. § 2–202.[358] Like Article 2, UCITA permits integrated writings to be supplemented by course of performance and by course of dealing and usage of trade. Courts may receive evidence of consistent additional terms unless the record states that it is "a complete and exclusive statement of the terms of the agreement."[359]

(1) Express Warranties

UCITA's express warranty provisions include both affirmation of act and promises that the software publisher or other licensor makes to its customer relating to the software, which is the "basis of the bargain" test. An express warranty is breached when claims are not supported or product fails to live to affirmative statements about its performance. UCITA's express warranty provisions for computer information transactions borrows extensively from U.C.C. § 2–313. Express warranties are not disclaimable because it would be fraud to make a statement about a digital product's performance and then later disclaim it.

---

[355] See e.g., Robert W. Gomulkiewicz, Getting Serious About User–Friendly Mass Market Licensing for Software, 12 GEO. MASON L. REV. 687, 687–88 (2004) (concluding that end user licenses (EULAs) are here to stay for the foreseeable future despite hundreds of articles criticizing this form of contracting).

[356] William Denny, The Joint Task Force of the Delaware State Bar Association Sections of Commercial Law, Computer Law, Intellectual Property, and Real and Personal Property Overview of the Uniform Computer Transactions Act (Jan. 5, 2000) at 11.

[357] Id.

[358] The parol evidence rule prohibits the introduction of extrinsic evidence in prior or contemporaneous agreements to alter the terms of an integrated and complete written contract. Where two contracts contain all the essential terms of the respective agreements, and neither contract is facially ambiguous, they must be viewed as integrated documents that are subject to the parol evidence rule. Under these circumstances, the terms of these contracts may not be varied by parol evidence unless they are somehow ambiguous.

[359] UCITA § 301.

Internet merchants create express warranties whenever they make definite statements about the software's performance in product packaging, banner advertisements, pop-up advertisements, and sales representations or demonstrations, whether on or off line. Website promotional materials, product descriptions, samples, or advertisements will also create express warranties. A breach of warranty claim has four elements: (1) a contract between the parties; (2) a breach of that contract; (3) damages flowing the breach; and (4) that the party stating the claim performed its own contractual obligations. UCITA divides warranties into two broad categories: warranties of non-infringement and warranties of quality. Common software licensing warranties include those of non-infringement, express warranties, the implied warranty of merchantability of a computer program, information content, fitness for licensee's purpose, and the warranty of system integration.[360] When applied to software, the concept of merchantability requires the software to perform at a level that is at least fair, average, and not objectionable in the software industry. Merchantability always references the specific industry. Software must have the minimal quality of similar code in the industry (which tolerates a certain amount of bugs) without objection. The mere fact there are problems in the software does not mean it is unmerchantable.[361]

UCITA's express warranty provisions include "not only affirmations of fact, but also promises made by the licensor to its licensee which relate to the software and become part of the basis of the bargain."[362] Affirmations of fact about software or other digital information creates express warranties to the extent that they form the "basis of the bargain."[363] A licensor makes an express warranty "if the licensor affirms a fact or makes a promise to the licensee."[364] Internet merchants create express warranties when they make definite statements about the software product packaging; banner advertisements; sales literature; and demonstrations—notwithstanding representations made by sales personnel to customers.

Website promotional materials, product descriptions, samples, or advertisements will also create express warranties. A statement that goes to the "basis of the fact" creates an express warranty. Express warranties in the online world are created through sales literature, seller's talk, website advertisements, and live demonstrations on the Internet. The question of whether an express warranty is breached is determined by whether the claims made by products are supportable. UCITA's express warranty

---

[360] Id. at §§ 401, 403–405.

[361] Id. (stating that "[t]he mere fact that some systemic performance failures occur does not prove breach of merchantability. The issue should be whether those failures are extraordinary as juxtaposed to ordinary users and performance of similarly complex programs").

[362] Baney Corp. v. Agilysys NV, LLC, 773 F. Supp. 2d 593, 603 (D. Md. 2011) (holding "that a provision in a license agreement for a multi-property management system computer program requiring defendant to correct program errors was a warranty under Maryland's Uniform Computer Information Transactions Act, but a disclaimer that correction of errors was not guaranteed was construed as requiring only a good faith effort to correct program errors.").

[363] Courts have held that an advertisement or packaging may create an express warranty. See e.g., Cipollone v. Liggett Group, Inc., 893 F. 2d 541, 575–76 (3d Cir. 1990) rev'd in part on other grounds 505 U.S. 504(1992) (concluding that cigarette advertisements representing that the cigarettes were safe could constitute an express warranty); Elias v. Ungar's Food Products, 252 F.R.D. 233, 252 (D.N.J. 2008) (packaging statements regarding fat and caloric content created express warranty).

[364] JANE K. WINN & BENJAMIN WRIGHT, THE LAW OF ELECTRONIC COMMERCE 13–30 (2001).

provisions for computer information transactions are substantially similar to U.C.C. § 2–313.

(2) Implied Warranty of Merchantability

As with U.C.C. Article 2, merchantability in software contracts are contextual and defined in large part by quality standards in the industry. The implied warranty of merchantability means that the software quality standards must be fit for its ordinary purpose. Software must be non-objectionable in the trade, be at least fair average, and be adequately packaged. Software vendors typically disclaim this warranty because of uncertainty as to the meaning of merchantability for software or digital products. Software is rarely, if ever, bug-free, so vendors do not want to be held accountable for minor errors. Information, software, or data, must have the minimal quality of similar code in the industry, which tolerates a certain amount of bugs without objection. Bug free software is not yet the industry standard and insubstantial defects in software may not defeat its merchantability.[365] Software or data need not be the best quality, but cannot be the worst either, in order to satisfy the merchantability standard.

(3) Fitness–Type Warranties

Courts subdivide implied warranties of quality into the implied warranty of merchantability and the systems integration warranty or fitness-type warranty. The concept of merchantability applies to the ordinary purposes of software, data, or information, whereas fitness or systems integration warranties signify interoperability standards or whether a given software application works on a specific computer system. The fitness for a particular purpose warranty has its genesis in U.C.C. § 2–315. Section 405 of UCITA recognizes two fitness-type warranties: (a) the fitness for particular purpose (Section 405(a)) and (c) the systems integration warranty (Section 405(c)). UCITA's fitness for a particular purpose warranty, Section 405(a), requires proof that the licensor knew or had reason to know of a particular purpose for which the information is required.

The licensee must demonstrate that it was relying upon the licensor, and that the computer software or other information was fit for a particular purpose. The fitness warranty is disclaimable and modifiable, arising whenever a licensee relies upon a "licensor's skill or judgment to select, develop, or furnish" software or other information. This implied warranty is that the software delivered is fit for the licensee's purpose. Subsection 405(a)(2) applies a reasonable effort standard for service-like obligations. The software fitness standard is less rigorous than that for the sale of goods.

The software fitness standard is less rigorous than that for the sale of goods. This fitness warranty is contextualized, which means that software may pass the merchantability hurdle, but may not be suitable for a licensee's needs.[366] In an illustrative case, a computer vendor delivered a computed topographer scan machine ("CT Scan") that was merchantable but still not suitable for the customer's particular purpose. The CT scanner met the standard of fair average quality but failed to pass the

---

[365] Id. (stating that "[t]he mere fact that some systemic performance failures occur does not prove breach of merchantability. The issue should be whether those failures are extraordinary as juxtaposed to ordinary users and performance of similarly complex programs.").

[366] BARKLEY CLARK & CHRISTOPHER SMITH, 1 THE LAW OF PRODUCT WARRANTIES § 6.2 (Nov. 2009).

contextual fitness test, as it was not suitable for the radiologists' practice, which used x-rays to create pictures of cross-sections of the entire body.

The fitness warranty issue arose because the radiologists had informed the vendor that they needed software for full body scans, not just head scans, therefore the fitness warranty was breached because the CT Scan software delivered could only accommodate head scans. Section 405(a) is the fitness warranty that applies "when a licensor has reason to know of the licensee's particular purpose in the transaction and that the licensee is relying on the licensor's expertise in selecting or developing information suitable for that purpose."[367] Section 405(a)(2) cuts back on the fitness for a particular purpose where the licensor is rendering services in a computer contract. Subsection 405(a)(2) "applies a reasonable effort standard for cases where the relationship appears to concern services-like obligations. Under prior law, the decision was based on whether a court viewed the transaction as a sale (result) or services (effort) contract."[368]

UCITA's fitness for a particular purpose warranty, Section 405(a) requires proof that the licensor knew or had reason to know of a particular purpose for which the information is required. The licensee must demonstrate that it was relying upon the licensor that the computer software or other information was fit for a particular purpose. The fitness warranty is disclaimable and modifiable; it arises when a licensee relies upon a "licensor's skill or judgment to select, develop, or furnish" software or other information.[369] This implied warranty is that software is fit for the licensee's purpose.

> If an agreement requires a licensor to provide or select a system consisting of computer programs and goods, and the licensor has reason to know that the licensee is relying on the skill or judgment of the licensor to select the components of the system, there is an implied warranty that the components provided or selected will function together as a system.[370]

In the illustrative medical products case discussed above a computer vendor delivered a CAT scan machine that was merchantable but was not suitable for the customer's particular purpose. The CAT scanner was of fair average quality but did not meet the contextual needs of the radiologists. The group of radiologists let their vendor know that they intended to use the product for body scanning, not just head scanning as the CAT Scan software was only fit for head scans and could not read full-body scans. In another software fitness case, a doctor charged that a computer vendor's billing system software was not fit for its particular purposes. The court found that the doctor's office failed to give its vendor notice of the problems and found the problem to be training staff on how to use the software rather than a defect in the software.

Software must not only be merchantable and fit for a particular purpose but also be interoperable with a given computer system or it is of no use to the licensee. "Section 405(c) creates a new implied warranty regarding system performance in cases of systems integration contracts. The warranty is that the selected components will

---

[367] UCITA, Id. at § 405(a).

[368] UCITA, Id. at § 405, cmt. 4.

[369] UCITA, Id. at § 405(a)(1).

[370] UCITA § 405(c)(2).

function as a system."[371] "This does not mean that the system, other than as stated in subsection (a) will meet the licensee's purposes, that it is an optimal system, or that it will not infringe third party rights. The warranty is merely that the system will functionally operate as a system."[372]

(4) Systems Integration Warranties

Systems integration warranties are more important in the business-to-business cases than the business-to-consumer context. UCITA § 405(c) creates an implied warranty of system integration for software that performs as part of a complex computer system. The systems integration warranty is a representation that a given component will interoperate with other components of a system. In a development contract, the commissioning party should require the licensor to give a compatibility warranty:

> Compatibility warranty—The software should be warranted to operate with any hardware or third party software the licensor recommends. This is especially important if the software will be used as a basis on which the licensee plans to build a particular function. Also, the warranty should specify that all upgrades and enhancements provided will operate with the licensed software without errors or malfunctions.[373]

The systems integration warranty often arises when a customer relies upon the expertise of the vendor who represents that a given component or program will work on a given system. For example, an online company could be making a systems integration warranty if it told a customer its software would perform on a Windows 8 platform.

(5) Information Content Warranties

UCITA recognizes an implied warranty for informational content that is unlike those found in either Article 2 or 2A of the UCC. Section 404, the information content warranty, is given only by merchant/licensors with a special relationship of reliance with the licensee that "collects, compiles, processes, provides or transmits informational content."[374] According to § 404(a), the merchant-licensor's duty as to information content is limited to inaccuracies "caused by the merchant's failure to perform with reasonable care."[375] UCITA § 404(b)(1) does not extend this warranty to encompass published content nor is it applicable to the subjective qualities of information. The information content warranty is inapplicable to published conduits or where licensor is simply a conduit, which does not provide editorial services.

UCITA's information content warranty is negligence-based, not predicated upon strict liability like the other warranties. Section 404, cmt. 2 states, "Reasonable efforts, not perfect results, provide the appropriate standard in the absence of express terms to the contrary."[376] Section 404(b) does not warrant the accuracy of published information.

---

[371] UCITA § 405, cmt. 6.

[372] Id.

[373] Marie Flores, Don't Settle For Just a Warranty, 19 NO. 10 E-COMMERCE L. & STRATEGY 1 (Feb. 2003).

[374] UCITA § 404.

[375] UCITA § 404(b)(1).

[376] UCITA § 404(b).

Licensors frequently limit any warranty representation to what they contributed to a database, software or other digital information to avoid being held legally responsible for the shortcomings of the entire system.

This warranty is more appropriate to database access agreements than to software licensing. "An 'access agreement' is an agreement that authorizes the user of software to access the provider's software via a data-transmission system, such as the Internet, or via a private network or another intermediary now known or hereafter developed."[377] Section 404(a) limits the warranty to merchant/licensors that have a special relationship of reliance with the licensee. This information-content warranty is limited to the statement that the content was not inaccurate due to anything that the licensor did in its processing. It is the information content creator, not the licensor, who would create inaccuracies in informational content. Therefore, this warranty gives little protection to the licensee against inaccuracies.

The merchant-licensor's duty as to information content is limited to inaccuracies "caused by the merchant's failure to perform with reasonable care."[378] UCITA devises an implied warranty for informational content that is unlike those found in either Article 2 or 2A of the UCC.[379] Virginia, one of only two states to enact UCITA, adopted the information content warranty:

> Unless the warranty is disclaimed or modified, a merchant that, in a special relationship of reliance with a licensee, collects, compiles, processes, provides, or transmits informational content warrants to that licensee that there is no inaccuracy in the informational content caused by the merchant's failure to perform with reasonable care.
>
> (b) A warranty does not arise under subsection (A) with respect to:
>
> (1) subjective characteristics of the informational content, such as the aesthetics, appeal, and suitability to taste;
>
> (2) published informational content; or
>
> (3) a person that acts as a conduit or provides no more than editorial services in collecting, compiling, distributing, processing, providing, or transmitting informational content that under the circumstances can be identified as that of a third person.
>
> (c) The warranty under this section is not subject to the preclusion . . . (b)(1) on disclaiming obligations of diligence, reasonableness, or care.[380]

UCITA's information content warranty is negligence-based not predicated upon strict liability like the other warranties. The information warranty is not what it is cracked up to be because it is not applicable to published content. "One who hires an expert cannot expect infallibility unless the express terms clearly so require. Reasonable efforts, not perfect results, provide the appropriate standard in the absence of express terms to the contrary."[381] Moreover, this warranty is more significant for

---

[377] Principles of the Law of Software Contracts, Id. at § 101(a).

[378] UCITA § 404(a).

[379] Id. at § 404.

[380] Va. Code § 59.1–504.4. (Implied warranty; informational content).

[381] UCITA § 404, cmt. 2.

what it does not do. Section 404(b) states, "merchant licensors give no warranty for the accuracy of published information content."[382] A lawyer representing a licensor in a contract where the customer delivers data should limit any warranty protection to the licensor's contribution to the inaccuracy. This warranty is more appropriate to database agreements than for software licensing.

The information content warranty focusing on accuracy of data has a limited sphere of application. First, only a merchant/licensor can give this warranty.[383] Second, the merchant/licensor must have a special relationship of reliance with the licensee.[384] Third, the warranty is limited to the statement that the content was not inaccurate due to the licensor's processing.[385] It is the information content creator, not the licensor, who would create inaccuracies in informational content. Therefore, this warranty gives little protection to the licensee against inaccuracies. This special warranty applies to merchant/licensors who deal in information transactions; it requires that the information transferred is accurate within the practice of reasonable care.[386]

The warranty for informational content does not arise for subjective aspects of the informational content, published content or when the licensor is merely acting as an information transfer conduit without providing editorial services.[387] This warranty may be disclaimed despite UCITA's general prohibition against disclaiming reasonableness and care.[388] The information content warranty does not extend to aesthetics, subjective quality, or marketability. No court has construed the meaning of the implied warranty for information content but presumably, the general standard for services applies.[389]

(6) Warranty Disclaimers & Limitations

UCITA allows the parties to disclaim or modify all implied warranties by words or conduct. The parties to a software license agreement must use specific language to disclaim warranties, although it may sometimes be disclaimed by circumstances. An express warranty once created is as "tenacious as a bulldog, and the only way to get rid of it is to see that it never takes hold."[390] Many license agreements attempt to disclaim express warranties, but the only way to avoid liability for express warranties is not to make them. As with U.C.C. Article 2, the implied warranty of merchantability is sufficient to disclaim the implied warranty of informational content. The vast majority of software license agreements disclaim the implied warranty of merchantability. A former Microsoft lawyer attributes this software industry contracting practice of

---

[382] UCITA § 404(b).

[383] UCITA § 404(a).

[384] Id.

[385] Id.

[386] Id.

[387] Id. at § 404(b).

[388] Id. at § 404(c).

[389] UCITA § 404, cmt. 1.

[390] Thomas M. Quinn, Uniform Commercial Code Commentary And Law Digest ¶2–313[A] 2–136 (1st ed. 1978).

disclaiming merchantability to the uncertain meaning of software merchantability. Why should software publishers take on a liability with 'unknown repercussions?'[391]

Just as in Article 2 of the U.C.C., UCITA allows the parties to disclaim or modify all implied warranties by words or conduct. "Any disclaimer of the implied warranty of non-infringement and quiet enjoyment must be by specific language or by circumstances . . . of the implied warranty of merchantability is also sufficient to disclaim the implied warranty of informational content."[392] In addition, the use of "as is" or like expressions may disclaim remedies with the "exception of the warranties of quiet enjoyment and non-infringement under UCITA § 401 or UCITA § 404,"[393] Warranties of noninfringement are only disclaimable by specific language. Similarly specific language is required to disclaim the warranty of accuracy, UCITA § 404.[394] Amazon, the Internet's largest bookstore, is typical of Internet vendors in disclaiming all warranties, express, or implied, including, but not limited to, implied warranties of merchantability and fitness for a particular purpose. Amazon also does not make any warranty as to its information, content, materials, products (including software), or services. Amazon also disclaims responsibility for viruses originating on its site using specific language.

UCITA's legal infrastructure legitimates the software industry practice of eliminating the implied warranty; licensors often follow Amazon.com's practice of offering its services on an "as-is" basis. In order to exclude the implied warranty of merchantability, the exclusionary language must mention the word "merchantability;" must be in writing; and must be conspicuous. Warranty limitations must not be unconscionable nor violate fundamental public policies. The Reporter for the Principles of the Law of Contracts provided by the American law Institute completed an empirical study concluding that fifty-three out of fifty-four Internet websites eliminated all warranty protection.[395] From the beginning of the software industry, vendors universally disclaimed implied warranties of merchantability and the fitness for a particular purpose. In the absence of a disclaimer, computer programs must be fit for their ordinary purpose.

Consumer software is subject to state law limitations. Some software publishers will place a legend on their warranty disclaimer that: "Certain state laws do not allow limitations on implied warranties or the exclusion or limitation of certain damages." The proviso might additionally state, "If these laws apply to you, some or all of the above disclaimers, exclusions, or limitations may not apply to you, and you might have additional rights to avoid undue scrutiny from the Federal Trade Commission or state attorneys general consumer protection divisions." Massachusetts' Chapter 106, 2–316A prohibits sellers as well as lessors to disclaim the implied warranty of merchantability and fitness for a particular purpose. Massachusetts' law makes it clear that attempted

---

[391] Robert W. Gomulkiewicz, The Implied Warranty of Merchantability in Software Contracts: A Warranty No One Dares to Give and How to Change That, 16 JOHN MARSHALL J. OF COMP. & INFO. L. 393, 393 (1998).

[392] 2 GEORGE B. DELTA & JEFFREY H. MATSURRA, LAW OF THE INTERNET 13–118 (2008).

[393] Id.

[394] JOHN EDWARD MURRAY & HARRY M. FLECTNER, SALES, LEASES, AND ELECTRONIC COMMERCE: PROBLEMS AND MATERIALS ON NATIONAL AND INTERNATIONAL TRANSACTIONS 146 (2003).

[395] Robert A. Hillman & Ibrahim Barakat, Warranties and Disclaimers in the Electronic Age, 11 YALE J. L. & TECH. 1, 3 (2009).

disclaimers of the implied warranties of fitness and merchantability in consumer transactions are unenforceable.

(7) Non–Infringement Warranty

The non-infringement warranty is a representation that the licensor warrants that it does not infringe a third party's patents, copyrights, trademarks, or trade secrets. The essence of this warranty is that the licensor represents that it has the intellectual property rights necessary to license the software or digital data. Most licensors are not willing to provide this broad non-infringement warranty and instead give a warranty that they have no knowledge of infringement.[396] Under this provision, a licensor that knowingly delivers infringing software or interferes with its customer's right to use software will be required to indemnify its customer. Any disclaimer of the implied warranty of non-infringement and quiet enjoyment must be done with specific language. UCITA adapts the warranty of quiet possession of information transfers from the law of real property.

The essence of the quiet enjoyment warranty is the right of a licensee to use information for the duration of the license without interference by a licensor or a third party. The quiet enjoyment warranty applies only to the acts or omissions of the licensor, not to third parties. A licensee receives "peace of mind" that it is not purchasing an intellectual property lawsuit along with the software code. The licensor is accountable if the software or other information product infringes title or intellectual property rights of others. UCITA's non-infringement warranty states:

> A licensor of information that is a merchant regularly dealing in information of the kind warrants that the information will be delivered free of the rightful claim of any third person by way of infringement or misappropriation, but a licensee that furnishes detailed specifications to the licensor and the method required for meeting the specifications holds the licensor harmless against any such claim that arises out of compliance with either the required specification or the required method except for a claim that results from the failure of the licensor to adopt, or notify the licensee of, a non-infringing alternative of which the licensor had reason to know.[397]

A licensor that delivers infringing software or interferes with its customer's right to use software will be required to indemnify its customer if its software infringes the intellectual property of third parties. Any disclaimer of the implied warranty of non-infringement and quiet enjoyment must be done with specific language. UCITA adapts the warranty of quiet possession of information transfers. This concept originated in real property transactions and later was applied to sales and leases of goods in the UCC.

UCITA imposes a strict liability standard, making the licensor accountable if the software or other information product infringes title or intellectual property rights of others. The software warranties for non-interference and non-infringement protect the licensee should the licensed software infringe the intellectual property rights of third parties. In states adopting UCITA, the licensor will have a duty to indemnify its

---

[396] H. WARD CLASSEN, A PRACTICAL GUIDE TO SOFTWARE LICENSING FOR LICENSEES AND LICENSORS 511 (2d ed. 2007).

[397] UCITA § 401(a).

customer if delivered software violates a third party's intellectual property rights.[398] Nevertheless, the licensor will seek to limit its indemnification duties to claims recognized under U.S. intellectual property rights existing at the time that the licensor delivers the software.[399] In addition to non-infringement, licensors also give a warranty of non-interference to their customers:

> for the duration of the license, that no person holds a rightful claim to, or interest in, the information which arose from an act or omission of the licensor, other than a claim by way of infringement or misappropriation, which will interfere with the licensee's enjoyment of its interest; and

> (2) as to rights granted exclusively to the licensee, that within the scope of the license:

> (A) to the knowledge of the licensor, any licensed patent rights are valid and exclusive to the extent exclusivity and validity are recognized by the law under which the patent rights were created; and

> (B) in all other cases, the licensed informational rights are valid and exclusive for the information as a whole to the extent exclusivity and validity are recognized by the law applicable to the licensed rights in a jurisdiction to which the license applies.[400]

(I) Performance of a License Agreement

Delivery in a software contract occurs when the software maker gives its customer electronic access to the licensed software. In a typical software license agreement, the licensor's delivery obligation may be to give its customer an activation key to enable access to the licensed software. In an Internet transmission, delivery frequently comes in the form of a download from a website. In a cloud-computing environment, a customer will access computing applications and data from a datacenter that provides services as opposed to tangible goods. Part 6 of UCITA extends commercial law concepts and methods to information performance standards. Section 605 applies a "material breach" standard in business-to-business transactions rather than the perfect tender rule, which is reserved for business-to-consumer transactions.[401] Licensors will generally prefer a fundamental or material breach standard for performance.

A material breach of a software license agreement "occurs when there is a breach of an essential and inducing feature of the contract."[402] The First Circuit U.S. Court of Appeals defined material breach to occur: "when there is a breach of an essential and inducing feature of the contract."[403] A material breach by one party excuses the other party from further performance under the contract, and once relieved from performance, the injured party is not liable for further damages incurred by the party in material breach. The legal significance of a material breach by either the licensor or

---

[398] UCITA § 401.

[399] H. WARD CLASSEN, A PRACTICAL GUIDE TO SOFTWARE LICENSING, Id. at 57.

[400] UCITA § 401(b) (stating non-interference warranty).

[401] UCITA § 605.

[402] Teragram Corp. v. Marketwatch.com, Inc., 444 F.3d 1, 26 (1st Cir. 2006).

[403] Id.

licensee "excuses the other party from further performance under the contract."[404] Software failure is "the occurrence of either deficient functionality, where the program fails to perform a required function, or deficient performance, where the program performs a required function too slow or in an insufficient manner"[405] UCITA's § 701 gives an aggrieved party the right to refuse a performance that is a material breach.[406] Under this section, a material breach is first determined by examining the agreement. Examples of breach would be repudiation of a contract, failure to perform a contractual obligation in a timely way, exceeding the scope of use, or failing to comply with other conditions expressed in the contract.

As with U.C.C. Article 2, it is a breach to repudiate a contract before the date of performance (anticipatory repudiation). UCITA's performance rules are functionally equivalent to U.C.C. Article 2 except for its articulation of a material breach standard for non-mass-market transactions. Section 703 imports U.C.C. § 2–508's concept of a cure. A federal appeals court affirmed damages for a software developer's failure to cure software defects in a 2006 case. The court found that a licensor failed to make any efforts to correct material failure and did not perform substantially in accordance with the software's documentation.[407] Section 704 adopts the material breach standard for defective tender of software. Section 707 imports the concept of revocation of acceptance from Article 2. Section 708 gives parties a right to an adequate assurance of performance, while Section 709 adopts the concept of anticipatory repudiation with similar provisions to U.C.C. Article 2, whereas retraction of anticipatory repudiation is found in Section 710.[408]

Defects in software may be difficult to detect unless engineers build in an extensive period of alpha testing. Newly developed software will often have latent design defects only detectable in certain applications. Software problems may not surface until the product interacts with a third party's software. The licensor will want to reallocate the risk if its product will not work with third party software. U.C.C. Article 2's perfect tender rule does not mesh well with developmental or customized software where bugs are worked out over a period of acceptance testing. A licensor will be concerned that a court will mechanically apply the "perfect tender" standard to software, so it is preferred that the parties agree to a material breach or fundamental breach standard to replace the perfect tender rule. Saba Software disclosed in a 10Q S.E.C. filing that they, like many other companies, are challenged by the problem of identifying design defects or errors in their software prior to release:

> Products as complex as ours often contain unknown and undetected errors or performance problems. Although our products are subject to rigorous testing and quality control processes, serious defects are frequently found during the period immediately following introduction and initial shipment of new products or enhancements to existing products. Although we attempt to resolve all errors that we believe would be considered serious by our customers before shipment to them, our products are not error-free. These errors or performance problems could result

---

[404] Id. at 27.

[405] See Daniel T. Perlman, Note, Who Pays the Price of Computer Software Failure?, 24 RUTGERS COMPUTER & TECH. L.J. 383, 387 (1998).

[406] UCITA § 701.

[407] Teragram Corp. v. Marketwatch.com, Inc., 444 F.3d 1, 29 (1st Cir. 2006).

[408] UCITA §§ 709, 710.

in lost revenues, reduced service levels, delays in customer acceptance on professional services products and would be detrimental to our business and reputation. As is typical in the software industry, with each release we have discovered errors in our products after introduction. We will not be able to detect and correct all errors before releasing our products commercially and these undetected errors could be significant. We cannot assure you that there are no undetected errors or performance problems.[409]

A software maker will find it difficult to comply with the "perfect tender rule." The parties must spell out the meaning of impaired functionality if they choose that test rather than "perfect tender." U.C.C. § 601, the perfect tender rule, permits a buyer to obtain substitute goods if the goods fail "in any respect to conform to the contract."[410] UCITA's material breach standard is functionally equivalent to Article 25 of the Convention for the International Sale of Goods ("CISG"). UCITA imports a large number of performance-related concepts such as tender, acceptance, rejection, revocation, cure repudiation, and retraction from U.C.C. Article 2, with minor adaptations. UCITA's concept of tender is that a licensor transmits a copy of software or otherwise enables use or access to software, databases, or other information. In a mass-market license agreement, the acceptance process will typically include downloading and using the software. As with the sale of goods, acceptance occurs if the customer fails to return software after using it. The customer may expressly communicate acceptance to the software publisher or failing to reject the software. The parties need to specify acceptance criteria for the customer's acceptance testing in its operational environment. The acceptance-testing period is a software industry practice where the software developer gives its customer a fixed period to evaluate the software and either accept or reject it.

UCITA adopts a material breach standard for performance in Section 701 that gives an aggrieved party the right to refuse a performance that is a material breach. Section 701 states a material breach is first determined by examining the agreement. "A breach occurs if a party without legal excuse fails to perform an obligation in a timely manner, repudiates a contract, or exceeds a contractual use term, or otherwise is not in compliance with an obligation placed on it by this [Act] or the agreement."[411] UCITA § 601(b)(1) excludes the material breach standard for copies of software or other information in a mass-market transaction. UCITA adopts the perfect tender rule for mass-market transactions but this rule does not extend to business-to-business or custom licenses.[412] UCITA defines a "mass-market" license to include "consumer contracts" but also any other license where the end-user licensee receives software on the same terms. Mass-market end-user licenses are offered by the licensor on the same terms for the same rights without individual negotiation. Part 6 of UCITA also sets forth the procedure for terminating a license agreement.

UCITA § 617 requires that the terminating party to give the other party a "reasonable notice of termination."[413] Termination is the legally operative stage that

---

[409] Saba Software Inc., 10–Q Filing to Securities & Exchange Commission (October 7, 2009).

[410] U.C.C. § 2–601.

[411] UCITA § 701.

[412] UCITA § 601(b)(1).

[413] UCITA § 617.

discharges obligations on the part of the licensor and the licensee. Nevertheless, in software license agreements, a licensee may have continuing obligations that survive termination unlike sales or leases of goods. The Joint Task Force of the Delaware State Bar Association Sections of Commercial Law, Computer Law, Intellectual Property, and Real and Personal Property summarizes UCITA Part Six as follows:

> Part 6 of UCITA adapts traditional rules as to what is acceptable performance to the context of computer information transactions, including providing rules for the protection of the parties concerning the electronic regulation of performance (Section 605), to clarify that the appropriate general rule is one of material breach with respect to cancellation (rather than so called "perfect tender") (see Section 601; see also Sections 701, 704, and 802), and to carry over the familiar rules of Article 2 when appropriate in the context of the tangible medium on which the information is fixed and for impracticability. Part 6 also supplies guidance in the case of certain specialized types of contracts for termination.[414]

UCITA adopts a substantial performance or material breach standard versus Article 2's parochial and unrealistic perfect tender rule for contract performance, which is adopted in no other country connected to the Internet. In contrast, the U.C.C. Article 2 perfect tender rule permits a buyer to obtain substitute goods if the goods fail "in any respect to conform to the contract."[415] Perfect tender is not a realistic performance standard for the sale of goods, and courts find ways to bypass this harsh doctrine. Perfect tender is a disaster for the software industry where software may be composed of millions of lines of code. A licensee should not be able to cancel a software contract because of a minor bug or errant line of code. The material breach standard parallels the fundamental breach of Article 25 of CISG.[416] The vast majority of material breach cases will be ones in which the software fails to substantially conform to its documentation.

UCITA imports a large number of performance concepts from U.C.C. Article 2, with minor adaptations. UCITA adapts U.C.C. Article 2 concepts such as tender, acceptance, rejection, revocation of acceptance, cure, anticipatory repudiation, and retraction of anticipatory repudiation from Article 2 of the UCC. UCITA's concept of tender is that a licensor transmits a copy of software or otherwise enables use or access to software, databases, or other information.[417] A licensor's right to cure is a major countervailing power to the licensee's right to reject software products. In Sun Microsystems technology development and distribution license, Microsoft had a thirty-day period for error correction if it failed to meet the compatibility requirements for Java programming language.[418] If Microsoft could not cure the problems in this period, Sun Microsystems had the right of termination.

Under U.C.C. Article 2, a buyer's refusal to permit the seller to cure the non-conforming tender was grounds for breach of the sales contract. In customized or development software agreements, the acceptance period is the functional equivalent of

---

[414] William Denny, The Joint Task Force of the Delaware State Bar Association Sections of Commercial Law, Computer Law, Intellectual Property, and Real and Personal Property Overview of the Uniform Computer Transactions Act (Jan. 5, 2000).

[415] U.C.C. § 2–601.

[416] CISG art. 25.

[417] U.C.C. §§ 2–601, 2–602.

[418] Sun Microsystems v. Microsoft Corp., 81 F. Supp.2d 1026, 1032 (N.D. Cal. 2000).

a cure. During the acceptance-testing period, the customer will have an opportunity to fix bugs, reconfigure interfaces, and make adjustments to improve compatibility. UCITA adapts U.C.C. Article 2's perfect tender rule to mass-market software licensing transactions.[419] UCITA § 601(b)(1) excludes the material breach standard for copies of software or other information in a mass-market transaction. "This "conforming tender" rule (sometimes described as the "perfect tender" rule) applies to cases involving delivery of a copy in mass-market transactions."[420]

UCITA defines a "mass-market" license to include "consumer contracts" but also any other license where the end-user licensee receives software on the same terms. Mass-market end-user licenses are offered by the licensor on the same terms for the "same information or informational rights in a retail transaction under terms and in a quantity consistent with an ordinary transaction in a retail market."[421] Part 6 of UCITA sets forth the procedure for terminating a license agreement. UCITA § 617 requires that the terminating party to give the other party a "reasonable notice of termination."[422] Termination is the legally operative stage that discharges obligations on the part of the licensor and the licensee. In software license agreements, a licensee may have continuing obligations that survive termination.

(J) Remedies for Licensors and Licensees

Part 7 of UCITA establishes the basic rules that govern breach of computer information transaction agreements. Even if a licensor tenders software with a substantial defect, it will have an opportunity to cure—a concept UCITA imports from U.C.C. § 2–508. A customer's failure to notify the vendor that it is rejecting software serves as a waiver of all remedies. Part 8 of UCITA imports many U.C.C. Article 2's remedies by adapting provisions to licensing. UCITA defines "'direct damages' as compensation for losses associated with the value of the contracted for performance itself as contrasted to loss of a benefit expected from use of the performance or its results."[423] The key UCITA sections measuring direct damages are Section 808 and 809 that are capped by the contracted-for price or market value for the performance as appropriate. Section 816 of UCITA limits licensor's ability to electronically repossess information or disable software.

UCITA gives the aggrieved party the right to seek a remedy for nonmaterial breaches as well as for material breaches. However, rescinding a software license agreement does not preclude the aggrieved party from pursuing other remedies. An aggrieved party may cancel a license agreement if there is an uncured material breach, but the breaching party has a right to notice before the non-breaching party cancels a software contract. UCITA tailored buyer and seller remedies to software transactions. UCITA § 804 is a carbon copy of U.C.C. § 2–718, the doctrine of liquidated damages, which defers to the parties' compensation clauses.

Parties may specify liquidated damages, sometimes called compensation clauses, in advance so long as they do not amount to a penalty clause. A compensation clause in

---

[419] UCITA § 601, cmt. 4.

[420] Id.

[421] U.C.C. § 1–201(44).

[422] UCITA § 617.

[423] UCITA § 102(22).

a license agreement may set both a floor and a ceiling for recovery by the non-breaching party (minimum and maximum recovery). The licensee can only change limited remedies on the narrow grounds of unconscionability, fundamental public policy, or the issue of mutuality of obligation. None of these tools are promising for addressing consumer protection problems such as one-sided choice of law, predispute mandatory arbitration, and limited but exclusive remedies.[424]

Section 803(b) adopts the doctrine of "sole and exclusive" remedy from U.C.C. Article 2. Xerox offers two remedies for its breach of warranty; (1) replace the non-conforming software or (2) give its customer a refund. The licensor must include the specific language "sole and exclusive" to the limited remedy provision in the license to ensure that the limited remedy displace all other remedies.

If a licensee can prove that "performance of an exclusive or limited remedy causes the remedy to fail of its essential purpose," it may pursue all licensee remedies under UCITA. UCITA's doctrine of the failure of essential purpose is the functional equivalent of U.C.C. § 2–719(2). Courts frequently employ the doctrine of the failure of essential purpose to strike down unreasonable limitations of damages in software licenses, as was the case in *RRX Industries. v. Lab–Con, Inc.*[425] In *RRX Industries,* the court invalidated a clause in a software license agreement that limited the licensee's recovery to actual fees paid under the license agreement. In *RRX,* the computer seller began installing the software system in January 1981 and completed it in June 1981. Bugs appeared in them soon after installation. The seller attempted to repair the bugs by telephone patching.

The licensor upgraded the system to make it compatible with hardware that was more sophisticated. However, the software maker was unable to iron out the bugs and the software did not perform according to the specifications. The court found that the computer maker failed to install an operational software system and to train the buyer's employees how to use it. The court upheld the district court's finding that the default of the computer seller was "so total and fundamental that its consequential damages limitation was expunged from the contract."[426]

UCITA § 803 permits an aggrieved licensee to have all UCITA remedies if the vendor's sole and exclusive remedy "fails of its essential purpose." Courts have struck down limited remedy clauses in license agreements where the licensee does not receive the benefit of the bargain.[427] As with most UCITA provisions, the parties to a license agreement have the freedom of contract to forge their own contract remedies. UCITA gives the aggrieved party the right to seek a remedy for nonmaterial breaches as well as for material breaches. However, rescinding a software license agreement does not preclude the aggrieved party from pursuing other remedies. An aggrieved party may cancel a license agreement if there is an uncured material breach, but the breaching party has a right to notice before the non-breaching party cancels a software contract.

---

[424] See generally, Jean R. Sternlight, Creeping Mandatory Arbitration: Is It Just?, 57 STAN. L. REV. 1631 (2005).

[425] 772 F.2d 543 (9th Cir. 1985).

[426] Id. at 547.

[427] RRX Industries, Inc. v. Lab-Con, Inc., 772 F.2d 543, 41 U.C.C. Rep. Serv. 1561 (9th Cir. 1985) (striking down a clause in a software license where the licensor agreed to correct programming "bugs" but limited the licensor's liability to an amount not in excess of the actual amounts paid to the licensor as license fees).

UCITA has essentially imported the buyer's and seller's remedies of Article 2 of the U.C.C. to software transactions.

Non-performance of the remedy leaves the licensee without what it bargained for under the contract, a functioning product.[428] For example, UCITA reasons that an agreed limited remedy provision is enforceable even if it does not afford a consumer (or other licensee) a "minimum adequate remedy."[429] The consumer's only tools for challenging TOUs will be on the narrow grounds of unconscionability, fundamental public policy, and the issue of mutuality of obligation.[430] None of these tools is promising in resolvingroblems such as one-sided choice of law and forum clauses.

If a licensee can prove that "performance of an exclusive or limited remedy causes the remedy to fail of its essential purpose," the licensee may pursue any other UCITA remedy.[431] Maryland's UCITA allows parties to choose the remedies for breach of contract "even to the point of eliminating judicial remedies and creating an "exclusive . . . sole remedy."[432] UCITA's doctrine of the failure of essential purpose is the functional equivalent of U.C.C. § 2–719(2) which provides: "Where circumstances cause an exclusive or limited remedy to fail of its essential purpose, remedy may be had as provided in this Act."[433] UCITA § 803 permits an aggrieved licensee to have all UCITA remedies if the vendor's sole and exclusive remedy "fails of its essential purpose."[434] This provision gives the licensee all of the remedies of UCITA if a limited, exclusive remedy fails.

§ 4.8   PRINCIPLES OF THE LAW OF SOFTWARE CONTRACTS

The American Law Institute ("ALI") initiated the Principles of the Law of Software Contracts ("Principles") to fill a gap left by the demise of UCITA and to bridge a gap in software contracting law.[435] The ALI approved the Principles in 2009 as "soft law" as opposed to UCITA, which was hard law as a state statute to be enacted by legislatures. The Principles are a Restatement-like template to guide courts, contractors, and policymakers. "Further, the near demise of the Uniform Computer Information Transactions Act ("UCITA") and the vague scope provision of amended Article 2 of the Uniform Commercial Code ("U.C.C.") (also unlikely to be widely adopted) exacerbate the confusion, calling attention to the current legal vacuum."[436] The purpose of the Principles is to harmonize and unify software contracting law whether denominated by a sale, a lease, license or other assignment. "Perhaps no other

---

[428] UCITA § 803 cmt. 5(a).

[429] UCITA § 803, cmt. 6.

[430] Id.

[431] Id. at § 803(b).

[432] Baney Corp. v. Agilysys NV, LLC, 773 F.Supp.2d 593, 605 (D. Md. 2011).

[433] U.C.C. § 2–719(2).

[434] Id.

[435] "Issues arising from the process of formation in the software environment share common themes with other kinds of contracts. One major set of questions involves whether to enforce contract terms that become available only after payment, or that are presented in a take-it-or-leave-it standard form, or both. Neither Article 2 of the U.C.C. nor the common law has satisfactorily resolved these issues, as evidenced by the amount of litigation, conflicting decisions, and ink spilled in the law reviews." Principles of the Law of Software Contracts, Introduction.

[436] Principles of the Law of Software Contracts Intro. (2010).

commercial subject matter is in greater need of harmonization and clarification" than software contracts."[437] The Principles bridge a gap in software law:

These Principles seek to clarify and unify the law of software transactions. In light of the many percolating legal issues that pertain to the formation and enforcement of software agreements, an attempt to "restate" this law would be premature. Reinforcing this view, software technology continues to develop, which influences methods of doing business and changes or creates new legal issues. Instead of restating the law, a "Principles" project accounts for the case law and recommends best practices, without unduly hindering the law's adaptability to future developments. For example, the "Principles" drafter can formulate the "black letter" rather broadly, with substantial elaboration in Comments. Further, although these Principles often employ prescriptive language, a "Principles" project is not the law unless and until a court adopts it. Courts can apply the Principles as definitive rules, as a "gloss" on the common law, U.C.C. Article 2, or other statutes, or not at all, as they see fit.[438]

The Principles aim at clear formulations of the law as it presently stands or might plausibly be stated by a court. In the absence of a software contracting law, courts stretch U.C.C. Article 2 and other bricks and mortar principles to digital information. The Reporters identified four issues that need to be resolved in a mature software contracting law:

Software contracts create a wide array of new issues on the substantive side. One central issue is whether contracting parties are free to broaden or narrow the protections afforded by federal and state intellectual property law. Resolution of this issue requires not only attention to contract law, but also sensitivity to the balance of rights created by intellectual property law. Another issue involves the limits of freedom of contract. What terms should be stricken on unconscionability, public policy, or related grounds? A third important issue involves the appropriate level of quality protection for users of software in light of the engineering challenges and diverse methods of producing it, on the one hand, and defective software's potential to cause calamitous harm, on the other. A fourth issue involves the permissible range of software remedies providers may employ, including self-help mechanisms and remedy limitations.[439]

To date, only a single court has cited the Principles of the Law of Software Contracts in a judicial opinion and no court has adopted any of its substantive provisions.[440] Nevertheless, the Principles provide a useful template for software contracts of all kinds: sales, leases, and licenses.[441] UCITA, in contrast, was a statute designed for

---

[437] Principles of the Law of Software Contracts, Id. at Intro. (2010).

[438] Id.

[439] Principles of the Law of Software Contracts Intro. (2010).

[440] Conwell v. Gray Loon Outdoor Mktg. Group, 906 N.E.2d 805, 811 (Ind. Sup. Ct. 2009) (refusing to apply U.C.C. Article 2 but noting that American Law Institute launched Principles of the Law of Software Contracts in affirming judgment in favor of Internet website designer who sued client, seeking payment for making website modifications and hosting client's website).

[441] "The Principles should apply to all software agreements supported by a consideration, including licenses, sales, and access contracts. To some extent, this approach eliminates heretofore contentious debates over the characterization of a transaction, and the resulting implications. For example, the application and reach of these Principles should not depend on whether a transferor labels a transaction a sale or a license. In this regard, the goal of the Principles is to make sure that the legal rights that flow from an agreement do

software licensors. Some critics of the ALI law reform project characterize it as provisions as being too pro-licensee, such as the nondisclaimable duty to warn users of hidden material defects.[442]   This was the opposite criticism of UCITA, which was perceived as pro-licensor.

Because of its burgeoning importance, perhaps no other commercial subject matter is in greater need of harmonization and clarification. Although the software industry is relatively young, it constitutes an increasingly important share of our economy. Further, the law governing the transfer of hard goods is inadequate to govern software transactions because, unlike hard goods, software is characterized by novel speed, copying, and storage capabilities, and new inspection, monitoring, and quality challenges. In short, parties to software transactions would greatly benefit from the clarification and improvement of this area of the law

These Principles seek to clarify and unify the law of software transactions. In light of the many percolating legal issues that pertain to the formation and enforcement of software agreements, an attempt to "restate" this law would be premature. Reinforcing this view, software technology continues to develop, which influences methods of doing business and changes or creates new legal issues. Instead of restating the law, a "Principles" project accounts for the case law and recommends best practices, without unduly hindering the law's adaptability to future developments. . . . The ALI has employed the "Principles" approach before in projects such as "Principles of Corporate Governance: Analysis and Recommendations" and "Principles of the Law of Family Dissolution: Analysis and Recommendations."[443]

Judges have little recourse but to stretch U.C.C. Article 2 to software but sales law "is inadequate to govern software transactions because, unlike hard goods, software is characterized by novel speed, copying, and storage capabilities, and new inspection, monitoring, and quality challenges."[444] The problem with extending U.C.C. Article 2 to software is that it does not fit this durable goods paradigm.[445] Title never passes with licensing unlike sales. Similarly, U.C.C. Article 2's warranty of title is inapplicable to software transactions. Software requires its own specialized legal infrastructure to

---

not depend solely on the label a party places on the agreement. Instead, legal rights are based on the legitimacy of the process of contracting and the meaning and appropriateness of the substantive terms in light of federal intellectual property law, public policy, and unconscionability concerns." Principles of the Law of Software Contracts 1, 2 Overview (2010).

[442] H. Ward Classen, who represents large-scale licensors, stated in his software licensing treatise, that the "Principles are perceived as licensee oriented and as incorporating consumer protections into commercial transactions. Many argue the Principles limit the freedom of contract, increasing vendor cost and uncertainty, leading to an increase in litigation . . . From the licensor's perspective, the most controversial provision addresses a non-disclaimable warranty of 'no hidden material defects.' This warranty may not be disclaimed. The warranty extends " to any party in the normal chain of distribution." H. WARD CLASSEN, A PRACTICAL GUIDE TO SOFTWARE LICENSING FOR LICENSEES AND LICENSORS, (4th ed. 2011) at 273.

[443] Principles of the Law of Software Contracts, Reporters' Introduction (2010).

[444] Id. at 1–2.

[445] The courts' strained efforts of applying the law of sales to the licensing of intangibles is like the television commercial in which two mechanics are trying to fit an oversized automobile battery into a car too small to accommodate it. The car owner looks on with horror as the mechanics hit the battery with mallets, trying to drive it into place. The owner objects and the mechanics say, "we'll make it fit!" The owner says, "I'm not comfortable with make it fit." Michael L. Rustad, Commercial Law Infrastructure for the Age of Information, 16 J. MARSHALL J. COMPUTER & INFO. L. 255, 274 (1997).

reflect its emblematic qualities in the borderline between intellectual property and the law of contracts.

   With soft law, courts have the discretion to apply the Principles as definitive rules, to supplement the common law or Article 2 of the UCC, or not use this template.[446] In the past, the ALI distilled the common law by developing Restatements of the Law such as the Restatement of Contracts and the Restatement of Torts. In contrast to UCITA or Article 2 of the UCC, the Principles of Software are not self-executing and do not apply unless a court adopts them. The Principles offer courts as well as attorneys representing clients a limited number of rules applicable to most software contracts.[447] Courts may also apply the Principles by analogy even though a given transaction is outside the sphere of application. The following is a roadmap of the topics covered by the Principles of the law of Software Contracts:

Chapters of Principles	Key Sections
Chapter 1, Definitions, Scope & General Terms (Sections 1.01–1.14)	Definitions in § 1.01; Scope in General, § 1.06; Scope of Embedded Software; § 1.07; Scope: Mixed Transfers, § 1.08, Enforcement of Terms under Federal intellectual property Law, § 1.09; Public Policy, § 1.10. Unconscionability, § 1.11; Relation to Outside Law, § 1.12 Choice of Law in Standard Form Transfers, Forum–Selection Clauses, § 1.14.
Chapter 2, Formation and Enforcement (Sections 2.01–2.04)	Formation Generally, § 2.01. Enforcement of the Standard Form, § 2.02; Contract Modification, § 2.03.
Chapter 3, Performance (Sections 3.01– 3.12)	Implied Indemnification vs. Infringement, § 3.01;

---

[446] Maureen O'Rourke, Software Contracting, SM088 ALI–ABA 27, American Law Institute American Bar Association, CLE (June 7–8, 2008) (presenting discussion draft).

[447] American Law Institute Reporters, Memorandum to Principles of Software Contracts (May 2010) at xix.

	Express Quality Warranties, § 3.02; Implied Warranty of Merchantability, § 3.03; Implied Warranty of Fitness for a Particular Purpose, § 3.04; Other Implied Quality Warranties, § 3.05; Disclaimer of Express & Implied Quality Warranties, § 3.06; and Third–Party Beneficiaries of Warranty, § 3.07.
Chapter 4 Remedies (Sections 4.01–4.06).	Contractual Modification or Limitation of Remedy, § 4.01; Liquidation and Limitation of Damages, § 4.02; Use of Automated Disablements, § 4.03; Cancellation, § 4.04; Expectation Damages, § 4.05; and Specific Performance, § 4.06.

(A) Sphere of Application

(1) Software Contracts for Consideration

The Principles apply to any transfer of any software, including sales, leases, and licenses, as long as the transfer of software is supported by consideration, which encompasses sales, leases, and licenses.[448] Apache License Version 2.0 grants the licensee a "perpetual, worldwide, non-exclusive, no-charge, royalty-free, irrevocable copyright license to reproduce, prepare Derivative Works of, publicly display, publicly perform, sublicense, and distribute the Work and such Derivative Works in Source or

---

[448] "These Principles address several sets of issues. The first issue involves the scope of the project. For a discussion of this difficult issue, see the Summary Overview to Chapter 1, Topic 2, that follows. We conclude that the appropriate scope of the project is agreements for the transfer of software or access to software for a consideration, i.e., software contracts. The project does not include the exchange of digital art or digital databases for reasons discussed in the Summary Overview to Topic 2 of this Chapter." American Law Institute Reporters, Introduction to Principles of Software Contracts (May 2010).

Object form."[449] The Principles' sphere of application excludes all open source software contracts that are royalty-free or without consideration.

The Principles of the Law of Software Contracts is a project aimed at all software contracts entered into for consideration, whether structured as licenses, transfers, assignments, or sales. The Restatement-like Principles address legal issues for transferring software for consideration, whether by lease, license or sale.

(2) Exclusions from the Principles' Sphere of Application

(a) Digital Content & Databases

"Section 1.01(j) defines software to exclude digital content (digital art and digital databases) and §§ 1.06 through 1.08 delineate the types of software transfers targeted by the Principles."[450]

(b) Embedded Software

The Principles exclude embedded software from its sphere of application.[451] The Principles are inapplicable to physical media on which software is stored or transferred such as a CD–ROM or firmware.[452] UCITA Article 2 is the applicable law for CD-ROMs and firmware, a result similar to UCITA's sphere of application.

(c) Open Source Software Contracts Without Consideration

Open source licenses[453] without licensing fees or other consideration, are outside the scope of the Principles.[454]

---

[449] Open Source Initiative, Open Source Initiative OSI—Apache License, Version 2.0:Licensing, Apache License Version 2.-0, http://www.opensource.org/licenses/apache2.0.php (last visited June 29, 2013).

[450] Id.

[451] "Software embedded in goods should less frequently raise issues concerning copying, transfer, support, maintenance, upgrade, inspection, monitoring, licensing restrictions, or remedial limitations (in any way distinct from the goods themselves). For example, embedded software typically is difficult to copy and special-purpose in nature so that the owner of one kind of goods with embedded software cannot easily copy the software and transfer it for use in another brand or kind of goods. In addition, "[w]hen software is embedded and marketed as an integral part of goods, many, if not most, people would consider the software to be part of the goods." Principles of the Law of Software Contracts 1, 2 Overview (2010).

[452] "Like UCITA, these Principles do not apply to transactions that involve telecommunication services, such as the distribution of audio and visual content either on cable or over the Internet, and do not apply to most transactions involving the motion picture and music industries. However, these Principles effectuate these exclusions, not by creating industry-specific carve-outs, but by limiting the scope to transfers of software as defined in § 1.01(j) and (m) and by utilizing the predominant-purpose test of § 1.08 for mixed transactions. Principles of the Law of Software Contracts 1, 2 Overview (2010). "Section 1.01(j), which defines software, and §§ 1.06 through 1.08, on scope, accomplish the goals set forth in this discussion. Section 1.01(j) defines software to exclude digital content (digital art and digital databases) and §§ 1.06 through 1.08 delineate the types of software transfers targeted by the Principles. The rules and Comments on scope that follow surely do not clearly place every transaction on one side or the other of the scope line. No scope provisions could achieve that goal. Instead, these Principles set forth a limited number of coherent rules on scope that courts can apply to most transactions and that identify the types of transfers these Principles target." Id.

[453] Red Hat, Inc. for example is a leading provider of open source software and related services to enterprise customers. Red Hat's open source software, used by Wall Street investment firms, hundreds of Fortune 500 companies, and the United States government, is outside the sphere of application of the Principles of the Law of Software Contracts.

[454] Jacobsen v. Katzer, 535 F.3d 1373, 1378 (Fed. Cir. 2008) ("Open source software licenses, or 'public licenses,' are used by artists, authors, educators, software developers, and scientists who wish to create collaborative projects and to dedicate certain works to the public.").

(d) Physical Tangible Medium

As with UCITA, Section 1.06(b)(1) of the Principles "does not apply to any disk, CD–ROM, or other tangible medium that stores the software. If a disk is defective so that the software is inaccessible, for example, Article 2 of the Uniform Commercial Code applies to determine the transferee's warranty and remedial rights."[455] The Reporters explain why a defective physical disk is outside the Principles' sphere of application:

A transfers a word-processing program to B on a CD–ROM. The CD–ROM is defective. These Principles apply to the transfer of the word-processing program but not to the defective CD–ROM. The warranty rules of Article 2 of the U.C.C. comfortably govern the quality of the CD–ROM, whereas these Principles directly address quality concerns relating to the software program.[456]

(3) Mixed Transactions

The Reporters acknowledge this "gravamen of the action" is anomalous in that U.C.C. Article 2 could apply to part of a transaction and the Principles of the Law of Software Contracts to the same transaction.[457] The Reporters focus on the special problems presented by the software component of mixed transactions. The Principles apply a "predominant purpose" test; or what the Convention for the International Sale of Goods conceptualizes as the "preponderant part" test. If a manufacturer embeds software in goods or software is part of a mixed transaction, courts ask whether the goods or software predominates. The Reporters state:

Software embedded in goods should less frequently raise issues concerning copying, transfer, support, maintenance, upgrade, inspection, monitoring, licensing restrictions, or remedial limitations (in any way distinct from the goods themselves). For example, embedded software typically is difficult to copy and special-purpose in nature so that the owner of one kind of goods with embedded software cannot easily copy the software and transfer it for use in another brand or kind of goods. In addition, "[w]hen software is embedded and marketed as an integral part of goods, many, if not most, people would consider the software to be part of the goods." For these reasons, these Principles exclude transfers of embedded software, except when the "predominant purpose" of the transaction is the transfer of the software, in which case the above issues are more likely to arise. Software issues may also arise when a party transfers non-embedded software along with any combination of goods, digital content, and services. These Principles apply to the software portion of these transactions unless any digital content or services predominate.[458]

---

[455] Principles of the Law of Software Contracts § 1.06 (2010), cmt.

[456] Principles of the Law of Software Contracts § 1.06 (2010), illust. 1.

[457] "Under subsection (b)(1) of this Section, these Principles do not apply to any disk, CD–ROM, or other tangible medium that stores the software. If a disk is defective so that the software is inaccessible, for example, Article 2 of the Uniform Commercial Code applies to determine the transferee's warranty and remedial rights. Although this approach creates the anomaly that two sets of rules may apply to the same transaction, such a result is appropriate and inevitable in a project that focuses on the special problems presented by the software component of mixed transactions. Further, such a treatment is not unique to software contracts." Principles of the Law of Software Contracts § 1.06, cmt. a (2010).

[458] Principles of the Law of Software Contracts 1, 2 Overview (2010).

(4) Application by Analogy

These Restatement-like Principles address legal issues for transferring software for consideration, whether by lease, license or sale. The Reporters suggest that courts may extend the sphere of the Principles' application by analogy: Courts facing difficult legal issues "involving digital-database and digital-art transactions can look to these Principles by analogy if appropriate."[459]

The Principles of the Law of Software Contracts

What's In its Sphere of Application	What's Outside its Sphere of Application
Sales, Leases, and Licenses of Software Contracts entered into with consideration.	Open Source and Other Software Contracts Software Contracts Where There is No Consideration.
	Digital Art, Digital Databases[460]
	Embedded Software

(B) Preliminary Concerns

The prefatory Principles (Chapter 1) provide a legal infrastructure including definitions, scope, and general terms, digital content, record, software, choice of forum, choice of law and unconscionability.[461] The Principles of the Law of Software Contracts makes it clear that the parties' choice of law must give way to federal intellectual property rules to the contrary. A software contract is unenforceable if it "(A) conflicts with a mandatory rule of federal intellectual property law, or (B) conflicts impermissibly with the purposes and policies of federal intellectual property law, or (C) would constitute federal intellectual property misuse in an infringement proceeding."[462] There is almost no case law on what kinds of software contracting terms would violate a fundamental public policy.

The Principles guide courts in policing unfair or unconscionable license agreements. Section 1.09, illus. #8 for example, would invalidate a provision in a license agreement where a transferee of a spreadsheet software program is asked to agree not to implement ideas or develop a competing program for 99 years. A few software licensors prohibit licensees from publicly criticizing software, a practice that is also challengeable under Section 109. The Principles make it clear software contracts are

---

[459] Principles of the Law of Software Contracts § 1.06, cmt. (f) (2010).

[460] "It [The Principles] does not include digital art or a digital database (digital content), as defined in § 1.01(f). However, courts can look to these Principles by analogy to resolve issues involving digital content if appropriate." Principles of the Law of Software Contracts § 1.06 cmt. a (2010)

[461] "A "standard form" is a record regularly used to embody terms of agreements of the same type." Principles of the Law of Software Contracts, § 1.01.

[462] Principles of the Law of Software Contracts § 1.09.

governed by state law and trumped by federal intellectual property law under the Supremacy Clause of the U.S. Constitution.[463]

(1) Anti–Reverse Engineering Clauses

Reverse engineering is a process by which a computer or software engineer works backward to determine how the software works. The Supreme Court defined reverse engineering broadly as "starting with the known product and working backwards to divine the process which aided in its development or manufacture."[464] Anti-reverse engineering clauses prohibit licensees from decompiling or reverse engineering licensed software such as games. Reverse engineering allows software developers to make better products. "Without this capacity, there is no guarantee that new programs will work together."[465] European courts would likely find that a licensor's strict prohibition against reverse engineering violates a public policy in favor of interoperability of computer systems.[466] Software developers will need to comply with European Union restrictions on interoperability. A Paris court ruled that Nintendo had no right to prevent flash cartridges from other software companies to work on their game systems.[467] The reverse engineering of software is a social good because it enables programmers to develop code that is interoperable with established platforms.

Section 118 of UCITA entitled Terms on reverse engineering, renders contractual prohibitions against reverse engineering as unenforceable.[468] UCITA's Reporter states that reverse engineering clauses in license agreements may be unenforceable if they prohibit tests for interoperability.[469] Reverse engineering is a process by which a computer or software engineer works backward to determine how the software works. The Supreme Court defined reverse engineering broadly as "starting with the known product and working backwards to divine the process which aided in its development or manufacture."[470] Anti-reverse engineering clauses prohibit licensees from decompiling or reverse engineering licensed software such as games.

---

[463] The Supremacy Clause provides that federal law shall be the supreme law of the land; and the judges in every state shall be bound thereby, anything in the Constitution or laws of any state to the contrary notwithstanding. U.S. Const. art. VI, cl. 2. Under this principle, Congress has the power to preempt state law. However, in considering whether a state statute is preempted, courts should assume that the historic police powers of the states are not superseded unless that was the clear and manifest purpose of Congress. U.S. CONST. art. VI, cl. 2.

[464] Kewanee Oil Co. v. Bicron Corp, 470 U.S. 470, 476 (1974) ("A trade secret law, however, does not offer protection against discovery by so-called reverse engineering, that is by starting with the known product and working backward to divine the process which aided in its development or manufacture.").

[465] RICHARD S. ROSENBERG, THE SOCIAL IMPACT OF COMPUTERS 511 (2004).

[466] Reverse engineering is necessary to attain interoperability of computer systems. The European Community recognizes a right to reverse engineering to prevent unfair competition or what we refer to as antitrust.

[467] Nintendo Loses Suit Against DS Flash Cards, ESCAPIST MAGAZINE (Dec. 4, 2009).

[468] UCITA § 118 (Amendments to Uniform Computer Transactions Act) (stating licensee "may identify, analyze, and use those elements of the program necessary to achieve interoperability of an independently created computer program with other programs including adapting or modifying the licensee's computer program.").

[469] The Reporter notes to Section 105(b) suggest that anti-reveres engineering clauses prohibiting tests for interoperability may violate a "fundamental public policy." ANDREA MATWYSHYN, HARBORING DATA: INFORMATION SECURITY, LAW AND THE CORPORATION 170 (2009).

[470] Kewanee Oil Co. v. Bicron Corp, 470 U.S. 470, 476 (1974) ("A trade secret law, however, does not offer protection against discovery by so-called reverse engineering, that is by starting with the known product and working backward to divine the process which aided in its development or manufacture.").

Blizzard, for example, requires users of its World of WarCraft online game to agree to the Battle.net Terms of Use ("TOU") by clicking on an "I Agree" button. The TOU is displayed when the user first accesses the Battle.net server. Internet users who do not click agreement to the TOU may return their CD–ROM game within thirty days of purchase and receive a full refund of the purchase price.[471] Blizzard's TOU prohibits users from disassembling, decompiling, or otherwise reverse engineering the game software or the Battle.net service; and "hosting or providing matchmaking services for the game."[472] Any license agreement is unenforceable when it: "(a) conflicts with a mandatory rule of federal intellectual property law; or (b) conflicts impermissibly with the purposes and policies of federal intellectual property law; or (c) would constitute federal intellectual property misuse in an infringement proceeding."[473]

(2) Public Policy Reasons Not to Enforce Licenses

The Principles guide courts to refuse to enforce license agreements if enforcement would violate important public policies.[474] As seen in the example above, a court will find a provision in a license agreement violative of public policy where a transferee of a spreadsheet software program is asked to agree not to implement ideas or develop a competing program for 99 years.[475] A court may refuse to enforce an online contract that violates fundamental public policies.[476] There is little case law on what kinds of contract terms a court may find to be contrary to a fundamental public policy. A court may likely find that the sale of hardcore pornography or human embryos on a website is a violation of public policy. A few software licensors prohibit licensees from publicly criticizing software. Clauses enjoining the criticism of software products have a chilling effect on free expression and may be prohibited by public policy considerations.[477]

It is unclear whether courts will use the "fundamental public policy" doctrine to invalidate unfair, oppressive, or surprising terms in mass-market agreements. UCITA seems to give the courts wide discretion to "avoid a result contrary to public policy, in each case to the extent that the interest in enforcement is clearly outweighed by a

---

[471] This description of the Blizzard Terms of Use is described in Davidson & Assocs. v. Internet Gateway, Inc., 422 F.3d 630, 635 (8th Cir. 2005).

[472] Id. (meaning that the user can creating environments allowing them to play against other users apart from the types of play permitted under the EULA).

[473] Principles of the Law of Software Contracts § 1.09.

[474] "The American Law Institute's project on Principles of the Law of Software Contracts suggests there are currently three possible ways to police unreasonable transfer and use restrictions. First, they might be pre-empted by federal law. Second and third, they also might be against public policy or unconscionable under state law. A fourth possibility is that state public policy judgments could be made by state statutes, making certain types of terms unenforceable in general, or unenforceable in mass-market transactions; state statutes also could provide minimum transfer and use rights and provide contract remedies, such as rejection or damages for failure to provide them." Jean Braucher, Contracting Out of the Uniform Commercial Code, Contracting Out of Article 2 Using a 'License' Label, A Strategy That Should Not Work for Software Products, 40 LOY. L.A. REV. 261, 274 (2006).

[475] Id. at § 1.09, illus. #8.

[476] UCITA § 105.

[477] "In the First Amendment context, litigants are permitted to challenge a statute not because their own rights of free expression are violated, but because of a judicial prediction or assumption that the statute's very existence may cause others not before the court to refrain from constitutionally protected speech or expression." Backpage.com, LLC v. McKenna, 881 F. Supp. 2d 1262, 1270 (W. D. Wash. 2012).

public policy against enforcement of the term," although the case law has yet to evolve.[478]

(3) Unconscionability

The Reporters have adopted U.C.C. Article 2's principle of unconscionability, which enables courts to police licensors that overreach in software licenses and other contracts. Courts require licensees to demonstrate both procedural unconscionability in contract formation and unfair or surprising terms (substantive unconscionability). A comment to § 1.1 states: "With some exceptions, courts usually require a showing of both procedural (defects in the contract-formation process) and substantive (the agreement or term unfairly surprises or oppresses one party)" before they will strike down a clause or license agreement.[479] "[G]ross inequality of bargaining power, together with terms unreasonably favorable to the stronger party, may confirm indications that the transaction involved elements of deception or compulsion, or may show that the weaker party had no meaningful choice."[480] The Reporters cite "[e]xamples of procedural unconscionability include conduct approaching misrepresentation or duress, as well as hidden, incomprehensible, or obscure terms. The Reporters cited examples of substantively unconscionable terms include a cross-collateral clause and a clause unreasonably limiting the time within which a buyer must notify the seller about claims involving latent defects."[481]

The Principles imported U.C.C. § 2–302's concept of unconscionability in § 1.11:

(a) If the court as a matter of law finds the agreement or any term of the agreement to have been unconscionable at the time it was made, the court may refuse to enforce the agreement, or it may enforce the remainder of the agreement without the unconscionable term, or it may so limit the application of any unconscionable term to avoid any unconscionable result.

(b) When it is claimed or appears to the court that the agreement or any term thereof may be unconscionable, the parties shall be afforded a reasonable opportunity to present evidence as to its commercial setting, purpose, and effect to aid the court in making the determination.[482]

The lesson from five decades of U.C.C. § 2–302 is that unconscionability applies to business-to-consumer transactions, but is rarely an issue in business-to-business transactions.[483] The Reporters' comment is that "[t]raditional unconscionability law should apply in the context of software agreements, and will likely be most relevant in

---

[478] Id. at § 105(b).

[479] Principles of the Law of Software Contracts § 1.11 cmt. b (2010).

[480] RESTATEMENT (SECOND) CONTRACTS § 208, cmt.

[481] Id. at § 1.11, cmt. c.

[482] Id. at § 1.11.

[483] Nevertheless, Aral v. EarthLink, Inc., 36 Cal.Rptr.3d 229, 238 (Ct. App. 2005) ("[T]erms . . . were presented on a 'take it or leave it' basis either through installation of the software or through materials included in the package mailed with the software with no opportunity to opt out. This is quintessential procedural unconscionability. With respect to substantive unconscionability, Aral alleged . . . that EarthLink began charging customers for DSL service as soon as they ordered [it] although the company knew or should have known that the service would not be available until after the modem was delivered, some weeks later. . . . [T]he gravamen of the complaint is that numerous consumers were cheated out of small sums of money through deliberate behavior. Accepting these allegations as true . . . the class action waiver must be deemed unconscionable under California law").

retail-like standard-form transfers."[484] The comments to Section 1.11 demonstrate that unconscionability is a doctrine targeting consumer transactions:

1. B, a consumer, buys a computer with pre-loaded software from A, a direct marketer, by telephone. A includes its standard form with the software, and displays the form on its website. The form includes 26 paragraphs. Paragraph 25 provides for arbitration in Chicago under the rules of the International Chamber of Commerce. Even assuming the transaction complies with § 2.02 of these Principles, a court might nonetheless hold the arbitration provision unconscionable if the arbitration clause is hidden in small print and arbitration in Chicago is unduly burdensome because, for example, Chicago is a distant forum and arbitration there or with the selected arbitrator is unduly expensive.

2. Company A markets software for preparing construction bids. In a negotiated exchange, Company A and Company B enter into an otherwise enforceable agreement in which B acquires the software and uses it to submit a bid. B loses a business opportunity because the software is defective and causes an inaccurate bid. The standard-form agreement limits consequential damages to the price of the software. The agreement is likely enforceable between the two commercial parties. See also § 4.01(c) of these Principles.[485]

The Reporters acknowledge that terms of service and other license agreements may be unconscionable, even if validly formed under Chapter 2 of the Principles.[486] Even if a standard form contract complies with the Principles formation requirements, "it should not be sheltered from an unconscionability challenge."[487] The Principles Reporters suggest, "[r]equiring a lesser degree of procedural unconscionability when terms are particularly onerous may help to counteract the market reality that transferees generally do not read terms, often do not understand them when they are aware of them, and underestimate the probability of a defective product."[488]

"Additionally, in the clickwrap context, consumers often do not consider the click as signifying the same assent as a signature. Thus, when a term is particularly onerous, the court should require a lesser showing of procedural unconscionability."[489] The Reporters compare substantive unconscionability to the European mandatory rule that courts will not enforce terms creating a significant imbalance in the bargain to the consumer's detriment. The European Commission's 1993 Directive on Unfair Contract Terms compiled "a nonexclusive list of terms that may be considered unfair when not individually negotiated."[490] The Principles of the Law of Software Contracts did not compile a list of unfair terms, but noted that the Directive's list may be a useful reference point for U.S. courts determining unconscionability.[491]

Nevertheless, these Principles opt to rely on traditional unconscionability doctrine rather than defining which terms are enforceable and which are not. A court may,

---

[484] Id. at § 1.11, cmt. c.

[485] Id. at § 1.11, illus. 1.

[486] Id. at § 1.11, cmt. 1.

[487] Id.

[488] Id.

[489] Id.

[490] Id.

[491] Principles of the Law of Software Contracts, Id. at § 1.11, cmt. c (2010).

however, find the European Union's Unfair Contract Terms Directive's ("UCTD") list useful in evaluating unconscionability claims. The annex to the Directive gives examples of terms that the EU considers unfair, deceptive, and unenforceable. Generally, terms that authorize the transferor to add spyware to a transferee's computer, allow the transferor to modify the contract without notice or an opportunity to object or consent, extend obligations automatically and without notice, allow the transferor to change the nature of the software unilaterally, or authorize cancellation without notice are suspect under these Principles.[492] Unlike the UCTD, the Reporters rejected the mandatory terms approach favored by the European Commission:

> So long as the formation process is reasonable, an important philosophy of these Principles is freedom of contract. The view that transferors understand their products and the risks of contracting better than lawmakers underscores this philosophy. In addition, regulators may misidentify the class of terms that are the product of market failures. These Principles therefore reject, in large part, adopting substantive mandatory rules for software agreements. Exceptions, in limited circumstances, include certain terms that apply to contract breakdown, such as choice of law, forum selection, the warranty of no material hidden defects, liquidated damages, and automated disablement.[493]

(4) Mixed Transactions

Software contracts frequently involve sales as well as services. In addition, services are often included in the licensing of software. The Reporters adopted a predominant purpose test for mixed transactions. Therefore, "the Principles exclude transfers of embedded software, except when the 'predominant purpose' of the transaction is the transfer of the software, in which case the above issues are more likely to arise."[494] Software issues may also arise when a party transfers non-embedded software along with any combination of goods, digital content, and services. These Principles apply to the software portion of these transactions unless any digital content or services predominate.

(C) Forum Selection Clauses

During the past four decades, U.S. courts have been predisposed to enforce the parties' choice of forum and law clauses. The Principles also presume that U.S. style choice of forum clauses are broadly enforceable.[495] Sections 114 of the Principles allow the parties to submit to jurisdiction and agree to an exclusive forum so long as it is not unfair or unreasonable. Section 114 states:

---

[492] Id.

[493] Principles of the Law of Software Contracts 2, 2 Overview (2010).

[494] Principles of the Law of Software Contracts 1, 2 Overview (2010).

[495] See e.g., Guadagno v. ETrade Bank, 592 F. Supp. 2d 1263, 1271–72 (C.D. Cal. 2008) (upholding a forum selection clause requiring users to waive their right to joining class action and submitting to pre-dispute mandatory arbitration); Eslworldwide.com, Inc. v. Interland, Inc., No. 06 CV 2503, 2006 WL 1716881, at 2 (S.D.N.Y. June 21, 2006) (upholding forum selection clause including in clickwrap agreement); Siebert v. Amateur Athletic Union of U.S., Inc., 422 F. Supp. 2d 1033, 1039 (D. Minn. 2006) (upholding forum selection clause for pre-dispute mandatory arbitration); Adsit Co., Inc. v. Gustin, 874 N.E.2d 1018, 1024 (Ind. Ct. App. 2007) (upholding Adsit's Terms of Use agreement containing a forum selection clause and choice of law clause where user was required to click on a button reading "I Accept" that was placed strategically at the bottom of the webpage containing the policy; clickwrap agreement also was displayed on an internet webpage).

The parties may by agreement choose an exclusive forum unless the choice is unfair or unreasonable. A forum choice may be unfair or unreasonable if:

(a) the forum is unreasonably inconvenient for a party;

(b) the agreement as to the forum was obtained by misrepresentation, duress, the abuse of economic power, or other unconscionable means;

(c) the forum does not have power under its domestic law to entertain the action or to award remedies otherwise available; or

(d) enforcement of the forum-selection clause would be repugnant to public policy as expressed in the law of the forum in which suit is brought.[496]

These provisions do not address the problem arising when the cost appearing in a forum exceeds what is stake. In these cases, the forum selection clause operates de facto as a liability shield because the plaintiff cannot exercise her rights.

(D) Formation of Software Contracts

(1) Liberal Formation Rules

Section 2.01 of the Principles "sets forth the general approach to formation issues. It is based on portions of both the original and amended U.C.C. §§ 2–204, 2–206, and 2–207, and the Restatement Second of Contracts §§ 18–34, 50–70."[497] Section 2.01 applies to negotiated software agreements and standard-form agreements, but the Section is subject to the separate rules of § 2.02 that govern standard-form transfers of generally available software. Section 2.01 therefore applies if the software transferor uses a standard form but the transfer is of a large number of copies of software, the right to access software is to a large number of end users, or the software is not generally available to the public under the same standard terms. The Principles adopt the liberal contract formation rules from U.C.C. Article 2. A software "contract may be formed in any manner sufficient to show an agreement, including by offer and acceptance and by contract."[498]

The U.C.C. Article 2 inspired formation rules apply to both negotiated software contracts and standard-form agreements. Section 2.01 covers standard form as well as customized software licenses. Software license agreements or other transfers may be made in any method as long as it shows the parties have reached an agreement. Additionally, the Principles validate "rolling contracts" even if presented to the consumer in a take-it-or-leave-it standard form. The Principles use the concept of electronic records as the functional equivalent of a physical writing to satisfy the Statute of Frauds.

Section 2.01 covers standard form as well as non mass-market transactions. Software license agreements or other transfers "may be formed in any manner sufficient to show agreement."[499] Section 2.01 states:

(a) Subject to § 2.02, a contract may be formed in any manner sufficient to show an agreement, including by offer and acceptance and by conduct.

---

[496] Principles of the Law of Software Contracts, § 1.1.

[497] Principles of the Law of Software Contracts § 2.01, cmt. (a) (2010).

[498] Principles of the Law of Software Contracts, § 2.01(a).

[499] Id. at § 2.01.

(b) A contract may be formed under subsection (a) even though

(1) one or more terms are left open, if there is a reasonably certain basis for granting an appropriate remedy in the event of a breach; or

(2) the parties' records are different. In such a case, the terms of the contract are

(A) terms, whether in a record or not, to which both parties agree;

(B) terms that appear in the records of both parties; and

(C) terms supplied by these Principles or other law.[500]

(2) Battle of the Forms Provision

U.C.C. § 2–207 governing the battle of the forms under Article 2 is one of the most complicated provisions of U.C.C. Article 2. That section is divided into three sections, each of which covers a different problem. U.C.C. § 2–207(1) recognizes that contracts may be formed despite having conflicting or additional terms. U.C.C. § 2–207(2)'s framework deals with what to do with conflicting or additional terms. U.C.C. § 2–207(3) presents a solution when there is no contract on the form but rather on the parties conduct. The Principles of the Law of Software Contracts have adopted a clear and easy to understand alternative to U.C.C. § 2–207 with § 2.01(b)(2)(A)-(C).[501] Under § 2.01(b)(2) of these Principles, the terms consist of terms common to both records, other terms the parties agreed to, and supplemental terms supplied by these Principles and outside law. Thus, if the parties' records differ insubstantially, courts can enforce the common terms under § 2.01(b)(2)(B). The contract first consists of the terms where both records agree and terms that appear in both records combined with supplemental principles.[502] Conflicting and additional terms falls out and are not part of the software contract. The Reporters illustrate the simple approach to battle of the forms with the following illustration:

B, a computer manufacturer, sends A, a software transferor, an order for 500 copies of a graphic-design software package. B's order provides that A warrants the software to be free from defects. A ships 500 copies of the software to B accompanied by a standard form disclaiming all express and implied warranties. B accepts delivery of the software. Under § 2.01(b), the parties' conduct shows that they formed a contract even though the records alone do not establish a contract. Section 2.01(b)(2)(A) and (B) do not apply to the issue of implied warranties because the disclaimer of implied warranties is not in both records and the parties did not agree on the treatment of implied warranties. Subsection (b)(2)(C) does apply, however, which looks to these Principles or outside law to supply terms. Under Sections 3.03 through 3.05 of the Principles, the agreement includes implied warranties. Further, under § 2.01(b)(2)(A), the contract also includes express warranties to the extent that A has made any promises, descriptions, and affirmations. B has agreed to such warranties by implication because B has

---

[500] Principles of the Law of Software Contracts § 2.01 (2010).

[501] In such a case, the terms of the contract are:

(A) terms, whether in a record or not, to which both parties agree;

(B) terms that appear in the records of both parties; and

(C) terms supplied by these Principles or other law.

Principles of the Law of Software Contracts § 2.01(2)(A)-(C) (2010).

[502] Id.

accepted the software and the warranties benefit B. The "free from defects" term in B's record drops out, however, because it is not in both records. Subsection (b)(2) also applies if one or both records include a provision such as "only our terms govern" and the parties perform the agreement.[503]

Section 2.02 addresses standard form transfers of generally available software. The contract rules for electronic and prepackaged software adopt an objective theory of contract formation[504] in Section 2.01(b) where a transferee is deemed to have adopted a standard form where a reasonable transferor would believe that the other party intends to be bound. Section 2.02 addresses standard form transfers of generally available software. Section 2.02 addresses standard form transfers of generally available software. The contract rules for electronic and prepackaged software adopt an objective theory of contract formation[505] in Section 2.01(b) where a transferee is deemed to have adopted a standard form where a reasonable transferor would believe that the other party intends to be bound.

(2) Formation Safe Harbor Provisions

The Principles validate mass-market license agreements such as clickwrap and shrinkwrap, but do not validate browsewrap because it does not give the licensee reasonable accessibility to terms prior to the transfer.[506] The Principles adopt the "opportunity to review" test in UCITA, which gives the licensee reasonable accessibility to terms prior to the transfer. Clickwrap, for example, should be structured so that the "I accept" radio button appears either at the end of, or adjacent to, the license to pass the "opportunity to review" test. Under § 2.02(d), a transferor of software must give the transferee the capacity to store and reproduce the license or other standard form.

The key to the Principles' formation safe harbor is whether "the standard form is reasonably accessible electronically prior to initiation of the transfer at issue."[507] "The safe harbor also requires a 'clickwrap' acceptance of terms, which means that the 'I accept' icon must appear at the end of, or adjacent to, the standard form."[508] For electronic contracts, the Principles' safe harbor requires that the "transferee can store and reproduce the standard form."[509] Contract formation is subject to limitations based upon public policy, unconscionability, and other invalidating defenses.[510] These terms are broadly admissible to "supplement a record."[511] The opportunity to review and

---

[503] Principles of the Law of Software Contracts § 2.01, illus. 6.b (2010).

[504] "Whether a meeting of the minds exists, however, is determined objectively by looking at the intent of the parties as expressed by their actual words or acts. A meeting of the minds cannot be determined on the undisclosed assumption or secret surmise of either party." Int'l Casings Group, Inc. v. Premium Std. Farms, Inc., 358 F. Supp. 2d 863, 869 (W.D. Mo. 2005).

[505] "Whether a meeting of the minds exists, however, is determined objectively by looking at the intent of the parties as expressed by their actual words or acts. A meeting of the minds cannot be determined on the undisclosed assumption or secret surmise of either party." Int'l Casings Group, Inc. v. Premium Std. Farms, Inc., 358 F. Supp. 2d 863, 869 (W.D. Mo. 2005).

[506] Id.

[507] Id. at § 2.02(c)(1).

[508] Robert A. Hillman & Maureen O'Rourke, Defending Disclosure in Software Licensing, 78 U. Chi. L. Rev. 95, 104 n. 53 (2011).

[509] Principles of the Law of Software Contracts, § 2.02(d)

[510] Id. § 2.02(d) (noting that the Principles is subject to "invalidating defenses supplied by these Principles or outside law, a standard term is enforceable if reasonably comprehensible.").

[511] Id. at § 3.08(g)(2).

manifestation of assent are also predicates for formation of mass-market licenses under UCITA.

(3) Parol Evidence Rule

In order to reduce fraudulent assertions of the existence of terms in license

It is the court's role to determine whether a given software contract is integrated. Under Section 3.08(f) of the Principles states, "unambiguous terms set forth in a fully integrated record may not be contradicted by evidence of any prior agreement or of a contemporaneous oral agreement." The Principles import a liberal rule from U.C.C. Article 2 that calls for the broad admissibility of evidence as to course of performance, course of dealing, and usage of trade. This broad admissibility of supplemental terms also applies to fully integrated agreements. Section 2.02 applies special rules for standard or mass-market transfers of generally available software. Section 3.08's parol evidence rule distinguishes between fully integrated and partially integrated records, drinking deeply from the wells of the Restatement (Second) of Contracts and U.C.C. § 2–202.[512] Fully integrated software contracts are "intended by the parties as a complete and exclusive statement of the terms of an agreement."[513] In contrast, a partially integrated record or records are a "complete and exclusive statement of one or more terms of an agreement."[514] As with U.C.C. Article 2, even fully integrated terms or agreements "may be explained by evidence of course of performance, course of dealing, usage of trade, and consistent additional terms."[515]

(4) Liberal Contract Formation

Section 201(a) provides that a software "contract may be formed in any manner sufficient to show an agreement, including by offer and acceptance and by conduct."[516] As with U.C.C. Article 2, a "software contract may be formed under subsection (a) even though(1) one or more terms are left open, if there is a reasonably certain basis for granting an appropriate remedy in the event of a breach; or (2) the parties' records are different."[517] Subsection (a) follows common-law and U.C.C. Article 2 formation principles. The Reporters comment notes, "The policy is to enforce agreements no matter how formed. A principal challenge in negotiated agreements is to distinguish pre-contract negotiations and preliminary drafts, on the one hand, from the formation of an enforceable agreement on the other."[518] The Principles adopt the objective test for contract formation also followed by the Restatement (Second) of Contracts. Thus, in a software license or other contract, the court bases contract formation "on what the

---

[512] The Reporters state that they are seeking "a middle ground between rigid enforcement of the parol-evidence rule and its abrogation. . . . Based on these sources, these Principles bar evidence only if (1) the parties intended a full integration or (2) the parties intended a partial integration and the evidence is of conflicting terms." Principles of the Law of Software Contracts § 3.08, cmt. (a) (2010). Id. at § 3.08, cmt. a.

[513] Id. at § 3.08(a).

[514] Id.

[515] Id.

[516] Principles of the Law of Software Contracts § 2.01(a) (2010).

[517] Principles of the Law of Software Contracts § 2.01(b)(1) (2010).

[518] Principles of the Law of Software Contracts § 2.01, cmt. b (2010).

circumstances *show*, not on what they subjectively believe."[519] The Reporters provide the following illustrations of how contract formation works in the non-retail setting:

1. A, a software transferor, enters a multiuser licensing agreement with B, an automobile manufacturer, which authorizes 4000 of B's employees to use the software. The agreement includes a three-year maintenance agreement. The software is generally available to the public. Section 2.01 applies, not § 2.02, because the magnitude of the transfer is inconsistent with a retail sale and because the terms of the multiuser agreement differ from those in a typical retail sale.

2. A, a software publisher, transfers one copy of accounting software to B, an automobile manufacturer. The transfer is by standard form, but does not include multiuser authorization. The software is generally available to the public under the same standard terms. Section 2.02 applies, not § 2.01, because the transfer is of only one copy and is therefore consistent with a retail sale, and the software is available to the public under the same terms.[520]

(5) Standard Form Software Contracts

"Section 2.01(a) encompasses both contract-formation routes. Not only can parties form a software contract by virtue of a traditional offer and acceptance, but they can also form one if their conduct shows their intention to contract, such as by delivering and accepting software despite the absence of an enforceable record."[521] Section 2.01 applies to negotiated software agreements as well as mass-market or standard-form agreements, "but the Section is subject to the separate rules of § 2.02 that govern standard-form transfers of generally available software."[522] Section 2.01 therefore applies if the software transferor uses a standard form but the transfer is of a large number of copies of software, the right to access software is to a large number of end users, or the software is not generally available to the public under the same standard terms.

(6) Modification of a Software Contract

Under the Principles, as with UCITA, a modification of a software contract requires no consideration to be binding. Section 2.03 validates no-oral-modifications clauses unless waived.[523] Section 2.03 also provides that contractual modifications require no particular form; they "may be formed in any manner sufficient to show an agreement."[524] For electronic transfers of software, e-notices of modification are enforcement provided the transferee receives a reasonable electronic notice of the modification and the transferee signifies agreement to the modifications electronically.[525]

---

[519] Id.

[520] Principles of the Law of Software Contracts § 2.01, illust. 1–2 (2010).

[521] Principles of the Law of Software Contracts § 2.01, illus. 3(b) (2010).

[522] Principles of the Law of Software Contracts § 2.01 cmt. (a) (2010).

[523] Id. at Topic 3, Contract Modification, Summary Overview, § 2.03.

[524] Id. at § 2.03(a).

[525] Id. at § 2.03(b).

(7) Supplemental Terms

The Principles recognize a hierarchy of contract terms, which begins with the language of the entire agreement but also considers the parties course of performance, course of dealing and usage of trade in that order. [526] If there is a disagreement over meaning of a term in a record, courts are to apply the standard of reasonable integration.[527] Section 3.10 articulates two exceptions to 3.09(a)'s objective interpretation rule.[528] The first exception is that if the parties to a software contract disagree over the meaning of words or conduct, "the meaning intended by one of them should be enforced if at the time the parties made the agreement that party did not know or have reason to know of any different meaning intended by the other party."[529] The second exception is that parties do not have an agreement where "the parties disagree over the meaning of a fundamental term or terms" but that applies only if the words or conduct are susceptible to more than one meaning.[530]

(E) Software Contracting Warranties

Section 3.01 is the functional equivalent of U.C.C. § 2–312 but gives licensees and other transferees a lesser infringement warranty than what buyers receive under Article 2. Section 3.01 gives licensees and other transferees a lesser infringement warranty. A licensor is not liable for transferring software infringing the patents of others absent knowledge of the infringing content. Licensors typically do not give the non-infringement warranty when the licensee uses the software in a way contrary to the agreement. A licensor may disclaim or limit implied warranties. Sections 3.02 through 3.07 in the Principles import warranties concepts from U.C.C. Article 2 and UCITA with some differences. Section 3.02 creates an express warranty if the licensor delivers software that fails to conform to the description in advertising or packaging. As with U.C.C. Article 2, courts are to distinguish between puffery or seller's talk and statements more definite or specific to constitute an enforceable express warranty.

(1) Express Warranties

The quality warranties outlined in Chapter 3 of the Principles closely track U.C.C. Article 2, while accommodating them to software commercial realities. Section 3.02 of the Principles makes the transferor liable for express warranties to any transferee in the distribution chain, including all intermediate parties and end users.[531] The creation of an express warranty is not dependent upon whether a transferor uses formal words such as "warrant" or "guarantee" or that it has a specific intention to make a warranty. A licensor's affirmation of the value of software is mere puffery and does not constitute an express warranty.

The Principles recognize express warranties but decline to adopt a "basis of the bargain" test for enforceability.[532] Instead, the Principles replace the "basis of the bargain" test with an objective test focusing on whether the representations made by the

---

[526] Id. at § 3.09.
[527] Id. at § 3.09(a).
[528] Id. at § 3.10(a)–(b).
[529] Id. at § 3.10(a).
[530] Id. at § 3.10(b)(1).
[531] Principles of the Law of Software Contracts § 3.02, cmt. a. (2009).
[532] Id. at § 3.02.

licensor about software are sufficiently definite so a licensee or other transferee can reasonably rely upon them. If the transferor makes a statement constituting an affirmation of fact, promise, or description, the statement constitutes an express warranty, so long as a licensee or assignee reasonably relies on the statement. As with U.C.C. Article 2, Express warranties survive unexpected disclaimers and the only way to disclaim them is not to make them. Reliance is not a formal requirement of Article 2 or UCITA but it is difficult for the plaintiff to prove an express warranty without a showing of reliance.

The Reporters borrow Section 3.02 of the Principles from both UCITA and Article 2 of the UCC. This section creates a cause of action for the licensee if the delivered software fails to conform to the description in advertising or packaging. If an employee of the software licensor demonstrates the software to a licensee, the software must conform to the demonstration. A licensor is potentially liable for express warranties to any transferee in the distributional chain, including intermediaries and end users.

(2) Implied Warranty of Merchantability

The Principles downsize U.C.C. Article 2's six-part test for merchantability to three quality standards in Section 3.01(b) for merchant transferors.[533] Merchantable software, at a minimum, must "(1) pass without objection in the trade under the contract description; (2) be fit for the ordinary purposes for which such software is used; and (3) be adequately packaged and labeled."[534] The Principles draw upon industry standards in setting minimal standards of merchantability. The implied warranty of merchantability is a flexible set of standards and can be calibrated for many different kinds of software. The Principles do not extend the implied warranty of merchantability to open source software because "developers have little control over quality."[535]

Software warranties determine the merchantability of software by referencing current software best practices. For example, a maker of Automated Teller Machine ("ATM") software must ensure that its product meets minimum industry standards for security. The leading ATM provider incorporates a Triple DES standard to encrypt customers' financial and personal data. Triple–DES is an encryption standard designed to make ATM transactions more secure. Software makers that fulfill this standard are similar to a seller of goods meeting a merchantability standard that goods "pass without objection in the trade under the contract."[506] The level of computer security is an example of an industry standard or usage of trade.

Software is merchantable if it complies with best practices like incorporating reasonable security. The software industry claims bug-free software is impossible to produce. Software makers may deliver software with minor defects and still satisfy the implied warranty of merchantability so long as the software would pass without objection in the trade and be fit for its ordinary purposes. Software consisting of millions of lines of code will violate merchantability if it does not perform its functionality. In development software projects, the licensee is given a period of

---

[533] Id. at § 3.01(b).
[534] Id.
[535] Id. at § 3.01, cmt. a.

acceptance testing to identify bugs, allowing the software maker an opportunity to correct them.

(3) Systems Integration & Fitness Warranties

The Principles, too, adopts a systems integration or fitness warranty. Section 3.04 of the Principles requires the licensor to know, or have a reason to know, of the particular purpose of the licensee to make a fitness type warranty. If a software developer warrants its software will function with a given computer system, the company will be liable for the warranty of fitness for a particular purpose under § 3.04. Section 3.04 requires the customer to prove that licensor or other vendor knew or had reason to know of the licensee's particular purposes for the software.

The concept of systems integration is a software engineering term meaning an engineer's ability to combine "software components into an integrated whole."[536] Systems integration and fitness for a particular purpose are closely related doctrines often used in custom software contracts. The Reporters imported Section 3.04 of the Principles from U.C.C. § 2–312 and UCITA § 405. Section 3.04 of the Principles requires the licensor know, or have a reason to know, of the particular purpose of the licensee to make a fitness type warranty. If a software developer warrants its software will function with a given computer system, the company will be liable for the warranty of fitness for a particular purpose under § 3.04. A licensor violates a fitness warranty when it selects software for the particular purpose of the licensee.

Fitness warranties may be created in part by product advertising or sales representations. Companies claiming that they are systems integration specialists may create fitness warranties. Vendors frequently must address system integration tasks to make hardware and software compatible. For example, systems integration is required to link a given firewall system with other security systems such as surveillance products. Systems integration is a software engineering term meaning an engineer's ability to combine software components so they work as an integrated whole, which is also known as interoperability.

Like the fitness warranty, systems integration depends upon a showing of reliance of the customer on the licensor's representation that software will work or is integrated with a given computer system. For example, if a software developer warrants that their software will function with Microsoft's Word 8 the license will be liable under the systems integration warranty. Systems integration is a common issue in software contracts because engineers will often need interfaces to make products interoperable. Customers would typically license software from diverse vendors employing a 'best of breed' strategy, purchasing different applications from several vendors. The customer is often in a position that they need computer consultants to help them achieve 'systems integration.'[537] In many instances, software engineers will need to write

---

[536] Carnegie Mellon, A Framework for Software Product Line Practice, Version 5.0, Software System Integration, http://www.sei.cmu.edu/productlines/frame_report/softwareSI.htm (last visited March 19, 2010).

[537] Companies will enter into "systems integrations" contracts with consultants who must compile engineering and process specifications and documentation to make systems work together. See e.g., Uop v. Consulting, 1997 Conn. Super. LEXIS 1090 (Conn. Super. Ct., April 24, 1997) (striking complaint for negligence in the performance of a systems integration consulting contract because of the economic loss doctrine).

custom code for interfaces that would allow components from different vendors to run together.[538]

It is sometimes difficult to predict whether systems integration can be achieved easily because programmers cannot always rely upon the same assumptions about how components work together.[539] Carnegie–Mellon's best practices for achieving integration states:

> In a product line, the effort involved in software system integration lies along a spectrum. At one end, the effort is almost zero. If you know all the products' potential variations in advance, you can produce an integrated parameterized template of a generic system with formal parameters. You can then generate final products by supplying the actual parameters specific to the individual product requirements and launching the construction tool (along the lines of the UNIX Make utility). In this case, each product consists entirely of core components; no product-specific code exists. This is the "system generation" end of the integration spectrum. At the other end of the spectrum, considerable coding may be involved to bring the right core components together into a cohesive whole. Perhaps the components need to be wrapped, or perhaps new components need to be designed and implemented especially for the product. In these situations, the integration more closely resembles that of a single-system project.[540]

Most software product lines occupy a middle point on the spectrum. Obviously, the closer to the generation side of the spectrum you can align your production approach, the easier integration will be and the more products you will be able to turn out in a short period.[541] A warranty of systems integration arises when a software developer represents that its product will work on a customer's computer system or when they attest that the software will work on certain platforms. Oracle's CEO likely made systems integration warranties in a famous press conference, assuming potential customers can prove reliance on his systems integration representations:

> The right model for enterprise software is "Here are all the pieces. They've all been engineered to work together. No systems integration required. You can install it in a matter of months in the largest and most complex operations. All the pieces are there: marketing, sales, web store, service, internet procurement, auctioning, supply chain automation, manufacturing, human resources, everything. And all the pieces fit together."
>
> So in the early stages—the very early stages of this release 11i, we're saying, 'We're right. The rest of the world is wrong'; where there's all this controversy where we can't show lots and lots of companies up and running—big companies up and running—they're just beginning to come live now, already we're getting tremendous traction in the market. And it will be far and away the biggest success in the history of our company, much bigger than the database.[542]

---

[538] In re Oracle Corp. Secs. Litig., 2009 U.S. Dist. LEXIS 50995 *11 (N.D. Cal., June 16, 2009).

[539] *Id.*

[540] Carnegie–Mellon, *Software System Integration, Id.*

[541] *Id.*

[542] In re Oracle Corp. Secs. Litig., *Id.* at *13.

In the Oracle Corporation Securities Litigation, the plaintiffs contended that Oracle released Suite 11i prematurely and that it did not work in different computing environments. Oracle's CEO, Larry Ellison, touted its applications as seamless at an "AppWorld" Conference: "In fact, we recommend that you start with, you try a component of the suite and then you add it in. Now the nice thing is it's like Lego blocks. Once you have one piece in, the other pieces just snap together. There's no systems integration required. . . . You just basically turn it on or snap it together. It is absolutely all the pieces within the suite are literally plug and play."[543] Oracle's Application Suite 11i is a program that integrates business processes planning such as accounting, human resources, and manufacturing.

Systems integration issues arise where customer require that specific software applications be compatible with specific software and hardware. Video drivers, for example, must work with a Windows7 platform.[544] A computer must also have the compatible hardware and systems requirement to run with the Window's 7 operating system or Apple's Mac OS X operating system.[545] The licensor or software vendor will either disclaim the systems warranty or limit software installation of the system, not its integration to the older system. In *Foundation Software v. Digital Equipment Corp.*,[546] the court held the vendor liable for promising that the software would run on the Micro Vax system when it was, in fact, incompatible. A U.S. software publisher, for example, would be making a systems integration warranty if it told a customer that its software would work on Microsoft's Windows Server 2003 platform.

Sales representative often claim that a licensor's software is compatible with other vendor's applications, which creates an enforceable systems integration warranty. Companies often claim that their software is compatible with other vendor's applications, which makes a systems integration warranty. In development contracts, systems integration is a quantifiable and nonquantifiable discriminator as to the difficulty of completing a software development or custom contract. The developed software might conform to its technical specifications during alpha testing, but fail a beta test in the customer's environment of use. In many software development projects, the difficulty is that software will not plug in and execute. Many projects fail because customized modules are incompatible with third party products. In a government contract, the contract will typically call for the vendor to install and integrate system elements. Systems integration includes making systems subsystems, components, support equipment, and software/data work together.

The vendor is frequently responsible for ensuring "that the total system will meet all requirements."[547] If a software developer warrants its software will function with a given computer system, the company will be liable for the warranty of "fitness for a particular purpose" under § 3.04.[548] Section 3.04 requires the customer to prove that licensor or other vendor knew or had reason to know of the licensee's particular purposes for the software. The free and open source licensing paradigm requires

---

[543] *Ind.* at *12.

[544] MICHAEL ALDRIDGE, MCTS MICROSOFT WINDOWS VISTA CLIENT CONFIGURATION EXAM 70–620 (2007) at 10.

[545] Id.

[546] 807 F. Supp. 1195 (D. Md. 1992).

[547] Fairchild Indus. v. United States, 71 F.3d 868, 871 (Fed. Cir. 1995).

[548] The Principles of the Law of Software Contracts, § 3.04.

licensors to give downstream users an opportunity to look under the hood so they "can easily understand and change those instructions."[549]

A counterhegemonic paradigm that distributes software in source code enables a community of collaborators to share improvements. Stephen Weber's 2004 book, *The Success of Open Source*, describes how the open source movement has changed the meaning of property in the information-based economy: "Property in open source is configured fundamentally around the right to distribute, not the right to exclude."[550] Open source programmers have developed a long list of products that includes Apache, the Linux operating system, "the scripting language PERL, and the popular email server Sendmail."[551] Section 3.04 of the Principles is a functional equivalent of U.C.C. § 2–312 and UCITA § 405.

(4) Non–Infringement Warranties

The Principles generally follow the contours of warranties set forth in Article 2 of the U.C.C.—except for the non-infringement warranty. Article 2 of the U.C.C. imposes a strict liability for transferring goods infringing the patents or other intellectual property rights of third parties while the Principles adopt a negligence standard. Section 3.01 of the Principles gives licensees and other transferees a lesser infringement warranty than U.C.C. Article 2's does § 2–312. The Principles also permits software vendors to disclaim their implied indemnification obligations consistent with U.C.C. § 2–312. A former Microsoft lawyer explains this software industry contracting practice results because software makers believe that taking on this liability will lead to unknown repercussions[552] Section 3.01 permits software transferors to exclude or modify the implied indemnification against infringement.[553] The UCC's non-infringement warranty does not depend upon the seller's knowledge because it is a strict liability-like obligation while the Principles adopt a negligence standard

Licensors routinely disclaim non-infringement warranties because of the uncertainties in the enforcement of software patents, which is a topic discussed in Chapter 13. Section 3.01(a) states that unless the parties otherwise agree, a transferor that deals in software of the kind and receives payment, agrees to "indemnify and hold the transferee harmless against any claim of a third party based on infringement of an intellectual property or like right."[554] A licensor is not liable for transferring software infringing the patents of others absent knowledge of the infringing content.[555] Transferors do not give the non-infringement warranty when the transferee uses the software in a way contrary to the agreement.

---

[549] Brief of *Amicus Curiae* Electronic Freedom Foundation, KSR Int'l Co. v. Teleflex Inc., 2004 U.S. Briefs 1350 Aug. 22, (2006).

[550] STEPHEN WEBER, THE SUCCESS OF SOURCE CODE 1 (2004).

[551] Jay P. Kesan & Rajiv C. Shah, Deconstructing Code, 6 Yale J. L. & Tech. 277, 350 (2003–2004) (retelling the story of the open source software movement and its accomplishments).

[552] Robert W. Gomulkiewicz, The Implied Warranty of Merchantability in Software Contracts: A Warranty No One Dares to Give and How to Change That, 16 JOHN MARSHALL J. OF COMP. & INFO. l. 393, 393 (1998).

[553] Id. (citing Section 3.01).

[554] Principles, § 3.01.

[555] U.C.C. § 2–312.

(5) Disclaiming Warranties

The Principles of the Law of Software Contracts draws upon industry standards in setting the standard of merchantability. Although the implied warranty of merchantability is a flexible set of standards, it varies within the software industry. The Principles do not extend the implied warranty of merchantability to open source software because "developers have little control over quality."[556] Furthermore, most software makers will disclaim the implied warranty of merchantability. A Texas court upheld the following disclaimer in a license agreement between sophisticated businesses:

> EXCEPT FOR [LICENSOR'S] OBLIGATIONS UNDER SECTION 1.1 BELOW (NON–INFRINGEMENT) AND SECTION 12 BELOW (CONFIDENTIALITY), [LICENSOR] MAKES NO REPRESENTATIONS, WARRANTIES OR GUARANTEES, EXPRESS OR IMPLIED, INCLUDING WARRANTIES OF MERCHANTABILITY OR FITNESS FOR ANY USE OR ANY PARTICULAR PURPOSE WITH REGARD TO THE SOFTWARE AND DOCUMENTATION. [LICENSOR DOES NOT WARRANTY THAT THE OPERATION OF THE SOFTWARE WILL BE UNINTERRUPTED OR ERROR–FREE ... THE SOFTWARE AND DOCUMENTATION IS LICENSED TO [LICENSEE] ON AN 'AS IS' BASIS.[557]

A former Microsoft lawyer contends that vendors disclaim these warranties because the "repercussions are unknown."[558] Software makers disclaim performance warranties such as merchantability and fitness for a particular purpose because of uncertainty as to what these warranties mean as to software:

> First, the doctrine of implied warranty of merchantability requires that goods must "pass without objection in the trade"; however, all programs are subject to criticism in the computer trade press. Second, the court would have to determine the standard to which the software would be compared. However, the dynamic nature of the software industry makes such a comparison difficult. Furthermore, such comparison would be difficult because computer software is generally perceived as a collection of unique ideas.[559]

(6) Nondisclaimable Warranty for Hidden Defects

Section 3.05(a) creates a nondisclaimable warranty that a licensor's software does not have hidden defects of which it is aware at the time of transfer; "The ALI Principles include three kinds of disclosure: disclosure of facts (concerning the quality of software), disclosure of terms (of standard forms), and disclosure of post-contract intentions (to pursue remote disablement of software)."[560] Section 3.05(b) provides that a party that transfers software by sale, license, or otherwise, and receives money or a

---

[556] Principles of the Law of Software Contracts § 3.01, cmt. a.

[557] I2Technologies, Inc. v. DARC Corp., 2003 WL 22205091 (N.D. Tex., Sept. 23, 2003) (quoting DARC's anti-disabling device warranty).

[558] Robert W. Gomulkiewicz, The *Implied Warranty of Merchantability in Software Contracts: A Warranty No One Dares to Give and How to Change That*, 16 JOHN MARSHALL J. OF COMP. & INFO. L. 393, 393 (1998).

[559] *Id.* at 234.

[560] Robert A. Hillman & Maureen O'Rourke, Defending Disclosure in Software Licensing, 78 U. CHI. L. REV. 95, 95 (2011).

monetary obligation warrants "that the software contains no material hidden defects of which the transferor was aware at the time of the transfer."[561] A software licensor makes a nondisclaimable warranty if its software does not have hidden defects of which it is aware at the time of transfer.[562] The Reporters are extending a products liability theory in requiring licensors to warn licensees of known dangers. This provision is well established in products liability: "The majority of states, either by case law or by statute, follow the principle that 'the seller is required to give warning against a danger, if he has knowledge, or by the application of reasonable, developed human skill and foresight should have knowledge of the danger.'" The software industry's response to this provision has been overwhelmingly hostile. The chief concern is that the provision is vague and will lead to disputes as to whether software bugs create a duty to inform customers. ALI Reporters Robert Hillman and Maureen O'Rourke contend that Section 3.05 does no more than incorporate existing contract law's duty to disclose and tort's fraudulent concealment law.[563] The anachronistic practice of the software industry is to disclaim all warranties including the implied warranty of merchantability and offer the dissatisfied purchaser, a limited and often inadequate remedy. The nondisclaimable warranty is the first modest step to mandatory minimum adequate remedies. Some proprietary software publishers who contend that this provision creates uncertainty as to the meaning of "material defect" oppose section 3.05.[564] Linux and other open source stakeholders oppose this warranty for free and open software ("FOSS").[565] Another critic of the non-disclaimable warranty of no defect provision recommends opting out of the Principles as in the clause below:

> This Agreement and all related disputes shall be governed by the laws of _____, without regard to the United Nations Convention on Contracts for the International Sale of Goods or the American Law Institute's Principles of the Law of Software Contracts ("Principles"). The parties agree that (i) the Principles shall have no application whatsoever to the interpretation or enforcement of this Agreement, and (ii) neither party shall invoke the Principles in whole or in part in any judicial or arbitral proceeding relating to this Agreement.[566]

(F) Software Performance Standards

(1) Breach and Material Breach

The Principles defines a breach as failure to perform without a legal excuse.[567] The material breach standard is more licensor oriented than U.C.C. Article 2's perfect tender rule. Customized software code will rarely be bug-free, and therefore the licensor will

---

[561] Principles of the Law of Software Contracts § 3.05(b).

[562] Id. at § 305(b).

[563] Hillman and O'Rourke, Defending Disclosure, Id. at 95.

[564] "A few software providers also worry about the meaning of "material defect." The comments to section 3.05(b) point out that the section simply captures the principle of material breach: Does the defect mean that the transferee will not get substantially what it bargained for and reasonably expected under the contract? The criticism that "materiality" is too vague, if accurate, would mean that contract law would have to abolish its material breach doctrine too." Robert Hillman, American Law Institute Approves Principles of the Law of Software Contracts, Concurring Opinions Blog, (June 2, 2009) http://www. concurringopinions. com/archives/2009/06/american-law-institute-approves-the-principles-of-the-law-of-software-contracts.html.

[565] Id. (response to Hillman's post by Ken Arromdee, June 2, 2009).

[566] Id. (response to Hillman's post by Sean Hogle, June 6, 2009).

[567] Principles of the Law of Software Contracts § 3.11(a).

violate Article 2's perfect tender rule most of the time. Material breach reflects the industry standard that developed software is almost never free of bugs. Software licensors should use the "material breach" standard so their customer will not pretextually reject software because of minor bugs that do not impair functionality or performance. The Reporters do not replicate other law on breach but instead focus "on what constitutes breach so as to entitle an aggrieved party to a remedy."[568]

The Principles did not include specialized rules for tender, acceptance, rejection, repudiation, "anticipatory repudiation, adequate assurance of performance, or other performance-related topics such as inspection."[569] These concepts are imported from well-travelled provisions of Article 2 of the U.C.C. and the common law without substantial reworking. Instead, the drafters developed rules not found in the common law and tailored them to the specific problems of software contracting. Courts consider the behavior of the party as well as the covenant of good faith and fair dealing.

(2) Material Breach

The Principles draw in large part from the Restatement (Second) of Contracts § 241 and UCITA § 701 in determining what constitutes a material breach. Section 3.11 defines a material breach as an electronic agent that allows the non-breaching party to declare the end of the contract. A material breach occurs where transferors breach the warranty of § 3.05(B) (duty to disclose material hidden defects), a limited remedy fails of its essential purpose (§ 4.01), or the transferor breaches the contract by failing to comply with § 4.03, which is the provision for electronic repossession or automatic disablement by planting malicious or disabling code.

UCITA was the contracting statute to displace the perfect tender rule with the material breach standard. Under Section 3.11, a material breach signifies the end of the contract whereas a non-breaching party may recover for non-material breach and the contract is still in force. UCITA adopted a substantial performance or material breach standard for development software contracts versus Article 2's parochial and unrealistic perfect tender rule. The most significant factors include: the terms of the agreement; (1) usage of trade, course of dealing, and (2) course of performance; (3) the extent which the aggrieved party will be deprived of the benefit reasonably expected; (4) the extent to which the aggrieved party can be adequately compensated for the part of the benefit deprived; (5) the degree of harm or likely harm to the aggrieved party; and (6) the extent to which the behavior of the party failing to perform or to offer to perform departs from standards of good faith and fair dealing.[570] The Reporters note also that a material breach occurs where transferors breach the warranty of § 3.05(b) (duty to disclose material hidden defects), a limited remedy fails of its essential purpose (§ 4.01); or the transferor breaches the contract by failing to comply with § 4.03, which is the provision for automatic disablement.[571]

(3) Right to Cure

Breaching parties have the right to cure at their own expense where the time for performance has not yet expired or there are reasonable grounds to believe the

---

[568] Topic 3, Breach, Summary Overview, Id. at 138.

[569] Id.

[570] Id. at § 3.11(c)(1)–(6).

[571] Id. at § 3.11(d).

nonconforming software would be acceptable to the licensee. Software licensors also often give licensees a period of acceptance testing in addition to the cure. The Principles of the Law of Software Contracts imported the concept of cure of breach from UCITA, which gives software licensors a second chance to get things right, if the software does not work as intended.[572] As with U.C.C. Article 2, breaching parties have the right to cure at their own expense where the time for performance has not yet expired or there are "reasonable grounds to believe the nonconforming performance would be acceptable."[573] Software licensors often give licensees a period of acceptance testing during which time the licensor may cure defects. The cure gives the breaching party a "further reasonable time after performance was due" to get things right.[574]

(G) Remedies for Breach of Software Contracts

(1) UCITA–Like Remedies

The Principles of Software Contracts validate the parties' agreements as to what the remedies should be much like UCITA and U.C.C. Article 2. The Reporters assume parties to software contracts will adapt well-established principles from sales such resale, market price, specific performance, and liquidated damages to software contracts. Software licensors should provide their customers with a minimally adequate remedy. In the absence of agreement, the drafters adopted the expectation theory of damages.[575] The non-breaching party is entitled to remedies for breach. The breach of a software contract may constitute copyright infringement as well as breach of contract. Copyright infringement is a cause of action arising out of interfering with an author's exclusive rights. Infringement is the reproduction, distribution, performance, public display, or creation of a derivative work without permission of the copyright owner.

(2) Use of Automated Disablement to Impair Use

The Principles of the Law of Software Contracts limit the ability of a software licensor to remotely remove or disable software. Electronic self-help is always a controversial provision because of the unbridled power it gives licensors over essential software to the customer's business. A disabling device is computer code that prevents users from accessing software.[576] The use of disabling devices is a very controversial practice in the software industry. A software licensor should not use disabling devices unless the licensee agrees to this remedy prior to entering into the license agreement.[577] Furthermore, a licensor should not disable software without providing notice to the licensee. For example, the electronic repossession of a business's billing software might deprive business of the ability to collect accounts. The principal concern of the licensee about disablement is that a licensor may repossess mission-critical

---

[572] Id. at § 3.12.

[573] Id.

[574] Id. at § 3.12(a)(2).

[575] Reporter's Memorandum at xxii.

[576] "Often inserted by a vendor to allow the vendor to prevent the end user from using the software after the license has expired. It may also refer to a virus, spider, worm, etc., that disables the software. Disabling code is often referred to as malicious code." H. WARD CLASSEN, A PRACTICAL GUIDE TO SOFTWARE LICENSING FOR LICENSEES AND LICENSORS (4th ed. 2011) at 396.

[577] UCITA § 605.

software where there is a *bona fide* dispute over a term in a software contract. Section 4.03 provides, "A transferor may not use automated disablement of the process results in the loss of rights granted in the agreement or the loss of use of other software or digital content."[578]

Section 4.03 balances the interests of licensors and licensees by permitting automated disablement under certain limited circumstances, but strictly prohibiting disablement as a self-help remedy. Electronic self-help is always a controversial provision because of the power it gives licensors over integral software in enterprises. Electronic disablement is strictly prohibited in standard form transfers of generally available software and all consumer transactions.[579] Licensors using electronic disablement contrary to the Principles are subject to liability for direct, incidental, and consequential damages.[580] In business-to-business transfers, disablement is permitted but subject to limitations such as "the term authorizing automated disablement is conspicuous; [and] the transferor provides timely notice of the breach" and gives the other party a reasonable right to a cure.[581] The Reporters also note how parties frequently tailor their own remedies with consequential damages exclusions, as limited remedies will fail of their essential purpose making consequential damages limitations unenforceable because they are unconscionable.

(3) Liquidated Damages

Section 4.02 provides for liquidated damages but these clauses may not be penal provisions i.e. "the amount must be reasonable in light of the anticipated harm or actual harm caused by the breach."[582] The guideposts in U.C.C. § 2–718 were imported to the Principles. If the court strikes down compensation or liquated damages clauses, the remedies are available had the clause not been included.[583] The Reporters decline to develop precise formulas for measuring damages in software contracts, but direct courts to U.C.C. Article 2 for guidance.[584]

(4) Cancellation & Expectancy Damages

Cancellation of the software contract is appropriate by the non-breaching party who provides that the other party committed a material breach.[585] As with U.C.C. Article 2, there is no right to cancel absent notice to the breaching party, which triggers their right to cure. Section 4.05 draws upon the common law of contract in recognizing that the non-breaching party has the right to "expectation damages."[586] Damages for loss expectancy include incidental and consequential damages less expenses saved that stem from the breach.[587]

---

[578] Id. at § 4.03.

[579] Id. at § 4.03(c).

[580] Id. at § 4.03(e).

[581] Id. at § 4.03(d)(1)–(3).

[582] Id. at § 4.02(a).

[583] Id. at § 4.02(b); see also, § 4.01, cmt. a, illus. 2.

[584] Id. at § 4.05, cmt. a.

[585] Id. at § 4.04.

[586] Id. at § 4.05.

[587] Id.

(5) *Specific Performance*

Section 4.06 recognizes the equitable remedy of specific performance where software "is unique or in other proper circumstances."[588] Specific performance is not available for personal services such as support by a particular programmer.[589] Specific performance, as with the sales of goods, is appropriate where the software is unique or in proper circumstances. This remedy, based upon equity, is discretionary and unavailable absent a showing of exceptional circumstances.

§ 4.9   CLOUD COMPUTING SERVICE LEVEL AGREEMENTS

The term, cloud computing, is a metaphor that describes public as well as private providers of software access or storage. Cloud computing is "used to describe a software-as-a-service ("SAAS") platform for the online delivery of products and services."[590] Despite the metaphor that services and software are stored in the clouds, cloud computing always has a physical location. "Cloud computing is a model for enabling convenient, on-demand network access to a shared pool of configurable computing resources (e.g., networks, servers, storage, applications, and services) that can be rapidly provisioned and released with minimal management effort or service provider interaction."[591] "Amazon, Google, Rackspace, and Microsoft are leading companies in the business of renting cloud computing and storage.[592] Cloud computing is in perpetual motion and the buzz is that it will displace traditional software licensing. Nevertheless, Richard Stallman, a founding father of the open source movement describes it as a trap for the unwary. He writes about how cloud computing raises the specter of unilateral control by proprietary companies: "It's stupidity. It's worse than stupidity: it's a marketing hype campaign. Somebody is saying this is inevitable—and whenever you hear somebody saying that, it's very likely to be a set of businesses."[593]   A litigator examines how cloud computing impacts discovery and jurisdiction:

> We have reached the point where some of us do not know where in the "cloud" our computer backup files reside. There are drive-through windows at fast food restaurants in the Midwest where orders are taken by call centers in the Southeast. We fly from Boston to Chicago, *for the day*, and stop along the way to eat dinner at the airport in Philadelphia. In short, nothing stops at a state border anymore.[594]

Companies as well as individuals are storing their data and using software in the clouds and therefore "no longer have direct physical access to the devices storing their

---

[588] Id. at § 4.06(a).

[589] Id. at § 4.06(a), cmt. a.

[590] Rearden LLC v. Rearden Commerce, 597 F. Supp. 2d 1006, 1021 (N.D. Cal. 2009).

[591] NATIONAL INSTITUTE OF STANDARDS & TECHNOLOGY, NIST CLOUD COMPUTING PROGRAM, http://www.nist.gov/itl/cloud/index.cfm (last visited May 23, 2013).

[592] Scott DeCarlo & Tomio Geron, America's Fastest Growing Tech Companies, FORBES (June 24, 2013).

[593] MICHAEL ARMBRUST, ARMANDO FOX, REAN GRIFFITH, ANTHONY D. JOSEPH, RANDY KATZ, ANDY KONWINSKI, GUNHO LEE, DAVID PATTERSON, ARIEL RABKIN, ION STOICA, AND MATEI ZAHARIA., ABOVE THE CLOUDS: A BERKELEY VIEW OF CLOUD COMPUTING (Feb. 10, 2009) at 1 (Executive Summary) (quoting Free Software pioneer Richard Stallman).

[594] ANDREW SCHULMAN A PRACTICAL GUIDE TO ORGANIZING A BUSINESS IN RHODE ISLAND (MCLE) § II-16.1(2013).

data."[595] A University of California–Berkeley Distributed Systems Laboratory research report describes the variegated service paradigm of cloud computing:

> Cloud Computing refers to both the applications delivered as services over the Internet and the hardware and systems software in the datacenters that provide those services. The services themselves have long been referred to as Software as a Service (SaaS). The datacenter hardware and software is what we will call a Cloud. When a Cloud is made available in a pay-as-you-go manner to the public, we call it a Public Cloud; the service being sold is Utility Computing. We use the term Private Cloud to refer to internal datacenters of a business or other organization, not made available to the public. Thus, Cloud Computing is the sum of SaaS and Utility Computing, but does not include Private Clouds. People can be users or providers of SaaS, or users or providers of Utility Computing. We focus on SaaS Providers (Cloud Users) and Cloud Providers, which have received less attention than SaaS Users. From a hardware point of view, three aspects are new in Cloud Computing.[596]

The service agreement by application service providers ("ASPs") emerged in the late 1990s as a model of distribution that did not involve installation at the customer's facility. For instance, Microsoft devised a method of distributed service that includes linking popular programs in a services package. Distributed service agreements reflect a new licensing model, which encompasses software as well as services. As with other licenses, the service provider makes it clear that it is retaining all proprietary rights and that the customer does not own the software or the media on which it is inscribed. Subscription based licenses frequently encompass services as well as the licensing of software such as 24/7 telephone support, installation, or maintenance. The leading cloud-based storage products are DropBox, SugarSync, and Pogoplug/Cloudstor. The U/Cal Berkeley Report identified hardware savings from cloud computing. The chief finding was that the appeal of cloud computing was the "the construction and operation of extremely large-scale, commodity-computer datacenters at low cost locations."[597] The chief savings for companies are the "cost of electricity, network bandwidth, operations, software, and hardware available at these very large economies."[598] The researchers identified three hardware-related aspects of cloud computing accounting for its appeal:

(1) The illusion of infinite computing resources available on demand, thereby eliminating the need for Cloud Computing users to plan far ahead for provisioning.

(2) The elimination of an up-front commitment by Cloud users, thereby allowing companies to start small and increase hardware resources only when there is an increase in their needs.

---

[595] JEFFREY FOLLETT, ET. AL., MCLE MASSACHUSETTS DISCOVERY PRACTICE § 20.1 (2012 ed.) (discussing electronic discovery).

[596] MICHAEL ARMBRUST, ARMANDO FOX, REAN GRIFFITH, ANTHONY D. JOSEPH, RANDY KATZ, ANDY KONWINSKI, GUNHO LEE, DAVID PATTERSON, ARIEL RABKIN, ION STOICA, AND MATEI ZAHARIA., ABOVE THE CLOUDS: A BERKELEY VIEW OF CLOUD COMPUTING (Feb. 10, 2009) at 1 (Executive Summary).

[597] Id.

[598] Id.

(3) The ability to pay for use of computing resources on a short-term basis as needed (e.g., processors by the hour and storage by the day) and release them as needed, thereby rewarding conservation by letting machines and storage go when they are no longer useful and storage by the day)[599]

(4) The illusion of infinite computing resources available on demand, thereby eliminating the need for Cloud Computing users to plan far ahead for provisioning.

(5) The elimination of an up-front commitment by Cloud users, thereby allowing companies to start small and increase hardware resources only when there is an increase in their needs.

(6) The ability to pay for use of computing resources on a short-term basis as needed (e.g., processors by the hour and storage by the day) and release them as needed, thereby rewarding conservation by letting machines and storage go when they are no longer useful and storage by the day) and release them as needed, thereby rewarding conservation by letting machines and storage go when they are no longer useful.

Cloud computing is a disruptive technology for traditional legal rules built upon a foundation of territorial sovereignty. "With the ubiquity of cloud computing, the government's reach into private data becomes even more problematic."[600] Cloud computing creates new legal dilemmas such as what constitutes electronic storage, an issue key to the Electronic Communications Privacy Act. How should the Stored Communications Act be tweaked to recognize that since the Act was enacted, e-mail and other messages are stored and accessed remotely by Internet users?[601] What should constitute electronic storage in an era of the synchronization of copies across countless servers that may also be cross-border or cross-national. Cloud-based services have become standard for personal use, business use, educational use, and even governmental use.

The cloud-computing infrastructure is undergoing the same revolution as commuter vehicles did in the 1960s, and telephone communications underwent before that. He describes the "computer utility" companies of the 1960s, which operated the first networks for scientific research, which foreshadowed the growth of cloud computing which, with more powerful and cheaper computers, has grown exponentially in use. The FCC has yet to treat cloud computing as a utility subject to its regulations.[602] In general, federal agencies do not regard Internet commercial institutions such as Google as utilities.

---

[599] Id.

[600] See United States v. Cotterman, 709 F.3d 952, 965 (9th Cir. 2013) (en banc).

[601] Nearly thirty years ago, the Stored Communications Privacy Act was enacted to fill a gap in the then relatively new ECPA. See Russell S. Burnside, The Electronic Communications Privacy Act of 1986: The Challenge of Applying Ambiguous Statutory Language to Intricate Telecommunication Technologies, 13 RUTGERS COMPUTER & TECH. L.J. 451, 516–17 (1987) (lamenting "the 1986 Act's circumscription of legal protections for electronic communications, E–Mail, and remote computer services.).

[602] Kevin Werbach, The Network Utility, 60 DUKE L.J. 1761 (2011).

(A) NIST Definition of Cloud Computing

Cloud computing is a model for enabling convenient, on-demand network access to a shared pool of configurable computing resources (e.g., networks, servers, storage, applications, and services) that can be rapidly provisioned and released with minimal management effort or service provider interaction."[603] The National Institute of Standards and Technology ("NIST") defines cloud computing as having the following qualities:

> Cloud computing is a model for enabling convenient, on-demand network access to a shared pool of configurable computing resources (e.g., networks, servers, storage, applications, and services) that can be rapidly provisioned and released with minimal management effort or service provider interaction. This cloud model promotes availability and is composed of five essential characteristics (On-demand self-service, Broad network access, Resource pooling, Rapid elasticity, Measured Service); three service models (Cloud Software as a Service ("SaaS"), Cloud Platform as a Service ("PaaS"), Cloud Infrastructure as a Service ("IaaS")); and, four deployment models (Private cloud, Community cloud, Public cloud, Hybrid cloud). Key enabling technologies include: (1) fast wide-area networks, (2) powerful, inexpensive server computers, and (3) high-performance virtualization for commodity hardware.[604]

(B) Qualities of Cloud Computing

Cloud computing "enabling technologies include: (1) fast wide-area networks, (2) powerful, inexpensive server computers, and (3) high-performance virtualization for commodity hardware."[605] ReDigi describes cloud computing as "the process involves "migrating" a user's file, packet by packet—"analogous to a train"—from the user's computer to the Cloud Locker so that data does not exist in two places at any one time."[606] Cloud computing is rapidly evolving encompassing both software and hardware. The cloud infrastructure can be viewed as containing both a physical layer and an abstraction layer. The physical layer consists of the hardware resources that are necessary to support the cloud services being provided, and typically includes server, storage and network components. The abstraction layer consists of the software deployed across the physical layer, which "manifests the essential cloud characteristics. Conceptually the abstraction layer sits above the physical layer."[607] NIST's definition of cloud computing explains its essential qualities:

> *On-demand self-service.* A consumer can unilaterally provision computing capabilities, such as server time and network storage, as needed automatically without requiring human interaction with each service provider.

> *Broad network access.* Capabilities are available over the network and accessed through standard mechanisms that promote use by heterogeneous thin or thick client platforms (e.g., mobile phones, tablets, laptops, and workstations).

---

[603] PETER MELL & TIMOTHY GRANCE, NAT'L INST. OF STANDARDS & TECH., U.S. DEP'T OF COMMERCE, SPECIAL PUBLICATION 800–145: NIST DEFINITION OF CLOUD COMPUTING (Draft), at 2 (2011).

[604] Id.

[605] Id.

[606] Capitol Records, LLC v. ReDigi Inc., 106 U.S.P.Q.2D (BNA) 1449, 1449 (S.D. N.Y. 2013).

[607] Id. at 2, n.2.

Resource pooling. The provider's computing resources are pooled to serve multiple consumers using a multi-tenant model, with different physical and virtual resources dynamically assigned and reassigned according to consumer demand. There is a sense of location independence in that the customer generally has no control or knowledge over the exact location of the provided resources but may be able to specify location at a higher level of abstraction (e.g., country, state, or datacenter). Examples of resources include storage, processing, memory, and network bandwidth.

Rapid elasticity. Capabilities can be elastically provisioned and released, in some cases automatically, to scale rapidly outward and inward commensurate with demand. To the consumer, the capabilities available for provisioning often appear to be unlimited and can be appropriated in any quantity at any time.

Measured service. Cloud systems automatically control and optimize resource use by leveraging a metering capability at some level of abstraction appropriate to the type of service (e.g., storage, processing, bandwidth, and active user accounts). Resource usage can be monitored, controlled, and reported, providing transparency for both the provider and consumer of the utilized service.[608]

(C) Software as a Service Paradigm

Service bureaus lease or sell data processing, computer time, online services, and access to software in return for subscription fees. Service bureaus are businesses that provide data processing, online services, and access to software through a direct connection over the Internet or WAN services for a fee. [609] A licensor will want a clause that addresses service bureaus. Service bureaus offer diversified software packages or target specific industries. Vendors have developed payroll interface software products that bridge between their software and payroll service bureaus. Service bureaus also offer credit-reporting software to customers. Service bureaus charge their customers pay access and storage charges. Credit or collection agencies depend upon the service bureau to have properly functioning software with the latest updates. Similarly, human relations or payroll departments will access software through service bureaus. Service bureaus increasingly support GNU/Linux and Free/Open Source Software. Cloud computing has evolved as the latest stage in software as a service.

Richard Raysman and Peter Brown, in their computer law treatise, explain that the service bureau will warrant that it will deliver a software system that meets its customer's needs and this also includes documentation, training, and the right of the customer to have a programmer at the services bureau.[610] In addition, the service bureau will warrant that its staff will have the "appropriate technical and application skills to enable them to perform their duties" under the service bureau agreement. Many service bureaus will agree to make modifications or enhancements available to their customers for no additional fee.[611]

---

[608] Peter Mell & Timothy Grance, The NIST Definition of Cloud Computing: Recommendations of the National Institute of Standards and Technology, Special Publication, 800–145 (Sept. 2011) at 1.

[609] PCMAG.com, Encyclopedia, Id.

[610] 2 Richard Raysman & Peter Brown, COMPUTER LAW: DRAFTING AND NEGOTIATING FORMS AND AGREEMENTS § 10.15A at 10–81 (2009).

[611] *Id.* at 10–76.

Cloud providers have developed the next generation of IT services, storing data and running applications and permitting users access data and collaborate on any device, from any location 24/7. Ideally, data or software can be accessed, edited, and shared securely from any location on any device. To date, cloud computing providers have adopted a services paradigm. A typical provision, for example, makes a term of service automatically renewable in perpetuity, subject only to written cancellation by the customer. The fees are generally in the form of monthly service fees with upgrades. Providers issue service credits to customer accounts to offset future billable services. Service credits are not typically transferable to other account holders.

(D) Service Level Agreements for Cloud Computing

I've looked at clouds from both sides now
From up and down, and still somehow
It's cloud illusion I recall
I really don't know clouds at all.
Joni Mitchell, *Both Sides Now*

This section presents the chief issues in negotiating, drafting, and litigating cloud computing service level agreements. The development of cloud computing creates new contracting issues such as whether reasonable security is an implied norm for off-site storage. Cloud computing, like out-sourcing data, exists in a legislative vacuum. Some of the same issues applicable to software licensing apply equally well to cloud computing. Lawyers representing providers and clients need to consider issues such as choice of law, choice of forum, jurisdiction, performance standards, security, and warranties such as systems integration and fitness for a particular purpose. In addition "some new issues come about because of the multi-tenant nature (information from multiple companies may reside on the same physical hardware) of cloud computing, the merger of applications and data, and the fact that a company's workloads might reside outside of their physical on-premise datacenter."[612] Some issues include data or software accuracy, quality, completeness, timeliness, responsiveness resource efficiency, metrics for measuring usage, auditing, privacy, security, interoperability, and what happens in the event of service interruption. Amazon's EC2 service and Google's Google App Engine are two of the best-known examples of cloud computing, which Gartner Inc., a technology research company, defines as a type of computing in which "massively scalable IT- enabled capabilities are delivered 'as a service' to external customers using Internet technologies."[613] Google set the stage for revolutionary technological concepts such as Cloud computing, which enables clients to access software and data stored in remote sites.

Cloud computing service level agreements ("SLAs") address issues such as data protection, data security, and storage services. For a provider, the goal of the SLA is to reallocate the risk of service interruptions and limit liability and exposure to consequential damages. Many providers offer "service credits" for interruptions to displace other remedies. From a customer's perspective, the SLA must provide "peace of mind" that it will have meaningful remedies in the event of loss of data or service

---

[612] Open Cloud Manifesto, Dedicated to the Principle That the Cloud Should Remain Open, http://www.opencloudmanifesto.org/ (last visited June 15, 2013).

[613] Jon Brodkin, Seven Cloud-Computing Risks, NETWORK WORLD (July 2, 2008) (reviewing Gartner Report on risks of cloud computing).

interruptions. SLAs need to address backup audits and assessments as well as backups in the event of service interruptions.

Neither Congress nor state legislatures have enacted new contracting law addressing cloud computing or service bureaus. This is another example of legal lag where the information technologies are evolving faster than the law. Cloud computing is a new paradigm of providing information technology services with diverse ideal types that include on-site private clouds, off-site private clouds, public clouds, or hybrids such as when a business places its website on a public cloud but retains a private cloud for its internal operations.[614] A 2011 survey of 3,000 CIO executives confirmed the importance of cloud computing in U.S. companies.[615] SITA, an air traffic transportation specialist, joined forces with Orange Business Services, to create a high performance cloud structure.[616] "The companies are attempting to build a highly resilient network by using high tier, redundant connections, failover sites, and intelligent re-routing; this will help them meet their service level commitments."[617]

In many respects, cloud-computing works like a utility such as water or electricity in that is measured, scaled out, and provides on demand services. NIST develops a paradigm of three service models:

Cloud Software as a Service ("SaaS"): The capability provided to the consumer to use the provider's applications running on a cloud infrastructure. The applications are accessible from various client devices through a thin client interface such as a Web browser (e.g., Web based email). The consumer does not manage or control the underlying cloud infrastructure including network, servers, operating systems, storage, or even individual application capabilities, with the possible exception of limited user specific application configuration settings.

Cloud Platform as a Service ("PaaS"): The capability provided to the consumer is to deploy onto the cloud infrastructure consumer created or acquired applications created using programming languages and tools supported by the provider. The consumer does not manage or control the underlying cloud infrastructure including network, servers, operating systems, or storage, but has control over the deployed applications and possibly application hosting environment configurations.

Cloud Infrastructure as a Service ("IaaS"): The capability provided to the consumer is to provision processing, storage, networks, and other fundamental computing resources where the consumer is able to deploy and run arbitrary software, which can include operating systems and applications. The consumer does not manage or control the underlying cloud infrastructure but has control over the operating

---

[614] Nathan Marke, Clearing the Clouds: What's Right For Your Business, CBR ROLLING BLOG, (June 17, 2011), http://www.cbronline.com/blogs/cbr-rolling-blog/clearing-the-clouds-whats-right-for-your-business-210611 (last visited May 23, 2013).

[615] Glenn Gruber, Six Questions Hoteliers Should Ask Providers of Cloud-Based Systems, TALKING TRAVEL TECH BLOG, (June 16, 2011), http://www.tnooz.com/2011/06/21/news/six-questions-hoteliers-should-ask-providers-of-cloud-based-systems/ (last visited May 23, 2013).

[616] Press Release, SITA and Orange Business Services Join Forces to Build a Global Cloud Computing Infastructure, MARKETWATCH.COM (June 22, 2011), (June 22, 2013), http://www.marketwatch.com/story/sita-and-orange-business-services-join-forces-to-build-a-global-cloud-computing-infrastructure-2011–06–22?reflink=MW_news_stmp (last visited May 30, 2013).

[617] Id.

systems, storage, deployed applications, and possibly limited control of select networking components (e.g., host firewalls).[618]

In addition to the private sector, approximately 25% of the federal government's eighty billion in IT spending is a potential target for cloud computing solutions.[619]

Lawyers representing cloud-computing customers will need to focus on the meaning of key terms in their contracts such as "availability, "access," and "outage." The first generation of service level agreement ("SLA") is the chief instrumentality for cloud computing contract law.[620] Service providers use SLAs to reallocating risks, disclaiming warranties, and limiting remedies to service credits.[621] In a service paradigm, the provider gives only a "best efforts" promise as opposed to strict liability-like express warranties that run with sales of goods or the Principles of the Law of Software Contracts. An exception to this tendency is the warranty-like protections given by AMS, a public peer exchange.[622]

Access and outage terms are two of the most important provisions in any SLA agreement.[623] Access is the *sine qua non* of cloud computing and therefore the agreement must carefully define how outage is to be measured.[624] Epocrates' SLA spells out what access means under the contract: "'Availability' is defined as the time when the infrastructure is available for users to access the BMJWebDxPremium Product. Availability is measured on a 24/7/365 basis and means when the BMJWebDxPremium Product is functioning correctly when accessed via the internet from outside the Epocrates network and includes being able to access the BMJWebDxPremium Product."[625] Epocrates' SLA also explains the operational structure for its cloud in its SLA:

> The Epocrates production facility has been architected as a highly available and highly scalable infrastructure. The site is monitored on a 24 7 365 basis for fault

---

[618] Id. at 17.

[619] Jill Tumler Singer, Is Cloud Computing For Real? Summary of Session By CIO of the National Reconnaissance Office at Cloud Expo New York, Sys-Con Media, http://www.sys-con.com/node/1878613 (last visited May 31, 2013).

[620] Risks of Cloud Computing, Queensland Government, 2011, http://www.business.qld.gov.au/technology-for-business/cloud-computing-business/cloud-computing-risks.html (last visited May 25, 2013).

[621] CIOs key questions for cloud providers concerned access, outages, and recovery of data. "Do you have SLAs on RTO (Recovery Time Object) / RPO (Recovery Point Objective)?" Other questions include whether cloud providers had data backups. If so, how far back in time may data be recovered? How quickly can data be recovered? Executives are also interested in availability terms, system integration, and the portability of data. Glenn, Gruber, Six Questions Hoteliers Should Ask Providers, Id.

[622] "AMS is a public peering hub—connects cloud providers together. Is now offering SLA guaranteed 100gbE connections, not just 'best effort' SLAs that most in industry currently use." David Sims, Amsterdam Peering Exchange Intros SLA for Guaranteed Bandwidth, TMCNET.COM, http://www.tmcnet.com/channels/voice-peering/articles/186546–amsterdam-peering-exchange-intros-sla-guaranteed-bandwidth.htm (last visited May 25, 2013).

[623] "Outages damage perception of reliability of the cloud." Robert Plant, Don't Get Stuck in the Cloud: Even if Your Data is Secure, One Glitch with a Cloud Provider Could Scare off your Customers, HARV. BUS. REV., http://www.businessweek.com/managing/content/jun2011/ca20110621_098805.htm (last visited May 23, 2013).

[624] "Access to cloud resources requires. . . access to the cloud." Id.

[625] Epocrates Material Contract in SEC Filing, Exhibit 10, July 16, 2010 (Data processing and preparation DATED 20th February 2007 (1) The BMJ Publishing Group- and -(2) Epocrates, Inc. Click for Enhanced Coverage Linking Searches Agreement for the Newdx Project).

and performance characteristics. Every effort is made to minimize the frequency and effects of planned and/or unplanned outages of the infrastructure.

The Service Level Agreement ("SLA") for the production infrastructure is as set out below:

The SLA sets out the time when the BMJWebDxPremium Product will be available for external user access. This includes access to the BMJWebDxPremium Product and NewDx Content included in that product and any other agreed content to the extent that Epocrates and its contractors host it. Epocrates agrees and undertakes to provide the Service Levels to the site in accordance with this Schedule. Epocrates further agrees that it shall monitor and measure the performance of the service and of the Service Levels and shall report the same to the BMJ as set out below.[626]

Cloud providers have developed software that measures usage, which is the basis for charging its customers[627] For example; a new software product by "Uptime Software" monitors cloud services and provides estimates on costs, uptime, and other benchmarks. This software signals a new era in contract enforcement as software monitors resources, determines cloud costs, and helps enforce SLAs.[628] Nevertheless, it is important for providers and clients to spell out how service level credits are computed and provide for auditing by both parties.[629] A FDIC official notes that SLA cloud computing is still in the process of evolution. He notes the difficulty of locking down the meaning of a cloud computing contract.[630] This FDIC specialist highlights the following key negotiating points:

How do you monitor that relationship? Who does the monitoring? What do you monitor? For example, are you looking at the business health of the service provider, the compliance with regulations and compliance with the bank's own internal policies? How is their security posture? Essentially, it's everything we'd want to see in the service level agreements.

For example, ensuring availability of your data, how do you know whether or not the cloud is really capable of providing you 100 percent up time? Is it a guarantee or is it a commitment? And we've seen some recent examples where cloud outages do occur, even though they may provide commitments 100 percent up time. The same goes for security. There have been a few instances where we've seen some cloud providers for data storage asserting that there is security, only to find out later that there really isn't security that they committed to.[631]

---

[626] Id.

[627] Jessica Davis, MSPs, SaaS Providers Get a Handle on Cloud Computing Costs With Uptime Software, ChannelInsider.com, http://www.channelinsider.com/c/a/Cloud-Computing/MSPs-SaaS-Providers–Get-a-Handle-on-Cloud-Computing-Costs-With-Uptime-Software-112268/ (last visited May 31, 2013).

[628] Id.

[629] Nathan Marke, Clearing the Clouds: What's Right For Your Business, CBR ROLLING BLOG,(June 17, 2011) http://www. cbronline.com/blogs/cbr-rolling-blog/clearing-the-clouds-whats-right-for-your-business-210611 (last visited May 30, 2013).

[630] Tracy Kitten, Cloud & Mobile: Vendor Weak Points: FDIC's Saxinger on Management and Contracts with Third Parties, BANKINFOSECURITY.COM, (June 22, 2011) http://www. bankinfosecurity. com/articles.php?art_id=3770 (last visited May 30, 2013).

[631] Id.

The SLA agreement must also provide for prompt hardware service in the event of outages in private clouds. The Society for Worldwide Interbank Financial Telecommunication ("SWIFT") provides a network that enables financial institutions worldwide to send and receive information about financial transactions in a secure, standardized and reliable environment. For the past forty years, SWIFT has averaged 99.999 uptime.[632] Security is the watchword for lawyers representing cloud computing clients:

> [B]e specific in the security protocols they require, keeping in mind that they must be reasonable and within the cloud provider's ability to implement. Schultz said organizations should insist on data loss prevention, but be prepared to pay more for it.

> Consider including penalty clauses for data security breaches in their cloud SLAs. Getting that requires a cloud provider serious enough about data security . . . It's nice to get money back if you have a breach. It won't cover your costs but you're getting someone who invests skin in the game.'

> The cloud provider must be obligated to return or destroy data as directed by the customer, and the contract should have a timeframe for accomplishing that.[633]

To effectively represent their clients, an attorney representing customers must spell out rights in the event cloud computing software or data is unavailable.[634] In addition, the parties to cloud computing SLAs must spell out: (1) Rights and Duties of provider and client; (2) Metrics / measurements to be used in measuring level of service, disruption, or maintenance; (3) Description and list of services provider is to deliver that will conform to terms (Clients should consider how measurement is reported), (4) Issues with SLA's where cloud provider outsources to another cloud provider; upstream SLA needs to give complimentary representations about level of service and other obligations.[635] An IBM White Paper sets forth ten issues that lawyers must consider in negotiating SLAs:

(1) *Business Level Objectives:* An organization must define *why* it will use the cloud services before it can define exactly what services it will use. This part is more organizational politics than technical issues: Some groups may get funding cuts or lose control of their infrastructure.

(2) *Responsibilities of Both Parties:* It is important to define the balance of responsibilities between the provider and consumer. For example, the provider will be responsible for the Software-as-a-Service aspects, but the consumer may be mostly responsible for his VM that contains licensed software and works with sensitive data.

---

[632] Karl Flinders, Bank App Store Part of Community Cloud Developments, COMPUTERWEEKLY.COM, (June 21, 2011) http://www.computerweekly.com/Articles/2011/06/21/247043/Bank-app-store-part-of-community-cloud-developments.htm (last visited May 30, 2013).

[633] Marcia Savage, Cloud Computing Contracts and Security's Role, TECHTARGET.COM, (June 22, 2011) http://searchcloudsecurity.techtarget.com/news/2240037158/Cloud-computing-contracts-and-securitys-role (last visited May 30, 2013).

[634] See discussion between IBM's John Easton and VMWare's Lee Dilworth regarding Cloud Computing, http://www.datacenterdynamics.com/focus/themes/cloud-computing/datacenter-discussions-ibm-and-vmware?SQ_DESIGN_NAME=print (last visited May 31, 2013).

[635] Id.

(3) *Business Continuity/Disaster Recovery:* The consumer should ensure the provider maintains adequate disaster protection. Two examples come to mind: Storing valuable data on the cloud as backup and *cloud bursting* (switchover when in-house datacenters are unable to handle processing loads).

(4) *Redundancy:* Consider how redundant your provider's systems are.

(5) *Maintenance:* One of the nicest aspects of using a cloud is that the provider handles the maintenance. But consumers should know, when providers will do maintenance tasks:

- Will services be unavailable during that time?

- Will services be available, but with much lower throughput?

- Will the consumer have a chance to test their applications against the updated service?

(6) *Data Location:* There are regulations that certain types of data can only be stored in certain physical locations. Providers can respond to those requirements with a guarantee that a consumer's data will be stored in certain locations only and the ability to audit that situation.

(7) *Data Seizure:* If law enforcement seizes a provider's equipment to capture the data and applications belonging to a particular consumer, that seizure is likely to affect other consumers that use the same provider. Consider a third party to provide additional backup.

(8) *Provider Failure:* Make contingency plans that take into account the financial health of the provider.

(9) *Jurisdiction:* Again, understand the local laws that apply to your provider as well as you do the laws that apply to you.

(10) *Brokers and Resellers:* If your provider is a broker or reseller of cloud services, you need to understand the policies of your provider and the actual provider.[636]

The SLA is a very different paradigm than standard software contracts with new risks.[637] A survey of senior information technology executives concluded that respondents were concerned about the lack of rights and remedies in SLAs.[638] IBM charges more for SLAs with meaningful warranties and remedies.[639] IBM's White Paper states that SLAs need to fulfill four objectives:

---

[636] IBM.com, Review and Summary of Cloud Service Level Agreements, http://www.ibm.com/developerworks/cloud/library/cl-rev2sla.html (last visited June 23, 2013).

[637] Id.; Ambrose McNevin, Death of the Datacenter?, DATACENTERDYNAMICS.COM, http://www.datacenterdynamics.com/focus/archive/2011/06/death-of-the-data-center (last visited May 30, 2013) ("Cloud computing will not do to the datacenter what the personal computer did to the mainframe; there are still many risks in moving to the cloud").

[638] The study described risks IT professionals and executives consider with cloud computing: Vendor lock-in, data security, compliance with regulation, lack of strong SLAs. Senior business executives were more concerned with contractual issues in SLAs than Senior IT executives. The Potential Storms of Cloud Computing, FINCHANNEL.COM (2011), http://finchannel.com/Main_News/B_Schools/88862_The_potential_storms_of_cloud_computing/ (last visited May 31, 2013).

[639] The Importance of Service Level Agreements, Perspectives on Cloud Computing, http://cloudbloggroup.tumblr.com/post/7045628090/the-importance-of-service-level-agreements.

- The list of services the provider will deliver and a complete definition of each service.

- Metrics to determine whether the provider is delivering the service as promised and an auditing mechanism to monitor the service.

- Responsibilities of the provider and the consumer and remedies available to both if the terms of the SLA are not met.

- A description of how the SLA will change over time.[640]

Another survey of cloud computing customers revealed dissatisfaction with the terms of cloud computing service agreements:

One critical element of cloud strategy revealed by the survey involves service levels: 'Survey respondents hold very low opinions of the service-level agreements they are getting from vendors,' . . ." That's why we believe that the first essential-but-unknown success factor in cloud implementations is a strong focus on SLAs."[641]

A study of cloud computing clients concluded that SLA agreements were an entirely new paradigm with unique negotiating points: "About one-third of service consumer respondents rate the effectiveness of their SLAs 3 on a scale of 1 ("very ineffective") to 5 ("generally very effective").[642] Only 16% of the respondents gave their SLAs the highest ratings though "49% say their providers deliver 95% to 100% compliance."[643] The cloud computing contracting survey also concluded that:

57% of service consumers rely on internal IT to monitor provider SLAs.

46% agree it's difficult to monitor service-level targets with public cloud service providers.

Most (79%) of SLA terms are negotiated.

The vast majority (96%) of SLAs did not fully meet the required service-level targets over the past year.

Most (57%) service consumers assess financial penalties on service providers when terms aren't met, yet only 10% say they receive full reimbursement.[644]

In the cloud computing legal environment, there is frequently a mismatch in service level agreements (SLAs) between existing systems (tomorrow's legacy) and what is being offered for cloud-based services.[645] "Despite supplier promises around availability, standard SLA targets still fall well short of current performance in more

---

[640] IBM.com, Review and Summary of Cloud Service Level Agreements, Id. at 1.

[641] Eileen Feretic, There's No Escaping the Cloud, BASELINEMAG.COM, (2011), http://www.baselinemag.com/c/a/IT-Management/Theres-No-Escaping-the-Cloud-595183/.

[642] Id.

[643] Id.

[644] Press Release, InformationWeek Analytics New Research Finds Only 4% of SLAs Met All Service–Level Targets Over the Past 12 Months, PRNEWSWIRE.COM, (June 24, 2011) http://www.prnewswire.com/news-releases/informationweek-analytics-new-research-finds-only-4–of-slas-met-all-service-level-targets-over-the-past-12–months-124485048.html (last visited May 31, 2013).

[645] Id.

traditional delivery models."[646] Security and privacy issues abound with cloud computing though Internet law has not yet evolved to address these issues.[647] Security priorities for cloud computing include: (1) Governance, Risk & Compliance, (2) Identity Management Infrastructure Security (3) Confidentiality of Data and (4) Data Protection.[648] As a U.S.-based company, Microsoft has to comply with the Patriot Act— which means that the U.S. government may access EU–Based cloud data potentially violating the EU Data Protection Directive.[649] Outsourcing data including personally identifiable information about European consumers may create unanticipated negative consequences as to the portability of data.[650]

§ 4.10 COMMERCIAL LAW OF INTERNET INTANGIBLES

The lesson of the past two decades is the protean qualities of U.C.C. Article 9. The law of secured transactions accommodates well to changing information technologies. Courts have had little difficulty in accommodating principles of secured transactions to cyberspace or to the transfer of intangible assets. In an information-based economy, software and intellectual property are a company's crown jewels. A leading law school casebook on the licensing of intellectual property notes that companies seeking financing will need to prove "the valuation of the company's intellectual property" before lenders will loan them money.[651] Bankruptcy trustees are disbursing internet assets such as domain names or IP addresses routinely:

> Bankruptcy trustees, debtors-in-possession, and receivers are seeing an increase in efforts to sell Internet Protocol (IP) addresses, also referred to "IP Numbers." IP Numbers are the unique numeric identifiers associated with computers connected to the Internet.. While sales of IP Numbers can deliver value to the estate, IP Numbers are unusual in that their value, use and transfer are enhanced by applicable contract and policy. Ignoring the contracts and policies can delay the sale process and reduce or negate the value of IP Numbers. This article seeks to provide an overview of issues associated with IP Number sales, as well as suggesting an approach for permissible and straightforward sales to obtain the highest value.[652]

---

[646] Andy Gallagher, An Evolutionary Approach to Cloud Computing, COMPUTERWEEKLY.COM (June 17, 2011), http://www.computerweekly.com/Articles/2011/06/17/247021/An-evolutionary-approach-to-cloud-computing.htm (last visited May 31, 2013).

[647] Jan De Clercq, Stay Safe in the Cloud: Focus on Security When Considering Cloud Adoption, WINDOWSITPRO, (June 24, 2011), http://www.windowsitpro.com/article/security/Stay%20Safe%20in%20 the%20Cloud-130060 (last visited May 31, 2013).

[648] Jan De Clercq, Stay Safe in the Cloud, Id.

[649] Zack Whittaker, Microsoft Admits Patriot Act Can Access EU-Based Cloud Data, ZDNET, http://www.zdnet.com/blog/igeneration/microsoft-admits-patriot-act-can-access-eu-based-cloud-data/11225 (last visited May 31, 2013).

[650] Stuart Wilson, Steve Bailey, CommVault, CHANNELEMEA.COM (June 24, 2011, http://www.channelemea.com/spip.php?article4301 (last visited May 30, 2013) ("What is less publicized . . . is the additional risk of outsourcing email for faculty and students who are European residents. The European Union (EU) has much stricter privacy laws than the US, which could require seeking permission from the parties prior to engaging a third-party to handle their email.").

[651] ROBERT W. GOMULKIEWICZ, XUAN–THAO NGUYEN, AND DANIELLE CONWAY–JONES, LICENSING INTELLECTUAL PROPERTY: LAW AND APPLICATION 529 (2008).

[652] Stephen M. Ryan, Matthew Martel, and Ben Edelman, Internet Protocol Numbers Internet Protocol Numbers and the American Registry for Internet Numbers: Suggested Guidance for Bankruptcy Trustees, Debtors-in-Possession and Receivers, BLOOMBERG BNA, BANKRUPTCY RESOURCE CENTER (Jan. 4, 2012).

A federal bankruptcy judge ordered that its founders purchase Bebo.com, once the third largest social media website.[653] Increasingly, trustees or debtors-in-possession view domain names as significant assets for secured lending and sales of assets.[654] To understand how to collateralize software and underlying intellectual property, it is necessary to briefly cover the basics of secured transactions. U.C.C. Article 9 is part of the Uniform Commercial Code, a state law, that covers financial obligations secured by interest in personal property and fixtures but not real property, which is covered by the state law of mortgages. Security agreements are contracts that create a security interest in collateral denominated by the debtor. Intellectual property rights are defined as general intangibles, a U.C.C. Article 9 category of collateral. Software is protectable by both patents and copyrights and the underlying intellectual property, which are general intangibles, can serve as collateral. For patents, which are general intangibles, perfection is accomplished by filing a UCC-1 or financing statement in the state where the debtor's headquarters are located. In contrast, copyrights are perfected by registration in the U.S. Copyright Office.

Security interests are consensual, as opposed to judicial or mechanical liens, which are created by law. U.C.C. Article 9 provides the legal infrastructure for assets-based financing where the assets are personal property. The idea is for a creditor to back up their right to payment (such as a promissory note) with the right to repossess and sell the debtor's collateral. UCC's sphere of application is spelled out in § 9–109(a)(1). Article 9 applies to "a transaction, regardless of its form, that creates a security interest in personal property or fixture."[655]   U.C.C. Article 9's unified concept of the security interest and methods of perfection that turn on the type of collateral applies equally well to Internet-related commercial and consumer financing of personal property. The chart below is a roadmap to the seven parts of U.C.C. Article 9. Creditors will need to consider how U.C.C. Article 9 priority rules apply to software.

---

[653] In re Bebo.com Inc., No. 2:13–bik-22205 (Bankr. Ct., C.D. Cal., July 13, 2013).

[654] Domain names are property that can be a valuable asset in secured lending. "Like their brick-and-mortar counterparts, "e-tailers" must have an attractive address online known as a "domain name." To establish their website's presence on the Internet, domain name holders contract with an Internet Service Provider, which provides the services necessary for registering a domain name. 'Domain names are unique; [they] are assigned on a first come, first serve basis." As a result, "there are no two identical names on the Internet.' In addition, domain names enable Internet users to locate a website using that name." Rachel Ehrlich Albanese and Avi Fox, Chapter 11.com: New Life for the Failed Retailer, BLOOMBERG BNA: ELECTRONIC COMMERCE AND THE LAW. (Aug. 23, 2010).

[655] U.C.C. § 9–109(a)(1).

Parts to Article 9 of the U.C.C.	Key Topics Covered
Part 1: § 9–100s: General Provisions	Definitions of General Concepts
Part 2: § 9–200s: Effectiveness and Attachment	General Effectiveness of Security Agreement, Attachment and Enforcement of Security Interest, After–Acquired Property Clauses; Future Advances;
Part 3: § 9–300s: Perfection and Priority	Law Governing the Perfection and Priority of Security Interests, Conflict of Law Rules, Types of Collateral and How They Determine Method of Perfection, Location of Debtor, Security Interests That Are Perfected Upon Attachment, Perfection by Possession, Perfection by Control, Priority Rules, Lien Creditors vs. Secured Creditors, Buyers of Goods, Licensees of Intangibles; Priorities Among Conflicting Security Interests, Future Advances, Priority of Purchase –Money–Security Interests, Priority of Security Interests in Transferred Collateral, Accessions, Commingled Goods, Rights of Banks and Relationship Between Bank and Secured Party when Deposit Accounts are Controlled
Part 4: § 9–400s: Rights of Third Parties	Alienability of Debtor's Rights, Security Agreements Cannot Prevent Transfers of the Debtor's Rights, Assignment & Anti–Assignment of Security Interests
Part 5: § 9–500s: Filing	Contents of the Financing Statement, Name of Debtor and Secured Party, Filing and Compliance with Other Laws, Effects of Errors & Omissions, Effect of Certain Events on Effectiveness of Financing Statement, Changes in Debtor's Name, Changes in Location of Collateral, New Debtors, Effectiveness of Filed Records, Amending Finance Statements, Termination Statements, What Constitutes Filing, Grounds for Refusing to Accept Financing Statements, Duties and Operation of Filing Office, Acceptance and Refusal to Accept Record, Uniform Forms of Financing Statements & Amendments, Fees, Filing Office Rules

Part 6: § 9–600s Default and Enforcement of Security Interests	Rights After Default, Rights and Duties of Secured Party in Possession and Control, Waiver and Variance of Rights and Duties, Secured Party's Right to Take Possession After Default, Disposition (sale, lease or licensing) of Collateral After Default, Notification Before Disposition of Collateral, Notification Forms, Contents and Form of Notification Before Disposition of Collateral: Consumer Goods Transaction; Application of Proceeds, Surplus & Deficiency, Rights of Transferees of Collateral, Rights & Duties of Certain Secondary Obligors; Full and Partial Satisfaction of Obligation, Notification of Proposal to Accept Collateral, Right of Redemption, Remedies for Secured Party's Failure to Comply with Article, Impact on Deficiency or Surplus, Determination of Whether Conduct was Commercially Reasonable.
Part 7: 9–700s: Transition	Effective Date, Savings Clause, Security Interest Perfected (and Unperfected) Before Effective Date, Continuation Statements

U.C.C. Article 9 provides the ground rules for how to create, perfect, and gain priority for security interests in Internet-related software and other intangible assets. U.C.C. Article 9 determines the rules for perfecting security interests in software, intellectual property and other information-based assets in every U.S. jurisdiction. Counsel securing Internet-related assets outside the U.S. will need to comply with foreign law. U.C.C. Article 9's rules of perfection are not followed outside the United States but many countries are beginning to adopt U.S. style central registries. The Reporters of the Principles of the Law of Software Contracts exclude the "transfer of a security interest in software" from its sphere of application.[656]

If the parties create a security interest in software, U.C.C. Article 9 applies, not the Principles. Article 9's major innovation was to create the legal invention of a "security interest" in personal property. A security interest is an interest in personal property that backs up the debtor's promise to pay or other payment obligation. Collateral means "any tangible or intangible asset belonging to the debtor in which the debtor grants a security interest to its secured party."[657] Secured parties are those who are the beneficiaries of the security interest. The granting clause gives the secured

---

[656] American Law Institute, Principles of the Law of Software Contracts (Proposed Final Draft, March 6, 2009) at § 1.06(b)(2).

[657] JAMES J. WHITE & ROBERT S. SUMMERS, UNIFORM COMMERCIAL CODE (St. Paul: West Publishing Co. 6th ed. 2010) at 1151.

party a security interest in designated collateral generally indicated by specific listing or collateral types such as software as a general intangible.[658]

Section 109 defines the scope of U.C.C. Article 9. Article 9 applies to any "transaction, regardless of its form, that creates a security interest in personal property or fixtures."[659] A security interest, in turn, is "an interest in personal property or fixtures which secures payment for performance of an obligation."[660] Obligations based upon realty other than fixtures are outside of U.C.C. Article 9's scope. The parties to a secured transaction create all of these security interests by contract. The security agreement is an advanced form of contracting which often has numerous conditions and covenants.

The typical security agreement has a granting clause giving the secured party rights in property owned by the debtor. In the clause below, the secured party grants a security interest in their copyright: "Big Software Company hereby grants to First National Bank (Secured Party) a security interest in their copyrighted software and agrees that Secured Party has and shall continue to have a security interest in the following property, including, without limitation, the copyrighted software described in the Exhibits attached." The debtor's property denominated under the security agreement is "collateral." The secured party gains numerous advantages over general creditors by obtaining a security agreement interests. The security agreement between the secured party (generally a bank) and the debtor (generally a borrower) creates a consensual security interest in software collateral. The debtor is generally a borrower in a credit transaction, while the secured party is the beneficiary of the security interest. The entire idea of a secured transaction is that the secured party has a security interest in designated collateral of the debtor that can be repossessed or realized in the event of a default. One of the common events of default is the failure of the debtor to pay a promissory note installment.

The security agreement between the secured party and debtor is a relational contract. The security agreement will typically be 50 to 100 pages long with extensive covenants, conditions, and restrictions tailored to the type of collateral and transactions. At a minimum, a security agreement includes the names of the parties, a granting clause, a reasonable description of the collateral, promises by the debtor and creditor, warranties, events of default, acceleration, remedies, and the signatures of the parties. In addition to the security agreement, a secured party will require the debtor's principals to sign a promissory note as accommodation parties. This means that if the debtor does not pay, the accommodation parties will. If debtor is a start-up company, the secured party or bank will typically ask the debtor's principals to sign in their personal capacity guaranties or sureties. The security agreement is the ultimate source as to whether software or other intangibles are included.

A licensor of software or other information may create an account classified as Article 9 collateral.[661] The account or the stream of payments can be collateral that the secured party will want to be part of the collateral covered by its security agreement with the debtor. In the example above, Article 9 covers consensual security interests

---

[658] See U.C.C. § 9–102(a)(72)(A); § 9–102(a)(73)(A).

[659] U.C.C. § 9–109(9).

[660] U.C.C. § 1–201(b)(35).

[661] U.C.C. § 9–102(a)(2).

created by the secured party and the licensor/debtor as a matter of contract law. In contrast, judicial liens or non-consensual liens are created as a matter of law. If a sheriff levied on a licensor's equipment such as its computers and office equipment because the company failed to pay taxes or a general creditor, this would be a right accorded by statute, not agreement. Lawyers representing Internet companies will need to determine what special steps need to be taken to perfect security interests in collateral. "If some of the secured party's collateral consists of rights to payment arising from copyrights, in whole or in material part, the secured party should" be sure that the security agreement and the financing statement perfect its security interest in the right of payment."[662] Increasingly, the federal law of bankruptcy will be determining the rights and liabilities of e-commerce companies seeking Chapter 7 or 11 protections. Internet assets such as websites will increasingly be collateralized as the economy emphasizes intangible assets.

§ 4.11   CROSS–BORDER ELECTRONIC COMMERCE

The Internet, by its very nature, is international, yet there is no uniform legal infrastructure for commercial transactions harmonized for the global marketplace.[663] However, an international commercial law is beginning to evolve:

> The way of the future in the increasingly global economy is to create greater uniformity in commercial standards of doing business across nations. Where differences in laws and languages create barriers to trade in the process of negotiating and translating complex written documents, short cuts provided by new systems will be needed to keep pace with international commerce and trade. Many recent uniform systems are evolving, based on mercantile law and industry practices, such as the INCOTERMS, the international (and generally accepted) system of commercial delivery terms.[664]

In the absence of international conventions, domestic law applies to license agreements and terms of service. There is great uncertainty as to whose law will govern online commerce, which knows no international borders. Uniform rules for safeguarding commercial information transfers would be a desirable international development. Contract law in cyberspace must take into account radically different social, economic, and legal systems. A growing number of companies are engaged in cross-border electronic commerce. The movement to devise uniform rules to be used in private international law has evolved rapidly over the past century. The United

---

[662] Edwin Smith, MCLE Taking and Enforcing Security Interests in Personal Property § 2.4.

[663] Robert A. Hillman of the Cornell Law School is the Reporter of the Principles of the Law of Software Contracts, while Maureen O'Rourke, the Dean of the Boston University Law School, the Associate Reporter, are distinguished legal academics who understand the globalized nature of software transaction. The Reporters also demonstrate their sophisticated understanding of software consumer issues when they acknowledge the different approach taken in the Principles from Europe's "pro-regulatory stance to consumer protection and contract terms specifically." Principles of the Law of Software Contracts, 2009 A.L.I., § 1.11, cmt. c. The Reporters acknowledge that they have considered the European approach to consumer transactions rejecting it in favor of the U.S.-based unconscionability doctrine. Id. The Reporters note that the annex to the Unfair Contract Terms Directive may be useful to courts "in evaluating unconscionability claims." Id. Finally, the Reporters acknowledge that it may be expensive for software makers to localize their contracts for the European consumer market. Id. This section demonstrates that Internet contracting practices must be localized because countries connected to the Internet have radically different legal cultures.

[664] MCLE Drafting and Enforcing Massachusetts Contracts § 3.11 (2013).

Nations Commission for International Trade ("UNCITRAL"); the International Institute for the Unification of Private Law ("UNIDROIT"); the Council on Europe (Council); and the International Chamber of Commerce ("ICC") have all spearheaded past efforts to create international commercial law.

The European Commission contends that E–Commerce will increase only if consumers are convinced they have a minimal adequate remedy when entering into cross-border sales and services.[665] UNCITRAL's Model Law on Electronic Commerce is consistent with UCITA's E–Commerce infrastructure in addressing business-to-business but not business-to-consumer rules. UNCITRAL's Model Law, like UCITA, validates the digital signature as the functional equivalent of the "pen and paper" signature. Article 7 of the UNCITRAL's model law on Electronic Commerce defines a signature as follows: "The only significant difference between a domestic contract and an international contract is that in the former all the relevant elements of the contract in question are connected with one country only."[666] The parties subject to an international contract law will need to consider jurisdictional choice of law and conflicts of law issues that arise when radically different legal cultures converge.[667]

Software licensing is increasingly a global enterprise, which creates new complications for an E–Commerce company.[668] Lawyers representing E–Commerce companies must tailor cross-border licensing to consider different consumer protection and contracting rules, as well as linguistic and cultural differences.[669] Internet companies targeting European consumers must comply with the Unfair Contracts Term Directive ("UCTD"); European courts will not enforce contractual provisions determined to be unfair under the Directive.[670] The Annex to the UCTD classifies many terms in standard-form TOUs as unfair and this includes disclaimers of warranties, limitations of licensor's liability, unilateral modifications to contract terms, and the acceptance of the license agreement by performance. If a given term in a license agreement is not addressed in the Annex of Suspect Terms, a European court may refuse to enforce it under a more general test of unfairness. Article 8 of the UCTD provides that Member States have the discretion to adopt provisions that are more stringent.

Europe is unique because the twenty-eight countries of the European Union enacted a *de facto* cross-border regime governing electronic commerce. The European

---

[665] "The [Directive on Consumer Rights] Proposal ensures a high level of consumer protection and aims at establishing the real retail internal market, making it easier and less costly for traders to sell cross border and providing consumers with a larger choice and competitive price." Europa, Proposal for a Directive on Consumer Rights, http://ec.europa.eu/consumers/rights/cons_ acquis_en.htm (last visited Sept. 3, 2012).

[666] UNILEX, UNIDROIT PRINCIPLES OF INTERNATIONAL COMMERCIAL LAW PRINCIPLES.

[667] A recent example of cultural clash is the French case against Twitter for enabling the transmission of anti-Jewish tweets. This action is going forward in a French court but would be dismissed at an early stage in the United States because of the First Amendment and Section 230 of the Communications Decency Act. See Eleanor Beardsley, French Twitter Lawsuit Pits Free Speech Against Hate Groups, NATIONAL PUBLIC RADIO (Jan. 22, 2013).

[668] There is relatively little case law on shrinkwrap, but a Scottish court upheld a shrinkwrap license in a business-to-business setting. Beta Computers (Europe) Limited v. Adobe Systems (Europe) Limited. FSR (1996) 367.

[669] MARK LEMLEY, ET AL., SOFTWARE AND INTERNET LAW 459 (2006) (noting the need for legal protection of software and computer technology in an environment "complicated in part because of differences among national legal rules, traditions, procedures, and institutional frameworks.").

[670] See generally, Michael L. Rustad & Vittoria Maria Onufrio, The Exportability of the Principles of Software: Lost in Translation?, 2 HASTINGS SCI. & TECH. L.J. 25, 51–52 (2010).

Commission ("EC") has powers of initiative, implementation, management, and control, which allows it to formulate harmonized regulations. The differences between the EU and the U.S. approaches to TOUs reflect different assumptions about the role of government in regulating markets.[671] Consumers throughout the EU have mandatory rights and remedies that are non-waivable, regardless of whether or not the consumer reads these terms. In Europe, the EU Commission has launched a quiet revolution giving European consumers rights across the Continent. During the past decade, the EC has approved Internet regulations such as the E–Commerce Directive; E–Signatures Directive; Distance Selling Directive; Data Protection Directive; Database Protection Directive; and the Copyright Directive. The right to protection of personal data is established by Article 8 of the Charter, and in Article 8 of the European Convention of Human Rights. The EU recognizes E–Commerce does not flourish without mandatory consumer protection across national borders. Reverse engineering is a right guaranteed to European licensees under the Software Directive for purposes of interoperability. Many of the U.S. style terms of service are invalid or questionable under mandatory European consumer protection rules.[672]

(A) EU Consumer Protection

Online businesses, including U.S. companies, must give European consumers accurate pre-contractual disclosures.[673] Online sellers are required to give consumers confirmatory disclosures before the delivery of computer software or other E–Commerce contracts. The seller's confirmation disclosure must explain the period in which a consumer can cancel the contract. Specifically, websites must give the consumer a right to cancel a distance contract. Further, a website seller must give European consumers a right of withdrawal period not shorter than seven working days. If an e-Business accepts orders via its website or other instrumentality, it will have only 30 days to fill the order. An E–Commerce seller must give European consumers precontractual disclosures including that they have the right to a refund payable within 30 days.

Sellers may not require European consumers to waive consumer rights under the Distance Selling Directive or Unfair Contract Terms Directive or any other mandatory rule. The European Union's Unfair Contract Directive gives, in effect, all European consumers a fundamental right to read, review, and understand standard terms before concluding a contract.[674] Simply put, mass-market license agreements where the

---

[671] Jane K. Winn & Brian H. Bix, Diverging Perspectives on Electronic Contracting in the U.S. and EU, 54 CLEV. ST. L. REV. 175, 183 (2006).

[672] Michael L. Rustad and Maria Vittoria Onufrio. Reconceptualizing Consumer Terms of Use for a Globalized Knowledge Economy. 14 U. PA. J. BUS. L. REV. 1085–1190 (2012).

[673] See e.g. Council Directive 93/13/EEC of 5 April 1993 on unfair terms in consumer contracts(5) and Directive 97/7/EC of the European Parliament and of the Council of 20 May 1997 on the protection of consumers in respect of distance contracts; Council Directive 84/450/EEC of 10 September 1984 concerning misleading and comparative advertising, Council Directive 85/374/EEC of 25 July 1985 on the approximation of the laws, regulations and administrative provisions concerning liability for defective products.

[674] "Terms that are found unfair under the Directive are not binding for consumers. The Directive also requires contract terms to be drafted in plain and intelligible language and states that ambiguities will be interpreted in favor of consumers." Unfair Contract Terms, EUROPA, http://ec.europa.eu/consumers/cons_int/safe_shop/unf_cont_terms/index_en.htm (last updated April 7, 2007). Member States vary in their treatment of unfair terms. "However, in some member states the contractual rights and obligations can generally be adjusted, not only concentrating on the specific unfair term. Furthermore, in some member states public bodies can request the incorporation of new terms in order to prevent a significant imbalance between the rights and obligations." Martin Ebbers, Unfair Contract Terms Directive (93/13), CONSUMER

consumer cannot view the terms prior to payment are invalid in all twenty-eight Member States of the EU under the Unfair Contract Terms Directive.[675]

(B) Electronic Commerce Directive

Member States are required to develop national legislation implementing the Electronic Commerce Directive ("E–Commerce Directive").[676] The E–Commerce Directive, which took effect on January 6, 2002, creates a legal framework for online service providers, commercial communications, electronic contracts, and limitations of liability of intermediary service providers. Article 1 states that the E–Commerce Directive seeks to contribute to the proper functioning of the internal market by ensuring the free movement of information society services between the Member States.[677] The E–Commerce Directive establishes rules such as the transparency and information requirements for online service providers, commercial communications, electronic contracts, and limitations of liability of intermediary service providers.[678] The E–Commerce Directive requires providers to list designated information on their website to qualify for immunities. Barclay's Bank for example, complies with the Directive disclosures in the following chart:[679]

Company name	Barclays Bank PLC.
Registered office	1 Churchill Place, London E14 5HP

LAW COMPENDIUM: COMPARATIVE ANALYSIS 5 (2007), available at http://www.eu-consumer-law.org/consumerstudy_ part2c_en.pdf (last visited June 8, 2012).

[675] Council Directive 93/13/EEC of 5 April 1993 on unfair terms in consumer contracts at art. 4(1):

Without prejudice to Article 7, the unfairness of a contractual term shall be assessed, taking into account the nature of the goods or services for which the contract was concluded and by referring, at the time of conclusion of the contract, to all the circumstances attending the conclusion of the contract and to all the other terms of the contract or of another contract on which it is dependent.

[676] The European Parliament and the European Council adopted the Directive on June 8, 2000.

[677] Id. at art. 1(1).

[678] Articles 10 through 21 of the E–Commerce Directive 'set forth the liability limitations for intermediary service providers and applicable take-down and put-back regimes for illegal material distributed through their facilities.' European ISPs are immunized for caching, hosting, and perfunctory tasks related to efficient transmission of digital data. The E–Commerce Directive does not impose liability on the ISP if it does not modify information transmitted by third parties, unless the ISP acquires actual or constructive notice of illegal content and fails to take prompt remedial steps. Article 15(1) makes it clear that Member States may not impose a duty on providers to investigate questionable e-mails or website posters. Article 15(2), however, permits Member States to enact legislation requiring providers to notify law enforcement when they discover illegal activities on their services. One of the complexities of the E–Commerce Directive's constructive notice provision is its insufficient guidance as to what circumstances and requirements place ISPs on notice. Michael L. Rustad & Thomas H. Koenig, Rebooting Cybertort Law, 80 WASH. L. REV. 335, 393 (2005). Article 17 of the Brussels Regulations provides that a consumer cannot waive her right to sue a supplier in her local court. A supplier, which includes U.S. software companies, directing their activities to the consumer's home state is automatically subject to jurisdiction because he has directed activities to that state as defined in Article 15. Finally, a consumer may enforce a judgment in any Member State upon completion of the formalities set forth in Article 53. Id. at arts. 15, 17, 53.

[679] Barclays, Barclays Complies with Electronic Commerce Directive, http://www.barclays.co.uk/ImportantInformation/The ElectronicCommerceDirective/P1242558133032.

(1) Intermediary Liability

The E–Commerce Directive applies only to service providers established within the twenty-eight Member States of the EU. The E–Commerce Directive exempts service providers from liability for intermediaries "where they play a passive role as a "mere conduit" of information from third parties and limits service providers' liability for other "intermediary" activities such as the storage of information."[680] Article 12 provides for immunity from liability for providers serving as a mere conduit, Articles 13 and 14 immunize providers for ministerial activities such as caching and hosting. Article 14, entitled "Hosting," states:

1. Where an information society service is provided that consists of the storage of information provided by a recipient of the service, Member States shall ensure that the service provider is not liable for the information stored at the request of a recipient of the service, on condition that:

(a) the provider does not have actual knowledge of illegal activity or information and, as regards claims for damages, is not aware of facts or circumstances from which the illegal activity or information is apparent; or

(b) the provider, upon obtaining such knowledge or awareness, acts expeditiously to remove or to disable access to the information.

2. Paragraph 1 shall not apply when the recipient of the service is acting under the authority or the control of the provider.

3. This Article shall not affect the possibility for a court or administrative authority, in accordance with Member States' legal systems, of requiring the service provider to terminate or prevent an infringement, nor does it affect the possibility for Member States of establishing procedures governing the removal or disabling of access to information.[681]

Article 14 establishes a procedure for taking down infringing or illegal content with delineated notice and takedown procedures. Internet services providers are not responsible for the content they host as long as (1) the acts in question are neutral intermediary acts of a mere technical, automatic and passive capacity; (2) they are not informed of its illegal character, and (3) they act promptly to remove or disable access to the material when informed of it.[682] In addition, Article 15 prevents EU Member States from requiring service providers to affirmatively monitor content for potentially illegal activities.[683] These E–Commerce service provider rules are functionally equivalent to the safe harbors of the Digital Millennium Copyright Act discussed in Chapter 10. The European Commission announced it "will clarify the procedures for taking down and blocking access to illegal content after complaints that the rules were unclear and resulted in illegal content staying online for too long."[684]

---

[680] Europa, Electronic Commerce: Commission Welcomes Final Adoption of Legal Framework Directive, Summary (2012).

[681] Id. at art 14.

[682] Id.

[683] Id. at art. 15.

[684] EU Commission Will Clarify Website Notice and Takedown Procedures, OUTLAW.COM (Jan. 12, 2012), http://www.out-law.com/en/articles/2012/january-/commission-will-clarify-website-notice-and-takedown-procedures/.

(2) Spam–E–Mail

Article 7 of the E–Commerce Directive requires service providers to "ensure that service providers undertaking unsolicited commercial communications by electronic mail consult regularly and respect the opt-out registers in which natural persons not wishing to receive such commercial communications can register themselves."[685] Article 7 requires Internet service providers to ensure that any unsolicited commercial communication sent by electronic mail is clearly and unambiguously identifiable as such as soon as the consumer receives it. Article 7(2) requires providers to comply with the EU opt-in rules for commercial e-mail.[686]

(3) Electronic Contracts

Article 9 of the E–Commerce Directive requires providers to recognize the validation of electronic or digital signatures.[687] Article 9(2)'s list of exceptions for electronic contracts is similar to the U.S. approach in UETA and E–SIGN. As in the United States, Internet service providers have no affirmative duty to monitor illegal or infringing content in the European Union.[688] Article 9 provides: "Member States shall ensure that their legal system allows contracts to be concluded by electronic means. Member States shall in particular ensure that the legal requirements applicable to the contractual process neither create obstacles for the use of electronic contracts nor result in such contracts being deprived of legal effectiveness and validity on account of their having been made by electronic means."[689]

Article 9 contains functionally equivalent provisions to EUTA and the E–Sign Act. Like these U.S. statutes, the European E–Commerce Directive provides that certain categories of contracts may not be concluded electronically: (a) real estate contracts except rental agreements, (b) contracts required to be in writing by courts or statutes, (c) contracts of suretyship or security agreements, and (d) contracts for family law or trusts/estates.[690]

(4) Duty to Respond to Report Illegal Activities

Article 15(2) gives Member States the option of establishing a duty of service providers to "inform the competent public authorities of alleged illegal activities undertaken or information provided by recipients of their service or obligations to communicate to the competent authorities, at their request."[691] This role is similar to the one of U.S. service providers who have a duty to report illegal activities, such as the distribution of child pornography and respond to subpoenas of courts of competent jurisdiction. The Directive requires seller to give consumers disclosures before electronic

---

[685] Id. at art. 7(1)(describing unsolicited commercial communications opt-out procedure).

[686] "Without prejudice to Directive 97/7/EC and Directive 97/66/EC, Member States shall take measures to ensure that service providers undertaking unsolicited commercial communications by electronic mail consult regularly and respect the opt-out registers in which natural persons not wishing to receive such commercial communications can register themselves." Id. at art. 7(2).

[687] Id. at art. 9.

[688] Id. at art. 15(1) ("Member States shall not impose a general obligation on providers, when providing the services covered by Articles 12, 13 and 14, to monitor the information which they transmit or store, nor a general obligation actively to seek facts or circumstances indicating illegal activity.").

[689] Id. at art. 9(1).

[690] Id. at art. 9(2).

[691] Id. at art. 15(2).

contracting on how to conclude online contracts, as well as the means of correcting errors. Article 10 gives consumers the right to store and retrieve contracts or they are unenforceable. Article 12 essentially immunizes ISPs for conduit activities much like the U.S. Digital Millennium Copyright Act's Section 512 discussed in Chapter 10. There are a number of requirements that must be met for a service provider to receive 17 U.S.C. § 512(c) safe harbor protection.

(5) Liability of Service Providers

The liability limitation for European service providers applies only if the service provider does not initiate or modify the transmission. Articles 13 and 14 of the Directive immunize a service provider's caching and hosting activities. Article 16 imposes no duty of providers to monitor their websites for illegal activities like the DMCA. Member States must develop legislation to inform the authorities of illegal activities. Member States are to develop legislation to encourage out of court settlements of disputes under Article 17.

(C) The Convention for the International Sale of Goods

(1) Sphere of Application

The Convention for the International Sale of Goods ("CISG") applies to business-to-business transactions where the buyer and seller are in different signatory states.[692] The purpose of the UNCITRAL was to modernize and harmonize the international law of sales. By January 1, 1988, when the United States became a signatory, the CISG was the applicable law for international sales contracts in more than sixty countries. As of May 2, 2012, 74 countries became CISG signatories, accounting for an even larger proportion of U.S. trading partners. CISG consists of four parts made up of three substantive parts and a fourth part containing final provisions. The CISG drafters divided the international sales statute into articles, which are subdivided into chapters in each part of the statute. Part I, entitled the "Sphere of Application and General Provisions," establishes CISG's sphere of application. Article 1 of CISG sets forth the basic rules on applicability of the international law to contracting states. Nationality is important in determining scope; the CISG's scope section uses "place of business" of a party and not "nationality, place of incorporation, or place of head office."[693]

(2) Exclusions & Overview of Scope

Nevertheless, the CISG excludes the following from the scope of its application: auction sales, the sale of securities, negotiable instruments, ships, aircraft, and the sale of electricity. CISG's Reporters excluded consumer transactions as well as all tort actions including causes of action for products liability. Because Europe has adopted the Products Liability Directive there is no need for CISG to cover those causes of action. The justification for CISG exclusions is that it would subject sellers to conflicting national laws or extant law. CISG Part I, Chapter 2, General Provisions, applies to both buyers and sellers in Articles 7 through 13. CISG Part II, spans Articles 14 through 24, and sets forth rules for the formation of the international sales contract.

---

[692] Final Act of the U.N. Conference on Contracts for the International Sale of Goods, Official Records, Annex I at 230 (April 10, 1980), U.N. Doc. A/ Conf.9 7/18, reprinted in 19 INT'L LEGAL MATERIALS 668 (1980), art. 3(2) [hereinafter CISG].

[693] CISG art. 1.

CISG Part III, Articles 25 through 88, covers topics such as breach, avoidance, party obligations, and remedies relevant in software licensing where the CISG is the governing law. CISG Part IV consists of final provisions, including reservations and legal provisions for becoming a signatory state. CISG differs from U.C.C. Article 2 in recognizing the concept of fundamental breach when either party may avoid a contract. U.C.C. Article 2 employs the "Perfect Tender Rule," which permits a buyer to reject a contract if it fails to conform in any respect to the contract.[694] The CISG, however, makes it more difficult to cancel an international sales agreement because of its Article 25 fundamental breach standard.

The CISG's exclusive jurisdiction bases itself upon the seller and buyer's places of business, as opposed to the nationality of the buyer and seller. The CISG applies unless the parties agree to opt out of the Convention under CISG Article 6. The CISG is also inapplicable if one of the parties is unaware that the other's place of business is a foreign CISG signatory state.[695] Article 10 of CISG applies if one of the parties has multiple places of business. Courts will likely exclude service-like transactions as well as contracts where sales are only incidental transactions. CISG leaves less room for creative judicial reforms, though some commentators believe that this statute should be stretched to software transactions, even though it is an intangible. CISG rules for international sales contracts apply in two circumstances: (1) when contracts for the sale of goods are between parties whose places of business are in different CISG Contracting States; or (2) "when the rules of private international law lead to the application of the law of a Contracting State."[696]

This provision applies when one party has a place of business in a CISG signatory state and the other party's place of business is located in a non-CISG state. A court deciding an international sales law dispute could make a decision that private international law leads to applying the law of the CISG or some other body of law. In this provision, the CISG is deferring to the court's application of its private international law principles, often referred to as conflict of law principles by U.S. courts.[697] Article 1(b) is not applicable to U.S. contracting parties because the U.S. entered a reservation derogating from this principle. The U.S. representatives to the Convention found this article to create uncertainty.

(3) CISG's Application to Computer Software

The CISG does not address the question of whether the Convention applies to the licensing of software. U.S. courts classify most software license transactions as falling under Article 2 of the U.C.C., governing the sale of goods,—even though these

---

[694] CISG art. 25. Under CISG, "breach of contract" covers all failures of a party to perform any of his obligations. However, a fundamental breach is more serious and may warrant cancellation:

A breach of contract committed by one of the parties is fundamental if it results in such detriment to the other party as substantially to deprive him of what he is entitled to expect under the contract, unless the party in breach did not foresee and a reasonable person of the same kind in the same circumstances would not have foreseen such a result.

[695] CISG art. 1(2).

[696] CISG art. 1.

[697] Rod N. Andreason, MCC–Marble Ceramic Center: The Parol Evidence Rule and Other Domestic Law Under the Convention on Contracts for the International Sale of Goods, 1999 B.Y.U. LAW REV. 351, 376 (1999) (arguing that private international law must also be consulted to resolve substantive issues of cross-border sales law).

transactions involve the transfer of information or digital data.[698] However, the exclusion of specific intangibles like electricity or shares of stock does not signal the "conclusion that the subject matter of a CISG sale must always be a tangible thing."[699] CISG applies to diverse forms of software licensing but goods, like software, frequently involve a mix of sales and services:

> Though we cannot see or touch it, a computer program is not really all that different from a tractor or a microwave oven, in that a program—designed and built to process words, bill customers or play games—is also a kind of "machine." In other words, a computer program is a *real* and very *functional thing*; it is neither "virtual reality" nor simply a bundle of (copyrighted) "information." Once we recognize the functional nature of a program, we begin to see that the CISG rules (on contract formation, obligations, remedies for breach etc.) are well-suited to regulate international sales of these particular things.[700]

Academic commentators contend that custom software, Internet downloads, and standard mass-market licenses are all within CISG's sphere.[701] Under CISG, "the goods referred to are conceived as movable assets; and the common-law tradition sets great store by noting that they have to be corporeal as well."[702] CISG "seems well-suited to the regulation of contracts for the sale of computer software."[703] Counsel representing parties in international licensing agreements need to consider whether they will opt out of CISG in the event a court extends CISG to international licensing agreements.

(4) CISG Formation Rules

Assuming that the CISG applies to the software contract, there are many differences in formation rules from U.C.C. Article 2. The CISG does not require a writing to be enforceable and thus CISG recognizes neither Statute of Fraud nor Parol Evidence Rule. Anglo–American contract theory follows an objective theory of contract. In contrast, Article 8 of the CISG interprets an international sales contract according to the party's intent. Unlike the parol evidence rule, a court may consider subjective intent as well as objective circumstances prior to or contemporaneous with any final writing, whether integrated or not. Article 8 also permits courts and tribunals to consider subjective intent as well as the reasonable interpretation of the parties' statements and conduct.[704]

---

[698] Robert B. Doe & Jen C. Salyers, Chapter 18 on Software Licenses in KATHRERYN A. ANDRESEN, LAW & BUSINESS OF COMPUTER SOFTWARE 18–5 to 18.6 (2008).

[699] Joseph Lookofsky, In Dubio Pro Conventione? Some Thoughts about Opt–Outs, Computer Software and Preëmption Under the CISG, 13 DUKE J. INT. & COMP. L. 258 (2003).

[700] Id. at 756.

[701] Id. at 278.

[702] FRITZ ENDERLEIN & DIETRICH MASKOW, INTERNATIONAL SALES LAW: UNITED NATIONS CONVENTION ON CONTRACTS FOR THE INTERNATIONAL SALE OF GOODS, CONVENTION ON THE LIMITATION PERIOD IN THE INTERNATIONAL SALE OF GOODS (New York: Oceana Publications, 1992) (visited Dec. 28, 2005) http://www.cisg.law.pace.edu/cisg/biblio/enderlein-art01.html.

[703] JOSEPH M. LOOKOFSKY, UNDERSTANDING THE CISG IN THE USA 61 (1995).

[704] MCC–Marble Ceramic Center, Inc. v. Ceramica Nuova d'Agostino, S.P.A., 144 F.3d 1384 (11th Cir. 1998).

(5) CISG's Warranty–Like Provisions

The CISG does not use the word "warranty," although all of the warranties found in U.C.C. § 2–313 to § 2–315 are found in Article 35. CISG Article 35 requires that the seller deliver goods of the quantity, quality, and description required by the contract.[705] Unlike the UCC, the CISG does not adhere to any formal requirements to disclaim warranties, such as a "conspicuous" disclaimer of the implied warranty of merchantability that expressly mentions the term merchantability.

(6) CISG's Fundamental Breach and Avoidance

Article 2 of the U.C.C. permits a buyer to reject a contract if it fails to conform in any respect to the contract, which is the milestone concept known as the "Perfect Tender Rule."[706] The CISG makes it more difficult to cancel an international sales agreement because of its Article 25 fundamental breach standard. Fundamental breach, in contrast, is the predicate for avoiding a CISG contract under Articles 49(1)(A) and 64(1)(A). Article 49(1)(A) gives the buyer a right to "avoid" the contract if the failure of the seller amounts to a fundamental breach. If there is a fundamental breach of contract by the seller, a buyer may require the seller to deliver substitute goods, which is a remedy found in Article 46(2). Article 25 gives some guidance as to the nature of a fundamental breach.

A breach is fundamental if it causes such "detriment to the other party" to "substantially deprive him of what he is entitled to expect under the contract."[707] Assuming there is an Article 25 fundamental breach, the buyer will have remedies even though the risk of loss has already passed from the seller. In contrast, if there is a mere non-fundamental breach, the buyer will be able to claim either monetary damages for the difference between the value of what was promised and delivered as provided for in Article 74. As with U.C.C. § 2–714, a buyer may accept goods notwithstanding their nonconformity and claim a price reduction.[708] In a software license, the CISG's fundamental breach is more pro-licensor than U.C.C. § 2–601's perfect tender rule and better suited for the "buggy nature" of software.

(7) Breach and Remedies

A buyer may require the seller to deliver substitute goods under CISG Article 46(2) if the seller fundamentally breaches the contract. U.C.C. Article 2's standard is one of perfect tender, U.C.C. § 2–601. CISG, unlike U.C.C. Article 2, does not require a Statute of Fraud nor does it adopt the parol evidence rule. Article 8 of CISG allows either party to introduce evidence of prior or contemporaneous agreements to interpret a contract. Assuming there is a fundamental breach under Article 25, the buyer will have remedies even though the risk of loss has already passed from the seller. Nevertheless, a buyer may seek monetary remedy for non-fundamental breaches. The difference between the value of what was promised and delivered, Article 74, is a buyer's fundamental remedy for accepted goods. The CISG enables a buyer to accept

---

[705] CISG art. 35.

[706] U.C.C. § 2–601.

[707] CISG art. 25.

[708] See CISG art. 50.

goods even though they do not conform to contract and claim a price reduction as an offset.[709]

(D) Europe's Doctrine of Exhaustion

In July of 2012, the European Court of Justice ("ECJ")[710] ruled against Oracle that only the right to distribute software is subject to the European Union's exhaustion doctrine, which is the equivalent of the first sale doctrine followed by U.S. courts.[711] Exhaustion is a synonym for first sale for all practical purposes. Oracle filed suit against UsedSoft in the *Landgericht München* I (Regional Court, Munich I) "seeking an order that UsedSoft cease the practices" of relicensing Oracle software. According to the *Bundesgerichtshof*, the actions of UsedSoft and its customers infringe Oracle's exclusive right of permanent or temporary reproduction of computer programs within the meaning of Article 4(1)(A) of Directive 2009/24. The German court reasoned:

Oracle filed suit against UsedSoft after it promoted an "Oracle Special Offer" in which it offered for sale "already used" licenses for Oracle software. UsedSoft represented that all licenses were current because the maintenance agreement concluded between the original license holder and Oracle was still in force. Oracle's principal method of distribution was to have its customers download software from the Internet. The original Oracle licenses were multi-user and exceeded the number of licenses needed by the first acquirer. UsedSoft would then purchase these licenses from organizations that had valid licenses but had stopped using the software. UsedSoft contended that its business model was authorized by Europe's exhaustion doctrine.[712] Oracle contended, "Exhaustion did not apply to downloading a computer program from the Internet, because there was no sale of a tangible object" only a license.[713] The ECJ opinion ruled that EU Directive permitted licensees to dispose of copies downloaded from the Internet so long as they do not retain a copy for themselves. The European Court of Justice decided that the Directive:

> must be interpreted as meaning that, in the event of the resale of a user license entailing the resale of a copy of a computer program downloaded from the copyright holder's website, that license having originally been granted by that right holder to the first acquirer for an unlimited period in return for payment of a fee intended to enable the right holder to obtain a remuneration corresponding to the economic value of that copy of his work, the second acquirer of the license, as well as any subsequent acquirer of it, will be able to rely on the exhaustion of the distribution right under Article 4(2) of that directive, and hence be regarded as lawful acquirers of a copy of a computer program within the meaning of Article

---

[709] For a full discussion of CISG and how it compares to U.C.C. Article 2, see Michael L. Rustad, THE CONCEPTS AND METHODS OF SALES, LEASES AND LICENSES IN A GLOBAL PERSPECTIVE (2007).

[710] EU Member States will refer issues to the ECJ and often cases are referred back to the national court for a final decision consistent with the ECJ ruling.

[711] In Case C–128/11, Bierbach, Administrator of UsedSoft GmbH v. Oracle International Corp., July 3, 2012, Judgment of the Court (Grand Chamber), Reference for a preliminary ruling under Article 267 TFEU from the Bundesgerichtshof (Germany), made by decision of 3 February 2011, received at the Court on 14 March 2011, in the proceedings.

[712] Directive 2009/24/EC of the European Parliament and of the Council of 23 April 2009 on the legal protection of computer programs.

[713] Id.

5(1) of that directive and benefit from the right of reproduction provided for in that provision.[714]

The court's decision was that the first sale or exhaustion doctrine applies equally well to downloading software from the Internet.

(E) Cross–Border Licensing

U.S. companies need to localize their licensing agreements tailored for diverse legal cultures as illustrated by *Micro Data Base Systems, Inc. v. State Bank of India*.[715] The key issue in *Micro Data Systems* turned on the territorial limits of the license's granting clause. In *Micro Data Base Systems*, the State Bank of Mumbai, India entered into an end-user agreement with the Indiana-based MDBS, the developer of the Database Management System. The license agreement did not contain geographic limitations on where the software could be used. MDBS's Runtime Distribution License Agreement permitted the India-based bank to copy and distributes MDBS modules so long as each copy incorporated tokens to track authorized users. The State Bank of India agreed to purchase tokens for each licensed copy of the software used by MDBS. The licensor charged royalties based upon the sale of tokens used in the shipment of each module.

State Bank of India installed the MDBS in 130 branches around the world. State Bank did not purchase tokens for all of the MDBS modules it used and distributed. In the early 1990s, State Bank used the MDBS software to drive a third-party banking program known as IBSnet. Morgan Laboratories created IBSnet and sold it to State Bank. MDBS filed suit against State Bank of India claiming copyright infringement and breach of the software license agreement. Since MDBS had imposed no territorial limitations, the court held the software license agreement covered locations both inside and outside of India. However, the *Micro Data Base Systems* court ruled that State Bank of India was liable for every software module they distributed without copy control tokens. The court computed damages by multiplying the number of unauthorized copies times the cost for 447 tokens, which totaled $447,000 plus interest. The court ruled that MDBS could not recover damages for copyright infringement since U.S. copyright law has no extraterritorial effect on infringing conduct occurring in India. The tracking system described in *Micro Data Base Systems, Inc.* enabled the licensor to monitor and control the copying, distribution, and use of its software.

(F) Cross–Border Payments

EBay initiated a payments system in Germany and Austria in which it "intermediated payments, receiving funds directly from buyers for items purchased from newly registered sellers on the localized eBay websites in those countries."[716] EBay reported that the German *Bundesanstalt fur Finanzdienstleistungsaufsicht* (BaFin) and the Austrian *Finanzmarktaufsicht* (FMA) required it to obtain a license as a condition of introducing this system. EBay's payment processing unit is based in

---

[714] Id. at clause 88.
[715] 177 F. Supp.2d 881 (N.D. Ind. 2001).
[716] EBay SEC 10–Q Filing (July 19, 2013).

Luxembourg, which does not require a license.[717] EBay faces regulations and licensure in other countries where it operates:

> In Australia, PayPal serves its customers through PayPal Australia Pty. Ltd., which is licensed by the Australian Prudential Regulatory Authority as a purchased payment facility provider, which is a type of authorized depository institution. Accordingly, PayPal Australia is subject to significant fines or other enforcement action if it violates the disclosure, reporting, anti-money laundering, capitalization, corporate governance or other requirements imposed on Australian depository institutions. In China, PayPal is affiliated with Shanghai Wangfuyi Information Technology Ltd., which is licensed as an Internet Content Provider and operates a payments service only for Chinese customers and only for transactions denominated in Chinese currency. The People's Bank of China (PBOC) has enacted regulations to establish a new type of license, called a Payment Clearing Organization (PCO) license, which will be required for non-bank payment services.[718]

The Internet poses new legal dilemmas for payments systems. One of the greatest risks for businesses is when a cybercriminal operating in a distant forum steal credentials from a commercial bank transfer or wire transfer. For consumers, the greatest risk is the interception of credit card information. By the time the Internet evolved, credit cards were well-established as a payment system. Consumers continue to use credit cards for most retail Internet purchases, though there is a recent shift to debit cards and ACH (automated clearinghouse) transfers.[719] ACH transfers for Internet purchases are growing exponentially since 2001.[720] Credit card providers and processers are stepping up their security for credit card processing.[721] The National Automated Clearing House Association (NACHA) rules now address "Internet-Initiated Entries."[722] Foreign and cross-border payments and mobile payments over a cell phone or other device, which are far more common in foreign countries such as Japan than in the U.S., are at the cutting edge of payments law. [723] However, the law governing Internet payments is lagging behind the staggering increasing in new mobile phone applications enabling payment.

---

[717] Id.

[718] Id.

[719] LYNN M. LOPUCKI, ELIZABETH WARREN, DANIEL KEATING, AND RONALD J. MANN, COMMERCIAL TRANSACTIONS: A SYSTEMS APPROACH 600 (5th ed. 2013)

[720] Id. at 607.

[721] Id.

[722] Id.

[723] Id.

Chapter 5

CONSUMER REGULATION IN CYBERSPACE

§ 5.1 OVERVIEW OF INTERNET–RELATED CONSUMER PROTECTION

This chapter provides an overview of consumer regulations in cyberspace. The Federal Trade Commission defines consumers as individuals purchasing goods or services online for personal, family, or household purposes.[1] Chapter 7 will address issues for protecting the privacy of consumers and the trend towards giving them greater control over the collection and use of their personal data. Google estimates that the advertising-supported Internet sustains about $300 billion of the U.S. economy. However, the proliferation of deceptive and fraudulent advertisements has become the seamy side of the internet with online lotteries, pyramid schemes, Nigerian e-mail swindles, spam emails, and Trojan horse programs, choking electronic commerce and bilking unwary consumers.[2] Trojan horse programs that choke electronic commerce and bilk unwary consumers.[3] The FTC's Bureau of Consumer Protection warns of the Tech Support Scam prettying upon consumers:

> Scammers call and claim to be computer techs associated with well-known companies like Microsoft. They say that they've detected viruses or other malware on your computer to trick you into giving them remote access or paying for software you don't need.[4]

The National Consumer League's Internet Fraud Watch warns online consumers about the dangers of downloading digital images, music, or software because of the risk

---

[1] The "consumer" is defined as an individual buying goods for "personal, family, or household purposes." For example, the term "consumer debt" in the federal bankruptcy statute is defined to include "debt incurred by an individual primarily for a personal, family, or household purpose." 11 U.S.C. § 101(8) (2000). "The definition [of consumer debt used in the bankruptcy act] is adapted from the definition used in various consumer protection laws." H.R Rep. No. 95–595, at 309 (1977), reprinted in 1978 U.S.C.C.A.N. 5963, 6266; S. Rep. No. 95–989, at 22 (1978), reprinted in 1978 U.S.C.C.A.N. 5787, 5808; See also, 15 U.S.C. § 2301(1) (2005) (defining term "consumer product" to include "any tangible personal property which is distributed in commerce and which is normally used for personal, family, or household purposes"). TILA's scope is limited to "consumer" credit transactions, which are defined as transactions in which "the money, property, or services which are the subject of the transaction are primarily for personal, family, or household purposes." 15 U.S.C. § 1602(h) (2000); 12 C.F.R. § 226.2(p) (2004).

[2] The Internet offers low-cost communication, the capacity to reach a global audience, and a presumptive veneer of credibility stemming from the anonymity of cyberspace. Thus, Internet users may find it hard to distinguish genuine sources of information from fraudulent sources, creating a fertile environment for all kinds of Internet fraud. Miriam R. Albert, E-Buyer Beware: Why Online Auction Fraud Should Be Regulated, 39 AM. BUS. L.J. 575, 578–79 (2002); see George P. Long, III, Comment, Who Are You?: Identity and Anonymity in Cyberspace, 55 U. PITT. L. REV. 1177, 1178–79 (1994).

[3] The Internet offers low-cost communication, the capacity to reach a global audience, and a presumptive veneer of credibility stemming from the anonymity of cyberspace. Thus, Internet users may find it hard to distinguish genuine sources of information from fraudulent sources, creating a fertile environment for all kinds of Internet fraud. Miriam R. Albert, E-Buyer Beware: Why Online Auction Fraud Should Be Regulated, 39 AM. BUS. L.J. 575, 578–79 (2002); see George P. Long, III, Comment, Who Are You?: Identity and Anonymity in Cyberspace, 55 U. PITT. L. REV. 1177, 1178–79 (1994).

[4] Federal Trade Commission, Consumer Protection Bureau, Tech Support Scam (2013).

of viruses or malware. The vendors of unwanted software and spam use at least four methods to install software on personal computers without obtaining the computer users' informed consent: (1) drive-by downloads; (2) installation via distribution partners; (3) installation through security holes; and (4) installation at a user's request without displaying a license agreement.[5]

The *modus operandi* of a "drive-by download" is to send misleading pop-up offerings to install software while the user is browsing. Recall that in Chapter 2, we discussed theories of Internet governance, and noted how governments are struggling to update consumer protection for the Internet. Lawrence Lessig notes, "To regulate well, you need to know (1) who someone is, (2) where they are, and (3) what they're doing . . . but because of the way the Internet was originally designed [and, more on this below], there was no simple way to know (1) who someone is, (2) where they are, and (3) what they're doing."[6] Lessig's broader point is that cyberspace is inherently less regulatable than the bricks and mortar world because of its unique geographically distributed architecture.[7] Through our discussion of consumer regulation in cyberspace, this chapter examines the difficulties of protecting consumer rights in a cross-border legal environment. As we have noted in prior chapters, online companies must comply with regulations in every country where their business operates. EBay acknowledges this reality in its SEC 10-Q filing:

> Numerous states and foreign jurisdictions, including the State of California, where our headquarters are located, have regulations regarding "auctions" and the handling of property by "secondhand dealers" or "pawnbrokers." Several states and some foreign jurisdictions have attempted to impose such regulations upon us or our users, and others may attempt to do so in the future. Attempted enforcement of these laws against some of our users appears to be increasing. In France, we were sued by *Conseil des Ventes*, the French auction regulatory authority, which has alleged that sales on our French website constitute illegal auctions that cannot be performed without its consent.[8]

§ 5.2   FTC AS CYBERSPACE CONSTABLE

Congress created the Federal Trade Commission ("FTC") in 1914 to prevent unfair methods of competition in commerce. The FTC is an independent agency of the United States Government created by statute.[9] The FTC enforces Section 5(a) of the FTC Act ("FTCA"), 15 U.S.C. § 45(a), which prohibits unfair or deceptive acts or practices. In the 1960s and 1970s, the FTC was widely perceived as an ineffective agency with a weak investigative branch.[10] Beginning with the Nixon Administration, the FTC received more resources and implemented meaningful reforms. In the late 1990s, the FTC ratcheted up enforcement in cyberspace focusing largely upon privacy policies of websites. In the United States, the FTC is the constable for cyberspace in filing suit against Internet

---

[5] Ben Edelman, 180solutions Installation Methods and License Agreement (2008), http://www.benedelman.org/spyware /180–affiliates/installation.html (last visited Aug. 1, 2013).

[6] LAWRENCE LESSIG, CODE: VERSION 2.0 (2006) at 24.

[7] Id.

[8] eBay SEC 10–Q Filing (July 19, 2013).

[9] 15 U.S.C. §§ 41–58.

[10] See generally, EDWARD F. COX, ROBERT C. FELLMETH, JOHN E. SCHULZ THE NADER REPORT ON THE FEDERAL TRADE COMMISSION (1970) (concluding that the FTC and relied upon consumers to report problems thus failing to detect and enforce violations).

wrongdoers for unfair and deceptive practices.[11] The FTC administers many Internet-related laws governing consumer rights in e-commerce including the Children's Online Privacy Protection Act, the Safe Web Act, and the Controlling the Assault of Non–Solicited Pornography and Marketing Act of 2003.[12] The FTC has yet to formulate a compliance program addressing unfair and deceptive terms of service agreements governing social media and cloud computing. Christopher Wolf and Winston Maxwell explain how the FTC's Consumer Protection Bureau operates:

> A major, if not defining characteristic of U.S. privacy law, comes from the targeted enforcement actions against bad (or negligent) actors—principally by the U.S. Federal Trade Commission—which has created a "common law" of what is expected from business when it comes to the collection, use, and protection of personal information. The FTC has authority to take enforcement action against "unfair or deceptive" practices. In the privacy context, this has resulted in enforcement actions against companies that have promised something in their privacy policies about the collection, use, or protection of personal information but in practice, handled the personal information in ways that differed from the promised treatment. Early examples include enforcement actions against Eli Lilly, Microsoft Passport, and Gateway, when each company made representations concerning its data practices—such as how data will be collected, shared, and protected—which were contrary to what actually happened.[13]

The FTC takes the position that the FTCA prohibition on unfair or deceptive acts or practices applies equally well to cyberspace considering three basic principles: (1) online advertisements must be truthful and not misleading, (2) online advertisers must have evidence to back up their claims ("substantiation"), and (3) they cannot be unfair. The FTC has filed hundreds of Section 5 actions to enjoin fraud and deception on the Internet. The FTC's Bureau of Consumer Protection is the principal FTC unit dedicated for enforcement and Internet-related regulations. Many state attorney generals also claim jurisdiction over Internet fraud affecting their citizens. In addition, many U.S. states have enacted deceptive trade practices acts, sometimes referred to as "little FTC acts." For example, Section 2 of Massachusetts' Chapter 93A makes it unlawful to engage in "unfair methods of competition and unfair or deceptive acts or practices." Massachusetts' Chapter 93A provides double or treble damages and attorneys' fees for unfair and deceptive trade practices.[14]

The Division of Advertising Practices enforces laws against "unfair, misleading, or false advertising."[15] The basic consumer protection statute enforced by the Commission is Section 5 of the FTCA, which stipulates, "unfair or deceptive acts or practices in or affecting commerce, are . . . declared unlawful."[16] The FTC considers three factors in

---

[11] Unfair and deceptive practices acts, at the state or federal level, requires three elements: (1) a deceptive act or unfair practice; (2) causation; and (3) actual damages.

[12] The FTC is authorized to initiate federal district court proceedings, by its own attorneys, to enjoin violations of the FTC Act and to secure such equitable relief as may be appropriate in each case. 15 U.S.C. § 53(b).

[13] Christopher Wolf and Winston Maxwell, So Close, Yet So Far Apart: The EU and U.S. Visions of a New Privacy Framework, 26 ANTITRUST ABA 8.9 (2012).

[14] MASS. GEN. LAWS ch. 93A § 11 (stating that unfair and deceptive trade practices may be punished by awards of up to three but not less than two times actual damages for willful or knowing violations of the act).

[15] AARON SCHWABACH, INTERNET AND THE LAW: TECHNOLOGY, SOCIETY, AND COMPROMISES 139 (2006) (describing the FTC's role in Internet consumer regulation).

[16] Federal Trade Commission Act. Section 5(a) of the Federal Trade Commission Act, 15 U.S.C. § 45(a).

determining whether a practice is unfair: (1) Does the practice injure consumers? (2) Does it violate public policy? (3) Is the practice unethical? Section 5 is sometimes referred to as the FTC's unfairness jurisdiction. Section 13(b) of the FTCA authorizes the Commission to file suit in any U.S. federal district court to enjoin an act or practice that violates Section 5 of the FTCA.

Academic commentators and courts referred to this section as the FTC's unfairness jurisdiction. Section 13(b) of the FTCA authorizes the Commission to file suit in any U.S. federal district court to enjoin an act or practice that violates Section 5 of the FTCA. The FTC considers three factors in determining whether a practice is unfair: (1) Does the practice injure consumers? (2) Does it violate public policy? (3) Is the practice unethical? Private as well as public attorneys generally can employ Section 5 of the FTCA to police unfair or deceptive clauses in software contracts.

The FTC looks for deception and unfairness in banner ads, pop ups, social media reviews, blogger endorsements, Geotagging offers, online targeted ads, and even in-game advertising. The FTC was one of the first federal agencies to address unfair and deceptive Internet-related activities. In *FTC v. Corzine*,[17] defendant Corzine ran online advertisements, offering a credit repair kit, on America Online. He represented that purchasers of his credit repair kit could legally establish a clean credit record. In 1994, the FTC filed a complaint, charging defendant with misrepresentations in violation of Section 5 of the FTCA.

The court entered an *ex parte* temporary restraining order freezing Corzine's assets. In addition, the Court entered a Consent Decree, enjoining Corzine from making misrepresentations concerning credit repair programs and requiring him to pay $1,917 to consumers. Two years later, the FTC charged another Internet entrepreneur with falsely representing a business opportunity to the public, offering that purchasers could earn $4,000 or more per month. The FTC entered into a consent order requiring this defendant to cease and desist from misrepresenting the earnings potential of business opportunities.[18]

In addition to the FTCA, the FTC administers diverse laws applicable to cyberspace activities including The Undertaking Spam, Spyware, and Fraud Enforcement With Enforcers Beyond Borders Act of 2006 ("Safe Web"). Safe Web amended Section 5's "unfair or deceptive acts or practices" to include "such acts or practices involving foreign commerce" causing reasonably foreseeable injury within the United States.[19] The Safe Web statute immunizes Internet Service Providers and consumer reporting agencies from liability for voluntary disclosures to the Commission about suspected online fraud or deception. The FTC takes the position that the Fair Credit Reporting Act[20] is applicable to those who aggregate information from social media sites.

In *Federal Trade Commission v. Commerce Planet*,[21] Commerce Planet's Online Supplier website used pop-up advertising on other websites to attract customers. The FTC contended that Commerce Planet:

---

[17] CIV–S–94–1446 (E.D. Cal. filed Sept. 12, 1994).

[18] FTC v. Timothy R. Bean, Docket No. C–3665 (final consent June 10, 1996).

[19] 15 U.S.C. § 45(a)(4)(A).

[20] 15 U.S.C. §§ 1681 et seq.

[21] 2012 WL 6052443 (C.D. Cal. July 17, 2013).

invited consumers to "activate FREE 7–DAY TRIAL—just pay S/H." Consumers were given two choices for shipping, either regular for $1.95 or Expedited for $7.95. The linked Terms of Membership explained that if the consumer did not cancel the OnlineSupplier.com membership within seven days, the consumer would be charged a monthly membership fee of $59.95.

Many consumers first learned about the recurring charges when they received their credit card bills with a Commerce Planet charge. Many consumers reportedly called the customer service telephone number or contacted Online Supplier by e-mail to cancel and obtain refunds, but most had difficulty doing so. Many customers had to call multiple times to cancel.[22] The FTC charged that Commerce Planet made it difficult for consumers to cancel and some cancelled only after threatening to retain an attorney, the Better Business Bureau or government authorities. "Some consumers were only able to stop the charges by contacting their credit card companies to reverse the charges or cancel their cards. It took some consumers several months to identify the source of the charges and extricate themselves from defendant Commerce Planet's plan."[23] Other consumers paid unauthorized charges of up to several hundred dollars.[24]

(A) Unfair & Deceptive Trade Practices

The FTC is the chief enforcer of federal privacy statutes, including the COPPA and the Controlling the Assault of Non–Solicited Pornography and Marketing Act of 2003 ("CAN–SPAM"). "In the United States legal landscape, sensitive information is accorded special recognition through a series of key privacy statutes."[25] The FTC has used its authority to patrol Internet websites for unfair and deceptive practices. The FTC filed suit against an Internet pornographer for unfair and deceptive billing practices. The pornographer billed telephone account holders for the adult entertainment service even if they did not actually use the service.[26] The court ruled the Commerce Planet's business practices constituted false advertising and awarded the Commission, $18.2 million in damages. Private as well as public attorneys generally can employ Section 5 of the Federal Trade Commission Act to police unfair or deceptive clauses in Internet contracts.

In *FTC v. Fortuna Alliance, L.L.C.*, et al.,[27] the FTC enjoined an Internet marketed pyramid scheme that defrauded 25,000 U.S. consumers. The defendants marketed their pyramid scheme as if it was a legitimate investment opportunity.[28] The

---

[22] Id.

[23] Id.

[24] Id.

[25] Helen Nissenbaum, Privacy as Contextual Integrity, 79 WASH. L. REV. 119, 129 (2004).

[26] FTC v. Verity Intern., 124 F. Supp. 2d 193 (S.D. N.Y. 2000).

[27] Civ. No. C96–799M (W.D. Wash. 1996).

[28] A Ponzi scheme, named after Boston's Charles Ponzi, is a fraudulent investment operation that pays returns to its investors from their own money or the money paid by subsequent investors. Many Ponzi schemes end because the promoter diverts investment dollars and has trouble paying the promised return for latter investors. The Securities and Exchange Commission states: "A Ponzi scheme is an investment fraud that involves the payment of purported returns to existing investors from funds contributed by new investors. Ponzi scheme organizers often solicit new investors by promising to invest funds in opportunities claimed to generate high returns with little or no risk. In many Ponzi schemes, the fraudsters focus on attracting new money to make promised payments to earlier-stage investors and to use for personal expenses, instead of engaging in any legitimate investment activity." Securities and Exchange Commission, Ponzi Schemes, Frequently Asked Questions, http://www.sec.gov/answers/ponzi.htm (last visited Aug. 1, 2013).

fraudulent scheme was, "nothing but a high-tech chain letter, with certain losses for the great majority of investors and tremendous profits for the defendants."[29] This pyramid scheme alone yielded $11 million from consumers. The defendants were able to transfer millions to an offshore bank account in Antigua. However, the FTC and the U.S. Department of Justice were able to freeze the Antigua accounts to recoup some of the illicit gains.[30] In *FTC v. PCCare247 Inc.*,[31] the FTC sought injunctive relief and damages against individual defendants in India that tricked American consumers into spending money to fix non-existent problems with their computers. Interestingly, the court approved FTC's serving process through the defendants' Facebook accounts. Nevertheless, the FTC also transmitted the summons and complaint to the Indian central authority for service under Article 5 of the Hague Service Convention. In addition, the FTC attempted process by email, FedEx, and personal service. The FTC also filed a lawsuit against Wyndham Hotels "to provide reasonable and appropriate security for the personal information collected and maintained" exposing "consumers' personal data to unauthorized access and theft."[32] The FTC amended complaint charges:

> Defendants' failure to maintain reasonable security allowed intruders to obtain unauthorized access to the computer networks of Wyndham Hotels and Resorts, LLC, and several hotels franchised and managed by Defendants on three separate occasions in less than two years. Defendants' security failures led to fraudulent charges on consumers' accounts, more than $10.6 million in fraud loss, and the export of hundreds of thousands of consumers' payment card account information to a domain registered in Russia. In all three security breaches, hackers accessed sensitive consumer data by compromising Defendants' Phoenix, Arizona datacenter. [33]

(B) Online Fraudulent Schemes

Consumer contracts are those entered into for personal, family, or household purposes. Daily reports of fraudulent online auctions, Nigerian money offers, deceptive

---

[29] Id.

[30] "Ponzi and pyramid schemes are closely related because they both involve paying longer-standing members with money from new participants, instead of actual profits from investing or selling products to the public." Id. Ponzi schemes require no recruiting and collapse more slowly than pyramid schemes. Id.

[31] FTC v. PCCare247 Inc., 2013 WL 841037 (S.D.N.Y. March 7, 2013).

[32] Amended Complaint, FTC v. Wyndham Worldwide Corp., No. CV 12–1365–PHXPGR (D. Ariz. Aug. 9, 2012).

[33] The FTC contends: "Since at least 2008, Defendants have disseminated, or caused to be

disseminated, privacy policies or statements on their website to their customers and potential customers. These policies or statements include, but are not limited to, the following statement regarding the privacy and confidentiality of personal information, disseminated on the Hotels and Resorts' website. The hotel website stated: "Currently, our Websites utilize a variety of different security measures designed to protect personally identifiable information from unauthorized access by users both inside and outside of our company, including the use of 128–bit encryption based on a Class 3 Digital Certificate issued by VeriSign Inc. This

allows for utilization of Secure Sockets Layer, which is a method for encrypting data. This protects confidential information—such as credit card numbers, online forms, and financial data—from loss, misuse, interception and hacking. We take commercially reasonable efforts to create and maintain "fire walls" and other appropriate safeguards to ensure that to the extent we control the Information, the

Information is used only as authorized by us and consistent with this Policy, and that the Information is not improperly altered or destroyed." Id. at 9–10. In reality, the Wyndham security was inadequate because it was improperly configured and implemented." Id. at 10.

work-at-home plans, and illegal pyramid schemes confirm the ubiquity of consumer fraud.[34] Consumer law is largely about giving consumers procedural protections, disclosures, remedies, and mandatory provisions.[35] The FTC's endorsement guidelines, for example, require bloggers and social media site posters to disclose any financial interest they have in goods or services in the new media. Since the mid-1990s, the FTC has taken the position that Internet sellers must comply with its rules on advertising. In addition, social media sites and other new media must comply with consumer laws governing Internet advertisements, the sale of securities, taxation, unfair and deceptive trade practices, pricing laws, and general state and federal consumer statutes. An online company must institute adequate policies, terms of service, and other related safeguards to ensure it does not violate state and federal consumer law. These policies apply in the "clicks" world just as in the "brick-and-mortar" world.

(C) Online Advertising & Marketing

The key issues for Internet-related advertising are how to resolve banner ads, pop ups, Yelp Reviews, blogger endorsements, Geotagging offers, online targeted ads, and in-game advertising. Long-standing FTC precedents treat advertisements as deceptive if they contain either a misrepresentation or omission that is likely to mislead consumers acting reasonably under the circumstances.[36].The FTC takes the position that the Federal Trade Commission Act's prohibition on "unfair or deceptive acts or practices" applies to Internet advertising, marketing and sales by stating, "Many Commission rules and guides are not limited to any particular medium used to disseminate claims or advertising, and therefore, apply to online activities."[37]

(1) Online Disclosures

The FTC enforces three basic principles about advertisements: (1) They must be truthful and not misleading; (2) Advertisers must have evidence to back up their claims ("substantiation"); and (3) Advertisements cannot be unfair. To comply with the FTC Dot.com disclosures, online advertisers, must:

> identify all express and implied claims that the ad conveys to consumers. When identifying claims, advertisers should not focus only on individual phrases or statements, but should consider the ad as a whole, including the text, product name, and depictions. If an ad makes express or implied claims that are likely to be misleading without certain qualifying information, the information must be disclosed. Advertisers must determine which claims might need qualification and what information should be provided in a disclosure. If qualifying information is necessary to prevent an ad from being misleading, advertisers must present the information clearly and conspicuously. A disclosure only qualifies or limits a claim, to avoid a misleading impression. It cannot cure a false claim. If a disclosure

---

[34] See e.g., Alexandra Frean, Mail–Order Degree Scam Closed Down, The Australian, March 12, 2003, at 19 ("[shutting] down a series of websites selling invalid degrees from bogus universities which used an address in Palmers Green, North London, to give their operation a cloak of respectability and defrauded hundreds of thousands of mostly American customers); E. Scott Reckard, AOL, Cendant Dismissed From Homestore Suit, L.A. TIMES, March 11, 2003, at 2 (reporting billions of dollars lost by investors in Internet fraud case).

[35] See generally, MICHAEL L. RUSTAD, EVERYDAY CONSUMER LAW (2008).

[36] Cliffdale Associates Inc., 105 F.T.C. 174 (1984).

[37] FEDERAL TRADE COMMISSION, DOT.COM DISCLOSURES 1 (2012).

provides information that contradicts a claim, the disclosure will not be sufficient to prevent the ad from being deceptive. In that situation, the claim itself must be modified.[38]

In *Chapman v. Skype,*[39] a respondent brief describes how Skype's terms of use comply with FTC dot.com guidelines:

---

[38] Id. at 3.

[39] 2013 WL 1499582 * 32 (Cal. Ct. of App., April 2, 2013) (citations to the record omitted) ("Further, the 2013 guidelines draw a distinction between "brick and mortar" and online stores. *Id.* at iii. If a product may be purchased from "brick and mortar" stores then any necessary disclosure "should be presented in the ad itself-that is, before consumers head to a store or some other online retailer." *Id.* As to purely online retailers, like Skype, the 2013 guidelines state retailers should among other things "[d]isplay disclosures before consumers make a decision to buy-e.g., before they 'add to shopping cart.' Also recognize that disclosures may have to be repeated before purchase *to ensure* they are adequately presented to consumers." *Id.* at ii-iii (emphasis added). Skype did both, repeatedly disclosing the Policy in its advertising and at the purchase page immediately above the "Buy now" button *to ensure* the terms are adequately presented to Skype's customers.").

FTC Guidance	Skype's Website
Place disclosures near, and when possible, on the same screen as the triggering claim.	The "Unlimited U.S. & Canada" subscription Chapman purchased "has a numerical superscript immediately present after the word 'UNLIMITED' in the title," linking to the Policy on the same page.
Use hyperlink styles consistently so that consumers know when a link is available.	Hyperlinks throughout Skype's website to the Policy consistently use the same blue font and an underline to 225.
Take consumers directly to the disclosure on the click-through page.	The numerical superscript "references a link at the bottom of the page to Skype's 'fair usage policy'," and a click on that takes the user directly to the Policy.
Display disclosures prior to purchase, but recognize that as well placement limited only to the order page may not always work.	Skype repeatedly displays the Policy at both the initial advertisement and at the order page, as other places on Skype's website.
Repeat disclosures, as needed, on lengthy Websites and in connection with repeated claims.	The Policy is disclosed no fewer than half a dozen times-four times on the page advertising monthly subscriptions (RA 9, 40), under the "I Agree" on the purchase page, in the Terms of Service, and in the "Important Legal Information" link.
Use clear language and syntax so that consumers understand the disclosures.[40]	The Policy states in clear language and syntax the subscription allowances are "10,000 minutes a month, with a maximum of 6 hours a day, and no more than 50 [different] numbers may be called a day."

The FTC has filed "over 100 law enforcement actions to stop fraud and deception online and is working to educate businesses about their legal obligations and consumers about their rights."[41] The FTC has filed civil actions against advertiser who did not honor consumer requests to opt out of future mailings.[42] The emphasis of the FTC enforcement is procedural, rather than substantive. Websites are most likely to be targeted by the FTC if they do not live up to their posted privacy policies.

---

[40] See generally, Federal Trade Commission Dot.com Disclosures: How to Make Effective Disclosures in Digital Advertising," available at http://www.ftc.gov/os/2013/03/130312dotcomdisclosures.pdf ("2013 guidelines") (last visited Aug. 1, 2013).

[41] Id.

[42] FEDERAL TRADE COMMISSION, PROTECTING CONSUMER PRIVACY IN AN ERA OF RAPID. CHANGE: RECOMMENDATIONS FOR BUSINESSES AND POLICYMAKERS 8 (March 2012).

(2) FTC Guidance on Online Endorsements

False or deceptive endorsements in a social media site or website also violate Section 5 of the FTCA. In December of 2009, the FTC issued new guidelines for online endorsements, prohibiting statements by bloggers and other online reviewers that would be deceptive if made by advertisers.[43] Specifically, endorsements "may not contain any representations which would be deceptive, or could not be substantiated if made directly by the advertiser."[44] The FTC guidelines apply equally well to social media sites and networks and thus any endorsements on these sites must be non-deceptive. The FTC includes several examples, applying various Guide provisions to new forms of consumer-generated media, such as the use of blogs in word of mouth marketing campaigns. Bloggers, or new media posters, have an affirmative obligation to disclose material connections if they endorse products or services. After the Comment period, the Commission clarified that the advertiser and the blogger both are subject to liability for misleading or unsubstantiated representations made in the course of the blogger's endorsement. The Commission cited the following example of how its endorsement rules apply to new media such as blogs:

> A skin care products advertiser participates in a blog advertising service. The service matches up advertisers with bloggers who will promote the advertiser's products on their personal blogs. The advertiser requests that a blogger try a new body lotion and write a review of the product on her blog. Although the advertiser does not make any specific claims about the lotion's ability to cure skin conditions and the blogger does not ask the advertiser whether there is substantiation for the claim, in her review the blogger writes that, the lotion cures eczema and recommends the product to her blog readers who suffer from this condition. The advertiser is subject to liability for misleading or unsubstantiated representations made through the blogger's endorsement. The blogger also is subject to liability for misleading or unsubstantiated representations made in the course of her endorsement. The blogger is also liable if she fails to disclose clearly and conspicuously that she is being paid for her services.[45]

The FTC tackles the problem of paid endorsements on Facebook and other social media in its updated guide:

> You do some research and find a glowing review on someone's blog that a certain resort is the most luxurious place they've ever stayed. If you found out that the hotel had paid that blogger to say great things about it or that the blogger had stayed there for a week for free, it would affect how much weight you'd give the blogger's endorsement.[46]

In *Legacy Learning Systems, Inc.*,[47] Legacy Learning Systems Inc. and its owner, Lester Gabriel Smith, deceptively advertised the "Learn and Master Guitar" program through online affiliate marketers who falsely posed as ordinary consumers or independent reviewers. The FTC entered into a consent order for $250,000 to settle

---

[43] 16 C.F.R. § 255(1)(A).

[44] Id.

[45] 16 C.F.R. § 255(1), example 5.

[46] FEDERAL TRADE COMMISSION, THE FTC'S REVISED ENDORSEMENT GUIDES: WHAT PEOPLE ARE ASKING 2 (2012).

[47] In re Legacy Learning Systems Inc., Federal Trade Commission, C–4323 (March 15, 2011).

charges that the company deceptively used online affiliate marketers that masqueraded as ordinary consumers, when in reality they were paid representatives. The defendants also agreed to maintain a system to review and monitor their affiliate marketers' representations and disclosures.

The FTC's call for greater disclosures on blogs or social media sites is because that the reader may not be aware that the poster has a paid relationship with the companies whose products are mentioned. The FTC could not have anticipated social media, such as Twitter, when it drafted its endorsement guides in 1980—nearly two decades before the launch of the World Wide Web. However, the FTC entered into a consent order prohibiting Twitter from misrepresenting the security, privacy, confidentiality, or integrity of any "nonpublic consumer information." The order requires Twitter to establish and maintain a comprehensive information security program that is designed to protect the security, privacy, confidentiality, and integrity of nonpublic consumer information.

(3) FTC Mandatory Website Disclosures

The FTC requires online advertisers "to ensure that consumers receive material information about the terms of a transaction . . . [and they] must be clear and conspicuous."[48] The placement of the disclosure as well as its proximity to the underlying claim applies to online advertisements. The FTC also requires Internet advertisers to consider:

> the prominence of the disclosure; whether items in other parts of the ad distract attention from the disclosure; whether the advertisement is so lengthy that the disclosure needs to be repeated; whether disclosures in audio messages are presented in an adequate volume and cadence and visual disclosures appear for a sufficient duration; and, whether language is understandable to the intended audience.[49]

The online advertiser should "place disclosures near, and when possible, on the same screen as the triggering claim."[50] The FTC recommends using "text or visual cues to encourage consumers to scroll down a Web page when it is necessary to view a disclosure."[51] The FTC suggests that advertisers do an audit to determine that banner and other advertisements meet the standard of conspicuousness. Advertisers must "evaluate the size, color, and graphics of the disclosure in relation to other parts of the Website."[52] The FTC raises the following issues with accommodating their regulations to social media and mobile devices:

- How can effective disclosures be made on social media platforms and mobile devices—including when they are used in commercial texting—that limit the space available for disclosure? For example, when consumers are paid or receive other benefits for providing an endorsement, how can they effectively disclose on platforms that allow only short messages or a simple sign of approval?

---

[48] FEDERAL TRADE COMMISSION, DOT.COM DISCLOSURES 1 (2012).
[49] Id.
[50] Id.
[51] Id. at 3.
[52] Id.

- When can disclosures provided separately from an initial advertisement be considered adequate? For example, if a consumer receives a location-based ad for a discounted cup of coffee on her mobile device because she is near a particular coffee shop, what terms must be disclosed in the mobile ad and what terms, if any, do not have to be disclosed until the consumer enters the coffee shop to make her purchase?

- What are the options when using devices that do not allow downloading or printing the terms of an agreement? For example, is providing consumers a means to send a copy of the agreement to themselves to read later an effective way to provide this information?

- How can disclosures that are made in the original advertisement be retained when the advertisement is aggregated (for example, on dashboards) or re-transmitted (through, for example, re-tweeting)?

- What are the disclosure opportunities and limitations of hyperlinks, jump links, hashtags, click-throughs, layered disclosures, icons, and other similar options? How should these options be evaluated in terms of placement and proximity?

- How can short, effective, and accessible privacy disclosures be made on mobile devices?

- What does the research show about how consumers' use of mobile and other devices can affect the effectiveness of disclosures on particular devices or platforms? And what does it show about the relationship between how consumers use mobile devices and their understanding of disclosures and advertising displayed on mobile devices? What does the research show about how consumers make decisions based on that information? Is there specific research on the effectiveness of disclosures on mobile devices, including layered disclosures and icons, and, if so, what are the implications of that research for disclosures such as offer terms and privacy practices?[53]

The FTC issued guidelines to ensure that products and services are described truthfully online. The FTC staff guidance document summarized the following guidelines for developing online advertisements:

The same consumer protection laws that apply to commercial activities in other media apply online, including activities in the mobile marketplace. The FTC Act's prohibition on "unfair or deceptive acts or practices" encompasses online advertising, marketing, and sales. In addition, many Commission rules and guides are not limited to any particular medium used to disseminate claims or advertising, and therefore, apply to the wide spectrum of online activities.

When practical, advertisers should incorporate relevant limitations and qualifying information into the underlying claim, rather than having a separate disclosure qualifying the claim.

Required disclosures must be clear and conspicuous. In evaluating whether a disclosure is likely to be clear and conspicuous, advertisers should consider its

---

[53] Federal Trade Commission, FTC Will Host Public Workshop to Explore Advertising Disclosures in Online and Mobile Media on May 30, 2012 (Feb. 29, 2012).

placement in the ad and its proximity to the relevant claim. The closer the disclosure is to the claim to which it relates, the better. Additional considerations include: the prominence of the disclosure; whether it is unavoidable; whether other parts of the ad distract attention from the disclosure; whether the disclosure needs to be repeated at different places on a website; whether disclosures in audio messages are presented in an adequate volume and cadence; whether visual disclosures appear for a sufficient duration; and whether the language of the disclosure is understandable to the intended audience.

To make a disclosure clear and conspicuous, advertisers should:

- Place the disclosure as close as possible to the triggering claim.

- Take account of the various devices and platforms consumers may use to view advertising and any corresponding disclosure. If an ad is viewable on a particular device or platform, any necessary disclosures should be sufficient to prevent the ad from being misleading when viewed on that device or platform.

- When a space-constrained ad requires a disclosure, incorporate the disclosure into the ad whenever possible. However, when it is not possible to make a disclosure in a space-constrained ad, it may, under some circumstances, be acceptable to make the disclosure clearly and conspicuously on the page to which the ad links.

- When using a hyperlink to lead to a disclosure, make the link obvious;
    o label the hyperlink appropriately to convey the importance, nature, and relevance of the information it leads to;
    o use hyperlink styles consistently, so consumers know when a link is available;
    o place the hyperlink as close as possible to the relevant information it qualifies and make it noticeable;
    o take consumers directly to the disclosure on the click-through page;
    o assess the effectiveness of the hyperlink by monitoring click-through rates and other information about consumer use and make changes accordingly.

- Preferably, design advertisements so that "scrolling" is not necessary in order to find a disclosure. When scrolling is necessary, use text or visual cues to encourage consumers to scroll to view the disclosure.

- Keep abreast of empirical research about where consumers do and do not look on a screen.

- Recognize and respond to any technological limitations or unique characteristics of a communication method when making disclosures.

- Display disclosures before consumers make a decision to buy—

- e.g., before they "add to shopping cart." Also recognize that disclosures may have to be repeated before purchase to ensure that they are adequately presented to consumers.

- Repeat disclosures, as needed, on lengthy websites and in connection with repeated claims. Disclosures may also have to be repeated if consumers have multiple routes through a website.

- If a product or service promoted online is intended to be (or can be) purchased from "brick and mortar" stores or from online retailers other than the advertiser itself, then any disclosure necessary to prevent deception or unfair injury should be presented in the ad itself—that is, before consumers head to a store or some other online retailer.

- Necessary disclosures should not be relegated to "terms of use" and similar contractual agreements.

- Prominently display disclosures so they are noticeable to consumers, and evaluate the size, color, and graphic treatment of the disclosure in relation to other parts of the webpage.

- Review the entire ad to assess whether the disclosure is effective in light of other elements—text, graphics, hyperlinks, or sound—that might distract consumers' attention from the disclosure.

- Use audio disclosures when making audio claims, and present them in a volume and cadence so that consumers can hear and understand them.

- Display visual disclosures for a duration sufficient for consumers to notice, read, and understand them.

- Use plain language and syntax so that consumers understand the disclosures.[54]

The FTC document emphasizes the importance of online advertisers making clear and conspicuous online disclosures and that "[t]he ultimate test is not the size of the font or the location of the disclosure, although they are important considerations; the ultimate test is whether the information intended to be conveyed is actually conveyed to consumers."[55]

(D) Unfair or Deceptive Online Practices

The FTC's Consumer Sentinel Database reveals that online auction sites and retail schemes are Petri dishes for virtual consumer fraud. The FTC found that the most pervasive online auction complaint is that the consumer did not receive the item they paid for online. Few Americans can resist a bargain for luxury goods such as Coach™ purses, Mont Blanc™ pens, or Gucci™ jewelry. The most typical fraud is for the seller to secure payment and then deliver knockoffs or obvious fakes. EBay and other online auction houses typically disclaim responsibility for fraudulent sales transactions.

Beginning in the mid-1990s, the FTC extended advertising regulations to the Internet using its authority under Section 5 of the FTCA. False and deceptive advertising will subject the online company to regulatory actions by the FTC. "Spyware software raises a host of privacy, security, and functionality issues for even the most savvy computer users. Installed on your computer without your consent, spyware

---

[54] Federal Trade Commission, .Com Disclosures, How to Make Effective Disclosures in Digital Advertising (2013), http://www.ftc.gov/os/2013/03/130312dotcomdisclosures.pdf.

[55] Id. at 1.

monitors or controls your computer use."[56] Spyware may be transmitted via pop-up ads where it redirects the user's computer to unwanted websites or records keystrokes. In recent years, the FTC filed hundreds of enforcement actions against spyware companies installing software on a consumer's computer altering their browsers, homepage, or search capabilities without the user's consent or knowledge.

The FTC classifies spyware as an unfair and deceptive trade practice under Section 5 of the FTCA. In *Legacy Learning Systems, Inc.*,[57] the Commission entered into a consent order for $250,000 to settle charges that the company deceptively used online affiliate marketers that masqueraded as ordinary consumers, when they were paid representatives. In *Reverb Communications, Inc.*,[58] the FTC entered into a consent order with a public relations agency, whose employees posed as consumers, in posting game reviews on the iTunes store site. In fact, the video game company had hired the reviewers who were working on behalf of the developers.

(1) Deceptive Pornographers

The FTC prohibits specific disreputable practices on the Internet such as "Negative Option Marketing"—the practice through which a customer is charged for a product or service they never intended to purchase. Online scammers sometimes ship merchandise to consumers who have not requested it, forcing the recipient to either pay for the merchandise or return it at her own expense or inconvenience.[59] In *FTC v. Audiotex Connection, Inc.*,[60] the defendants maintained adult entertainment sites at: www.beavisbutthead.com, www.sexygirls.com, and, www.1adult.com. Consumers who visited one of these sites were solicited to download a viewer program, called "david.exe," in order to view "free" images.

When downloaded and executed, the program disconnected the computer from the consumer's own access provider, turned off the consumers' modem speakers, dialed an international telephone number, and reconnected the computer to a remote foreign site. The international call was billed to consumers at more than $2 per minute. The cybercriminals' software caused the charges to keep accruing until the consumer shut down his computer entirely. Consumers received telephone bills for calls purportedly made to Moldova when the calls actually went only as far as Canada. The court entered an *ex parte* order freezing the defendant's assets and created a $1 million escrow fund for potential redress to victims of this insidious scheme.

(2) Nigerian 419 E–Mail Swindles

Nigerian 419 e-mail swindles, named after Section 419 of the Nigerian criminal code, typically begin with an e-mail offer to transfer millions of dollars into the victim's bank account. In these e-mail frauds, a purported third world official or business representative typically offers to share his family's fortune with an Internet user in return for supposedly circumventing his country's currency restrictions by moving assets outside his country to a safe banking haven. One ongoing Internet swindle is the

---

[56] Federal Trade Commission, Spyware (2008).

[57] Federal Trade Commission, C–4323 (March 15, 2011).

[58] Federal Trade Commission, C–4310 (Aug. 26, 2010).

[59] FTC v. Crescent Pub. Group, Inc., 129 F. Supp. 2d 311 (S.D. N.Y. 2001) (ordering injunction where consumers' credit cards were automatically charged for "free tour" of pornographic website).

[60] CV–97–0726 (E.D.N.Y. filed Feb. 13, 1997).

"Nigerian letter fraud scheme, in which an e-mail message appearing to come from the Nigerian Government promises the potential victim a share of a substantial amount of money in exchange for the use of the victim's bank account."[61] In one variation of the scheme, the scammer instructs the consumer to set up a bank account in the scammer's name with a good faith deposit that soon vanishes.

Another variation involves an e-mail purporting to be from a Nigerian banker offering the recipient the opportunity to earn hundreds of thousands of dollars if they send their banking information. Many variants of the Nigerian money swindles are carried out on the Internet where they "[c]ontinue to victimize American consumers"[62], causing thousands of consumers fall victim. The U.S. Department of Justice filed a lawsuit against AT&T in 2012 alleging that it knew that its government-subsidized service for the hearing-impaired was "a haven for Nigerian scam artists."[63]

The Federal Communications Commissioncharged AT&T with billing them $16 million for hearing-impaired calls, when "as much as 95% of which was provided to international callers attempted to defraud U.S. merchants."[64] The IP Relay Service enables the hearing impaired "to place telephone calls by typing messages over the Internet," and to "read aloud to parties on the other end of the line by call-center employees."[65] Scammers used the IP relay service to purchase goods and services using stolen credit cards. The U.S. Justice Department filed suit shortly after a study found that ten out of twelve users of the service were foreign—mostly from Lagos, Nigeria. AT&T's role in the fraud is one of negligent enablement for not taking measures to reduce the fraud.

(3) Dot.Cons

The FTC asserts broad investigative and law enforcement authority through the Federal Trade Commission Act ("FTCA") to police fraud on the borderless Internet. The FTC has the statutory authority to initiate an enforcement action if it has the "reason to believe" a defendant has violated the FTCA.[66] The FTC "e-cops" search the Internet for unfair or deceptive practices and often uncover victims of "dot cons." FTC's web-surfing enforcers have identified the top ten dot cons: (1) Internet Auctions, (2) Internet Access Services, (3) Credit Card Fraud, (4) International Modem Dialing, (5) Web Cramming, (6) Multilevel Marketing Plans/Pyramids, (7) Travel and Vacation Schemes, (8) Business Opportunities, (9) Investments, and (10) Health Care Products/Services.[67]

(4) Mousetrappers

Mousetrappers or page jackers use malware to obstruct surfer's ability to either close the browser, or go back to the previous web page when a consumer accesses an adult entertainment site. In 2002, the FTC filed suit against John Zuccarini a notorious "cybersquatter" who was in the practice of "mousetrapping" Internet users. A federal court found Zuccarini violated the trademark rights of third parties by registering

---

[61] DEBORAH MORLEY, UNDERSTANDING COMPUTERS IN CHANGING SOCIETY 187 (2008).

[62] Federal Trade Commission, FTC Details Efforts to Halt Internet Scams (2004).

[63] Anton Troianovski & Brent Kendall, AT&T Tied to Nigerian Scam, WALL. ST. J. (March 23, 2012) at B1.

[64] Id.

[65] Id.

[66] 15 U.S.C. § 45(B) (2012).

[67] Federal Trade Commission, Dot Cons (2000).

Internet domain names that are misspellings of legitimate domain names or that incorporated transposed or inverted words or phrases.[68] In a 2005 case, the FTC charged Odysseus Marketing, Inc. and its principal, Rines, with luring consumers to their website by offering free software including a program that supposedly allowed them to engage in anonymous peer-to-peer file sharing. The bogus software was bundled with spyware that intercepted and replaced search results and barraged consumers' computers with pop-up ads.

The FTC alleged that the defendants' software captured consumer's personal information and transmitted the information to the defendants' servers. Consumers were unable to locate or uninstall the spyware through reasonable means. A federal court "ordered a preliminary halt to these practices pending trial and in October 2006 Odysseus and Rines settled the charges by stipulating to a permanent injunction."[69]

(5) *The Cybersex Wonderland*

The Internet has reshaped the commercial sex industry in profound ways. Whether it is pornography or prostitution, the Internet red light district contains hundreds of websites that routinely flout community standards of obscenity. One of the unsettled issues in Global Internet Law is to determine what community standards apply in cyberspace. The commoditization of cybersex continues to evolve as indicated by the rise of websites enabling prostitution. The Craigslist murder committed by a Boston University medical student raised consciousness about how the Internet was changing the face of prostitution. Backpage.com operates an online classified advertising service located at www.backpage.com. It is the second largest online advertising service and hosts millions of advertisements per month throughout the country."[70] A journalist concluded that Backpage devolved into "[a] godsend to pimps, allowing customers to order a girl online."[71] ".A Brooklyn sex-trafficking unit found typical victims to be aged 12 to 25 and "most cases included girls marketed through Backpage ads."[72]

State attorneys general identified "cases in twenty-two different states in which pimps peddled underage girls through Backpage.com."[73] The FTC has not stepped into the enforcement breach addressing this issue. State attorneys general pressured Craigslist.org to stop accepting advertising for illicit services. The majority of state attorneys general have mounted a campaign against Backpage.com. "Although Backpage.com screens adult ads prior to posting, ads depicting minors still appear online."[74] Authorities found a 15–year-old girl depicted in an advertisement to have arranged to have sexual intercourse with a man for $80."[75] A Tennessee federal court depicted the Internet as a commercial sex marketplace:

---

[68] Federal Trade Commission v. John Zuccarini, 2002 WL 1378421 (E.D. Pa. 2002).

[69] Federal Trade Commission, FTC Asks Court to Hold Internet Pagejacking Defendants in Contempt; Previous FTC Order Barred Phishing, Pagejacking, and Mousetrapping (Jan. 31, 2008).

[70] Backpage.com, LLC v. McKenna, 881 F. Supp. 2d 1262, 1262 (W.D. Wash. 2012).

[71] Nicolas D. Kristof, How Pimps Use the Web to Sell Girls, N.Y. TIMES (Jan. 25, 2012).

[72] Nicolas Kristof, How Pimps Use the Web to Sell Girls, Id.

[73] Attorneys General to Backpage.com: prove you're fighting human trafficking. WASHINGTON STATE OFFICE OF THE ATTORNEY GENERAL (Aug. 31, 2011). http://www.atg.wa.gov/pressrelease. aspx?id=28896.

[74] Id. at 1267.

[75] Id.

The Internet has become a favored means of advertising the availability of children for sex because advertisements can be purchased more rapidly than in other media, allowing pimps to move victims to different locations quickly. TBI Assistant Special Agent Margie Quin has supervised or consulted in more than twenty-five investigations of commercial child sexual exploitation since 2009. In most of the child prostitution investigations in which she has been involved, pimps have used online advertising services—including Backpage.com—to reach potential Johns. In 2008, Craigslist—then the leading operator of online adult-oriented advertising—entered into an agreement with the attorneys general of forty-three states in which the website agreed to screen and tag objectionable advertisements, and require telephone number and credit card verification for advertisements in its "erotic services" category. Another study published in early 2011 found that approximately 83 percent of prostitutes in New York City maintained a Facebook page to promote their services and that, as early as 2008, used that website to connect with 25 percent of their regular clients. The study's author predicted Facebook would become "the leading online recruitment space" for prostitution.[76]

Beginning in 2009, the state attorneys general began an investigation of Backpage.com regarding concerns over its "adult" section advertisements. A federal court described the coordinated campaign of state attorneys general against Backpage.com's sex-related advertisements:

> When Backpage.com began charging for advertisements in its adult category sometime between 2009 and late 2010, ads for prostitution migrated to the website's free personal ads section. As a result, Backpage.com began charging for personal ads, as well. In September 2010, the same month that craigslist eliminated its adult services section, twenty-one state attorneys general sent Backpage.com a letter urging it to shut down its adult section. On August 31, 2011, forty-six state attorneys general sent another letter to Backpage.com, decrying the continued appearance of prostitution ads on the website and asking the website to share information about its screening policies and data on the number of adult section ads it received and blocked. The 2011 letter reminded Backpage.com of the officials' earlier request that the website shutter its adult section.[77]

In January 2012, Washington State became the first state legislature to address sex ads on the Internet. The Washington statute would have created criminal liability for a person who "knowingly sells or offers to sell an advertisement that would appear to a reasonable person to be for the purpose of engaging in what would be commercial sexual abuse of a minor, if occurring in this state."[78] The Washington statute made it an affirmative defense if the website attempted to ascertain the age of models depicted in online advertisements.[79] Backpage.com filed suit against the Washington state seeking an injunction, "claiming the law was preempted by the federal

---

[76] Backpage.com, LLC v. Cooper, 2013 WL 1558785 *3–*4 (M.D. Tenn., Jan. 3, 2013).

[77] Id. at *4.

[78] Id.

[79] Id.

Communications Decency Act and violated the First Amendment and Commerce Clause of the U.S. Constitution."[80]

Several other investigations uncovered cases where minors were depicted in Backpage advertisements and engaged in prostitution services.[81] In 2013, the federal court in *Backpage.com, LLC v. Cooper*[82] the court issued an injunction against a Tennessee statute that defined the felony offense of advertising for the commercial abuse of a minor.

(E) Magnuson–Moss Consumer Warranty Act & Software

The Federal Trade Commission has another tool to police Internet-related contracts, the Magnuson–Moss Warranty Act. Congress enacted the Magnuson–Moss Act in 1975 to provide consumers with better information about warranties for the sale of goods.[83] Congress's purpose was to "improve the adequacy of information available to consumers, prevent deception, and improve competition in the marketing of consumer products."[84] The Magnuson–Moss Warranty Act aims to deter the seller's unsavory practice of lulling buyers into complacency by drafting fancy-looking anti-warranties that, in effect, deprived consumers of a meaningful remedy. Congress was redressing the seller's deceptive practice of offering consumers "paper with the filigree border bearing the bold caption 'Warranty' or 'Guarantee' was often of no greater worth than the paper it was printed on."[85] Congress also sought to create incentives for sellers to perform their warranty obligations in a timely and thorough manner and to resolve disputes with a minimum of delay and expense to consumers.

(1) The Magnuson–Moss Act and Software

The Magnuson–Moss Warranty Act applies to the sales of consumer products defined as "tangible personal property which is distributed in commerce and which is normally used for personal, family, or household purposes."[86] Software is an intangible; however that has not prevented numerous courts from applying U.C.C. Article 2 sales of goods provisions to the licensing of software. The fact that software makers license rather than sell goods does not mean that software is outside the Act's sphere of application. The American Law Institute's May 2009 approval of the Principles of Software Contracts "increase[s] the likelihood that courts will apply the Magnuson–Moss Warranty Act to packages software because nothing turns on transferors labeling their transactions as licenses."[87] Where it is unclear whether a particular product is covered under the definition of consumer product, any ambiguity will be resolved in

---

[80] Backpage.com, LLC v. McKenna, No. C12–954–SM, 2012 WL 304543 (W.D.Wash. July 27, 2012) (entering an injunction).

[81] Id. at 1268.

[82] 2013 WL 1558785 (M.D. Tenn., Jan. 3, 2013) (entering injunction against enforcement of statute that would have added add an offense for the sale or the offer to sell "an advertisement that would appear to a reasonable person to be for the purpose of engaging in what would be a commercial sex act . . . with a minor.").

[83] See 15 U.S.C. §§ 2301–2312.

[84] 15 U.S.C. § 2302(a).

[85] H.R. REP. No. 93–1107 (1974).

[86] 15 U.S.C. § 2301(1).

[87] Overview, Chapter 3 Performance (Principles of the Law of Software Contracts, (Proposed Final Draft, March 16, 2009) at 162.

favor of coverage.[88] The statutory interpretation rule of *contra preferentem* suggests that courts will apply Magnuson–Moss to consumer software. Courts willing to recognize the federal consumer warranty act's applicability to software may certify class actions assuming jurisdictional requirements are met.[89] In addition, individual consumers may bring civil actions for damages and recover attorney's fees against software makers.[90]

(2) The Path of the Magnuson–Moss Warranty Act

The New Jersey Law Commission found neither the Magnuson-Moss Warranty Act nor FTC Regulations addressed the applicability of the Act to software. Their research found no court prior to 2000 applied Magnuson-Moss to mass-market software licenses. The Commission summarized a FTC ruling that Gateway violated the Magnuson Moss Warranty Act by: (1) failing to inform consumers that some states do not allow for excluding liability for incidental or consequential damages, (2) failing to disclose that consumers may have legal rights in addition to the warranty, (3) disclaiming any implied warranty except as provided by the Act and (4) failing to make the text of the warranty available prior to sale.[91] The New Jersey Commission notes that consumers will have the following federal rights if Magnuson–Moss applies to software and other information-based products: "(1) the implied warranty cannot be excluded but only limited in duration; (2) the persnickety disclosure requirements may provide federal claims against careless warrantors and (3) warranties must be made available prior to sale."[92] Vendors may also want to consider including a provision in their licenses that some states do not permit excluding liability for incidental or consequential damages. The current practice of "pay now, terms later" violates the consumer protection principle of making the text of a warranty available prior to a sale.

A few courts have also signaled their willingness to apply the act to consumer software transactions. In *Microsoft v. Manning*,[93] the Texas Appeals Court affirmed the certification of a class action against Microsoft for breaches of express warranty and the implied warranty of merchantability, as well as for violation of the Magnuson-Moss Warranty-Federal Trade Commission Improvement Act. In the certified class action, the plaintiffs contended that Microsoft software was defective because it sometimes destroyed data.[94] The plaintiffs in the class action sought recovery of the cost of an upgrade that would remediate the data destruction problem.[95]

A California Court extended the Magnuson–Moss Warranty Act to the software warranty provisions of Apple's iPhone in *In re Apple & AT & T Antitrust Litigation*.[96] The class action complaint challenged Apple's iPhone policy of voiding warranties for

---

[88] 16 C.F.R. 700.1(a).

[89] 15 U.S.C. § 2310(d).

[90] 15 U.S.C. § 2310(d).

[91] Staff, UCITA & Magnuson–Moss Warranty–Federal Trade Commission Improvement Act (Februay 14, 2000 Memorandum.

[92] Id.

[93] 914 S.W.2d 602 (Tex. App. Texarkana 1995).

[94] Id. at 606.

[95] Id.

[96] 596 F.Supp.2d 1288 (N.D. Cal., Oct. 1, 2008).

the device if customers downloaded competing applications. The consumers contended that Apple refused to honor warranties of iPhone customers whose phones were damaged when they installed "unlocking software for the specific purposes of using non-ATTM SIM cards and unapproved TPAs on their iPhones."[97] The court ruled that the plaintiffs alleged sufficient facts to state a Magnuson–Moss Act claim "because it alleges that Apple refused to honor the warranties of customers who used iPhone applications and cellular service not approved by Apple."[98] Software licensors marketing products for the consumer market need to do a complete audit to determine whether their practices comply with the Magnuson-Moss Warranty Act.

(3) Disclaimability of Implied Warranties

Software makers routinely disclaim the implied warranty of merchantability in consumer transactions. Put simply, the Magnuson–Moss Act does not permit sellers to eliminate the implied warranty of merchantability if they make a written warranty or enter into a service agreement at the time of sale or ninety days after.[99] The Magnuson-Moss Act does permit licensors to limit the duration of an implied warranty so long as the limitation is set forth in clear and "unmistakable language." Implied warranties may be limited in duration only if they display "clear and unmistakable language on the face of the warranty."[100]

A New York State court dismissed a Magnuson–Moss Act claim against a software maker for not delivering a product that was Year 2000 compliant ("Y2K"). The court ruled that the plaintiff's Y2K breach of warranty and Magnuson–Moss Act claims were properly dismissed "in view of defendant's disclaimer of all implied warranties and plaintiff's use of the software without any problems during the 90–day warranty period."[101] This case demonstrates that a software maker can limit its exposure by offering consumers a minimum warranty period. In short, where written warranties are given, the Magnuson–Moss Act invalidates attempts to disclaim implied warranties.[102] If a seller gives written warranties, it may not entirely disclaim implied warranties.[103] If the FTC applies the Magnuson-Moss Act to consumer software, software maker must do three things:

> (1) Designate or title, their written warranty as either 'full' or 'limited;' (2) Provide certain specified information about the coverage of the offered warranty in a single, clear, and easy-to-read document; (3) Sellers must make warranties available where their consumer products are sold so that consumers can read them before buying.

---

[97] Id. at 1313.

[98] Id. (ruling that the complaint stated a sufficient cause of acton under 15 U.S.C. § 2302(c) that states: "[n]o warrantor of a consumer product may condition its written or implied warranty of such product on the consumer's using, in connection with such product, any article or service (other than article or service provided without charge under the terms of the warranty) which is identified by brand, trade, or corporate name." 15 U.S.C. § 2302(c).

[99] 15 U.S.C. § 2308(a)(1)(2).

[100] 15 U.S.C. § 2308(b).

[101] Against Gravity Apparel, Inc. v. Quarterdeck Corp., 699 N.Y.S.2d 368 (N.Y.A.D. 1 Dept.,1999).

[102] 15 U.S.C. § 2398(a).

[103] Id.

(4) Labeling of Consumer Warranties

Since software makers for the consumer market typically make written warranties, they must designate them as either a "Full Warranty" or "Limited Warranty."[104] The Magnuson–Moss Act defines minimum content standards for such warranties requiring a seller to label either the warranty as "full" or "limited." [105] The term "full" means that the seller is required to give the federal minimum consumer warranty standards.[106] A full warranty comes with a lemon consumer goods provision. If a consumer product defect or malfunction cannot be remediated "after a reasonable number of attempts," the consumer receives a full refund or replacement without charge.[107] Consumer buyers are not required to do anything other than notify the seller or supplier to obtain remedies for a breach of a full warranty.[108]

A "Limited Warranty" under the Magnuson-Moss Act is a warranty that does not meet the federal minimum standards for warranties statutory and regulatory requirements for disclosure and must satisfy the pre-sale availability rule. Standard-form vendors need to label either their written product warranties as "limited" or "full" or face the possibility of consumer class actions. The Magnuson-Moss Act requires the supplier to conspicuously label consumer warranties as either full or limited. The phrase "Limited Warranty" is key to compliance with the Magnuson-Moss Act in the event a court extends the federal warranty act to software. Software licensors should include the phrase "Limited Warranty" in describing their warranties. Few software vendors are willing to give a "Full Warranty" that requires warrantors to fulfill a number of minimum standards.[109] The Magnuson–Moss Act gives consumers' remedies if the seller fails to comply with the Act's labeling requirements.[110] A web-based product addresses the Magnuson–Moss Act in its license agreement by first stating that it was their understanding that the Magnuson–Moss Act did not apply to their web-based software program. The software maker then included a clause that provided for limited warranties in the event a court applied the federal consumer act by analogy.[111] The licensor of vacation management software has a similar provision:

> The Software is not a "consumer product." However, should a court of competent jurisdiction determine that the software is a "consumer product" under the Magnuson–Moss Warranty—Federal Trade Commission Improvement Act, and then implied warranties, if any, are limited in time to a period of thirty (30) days after you receive the software. After that period, all implied warranties are expressly disclaimed. Some states do not allow limitations on how long an implied warranty lasts, so the above limitations may not apply to you.[112]

---

[104] 15 U.S.C. 2303(a).

[105] 15 U.S.C. § 2302(a).

[106] 15 U.S.C. § 2304.

[107] 15 U.S.C. § 2304(a)(4).

[108] 15 U.S.C. § 2304(b)(1).

[109] 15 U.S.C. § 2304.

[110] 15 U.S.C. §§ 2301–2312.

[111] TradeAHome, End User License Agreement, http://www.tradeahome.com/eula.php (last visited July 5, 2013).

[112] Vacationrentalmanagementsoftware.com, End–User Software License Service Agreement, http://74.125.47.132/search?q=cache:Rah0zzq4lx8J:www.vacationrentalmanagementsoftware.com/content/eul

The advantage of these provisions is that they satisfy the FTC's minimum labeling requirements for consumer goods covered by the Magnuson–Moss Warranty Act. Further, the license provision that the parties do not believe that Magnuson–Moss applies to their transaction may persuade a court not to apply the federal act by analogy. Of course, this provision does not address unfair and deceptive trade practices statutes. Software makers are subject to little FTC action but cannot bypass their provisions through creative contract clauses.

(5) Limited Warranty

The Magnuson-Moss Act requires consumer goods costing greater than $10 to be labeled with either "full" or "limited" warranties. Products costing greater than $15 are subject to other disclosure requirements for full or limited warranties. The broad language of the statute applies to written warranties for consumer products sold over the Internet. Courts will also apply the Magnuson–Moss to hybrid transactions where computer hardware is the preponderant part of the transaction. Courts will extend U.C.C. Article 2 to computer contracts where services are only incidental.[113] However, because software is classified as an intangible good, it is unclear whether the Magnuson–Moss applies to computer software transactions.

The test for inclusion or exclusion from Article 2 is "whether their predominant factor is that of a sale versus services which are governed by the common law."[114] Courts look to the substance of the agreement as opposed to whether a given agreement is labeled as a sale. A developer's agreement to design software for a customer from scratch is likely to be classified as services, especially if the developer is paid for time and materials.[115] Conversely, development license agreements, where software makers customize code, are more likely to be classified as services as opposed to the sale of goods. Once the predominant purpose of the contract is established as a transaction in goods, Article 2 applies to the entire transaction.[116] However, the Magnuson–Moss does not apply to merchant-to-merchant sales and is solely a consumer protection statute.

Under the Magnuson-Moss Act, the implied warranty of merchantability is not completely disclaimable. The Magnuson-Moss Act provides that a supplier may not disclaim or modify any implied warranty to a consumer if (1) the supplier makes any written warranty to the consumer or, (2) at the time of the sale or within 90 days thereafter, the supplier enters into a service contract with the consumer relative to the consumer product.[117] If a seller gives only a limited warranty, the implied warranty of merchantability may be limited for the duration of a limited written warranty. However, the limited duration period must be conscionable and explained in clear and unmistakable language.

---

a_11_06.doc+magnuson-moss+software+license+agreement&cd=7&hl=en&ct=clnk&gl=us&ie=UTF-8   (last visited July 5, 2013).

[113] See e.g., Chatlos Sys., Inc. v. Nat'l Cash Register Corp., 479 F. Supp. 738, 742 (D.N.J. 1979) (applying U.C.C. Article 2 to computer contract where services were incidental to the lease agreement).

[114] Bonebrake v. Cox, 499 F.2d 951, 960 (8th Cir. 1974) (contract for sale of goods including substantial amounts of labor covered by Article 2).

[115] Pearl Invs. LLC v. Standard I/O, Inc., 257 F. Supp. 326, 353 (D. Me. 2003) (classifying development software agreement as services).

[116] Colonial Life Ins. Co. v. Electronic Data Systems Corp., 817 F. Supp. 735 (D.N.H. 1993).

[117] 15 U.S.C. § 2308(a)(1), (2).

If a manufacturer of computer hardware has not corrected or cured problems in its computer system after a reasonable number of attempts, the consumer must receive a refund or replacement without charge plus reasonable expenses. The Magnuson–Moss would provide a remedy to consumers in cases where there are "repeated failures to pass agree acceptance tests," as well as failure to provide deliverables such as source codes that caused the licensee to withhold payment. If courts or Congress extends the Magnuson–Moss Act to software or Internet-related licenses, license agreements will need to be modified.

§ 5.3   REGULATION OF ONLINE SPAM

Spam is defined as unsolicited bulk e-mail ("UBE"), or, unsolicited commercial e-mail ("UCE"). The term spam was inspired from a 1970 Monty Python Flying Circus sketch where a waiter recited a menu where every breakfast dish included spam. A self-proclaimed spam king bragged: "When you're sending out 250 million e-mails, even a blind squirrel will find a nut." "E-mail's open architecture and low marginal costs thus combine to create a forgiving cost structure. A spammer can make money with as low as a 0.005% response rate, or even a 0.000005% response rate."[118]

In a typical day, the average consumer has an e-mail inbox full of offers to make fast money or other fraudulent solicitations. Congress extended The Telephone Consumer Protection Act of 1991 ("TCPA") to Internet telemarketing.[119] Primarily, the TCPA governs telemarketing.[120] In April of 2013, the mobile social network provider, Path, was targeted by an Illinois class action for sending unsolicited text ads. The class action contends that Path violated the TCPA by using automated services to transmit SMS messages without the recipient's consent. The Federal Communications Commission ("FCC") is the chief agency that enforces the TCPA, although state attorneys general can also file suit.

The FTC is in the process of revising anti-spam guideposts to address the growing problem of junk messages on mobile devices and in cloud computing. The FCC has authority to collect complaints and institute enforcement actions against violators of the TCPA. A 2011 study by IBM found that companies are reducing spam by "improved vulnerability patching, but attackers are now targeting mobile devices and the cloud."[121] The FTC will need to modify its anti-spam guides to address the growing problem of spam on mobile devices and in cloud computing. Cybercriminals and scammers are constantly adapting and developing new technologies to exploit lags in the law.

Congress enacted the Controlling the Assault of Non–Solicited Pornography and Marketing Act of 2003 ("CAN–SPAM").[122] CAN–SPAM prohibits fraudulent, abusive and deceptive commercial e-mail.[123] The CAN–SPAM Act requires that any commercial electronic mail message provide (i) clear and conspicuous identification that the

---

[118] Rebecca Bolin, Opting Out of Spam: A Domain Level Do Not Spam Registry, 24 YALE L. & POL'Y REV. 399, 401 (2006).

[119] 47 U.S.C. § 227.

[120] 47 U.S.C. § 227 (2012).

[121] Jeffrey Burt, IBM: Security is Improving, but Cyber-Criminals Are Adapting, EWEEK.COM (March 22, 2012).

[122] 15 U.S.C. §§ 7701–7713 (2003).

[123] 15 U.S.C. §§ 7703, 7704.

message is an advertisement or solicitation; (ii) clear and conspicuous notice of the opportunity to decline to receive further commercial electronic mail messages from the sender; and (iii) a valid physical postal address of the sender.[124] The CAN–SPAM statute recognizes private causes of action by service providers in addition to criminal sanctions. A provider of an Internet access service adversely affected by violations of particular provisions of the CAN–SPAM Act may bring a civil action.[125] Private citizens may not file CAN–SPAM actions, rather "only the FTC, various other federal agencies, a state attorney general on behalf of residents, or providers of Internet access services may bring lawsuits enforcing the CAN SPAM Act."[126] Under CAN-SPAM, a plaintiff may elect to recover monetary damages in an amount equal to the greater of actual losses or statutory damages specified by the CAN–SPAM Act.[127] CAN-SPAM statutory damages area computed as follows:

(A) In general. For purposes of paragraph (1)(B)(ii), the amount determined under this paragraph is the amount calculated by multiplying the number of violations (with each separately addressed unlawful message that is transmitted or attempted to be transmitted over the facilities of the provider of Internet access service, or that is transmitted or attempted to be transmitted to an electronic mail address obtained from the provider of Internet access service in violation of section 5(b)(1)(A)(i) [15 USCS § 7704(b)(1)(A)(i)], treated as a separate violation) by—

(i) up to $ 100, in the case of a violation of section 5(a)(1) [15 USCS § 7704(a)(1)]; or

(ii) up to $ 25, in the case of any other violation of section 5 [15 USCS § 7704].

(B) Limitation. For any violation of section 5 [15 USCS § 7704] (other than section 5(a)(1) [15 USCS § 7704(a)(1)]), the amount determined under subparagraph (A) may not exceed $ 1,000,000.

(C) Aggravated damages. The court may increase a damage award to an amount equal to not more than three times the amount otherwise available under this paragraph if—

(i) the court determines that the defendant committed the violation willfully and knowingly; or

(ii) the defendant's unlawful activity included one or more of the aggravated violations set forth in section 5(b) [15 USCS § 7704(b)].[128]

The CAN-SPAM Act offers an extremely restrictive private right of action that bars consumers and other victims of spam. CAN-SPAM states: "A provider of Internet access service adversely affected by a violation of [the Act] . . . may bring a civil action in any district court[,]" to protect itself from further harm or to recover actual or statutory damages.[129] An Internet access service is defined under Section 7702(11) of the CAN–SPAM Act as, "a service that enables users to access content, information, electronic mail, or other services offered over the Internet, and may also include access

---

[124] 15 U.S.C. § 7704(a)(5).

[125] 15 U.S.C. § 7706(g)(1).

[126] Martin v. CCH, Inc ., 784 F.Supp.2d 1000, 1004 (N.D.Ill.2011).

[127] 15 U.S.C. §7706(g)(1).

[128] 15 U.S.C. § 7706(g)(3).

[129] 15 U.S.C. § 7706(g)(1).

to proprietary content, information, and other services as part of a package of services offered to consumers. Such term does not include telecommunications services."[130] Courts have determined that administrators of e-mail accounts qualify as access providers.[131] If they qualify as an Internet access service provider, the CAN–SPAM plaintiff may pursue actual or statutory damages, whatever is greater.[132]

To state a claim under the CAN–SPAM Act,[133] a plaintiff must allege that the defendant sent e-mail containing "materially false or materially misleading" header information.[134] A "header" is called "header information" in CAN–SPAM and defined as "the source, destination, and routing information attached to an electronic mail message, including the originating domain name and originating electronic mail address, and any other information that appears in the line identifying, or purporting to identify, a person initiating the message."[135] CAN-SPAM defines false or materially misleading headers to include "information that is technically accurate but includes an originating electronic mail address, domain name, or Internet Protocol address the access to which for purposes of initiating the message was obtained by means of false or fraudulent pretenses or representations shall be considered materially misleading."[136] CAN–SPAM prohibits false or misleading transmission of information, deceptive headers, and requires e-mails to provide an easy to use opt out method. Section 7704(a)(1) of the CAN–SPAM, which addresses Header Violations, states:

> It is unlawful for any person to initiate the transmission, to a protected computer, of a commercial electronic mail message, or a transactional or relationship message, that contains, or is accompanied by, header information that is materially false or materially misleading . . . [h]eader information shall be considered materially misleading if it fails to identify accurately a protected computer used to initiate the message because the person initiating the message knowingly uses another protected computer to relay or retransmit the message for purposes of disguising its origin.[137]

Section 7704(a)(1), further states:

> It is unlawful for any person to initiate the transmission of any commercial electronic mail message to a protected computer unless the message provides—(i) clear and conspicuous identification that the message is an advertisement or solicitation; (ii) clear and conspicuous notice of the opportunity under paragraph (3) to decline to receive further commercial electronic mail messages from the sender; and (iii) a valid physical postal address of the sender.[138]

---

[130] 15 U.S.C. § 7702(11).

[131] See e.g., White Buffalo Ventures, LLC v. Univ. of Texas at Austin, 420 F.3d 366, 373 (5th Cir. 2005) (ruling that University of Texas' administration of email accounts and email access was classifiable as CANSPAM's definition of an Internet access service) Cf. Gordon v. Virtumundo, Inc., 575 F.3d 1040, 1051–52 (9th Cir. 2009) (finding that individual plaintiff did not have standing under the CAN–SPAM Act as an Internet Access service provider simply by registering a domain name and using an ordinary Internet connection to set up email accounts).

[132] 15 U.S.C. § 7706(g)(1)(B).

[133] 15 U.S.C. §§ 7701 et seq.

[134] 15 U.S.C. § 7704(A)(1).

[135] 15 U.S.C. § 7704.

[136] 15 U.S.C. § 7704(a)(1)(A).

[137] 15 U.S.C. §§ 7704(a)(1), 7704(a)(1)(C).

[138] 15 U.S.C. § 7704(a)(5).

The conduct prohibited by section 7704(a)(5) is referred to in this order as "Content Violations." The CAN–SPAM Act provides statutory damages against parties who engage in a pattern or practice in violation of § 7704(a)(5).[139]

In its first decade, CAN–SPAM has not been effective in stemming the ocean of spam e-mail. As mentioned above, CAN–SPAM does not authorize private lawsuits by aggrieved consumers. Furthermore, the new federal anti-spam statute preempts all state anti-spam legislation, even those providing consumers with a cause of action against commercial e-mailers.[140] Accordingly, CAN–SPAM is a cause of action normally pursued by FTC enforcers and service providers.

Nevertheless, service providers must prove they were "adversely affected" by spam. Adverse effects include spam-related network crashes, a higher bandwidth utilization because of the flood of messages, and increased costs for hardware and software upgrades, network expansion, as well as the costs of additional people responding to complaints. The FTC does not permit state attorneys general to file anti-spam lawsuits if there is a pending federal civil or administrative enforcement action.

Transactional or relationship messages based on a preexisting relationship such as a bank customer relationship are exempt from CAN–SPAM, but the messages cannot be either false or misleading.[141] Commercial e-mails using false or misleading headers, or violating CAN–SPAM's other provisions, are subject to fines of up to $11,000 for each unsolicited e-mailing. A federal court ordered a California direct marketer to pay $3.4 million in fines for spam sent to a school district. To put it bluntly, the victims of spam, e-mail recipients, have no right to pursue CAN–SPAM remedies against spammers. In many respects, CAN–SPAM has resulted in more spam because its provisions preempted state anti-spam statutes.

The formula for statutory damages is computed by multiplying the number of violations (with each separately addressed unlawful message over the access providers services), Each violation of Section 7704(b)(1)(A)(i) is classified as a separate violation "by—(i) up to $100, in the case of a violation of section 7704(a)(1) . . . or (ii) up to $25, in the case of any other violation of Section 7704 of this title."[142] Finally, Section 7706(3)(C) gives the court the discretion to increase CAN–SPAM damages up to three times if they find the defendant willfully and knowingly committed a violation of Section 7704.[143] Under the CAN–SPAM Act, courts have the discretion to award aggravated damages where the defendant "use[d] scripts or other automated means to register for multiple electronic mail accounts or online user accounts from which to transmit to a protected computer, or enable another person to transmit to a protected computer, a commercial electronic mail message."[144] Under these circumstances "[t]he

---

[139] 15 U.S.C. § 7706(g)(1).

[140] Gordon v. Doe, 459 Fed. Appx. 681 (9th Cir. 2011) (affirming summary judgment in favor of defendant because private litigant is not an Internet service access provider and his action under the Washington Commercial Email Marketing Act (the "CEMA") was preempted because plaintiff "failed to raise a genuine dispute of material fact as to whether this claim involved fraud or deception necessary to exempt it from the CAN–SPAM Act's preemption clause").

[141] Id.

[142] Anytime Fitness, LLC v. Roberts, 2013 U.S. Dist. LEXIS 58906 (D. Minn. April 24, 2013) at *10 (discussing remedies provisions of CAN–SPAM).

[143] 15 U.S.C. § 7706(g)(3)(C).

[144] 15 U.S.C. § 7704(b)(2); 15 U.S.C. § 7706(g)(3)(C).

court may increase a damage award to an amount equal to not more than three times the amount otherwise available."[145]

In 2008, the FTC issued a CAN–SPAM rule that addressed four topics: "(1) an e-mail recipient cannot be required to pay a fee, provide information other than his or her e-mail address and opt-out preferences, or take any steps other than sending a reply e-mail message or visiting a single Internet Web page to opt out of receiving future e-mail from a sender; (2) the definition of "sender" was modified to make it easier to determine which of multiple parties advertising in a single e-mail message is responsible for complying with the Act's opt-out requirements; (3) a "sender" of commercial e-mail can include an accurately-registered post office box or private mailbox established under United States Postal Service regulations to satisfy the Act's requirement that a commercial e-mail display a "valid physical postal address"; and (4) a definition of the term "person" was added to clarify that CAN–SPAM's obligations are not limited to natural persons."[146]

The CAN–SPAM Act regulates the manner in which commercial e-mail transmits, and regulates the various activities related to commercial e-mail, such as prohibiting the use of false, misleading, or deceptive information, prohibiting the use of automated bots to create multiple e-mail accounts, and requiring certain contact information in commercial electronic mail messages.[147] The terms of service will generally prohibit the use of scrapers, robots, spiders, and other means of data mining by any form of automated device or software tool without consent. A web robot or bot gathers data and mines it for "data aggregators."

The CAN–SPAM Act contains an explicit preemption clause, which states: "This chapter supersedes any statute, regulation, or rule of a State . . . that expressly regulates the use of electronic mail to send commercial messages, except to the extent that any such statute, regulation, or rule prohibits falsity or deception in any portion of a commercial electronic mail message or information attached thereto."[148] CAN–SPAM also contains an express provision that limits the scope of its preemption. It states: "[t]his chapter shall not be construed to preempt the applicability of: (A) State laws that are not specific to electronic mail, including State trespass, contract, or tort law; or (B) other State laws to the extent that those laws relate to acts of fraud or computer crime." "CAN–SPAM thus expressly preempts any state statute that regulates the use of e-mail for commercial messages unless the statute prohibits "falsity or deception" in commercial e-mails" or fraud and computer crime.[149] This federal statute preempts state anti-spam statutes but not common law tort actions such as trespass to chattels or intentional misrepresentation.[150] Prior to CAN-SPAM, California enacted an anti-spam statute the prohibited e-mails with false headings. In *Gordon v. Virtumundo*,

---

[145] 15 U.S.C. § 7706(g)(3)(C).

[146] Federal Trade Commission, FTC Approves New Rule Provision Under the CAN–SPAM Act, http://www.ftc.gov/opa/2008/05/canspam.shtm (last visited May 17, 2013).

[147] 15 U.S.C. § 7704 (2003).

[148] Hafke v. Rossdale Group, LLC, 2011 U.S. Dist. LEXIS 116003 *4 (W.D. Mich, Oct 7, 2011) (citing 15 U.S.C. § 7707(b)(2)).

[149] Id.

[150] Hypertouch, Inc. v. Azoogle.com, Inc., 2009 WL 734674 (N.D. Cal., Mar. 19, 2009).

Inc.,[151] the Ninth Circuit ruled that CAN-SPAM preempted the state statute because Congress enacted the federal statute to regulate spam e-mail on a nationwide basis.

In *White Buffalo Ventures v. University of Texas,*[152] the Fifth Circuit considered a challenge by an unsolicited e-mailing company alleging the University of Texas anti-spam policy violated the First Amendment. White Buffalo operated several online dating services, including one, called "longhornsingles.com" that targeted University of Texas students. The commercial e-mailer, White Buffalo, made a Freedom of Information Act request to obtain the e-mail addresses of all of the University of Texas students. In return, the University blocked e-mail messages from White Buffalo because it violated the University's anti-solicitation policies banning unwelcome bulk commercial e-mails. The Fifth Circuit ruled that the University was a state actor and that its concerted effort in blocking unsolicited commercial e-mail constituted a state regulation subject to CAN–SPAM's preemption clause.[153] Nevertheless, the court found that Section 7707(C) of the CAN–SPAM Act did not preempt the University of Texas's blocking of spam e-mail. The court rejected the online dating service's contention the federal CAN–SPAM preempted the university's anti-solicitation policy. CAN–SPAM "supersedes any statute, regulation, or rule . . . that expressly regulates the use of electronic mail to send commercial messages" to the extent that these rules prohibit "[f]alsity or deception in any part of a commercial electronic mail messages."[154] The *White Buffalo* court did not find CAN–SPAM expressly preempted the University's policy, but instead found a presumption against preemption.

In formulating its opinion, the court reviewed three questions. First, did the University of Texas violate the First Amendment when it blocked delivery of unsolicited commercial e-mail or spam from White Buffalo? Second, did the University of Texas violate the Constitution of the United States when it blocked access from its on-campus network to White Buffalo? Third, did the CAN–SPAM Act preemption provision preempt the University of Texas at Austin's anti-spam policy? The theory of preemption derives from the Supremacy Clause of the United States Constitution, which provides that the laws of the United States "shall be the supreme Law of the Land; . . . anything in the Constitution or Laws of any state to the Contrary notwithstanding."[155]

Central to the principle of preemption generally is the value of providing for legal uniformity where Congress has acted nationally.[156] The *White Buffalo* court explained that CAN–SPAM did not prevent the University from installing spam filters to conserve server space and save time and resources. CAN–SPAM does not preempt the Regents' e-mail rules, because it is in tension with plain text found elsewhere in the Act, and that tension triggers the presumption against preemption. The *White Buffalo* court also rejected the commercial e-mailer's claim that their messages were protected as commercial speech. Commercial speech, while protected under the First Amendment, is afforded less protection that other forms of constitutionally protected expression.

---

[151] 575 F.3d 1040, 1061-1062 (9th Cir. 2009).

[152] 420 F.3d 366 (5th Cir. 2005).

[153] Id. at 573.

[154] CAN–SPAM Act § (8)(B) (2003).

[155] Altria Group, Inc. v. Good, 555 U.S. 70, 76 (2008) (quoting U.S. Const. art. VI, cl. 2).

[156] Barclays Capital Inc. v. Theflyonthewall.com, Inc., 650 F.3d 876 (2d Cir. 2011).

Under a *Central Hudson* test, a court first must determine whether the commercial speech concerns unlawful activity, or that it is inherently misleading.[157]

If the speech is either unlawful or misleading, then the First Amendment does not protect it. Nevertheless, if the speech is neither unlawful nor misleading, then the challenged speech regulation violates the First Amendment unless government regulators can establish that: (1) they have identified a substantial government interest; (2) the regulation "directly advances" the asserted interest; and (3) the regulation "is no more extensive than is necessary to serve that interest."[158] "The 'core notion' of commercial speech includes "speech that does no more than propose a commercial transaction" and is entitled to less protection than non-commercial speech.[159] The Supreme Court in *Central Hudson Gas & Elec. Corp. v. Public Serv. Comm'n*[160] defined commercial speech as "expression related solely to the economic interests of the speaker and its audience."[161] In order to qualify for commercial speech under the *Central Hudson* test for First Amendment protection, commercial speech must concern lawful activity and not be misleading. The *White Buffalo* court applied Central Hudson's four-part test to evaluate the legality of the University's commercial speech regulation: (1) whether the speech is unlawful or misleading; (2) whether the government's expressed interest is substantial; (3) whether the state action directly promotes that interest; and (4) whether the state action is more extensive than necessary to promote that interest.

The court found both parties agreed that White Buffalo's commercial solicitations were legal, contained factually accurate information, and therefore passed the first part of the *Central Hudson* test. The court also found that the University's interest in stopping spam from clogging up its servers to be a substantial interest. The third part of the *Central Hudson* test asks whether the speech restriction directly and materially advances the asserted governmental interest. The *White Buffalo* court also found the university anti-spam regulations passed the third prong because they promoted a substantial interest. The *White Buffalo* court held the University of Texas' policy in blocking e-mail was no more extensive than what was necessary to secure the state's substantial interest in blocking unwanted spam. "For an Internet server efficiency rationale to pass muster under the fourth prong of *Central Hudson*, e-mail spam filters must block a set of spam that poses a legitimate threat to server efficiency."[162]

> In a 2010 complaint, Facebook noted how spammers, "represented that in order to qualify for certain fake or deceptive offers, people had to spam their friends, sign up for automatic mobile phone subscription services, or provide other information. We claim that by doing this, they violated the U.S. Computer Fraud and Abuse Act, the Controlling the Assault of Non-Solicited Pornography and Marketing Act (CAN-SPAM), and other state and federal laws."[163] Facebook won the largest anti-spam award in history with an $873 million judgment against Adam Guerbuez

---

[157] Central Hudson Gas & Electric Corp. v. Public Service Comm'n, 447 U.S. 557, 566 (1980).

[158] Id.

[159] Bad Frog Brewery, Inc. v. N.Y. State Liquor Auth., 134 F.3d 87, 97 (2d Cir. 1998).

[160] 447 U.S. 557, 561 (1980).

[161] Id at 561.

[162] White Buffalo Ventures v. University of Texas at Austin, 420 F.3d 366, 377 (2005).

[163] Facebook, Updates in Facebook's Fight Against Spam and Spammers (Oct. 10, 2010), http://www.facebook.com/note.php?note_id=442722120765 (last visited Nov. 14, 2013).

and Atlantis Blue Capital.[164] Additionally, in *Facebook v. Guerbuez*,[165] a court awarded Facebook $873 million against a Facebook member who had sent four million spam emails to Facebook users. The court awarded half of the maximum statutory damages, "$50 per wrongful communication," declining to award treble damages under the given the size of the CAN–SPAM award.[166] In another huge anti-spam case, a federal court "awarded Facebook $360,500,000 in statutory damages and issued a permanent injunction against notorious spammer, Philip Porembski,[167]

Facebook received nearly $711 million in damages against Sanford Wallace, "the King of Spam"[168] In W*allace,* the defendants engaged in a phishing and spamming scheme that operated as follows:

> Defendants send out emails to multiple Facebook users. The emails appear to be legitimate messages and ask the recipients to click on a link to another website. That website is a phishing site designed to trick users into divulging their Facebook login information. Once users divulge the information, Defendants then use it to send spam to the friends of the users, and as the cycle repeats the number of compromised Facebook accounts increases rapidly. Facebook also alleges that certain spam messages redirect users to websites that pay Defendants for each user visit.[169]

Facebook filed suit against the defendants alleging that the phishing operation violated CAN–SPAM, the Computer Fraud and Abuse Act, and California state law.[170] The court entered a temporary injunction against the defendants and the plaintiff sought statutory damages.[171] The court awarded the plaintiff $710,737,650 in damages calculated by multiplying the number of emails by "$50.00 per violation of the CAN–SPAM Act."[172] The court determined that it should award $50.00 per violation, based upon an examination of statutory factor.[173] Specifically, the court stated that "[t]he record demonstrates that Wallace willfully violated the statutes in question with blatant disregard for the rights of Facebook and the thousands of Facebook users whose accounts were compromised by his conduct."[174] In that case, the defendant's conduct included violating a temporary restraining order and preliminary injunction.[175] In 2008, "Wallace was ordered to pay MySpace.com $234 million following a trial at

---

[164] Id.

[165] No. C08–03889 (N.D.Cal. decided Nov. 21, 2008),

[166] 15 U.S.C. § 7704(A)(1) (2003).

[167] Facebook, Updates in Facebook's Fight Against Spam and Spammers (Oct. 10, 2010), http://www.facebook.com/note.php?note_id=442722120765 (last visited Nov. 14, 2013).

[168] Steven Musil, Facebook Awarded $711m in Spam Lawsuit, CBS NEWS http://www.cbsnews.com/2100–503063_162–5455847. html (Oct. 9, 2011); See also, See Facebook v. Fisher, No. C 09–05842 JF (PSG), 2011 WL 250395, at *2 (N.D.Cal. Jan. 26, 2011) (reducing the statutory award and declining to award treble damages where the $2 billion requested damages award was not proportionate to the gravity of the defendants' acts).

[169] Id. at *1.

[170] Id.

[171] Id. at *2.

[172] Id.

[173] Id.

[174] Id.

[175] Id.

which he repeatedly failed to turn over documents or even show up in court." In *MySpace v. Wallace,[176]* the court awarded MySpace $223 million against Wallace who had sent nearly 400,000 messages and posted 890,000 comments from 320,000 "hijacked" MySpace.com user accounts.

Moreover, a federal court in *Yahoo! Inc. v. XYZ Companies,*[177] awarded a $600 million damage award against a spam e-mailer that used Yahoo!'s marks in over eleven million fraudulent e-mails.[178] The Nigerian advance fee fraud is an Internet update of a swindle developed first in the 1920s using the postal service. The Internet spam swindle involves sending massive amounts of spam to consumers:

> The *Yahoo! Inc. v. XYZ Companies et al.* case involved Nigerian, Thai and Taiwanese spammers who sent millions of e-mails purporting to be from or sent on behalf of Yahoo! and contained Yahoo! trademarks. The e-mails notified the victims that they had just won a Nigerian lottery with which Yahoo! appeared to be affiliated. In order to collect those winnings, the e-mail required its recipients to pay some up-front fees (thus the "advance fee" fraud moniker).[179]

The CAN–SPAM verdict arising out of the Nigerian Advance Free Fraud is likely not collectible.[180] At present, while most countries have anti-spam laws, there is relatively little enforcement across national borders.

§ 5.4   FEDERAL COMMUNICATIONS COMMISSION

Congress enacted The Telecommunications Act of 1996 ("TCA") as "an omnibus overhaul of the federal regulation of communications companies," the purpose of which is to, "provide for a pro-competitive, deregulatory national policy framework designed to accelerate rapidly private sector deployment of advanced telecommunications and information technologies and services . . . by opening all telecommunications markets to competition."[181] The first smartphones, for example, were not developed until 1999 enabling high speed Internet and data access. By 2013, smartphones outsold landline phones by a large margin with Android and iPhone as the leading sellers. Gradually, the Federal Communications Commission (FCC) is addressing the rise of the Internet and mobile telephones. In *National Cable & Telecommunications Association v. Brand X Internet Services,*[182] the United States Supreme Court upheld the FCC's authority to classify methods of broadband Internet access into pre-existing definitions of the TCA. In that case, the Court upheld the FCC's classification of broadband cable Internet service as an "information service," and the FCC's conclusion that broadband cable Internet service was not a "telecommunications service."[183] In late 2012, the releases a new Smartphone Security Checker to help consumers protect themselves from mobile cyber threats. In July of 2012, the FCC's Enforcement Bureau entered into a $1.25 million consent decree with

---

[176] 2008 U.S. Dist. LEXIS 75752 (C.D.Cal. May 28, 2008).

[177] No. 08–4581 (S.D. N.Y., Dec. 5, 2011).

[178] Yahoo! Gets $610 Million From Hoax Perpetrator, ELEC. COM. & L. REP. (BNA) (Dec. 5, 2011).

[179] Id.

[180] Id.

[181] Sprint Spectrum, L.P. v. Willoth, 176 F.3d 630, 637 (2d Cir. 1999).

[182] 545 U.S. 967 (2005).

[183] Id.

Verizon Wireless that "resolves an investigation into whether the company had fully complied with the FCC's 'C Block rules,' requiring licensees of C Block spectrum to allow customers to freely use the devices and applications of their choosing."[184]

(A) The Communications Act of 1934

The Federal Communications Commission ("FCC") is an independent United States government agency established by the Communications Act of 1934.[185] The FCC regulates interstate and international communications through radio, television, wire, satellite, and cable. The FCC jurisdiction covers the fifty states, the District of Columbia, and unincorporated territories. The 1934 Act combined previous statutes governing telephone voice service and radio broadcasting. The Telecommunications Act of 1996 amended and updated the 1934 Act with the goal of promoting competition in all communications sectors.

(B) Net Neutrality

The policy debate over "net neutrality" concerns what role the government should have in regulating broadband Internet providers transmitting and delivering Internet traffic over their networks. A telecommunications carrier violated network neutrality when they block Web traffic over their networks. Network neutrality is the key to generative capacity in enabling innovation. Google is a strong supporter of neutrality, which it defines as "equal access to the Internet."[186] The search engine mogul contends, "Broadband carriers should not be able to discriminate against competing applications or content."[187] "Just as telephone companies are not permitted to tell consumers who they can call or what they can say, broadband carriers should not be allowed to use their market power to control activity online."[188] The major policy issue centers on what types and degrees of control the government should impose on broadband providers.[189] The consumer interest in net neutrality is to prevent broadband providers from blocking or slowing traffic based upon content or the type of customer.

In his U.S. Senate testimony, Lawrence Lessig noted how broadband providers point to the efficiency of tiered pricing depending upon customers and content. He stated, "Network neutrality is more broadly an environment or platform permitting minimum interference by the network or platform owner."[190] Lessig drew upon American history to describe how the interests of the United States imposed limits on the freedom of infrastructure providers to enhance the public good. The electricity grid signifies neutral network norms because electricity providers are not permitted to discriminate among

---

[184] Federal Communications Commission Document, Verizon Wireless to Pay $1.25 Million to Settle Investigation (July 31, 2013), http://www.fcc.gov/document/verizon-wireless-pay-125-million-settle-investigation.

[185] 47 U.S.C. § 151.

[186] GOOGLE, A GUIDE TO NETWORK NEUTRALITY (2008).

[187] Id.

[188] Id.

[189] Marc S. Martin, Net Neutrality Update, ABA Business Law Section, Cyberspace Committee Forum (Washington, D.C. 2007).

[190] Lawrence Lessig, Hearing on The Future of the Internet. Testimony Before the U.S. Senate Committee on Commerce. Science & Transportation (April 28, 2008) at 2.

users or applications for electricity. Network discrimination will have a chilling impact on Internet entrepreneurs and constrain new applications.[191]

Lawrence Lessig's testimony cites the dangers of privatizing Internet infrastructure. He described how the U.S. Post Office jump-started the development of newspapers and periodicals. Network owners "have the ability to, in effect open the Internet's letters to peek inside the packets and choose which go faster or which get blocked."[192] The Republican Party platform in the 2012 election proposed to repeal the FCC's net neutrality rules and to auction the government-controlled spectrum to spread high-speed Internet access.[193]

Congress should articulate network neutrality principles to ensure networks implement norms, to facilitate the qualities of abundance and neutrality. Regulatory policies should incentivize network providers to develop "broadband abundance" supporting a "wide range of economic and social activity." In contrast, federal regulations allowed cable owners an "almost unlimited range of freedom" in determining pricing structures, which resulted in "significant price increases" and a "radical drop in independently produced television."[194] Lessig proposes that Congress direct the FCC to implement network neutrality.

Lessig proposes that Congress direct the FCC to implement network neutrality. He concludes Congress must act to ensure "both technical and legal control over innovation on the Internet."[195] The FCC, the chief federal agency concerned with net neutrality, investigated Comcast and Cox Communications for allegedly blocking the traffic of customers.[196] The concept of network neutrality assumes a relative autonomy of users in controlling the content they view as well as applications they use on the Internet. A.R.C. Networks summarized a 2005 FCC policy on net neutrality and speculated on the future path of the law in a 2013 SEC filing:

> In August 2005, the FCC adopted a policy statement that outlined four principles intended to preserve and promote the open and interconnected nature of the Internet. The FCC, the Obama Administration, and Congress have expressed interest in imposing these so-called "net neutrality" requirements on broadband Internet access providers, which address whether, and the extent to which, owners of network infrastructure should be permitted to engage in network management practices that prioritize data packets on their networks through commercial arrangements or based on other preferences.

In 2005, The Federal Communications Commission ("FCC") adopted a policy statement expressing its view that consumers are entitled to access lawful Internet content and to run applications and use services of their choice, subject to the needs of

---

[191] Id. at 8 (testifying that broad band providers are engaging in censorship of Internet content).

[192] Id.

[193] Rep. Paul Ryan (R–Wis.), the 2012 Republican Vice Presidential nominee "has been among the most outspoken critics of the FCC's net neutrality rules, which prohibits Internet service providers from discriminating against traffic that travels over their networks. In 2011, Ryan voted for a resolution disapproving the rules and, in 2006, voted against a Democratic-sponsored amendment to a bill that would have codified basic network neutrality principles in law." Paul Barbagallo, Republican Platform Blasts Obama Policy on Spectrum, Net Neutrality, BLOOMBERG BNA, ELECT. COMM. & LAW REPORT (Aug. 29, 2012).

[194] Id.

[195] Id.

[196] Network Neutrality Practices, BLOOMBERG BNA, ELECT. COMM. & LAW REPORT, (May 21, 2008).

law enforcement and reasonable network management. In an August 2008 decision, the FCC characterized these net neutrality principles as binding and enforceable and stated that network operators have the burden to prove that their network management techniques are reasonable. In that order, which was overturned by a court decision in April 2010, the FCC imposed sanctions on a broadband Internet access provider for managing its network by blocking or degrading some Internet transmissions and applications in a way that the FCC found to be unreasonably discriminatory. In December 2010, the FCC issued new rules to govern network management practices and prohibit unreasonable discrimination in the transmission of Internet traffic. These rules have not taken effect and are currently being challenged in court. It is not possible to determine what specific broadband network management techniques or related business arrangements may be deemed reasonable or unreasonable in the future.[197]

The FCC needs to conceptualize Internet connectivity and cloud computing from a mere service into a full-fledged utility. The cloud-computing infrastructure has undergoing the same revolution as commuter vehicles did in the 1960s, and telephone communications underwent before that. The FCC has yet to treat cloud computing as a utility subject to its regulations.[198] In general, federal agencies do not regard Internet commercial institutions such as Google as utilities.

§ 5.5   SECURITIES & EXCHANGE RULES FOR THE INTERNET

The Securities and Exchange Commission ("SEC") regulates the sale of securities subject to the registration requirements of the Securities Act of 1933. The SEC Office of Internet Enforcement ("OIE") administers the SEC Enforcement Division's Internet program. Internet "road shows" or webcasts must comply with SEC regulations. The SEC, for example, protects consumers by policing websites offering securities, soliciting securities transactions, or advertising investment services offshore. Under the Securities Act of 1934, the SEC formulated proxy rules permitting issuers and other persons to furnish proxy materials to shareholders by posting them on an Internet website—if shareholders receive notice that the proxy materials are available in hard copy form. Issuers must make copies of the proxy materials available to shareholders on request and at no charge.[199] One of the unsettled issues is whether companies have a duty to disclose cyber-attacks. The SEC issued a voluntary disclosure plan, which is creating a *de facto* standard that companies disclose cyber-attacks in their SEC filings.[200] A Bloomberg report noted:

> Google, the world's biggest search engine, agreed in May to put its previously disclosed cyber-assault in an earnings report. American International Group Inc. (AIG), Hartford Financial Services Group Inc. (HIG), Eastman Chemical Co. (EMN) and Quest Diagnostics Inc. (DGX) were also prodded to improve disclosures of cyber-risks, according to SEC letters available on the regulator's website.[201]

---

[197] A.R.C. Systems, SEC S-1/A Filing (June 5, 2013).

[198] Kevin Werbach, The Network Utility, 60 DUKE L.J. 1761 (2011).

[199] SEC, Internet Availability of Proxy Materials, RIN 3235-AJ47 (March 30, 2007).

[200] Linda Sandler, SEC Guidance on Cyber–Disclosure Becomes Rule for Google, BLOOMBERG (Aug. 29, 2012).

[201] Id.

In 2011 the SEC's Division of Corporation Finance issued "CF Disclosure Guidance: Topic No.2, Cybersecurity," that gives publicly owned companies guidance on their reporting duties for cyber-attacks under the Securities Act of 1933 and the Securities Exchange Act of 1934.[202] "Registrants are required to report remediation costs, increased cybersecurity protection costs, lost revenues, litigation, and reputation damages.[203] Risk factor disclosures include cybersecurity risks to business or operations.[204]

The greater the risk of cyber incidents, the greater the duty in reporting security breaches and to implement reasonable precautions. The Securities and Exchange Commission entered into an agreement where NASDAQ Stock Market LLC, "agreed to pay a record $10 million penalty to settle administrative charges stemming from its 'poor systems and decision-making' during the initial public offering and secondary market trading of Facebook Inc."[205] In February of 2012, the Commodity Futures Trading Commission ("CFTC") and the SEC proposed Identity Theft Red Flags Rules which will require financial institutions to "develop and implement an identity theft prevention program that is designed to detect, prevent and mitigate identify theft." The obligation to develop identity theft programs applies to "certain existing accounts or the opening of new accounts."[206]

The Identity Theft Red Flag Rules will amend section 615(e) of the Fair Credit Reporting Act ("FCRA"). The rule requires financial institutions and creditors to "develop and implement a written identity theft program . . . designed to detect, prevent, and mitigate identity theft in connection with certain existing accounts or the opening of new accounts."[207] The Commission proposes guidelines to assist entities in tailoring Red Flags to the size and complexity of their organization. A supplement to the Rule cites many examples of Red Flags that organizations should take into account. In February of 2012, the SEC ruled that publicly owned wireless providers must allow resolutions on network neutrality to be included on their annual shareholder ballots and proxy statements. In 2012, the SEC "issued guidelines that require public companies to disclose the risk of cyber incidents if they materially affect a registrant's products, services, relationships with customers or suppliers, or competitive conditions, or if they make an investment in the company speculative or risky."[208] A recent corporate governance survey concluded that senior management and their boards "still are not exercising appropriate governance over the privacy and security of their digital assets."[209]

---

[202] U.S. Securities and Exchange Commission, Division of Corporate Finance Securities and Exchange Commission, CF Disclosure Guidance: Topic No. 2, Cybersecurity (Oct. 13, 2011). http://www.sec.gov/divisions/corpfin/guidance/cfguidance-topic2.htm (last visited Nov. 16, 2013).

[203] Id.

[204] Id.

[205] Phyllis Diamond, NASDAQ to Pay Record $10M Over Glitches In Facebook IPO, Secondary Market Trading, BNA BLOOMBERG BNA: ELECTRONIC COMMERCE & LAW (May 31, 2013), (discussing In re Nasdaq Stock Market LLC, SEC, Admin. Proc. File No. 3–15339, (May 29 2013)).

[206] Securities and Exchange Commission, Identity Theft Red Flags Rule (2012).

[207] Id.

[208] JODY R. WESBY, GOVERNANCE OF ENTERPRISE SECURITY: CYLAB 2012 REPORT (2012).

[209] Id.

§ 5.6   INTERNET TAXATION

(A) Federal Tax Law

Cyberspace is the fastest growing free-trade zone, but governments have found it difficult to determine how to tax Internet-related transactions. Internet trade is multi-hemispheric, as the sun never sets on a Website that stands ready to communicate with customers 24/7 in all countries connected to the World Wide Web. The Internet Tax Freedom Act imposed a "temporary moratorium on Internet specific taxes" by states and localities to avoid "stunt[ing] the growth of electronic commerce."[210] This statute does not create "tax freedom" for transactions on the Internet but instead forbids multiple or discriminatory taxes on electronic commerce. "Section 1105(6) says that a multiple tax means two states taxing the same thing without a tax credit."[211] Section 1106(C) drives that point home by stating that sales and use taxes on tangible personal property are valid even if they otherwise would be called multiple taxes.[212]

Congress prohibited: (1) all state and local taxes on "Internet access" (unless grandfathered) and (2) all discriminatory taxes on "electronic commerce," including the provision of "Internet access."[213] Congress has extended a "moratorium on state and local taxation of Internet access or multiple or discriminatory taxes on ecommerce has been extended through November 2014."[214] This moratorium does not prohibit federal, state, or local authorities from collecting taxes on our income or from collecting certain taxes that were in effect prior to the enactment of the moratorium and/or one of its extensions.

(B) State Internet Taxes

The rules for indirect taxes (i.e., sales and use tax, value-added tax ("VAT"), goods and services tax, business tax and gross receipt tax) to e-commerce are in flux and still evolving. EBay is a global Internet business that acknowledges the law is evolving because states "are increasingly looking for ways to increase revenues, which has resulted in discussions about tax reform and other legislative action to increase tax revenues, including through indirect taxes."[215] EBay concludes that a growing number of jurisdictions have either implemented or are considering addressing at least some aspect of e-commerce transactions:

> Some jurisdictions have implemented or may implement laws specifically addressing the Internet or some aspect of ecommerce. For example, the State of New York has passed legislation that requires any out-of-state seller of tangible personal property to collect and remit New York use tax if the seller engages affiliates above certain financial thresholds in New York to perform certain business promotion activities. In March 2013, the New York Court of Appeals

---

[210] S. Rep. No. 105–184, at 1–2 (1998).

[211] City of Chicago v. StubHub!, Inc., 624 F.3d 363, 366 (7th Cir. 2010).

[212] Id.

[213] ITFA §§ 1101(A), 1105(3).

[214] eBay SEC 10–Q Filing (July 20, 2013).

[215] Id.

(New York State's highest court) upheld this legislation in *Amazon.com, LLC and Overstock.com, Inc. v. New York State Department of Taxation and Finance.*[216]

In September 2012, California enacted a new law, which is similar to the law passed in New York, but excludes certain forms of Internet marketing and is limited to retailers who exceed prescribed sales volume thresholds. EBay also found that the Pennsylvania Department of Revenue ruled that online retailers such as eBay or PayPal could have a nexus to the state.[217] The central issue in Illinois, for example, is whether a company such as eBay will have a duty to collect use taxes. Colorado enacted a statute that imposes tax notice and reporting requirements on online companies:

> The law is designed to aid Colorado in collecting use tax from Colorado residents who purchase taxable items from out-of-state retailers. The regulation promulgated by the Colorado Department of Revenue excludes from these reporting obligations businesses that sell $100,000 or less into the state in a calendar year, thus limiting the impact on our sellers. A number of out-of-state retailers have challenged the law and a Federal District Court issued an injunction blocking enforcement of the regulations pending a resolution of the case. In March 2012, a federal judge struck down the Colorado law as unconstitutional, finding that it discriminated against interstate commerce, and the State of Colorado has not appealed this decision. Oklahoma has enacted a similar law but has not taken any published enforcement action to date.[218]

It is unclear whether courts will uphold new sales and use tax collection. In *Nat'l Bellas Hess v. Dept. of Revenue of State of Ill.,*[219] the U.S. Supreme Court held it was a violation of the Due Process Clause to require a mail order retailer, without offices or sales agents in Illinois, to pay a use tax. In this pre-World Wide Web case, the Court expressed concern that local tax collectors could restrain interstate commerce if the mail order retailer was subject to a tax. A quarter century later, the U.S. Supreme Court ruled states could not compel businesses to pay a sales tax unless the company had a physical presence in the state. In *Quill Corporation v. North Dakota,*[220] Quill, a Delaware corporation with a physical presence in Illinois, California, and Georgia, sold $1 million in mail-order office supplies to 3,000 customers in North Dakota. North Dakota wanted to charge sales tax on this income. The Supreme Court held that such a tax would not violate the Due Process Clause of the Constitution because, "Quill . . . purposefully directed its activities at North Dakota residents, the magnitude of those contacts [were] more than sufficient for due process purposes, and . . . the use tax [was] related to the benefits Quill receives from access to the State."[221]

The Court, however, held the Commerce Clause does not allow individual states to interfere with interstate commerce when the "only connection with customers in the [taxing] State is by . . . mail."[222] Therefore, North Dakota could not impose its sales tax on Quill. The Court's decision means that states may not require retailers to collect sales

---

[216] 81 A.D.3d 183, 20 N.Y.3d 590 (2013).

[217] Id.

[218] Id.

[219] 386 U.S. 753 (1967).

[220] 504 U.S. 298 (1992).

[221] Id. at 308.

[222] Id. at 298.

taxes unless they have a physical presence in that state. The problem of developing an Internet or even a nationwide point-of-deliver tax collection system is not even on the drawing boards at either the federal or the state levels.[223]

The Streamlined Sales and Use Tax Agreement ("SSUTA") joins twenty-four states to simplify and make more uniform sales and use tax collection and administration by retailers and states. SSUTA proposes to require collection and remittance of remote sales tax by out-of-state sellers. The SSUTA is a legislative initiative of the National Conference of State Legislatures ("NCCUSL") intended to reduce the cost and administrative burdens on retailers that collect the sales tax, particularly retailers operating in multiple states.[224] SSUTA changes local sales taxes from:

> an origin-based system to a destination-based system, providing amnesty for remote sellers who voluntarily begin collecting sales tax, providing compensation for certified service providers that will coordinate and process the sales tax reported by remote sellers, and providing assistance for small businesses that need to adapt to destination-based sales tax.[225]

Under SSUTA, Internet businesses that deliver products to customers, either directly from their stores or from warehouses have a duty to "code the local sales tax to that of the destination city or unincorporated county."[226] One of the gaps in SSUTA is that only twenty-four of the fifty-one jurisdictions have passed this state tax collection statute. This failure to harmonize state tax law obligations creates significant costs for online retailers such as Overstock.com, who spent $1.3 million implementing software in order to add a single state to its point-of-delivery tax collection.[227] The city of Chicago, Illinois, filed suit against eBay and its subsidiary, Stub Hub, for failing to collect that city's amusement taxes on concert and sporting event tickets sold through their websites. EBay takes the position that the city's amusement tax is inapplicable to the Internet reselling of sports and entertainment tickets.[228]

Municipalities have begun to file actions against large Internet businesses to collect local taxes. In *City of Chicago v. StubHub!, Inc.*,[229] the city of Chicago, Illinois, filed suit against eBay and its subsidiary, Stub Hub, for failing to collect that city's amusement taxes on concert and sporting event tickets sold through their websites. EBay contended that the city's amusement tax is inapplicable to the Internet reselling of sports and entertainment tickets.[230] The Seventh Circuit ruled that StubHub was not required to collect and remit a city amusement tax.

The city of Chicago also filed suit against Hotels.com for failing to remit city hotel taxes. New York State already compels online retailers to collect sales taxes on goods sold over the Internet to New York residents even though the retailer does not have a physical presence in that state. Utah based Overstock.com challenged the

---

[223] See Patrick M. Byrne and Jonathan E. Johnson III, The Rights and Wrongs of Taxing Internet Retailers, WALL ST. J. (July 24, 2012) at A15.

[224] Washington State Department of Revenue, Streamlined Sales and Usage Tax Agreement (2012).

[225] Id.

[226] Id.

[227] Byrne and Johnson, The Rights and Wrongs of Taxing Internet Retailers, Id.

[228] SiliconValley.com, Chicago Sues eBay Over Concert Ticket Sales (May 20, 2008).

[229] 624 F.3d 363 (7th Cir. 2010).

[230] SiliconValley.com, Chicago Sues eBay, Id.

constitutionality of the New York statute.[231] State and local taxes vary significantly in what they tax and what they exempt. These "complexities reduce the likelihood that Congress will exercise its authority under the Commerce Clause to require remote vendors to collect sales tax on all sales, unless the rules . . . [are] simplified."[232] With cloud computing, there are questions of where the sites for taxable presence should be determined. Other tax issues include "the nature of the transaction (services, purchase or license of software, access to intangibles), and where income should be sourced."[233]

In 2012, Amazon.com entered into a contract with the state of Nevada to collect sales tax revenues on the online bookstore sales to Nevada customers. Cities have begun to file actions against large Internet businesses. In *City of San Antonio v. Hotels.com*,[234] a Texas "jury found the defendants had been controlling occupancy of the hotel rooms, but had not converted tax revenues. The plaintiffs were awarded a total of $20,162,383, which included $6,169,040 from Expedia, $7,272,059 from Hotels.com, $1,667,993 from Hotwire, $417,103 from Internetwork and Trip Network, $1,114,357 from Orbitz, $1,913,236 from Priceline, $161,208 from Site59, $1,332,117 from Travelocity, $115,270 from Travelweb."[235] The City of San Antonio "filed a class action suit on behalf of itself and 172 other Texas municipalities against the 11 Internet corporations, alleging violations of the Texas Tax Code and conversion."[236]

The cities claimed the Internet websites "purchased rooms at city hotels for discount rates and then sold those rooms to customers at higher retail rates, but paid local hotel occupancy taxes based on the discount rate."[237] The defendants contended, "The hotels controlled occupancy of the rooms, not them, and claimed none of them had sufficient physical presence in Texas to be subject to the occupancy taxes."[238] The Internet businesses argued that the City's imposition of tax on them but not travel services violated the Commerce Clause because it "constituted illegal discrimination against Internet commerce."[239] In *City of Chicago v. StubHub!, Inc.*,[240] the Seventh Circuit also ruled that StubHub was not required to collect and remit a city amusement tax.

§ 5.7   STATE CONSUMER PROTECTION

The states play a critical role in protecting consumers in cyberspace. The mission of a state attorney general is to protect consumers injured by unfair and deceptive practices. State attorneys general are the chief legal officers of the state and the chief constables for cyberspace state enforcement. Each state has a "Little FTC" statute punishing defendants for unfair or deceptive trade practices. A state deceptive trade practice act has three elements: (1) the business is engaged in trade or commerce; (2) the business has committed unfair or deceptive acts or practices in the trade or commerce in

---

[231] Reuters, Overstock.com Sues N.Y. Over Internet Tax (May 30, 2008).

[232] Annette Nellen, Overview of Internet Taxation Issues (BNA, 2012).

[233] Id.

[234] 2009 WL 3864822 (W.D. Tex., Oct. 30, 2009).

[235] Id.

[236] Id.

[237] Id.

[238] Id.

[239] Id.

[240] 624 F.3d 363 (7th Cir. 2010).

which they are engaged; and (3) the consumer proves a financial injury and is seeking damages. The phrase "unfair or deceptive practices" applies to a wide range of practices in online sales or services. The Washington State Attorney General, for example, filed a claim against Movieland.com for its abusive use of pop-up ads.

In *Movieland*, the consumer was given a trial period of the service then was bombarded with pop-up ads appearing hourly subjecting the consumer to a forty second payment demand that would not close. The consumer could not delete these persistent messages without paying a fee ranging from $19.95 to $100.00. The court ruled Movieland.com's scheme was an unfair and deceptive method of generating online revenue. Washington is one of the few states to have an anti-spyware amendment to its computer crime statute. Washington imposes fines up to $2 million for deceptive practices such as planting software appearing whenever a consumer launches an Internet browser. This anti-spyware statute also makes it unlawful to use deceptive means to harvest personally identifiable information or to record keystrokes made by a consumer and transfer information to a business.

In *State of Texas v. Ernst*,[241] Auto Depot maintained a website and advertised on Craigslist and in the local newspaper, promising used vehicles at low prices with a full one-year warranty. In *Ernst*, the consumer sought a car with a full warranty because she needed reliable transportation for her job.[242] Auto Depot "sold her a 2003 Honda Civic, claiming that it needed minor repairs but would be a better car." The salesman indicated that the vehicle would be "better than new,' and would have the full warranty."[243] "When the consumer demanded to see the Honda Civic automobile she had purchased, she allegedly learned Auto Depot was actually removing parts from the car instead of repairing it."[244] The consumer demanded her money back, but allegedly was told by the online seller that he did not have her money to refund as he had used it to pay the mortgage.[245]

In December 2011, Auto Depot reportedly notified a consumer that her Lexus was ready, but when she went to pick up the car, she allegedly found that it had transmission and brake problems so she returned the vehicle.[246] When she "stopped by to check on the car, she reportedly learned that it had been provided to another consumer as a loaner and that it was listed on Craigslist as available for purchase from Auto Depot."[247] The state of Texas "contended that Auto Depot had failed to provide titles to the vehicles it sold in a timely fashion, sold vehicles that had problem titles, such as salvage titles, without disclosing the problems to consumers, and ran a used car lot without a proper license."[248] Texas charged the dealer with engaging in false, misleading and deceptive actions and practices in violation of the Texas Deceptive Trade Practices Act ("DTPA").[249] The dealer and the State of Texas entered a settlement, which required the dealer "to pay restitution to various consumers in the

---

[241] 2013 WL 1790693 (Tex.Dist. Feb. 22, 2013).

[242] Id.

[243] Id.

[244] Id.

[245] Id.

[246] Id.

[247] Id.

[248] Id.

[249] Id.

total amount of $57,678, $200,000 to the state for civil penalties and $55,000 to the plaintiff for attorney fees."[250]

§ 5.8   COMMERCE CLAUSE CHALLENGES

In *Gibbons v. Ogden*,[251] the U.S. Supreme Court first recognized the power of Congress to regulate Interstate Commerce. New York state law gave two individuals, Robert Livingston and Robert Fulton, the exclusive right to operate steamboats on waters within New York State for a thirty-year period beginning in 1808. A court issued an injunction against Gibbons from navigating steamboats in the waters between New York and New Jersey because it violated the exclusive license New York granted to Livingston and Fulton. Gibbons contended that the New York license violated an act of Congress, which regulated trade and fisheries. The Court held that "commerce" included more than just the "traffic" of goods from one state to another; it also included the regulation of commercial "intercourse," such as navigation on the country's waterways.[252] The Court ruled that the New York law prohibiting vessels from navigating the waters of the state was repugnant to the Constitution and void.

The Court ruling meant that Gibbons had the right to operate his steamboat on the Hudson River between New York and New Jersey. *Gibbons* stands for the proposition that Congress could preempt state law and for its articulation of the Commerce Clause.[253] The positive Commerce Clause in Article 1 of the U.S. Constitution gives Congress powers to regulate commerce. The Commerce Clause provides authority to Congress to regulate commerce among the several states but it also carries negative or implicit consequences for states' authority to regulate interstate commerce, a negative Commerce Clause.[254] Under the "dormant" or negative Commerce Clause, a state may not enact legislation that has the practical effect of regulating commerce that takes place wholly outside of its borders, whether or not the commerce has effects within the state, and whether or not the statute's extraterritorial scope was intended by the lawmakers. The Washington State Supreme Court articulates the test for whether a statute violates the dormant commerce clause:

> If Congress has not granted the states authority to regulate a matter affecting interstate commerce, the dormant Commerce Clause applies, and court must determine (1) whether the language of challenged state statute openly discriminates against out-of-state entities in favor of in-state ones or (2) whether the direct effect of the statute evenhandedly applies to in-state and out-of-state entities. U.S. Const. art. 1, § 8, cl. 3.[255]

---

[250] Id.

[251] 22 U.S. 1 (1824).

[252] Id. at 189–190.

[253] Id. at 9.

[254] "The dormant Commerce Clause sets two complementary boundaries for states' regulatory powers over commerce: (1) on one hand, states cannot interfere with Congress's constitutional authority over interstate commerce by enacting laws that seriously impede interstate commerce, even when Congress has not acted, but (2) on the other hand, states retain authority under their general police powers to regulate matters of legitimate local concern, even though interstate commerce may be affected." IMS Health Inc. v. Mills, 616 F.3d 7, 28 (1st Cir. 2010).

[255] Rouso v. State, 170 Wash.2d 70, 239 P.3d 1084, 1087 (2010) (ruling that state regulation on Internet gambling did not violate the U.S. Commerce Clause).

(A) American Libraries Assoc. v. Pataki

The Internet raises difficult issues in determining the power of a state to prescribe conduct outside its borders. States prohibiting the distribution of indecent materials to minors raise Commerce Clause concerns. In these cases, the court must determine whether the burden on interstate commerce outweighs the benefit of protecting minors. The Commerce Clause contains an express authorization for Congress to "regulate Commerce with foreign Nations, and among the several States." The U.S. Supreme Court has long recognized the so-called Dormant Commerce Clause, which prevents states from regulating or taxing to discriminate, or materially burden interstate commerce. The Dormant Commerce Clause thus "limits the power of the States to erect barriers against interstate trade."[256] The idea behind this "negative" Dormant Commerce Clause is to prevent local authorities from burdening Interstate commerce activities.

The court in *American Libraries Association v. Pataki*,[257] traced the Dormant Commerce Clause back to Justice Johnson's 1824 concurring opinion in *Gibbons v. Ogden*,[258] where the issue was whether New York could restrain the navigation of out-of-state steamboats in its waters. The *Pataki* court noted how the Commerce Clause prohibits state regulations that discriminate or unduly burden interstate commerce, even if they are facially nondiscriminatory. A "dormant" or "negative" aspect of this grant of power is a state's power to impinge on interstate commerce may be limited in some situations.[259] In *Pataki*,[260] plaintiff libraries challenged the constitutionality of a New York state statute attempting to keep people from transmitting material harmful to minors via the Internet. The librarians filed a lawsuit seeking declaratory and injunctive relief and contended that the state statute violated the First Amendment and burdened interstate commerce, violating the Commerce Clause. The court granted the preliminary injunction, holding that the plaintiffs showed a likelihood of success on the merits because the New York State represented an unconstitutional intrusion into interstate commerce.

The court compared the Internet to highways and railroads in reaching its decision. Courts evaluate state regulations under a balancing test, requiring them to uphold a state regulation serving an important public interest—unless the benefits of the regulation outweigh the burden placed on interstate commerce. In this case, the burden on interstate commerce exceeded the benefits of preventing indecent materials from being available to minors. The *Pataki* case stood for the proposition that almost any attempt by the states to regulate cyberspace conduct was challengeable under the dormant commerce clause.

(B) Internet Sales of Alcohol

In *Healy v. Beer Institute Inc.*,[261] the U.S. Supreme Court ruled the Commerce Clause prohibits state regulations attempting to govern conduct "that takes place wholly

---

[256] Dennis v. Higgins, 498 U.S. 439, 446 (1991).

[257] Id.

[258] 22 U.S. 1 (1824).

[259] Quill Corp. v. North Dakota, 504 U.S. 298 (1992).

[260] 969 F. Supp. 160 (S.D. N.Y. 1997).

[261] 491 U.S. 324, 336 (1989).

outside of the State's borders, whether or not the commerce has effects within the State."[262] In *Beer Institute*, Connecticut enacted a statute requiring out-of-state beer shippers to affirm that their posted prices for products sold to Connecticut wholesalers are no higher than the prices at which those products sell in bordering New England states. A brewers trade association, as well as major producers and importers of beer, challenged the statute under the Commerce Clause.

A brewers trade association, as well as major producers and importers of beer, challenged the statute under the Commerce Clause.

The court upheld the Connecticut pricing statute, but the Second Circuit reversed; holding the statute violated the Commerce Clause by controlling the prices at which out-of-state shippers could sell beer in other States. The Dormant Commerce Clause is a legal doctrine that restricts the states' power to enact anticompetitive laws that discriminate against sellers in other states. The U.S. Supreme Court ruled the pricing statute had the practical effect of controlling commercial activity wholly outside Connecticut. The Court also found the statute violated the Commerce Clause on its face and discriminated against interstate commerce. It applied only to brewers and shippers engaged in interstate commerce—not solely Connecticut sales—because it was not justified by a valid purpose unrelated to economic protection.

In the 2005 case of *Granholm v. Heald*,[263] the U.S. Supreme Court struck down Michigan and New York statutes permitting in-state wineries, but not out-of-state wineries, from shipping alcohol to customers on the grounds the statutes violated the Dormant Commerce Clause. Michigan and New York argued their statutes were valid exercises of state power under the Twenty First Amendment that ended federal Prohibition but left it to the states to regulate alcohol importation. The U.S. Supreme Court accepted certiorari because of a split between the Sixth and Second Circuits as to whether the respective statutes violated the Commerce Clause. The U.S. Supreme Court held both states' laws violated the Dormant Commerce Clause because the regulations favored in-state wineries at the expense of out-of-state wineries and that the Twenty First Amendment did not authorize this discrimination. The *Granholm* Court reasoned that the ability to sell wine over the Internet helped make direct shipments an attractive sales channel for the small wineries. The Court ruled the states did not establish a legitimate purpose to justify their discriminatory treatment.

(C) State Anti–Spam Statutes

States can use their unfair trade practices acts, often called "Little FTC Acts, against spam so long as it is not preempted by CAN-SPAM. Many U.S. states enacted anti-spam statutes prior to CAN-SPAM. In addition, litigants deployed state tort causes of action such as the trespass to chattels to spam e-mail. Chapter 6 examines the use of personal property torts to spam in detail. In *Washington v. Heckel*,[264] the Washington Supreme Court held that Washington's Anti–Spam Act did not violate the Commerce Clause—reversing a lower court's decision that the statute was unconstitutional. The CAN-SPAM preempts state anti-spam provisions that conflict with

---

[262] Id.

[263] 544 U.S. 460 (2005).

[264] 143 Wn.2d 824, 24 P. 3d 404, 409–411 (Wash. 2001).

the federal law.[265]   In the aftermath of CAN-SPAM, the states may prohibit deception and false information in commercial e-mail.[266]

(D) State Regulation for Online Gambling

The Washington Supreme Court ruled that a Washington statute regulating online gambling did not violate the U.S. Commerce Clause. In *State v. Rousso,* an amateur poker enthusiast, who enjoyed playing poker in virtual gaming rooms, filed for a declaratory judgment action, seeking a declaration that a Washington statute, which criminalizes the knowing transmission and reception of gambling information by various means, including use of the Internet was unconstitutional. "The Unlawful Internet Gambling Enforcement Act of 2006 ("UIGEA") "prohibited any person engaged in the business of gambling from accepting money in any form for participation in *unlawful* Internet gambling." The court held that the statute does not "have a direct discriminatory effect on interstate commerce.

The statute prohibits Internet gambling evenhandedly, regardless of whether the company running the website is located in or outside the state of Washington."[267] The court found that the UIGEA did not have different effects on "in-state and out-of-state entities engaging or that would engage in Internet gambling."[268] The court also found the state's interest in enacting UIGEA to be significant:

> Internet gambling introduces new ways to exacerbate these same threats to health, welfare, safety, and morals. Gambling addicts and underage gamblers have greater accessibility to on-line gambling—able to gamble from their homes immediately and on demand, at any time, on any day, unhindered by in-person regulatory measures. Concerns over ties to organized crime and money laundering are exacerbated where on-line gambling operations are not physically present in state to be inspected for regulatory compliance. Washington has a legitimate and substantial state interest in addressing the effects of Internet gambling.[269]

The court also rejected challenges on diverse constitutional grounds including arguments that the UIGEA violated the First Amendment, was void for vagueness, and that it excessively burdened interstate commerce.

§ 5.9   INTERNET PAYMENTS SYSTEMS

Online banking services, now well-established, permit customers to pay bills, make payments, manage accounts, transfer funds, and even view images of cleared checks. Increasingly, Americans are doing much of their banking online, rarely venturing into a brick-and-mortar bank. In addition to traditional banking systems, the Internet has created Internet based alternative payment systems such as PayPal (owned by eBay).

---

[265] CAN–SPAM contains an express preemption provision superseding "any statute, regulation, or rule of a State . . . that expressly regulates the use of electronic mail to send commercial messages, except to the extent that any such statute, regulation, or rule prohibits falsity or deception in any portion of a commercial electronic mail message or information attached thereto." 15 U.S.C. § 7707(b)(1).

[266] In addition, Congress stated that the preemption clause should not be construed to preempt the applicability of state laws that are not specific to email or "[s]tate laws to the extent that those laws relate to acts of fraud or computer crime." *See* 15 U.S.C. § 7707(b)(2).

[267] Id.

[268] Id.

[269] Id. at 1090.

Federal law also covers credit cards, the most important Internet payments system. In 1968, Congress enacted The Truth-in-Lending Act ("TILA") as Title 1 of the Consumer Credit Protection Act.[270]

The federal Truth in Lending Act establishes a $50 maximum liability for the unauthorized use of credit cards. Regulation Z comprises the Federal Reserve Bank's regulations for TILA. Regulation Z is primarily a disclose statute where card issuers must follow protocol in disclosing the terms and conditions to cardholders. Congress enacted the Fair Credit Billing Act ("FCBA"),[271] to prescribe an orderly procedure for identifying and resolving disputes between a cardholder and a card issuer as to the amount due at any given time. Additionally, in 2009, President Obama signed the Credit Card Accountability, Responsibility, and Disclosure Act.

As noted in Chapter 4, consumers use credit cards in the vast majority of consumer payments on the Internet. PayPal members can transfer money to other people or businesses for online auctions or purchases. In September of 2006, twenty-eight state attorneys general entered into a settlement with PayPal arising out of a complaint alleging that PayPal did not disclose funding sources for each purchase. The state attorneys general charged PayPal with withdrawing money from consumers' bank accounts even if users submitted their credit card information when signing up. A payee needs an e-mail account and a checking account, which enables PayPal to disburse funds.[272]

The consumers registered complaints with their state attorney general after receiving their monthly bank statements and learning that money had been withdrawn from their bank accounts .This financial transaction conflicted with their intention to use a credit card as opposed to withdrawing money from their bank account. Other consumers complained PayPal placed a hold on funds held in the user's PayPal account. Still others were confused about how to use PayPal's in-house dispute resolution programs and chargeback features. The settlement requires PayPal to provide clear and conspicuous disclosures about the important terms and conditions before a consumer becomes a PayPal member. PayPal employs the "technology of the Website to facilitate the use of conventional payment networks."[273] In January 2012, the Consumer Financial Protection Bureau, the new federal consumer protection agency, "finalized new rules under Regulation E, mandated by the Dodd–Frank Act, which will require PayPal, starting in October 2013, to provide additional disclosures, error resolution rights and cancellation rights to U.S. consumers who make international remittance payments.[274]

In 2010, Twitter's co-founder developed Square a mobile payment ("m-payment") system that "allows merchants to directly accept credit card payments through a small device attached to a cell phone."[275] For m-payment systems, three basic questions comprise the policy debate:

---

[270] 15 U.S.C. §§ 1601 et seq.

[271] 15 U.S.C. §§ 1666–1666j.

[272] LYNN LOPUCKI, ET AL., COMMERCIAL TRANSACTIONS: A SYSTEMS APPROACH 340 (2012).

[273] Id.

[274] EBay, SEC 10–Q Filing (July 19, 213).

[275] Colin Hector & Liz Eraker Public Citizen, Highlights from Mobile Payments: Global Markets, Empowered Consumers and New Rules, PUBLIC CITIZEN (Dec. 1, 2010).

First, to what extent will mobile payment systems develop as an independent payment system? Second, what are the consumer expectations concerning the security and integrity of m-payment systems? Finally, what regulatory models appropriately reflect these expectations while ensuring the continued development of this burgeoning technology?[276]

Under U.C.C. Article 4A, a bank receiving a payment order ordinarily bears the risk of loss of any unauthorized funds transfer. Nevertheless, banks often use indemnity agreements to shift the loss back to the customer. In *Patco*, the e-bank's predecessor in interest authorized six apparently fraudulent withdrawals from plaintiff's account after the perpetrators correctly supplied plaintiff's security answers. These high-risk transfers were approved even though the bank's security system flagged the transactions as unusually high-risk. The court stated:

> On May 11, 12, and 13, unknown third parties initiated further withdrawals from Patco's account in the amounts of $99,068, $91,959, and $113,647, respectively. Like the prior fraudulent transactions, these transactions were uncharacteristic in that they sent money to numerous individuals to whom Patco had never before sent funds, were for greater amounts than Patco's ordinary third-party transactions, were sent from computers that were not recognized by Ocean Bank's system, and originated from IP addresses that were not recognized as valid IP addresses of Patco. As a result of these unusual characteristics, the transactions continued to generate higher than normal risk scores. The May 11 transaction generated a risk score of 720, the May 12 transaction triggered a risk score of 563, and the transaction on May 13 generated a risk score of 785. The Bank did not manually review any of these transactions to determine their legitimacy or notify Patco.[277]

The plaintiff's in *Patco* contended that the financial institution's computer security did not comply with the standard of commercial reasonableness under U.C.C. Article 4A, which governs wire transfers. The plaintiffs contended that the predecessor bank substantially increased the risk of fraud by asking for security answers for every transaction for customers with frequent, regular, high dollar transfers. Then, when it had warning that such fraud was likely occurring, it neither monitored nor provided notice to customers before allowing the transaction to be completed. The First Circuit agreed and reversed the lower court finding that the security system was negligently designed and refused to enforce the indemnification agreement that would shift the loss back to the commercial customer. In August of 2012, a number of national stores including Wal-Mart, Target, 7-Eleven, and Sunoco joined forces "to develop a mobile payment network that would battle similar services from Google Inc. and other companies."[278] The "digital wallet" will enable shoppers to use their phones much like credit or debit cards.[279] Businesses are increasing the use of eBanking for their commercial checking accounts. Banks will allow eBanking commercial customers to make electronic funds transfers through them via the Automated Clearing House ("ACH") network, a system used by banks to transfer funds electronically between accounts. Article 4A of the Uniform Commercial Code governs wholesale wire transfers

---

[276] Id.

[277] Id. at 19.

[278] Robin Sidel, Payments Network Takes on Google, Retailers Including Wal-Mart, Target and 7-Eleven to Unveil Mobile System Employing Smartphones, WALL ST. J. (Aug. 15, 2012) at C1.

[279] Id.

and commercial ACH transfers, generally between businesses and their financial institutions. In *Patco Constr. Co. v. People's United Bank*,[280] the First Circuit reversed the lower court ruling that a Maine company had a cause of action against its bank under U.C.C. Article 4A, which governs electronic funds transfers.

§ 5.10 PREDISPUTE MANDATORY ARBITRATION IN CONSUMER ACTIONS

U.S. federal courts are inclined to enforce predispute mandatory arbitration clauses in consumer cases. Courts compel arbitration under the Federal Arbitration Act ("FAA") if two issues are resolved: "(i) whether a valid agreement or obligation to arbitrate exists, and (ii) whether one party to the agreement has failed, neglected, or refused to arbitrate."[281] Arbitration is a matter of contract law so the license agreement must indicate that the parties have agreed to arbitrate disputes. Before compelling an unwilling party to arbitrate, a court must engage in a limited review to determine whether the dispute is arbitrable; meaning that a valid agreement to arbitrate exists between the parties and that the specific dispute falls within the substantive scope of that agreement. In the United States, predispute mandatory arbitration agreements are enforceable in business-to-consumer transactions. In Europe and much of the rest of the world, predispute mandatory arbitration agreement is enforceable in business-to-business transactions.

U.S. courts enforce mass-market license agreements so long as the consumer has notice of the existence of the agreement; an opportunity to read the agreement; and the consumer performs some act that manifests assent. Courts will not enforce agreements where a licensor makes little effort to draw attention to pro-licensor terms such as "arbitration." In *Bragg v. Linden Research, Inc.*, the developer of "Second Life," an online virtual world developed by the defendant, confiscated the plaintiff's virtual property and deported him from their virtual world.[282] The plaintiff filed suit and Linden Research filed a motion to compel arbitration based on their arbitration agreement. The court found the arbitration agreement to be procedurally and substantively unconscionable because it was buried in a take-it-or-leave-it terms of service agreement.

The *Bragg* court found lack of mutuality and that Second Life failed to give Bragg sufficient information on the costs and rules of arbitration according to rules of the International Chamber of Commerce.[283] The court reasoned that Second Life could have explained the arbitration procedure in either the terms of use or a hyperlink to another page. In *Scarcella v. America Online*,[284] a New York trial court refused to enforce a forum selection clause in a clickwrap license because it violated a New York state policy favoring the simplified proceedings of small claims court for low-value disputes. These cases are the exception, as most U.S. courts will enforce choice of forum clauses that divest consumers of their right to litigate in their home court.

By incorporating predispute mandatory arbitration clauses into their terms of service, a large and growing number of Internet companies are divesting users of their

---

[280] 684 F.3d 197 (1st Cir. 2012).

[281] PaineWebber, Inc. v. Bybyk, 81 F.3d 1193, 1198 (2d Cir. 1996).

[282] 487 F. Supp. 2d 593, 593 n. 4 (E.D. Pa. 2007).

[283] Id. at 606.

[284] 798 N.Y.S.2d 348 (2004).

rights to civil recourse against providers who violate their privacy, commit torts, or infringe their intellectual property rights.[285] Social Network Site ("SNS") users around the world are required to agree to predispute mandatory arbitration as a condition of joining social networking communities.[286] SNS users that enter into clickwrap or browsewrap terms of service agreements waive their right to a jury trial, discovery, and appeal, without reasonable notice that they are waiving these important rights. In the first empirical study of the use of arbitration in social network terms of use,[287] the researchers found "mandatory arbitration to be the exclusive dispute resolution mechanism for forty-six percent (n=17) of the terms of service and privacy policies that contained arbitral clauses."[288] "Nearly one in four SNSs in the sample incorporated some form of arbitration clause either in the terms of service agreement or in the privacy policy (37 of 157 or 24%).[289]

Sixty-two percent of the social media sites' terms of service agreements that specified arbitration incorporated some form of mandatory arbitration. (n=23).[290] Four arbitral clauses permitted either party to elect arbitration, and ten others allowed the election if the claim is below a threshold amount. These clauses may take the form of

---

[285] Civil wrongs committed on social media sites are difficult to litigate because of problems such as the anonymous poster, the distant forum, the problem of finding representation, and arbitral clauses. Given that there are billions of social media sites, lawsuits are rare despite the huge potential for intentional torts, infringement, and employment-related disputes. Cf. K.D. v. Facebook, Inc., No. 3:11–cv-461 (S.D. Ill, March 8, 2012) (enforcing the forum-selection clause in Facebook's Terms of Service); Claridge v. RockYou Inc., 785 F. Supp. 2d 855 (N.D. Cal. 2011) (settling class action for failure of the site to secure user's privacy and security); Cohen v. Facebook, Inc., 798 F. Supp. 2d 1090 (N.D. Cal. 2011) (holding that Facebook users did not consent to the SNS using their names and likenesses to promote service and ruling that the plaintiffs sufficiently stated a claim for appropriation of their names and likenesses for an advantage, but ruling that the plaintiffs were unable to prove damages); In re Facebook Privacy Litigation, 791 F. Supp. 2d 705 (N.D. Cal. 2011) (dismissing class action by Facebook users based upon the Electronic Communications Privacy Act as well as California state law); Hubbard v. MySpace, Inc., 788 F. Supp. 2d 319 (S.D.N.Y. 2011) (filing class action against MySpace for alleged violation of the Stored Communications Act); In re Google Buzz Privacy Litigation, 2011 WL 7460099 (N.D. Cal. 2001) (approving $8 million settlement in class action brought by Gmail users arising out of Google's disclosure of personally identifiable information without authorization through the defunct site, Google Buzz).

[286] The researchers studied a sample 157 social networking sites broadly representative of the universe of social media in 2012. "Generalist sites, such as Facebook and MyLife, target connections between friends, family, and acquaintances. In contrast, niche sites include those designed for educational, career, or professional development such as LinkedIn. Sites that enable meetings in major cities for shared interest groups are included in the sample. Social media websites targeting specific age, racial, cultural, or status-oriented groups are also part of the SNS sample. Sites appealing to rating, dating, mating, and sexual fetishism are included in the sample, as are sites dedicated to entertainment (anime, video sharing, book reviews, and movies) and highlighting talent." Michael L. Rustad, Richard Buckingham, Diane D'Angelo, & Kate Durlacher, An Empirical Study of Predispute Mandatory Arbitration Clauses in Social Media Terms of Service, 34 U. ARK. LITTLE ROCK L. REV. 643, 649 (2012).

[287] "To obtain a more comprehensive understanding of the incidence of mandatory arbitration clauses in the rapidly evolving arena of SNSs, we selected a sample of 157 United States and international SNSs based in large part on Wikipedia's list of Social Networking Sites. Each site from the Wikipedia list was accessed and reviewed by the research team to determine whether it was predominantly an SNS at the time of coding. In addition to the Wikipedia master list, we included two of the most popular social media sites, YouTube and Second Life, and popular online dating sites Match.com and eHarmony. The websites chosen in the sample all provide users with a place to form networks and connect with persons with shared interests or other affinities. Social networking enables consumers to reach out and form connections with friends, families, colleagues, and persons sharing interests or attributes. While there is no exhaustive listing of the social media universe, it is likely this sample is broadly representative of the universe of social networking sites in late 2011 and early 2012." Id at 647–48.

[288] Id.

[289] Id. at 653.

[290] Id. at 654.

an elected remedy, but if the SNS "elects" arbitration, they are functionally equivalent to pure mandatory arbitration clauses.[291] The chart below demonstrates the arbitral providers selected by the social media sites as specified in their terms of use or service.

American Arbitration Association (AAA)	16	43.2%
U.S. Arbitral Provider TBD	12	32.4%
Judicial Arbitration and Mediation Services (JAMS)	3	8.1%
Foreign Provider TBD	3	8.1%
United States Arbitration & Mediation (USA&M)	1	2.7%
Arbitration and Mediation Institute of Canada (AMIC)	1	2.7%
Hong Kong International Arbitration Center (HKIAC) or Singapore International Arbitration Center (SIAC)	1	2.7
Total	37	100%

The most popular arbitral forum was the American Arbitration Association. Two-thirds of the providers provided for arbitration in the U.S., but in one-third of the terms of use agreements, the arbitral provider was not chosen. In other words, the provider had the discretion to select the forum and the provider. Five providers required users to submit to foreign arbitral providers. For example, the sexual fetishism site FetLife requires consumers to settle their claims by binding arbitration in accordance with the rules of the Arbitration and Mediation Institute of Canada (AMIC)."[292] "Gays.com's terms of service establishes the site of arbitration in Hong Kong, and requires arbitrators to apply Hong Kong law."[293] Mouthshut, a site located in India, has a terms of service agreement stating:

> This Agreement is governed in all respects by the laws of Republic of India as such laws are applied to agreements entered into and to be performed entirely within India between Indian residents. Any controversy or claim arising out of or relating to this Agreement or the MouthShut.com site shall be settled by binding arbitration in accordance with the Indian Arbitration Act 1996. Any such controversy or claim shall be arbitrated on an individual basis, and shall not be consolidated in any arbitration with any claim or controversy of any other party. The arbitration shall be conducted in Mumbai, India and judgment on the arbitration award may be entered into any court having jurisdiction thereof.[294]

Three of the foreign SNSs (eight percent of the sample) did not make known the arbitral provider. One foreign SNS specified a Hong Kong or Peoples Republic of China-based provider depending upon the geographical origin of the user."[295] The

---

[291] Id.

[292] Id. at 645.

[293] Id.

[294] Terms of Service, Mouthshut.com, http://www.mouthshut.com/help/tos.php (last visited May 25, 2013).

[295] Id. at 655.

predispute mandatory arbitration clauses employed by the most popular social media sites did not disclose the cost or information such as a link to the rules for consumer arbitration.

The researchers completed a content analysis of the agreements finding "the word count for arbitration clauses in the sample ranges from 50 to 2565 words. The average (mean) arbitration clause is 318 words in length whereas the median is 204 words. Forty-six percent of the arbitral clauses are under 200 words and did not explain rights in clear terms."[296] U.S. courts recognize a consumer's duty to read, though empirical research confirms that consumers rarely read, let alone, study terms of use.[297] Nevertheless, even if a consumer studied these agreements, they would not find them illuminating. The researchers' content analysis found that the social media terms of service agreements were inconspicuous:

> The research team completed a content analysis of each terms of service agreement to determine whether the arbitration clause was presented in a conspicuous manner according to the standards of the Uniform Commercial Code ("UCC"), which is the chief statute governing commercial transaction in the United States. An arbitration clause was conspicuous if it met any of the U.C.C. guideposts, such as contrasting type, font, color, or language that called attention to the clause. Our content analysis of the placement of arbitral clauses revealed that only six of the thirty-seven clauses (sixteen percent) met any of the minimal U.C.C. standards for conspicuousness. The preponderance of social media websites was inconspicuous because they did not attempt to draw the social media user's attention to the provisions of arbitration clauses. . . . Users of SNSs who submit to arbitration waive their right to discovery entirely or may have limited discovery at the sole discretion of the arbitrator. Only one of the thirty-seven arbitration clauses (three percent) mentioned that by agreeing to arbitration users waived their right to unconditional discovery.[298]

There is a growing tendency of social media providers to couple anti-class action (class action waiver) clauses with predispute mandatory arbitration clauses. Ten social media providers required users to waive the right to join class actions entirely, while the Tagged.com site reserved its right to consolidate cases:

> At any time and in its sole discretion Tagged may direct the AAA to consolidate any and all pending individual arbitration claims that (i) arise in substantial part from the same and/or related transactions, events and/or occurrences, and (ii) involve a common question of law and/or fact which, if resolved in multiple individual and non-consolidated arbitration proceedings, may result in conflicting and/or inconsistent results. In said event, you hereby consent to consolidated arbitration, in lieu of individual arbitration, of all claims you may have against tagged and the AAA rules set forth herein shall govern all parties.[299] The chart

---

[296] Id. at 656.

[297] "[C]onsumers rarely read or understand" predispute mandatory arbitration agreements. Amy J. Schmitz, Consideration of "Contracting Culture" in Enforcing Arbitration Provisions, 81 St. John's L. Rev. 123, 160 (2007).

[298] Rustad, et. al, Empirical Study of Predispute Mandatory Arbitration in Social Media Sites, Id. at 657–58.

[299] Id. at 660.

below is a cross-tabulation of class actions in terms of service agreements requiring predispute mandatory arbitration.

Class Actions Prohibited	N=10	27%
Class Actions Not Prohibited	N=26	70.3%
Class Actions Prohibited for Users but Not SNS	N=1	2.7%
Total[300]	N=37	100%

The predispute mandatory arbitration agreement was by far the most popular choice for alternative dispute resolution for social media sites in the sample. Sixty-two percent of the terms of service agreements with arbitral clauses incorporated some form of mandatory agreement clause (n=23).[301] None of the providers gave social media users the option to pursue arbitration, while retaining their jury trial right. Mandatory arbitration requires consumers to agree in advance to submit disputes to a private arbitral provider and divests consumers of important rights that would otherwise be available, such as their Seventh Amendment right to a jury trial, discovery, and appeal."[302] In addition, arbitrators conducting consumer arbitrations have perverse incentives to favor repeat corporate player clients over individual users. Because it is the SNS selecting the arbitrator, a victory in favor of a consumer favors pro-SNS arbitrators. A federal bankruptcy court described the abuses of mandatory arbitration in consumer transactions as a "putrid odor which is overwhelming to the body politic."[303] In the U.S., the courts are disposed to enforce predispute mandatory arbitration clauses.[304] The AAA's Consumer Due Process Protocol requires social media providers to "undertake reasonable measures to provide Consumers with full and accurate information regarding Consumer ADR Programs."[305]

To comply with the AAA consumer standard, a social media site employing consumer arbitration must give the consumer "(1) clear and adequate notice regarding

---

[300] Id.

[301] Id. at 663.

[302] Id.

[303] Id. (quoting In re Knepp, 229 B.R. 821, 827 (Bankr. N.D. Ala. 1999).

[304] Compulsory arbitration clauses in mass-market license agreements, computer contracts, or terms of service have been upheld by numerous United States courts. See e.g., Chandler v. AT&T Wireless Servs., Inc., 358 F. Supp. 2d 701, 706 (S.D. Ill. 2005) (ordering arbitration in case where predispute arbitration clause was added to the consumer's contract for wireless services); Lieschke v. RealNetworks, Inc., No. 99C7274, 2000 U.S. Dist. LEXIS 1683 (N.D. Ill. Feb. 10, 2000) (enforcing arbitration clauses in terms of service agreement); Westendorff v. Gateway 2000, Inc., 2000 WL 307369 (Del. Ch. March 16, 2000), aff'd, 763 A.2d 92 (Del. 2000); Caspi v. Microsoft Network, L.L.C., 732 A.2d 528, 530, 532–33 (N.J. 1999) (validating forum selection clause where subscribers to online software were required to review license terms in scrollable window and to click "I Agree" or "I Don't Agree"); Brower v. Gateway 2000, Inc., 676 N.Y.S.2d 569 (1998) (ordering enforcement of arbitration clause in Gateway's standard computer contract); Barnett v. Network Solutions, Inc., 38 S.W.3d 200, 203–04 (Tex. App. 2001) (upholding forum selection clause in online contract for registering Internet domain names that required users to scroll through terms before accepting or rejecting them); cf. Specht v. Netscape Commun. Corp., 306 F.3d 17 (2d Cir. 2002) (holding that user's downloading software where the terms were submerged did not manifest assent to arbitration clause); Klocek v. Gateway, Inc., 104 F. Supp. 2d 1332 (D. Kan. 2000) (declining to enforce arbitration clause on grounds that user did not agree to standard terms mailed inside computer box).

[305] Consumer Due Process Protocol: Statement of Principles of the National Consumer Disputes Advisory Committee, American Arbitration Association, http://www.adr.org/aaa/ShowPDF?doc=ADRSTG_005014 (last visited May 28, 2013).

the ADR provisions, including a statement indicating whether participation in the ADR Program is mandatory or optional, and (2) reasonable means by which Consumers may obtain additional information regarding the ADR Program."[306] Nearly every social media arbitral clause specifies whether the arbitration is compulsory or voluntary, though several of the agreements in our sample were indefinite. With few exceptions, however, the social media sites do not provide consumers with a means of obtaining additional information regarding the ADR provider, fees, or the rights affected by the arbitral clause.[307]   The above-referenced study of social media terms of service agreements concluded that most agreements violated the AAA protocol for consumer arbitration agreements:

> The SNS arbitration clauses in our sample are not only brief but also often indeterminate, making it all but impossible for the ordinary consumer to understand. The SNS arbitral clauses fall short of the AAA's protocol standard because they fail to provide a cogent explanation of arbitration and its consequences. Forty-six percent of the arbitral clauses are 181 words or less. The vast majority of terms of service provide no elucidation of the consequence of arbitration except self-serving declarations that the proceedings were more efficient and cost-effective than court resolutions. The typical social media site neither attempts to explain what arbitration involves nor does it provide links to access additional information. Only five out of thirty-seven providers surveyed attempted to explain any aspect of arbitration. The arbitral provider is named in nearly two-thirds of the cases (sixty-two percent, n=23). In fourteen cases, the social media arbitral clause did not specify or even make mention of the provider. In less than one in three cases, social media sites centered in the United States did not disclose the arbitral provider. Three of the foreign SNSs (eight percent of the sample) did not identify the provider. One foreign SNS specified a Hong Kong or Chinese provider, depending upon the geographical area of the user.[308]

Arbitration agreements drafted by providers did not minimally give consumers notice of the ground rules for conducting arbitration. "Five social media providers chose the AAA consumer rules to govern arbitration proceedings. Twelve of the social media site agreements mentioned the AAA, but did not explain whether consumer or commercial rules were applicable. A few social networking sites required that mandatory arbitration be settled according to commercial arbitration rules.

"Focus, a photo-sharing site, required arbitrations to be conducted in San Francisco under the AAA's commercial law rules."[309] At present, users of SNSs do not have minimum access to the information they need to make a rational decision about whether to agree to arbitration, which violates the AAA's consumer due process principle of full and adequate disclosures. Predispute mandatory arbitration clauses as well as other U.S. style terms of service are not likely enforceable throughout the

---

[306] Id.

[307] Id.

[308] Michael L. Rustad, Richard Buckingham, Diane D'Angelo, & Kate Durlacher, An Empirical Study of Predispute Mandatory Arbitration Clauses in Social Media Terms of Service, 34 U. ARK. LITTLE ROCK L. REV. 643, 665–66 (2012).

[309] Id.

twenty-eight countries of the European Union as the next section demonstrates.[310] Social media providers such as Facebook with more than a billion users will need to comply with consumer law in radically different legal cultures.

§ 5.11 GLOBAL CONSUMER ISSUES

The Internet is truly a global consumer market so ideally protection should extend across national borders. Much of the cross-border Internet is devoid of cross-border consumer protection. Social media sites, for example, have self-serving terms of service that essentially strip a consumer of any meaningful remedy for the invasion of privacy. Facebook is approaching a billion subscribers and is currently available in seventy languages. To date, there is no movement toward affording consumers minimum adequate remedies when they are victimized on the Internet. However, consumer protection in the European Union affords a possible model for global consumer protection as the European Commission has enacted a large number of e-commerce regulations for all of its twenty-eight Member States.[311] Europe already provided minimum consumer remedies in the twenty-eight countries of the Eurozone, .and now Europeans enjoy the same consumer rights and remedies in an online transaction with a seller in another EU country as their home country.

Through Europe, welfarism in contract law has taken the form of mandatory terms and the power to strike down unfair contracts. The Unfair Contract Terms Directive ("UCTD") Annex of Unfair Terms illustrates the divergence between U.S. and European consumer rules. The Annex to the UCTD is a nonexclusive list of terms considered suspect under Article 3(3). This UCTD list presumptively invalidates many widely used American-style licensing terms providing disclaimer of warranties, limitation of licensor's liability, limitation of remedies for consumer, unilateral modifications to contract terms, and contract acceptance by performance. Mandatory minimum consumer protection is non-waivable and applies throughout the Eurozone.

Many private industry stakeholders believe that mandatory consumer rules are not the answer to Internet governance and governments should defer to the market. This chapter has examined the differences between U.S.-style Internet contracts, and the mandatory consumer rules followed in Europe and in other countries connected to the Internet. Chapter 3 introduced the Brussels Regulation, governing choice of forum

---

[310] This may not be true, however, under the laws of other countries. A French court of appeals recently ruled that a Facebook user is not bound by the provision that requires disputes to be brought exclusively in a state or federal court located in Santa Clara County. Sébastien R. v. Société Facebook, Inc., Cour d'appel [CA][regional court of appeal] Pau, March 23, 2012. The court ruled that the provision violates Article 48 of the French Code of Civil Procedure, which requires that such a clause be highly visible. The court also found that such a restrictive clause is only valid between businesses.

[311] See Council Directive 2000/31/EC of 8 June 2000 on Certain Legal Aspects of Information Society Services, in Particular Electronic Commerce, in the Internal Market ('Directive on Electronic Commerce'), 2000 O.J. (L 178) [hereinafter E–Commerce Directive] (discussing certain legal aspects of information society services, in particular electronic commerce, in the internal market of the European Community), available at http://europa.eu.int/eur-lex/pri/en/oj/dat/2000/l_178/l_17820000717en00010016.pdf (last visited April 24, 2005). The E–Commerce Directive harmonizes rules for all European countries for commercial communications, electronic contracts, and limitations of liability of intermediary service providers. The European Union (EU) is an international organization of European countries that forms common institutions. Europa, The European Union at a Glance, at http:// europa.eu.int/abc/index_en.htm (last visited April 24, 2005). The EU's five major institutions are the European Parliament, Council of The European Union, European Commission, Court of Justice, and Court of Auditors. Id. EU decisions and procedures are based on treaties between the Member States. Id. Directives require all EU member states to enact legislation to implement policies by a given date. Id.

clauses for consumer transactions, and Rome I, and governing choice of law. Europe's mandatory rule is that the consumers have a right to litigate in their home court or forum under their jurisdiction's consumer protection. In contrast, the U.S. approach to consumer law is market-based predicated upon the legal fiction of freedom of contract. This freedom of contract influenced approach contrasts with the European Community's mandatory terms approach. The result is that the U.S. approach to consumer protection is piecemeal and sectorial whereas European consumers have comprehensive protection throughout the EU.

Unlike the U.S. approach, the European approach is comprehensive and applies across borders in the Eurozone. None of the providers gave social media users the option to pursue arbitration, while retaining their jury trial right. The U.S. policy governing spam, for example is a system of opt-out of commercial e-mail. The European approach is diametrically opposed in that it is an opt-in policy. European consumers do not receive spam e-mail unless they specifically opt in. Governments connected to the Internet have not been able to reach agreement with adopting mandatory consumer rules. Consumer fraud largely goes unpunished when cybercriminals operate in offshore havens. Just as in the brick-and-mortar world, immunity breeds irresponsibility. Internet governance also "has profound implications for competition and trade, democratization, free expression, and access to information."[312]

(A) Unfair Online Advertising

The European Union adopted the Unfair Commercial Practices Directive ("UCPD") on May 11, 2005.[313] The UCPD regulates commercial practices from business-to-consumer, replacing the Misleading Advertising Directive. The UCPD prohibits misleading advertising distorting economic behavior.[314] This directive covers misleading actions (Article 6), misleading omissions (Article 7), and aggressive commercial practices (Article 8) on the advertiser's behalf. The European Parliament's 2009 implementation of the 2005 Misleading Advertising Directive stresses the importance of making consumers and traders more confident in cross-border transactions in the internal market.[315] The EU completed an Airlines Sweep and EU Ringtones Sweep to begin monitoring the implementation and enforcement of the internal market legislation. The UCPD applies equally well to social media sites and other Internet contracts.

(B) Unfair Consumer Contracts Directive

The Directive on Unfair Terms in Consumer Contracts ("UCTD") applies generally to Internet-related consumer transactions, which means transactions with persons outside their profession or occupation. Online contractual terms classified as unfair under the UCTD are not binding on consumers.[316] European consumer contracts are not

---

[312] Amy E. Bivins, Internet Governance Bono Mack Urges Senate to Take Up House Internet Governance Bill After August Recess, ELEC. COMM. L. REPORT (Aug. 15, 2012) (quoting H. Cong. Res. 127).

[313] Directive 2005/29/EC.

[314] Id. at art. 5.2(B).

[315] The European Union uses the concept of the internal market to refer to the ideal where "the free movement of goods, services, capital and persons is ensured and in which European citizens are free to live, work, study and do business." Europa, Summaries of European Legislation (2012). "The European Union is working towards further simplification of the regulations which still prevent citizens and businesses from making the most of the advantages of the single market." Id.

[316] A growing body of European case law proves our point that click-wrap agreements are suspect under the Unfair Contract Terms Directive as well as national law. See e.g., Giudice di pace di Partanna n.

enforceable unless drafted in plain and intelligible language. The language of Directive 93/13 compels courts to apply a two-part test to determine whether a given contractual provision is unfair.[317] To qualify as an unfair contract, there must be a significant imbalance to the detriment of the consumer and that imbalance should be "contrary to good faith."[318] Nevertheless, the prevailing—and more correct interpretation of Directive 93/13—is that any contractual term in a consumer contract causing a significant imbalance is by definition contrary to the principle of good faith.[319] Under this interpretation, a court, consumer administrative agency or authority will deploy the Directive to strike down oppressive terms in consumer contracts such as terms of service ("TOS") agreements. The language in Article 3 of the Directive addresses newly emergent terms not found in the Annex. An Annex to Directive 93/13 is a non-exclusive list of terms considered suspect under Article 3(3)

This list invalidates many common terms in U.S.-style TOS agreements: disclaimer of warranties, limitations of licensor's liability, rolling contracts, and the acceptance of the license agreement by performance. If a given term in a license agreement is not addressed in the Annex of suspect terms, the court will strike down terms deploying a more general test of unfairness. Article 8 makes it clear that the Directive is the floor but not the ceiling for consumer protection providing that Member States have the discretion to adopt provisions that are more stringent.[320] Individual EU countries could, for example, transform the gray list into a black list.[321] European courts and consumer agencies have the power to review all non-negotiated contracts to determine if they are unfair:

> taking into account the nature of the goods or services for which the contract was concluded and by referring, at the time of conclusion of the contract, to all the circumstances attending the conclusion of the contract and to all the other terms of the contract or of another contract on which it is dependent.[322]

However, Article 4(2) provides that this test does not apply to core terms, including "neither . . . the definition of the main subject matter of the contract nor . . . the adequacy of the price and remuneration."[323] Directive 93/13 is a robust tool for European courts seeking to strike down one-sided TOUs with hidden terms. Few U.S.

15/2002, case No. 206/2001 R.G.A.C. available at http://www.infogiur.com/giurisprudenza/ g_d_p&uscore;partanna_15_2002.asp; Union Fédérale des Consommateurs v. AOL France, R.G. N 02/03156, Tribunal de grande instance [T.G.I.] [ordinary court of original jurisdiction] Nanterre, le ch., June 2, 2004, tgin020604 (Fr.), available at http://www.clauses-abusives.fr/juris/tgin020604.pdf, aff.'d AOL France v.UFC Que Choisir, R.G. N [degree] 04/05564, Cour d'appel [CA] [regional court of appeal] Versailles, le ch., Sept. 15, 2005, J.C.P. IV 150905, available at /attachment.html/1694/AOL+ France+v.+UFC+Que+Choisir'+R.G.+ N+0405564.pdf.

[317] James R. Maxeiner, Standard–Terms Contracting in the Global Electronic Age: European Alternatives, 28 YALE J. INT'L L. 109, 134 (2003).

[318] Id. at 135.

[319] Id.

[320] Article 8 of Council Directive 93/13 provides: "Member States may adopt or retain the most stringent provisions compatible with the Treaty in the area covered by this Directive, to ensure a maximum degree of protection for the consumer." Council Directive 93/13, at art. 8.

[321] A contractual term appearing on a gray list is essentially a presumption of unfairness that can be overcome by contrary evidence. In contrast, black list terms are prohibited outright and are per se regarded as unfair. WADE JACOBY, THE ENLARGEMENT OF THE EUROPEAN UNION AND NATO: ORDERING FROM THE MENU IN CENTRAL EUROPE 71 n.32 (2005).

[322] Council Directive 93/13, Id. at art. 4(1).

[323] Id. at art. 4(2).

companies have constructed terms of service or license agreements that will satisfy the pro-consumer rules of the Directive 93/13. The UCTD instructs courts to interpret ambiguities in favor of consumers. Under Article 3 of the UCTD: "[A] term is unfair if, contrary to the requirements of good faith, it causes a significant imbalance in the parties' rights and obligations arising under the contract, to the detriment of the consumer."[324] Unfair terms are to be determined at the conclusion of the contract. In contrast, U.S. courts enforce contract terms disadvantaging consumers such as the disclaimer of all remedies, adverse choice of law and forum clauses, and limitation of meaningful remedies. "Even those firms without market power exploit the cognitive failures of their customers through the "shrouding" of terms and similar techniques."[325]

Thus, Europe has a more comprehensive view of consumer rights in cyberspace than the U.S. piecemeal approach. Further, The UCTD provides Europe with a tool for consumer groups and courts to strike down one-sided Internet terms of service agreements. "Rolling contracts" are not widely accepted in the Eurozone and courts and regulatory agencies have struck down many U.S. style terms.

(C) Distance Selling Directive

The European legislature enacted the Distance Selling Directive to guarantee that all consumers in the twenty-eight Member States of the European Union have the same rights whether they purchase goods in person or through distance communications.[326] The European Legislature defines "Distance Selling" as "the conclusion of a contract regarding goods or services whereby the contract between the consumer and the supplier takes place by means of technology for communication at a distance."[327] The Distance Selling Directive sets forth minimum mandatory disclosures that cover (a) the price of the goods or services including all taxes, (b) delivery costs, where appropriate, (c) the arrangements for payment, delivery or performance, (d) the existence of a right of withdrawal, (e) the cost of using the means of distance communication, where it is calculated other than at the basic rate, (f) the period for which the offer or the price remains valid, and, where appropriate, (g) the minimum duration of the contract in the case of contracts for the supply of products or services to be performed permanently or recurrently.[328]

European consumers have the absolute right to cancel a distance sale if the seller is unable to deliver the goods or services within thirty days.[329] However, the European Directive did exempt certain distance sales from its application. Examples of distance sales covered by the Distance Selling Directive include construction contracts, financial services, contracts made by vending machines, auctions, and public pay telephones.[330] A remote software licensor must inform European consumers of their right of withdrawal and offer a refund payable within 30 days.[331] Article 2 of the Distance

---

[324] 97/7/EC, Id. at art. 3.

[325] Ronald J. Mann & Travis Siebeneicher, Just One Click: The Reality of Internet Retail Contracting, 108 COLUM. L. REV. 984, 985 (2008).

[326] Council Directive 97/7/EC of the European Parliament and of the Council of 20 May 1997 on the Protection of Consumers in Respect of Distance Contracts, 1997 O.J. (L 144) (June 4, 1997).

[327] Id. at art. 2.

[328] Id. at 5

[329] Id. at 2.

[330] Id. at art. 3.

[331] Council Directive 973/13 at art. 7(2).

Selling Directive states the basic definitions key to the sphere of operation of the directive:

(1) "distance contract" means any contract concerning goods or services concluded between a supplier and a consumer under an organized distance sales or service-provision scheme run by the supplier, who, for the purpose of the contract, makes exclusive use of one or more means of distance communication up to and including the moment at which the contract is concluded;

(2) "consumer" means any natural person who, in contracts covered by this Directive, is acting for purposes, which are outside his trade, business or profession;

(3) "supplier" means any natural or legal person who, in contracts covered by this Directive, is acting in his commercial or professional capacity;

(4) "means of distance communication" means any means, which, without the simultaneous physical presence of the supplier and the consumer, may be used for the conclusion of a contract between those parties. An indicative list of the means covered by this Directive is contained in Annex I;

(5) "operator of a means of communication" means any public or private natural or legal person whose trade, business or profession involves making one or more means of distance communication available to suppliers.[332]

Any E–Business or software company targeting European consumers must comply with the Distance Selling Directive. This requires the seller to give mandatory pre-contractual disclosures as well as confirmatory disclosures no later than the time it delivers its products. The Directive provides a list of uniform pre-contractual terms that the seller must disclose to the consumer before the conclusion of the contract including: the main characteristics of the goods or services, the identity of the trader, the geographical address at which the trader is established, the trader's contact information, the total price of the goods or services including all taxes and additional delivery or postal charges, and whether any returns charges are payable by the consumer.[333]

The seller also must inform the consumer about whether they have a right of withdrawal.[334] Where a right of withdrawal exists, the conditions and procedures for exercising that right must be specified.[335] Conversely, the circumstances under which the consumer will lose his right of withdrawal must also be explained.[336] The trader must also inform the consumer of any technical protection measures of digital content, which includes not only digital rights management but also more invasive technologies such as DVD regional codes or tracking and monitoring tools.[337] In addition, the trader must inform the consumer of any relevant interoperability of digital content with hardware and software that the trader has knowledge or a reason to know of its

---

[332] Id. at art. 2.

[333] Id. at art. 6(a)-(g).

[334] Id. at art. 6(h).

[335] Id.

[336] Id. at art. 6(k).

[337] Id. at art. 6(r).

existence.[338] Under the new Directive, the original period of seven days to withdraw from a distance contract is extended to fourteen days starting the day on which the consumer acquires physical possession of the goods.[339]

If the Internet vendor has not provided the consumer with the information on the right of withdrawal, the withdrawal period shall expire twelve months from the end of the initial withdrawal period.[340] The Directive's provision on the right of withdrawal does not apply to the supply of sealed audio or video recordings and sealed computer software that are unsealed by the consumer after delivery.[341] They also do not apply to digital content not supplied on a tangible medium if the performance began with the consumer's prior express consent regarding loss of his right of withdrawal.[342] The problem of legal lag is a continual one as technologies outgrow Directives and Regulations. In response to this legal lag, the EC has approved a new Directive on Consumer Rights, which will update the Distance Selling Directive and other consumer protections for Internet-related consumer transactions. In *Content Services Ltd v. Bundesarbeitskammer,*[343] the European Court of Justice ruled that a website that provided consumer information by a hyperlink did not meet the requirements of the Distance Selling Directive. A favorite question that Chief Justice Burger posed to counsel appearing before the Court was, "If it doesn't make good sense, how can it make good law?" To update Chief Justice Burger: "How can it be good law to apply a fifty-year-old law designed for durable goods to the Internet?"

In 2011, EU Council and the European Parliament approved the New Consumer Rights Directive.[344] An Internet contract almost never involves direct contact with the merchandise, let alone the seller and is conducted computer-to-computer. Accordingly, the Directive on Consumer Rights displaces both the 97/7/EC distance-selling directive, and the 85/577/EC directive on the protection of consumers regarding contracts negotiated away from business premises by providing a standard set of EU-wide consumer rights. The new EU directive on consumer rights creates uniform minimum protection for consumers conducting distance sales such as ordering goods and services over the Internet. The Directive was approved by the Parliament on June 23, 2011 and

---

[338] Id. at art. 6(s).

[339] Id. at art. 9.

[340] Id. at art. 10.

[341] Id. at art. 16(1).

[342] Id. at art. 16(m).

[343] E.C.J., No. C–49/11, July 5, 2012.

[344] Directives must be implemented by each Member State. For example, the United Kingdom's 1998 Data Protection Act implemented the REC Data Protection Directive (95/46/EC). See Council Directive 95/46/EC of the European Parliament and of the Council of 24 Oct. 1995 on the Protection of Individuals with Regard to the Processing of Personal Data and on the Free Movement of Such Data, 1995 O.J. (L 281) 31, available at http://europa.eu.int/eur-lex/lex/LexUriServ/LexUriServ.do?url=CELEX:31995L0046:EN:HTML (last visited June 15, 2013). The Council of European Union is a key decision-making institution that is responsible for foreign affairs, farming, industry, transport, and other emergent issues. See Gateway to the European Union, http://europa.eu/index_en.htm (last visited June 17, 2013). The Council, known even as the Council of Ministers, is the principal legislative and decision-making body in the EU. The Council includes ministers of the governments of each of the Member States and is divided into different functional areas called formations. European citizens directly elect the European Parliament every five years. The Parliament consists of 785 Members of the European Parliament ("MEP"), representing nearly 500 million European citizens. The European Council and the Parliament are principally responsible for the legislative functions of the single EU market. The MEP is divided into political groups rather than representing national blocs. Each political group reflects its parties' political ideology as opposed to national political ideologies. Some MEPs are not attached to any political group. Id.

by the Council on October 11, 2011. After the entry into force of the Directive, the Member States shall have two years to implement its provisions into their national law. Consumer groups were generally satisfied with the new regulation as it strikes a fair balance between consumer rights and business interests.[345]

(D) "Rolling Contracts" in the Eurozone

Courts have recognized a "layered" or "rolling" system of electronic contract formation, which is an extension of the layered contract formation used in durable goods sales. With a layered contract, licensors structure their agreements so that a customer will manifest assent to different terms at different points in time. For example, a cell phone contract may introduce new terms after the initial monthly agreement by posting them on a website. Terms of service agreements for social media sites typically reserve the right to unilaterally alter or modify terms of use or service by simply posting a changed privacy policy on a website. Instagram, for example, altered its position as to the intellectual property rights of photographs posted on its service, creating a firestorm of protest in the user community. In response to the blowback from its users, Instagram revoked its unilateral modification of its IP policy. Nevertheless, the recent trend in judicial decisions is that courts enforce "cash now, terms later" licenses so long as the licensor gives reasonable notice to the user and an opportunity to decline the terms.

The "pay now" and "terms later" contracting practice evolved as a mass-market software industry standard in the 1990s. However, the post payment disclosure of contract terms is a practice not well accepted outside of the United States.[346] Internet contracts, enforceable in the United States, are not enforceable in the European Union countries and perhaps other countries around the world.[347] The Norwegian Consumer Agency challenged the iTunes TOS, which was structured as a rolling contract. Specifically, the Norwegian consumer authorities objected to an iTunes rolling contract provision allowing iTunes to modify the terms of services and to impose new or additional rules, policies, terms, or conditions. The Norwegian consumer advocate also objected to the iTunes full disclaimer of liability for loss of data, corruption, attack, viruses, interference, hacking, or other security intrusions. On January 25, 2006, the Norwegian Consumer Council filed a complaint with the Consumer Ombudsman against iTunes for violating fundamental consumer rights. Norwegian Consumer Ombudsman, Bjørn Erik Thon, contended that some of iTunes terms of service were unreasonable, violating Section 9(A) of the Norwegian Marketing Control Act.

---

[345] SMEs Balk at New Consumer Rights Directive, EurActiv (June 27, 2011), http:// www. euractiv. com/consumers/smes-balk-new-consumer-rights-directive-news-505974 (last visited June 8, 2013).

[346] See e.g., Pro CD, Inc. v. Zeidenberg, 86 F. 3d 1447 (7th Cir. 1996); Hill v. Gateway 2000, Inc., 105 F. 3d 1147 (7th Cir., 1997); I.LAN Systems, Inc. v. Netscout Service Level Corp., 183 F. Supp. 2d 328 (D. Mass. 2002); M.A. Mortenson Co. Inc. v. Timberline Software Corp., 1998 P. 2d 328 (Wash. 1999); Brower v. Gateway 2000, Inc., 676 N.Y.S. 2d 569 (N.Y.A.D., 1998). Cf. Step-Saver Data Systems v. Wyse Technology, 939 F. 2d 91 (3dCir. 1991).

[347] David Naylor & Cyril Ritter, B2C in Europe and Avoiding Contractual Liability: Why Businesses with European Operations Should Review Their Customer Contracts Now, Legal Updates & News, http://www.mofo.com/news/updates/files/update1297.html (Last visited Nov. 8, 2009); Robert L. Oakley, Fairness in Electronic Contracting: Minimum Standards for Non–Negotiated Contracts, 42 HOUS. L. REV. 1041, 1067 (2005) (asserting that "the Directive also specifically provides that consumers in member states should not lose the protection of the Directive by virtue of a choice-of-law provision in a non-member country. That would make, for example, the choice of Virginia law in an AOL contract inapplicable within the European Union.").

Apple's iPhone5, iPod, and Macs are popular in Europe as well as in the United States. Apple modified many of its clauses in its terms of service agreements used in the European consumer marketplace in response to a 2006 consumer advocate's complaint that its standard form was unfair. Nevertheless, the Norwegian consumer agency renewed its complaint against iTunes in 2008 because Apple's digital rights management software prevented their services from being "interoperable so that you can play music bought on iTunes on other devices, including mobile phones."[348] Nevertheless, in February of 2009, the Norwegian ombudsman dropped the complaint against Apple after it agreed that not all of its songs would include DRM locks. Content providers are using the digital rights management technology contained in DRM software.

In *Union Federale de Consommateurs v. AOL France,* the French court struck down thirty-six clauses in AOL France's (hereinafter AOL) standard TOU agreement, and further required the online provider to remove those clauses from their TOUs within one month. Additionally, the court fined AOL for each day it delayed removing the objectionable clauses.[349] The French court ruled that AOL had a duty to notify its French customers of the resulting changes to its terms of use and imposed a fine of €30,000 against AOL; ordering the online provider to publish the substantive parts of the court's judgment on its website and in three national daily newspapers. Some of the unenforceable terms in the America Online contract were those that:

> entitle the ISP to unilaterally modify the offered service without the consumer's express consent (except where allowed by law); entitle the ISP to unilaterally modify the amount of the service fees in fi ex-term agreements without the consumer's express consent, even if the consumer may terminate the agreement; limit all obligations of the ISP to best effort obligations; exonerate the ISP from its obligation to ensure access to the offered service in the event of a breakdown; allow the ISP to terminate the agreement in the event of the consumer in the even "imprecise" obligations (e.g., "abnormal use of service") or the consumer's refusal to pay, even if such refusal is justified; make the consumer liable both for liquidated and normal damages in the event of termination of the agreement for breach; and provide that notices sent by e-mail are effective after the expiration of an excessively short period of time (e.g., two weeks), even if the consumer did not consult them.[350]

The AOL France case is not an isolated case but reflects a larger trend of European courts and consumer authorities to refuse to enforce U.S. style software contracts. In Germany, consumers associations have challenged successfully the terms of CompuServe, AOL, and Microsoft: the first one was subject to a default judgment; the other two agreed to a binding cease-and-desist declaration. All three American companies have entered into settlement agreements agreeing to change their marketing practices. The implications of these cases are that practices validated by the Principles of Software Contract expose U.S. companies to a heightened litigation risk in Europe.

---

[348] Reuters News Service, Norway Consumer Body Challenges iTune DRM (Sept. 30, 2009).

[349] Bradley Joslove & Andréi Krylov, Standard American Business-to-Consumer Terms and Conditions in the EU, 18 MICH INT'L L. 1, 2–3 (2005).

[350] Id.

Most U.S. courts would find the same clauses struck down by the French court in the AOL case to be generally enforceable.[351] The golden age of the broad enforcement of U.S. style EULAs may be ending because of the increasingly flattened world where U.S. companies license content to European consumers. The U.S. is like Mars—and Europe is like Venus—when it comes to consumer rights for EULAs. Europe rejects freedom of contract in consumer transactions recognizing this is a legal fiction in non-negotiated standard form contracts. In this regard, Europe has breached the citadel of regressive software licensing practices in enacting Community-wide directives and regulations to protect consumers against abuses by dominant software companies.

(E) Mandatory Terms in Consumer Contracts[352]

The following table demonstrates how U.S. style standard form contracts used in Internet transactions violate mandatory European consumer directives and regulations. The illustrative clauses in the table highlight diametrically opposed mass-market licensing paradigms between the United States and Europe. The European Directive on Unfair Contract Terms ("UCTD") seeks to prevent significant imbalances in the rights and obligations of consumers on the one hand and sellers and suppliers on the other hand. "This general requirement is supplemented by a list of examples of terms that may be regarded as unfair. Terms that are found unfair under the Directive are not binding for consumers."[353] The U.S. market-based approach to terms of use is antithetical to the European consumer law, which provides consumers with minimum procedural and substantive protection.

---

[351] In Union Fédérale des Consommateurs v. AOL France, AOL's terms of service agreement was struck down. The AOL France case is not an isolated case but reflects a larger trend to challenge U.S. style software contracts. In Germany, consumers associations have challenged successfully the terms of Compuserve, AOL, and Microsoft: the first one was subject to a default judgment; the other two agreed to a binding cease-and-desist declaration. All three American companies have entered into settlement agreements agreeing to change their marketing practices. The implications of these cases are that practices validated by the Principles of Software Contract expose U.S. companies to a heightened litigation risk in Europe. Michael L. Rustad & Vittoria Maria Onufrio, The Exportability of the Principles of Software: Lost in Translation?, 2 HASTINGS SCI. & TECH L. J. 25, 79 (2010) (internal footnote omitted).

[352] The section on Mandatory Terms in Consumer Contracts was co-authored with Vit Svejkovsky, a 2012 LL.M. graduate of Suffolk University Law School.

[353] European Commission, Unfair Contract Terms, http://ec.europa.eu/justice/consumer-marketing/rights-contracts/unfair-contract/index_en.htm (last visited June 28, 2013).

U.S. Style Standard Form Provisions Favoring Licensor	European Union Mandatory Consumer Rules Applicable to Standard Form Licenses[354]
Compulsory Jurisdiction or Choice of Forum Clause: You will resolve any claim, cause of action or dispute (claim) you have with us arising out of or relating to this [terms of service, shrinkwrap, clickwrap agreement, or browsewrap agreement] exclusively in a state or federal court located in [in a U.S. city county]. You agree to submit to the personal jurisdiction of the courts located in [in a U.S. county and state] for litigating all such claims.	*European Consumers Home Court Rule: As Adopted by Articles 15–17 of the Brussels Regulation.*[355] Consumer home court rules apply, "In matters relating to a contract concluded by a person, the consumer, for a purpose which can be regarded as being outside his trade or profession."[356] The consumer home court rules apply to contracts "concluded with a person who pursues commercial or professional activities in the Member State of the consumer's domicile or, by any means, directs such activities to that Member State or to several States."[357] Article 17 makes this provision non-waivable.[358]
Typical U.S. Choice of Law Clause: The laws of the State of ___ will govern this terms of use agreement, as well as any claim that might arise between you and us, without regard to conflict of law provisions.	*Mandatory EU Consumer Home Court Rule:* Article 6 of the Rome I Regulation governing choice of law prohibits one-sided choice of law clauses in consumer transactions. The governing law has to be the law of the member state where the consumer is domiciled.[359]

---

[354] Article 17 of the Brussels Regulations, for example provides that a consumer cannot waive her right to sue a supplier in her local court. A supplier, which includes U.S. software companies, directing their activities to the consumer's home state is automatically subject to jurisdiction because he has directed activities to that state as defined in Article 15. Finally, a consumer may enforce a judgment in any Member State upon completion of the formalities set forth in Article 53. Id. at arts. 15, 17, 53. Council Regulation (EC) No 44/2001 of 22 December on jurisdiction and the recognition and enforcement of judgments in civil and commercial matters ("Brussels Regulation").

[355] Id.

[356] Id. at art. 15(1)(C).

[357] Id.

[358] Id. at art. 17.

[359] Regulation (EC) No 593/2008 OF THE EUROPEAN PARLIAMENT AND OF THE COUNCIL of 17 June 2008 on the law applicable to contractual obligations (Rome I) at art. 6 (stating that choice of law may not deprive consumers of consumer protection in their home court or forum).

Typical U.S. Clause Eliminating All Warranties: WE ARE PROVIDING [data, website content, software etc.] WITHOUT ANY EXPRESS OR IMPLIED WARRANTIES INCLUDING, BUT NOT LIMITED TO, IMPLIED WARRANTIES OF MERCHANTABILITY, FITNESS FOR A PARTICULAR PURPOSE, AND NON–INFRINGEMENT.	*The Unfair Contract Terms Directive ("UCTD") prohibits clauses that eliminate warranties and remedies where . . . there is a "significant imbalance in the rights and obligations of consumers on the one hand and sellers and suppliers on the other hand."*[360] Term (b) in the Annex to the UCTD provides: "1. A contractual term which has not been individually negotiated shall be regarded as unfair if, contrary to the requirement of good faith, it causes a significant imbalance in the parties' rights and obligations arising under the contract, to the detriment of the consumer."[361]
Browsewrap Agreement are Broadly Enforceable in the United States: By using the Products and Services, you agree, without limitation or qualification, to be bound by, and to comply with, these Terms and Conditions and any other posted guidelines or rules applicable to [website] or any Product or Service.	*Browsewrap-type are challengeable by European Consumers Under the UCTD.* Browsewrap violates term (i) to the annex which provides that terms are unenforceable where they "irrevocably binding the consumer to terms with which he had no real opportunity of becoming acquainted before the conclusion of the contract."[362]
In the U.S., Rolling Contracts or Asserting the Dominant Party's Unilateral Right to Change Terms After the Conclusion of the Consumer Contract: We can change [terms of use, shrinkwrap, clickwrap or browsewrap] if we provide you notice (by posting the change on our website). Your continued use of [our website] following changes to our terms constitutes your acceptance of our	*European Rolling Contracts in Consumer Licensing or Terms of Use Violates the UCTD and Several Terms in the Annex Address the Issue.* Term (c) in the annex to the UCTD prohibits making agreements "binding on the consumer whereas provision of services by the seller or supplier is subject to a condition whose realization depends on his own will alone."[363] Term (j) prohibits sellers or suppliers from altering "the terms of the contract unilaterally without a valid reason which is specified in the contract."[364] Rolling contracts also violate term (i) to the

---

[360] Council Directive 93/13/EEC of 5 April 1993 on unfair terms in consumer contracts ("UCTD")

[361] Id. at annex at term (b).

[362] Id. at annex at term (i).

[363] Id. at annex at term (c).

[364] Id. at annex at term (j).

amended terms.	UCTD because they bind the consumer without giving them an "opportunity of becoming acquainted before the conclusion of the contract.[365] Finally, rolling contracts violate term (k) of the UCTD because the seller or supplier is "unilaterally altering the contract terms without a valid reason as to any of the characteristic of the product or service to be provided."[366]
Pre–Dispute Mandatory Arbitration Clauses are broadly enforceable in the United States:[367] Any controversy or claim arising out of or relating to these Terms and Conditions or any user's use of the Products and Services shall be settled by binding arbitration in accordance with the commercial arbitration rules of the [arbitral provider]. The arbitration shall be conducted in [dominant party's home court], and judgment on the arbitration award may be entered into in any state or federal court in [dominant party's jurisdiction]. Any party seeking temporary or preliminary injunctive relief may do so in any state or federal court in [dominant party's jurisdiction].	*Predispute Mandatory Arbitration Provision Could Violate the Brussels Regulation's Mandatory Home Court Rules for Consumers Found in Articles 15–17[368] as well as the UCTD.* Term (q) of the annex to the UCTD prohibits the dominant party from: excluding or hindering the consumer's right "to take legal action or exercise any other legal remedy, particularly by requiring the consumer to take disputes exclusively to arbitration not covered by legal provisions, unduly restricting the evidence available to him or imposing on him a burden of proof which, according to the applicable law, should lie with another party to the contract."[369] Predispute mandatory arbitration rules that reserve the right for the dominant party to exercise their legal rights but deny that right to the consumer is "significantly imbalanced" and violate term (b) of the annex to the UCTD.[370] Predispute mandatory arbitration clauses also provide consumers

---

[365] Id. at annex at term (i).

[366] Id. at annex at term (k).

[367] Compulsory arbitration clauses in mass-market license agreements, computer contracts, or terms of service have been upheld by numerous United States courts. See e.g., Chandler v. AT&T Wireless Servs., Inc., 358 F. Supp. 2d 701, 706 (S.D. Ill. 2005) (ordering arbitration in case where predispute arbitration clause was added to the consumer's contract for wireless services); Westendorff v. Gateway 2000, Inc., 2000 WL 307369 (Del. Ch. March 16, 2000), aff'd, 763 A.2d 92 (Del. 2000); Brower v. Gateway 2000, Inc., 676 N.Y.S.2d 569 (1998) (ordering enforcement of arbitration clause in Gateway's standard computer contract).

[368] Brussels Regulation, Id. at arts. 15–17.

[369] Id. at annex at term (q).

[370] Council Directive 93/13/EEC of 5 April 1993 on unfair terms in consumer contracts, Id. at annex at term (b) ("inappropriately excluding or limiting the legal rights of the consumer vis-à-vis the seller or supplier or another party in the event of total or partial non-performance or inadequate performance by the seller or supplier of any of the contractual obligations, including the option of offsetting a debt owed to the seller or supplier against any claim which the consumer may have against him").

	with little or no information about the consequences of the clause or the cost of deciding disputes thus violating term (i) of the annex to the UCTD.[371]
Anti–Class Action Waivers Are Broadly Enforceable in the United States: You are prohibited from entering into disputes that are the subject of purported class action litigation in which you are not a member of a certified class.[372]	*Anti–Class Action Clauses could violate the UCTD in the European Union.* European consumers with identical complaints arising out of a license agreement or terms of use may join in a class suit or representative action in U.S. or European courts recognizing the aggregation of cases. Anti-class action waivers do not permit the consolidation of complaints into a single proceeding. This provision is significantly imbalanced in favor of the dominant party. Some anti-class waivers reserve the right of the dominant party to consolidate actions, which is an imbalanced provision. Anti-class action waivers likely violate term (b) of the annex to the UCTD.[373]
Limitations of Remedy; No Minimum Adequate Remedy Are Broadly Enforceable in the United States: UNDER NO CIRCUMSTANCES SHALL [provider] BE LIABLE ON ACCOUNT OF MEMBER'S USE OR MISUSE OF THE [. . . .] WEBSITE OR THE SERVICES, WHETHER THE DAMAGES ARISE FROM USE OR MISUSE OF THE [. . . .] WEBSITE OR THE SERVICES, FROM INABILITY TO USE THE	*Mandatory arbitration clauses violate the UCTD, the Brussels Regulation, and the Rome I Regulation* Limitations of remedies common in U.S. style standard term agreements are significantly imbalanced in favor of the dominant party and thus violate the UCTD.[374]

---

[371] Term (i) provides that it is an unfair term to irrevocably bind "the consumer to terms with which he had no real opportunity of becoming acquainted before the conclusion of the contract." Id. at annex at term (I).

[372] A class action by consumers produces several salutary byproducts, including a therapeutic effect upon those sellers who indulge in fraudulent practices, aid to legitimate business enterprises by curtailing illegitimate competition, and avoidance to the judicial process of the burden of multiple litigation involving identical claims. The benefit to the parties and the courts would, in many circumstances, be substantial. European class actions to remediate consumer grievances are still in their infancy. It is likely that anti-class action waivers would violate term (b) of the annex to the UCTD, because these waivers exclude or limit legal rights of consumers. Council Directive 93/13/EEC of 5 April 1993 on unfair terms in consumer contracts, Id. at annex at term (b) ("inappropriately excluding or limiting the legal rights of the consumer vis-à-vis the seller or supplier or another party in the event of total or partial non-performance or inadequate performance by the seller or supplier of any of the contractual obligations, including the option of offsetting a debt owed to the seller or supplier against any claim which the consumer may have against him").

[373] Id.

[374] Id.

WEBSITE OR THE SERVICES, OR THE INTERRUPTION, SUSPENSION, MODIFICATION, ALTERATION, OR TERMINATION OF THE WEBSITE OR THE SERVICES. SUCH LIMITATION SHALL ALSO APPLY WITH RESPECT TO DAMAGES INCURRED BY REASON OF OTHER SERVICES OR PRODUCTS RECEIVED THROUGH OR ADVERTISED IN CONNECTION WITH THE [. . .] WEBSITE OR THE SERVICES OR ANY LINKS ON THE WEBSITE, AS WELL AS BY REASON OF ANY INFORMATION OR ADVICE RECEIVED THROUGH OR ADVERTISED IN CONNECTION WITH THE WEBSITE OR THE SERVICES OR ANY LINKS ON THE [. . .] WEBSITE. THESE LIMITATIONS SHALL APPLY TO THE FULLEST EXTENT PERMITTED BY LAW.	

As the comparisons above confirm, many standard provisions in U.S. style terms of use or other Internet license agreements are unenforceable in Europe. The European Union does not follow the U.S. free market approach to consumer transactions. The European Commission takes the position that even if a consumer assents to an abusive term, it is unenforceable as a matter of law and European consumers, unlike their American counterparts, cannot be hauled into distant forums and be divested of mandatory consumer protection. The EU's purpose was to create a seamless body of consumer protection, providing certainty for consumers and predictability for the business community.

Countries outside of Europe have adopted similar approaches to mass-market licenses. Under the Japanese law, for example, shrinkwrap agreements are likely to be unenforceable,[375] unless the consumer is aware of the license terms and consents to them before purchasing the software. It generally happens when the licensor prints the licensing contract out of the box by giving consumers the opportunity to read the license terms. However, even in this scenario, if terms in standard form contracts are unreasonably unfavourable to the consumer, they can be struck down by the courts.[376] In fact, Japan, as well as other modern economies like Europe, New Zealand and Canada, provides a consumer legislation, which makes void unfair contract terms. That

---

[375] Tsuneo Matsumoto, Article 2B and Mass-Market License Contracts: A Japanese Perspective, 13 BERKELEY TECH. L.J. 1283, 1284 (1998).

[376] Id., at 1285.

means that, unfair terms cannot be enforceable against the consumer, even when he had the opportunity to read and assent to them.

The Japanese consumer contract law, as well as the European Directive on unfair contract terms, includes a grey list of unfair terms.[377]   However, none of the terms listed seem to address whether a contract may limit the users' rights, which copyright law would ordinarily permit.[378]   Professor Matsumoto explains that if copyright law establishes a set of mandatory provisions, any license term inconsistent with them will be unenforceable, regardless of the fact that the term was individually negotiated or standardized.[379]   Unfortunately, in Japan few copyright provisions are mandatory. As a result, when default copyright provisions are at stake, it would be possible to negotiate individually contracts limiting the users' rights. However, some scholars believe that, at least in standardized contracts, the default rules could be used to determine the unfairness of a particular license term.[380]   Thus, in the case of standard form contracts, Japanese courts may strike down a term if it would limit rights that copyright law allows users.[381]

It seems that the Japanese legislature, as well as the European legislature, doubts that a pure economic regulation could provide enough support for the online consumer market. This is the likely reason why they enacted consumer legislation able to maintain a certain degree of consumer protection. By contrast, the U.S. embraced a much lower minimum level of protection, requiring individuals to bear more risk in consumer transactions. The Japanese and the European experiences show that the U.S. is falling behind its competitors in protecting the consumers' rights in online transactions. U.S. companies targeting foreign countries on the Internet must localize their contracts to avoid enforcement actions by public regulators. The lessons drawn from European mandatory consumer law apply to other countries around the globe. At a minimum, U.S. companies must tailor their Internet-related contracts exported to foreign business to consumer and business-to-business transactions.

(F) Foreign Taxation of Online Services

Global Internet businesses, such as eBay, do not collect taxes on the goods or services sold by users of their services. As with U.S. states and cities, many foreign countries are seeking to require online companies to collect, report, or record taxes. One or more states, the federal government or foreign countries may seek to impose a tax collection, reporting or record-keeping obligation on companies that engage in or facilitate ecommerce. EBay's subsidiaries, for example, have received a tax assessment "for tax years 2001-2005 from the Canadian Revenue Agency (CRA), which assert goods and service tax (GST) and harmonized sales tax (HST) on [eBay's] fees charged to Canadian users."[382]   EBay successfully challenged these reassessments and the Canadian tax authorities ruled that no tax was due.[383]   EBay also successfully

---

[377] Id.

[378] Id.

[379] Id., at 1286.

[380] Id., (quoting SHOJI KAWAKAMI, YAKKAN KISEI NO HORI, The Theories For Control Of Standardized Contracts, 383 (1988)).

[381] Id. at 1286.

[382] eBay SEC Q-1 Filing (July 19, 2013).

[383] Id.

challenged Korean tax authorities who "asserted that certain coupons and incentives available on our sites should not be deducted when computing taxes on our fees."[384] In their filing, eBay stated:

> We challenged these assessments and in June 2012, the National Tax Tribunal issued a final ruling in our favor with respect to item incentives from June 2006 onward. The assessments on coupons and incentives up to May 2006 are being reviewed by the Seoul High Court following the lower court's ruling in our favor in January 2013. Should any new taxes become applicable to our fees or if the taxes we pay are found to be deficient, our business could be harmed.[385]

The Internet has also spawned entirely new peer-to-peer businesses, such as sharing housing accommodations. One estimate is that the peer-to-peer rental market is now worth $26 billion.[386] Another unsettled issue is whether these rentals will be subject to room use taxes. In Amsterdam, "officials are using Airnb listings to track down unlicensed hotels."[387] The peer-to-peer sharing economy enabled by the Internet is yet another example of how this remarkable technology disrupts regulators, courts, and companies.[388]

---

[384] Id.

[385] Id.

[386] The Rise of the Sharing Economy, THE ECONOMIST (March 9, 2013) at 9.

[387] Id.

[388] Id.

Chapter 6

GLOBAL INTERNET TORTS

§ 6.1 OVERVIEW OF CYBERTORTS

(A) What Cybertorts Are

Tort law needs to be continually updated to address emergent technological and social changes.[1] Prior to the industrial revolution, tort law adjusted relations between neighbors and families in the local community. Tort law as a substantive field of law did not evolve until the nineteenth-century with the rise of negligence.[2] Negligence evolved in response to new large-scale risks created by the rise of large-scale manufacturing, railroads, and steamboats.[3] Tort law in the real-space world was slow to develop during the Industrial Revolution, The rise of the automobile, for example, required courts and legislatures to rework the law of torts.[4] Injury law has evolved over the past two and one half millennia in the Western world, generating "a broad and ever-developing framework of injury law,"[5] and the latest iteration is civil wrongs on the Internet.

William L. Prosser, in his classic tort treatise, described tort law as a "battleground of social theory."[6] This is an apt description of Internet-related torts in the first decades of the twenty-first century. The Internet is the leading edge for culture, countercultures, and libertinage, but its back alley is a zone for rogues,

---

[1] Professor Ogburn's argument was that "the various parts of modern culture are not changing at the same rate, some parts are changing much more rapidly than others; and that since there is a correlation and interdependence of parts, a rapid change in one part of our culture requires readjustments through other changes in the various correlated parts of culture." SOCIAL SCIENCE QUOTATIONS: WHO SAID WHAT, WHEN & WHERE 175 (David L. Sills & Robert K. Merton eds., 2000) [hereinafter SOCIAL SCIENCE QUOTATIONS] (reporting survey of American life commissioned by President Herbert Hoover and published during Franklin Roosevelt's presidency).

[2] G. Edward White, The Intellectual Origins of Torts in America, 86 YALE L.J. 671, 678–83 (1977).

[3] MORTON J. HORWITZ, THE TRANSFORMATION OF AMERICAN LAW, 1780–1860 209–10 (1977).

[4] By way of example, products liability was a field that owes its origins to automobile law cases. The field of products liability took form in large part through a series of groundbreaking automobile liability cases. Judge Benjamin Cardozo, in MacPherson v. Buick Motor Co., 111 N.E. 1050 (1916), was the first judge to lay the foundation for the field of products liability when he creatively sidestepping the harsh doctrine of privity permitting a consumer to recover for injuries caused by a collapsed wheel on his Buick roadster. In his famous ruling, Judge Cardozo declared that "if [the manufacturer] is negligent, where danger is to be foreseen, a liability will follow." Id. at 1053. The citadel of privity finally collapsed in yet another automobile liability case forty-four years later. See Henningsen v. Bloomfield Motors, 161 A.2d 69, 99–100 (1960) (finding no contractual privity for breach of warranty in accident arising out of a malfunctioning automobile steering system). The first one hundred-million dollar award for punitive damages was in the Ford Pinto case of Grimshaw v. Ford Motor Co., 174 Cal. Rptr. 348, 348 (Cal. Ct. App. 1981) (remitting the $ 125 million punitive damages to $ 3.5 million). The jurisprudence of strict liability was in large part a judicial solution to the problem of reallocating the cost of accidents caused by defective automobiles. For example, the manufacturer's duty to recall or retrofit defective products was directly impacted by automobile law. Michael L. Rustad & Thomas H. Koenig, Cybertorts and Legal Lag: An Empirical Analysis, 13 S. CAL. INTERDIS. L. J. 77, 79 (2003). The invention of the automobile spurred changes in jurisdiction, state warranties, and the certificates of title rules enacted to trace stolen automobiles.

[5] MARSHALL S. SHAPO, AN INJURY LAW CONSTITUTION 22 (2012).

[6] W. Page Keeton, et al., Prosser and Keeton on the Law of Torts, § 3 (5th ed. 1984) at 15.

fraudsters, stalkers, and predators—the motliest assortment of tortfeasors. The viciousness with which ex-husbands and lovers destroy reputations and inflict emotional injuries with impunity is part of the Internet's seamy side. Cybertorts are primarily about defective information that harms economic, privacy, and reputational interests. Virtual torts or cybertorts are civil actions to recover chiefly economic, reputational, or privacy-based damages arising from Internet communications; such as e-mail, blogs, or website postings.

Technorati, for example, uncovered 112 million blogs worldwide—this number does not include the estimated 72 million bloviators in the Chinese blogosphere. Bloggers and their audiences collide, collaborate, and enter into highly charged feuds that sometimes end in litigation. Cybertorts supplement but do not supplant the regulation of cyberspace.[7] Anonymous cyber mobs terrorize women "with threats of sexual violence and doctored photographs, often encouraging others to physically assault individuals and providing their home addresses."[8] Since the mid-1990s, most Internet tort cases have been business or publication torts, filed by companies to protect their intangible assets, reputation, and e-market share. Relatively few consumers have been able to recover for virtual injuries arising out of Internet publication torts.[9] For most Internet-related torts against individuals, the preferred remedy is to mitigate the damage to the plaintiff's reputation or peace of mind, with obtaining a monetary settlement being of secondary importance

The chief controversy for Internet torts is whether websites should continue to be shielded from most tort liability.[10] The argument for a broad immunity is that website entrepreneurs enjoy a subsidy enabling them to publish materials that benefit the public. Nevertheless, cyberspace may well constitute a "tort-free zone" for service providers and ultimately shield wrongdoers.[11] In addition, jurisdiction, for example, is often difficult to establish in cybertorts because of the lack of clarity as to where a virtual injury occurs. In this chapter, the term "cybertort" is used to describe torts arising out of e-mail, social media sites, and other computer related contexts.

Among the subjects covered in this chapter are intentional torts; personal property torts; information-based torts; privacy; negligent security; information products liability; foreign Internet torts, or, *delicts*; common law defenses; and Section 230 of the Communications Decency Act ("CDA"). The CDA shields interactive computer services

---

[7] Michael L. Rustad, Torts as Public Wrongs, 38 Pepperdine L. Rev. 433, 440 (2011) ("While the manifest function of tort law is civil recourse or compensation, its latent function is vindicating public wrongs.").

[8] Danielle Keats Citrone, Civil Rights in our Information Age, Chapter 2 in THE OFFENSIVE INTERNET: PRIVACY, SPEECH, AND REPUTATION (ed. Saul Levmore & Martha C. Nussbaum) 31, 33 (2010).

[9] Michael L. Rustad & Thomas H. Koenig, Cybertorts and Legal Lag: An Empirical Analysis, 13 S. CAL. INTERDISC. L.J. 77, 128 (2003) (presenting empirical research on the incidence of cybertorts).

[10] Nigel Shadbolt & Tim Berners Lee, Web Science Emerges, SCI. AM. (Oct. 2008) at 79 (citing Technorati study).

[11] Professors Ronald J. Mann and Jane K. Winn define the term "ISP" to subsume "a variety of activities: from the wholly anonymous transmission of a backbone provider, to the wholly transmissive service that a commercial ISP provides to a domain like utexas.edu, to the partially content-based activity that a provider like AOL, MSN, or Yahoo! provide to one of their subscribers." RONALD J. MANN & JANE K. WINN, ELECTRONIC COMMERCE 177 (2d ed. 2005). For purposes of the Digital Millennium Copyright Act, an Internet "service provider," or ISP, is "a provider of online services or network access, or the operator of facilities therefore." 17 U.S.C. § 512(k)(1)(B).

from claims that seek to treat him or her as the publisher or speaker of information provided by another information content provider.[12]

(B) The Unique Qualities of Virtual Torts

In virtual space, all torts are, in an important sense, information-based.[13] In virtual space, all torts are, in an important sense, are information-based. Cybertorts serve as a gap-filler that supplements the criminal law and the limited regulations of cyberspace torts that complement regulation by serving a[14] Torts in cyberspace are referred to as e-torts, cybertorts, or Internet torts. Internet-related torts arise on Twitter, blogs, e-mail transmissions, and website postings. This is in contrast to traditional categories of injury such as automobile accidents, slip and fall mishaps, medical malpractice, or injuries due to dangerously defective products. The largest numbers of Internet tort cases are publication torts filed by companies to protect their interests. Repeat players such as terms of service providers require consumers to submit to one-sided mandatory arbitration clauses, which are in effect, an anti-remedy.[15] As a result, few consumers have been able to recover for virtual injuries arising out of Internet publication torts. Internet tort cases have given rise to new questions of liability. For example, if an intruder or virus exploits a website, destroys or misappropriates trade secrets or other data belonging to third parties, does the company's failure to have a contingency plan make it liable? Negligent computer security is a cause of action that has been slow to develop. In the first two decades of Internet torts, negligence cases have been rare, as the legal landscape has been dominated by intentional torts.

The potential for Internet-related intentional torts in the blogosphere is staggering. Internet torts are not just old wine in new bottles but create unique injuries or harm. Each day Internet users leave digital trails that may be classified as torts or civil wrongs. .Online mobs use Google bombing to ensure that anyone searching a particular's

---

[12] The Communications Decency Act ("CDA"), 47 U.S.C. § 230(c)(1), "precludes courts from entertaining claims that would place a computer service provider in a publisher's role," and therefore bars "lawsuits seeking to hold a service provider liable for its exercise of a publisher's traditional editorial functions—such as deciding whether to publish, withdraw, postpone, or alter content." Zeran v. America Online, Inc., 129 F.3d 327, 330 (4th Cir. 1997). The CDA defines "interactive computer service" as "any information service, system, or access software provider that provides or enables computer access by multiple users to a computer server, including specifically a service or system that provides access to the Internet and such systems operated or services offered by libraries or educational systems." 47 U.S.C. § 230(f)(2).

[13] Nicolas P. Terry, Cyber–Malpractice: Legal Exposure for Cybermedicine, 25 AM. J. L. & MED. 327, 332 (1999).

[14] Id.

[15] See Michael L. Rustad & Thomas H. Koenig, Rebooting Cybertort Law, 80 WASH. L. REV. 335, 351 (2005) ("Repeat players such as ISPs have no qualms about protecting their rights through Internet lawsuits over intellectual property, tort, and contract rights, all of which are primarily resolved in federal courts."). In contrast consumers, are often required to submit their claims to one-sided arbitral providers. Mark E. Budnitz, Arbitration of Disputes Between Consumers and Financial Institutions: A Serious Threat to Consumer Protection, 10 OHIO ST. J. ON DISP. RESOL. 267, 310, 318, 326–330 (1995) (arguing that consumer arbitration favors repeat players). See also, Edward A. Dauer, Judicial Policing of Consumer Arbitration, 1 PEPP. DISP. RESOL. L.J. 91 (2000); Zev J. Eigen, Nicholas F. Menillo and David Sherwyn, Shifting the Paradigm of the Debate: A Proposal to Eliminate At–Will Employment and Implement a "Mandatory Arbitration Act," 87 IND. L.J. 271, 273 (2012) (arguing that those favoring and opposing mandatory arbitration are entrenched and polarized and noting that "detractors are making this erroneous presumption about mandatory arbitration."); Theodore Eisenberg & Geoffrey P. Miller, The Flight from Arbitration: An Empirical Study of Ex Ante Arbitration Clauses in the Contracts of Publicly Held Companies, 56 DEPAUL L. REV. 335, 336–37 (2007) (arguing that these clauses were included in consumer contracts to side-step class actions).

woman's name will see defamatory or damaging statements.[16] Social networks "leverage trust and vouching, lending credibility to hurtful materials posted."[17] In the brick-and-mortar world, torts are largely about accident law where there is a potentially large sum of compensatory damages at stake. For most Internet-related torts, the individual plaintiff's goal, generally, is to restore his or her reputation or peace of mind with a monetary settlement being a subsidiary concern. For corporate plaintiffs, Internet torts are primarily about protecting a company's reputation, business, or intellectual property.

A virtual hate posting or online stalking is the viral gift that keeps on giving. Plaintiffs in virtual injury cases will find that an injurious comment is difficult to expunge from the Internet, unlike a newspaper where a retraction and the passage of time may reduce the radius of the injury significantly. Virtual torts—such as the invasion of privacy, or defamation—are frequently difficult to expunge once they go into a viral spiral.[18] Retractions on the Internet by bloviators or other tortfeasors will rarely be effective even with the help of companies such as Reputation Defender that will attempt to expunge tortious postings. Once an injurious comment has been posted, it may be mirrored on other sites, or be captured by companies using Wayback Machines that capture content from a given period.[19] The Wayback Machine seeks to catalogue all websites on the Internet and currently has a database spanning more than a decade. Images from the Wayback Machine must still be authenticated before legal action can be undertaken.

To authenticate a screenshot, the government will typically call a witness to "testify about how the Wayback Machine website works and express an opinion about the reliability of its contents."[20] The Wayback Machine enables users to "browse through over 150 billion web pages archived from 1996 to a few months ago."[21] The user types in the web address of a site or page where they would like to start, and presses enter.[22] Users "select from the archived dates available. The selected pages, in turn point to other archived pages at as close a date as possible."[23]

Another digital treasure trove, the Internet Archive, "collects, stores, and provides access to approximately 160 billion web pages."[24] It is unclear how a defamation defendant would retract a libelous posting given the multiplicity of these sites. There is

---

[16] Id. at 34.

[17] Anita Bernstein, Real Remedies for Virtual Injuries, 90 N.C. L. REV. 1, 14 (2012).

[18] What Justice Benjamin Cardozo wrote about defamation is especially true about the Internet: "Reputation . . . is a plant of tender growth, and its bloom, once lost, is not easily restored." People ex rel Karlin v. Culkin, 248 N.Y. 464, 478 (1928) (J. Cardozo).

[19] "Browse through over 240 billion web pages archived from 1996 to a few months ago. To start surfing the Wayback, type in the web address of a site or page where you would like to start, and press enter. Then select from the archived dates available. The resulting pages point to other archived pages at as close a date as possible. Keyword searching is not currently supported. http://archive.bibalex.org, the Internet archive at the New Library of Alexandria, Egypt, Mirrors the Wayback Machine." http://archive.org/web/web.php (last visited June 14, 2013).

[20] United States v. Bansal, 663 F.3d 634, 668 (3dCir. 2011); Novak v. Tucows, Inc., No. 06–CV–1909, 2007 U.S. Dist. LEXIS 21269, 2007 WL 922306, at *5 (E.D.N.Y. March 26, 2007) (striking Wayback Machine evidence in the absence of any authentication of plaintiff's internet printouts).

[21] Internet Archive, About the Wayback Machine, http://archive.org/web/web.php.

[22] Id.

[23] Id.

[24] Id.

no procedural mechanism for expunging ongoing Internet-related torts—let alone giving plaintiffs the right to remove postings that create ongoing injuries. To date, despite an epidemic of computer security flaws, no plaintiff has recovered damages for negligent Internet security under either a tort or a contract cause of action.[25]

Yet, most security incidents result from hackers exploiting known vulnerabilities arising out of grossly inadequate software engineering practices. Too many Internet websites fail to reduce the radius of the risk of known security flaws in their products before releasing them into the stream of cyberspace commerce. Worse yet, plaintiffs have no legal right to compel a website to remove material that constitutes an ongoing tort or crime. It is often expensive and difficult to unveil anonymous posters and, as Chapter 3 illustrated, personal jurisdiction is often problematic when pursuing tortfeasors across borders. Another unique feature of cybertorts is that injunctive relief and other equitable remedies are often more important than monetary damages, which is the remedy of choice for bricks and mortar torts.[26]

(C) Cyber Liability Insurance

Risk averse companies will seek indemnification or insurance to reallocate the risks of cybertort liability but the vast majority of cybertorts are intentional torts, which are not insurable.[27] Many U.S. states take the position that insuring against punitive damages creates a moral hazard and therefore should not be permitted on public policy grounds. Insurance policy options include coverage for information-based torts such as defamation, Internet security breaches, theft of consumer data, property damage, errors and omissions (such as professional liability for computer programming errors), directors' and officers' liability, extortion coverage, and group personal liability. Insurers have not yet offered business interruption policies because they have too little data on the risk factors.

Internet crime liability requires an assessment of first and third party risks. For example, the "distributed-denial-of-service-attack on Yahoo, eBay, and *E-Trade on February 8, 2000, generated a turnover loss of $250 million."[28] A growing number of states have enacted data breach statutes in addition to common law tort liability. The California Senate approved a proposal to extend their data protection statute to

---

[25] See Michael L. Rustad & Thomas H. Koenig, Taming the Tort Monster: The American Civil Justice System as a Battleground of Social Theory, 68 BROOK. L. REV. 1, 6 (2002) (explaining that "[t]orts in cyberspace have been slow to develop, partially as the result of tort reform and new judicial subsidies benefiting Internet service providers, telecommunications giants and media moguls" and arguing that "[t]ort rights and remedies must be strengthened so that they can play their traditional social control role in the information age.").

[26] In many substantive fields of cyberspace law, injunctive or equitable relief is the primary objective of the plaintiff. For example, in the leading constitutional cases in cyberspace, the whole point is to enjoin enforcement of a statute. See e.g., Ashcroft v. ACLU, 535 U.S. 564 (2002) (enjoining enforcement of the Child Online Protection Act which incorporated community standards to identify material harmful to minors). See also Reno v. ACLU, 521 U.S. 844 (1997) (holding portions of the Communications Decency Act of 1996 to be unconstitutional). Injunctive relief is the chief remedy sought in anti-spam cases. See e.g., America Online, Inc. v. Nat'l Health Care Disc., Inc., 174 F. Supp. 2d 890 (N.D. Iowa 2001) (entering preliminary injunction against mass commercial e-mail firm violating AOL's terms of service agreement). Many of the tort cases in cyberspace also focus on injunctive relief. See Register.com, Inc. v. Verio, Inc., 126 F. Supp. 2d 238 (S.D. N.Y. 2000) (demonstrating a likelihood of success on the merits and irreparable harm without such relief based upon contract law, trespass to chattels, and violations of computer fraud and trademark laws).

[27] Steven Shavell, Liability for Harm Versus Regulation of Safety, 13 J. LEGAL STUDIES 357 (1984).

[28] Torsten Grzebiela, Insurability of Electronic Commerce Risks, PROCEEDINGS OF THE 35TH HAWAII INTERNATIONAL CONFERENCE ON SYSTEM SCIENCES (2002) at 1.

address "email addresses, passwords, user names, and security questions and answers for online accounts."[29] The problem that insurers face is the lack of long-term project data on the radius of the risk of E–Commerce specific risks.[30] Cyber risks are losses "relating to malfunction of or injury to computers (hardware and software), as well as the failure of electronic systems and communication systems, including e-mail and the Internet."[31]

The chief Internet-related torts are information-based virtual injuries—such as defamation, the invasion of privacy, business torts, and personal property torts. Torts such as defamation, trade secret misappropriation, the right of publicity, publication of private facts, false light and intrusion into seclusion apply equally well to bloggers and posters on social networking sites.[32] Traditional insurance policies do not afford much coverage for cyber risks because they tend to be oriented towards insuring tangible property as opposed to data or intangibles. Increasingly, insurers are offering coverage for E–Commerce activities but many companies are still self-insured or running with the risk of theft of information and data. Insurance policy coverage options include coverage for the risks of cybercrimes, property damage, errors and omissions (such as professional liability for computer programming errors), directors and officers liability, employment practices liability, business interruption, extortion coverage, group personal liability, and key person life coverage.[33]

Insurance for cyberspace activities is in its infancy and insurers do not have long tail data on security and other cybertort risks. Insurers are collecting data on cybercrimes to determine whether they will offer cybercrime coverage. Thus, insurers have yet to play a significant role in enforcing safety standards or stimulating industry standards to reduce the radius of the risk. The earliest indemnification cases were claims by customers of service providers. In *America Online, Inc. v. St. Paul Mercury Ins. Co.*,[34] the federal court determined that liability associated with loss of use of consumers' computers was excluded from coverage under AOL's general liability policy's impaired property exclusion. The court reasoned the consumers' underlying complaint to be that AOL's proprietary software was a defective product that caused the loss of computer use. The court found that defective products claims were barred since harm to property that was not physically damaged was excluded from coverage where it was caused by a faulty or dangerous product.

---

[29] Data Breaches: California Data Breach Notice Law Would Apply to User Names, Passwords, BLOOMBERG BNA, ELECTRONIC COMMERCE & LAW REPORT (May 22, 2013).

[30] Id. at 2.

[31] JEFFREY STEMPEL, STEMPEL ON INSURANCE CONTRACTS, § 23.01 (3rd ed. 2005).

[32] "In the brick-and-mortar world, negligence-based cases dominate the legal landscape. The most frequent type of traditional tort case involves an individual suing another individual (47%), followed by an individual suing a business (37%). The universe of Internet torts, in sharp contrast, continues to be doctrinally rooted in personal property torts that originated during England's feudal period, such as conversion and trespass to chattels. An astonishing 101 of the 143 cybertort plaintiffs (71%) based their claims on intentional torts. In our sample, plaintiffs in only four cases asserted negligence or malpractice causes of action. Corporations, rather than individual litigants, filed three-quarters of the cybertort cases in which negligence was at issue." Michael L. Rustad & Thomas H. Koenig, Rebooting Cybertort Law, 80 Wash. L. Rev. 335, 358 (2005); See e.g., Daniel Nemet–Nejat, Hey, That's My Persona!: Exploring the Right of Publicity for Blogs and Online Social Networks, 33 COLUM. J.L. & ARTS 113, 129 (2009).

[33] Dennis Drouin, Cyber Risk Insurance, GIAC SECURITY ESSENTIAL CERTIFICATION (Feb. 9, 2004).

[34] 207 F. Supp.2d 459 (E.D. Va. 2001).

§ 6.2   INTENTIONAL CYBERTORTS AGAINST THE PERSON

(A) Assault and Battery

Intentional torts are injuries committed with the purpose to bring about a desired result or a substantial certainty that a desired consequence will occur: "One who intentionally causes injury to another is subject to liability to the other for that injury, if his conduct is generally culpable and not [privileged]."[35] To establish a *prima facie* case for an intentional tort, a cybertort plaintiff must prove three things: (1) an act by the defendant; (2) intent, which means that the defendant desires or it is substantially certain that an act will occur; and (3) causal connection between the defendant's act and some injury. Intentional torts such as battery; assault; false imprisonment; or trespass to land are not likely to be well developed in cyberspace. Assault is unlikely to arise out of cyberspace activities.[36] To prove assault, a plaintiff must prove some act by the defendant creating a reasonable apprehension in plaintiff of immediate harmful or offensive contact to the plaintiffs' person.

As with any intentional tort, the plaintiff must prove the defendant intended an act causally connected to her injury. Words alone do not make the actor liable for assault unless the plaintiff is placed in reasonable apprehension of an imminent harmful or offensive contact with his person. Battery, too, is virtually impossible to be developed in cyberspace because there can be neither a harmful or offensive contact nor an imminent apprehension of such a contact in cyberspace.[37] Using texting or social media to create violent mobs creates the potential for liability for assault and battery. In Chicago, "a mob action [goes] along Michigan Avenue in March. They say several hundred people—most of them teenagers—ran up and down the upscale shopping area, yelling and bumping into people."[38] To date, intentional tort actions have seldom been asserted in Internet-related cases and where they have been asserted no plaintiff has been successful.[39]

(B) Intentional Infliction of Emotional Distress

ort remedies need to be developed to protect against cyberstalking and threatening e-mail transmissions from angry ex-husbands, spurned boyfriends, or infatuated strangers. No reported case has yet granted redress for online stalking. Internet wrongdoers have harmed women by, among other things, maliciously posting personal information on sadomasochistic web sites and by using new morphing technologies to superimpose their victim's face on pornographic images. Intentional torts are injuries committed to bring about a desired result. Under the law of torts, the substantial

---

[35] RESTATEMENT (SECOND) TORTS § 870 (1979).

[36] The problem for the plaintiff in proving assault is that a plaintiff must be placed in reasonable apprehension of immediate harmful or offensive contact. Similarly, the elements of false imprisonment will not be present unless an act of the defendant either confines or restrains the plaintiff in a bounded area. Trespass to land is also not likely to arise out of an Internet interaction. To establish a prima facie case for trespass to land, there must be proof of a physical invasion of real property along with intent and causation.

[37] See RESTATEMENT THIRD OF TORTS: LIABILITY FOR PHYSICAL AND EMOTIONAL HARM § 18, § 21 (2009).

[38] Illinois Cracks Down on Social Media Flash Mob, CHICAGO DAILY HERALD (May 18, 2013).

[39] Erin S. Davis, A World Wide Problem on the World Wide Web: International Responses to Transnational Identity Theft via the Internet, 12 WASH. U. J.L. & POL'Y 201, 201 (2003) (stating that the difficulty of developing cyberspace remedies lies in the radically divergent legal traditions of countries connected to the Internet).

certainty doctrine is a legal theory that assumes the required tortious intent even if the actor did not intend the result, but knew with substantial certainty that the desired consequences would occur. "One who intentionally causes injury to another is subject to liability to the other for that injury, if his conduct is generally culpable and not [privileged]."[40] Battery, assault, false imprisonment, intentional infliction of emotional distress, conversion, trespass to land, and trespass to chattels are examples of intentional torts. "One who intentionally causes injury to another is subject to liability to the other for that injury, if his conduct is generally culpable and not [privileged]."[41] The intentional infliction of emotional distress ("IIED") tort of outrage is often asserted in cybertort actions but seldom successful.[42] To support the IIED, conduct must be so outrageous in character, and so extreme in degree, as to go beyond all possible bounds of decency.[43] The intentional infliction of emotional distress and the invasion of privacy are the intentional torts most often pleaded in stalking cases.[44] IIED actions arise out of "Internet websites, chat rooms, instant messaging, text, and picture messaging on phones and blogs to harass or intimidate others."[45] States following Section 46 of the Restatement (Third) of Torts require only a showing of recklessness to prove IIED. Other states require the plaintiff to prove intent.[46]

---

[40] RESTATEMENT (SECOND) TORTS § 870 (1979).

[41] Id.

[42] "The ugly side of the Internet is illustrated by the increasing occurrence of harassment and stalking in the online environment. One woman, after dating a man whom she had met online, could not escape his harassing contacts for months despite changing her phone number and relocating her residence. Such cases may lead to liability for intentional infliction of emotional distress. The RESTATEMENT (SECOND) OF TORTS provides: 'One who by extreme and outrageous conduct either intentionally or recklessly causes severe emotional distress to another is subject to liability for such distress and if bodily harm to the other results from it, for such bodily harm.' . . . Dozens of recent articles reference the prevalence of stalking on the Internet and the rise in related court cases. A recent poll indicates that a full eighty percent of Americans worry about "virtual stalking." Threats in Cyberspace can be as disturbing as threats in the physical world. While many threats do not rise to this level, courts should, nevertheless, allow Cyberspace victims to sue for assault in appropriate circumstances. The tort of assault requires threatening words to be used against a person in a context where the recipient could reasonably fear that a physical attack was imminent. At least one case has held that threats from a telephone user one room away can constitute assault. Arguably, a court may find assault where threatening words are received over the Internet, as the recipient may know, or have no way of knowing, whether the sender is nearby." Michael L. Rustad, Legal Resources for Lawyers Lost in Cyberspace, 30 SUFFOLK U. L. REV. 317, 342–43 (1996). In the decade and a half since the World Wide Web went online, only a handful of plaintiffs have succeeded in asserting an intentional infliction of emotional distress claim. Few of these plaintiffs have recovered a single dollar from spiteful individuals who perpetrate outrageous actions beyond the reach of tort law. Section 230, for example, shields websites from liability for third party postings that amount to the tort of outrage. Revenge porn websites, for example, have no liability under the current law for postings and photographs of third parties.

[43] RESTATEMENT (THIRD) OF TORTS § 46.

[44] Cause of Action by Victim of Stalking Against Stalker and Third Parties, 32 CAUSES OF ACTION 2d 487 (2006).

[45] Eric Y. Drogin, et al. Psycholegal Aspects of Cyberbullying: The Dark Side of Social Networking, THE SCITECHLAWYER (Spring 2012) at 5.

[46] "[T]he rigor of the outrageousness standard is well-established." Mesa v. City of N.Y., No. 09 Civ. 10464(JPO), 2013 WL 31002, at *28 (S.D.N.Y. Jan. 3, 2013). Conduct must have been "so outrageous in character, and so extreme in degree, as to go beyond all possible bounds of decency, and to be regarded as atrocious, and utterly intolerable in a civilized society." Sullivan v. Andino, No. 09 Civ. 3668(VB), 2012 WL 4714766, at *7 (S.D.N.Y. Sept. 18, 2012) (citing Murphy v. Am. Home Prods. Corp., 58 N.Y.2d 293, 303 (N.Y.1983)). Recovery for IIED claims is available "only where severe mental pain or anguish is inflicted through a deliberate and malicious campaign of harassment or intimidation." Hanly v. Powell Goldstein, LLP, No. 05 Civ. 5089(KMW), 2007 WL 747806, at *6 (S.D.N.Y. March 5, 2007)

The Restatement (Third) illustrates IIED, or the tort of outrage, arising out of vicious postings on websites by high school students bullying and stalking a classmate.[47] A Georgia girl filed an IIED and libel action against two classmates and their parents in a Facebook cyberbullying case. Her classmates created a fake Facebook page in her name, with photos and posts that were distorted to make her appear to be obese, racist, sexually active, and an illegal drug user. Even though the website that masqueraded as the plaintiff's was a cruel hoax, her IIED lawsuit is unlikely to succeed because of the difficulty of proving the conduct was so extreme to violate all bounds of decency or that it caused her such extreme distress that she needed to seek counseling.

IIED is not cognizable for "demeaning comments" that a company made on an ex-employee's Facebook page. In *Murdock v. L.A. Fitness*[48], the plaintiff based his IIED claim on L.A. Fitness employees "humiliating, bullying, making racially offensive statements . . . [and] posting demeaning comments on its Facebook [page]."[49] The court stated that while these comments were insensitive, they do not amount to extreme or outrageous conduct. To be held liable for the tort of outrage, the Internet actor "must do more than intentionally or recklessly cause emotional harm. The actor must act in a ways that is extreme and outrageous."[50]

Some states following Section 46 of the Restatement (Second) of Torts require only a showing of recklessness for IIED. The tort of outrage causes of action is often difficult to pursue because cyberattacks are often anonymous. A social networking site, Autoadmit, featured a message board "generating hundreds of threatening, sexually explicit and damaging statements about female law students."[51] One anonymous poster[52] wrote, "I'll force myself on [the identified student] and sodomize her repeatedly."[53] Most online cyber mob bullying never ripens into a tort lawsuit even though online IIED "produces serious emotional and physical suffering" as well as "sustained loss of personal security."[54] Jacqueline Lipton tells the story of how a child's humiliating video went viral causing him such extreme emotional distress that he was institutionalized in a children's psychiatric facility:

> Consider the fate of "Star Wars Kid," a Canadian teenager who filmed himself playing with a golf ball retriever as if it was a light-saber from the *Star Wars* movies. . . . His video was posted to the Internet without his authorization. A variety of amateur video enthusiasts then adopted it on services such as YouTube. They created many popular, but extremely humiliating, mash-up videos of the youth. The young man ended up dropping out of school. He also required psychiatric care, including a period of institutionalization at a children's psychiatric facility.[55]

---

[47] See RESTATEMENT (THIRD) OF TORTS, § 46, illus. 1.

[48] 2012 WL 5331224 (D. Minn. Oct. 29, 2012).

[49] Id. at *1-*3.

[50] RESTATEMENT (THIRD) OF TORTS, § 46, cmt. d.

[51] Danielle Keats Citrone, Civil Rights in Our Information Age, Chapter 2 in THE OFFENSIVE INTERNET: PRIVACY, SPEECH, AND REPUTATION (ed. Saul Levmore & Martha C. Nussbaum) 31, 43 (2010).

[52] A victim of these sites could theoretically file a John Doe subpoena requesting IP addresses to identify the anonymous posters, but his is rarely successful.

[53] Danielle Citrone, Civil Rights in Our Information Age, Id. at 34.

[54] Id. at 37.

[55] Jacqueline Lipton, We, the Paparazzi: Developing a Privacy Paradigm for Digital Video, 95 IOWA L. REV. 919, 921–922 (2010).

Tammy S. Blakey, Continental Airlines' first female captain, filed sexual harassment and hostile work environment claims against Continental based in part on sexually demeaning Internet postings by some male pilots on the Crew Members Forum.[56] A jury awarded Blakey $480,000 in back pay, $15,000 in front pay and $500,000 for emotional damages.[57] The trial court granted summary judgment in favor of Continental Airlines in large part because the employer did not have control of postings by the pilots on the online bulletin board. In reversing and remanding, the New Jersey Supreme Court instructed the trial court to consider whether the bulletin board may "have been so closely related to the workplace environment and beneficial to [the employer] that a continuation of harassment on the forum should be regarded as part of the workplace."[58]

Amanda Butler, a second female pilot who alleged a parallel pattern of online sexual harassment also sued Continental Airlines. In *Butler v. Cont'l Express, Inc.*,[59] Rainer Krebs, a pilot for Continental Express, used a software application to superimpose Ms. Butler's face onto nude pictures of women in sexually suggestive poses. He posted these pornographic images on the Internet and the airline's intranet. Ms. Butler received a jury award predicated upon defamation per se, IIED, invasion of privacy, and punitive damages. The virtual injury suffered by Amanda Butler involves an entirely new category of intensified injury due to objectionable images distributed online; this malignant behavior went far beyond the verbal bantering found in a traditional workplace. The jury awarded punitive damages against the airline for not taking prompt remedial disciplinary action after gaining knowledge of the harassment, as well as $360,198 to compensate Ms. Butler for mental anguish and damage to her reputation. Cyberbullying requires a showing of extremely outrageous behavior calculated to cause extreme emotional distress.

A Michigan federal jury awarded $4.5 million to the University of Michigan's first openly gay student body president arising out of Internet postings by a former Michigan assistant attorney general.[60] The "jury ruled in favor of Christopher Armstrong, who claimed he suffered distress after a blog created by Andrew Shirvell accused him of enticing minors with alcohol and recruiting people to become homosexual."[61] "Armstrong accused Shirvell of defamation as well as emotional distress for his actions on the blog, in Facebook posts and during visits to the Ann Arbor campus."[62] The jury award was predicated upon the torts of the intentional

---

[56] Blakey v. Continental Airlines, Inc., 164 N.J. 38 (2000). See also, Blakey v. Cont'l Airlines, 730 A.2d 854 (N.J. Sup. Ct. 1999) (dismissing a female airline pilot's defamation lawsuit for statements made on Continental Airline's internal electronic bulletin board since there was no evidence that defendant-pilots targeted their postings at plaintiff).

[57] Id. at 54.

[58] Id.

[59] 2002 NLP IP Company–American Lawyer Media, J: 98: 05227, No. 96–1204096 (Montgomery, Texas June 8, 1998).

[60] Tom Watkins, Jury Orders Lawyer to Pay $4.5 Million to Gay University of Michigan Alumnus, CNN JUSTICE (Aug. 17, 2012).

[61] Jeff Karoub, Lawyer Ordered to Pay $4.5 Million to Gay University of Michigan Student, Associated Press, (August 17, 2012).

[62] Id.

infliction of emotional distress, the invasion of privacy, and defamation.[63] The recent trend is "incorporating criminal liability, in addition to civil tort liability."[64]

(C) Malicious Prosecution

Plaintiffs must demonstrate three to prove malicious prosecution: a plaintiff must demonstrate that the prior action (1) was commenced by or at the direction of the defendant and was pursued to a legal termination in the plaintiff's favor; (2) was brought without probable cause; and (3) initiated with malice. The victims of frivolous cybertort lawsuits may file malicious prosecution claims. "A litigant will lack probable cause for his action either (1) if he relies upon facts which he has no reasonable cause to believe to be true, or (2) if he seeks recovery upon a legal theory which is untenable under the facts known to him."[65] In *Xcentric Ventures L.L.C. v. Borodkin,*[66] the defendants in a malicious prosecution action sued RipOffReport.com for a RICO racketeering claim and lost. Ripoff Report then filed suit against the unsuccessful plaintiffs for malicious prosecution and aiding and abetting tortious conduct.[67] The court found that while the plaintiffs' case was tenuous that there was probable cause to file the complaint so the claim for malicious prosecution failed.[68] The court also found no basis for an aiding and abetting claim.[69]

In a Massachusetts case, an attorney convinced a state trial court to assign him Ripoff's copyright in the aftermath of a defamation lawsuit against the website.[70] A Massachusetts trial judge issued an opinion issuing an injunction against Ripoff naming the plaintiff as copyright owner with the power to take all steps and action necessary or appropriate in the name and place "of the defendant to get the report taken down."[71] After receiving an assignment of the copyright, he filed suit against Ripoff for copyright infringement for the defamatory posting about him.[72] It is unlikely, however, that this order will survive scrutiny upon review because it is not a valid assignment or transfer under the U.S. Copyright Act.

(D) Intentional Cybertorts & the First Amendment

Cybertorts frequently trigger the First Amendment because most actions are information-based torts such as the invasion of privacy or defamation.[73] These cases present courts with difficult issues in balancing state tort causes of action against expression protected by the First Amendment. In *Draker v. Schreiber*, a Texas court dismissed a Vice–Principal's claims for IIED against students who created a fake

---

[63] Watkins, Jury Orders Lawyer to Pay $4.5 Million, Id.

[64] Drogin, Cyberbullying, Id.

[65] Sangster v. Paetkau, 80 Cal.Rptr.2d 66, 75 (Cal.Ct.App.1998).

[66] No. 2:12–cv–01426–GMS (D. Az., June 13, 2013).

[67] Id.

[68] Id.

[69] Id.

[70] Sheri Qualters, Attorney Uses Copyright to Attack Unflattering Post, NATIONAL LAW JOURNAL (July 18, 2013).

[71] Id.

[72] Id.

[73] In Cyber Promotions, Inc. v. America Online, Inc., 948 F. Supp. 436, 447 (E.D. Pa. 1996), the court ruled that a private company did not have a First Amendment right to send massive amounts of unsolicited, commercial e-mail to Internet subscribers.

MySpace website masquerading as the school official.[74] A student's website contained the Vice President's name, photo, and place of employment, and made explicit and graphic sexual references, falsely describing her as a lesbian. The court first entered a summary judgment motion against the Vice-Principal because the derogatory statements were not statements of fact. The *Draker* court entered summary judgment against the plaintiff's IIED claim also because this cause of action overlapped with facts pleaded in his defamation claim. Cybertort plaintiffs must demonstrate a defendant's extreme misconduct violating important social norms, illustrating Lessig's argument about how social norms and the law interrelate.

Torts, such as the intentional infliction of emotional distress and false light privacy, are also subject to the constraints of the First Amendment of the U.S. Constitution as confirmed in later cases. The leading non-defamation case arose out of a lawsuit that evangelist Jerry Falwell filed against Larry Flynt, publisher of Hustler Magazine, alleging defamation, invasion of privacy and the intentional infliction of emotional distress for a parody that purported to describe Falwell's first sexual experience, with his mother in an outhouse.[75] Parody is also a First Amendment defense to federal Lanham Act actions, a topic discussed in Chapter 11. The U.S. Supreme Court ruled that Falwell was a public figure and there could be no tort liability under *New York Times v. Sullivan*'s actual malice standard discussed in the defamation section of this chapter. Thus, the First Amendment poses a major obstacle to the development of information-based cybertorts.[76]

(E) Trespass to Virtual Chattels

To constitute a trespass to chattels on the Internet, courts must stretch the ancient tort of trespass to include virtual property not just tangibles such as cattle, sheep or pitchforks.[77] This personal property tort was formulated for tangible goods, not intangible information. U.S. courts have not been reticent to stretch trespass to chattels to apply to intangibles such as websites spyware, or spam-email. Trespass to chattels and conversion were "private wrongs" mentioned by Sir William Blackstone in his famous *Commentaries on the Law of England*, 1762–1765.[78] The intentional torts

---

[74] 2008 WL 3457023 (Tex. App. Ct. 2008).

[75] Hustler Magazine, Inc. v. Falwell, 485 U.S. 46 (1988).

[76] Sanders v. Acclaim Entm't, Inc., 188 F. Supp. 2d 1264 (D. Colo. 2002) (dismissing actions based on negligence and strict liability in lawsuit filed in the Columbine school shooting case in which it was claimed that the killers were "fanatical consumers of violent video games and movies distributed on the Internet"); James v. Meow Media, Inc., 90 F. Supp. 2d 798, 819 (W.D. Ky. 2000) (dismissing product liability claims, finding that information "products" were not encompassed in Kentucky's strict products liability statute "because thoughts, ideas, and expressions contained within defendants' movie, games, and website materials did not constitute a 'product' within the realm of the strict liability doctrine.").

[77] See Hotmail Corp. v. Van$ Money Pie, Inc., No. C98–20064, 1998 U.S. Dist. LEXIS 10729 (N.D. Cal. April 16, 1998) (applying trespass to chattels theory to spam e-mail and finding injury requirement fulfilled by the added costs for personnel in eliminating or responding to e-mail); CompuServe Inc. v. Cyber Promotions, Inc., 962 F. Supp. 1015, 1021–28 (S.D. Ohio 1997) (ruling that spam e-mail constitutes intermeddling with provider's computer system).

[78] "This action of trover and conversion was in its original an action of trespass upon the case, for recovery of damages . . . of any of his chattels, or making them in a worse condition than before." The SIR WILLIAM BLACKSTONE, COMMENTARIES OF SIR WILLIAM BLACKSTONE, KNIGHT, ON THE LAWS AND CONSTITUTION OF ENGLAND (COMMENTARIES ON THE LAWS OF ENGLAND (Aba Classics) (1763–65) at 284 (describing trespass and conversion as wrongs and distinguishing between torts committed with and without force); Sir William Blackstone published Commentaries on the Laws of England from 1765–1769. Volume III of the Commentaries, entitled Private Wrongs, covers the tort law of the mid-eighteenth century. See John

protecting personal property described by William Blackstone serve a special function in the age of the Internet. In eighteenth-century England, the action for trespass to chattels was used to provide compensation for the dispossession of tangible personal property. Today, this ancient remedy has been resurrected to apply to invasions of websites by spam e-mailers, web scrapers, and other virtual trespassers. Electronic signals generated and sent by computer have been held to be sufficiently physically tangible to support a trespass cause of action."[79]

The traditional elements of trespass to chattels require the plaintiff to prove: (1) there must be a disturbance of the plaintiff's possession and (2) the disturbance may be by an actual taking, a physical seizing, and taking hold of the goods, removing them from their owner, or by exercising a control or authority over them inconsistent with the owner's possession.[80] To establish a *prima facie* case of cybertrespass to chattels, the biggest obstacle will be establishing damages. Courts have had little difficulty finding that spreading viruses or transmitting spam can constitute intermeddling or even dispossession of a plaintiff's computer system. Trespass to chattels is conversion's little brother and differs only in the substantiality of damages. Courts have "perused our ancient authors for out of the old fields must come the new corn."[81]

Courts have developed new applications for the ancient personal property torts of the trespass to chattels and conversion. To update Frederic Maitland, "The forms of action we have buried but they rule us from their graves."[82] "In recent years, trespass to personal property, which had been largely relegated to a historical note in legal textbooks, has reemerged as a cause of action in Internet advertising and e-mail cases."[83] "To constitute a trespass to chattels, there must be an interference that proximately causes some injury to the chattel or the plaintiff's rights to it. The owner may recover only the actual damages suffered because of the impairment of the property or the loss of its use. Some actual injury must have occurred in order for a trespass to chattels to be actionable."[84] Plaintiffs in Internet cases often find it difficult to prove actual damages.[85]

(1) Spam E–Mail

Internet service providers such as America Online, Hotmail, and Prodigy were pioneers in using the tort of cybertrespass to chattels to address website intrusions by spyware, spam e-mailers, and web scrapers.[86] The first court opinion to rule that spammers had no First Amendment right to send unsolicited e-mail was handed down in

---

H. Langbein, Introduction to 3 BLACKSTONE COMMENTARIES ON THE LAWS OF ENGLAND (photo. reprint 1979) (1768).

[79] Thrifty–Tel, Inc. v. Bezenek, 46 Cal. App. 4th 1559, 1567 (1996).

[80] Id.

[81] Coke, 4 Inst. 409.

[82] FREDERIC W. MAITLAND, THE FORMS OF ACTION AT COMMON LAW 296 (1909).

[83] Sotelo v. DirectRevenue, Inc., 384 F. Supp. 2d 1219, 1234 (N.D. Ill. 2005).

[84] Intel v. Hamidi, 30 Cal. 4th 1342, 1351, 71 P.3d 296, 302 (2003).

[85] See e.g., Ticketmaster Corp. v. Tickets.com, Inc., 2000 U.S. Dist. LEXIS 12987, 2000 WL 1887522 (2000) (finding insufficient evidence of harm to the chattel to constitute an actionable trespass).

[86] America Online, Inc., v. National Healthcare Disc., Inc., 174 F. Supp. 2d 890 (N.D. Iowa 2001) (awarding $ 319,500 in compensatory damages and $ 100,000 in punitive damages where a defendant defaulted in a judgment based upon trespass to chattels where the commercial e-mailer ignored repeated requests to stop the sending of junk e-mail to AOL and its members).

1996.[87] The first court to apply trespass to chattels to spamming was *CompuServe v. Cyberpromotions, Inc.*[88] In that case, CompuServe filed for a preliminary injunction against Cyberpromotions, a bulk e-mailer. CompuServe was then one of the major national commercial online computer services operating a proprietary nationwide computer network. CompuServe also provided its subscribers with the ability to send and receive e-mails. Cyberpromotions, Inc. and its president Sanford Wallace sold spam e-mail advertisements on behalf of themselves and their clients to hundreds of thousands of CompuServe subscribers. CompuServe notified Cyberpromotions and Sanford that they are prohibited from using CompuServe to process, store or send unsolicited e-mail.

In response, the spammers increased the frequency of e-mail solicitations to CompuServe subscribers. CompuServe was unable to block the spam e-mail and filed suit seeking injunctive relief against the spammer. The spammer defendant defended the claim because it had a First Amendment right to commercial speech. The *CompuServe* court rejected this First Amendment defense. The court found the:

> "defendants engaged in a course of conduct of transmitting a substantial volume of electronic data in the form of unsolicited e-mail to plaintiff's proprietary computer equipment, where defendants continued such practice after repeated demands to cease and desist, and where defendants deliberately evaded plaintiff's affirmative efforts to protect its computer equipment from such use, plaintiff has a viable claim for trespass to personal property and is entitled to injunctive relief to protect its property."[89]

The court ruled Cyberpromotions' spamming activities exceeded consent and constituted a trespass because the defendant bypassed CompuServe's spam blocking software. The *CompuServe* court explained that a plaintiff could sustain an action "for trespass to chattels, as opposed to an action for conversion, without showing a substantial interference with its right to possession of that chattel."[90] The court also found Cyberpromotion's falsification of point of origin information to be evidence it had trespassed on CompuServe's computer network.[91] The use of false header information was calculated to bypass CompuServe's access controls. The court premised the "injury element" of trespass to chattels on the spammer's drain on the processing speed and disk space of the computers. Under this logic, the personal property tort's physical contact element is satisfied by the mere reception of electrons. "Unwanted telephone callers would seem to be engaging in trespass to chattels; the telephone call sends signals

---

[87] Cyber Promotions, Inc. v. America Online, Inc., 1996 U.S. Dist. LEXIS 19073, 1996 WL 633702, *9 (E.D.Pa. 1996). (ruling that Cyber Promotions had the First Amendment right to send unobstructed e-mail to AOL subscribers and that America Online was not equivalent to a company town where a private entity was exercising municipal powers).

[88] 962 F. Supp. 1015 (S.D. Ohio 1997).

[89] Id. at 1017.

[90] Id.

[91] The tort of trespass to chattel encompasses unauthorized access to a computer system where "(1) defendant intentionally and without authorization interfered with plaintiff's possessory interest in the computer system; and (2) defendant's unauthorized use proximately resulted in damage to plaintiff." eBay, Inc. v. Bidder's Edge, Inc., 100 F.Supp.2d 1058, 1069–70 (N.D.Cal.2000); Thrifty–Tel, Inc. v. Bezenek, 46 Cal.App.4th 1559, 1566 & n. 6, 54 Cal.Rptr.2d 468 (1996) (among the first cases to apply this tort in an electronic context).

to the instrument of the recipient. So, too, with fax machines that receives unwelcome transmissions."[92]

(2) Bots as Trespassers

A web robot, or "bot," gathers and mines data from third party websites. Most bot related trespass to chattels cases arise out of a competitor's misuse or abuse of bots. In *eBay Inc. v. Bidder's Edge, Inc.*,[93] the online mogul, eBay, filed suit against Bidder's Edge ("BE"), an aggregate auction website that enables consumers to do comparison-shopping. EBay sought a preliminary injunction against BE for trespassing on its website—trespass to chattels—as well as a variety of other business torts including trade libel and interference with prospective advantage.[94] In that case, Bidder's Edge operated an auction aggregation site, accessing the eBay site about 100,000 times per day, accounting for between 1 and 2 percent of the information requests received by eBay and a slightly smaller percentage of the data transferred by eBay.[95]

The district court rejected eBay's claim that it was entitled to injunctive relief because of the defendant's unauthorized presence alone or because of the incremental cost, the defendant had imposed on operation of the eBay site but found sufficient proof of *threatened* harm in the potential for others to harm.[96] The court reasoned: "If BE's activity is allowed to continue unchecked, it would encourage other auction aggregators to engage in similar recursive searching of the eBay system such that eBay would suffer irreparable harm from reduced system performance, system unavailability, or data losses."[97] The court held the evidence of injury to eBay's computer system sufficient to support a preliminary injunction:

> If the court were to hold otherwise, it would likely encourage other auction aggregators to crawl the eBay site, potentially to the point of denying effective access to eBay's customers. If preliminary injunctive relief was denied, and other aggregators began to crawl the eBay site, there appears to be little doubt that the load on eBay's computer system would qualify as a substantial impairment of condition or value."[98]

(3) Intel v. Hamidi

Trespass to chattels requires the plaintiff to demonstrate a concrete injury, which is not a requirement for trespass to land where nominal damages suffice to pursue a cause of action. Plaintiffs in trespass to chattels case frequently lose their case because they cannot establish concrete damages from a defendant's intermeddling with their website or computer system. This issue of proving concrete damages arose in a trespass to chattels case in which the Intel Corporation filed suit against Ken Hamidi, an

---

[92] Dan J. Burk, The Trouble With Trespass, 3 J. SMALL & EMERGING BUS. L. 1 (1998).

[93] 100 F. Supp. 2d 1058 (N.D. Cal. 2000).

[94] The court held that bots or automated data collection from a company's publicly accessible Website is a trespass on the company's computer system. EBay, Inc. v. Bidder's Edge, Inc., 100 F. Supp. 2d 1058, 1069–1072 (eBay); See also Register.com, Inc. v. Verio, Inc., 126 F. Supp. 2d 238, 248–251 (S.D.N.Y. 2000); Ticketmaster Corp. v. Tickets.com, Inc., supra, 2000 U.S. Dist. LEXIS 12987 at *17, 2000 WL 1887522 at p. *4.) (finding a sufficient injury by taxing computer equipment of websites).

[95] EBay, Inc. v. Bidder's Edge, Inc., Id. at 1061–63.

[96] Id. at 1065–66.

[97] Id. at 1066.

[98] Id. at 1071–72.

ex-employee. In *Intel Corp. v. Hamidi*,[99] the California Supreme Court held that Hamidi's e-mails to current Intel employees, despite requests by Intel to stop sending messages, did not constitute trespass of Intel's e-mail system. Ken Hamidi created an anti-Intel website, transmitting messages critical of Intel's employment practices to over 30,000 Intel employees on six separate occasions. Intel demanded Hamidi stop sending the messages, but he refused and bypassed Intel's firewall[100] that employed routers to filter and transfer information between Intel's internal network and the Internet.

When Intel was unable to block or otherwise filter out the messages, it sent a letter demanding that Hamidi stop sending the mass e-mails to current employees. After Hamidi refused to heed this warning, Intel sought injunctive relief based upon the tort actions of nuisance and trespass to chattels. Intel ultimately dropped its nuisance theory and claim for damages, and only sought injunctive relief.[101] The California Superior Court issued a preliminary injunction, enjoining Hamidi from sending e-mail messages to Intel employees. The California Court of Appeals upheld the injunction, prohibiting Hamidi and his nonprofit organization from sending unsolicited e-mail to Intel's employees. The appeals court found Intel was likely to prevail on its claim that Hamidi trespassed onto Intel's computer system.

Trespass to chattels based upon computer intrusions do not allow "an action for nominal damages for harmless intermeddling with the chattel."[102] The California Supreme Court rejected Intel's trespass to chattels claim on the grounds it had proven no damages.[103] The court found Hamidi's e-mails interfered with, but did not dispossess Intel of their computer system. Intel's computer system was not slowed down by Hamidi's e-mail messages nor did he damage the physical quality or value of Intel's computer equipment.[104]

The court compared Hamidi's unwelcome e-mails to an unpleasant letter, which clearly does not cause injury to the recipient's mailbox.[105] The substantiality of damages was also at issue in another case where the court ruled that a plaintiff failed to establish trespass to chattels because of the inconvenience of deleting the defendant's pop-up advertisements on several occasions.[106] Plaintiffs' attorneys have unsuccessfully

---

[99] 30 Cal.4th 1342 (2003).

[100] A firewall is software at the perimeter controlling access by examining packet headings to authenticate and identify users.

[101] In many fields of global Internet law, injunctive or equitable relief is the primary objective of the plaintiff. For example, in the leading constitutional cases in cyberspace, the whole point is to enjoin enforcement of a statute. See e.g., Ashcroft v. ACLU, 535 U.S. 564 (2002) (enjoining enforcement of the Child Online Protection Act which incorporated community standards to identify material harmful to minors). See also Reno v. ACLU, 521 U.S. 844 (1997) (holding portions of the Communications Decency Act of 1996 to be unconstitutional). Injunctive relief is the chief remedy sought in anti-spam cases. See e.g., America Online, Inc. v. Nat'l Health Care Disc., Inc., 174 F. Supp. 2d 890 (N.D. Iowa 2001) (entering preliminary injunction against mass commercial e-mail firm violating AOL's terms of service agreement). Many of the tort cases in cyberspace also focus on injunctive relief. See Register.com, Inc. v. Verio, Inc., 126 F. Supp. 2d 238 (S.D. N.Y. 2000) (demonstrating a likelihood of success on the merits and irreparable harm without such relief based upon contract law, trespass to chattels, and violations of computer fraud and trademark laws).

[102] Intel Corp. v. Hamidi, 30 Cal. 4th 1342, 1 Cal. Rptr. 3d 32, 71 P. 3d 296, 302 (Cal. 2003).

[103] 71 P.3d 296 (Cal. 2003).

[104] "[T]he tort does not encompass . . . an electronic communication that neither damages the recipient computer system nor impairs its functioning." Id.

[105] 30 Cal.4th 1342, 1347 (2003).

[106] DirecTV, Inc. v. Chin, 2003 WL 22102144 (W.D. Tex. 2003).

attempted to overcome the "present injury" barrier by arguing that consumers are at risk of being victims of identity theft in the future. No plaintiff has been successful in receiving an award to compensate for lost data where identity theft has not yet occurred.[107]

(4) Spyware as Trespass to Chattels

In *Sotelo v. DirectRevenue*,[108] the plaintiff sued the defendant for surreptitiously installing spyware on its computers. Direct Revenue's spyware delivered advertisements to consumers' computer screens through the Internet. To induce consumers to view the ads, the company offered popular software applications, such as screensavers, or games, for no charge. When the consumer downloaded the application, another piece of software known as an "advertising client" that generated the pop-up ads was also installed. The ads could be discarded by clicking on an "X" in the upper right-hand corner of the display-box in which they appeared. In *Sotelo*, the plaintiff claimed the spyware caused its computers to slow down and took up bandwidth, resulting in increased Internet charges. The *Sotelo* court refused to dismiss the plaintiff's trespass to chattels claim finding that unleashing spyware met the injury requirement. The court found that the spam e-mailers caused an actionable injury. The court also refused to dismiss the plaintiff's Illinois Consumer Fraud Act and negligence claim that Direct Revenue breached its duty not to harm its computers, as well as a computer-tampering claim.

(F) Conversion in Cyberspace

"The tort of conversion has been confined to those major interferences with the chattel, or with the plaintiff's rights in it, which are so serious, and so important, as to justify the forced judicial sale to the defendant which is the distinguishing feature of the action. Conversion is an intentional exercise of dominion or control over a chattel which so seriously interferes with the right of another to control it that the actor may justly be required to pay the other the full value of the chattel."[109] Cyberconversion is the wrongful exercise of dominion over personal property on the Internet.

This tort is committed by: (1) intentionally dispossessing another of a chattel; (2) intentionally destroying or altering a chattel in the actor's possession; (3) using a chattel in the actor's possession without authority; (4) receiving a chattel pursuant to sale, lease, pledge, gift or other transaction intending to acquire for himself or for another a proprietary interest in it; (5) disposing of a chattel by a sale, lease, pledge, gift or other transaction intending to transfer a proprietary interest in it; (6) misdelivering a chattel; or (7) refusing to surrender a chattel on demand.[110]

Trespass to chattels is the remedy for reparable personal property whereas conversion applies if there is a complete destruction or dispossession of the personal property. The chief difference between conversion and the trespass to chattels is the

---

[107] Plaintiffs have failed to demonstrate a cognizable injury in a number of negligent computer security cases in which data was lost or stolen. See e.g., Giordano v. Wachovia Sec., 2006 U.S. Dist. LEXIS 52266 (D.N.J. 2006); Bell v. Acxiom Corp., 2006 U.S. Dist. LEXIS 72477 (E.D. Ark. 2006); Key v. DSW, Inc., 454 F. Supp. 2d 684 (S.D. Ohio 2006) and Stollenwerk v. Tri–West Healthcare Alliance, 2005 WL 2465906 (D. Ariz. 2005).

[108] 384 F. Supp. 2d 1219 (N.D. Ill. 2005).

[109] Platte Valley Bank v. Tetra Fin. Group, LLC, 682 F.3d 1078, 1084 (8th Cir. 2012).

[110] Heidtman Steel Prods. v. Compuware Corp., 1999 U.S. Dist. LEXIS 21700 *39 (N.D. Ohio Feb. 15, 1999).

seriousness of the interference or consequences to a computer system. If a virus causes a computer system to go down, this is a substantial and involuntary interference. Conversion can be proven if the defendant seriously invades another's chattel interest in a domain name or a website. A wrongful transfer of a domain name can constitute conversion or substantially changing a website or severely damaging or destroying it can also be a conversion. The standard remedy for conversion is the fair market value of whatever was converted.

The tort of conversion is an aggravated interference with personal property and the remedy is a "forced sale" for the full value of the chattel at the time of dispossession. In contrast, the remedy for trespass to chattels is compensation for the loss of value due to the defendant's interference. Most U.S. "jurisdictions allow the plaintiff to recover for loss of use damages when property is destroyed and limit such recovery loss of use during repair."[111] Conversion is a personal property tort redressing a defendant's unlawful exercise of domain, control, or withholding possession of chattels. Conversion is not cognizable in most jurisdictions unless the personal property owner makes a formal demand to the defendant for return of her property. No court has extended conversion to intellectual property misappropriation because federal or state statutes in most instances preempt this tort action.

(1) Cyberconversion of Domain Names

Every computer connected to the Internet has a unique Internet Protocol ("IP") number, which is an address that allows connected computers to receive information through the network. Because the IP number was difficult to recall, the Domain Name Service ("DNS") associates the number with more easily remembered alphanumeric addresses. A unique domain name arising from the Internet Protocol has qualities of being an intangible. Conversion was originally a remedy for the wrongful taking of the lost goods of another person, so it applied only to tangible property. In *Kremen v. Cohen*,[112] ex-convict Stephen Cohen forged a letter to a domain name registrar, Network Solutions. In the letter, a confederate claimed he was the new contact person for Online Classifieds, Inc., the owner of the domain name, and requested Network Solutions to deregister sex.com. Network Solutions made no effort to determine the authenticity of the letter and instead transferred the domain name, sex.com, to the defrauder, Cohen.[113] After Gary Kremen contacted Network Solutions some time later about the transfer of the domain name to Cohen, an administrator informed him it was too late to undo the transfer. Cohen went on to build sex.com into a cyberporn empire.[114]

Kremen filed suit against Cohen, seeking damages and return of the domain names. A federal court awarded him $40 million in compensatory damages and another $25

---

[111] WILLIAM M. TABB & ELAINE W. SHOBEN, REMEDIES IN A NUTSHELL 143 (2005).

[112] 337 F.3d 1024 (9th Cir. 2003).

[113] Kremen v. Cohen, 337 F.3d 1024, 1027 (9th Cir. 2003).

[114] See generally, KIEREN MCCARTHY, SEX.COM: TWO MEN, TWELVE YEARS AND THE BRUTAL BATTLE FOR THE JEWEL IN THE INTERNET'S CROWN (2007) ("With five million page views every day, sex.com was the most valuable piece of virtual real estate on the planet during the first years of the Internet. But the fact that it didn't physically exist didn't mean that it couldn't be stolen. With an ingenious scam—the full details of which have never been revealed until now—lifelong con man Stephen Cohen was able to snatch the domain name and walk into a life of untold wealth and luxury. But Cohen underestimated the determination of Gary Kremen—sex.com's original owner—to get his property back. The efforts took ten years and millions of dollars, but Kremen eventually saw Cohen finally pay for his crimes.").

million in punitive damages. The court ordered Cohen, the primary wrongdoer, to disgorge profits from using the sex.com domain name and invoked a constructive trust over the ill-gotten gains. Cohen fled to Mexico, hiding his profits in offshore locations beyond the reach of the legal process. Kremen next filed suit against Network Solutions for the tort of conversion. The U.S. district court concluded the letter to Network Solutions was a forgery. The district court, however, reasoned Network Solutions was not liable for conversion because domain names were intangibles and therefore not personal property. The Ninth Circuit reversed the lower court's decision with its holding that the defendant converted a domain name despite its intangible nature.[115] This appellate case was the first time in that a court stretched the tort of conversion to the misappropriation of a domain name. The court reasoned that corporations could be liable when they take away someone's shares, which are pieces of paper symbolizing intangible assets.[116] Since *Kremen*, other California courts have held that a domain name could be converted under California tort law despite it being an intangible.[117] Few other U.S. jurisdictions have followed suit.

(2) Conversion of Websites

In the past twenty-five years, plaintiffs have rarely asserted causes of action for conversion arising out a takeover of the website or its intangible assets. In *Budsgunshop.com v. Security Safe Outlet, Inc.*,[118] a federal court ruled that the U.S. Copyright Act did not preempt a plaintiff's tort of conversion claim arising out of the dispute over the ownership of a website. Security Safe Outlet ("SSO") and its officer expanded its online business selling firearms and its accessories through the www.budsgunshop.com website.[119] SSO hired a consultant to oversee and improve its websites. The consultant and a co-defendant "began the process of spinning out the online business operations of SSO as a separate business entity." This action constituted SSO's proposed third-party claims against the defendant; for conversion, breach of fiduciary duty, and diverting SSO's corporate assets and opportunity, as well as its third-party claims for aiding and abetting this alleged misconduct.[120] Budsgunshop.com ("BGS") filed a multiple count claim against SSO. SSO responded with a counterclaim against BGS asserting a conversion claim centering on three items of property:

> (1) The www.budsgunshop.com website and all data pertaining to that website, including the e-mail database; (2) the data stored on the SSO server located in Paris, Kentucky, which also includes contact information for customers and other

---

[115] Id.

[116] Id. at 1035 (analogizing to cases where corporations are liable for converting shares of stock belonging to someone other than the true owner).

[117] CRS Recovery, Inc. v. Laxton, 600 F.3d 1138, 1142 (9th Cir. 2010) ("Domain names are intangible property subject to conversion claims. To this end, courts generally hold that domain names are subject to the same laws as other types of intangible property. The court has previously explained the logic of California understanding domain names as intangible property because domain names are well-defined interests, exclusive to the owner, and are bought and sold, often for high values. Domain names are thus subject to conversion under California law, notwithstanding the common law tort law distinction between tangible and intangible property for conversion claims").

[118] 2012 U.S. Dist. LEXIS 72575 (E.D. Ky., May 23, 2012).

[119] Id. at *2.

[120] Id. at *3.

dealers; and (3) the www.Security SafeOutlet.com website and all data and electronic information stored within and pertaining to that website.[121]

BGS contended that "websites, databases, data, and other electronic information to be within the scope of copyright law the [U.S. Copyright Act]," preempted SSO's conversion claim."[122] The federal court ruled the U.S. Copyright Act did not preempt SSO's conversion claim, finding no authority that disputes over the ownership of websites were even addressed by the federal statute.[123] "However, BGS does not point courts to any authority holding that all websites are necessarily within the scope of copyright law, simply by virtue of being a website."[124] The court ruled that it lacked the information it needed to determine whether the U.S. Copyright Act preempted website conversion actions.[125] The Kentucky ruling that the U.S. Copyright Act does not preempt conversion claims is a cautious first step toward recognizing broader cyberconversion claims arising out of intermeddling or taking over websites and virtual data. California and New York are the sole U.S. jurisdictions holding such claims cognizable.[126]

§ 6.3   INTENTIONAL BUSINESS TORTS IN CYBERSPACE

The vast majority of business torts in cyberspace are based upon intentional misconduct rather than negligence or strict liability. Corporate plaintiffs file cybertort cases pleading business torts, which include interference with contract, fraud, misrepresentation, trade libel, and the misappropriation of trade secrets. Misappropriation is defined as either acquisition of a trade secret by improper means or disclosure of a trade secret without permission. Business torts typically arise out of online commercial or consumer contracts.

Misappropriation is defined as either acquisition of a trade secret by improper means or disclosure of a trade secret without permission. In addition to the tort of misappropriation for trade secrets covered in Chapter 12, there is also a tort action for breach of confidence, sometimes asserted in disputes over website development. Business torts typically arise out of online commercial or consumer contracts. Business torts include interference with contract, fraud, misrepresentation, trade libel, and the misappropriation of trade secrets.[127]

To prevail in a breach of confidence claim, the plaintiff must show that: (1) it conveyed confidential and novel information; (2) defendants had knowledge that the information was being disclosed in confidence; (3) there was an understanding between plaintiff and defendants that the confidence be maintained; and (4) there was disclosure or use in violation of the understanding.[128] Amazon.com and Wal–Mart

---

[121] Id. at *35.

[122] Id. at *33.

[123] Id. at *33–34.

[124] Id. at *34.

[125] Id. at *41.

[126] Deborah F. Buckman, Annotation, Conversion of Electronic Data, Including Domain Names, 40 A.L.R.6th 295, 306–12 (2008).

[127] The first empirical study of cybertort revealed that business torts constituted 35% of all decided cases and defamation comprised another 27% of the cases. See Michael L. Rustad & Thomas H. Koenig, Cybertorts and Legal Lag: An Empirical Analysis, 13 S. CAL. INTERDISC. L.J. 77, 92 (2003).

[128] Cinebase Software v. Media Guaranty Trust, Inc., 1998 U.S. Dist. LEXIS 15007 (D. N.D. Calif. Sept. 21, 1998).

Stores settled a trade secrets case in which Amazon was charged with hiring Wal–Mart's Essential Computer Systems Managers in order to steal trade secrets.[129] Trade secrets protect proprietary information such as customer lists, technology, and processes, in addition to source codes.[130] In addition to the tort of misappropriation for trade secrets, a company may also have a breach of confidence claim in software development cases. Chapter 12 examines the concepts and methods of trade secrets in cyberspace in detail.

(A) Unfair Competition

The Restatement (Third) of Unfair Competition treats the appropriation of another company's intangible assets as unfair competition. Courts subdivide state unfair competition claims arising out of the defendant's misuse of trademarks into two general types: (1) consumer confusion as to the source of products, and (2) unfair trade practices, a residual category of unfair competition laws. Historically, trademark infringement was a tort; today it is governed by statute. Chapter 11 will cover trademark-related unfair competition causes of action.

The FTC may initiate enforcement actions against palming off, reverse palming off, or other unfair competition in cyberspace cases. Unfair competition occurs when the defendant makes representations deceiving the public such as "palming off" on the trademarks of others. "Palming off" occurs when a defendant uses symbols that are substantially similar to that of a trademark owner. Moreover, reverse passing off typically involves removing or obliterating an original trademark on the plaintiff's goods, without authorization, before reselling those goods. The defendant is masquerading in trademark or trade dress of the plaintiff who actually produced the goods or services.

Misstatements in advertisements and palming off are regarded as frauds against the consuming public.[131] The federal Lanham Act and state trademark law are the sources of law for protecting trademarks, service marks or trade names. Section 43(A) of the Lanham Act provides remedies for false designation of original, false or misleading description of fact that are likely to cause confusion.[132] To state a claim for false designation of origin and false advertising under the Lanham Act, a plaintiff must allege that the defendant in connection with goods or services used in commerce the plaintiff's mark in a manner likely to confuse consumers about the source or sponsorship of the goods or services.[133] In addition, the FTC may prosecute unfair competition cases through its powers to prevent unfair or deceptive trade practices.[134]

---

[129] Associated Press, Amazon and Wal–Mart Settle Accusations Online Bookseller Stole Trade Secrets, BOSTON GLOBE, (April 5, 1999).

[130] "Proprietary Information" means Inventions, Works, Intellectual Property, and any and all confidential, proprietary or secret information, including, without limitation, information relating to products, best-practices, templates, methodologies, research, technology, developments, services, clients, End Customers, suppliers, employees, business, operations or activities, and also similar information of any third party also divulged by the disclosing Party." Control4 Corp., SEC S-1–A Filing (July 18, 2013) (defining proprietary information in licensing agreements).

[131] Id.

[132] 15 U.S.C. § 1125(a).

[133] Lanham Act, § 43(a), 15 U.S.C. § 1125(a).

[134] 15 U.S.C. § 45(B).

(B) Misappropriation of Intangible Data

Misappropriation is the only "unfair competition tort which protects against the simple unfair copying of intellectual creations."[135] Like human beings, all torts have a birthday and the birth of misappropriation was in 1918 when a court first recognized this cause of action. In *International News v. Associated Press*, a court recognized the misappropriation of intangible data for the first time in a case that arose out of the dispute between two news services.[136] The plaintiff, Associated Press ("AP"), had a news wire and sold subscription services to individual newspapers. International News ("INS") would copy AP's "hot news" stories and dispatch them to its customers. The U.S. Supreme Court recognized that this copying constituted unfair competition,[137] stating, "You cannot reap where you have not sown."[138]

The Restatement (Third) of Unfair Competition treats the appropriation of another company's intangible assets as a form of unfair competition. In *Reed Construction Data v. McGraw Hill Companies*,[139] an information provider for the construction industry filed suit against a McGraw–Hill subsidiary, charging that it misappropriated trade secrets masquerading as customers. Reed's complaint cited multiple counts of misconduct by Dodge, an employee of McGraw–Hill, including fraud; misappropriation of trade secrets; misappropriation of confidential information; unfair competition; tortious interference with prospective economic advantage; violation of New York's general business law; violation of the RICO Act; RICO conspiracy; monopolization; attempted monopolization; and unjust enrichment. The parties settled this case before there was a published court opinion. Few countries outside the United States recognize the misappropriation tort. Nevertheless, the Anglo–Australian legal system may soon recognize the virtual misappropriation tort for "reaping without sowing."[140]

(C) Interference with Business Contracts

"Interference with contract" is a tort action for a defendant that convinces a party to breach their contract with the plaintiff or makes it impossible for the plaintiff to carry out its contractual obligations. Five elements are necessary to support a claim for tortious interference with contract or contractual relations: (1) existence of a valid and enforceable contract; (2) defendant's knowledge of that contract; (3) defendant's intentional inducement to breach that contract; (4) the absence of justification; and (5) damages resulting from the breach. In contrast, the interference with prospective contractual relations requires the plaintiff to prove: (1) the defendant intentionally interfered with the plaintiff's existing or potential economic relations (2) for an improper purpose or by improper means and (3) caused injury to the plaintiff. Plaintiffs deploy this tort in pop-up cases on the theory that these advertisements interfere with prospective economic relations.[141] To state a claim for intentional interference with prospective economic advantage, a plaintiff must prove the following:

---

[135] Estelle Derclaye, The Legal Protection of Databases: A Comparative Analysis 226 (2008).

[136] International News v. Associated Press, 248 U.S. 215 (1918).

[137] See generally, Shyamkrishna Balganesh, 'Hot News': The Enduring Myth of Property in News, Colum. L. Rev. 111 (2011).

[138] International News v. Associated Press, 248 U.S. 215, 239 (1918).

[139] No. 09–8578 (S.D.N.Y. September 14, 2010).

[140] Huw Beverley-Smith, The Commercial Appropriation of Personality 112 (2002).

[141] See e.g., Overstock.com v. Smartbargains, Inc., 192 P.3d 858 (Utah 2008).

(1) an economic relationship between the plaintiff and some third party, with the probability of future economic benefit to the plaintiff; (2) the defendant's knowledge of the relationship; (3) intentional acts on the part of the defendant designed to disrupt the relationship; (4) actual disruption of the relationship; and (5) economic harm to the plaintiff proximately caused by the acts of the defendant. The tort of intentional interference with prospective economic advantage does not require a plaintiff to plead that the defendant acted with the specific intent, or purpose, of disrupting the plaintiff's prospective economic advantage. Instead, to satisfy the intent requirement for this tort, it is sufficient to plead that the defendant knew that the interference was certain or substantially certain to occur because of its action.[142]

The tort of prospective economic advantage requires the plaintiff to prove specific persons or entities that were interrupted by the defendant's actions. Courts will not permit a cause of action to accrue where the plaintiff merely lost business on the Internet absent proof of definite contracts interrupted.

A court found that the defendant interfered with prospective contracts and breached a contract in a Pennsylvania case involving ConsulNet, a Canadian eBusiness that designed websites for realtors.[143] The defendant applied for membership, pretending to be a RE/Max real estate broker interested in building a real estate website. His true purpose was to steal the plaintiff's copyrighted software code. The defendant copied copyrighted code from the site and used the purloined software to create a substantially similar real estate web building service. In addition to the tort of intentional interference with contract, there is a closely related tort of "interference with prospective economic advantage."[144] "The tort of intentional or negligent interference with prospective economic advantage imposes liability for improper methods is disrupting or diverting the business relationship of another which falls outside the boundaries of fair competition."[145]

An Ohio federal jury awarded $10,000 in favor of a website that "developed and hosted custom-built websites for dealers of "power sport" vehicles, such as all-terrain vehicles, snowmobiles, motorcycles and related equipment and accessories."[146] Powersports ("PSN") entered into a website development and hosting contract with Ohio-based W.W. Cycles. The website development agreement allegedly stated that PSN would be the sole owner of the website and any software or databases used in the development and operation of the site.[147]

---

[142] Korea Supply Co. v. Lockheed Martin Corp., 29 Cal. 4th 1134, 1153 (Cal. 2003).

[143] ConsulNet Computing, Inc. v. Moore, 2007 WL 2702446 (E.D. Pa. 2007).

[144] THE RESTATEMENT (SECOND) OF TORTS, Section 766(B) provides: One who intentionally and improperly interferes with another's prospective contractual relation (except a contract to marry) is subject to liability to the other for the pecuniary harm resulting from loss of the benefits of the relation, whether the interference consists of:

(A) inducing or otherwise causing a third person not to enter into or continue the prospective relation or

(B) preventing the other from acquiring or continuing the prospective relation.

RESTATEMENT (SECOND) OF TORTS, § 766(B) (1979).

[145] Settimo Associates v. Environ Systems, Inc., 14 Cal.App.4th 842 (1993).

[146] Powersports Network v. W.W. Cycles Inc., 2006 WL 1976070 (E.D.Wis., May 31, 2006).

[147] Id.

"W.W. Cycles would then be provided with the site and have use of the services as long as they remained under contract and paid invoices from PSN on time. W.W. Cycles terminated the agreement."[148] "The smoking gun was that an Ohio-based website developer, "accessed the PSN server Oct. 17, 2003, and copied the content of both the PSN-hosted W.W. Cycles' website and the additional catalogs PSN had added to the website that same day."[149] The jury concluded, "W.W. Cycles breached the contract and the implied covenant of good faith and fair dealing with PSN, and was unjustly enriched by their actions," but "did not tortiously interfere with PSN's contract with W.W. Cycles, did not conspire with W.W. Cycles and was not unjustly enriched."[150]

(D) Negligent Interference with Contract

The "tort of negligent interference with economic relationship arises only when the defendant owes the plaintiff a duty of care."[151] The biggest obstacle to a negligent interference with contract claim is establishing a duty. "Among the criteria for establishing a duty of care is the blameworthiness of the defendant's conduct. For negligent interference, a defendant's conduct is blameworthy only if it was independently wrongful apart from the interference itself."[152]

§ 6.4   INTENTIONAL INFORMATION–BASED TORTS

(A) Cyberfraud

The intentional torts of fraud, deceit, or misrepresentation are information torts because the plaintiff has suffered loss in relying upon false or misleading statements made by defendants. The elements of an intentional misrepresentation claim in cyberspace are the same as in the brick and mortar world: (1) a knowingly false representation by the defendant; (2) an intent to deceive or induce reliance; (3) justifiable reliance by the plaintiff; and (4) resulting damages. Fraud or misrepresentation includes willfully deceiving another with intent to induce a person to alter their position to their detriment. Cyberfrauds are enabled by anonymity of the Internet and difficulty of locating the wrongdoer. Despite the ubiquity of fraud on the Internet, relatively few plaintiffs have been successful in the first generation of Internet torts.

Companies have a fraud claim when they pay for click on ads where "website owners use robots or boiler rooms in third world countries where people are paid pennies to repeatedly click on ads hosted on the Internet."[153] In a Texas case, a seller of a computer system was liable for fraudulent inducement for convincing a buyer to enter into a computer contract. The seller's false representation was that untrained personnel could operate the computer system and that the software would be "bug-free."[154] The plaintiff prevailed because neither of these statements was true.

---

[148] Id.

[149] Id.

[150] Id.

[151] LiMandri v. Judkins, 52 Cal.App.4th 326, 348 (1997).

[152] Lange v. TIG Ins. Co., 68 Cal.App.4th 1179, 1187 (1998).

[153] Miller Barondess, LLP, Pay Click Fraud, http://www.syversonlaw.com/Internet-Law/Internet-Class-Actions.shtml.

[154] Integrated Title Data Systems v. Delaney, 800 S.W.2d 336 (Tex. App. El Paso 1990).

(B) Online Defamation

(1) Defamation for Individuals & Businesses

Online defamation is the use of e-mail or Internet web sites to transmit false and damaging information about persons. When corporations or other entities are disparaged by false or misleading information transmitted online, they seek relief through the allied torts of trade libel or injurious falsehoods. A defamatory statement harms the reputation of another in a way that lowers the estimation of the community about that person or deters third persons from associating or dealing with him.[155] "In order to recover for defamation, a plaintiff must allege that the defendant caused injury to the plaintiff by making false, defamatory statements of or concerning the plaintiff, which were published to a third person."[156] It is the *sine qua non* of defamation that a publication consists of a false statement of fact rather than opinion. Nevertheless, a stated opinion may also be actionable if it implies the allegation of undisclosed defamatory facts as the basis for the opinion. Even if the speaker states correct facts upon which he bases his opinion, he may be liable for defamation because the facts were incomplete or incorrect or the statement implied a false assertion of fact.

Publication of a defamatory statement requires communication of the statement to some third person who understands both the defamatory meaning of the statement and its application to the person to who reference is made. When deciding whether a statement is defamatory, a court must consider not only what the defendant explicitly states but also the meaning that is insinuated or implied. The result is driven by the totality of circumstances in the case at hand, beginning with the language of the statement itself and then considering the context in which the statement was made.

Cybersmearing is broadly defined as anonymous or pseudo-anonymous defamation on the Internet.[157] In the bricks and mortar world, a defamatory statement is one that is false and: (1) injures another person's reputation; (2) subjects the person to hatred, contempt or ridicule; or (3) causes others to lose good will or confidence in that person.[158] Defendants can defame plaintiffs on Twitter just as in the brick-and-mortar world. Courtney Love, founding member of the band Hole and widow of Nirvana's Kurt Cobain, posted a tweet that alleged that Dave Grohl, former Nirvana drummer, tried to

---

[155] RESTATEMENT (SECOND) OF TORTS, § 559 (1977).

[156] Boyce & Isley v. Cooper, 153 N.C.App. 25, 29, 568 S.E.2d 893, 897 (2002).

[157] See Roger M. Rosen & Charles B. Rosenberg, Suing Anonymous Defendants for Internet Defamation, 19 THE COMPUTER & INTERNET LAWYER 9 (2002).

[158] Romaine v. Kallinger, 109 N.J. 282, 289, 537 A.2d 284 (1988); Courts vary in defining defamation, and often a particular definition or rule is peculiar to a small number of jurisdictions. W. PAGE KEETON ET AL., PROSSER AND KEETON ON THE LAW OF TORTS § 111, at 773 (5th ed. 1984). Defamation is "that which tends to injure 'reputation' in the popular sense; to diminish the esteem, respect, goodwill or confidence in which the plaintiff is held, or to excite adverse, derogatory or unpleasant feelings or opinions against him." Id. Keeton describes the prima facie case as follows: it has always been necessary for the plaintiff to prove as a part of his prima facie case that the defendant (1) published a statement that was (2) defamatory (3) of and concerning the plaintiff. In a typical case of defamation, the publisher (1) realized that the statement made was defamatory, (2) intended to refer to the plaintiff, and (3) intended to communicate it to a third person or persons. Id. § 113, at 802. A business defamation lawsuit occurs when an untrue statement is communicated which "prejudice[s] [the business entity] in the conduct of its business and deter[s] others from dealing with it." A.F.M. Corp. v. Corp. Aircraft Mgmt., 626 F. Supp. 1533, 1551 (D. Mass. 1985); See e.g., Amway Corp. v. Proctor & Gamble Co., 1:98–CV–726, 2000 U.S. Dist. LEXIS 372, at *15–16 (W.D. Mich. Jan. 6, 2000) (ruling that Amway made prima facie showing that P & G's website was aimed at forum and caused harm to its business reputation).

seduce her teenage daughter, Frances Bean Cobain. Grohl described Love's as false statements that were extremely upsetting.[159]

Love settled this and another Twitter defamation case filed by her dress designer, Dawn Simorangkir, with a payment of $430,000.[160] Love's statements would likely have constituted libel per se. After several highly publicized claims against her, Ms. Love closed her Twitter account. In *Tabor v. McKinney,*[161] a Georgia woman made defamatory statements to newspaper and TV reporters and published defamatory statements on the Internet regarding a couple and their business after the business brought a lawsuit against the woman's husband. The defendants "wrote and published blogs on the Internet stating John ran a window scam on them, possibly resulting in hundreds of thousands of dollars in profits going into [the plaintiff's pocket]; that plaintiff had cheated on his property tax bills through a property tax scam . . . and had willingly lied under oath during litigation of a case."[162]

In addition, the defendant "reportedly wrote and published blogs accusing the plaintiff of spoliation of evidence, cocaine use and sexual improprieties.[163] The jury found the defendant "published defamatory statements, the statements were substantially false, the statements made about [the plaintiff] were published with constitutional malice, and the plaintiffs were injured by publication of the statements."[164] The jury awarded the primary plaintiff $550,000 and his wife $350,000 for damages suffered from publication of the statements.[165] The jury found that the plaintiffs proved the elements of defamation:

> The general elements of an action for defamation are: (1) a false and defamatory statement concerning another; (2) some negligence, or greater fault, in publishing the statement; (3) publication to at least one third person; (4) lack of privilege in publication; (5) special damages, unless actionable per se; and (6) some actual harm to warrant compensatory damages.[166]

"Publication is a term of art, signifying communication of the defamatory statement to a third party."[167] A plaintiff making a claim for product disparagement or trade libel has a similar burden to defamation. The company plaintiff must prove: (1) a false statement; (2) published to a third party; (3) derogatory to the plaintiff's business in general, to the title to his property, or its quality; (4) through which the defendant intended to cause harm to the plaintiff's pecuniary interest, or either recognized or should have recognized that it was likely to do so; (5) with malice; and (6) thus, causing special damages. To prevail in a defamation action, "the plaintiff must establish that it

---

[159] Amelia Proud, "Twitter Should Ban My Mother!" Frances Bean Cobain Slams Courtney Love's "Gross" Allegation That Dave Grohl Tried to Seduce Her, MAILONELINE (April 14, 2012).

[160] Courtney Love's Twitter Rants Cost Her $430,000, MEDIABISTRO.COM, http://www.mediabistro.com/alltwitter/courtney-loves-twitter-rants-cost-her-430000_b4046 (last visited July 25, 2013).

[161] 2012 WL 3986236 (Ga. Super., Feb. 17, 2012).

[162] Id.

[163] Id.

[164] Id.

[165] Id.

[166] RESTATEMENT (SECOND) OF TORTS, § 558 (1965).

[167] Rossignol v. Silvernail, 146 A.D.2d 907 (3dDept. 1989).

was she who was defamed and the defendant was the one who caused it, even if the defendant had no intent to defame the plaintiff."[168]

Online defamation is the use of e-mail or Internet websites to transmit false and damaging information about persons. When corporations or other entities are disparaged by false or misleading information transmitted online, they seek relief through the allied torts of trade libel or injurious falsehoods. "Trade libel requires proof of special damages; while libel per se, even if based on disparagement in business, requires no such proof of special damages."[169] Ola Lewis, a North Carolina judge up for reelection in 2012 filed a libel per se lawsuit.[170] Judge Lewis endorsed a state senate candidate and was allegedly libeled by an opposing candidate's supporter. The defendant "posted a blog entry on Carolina Talk Network and on Facebook, which was entitled 'Dirty Politics by the Good Ol Boys.'"[171] The post criticized a candidate that Judge Lewis endorsed and stated that her endorsement also violated North Carolina's state judicial conduct code.[172]

The plaintiff's attorney immediately contacted Rapp and advised him that he was mistaken. The defendant "posted a second blog entry a couple of days later under the title of 'Apologies, Corrections, Explanations and Amplifications on My Blogs,' but continued to imply that plaintiff's actions were unethical."[173] The North Carolina jury verdict was in favor of Judge Lewis for $105,000, based upon a finding of libel per se. Libel per se, unlike garden-variety libel, does not require proof of special damages. Damages are presumed if the communication is classifiable as defamation per se.

Online defamation claims commonly arise out postings on websites or incendiary exchanges in e-mails. In a 2003 Massachusetts case, a member of the Board of Selectman for the town of Dracut, Mass., and controller of the Dracut's Weekly Roundtable Website allegedly made defamatory statements about a woman in e-mails he posted on the site.[174] The plaintiff had previously accused the Selectman of sexually assaulting her on two occasions and publishing statements about him on a Talk of the Town forum, which led the defendant to file a counterclaim for defamation.[175]

The plaintiff filed an action against the Selectman for the intentional torts of defamation and infliction of emotional distress. To support her defamation action, she argued that the defendant "knew or should have known that his remarks were false, that he published the remarks in two e-mails and that the e-mails were read by third parties."[176] She contended that the defendant "exhibited extreme and outrageous conduct and that she suffered extreme emotional distress as a result."[177] A Massachusetts state court jury returned a verdict for the defendant on the plaintiff's claim finding that the Selectman did not "commit an assault and battery upon DuPont,

---

[168] Bettina M. Chin, Regulating Your Second Life: Defamation in Virtual Worlds, 72 BROOKLYN L. REV. 1303, 1332 (2007).

[169] The Penn Warranty Corp. v. Digiovnni, No. 600659/04 (N.Y. Supreme Court, Oct. 28, 2005) at 7.

[170] Lewis v. Rapp, 2013 WL 940220 (N.C. Super. Jan 1, 2013).

[171] Id.

[172] Id.

[173] Id.

[174] DuPont v. Williams, 2006 WL 4706993 (Mass. Super., Sept. 26, 2006).

[175] Id.

[176] Id.

[177] Id.

but that DuPont did publish defamatory statements about Williams."[178] However, "the jury did not award Williams damages because he failed to establish that he suffered damages as a result of her defamatory statements."[179]

(2) Publishers, Conduits & Distributors

At common law, defendants that "publicize another's libel may be treated in one of three ways: as primary publishers (such as book or newspaper publishers); as conduits (such as a telephone company); or as distributors (such as a book store, library, or news dealer)."[180] The definition of a publisher becomes more complicated "[b]ecause "they cooperate actively in the publication," [and] primary publishers, also known as "original publishers," are generally held to a strict standard of liability comparable to that of authors."[181] An example of a conduit is the telephone company or an Internet service provider.

Distributors (sometimes known as "secondary publishers"), whose ability to control defamatory speech lies somewhere between that of primary publishers and conduits, are subject to an intermediate standard of responsibility and may only be held liable as publishers if they know or have reason to know of the defamatory nature of matter they disseminate.[182]

Distributors are not liable for defamatory statements absent such knowledge or reason to know of the contents. One who republishes a defamatory statement may be liable to the same extent as the original speaker because each publication causes a new harm to the plaintiff's reputation. However, a republisher is liable only if the original statement is defamatory. Libel *per quod* applies to a communication—which may not be defamatory on its face—that is defamatory when connected with other facts. If the court must resort to innuendo or extrinsic evidence to determine that a statement was defamatory, then it is "libel per quod" and requires proof of injury and damages.

(3) Internet Posting is Libel

With hundreds of different legal cultures connected to the Internet, it is unclear how courts should define community for purposes of libel. "Defamation is the injury to one's reputation either by written expression, which is libel, or by oral expression, which is slander."[183] In order to prevail, a plaintiff must prove: (1) that the defendant made a false and defamatory statement concerning plaintiff; (2) that the defendant published the statement without privilege to a third party; (3) that the defendant's fault in publishing the statement amounted to at least negligence; and (4) either that the statement was actionable as a matter of law irrespective of special harm or that its publication caused plaintiff special harm.

Nevertheless, what community applies when to a libelous blog posting or tweet? If a defamatory statement is actionable per se, then under common law principles, the law presumes the defendant acted with common law malice and awards general damages. Courts classify Internet postings such as those addressed in the *Dirty World* case as

---

[178] Id.

[179] Id.

[180] Barrett v. Rosenthal, 112 Cal. App. 4th 749, 762 (Cal. Ct. of App. 2003).

[181] Id.

[182] See RESTATEMENT (SECOND) OF TORTS, § 581(1).

[183] Biro v. Condé Nast, 883 F.Supp.2d 441, 456 (S.D.N.Y.2012).

being libelous rather than being slanderous. Publication means the defendant posted the allegedly defamatory statement on a website or transmitted the statements in e-mails. The law of defamation requires factual statements, as opposed to mere opinions.

In *Hammer v. Amazon.com*,[184] a self-published author filed a defamation lawsuit against Amazon.com in relation to unfavorable reviews of his books on their website. The court dismissed the action because the reviews were of pure opinion and therefore protected. Websites such as Ratemyprofessor.com enable anonymous posters to make incendiary statements about their professors. In addition, dissatisfied clients sometimes create websites targeting lawyers, doctors, or other professional reputations. A former client on a website targeted Michael Baumer, a Texas bankruptcy attorney. The former client's postings led him to file a defamation lawsuit in *Baumer v. Morris*.[185]

The bankruptcy attorney filed a Chapter 7 bankruptcy filing on behalf of his client, Scott Morris.[186] "Baumer and Morris apparently agreed that Baumer's fee for handling the bankruptcy would be $3,300. Morris allegedly did not have enough cash to pay the fee, so Morris offered to pay with $800 in cash and a watch."[187]

The parties disagreed about whether the watch was collateral for a security agreement.[188] The client filed a complaint with the State Bar of Texas, claiming that Baumer stole his watch. "The State Bar of Texas apparently conducted an investigation and determined that Baumer had not stolen anything from Morris."[189]The former client then "launched two websites, www.michaelbaumer.com and www.michaelbaumer.info, which made several false claims regarding Baumer. The allegedly defamatory statements included one that stated that the: 'Texas Bar [was] investigating Michael Baumer' and 'we had a deal and he reneged, lied, and stole from me.'"[190] "The websites apparently appeared as some of the top listed unsponsored websites when a search for Baumer was performed on the Internet and caused Baumer to receive unsolicited inquiries regarding the truth of the assertions included on the websites from the general public, prospective clients, and other attorneys."[191]

The attorney suffered a 27% decrease in bankruptcy business after the websites.[192]The attorney contended that his former client "committed tortious interference with prospective business relations in that he had intentionally interfered with his business relationships with third persons, causing the injury and actual damages to the plaintiff."[193] The plaintiff also sought damages "for business disparagement, defamation, cyber defamation, slander and libel against the defendant."[194]The plaintiff sought recovery of his actual damages, exemplary damages, pre and post-judgment interest, attorney fees and court costs.

---

[184] 392 F. Supp. 2d 423 (E.D. N.Y. 2005).
[185] 2013 WL 830444 (Tex. Dist., Jan. 22, 2013).
[186] Id.
[187] Id.
[188] Id.
[189] Id.
[190] Id.
[191] Id.
[192] Id.
[193] Id.
[194] Id.

In addition to monetary damages, the plaintiff also requested temporary and permanent injunctions enjoining his former client, his agents, assigns, employees, officers, directors, attorneys, subsidiaries and related entities from continued publication of the websites, and from interfering, disparaging, making false oral and written statements, attacking, slandering, libeling or tortiously commenting upon the plaintiff, the plaintiff's business and the plaintiff's reputation. The court "awarded the plaintiff $115,000 in damages, along with pre and post-judgment interest" and permanently restrained the continued publication of the websites.[195]

(4) Libel Per Se

In order to be libelous per se, defamatory words must be susceptible of only one meaning so that a court may presume, as a matter of law, that the defendant intended to disgrace and degrade the plaintiff, holding them out to public hatred, contempt or ridicule. Libel per se in the blogosphere is the same as for traditional torts.[196] A plaintiff need not prove actual damages with libel per se because courts presume damages. Under the common law, it was libelous per se, that is, without need of proof of malice or actual damages, to: (1) accuse a person of commission of crime; (2) impute unchastity to a woman; (3) state that a person had a loathsome disease—e.g. AIDS, mental illness etc.; or (4) make any statement that would damage a person in his business or standing in the community—e.g. crooked lawyer.[197]

Several Internet-related cases reflect the increased incidence of defamation lawsuits in blogospheres and peer networking websites such as MySpace.[198] A pair of Texas patent litigators sued Cisco for allegedly defamatory statements made by a company employee on the "Troll Tracker" blog. Courts must evaluate words within their context in determining whether a given statement is defamatory.[199] A publication is libelous, or actionable per se, if, among other things, it tends to harm one in their business or occupation, or imputes to them some criminal offense involving moral turpitude.

Postings by ex-spouses have led to jury awards based upon defamation per se. An Arizona jury awarded $200,000 arising out of a former husband's spouse's posting of defamatory statements concerning allegations of child abuse on a public website in _LaRue v. Brown_[200] A jury returned a verdict in which "the plaintiffs received $150,000 from the defendants for compensatory damages and $50,000 from defendant Sarah

---

[195] "Along with the monetary damages, the court also ordered that the defendant, his agents, employees, officers, directors, attorneys, subsidiaries and related entities, including Host Gator or the current hosting entity of the websites, were permanently restrained from continued publication of the websites and from interfering, disparaging, making false oral and written statements, attacking, slandering, libeling or tortiously commenting upon the plaintiff, the plaintiff's business and the plaintiff's reputation." Id.

[196] Blue Ridge Homes, Inc. v. Thein, 191 P.3d 374, 378, 382 (Mont. 2008).

[197] "Libel per se is not limited to the four categories of statements considered slanderous per se." Burrill v. Nair, 2013 WL 3087613 (Ct. of App. 3rd Dist., June 3, 2013).

[198] See e.g., Allstate Ins. Co. v. Cooper, 2008 WL 1990785 (W.D. Pa. 2008) (reporting action by high school principal filed student against students for defamatory MySpace postings).

[199] Lewis v. Rapp, 2012 WL 1512110 (N.C. App. Ct., May 1, 2012).

[200] 2012 WL 6915097 (Ariz.Super., Nov. 1, 2012) (The plaintiffs "filed a lawsuit against David and Sarah Brown in the Maricopa County Superior Court. The plaintiff asserted claims of defamation, intentional infliction of emotional distress, aiding and abetting, invasion of privacy, civil conspiracy and injurious falsehood. They claimed the matter was brought to the attention of family court and the defendants denied any involvement. Counsel for the website allegedly informed the plaintiff that the postings had been written by Sarah").

Brown for punitive damages."[201] The court assessed jury fees against the defendants for $1,272.15 and awarded the plaintiffs $2,227.50 in attorney's fees. In that case, the court determined that the false statement that the plaintiff had sexually abused his daughter constituted defamation.

(5) Special Damages & Libel

Defamatory communications "tend to harm the reputation of another as to lower him in the estimation of the community or deter third persons from associating or dealing with them."[202] If the statement is writing, then the defamation is libel. If the statement is oral, the defamation is slander. The emblem of defamation is that it subjects the plaintiff to hatred, contempt, or ridicule, or causes others to lose good will or confidence in that person. A defamation action requires proof of four elements: (1) a false statement, (2) publication, (3) fault, and (4) damages. Damage awards in defamation cases can be for (1) general damages for harm to reputation, wounded feelings, and humiliation; or (2) special damages for "the loss of something having economic or pecuniary value[203] One difficult issue for courts is measuring where the plaintiff's injury occurred and how to determine the meaning of a significant segment of the community in cyberspace.

Courts have yet to determine the meaning of the loss of online reputation in the relevant community of blogosphere or social network sites. If the defamation is not actionable per se, then, at common law, the plaintiff must plead and prove actual malice and special damages. Actual malice exists when the defendant publishes a defamatory statement with knowledge that it was false or with reckless disregard of whether it was false or not. A defendant acts with "actual malice," as must be shown in a defamation action by a public figure plaintiff, when the defendant knows the statement is false or recklessly disregards its probable falsity. To demonstrate reckless disregard, there must be sufficient evidence to permit the conclusion that the defendant, in fact, entertained serious doubts as to the truth of his publication, or offer proof that the false publication was made with a high degree of awareness of their probable falsity. Malice is difficult to prove because it requires evidence of the defendant's actual state of mind.

(6) State Action

The First Amendment does not regulate the conduct of private parties; a party may not allege a constitutional violation without alleging the conduct of a state actor.[204] Generally, the First Amendment does not apply to speech on private property, such as a company's website. A person using the Internet to distribute or download copyrighted music without authorization is not entitled to have his identity protected from disclosure under the First Amendment.[205] A governmental entity does not create a public forum when it establishes an Internet connection—even if access to the Internet connection is located in a public building and is open for use by the public.[206] In *Noah*

---

[201] Id.

[202] RESTATEMENT (SECOND) OF TORTS, § 559 (1965).

[203] 1 D. HAGGARD, COOLEY ON TORTS § 164, p. 580 (4th ed. 1932).

[204] Hammer v. Amazon.com, 392 F. Supp. 2d 423, 432 (E.D. N.Y. 2005).

[205] Interscope Records v. Does 1–14, 558 F. Supp.2d 1176, 1178 (D. Kan. 2008).

[206] United States v. American Library Association, Inc., 539 U.S. 194, 205 (2003).

v. AOL Time–Warner, Inc.,[207] the Virginia district court ruled that AOL's termination of an Internet service account because of pro-Islamic statements raised no First Amendment claim because the Constitution does not protect against actions taken by private entities. Public entities, in contrast, are subject to First Amendment actions.

(7) Publishers, Distributors, and Conduits

A publisher is liable for defamatory statements in its works and the plaintiff need not prove the publisher had knowledge of the defamatory content. In contrast, distributors are not liable for defamatory statements contained in materials unless they distribute without proof of actual knowledge of the defamatory statements. Distributors are subject to an intermediate standard between publishers and conduits.[208] A distributor is only liable if they knew, or had reason to know, of the defamatory content of what they were disseminating.[209] Conduits are common carrier type defendants, who are generally not liable for defamatory content since they have no ability to screen or control defamatory material. A conduit is viewed by courts like a pipe as opposed to a newspaper or other publisher.

Section 230 of the Communications Decency Act (covered later in this chapter) treats websites as conduits so relatively few lawsuits for online defamation have been successful, even though there are a seemingly infinite websites rating local businesses, law professors, medical doctors, neighbors, and dates. The Internet has given estranged spouses and spurned lovers a worldwide forum for online attacks. Millions of YouTube visitors watched a video in which a woman "attacked her ex-husband for everything from his alleged shortcomings in bed to what she couldn't stand about his family."[210] Websites are immunized by Section 230 for the postings of third parties. While providers are not liable for negative postings on sites such as DontDateHimGirl.com, the poster may be liable for false statements.

(8) Anonymous Speech and Subpoena Duces Tecum

Anonymous speech in blogs or chartrooms is entitled to First Amendment protection. This protection extends to anonymous Internet speech. "It is well understood that the right of free speech is not absolute at all times and under all circumstances"[211] and does not extend to defamatory postings. The degree of scrutiny courts give to impositions on speech "varies depending on the circumstances and type of speech at issue," and thus "the nature of the speech should be a driving force in choosing a standard by which to balance the rights of anonymous speakers in discovery disputes."[212] Anonymous website postings make it difficult to pursue online libel lawsuits.[213]

---

[207] 261 F. Supp.2d 532, 546 (E.D. Va. 2003).

[208] Conduit is a term used in defamation cases to connote some neutral distribution mechanism "such as a telephone line or computer network that is used to disseminate a defamatory statement." IT Law Wiki, Conduit (2012).

[209] Austin v. CrystalTech Web Hosting, Inc., 125 P.3d 389 (Ariz. Ct. App. 2005).

[210] Anita Hamilton, Outsmart Your Haters, TIME (Oct. 6, 2008) at 67.

[211] Chaplinsky v. State of New Hampshire, 315 U.S. 568, 572 (1942).

[212] In re Anonymous Online Speakers, No. 09–71625, 2011 WL 61635, at *2, *6 (9th Cir. Jan. 7, 2011).

[213] See e.g., First Time Videos, LLC v. Does, No. C 11–01675 LB, 2011 U.S. Dist. LEXIS 42376, at *7 (N.D. Cal. April 14, 2011) (ruling that copyright owner of pornographic videos and photographs had good cause to unveil names and addresses of peer-to-peer users who distributed content without their permission).

In *Obsidian Finance Group v. Cox*,[214] the court ruled that the Oregon's state shield law protects journalists, but not bloggers from complying with subpoenas revealing anonymous sources. The shield does not protect the substantive content of the allegedly defamatory materials, only the source. Courts in other states are likely to follow Oregon in requiring bloggers and other online journalists to have a formal, established media source affiliation. Companies apply to courts to serve a John Doe subpoena directed to Internet service providers in order to unmask anonymous posters.[215] The computer manufacturer Compaq filed a John Doe subpoena against an ISP, ordering it to disclose the identity of anonymous posters whose inaccurate and libelous information depressed the company's stock price.

A Seattle company filed a libel lawsuit against users of Yahoo! message boards who were later unveiled with the help of John Doe subpoenas. Copyright owners sought John Doe subpoenas to reveal Verizon's customers who allegedly downloaded copyrighted music or video without authorization. A standard discovery request will be for electronic files, e-mail messages (with attachments), Instant Message communications, and/or other communication transmitted on a provider's service for a designated period.[216]

Many courts follow the test articulated in *Dendrite Int'l, Inc. v. Doe*.[217] The *Dendrite* court held that a plaintiff seeking to unveil an anonymous speaker must: (1) give notice; (2) identify the exact statements that constitute allegedly actionable speech; (3) establish a *prima facie* cause of action against the defendant based on the complaint and all information provided to the court; and (4) produce sufficient evidence supporting each element of its cause of action, on a *prima facie* basis, prior to a court ordering the disclosure of the identity of the unnamed defendant. Assuming the plaintiff establishes a *prima facie* cause of action; the court must "balance the defendant's First Amendment right of anonymous free speech against the strength of the *prima facie* case presented and the necessity for the disclosure of the anonymous defendant's identity to allow the plaintiff to properly proceed."[218] Courts are disinclined to issue a John Doe subpoena unless the ISP gives notice to the anonymous speaker and gives him or her an opportunity to be heard.

In *United States v. Doe (In re Grand Jury Subpoena Duces Tecum)*,[219] a John Doe was served with a subpoena *duces tecum,* requiring him to appear before a Northern District of Florida grand jury and produce the unencrypted contents located on the hard drives of Doe's laptop computers and five external hard drives. Doe informed the United States Attorney for the Northern District of Florida that when he appeared before the grand jury, he would invoke his Fifth Amendment privilege against self-incrimination and refuse to comply with the subpoena. In another case, the Eleventh Circuit reversed a federal district court order requiring the defendant, a child pornography suspect, to decrypt his hard drives. John Doe subpoenas to unveil

---

[214] 2011 WL 5999334 (D. Ore. November 30, 2011).

[215] See generally, Matthew Mazzotta, Balancing Act: Finding Consensus on Standards for Unmasking Anonymous Internet Speakers, 51 B. C. L. REV. 833 (May 2010).

[216] See e.g., First Time Videos v. Does, No. C 11–01675 LB, 2011 U.S. Dist. LEXIS 42376, at *7 (N.D. Cal., April 14, 2011) (ruling that copyright owner of pornographic videos and photographs had good cause to unveil names and addresses of peer-to-peer users who distributed content without their permission).

[217] 775 A.2d 756 (N.J. Super. Ct. App. Div. 2001).

[218] Id.

[219] 2012 U.S. App. LEXIS 3894 (11th Cir. 2012).

anonymous Internet speakers raise troubling privacy issues when corporations use them to unmask whistleblowers and restrain corporate critics.

The danger is that will seek *subpoenas duces tecum* in order to stifle critics of their products and services. Courts issuing these subpoenas must balance the rights of anonymous speakers against the right to vindicate tort rights and remedies. Courts outside of the United States are reluctant to order service providers to reveal subscriber data.[220] In addition, copyright owners representing the film and music industry are increasingly seeking to unveil anonymous file sharers.[221] A Chilling Effects.org Report documents an increase in the use of John Doe subpoenas by the Recording Industry Association of America to unveil anonymous infringers sharing copyrighted content:

> Although the RIAA presents evidence of copyright infringement by *some* anonymous defendants in its court filings before it issues subpoenas, the RIAA subpoenas the names of far more defendants solely based on its allegations. As in the case of message board subpoenas, some ISPs notify subscribers before identifying them, giving them a chance to object, but not all ISPs do so. The RIAA has been saving itself court costs by filing a single lawsuit against all alleged infringers who subscribe to the same ISP, regardless of the probable physical location of the alleged infringers; therefore, subscribers who are notified of a subpoena by their ISP and wish to object may be forced to interact with a court on the other side of the country. In short, subpoenas issued in "John Doe" lawsuits are shifting the burden to anonymous internet users to fight for their anonymity.[222]

Social media sites are the latest battleground for unveiling anonymous speakers. Twitter revealed "data identifying users to French authorities in response to a January ruling by a French court regarding anti-Semitic tweets posted in October 2012 under the hashtag #unbonjuif (#agoodjew).[223] In October of 2012, "the hashtag #unbonjuif (#agoodjew) was trending as the third-most tweeted subject in France. Users jumped on the chance to tweet phrases like 'a good Jew is a dead Jew,' ultimately forcing the French Jewish students' union ("UEJF") to file a lawsuit against Twitter for allowing that content to appear."[224]

---

[220] The European Court of Justice in a 2012 decision ruled that EU Member States "may, but do not have to, require electronic communications services to disclose subscriber account data to intellectual property owners pursuing copyright infringement litigation." Amy E. Bivins, ECJ: Member States May Require ISPs to Disclose Account Data in Copyright Suits, BLOOMBERG BNA, ELECT. COMM. & LAW REPORT (May 21, 2012) (discussing Bonnier Audio AB v. Perfect Communication Sweden AB, E.C.J., No. 10–461, April 19, 2012).

[221] See e.g., First Time Videos, LLC v. Does, No. C 11–01675 LB, 2011 U.S. Dist. LEXIS 42376, at *7 (N.D. Cal. April 14, 2011) (ruling that copyright owner of pornographic videos and photographs had good cause to unveil names and addresses of peer-to-peer users who distributed content without their permission).

[222] Chilling Effects.org, John Doe Anonymity: Meet John Doe, http://chillingeffects.org/johndoe/ (last visited June 17, 2013).

[223] Twitter Releases User Data to France After Lawsuit Over Anti-Semitic Tweets (July 12, 2013), http://www.jns.org/news-briefs/2013/7/12/twitter-releases-user-data-to-france-after-anti-semitic-tweets-lawsuit (July 13, 2013).

[224] Alina Dain Sharon, A Web of Hate: European, U.S. Laws Clash on Defining and Policing Online Anti-Semitism, JNS.ORG (Feb. 24, 2013).

(C) Defenses in Defamation

(1) Public Official

The key principle in defamation/free expression cases is the "profound national commitment to the principle that debate on public issues should be uninhibited, robust, and wide-open."[225] Where the plaintiff is a public official and the allegedly defamatory statement concerns official conduct, the official must prove that the statement was made with actual malice; that is, with knowledge that it was false or with reckless disregard of whether it was false or not. The rule requiring public officials to prove actual malice is based on First Amendment principles reflecting the U.S. Supreme Court's consideration of the national commitment to robust and wide-open debate of public issues. The Court, in *New York Times v. Sullivan*,[226] was the first to rule that a state defamation case violated the First Amendment of the U.S. Constitution. The Court's *Sullivan* decision was the most important defamation case in American history because of its holding that the state tort of defamation was subject to the constraints of the First Amendment.

The *Sullivan* Court noted that public questions are protected as a freedom of expression under the First Amendment. The Court's ruling that a public official cannot recover damages for defamation absent proof of actual malice was necessary to encourage robust debate on public issues. After *Sullivan*, the Court required a public official to prove defamation by a malice standard as opposed to a lesser standard, such as negligence. If a plaintiff is a public official, he or she must show by clear and convincing evidence that a false and defamatory statement was made against him or her with actual malice— in other words, the defendant knew the statement either was false or acted with reckless disregard as to the truth or falsity of the statement. The significance of the *Sullivan* case is that it recognized for the first time that torts could clash with the First Amendment.

In *Corcept Therapeutics, Inc. v. Rothschild*,[227] Corcept Therapeutics filed a lawsuit in California state court for defamation, intentional infliction of emotional distress ("IIED"), and interference with prospective business relations against Rothschild. Rothschild removed the suit to federal court and filed a special motion to strike the plaintiff's complaint pursuant to California's anti-SLAPP (Strategic Lawsuits against Public Participation) statute.[228] SLAPPs "masquerade as ordinary lawsuits but are intended to deter ordinary people from exercising their political or legal rights or to punish them for doing so."[229] The defamation portion of the plaintiff's complaint alleged that Rothschild made defamatory postings on Yahoo! message boards regarding Corcept, its founders, and its principal product—a drug named Corlux.

The plaintiff's remaining claims arose from the Yahoo! postings as well as a series of harassing phone calls allegedly made by Rothschild. The Ninth Circuit concluded

---

[225] New York Times Co. v. Sullivan, 376 U.S. 254, 270 (1964).

[226] 376 U.S. 254 (1964).

[227] 339 Fed. Appx. 789 (9th Cir. 2009).

[228] "SLAPP is an acronym for Strategic Lawsuit Against Public Participation. SLAPP litigation, generally, is litigation without merit filed to dissuade or punish the exercise of First Amendment rights of defendants. " Lafayette Morehouse, Inc. v. Chronicle Publishing Co., 37 Cal. App. 4th 855, 858 (1995).

[229] Makaeff v. Trump University, LLC, 715 F.3d 254, 261 (9th Cir. 2013).

that the court correctly denied Rothschild's anti-SLAPP motion and affirmed with respect to all claims. The appellate court upheld the district court's finding that Corcept and its founders showed a probability they would be able to prove at trial that several of the statements in Rothschild's postings were made with knowledge of or a reckless disregard for the falsity of the statements, which is the standard for public figures. "To prevail on an anti-SLAPP motion, the moving defendant must make a *prima facie* showing that the plaintiff's suit arises from an act in furtherance of a constitutional right to free speech."[230]

(2) Public Figures, Limited Public Figures

(a) General Purpose Public Figure

Public figures are plaintiffs who are famous or celebrities who have earned fame or notoriety. Limited public figures are those who have voluntarily injected themselves into a particular public controversy; they become public figures for that limited range of issues. A public figure suing for defamation must demonstrate actual malice by clear and convincing evidence, where "actual malice" requires a showing that the allegedly false statement was made with knowledge that it was false or with reckless disregard of whether it was false or not. The "reckless disregard" standard requires a high degree of awareness of probable falsity. "Few people," however, "attain the general notoriety that would make them public figures for all purposes."[231] In 1967, the Court expanded Sullivan's constitutional limitations from public officials to public figures in *Curtis Publ'g Co. v. Butts*.[232] The Court in *Gertz v. Robert Welch, Inc.*,[233] distinguished between general purpose public figures and limited public figures. A general-purpose public figure has such "pervasive fame or notoriety so that she is a public figure for all purposes and in all contexts."[234]

General purpose public figures include celebrities who are famous featured in salacious supermarket tabloids. "Defining "public figures," a federal judge once said, "is much like trying to nail a jellyfish to the wall." "The defendant who can show that his plaintiff is a public figure can hold that plaintiff to a higher standard of proof, forcing him to prove that the defendant was reckless, rather than negligent."[235] To be liable for the defamation of a public figure, a distributor of allegedly defamatory material must act with actual malice—that is, with knowledge that the material was false or with reckless disregard of whether it was false or not.[236]

(b) Limited Purpose Public Figure

In *Gertz v. Robert Welch, Inc.*,[237] the U.S. Supreme Court distinguished between two categories of public figures: an "all purpose" public figure and a "limited purpose"

---

[230] Id.

[231] Waldbaum v. Fairchild Publn's, Inc., 627 F.2d 1287, 1296 (D.C.Cir.1980).

[232] Curtis Publ'g Co. v. Butts, 388 U.S. 130 (1967).

[233] 418 U.S. 323 (1974) (ruling that Robert Welch of the John Birch Society was not either a public official as in Sullivan or a general public figure as in Curtis, but was a limited public figure because he thrust himself into the vortex of a public issue).

[234] Id. at 345.

[235] Thomas D. Brooks, Catching Jellyfish in the Internet: The Public–Figure Doctrine and Defamation on Computer Bulletin Boards, 21 RUTGERS COMPUTER & TECH L. J. 461, 461 (1995).

[236] Curtis Publ'g Co. v. Butts, 388 U.S. 130 (1967).

[237] 418 U.S. 323 at 351.

public figure.[238] Limited public figures in cyberspace, like those in the bricks and mortar world, are those who have "assume[d] special prominence in the resolution of public questions."[239] The D.C. Circuit "formulated a three-part test for identifying a limited-purpose public figure, requiring (1) that there have been a public controversy; (2) that the plaintiff have played a sufficiently central role in the controversy; and (3) that the alleged defamatory statement have been germane to the plaintiff's participation in the controversy."[240] A "limited purpose" public figure in cyberspace will generally be a blogger or someone who "voluntarily injects herself or is drawn into a particular public controversy and thereby becomes a public figure for a limited range of issues."[241]

> When a libel action involves a speech of public concern, a plaintiff must show that the defendant published a defamatory statement about the plaintiff, the defamatory statement was false, the defendant was at fault in publishing it, and the plaintiff suffered actual injury from the statements.[242]

"Limited purpose" public figures are only public figures on issues where they inject themselves into a public controversy. The U.S. Supreme Court created the "limited purpose" public figure classification to "define the proper accommodation between the law of defamation and the freedoms of speech and press protected by the First Amendment."[243] Whether an individual is a public official, public figure, limited public figure, or private person is a question of law for the court to resolve. It is unclear whether the mere posting of comments on a website voluntarily thrusts a plaintiff into a public controversy, and thus categorize the plaintiff as a limited purpose public figure. Courts are beginning to regard websites as public forums.

The California Supreme Court held that websites accessible to the public are "public forums" for the purposes of the Anti–SLAPP statute.[244] In a Minnesota case, a court ruled that a community blogger was a limited public figure who committed defamation, intentionally interfered with former community leader's employment contract by his blog, and associated comments.[245] In *Moore*, the plaintiff was the executive director of a Minnesota housing agency and the defendants were board members. The board ousted Moore and he filed suit against the board members. Moore found new employment at the University of Minnesota's Urban Research and Outreach/Engagement Center ("UROC") to study mortgage foreclosures. When Hoff a neighborhood blogger learned of this position, he blogged that Moore was involved with a fraudulent mortgage.

Hoff's blog stated: that there was, "[r]epeated and specific evidence in Hennepin County District Court shows Jerry Moore was involved with a high-profile fraudulent mortgage at 1564 Hillside Ave. N." Moore said he was also alleged to have received a

---

[238] Id.

[239] Gertz v. Robert Welch, Inc., 418 U.S. 323, 352 (1974) ("Under the First Amendment there is no such thing as a false idea . . . (it) requires that we protect some falsehood in order to protect speech that matters.").

[240] Clyburn v. News World Commc'ns, Inc., 903 F.2d 29, 31 (D.C.Cir.1990).

[241] Curtis Publ'g Co. Id. at 351.

[242] Mathis v. Cannon, 573 S.E.2d 376, 381 (Ga. 2002).

[243] Gertz, Id. at 325.

[244] Barrett v. Rosenthal, 40 Cal.4th 33, 41, fn. 4, 51 Cal. Rptr. 3d 55, 146 P.3d 510 (2006).

[245] Moore v. Allen, 27–CV–09–17778, (D. Ct. Minn.,4th Jud. Dist., March 11, 2011).

$5,000 check for new windows at that location."[246] Moore "alleged Hoff, through his blog and the blog's comment section, had created a "defamation zone" that made him responsible for any defamatory remarks made on the blog and in the related comments section, particularly comments made anonymously or by those who used monikers to hide their true identities."[247] The jury found that Hoff's statement that Moore was involved in a fraudulent mortgage was not false, but did find that Hoff intentionally interfered with Moore's contract with the University of Minnesota.[248] The jury awarded the plaintiff $35,000 in economic damages and $25,000 to compensate him for actual harm to reputation and emotional injuries.[249]

(3) Standard for Private Persons

In online defamation cases against ordinary private individuals, the plaintiff must prove: (1) a false and defamatory statement concerning another, (2) unprivileged publication to third party, (3) fault amounting to at least negligence on the publisher's part, and (4) either actionability of statement irrespective of special harm, or existence of special harm caused by publication. A New Hampshire Jane Doe plaintiff filed suit against Friendfinder.com, an adult networking site, for defamatory third party postings under the screen name "petra03755" which depicted her as a "swinger." The anonymous poster created a false defamatory profile of the Jane Doe plaintiff.

The court granted Friendfinder.com's motion to dismiss the plaintiff's claims for invasion of privacy and defamation on grounds of the federal immunity under Section 230 of the Communications Decency Act. The federal court ruled that Friendfinder.com was an interactive service provider and not a content creator because an unrelated content provider provided the allegedly defamatory profile page. The court ruled Friendfinder.com was not transformed into a content provider merely because it changed the wording about the age of Jane Doe's profile from age 40 or 41 to the "early forties." However, a website operator making extensive editorial modifications risks losing its Section 230 immunity.[250]

(4) Truth as a Complete Defense

To be actionable in either a defamation or trade libel case, the defamatory statement must be a false statement of fact; statements of opinion alone will not support a cause of action for trade libel. In defamation actions, where the protected interest is personal reputation, truth is an absolute defense. In U.S. defamation actions, "the defense of truth is constitutionally required where the subject of the publication is a public official or public figure; moreover, the defamed public official or public figure must prove not only that the publication is false but that it was knowingly so or was circulated with reckless disregard for its truth or falsity."[251] Journalists and other functionally equivalent commentators may also defend on the grounds of fair comment for matters of public interest. In addition, the spousal,

---

[246] Id.

[247] Id.

[248] Id.

[249] Id.

[250] See Doe v. Friendfinder Network Inc., 2008 WL 2001745 (D.N.H. 2008).

[251] Cox Broadcasting Corp. v. Cohn, 420 U.S. 469, 491 (1975).

legislative, and judicial immunities apply to Internet defamation cases, just as in the bricks and mortar world.

(5) First Amendment Defenses

In an online defamation dispute, a defendant is unlikely to be able to assert a First Amendment defense because there will be no state action in social networking sites or websites. Facebook and other social media sites are private forums and therefore plaintiffs will not have First Amendment rights. In contrast, if a governmental unit restrains a social media site or blog, there is state action.[252] A New York trial court ruled that the First Amendment forbids a suit against a website that criticizes an insurer's products or services, for torts arising out of statements he made on his "gripe site" because they were opinions about the quality of service and thus protected.[253] The website made negative comments about car service warranties, the auto insurance industry, and the New Jersey judiciary, but much of the content was about the customer's New Jersey small claims court action.[254]

The insurer sought an injunction to shut down the gripe site asserting six causes of action: "(1) intentional interference with prospective economic advantage; (2) coercion, harassment, extortion; (3) trade libel; (4) Civil RICO; (5) infringement: false designation of origin and unfair competition, and (6) a permanent injunction against the publishing of a certain website and otherwise publishing certain speech."[255]

(6) Privileges and Qualified Privileges

A qualified privilege of common interest applies to communications made in good faith on any subject matter in which the party making the communication has an interest or in reference to which he has a duty, public or private, legal, either moral, or social, if made to a person having a corresponding interest or duty. An ex-employer giving an evaluation of an ex-employee will have a qualified privilege.

(7) Anti–SLAPP Suit Statutes

Strategic Lawsuits Against Public Participation ("SLAPP") lawsuits are questionable or frivolous lawsuits filed by companies and individuals to stifle speech and expression.[256] The purpose of a SLAPP lawsuit is to intimidate critics into silence by filing a lawsuit that is expensive and time-consuming. A number of U.S. jurisdictions have enacted Anti–SLAPP Statutes that give a cause of action to a person who is sued while exercising her right of petition or free speech under the United States or a state constitution in connection with a public issue. California's Anti–

---

[252] See generally, Layshock v. Hermitage Sch. Dist., No. 07–4465, 2011 U.S. App. LEXIS 11994, at *42 (3d Cir., Jun. 13, 2011) (Jordan, J., concurring) ("For better or worse, wireless Internet access, SMARTPHONEs, tablet computers, social networking services like Facebook, and stream-of-consciousness communications via Twitter give an omnipresence to speech that makes any effort to trace First Amendment boundaries along the physical boundaries.").

[253] The Penn Warranty Corp. v. Digiovnni, No. 600659/04 (N.Y. Supreme Court, Oct. 28, 2005).

[254] Id. at 5.

[255] Id. at 2.

[256] Global Telemedia Int'l, Inc. v. Doe 1, 132 F. Supp. 2d 1261, 1263 (C.D. Cal. 2001) (granting defendant's motion to dismiss on grounds that California's Anti-SLAPP (Strategic Litigation Against Public Participation) provisions applied and defendant's postings about company were protected as exercise of free speech in connection with public issue).

SLAPP Statute[257] was enacted in reply to a "disturbing increase in lawsuits brought primarily to chill the valid exercise of the constitutional rights of freedom of speech."[258] Anti–SLAPP statutes in California and other states have been deployed to dismiss Internet-related trade libel lawsuits. The statute allows the dismissal of meritless claims that a plaintiff files to constrain expression. In order to dismiss a cause of action under California's Anti–SLAPP Statute, the court must determine two things:

> First, the court must decide whether the defendant has made a sufficient threshold showing that the challenged cause of action is subject to a special motion to strike. Second, if the threshold showing has been made, the court must determine whether the plaintiff has demonstrated sufficient minimal merit to be allowed to proceed. . . . Nothing outside of this two-step process is relevant.[259]

A California appellate court ruled that websites were accessible to the public—thus being public forums for the purposes of California's Anti–SLAPP statute.[260]

(8) Retraction Statutes

When a plaintiff is required to give the defendant an opportunity to retract a defamatory statement, it works like a prelitigation notice.[261] Thirty-one states have enacted retraction statutes that enable a defendant to retract a defamatory statement. Retraction statutes require the plaintiff to demand a retraction before filing a libel lawsuit. Retraction statutes are effective for many defamed individuals who are merely seeking to have their reputation repaired while avoiding costly and invasive litigation. Thus, in many instances, "a correction, retraction or apology is often adequate" to resolve the harm to reputation caused by a defamatory statement when applied with some consistency.[262]

(9) Single Publication Rule

Under U.S. law, a single publication will prevent a plaintiff from bringing repetitive defamation claims against a publisher. Under the single publication rule, separate publications of the original content cannot be the basis for separate defamation claims. "The single-publication rule limits tort claims premised on mass communications to a single cause of action that accrues upon the first publication of the communication, thereby sparing the courts from litigation of stale claims when an offending book or magazine is resold years later."[263]

> Thus, for purposes of the statute of limitations in defamation claims, a book, magazine, or newspaper has one publication date, the date on which it is first generally available to the public. Copies of the original are still part of the single

---

[257] Cal. Civ. Proc. § 425.16(A) (2011).

[258] Manufactured Home Communities, Inc. v. County of San Diego, 544 F.3d 959, 963 (9th Cir. 2008).

[259] Weinberg v. Feisel, 110 Cal.App.4th 1122, 1130 (2003).

[260] See also, Kronemyer v. Internet Movie Database Inc., 150 Cal. App. 4th 941 (Cal. Ct. of App. 2007).

[261] The issue is how retraction should work for the Internet, where it is unclear how to retract a defamatory statement where there are mirror sites and Wayback Machines that capture earlier versions of websites.

[262] Allison E. Horton, Beyond Control?: The Rise and Fall of Defamation Regulation on the Internet, 43 VAL. U.L. REV. 1265, 1295–96 (2009).

[263] Roberts v. McAfee Inc., 660 F.3d 1156, 1168 (9th Cir. 2011).

publication but republication in a new edition creates a new publication on the rationale that the intent is to reach a new audience.[264]

Courts have had no difficulty extending the single publication rule to an Internet posting. The Ninth Circuit in *Yeager v. Bowlin*,[265] extended the single publication rule to a statement on a website that had not been modified since 2003. The court reasoned that because other materials on the website had been modified; this did not restart the statute of limitations for the postings that had been unchanged since 2003. "Under the single-publication rule, the statute of limitations is reset when a statement is republished; a statement in a printed publication is republished when it is reprinted in something that is not part of the same single integrated publication."[266] In print and on the Internet, statements generally are considered "published" when they are first made available to the public. Under a single publication rule, "once a defendant publishes a statement on a website, the defendant does not republish the statement by simply continuing to host the website."[267] Nevertheless, Chapter 3's discussion of Australian defamation law confirms that not every country follows the single publication rule.[268]

(D) Privacy Based Cybertorts

The misuse of Internet-based surveillance tools threatens our society as much as telephone wiretaps in the first decades of the twentieth-century when the tort of privacy was first recognized. Privacy-based torts have yet to evolve to address the widespread surveillance of Internet usage in the U.S. workplace. Courts have universally rejected the claim that employees have an expectation of privacy in their e-mail communications. The development of new technologies for harvesting personal information creates the potential for widespread invasions of privacy. The rise of the Internet and e-mail threatens privacy today just as the invention of the telephone or photography did in the early twentieth century. Eavesdropping, wiretapping, or intercepting e-mails could qualify as an intrusion upon seclusion. Despite daily reports about covert data mining, online espionage, and identity theft, only a handful of plaintiffs have received an injunction or money damages for invasion of privacy.

Louis Brandeis and his law partner, Samuel Warren, first proposed a new tort action for the invasion of privacy in a law review article in 1890.[269] The U.S. Supreme Court drew upon Warren and Brandeis in articulating the right to privacy as "the right to be let alone."[270] Courts and state legislatures began to recognize the right of privacy

---

[264] Jankovic. v. Int'l Crisis Group, 494 F.3d 1080, 1087 (D.D.C. 2011) (dismissing complaints for defamation, tortious interference with business expectancy, and false light invasion of privacy against International Crisis Group and one of its employees, James Lyon, for posting documents "that allegedly link Philip Zepter and his business interests to Serbian president Slobodan Milosevic, who was put on trial as a war criminal before his death.").

[265] 2012 WL 3892903 (Sept. 10, 2012).

[266] Id. at *4.

[267] Id.

[268] See e.g., Churchill v. New Jersey, 876 A. 2d 311 (N.J. Super. Ct. App. Div. 2005) (applying the single publication rule to publication on the Internet and ruling that a defamation complaint should be dismissed because it was filed almost two years after initial publication because New Jersey has a one-year statute of limitations for defamation actions).

[269] Samuel Warren & Louis Brandeis, The Right to Privacy, 4 HARV. L. REV. 193 (1890).

[270] Katz v. United States, 389 U.S. 347, 511 n.6 (1967).

shortly after this publication.[271] "It has been said that a 'right of privacy' has been recognized at common law in thirty states plus the District of Columbia and by statute in four States."[272]

Causes of action for invasion of privacy are comprised of four analytically distinct torts: (1) intrusion upon seclusion, (2) appropriation of name or likeness, (3) publicity given to private life, and (4) publicity placing person in false light.[273] Not all jurisdictions recognize all four forms of this privacy-based tort.[274] Some U.S. jurisdictions have enacted privacy statutes recognizing the common law torts. Courts have been unwilling to find the publishing of disciplinary action on a website to be an invasion of privacy where the information is part of a public record. Selling, transferring, transmitting, and manipulating personal data is the life-blood of e-commerce and such activities are mostly beyond the reach of tort actions. Courts have largely been disinclined to stretch the tort of privacy to the Internet.

In the first generation of Internet torts, few plaintiffs have been successful in receiving civil recourse in large part because of the shield provided by Section 230. A commentator describes teens and young adults "living their lives as if in a fishbowl" because of the Internet.[275] Internet sites specialize in collecting "revenge porn" depicting ex-wives and ex-girlfriends in sexual situations.[276] In one case an ex-boyfriend distributed nude pictures of a high school girl, which led to harassment by her classmates; later she committed suicide.[277] Plaintiffs filing tort lawsuits in response to Revenge Porn postings have been successful.[278] To date, few plaintiffs have recovered damages for abuses in the Internet fishbowl. California enacted a statute that makes it a crime to distribute private images with the intent to harass or annoy.[279] One of the difficulties of anti-revenge porn statutes is to frame them so they do not have a chilling effect on legitimate speech.

---

[271] The U.S. Supreme Court in Time Inc. v. Hill, 385 U.S. 74 (1967) noted how New York's statute was enacted a year after Roberson v. Rochester Folding Box Co., 171 N.Y. 538, 64 N.E. 442 (1902). The New York Court of Appeals traced the development of the right to privacy to a "celebrated article of Warren and Brandeis, entitled The Right to Privacy. . . The Court of Appeals, however, denied the existence of such a right at common law but observed that 'the legislative body could very well interfere and arbitrarily provide that no one should be permitted for his own selfish purpose to use the picture or the name of another for advertising purposes without his consent" . . . Id. at 380–81. The court observed that New York's privacy statute was a direct response to Warren and Brandeis' law review article.

[272] Time Inc. v. Hill, 385 U.S. 374, 384 (1967) (citing Prosser).

[273] Many states recognize four types of interests protected by a person's right to privacy: (1) unreasonable intrusions upon the seclusion of another, (2) appropriation of the other's name or likeness, (3) unreasonable publicity given to the other's private life, and (4) publicity that unreasonably places the other in a false light before the public. RESTATEMENT (SECOND) OF TORTS § 652(B) (1977). See also, RESTATEMENT (SECOND) OF TORTS, § 652A (1965).

[274] Colorado, for example, does not recognize false light privacy. Shrader v Beann, 2012 U.S. App. LEXIS 24587 (10th Cir., Nov. 29, 2012) (applying Colorado law).

[275] Anupam Chander, Youthful Indiscretion in an Internet Age, in SAUL LEVMORE & MARTHA C. NUSSBAUM, THE OFFENSIVE INTERNET: PRIVACY, SPEECH, AND REPUTATION (2010).

[276] Id. at 126.

[277] Id.

[278] Woodrow Hartog, How to Fight Revenge Porn, Stanford University, Center for Internet and Society (May 10, 2013) (citing reasons for lawsuit failure such as the CDA Section 230 immunity and the difficulty of identifying wrongdoers; recommending action based upon breach of confidence).

[279]

(1) Intrusion Upon Seclusion

To establish liability for intrusion upon seclusion, a plaintiff must plead, and prove, that: In cases involving an unreasonable intrusion, a plaintiff must show: (1) the defendant intentionally intruded, physically or otherwise, upon the solitude or seclusion of the plaintiff or his private affairs or concerns, and (2) the intrusion would be highly offensive to a reasonable person. The Restatement (Second) of Torts requires the plaintiff to prove four things: (1) the defendant committed an unauthorized intrusion or prying into the plaintiff's seclusion; (2) the intrusion would be highly offensive or objectionable to a reasonable person; (3) the matter intruded upon was private; and (4) the intrusion caused the plaintiff anguish and suffering.[280] A plaintiff must prove that they had an actual expectation of seclusion, or objectively reasonable solicitude. Companies do not have privacy claims so they may not assert this cause of action for website postings about a business such as a customer gripe site.[281]

In *Murphy v. Spring*,[282] the Oklahoma federal court found a public school administration's unreasonable intrusion into an administrative assistant's private email account constituted intrusion upon seclusion. In *Spring*, the school administrators intentionally accessed the administrative assistant's private email account "in order to garner evidence in support of their recommended termination, which was made in retaliation for [the assistant's] whistle blowing on their illegal conduct."[283] The court found this intrusion to be "highly offensive to a reasonable person" for purposes of an invasion of privacy claim and/or "outrageous" for purposes of an IIED claim."[284] It is certainly different from passively reading or watching a communication that someone else illegally intercepted from the plaintiff.

An emblematic case was *Varian Medical Systems, Inc. v. Delfino*.[285] In *Delfino*, the employers received a series of threats over the Internet—via email to Delfino and postings on a Yahoo! Inc. message board. The unknown perpetrator used pseudonyms, most often "crack_smoking_jesus." The threats were ugly and frightening. For example:

"It's coming, motherfucker, and you won't see it. I seriously hope you have health insurance because you're going to get your ass stomped by me and some friends. . . . You can look forward to all of your fingers getting broken, several kicks to the ribs and mouth, break some teeth, and a cracked head. Also, your car will be trashed and your computer destroyed. Maybe set your place on fire." A California jury found the "defendants liable for libel, invasion of privacy (appropriation of name), breach of contract, and conspiracy, and awarded plaintiffs a total of $425,000 in compensatory

---

[280] In order to establish a claim for intrusion upon seclusion, a plaintiff must prove: "(1) an intentional intrusion, physical or otherwise, (2) upon the plaintiff's solitude or seclusion or private affairs or concerns, (3) which would be highly offensive to a reasonable person." Mauri v. Smith, 324 Ore. 476, 482,-83, 929 P.2d 307, 310 (1996). See generally, RESTATEMENT (SECOND) OF TORTS, § 652 (1965)

[281] Seaton v. TripAdvisor, 728 F.3rd 592 (6th Cir. 2013) (holding that hotel owner could not assert false light invasion of privacy claim against website for placing hotel on it 'Dirtiest Hotel' list since owner was not personally named on list and hotel was a business).

[281] Id. at *11.

[282] 2013 WL 5172951 (W.D. Okla., Sept. 12, 2013).

[283] Id. at *11.

[284] Id.

[285] Varian Medical Systems, Inc. v. Delfino, 106 P.3d 958 (2005).

damages. The jury further found that defendants acted with malice, fraud, or oppression, and awarded the plaintiffs $350,000 in punitive damages. The trial court also issued a permanent injunction against defendants."[286]

Courts have been unreceptive to consumer lawsuits, alleging that spyware is an intrusion upon seclusion. Google collects street views by having a car with a mounted camera go around the neighborhood and snap pictures. In *Boring v. Google, Inc.*,[287] the plaintiffs sued Google for invasion of privacy and trespass. Google's Street View car drove down their private road taking pictures of their house and pool and displayed them in Google's Street View feature. The court dismissed the plaintiffs' intrusion upon seclusion and right to publicity claims because no reasonable person would find that Google's car driving down their road and taking pictures to be "highly offensive." Nevertheless, the Third Circuit reversed the federal trial court on the trespass claim and allowed it to stand. Foreign courts and consumer protection agencies have fined Google for invasion of privacy arising out of its Street View data collection in France and the United Kingdom.

(2) *Appropriation & Right of Publicity*

The right of publicity evolved out of the right to privacy torts, specifically, from the tort of "invasion of privacy by appropriation."[288] The first case to describe this protection as a "right of publicity" was *Haelan Labs., Inc. v. Topps Chewing Gum, Inc.*,[289] which concerned the rights of professional baseball players whose images were used in baseball cards without their consent. The common law elements of the tort of the right of publicity are: (1) the defendant's use of the plaintiff's identity; (2) the appropriation of plaintiff's name or likeness to defendant's advantage, commercially or otherwise; and (3) the plaintiff has not given the defendant consent.[290] The tort of right of publicity, sometimes called the tort of commercial appropriation, protects the "inherent right of every human being to control the commercial use of his or her identity."[291]

The right of publicity applies to "[o]ne who appropriates the commercial value of a person's identity by using without consent the person's name, likeness, or other indicia of identity for purposes of trade is subject to liability."[292] Most appropriation or right of publicity claims arising out of a defendant's use of a person's name or likeness to advertise the defendant's product or when the defendant impersonates the person for gain. The misappropriation tort is an intellectual property right in protecting the value of one's name rather than one's name per se.

The right of publicity or appropriation tort is the only property-based action of the four privacy-based torts. In *C.B.C. Distribution and Mktg., Inc. v. Major League Baseball Advanced Media, L.P.*,[293] CBC marketed fantasy sports leagues on the Internet as well

---

[286] Id. at 963.

[287] 2010 U.S. App. LEXIS 1891 (3dCir., Jan. 25, 2010).

[288] J. THOMAS MCCARTHY, THE RIGHTS OF PUBLICITY AND PRIVACY, § 1:23 (2d ed. 2012).

[289] 202 F.2d 866 (2d Cir. 1953).

[290] "Under California law, to state a common law cause of action for misappropriation, a plaintiff must plead sufficient facts to establish: (1) defendant's use of plaintiff's identity; (2) the appropriation of plaintiff's name or likeness to defendant's advantage, commercially or otherwise; (3) lack of consent; and (4) resulting injury." Fraley v. Facebook, 830 F. Supp.2d 785 (N.D. Ca. 2011).

[291] J. THOMAS MCCARTHY, THE RIGHTS OF PUBLICITY AND PRIVACY, ' 1.2, 1–8 (1992).

[292] RESTATEMENT (THIRD) OF UNFAIR COMPETITION § 46 (2005).

[293] 505 F.3d 818 (8th Cir. 2007).

as by regular mail and telephone. Fantasy league participants form teams by drafting players from various Major League Baseball ("MLB") teams and use the cumulative statistics of the teams' players in actual games to determine the fantasy team's success. The MLB players were unable to prove the fantasy league exploited their identity without their consent and for the purpose of commercial gain. The Eighth Circuit ruled that the MLB players' "right of publicity" does not include personal statistics used in fantasy baseball leagues. CBC used "players' identities . . . for purposes of profit . . . and their identities [were] being used for commercial advantage," which satisfied the elements of right to publicity.[294]

The court, however, ultimately decided the company's right to free speech outweighed the players' right to publicity, because the "line between the informing and the entertaining is too elusive for the protection of that basic right."[295] "The right of publicity as recognized by statute and common law is fundamentally constrained by the public and constitutional interest in freedom of expression."[296] In *Hart v. Electronic Arts, Inc.*,[297] a former Rutgers University football player filed a class action against a video game developer, alleging misappropriation of the likeness and identity of him and others incorporated in a NCAA football-related video game. The video game maker was able to remove the action to federal court where the court granted summary judgment in favor of a video game developer because the First Amendment protected it. The Third Circuit reversed in favor of the college football players when a game maker used their likenesses and statistics in a video game.[298] The federal circuit court framed the principal issue as developing "a definitive methodology for balancing the tension between the First Amendment and the right of publicity, . . . a case of first impression."[299] The court rejected the predominant purpose test, which asked whether the product sold "predominately" exploits the plaintiff's identity.[300] Instead, the appeals court imported the "transformative use" test first developed in copyright law to the right of publicity.[301] The court noted:

> The Transformative Use Test maintains a singular focus on whether the work sufficiently transforms the celebrity's identity or likeness, thereby allowing courts to account for the fact that misappropriation can occur in any market segment, including those related to the celebrity.[302]

The court found that the college athletes had a right of publicity because the avatars representing them were not sufficiently transformative:

> Considering the context within which the digital avatar exists—effectively, looking at how Appellant's identity is "incorporated into and transformed by" . . . provides little support for Appellee's arguments. The digital Ryan Hart does what the actual Ryan Hart did while at Rutgers: he plays college football, in digital recreations of college football stadiums, filled with all the trappings of a college

---

[294] Id.
[295] Id.
[296] RESTATEMENT (THIRD) OF UNFAIR COMPETITION, § 47, cmt.
[297] 2011 WL 4005350 (D.N.J. Sept. 9, 2011).
[298] Hart v. Electronic Arts, Inc., 2013 WL 2161317 (3d Cir. May 21, 2013).
[299] Id. at *7.
[300] Id. at *9.
[301] Id. at *13.
[302] Id. at *17.

football game. This is not transformative; the various digitized sights and sounds in the video game do not alter or transform the Appellant's identity in a significant way.[303]

The court held that the NCAA football videos violated the college athletes' right of publicity.[304] The court concluded that the "overall claim for violation of his right of publicity should have survived the video game makers' motion for summary judgment.[305]

The tort of the right of publicity is the unauthorized taking of another's name or likeness.[306] This was the first form of an invasion of privacy tort recognized by courts. There have been several cases where plaintiffs have sued for right of publicity based on their likenesses appearing on the Internet.[307] The federal district court enjoined an adult entertainment website from distributing the video sex tape of Pamela Anderson Lee and musician Brett Michaels on its subscription website.[308] The court found the site liable for copyright infringement, and for infringing the celebrities' rights of privacy and publicity. The Ninth Circuit in *Perfect 10, Inc. v. CCBill*,[309] stretched Section 230 of the Communications Decency Act to immunize websites for claims based upon the right of publicity and other state intellectual property rights. In *Perfect 10*, the plaintiff, a modeling agency, charged a website with violating its models' rights of publicity when it allowed third parties to post infringing copyrighted images on the site. The gist of Perfect 10's right of privacy claim was the unauthorized commercial use of the models' names and images. The defendant website responded with a claim that Section 230 of the CDA[310] immunized them from the claim and the Ninth Circuit agreed.

California is representative of states that have a statutory-based publicity right. In *Yeager v. Bowlin*,[311] the Ninth Circuit applied the single publication rule to a statement on a website that allegedly violated an aviation public figure's right to

---

[303] Id. at *19.

[304] Id. at *22.

[305] Id.

[306] "One who appropriates to his own use or benefit the name or likeness of another is subject to liability to the other for invasion of privacy." RESTATEMENT (SECOND) OF TORTS, § 652C. The comments also make clear that "the right created by [the rule in §652C] is in the nature of a property right." Id.§ 652C cmt. a.

[307] Lee v. Internet Entm't Group, Inc., 33 Fed. Appx. 886 (9th Cir. 2002) (finding an issue of material fact as to whether a settlement and release entered into by celebrities and an entertainment organization covered only Internet distribution of an allegedly stolen videotape depicting them engaged in intimate acts or whether it extended to distribution of the tape on VHS and DVD via retail stores).

[308] Michaels v. Internet Entertainment Group Inc., 5 F. Supp. 2d 823 (C.D. Cal. 1998); See also Lee v. Internet Entm't Group, Inc., 33 Fed. Appx. 886 (9th Cir. 2002) (finding an issue of material fact as to whether a settlement and release entered into by celebrities and an entertainment organization covered only Internet distribution of an allegedly stolen videotape depicting them engaged in intimate acts or whether it extended to distribution of the tape on VHS and DVD via retail stores).

[309] 488 F.3d 1102 (9th Cir. 2007).

[310] Chapter 9 sets forth the statutory framework immunizing websites from torts. Section 230(e)(3) further provides that: "No cause of action may be brought and no liability may be imposed under any State or local law that is inconsistent with this section." 47 U.S.C. § 230(e)(3). Section 230 defines interactive computer services broadly to include: "any information service, system, or access software

provider that provides or enables computer access by multiple users to a computer server, including

specifically a service or system that provides access to the Internet and such systems operated or

services offered by libraries or educational institutions" 47 U.S.C. § 230(e)(3). Section 230(c) shields websites and service providers from secondary tort liability or torts committed by third parties.

[311] 2012 WL 3892903 (Sept. 10, 2012).

privacy and California's statutory right to publicity. The court ruled that both claims were subject to a two-year statute of limitations and were dismissed as timely.[312] In that case, the court found "no evidence in the record that the Bowlins, who ran the sports memorabilia company, added any information about Chuck Yeager, or modified any of the challenged statements about Yeager on their website, after October 2003."[313]

In *Fain v. Silkening Techns.*,[314] a Florida jury award concluded that a company used the plaintiff model's image on online hair care product advertisement without authorization. The plaintiff was a model and "actress, [who] permitted Krush Models to use her image for advertisement but later discovered her image was being used by Silkening Technologies on its website to advertise its hair care products."[315] The plaintiff claimed the defendants' use of her image was not authorized and that the "defendants attempted to purchase the photo from another modeling agency she was associated with after she had already discovered the unauthorized use."[316] A Florida jury returned a verdict in favor for the plaintiff for $100,000 in damages for loss based on the unauthorized use of her image.[317]

(3) Public Disclosure of Private Fact

To pursue a public disclosure of private facts, the plaintiff must plead that: (1) publicity was given to the disclosure of private facts; (2) the facts were private, not public; (3) the matter made public was such as to be highly offensive to a reasonable person; and (4) the matter publicized was not one of legitimate public concern. "The tort of public disclosure of private facts is meant to protect against the disclosure of "intimate . . . details the publicizing of which would be not merely embarrassing and painful but deeply shocking to the average person subjected to such exposure."[318]

Unlike invasion of privacy for publicity given to private life, invasion of privacy for publicity placing person in false light does not require proof that matter giving rise to plaintiff's claim be restricted to one of private concern. A federal judge dismissed a public disclosure of private facts for derogatory comments posted about a Missouri woman. The court reasoned that since the posting consisted of outright fabrications, there was no invasion of privacy.[319] In *In re Google Buzz Privacy Litigation*,[320] a federal court approved an $8.5 million settlement in a class action suit brought by Gmail users who contended that Google exposed their personal information without authorization through "Google Buzz," now a defunct social networking site.

The plaintiffs in Google Buzz asserted a claim for the Public Disclosure of Private Facts as recognized by California common law. In order to state a claim for public

---

[312] Id. at *3.

[313] Id.

[314] 2012 WL 7004385 (Fla. Cir. Ct., Sept. 24, 2012).

[315] Id.

[316] Id.

[317] Id.

[318] Chisholm v. Foothill Capital Corp., 3 F. Supp. 2d 925, 940–41 (N.D. Ill. 1998).

[319] Donald Brown, Federal Judge Rules "Dirty" Website Not Libel for Inflammatory Comments, FIRST AMENDMENT COALITION (June 7, 2011) (reasoning "that there was no valid claim for public disclosure of private facts because Dirty World LLC did not reveal any private truths since the comments were fabrications according to the woman.").

[320] 2011 WL 7460099 (N.D. Cal. 2011).

disclosure of private facts, the facts must not only be private, but the matter revealed must be highly offensive to a reasonable person.[321] A California Appeals Court ruled that a preliminary injunction prohibiting an ex-wife from posting "false and defamatory statements and/or confidential personal information" on the Internet was an unconstitutional prior restraint.[322] In a Maine case, the court considered a case in which a plaintiff filed a public disclosure of private facts case against a former classmate who published a book about their prolonged high school feud called, "Help Us Get Mia." The court rejected the plaintiff's claim for public disclosure for private facts, finding many of the statements posted by the plaintiff on her MySpace page.[323]

(4) False Light

The fourth privacy-based tort is placing the plaintiff in a false light. A defendant who gives publicity to a matter concerning the plaintiff that places the plaintiff in a false light if: the other (1) would be highly offensive to reasonable person; and (2) had knowledge of or acted in reckless disregard as to falsity of publicized matter and false light in which other was placed.[324] False light is not a strict liability tort. The defendant must have knowledge of or have acted in reckless disregard as to the falsity of the published facts to be liable. In *Meyerkord v. Zipatoni,*[325] a former employee sued his former employer when the employer failed to remove the employee's name as the registrant from a website the employer created that launched a viral internet marketing campaign for a gaming system.[326] "Shortly after the marketing campaign became active, bloggers, consumers, and consumer activist groups began voicing their concern, suspicion, and accusations over the campaign and those associated with it, including the former employee, on blogs and websites."[327] The employee filed a false light invasion of privacy action because his former employer failed to remove his name as a registrant and let the viral marketing campaign be publicly attributable to him.[328] The plaintiff claimed emotional distress and loss of reputation in his community as damages that would be ongoing as this information would be on blogs and websites criticizing him and be difficult to erase from the Internet.[329] The court found a sufficient basis for false light distinguishing this claim from defamation.[330]

A typical false light case arose out of a chiropractor's former patient posting of negative reviews of his San Francisco chiropractic services on Yelp.com. The defendant's postings suggested that the chiropractor was dishonest and engaged in insurance fraud through dishonest "time of service" billing practices. The plaintiff contended that the postings placed him in a false light in the public light and defamed

---

[321] RESTATEMENT (SECOND) OF TORTS, § 652D (1965).

[322] Evans v. Evans, 76 Cal. Rptr.3d 859 (Ct. App. 2008).

[323] Sandler v. Calcagni, 565 F. Supp.2d 184 (D. Me. 2008).

[324] RESTATEMENT (SECOND) OF TORTS § 652C (1965).

[325] 276 S.W.3d 319 (Mo. App. E.D. 2008).

[326] Id. at 321.

[327] Id.

[328] Id. at 321-322.

[329] Id. at 322 ("The employee alleged his privacy had been invaded, his reputation and standing in the community was injured, and he suffered shame, embarrassment, humiliation, harassment, and mental anguish. *Id.* at 322. The employee further alleged his injuries would be ongoing because blogs and websites criticizing him would remain on the internet and were available for searching and viewing for an indefinite period of time").

[330] Id.

him, contending that the publicity created by the Yelp.com posting was offensive and objectionable to "a reasonable person of ordinary sensibilities. The plaintiff also contended that the posting was done with malice in made either knowledge of its falsity or in reckless disregard of the truth."[331] In *Patterson v. Grant-Herms*,[332] an operations agent employed by Southwest Airlines, filed an action against the defendant asserting causes of action for slander, defamation, libel, and false light invasion of privacy. The plaintiff contended that the defendants made untrue statements and posted false and defamatory comments about her on Facebook and Twitter relative to a confrontation between the two when Ms. Grant–Herms and her three children attempted to board a plane in violation of Southwest Airlines policy. The lower court granted summary judgment to the defendant on all of the agent's claims. The court ruled that the agent's claim of false light invasion of privacy, holding that the language "was not highly offensive to a reasonable person." The Tennessee appeals court reversed this finding observing that "a reasonable person could find, under the entire circumstances of the incident, that Ms. Grant–Herms' posting of selective facts placed Ms. Patterson in a false light by implying that Ms. Patterson was rude and a bad service agent, one who was more concerned with adherence to the airline rules and procedures than the welfare of the child, and that these implications caused injury to her."[333] False light claims often raise First Amendment concerns although some courts do not extend the *Sullivan* framework to this privacy-based tort.[334]

§ 6.5 NEGLIGENCE BASED ACTIONS

(A) Internet Related Negligence

The traditional formula for negligence asks whether: the defendant owed a duty to the foreseeable plaintiff; the defendant breached that duty to the plaintiff; the plaintiff suffered an injury; and the breach of the duty was the proximate cause of the injury. In practice, however, the courts often blend the concepts of duty and proximate cause by asking whether a duty is owed to the plaintiff. The central question in duty or proximate cause cases has to do with the expansion or retraction of liability. "Under these rubrics, a standard problem is whether the negligent defendant can be held liable for unforeseeable consequences or to unforeseeable plaintiffs."[335] The California Supreme Court in *Dillon v. Legg* acknowledged that duty was "a shorthand statement of a conclusion, rather than an aid to analysis in itself."[336] The court in *Rowland v. Christian*[337] acknowledged that policy factors such as the policy of preventing future harm or availability of insurance entered into the determination of whether a duty was owed.

---

[331] Complaint in Biegel v. Norberg, No. 08–472522 (Super. Ct. S.F., July 25, 2008).

[332] 2013 WL 5568427 (Tenn. Ct. App. Oct. 8, 2013); See also Perez v. Factory Direct of Secaucus, LLC, 2013 WL 5770734 (D.N.J., Oct. 23, 2013) (finding that blog postings about legal standard in employment lawsuit did not place the plaintiff in a false light).

[333] Id.

[334] Farrow v. Saint Francis Medical Center, 407 S.W.3d 579, 601 (Mo. App. 2013) (explaining differences between false light and defamation cases in view of First Amendment).

[335] Ernest J. Weinrib, Causation and Wrongdoing, 63 CHI–KENT L. REV. 407, 439 (1987).

[336] Dillon v. Legg, 441 P.2d 912 (Cal. 1968).

[337] 443 P.2d 651 (Cal. 1968).

Judges used the allied concepts of duty and proximate cause as devices to exclude categories of plaintiffs where the risk was so unforeseeable that the line was drawn on liability.[338] More importantly, these doctrinal tools permit judges to make evaluations of risk-creation in cyberspace just as in the age of industrialization. The law of torts imposes no general duty to control the conduct of third persons or to prevent dangerous individuals from doing harm to others.[339] However, courts will use the language of foreseeability to create a "special duty" where the plaintiff is particularly sympathetic, or where strict interpretation of the no duty rule is particularly harsh. Courts are just beginning to determine whether given entities have a duty to cyberspace users.

In one of the largest empirical studies of tort litigation, the Institute for Civil Justice found that negligence-based motor vehicle claims accounted for almost two in three cases.[340] Negligence is conduct that departs from the reasonable standard of care imposed by law for the protection of others.[341] Ninety percent of tort law is about negligence in the brick-and-mortar world but in cyberspace, negligence-based causes of action are rare. Courts often come to recognize new duties to address increasing or emergent risks such as the development of medical malpractice and products liability in the 1960s. Negligence is just beginning to promote deterrence in cyberspace and will have even greater salience as data breaches and computer intrusions become foreseeable.

Courts have been unwilling to recognize new duties of care for cyberspace activities, perhaps because of a fear of "opening the floodgates" to a tidal wave of litigation. To prove negligence based cybertorts, a plaintiff must prove, by a preponderance of the evidence, each element of negligence: duty, breach of duty, cause-in-fact,[342] proximate cause, and damages. Duty is a legal obligation to conform to a reasonable person standard of care in order to protect others against unreasonable risks of harm.[343] A breach of the duty of care is the failure of a defendant to conform to the standard of reasonable care. Courts construct tests for reasonable care such as whether the defendant has violated a statute, industry standard, or customary usage of trade.[344]

---

[338] E. Wayne Theode, Tort Analysis: Duty–Risk v. Proximate Cause and the Rational Allocation of Functions Between Judge and Jury, 1977 UTAH L. REV. 1, 33 (1977).

[339] RESTATEMENT (SECOND) OF TORTS § 315 (1965).

[340] Marc Galanter, Real World Torts: Antidote to Anecdote, 55 MD. L. REV. 1093, 1102 (1996).

[341] Michael J. Rustad & Thomas H. Koenig, Extending Learned Hand's Negligence Formula to Information Security Breaches, 3 I/S: J.L. & POL'Y FOR INFO. SOC'Y 237, 239–40 (2007) ("[C]ompanies have a duty to provide reasonable information security practices under the common law of torts.").

[342] "'But for' causation is a short way of saying the defendant's conduct is a cause of the event if the event would not have occurred but for that conduct. It is sometimes stated as sine qua non causation, i.e., without which not. In determining whether a particular factor was a but-for cause of a given event, a court begins by assuming that the factor was present at the time of the event, and then asks whether, even if that factor had been absent, the event nevertheless would have transpired in the same way." UMG Recordings, Inc. v. Veoh Networks, Inc., 106 U.S.P.Q.2D (BNA) 1253 (9th Cir. 2013).

[343] Unreasonable risks are those of "such magnitude as to outweigh what the law regards as the utility of the act . . . ." RESTATEMENT (SECOND) OF TORTS, § 291 (1965). The Restatement (Second) uses a risk/utility test that draws in large part from the famous Learned Hand risk-benefit model. See RESTATEMENT (SECOND) OF TORTS, § 291 & cmt. d (1965). The Hand formulation finds a defendant such as Cameron in breach if the burden of taking measures to avoid the harm would be less than the multiple of the likelihood that the harm will occur times the magnitude of the harm should it occur: $B < P \cdot L$ United States v. Carroll Towing Co., 159 F.2d 169, 173 (2d Cir. 1947).

[344] A wide variety of standards are evolving in the data security field. In a high security environment such as the military or banking, for example, the standard may be fingerprint recognition. Assa Abloy, ITG Introduces Smart Card Reader with Fingerprint Recognition, Product News Network, June 6, 2007, at 1. Another example of a security standard is the threefold authentication system "via card, pin, and

To date, consumers have rarely prevailed in negligent Internet security cases because they are unable to prove a present injury. None of the millions of consumers whose credit card numbers were stolen in the T.J. Maxx data heist will have a cause of action unless they can prove a concrete loss from the theft.[345] The recognition of new tort duties is inevitably a policy-based determination.[346] The judiciary balances such factors as the foreseeability of the harm of computer viruses, or other breaches of security; the degree of certainty between software vulnerabilities and harm; the connection between lax Internet security practices and the injury suffered by a computer user; the policy of preventing future intrusions; the burden on the information industry and the consequences to the community of imposing a duty to maintain adequate security; and the availability, costs, and prevalence of security solutions and insurance.

Negligent security policy is at the heart of recent data theft disasters involving identity fraud and the misappropriation of electronic information. Several statutes already give the state attorneys general or federal officials the right to seek penalties against any company that fails to disclose security breaches when consumer data has been compromised. However, no state or federal security breach notification statutes give the victims of data theft a private cause of action for data theft. [347]At present, the combination of the economic loss rule,[348] present injury requirements,[349] and the lack of a judicially created duty to secure data, presents an insurmountable barrier to individual recovery for negligent data handling. Companies use contractual devices such as "hold harmless" clauses and indemnification to shift the costs of data theft to users.[350]

Plaintiffs in Internet security cases, whether individuals or entities, are subject to user defenses such as the assumption of risk and contributory negligence as well as the doctrine of avoidable consequences or the duty to mitigate a loss once it occurs. Clifford

---

fingerprint." Id. Industry standards are rapidly evolving as vendors market new technologies to ensure authentication, access control and data protection. See, e.g., Press Release, Trapeze Smart Mobile, Trapeze Network Joins Support Trusted Network Connect Initiative (Sept. 19, 2006).

[345] Florida criminals hacked into TJX Company computers and compromises 45.5 million customer credit and debit accounts. Larry Greenemeier, T.J. Maxx Parent Company Data Theft is the Worst Ever, INFO WK. (March 29, 2007).

[346] Michael L. Rustad & Thomas H. Koenig, The Tort of Negligent Enablement of Cybercrime, 20 BERKELEY TECH. L.J. 1553, 1598 ("[T]he overarching goal of tort law is to control the costs of accidents rather than to eliminate them.").

[347] A consumer injured by a company's failure to give notice of a security breach already has a negligence per se cause of action. However, no court has permitted a consumer to use federal or state statutes in a lawsuit based upon the failure to implement reasonable security. One commentator contends that companies already have a duty to provide reasonable computer security and a duty to disclose data breaches should they occur. Thomas J. Smedinghoff, Security Breach Notification-Adapting to the Regulatory Framework, THE REVIEW OF BANKING & FINANCIAL SERVICES, Dec. 2005, at 12,

[348] Sidney R. Barrett, Jr., Recovery of Economic Loss in Tort for Construction Defects: A Critical Analysis, 40 S.C. L. REV. 891, 894-95 (1989) ("The economic loss doctrine marks the fundamental boundary between contract law, which is designed to enforce the expectancy interests of the parties, and tort law, which imposes a duty of reasonable care and thereby encourages citizens to avoid causing physical harm to others.").

[349] Plaintiffs have failed to demonstrate a cognizable injury in a number of other cases in which data was lost or stolen. See, e.g., Giordano v. Wachovia Sec., LLC, 2006 U.S. Dist. LEXIS 52266 (D.N.J. 2006); Bell v. Acxiom Corp., 2006 U.S. Dist. LEXIS 72477 (E.D. Ark. 2006); Key v. DSW, Inc., 454 F. Supp. 2d 684 (S.D. Ohio 2006).

[350] See generally, Michael L. Rustad, Thomas H. Koenig, Extending Learned Hand's Negligence Formulat to Information Security Breaches, 3 I/S: J. L. & POL'Y FOR INFO. SOC'Y 237 (2007) (Symposium: Cybersecurity Policy).

Stoll stresses the importance of changing user passwords to protect against hackers: "Treat your password like your toothbrush. Don't let anybody else use it, and get a new one every six months."[351] Defendants in Internet security cases can defend because users were not careful about protecting their cybertort. Comparative negligence is also measured by a risk utility test. In cybertort cases, as in the brick and mortar world, negligence is determined by a finding of excessive preventable dangers. The Restatement (Second) of Torts adopts a risk/utility test to measure breach of the standard of care.[352] Courts applying the risk/utility test, first articulated in *United States v. Carroll Towing Co.*,[353] determine breach of the standard of care by weighing the defendant's burden of precautions against the expected costs of accidents or injuries. The Learned Hand formula dictates a finding of negligence "if the probability be called P; the injury, L; and the burden, B; liability depends upon whether B is less than L multiplied by P: i.e., whether $B < P * L$."[354] The party that is the least cost avoider or who can best avoid the harm should bear the costs of that harm. If the damage could have been avoided by taking precautions at very little cost, then, even if the risk is slight, the safety step is cost-justified because the burden, B, is less than the probability of the accident multiplied by the gravity of the injury.

The American Law Institute adopted a modified version of the Learned Hand test in the Restatement (Second) of Torts, which defines negligence as an activity in which the magnitude of the risk outweighs the utility.[355]The Learned Hand formula is flexible enough to serve as the standard for a broad range of risky scenarios for cyberspace activities.[356] To set a standard of care for computer security, for example, the total costs and probability of computer security breaches can be compared to the cost of instituting strong security measures.[357] Negligent security cases should be recognized where precaution costs are inexpensive and the risk of harm great. Nevertheless,

---

[351] Clifford Stoll Quotes, http://www. brainyquote.com/quotes/authors/c/clifford_stoll.html. http://www. brainyquote.com/quotes/ authors /c/clifford_stoll.html#zqvCRv9gqvTGmwkY.99.

[352] A user that does not implement or update security would theoretically be subject to user defenses such as the assumption of risk and contributory negligence. Comparative negligence jurisdictions vary depending on whether they are "modified" or "pure" regimes. In a modified system, negligent plaintiffs may recover provided their negligence is neither equal to nor greater than that of the defendant. In a pure comparative negligence regime, the plaintiff's recovery diminishes by the degree of negligence, even if it is greater than or equal to that of the defendant. In a modified comparative negligence jurisdiction following the fifty-fifty rule, a plaintiff may not recover if his fault was fifty percent or more in contributing to his injury. In a pure comparative negligence jurisdiction, the plaintiff's recovery reduces by the degree of his or her own negligence. In order for there to be assumption of risk, there must be a knowing and voluntary embracing of a risk. Most U.S. jurisdictions follow some form of modified comparative negligence though a few states still follow the regressive doctrine of contributory negligence.

[353] 159 F.2d 169 (2d Cir. 1947).

[354] Id. at 173. ("if the probability be called P; the injury, L; and the burden, B; liability depends upon whether B is less than L multiplied by P: i.e., whether B less than PL").

[355] Unreasonable risks are those of "such magnitude as to outweigh what the law regards as the utility of the act." RESTATEMENT (SECOND) OF TORTS § 291 (1965).

[356] "The Learned Hand formula is of greater analytical than operational significance because precise empirical data for "operationalizing" these variables rarely exists." Michael L. Rustad & Thomas H. Koenig, Extending Learned Hand's Negligence Formula To Information Security Breaches, 3 I/S: A JOURNAL OF LAW & POLICY INFO. SOC. 237, 244 (2007).

[357] "By making the actor strictly liable-by denying him in other words an excuse based on his inability to avoid accidents by being more careful-we give him an incentive, missing in a negligence regime, to experiment with methods of preventing accidents that involve not greater exertions of care, assumed to be futile, but instead relocating, changing, or reducing (perhaps to the vanishing point) the activity giving rise to the accident." Ind. Harbor Belt R. Co. v. Am. Cyanamid Co., 916 F.2d 1174, 1177 (7th Cir. 1990).

sometimes the cost of precaution far exceeds the risk. Scott Adams' *Dilbert* featured a cartoon in which a corporation purchased laptop computers for their employees to use while traveling—then the chief information officer permanently attached the laptops to the employees' desks to prevent theft. A software company's 10–K filing described how security issues potentially influenced their business:

> Security experts have identified computer worm programs that target handsets running on certain operating systems. Although these worms have not been widely released and do not present an immediate risk to our business, we believe future threats could lead some end-users to seek to reduce or delay future purchases of our products or reduce or delay the use of their handsets. Wireless carriers and handset manufacturers may also increase their expenditures on protecting their wireless networks and mobile phone products from attack, which could delay adoption of new handset models. Any of these activities could adversely affect our revenues and this could harm our business, operating results and financial condition.[358]

Companies that do not implement reasonable security measures to thwart hackers may be liable for negligent enablement of cybercrimes. The conventional wisdom is that employees, ex-employees and consultants do most data thefts—the enemy within. However, Verizon's Risk Team conducted a 2012 study that concluded that hackers, not current or ex-employees, perpetrated eighty-one percent of the data breaches in their study. The biggest barrier to enablement claims is for plaintiffs to demonstrate a nexus between substandard security and a concrete injury. Courts have been slow to recognize new duties of care for cyberspace actors. Cybercriminals may easily exploit several vulnerabilities at the server level.[359] The best analytical approach for creating this new duty involves determining whether the burden of a comprehensive security solution is less than the magnitude of the damages caused by lost or stolen data, multiplied by the probability of occurrence. A major consideration in the decision to impose liability for negligent security is whether a company could have foreseen the particular harm resulting from its existing security precautions and whether cost effective measures would have significantly reduced the risk.

(B)　Negligent Enablement of Cybercrime

The negligent enablement of identity fraud or cybercrimes requires the plaintiffs to demonstrate a breach of the duty of care. Under this negligence-based theory, a website would be liable for failing to implement reasonable security or to monitor their computer systems to thwart cybercriminals or criminals from misappropriating customer data for identity fraud.[360] Robert Rabin first developed the concept of enabling liability for industries that facilitate third party crimes and other injuries to third parties.[361] Most jurisdictions have declined to recognize the negligent enablement

---

[358] Mandalay Media, Inc., 10–K filing, Securities & Exchange Commission, March 31, 2008.

[359] See Michael L. Rustad & Lori Eisenschmidt, The Commercial Law of Internet Security, 10 J. OF HIGH TECH. L. 213, 216 (1995).

[360] Michael L. Rustad & Thomas H. Koenig, The Tort of Negligent Enablement of Cybercrime, 20 BERKELEY TECH L. J. 1553 (2005) (proposing a new tort to hold software vendors accountable for defective products and services that pave the way for third-party cybercriminals).

[361] Robert L. Rabin, Enabling Torts, 49 DEPAUL L. REV. 435, 452 (1999) (formulating negligent enablement cause of action against handgun manufacturers for marketing products "inviting misuse and consequent harm to innocent victims").

of cybercrime as a cause of action.[362] Negligence is a tort where the plaintiff must prove actual damages—unlike some intentional torts such as trespass to land. Plaintiffs in Internet-related negligence cases often have a difficult time establishing concrete injuries or damages.

China launched a sophisticated cyberattack on Google's corporate infrastructure in 2010. In this case, the Chinese government was seeking to access the Gmail accounts of Chinese human rights activists. The attackers planted malicious code in Google's corporate networks, which also resulted in the theft of Google's intellectual property. In the aftermath of the attack, Google fortified its security by implementing encryption in its e-mail system and threatened to leave China.[363] Yahoo!, Intel, and scores other companies have been targets of similar attacks originated in China. LinkedIn.com, for example, used outdated methods to secure information of subscribers that enabled 6.5 million passwords to be purloined by some unknown cybercriminal. On June 6, 2012, the hackers posted millions of LinkedIn users' passwords on the Internet. Shortly after, LinkedIn "released a statement on its blog stating that it had recently completed a switch of its password encryption method from a system that stored member passwords in a hashed format to one that used both salted and hashed passwords for increased security."[364] The court held that LinkedIn was not liable for negligent security in a class action where the customers of the social media website argued that they faced increased risk of future harm as result of hacking incident. The court found that the hackers' posting of passwords on the Internet did not "demonstrate that [the LinkedIn users] sustained economic harm."[365] The court found that the plaintiffs had not satisfied the standing requirement for the class action "based on website's failure to adequately protect customers' personal information."[366] The defect in the complaint was that the plaintiffs "failed to allege facts demonstrating that the posting of the password on the internet amounted to a legally cognizable injury."[367] Nevertheless, the foreseeability of cybercrime, cyber espionage and cyberwarfare raises the issue of whether U.S. companies and Internet providers owe a duty to secure their websites to protect the data or trade secrets of third parties. Courts do not recognize a consumer's risk of being an identity theft victim because of a data breach as compensable damages.

The First Circuit recognized that plaintiffs had standing based upon money they spent to replace credit cards and theft insurance in *Anderson v. Hannaford Bros. Co.*[368] Courts are just beginning to hold data intermediaries such as software licensors, financial service companies, and other defendants liable for inadequate computer security that enables the theft of data. Negligent security policy is at the heart of Internet-related data disasters constituting identity fraud and the misappropriation of

---

[362] See e.g., Huggins v. Citibank, N.A., 355 S.C. 329, 331, 334, 585 S.E.2d 275 (S.C. 2003) (holding that "South Carolina does not recognize the tort of negligent enablement of imposter fraud."); Polzer v. TRW, Inc., 256 A.D.2d 248 248, 682 N.Y.S.2d 194 (N.Y. App. Div. 1998) (declining to recognize "a cause of action for "negligent enablement of impostor fraud").

[363] This high profile incident was described in EPIC's appellant brief in The Electronic Privacy Information Center v. U.S. National Security Agency, 2012 WL 13532 (D.D.C., Jan. 3, 2013).

[364] In re Linked in Privacy Litigation, 932 F. Supp.2d 1089, 1091 (N.D. Cal. 2013).

[365] Id.

[366] Id.

[367] Id.

[368] 2011 WL 5007175 (1st Cir. Oct. 20, 2011).

electronic information. The largest Internet-related data heist in history targeted T.J. Maxx, whose parent company is TJX Companies, Inc.

The Massachusetts retail company reported in January of 2007 hackers compromised at least 45.7 million credit cards through a breach of its computer system. The U.S. Justice Department indicted eleven defendants for illegally installing programs to capture card numbers, passwords and account information and then transmitting the purloined data to servers in the United States and Eastern Europe. The government charged the hackers with many federal crimes including violations of the CFAA and the ECPA, as well as statutes governing money laundering, credit card theft, identity theft, and conspiracy. Consumers, whose credit card information was compromised, filed a civil action against TJX Maxx for conversion on the theory that TJX enabled the hackers by failing to secure its computer system. The Massachusetts federal court dismissed the conversion count, ruling, "conversion relates to interference with tangible rather than intangible property," such as electronic records.[369]

In *In re Heartland Payment Systems Inc. Customer Data Sec. Breach Litigation*,[370] Heartland Payment Systems publicly disclosed that unknown hackers had breached its computer system and obtained access to confidential payment-card information for 100 million consumers. The Judicial Panel on Multidistrict Litigation divided the lawsuits into consumer plaintiffs and a track for financial institution plaintiffs. The federal court dismissed claims that Key Bank acted negligently by failing to ensure that Heartland complied with the Payment Card Industry Data Security Standards in a security breach case. The court also rejected the financial institution's breach of contract claim in that the court found no third party rights from a contract between Key Bank and Heartland. Finally, the court rejected the financial institution's breach of fiduciary duty claim in its finding that the financial institutions were not co-venturers.

U.S. courts have been reluctant to construct a duty to maintain reasonable computer security.[371] The watchword of negligence liability is risk; the greater the risk, the greater the duty. The failure to implement reasonable cybersecurity poses great risks to our networked society. Increasingly, the world's infrastructure is software-driven and networked which creates new vulnerabilities. A Congressional Research Service report was issued on pipeline cybersecurity:

> The vast U.S. network of natural gas and hazardous liquid pipelines is integral to U.S. energy supply and has vital links to other critical infrastructure. While an efficient and fundamentally safe means of transport, this network is vulnerable to cyber-attacks. In particular, cyber infiltration of supervisory control and data acquisition (SCADA) systems could allow successful "hackers" to disrupt pipeline service and cause spills, explosions, or fires—all from remote locations. In March 2012, the Department of Homeland Security (DHS) reported ongoing cyber intrusions among U.S. natural gas pipeline operators. These intrusions have

---

[369] In re TJX Companies Retail Sec. Breach Litigation, 527 F. Supp. 2d 209, 212 (D. Mass. 2007).

[370] 2012 WL 896256 (S.D. Tex. Mar. 4, 2012).

[371] Michael L. Rustad, The Negligent Enablement of Trade Secret Misappropriation, 22 SANTA CLARA COMPUTER & HIGH TECH. L.J. 455, 458 (2006).

heightened congressional concern about cybersecurity in the U.S. pipelines sector.[372]

Since September 11, 2001, terrorist groups have targeted pipelines as relatively soft targets.[373] The U.S. Department of Homeland Security has documented "ongoing cyber intrusions among U.S. natural gas pipeline operations" that have the potential of creating catastrophic property damage, economic loss, and personal injuries and death.[374] The immediate risk is that a cyber-attack could disrupt service or damage pipeline equipment or lines by using Trojan horse (malicious software) to create excessive line pressure or even gain control of the SCADA system.[375] Supervisory control and data acquisition ("SCADA") systems, software-based industrial control systems, go far beyond pipelines and manage "railways, utility power grids, water and sewer systems."[376] The preventive law lesson is that courts will likely recognize a duty to take reasonable measures to protect against cyber-attack that could disrupt service or damage pipeline equipment or lines.[377]

Courts have been slow to recognize a company's duty to secure their website or computers system to prevent hackers from compromising their computer system. Plaintiffs in inadequate computer security cases are customers harmed when data is compromised. In *Lone Star Nat. Bank, N.A. v. Heartland Payments Systems*,[378] the Fifth Circuit applying New Jersey law held that the economic loss doctrine did not bar credit card issuer banks' negligence claim against the processer of credit card transactions. The *Heartland Payments* case arose out of a group of hackers' breach of Heartland Payment Systems, Inc.'s data systems, compromising confidential information belonging to customers of the plaintiff banks. (Issuer Banks).[379] The district court dismissed the Issuer Banks' claims but the Fifth Circuit reversed and remanded the claim because Heartland was negligent.[380]

The lower court reasoned that there was no contractual relationship between the issuing banks and Heartland and that no common law negligence claim could go forward because of the economic loss doctrine. The Fifth Circuit reversed, reasoning that it was foreseeable that the issuing banks would be harmed if the processors 'computer systems were compromised by hackers. The court ruled issuer banks constituted an identifiable class and that the credit card processor had reason to foresee that the banks would be entities to suffer economic losses if it were negligent.

---

[372] PAUL W. PARFOMAK, PIPELINE CYBERSECURITY: FEDERAL POLICY, CONGRESSIONAL RESEARCH REPORT (Aug. 12, 2012).

[373] Id. at 1.

[374] Id.

[375] Id. at 4.

[376] Id. at 3.

[377] Id. at 4.

[378] 2013 WL 4728445 (5th Cir., Sept. 3, 2013).

[379] "The Issuer Banks have contracts with Visa and MasterCard that allow them to issue payment cards, including both credit and debit cards, to their customers. When a customer uses one of these cards at a merchant, the card information is first sent to a bank with whom the merchant contracts, known as the "acquirer bank." The acquirer bank then sends the information to a processor, such as Heartland, and the processor sends the information to the issuer bank that issued the card. The approval or disapproval of use of the card is then transmitted back to the merchant through this chain." Heartland, Key Bank, and other acquiring banks were members of the Visa and MasterCard Networks. Id. Heartland contrated with the Acquiring Banks to process their transactions. " Id.

[380] Id. at *1.

The issuing banks suffered losses in replacing their customer's cards and reimbursing them for fraudulent purchases causally connected to the security breach. The court also observed that in the absence of a tort remedy issuer banks would be left with no remedy for processor's alleged negligence defying notions of fairness and common sense. Moreover, the court noted that the allocation of risk could have been the subject of negotiations between issuer banks and processer by way of contracts with credit card companies.[381]

(C) Negligence Per Se

Elements of a common law negligence claim are: (1) the defendant owed a duty of care to the plaintiff, (2) breach of that duty, (3) injury to the plaintiff, and (4) legal causation between the defendant's breach and the plaintiff's injury. In a negligence per se case, the radius of the risk of data intrusion has dramatically increased with the rise of computer-based data networks and thus, the burden of precaution can be staggering. While the cost of encrypting data may be easily cost-justified, many other measures such as enhanced employee training, outside security consultancies, data monitoring, and security audits of every party in a data transmission stream are enormously expensive. While reliable data on the incidence of security intrusions is not available, courts can take judicial notice of the number of high profile data intrusions in recent years.

At present, consumers and companies have no meaningful remedy for injuries such as the theft of personal data, computer viruses or Internet fraud enabled by software failure. A company's failure to secure financial data, which results in injury to a consumer, will violate the Gramm-Leach-Bliley Act if the company has not implemented a comprehensive information security program.[382] Consumers may use a company's failure to implement reasonable security to argue that a company's actions are negligent per se. Negligence per se is a particularly powerful tool in the hands of a plaintiff because the statutory violation is used to prove both the duty and the breach of the standard of care for information security. No plaintiff has successfully employed a negligence per se argument in a computer security case. In the absence of a statutorily defined duty to maintain adequate website or computer security, injured consumers will likely turn to the common law of negligence.

The plaintiff must prove three things to establish negligence per se: (1) the injury must have been caused by the violation, (2) the injury must be the type intended to be prevented by the statute, and (3) the injured party must be one of the class intended to be protected by the statute.[383] The negligence per se doctrine is based on the rule that a presumption of negligence arises from the violation of a statute that was enacted to protect a class of persons—of which the plaintiff is a member—against the type of harm the plaintiff suffered as a result of the violation. Establishing duty is often the

---

[381] The issuer banks did not have a contractual relationship with Heartland, only the acquiring banks.

[382] 15 U.S.C. §§ 6801, 6805.

[383] Michael L. Rustad & Thomas H. Koenig, The Tort of Negligent Enablement of Cybercrime, 20 BERKELEY TECH. L. J. 1553, 1592–93 (2005) ("Although courts vary in what impact a statutory violation has on the adjudication of negligence, they may employ civil statutes to set standards in negligent enablement lawsuits. An unexcused violation of a statute requiring reasonable security is itself negligence, that is, negligence per se.").

most difficult issue in an Internet negligence case.[384] The advantage of negligence per se is that the breach of the statute satisfies both duty and breach. In addition to the duty to exercise ordinary care, there are also duties imposed by statutes. A party who seeks to prevail on a cause of action premised on the negligence per se doctrine must establish, among other elements that the party is one of the class of persons who is protected by the statute, ordinance, or regulation. Defendants may use negligence per se to demonstrate a plaintiff's contributory negligence, if it had violated a statutory duty to secure its computer system or Internet passwords.[385] Jurisdictions vary as to whether the violation of the statute is conclusive proof, presumptive proof, or just evidence of negligence.

Negligence per se is a particularly powerful tool in the hands of a plaintiff because the statutory violation satisfies both the elements of duty and breach. However, some jurisdictions treat the statutory violation as only some evidence of the breach as opposed to a *presumption* of breach. In jurisdictions where the statutory violation is a presumed breach, negligence per se is the practical equivalent of strict liability. The plaintiff will prevail by showing the statutory breach so long as the defendant produces no evidence of an excuse. The ISO 27001 standard is certifiable security governance standard:

> ISO 27001 provides organizations with a guidebook to help formulate security requirements to improve security and operations and ensure that specific security objectives are met. Specifically, it requires organizations to be competent in four security management areas including asset identification and valuation, risk assessment and acceptance criteria, management and acceptance of these items, and the continual improvement of an organization's overall security program.[386]

If the federal government required websites to implement international best practices regarding data privacy and data security, it could be the basis of a negligence per se action. A growing number of websites are seeking to become International Standards Organization (ISO 27001 certified). If a company's privacy or data security measures fail to comply, they would be subject to a negligence per se claim.

(D) Premises Liability in Cyberspace

Premises liability was first recognized in the early 1970s in the brick-and-mortar world as courts began to hold commercial property owners liable for the failure to provide reasonable security to protect their tenants. Later, the courts stretched the duty to prevent third party crimes that originated in apartment complexes to shopping malls, parking lots, retail establishments, day care centers, and other settings. Courts have

---

[384] Michael L. Rustad & Lori E. Eisenschmidt, The Commercial Law of Internet Law, 10 HIGH TECH. L.J. 213 (1995) (arguing that duties of care should extend to Internet security). See also Stephen E. Henderson & Matthew E. Yarbrough, Suing the Insecure?: A Duty of Care in Cyberspace, 32 N.M. L. REV. 11 (2002) (arguing that websites owe a duty of care to third parties injured by distributed denial of service attacks).

[385] Today, "software is defined as '[a] set of computer programs, procedures, and possibly associated documentation concerned with the operation of a data processing system, e.g., compilers, library routines, manuals, circuit diagrams.'" Michael D. Scott, Tort Liability for Vendors of Insecure Software: Has the Time Finally Come?, 67 MD. L. REV. 425, 430 (2008) (quoting U.S. Copyright Office, Compendium of Copyright Office Practices II, 300-34 (1984)).

[386] Websense ISO 27001 Certification, What is ISO 27001 Certification? http://www.websense.com/assets/datasheets/datasheet-websense-iso27001–certification.pdf (last visited July 21, 2013).

reworked the doctrine of premises liability to reflect societal changes. Until the last three decades, courts denied recovery to the victims of third-party criminal attacks on the grounds of no duty owed.[387] Courts overcame this "no duty" rule on public policy grounds of fairness and the law and economics principle of placing the burden of precaution on the least cost avoider. The property owner's duty to minimize the risk of crimes to tenants has served as a viable legal theory where inadequate security enables criminals to attack customers. To prevail in a premises liability lawsuit, a plaintiff must establish that: (1) the defendant owed a duty to protect the injured crime victim; (2) the defendant breached that duty; and (3) the breach of the duty was a proximate cause of the criminal act and the victim's injuries.[388]

To date, no court has extended premises liability to websites. The analogy to premises liability is that the seller of inadequately configured software may expose its customers to cybercriminals—much like a shopping mall located in a high crime area that fails to implement reasonable security such as hiring guards. Courts have largely been unreceptive to negligent security claims. The most significant doctrinal obstacle to extending premises liability to the Internet is that this is a borderless instrumentality without a nexus to land or premises. Nevertheless, the intangible nature of cyberspace has not prevented courts from stretching personal property torts like trespass to chattels and conversion to intangibles. The courts' ability to cut off new channels of liability through a "no duty" determination is the ultimate form of judicial contraception against cybertort expansion. Even if an Internet defendant negligently injures a consumer, there is no liability unless a court is willing to find that duties of care exist for web site activities.

The first wave of computer security lawsuits stemmed from claims alleging that defective software offers inadequate security, and is unreliable in protecting network perimeters. A software maker may be liable for tort liability for racing to market with software with grossly inadequate testing. A software company that releases software into the marketplace with known design defects may have liability under the law of torts. In December of 2009, a number of restaurants filed suit against a point-of-sale software manufacturer because their inadequately secured software enabled data heists from Romanian cybercriminals.[389] The restaurants filed suit against the hardware and software makers as well as the service provider. The plaintiffs contend that the software did not include standard security measures, which enabled the cybercriminal to load keylogger code that enabled the Romanian cybercriminals to steal customer's credit card numbers.[390]

Plaintiffs filed a class action lawsuit against CardSystems Solutions, Inc., alleging that the company's lax computer security led to the wholesale misappropriation of

---

[387] See, e.g., Nigido v. First Nat'l Bank, 288 A.2d 127 (Md. 1972).

[388] David G. Owen, Idea: The Five Elements of Negligence, 35 HOFSTRA L. REV. 1671, 1681 (2007) (defining proximate cause as "a reasonably close connection between a defendant's wrong and the plaintiff's injury, a connection that is not remote.").

[389] Alan J. Liddle, Restaurants Sue POS Firms Over Data Theft, NATION'S RESTAURANT NEWS (Dec. 4, 2009) at 1.

[390] Id (noting that the restaurants were "seeking to recover on behalf of operators are those related to hiring forensic auditors and information technology consultants; card company fines for non-compliance with data security standards; charge-back assessments related to goods purchased illegally using card numbers stolen from their restaurants; reimbursement for business lost, if any, as a result of adverse publicity tied to the data thefts; and attorneys' fees.").

credit and debit cards.[391] Committing one of the largest cybercrimes in history, intruders gained unauthorized access to forty million credit cards and transferred data from 200,000 cards from CardSystems's computer network. In the CardSystems Solutions litigation, the plaintiffs contended that the CardSystems computer security was inadequate enabling cybercriminals to compromise customers' credit card accounts.

The complaint charged CardSystems with numerous negligent acts, including insecure data handling practices, failure to maintain properly configured firewalls, failure to encrypt confidential customer data, and violations of reasonable internet security standards. The complaint also charged the financial services firm with violating a California state statute requiring it to inform customers of computer intrusions that compromise their personal data. The *CardSystems* class-action lawsuit is one of the first cases in which data handlers have been sued for negligent computer security practices.[392] Tort actions arising out of defective designed software are subject to the limitations of the economic loss rule. Under the economic loss rule, economic damages are not recoverable unless they are accompanied by actual physical harm to persons or their property.

Section 314A of the Restatement (Second) lists a number of special relationships that create a duty to render aid; such as that of a common carrier (e.g. railroad, airlines) to its passengers; an innkeeper to their guest; or possessors of land.[393] Plaintiffs are frequently left with no practical recourse but to file suit against a defendant business for failing to protect them from the direct criminal, who is unavailable or judgment-proof. Courts recognizing a duty to protect customers against third party criminals will often impose a foreseeability requirement such as "whether there were similar crimes on the property of that business."[394] Other courts apply a "totality of the circumstances [test] when analyzing the foreseeability of third-party harm."[395]

These personal property torts give the plaintiff recovery for damaged and destroyed property. Can virtual property be converted or intermeddled within Second Life, World of WarCraft or a wide variety of other virtual settings? Courts have yet to find data intermediaries liable for the foreseeable cybercrimes of third persons—as in premises liability actions. However, it would not be surprising if this new duty came to be recognized in the near future since intermediaries are often the least cost avoider. The intermediary is often in the best position to take cost effective measures of preventive vigilance. Negligent security claims argue that websites have a duty to certain categories of users.

---

[391] Complaint for Declaratory and Injunctive Relief, Parke v. CardSystems Solutions, Inc., No. CGC05–442624 (Cal. Super. Ct., July 5, 2005), available at http://www.techfirm.com/cardsystems.pdf [hereinafter CardSystems Complaint]; see also David Bank, Security Breaches of Customers' Data Trigger Lawsuits, WALL ST. J., July 21, 2005, at B1.

[392] For an exhaustive survey of tort liability for bad software See Michael L. Rustad & Thomas H. Koenig, The Tort of Negligent Enablement of Cybercrime, 20 BERKELEY TECH. L. J. 1553, 1155–56 (2005).

[393] RESTATEMENT (SECOND) OF TORTS § 321 (1965).

[394] ROGER E. SCHECHTER, A SHORT AND HAPPY GUIDE TO TORTS 77 (2012).

[395] Id.

A social media or commercial website could, theoretically, be liable for the reasonably foreseeable harm caused by third parties that injure customers.[396] A court adopting either of these approaches should look first at whether computer security is configured to enable cybercrimes or other computer intrusions. Next, the court should consider all other relevant circumstances including prior similar intrusions. Courts should examine factors such as: (1) whether there have been prior similar cybercrimes; (2) the cost of increased Internet security measures; and (3) the degree to which intermediaries can reduce the radius of the cybercrime problem. In the absence of a history of similar intrusions and security breaches, foreseeability is based on all facts and circumstances.

The Fifth Circuit rejected a plaintiff's claim that the law of premises liability for owners of real property applied to a website. In *Doe v. MySpace, Inc.*,[397] the plaintiff contended that MySpace was liable under a premises liability theory for failing to prevent sexual predators from harming minors using its services. In *MySpace*, a 13–year-old girl represented that she was 18 when she created a MySpace profile. As a result, her profile was automatically set to "public," and she met a 19–year-old man on MySpace a year later, when she was 14.[398] The two arranged an off-line meeting where the predator sexually assaulted her. The young girl and her mother filed suit in an attempt to hold MySpace liable for failing to implement basic safety measures to protect minors from adult predators whom they meet on MySpace.[399]

The federal appeals court upheld a federal district court's dismissal with prejudice of the plaintiffs' complaint.[400] The *MySpace* court applied Section 230 despite the fact that this statute immunizes publisher's liability rather than negligence. The court found the law of premises liability "germane to owners of real property," was inapplicable "to publishers and Internet service providers operating in the virtual world of cyberspace."[401] The court refused to divest MySpace of its Section 230 immunity despite its role in constructing profiles. The Fifth Circuit affirmed the federal district court's finding Section 230 of the CDA immunized MySpace for liability.[402]

(E) Professional Negligence

Cyber malpractice is a new category arising out of doctors giving medical advice to online visitors.[403] It is unclear how courts will apply principles of professional malpractice to telemedicine.[404] Many traditional tort categories have been stillborn because courts are unwilling to expand duties of care to redress wrongdoing that does

---

[396] RESTATEMENT (SECOND) OF TORTS § 281(b), cmt. e (1965) ("Conduct is negligent because it tends to subject the interests of another to an unreasonable risk of harm. Such a risk may be made up of a number of different hazards, which frequently are of a more or less definite character. The actor's negligence lies in subjecting the other to the aggregate of such hazards.").

[397] 528 F.3d 413 (5th Cir. 2008).

[398] Id. at 416.

[399] Id. at 417.

[400] Id.

[401] Id.

[402] Doe v. MySpace, Inc., 528 F.3d 413 (5th Cir. 2008).

[403] Nicolas P. Terry, Cyber–Malpractice: Legal Exposure for Cybermedicine, 25 AM. J.L. & MED. 327 (1999); Nicolas P. Terry, Structural and Legal Implications of e-Health, 33 J. HEALTH L. 605 (2000).

[404] "The Institute of Medicine has defined telemedicine to encompass telephone, video and electronic transmission of medical information using telephone or digital technology." Alissa R. Spielberg, Online Without a Net: Physician-Patient Communication by Electronic Mail, 25 AM. J.L. & MED. 267, 287–88 (1999).

not squarely fit within the boundaries of well-established torts. At present, the judiciary is wary of expanding or modifying new causes of action for negligent Internet security, computer malpractice, or strict liability for information products.[405] No U.S. court has recognized an action for computer or Internet security malpractice. Courts are just beginning to construct new duties for Internet security so it is unlikely computer malpractice will be a cognizable action.[406] U.S. courts have held that computer consultants are not professionals for purposes of computer professional negligence.[407] As Internet law matures, it is likely that software developers, website designers and Internet security specialists will begin to professionalize by developing industry standards of care. As of late 2013, no court has recognized an action for professional negligence filed against software engineers who construct insecure web sites.

(F) Negligent Data Brokering

Negligent data brokering imposes liability on a website that sells information to a client pertaining to a third party. Websites that act as information brokers may owe a duty of care if they sell information to a person who harms the plaintiff. The typical information brokering fact pattern involves a stalker who purchases information in order to harm the plaintiff. In these cases, it is the unauthorized distribution of Social Security numbers or other personal information that subjects the plaintiff to a foreseeable risk of fraud or personal harm. The liability of a website ultimately rests upon foreseeability and the likelihood, and severity of harm for information supplied to help a stalker or fraudulent actor track the plaintiff. The emblematic data broker cases was *Remsburg v. Docusearch, Inc.,*[408] In *Remsburg,* the New Hampshire Supreme Court held an online data broker liable for providing personal data to a criminal who used the information to track down and murder a former high school classmate. The court held the Internet data broker owed a duty to the victim because a data broker sold her contact information foreseeably endangering her. In *Remsburg*, the representative of the decedent, a young female murder victim, filed a lawsuit against an Internet-based investigative service, which had sold the victim's personal information to her killer.[409] Causes of action were based on intrusion upon seclusion, commercial appropriation of private information and violations of the Federal Fair Credit Reporting Act and the

---

[405] As the field of information technology matures, it is likely that software developers, web site designers and Internet security specialists will begin to professionalize by developing industry standards of care. The judiciary is wary of expanding or modifying new causes of action for negligent Internet security, computer malpractice, or strict liability for information products. Many traditional tort categories have been stillborn because courts are unwilling to expand duties of care to redress wrongdoing that does not squarely fit within the boundaries of well-established torts.

[406] Michael L. Rustad & Thomas H. Koenig, "Negligent Entrustment for Outsourced Data", in DATA PRIVACY AND PROTECTION: ISSUES AND PERSPECTIVES (2009). The court refused to recognize a computer malpractice court in Triangle Underwriters, Inc. v. Honeywell, Inc., 604 F. 2d 737 (2d Cir. 1979) and Chatlos Systems, Inc. v. National Cash Register Corp., 479 F. Supp. 738 (D. N.J. 1979). aff'd, 635 F.2d 1081 (3d Cir. 1980).

[407] See e.g., Racine County v. Oracular Milwaukee, Inc., 767 N.W.2d 280, 289 (Wis. Ct. App. 2009); Rapidigm, Inc. v. ATM Mgmt. Servs., 63 Pa. D. & C. 4th 234, 240–49 (Ct. Com. Pl. 2003) ("Most courts which have considered professional negligence claims raised against computer consultants have ruled that claims for economic loss should be governed only by contract law."); Nielsen Media Research, Inc. v. Microsystems Software, Inc., No. 99 CIV. 10876 (LAP). 2002 WL 31175223, at *8 (S.D.N.Y. Sept. 30, 2002) (holding that claim labeled "negligence" but included language of "reasonable care . . . in accordance with applicable professional standards" was really an impermissible attempt to plead professional negligence against a computer consultant, a non-professional under New York law).

[408] 816 A.2d 1001 (N.H. 2003).

[409] Id. at 152-54.

New Hampshire Consumer Protection Act. The ISP was found to be immune from tort liability under Section 230 of the CDA, but the court refused to dismiss the action, ruling that there was a sufficient basis for personal jurisdiction. In addition, the court found that the plaintiff had established a basis for the claim of invasion of the murder victim's privacy. Negligent enablement torts have yet to develop to address Internet wrongdoing. To address the invisibility of, and consumers' lack of control over, data brokers' collection and use of consumer information, the FTC supports targeted legislation "that would provide consumers with access to information about them held by a data broker."[410]

> To further increase transparency, the Commission calls on data brokers that compile data for marketing purposes to explore creating a centralized website where data brokers could: (1) identify themselves to consumers and describe how they collect and use consumer data and (2) detail the access rights and other choices they provide with respect to the consumer data they maintain.[411] If Congress enacts legislation imposing new duties on data brokers beyond individual sectors such as healthcare or financial services, this could be the basis for a negligence per se claim for the consequences of data breach.

(G) Negligent Misrepresentation

"To state a cause of action for negligent misrepresentation, a plaintiff must show: (1) the defendant made a misrepresentation of material fact that he believed to be true but which was in fact false; (2) the defendant was negligent in making the statement because he should have known the representation was false; (3) the defendant intended to induce the plaintiff to rely and [sic] on the misrepresentation; and (4) injury resulted to the plaintiff acting in justifiable reliance upon the misrepresentation."[412] A claim for either intentional or negligent misrepresentation requires the plaintiff to demonstrate that they justifiably relied on the erroneous information. "The liability of one who is under a public duty to give the information extends to loss suffered by any of the class of persons for whose benefit the duty is created, in any of the transactions in which it is intended to protect them."[413] The emblem of misrepresentation is justifiable reliance, which means that the principles of comparative negligence apply to this tort.[414]

The potential to incur liability for supplying incorrect information on a website or other online activity seems infinite. The emblem of fraud is the deliberate suppression of a fact by one who is bound to disclose it or by the disclosure of information likely to mislead. Negligent misrepresentation differs from intentional misrepresentation in that the plaintiff need not prove the defendant's intent to deceive as part of the *prima facie* case. However, to date, few plaintiffs have been successful in asserting negligent misrepresentation actions. The Section 552 of the Restatement (Second) Torts is entitled: "Information Negligently Supplied for the Guidance of Others. Section 552(1) states:

---

[410] FEDERAL TRADE COMMISSION, PROTECTING CONSUMERS PRIVACY IN AN ERA OF RAPID CHANGE (March 2012) at IX.

[411] Id.

[412] Specialty Marine & Indus. Supplies v. Venus, 66 So. 3d 306, 309 (Fla D. Ct. App. 2011).

[413] Id. at § 552(3).

[414] Id. at 310.

One who, in the course of his business, profession or employment, or in any other transaction in which he has a pecuniary interest, supplies false information for the guidance of others in their business transactions, is subject to liability for pecuniary loss caused to them by their justifiable reliance upon the information, if he fails to exercise reasonable care or competence in obtaining or communicating the information.[415]

The Restatement states that liability for losses "is limited to loss suffered:

(a) by the person or one of a limited group of persons for whose benefit and guidance he intends to supply the information or knows that the recipient intends to supply it; and

(b) through reliance upon it in a transaction that he intends the information to influence or knows that the recipient so intends or in a substantially similar transaction."[416] Negligent misrepresentation is a tort action positing a limited duty because of the possibility of cascading liability to unknown and unknowable persons.[417]

The Restatement illustration states:

Although liability under the rule stated in this Section is based upon negligence of the actor in failing to exercise reasonable care or competence in supplying correct information, the scope of his liability is not determined by the rules that govern liability for the negligent supplying of chattels that imperil the security of the person, land or chattels of those to whom they are supplied, . . . or other negligent misrepresentation that results in physical harm. . . . When the harm that is caused is only pecuniary loss, the courts have found it necessary to adopt a more restricted rule of liability, because of the extent to which misinformation may be, and may be expected to be, circulated, and the magnitude of the losses which may follow from reliance upon it.[418]

In *Smallwood v. NCSOFT Corp.*,[419] an Internet user claimed negligent misrepresentation by a virtual game maker after he became physically and mentally ill after playing Linneage II, an online game, for 20,000 hours. The plaintiff filed suit after he was locked out of the game and contended that the game maker was liable for a false misrepresentation advertising, "that it was a safe game," and a "fair game."[420] The plaintiff's claim was for negligent misrepresentation, as he could not prove the game publisher's actions were intentional. The court held that Smallwood stated a cause of action for negligent misrepresentation based upon his claim that the game maker supplied false information but dismissed Smallwood's defamation claim.

---

[415] RESTATEMENT (SECOND) OF TORTS § 552(1).

[416] Id. at § 552(2).

[417] "By limiting the liability for negligence of a supplier of information to be used in commercial transactions to cases in which he manifests an intent to supply the information for the sort of use in which the plaintiff's loss occurs, the law promotes the important social policy of encouraging the flow of commercial information upon which the operation of the economy rests. The limitation applies, however, only in the case of information supplied in good faith, for no interest of society is served by promoting the flow of information not genuinely believed by its maker to be true." Id. at § 552, cmt. a.

[418] Id

[419] 2010 U.S. Dist. LEXIS 82484 (D. Hawaii, Aug. 4, 2010).

[420] Id.

(H) Negligent Entrustment

In the brick-and-mortar world, negligent entrustment evolved to address cases such as parents allowing young children to drive farm machinery, use firearms, or set off fireworks. Under the "negligent entrustment" theory, the lender of an automobile, for example, is not responsible for the negligence of the borrower, unless he or she had or should have had knowledge that the borrower was physically or mentally incompetent to drive. Courts have been reluctant to stretch negligent entrustment to Internet causes of action. Nevertheless, in *Finkel v. Dauber*,[421] Facebook users filed a defamation suit against adolescent members of a secret group, but also included a count for negligent entrustment against their parents. The trial court for Nassau County held that the website postings did not contain statements of fact required for defamation claims, and that the computer was not dangerous instrument required for negligent entrustment claims.

(I) Private and Public Nuisance

Public nuisance theory, which has its origins in criminal law, does not mesh well with Internet websites because they are not land-based. To date, no governmental unit has sought abatement of the nuisance of an annoying website. For a public nuisance to exist there must be proof that the activity substantially interferes with the common rights of the public at large.[422] Generally, the plaintiff in a public nuisance action is a public official such as a state attorney general, who is seeking a remedy for violation of a public right. Private individuals may also sue for public nuisance, but only if they can demonstrate an injury separate and apart from the injury suffered by the public. Nuisance is a protean tort cause of action that has yet to be stretched to cyberspace. No plaintiffs have successfully asserted either private or public nuisance causes of action against a website.

For a private plaintiff to sue, she must demonstrate that she has standing by showing she has suffered an injury that is distinct from the general public.[423] A federal court found Craigslist to be immune from a public nuisance action in *Dart v. Craigslist, Inc.*[424] In *Dart*, a Cook County Illinois sheriff sought to hold Craigslist responsible for allegedly illegal content posted by users in Craigslist's erotic services section based upon public nuisance because it enabled prostitution. The federal court held that Craigslist was not susceptible to suit because of CDA Section 230(C)(1). Dan Burk favors recognition of the tort of cyberspace nuisance concluding "a healthy dose of real property doctrine might better accommodate the peculiar calculus of benefits and harms in cyberspace."[425]

---

[421] 906 N.Y.S. 2d 697 (2010).

[422] Daniel P. Larsen, Combating the Exotic Species Invasion: The Role of Tort Liability, 5 DUKE ENVTL. L. & POLY. F. 21, 40 (1995).

[423] Soap Corp. of Am. v. Reynolds, 178 F.2d 503, 506 (5th Cir. 1949); See also, RESTATEMENT (SECOND) OF TORTS § 821B (1) (1965) (defining public nuisance as an unreasonable interference with a right common to the public).

[424] 665 F. Supp. 2d 961 (N.D. Ill. 2009) (holding that Craigslist was immune from a suit for public nuisance created by the posting of prostitution advertisements on the Craigslist website because the elements of public nuisance required that Craigslist be considered the equivalent of a publisher in order to be held liable).

[425] Dan L. Burk, Trouble With Trespass, 4 J. SMALL & EMERGING BUS. L. 27, 4, 5 (2000).

(J) Negligent Failure to Warn

Negligent failure to warn cases arise out of a claim that a website owes a duty of care to its users, however, these cases are difficult to pursue because of CDA Section 230. In *Doe v. MySpace Inc.*,[426] the Fifth Circuit affirmed that Section 230 of the CDA barred claims alleging that MySpace negligently failed to keep minors off its website or to take measures to keep predators from communicating with minors. In *Robinson v. Match.com LLC*,[427] the court held that a website operator' relationship with a paying subscriber is an ordinary commercial contract relationship that creates no special duty of care. In *Beckman v. Match.com*,[428] a victim of a sexual assault and stabbing sued the online dating service for negligence in allowing a predator to use their services. "In plaintiff's claims for negligence and negligent infliction of emotional distress, plaintiff argues that Match.com failed 'to protect her from individuals trolling the website to further criminal activity' by 'exposing Plaintiff to a serial murderer who used the website as a vessel to facilitate attacks on unsuspecting women,' and 'by exposing Plaintiff to a serial killer who used Defendant's service to" brutally attack her.[429]

The court rejected the plaintiff's causes of action for the failure to warn or negligent misrepresentation. The problem with plaintiff's attempt to focus on Match.com's alleged failure to warn or alleged negligent misrepresentation "is that all of Match.com's conduct must trace back to the publication of third-party user content or profiles. Match.com is a website that publishes dating profiles."[430] The court found the plaintiff's cause of action were based entirely "third-party content published by Match.com on its website."[431] The court ruled that Section 230 of the CDA precluded a lawsuit for enabling a sexual predator "to post a profile on its website that plaintiff ultimately saw and responded to, thus leading to the predator assaulting her.[432]

§ 6.6   STRICT LIABILITY IN CYBERSPACE

Strict products liability cases are the third branch of traditional tort law. In contrast, no cybertorts-plaintiff has received either an equitable or a legal remedy based upon any theory of strict liability.[433] No court has recognized strict liability as a cause of action in a cybertort case and there are relatively few cases predicated upon negligence.[434] Moreover, judges have steadfastly refused to extend strict products liability to software, media products, or other intangibles in general. Courts have yet to extend products liability theories to defective software, computer viruses, or web sites with inadequate security or defective design. Courts have been reluctant to extend strict products liability to software, media products, or other intangibles in general.

---

[426] 528 F.3d 413 (5th Cir. 2008).

[427] No. 10–2651 (N.D. Tex. Aug. 10, 2012).

[428] 2013 WL 2355512 (D. Nev. May 29, 2013).

[429] Id. at *4.

[430] Id. at *5.

[431] Id.

[432] Id. at *3.

[433] Winter v. G.P. Putnam's Sons, 938 F. 2d 1033, 1036 (9th Cir. 1991) (observing that courts distinguish between the tangible containers of ideas from their communicative element for purposes of strict liability).

[434] It is unclear whether the concept of products liability can be extended to defective information on websites. Nathan D. Leadstrom, Internet Web Sites as Products Under Strict Products Liability: A Call for an Expanded Definition of Product, 40 WASHBURN L.J. 532, 534 (2001).

Additionally, courts have yet to extend products liability theories to bad software, computer viruses, or websites with inadequate security or defective design.[435] Furthermore, no court has applied the venerable doctrine of *Rylands v. Fletcher*[436] to software vendors that infect their user's computers with viruses.[437] A few courts have recognized strict liability for defective information.[438] To date, no plaintiff has successfully deployed a strict liability-like standard such as *res ipsa loquitur*[439] to failed computer vendors, programmers and others participating in the construction of software.[440] Products liability for defective Internet information is undeveloped as a cause of action even though websites are replete with rumors, misinformation, and outright lies.

(A) Information as Defective Products

(1) 3–D Product Manufacturing

The greatest potential for product liability arising out of the Internet is for durable goods. The technology of three-dimensional printing poses the possibility of products liability in the future. If a producer of a defective product used their 3–D printer for personal, household or family use, there would be no products liability. The missing element is a professional seller who releases products into the stream of commerce. Similarly, there would no warranty liability for merchantability under this fact pattern, as the 3–D operator is not a professional seller. As 3–D printing becomes more developed, it is probable that these technological innovations will be used for mass production. In a mass-produced unit, there would be traditional products liability if defective software caused a product to be defectively designed. Gerard Magliocca argues that 3D defective products may revitalize the common law of products liability:

> In a world of 3D printing, anyone could be a manufacturer. Let's say I make something from scratch in my 3D printer at home and that product (a toy, a cookie, a tool, a spare part) injures someone. Should we apply the same principles of product liability to that person that we would to a firm? Yes and no, I think. We probably won't require individuals to put warnings on what they make, but we may say that a design or manufacturing defect should lead to strict liability. Or would we say that a negligence standard should apply to homemade products?

---

[435] "No consumer was awarded punitive damages in a products liability action for bad software, the transmittal of a virus, or a faulty Internet security product." Michael L. Rustad, Punitive Damages in Cyberspace: Where in the World is the Consumer?, 7 CHAP. L. REV. 39, 47 (2004) (concluding from an empirical study of early cyberspace-related lawsuits from 1992–2002 that liability for defective software or information-based products was non-existent).

[436] [1868] UKHL 1.

[437] GRAHAM J. H. SMITH, INTERNET LAW & REGULATION 355 (4th ed. 2007).

[438] See Fluor Corp. v. Jeppesen & Co., 170 Cal. App. 3d 468, 476 (Ct. App. 1985) ("[A] sheet of paper might not be dangerous, per se, it would be difficult indeed to conceive of a salable commodity with more inherent lethal potential than an aid to aircraft navigation that, contrary to its own design standards, fails to list the highest land mass immediately surrounding a landing site.").

[439] To prove res ipsa loquitur, a plaintiff must establish the existence of the following three facts: (1) an injury of the type which usually does not occur in the absence of negligence, (2) caused by an instrumentality within the exclusive control of the defendant, and (3) which was not a result of an act or omission by the plaintiff.

[440] See Vincent M. Brannigan & Ruth E. Dayhoff, Liability for Personal Injuries Caused by Defective Medical Computer Programs, 7 AM. J. L. & MED. 123, 143 (1981).

Now try this one on for size. I upload a file that will make some something to a website. Someone downloads my file, makes the item, and this injures someone. Is the author of the file on the hook for a design defect claim? What about the website? While this could depend on a number of factors, courts will again need to think hard about how product liability rules should be adapted to this ecosystem.[441]

Failure to warn or inadequate warning cases could arise if the 3–D manufacturer acquired knowledge of a known or developing profile of danger. It is possible t single 3–D product could be defective as part of a bad batch, which would be analogous to a manufacturing defect. A New York statute would prohibit the production of "firearms via 3D printer unless the maker is a licensed gunsmith. Additionally, the gunsmith would have to notify the NYPD and register the 3D-printed weapon within 72 hours of its creation."[442]

(2) Cybercrime & FDA Regulated Medical Products

The duty to implement reasonable Internet security or features to thwart cybercriminals is rapidly evolving. Section 420 of the Restatement (Second) of Torts provides for strict liability when a product is in a "defective condition unreasonably dangerous to the user or consumer" and applies even though the manufacturer or seller "has exercised all possible care in the preparation" of the product. Chapter 7 surveys the HIPPA,[443] Gramm Bliley,[444] and other federal statutes requiring the implementation of reasonable security. The latest iteration is the duty to equip databases with firewalls and other perimeter defenses. The next issue to evolve will be whether a failure to implement reasonable security constitutes products liability. Traditional products liability lawsuits based upon design defect or failure of warn are likely given that many medical devices are vulnerable to remote disablement or viruses. A 2013 FDA Report documents that medical products have computer security vulnerabilities:

- Network-connected/configured medical devices infected or disabled by malware;

- The presence of malware on hospital computers, smartphones and tablets, targeting mobile devices using wireless technology to access patient data, monitoring systems, and implanted patient devices;

- Uncontrolled distribution of passwords, disabled passwords, hard-coded passwords for software intended for privileged device access (e.g., to administrative, technical, and maintenance personnel);

- Failure to provide timely security software updates and patches to medical devices and networks and to address related vulnerabilities in older medical device models (legacy devices);

---

[441] Gerard Magliocca, Product Liability and 3–D Printing, Concurring Opinions, March 5, 2013), http://www.concurringopinions.com/archives/2013/03/product-liability-and-3d-printing.html (last visited June 15, 2013).

[442] Zach Sokol, NYC's New Bill to Regulate 3–D Printed Guns Is Just the Beginning, MOTHERBOARD.COM, June 13, 2013.

[443] See Health Insurance Portability and Accountability Act of 1996 ("HIPAA), 42 U.S.C. §§ 1320d–1320d-8.

[444] Gramm-Leach-Bliley Act (GLB), also known as the Financial Services Modernization Act of 1999, (Pub.L. 106–102, 113 Stat. 13, 315 U.S.C. §§ 6801 et seq.)

- Security vulnerabilities in off-the-shelf software designed to prevent unauthorized device or network access, such as plain text or no authentication, hard-coded passwords, documented service accounts in service manuals, and poor coding/SQL injection.[445]

The *FDA Alert* on the possibility of computer viruses injuring patients raises an issue whether product manufacturers have a duty to design reasonable security into their products. A FDA senior office of the FDA's Medical Device unit acknowledged awareness that "hundreds of medical devices have been infected by malware."[446] The FDA states that is a duty of all medical device makers to design for safety by reducing the radius of risk of cybersecurity threats:

> Manufacturers are responsible for remaining vigilant about identifying risks and hazards associated with their medical devices, including risks related to cybersecurity, and are responsible for putting appropriate mitigations in place to address patient safety and assure proper device performance. The FDA expects medical device manufacturers to take appropriate steps to limit the opportunities for unauthorized access to medical devices. Specifically, we recommend that manufacturers review their cybersecurity practices and policies to assure that appropriate safeguards are in place to prevent unauthorized access or modification to their medical devices or compromise of the security of the hospital network that may be connected to the device The extent to which security controls are needed will depend on the medical device, its environment of use, the type and probability of the risks to which it is exposed, and the probable risks to patients from a security breach.[447]

While the FDA has not enacted regulations governing the cybersecurity of medical devices, it states that medical product makers are to consider the following guidelines for computer security:

- Take steps to limit unauthorized device access to trusted users only, particularly for those devices that are life sustaining or could be directly connected to hospital networks.

- Appropriate security controls may include: user authentication, for example, user ID and password, smartcard or biometric; strengthening password protection by avoiding hard-coded passwords and limiting public access to passwords used for technical device access; physical locks; card readers; and guards.

- Protect individual components from exploitation and develop strategies for active security protection appropriate for the device's use environment. Such strategies should include timely deployment of routine, validated security patches and methods to restrict software or firmware updates to authenticated code. *Note: The FDA typically does not need to review or approve medical device software changes made solely to strengthen cybersecurity.*

---

[445] Food and Drug Administration, FDA Safety Communication: Cybersecurity for Medical Devices and Hospital Networks, http://www.fda.gov/MedicalDevices/Safety/AlertsandNotices/ucm356423.htm (last visited June 15, 2013).

[446] Christopher Weaver, Patients Put at Risk by Computer Viruses, WALL ST. J (June 14, 2013) at 1.

[447] FDA Alert, Cybersecurity for Medical Devices, Id.

- Use design approaches that maintain a device's critical functionality, even when security has been compromised, known as "fail-safe modes."

- Provide methods for retention and recovery after an incident where security has been compromised. Cybersecurity incidents are increasingly likely and manufacturers should consider incident response plans that address the possibility of degraded operation and efficient restoration and recovery.[448]

The FDA's 2013 report is the first step in making reasonable cybersecurity a standard design feature. The FDA urges that companies develop prompt remedial measures to recover from intrusions in advance and recognizes a duty to report security failures. To date, there have been no injuries or deaths due to deficits in Internet or computer security; however, with the digitalization of devices, such incidents are foreseeable.[449] Nevertheless, the medical device makers are on notice that they must reduce the radius of risk of Internet security threats in their products. Products liability is more likely to evolve for durable goods that have cybersecurity vulnerabilities than for pure software or information-based products. Products liability lies in the borderland between the law of contracts and of torts, reallocating the cost of injuries to those who supply dangerously defective "goods or products for the use of others."[450] Plaintiffs frequently plead multiple theories including strict liability, negligence, and warranty.

(3) Video Games as Products

Products liability has been slow to develop in cybertort cases. The Sixth Circuit rejected a products liability claim arising out of a Kentucky school shooting. The plaintiffs contended the school shooter "regularly played video games, watched movies, and viewed Internet sites produced by the firms."[451] They contended that the defendant's games "desensitized the shooter to violence" and caused the shooter to attack his classmates. Courts have generally been reluctant to classify Internet transmissions as "products" for purposes of products liability. The 24/7 virtual marketplace makes it even more likely that products liability cases will originate from a website sale.[452] The failure to report security intrusions may also result in liability

---

[448] Id. (italics in the original).

[449] Id.

[450] W. PAGE KEETON ET AL., PROSSER AND KEETON ON THE LAW OF TORTS, § 95, at 677–78 (5th ed. 1984).

[451] James v. Meow Media, Inc., 300 F.3d 683, 688 (6th Cir. 2002) (affirming lower court's dismissal of product liability claims, finding that information "products" were not encompassed in Kentucky's strict products liability statute "because thoughts, ideas, and expressions contained within defendants' movie, games, and website materials did not constitute a "product' within the realm of the strict liability doctrine"); See also Sanders v. Acclaim Entm't, Inc., 188 F. Supp. 2d 1264 (D. Colo. 2002) (dismissing actions based on negligence and strict liability in lawsuit filed in the Columbine school shooting case in which it was claimed that the killers were "fanatical consumers of violent video games and movies distributed on the Internet").

[452] The U.S. consumer marketplace already exports a large percentage of products from China, where product safety standards are not at the level of U.S. manufacturers. Andrew Popper describes the radius of the risk of dangerously defective products made in countries without a strong tort system or safety standards:
Daiso children's jewelry manufactured in China was recalled because of excessive levels of lead. Wendy Bellissimo Hidden Hills Collection Cribs manufactured in China were recalled because of a crib-slat strangling hazard. Mini Chef Complete Toy Kitchens manufactured in Thailand were recalled because of a choking hazard. MindWare's Animal Tracking Explorer Kit manufactured in China was recalled because it failed to warn of the presence of chemical calcium hydroxide. The Adventure Play Set manufactured in China was recalled because of weak chains that led to breaking and injury.

for product makers as well as customers. The FDA alert makes it clear that companies and customers have a duty to report security incidents:

> Prompt reporting of adverse events can help the FDA identify and better understand the risks associated with medical devices. If you suspect that a cybersecurity event has affected the performance of a medical device or has impacted a hospital network system, we encourage you to file a voluntary report through Med Watch, the FDA Safety Information and Adverse Event Reporting program.[453]

(4) Defective Navigational Charts

Relatively few courts have found suppliers of information such as maps or charts liable under a products liability theory. Products liability evolved to address personal injuries caused by defects to tangible goods, not intangible information. But in a case from the early 1980s, the Second Circuit stretched strict product liability to accommodate a defective air navigational chart in *Salome v. Jeppesen & Co.*[454] The court found that the trial court did not err in classifying appellant's navigational charts as products, rather than services, comparing the charts to mass-produced products that "reached customers without any individual tailoring or substantial change in contents." In the *Jeppesen* case, "Captain Willard Vernon Wahlund, a Braniff International pilot with approximately seven thousand hours of flight experience, departed from an airport at Charleston, West Virginia, on a flight to Danbury, Connecticut."[455] The Braniff International pilot "was off-duty and was piloting his own Beechcraft Sierra; the plane was equipped with a King 214 receiver for instrument flight purposes and carried ample fuel."[456] "The flight was one leg of a trip which originated in Dallas and which was slated to end in Danbury. Wahlund's father and Erik, Wahlund's six-year-old son, accompanied him."[457] The plane crashed and the passengers were killed on impact. The court ruled that a mass-produced navigational map constituted a "products" under products liability law. By publishing and by "selling the charts, Jeppesen undertook a special responsibility, as seller, to insure that consumers will not be injured by the use of the charts."[458] Jeppesen, the mapmaker, "is entitled-and encouraged-to treat the burden of accidental injury as a cost of production to be covered by liability insurance."[459] The court further stated" that "the mass production and marketing of these charts requires Jeppesen to bear the costs of accidents that are proximately caused by defects in the charts."[460] The jury specifically found "that Jeppesen's area chart was defective in designating Martinsburg as having a full instrument landing system-through the designation ILS-and that Jeppesen was negligent in the manufacture or inspection of that chart."[461] Plaintiffs claiming

---

ANDREW F. POPPER, WHITE PAPER, DEFECTIVE PRODUCTS IN THE UNITED STATES: ISSUES AND DISCUSSION (American University, Washington College of Law, Nov. 14, 2008).

[453] Id.

[454] 707 F.2d 671 (2d Cir. 1983).

[455] Id. at 672.

[456] Id.

[457] Id.

[458] Id. at 677.

[459] Id.

[460] Id.

[461] Id.

physical injury or economic loss due to defective software may make a similar argument if the software is mass-market as opposed to customized.

(B) Internet–Related Products Liability

(1) Definition of Products Liability

Products liability verdicts are rare in cybertort cases.[462] The term "products liability action" is broadly defined to include any action against a manufacturer or seller for recovery of damages, or other relief for harm allegedly caused by a defective product, whether the action is based on strict products liability; negligence; misrepresentation; breach of express or implied warranty; or any other theory or combination of theories, and whether the relief sought is recovery of damages or any other legal or equitable relief, including a suit for: (1) injury, damage to or loss of real or personal property; (2) personal injury; (3) wrongful death; (4) economic loss; or (5) declaratory, injunctive, or other equitable relief. Section 402A of the Restatement (Second) of Torts holds a manufacturer strictly liable for harm to person or property caused by "any product in a defective condition unreasonably dangerous to the user."[463] The Restatement (Third) of Torts represents a retreat from strict liability making it more difficult for plaintiffs to prevail.[464]

(2) Three Types of Product Defects

The courts have recognized three paradigmatic types of defects in products litigation: (1) manufacturing defects, (2) design defects, and (3) the failure to warn or inadequate warnings.[465] A defect in a products liability case is as necessary as a hole in

---

[462] "In more than a decade of Internet cases, only one company has been forced by a court to make any restitution for the sale of defective goods on its website. This sole successful products liability action, a 2003 case, arose out of the website sale of a field-monitoring device for tracking criminals under house arrest. The manufacturer's website advertised that its field-monitoring unit in the offender's home would detect any tampering. However, when a murderer cut off the ankle device, he was out of range of the monitoring unit, so the home unit did not detect the tampering. The court refused to impose a legal duty on the manufacturer to make a tamper-proof field-monitoring device. Similarly, the court found that the monitoring device did not breach any express or implied warranty, nor was it defectively manufactured. The victim's estate successfully brought an action only for misrepresentation based on false statements about the field-monitoring unit on the company's website." Michael L. Rustad & Thomas H. Koenig, Rebooting Cybertort Law, 80 Wash. L. Rev. 355, 359 (2005) (discussing Kirby v. B.I. Inc., No. CIV.A.4:98– CV–1136–Y, 2003 U.S. Dist. LEXIS 16964, at 49–50 (N.D. Tex. Sept. 26, 2003).

[463] The Restatement (Second) of Torts § 402A sets forth the elements of a claim for strict product liability:

(1) One who sells any product in a defective condition unreasonably dangerous to the user or consumer or to his property is subject to liability for physical harm thereby caused to the ultimate user or consumer, or to his property, if

(a) the seller is engaged in the business of selling such a product, and

(b) it is expected to and does reach the user or consumer without substantial change in the condition in which it is sold.

(2) The rule stated in Subsection (1) applies although

(a) the seller has exercised all possible care in the preparation and sale of his product, and

(b) the user or consumer has not bought the product from or entered into any contractual relation with the seller.

[464] It seems unlikely that the courts adopting the Restatement will be receptive to stretching product liability concepts to software, digital information, and other intangibles." Michael L. Rustad & Thomas H. Koenig, The Tort of Negligent Enablement of Cyberspace, 20 Berkeley Tech. L.J. 1553, 1577 (2005).

[465] The Restatement (Third) of Products Liability recognizes three paradigmatic defects: manufacturing, design, and warning. A defect is determined if "at the time of sale or distribution, it contains

a donut. Courts have largely displaced the consumer expectation test with the risk utility test but California and a few other jurisdictions permit jury instructions on both tests.[466] The Restatement (Third) of Torts: Products Liability requires the plaintiff to prove there is a reasonable alternative design that would avert the risk of impugned design. The product may lack adequate warnings or instructions.[467] Products liability applies to distributors of defective computer hardware and may apply to software. Software malfunctions of key infrastructure may have latent defects that prove deadly. The consumer expectations test holds a manufacturer strictly liable for any condition not contemplated by the ultimate consumer that will be unreasonably dangerous to him or her. In contrast, the risk-utility analysis weighs a product's risks against its benefits.

If a product's utility, as designed, outweighs its risks, the product's design is not defective. Section 1 of the Restatement (Third) of Torts: Products Liability makes each seller in the chain of distribution liable if there is proof that the product was sold with a defect.[468] The American Law Institute approved the Restatement (Third) of Products Liability in 1997, which replaces the Restatement (Second)'s strict products liability with negligence-based standards in design and failure to warn cases. Section 2 defines a "design defect" as that which occurs when the foreseeable risks of harm posed by the product could have been reduced or avoided by the adoption of a "reasonable alternative design." The definition replaces Section 402A of the Restatement (Second)'s "consumer expectation" test with the "risk/utility test." Similarly, Section 2(C) imposes a negligence-like standard in failure to warn cases. A product is defective if "the foreseeable risks of harm posed by the product could have been reduced or avoided by the provision of reasonable instructions or warnings by the seller."[469]

Courts are hesitant to recognize new duties of care for digital data or information based injuries. No U.S. court, for example, recognizes an action for digital products liability. The duty to warn licensees of known latent defects gives the customer the

---

a manufacturing defect, is defective in design, or is defective because of inadequate instructions or warnings." RESTATEMENT (THIRD) OF TORTS: PROD. LIAB. § 2 (1998). Section 2 defines the three categories of product defects:

(A). [a product] contains a manufacturing defect when the product departs from its intended design even though all possible care was exercised in the preparation and marketing of the product;

(B) [a product] is defective in design when the foreseeable risks of harm posed by the product could have been reduced or avoided by the adoption of a reasonable alternative design by the seller or other distributor, or a predecessor in the commercial chain of distribution, and the omission of the alternative design renders the product not reasonably safe;

(C) [a product] is defective because of inadequate instructions or warnings when the foreseeable risks of harm posed by the product could have been reduced or avoided by the provision of reasonable instructions or warnings by the seller or other distributor, or a predecessor in the commercial chain of distribution, and the omission of the instructions or warnings renders the product not reasonably safe. Id.

[466] In Barker v. Lull Engineering Co., 573 P.2d 443, 453 (1978), the California Supreme Court allowed plaintiffs in defective products case to interpose either the consumer expectation test of Section 402A or risk utility. The court suggested the court instruct the jury "that a product is defective in design (1) if the plaintiff demonstrates that the product failed to perform as safely as an ordinary consumer would expect when used in an intended or reasonably foreseeable manner, or (2) if the plaintiff proves that the product's design proximately caused his injury and the defendant fails to prove . . . that on balance the benefits of the challenged design outweighed the risk of danger inherent in such a design."

[467] Id. at 452, 454.

[468] RESTATEMENT THIRD OF TORTS: PRODUCTS LIABILITY § 1 (1998).

[469] See RESTATEMENT (THIRD) OF TORTS, 2(c) (2003).

knowledge they need to protect themselves—much like the consumer of products. The Principles of Software Contracts would also hold a computer vendor liable for statements made about software performance. In *Doe II v. MySpace Inc.*,[470] the parents of teenage girls filed strict products liability and negligence claims against MySpace, alleging that men they met through the site sexually assaulted them. The court sustained MySpace's demurrers without leave to amend and dismissed the complaints. The Court of Appeals affirmed and held that the website, as a publisher of third-party content, had immunity under the Communications Decency Act, and that it wasn't an "information content provider."

(C) Economic Loss Rule

The economic loss rule ("ELR") draws the boundary between torts and the law of contracts. The ELR originated in the field of products liability but courts have stretched this doctrine beyond defective products cases to negligence, fraud, and virtually every other tort.[471] The ELR shields design professionals from negligence claims for "purely economic losses by both those in privity and those not in privity with the professional."[472] Courts must first determine as a question of law whether negligence has resulted in purely "economic loss" in which case the action is contractual, rather than a tort.[473] Even if the plaintiff can prove the elements of negligent security, courts apply the ELR where the breach of a duty merely restates a contractual obligation. The economic loss doctrine in tort law is a response to efforts by plaintiffs to avoid contract law and its limitations by trying to transform breaches of contract into torts.[474]

The ELR is a barrier against recovery for lost proprietary data, trade secrets, and lost profits where there is a contractual nexus between the data handler and data entruster. Defendants in Internet security cases use the economic loss doctrine as a shield from liability. The ELR bars claims for "consequential, or indirect, economic losses attributable to the product defect, such as lost profits resulting from the inability

---

[470] 175 Cal. App. 4th 561, 96 Cal. Rptr. 3d 148 (2009).

[471] The Economic Loss Rule (ELR) bars recovery in products liability actions where the loss is purely economic, that is, direct economic loss to the product itself as opposed to personal injury or damage to other property. If the product itself is harmed, the purchaser must seek a remedy in contract, not tort. See, e.g., Imaging Fin. Servs. v. Lettergraphics Detroit, Inc., 1999 U.S. App. LEXIS 2405 (6th Cir. Feb. 9, 1999). See also Neibarger v. Universal Coops., Inc., 486 N.W.2d 612, 615 (1992) (observing that the economic loss rule "provides that where a purchaser's expectations in a sale are frustrated because the product he bought is not working properly, his remedy is said to be in contract alone, for he has suffered only 'economic' losses"); Nielsen Media Research, Inc. v. Microsystems Software Inc., 2002 U.S. Dist. LEXIS 18261 (S.D. N.Y. 2002) (holding that a plaintiff could recover for breach of warranty if it is determined that the contract was for goods, but could not recover for negligence). See generally, East River Steamship Corp. v Transamerica Delaval, Inc., 476 U.S. 858 (1986).

[472] GEORGE G. BACHRACH, SALVAGE BY THE SURETY 225 (1999).

[473] The Economic Loss Rule ("ELR") bars recovery in products liability actions where the loss is purely economic, that is, direct economic loss to the product itself as opposed to personal injury or damage to other property. If the product itself is harmed, the purchaser must seek a remedy in contract, not tort. See e.g., Imaging Fin. Servs. v. Lettergraphics Detroit, Inc., 1999 U.S. App. LEXIS 2405 (6th Cir. Feb. 9, 1999). See also Neibarger v. Universal Coops., Inc., 486 N.W.2d 612, 615 (1992) (observing that the economic loss rule "provides that where a purchaser's expectations in a sale are frustrated because the product he bought is not working properly, his remedy is said to be in contract alone, for he has suffered only "economic' losses"); Nielsen Media Research, Inc. v. Microsystems Software Inc., 2002 U.S. Dist. LEXIS 18261 (S.D. N.Y. 2002) (holding that a plaintiff could recover for breach of warranty if it is determined that the contract was for goods, but could not recover for negligence).

[474] First Internet Bank of Indiana v. Lawyers Title Ins. Co., 2009 U.S. Dist. LEXIS 59673, at *25 (S.D. Ind. July 13, 2009).

to make use of the product."[475] Negligent misrepresentation, fraud, and other tort claims arising out of data breaches are barred by the ELR. The ELR, present injury requirement, and the lack of a judicially created duty to secure data limit defendants' liability for negligent data handling. An Internet website with lax computer security, enabling the theft of consumers' personally identifiable information such as credit card numbers, could be liable for facilitating the data heist.

Negligent computer security or Internet security may result in cascading economic losses to companies or consumers. Physical injury torts, in contrast, have a more predictable outcome. The ELR bars recovery in products liability actions where the loss is purely economic, that is, direct economic loss to the product itself as opposed to personal injury or damage to other property. An actor has a duty of care when engaged in activities posing a risk of physical harm. An actor's liability for the negligent infliction of economic loss is narrower than for physical injuries and recognized in narrow, specific circumstances. The reasoning behind limitations on recovery of economic loss is that the harm is often indeterminate and disproportionate.

(D) Negligent Information Liability

In negligence-based cases for information products, courts will typically find that the defendant owed the plaintiff no duty and dismiss the cases.[476] Courts are reluctant to find a defendant owes a duty for information presented in a website or in software. In *James v. Meow Media, Inc.*,[477] a federal court dismissed the plaintiffs' products liability claims based on the argument that violent Internet games caused school killings because thoughts, ideas, and expressions contained within defendants' movie, games, and website materials were not "products" "within the realm of the strict liability doctrine."[478] In *Davidson v. Time Warner, Inc.*,[479] the court dismissed the plaintiff's action based on the argument that violent rap music had led to the murder of a state trooper. The court explained that, because the element of foreseeability was absent under Texas' balancing test, no duty existed. "No duty" rules are based upon public policy and generally benefit the defendant because they either eliminate, or modify, a duty of care; thus, the lower the foreseeability, the more likely an information products case will be dismissed. A very high degree of foreseeability is required when the great burden is on society of preventing "harm" by restraining or punishing artistic expression. The "countervailing policies" that arise out of the First Amendment have substantial bearing upon the imposition of liability.[480]

---

[475] MICHAEL D. SCOTT, INTERNET AND TECHNOLOGY DESK REFERENCE (2007) at 335.

[476] To establish a negligence claim, a plaintiff must satisfy four elements: (1) the existence of a duty of care, (2) breach of that duty, (3) legal causation, and (4) damages. Sanchez ex rel. Sanchez v. Wal–Mart Stores, Inc., 221 P.3d 1276, 1280 (Nev.2009). Whether a duty of care exists is "a question of law" for the court to decide. Id. In general, "no duty is owed to control the dangerous conduct of another or to warn others of the dangerous conduct." Id. (citation omitted). An exception exists when (1) there is a special relationship between the parties; and (2) the harm created by the defendant's conduct is foreseeable. Id. at 1280–81.

[477] 90 F. Supp. 2d 798, 811 (W.D. Ky. 2000).

[478] Id.

[479] 1997 U.S. Dist. LEXIS 21559 (S.D. Tex. 1997).

[480] McCollum v. CBS, Inc., 202 Cal.App.3d 989 (1988) (dismissing claim on grounds of foreseeability that Ozzie Osbourne's song, entitled "Suicide Solution," caused a 19 year-old boy to commit suicide).

(E) Innominate Torts in Cyberspace

Courts could recognize remedies for cyberwrongs that do not fit established tort categories by adopting the concept of the *prima facie* tort.[481] A *prima facie* tort, sometimes called an innominate tort, was adopted in the Restatement (Second) of Torts as a residual category of liability for intentional injuries where the defendant can demonstrate no justification or excuse.[482] Comment (d) to Section 870 notes that "a prime example of a tort presently not fully developed is intentional infliction of emotional distress; its contours are not yet fully clear. While the Restatement recognizes this *prima facie* tort, few jurisdictions have adopted it. Other categories of recent development include injurious falsehood, interference with contractual relations and interference with prospective economic advantage. The more mature the stage of the development the more definite the contours of the tort and of the privileges that may be defenses to it."[483] Few courts have adopted this innominate intentional tort, which would permit recovery where the defendant has been malicious but where not all of the elements of a traditional intentional tort are present.[484] The development of the Internet is too recent for cybertorts to have evolved definite contours.

§ 6.7 SECONDARY TORT LIABILITY

Secondary tort liability requires the plaintiff to demonstrate that the secondary tortfeasor played some significant role in further a tort.[485] The common law doctrine of *respondeat superior* makes an employer liable for cybertorts and even punitive damages if the plaintiff shows the employee's action was committed within the scope of the employment. Secondary, or indirect tort liability, is not well developed in tort law beyond vicarious liability. Online companies face a substantial risk for secondary tort liability. For example, partners have joint and several liability for torts committed by the partnership. Therefore, the plaintiff may bring action against partners individually; they do not have to sue partnership first. The Restatement (Second) provides that a party is liable for another's tort if the party "knows that the other's conduct constitutes a breach of duty and gives substantial assistance or encouragement to the other so to conduct himself."[486] "Agency is the fiduciary relationship that arises when one person (a 'principal') manifests assent to another person (an 'agent') that the agent shall act on the principal's behalf and subject to the principal's control, and the agent manifests assent or otherwise consents so to act."[487] The courts have yet to expand cybertort liability for breach of confidence by fiduciaries.

---

[481] New York has adopted the "prima facie tort" but has added additional elements to restrict this action. Kenneth J. Vandevelde, Prima Facie Tort, 19 HOFSTRA L. REV. 447, 494 (1990).

[482] See e.g., RESTATEMENT (SECOND) OF TORTS 870 (1979).

[483] RESTATEMENT (SECOND) OF TORTS 870, cmt. d (1979).

[484] New York has adopted the "prima facie tort" but has added additional elements to restrict this action. Kenneth J. Vandevelde, Prima Facie Tort, 19 HOFSTRA L. REV. 447, 494 (1990).

[485] See RESTATEMENT (SECOND) TORTS § 876(a), cmt. c (2011) (a party that "innocently, rightfully and carefully does an act that has the effect of furthering the tortious conduct or cooperating in the tortious design of another is not for that reason subject to liability").

[486] RESTATEMENT (SECOND) OF TORTS § 876(b) (1979).

[487] RESTATEMENT (THIRD) OF AGENCY § 1.01 (Tentative Draft).

§ 6.8   CYBERTORT PUNITIVE DAMAGES

All but a few U.S. jurisdictions allows plaintiffs to seek punitive damages. Punitive damages are recoverable in most jurisdictions if the plaintiff can prove reckless indifference. Punitive damages in cyberspace cases are more likely to be in business-to-business disputes versus in business-to-consumer transactions. In a study of Internet tort awards from 1992–2004, nearly half of the punitive damages awards (45%), included actions for the intentional interference with contract, unfair and deceptive trade practices, intentional interference with economic opportunities, intentional interference with noncommercial opportunities, unfair competition, fraudulent misrepresentation, and the misappropriation of trade secrets. All but a few of the Internet-related business tort cases involved large companies suing rivals or other companies interfering with their businesses.[488]

Punitive damages awarded in favor of individuals arose out of non-consumer contexts such as the employment relationship or in disputes between individuals. When punitive damages were awarded to individuals, it was often in the context of incendiary exchanges on listservs, web sites, or e-mails.[489] The category of cases awarding punitive damages to individuals involved online stalkers, vengeful neighbors, and sexual harassers. For example, when a neighbor published derogatory statements on an Internet web page about a family, the target obtained punitive damages in a Florida court. In that case, the defendant also published photographs of the plaintiff's minor child as well as the child's name, address, and telephone number on the web site. The plaintiff's punitive damages award was based on the common law torts of trespass, slander, nuisance, and intentional infliction of emotional distress.[490] In the formative era of cybertorts, many large punitive damage awards were uncollectible. In *John Does v. Franco Productions*,[491] the jury awarded a group of Illinois State University athletes, $46 million in compensatory damages and $460 million punitive damages. This large award was against an adult entertainment website that posted secret videos of the athletes in various states of undress. In that case, the website was not reachable by legal process. In *Konanykhine v. Izvestia Newspaper*,[492] a trial court entered a default judgment of $3.5 million in compensatory damages and $30 million in punitive damages in an online defamation case but this award is also uncollectable since the defendant has no reachable assets.

Beginning in the 1990s, the U.S. Supreme Court began to place due process limits on the size of punitive damages.[493] In *BMW of North America, Inc. v. Gore*,[494] a 5-4 majority struck down a $2 million punitive damages award by holding that the award was excessive and violated the Due Process Clause in a case where the actual damages

---

[488] Michael L. Rustad, Punitive Damages in Cyberspace: Where in the World is the Consumer? 7 CHAPMAN L. REV. 39 (2004) (concluding from an empirical study of early cyberspace-related lawsuits from 1992-2002 that liability for defective software or information-based products was non-existent).

[489] See, e.g., Butler v. Krebs, No. 96-1204096, 1998 WL 2023763 (Tex. Dist. Ct., June 8, 1998) (reporting jury verdict in favor of female Continental Express Pilot whose co-workers superimposed her photo on nude images and transmitted them on an intranet).

[490] Bagwell v. Phillips, No. 97-13631, 1998 WL 1656174 (Fla. Cir. Ct., Nov. 23, 1998).

[491] 2002 U.S. Dist. LEXIS 24032 (N.D. Ill. Nov. 25, 2002) (invasion of privacy).

[492] 2000 JAS Publications, Metro Verdicts Monthly (Arlington City, (Va. Dec. 13, 1999) (defamation). (on file with authors)

[493] Michael Rustad, The Closing of Punitive Damages' Iron Cage, 38 LOY. L.A. L. REV. 1297 (2005).

[494] BMW of N. Am., Inc. v. Gore, 517 U.S. 559, 585-86 (1996).

were only $4,000. The *BMW* Court created three guideposts to determine whether a given punitive damages award comports with due process: "(1) the degree of reprehensibility of the defendant's misconduct; (2) the disparity between the actual or potential harm suffered by the plaintiff and the punitive damages award; and (3) the difference between the punitive damages awarded by the jury and the civil penalties authorized or imposed in comparable cases."[495]

The Court continued to reshape the remedy of punitive damages in the 2007 case of *Philip Morris v. Williams*.[496] The punitive damages award in Philip Morris arose out of the claim of the death of Jesse Williams; a heavy cigarette smoker whose estate claimed Williams was lured into complacency by misleading advertisements. The estate contended that Williams smoked throughout his life because the cigarette maker knowingly and falsely led him to believe that cigarette smoking was safe. The Philip Morris jury awarded the decedent's estate compensatory damages of "about $821,000 (about $21,000 economic and $800,000 non-economic damages) along with $79.5 million in punitive damages," which the Supreme Court struck.

Writing for the majority, Justice Stephen Breyer stated: "[T]he Constitution's Due Process Clause forbids a State to use a punitive damages award to punish a defendant for injury that it inflicts upon non-parties or those whom they directly represent, i.e., injury that it inflicts upon those who are, essentially, strangers to the litigation."[497] The *Williams* case makes it difficult for plaintiffs to recover punitive damages in cybertort cases except in online stalking or intentional cybertorts because it is rare that cyberwrongs are directed at a single individual. The U.S. Supreme Court's holding that the Due Process Clause of the U.S. Constitution forbids juries from awarding punitive damages designed to punish a cybertort defendant for harming a non-party in other prior or pending cases outside the scope of the immediate lawsuit. The idea that punitive damages should be based upon a defendants patterns and practice of corporate wrongdoing goes to the heart of a typical spam email case or fraudulent e-mail swindle. The Court makes it clear that jurors were not to consider harm to non-parties when setting the amount of the punitive damages: "a jury may not go further than this and use a punitive damages verdict to punish a defendant directly on account of harms it is alleged to have visited on non-parties."[498]

It will be difficult to instruct juries in applying the *Williams* Court's newly minted standard, which treats a defendant's other bad acts as material to reprehensibility but inadmissible for purposes of setting the dollar amount of punitive damages. It is unclear how a trial court will draft or modify jury instructions in most cybertort actions. The problem with the Court's pattern and practice restrictions is that reprehensibility is both the measure of whether punitive damages should be awarded and in what amount. In fact, reprehensibility is the decisive test of the reasonableness of a punitive damages award. Historically, juries have been permitted to consider a defendant's nationwide pattern of misconduct. Now, juries are instructed to think about those acts as a determination of reprehensibility (the most important indication of the appropriateness of a punitive damage award) and, at the same time, are

---

[495] Id. at 575.

[496] Philip Morris v. Williams, 127 S.Ct. 1057 (2007).

[497] Id. at 1063.

[498] Id. at 1064.

instructed not to consider those bad acts as a basis for awarding or determining an amount of punitive damages.

§ 6.9   CYBERTORT DEFENSES

The deterrent effect of cyber liability rules has largely failed because websites are generally shielded for the torts of third parties. Cyberspace provides an ideal legal environment for tortfeasors and online criminals because Internet Service Providers (ISPs) have no duty to mitigate harms caused by ongoing torts, crimes, and infringing acts. Courts have stretched Congress's express language in § 230 of the Communications Decency Act from the narrow purpose of immunizing ISPs as publishers to the expanded purpose of shielding them from all tort liability. Section 230 preempts all tort claims and thus is a powerful immunity for websites insulating from liability for third party's tortious postings. Online intermediaries such as Internet service providers and websites do, however, have liability for their own direct torts, such as personal property torts, the invasion of privacy, negligently enabling the spread of viruses, or failing to prevent cybercrimes.[499]

The further expansion of ISP tort liability, the recognition of new duties of care, and the extension of traditional tort theories to new cyberspace injuries are necessary developments for the long-term welfare of consumers and other users. The chief controversy for Internet torts is whether websites should continue to be shielded from most tort liability.[500] Nevertheless, cyberspace may well constitute a "tort-free zone" for service providers.[501] Jurisdiction, for example, may be difficult to establish in cybertorts because of the lack of clarity as to where a virtual injury occurs. Just as automobile law reshaped the legal landscape in the 1920s and 1930s, cyberspace is beginning to have a major impact on the tort landscape.[502]

(A) Section 230 of the CDA

Internet torts have been slow to evolve because websites are largely protected from liability for third party postings by Section 230 of the Communications Decency

---

[499] "When a consumer experiences financial loss, identity theft, or the malicious meltdown of their personal computer, the online cybercriminal almost always defaults or is not locatable. The primary wrongdoer is generally beyond the reach of jurisdiction, particularly because the ISP has no duty to aid in locating the origin of the illegal posting. Many consumer frauds, for example, originate in the new Russian Republics, which have become "a popular venue for innovative cyberscams involving credit card numbers stolen from websites." While repeat players enjoy a favorable legal environment, consumers have no recourse against web hosts, websites, or service providers that benefit from selling advertising or providing other services for cybercriminals. Consumers are left defenseless in cyberspace because immunized service providers are the only identifiable deep pocket. ISPs currently have no duty to police the Internet or to develop technologies to track down off-shore posters of objectionable materials." Michael L. Rustad & Thomas H. Koenig, Rebooting Cybertort Law, 80 WASH. L. REV. 335, 350–51 (2005).

[500] Nigel Shadbolt & Tim Berners Lee, Web Science Emerges, SCI. AM. (Oct. 2008) at 79 (citing Technorati study).

[501] Professors Ronald J. Mann and Jane K. Winn define the term "ISP" to subsume "a variety of activities: from the wholly anonymous transmission of a backbone provider, to the wholly transmissive service that a commercial ISP provides to a domain like utexas.edu, to the partially content-based activity that a provider like AOL, MSN, or Yahoo! provide to one of their subscribers." RONALD J. MANN & JANE K. WINN, ELECTRONIC COMMERCE 177 (2d ed. 2005). For purposes of the Digital Millennium Copyright Act, an Internet "service provider," or ISP, is "a provider of online services or network access, or the operator of facilities therefore." 17 U.S.C. § 512(k)(1)(B).

[502] Richard M. Nixon, Changing Rules of Liability in Automobile Accident Litigation, 3 LAW & CONTEMP. PROBS. 476, 485 (1936).

Act of 1996.[503]") The CDA sought to preserve the "vibrant and competitive free market" of ideas on the Internet. This broad shield from tort liability was originally restricted to publisher's liability for defamation but federal courts have stretched it a variety of other tort contexts.[504] The chart below is a sampling of cases where websites have prevailed by non-publisher causes of action.

Case Name and Citation	Brief Recitation of Facts	Types of Section 230 Cases
Klayman v. Zuckerberg, 910 F. Supp.2d 314 (D.D.C. 2012).	Plaintiff alleged that the defendants marketed, used and allowed Facebook to be be used to intentionally, violently, and without cause" to assault the plaintiff. The plaintiff also contended that Facebook violated a duty of care by allowing and furthering death threats by the Palestinian Intifada.	Assault and Negligence Claims Shielded by CDA Section 230.
Chicago Lawyers' Committee for Civil Rights Under Law v. Craigslist, Inc., 519 F.3d 666 (7th Cir. 2008).	The plaintiff charged Craigslist with unlawful discrimination.	Fair Housing Act Claim Shielded by CDA Section 230. Section 230 of the CDA provided a safe harbor for Internet service providers that "publish" classified advertisements on Craigslist that violate the FHA, which (among other things) prohibits discriminatory advertisements for housing.
Xcentric Ventures,	RICO racketeering claims against	Motion to dismiss civil

[503] The CDA shield has been extended to diverse causes of action. See e.g. Shrader v. Beann, 2012 U.S. App. LEXIS 24587 (10th Cir., Nov. 29, 2012) (affirming dismissal of dismissing his claims of defamation, false-light invasion of privacy, intentional infliction of emotional distress, and civil conspiracy on grounds of Section 230 of the CDA).

[504] Ben Ezra, Weinstein, & Co. v. America Online, Inc., 206 F.3d 980, 985 (10th Cir. 2000) (holding Internet access provider was immunized for providing access to misleading stock information); OptInRealBig.com, LLC v. IronPort Sys., Inc., 323 F. Supp. 2d 1037, 1047 (N.D. Cal. 2004) (denying injunction in favor of spam e-mailer, ruling that spam complaint website was immunized from liability under CDA); Ramey v. Darkside Prods., No. CIV.A.02–730 (GK), 2004 U.S. Dist. LEXIS 10107, at *12–21 (D.D.C. May 17, 2004) (ruling that online advertising guide for adult entertainment was immunized by CDA in claim by woman that unauthorized photos were used on advertisement on website); PatentWizard, Inc. v. Kinko's, Inc., 163 F. Supp. 2d 1069, 1072 (D.S.D. 2001) (extending CDA immunity to copy center that permitted third-party users to send e-mails and other electronic communications anonymously).

L.L.C. v. Borodkin, 2013 WL 3034267 (D. Ariz., June 17, 2013).	Xcentric predicated on attempted extortion. The AEI Plaintiffs allegedly contacted Xcentric after the Ripoff Reports appeared on the website and learned that Xcentric "would not remove the defamatory posts even if they were false." Xcentric informed the AEI Plaintiffs that they could file a free rebuttal or, if they remained unsatisfied, join the Corporate Advocacy Program for a price of $5,000 per month per monitoring costs.	RICO claim granted because of Section 230 immunity.[505]
Okele v. Cars.com, 2013 WL 2321672, 2013 N.Y. Slip Op. 23174, (N.Y. City Civ. Ct., May 28, 2013).	Cars.com negligently failed to incorporate security features to prevent fraudulent sales	Ruled that Section 230 shielded Cars.com from negligence claim filed by consumer who paid for a truck but never received it.
Beckman v. Match.com, 2013 WL 2355512, (D. Nev., May 29, 2013)	Match.com negligently exposed plaintiff to a serial murderer on online dating service.	Held that Section 230 precluded negligence claims against operators of the Match.com online dating site. Applying Section 230 immunity to negligence claim against online dating suit by plaintiff assaulted by serial murderer she met through website; negligent claim arose out Match.com's warning and screening activities).
Doe v. MySpace Inc.,	Doe, a thirteen year old girl lied	Affirmed that Section

---

[505] See also, Asia Economic Institute v. Xcentric Ventures LLC, 2:10–cv-01360–SVW -PJW (C.D. Cal. May 4, 2011) (ruling that Section 230 shielded Ripoff Report from civil actions that included unfair business practices under Cal. Bus. & Prof. Code §§ 17200 et seq.; defamation; defamation per se; false light; intentional interference with prospective economic relations; negligent interference with prospective economic relations; and negligent interference with economic relations because the allegedly tortious postings were by third parties).

528 F.3d 413 (5th Cir. 2008).	about her age, representing that she was eighteen years old, and created a profile on MySpace.com. In April 2006, a nineteen-year-old male (Pete Solis) contacted her through the site. The two parties communicated offline and formed a relationship. They met in person on May 12, 2006, and Solis sexually assaulted Doe.	230 of the CDA barred claims alleging that MySpace Negligently failed to keep minors off its website or to keep predators from communicating

Information service providers have prevailed in nearly every cybertort related case in the last decade and a half. Section 230 provides:

(c) Protection for "good samaritan" blocking and screening of offensive material

(1) Treatment of publisher or speaker.

No provider or user of an interactive computer service shall be treated as the publisher or speaker of any information provided by another information content provider.

(2) Civil liability

No provider or user of an interactive computer service shall be held liable on account of-

(A) any action voluntarily taken in good faith to restrict access to or availability of material that the provider or user considers to be obscene, lewd, lascivious, filthy, excessively violent, harassing, or otherwise objectionable, whether or not such material is constitutionally protected; or

(B) any action taken to enable or make available to information content providers or others the technical means to restrict access to material described in paragraph (1).[506]

CDA Section 230 provides that "No provider or user of an interactive computer service shall be treated as the publisher or speaker of any information provided by another information content provider."[507] Further, Section 230 defines "interactive computer service" as "any information service, system, or access software provider that provides or enables computer access by multiple users to a computer server, including specifically a service or system that provides access to the Internet and such systems operated or services offered by libraries or educational institutions."[508] The statute also defines "information content provider" as "any person or entity that is responsible, in whole or in part, for the creation or development of information provided through the Internet or any other interactive computer service." The CDA sought to preserve the "vibrant and competitive free market" of ideas on the Internet.[509] Congress enacted the CDA to shield websites from information-based torts in the United States in the wake

---

[506] 47 U.S.C. § 230(c).

[507] 47 U.S.C. § 230(c)(1).

[508] 47 U.S.C. § 230(f)(2).

[509] 47 U.S.C. § 230(b)(2).

of a New York trial court decision that classified a website as a publisher in a defamatory third party postings case. Prior to Section 230, there was a cloud of uncertainty as to whether websites were liable for the defamatory postings of users.[510]

Section 230 of the CDA precludes plaintiffs from making interactive computer service providers liable for the publication of information created by third parties. To fall within the protection of the Section 230 of the CDA, a website must show: "(1) [it is] a provider or user of an interactive computer service; (2) the cause of action treat[s] the defendant as a publisher or speaker of information; and (3) the information at issue [is] provided by another information content provider."[511] Since Congress enacted the CDA in 1996, federal courts have stretched Section 230's immunity for publisher liability to cover every conceivable tort thus violating a basic principle that a responsible website is an answerable one.[512] What was originally only a narrow statutory immunity for publisher liability for third party content is now a shield for every tort and civil actions outside of tort.

By July 1, 2013, an astonishing 1,086 court decisions cited Section 230 of the CDA. Defendant websites have prevailed in cases where plaintiffs filed lawsuits for third party content. Those targeted by online mobs—often women and minorities—have no recourse against service providers because of Section 230, which immunizes websites for third party postings. It is often difficult to unveil the direct perpetrator who is often beyond the reach of legal process.[513]

The CDA immunity for service providers parallels the nineteenth century legal subsidies that insulated the railroad, steamboat companies, canal builders, and other builders of the nineteenth century industrial economy.[514] Immunity breeds irresponsibility because website operators have no legal incentive "to take down false or injurious materials or to collect and retain identities of posters."[515] The statutory purpose of Section 230 was to protect service providers by shielding them from defamation liability as publishers.[516] "Internet publishers are treated differently from corresponding publishers in print, television and radio."[517] As the next sections

---

[510] Stratton Oakmont, Inc. v. Prodigy Services Co., 1995 WL 323710 (N.Y. Sup. Ct. 1995) (finding ISP liable for defamatory statements because it exercised some editorial control and did not promptly take down statement made on Internet forum labeling company's stock option as fraudulent and its actions as criminal); But See Cubby, Inc. v. CompuServe, Inc., 776 F. Supp. 135 (S.D. N.Y. 1991) (finding that ISP was not liable for statements made in electronic bulletin board since it did not exercise editorial control).

[511] Delfino v. Agilent Technologies, Inc. 145 Cal. App.4th 790, 804–805 (2006).

[512] Michael L. Rustad & Thomas H. Koenig, Rebooting Cybertort Law, 80 WASH. L. REV. 335, 371 (2005) ("An activist judiciary, however, has radically expanded § 230 by conferring immunity on distributors. Section 230(c)(1) has been interpreted to preclude all tort lawsuits against ISPs, websites, and search engines. Courts have . . . haphazardly lump[ed] together web hosts, websites, search engines, and content creators into this amorphous category.").

[513] Danielle Keats Citrone, Civil Rights in our Information Age, Chapter 2 in THE OFFENSIVE INTERNET: PRIVACY, SPEECH, AND REPUTATION (ed. Saul Levmore & Martha C. Nussbaum) 31, 48 (2010).

[514] See MORTON HORWITZ, THE TRANSFORMATION OF AMERICAN LAW 1780–1860, at 99–101 (1977).

[515] Id. at 49.

[516] "Congress enacted § 230 to expressly overrule courts that would hold ISPs liable as publishers for materials posted by third parties.[Congress] worried that such a rule would deter a provider of an interactive computer service from removing objectionable material from its services that are frequented by minors because removing the material would subject the service provider to publisher liability. In response, Congress enacted 47 U.S.C. § 230 as part of the CDA." Ryan W. King, Online Defamation: Bringing the Communications Decency Act of 1996 in Line with Sound Public Policy, 2003 DUKE L. & TECH. REV. 0024, P 4, at http://www.law.duke.edu/journals/dltr/articles/PDF/2003DLTR0024.pdf.

[517] Carafano v. Metrosplash.com, Inc., 339 F.3d 1119, 1122 (9th Cir.2003).

demonstrate, the federal courts have interpreted Section 230 to shield providers from distributor liability as well as other torts.

(1) Distributor Liability

A strict reading of Section 230 would seemingly restrict a website or service provider's shield to publisher liability for defamation. Federal courts have stretched the long arm of Section 230 immunity to distributor liability.[518] How did websites and online providers get a complete shield from secondary tort liability, when Section 230 only mentions liability as publishers? Courts have long distinguished between primary publishers—i.e. newspapers or book publishers—and secondary publishers or distributors—i.e. bookstores, libraries, or newsstands—in common law defamation lawsuits.[519]

A newspaper is a republisher with the same liability as the person who originally published a story or article if the newspaper has notice of any defamatory content. Republishers are classified as primary publishers held to the same liability standard as the author of a defamatory work because of their active role in the publication. Distributors traditionally encompass mere conduits such as "telegraph and telephone companies, libraries, and news vendors."[520] Under the common law of defamation, distributors are not liable for content created by others unless they have knowledge of the defamatory content for materials distributed. A bookstore owner, for example, is not liable for defamatory statements if the store sold the books without actual knowledge of

---

[518] Zeran v. America Online, 129 F.3d 327, 330–31 (4th Cir. 1997) (in enacting § 230, Congress sought "to encourage service providers to self-regulate the dissemination of offensive material over their services" and to remove disincentives to self-regulation).

[519] Distributors include conduits such as "telegraph and telephone companies, libraries and news vendors." DAN B. DOBBS, THE LAW OF TORTS § 402, at 1123 (2000). Distributors do not have liability for content created by others unless "the distributor knows or should know of the defamatory content in materials he distributes." Id. A bookstore owner, for example, would not be liable for defamatory statements made in books the store sold absent actual knowledge. "ISPs and other distributors of information (e.g., bookstores) only assume liability when they acquire knowledge of the material they are handling." Brian C. Lewis, Note, Prevention of Computer Crime Amidst International Anarchy, 41 AM. CRIM. L. REV. 1353, 1368 (2004) (citing 47 U.S.C. § 230 (2000)). The common law rule makes a distributor liable where it has knowledge of the facts and circumstances that are producing clearly libelous activity, but takes no action to remove the material. See e.g., Lerman v. Chuckleberry Publ'g, Inc., 521 F. Supp. 228, 235 (S.D.N.Y. 1981) ("[D]istributors of defamatory publications are not liable if they neither know nor have reason to know of the defamation."), reversed on other grounds, Lerman v. Flynt Distrib. Co., Inc., 745 F.2d 123 (2d Cir. 1984). The Restatement Second of Torts explains:

> [A] news dealer is not liable for defamatory statements appearing in the newspapers or magazines that he sells if he neither knows nor has reason to know of the defamatory article. The dealer is under no duty to examine the various publications that he offers for sale to ascertain whether they contain any defamatory items. Unless there are special circumstances that should warn the dealer that a particular publication is defamatory, he is under no duty to ascertain its innocent or defamatory character. On the other hand, when a dealer offers for sale a particular paper or magazine that notoriously persists in printing scandalous items, the vendor may do so at the risk that any particular issue may contain defamatory language.

RESTATEMENT (SECOND) OF TORTS § 581 cmt. d (1977).

[520] Traditional defamation law categorized information disseminators into three groups to which very different legal standards were applied to determine defamation liability related to third-party content: (1) publishers (e.g., newspapers) exercise great control over final content and were therefore subject to strict liability; (2) distributors (e.g., booksellers) merely distribute content and were therefore subject to liability only upon a showing of knowledge or negligence; and (3) common carriers (e.g., telephone companies) only transmit information with no control over content and were therefore not liable at all. Jae Hong Lee, Note, Batzel v. Smith & Barrett v. Rosenthal: Defamation Liability for Third-Party Content on the Internet, 19 BERKELEY TECH. L.J. 469, 471 (2004); see generally, DAN B. DOBBS, THE LAW OF TORTS 1123 (2000).

the statements. Similarly, websites and other online defendants are not liable for the defamatory postings of third parties absent proof of knowledge or notice of the objectionable materials. In *Cubby v. CompuServe*,[521] the Ohio federal court ruled the service provider was not liable for content posted on its bulletin board.[522] The *Cubby* court held the service provider was merely a distributor akin to a bookstore, library, or newsstand and therefore was not liable for defamatory content.[523] CompuServe, Inc. made no effort to monitor content or provide any editorial services. It loaded text and databases instantaneously without any means to filter out objectionable content.[524]

Section 230 adopted the *Cubby* court's view that websites are distributors, not publishers. Since the CDA, courts have bloated ISP immunity to include distributor liability as well as every other information related tort, including the invasion of privacy, and negligence. The result has been that ISPs have prevailed in nearly every tort related case in the last decade. In 1995, a New York case, however, found the online BBS Prodigy to be a publisher subject to libel liability.[525] CDA Section 230 adopted the CompuServe approach to online intermediary liability as opposed to the New York trial court's ruling that intermediaries could be liable for third party postings.

(2) Failure to Remove Content

U.S. courts have ruled consistently that service providers are not liable for ongoing torts (or crimes) committed by third parties on their services even after they have received notice from the victim.[526] Providers have no duty to remove or take down content that constitutes an ongoing tort so long as they are not classifiable as a content creator. For example, in *Directory Assistants, Inc. v. Supermedia, LLC*,[527] a Connecticut-based advertising consulting agency, filed a defamation and tortious interference with contract claim against SuperMedia, LLC, and three of its employees arising out of that company's distribution of hyperlinks to allegedly defamatory material in Ripoff Report and another site. Directors Assistants also alleged that Supermedia sent these hyperlinks to third party customers and potential customers. The court dismissed all claims based upon Section 230 immunity.

---

[521] 776 F. Supp. 135 (S.D. N.Y. 1991).

[522] "CompuServe has no opportunity to review Rumorville's contents before DFA uploads it into CompuServe's computer banks, from which it is immediately available to approved CIS subscribers. CompuServe receives no part of any fees that DFA charges for access to Rumorville, nor does CompuServe compensate DFA for providing Rumorville to the Journalism Forum; the compensation CompuServe receives for making Rumorville available to its subscribers is the standard online time usage and membership fees charged to all CIS subscribers, regardless of the information services they use. CompuServe maintains that, before this action was filed, it had no notice of any complaints about the contents of the Rumorville publication or about DFA." Id. at 137. The court was persuaded that CompuServe was a distributor because it exercised almost no editorial control over anything posted on its message boards or electronic bulletin boards. Id. The federal court reasoned that, because it exercised no control, it could only be liable for torts if the plaintiff proved that the ISP had actual or constructive knowledge of defamatory materials. Id. at 141.

[523] Id. at 137, 140 (ruling that ISP was not publisher and was therefore analogous to mere conduit such as newsstand or bookstore).

[524] Id. at 140.

[525] See Stratton Oakmont, Inc. v. Prodigy Servs. Co., 63 U.S.L.W. 2765 (May 24, 1995), reargument denied, 1995 WL 805178 (N.Y. Sup. Dec. 11, 1995).

[526] See Michael L. Rustad & Thomas H. Koenig, Rebooting Cybertort Law, 80 WASH. L. REV. 335, 351 (2005) ("Repeat players such as ISPs have no qualms about protecting their rights through Internet lawsuits over intellectual property, tort, and contract rights, all of which are primarily resolved in federal courts.").

[527] 2012 WL 3329615 (E.D. Va. May 30, 2012).

Courts have yet to recognize that ISPs have a duty to remove content constituting ongoing torts or even crimes. "In fact, under the CDA, ISPs can apparently continue to host defamatory content that the original author wishes to have removed."[528] The leading case for "no liability" for failing to remove content is *Zeran v. America Online.*[529] A spiteful anonymous poster instructed members of the public to call Kenneth M. Zeran, a Seattle resident, to order merchandise with tasteless slogans celebrating the 1995 bombing in Oklahoma City of the Alfred P. Murrah Federal Building.[530] The messages listed Zeran's name and telephone number. An Oklahoma City radio announcer repeated some of these provocative messages on the air. In the aftermath of the radio broadcast, Zeran was deluged with hostile telephone calls and death threats but could not change his number because it was also used for his business. Zeran contended that AOL was negligent in failing to remove the incendiary posting and allowed the third party to post repeatedly, even after AOL had been made aware of their falsity.

In *Zeran*, the Fourth Circuit ruled a service provider was immunized from both publisher and distributor defamation lawsuits.[531] The *Zeran* court reasoned that the Communications Decency Act ("CDA"), 47 U.S.C. § 230(c)(1), "precludes courts from entertaining claims that would place a computer service provider in a publisher's role," and therefore bars "lawsuits seeking to hold a service provider liable for its exercise of a publisher's traditional editorial functions—such as deciding whether to publish, withdraw, postpone, or alter content."[532] AOL defended on grounds of Section 230 and the Fourth Circuit agreed, reasoning that the Congressional intent of 230 was to immunize internet communication providers from tort liability; to maintain robust Internet communications. The Fourth Circuit reasoned:

> If computer service providers were subject to distributor liability, they would face potential liability each time they receive notice of a potentially defamatory statement from any party, concerning any message. . . . Because service providers would be subject to liability only for the publication of information, and not for its removal, they would have a natural incentive simply to remove messages upon notification, whether the contents were defamatory or not.[533]

The *Zeran* court held that the plain language of Section 230 creates a "federal immunity to any cause of action that would make service providers liable for information originating from a third-party user of the service."[534] The *Zeran* ruling held that the service providers are not liable for refusing to remove the defamatory postings of third parties even after receiving notice of illegal content.[535] Another lesson of the *Zeran*

---

[528] Rebecca Tushnet, Power Without Responsibility: Intermediaries and the First Amendment, 76 GEO. WASH. L. REV. 986, 1002 (2008).

[529] 129 F.3d 327 (4th Cir. 1997).

[530] Id. at 329.

[531] Emily K. Fritts, Note, Internet Libel and the Communications Decency Act: How the Courts Erroneously Interpreted Congressional Intent with Regard to Liability of Internet Service Providers, 93 KY. L.J. 765, 777 (2004) ("[I]n Zeran the Fourth Circuit mixed distributor liability with publisher liability. . . . Rather than recognizing the distinct categories of "publisher" and "distributor" that are a traditional staple of defamation law, the court manipulated the term "publication" . . . instead of looking to cases for resolution of the distinction.").

[532] Id. at 330.

[533] Zeran, Id. at 333.

[534] Id.

[535] "The specter of tort liability in an area of such prolific speech would have an obvious chilling effect. It would be impossible for service providers to screen each of their millions of postings for possible problems.

case is that intermediaries have no obligation to take down information posted by third parties, which is unlike their duty under copyright law under the Digital Millennium Copyright Act. The significance of *Zeran* was that it was the first case where the court stretched Section 230 beyond publisher's liability as stated in the statutory language to immunize a defendant for distributor's liability. As the court noted, "[b]y its plain language, § 230 creates a federal immunity to any cause of action that would make service providers liable for information originating with a third party user of the service."[536] The court's reasoning was that distributor liability is merely a subset of publisher liability, which is not consistent with the common law, where distributors only had liability with notice of defamatory content. Nevertheless, hundreds of courts with approval have cited Zeran.

(3) Immunity When Websites Exercise Editorial Control

In *Blumenthal v. America Online*,[537] commentator Matt Drudge issued a false report on AOL that Sidney Blumenthal, an aide to President Clinton, had a history of spousal abuse. Matt Drudge and AOL entered into an agreement by which the service provider paid him royalties for publishing the Drudge Report on its service. Drudge later retracted the story and AOL published the retraction on its service. Blumenthal contended AOL should be liable for the defamatory communication even though it conceded AOL was an interactive computer service. In *Blumenthal v. Drudge*,[538] Blumenthal argued that Drudge was "not just an anonymous person who sent a message over the Internet" because of his license agreement with AOL.[539] AOL was also entitled under its contract to edit the content of the column.[540] Nevertheless, the court held that AOL was immune under section 230.[541]

Blumenthal contended AOL's editorial role made it a content provider, divesting it of its Section 230 immunity because the ISP not only sponsored the site but also paid Drudge $3,000 monthly royalty payments for posting his column on its online service. The *Blumenthal* court found that AOL had no editorial role—even though it had the right to edit, update, manage, or even remove objectionable content in its agreement to publish the Drudge Report. AOL had advertised that it hired Matt Drudge and was teaming up with his service in separate press releases.[542] The agreement made the Drudge Report available to all members of AOL's service for a period of one year. In exchange, defendant Drudge received a flat monthly 'royalty payment' of $3,000 from AOL. During the time relevant to this case, defendant Drudge has had no other source of income."[543] AOL also set the terms for Drudge's creation, editing, and management of the online Drudge Report.[544]

Faced with potential liability for each message republished by their services, interactive computer service providers might choose to severely restrict the number and type of messages posted." Id. at 331.

[536] Id. at 333.

[537] 992 F. Supp. 44 (D.D.C. 1998).

[538] Id.

[539] Id. at 51.

[540] Id.

[541] Id. at 49.

[542] Id. at 52 (acknowledging that Section 230 addresses the issue of publisher liability on a service provider for the exercise of its editorial and self- regulatory functions).

[543] Id. at 47.

[544] Id.

The court classified AOL as an interactive computer service entitled to a Section 230 liability shield. The court stated, "Congress has conferred immunity from tort liability as an incentive to Internet service providers to self-police the Internet for obscenity and other offensive material, even when the self-policing is unsuccessful or not even attempted."[545] The court's expansive interpretation of Section 230 protected AOL even though it had many attributes of a content creator. Another lesson learned from Blumenthal is that a website can assume some editorial role over content and still enjoy the secondary tort liability shield.[546] In *Ben Ezra, Weinstein & Co. v. America Online, Inc.*,[547] the Tenth Circuit stated that "Congress clearly enacted § 230 to forbid the imposition of publisher liability on a service provider for exercise of its editorial and self-regulatory functions."[548]

(4) Refusal to Remove Link

U.S. tort law recognizes no duty to take down tortious content because of the court's broad and liberal interpretation of the Section 230 shield. Courts have ruled that a website is not liable for failing to remove a link to tortious or other illegal content. An illustrative case is *Mmubango v. Google, Inc.*,[549] where a federal court ruled that Google was immunized by Section 230 for publishing (and refusing to remove) a link to a wikiscams.com website alleging defaming the plaintiff. The court ruled that Google was not an "information content provider" with respect to the allegedly defamatory material because Google did not create the content. A federal court in *Stevo Design Inc. v. SBR Marketing Ltd.*,[550] applied the Section 230 immunity to an offshore, sports-handicapping website's practice of awarding loyalty points to users who posted content on their website. The court noted that the test for liability "is whether the duty that the plaintiff alleges the defendant violated derives from the defendant's status or conduct as a publisher or speaker. If it does, 47 U.S.C. § 230(c)(1) precludes liability."[551]

(5) Exceptions to Section 230 Immunity

In *Fair Housing Council of the San Fernando Valley v. Roommates.com*,[552] the Ninth Circuit, sitting *en banc*, ruled by an 8–3 vote that Section 230 did not immunize a roommate-matching website specifically because it was a content creator. The Ninth Circuit held that an online roommate-matching service was not entitled to CDA immunity for discrimination because it required its users to divulge their sex, family

---

[545] Id. ("In some sort of tacit quid pro quo arrangement with the service provider community, Congress has conferred immunity from tort liability as an incentive to Internet service providers to self-police the Internet for obscenity and other offensive material even where the self-policing is unsuccessful or not even attempted.").

[546] Since Blumenthal, a number of courts have applied the Section 230 shield where websites exercised some traditional editorial tasks such as content creation. See e.g., Whitney Info. Network, Inc. v. Xcentric Ventures, LLC, 2008 U.S. Dist. LEXIS 11632, No. 2:04–cv-47–FtM-34SPC at *35–36 (M.D. Fla. Feb. 15, 2008) (ruling that merely "provid[ing] categories from which a poster must make a selection in order to submit a report on the ROR Website is not sufficient to treat [d]efendants as information content providers of the reports").

[547] 206 F.3d 980 (10th Cir. 2000).

[548] Id. at 986.

[549] 2013 U.S. Dist. LEXIS 24989 (E.D. Pa. Feb. 22, 2013).

[550] 105 U.S.P.Q.2D (BNA) 1925 (D. Nev., Jan 25, 2013).

[551] Id.

[552] 521 F.3d 1157, 1162 (9th Cir. 2008).

status, and sexual orientation, information that third parties allegedly used to discriminate in roommates selection.[553] The Ninth Circuit found that the website was the 'information content provider' as to the questions and thus was not immunized under the CDA.[554]

As a condition of searching listings or posting housing openings, subscribers were required to answer questions disclosing their sex and sexual orientation. Roommates.com's questionnaire asked whether applicants would bring children to a household. The site also encouraged subscribers to post additional comments.[555] The court agreed the website operator designed the discriminatory registration process for locating roommates and was undoubtedly the "information content provider" with regard to the questions.[556] The *Fair Housing Council* court reasoned websites could be both a service provider and content provider only if it passively displays content that is created entirely by third parties. In this instance, it is only a service provider with respect to that content.[557]

The Ninth Circuit noted a website is a content provider for postings "that it creates itself, or is responsible, in whole or in part for creating or developing."[558] The court concluded a website might be immune from liability for some of the content it displays to the public but be subject to liability for other content. The court found Roommates.com to be "forcing subscribers to answer [questions] as a condition of using its services" and that made them, in effect, content creators.[559] Nevertheless, Roommates website was entitled to immunity with regard to additional comments posted by subscribers since it provided no guidance and encouraged no discriminatory preferences.[560] To date, Roommates.com stands as a solitary pine representing liability in a in a forest of decisions for defendant websites.[561] Section 230 of the CDA immunizes Internet publishers for publisher liability for the content of third parties, but not for their own wrongful conduct. In *Anthony v. Yahoo!*,[562] the court refused to shield Yahoo! for posting stale profiles on its dating website to deceive consumers and gain subscribers stating:

> Admittedly, third parties created these profiles. Nevertheless, the CDA only entitles Yahoo! not to be "the publisher or speaker" of the profiles. It does not absolve Yahoo! from liability for any accompanying misrepresentations. Because

---

[553] Id. at 1164.

[554] Id.

[555] Id.

[556] "Roommates, of course, does much more than encourage or solicit; it forces users to answer certain questions and thereby provide information that other clients can use." Id. at 1166.

[557] Id.

[558] Id.

[559] Id. at 1165.

[560] Id. at 1164.

[561] The Seventh Circuit on similar facts to Roommates.com decided that a website was shielded from secondary tort liability. Chicago Lawyers' Committee for Civil Rights Under Law v. Craigslist, Inc., 519 F.3d 666 (7th Cir. 2008). In Chicago Lawyers Committee for Civil Rights, the Seventh Circuit found Craigslist not responsible for the open-ended "Additional Comments" form on their website. The Craigslist court held that, "[n]othing] in the service craigslist offers induces anyone to post any particular listing or express a preference for discrimination; for example, craigslist does not offer a lower price to people who include discriminatory statements in their postings." Id. at 671–672.

[562] 421 F.Supp.2d 1257 (N.D. Cal. 2006).

Anthony posits that Yahoo!'s manner of presenting the profiles—not the underlying profiles themselves—constitutes fraud, the CDA does not apply.[563]

A few courts have ruled that Section 230 immunity is not available if a website is too closely involved with the creation of content posted by third parties. The CDA protects providers of interactive computer services against liability arising from content created by third parties.

(6) ISPs & Rights of Publicity

The Ninth Circuit held Matchmaker.com was not liable when an unidentified party posted a false online personal profile for a former Star Trek actress on its service.[564] In *Carafano*, a former Star Trek Actress was the victim of an identity theft hoax perpetrated by an anonymous Matchmaker.com subscriber who created a fake profile on the defendant's service. The anonymous tortfeasor included the plaintiff's photograph, home address and other personally identifiable information resulting with the plaintiff being deluged with sexually explicit e-mails, telephone calls, and faxes at her home.[565] The actress filed suit against Matchmaker.com, charging it with a host of torts including defamation, right of publicity, invasion of privacy, and negligence. The Ninth Circuit held that the defendant was insulated from all liability because it was an interactive computer service.[566]

(7) The Case For & Against Section 230

Section 230's shield has thus been impervious to frontal assault by diverse plaintiffs including governmental attorneys. However, immunity also leads to irresponsibility especially in cases where websites benefit from endemic postings of revenge porn, trade libel or other illegal content. South Dakota's Attorney General, through the National Association of Attorney Generals, has asked state attorneys general throughout the U.S. "to sign on to a letter calling on Congress to amend the exemptions under Section 230 of the Communications Decency Act to give state officials greater authority in pursuing what he called 'certain egregious website conduct.'"[567] The proposed Section CDA Amendment favored by the state attorneys general would be unlikely to survive constitutional scrutiny because of overbreadth and vagueness. Nevertheless, the Fordham Law School Center on Law and Information Policy Research ("CLIP") Report on Section 230 confirms widespread criticism by academic observers and calls for reforms.[568] The CLIP report surveyed all academic articles and cases that followed and extended *Zeran* decided since 1996.

---

[563] Id. at 1263.

[564] Carafano v. Metrosplash.com. Inc., 339 F.3d 1119, 1122 (9th Cir. 2003).

[565] Id. at 1122 ("Through Section 1230 of the CDA], Congress granted most Internet services immunity from liability for publishing false or defamatory material so long as the information was provided by another party.").

[566] Id. at 1124 (ruling that matchmaker.com was entitled to a Section 230 immunity since it did not create or develop content in user profiles because of its questionnaire).

[567] Attorneys General Urged to Sign Onto Amendment to CDA Section 230, BLOOMBERG BNA ELECTRONIC COMMERCE AND THE LAW (June 18, 2013).

[568] Joel Reidenberg, et. al. Center on Law and Information Policy, Fordham Law School (April 25, 2012).

The research team performed a content analysis of all Section 230 cases and concluded that most courts interpreted the shield broadly.[569] In contrast, the Fordham CLIP team found "a majority of the scholarly literature identified is critical of Section 230."[570] Academic commentators have levied criticism at Congress that was creating too broad of shield from secondary tort liability and the courts for being too aggressive in expanding the immunity.[571] Section 230 immunizes websites for third party harassment, stalking, bullying and other cybertorts.[572] Academic critics of Section 230 contend that common law standards of liability should be restored.[573] Another criticism of Section 230 is that it leaves victims of cybertorts with no recourse because the intermediary is often the only locatable or solvent defendant.[574] A number of critics contend that Section 230 is no longer necessary because the Internet is no longer in its infancy.[575] Another criticism is that courts have difficulty drawing the line between the publisher and content provider.[576] Commentators, however, do not agree on whether it is the courts or Congress' job to reform Section 230.[577]

Too much cybertort liability will chill expression and stifle innovation. However, courts have expanded the meaning of "interactive computer services" in Section 230 to preclude nearly all tort lawsuits against ISPs, websites, and search engines.[578] The principal argument for a broad immunity is that it enables entrepreneurs to post third party content. Section 230 serves as a subsidy for websites because it lowers costs in defending against lawsuits. Eric Goldman favors retaining a broad immunity for websites and thus opposes the state attorneys general proposal to reform CDA Section 230. He writes:

> In 1996, Congress enacted 47 U.S.C. 230 (Section 230), which says that websites aren't liable for UGC ("user generated content") or other third party content—even if the website ignores takedown notices, and even if the website has exercised editorial control over the UGC. Section 230 is a globally unique policy solution; no other country has laws so protective of UGC website operators. As a result, Section 230 provides the foundation for our burgeoning domestic UGC industry,

---

[569] Id. at 8.

[570] Id. at 9.

[571] Id. at 25.

[572] Id.

[573] Id. at 27.

[574] Id. at 29.

[575] Id.

[576] Id.

[577] "One of the unintended consequences of 42 U.S.C. § 230, the Communications Decency Act of 1996 ("CDA"), is that it immunizes unfair, deceptive, and predatory practices in cyberspace. One of the statutory purposes of § 230 was to protect the "infant industry" of online service providers, such as America Online, CompuServe, and Prodigy, from tort liability arising out of postings by customers. Section 230 of the CDA immunizes ISPs for torts committed by subscribers and third parties. The long-term consequence of § 230 is to grant blanket immunity to ISPs for many torts in cyberspace. The courts have extended ISP immunity to nearly every conceivable information-related tort, including invasion of privacy; and negligence. The result has been that ISPs have prevailed in nearly every tort-related case in the last decade. This broad immunity lessens the incentive for ISPs to develop technologies that will detect or control third party wrongdoing on their systems." Michael L. Rustad, Punitive Damages in Cyberspace: Where in the World is the Consumer, 7 CHAPMAN L. REV. 39, 77 (2004).

[578] See Michael L. Rustad & Thomas H. Koenig, Rebooting Cybertort Law, 80 WASH. L. REV. 355, 371 (2005).

and it gives the United States global competitive advantages both in launching and operating UGC websites and in the social benefits these sites provide.[579]

Supporters of CDA Section 230 contend that this immunity "has played an essential role in the Internet's success in shielding UGC websites from third party torts.[580] He argues that without a robust Section 230, services such as Google, eBay, Twitter, and Pinterest "may not exist at all, or they would exist in a radically different form that would be more expensive and less helpful to users."[581]

(8) Shielding Against Website Negligence

Section 230 of the CDA shields interactive computer services from claims that seek to treat them as the publisher or speaker of information provided by another information content provider. CDA defines "interactive computer service" as "any information service, system, or access software provider that provides or enables computer access by multiple users to a computer server, including specifically a service or system that provides access to the Internet and such systems operated or services offered by libraries or educational systems."[582] Courts have stretched the CDA Section 230 to apply to negligence claims asserted against websites based upon inadequate security.

(B) Government Immunities

In 2005, a plaintiff discovered that his name was posted on a sex offender website, even though he was not a convicted sex offender. The plaintiff sued the city for violations of his civil rights, deprivation of due process, slander, libel and intentional infliction of emotional distress. The plaintiff "argued that he was subjected to ridicule. He called the posting 'disgusting,' derogatory and an 'outright lie.'"[583] Nevertheless, the court dismissed all claims, ruling that governmental immunity banned the law claims. He granted the defense motion for summary judgment and dismissed the case. In a similar Massachusetts case, a jury awarded the plaintiff $40,000 in a similar Massachusetts case and required the Commonwealth of Massachusetts to send a letter of apology.[584] Justice Holmes' cogent comment, "in moving water there is life and health; in stagnant pools, decay and death," is applicable to cybertorts. Judicial stagnation, tort reform, and Section 230 of the CDA have prevented the common law of torts from readily accommodating to the Internet. Cybertort remedies must expand in order to perform their traditional function of social control in the information age, an era in which the nature of injuries is being transformed. Even in cyberspace, tort law exists to vindicate, not veto, consumer protection.

---

[579] Eric Goldman, Excluding State Crimes from 47 U.S.C. 230 Immunity Would Be a Disaster (July 2013) at 1, http://papers.ssrn.com/sol3/papers.cfm?abstract_id=2287622&download=yes (last visited July 2, 2013).

[580] Id. at 4.

[581] Id. at 5.

[582] 47 U.S.C. § 230(f)(2).

[583] Bedwell v. City of Big Spring, Texas and Other Unknown Parties, 2007 WL 4788582 (W. D. Tex., Dec. 20, 2012).

[584] Allen v. Sexual Offender Board, 2011 WL 3915956 (Mass.Super., April 13, 2011).

§ 6.10   TRANSBORDER TORTS

In American society, tort serves as the default regulator of safety and economic power. The strong administrative state in Europe is an alternative to a strong cybertort regime. In Sweden, claimants look to insurance first and to torts second. Additionally, in Sweden, the tort system serves as a backup for those few individuals, such as foreigners, not covered by the nation's social security compensation agency, also called the *Forsakringskassan*. In Europe, cybertorts are patrolled by consumer regulatory agencies, not private litigants. The United States is the only country connected to the Internet that depends upon the tort system to fulfill public law functions. The countries of the European Union, for example, arm consumer regulatory agencies with roving powers to protect privacy and other rights of persons outside their profession or trade.

(A) Privacy–Based Litigation

Actions that do not invade privacy rights in the United States violate Eurozone privacy rules.[585] Google was assessed a fine of one hundred thousand euros in France for its Street View filming practices. "In November 2010 the UK Information Commissioner's Office [official website] found that Google had committed a 'significant breach "of the Data Protection Act and required that Google delete the payload data it collected in the UK and implement employee training on privacy principles, security awareness and the Data Protection Act."[586] Google has also been investigated in Canada, Australia, and Spain for allegations that its Street View filming violated consumers' privacy.[587]

(B) Cross–Border Internet Libel Law

Cyberlibel cases are just beginning to be filed in foreign courts. Libel tourism is a term that refers to U.S. publishers and writers being sued in foreign courts where defamation rules are akin to strict liability.[588] In 2003, Forbes Magazine was the defendant in a United Kingdom lawsuit arising out of an article they published about Boris Berezovsky, entitled "Godfather of the Kremlin." The *Forbes* article: "described the climate of violence that surrounded Russia's transition from a planned to a capitalist economy. It said that Berezovsky had been investigated in connection with the murder of Vladislav Listiev. It also said that Nikolai Glouchkov, a Berezovsky ally and an executive of the Russian airline Aeroflot, had been convicted of theft."[589] The United Kingdom's House of Lords ruled that the case could be decided under English libel law rather than Russian or U.S. law.[590] "The English court ruled that under

---

[585] Michael L. Rustad & Sandra R. Paulson, Monitoring Employee e-mail and Internet Usage: Avoiding the Omniscient Electronic Sweatshop: Insights from Europe, 7 U. PA. J. LAB. & EMP. L. 829, 904 (2005) (concluding that U.S. companies that monitor e-mail and Internet Communications violate European data privacy law and human rights law).

[586] Id.

[587] Jerry Votava, European Privacy Regulators Express New Concern Over Google Street View Data Collection, JURIST (May 3, 2012).

[588] Samuel A. Abady and Harvey Silvergate, 'Libel Tourism" and the War on Terror, BOSTON GLOBE (Nov. 7, 2006).

[589] Forbes, Berezovsky vs. Forbes (March 31, 2003), http://www.forbes.com/forbes/2003/0331/022.html (last visited July 13, 2013).

[590] Id.

English libel law the article's description of the Listiev case was tantamount to stating that Berezovsky was guilty of murder and that he was a gangland leader running a mafia-style operation."[591] The first Internet-related jurisdiction case for India, for example, was *SMC Pneumatics (India) Pvt. Ltd. v. Jogesh Kwatra*.[592] An Italian court ruled in favor of Wikipedia in a libel suit filed by a past associate of the former Italian Prime Minister, Silvio Berlusconi. The court applied reasoning similar to Section 230 of the CDA. It ruled that Wikipedia's Foundation could not be liable for libelous postings made by third parties.[593]

(1) Reforming UK Internet Defamation Law

During the first fifteen years of the World Wide Web, forum shopping was ubiquitous in cyberlibel cases and the United Kingdom was perceived as a favorable forum for plaintiffs. Recently, the UK has reformed its defamation law and updated it for the Internet. Section 14 abolishes the Slander of Women Act of 1891.[594] The United Kingdom's 2013 Defamation Act creates special rule for website operators. The 2013 UK defamation statute has the following features:

> Includes a requirement for claimants to show that they have suffered serious harm before suing for defamation.
>
> Removes the current presumption in favour of a jury trial.
>
> Introduces a defence of 'responsible publication on matters of public interest.'
>
> Provides increased protection to operators of websites that host user-generated content, providing they comply with the procedure to enable the complainant to resolve disputes directly with the author of the material concerned.
>
> Introduces new statutory defences of truth and honest opinion to replace the common law defences of justification and fair comment.[595]

The new statute creates a defense for website operators when a third party makes a defamatory statement.[596] Section Five of the 2013 Defamation Act addresses website operator liability for defamation for third party postings.[597] The Defamation Act of 2013 contemplates that the Secretary of State may promulgate regulations to:

---

[591] Id.

[592] "India's first case of cyber defamation, the High Court of Delhi assumed jurisdiction over a matter where a corporation was being defamed through e-mail messages and granted an ex-parte injunction. In that case, an employee, Kwatra was sending defamatory, derogatory, and vulgar messages about the company and its managing director. This case was the first one in which an Indian court exercised jurisdiction over cyber defamation." GEORGE B. DELTA AND JEFFREY H. MATSUURA. LAW OF THE INTERNET, § 3.04 Foreign Principles of Jurisdiction.

[593] "On June 20, 2013, the Civil Court of Rome ruled—unsurprisingly—that the Wikimedia Foundation is to be considered a hosting provider rather than a content provider, however, and thus could not be held liable for articles drafted by individual contributors." Wikipedia Prevails in Italian Lawsuit Brought by Berlusconi Ally Over 'Defamatory' Wikipedia Article, TNW, the Next Web (June 27, 2013), http://thenextweb.com/eu/2013/06/27/wikimedia-prevails-in-italian-lawsuit-brought-by-longtime-berlusconi-ally-over-inaccurate-wikipedia-entry/.

[594] Defamation Act of 2013, Id. at § 14, http://www.legislation.gov.uk/ukpga/2013/26/section/14.

[595] Summary of the Defamation Act 2013, http://services.parliament.uk/bills/2012–13/defamation.html (last visited May 15, 2013).

[596] Defamation Act 2013, § 5(2) (It is a defence for the operator to show that it was not the operator who posted the statement on the website).

[597] Id. at § 5(1).

make provisions as to the action required to be taken by an operator of a website in response to a notice of complaint (which may in particular include action relating to the identity or contact details of the person who posted the statement and action relating to its removal); (b) make provision specifying a time limit for the taking of any such action; (c) make provision conferring on the court a discretion to treat action taken after the expiry of a time limit as having been taken before the expiry; and make any other provision.[598]

Parliament promulgated two exceptions to the website operator's defense. First, the website operator cannot assert this defense for third party postings where the third party cannot be identified.[599] The statute states that it is possible to identify a person only if the complainant has sufficient information to bring a claim.[600] Second, the defense is not available where the complainant (typically the victim of libel) has given a notice of a complaint and failed to respond to the complaint.[601] Section 5(5)(b) contemplates regulations for time limits for the takedown notice provisions of the statute.[602]

Section 6 of the updated UK defamation statute specifies that a notice of complaint is a notice which—"(a) specifies the complainant's name, (b) sets out the statement concerned and explains why it is defamatory of the complainant, (c) specifies where on the website the statement was posted, and (d) contains such other information as may be specified in regulations."[603] In addition, the website operator defense for secondary tort liability is not available "if the claimant shows that the operator of the website has acted with malice in relation to the posting of the statement concerned."[604] Section 12 of the new statute states that the operator's defense "is not defeated by reason only of the fact that the operator of the website moderates the statements posted on it by others."[605] The new statute does not impose liability for frivolous takedown notices. Section 13 contemplates that courts may order websites to remove defamatory postings or non-parties to stop distributing objectionable content.[606]

The 2013 reforms to UK's defamation law closely track Section 521(c) of the Digital Millennium Copyright Act. Like the UK's takedown policy for defamation, the DMCA requires the complaint to identify the copyrighted work claimed to be infringing. The UK statute's requirement that the complaint specify where on the website the defamatory material is loaded is similar to the DMCA's requirement that the copyright owner specify information reasonably sufficient to permit the service provider to locate the material. Similarly, the UK requirement that the complaint explain why a statement is defamatory is similar to a DMCA complaint who must attest that "the website posting or use of the material in the manner complained of is not authorized by the copyright owner, its agent, or the law."[607] The UK defamation act is at odds with

---

[598] Id. at § 5(5).

[599] Id. at § 5(3)(a).

[600] Id. at § 4.

[601] Id. at § 5(3)(b)(c).

[602] Id. at § 5(b).

[603] Id. at § 6(a)–(d).

[604] Id. at § 11.

[605] Id. at § 12.

[606] Id. at § 13.

[607] 17 U.S.C. § 521(c).

U.S. law, which does not impose an obligation for ongoing defamation or other torts.[608] Nevertheless, the U.S. recognizes a notice and take down obligation for copyright infringement under the Digital Millennium Copyright Act. All of the EU Member States have a notice and takedown policy under the Electronic Commerce Directive.

(2) Harmonization of Internet Libel Law

No foreign countries impose constitutional limitations on tort actions such as defamation, false light privacy, and the intentional infliction of emotional distress. *The Wall Street Journal,* for example, was the defendant in a United Kingdom lawsuit over its republication of an April Fool's Day prank press release disseminated by Harrods Department Store on its website and print editions.[609]The newspaper issued a mock press release stating it planned to "float" its department store by building a ship version of the store and offered to sell shares in the venture. Upon learning the announcement had been a prank, the *Journal* countered with a story stating: "If Harrods, the British luxury retailer, ever goes public, investors would be wise to question its every disclosure."[610] Harrods, and its then-owner, Mohamed Al–Fayed, filed a libel suit in London's High Court of Justice.

It was not until 1994 that a plaintiff anywhere in the world prevailed in an Internet tort case. In *Rindos v. Hardwick*,[611] the University of Western Australia denied acting head of the Archaeology department, Dr. David Rindos, tenure. Gil Hardwick, an anthropologist, posted a rabble-rousing statement supporting the university's tenure decision and falsely accusing Dr. Rindos of being a pedophile. In addition, Hardwick stated that Dr. Rindos conducted anthropological research harming aboriginal peoples. Australia was the first country where a plaintiff was successful in recouping damages in an Internet-related case. Although an Australian court assessed this first damages award in an Internet tort case, the vast majority of subsequent cybertorts have been litigated in America.

Davison v Habeeb[612] was a case where plaintiffs sued three ISPs, including AOL, for allowing access to the Internet to those defaming them. In that case, the court applied English common law principles finding that the ISPs were mere conduits or facilitators, analogous to the postal service. The England and Wales High Court of Justice, Chancery Division held that Google Inc. was not liable for libel by hosting on its blogger web publishing service an article about a former intelligence services officer. Former UK intelligence officer, Andrea Davison, contended that Google, as owner of blogger, was liable for an article that linked her to a criminal conspiracy that included theft and fraud. The court found "no realistic prospect of the claimant establishing that the notification of her complaint fixed the fifth defendant [Google] with actual knowledge of unlawful activity or information, or made it aware of facts or circumstances from which it would have been apparent to it that the activity or information was unlawful."[613]

---

[608] 17 U.S.C. § 230.

[609] Dow Jones & Co., Inc. v. Harrods, Ltd., 237 F. Supp. 2d 394 (S.D. N.Y. 2002).

[610] Id.

[611] No. 940164 (Sup. Ct. W. Austl. March 31, 1994).

[612] [2011] EWHC 3031 (QB). Bunt v Tilley [2007] 1 WLR 1243.

[613] Id.

Dow Jones & Company, Inc. v. Gutnick,[614] illustrated the clash of different defamation regimes in the U.S. and Australia. In October 2000, the online edition of *Barron's Magazine*, a Dow Jones publication, posted an article "Unholy Gains" about Joseph Gutnick's questionable financial activities. Gutnick filed a defamation lawsuit in a Victoria, Australia court contending the story was untrue. The High Court held that *Dow Jones* could be sued in Victoria, which was the place of publication. Dow Jones argued that the Australian High Court should adopt the U.S. "single publication rule," which would allow the plaintiff to file only a single defamation case in New Jersey, the place of publication. The tort of defamation in Australia "focuses upon publications causing damage to reputation. It is a tort of strict liability, in the sense that a defendant may be liable even though no injury to reputation was intended and the defendant acted with reasonable care."[615]

The majority of the U.S. states have adopted some version of the single publication rule.[616] In contrast, Australia rejects the single publication rule and imposes liability standards making it easier to win defamation lawsuits. Australia considers defamation to be a strict liability tort, whereas the U.S. considers it a fault-based tort. The *Dow Jones* case ultimately settled for $44,000 and legal fees in November of 2004.[617] This decision leaves U.S. media companies—including social networking sites—liable for defamation in any jurisdiction where the content downloads. In 2013, the United Kingdom enacted the single publication rule.[618] *Gutnick* is a case study of clashing legal approaches about rules of jurisdiction and substantive tort law rules. The rise of the Internet ensures that different legal cultures will approach the same tort action differently.

---

[614] HCA 56 (Austl. 2002).

[615] Id.

[616] Id.

[617] David Rolph, "The Message, Not the Medium: Defamation, Publication and the Internet in Dow Jones & Co. v. Gutnick" (2002) 24 SYDNEY L. REV. 263.

[618] "This section applies if a person—

(A) publishes a statement to the public ("the first publication"), and

(B) subsequently publishes (whether or not to the public) that statement or a statement which is substantially the same.

(2) In subsection (1) "publication to the public" includes publication to a section of the public.

(3) For the purposes of section 4A of the Limitation Act 1980 (time limit for actions for defamation etc.) any cause of action against the person for defamation in respect of the subsequent publication is to be treated as having accrued on the date of the first publication.

(4) This section does not apply in relation to the subsequent publication if the manner of that publication is materially different from the manner of the first publication.

(5) In determining whether the manner of a subsequent publication is materially different from the manner of the first publication, the matters to which the court may have regard include (amongst other matters)—

(A) the level of prominence that a statement is given;

(B) the extent of the subsequent publication.

(6) Where this section applies—

(A) it does not affect the court's discretion under section 32A of the Limitation Act 1980 (discretionary exclusion of time limit for actions for defamation etc.), and

(B) the reference in subsection (1)(A) of that section to the operation of section 4A of that Act is a reference to the operation of section 4A together with this section." Defamation Act (2013), § 7.

(3) Jurisdiction and Discovery

Accessing data located on web servers in the clouds raises new challenges for cybertort litigators when the data is stored outside the United States. A litigator discusses how the Internet has changed discovery and the meaning of cross-border subpoenas:

> We have reached the point where some of us do not know where in the "cloud" our computer backup files reside. There are drive-through windows at fast food restaurants in the Midwest where orders are taken by call centers in the Southeast. We fly from Boston to Chicago, *for the day*, and stop along the way to eat dinner at the airport in Philadelphia. In short, nothing stops at a state border anymore.[619]

One of the problems is that civil procedure is still predicated upon territorial sovereignty and has not been updated for cloud computing where the location of data or servers may be outside the jurisdiction.

(4) EU Service Provider Liability

European service providers do not enjoy the near absolute immunity of their American counterparts. Although they have no duty to monitor content, they have a duty to remove tortious, infringing, or other illegal content. Congress has devised separate liability rules for ISPs for tort and copyright liability and has not enacted ISP rules as to trademark infringement or other illegal content. It is good to be an ISP in the United States compared to the duties imposed on ISPs in Europe to remove illegal content once they have notice. The Electronic Commerce Directive promulgated rules for content. The European Commission adopted the Electronic Commerce Directive to establish an Internal Market framework for electronic commerce.[620] The Electronic Commerce Directive "establishes harmonised rules on issues such as the transparency and information requirements for online service providers, commercial communications, electronic contracts and limitations of liability of intermediary service providers"[621] The Directive establishes a safe haven regime for hosting providers. Service providers, however, must remove tortious or other objectionable conduct without notice.[622] Nevertheless, service providers have no duty to affirmatively monitor third party content on their websites or other services.[623] A UK court ruled that Google could be liable for failing to remove libelous postings expeditiously after receiving notice.[624]

---

[619] Andrew Schulman A Practical Guide to Organizing a Bus in RI (MCLE) § II-16.1(2013).

[620] Directive 2000/31/EC of the European Parliament and of the Council of 8 June 2000 on certain legal aspects of information society services, in particular electronic commerce, in the Internal Market ("E–Commerce Directive").

[621] Id.

[622] Id. at art. 14.

[623] Id. at art. 15.

[624] Lisa Carroll, Google Must Act Quickly on Libellous Blogger posts, Says Appeal Court

Landmark Ruling That Tech Giant Could be Liable for Comments if it Has Been Notified of Them and Failed to Remove Them, THE GUARDIAN (Feb. 14, 2013) ("A conservative member of parliament,Tamiz, had initiated proceedings against Google Inc and Google UK after the company failed to promptly remove remarks about him on the London Muslim blog in July 2011. Tamiz subsequently settled his claim against Google UK but obtained permission to serve his claim in a London court against Google Inc.").

(5) Negligence

Louis Vuitton, Christian Dior Couture, Givenchy, Guerlain, Malletier and other French companies prevailed in a negligence-based action against eBay in the Paris Court of Commerce. The French designer's complaint contended that eBay and eBay International violated "French tort law by negligently broadcasting listings posted by the parties offering" counterfeit goods.[625] The companies also contended that eBay interfered with their distribution of goods in France by allowing listings for counterfeited goods. In 2008, the Paris Court of Commerce ruled that eBay and eBay International AG were "liable for failing to prevent the sale of counterfeit items on its website and traded on the plaintiffs' brand names, thus interfering with their businesses.[626] The court awarded plaintiffs 38.6 million euros and issued an injunction with daily fines of up to 100,000 euros for all sales of perfumes bearing the designers trade names. The court later reduced this award, but upheld eBay's liability for negligently failing to prevent listings for counterfeits.[627]

(C) Products Liability Directive

Europe adopted a strict liability-based directive in the 1980s.[628] Consumers throughout the European Union have the same level of legal protection and remedies for defective products. Article 1 of the Directive defines "product" to encompass "all movables, with the exception of primary agricultural products and game, even though incorporated into another movable or into an immovable."[629] The purpose of the Directive is "to protect the physical well-being and property of the consumer, the defectiveness of the product should be determined by reference not to its fitness for use but to the lack of the safety which the public at large is entitled to expect."[630] The Directive recognizes product misuse, "which is not reasonable under the circumstances."[631] The Directive also permits the defendant to introduce exonerating circumstances if the consumer is also at fault as well as contributory negligence to either reduce or exclude liability.[632] Furthermore, the Directive recognizes compensation for wrongful death as well as personal injury recovery that also includes non-economic damages or pain and suffering, but not punitive damages.[633]

Article 4 of the Directive closely tracks Section 402A of the Restatement of Torts setting forth the *prima facie* case: "The injured person shall be required to prove the damage, the defect and the causal relationship between defect and damage."[634] Article 5 adopts the doctrine of joint and several liability where there are multiple defendants

---

[625] eBay SEC Q-1 Filing (July 19, 2013).

[626] Id.

[627] Id.

[628] 85/374/EEC, Directive of the Council of the European Communities of 25 July 1985 on the approximation of the laws, regulations, and administrative provisions of the member states concerning liability for defective products.

[629] Id. at art. 1.

[630] Id. at prefatory whereas clauses.

[631] Id.

[632] Id.

[633] Id.

[634] Id. at art. 4.

in a European defective products case.[635] Under the European product liability directive:

1. A product is defective when it does not provide the safety, which a person is entitled to expect, considering all circumstances, including:

(a) the presentation of the product;

(b) the use to which it could reasonably be expected that the product would be put;

(c) the time when the product was put into circulation.

2. A product shall not be considered defective for the sole reason that a better product is subsequently put into circulation.[636]

Article 8 recognizes the doctrine of contribution for producers.[637] Article 9 recognizes recovery for:

(a) damage caused by death or by personal injuries;

(b) damage to, or destruction of, any item of property other than the defective product itself, with a lower threshold of 500 ECU, provided that the item of property:

(i) is of a type ordinarily intended for private use or consumption, and

(ii) was used by the injured person mainly for his own private use or consumption.[638]

Products liability in Europe is predicated upon strict liability whereas recently the United States is moving towards a negligence-based regime.[639] Traditional best practices to limit tort liability will not work in a global information-based economy. In addition, preventive law that works well in the United States or in another single country may not necessarily work in other countries, which do not share the assumption that service providers work in a liability-free zone.[640] Differences in language, culture and norms require e-businesses, like other global innovators to be flexible and incorporate iterative learning in their project management.[641] Lawyers representing global e-businesses need to develop policies to minimize torts on multiple sites. E-businesses must tailor privacy policies for cross-cultural collocations and that is the subject of Chapter Seven.

---

[635] Id. at art. 5.

[636] Id. at art. 6.

[637] Id. at art. 8.

[638] Id. at art. 7.

[639] RESTATEMENT (THIRD) TORTS: PRODUCTS LIABILITY.

[640] The theme that solutions working in a single location may not work for one dispersed across many sites around the world was a theme in a recent Harvard Business Review study of global innovation management. Keeley Wilson and Yves L. Doz, 10 Rules for Managing Global Innovation, HARV. BUS. REV. 85 (Oct. 2012).

[641] Id. at 86.

Chapter 7

INTERNET–RELATED PRIVACY

§ 7.1 OVERVIEW OF ONLINE PRIVACY

> As a result of the ubiquitous nature of the Internet, data rarely stays in only one jurisdiction. Rather, the Internet, social media, and Cloud computing cross national borders, allowing data to be transmitted to any location in the world. As such, the privacy problem is not restricted to any one jurisdiction. Indeed, the wonder of modern technology is the ability of people to access information and entertainment from virtually anywhere, and to send information globally. Thus, one would expect nations of the world to focus on a global standard of protection, and to harmonize existing laws.

Christopher Wolf and Winston Maxwell[1]

This chapter examines the most significant online privacy issues including the problem of transborder data protection, where the legal norms are in flux. In the late 1900s and early twentieth-century, privacy-based torts, along with remedies for misuse of novel technologies such as "instantaneous photographs," were being born. In the new millennium, American society is once again undergoing a technological revolution of great consequence. This time, America is evolving from a durable commodities-based economy to one based on the licensing of software, intellectual property, and other intangibles. Cisco Systems regards privacy as "a global issue without national borders and policymakers around the world are struggling to determine the best way to protect consumers' online."[2] Cyberspace privacy laws are in flux as legislatures attempt to accommodate to the omnipresent global Internet. Notably, Chief Justice William Rehnquist commented, "We are placed in the uncomfortable position of not knowing who might have access to our personal and business e-mails, our medical and financial records, or our cordless and cellular telephone conversations."[3] In 2012, the FTC entered into a $22.5 million settlement with Google, requiring the social networking giant to implement comprehensive privacy programs.

Apple was the target of a large number of class action lawsuits arising out of Apple-approved apps that collected personally identifiable information from iPhone, iPad, and iPod Touch users. The class action charged that Apple violated users' privacy by transmitting this information to third parties. Internet privacy laws are in flux as legislatures attempt to accommodate an ever-changing Internet. In June of 2013, President Obama acknowledged that "highly classified surveillance programs [were] necessary to protect Americans at the price of only 'modest encroachments' on personal

---

[1] Christopher Wolf and Winston Maxwell, So Close, Yet So Far Apart: The EU and U.S. Visions of a New Privacy Framework, 26 ANTITRUST ABA 8 (2012).

[2] Cisco Systems, Defining the Issue: Privacy, http://www.cisco.com/web/about/gov/issues/privacy.html (last visited Sept. 23, 2013).

[3] Bartnicki v. Vopper, 532 U.S. 514, 541 (2001) (Rehnquist, C.J, dissenting).

privacy."[4] Prism, the National Security Agency's program is "an Internet surveillance program collects data from online providers including e-mail, chat services, videos, photos, stored data, file transfers, video conferencing and log-in. The National Security Agency ("NSA")[5], relying upon the U.S. Patriot Act routinely collected phone records of millions of cell phone users."[6] The NSA obtained hundreds of millions of U.S. phone records. Under the Bush Administration, the government also engaged in widespread database creation and access to phone records. Google, Facebook Apple, and other Internet moguls are cooperative in NSA's PRISM program that monitors cyberspace.[7] The NSA invested billions of dollars to fund projects such as supercomputers to crack encryption and digital scrambling in its classified program, Bullrun.[8]

Congress must update federal privacy laws to improve protection of digital communication "where cell phones, e-mail and online social networking have come to rule daily life."[9] The Internet has lifted the veil of privacy, where the division between front stage and back stage has melted away. Sociologist Erving Goffman's dramaturgical theory employed theatre as a model for understanding the presentation of self as divided into the front stage and the back stage. Goffman's dramaturgical studies were about how waiters, hospital staff, sex workers, and other service providers separated their "front stage," publicly visible, actions from "back stage" or hidden behaviors.[10] Backstage tweets may express unfiltered thoughts that are normally only observed by close companions and confidents. For millions of users of social media, the boundaries between front stage and back stage have melted away. Jeffrey Rosen, a leading privacy scholar, describes how the dichotomy between front stage and back stage blurs when we adopt a "self-conscious formality" that melds the formal front stage with the informal back stage.[11]

Marshall McLuhan's argument was that the "medium is the message." Social media postings about a consumer's rating, dating, and mating confirms the wisdom of Marshall McLuhan's observation that "publication is a self-invasion of privacy."[12] McLuhan, a founder of media ecology, wrote about how new technologies create an "extension of us" on a grand scale. Facebook has become an obsession, permitting narcissists to broadcast their most private thoughts twenty-four hours every day. For

---

[4] Peter Nicholas & Sioban Gorman, Obama Defends Surveillance: In Rare Acknowledgement of Antiterror Tactics, President Cites 'Modest Encroachments' in Name of Security, WALL ST. J. (June 8–9, 2013) at 1.

[5] The National Security Agency ("NSA") formed in 1952 as a separately organized agency within the Department of Defense." The NSA has two identified missions: (1) the Signals Intelligence ("SIGINT") mission, to "collect, process, analyze, and disseminate SIGINT information for national foreign intelligence and counterintelligence purposes and to support military operations" and (2) the Information Assurance mission, to "confront the formidable challenge of preventing foreign adversaries from gaining access to sensitive or classified national security information." The NSA/CSS Mission, NSA/CSS, http://www.nsa.gov/about/mission/index.shtml (June 13, 2013).

[6] Charlie Savage Edward Watt & Peter Baker, U.S. Confirms That It Gathers Online Data Overseas, THE N.Y. TIMES (June 6, 2013).

[7] Id.

[8] Nicole Perlroth, Jeff Larson, and Scott Shane, N.S.A. Able to Foil Basic Safeguard of Privacy on Web, THE N.Y. TIMES (Sept. 5, 2013) (citing N.S.A. memorandum confirming that the agency spent billions to "break widely used Internet technologies").

[9] Editorial, The End of Privacy? Federal Laws Are Too Weak for New Forms of Surveillance of Our Plugged-in-Lives, N.Y. TIMES 10 (July 15, 2012).

[10] ERVING GOFFMAN, THE PRESENTATION OF SELF IN EVERYDAY LIFE (1959).

[11] JEFFREY ROSEN, THE NAKED CROWD 186 (2004).

[12] MARSHALL MCLUHAN, UNDERSTANDING MEDIA: THE EXTENSIONS OF MAN (1964).

social network sites, the greatest privacy threats are from self-disclosure and disclosures by friends, families, or social network contacts:

> Another reason why privacy expectations directed at social media companies tend to be misguided is that in the social media context, it is rarely the social media company that invades your privacy. What haunts people is typically user-generated content, i.e., information that people themselves, their friends, and other social media users upload. If other social media users disseminate offensive information, you may have claims against them under tort laws against libel and invasion of privacy. But, social media platform providers are not directly responsible for user generated privacy invasions. They can claim broad exemptions from contributory liability under existing laws that were intended to protect Internet service providers.[13]

In an era where cameras are standard features of mobile telephones, new websites such as People of Walmart.com have appeared. People of Wal-Mart has the feel of a Fellini-grotesque movie with its collection of grossly overweight, strangely dressed, or surrealistic shoppers at Wal-Mart.[14] These online pictures, taken by fellow customers, are the modern equivalent of Tod Browning's 1932 movie, *Freaks*, featuring bearded women and conjoined twins. Millions on social media sites such as Facebook and Twitter view People of Wal-Mart. The Wal-Mart customers who are the target of ridicule by millions of social media users have no right to demand that their pictures be taken down. At present, there is no right to forget. Social media sites' entire revenue model is based upon the commoditization of the self from users' widespread self-disclosure.

A federal court described a new GPS application, entitled Girls Around Me: the 'Stalker App:"

> The Girls Around Me app, which surfaced in March 2012, represents a highly disturbing manifestation of geolocation technology. The program drew data from the web service "Foursquare," through which users got "virtual rewards" (such as online badges) for checking in at various public establishments identified via their smartphone's GPS location software. Their location, in turn, would be broadcast to other users in an effort to both promote these establishments and create opportunities for social interaction. The Girls Around Me app correlated this geolocation data with personal identifiers publicly available on Facebook to perform an unusual function: by clicking on the Girls Around Me icon (a James Bond film-like silhouette against the backdrop of a radar screen), the user was presented with a map showing photographs and personal details of young women located nearby, including their names, ages, marital status, dates of birth and interests. After a prominent blogger wrote about the Girls Around Me app, it made national news, and the growing infamy led to its withdrawal. Yet, as the developers of the app noted in a defense of their efforts, the app did nothing more

---

[13] Lothar Determann: Social Media Privacy: A Dozen Myths and Facts, STANFORD TECHNOLOGY LAW. REVIEW. ¶ 1 (2012).

[14] "The People of Walmart invites users to post photos of shoppers with a questionable sense of style: bad hairdos, excessive tattoos or ill-fitting clothing are particular targets." Sarah LeMasson, People of Walmart Among Most Searched Websites, The TELEGRAPH (Sept. 4, 2009).

than aggregate (though in a highly distasteful manner) geolocation and personal information already available to the public.[15]

Users are required by the terms of service to indemnify Facebook and pay their own attorney's fees if a lawsuit is brought against the social media site for actions, content or information posted by these third parties. Foreign users of Facebook "consent to having [their] personal data transferred to and processed in the United States."[16] One observer characterized Facebook's revisions to their TOU agreement: "We Can Do Anything We Want with Your Content. Forever."[17] Companies have new legal obligations to comply with European Union and other country's privacy laws because data often involves personally identifiable information

§ 7.2   OVERVIEW OF THE LACK OF ONLINE PRIVACY

(A) No Privacy in Internet Searches

The Internet is an open bulletin board; there is no privacy for Internet activities by consumers. By June of 2009, "Americans conducted 13 billion searches a month on the Internet."[18] "Internet users have no expectation of privacy in the to/from addresses of their messages or the IP addresses of the websites they visit because they should know that this information is provided to and used by Internet service providers for the specific purpose of directing the routing of information."[19] Americans have no privacy information in Internet subscriber information or in IP addresses.[20] Websites publish mug shots of persons arrested, but never convicted of crimes and demand a large fee to remove a given photograph. The Internet Crime Complaint Center reports that it has received hundreds of complaints from individuals:

> claiming they located their mug shots on 20 different websites, all of which allegedly use similar business practices. Some victims reported they were juveniles at the time of the arrests and their records were sealed. Therefore, their information should not be available to the public. Others stated the information posted on the sites was either incorrect or blatantly false. Complainants who requested to have their mug shot removed, had to provide a copy of their driver's license, court record and other personal identifying information. However, providing such information puts those at risk for identify theft. Complainants were also subject to paying a fee to have their mug shot removed. Although they paid the fee, some of the mug shots were not removed. If they were removed, the mug shots appeared on similar websites. If the victim threatened to report the

---

[15] In re Smartphone Geolocation Data Application, 2013 U.S. Dist. LEXIS 62605 (May 1, 2013) at *31.

[16] Facebook, Terms of Use, Id. at. 16.

[17] Daniel Nemet–Nejat, Hey, That's My Persona!: Exploring the Right of Publicity for Blogs and Online Social Networks, 33 COLUM. J.L. & ARTS 113, 129 (2009).

[18] Scott Canon, Google Finds Itself With Competition from Bing, KANSAS CITY STAR (June 8, 2009) at 1–A.

[19] United States v. Forrester, 512 F.3d 500, 510 (9th Cir.2008),

[20] See also United States v. Bynum, 604 F.3d 161 (4th Cir.2010) (no privacy interest in internet subscriber information); United States v. Qing Li, 2008 WL 789899, *4–5 (S.D.Cal.2008) (Fourth Amendment does not bar government from obtaining destination IP addresses under the SCA).

websites for unlawful practice, the websites' owners threatened to escalate the damaging information against the victim.[21]

In the bricks and mortar world, mug shots are generally restricted to use by law enforcement, though publicizing photographs of sex offenders and other criminals is a recent trend. Nevertheless, the business model of distributing mug shots of those merely arrested stigmatizes individuals beyond local publication. Future employers, who routinely screen job applicants by doing Google searches will screen out individuals because the mug shots are so easily available.

(B) No Privacy Rights Against Data Dredgers

Scott McNealy, the former CEO of Sun Microsystems, stated, "You have zero privacy anyway. Get over it."[22] Two out of three Internet users utilize Google's search engine. Google collects information by planting cookies when users visit websites or interact with the service's ads and contents.[23] In *In re DoubleClick Privacy Litigation*,[24] the federal district court found no cause of action in favor of Internet users whose personal information such as names, e-mail addresses, telephone numbers, searches performed and the defendant's cookies were systematically collecting other personal information. The court dismissed all federal and state claims finding it implausible that website visitors did not consent to the use of cookies.[25] Consumers' names, e-mail addresses, telephone numbers and credit card accounts, among other personal information, may be gathered. Google also harvests data through premium services such as its ad keywords, social media (Google+), e-mail, googlets, and search requests. If a consumer creates a Google profile, for example, the service will distribute a publicly visible Google Profile, which may include one's name and photo.

On March 1, 2012, Google revised its privacy policy, which now permits the company to collect device and mobile network information including the hardware model, operating system version, unique device identifiers, and the consumer's phone number. Each time a consumer accesses a location-enabled Google service; the service may collect and process information about her actual location.[26] This information includes telephone numbers, calling-party numbers, forwarding numbers, the time and date of calls, duration of calls, SMS routing information and types of calls.[27] Google is able to store search queries by using cookies in order to identify the consumer's browser or account. Each time a consumer accesses a location-enabled Google service, the service may collect and process information about your actual location, like GPS signals sent by a mobile device.[28] Google employs "various technologies to determine location, such as sensor data from your device that may, provide information on nearby

---

[21]   Internet   Crime   Complaint   Center   (IC3),   Scam   Alert,   June   13,   2013, http://www.ic3.gov/media/2013/130619.aspx (last visited July 13, 2013).

[22] Polly Springer, Sun on Privacy: 'Get Over It.' WIRED (Jan. 26, 1999).

[23] Google, Policies & Privacy (March 1, 2012).

[24] 154 F. Supp. 2d 497, 500 (S.D. N.Y. 2001).

[25] Cookies "are computer programs commonly used by websites to store useful information such as usernames, passwords, and preferences, making it easier for users to access Web pages in an efficient manner. [The DoubleClick] cookies collect . . . [personal] 'information such as names, e-mail addresses, home and business addresses, telephone numbers, searches performed on the Internet, Web pages or sites visited on the Internet . . .'" Id. at 502.

[26] Google, Policies & Privacy, Id.

[27] Id.

[28] Id.

Wi–Fi access points and cell towers."[29] In addition, Google is able use these identifiers each time a consumer identifies with one of its partners.[30] A federal court in *In re Smartphone Geolocation Data Application*,[31] described how GPS affects privacy:

> One important aspect of smartphone technology is the ability of these devices to identify, on real time, their geographic location, which data can be shared with certain programs and providers to enable advanced functions. At present, three techniques are used to generate this information. The collection of cell-site data— the identification of the radio cell tower or towers nearest to the device—is the oldest geolocation technology and the one at issue in this case. Cell-site location is arguably the least precise of the three methods currently used, though that precision can be substantially enhanced through triangulation of signals from multiple towers.
>
> Global Positioning System ("GPS") data is a technique by which radio signals are received by the smartphone from a system of satellites in geosynchronous orbit and interpreted by programs to provide highly accurate location data. Wireless geolocation operates by comparing the access points used by the smartphone to connect to the Internet against a database of known router locations. Depending on the quality of the information in the database, this method, though similar to cell-site location, can be far more accurate because wireless transmissions have a shorter range than cellular transmissions. Additional emerging geolocation technologies, including Bluetooth beacons, reportedly have the potential to pinpoint the location of a phone to a matter of inches.[32]

(C) No Privacy in Social Networks

It is increasingly true that Internet users have inadequate privacy protection when making self-disclosures on social media websites. Over the past few years, a quiet revolution has begun, as many social networking sites ("SNSs") require users to enter into two kinds of contractual relationships, terms of service agreements and privacy policies, as a condition for accessing their websites. For hundreds of millions of consumers, the terms of use cabin and constrain their right to privacy. After a consumer has registered or accessed a site, SNSs reserve the right to modify substantive terms, sometimes without notifying users. An SNS, website, or other brick-and-mortar company can reduce transaction costs by using a predispute mandatory arbitration clause because it need not defend lawsuits in state or federal court but in a forum where it can choose the arbitral provider and rules to govern the dispute. In the first empirical study of social media sites' terms of use agreements, the researchers found nearly one in four SNSs in the sample incorporated some form of arbitration clause either in the terms of service agreement or in the privacy policy (37 of 157 or

---

[29] Id.

[30] Id.

[31] In re Smartphone Geolocation Data Application, 2013 U.S. Dist. LEXIS 62605 (E.D. N.Y. May 1, 2013).

[32] Id. at *20–*22.

nearly one in four agreements.[33] Lothar Determann uncovered twelve misconceptions about privacy on social network websites:

Myth 1: You Have Privacy Rights Against Social Media Companies

Myth 2: You Own Personal Data About You

Myth 3: European Privacy Laws Are Better, And The United States Has To Catch Up

Myth 4: Social Media Companies Threaten Your Privacy

Myth 5: Advertisers Threaten Your Privacy

Myth 6: Law Enforcement Should Be Kept Out Of Social Media In The Interest Of Better Privacy Protection

Myth 7: Technologies Threaten Your Privacy

Myth 8: You Have A Right To Be Forgotten

Myth 9: You Have A Right To Remain Anonymous On The Internet

Myth 10: Social Networks Are Not—But Should Be—Subject To Laws

Myth 11: Social Media Usage Isn't, Can't Be, Or Shouldn't Be Regulated By Employers

Myth 12: Consumers Care About Privacy[34]

Facebook's current privacy policy consigns "certain personal information, such as a user's name, profile pictures, current city, gender, networks, and pages that user is a 'fan' of (now, pages that user 'likes') is deemed "publicly available information."[35] To date, the United States has not developed specialized legislature addressing privacy on social network websites. Private ordering, as opposed to legislation, enables Facebook to develop an evolving privacy policy advancing its business model.[36] Facebook, for example, has extensive guidelines for personalization, which is a growing trend on social media and other sites. Facebook's privacy policy explains its personalization guidelines:

> To join the instant personalization program, a potential partner must enter into an agreement with us designed to protect your privacy. For example, this agreement requires that the partner delete your data if you turn off instant

---

[33] Michael L. Rustad, Richard Buckingham, Diane D'Angelo, and Katherine Durlacher, An Empirical Study of Predispute Study of Predispute Mandatory Arbitration Clauses in Social Media Terms of Service Agreements, 34 U. ARK. LITTLE ROCK L. REV. 643, 644 (2012).

[34] Lothar Determann: Social Media Privacy: A Dozen Myths and Facts, STANFORD TECH L REV. (2012).

[35] Michael J. Kasdan, Is Facebook Killing Privacy Softly? The Impact of Facebook's Default Privacy Settings on Online Privacy, 2 N.Y.U. INTELL. PROP. & ENT. LAW LEDGER 107, 111 (2011).

[36] "Facebook's privacy policy has undergone a significant shift over its relatively short existence. Its original policy limited the distribution of user information to a group of that user's choice (thus creating a private space for user communication). By contrast, its current policy makes much user information public by default and requires other information to be public. This public information is accessible by Facebook and its business partners and advertisers. The shift in Facebook's default privacy settings over time is perhaps most strikingly illustrated by an info-graphic created by Matt McKeon, a developer at the Visual Communication Lab at IBM Research. The blue shading indicates the extent that the viewing of various categories of information is limited to a user's friends, friends of friends, all Facebook users, or the entire Internet. Heavier shading towards the outer part of the circle indicates that the information is more widely accessible. Id. at 110–111.

personalization when you first visit the site. It also prevents the partner from accessing any information about you until you or your friends visit its site.

Instant personalization partners sometimes use an email hash process to see if any of their users are on Facebook and get those users' User IDs. This process is similar to searching for someone on Facebook using an email address, except in this case the email addresses are encrypted so no actual email addresses are exchanged. The partner is also contractually required not to use your User ID for any purpose (other than associating it with your account) until you or your friends visit the site.

When you visit an instant personalization site, we provide the site with your User ID and your friend list (as well as your age range, locale, and gender). The site can then connect your account on that site with your friends' accounts to make the site instantly social. The site can also access public information associated with any of the User IDs it receives, which it can use to make the site instantly personalized. For example, if the site is a music site, it can access your music interests to suggest songs you may like, and access your friends' music interests to let you know what they are listening to. Of course it can only access you or your friends' music interests if they are public. If the site wants any additional information, it will have to get your specific permission.[37]

The Federal Trade Commission has yet to collect empirical evidence on the uses and abuses of privacy in cyberspace and some of the neglected issues include:

Collecting current data on the privacy and data-management practices of major websites. The most recent data referenced in the Staff Report are from 2000.

Producing systematic evidence showing whether current practices are harming consumers. Although the Staff Report rejects a harm-based approach, the proposed framework will only produce benefits to the extent it alleviates identified harms.

Reviewing what is known about how consumers value privacy and undertaking additional studies as a basis for estimating the benefits of a new privacy framework.

Estimating the costs of the proposed framework and alternatives, including direct pecuniary costs to firms from devoting more resources to privacy and the indirect costs of having less information available. The Staff Report does not acknowledge that its proposal would entail any costs.

Producing sufficient evidence of a reasonable expectation that the benefits of the proposal are greater than the costs. Otherwise, the proposal should not be adopted.[38]

Facebook, alone, has one billion users, so by definition it is cross-border and cross-national. One of the dangers of a national sovereignty approach to privacy is the possibility that data will be cabined and contained contrary to the norm of

---

[37] Facebook, Data Use Policy (2013).

[38] Thomas M. Lenard & Paul H. Rubin, The FTC and Privacy: We Don't Need No Stinking Data, 12–1 ANTITRUST SRC. (2012).

interoperability. Wolf and Maxwell call for international standards governing privacy and data protection:

> One basis for the hoped-for interoperability is the wide agreement around the world, as there has been for decades, on the basics of what it means to protect privacy in an information age. The so-called 'Fair Information Practice Principles,' or 'FIPPs,' focus on empowerment of people to control their personal information and on safeguards to ensure adequate data security. FIPPs form the core of the 1980 OECD privacy guidelines on which both the U.S. and European models are based, and that were adopted 'to harmonise national privacy legislation and, while upholding [ ] human rights, [ ] prevent interruptions in international flows of data.'[39]

§ 7.3   EMPLOYMENT & THE INTERNET AS FRONT STAGE

(A) Employment–Related Online Privacy

The Internet is an information device that has created a permanent and pervasive treasure trove of private information beyond any scale created by prior technologies such as television, radio, or the telephone.[40] Internet users increasingly live their private lives in public through the self-immolation of their own privacy. E-mail, texting, instant messaging, and posting on social media sites obliterate the division between the public and the private spheres. In general, blogs are composed of narrative and commentary posted in reverse chronological order, while microblogging is a variant of blogging that allows users to send and follow brief text updates.[41] Bebo, which stands for *Blog Early, Blog Often,* is an example of a blogging site that permits users to post blogs, photographs, music, videos, and questionnaires for other users.[42] Twitter, a micro-blogging service, is an in vogue social networking site that permits consumers to send "tweets," or text-based posts no greater than 140 characters via instant messaging or cell phone text messaging. Employers routinely screen Facebook and Twitter for postings about their companies or organizations.

A growing number of employers are disciplining employees for anti-corporate or incendiary postings on social media sites. Employers are also monitoring social networking sites because of the risk that employees will misappropriate trade secrets.[43] The path of Internet privacy law forged by U.S. courts has a pro-employer's spin leaving employees without meaningful remedies for abuses of electronic e-mail and social media surveillance. The U.S. courts' mechanical jurisprudence is based upon a theory of property rights, which reasons that since business computers are the property of the employer they have an unfettered right to monitor usage. The employers' unfettered right to monitor gives employers the perverse incentive to pretextually terminate employees to save the money from paying retirement or severance benefits.

---

[39] Christopher Wolf and Winston Maxwell, So Close, Yet So Far Apart: The EU and U.S. Visions of a New Privacy Framework, 26 ANTITRUST ABA 8, 9 (2012).

[40] See generally, MARSHALL McLUHAN, UNDERSTANDING MEDIA: THE EXTENSIONS OF MAN (1964).

[41] Margaret M. DiBianca, Ethical Risks Arising from Lawyers' Use of (and Refusal to Use) Social Media, 12 DEL. L. REV. 179, 181 (2011) (internal citation omitted).

[42] BEBO, http://www.bebo.com (last visited June 30, 2013).

[43] Sandra A. Jeski, Leading Lawyers on Examining Privacy Issues, Addressing Security Concerns and Responding to Recent IT Trends, ASPATORE, 2011 WL 3020561 (2011).

It is common for universities and colleges to cybervet publicly available information about prospective faculty candidates. Ratemyprofessor.com, for example, gives faculty recruitment committees publicly available, although certainly not statistically representative, information about a candidate's teaching evaluations. Prospective employees troll the Internet, studying Facebook profiles, Twitter postings, or other publicly available information to gain intelligence on job candidates—a process called cybervetting. The most recent trend is for employers to ask job candidates for their Facebook or other social networking passwords, without giving them time to edit these pages, so that the company can view private profiles, timelines, and friends.[44] Self-immolation of privacy is emblematic of the world of social networks. "[I]t is not possible to claim back anything because we do not have control of our data in a social network, for example. It is like being naked in the village square. In these circumstances, to exercise the *fus prohibendi* to protect privacy is almost impossible."[45]

American companies may use third party software to track social media and Internet postings. Companies are increasingly exploiting social media as a window onto the back stage or the middle ground between front and back stage in "requesting" job applicants send friend requests to managers so they can learn more about the moral fitness of applicants and employees. U.S. Senator Richard Blumenthal (D. Conn.) proposed a federal statute to prohibit employers from requiring job applicants to make such personal disclosures. A California state senator is proposing an amendment to a state statute that would ban employers from asking either current employees or job applicants for their social media user names or passwords.[46] Facebook made password sharing a violation of their terms of service in 2012.

Maryland and Illinois have both enacted a state statute that "prohibits firms from demanding access to the private social networking profiles of job applicants and employees. It's a huge leap forward for privacy and a great guidepost for businesses, but its limited scope only highlights the need for more comprehensive reform."[47] Facebook, Yelp, and Twitter, were among twelve other corporate defendants in a high profile privacy lawsuit.[48] The complaint alleged that the social media companies installed apps that harvested data without the consumer's knowledge or consent.[49] The class action, on behalf of mobile app users, seeks injunctive relief and damages to prohibit "technology firms such as Facebook, Twitter, Yelp and Apple as well as Angry Birds and Cut the Rope games, from accessing confidential data without permission."[50]

---

[44] Manuel Valdes and Shannon McFarland, Job Seekers Being Asked for Facebook Passwords, SCI–TECHN–TODAY.COM (March 21, 2012).

[45] Bernard Perinan, The Origin of Privacy as a Legal Value: A Reflection on Roman and English Law, 52 AM. J. LEGAL HIST. 183, 186 (2012).

[46] Associated Press, U.S. Senator, Employers Shouldn't Ask Job Applicants for Facebook, Social Media Passwords, ASSOCIATED PRESS (March 22, 2012).

[47] Chad Bascombe, Social Network Protection Laws Are Not Enough, MEDIA, TECH. & SOCIAL MEDIA (Aug. 14, 2012).

[48] Beluga, Burbn, Instagram, Foursquare Labs, Gowalla, Foodspotting, Hipster, LinkedIn, Path, Rovio Mobile, ZeptoLab, Chillingo, Electronics Arts, and Kik Interactive were social media and gaming sites named as defendants in a class action in Texas.

[49] Jaikumar Vijayanj, 18 Firms Sued for Using Privacy–Invading Mobile Apps, COMPUTERWORLD (March 12, 2012).

[50] Lawsuit Filed Against Mobile App Providers, RTT NEWS (March 16, 2012).

(B) E–Mail & Internet Usage Monitoring

Employers have successfully defended against claims by employees based upon common law and statutory causes of actions. Courts have only been receptive to privacy claims in the workplace in exceptional circumstances where the employer is prying into intensely private matters. The e-mail system is an efficient means for forwarding documents, including pornographic or obscene messages, and it is a common practice to forward off color jokes or other objectionable materials to multiple recipients. The simple act of an employee forwarding these jokes may unwittingly expose a company to a discrimination lawsuit under Title VII of the Civil Rights Act of 1964 and state discrimination laws as well as cybertort litigation. Employees not only e-mail or surf the web but also contribute to blogs or participate in social networks such as Facebook while at work. Employees in the private sector have no recourse if their employer terminates them for blogging about the company. The reason is that private sector employees have no First Amendment right to criticize their company or employer as there is no state action. A state actor is someone acting on behalf of a governmental body and thus subject to the Bill of Rights, which includes the First Amendment. Under the doctrine of incorporation, the First Amendment as well as the Fourth and Fifth Amendment, also extends to state governmental actors.[51]

In contrast, the First Amendment gives public employees a qualified immunity if they are blogging about matters of "public concern." Employers engage in social media "listening" to gather intelligence on applicants for employment and to control the firm's reputation management.[52] An information technology company has many reasons for electronic surveillance or monitoring of e-mail or Internet usage of its employees to prevent its employees' from committing torts or crimes, misappropriating trade secrets of the company, or preventing lawsuits for discrimination or harassment, or other online torts.[53] American employees monitor e-mail or Internet usage without notice to their employees with impunity, whereas European companies are liable for violations of human rights for the same policy by the European Court of Human Rights. E-mail monitoring software is so sophisticated that it can detect and correctly categorize

---

[51] Constitutional protections such as the Fourth Amendment depend upon the plaintiff's demonstrating state action. With e-mail monitoring the plaintiff has the burden of proving that the state directed or controlled electronic surveillance in order for constitutional rights to be triggered. Central to the understanding of privacy rights in the American workplace is the public/private distinction. Simply put, the extent of employees' privacy rights in the workplace depends on whether they work in the public sector or private sector. Because constitutional rights operate primarily to protect citizens from the government, "state action" is required before a citizen can invoke a constitutional right. The manner in which a government employer treats its employees is by definition state action. Because of this dichotomy, public-sector employees enjoy far greater privacy rights than do private sector employees. For example, the Fourth Amendment protects all government workers from unreasonable searches and seizures by the government." S. Elizabeth Wilborn, Revising the Public/Private Distinction: Employee Monitoring in the Workplace, 32 GA. L. REV. 825, 829 (1998); Kevin J. Conlon, Privacy in the Workplace, 72 CHI.–KENT L. REV. 285, 285 (1996) ("The Court has been reluctant to find state action in the private sector. . . ."); See also, MacDonald v. Eastern Wyoming Mental Health Center, 941 F.2d 1115, 1118 (10th Cir. 1991) ("Absent any showing that the state directed, controlled, or influenced this particular personnel decision", proof that the private agency was subject to pervasive state regulation and monitoring of its personnel standards and received substantial state funds was not sufficient to show state action.).

[52] Amy E. Bevins, Privacy Attorneys Share Tips to Avoid Pitfalls When Mining Social Network Data, ELEC. COM. & L. REP. (BNA) (March 8, 2011).

[53] See generally, Sally Greenberg, Threats, Harassment, & Hate On–Line: Recent Developments, 6 B. U. PUB. INT. L. J. 673 (1997).

employees' facial expressions.[54] None of the EU countries would permit this form of intrusive monitoring acceptable in the United States.

Computer monitoring software permits workplace surveillance without the employees' knowledge. Current U.S. law imposes no duty on the part of employers to notify employees before implementing monitoring software.[55] In the United States, many companies have installed GPS, web cams, and other software to monitor their workers' e-mail and Internet usage. Companies employ electronic surveillance for diverse reasons including: (1) preventing the misuse of bandwidth as well as the loss of employee efficiency when employees surf the Internet; (2) ensuring that the company's networking policies are being implemented; (3) preventing lawsuits for discrimination, harassment or other online torts; (4) preventing the unauthorized transfer of intellectual property and avoiding liability due to employees making illegal copies of copyrighted materials; (5) safeguarding company records which must be kept to comply with federal statutes; (6) deterring the unlawful appropriation of personal information, and potential spam or viruses; and (7) protecting company assets including intellectual property and business plans.

Extensive e-mail monitoring and surveillance by employers is the functional equivalent of an "electronic sweatshop."[56] Employers without even giving their employees notice, monitor American workers on an unfathomable scale.[57] Electronic monitoring software sales increased exponentially from $ 139 million in 2001 to $ 662 million by 2006.[58] A 2004 survey of employer monitoring verified that "70% of responding employers have implemented a written e-mail policy governing use and content, 74% monitor employee outgoing and incoming e-mail, and 60% monitor employee Internet connections."[59] Nearly all computer monitoring software permits workplace surveillance without the employees' knowledge, and current law imposes no duty on the part of employers to notify employees before implementing monitoring software. American courts have given employers the right to monitor in virtually every case decided over the last decade and have held that employees have no expectation of

---

[54] Martha Neil, New "Big Brother" Software Will Monitor Workers' Facial Expressions, ABA J. (Jan. 16, 2008).

[55] See Michael L. Rustad & Sandra R. Paulsson, Monitoring Employee E-mail and Internet Usage: Avoiding the Omniscient Electronic Sweatshop: Insights From Europe, 7 U. PA. J. LAB. & EMP. L. 829, 898 (2005) ("In this era of information technology, where the fixed workplace is being rapidly displaced by a more protean electronic environment, wireless network connections create a seamless workplace. In a telecommuting world, an employee's workplace may be anywhere and everywhere.").

[56] Barbara Garson in The Electronic Sweatshop (1988), first conceptualized the term electronic sweatshop in reference to the impact of computers (arguing the ways that computers infringe upon privacy). See also, Laurie Thomas Lee, Watch Your E-Mail! Employee E–Mail Monitoring and Privacy in the Age of the "Electronic Sweatshop," 28 J. MARSHALL L. REV. 139, 139 (1994) (noting that e-mail is the "fastest growing form of electronic communication in the workplace"); Robert G. Boehmer, Artificial Monitoring and Surveillance of Employees: The Fine Line Dividing the Prudently Managed Enterprise from the Modern Sweatshop, 41 DEPAUL L. REV. 739, 808 (1992).

[57] Michael L Rustad & Sandra R Paulsson, Monitoring Employee E–Mail and Internet Usage Avoiding the Omniscient Electronic Sweatshop. Insights from Europe, 7 U. PA. J. LAB. & EMP L 829 (2005).

[58] Robin L. Wakefield, Computer Monitoring and Surveillance: Balancing Privacy with Security, 74 CPA J. 52 (July 1, 2004) (quoting an International Data Corporation study).

[59] Reginald C. Govan & Freddie Mac, 33rd Annual Institute on Employment Law: Workplace Privacy, 712 PLI/Lit 245, 251 (2004), available at WESTLAW, TP–ALL Library.

privacy in their electronic communications at work.[60] A comparative study of e-mail monitoring argued for enhanced protection for U.S. employees:

> Two in three U.S. corporate workplaces have no policy requiring their employees to manifest consent to electronic monitoring or acknowledging their workplace monitoring activities. The pervasive practice of employers monitoring e-mail or Internet usage without notice threatens the fundamental rights of American workers. It is a widespread misconception that 'e-mail is as private and confidential as communication via the U.S. Postal Service . . . Most e-mail, voice-mail and computer systems are in fact anything but private and confidential.' F. Scott Fitzgerald's The Great Gatsby has been described as "The Great American Novel," because it is the "quintessential work which captures the mood of the 'Jazz Age.'" The second chapter in Fitzgerald's novel describes an outsized billboard advertising optical services. The billboard sign, with its faceless blue eyes gazing out at the valley of ashes, today would be symbolic of the loss of privacy in the electronic workplace.[61]

The omniscient eyes on Dr. Eckleberg's billboard are now locked on workers in the electronic workplace where network administrators indiscriminately copy screen shots in real time, scan data files, read e-mail, analyze keystroke performance, and even overwrite passwords. The Remotespy.com website touts the following products:

> Internet Conversation Logging—Record both sides of all chat and instant message conversations (unlike basic keyloggers) for AOL, ICQ, MSN (Windows Live), AIM, Yahoo, GoogleTalk, Skype, PalTalk and XFire Instant Messengers. Find out who your employee, child or spouse is speaking with online while using your computer.

> Screenshot Logging—Capture full-size computer monitoring screenshots of your computer's desktop. Visually see exactly what is occurring on your monitored computer at regular intervals.

> Advanced Password Logging—Uncover and store usernames and passwords used on your computer even if the data is already present behind asterisks (***). Works for both windows applications and Internet Explorer websites featuring a password box. This is extremely useful in the case of a computer crash when you've lost your data and have no other way to recover your valuable passwords and usernames: RemoteSpy can be your backup solution!

> Window Activity Logging—Capture information on every window viewed and interacted with for maximum proof. All window titles will be captured secretly.

---

[60] Courts routinely rule that e-mail or Internet systems owned by companies are company property and therefore employees have no reasonable expectation of privacy in stored messages. See, e.g., Privacy Claim Rejected in Employer Access to E-mail Files, 16 Comp. & Online Litig. Rep. 9 (June 15, 1999). See, e.g., McLaren v. Microsoft Corp., 1999 Tex. App. LEXIS 4103 (Tex. Ct. App. 5th Dist. May 28, 1999) (rejecting employee's privacy claim against company for "breaking into" personal folders on his company computer). See also Smyth v. Pillsbury Co., 914 F. Supp. 97, 101 (E.D. Pa. 1996) (holding that plaintiff has no reasonable expectation of privacy in e-mail message stored on company owned computer system). See also, Smyth v. Pillsbury Co., 914 F. Supp. 97 (E.D. Pa. 1996) and Restuccia v. Burk Technology, Inc., No. 95–2125 (Mass. Supr. Ct. 1996).

[61] Michael L. Rustad & Sandra R. Paulsson, Monitoring Employee E-mail and Internet Usage: Avoiding the Omniscient Electronic Sweatshop: Insights from Europe, 7 U. PA. J. LAB. & EMP. L. 829, 830 (2005).

Application Activity Logging—Track every application/executable that was executed and interacted with on your computer. If they open an application on your PC, it will be recorded.

Keystroke Monitoring—Track all keystrokes pressed via a built-in keylogger [including hidden system keys!] and which windows they were pressed in. Keystrokes can also be passed through a formatter for easy viewing/exporting.

Website Activity Logging—Log all website titles and addresses that were visited on your PC. All information is recorded invisibly for you to view anytime! Supported browsers include Internet Explorer, Firefox, Netscape, Opera, Chrome and more![62]

Electronic surveillance by employers is "the merciless electronic whip that drives the fast pace of today's workplace." Just as the use of e-mail and the Internet is nearly universal, so is the inevitability of an electronic sweatshop where U.S. workers have no privacy.[63] Tools such as RemoteSpy amount to an electronic leash on workers. At present, U.S. employees in the private workplace have no constitutional, common law or statutory protection against abusive e-mail monitoring practices. In effect, American workers are divested of their privacy as soon as they log onto their workplace computer because U.S. courts have formalistically applied a property rights regime to electronic surveillance of e-mail and Internet usage. Computer monitoring software permits workplace surveillance without the employees' knowledge. Current U.S. law imposes no duty on the part of employers to notify employees before implementing monitoring software. Many U.S. companies have installed GPS, web cams, and other software to track location or monitor their workers' e-mail and Internet usage. American employers monitor e-mail or Internet usage without notice to their employees with impunity, whereas European companies are liable for violations of human rights for the same policy according to rulings by the European Court of Human Rights.

§ 7.4 WORKPLACE PRIVACY ISSUES

(A) National Labor Relations Act

Employer's monitoring of social media website postings raises the issue of whether this secret surveillance violates federal labor law. The National Labor Relations Act ("NLRA") considers it be an unfair labor practice to engage in surveillance of employees who are participating in "protected concerted activity" under section 7 of the NLRA.[64] The National Labor Relations Board ("NLRB") is of the opinion that an employer violates Section 8(a)(1) of the National Labor Relations Act when it maintains a work rule that reasonably chills employees in the exercise of their Section 7 rights, including the right to discuss discipline or disciplinary investigations involving their fellow employees on social media sites.[65]

---

[62] Expert Report of Fred Cate, Federal Trade Commission v. Cyberspy Software, LLC, 2009 WL 6667648 (M.D. Fla. June 9, 2009) (filed).

[63] Rustad & Paulsson, Monitoring Employee E–Mail and Internet Usage, Id. at 831–32.

[64] 29 U.S.C. § 1757.

[65] Alan L. Friel, Akash Sachdeva, Jesse Brody, and Jatinder Bahra, Safeguarding Brand Reputation in Social Media, CORPORATE COUNSEL (June 13, 2013) (discussing risks of blanket prohibition and the need to tailor policies so they do not infringe employees' rights to expression and the right to organize under the NLRA).

Companies create new risks for National Labor Relations Act violations when they apply a nuclear approach, prohibiting consumers from mentioning the company or its products and services online in its employment handbook or other policies. Nevertheless, employment handbook provisions that prohibit employees from mentioning the company online do not violate the First Amendment of the U.S. Constitution, as there is no state action. However, such a policy may violate section 7 of the NLRA. A blanket prohibition exposes companies to actions under the National Labor Relations Board protecting the right to organize.[66]

The NLRA protects employees' rights to engage in concerted activities for the purpose of collective bargaining or other mutual aid or protection. Section 7 of the NLRA gives employees the right to "engage in . . . concerted activities for the purpose of . . . mutual aid or protection."[67] Congress drafted the NLRA in the 1930s but it needs to update this statute to address social media. An employer monitoring e-mail or Internet communications for the purposes of constraining "concerted activity" will violate the NLRA. "Millions of people have begun chronicling their lives through online diaries and social networks. Sometimes they disclose too much information: describing past drug use, allowing pictures of themselves drunk at parties to be displayed, and griping about work. More and more of these "bloggers" are being fired because of what they publish online."[68] President Obama's National Labor Relations Board ("NLRB") has been vigilant in protecting employees who blog or post comments on social media sites about their workplace conditions.

(B) Concerted Activities

The NLRA grants employees the right to "form, join, or assist labor organizations, to bargain collectively through representatives of their own choosing, and to engage in other concerted activities for the purpose of collective bargaining or other mutual aid or protection"[69] Section 8(A)(3) of the NLRA makes it is unlawful for an employer by discrimination in terms of employment to discourage "membership in any labor organization," which includes discouraging "participation in concerted activities . . . such as a legitimate strike."[70] Section 7 of the NLRA protects workers posting on Facebook or e-mailing co-workers attempting to improve workplace conditions. President Obama's NLRB construes such activities as concerted but this could change under a different Administration. Employees making derogatory comments about their employers and are fired have no remedy unless they can demonstrate that they are engaged in concerted activities. Employees have no First Amendment right to criticize their employer or co-workers on Facebook or other forums. Amy J. Zdravecky, speaking at the ABA Section of Labor and Employment Law conference advised employers to consider the following factors in determining whether social media use qualified as concerted activity, protected by the NLRA:

---

[66] Alan L. Friel, Akash Sachdeva, Jesse Brody, and Jatinder Bahra, Safeguarding Brand Reputation in Social Media, CORPORATE COUNSEL (June 13, 2013) (discussing risks of blanket prohibition and the need to tailor policies so they do not infringe employees' rights to expression and the right to organize under the NLRA).

[67] Id.

[68] Robert Sprague, Fired for Blogging: Are There Legal Protections for Employees Who Blog? 9 U. PA. J. LAB. & EMP. L. 355, 355 (2007).

[69] 29 U.S.C. § 157.

[70] NLRB v. Erie Resistor Corp., 373 U.S. 221, 233 (1963).

- An employee's individual posting suggested collective action by employees;

- The posting referenced prior discussions among employees that could indicate the individual posting is concerted in nature;

- Other employees responded to the individual's posting;

- The online response of other employees indicated agreement with the individual's complaint or statement about work or working conditions, which could indicate concerted activity, or whether the response indicated no more than an expression of sympathy concerning a personal non-concerted complaint;

- The employee posting an online comment made any comments acknowledging that a gripe was purely personal or admitting the employee was not trying to enlist co-workers in group action; and,

- Employees took action after the posting such as engaging in further discussion of a complaint offline.[71]

The NLRB is likely to find social media postings directly related to conditions of employment as concerted activity than postings that are less central to workplace issues. During the period between June 2009 and April 2011, the NLRB "received approximately one hundred charges of unfair labor practices arising from social media activities and policies."[72] Merely complaining about co-employees or an incident at work is not concerted activity.[73] Four elements are required to prove concerted activity:

(1) online postings must relate to terms and conditions of employment; (2) there must be evidence of concert—i.e. there must be discussions among employees of the posts or coworker responses to the posts; (3) there must be evidence the employee was seeking to induce or prepare for group concerns; and (4) the posts must reflect an outgrowth of employees' collective concerns.[74]

(C) NLRA Section 8(a)(1)

In a series of rulings, the National Labor Relations Board has held that employee' Facebook postings about job performance and staffing are protected concerted activities. In a 2010 case, the NLRB found that a nonprofit social services provider unlawfully "terminated employees who posted comments on Facebook relating to allegations of poor job performance as previously expressed by one of their coworkers— a domestic violence advocate."[75] The Board ruled that the discharged employees' postings on Facebook were concerted activity under the *Meyers* case.[76] The NLRB explained that an activity is concerted when an employee acts "with or on the authority

---

[71] Lawrence E. Dube, Social Media: Workers Like Facebook, Other Social Media; Firms Scramble to Understand NLRA Rights, BLOOMBERG BNA, ELECT. COMM. & LAW REPORT (Feb. 29, 2012).

[72] Robert Sprague, Facebook Meets the NLRB: Employee Communications and Unfair Labor Practices, U. PA. J. BUS. LAW, 957, 963 (2012).

[73] Id. at 999.

[74] Id. at 999–1000.

[75] National Labor Relations Board, Office of the General Counsel, Memorandum OM 11–74 (Aug. 18, 2011) at 3.

[76] Meyers Industries (Meyers I). 268 NLRB 493 (1984), revd. sub nom, Prill v. NLRB, 755 F.2d 941 (D.C. Cir. 1985).

of other employees, and not solely by and on behalf of the employee himself."[77] In another case, the NLRB ruled that an employer's blogging and Internet policy that prohibited employees from depicting the company in any manner violated federal labor law.

Section 8(a)(1) of the NLRA makes it an unlawful or unfair labor practice for an employer to "interfere with, restrain, or coerce employees" with respect to their NLRA Section 7 organizational rights. An employer violates Section 8(a)(1) if the rules in place "would reasonably tend to chill employees in the exercise of their Section 7 rights."[78] The NLRB applies a two-step test to determine if an employer's social media policy or other work rule violates Section 8(a)(1):

> First, a rule is clearly unlawful if it explicitly restricts protected activities. If it will only violate Section 8(a)(1) upon a showing that: (1) employees would reasonably construe the language to prohibit Section 7 activity; (2) the rule was promulgated in response to union activity; or (3) the rule has been applied to restrict the exercise of Section 7 rights.[79]

The NLRB interprets the NLRA to protect employees from retaliation for complaining about abusive management practices on websites, including social media sites. In *G4S Secure Solutions (USA) Inc., and International Union, Security Police and Fire Professionals of America*, the Administrative Law Judge ("ALJ") examined a company's social networking policy and found it a violation of the NLRA to outright prohibit employees from "commenting on "work-related legal matters" without the permission of the company's legal department."[80] The NLRB upheld a second provision that prohibited employees from "posting any pictures or videos of employees in uniform or employees on a job site."[81] The ALJ stated, "No comment on work-related legal matters provision was overly restrictive of employees' rights to engage in protected concerted activity."[82] The NLRB makes it clear that employer's social media policy should not be overly broad to prohibit protected activities. Thus, an employee's discussion of wages or working conditions with other Facebook friends is generally protected activity.

The *2012 NLRB Report on Social Media* reviewed cases of protected activities and the concerted nature of employee postings on Facebook and other social media sites. The NLRB addressed the lawfulness of employer's rules prohibiting employees from "disparaging" the employer in any media. The NLRB found it unlawful for a collection agency to terminate an employee for posting critical comments on Facebook. The complainant posted a status update on her Facebook page using expletives and stating that her employer had messed up and that "she was done being a good employee."[83] The NLRB concluded that the employer's rule prohibiting disparaging comments was

---

[77] Id.

[78] Lafayette Park Hotel, 326 NLRB 824, 825 (1998).

[79] NATIONAL LABOR RELATIONS BOARD, THE 2012 NLRB REPORT ON SOCIAL MEDIA (Jan. 24, 2012) at 4 ("2012 NLRB Report on Social Media").

[80] Second ALJ Decision on Social–Media Policies under the NLRA, LABOR AND EMPLOYMENT LAW (April 13, 2005). For the full ALJ decision on G4S Secure Solutions (USA) Inc., See 2012 WL 1065721.

[81] Id.

[82] NATIONAL LABOR RELATIONS BOARD, THE 2012 NLRB REPORT ON SOCIAL MEDIA (2012).

[83] Id.

unlawful and that the collection agency violated the NLRA when it terminated the charging party for her protected concerted Facebook postings and pursuant to the rule.

An Administrative Law Judge found that a "nonprofit organization unlawfully discharged five employees after they posted comments on Facebook concerning working conditions, including work load and staffing issues."[84] The ALJ ordered that Hispanics United reinstate the five employees and awarded the employees back pay. In contrast, the NLRB has found individual gripes that do not encourage coworkers to engage in-group action to be unprotected and not concerted activity. The *2012 NLRB Report on Social Media* found the following emerging issues in social media-related cases:

(1) Collection agency's discharge of employee for Facebook comments and for violating non-disparagement rule was unlawful. Employee used expletives in status update expressing frustration with her supervisor. Charging party had 10 coworker friends and therefore the gripes were an exercise of NLRA, Section 8(A)(1) rights. The NLRB ruled that the employer's social media policy violated Section 7 of the NLRA because it restricted protected activities.

(2) Home improvement stores that discharged employee for Facebook comments was lawful but social media policy and no-solicitation rules were overly broad.[85]

An "employee's comments that are posted on social media are generally not protected if they are mere gripes not made in relation to group activity among employees."[86] Similarly, the NLRA does not offer any protection of an employee's Facebook postings about an irritating coworker. *The 2011 NLRB Report on Social Media* found the following activities to be protected in its rulings:

(1) Facebook postings about job performance staffing in a nonprofit organization constituted protected concerted activity;

(2) Employer's policies on Internet, Blogging, and the Discharge of an Employee for a Facebook Posting were unlawful;

(3) Luxury automobile dealership violated NLRA when it discharged a sales clerk for posting Facebook page photography and criticizing the dealer's sales event because the postings were protected, concerted activities;

(4) Sports Bar and Restaurant discharge of employees because of Facebook postings about their tax withholding practices were protected concerted activity;

(5) Union violated Section 8(b)(1)(A) by posting "Interrogation" Videotape on YouTube and Facebook. Union's posting of an edited version of videotape of workplace was not protected;

(6) Hospital's social media policy was overly broad;

(7) Employee Handbook rules on social policies were overly broad;

---

[84] Id.
[85] Id.
[86] NATIONAL LABOR RELATIONS BOARD, THE 2012 NLRB REPORT ON SOCIAL MEDIA (2012).

(8) Supermarket Chain's pressuring coworkers to use social media was lawful, but other prohibitions were over broad. Policy that no employee should be pressured to friend co-workers was lawful and did not restrict Section 7 concerted activity.[87]

An analysis of cases concluded that most social media-related NLRB cases "are merely gripes" and most do not "express a collective concern that has been or will soon be brought to the attention of management."[88] Nevertheless, employers may have a right, and even a duty to monitor social media communications to protect the personally identifiable information of third parties, trade secrets, and to investigate sexual or racial harassment. However, if they monitor social media, they must also minimize any exposure to claims that are chilling expression or restraining legitimate unionization efforts.

(D) Harassment by Co–Employees

Title VII of the Civil Rights Act of 1964 provides that it is unlawful to discriminate against an individual with respect to the terms of employment because of sex or race. Plaintiffs filing harassment claims may have tort actions as well. Courts have determined that employees may establish a "hostile workplace" claim if: (1) the conduct in question was unwelcome; (2) the harassment was sex or race-linked; (3) the sexual or racial harassment was severe and (4) there was a causal connection to the employer. Employee may base a hostile workplace claim upon an employer's failure to take prompt remedial responses to complaints about Internet harassment. For example, a federal court in California found Continental Express Airlines responsible for sexual harassment in a hostile workplace claim filed by a female pilot.[89] In *Butler*, co-employees depicted a female pilot in pornographic poses on the airline's intranet. The jury found Continental liable to the plaintiffs under theories of a hostile work environment and for ratification of sexual harassment.

In *Espinoza v. Orange County*,[90] a disabled employee of the Orange County probation department won a judgment for harassment based upon the California Fair Employment and Housing Act. The action arose from a co-employees' postings on a probation blog. Espinoza has no fingers on his right hand but has only two small stubs due to a birth defect. Espinoza was self-conscious about people seeing it and often kept his hand in his pocket.[91] An anonymous poster, who turned out to be a co-employee wrote, "I will give anyone 100 bucks if you get a picture of the claw."[92] The anonymous poster also wrote, "Do I still get the $100 if I get a picture of the claw with a blue glove dangling off it?"[93]

---

[87] Reports of the General Counsel Concerning Social Media Cases, Memorandum OM 11–74 (August 18, 2011).

[88] Robert Sprague, Facebook Meets the NLRB: Employee Communications and Unfair Labor Practices, U. PA. J. BUS. LAW, 957, 1011 (2012).

[89] Butler v. Krebs & Continental Express, Inc., 100 F. Supp. 2d 1058 (N.D. Cal. 2000).

[90] 2012 WL 420149 (Cal. App. Ct. February 9, 2012) (reporting that Espinoza's action was against Orange County and four members of the probation department was for harassment based on disability and failure to prevent harassment under the California Fair Employment and Housing Act).

[91] Id.

[92] Id. at 4.

[93] Id.

The next day the same poster again referred to the $100 for a picture of "the one handed bandit."[94] Espinoza based his complaint against the probation department on disability, retaliation, failing to prevent harassment, wrongful termination and the tort of the intentional infliction of emotional distress. The court granted a motion for non-suit as to the wrongful termination and intentional infliction causes of action against defendant. The appellate court upheld a verdict against Orange County and awarded the plaintiff over $820,000. The amount consisted of $700 for medical expenses, $320,000 in lost earnings, and $500,000 for mental distress. For there to be liability for harassment, the "conduct . . . [must be] severe or pervasive enough to create an objectively hostile or abusive work environment."[95] The bottom line is that an "employers do not have a duty to monitor private communications of their employees; employers do have a duty to take effective measures to stop co-employee harassment when the employer knows or has reason to know that such harassment is part of a pattern of harassment that is taking place in the workplace and in settings that are related to the workplace."[96]

(E) Social Media Employer Snooping — *Can schools do that*

The Social Networking Online Protection Act ("SNOPA") is a proposed federal statute that will prohibit employers and schools from demanding passwords so they can read private social media postings of students or prospective employees. Maryland enacted legislation in 2012 preventing employers from "demanding applicants hand over social networking log-in credentials. At least seven others states are considering similar legislation."[97]

(F) Public Employee's First Amendment Interests

In *Mattingly v. Milligan,*[98] an Arkansas county court employee used her mobile phone to make multiple postings on her Facebook wall referring to the firing of co-employees. "Two minutes after this post, Mattingly posted another comment: 'I am trying [sic] my heart goes out to the ladies in my office that were told by letter they were no longer needed . . . It's sad.'" The court found that these work-related postings to be constitutionally protected speech.[99] "Facebook posts were made primarily to further her private interest in receiving emotional support and affirmation; the fact remains that she did not make them as an employee but as a citizen." As a result, the court held that the speech was protected and denied the clerk's motion against the free speech claim. In public employment cases like *Mattingly*, the court applies a two-step analysis. The first step is whether the speech is classifiable as a "matter of public concern." The second step is to balance the employee's First Amendment right against the employer's rights. The court found that the employee's postings on Facebook were protected and no evidence that the postings disrupted the county clerk's office.

---

[94] Id.

[95] Lyle v. Warner Brothers Television Productions, 38 Cal.4th 264, 283 (2006).

[96] Blakey v. Continental Airlines, 164 N.J. 38, 61, 751 A.2d 538 (2000).

[97] John Fontana, SNOPA Legislation Would Bar Employers From Social Network Passwords, ZDNET (April 27, 2012).

[98] 2011 WL 5184283, at *1 (E.D. Ark. 2011).

[99] Id. at *3–*4.

In *Gresham v. City of Atlanta,*[100] the governmental employee posted: "Who would like to hear the story of how I arrested a forgery perpetrated at Best Buy online to find out later at the precinct that he was the nephew of an Atlanta Police Investigator . . . ?" The district court adopted the Magistrate recommendation that although the statement was a close question, it constituted enough speech to be considered speaking out as a matter of public concern. Nevertheless, in *Bland v. Robert,*[101] The plaintiff contended that in late 2009, the incumbent Sheriff learned that a number of his employees were actively supporting one of the Sheriff's opponents in the election.[102] The Sheriff learned that each of plaintiffs affirmatively expressed their support for his political opponent "by informing other individuals of their support, attending a cookout that the Sheriff's opponent also attended and 'liking' his Facebook page."[103] "According to the Plaintiffs, after learning of their support of his opponent, the Sheriff called a meeting in which he informed his employees that they should get on the "long train" with him rather than riding the "short train" with his opponent."[104]

After the Sheriff was reelected, he terminated the plaintiffs who filed a retaliation lawsuit charging that they were not reappointed for exercising their right of speech by liking his opponent on Facebook.[105] The court applied a three-part test; "[T]o determine whether a public employee has stated a claim under the First Amendment for retaliatory discharge, we must determine (1) whether the public employee was speaking as a citizen upon a matter of public concern or as an employee about a personal matter of personal interest; (2) whether the employee's interest in speaking upon the matter of public concern outweighed the government's interest in providing effective and efficient services to the public; and (3) whether the employee's speech was a substantial factor[106] in the employee's termination decision."[107] The first prong of this test necessarily requires that speech exists before an evaluation of the remaining prongs can occur. The court found that the plaintiffs' claims failed as a matter of law reasoning that several of the plaintiffs did not sufficiently alleged that they engaged in expressive speech, and another plaintiff did not prove that his alleged speech touched upon a matter of public concern.[108] The court distinguished the facts from Mattingly and Gresham where the plaintiffs made actual statements, not just clicking "like" on Facebook.[109] The court stated that "[s]imply liking a Facebook page is insufficient. It is not the kind of substantive statement that has previously warranted constitutional protection. The Court will not attempt to infer the actual content of . . . posts from one click of a button on [the Sheriff's opponents'] Facebook page.[110] The court did concede that "Facebook posts *can* be considered matters of public concern; however, the Court

---

[100] No. 1:10–CV–1301–RWS–ECS, 2011 WL 4601022 (N.D. Ga. Aug. 29, 2011).

[101] 857 F. Supp. 2d 599 (E.D. Va. 2012).

[102] Id. at 601.

[103] Id.

[104] Id.

[105] Id. at 602.

[106] Under tort law, the substantial factor test applies in negligence actions situations where more than one independent negligent act may be responsible for a plaintiff's injury; under the substantial factor test, an action is viewed as the cause of an injury only if the action was a substantial factor in bringing about plaintiff's injury.

[107] Id. at 603.

[108] Id.

[109] Id. at 604.

[110] Id.

does not believe" these plaintiffs "have alleged sufficient speech to garner First Amendment protection."[111] This case is emblematic of a growing number of disputes where torts conflict with First Amendment interests.

(G) Telecommuting

Telecommuting jobs such as "medical billing and coding, medical transcribing, and customer service are becoming commonplace with the advent of the Internet. Nearly one in ten Americans telecommutes "at least one day per week in 2010, an increase of approximately 18 percent from 2005."[112] The privacy issues for telecommuting include:

> security breaches of information in transit and malicious hacking; improper access to data by nonemployees in the home (e.g., spouses, housemates) or to other third parties resulting from lax procedures, improper data-sharing, or careless use of portable media, such as thumb drives (which may trigger employer obligations under state data breach notification laws if covered personal information is involved); unauthorized release by the employee of information; and, worst of all, misappropriation of the employer's confidential and proprietary information resulting in great harm to the employer's business.[113]

Attorneys representing companies recommend that companies have telecommuting policies as well as software controls such as firewall to minimize telecommuting liability for breach of security.[114]

§ 7.5 FOURTH AMENDMENT & INTERNET TECHNOLOGIES

In *In re Warrant to Search a Target Computer at Premises Unknown*,[115] the government sought a search and seizure warrant targeting a computer allegedly used to violate federal bank fraud, identity theft, and computer security laws. The government contended that unknown persons committed these crimes using a particular email account via an unknown computer at an unknown location. "The search would be accomplished by surreptitiously installing software designed not only to extract certain stored electronic records but also to generate user photographs and location information over a 30 day period."[116] The Government's warrant sought permission to hack the computer to seek the following information:

(1) Records existing on the Target Computer at the time the software is installed, including:

(2) Records of Internet Protocol addresses used;

(3) Records of Internet activity, including firewall logs, caches, browser history and cookies, "bookmarked" or "favorite" Web pages, search terms that the user

---

[111] Id.

[112] Linda B. Dwoskin & Jane Patullo, It's 9 a.m. Do You Know Where Your Employees Are At? The Legal Implications of Telecommuting, BLOOMBERG BNA: ELECTRONIC COMMERCE AND THE LAW (May 30, 2013),

[113] Id.

[114] Id; See also, Diana J.P. McKenzie, Information Technology Policies: Practical Protection in Cyberspace, 3 STAN. J.L. BUS. & FIN. 84 (Winter 1997).

[115] 2013 U.S. Dist. LEXIS 57608 (S.D. Tex., April 22, 2013).

[116] Id. at *1.

entered into any Internet search engine, and records of user-typed Web addresses;

(4) Records evidencing the use of the Internet Protocol addresses to communicate with the [victim's bank's] e-mail servers;

(5) Evidence of who used, owned, or controlled the TARGET COMPUTER at the time the things described in this warrant were created, edited, or deleted, such as logs registry entries, configuration file, saved user names and passwords, documents, browsing history, user profiles, e-mail contents, e-mail contacts, "chat," messaging logs, photographs, and correspondence;

(6) Evidence of software that would allow others to control the TARGET COMPUTER;

(7) Evidence of times the TARGET COMPUTER was used; and

(8) Records of applications run.[117]

The prospective data sought during a thirty day monitoring period included:

(1) Prospective data obtained during a 30–day monitoring period, including:

(2) accounting entries reflecting the identification of new fraud victims;

(3) Photographs (with no audio) taken using the TARGET COMPUTER's built-in camera after the installation of the NEW SOFTWARE, sufficient to identify the location of the TARGET COMPUTER and identify persons using the TARGET COMPUTER;

(4) Information about the TARGET COMPUTER's physical location, including latitude and longitude calculations the NEW SOFTWARE causes the TARGET COMPUTER to make; and

(5) Records of applications run.[118]

The federal magistrate characterized the government's search request as involving a case of first impression in the digital information being sought:

The 'search' for which the Government seeks authorization is actually two-fold: (1) a search for the Target Computer itself, and (2) a search for digital information stored on (or generated by) that computer. Neither search will take place within this district, so far as the Government's application shows. Contrary to the current metaphor often used by Internet-based service providers, digital information is not actually stored in clouds; it resides on a computer or some other form of electronic media that has a physical location. Before that digital information can be accessed by the Government's computers in this district, a search of the Target Computer must be made. That search takes place, not in the airy nothing of cyberspace, but in physical space with a local habitation and a name. Since the current location of the Target Computer is unknown, it necessarily follows that the current location of the information on the Target Computer is also unknown.[119]

---

[117] Id. at *3–*4.
[118] Id. at *4.
[119] Id. at *7–*8.

The court found that the warrant was not supported by the application denying it.[120] The court was troubled by the government's use of a targeted computer to seek information about counterfeit e-mail addresses finding that the warrant violated the Fourth Amendment's particularity requirement.[121] The risk is that the government could be monitoring innocent computers where the cybercriminals have "spoofed" Internet Protocol addresses to cover their tracks.[122] The warrant used a built-in camera to capture information on third parties:

> [T]he Government's data extraction software will activate the Target Computer's built-in-camera and snap photographs sufficient to identify the persons using the computer. The Government couches its description of this technique in terms of "photo monitoring," as opposed to video surveillance, but this is a distinction without a difference. In between snapping photographs, the Government will have real time access to the camera's video feed. That access amounts to video surveillance.[123]

The federal magistrate noted that this type of digital photographic surveillance requires Safeguard in order to comply with the Fourth Amendment warrant requirement:

In order to comply w/ 4th Amdmt

> Under those standards, a search warrant authorizing video surveillance must demonstrate not only probable cause to believe that evidence of a crime will be captured, but also should include: (1) a factual statement that alternative investigative methods have been tried and failed or reasonably appear to be unlikely to succeed if tried or would be too dangerous; (2) a particular description of the type of communication sought to be intercepted, and a statement of the particular offense to which it relates; (3) a statement of the duration of the order, which shall not be longer than is necessary to achieve the objective of the authorization nor, in any event, longer than 30 days, (though extensions are possible); and (4) a statement of the steps to be taken to assure that the surveillance will be minimized to effectuate only the purposes for which the order is issued.[124]

The federal magistrate found that the government failed to demonstrate that it was minimizing its request and whether there were reasonable less intrusive methods.[125] The court reasoned that the government's overly expansive request violated the Fourth Amendment.[126] The lesson of the case is that the government needs

---

[120] Id.

[121] The Government's application contains little or no explanation of how the Target Computer will be found. Presumably, the Government would contact the Target Computer via the counterfeit email address, on the assumption that only the actual culprits would have access to that email account. Even if this assumption proved correct, it would not necessarily mean that the government has made contact with the end-point Target Computer at which the culprits are sitting. It is not unusual for those engaged in illegal computer activity to "spoof" Internet Protocol addresses as a way of disguising their actual on-line presence; in such a case, the Government's search might be routed through one or more "innocent" computers on its way to the Target Computer. The Government's application offers nothing but indirect and conclusory assurance that its search technique will avoid infecting innocent computers or devices. Id. at *12–*13.

[122] Id. at *11–*12.

[123] Id. at *14–*15.

[124] Id. at *15–*16.

[125] Id. at *16.

[126] Id. at *12.

to explain how a target computer will be used to trap third parties without invading the privacy of innocent persons. The court states:

> Nor does the Government explain how it will ensure that only those "committing the illegal activity will be . . . subject to the technology." What if the Target Computer is located in a public library, an Internet café, or a workplace accessible to others? What if the computer is used by family or friends uninvolved in the illegal scheme? What if the counterfeit email address is used for legitimate reasons by others unconnected to the criminal conspiracy? What if the email address is accessed by more than one computer, or by a cell phone and other digital devices? There may well be sufficient answers to these questions, but the Government's application does not supply them.[127]

The *Unknown Premises* court was critical of the government's conclusory statements and inadequate attempts to explain what was being sought, thus violating the particularity requirement:

> Software that can retrieve this volume of information—Internet browser history, search terms, e-mail contents and contacts, "chat", instant messaging logs, photographs, correspondence, and records of applications run, among other things—is not fairly described as capturing "only limited amounts of data." Finally, given the unsupported assertion that the software will not be installed on "innocent" computers or devices, there remains a non-trivial possibility that the remote camera surveillance may well transmit images of persons not involved in the illegal activity under investigation.[128]

The *Unknown Premises* decision highlighted the incongruity between cloud computing and the Fourth Amendment. The court highlighted the importance of place in traditional Fourth Amendment jurisprudence and how the metaphor of cloud computing creates the illusion that place is no longer relevant:

> Contrary to the current metaphor often used by Internet-based service providers, digital information is not actually stored in clouds; it resides on a computer or some other form of electronic media that has a physical location.[4] Before that digital information can be accessed by the Government's computers in this district, a search of the Target Computer must be made. That search takes place, not in the airy nothing of cyberspace, but in physical space with a local habitation and a name. Since the current location of the Target Computer is unknown, it necessarily follows that the current location of the information on the Target Computer is also unknown. This means that the Government's application cannot satisfy the territorial limits of Rule 41(b)(1).[129]

The rise of the Internet creates an increasing number of cases where place is indeterminate, unknown and perhaps unknowable. The Fourth Amendment protects a person in the governmental workplace only if she has proved a subjective as well as an objective expectation of privacy in the place searched. The Fourth Amendment of the United States Constitution provides that:

---

[127] Id. at *13.

[128] Id. at *18.

[129] Id. at *7–*8.

[t]he right of the people to be secure in their persons, houses, papers, and effects, against unreasonable searches and seizures, shall not be violated, and no Warrants shall issue, but upon probable cause, supported by Oath or affirmation, and particularly describing the place to be searched, and the persons or things to be seized.

In *Leventhal v. Knapek*,[130] a Department of Transportation investigation uncovered evidence of an employee's misuse of a computer. The Second Circuit recognized that the employee had a reasonable expectation of privacy, but concluded that the investigatory search did not violate his Fourth Amendment rights because the government's legitimate purpose outweighed the employee's privacy interest in conducting the search.[131] The Fourth Amendment does not apply to a search unless the governmental intrusion infringes on the plaintiff's reasonable expectation of privacy, which is the legally protectable interest.

The *Knapek* court validated the government's investigatory search because it was reasonable in scope and advanced the employer's legitimate objective of searching for evidence of employee misfeasance.[132] This case illustrates how U.S. courts apply a balancing test that weighs privacy against the employer's interest in the public sector. This weighing of privacy versus the employer's need to investigate is inapplicable to the U.S. non-governmental workplace because the Fourth Amendment only applies to governmental actions by law enforcement or other public law entities, which is the doctrine of state action. State action is a predicate for all constitutional rights. Without a showing of state action, a plaintiff in a private workplace has no cause of action. Thus, the Fourth Amendment search-and-seizure provisions are not applicable to corporate invasions of privacy. Under U.S. law there is no freestanding privacy right for employees working in the private sector.[133] This is not the case in Europe where employees do have rights against secret surveillance by their private sector employers. E-mail monitoring and surveillance of Internet communications is permitted freely under U.S law but not in Europe.[134]

In the rare case, law enforcement cooperates with private companies in initiating a search. In these hybrid searches, there may be state action. If there is state action (a government agent taking the lead with the cooperation of the company), law enforcement officers must obtain a warrant before installing or executing electronic surveillance or conducting a search or seizure absent a showing of exigent exigent

---

[130] 266 F.3d 64 (2d Cir.,2001) (finding that investigatory searches by agency did not violate employee's Fourth Amendment rights).; Cf. O'Connor v. Ortega, 480 U.S. 709 (1987) (holding that the test of "reasonableness" applies to public employers, rather than the usual Fourth Amendment requirement of a warrant supported by "probable cause").

[131] Id. at 75.

[132] Id.

[133] ANUPAM CHANDER, LAUREN GELMAN, MARGARET JANE RADIN, SECURING PRIVACY IN THE INTERNET AGE 273 (2008) (noting that privacy in the U.S. does not rest upon a constitutional foundation but upon "fragile reeds of statutes that create a fragile and disjointed and often uncertain rights of privacy in specific types of data.").

[134] Michael L. Rustad & Sandra R. Paulsson, Monitoring Employee E-mail and Internet Usage: Avoiding the Omniscient Electronic Sweatshop: Insights from Europe, 7 U. PA. J. LAB. & EMP. L. 829, 866 (2005) ("European countries have formulated an all-encompassing cultural and legal response to privacy-based actions as compared to the United States, which continues to delineate a sharp distinction between private and public workplaces.").

circumstances or another exception to the exclusionary rule.[135] The exclusionary rule excludes all evidence collected without a valid warrant unless an exception applies. The U.S. Constitution also, has no extraterritorial effect and therefore does not constrain foreign law enforcement officers from monitoring the Internet activities of U.S. citizens. In *Katz v. United States*,[136] federal law enforcement officers attached an electronic eavesdropping device to a telephone booth in order to listen to conversations of a suspected illegal gambler. The Fourth Amendment applies to governmental actions where the intrusion infringes on the plaintiff's reasonable expectation of privacy.[137] Courts compel the plaintiff to prove that she had a subjective as well as an objective expectation of privacy in the place searched. The citizen's reasonable expectation of privacy is a requirement for any Fourth Amendment protection. The *Katz* Court held the Fourth Amendment protected people, not places, and that the defendant in *Katz* had a reasonable expectation of privacy when he shut the door on the telephone booth and made a telephone call. The Court rejected the government's argument that it did not violate Katz's constitutional rights since it committed no technical trespass in its electronic surveillance. The U.S. Supreme Court also applies the reasonable expectation of privacy test when deciding whether a public employer violates an employee's Fourth Amendment when it conducts a workplace search. As in public law enforcement, courts balance the employer's legitimate reasons for searches against the employee's reasonable expectation of privacy.[138] Whether a defendant has a constitutionally protected reasonable expectation of privacy involves two questions: (1) whether a defendant is able to establish an actual, subjective expectation of privacy with respect to the place being searched or items being seized, and (2) whether that expectation of privacy is one which society recognizes as reasonable.

(A) Internet–Related Search & Seizures

The Fourth Amendment's requirement of probable cause for the issuance of a search warrant "safeguards an individual's interest in the privacy of his home and possessions against the unjustified intrusion of the police."[139] The Fifth Circuit upheld the denial of a motion to suppress evidence arising out of the search of a Texas fire marshal's office computer containing images of child pornography from a newsgroup titled "alt.erotica.xxx.preteen."[140] Investigators uncovered child pornography on each of the defendant's hard drives, and all together, these hard drives contained thousands of files with such images. "The zip disk from Slanina's office contained more than one hundred files of child pornography."[141] The court found Slanina exhibited a subjective expectation of privacy in images of child pornography by storing them in containers away from plain

---

[135] See e.g., Katz v. United States, 389 U.S. 347, 357 (1967).

[136] Id.

[137] The Fourth Amendment provides "[t]he right of people to be secure in their persons, houses, papers and effects, against unreasonable searches and seizures. . . ." U.S. Const. Amend IV. Katz v. United States, 389 U.S.347, 361 (1967) (Harlan, J., concurring) (explaining the subjective and objective dimensions of the concept of a reasonable expectation of privacy); See O'Connor v. Ortega, 480 U.S. 709, 716 (1987) (applying the Fourth Amendment to searches in public sector workplaces).

[138] O'Connor v. Ortega, 480 U.S. 709 (1987) (holding a psychiatrist employed in a state hospital had a reasonable expectation of privacy in his office and was entitled to Fourth Amendment protection with respect to the search of his office by hospital officials).

[139] Steagald v. United States, 451 U.S. 204, 213 (1981).

[140] Slanina v. United States, 283 F.3d 670 (5th Cir. 2002).

[141] Id. at 675.

view. "To limit access to his computer files, he installed passwords, thereby making it more difficult for another person to get past the screen saver and reboot his computer."[142]

The federal appeals court found the supervisor's search of Slanina's computer was reasonable under the standard established in *O'Connor v. Ortega.*[143] The supervisor who conducted the search in *Slanina* had already learned about the accessing of child pornography newsgroups, which was evidence of the employee having downloaded child pornography onto his computer. The *O'Connor* court found the supervisor was justified in conducting an investigation into his employee's use of pornography because access to pornography violated city policy. Accordingly, the supervisor was legally permitted to conduct a full investigation to determine the extent of its employee's violations and therefore there was no Fourth Amendment violation.

(1) Smyth v. Pillsbury

Smyth v. Pillsbury[144] was the first reported case where a U.S. federal court upheld an employer's secret surveillance of employees' e-mails and Internet usage. In *Pillsbury*, a federal court held a company's interest in preventing inappropriate e-mail activity on its own system outweighed any employee privacy interest. Pillsbury maintained an e-mail system to enable communications with its employees. The company had previously assured its employees that e-mail communications could not be intercepted. Smyth, a regional operations manager, sent a combustible e-mail attacking management to his supervisor that, threatened to "kill the backstabbing bastards."[145] Pillsbury terminated Smyth's employment for "inappropriate and unprofessional comments over defendant's e-mail system."[146] The *Smyth* court ruled the employee had no expectation of privacy in online messages and, in any case, the employer's reading of these messages was not a "substantial and highly offensive" invasion of his privacy. The court reasoned that Pillsbury's right to prevent unprofessional and illegal activity outweighed any privacy interest of its employee in e-mail comments. The court ruled Smyth's termination did not violate a public policy based upon right of privacy.[147]

(2) Garrity v. John Hancock

John Hancock terminated two middle-aged female employees for forwarding sexually explicit e-mails from Internet joke websites and from other third parties in violation of the insurer's Internet usage policy.[148] One of their co-employees complained to management after receiving a forwarded e-mail with off-color jokes from the plaintiffs. John Hancock promptly began an investigation of the plaintiffs' e-mail folders, as well as the folders of those to whom the plaintiffs e-mailed on a regular basis. The ex-employees disputed the insurer's characterization of the e-mails in question as sexually explicit or in any way in violation of the policy language. The *Garrity* court found the plaintiffs' off color e-mail violated the insurer's e-mail policy. The Massachusetts federal court

---

[142] Id.

[143] 480 U.S. 709 (1987).

[144] 914 F. Supp. 97 (E.D. Pa. 1996).

[145] Id. at 99.

[146] Id. at 100.

[147] See Smyth v. The Pillsbury Co., 914 F. Supp. 97 (1996) (holding that even if the employee had a reasonable expectation of privacy, a reasonable person would not find the interception of such communications to be intrusive).

[148] Garrity v. John Hancock Mut. Life Ins. Co., 2002 WL 974676 (D. Mass. 2002).

dismissed the plaintiffs' privacy-based actions since the Hancock employees had no reasonable expectation of privacy in e-mails transmitted on John Hancock's e-mail and Internet usage policy.

To determine whether a contract is unconscionable, a court will typically examine "the commercial setting of the transaction, the use of fine print in the contract, and the use of high-pressure contracting tactics." John Hancock's policy made it clear that all information stored e-mail system was property owned by the insurer. "Even in the absence of a company e-mail policy, employees do not have a reasonable expectation of privacy in their work e-mail."[149] Further, the court said the interest of the employer to take affirmative steps against harassment outweighed the plaintiffs' privacy interest. U.S. courts' property-based approach to computer systems makes it difficult for plaintiffs to prevail even where employers' are engaging in egregious practices.[150] In the past two decades, not a single plaintiff has prevailed in a case arising out of an employer's surveillance of Internet or e-mail usage in the workplace. As noted earlier, this is an example of U.S. courts taking a formalistic property rights approach to monitoring. The courts' approach is that since the employer owns the computer system, it has a right to conduct secret surveillance. Secret surveillance in the workplace is strictly prohibited by European law, which is a topic discussed at the end of this chapter.

(B) Search and Seizure of Text Messages[151]

(1) The Ubiquity of Text Messaging and Electronic Messaging

A report by Congressman Ed Markey of Massachusetts found that in 2011 law enforcement agencies made 1.3 million requests for consumer phone information—including text messages—from the nine largest cellular carriers in 2011.[152] Stated succinctly, "[c]ell phones now represent a powerful tool . . . to cull information on a wide range of crimes."[153] Cell phones and text messages are now ubiquitous form of communication. "[Eighty-three percent] of American adults or greater than four out of five American now own a cell phone."[154]

The cell phone has "moved beyond a fashionable accessory and into the realm of life necessity."[155] "Text messages, [or] short electronically transmitted written communications between mobile devices, are closely intertwined with the popularity and adoption of cell phones."[156] For context, "an average of 4.1 billion text messages are

---

[149] Id. at *6.
[150] See e.g., Smyth v. Pillsbury Co., 914 F. Supp. 97 (E. D. Pa. 1996) (finding company's interest in preventing inappropriate e-mail activity on its own system outweighs any employee privacy interest); McLaren v. Microsoft Corp., 1999 Tex. App. LEXIS 4103 (Tex. App. Dallas May 28, 1999) (holding that employee had no reasonable expectation of privacy in e-mail messages transmitted over the company's network accessible by third parties); Garrity v. John Hancock Mut. Life Ins. Co., 2002 U.S. Dist. LEXIS 8343 (D. Mass., May 7, 2002) (granting summary judgment in favor of employer in case where e-mails were read by management).
[151] This practice pointer was authored by Carl Alexander Chiulli, Suffolk University Law School, 2013.
[152] Id. (citing Press Release, Congressman Ed Markey, Markey: Law Enforcement Collecting Information on Millions of Americans from Mobile Phone Carriers (on congressman's website)).
[153] Id.
[154] Pew Research Center, Americans and text messaging (Sep 19, 2011).
[155] State v. Patino, 2012 R.I. Super. LEXIS 139 at * 76 (Super. Ct. R.I., Sept. 4, 2012).
[156] Id. at *77.

exchanged daily [nationwide]."[157] "Text messages are frequently used to convey information that formerly would have been subject to an oral conversation."[158] Consequently, "[a]s Americans have turned to their cell phones to communicate, law enforcement has taken notice."[159] This raises a number of issues as to the Fourth Amendment protections that are afforded to cell phones, text messages, and electronic communications in general.

(2) The Fourth Amendment and the Katz Balancing Test

The Fourth Amendment "protects people from unreasonable government intrusions into their legitimate expectations of privacy."[160] The *sine qua non* of a Fourth Amendment inquiry is therefore "whether the search or seizure was reasonable under the totality of the circumstances." [161] The concept of the reasonable expectation of privacy does not descend from the legal heavens, but was instead promulgated in countless U.S. Supreme Court decisions that contemplated the Fourth Amendment in light of contemporary contextual, sociological, and technological circumstances.[162] Illustrative of the Fourth Amendment's necessary evolution is that it was considered constitutionally permissible to conduct warrantless telephone surveillance because there was no physical penetration of the telephone booth.[163] However, in *United States v. Katz,*[164] the Supreme Court rejected this logic, and fundamentally shifted its Fourth Amendment ideology, in holding that the Fourth Amendment protects "people, not places."[165] Justice John Harlan, in his seminal *Katz* concurrence, thus effectively set the stage for forthcoming Fourth Amendment jurisprudence by construing the now well-established legal standard that a warrant is required if the government is confronted with person's "reasonable expectation of privacy."[166]

Accordingly, and procedurally, a person may challenge the constitutional character of the government's search and/or seizure only after he or she has displayed a "reasonable expectation of privacy" in the area(s) searched or item(s) seized.[167] Justice Harlan's delineation was a two-pronged test requiring (1) a person to possess a subjective expectation of privacy in the item or area at issue and (2) that society be willing to recognize that expectation as reasonable."[168] The exclusionary rule suppresses evidence secured by the government without a warrant or exception to the

---

[157] Id. at *78 (citing Brief of Electronic Frontier Foundation et. al. as Amici Curiae in Support of Resp'ts, City of Ontario, Cal. v. Quon, 130 S. Ct. 2619 (2010), at 7.

[158] Id.

[159] Id.

[160] United States v. Chadwick, 433 U.S. 1, 7 (1977).

[161] State v. Patino, 2012 R.I. Super. LEXIS 139 at *84 (citing Cooper v. California, 386 U.S. 58, 59 (1967)).

[162] See e.g., Payton v. New York, 445 U.S. 573, 589–90 (1980) (applying search and seizure law to the use of thermal imagers to view the "the relative heat of various rooms in the home").

[163] Olmstead. v. United States, 277 U.S. 438, (1928) (ruling that the Fourth Amendment was not foreclosed by the interception of electronic communications).

[164] 389 U.S. 347 (1967)

[165] Id. at 351.

[166] Id. at 361 (Harlan, J., concurring).

[167] Id.

[168] Id.

warrant requirement. The U.S. Constitution's Fourth Amendment recognizes that all Americans have a legally recognized expectation of privacy.[169]

(3) Fourth Amendment Stretched to Text Messaging

In *City of Ontario v. Quon*,[170] the United States Supreme Court recognized that in deciding questions of reasonableness, courts should consider "rapid changes in the dynamics of communication and information transmission . . . not just [in] the technology itself but in what society accepts as proper behavior."[171] The issue before the Supreme Court in *Quon* was "whether text messages should be afforded Fourth Amendment privacy protection."[172] "But the Supreme Court declined, choosing instead to decide the case on narrower grounds and allow this question to percolate in the lower courts."[173] The lower courts give guidance on how search and seizure should be applied to cell phones and text messages.[174]

In *State v. Smith*,[175] the Ohio Supreme Court found that the data contained within a cell phone, *i.e.* text messages, was protectable under the Fourth Amendment because a cell phone is not a container and therefore cannot be searched incident to arrest. In *State v. Clampitt*,[176] a Missouri Appellate Court found that text messages stored on the defendant's phone, sent and received, were entitled to Fourth Amendment protection because text messages are a substitute for telephone calls and letters and accordingly worthy of the same protections. In *State v. Hinton*,[177] a Washington Appellate Court found that the Fourth Amendment protects text messages but only in conjunction with cell phones. Similarly, in *United States v. Finley*,[178] the Fifth Circuit held that cell phones and text messages should be treated the same for purposes of analyzing standing and protection under the Fourth Amendment.

While reaching these holdings, the presiding courts were presented with a number of interconnected sub-issues. One of the foremost issues that courts have considered is whether text messages are a separate and distinct entity from a cellular phone. To make this determination courts must determine whether a cell phone is a container under its traditional legal definition.[179] This determination or lack thereof, is important because if a cell phone is a container, then its text messages are, logically, its contents.[180] The expansive body of Fourth Amendment law for searching of

---

[169] See generally, 3 WAYNE LaFAVE, SEARCH & SEIZURE § 5.5 (4th ed.)

[170] City of Ontario v. Quon, 130 S. Ct. 2619 (2010).

[171] State v. Patino, 2012 R.I. Super. LEXIS 139 at *74 (citing Quon 130 S. Ct at 2629).

[172] Quon, 130 S. Ct. at 2629.

[173] Id. at 2629–30 (assuming, though not holding, that a reasonable expectation of privacy existed in text in the course of reaching a conclusion that a search of his government-issued pager by a government employer was not a violation of the Fourth Amendment considering the special needs of the workplace).

[174] U.S. Const. amend. IV ("The right of the people to be secure in their persons, houses, papers, and effects, against unreasonable searches and seizures, shall not be violated, and no Warrants shall issue, but upon probable cause, supported by Oath or affirmation, and particularly describing the place to be searched, and the persons or things to be seized.").

[175] 920 N.E.2d 949, 954 (Ohio 2009).

[176] 364 S.W.3d 605 (Mo. Ct. App. 2012).

[177] 2012 WL 2401673 (Wash. App. Div. June 26, 2012).

[178] 477 F.3d 250 (5th Cir. 2007).

[179] See State v. Patino, 2012 R.I. Super. LEXIS 139 at *95–102.

[180] Id.

containers would then apply to cell phones.[181] The second issue that courts have weighed is the rigidity with which to apply the third-party doctrine.

The third party doctrine states that an individual's expectation of privacy for information dissipates upon that information being voluntarily exposed or communicated to a third party.[182] Courts taking an overly formalistic perspective on the third-party doctrine vitiate any expectation of privacy for text messages because electronic communications necessarily pass through a service provider's network during their transmission. Thus, the third-party doctrine is always activated for electronic communications if it is applied absolutely. Another critical issue before courts is the proper use of analogies during the adjudication process.[183] Courts must decide if certain communication forms are similar enough to text messaging for it to be appropriate to glean law.[184] Difficulty arises because analogies to communications such as letters, emails, and phone conversations are frequently imperfect due to the evolutionary nature of technology. Electronic communications, in their current state, share the characteristics of many communication mediums. It is thus becoming increasingly difficult for courts to draw law from analogies without committing an analytical error.

(4) Warrantless Searches for Text Messages

Law enforcement officers routinely track cell phones and attempt to introduce text messages as probative evidence.[185] To date, courts have found no Fourth Amendment reasonable expectation of privacy in cell phone location data. *In re Smartphone Geolocation Data Application*,[186] the court authorized law enforcement using this data finding no violation of the Fourth Amendment:

> The advent of the smartphone has dramatically changed the ways in which we use and understand cellular telephone devices. Manufacturers modeled early cell phones on traditional landline telephones, to wit: a device used to communicate via audio conversation. Smartphones represent an entirely different paradigm. Contemporary smartphones, which continue to evolve,[4] are equipped with a panoply of technologies, allowing users not only the ability to make and receive audio calls, but also access to the Internet, text messages, video calls, email and thousands of software applications. Many of these features are akin to those formerly associated with a personal computer.[187]

In *State v. Patino*,[188] a Rhode Island trial court examined the question whether a criminal defendant had a right to privacy in text messages exploring the search and

---

[181] See generally, 3 WAYNE LaFAVE, SEARCH & SEIZURE § 5.5 (4th ed.).

[182] See id.

[183] See Patino, 2012 R.I. Super. LEXIS 139 at *128–46.

[184] Id.

[185] "Police efforts to obtain cell phone data are apparently common. Following an article published last April in the New York Times, reporting that law enforcement agencies routinely track cell phones with little or no court oversight, Representative Ed Markey (D-Mass) sent letters to major mobile carriers asking them about the number of requests they receive each year. The answer was more than 1.3 million requests in 2011, often without the knowledge of the person whose phone records are sought." Marie Andree Weis, Warrantless Text Message Search Threatens to Scuttle Murder Case, Digital Media Law (Sept. 24, 2012).

[186] 2013 U.S. Dist. LEXIS 62605 (E.D. N.Y. May 1, 2013).

[187] Id. at *21.

[188] 2012 R.I. Super. LEXIS 139 (R.I. Superior Ct., Sept. 4, 2012).

seizure of text messages and its interconnected sub-issues in detail. The state indicted Michael Patino for the murder of his girlfriend's six-year-old son based upon a series of text messages that he exchanged with the mother of the child. [189] Patino, in a motion to suppress, contended that the Cranston, Rhode Island police department violated his Fourth Amendment rights when they searched his girlfriend's cell phone and obtained his text messages without a warrant.[190] Applying the *Katz* test, the court first determined that Patino had the necessary standing to challenge the constitutionality of the Cranston Police Department's search and seizure of the defendant's text messages from his girlfriend's cellular phone.[191]

To reach this holding, the court dealt with a number of sub-issues including (1) whether cell phones are containers with text messages as their contents, (2) the appropriate application of the third-party doctrine to electronic communications, and (3) the ripe with pitfalls practice of too directly analogizing text messages to other forms of communication. Upon establishing Patino's standing, the court proceeded to hold that the Cranston Police Department's search of the cell phone of Patino's girlfriend violated the Fourth Amendment because it occurred without a warrant and outside of any established exception to the warrant requirement.[192] Consequently, the court ruled that the text messages at-issue, as well as a large amount of connected evidence, must be suppressed from Patino's murder trial because of the exclusionary rule and the fruit of the poisonous tree doctrine.[193] His written confession would not have been obtained but for the police's exploitation of the text messages in dispute.

(5) Cellular Phones as Containers

One of the most unsettled issues before courts is whether a mobile phone is classifiable as a container and thus subject to the containers exception to the Fourth Amendment. The *Patino* court classified the cell phone as an access point, rather than as a container, reasoning:

> A cell phone is the device by which text messages are sent, received, and stored. It is not, on accord of its physical dimensions or functionality, a closed container. Also, text messages are not a tangible object that fit within a cell phone. They are, in fact, information born in non-tangible digital form. In this Court's view, therefore, a cell phone is better thought of not as a container but as an "access point" to potentially boundless amounts of digital information.[194]

This is significant because containers, as defined by the law in *New York v. Belton*,[195] may be searched without a warrant pursuant to various well-established exceptions.[196] The U.S. Department of Justice urges its investigators to treat computers like closed containers:

---

[189] Id. at *1.

[190] Id. at *1–3.

[191] Id. at *145–6.

[192] Id. at *181.

[193] Id. at *309–11.

[194] Patino, 2012 R.I. Super. LEXIS 139 at *98.

[195] 453 U.S. 454, 460 (1981) (defining a container as "any object capable of holding another object" and thus implying physical dimensions).

[196] The six possible bases for a warrantless search of containers are as follow:

[I]t helps to treat the computer like a closed container such as a briefcase or file cabinet. The Fourth Amendment generally prohibits law enforcement from accessing and viewing information stored in a computer if it would be prohibited from opening a closed container and examining its contents in the same situation.[197]

The U.S. Justice Department acknowledges that the analogy between computer devices and closed containers is imperfect.[198] The *Patino* court reasoned that the similarities between a cell phone and a "container" were too tenuous to altogether apply the associated body of law. The court, in practical effect, precluded Rhode Island law enforcement from justifying the search and seizure of text message through the multiple warrantless exceptions that are recognized for containers; more is now necessary.

(6) The Third–Party Doctrine and Text Messaging

In the Internet age, it is common that individuals who retain a reasonable expectation of privacy in stored electronic information under their control may lose Fourth Amendment protections when they relinquish that control to third parties. For example, an individual may offer a container of electronic information to a third party by bringing a malfunctioning computer to a repair shop or by shipping a floppy diskette in the mail to a friend. Alternatively, a user may transmit information to third parties electronically, such as by sending data across the Internet, or a user may leave information on a shared computer network. When law enforcement agents learn of information possessed by third parties that may provide evidence of a crime, they may

---

(1) search of the object incident to the arrest of its possessor on the ground that it is within his "immediate control"; (2) inventory of the object subsequent to the arrest of its possessor; (3) search of the object on probable cause in exigent circumstances; (4) reasonable search of the object for reasons unrelated to the obtaining of evidence of crime; (5) search following a "controlled delivery" of the object by police or a police agent to a suspect; and (6) search of a container permitting a view or inference of its contents.

3 WAYNE LAFAVE, SEARCH & SEIZURE § 5.5 (4th ed.).

[197] The U.S. Department of Justice states further:

The most basic Fourth Amendment question in computer cases asks whether an individual enjoys a reasonable expectation of privacy in electronic information stored within computers (or other electronic storage devices) under the individual's control. For example, do individuals have a reasonable expectation of privacy in the contents of their laptop computers, USB drives, or cell phones? If the answer is "yes," then the government ordinarily must obtain a warrant, or fall within an exception to the warrant requirement, before it accesses the information stored inside. When confronted with this issue, courts have analogized the expectation of privacy in a computer to the expectation of privacy in closed containers such as suitcases, footlockers, or briefcases. Because individuals generally retain a reasonable expectation of privacy in the contents of closed containers.

See United States v. Ross, 456 U.S. 798, 822–23 (1982). They also generally retain a reasonable expectation of privacy in data held within electronic storage devices. U.S. DEPARTMENT OF JUSTICE, COMPUTER CRIME AND INTELLECTUAL PROPERTY, CRIMINAL SECTION SEARCHING AND SEIZING COMPUTERS & OBTAINING ELECTRONIC EVIDENCE IN CRIMINAL INVESTIGATIONS 3 (2009).

[198] "Although courts have analogized electronic storage devices to closed containers, some courts have also noted characteristics of computers which distinguish them from other closed containers. In United States v. Walser, 275 F.3d 981, 986 (10th Cir. 2001), the Tenth Circuit observed that "[t]he advent of the electronic age and . . . the development of desktop computers that are able to hold the equivalent of a library's worth of information, go beyond the established categories of constitutional doctrine. Analogies to other physical objects, such as dressers or file cabinets, do not often inform the situations we now face as judges when applying search and seizure law." See also United States v. Stierhoff, 477 F. Supp. 2d 423, 445 (D.R.I. 2007) ("analogizing a computer file to a closed container is a logical, if not entirely accurate, starting point for addressing the plain view doctrine's application to computer files"). Id. at 4, n.1.

wish to inspect it. Whether the Fourth Amendment requires them to obtain a warrant before examining the information depends in part, upon whether the third-party possession has eliminated the individual's reasonable expectation of privacy. The *Patino* court also weighed in on how the third-party doctrine applies to text messages, which is a form of electronic communications.

In the court's view, the third-party doctrine does not destroy an expectation of privacy in text messages because the doctrine is "ill-suited for contemporary forms of communication and thus should not wholly defeat an individual's expectation of privacy in the contents of his or her text messages."[199] The "third-party doctrine, in theory, seeks to strike a balance between the Fourth Amendment privacy rights of citizens and the investigative needs of the government."[200] The court determined that "in an era before the advent of cell phones, that the exchange of content of the text messages . . . would never have been public."[201] "The messages would have been exchanged [between parties] in person or via landline phone outside the view of law enforcement."[202]

Alternatively, the court reasoned that "the third-party doctrine is impliedly based on a theory of assumption of risk—*i.e.*, the theory that a sender of a text message assumes the risk that the recipient of that message will disclose its substance to a third party."[203] The court held that this "theory of assumption of risk does not match today's realities of electronic communications" because "to not partake in the medium is tantamount to actively choosing not to communicate."[204] In the court's words, "unless an individual is ready to relinquish his or her ability to effectively communicate in today's technological climate, the risk of surveillance is not a choice, but an undeniable reality."[205] These holdings take a logical stance on the third-party doctrine within the context of modern electronic communication. The court's duel holdings carefully outlay the purpose and reasoning of the third-party doctrine to prevent an individual's Fourth Amendment rights from being dissolved because of a doctrinal misunderstanding.

(7) Imperfect Analogies for Text Messaging

The *Patino* court acknowledged that courts frequently compare text messages to oral communications and letters but concluded:

> the usual tropes [ ] through which courts have viewed the limits of a reasonable expectation of privacy in text messages are of only limited use as they are largely predicated on a misconception regarding the technology's nature and use in contemporary society."[206]

Text messages, the court held, "are not letters, email, or even an oral communication alone—they are a technological and functional hybrid."[207] The court reasoned that text messages must be accommodated to the Fourth Amendment and

---

[199] State v. Patino, 2012 R.I. Super. LEXIS 139 at *128.
[200] Id. at *119.
[201] Id. at *125.
[202] Id.
[203] Id. at *126.
[204] Id.
[205] Id. at *127.
[206] Id. at *142.
[207] Id. at *143.

must reflect this reality and not be based on an incorrect analogy.[208] The *Patino* court, in making this point, impliedly cautioned other courts against extending extant law in a cursory manner without first considering the unique qualities of evolving technologies. The court expressed its opinion as to the virtues, if not necessity, of carefully considering the factual realities surrounding technology—as also advocated by the Supreme Court in *Quon*—before employing already developed but perhaps ill-fitting legal principles.

(8) Relevance of State v. Patino

State v. Patino[209] represents the first systematic analysis of the search and seizure of text messages. The *Patino* court's "thoughtful consideration of the [text messages and the Fourth Amendment] could help clear up some of the [current] uncertainty by providing state and district courts, as well as the Supreme Court, with the kind of analysis necessary to reach a consensus on the legality of text message interception and other types of surveillance, including GPS and cell phone tracking."[210] The *Patino* court has, in effect, brought common sense to the common law in updating the Fourth Amendment to extend to text messages. However, the manner in which the Fourth Amendment and electronic communications intersect is not yet settled law. Rulings from numerous appellate and high courts, potentially even the United States Supreme Court, are most likely necessary to find resolution for this increasingly common dilemma for law enforcement. Cases like *U.S. v. Patino* send a clarion call for police departments to obtain a search warrant before searching cell phones.[211] Courts are deeply divided about the necessity of obtaining a search warrant for text messages.[212]

(C) Global Positioning System ("GPS") Surveillance

Another unsettled issue is the extent of Fourth Amendment protection for the government's use of GPS in surveillance. In *United States v. Jones*,[213] the United States Supreme Court held that the installation of a GPS device on a person's car for the purpose of gathering information, along with the use of the device to track the car's movements, constituted a Fourth Amendment search. In Jones, police officers were investigating Antoine Jones, owner and operator of a nightclub in the District of Columbia, who was under suspicion of trafficking in narcotics. Police officers used multiple techniques "including visual surveillance of the nightclub, installation of a camera focused on the front door of the club, and a pen register and wiretap covering

---

[208] Id.

[209] State v. Patino, 2012 R.I. Super. LEXIS 139.

[210] Allison Grande, R.I. Text Message Ruling Fuels Police Surveillance Debate, Law 360, New York (September 6, 2012 10:14 PM EST).

[211] See e.g., People v. Wilson, 2013 WL 2360239 (Mich. App., May 30, 2013) (noting that police treated cell records as records seeing search warrant).

[212] United States v. Hill, 2011 WL 90130 (N. D. Cal. Jan. 10, 2011) (upholding warrantless search of iPhone photos incident to arrest); United States v. Finley, 477 F.3d 250, 259–60 (5th Cir.2007) (upholding warrantless search of cell phone incident to arrest); Cf. United States v. Park, 2007 WL 1521573 (N. D. Cal. May 23, 2007) (same); United States v. Lasalle, 2007 WL 1390820 (D. Hawai'i May 9, 2007) (ruling that warrantless search of cell phone phones was not incident to arrest as it was not on defendant's person); See also, State v. Smith, 124 Ohio St.3d 163, 920 N.E.2d 949 (2009) (suppressing warrantless cell phone search).

[213] 132 S.Ct. 945, 949 (2012).

Jones's cellular phone."[214] The government conceded that it did not seek a warrant to place a GPS on the defendant's vehicle:

> [A]gents installed a GPS tracking device on the undercarriage of the Jeep while it was parked in a public parking lot. Over the next 28 days, the Government used the device to track the vehicle's movements, and once had to replace the device's battery when the vehicle was parked in a different public lot in Maryland. By means of signals from multiple satellites, the device established the vehicle's location within 50 to 100 feet, and communicated that location by cellular phone to a Government computer.[215]

The defendant was charged with cocaine distribution causally connected to the information provided by the GPS. The Court held that tracking an automobile's whereabouts using a physically mounted GPS constituted a Fourth Amendment search.[216] The Court held that "the Government's installation of a GPS device on a target's vehicle, and its use of that device to monitor the vehicle's movements, constitutes a search."[217]Justice Scalia, writing for the majority, reasoned that by installing the device, "[t]he Government physically occupied private property for the purpose of obtaining information."[218]

In *Cunningham v. N.Y State Dept. of Labor*,[219] the New York Court of Appeals ruled that a State Inspector General's attaching a GPS device to a Department of Labor employee's personal car constituted a search within the meaning of the Fourth Amendment and the New York Constitution. The search in question was conducted by New York's Inspector General as part of an investigation of an employee's alleged unauthorized absences and submission of false time reports. The court described the GPS nonstop surveillance:

> The GPS device, known as a "Q-ball," once attached to the van, operated in conjunction with numerous satellites, from which it received tracking data, to fix the van's location. The Q-ball readings indicated the speed of the van and pinpointed its location within 30 feet. Readings were taken approximately every minute while the vehicle was in motion, but less often when it was stationary. The device's battery required replacement during the monitoring period, which resulted in yet another nocturnal visit by the investigator to the van's undercarriage. To download the location information retrieved by the Q-ball, the investigator would simply drive past the van and press a button on a corresponding receiver unit, causing the tracking history to be transmitted to and saved by a computer in the investigator's vehicle.[220]

The court ruled that the government's search did not require a warrant because it was under the workplace exception, but nevertheless did not comply with either the New York or U.S. Constitution because it was not a reasonable search. New York's

---

[214] Id. at 947.

[215] Id. at 948.

[216] Id. at 949.

[217] Id.

[218] Id.

[219] 2013 WL 3213347 (N.Y., June 23, 2013).

[220] Id. at 1195.

highest court previously decided in *People v. Weaver*[221] that a state police officer's placement of a GPS tracking device on the defendant's car, and the retrieval of data indicating car's location over period of approximately two months, constituted "search" requiring warrant under New York Constitution. In *Weaver*, the court did acknowledge that the defendant's reasonable expectation of privacy was diminished while in vehicle on public thoroughfare, but was not reduced to zero and that no exigent circumstances justified the officer's actions.[222] The court reasoned:

> Technological advances have produced many valuable tools for law enforcement and, as the years go by, the technology available to aid in the detection of criminal conduct will only become more and more sophisticated. Without judicial oversight, the use of these powerful devices presents a significant and, to our minds, unacceptable risk of abuse. Under our State Constitution, in the absence of exigent circumstances, the installation and use of a GPS device to monitor an individual's whereabouts requires a warrant supported by probable cause.[223]

§ 7.6 FEDERAL STATUTES GOVERNING INTERNET PRIVACY

(A) Privacy Act of 1974

Congress enacted the U.S. Privacy Act to prevent federal government from collecting unnecessary private information from individuals. This statute, enacted in the aftermath of Watergate, was concerned about the U.S. Governmental abuses as opposed to private companies. The federal statute specified the following fair information policies:

- There must be no personal data record-keeping systems whose very existence is secret;

- There must be a way for an individual to find out what information is in his or her file and how the information is being used;

- There must be a way for an individual to correct information in his or her records;

- Any organization creating, maintaining, using, or disseminating records of personally identifiable information must assure the reliability of the data for its intended use and must take precautions to prevent misuse; and

- There must be a way for an individual to prevent personal information obtained for one purpose from being used for another purpose without his or her consent.[224]

In *FAA v. Cooper*,[225] the U.S. Supreme Court held that the Privacy Act does not authorize damages for mental or emotional distress, and therefore does not waive the

---

[221] 12 N.Y.3d 433 (2009).

[222] Id. at 444 (The residual privacy expectation defendant retained in his vehicle, while perhaps small, was at least adequate to support his claim of a violation of his constitutional right to be free of unreasonable searches and seizures. The massive invasion of privacy entailed by the prolonged use of the GPS device was inconsistent with even the slightest reasonable expectation of privacy.").

[223] Id. at 447.

[224] Center for Democracy & Technology, Updating the Privacy Act of 1974 (June 5, 2009) (arguing that 1974 Privacy Act must be reformed to accommodate to the technological realities of the Internet).

government's sovereign immunity from liability for such harms. In *Cooper*, the Department of Transportation, and the SSA, in turn, provided the DOT with a spreadsheet containing investigations of a pilot for not disclosing his HIV status to the FAA. The FAA revoked the pilot's certificate and the U.S. Department of Justice indicted him for making false statements to a government agency. Cooper pleaded guilty and was fined and sentenced to probation. He then filed suit, alleging that the FAA, DOT, and SSA violated the Privacy Act of 1974, which contains a detailed set of requirements for the management of federal records. The Court's holding that plaintiffs could not pursue non-pecuniary damages   gives the U.S. Government a liability shield against most Internet-related claims, since the invasion of privacy action is seldom about money and largely about emotional injuries. *not consistg of*

(B) Children's Online Privacy Protection Act of 1998

The Children's Online Privacy Protection Act ("COPPA")[226] protects the privacy of children under 13 by making it illegal for companies to harvest personally identifiable information without their parents' consent.[227]COPPA's sphere of application is any website or online service that targets children 13 or younger. The FTC's COPPA rules went into effect on April 21, 2000.[228] The FTC issued new regulations, effective July 13, 2013, that expands COPPA to new information technologies such as plug-ins. The FTC initiated a comprehensive review of COPPA in 2010 to "ensure that the COPPA Rule keeps up with evolving technology and changes in the way children use and access the Internet, including the increased use of mobile devices and social networking."[229] The revised COPPA amendments provide:

- Modify the list of "personal information" that cannot be collected without parental notice and consent, clarifying that this category includes geolocation information, photographs, and videos;

- Offer companies a streamlined, voluntary and transparent approval process for new ways of getting parental consent;

- Close a loophole that allowed kid-directed apps and websites to permit third parties to collect personal information from children through plug-ins without parental notice and consent;

- Extend coverage in some of those cases so that the third parties doing the additional collection also have to comply with COPPA;

- Extend the COPPA Rule to cover persistent identifiers that can recognize users over time and across different websites or online services, such as IP addresses and mobile device IDs;

- Strengthen data security protections by requiring that covered website operators and online service providers take reasonable steps to release

---

[225] 132 S. Ct. 1441 (2012).

[226] 15 U.S.C. § 6501.

[227] 15 U.S.C. §§ 6501 et seq.

[228] 16 C.F.R. § 312.

[229] Federal Trade Commission, FTC Strengthens Kids' Privacy, Gives Parents Greater Control Over Their Information By Amending Children's Online Privacy Protection Rule Being Modified to Keep Up with Changing Technology (2013) http://www.ftc.gov/opa/2012/12/coppa.shtm (last visited June 17, 2013).

children's personal information only to companies that are capable of keeping it secure and confidential;

- Require that covered website operators adopt reasonable procedures for data retention and deletion; and

- Strengthen the FTC's oversight of self-regulatory safe harbor programs.[230]

The 2013 revisions to COPPA updated the following definitions:

- The definition of an *operator* has been updated to make clear that the Rule covers a child-directed site or service that integrates outside services, such as plug-ins or advertising networks, that collect personal information from its visitors. This definition does not extend liability to platforms, such as Google Play or the App Store, when such platforms merely offer the public access to child-directed apps.

- The definition of a *website or online service directed to children* is expanded to include plug-ins or ad networks that have actual knowledge that they are collecting personal information through a child-directed website or online service. In addition, in contrast to sites and services whose primary target audience is children, and who must presume all users are children, sites and services that target children only as a secondary audience or to a lesser degree may differentiate among users, and will be required to provide notice and obtain parental consent only for those users who identify themselves as being younger than 13.

- The definition of *personal information* now also includes geolocation information, as well as photos, videos, and audio files that contain a child's image or voice.

- The definition of *personal information* requiring parental notice and consent before collection now includes "persistent identifiers" that can be used to recognize users over time and across different websites or online services. However, no parental notice and consent is required when an operator collects a persistent identifier for the sole purpose of supporting the website or online service's internal operations, such as contextual advertising, frequency capping, legal compliance, site analysis, and network communications. Without parental consent, such information may never be used or disclosed to contact a specific individual, including through behavioral advertising, to amass a profile on a specific individual, or for any other purpose. The final amended Rule also adds a process allowing industry to seek formal approval to add permitted activities to the definition of *support for internal operations*.

- The definition of *collection* of personal information has been changed so that operators may allow children to participate in interactive communities without parental consent, so long as the operators take reasonable measures to delete all or virtually all children's personal information before it is made public.[231]

---

[230] Id.
[231] Id.

The FTC mandates that the site operator obtain verifiable parental consent and give conspicuous notice of their information practices.[232] Parents have a right to review personal information provided by a child and delete the information or have it deleted. A website may not condition a child's use of the website upon the successful collection of personal information. The FTC requires that a website give a child's parents the opportunity to restrain further use or collection of information. A website must have reasonable security to protect the confidentiality, security, and integrity of personal information collected from children. The Revised COPPA rule modifies rules and the machinery for complying with parental consent:

> The FTC considered numerous comments on the 'sliding-scale mechanism of parental consent," otherwise known as "email plus.' Under this method, operators that collect children's personal information for internal use only may obtain verifiable parental consent with an e-mail from the parent, as long as the operator confirms consent by sending a delayed e-mail confirmation to the parent, or calling or sending a letter to the parent. After considering the comments on 'email plus,' the FTC concluded that it remains a valued and cost-effective consent mechanism for certain operators. The Final Rule retains email plus as an acceptable consent method for operators that collect personal information only for *internal* use.

> To encourage the development of new consent methods, the Commission establishes a voluntary 120–day notice and comment process so parties can seek approval of a particular consent method. Operators participating in a Commission-approved safe-harbor program may use any consent method approved by the program.[233]

The revised COPPA incorporates a reasonable security standard for service providers:

> The amended Final Rule requires operators to take reasonable steps to make sure that children's personal information is released only to service providers and third parties that are capable of maintaining the confidentiality, security, and integrity of such information, and who assure that they will do so. The Rule also requires operators to retain children's personal information for only as long as is reasonably necessary, and to protect against unauthorized access or use while the information is being disposed of.[234]

The FTC is seeking greater compliance with its parental consent rules by requiring providers to submit audits annually to the Commission.[235] Annual reports from providers will allow the Commission to gauge the need for enforcement. The FTC's COPPA Rule provides websites with safe harbor if they comply with approved self-regulatory guidelines formulated by marketing or online industries. Self-regulatory guidelines must subject operators to the same or greater protections for children as contained in Sections 312.2 through 312.9 of the FTC's COPPA Rule. The site is required to conduct periodic reviews of subject operators' information practices. The website operator must first

---

[232] 16 C.F.R. §§ 312.4, 312.5.

[233] Federal Trade Commission, FTC Strengthens Kids' Privacy, Gives Parents Greater Control Over Their Information By Amending Children's Online Privacy Protection Rule Being Modified to Keep Up with Changing Technology (2013) http://www.ftc.gov/opa/2012/12/coppa.shtm (last visited June 17, 2013).

[234] Id.

[235] Id.

determine whether the website is targeting children under the age of 13. The FTC states the website must comply with COPPA if the operator has a "general audience website and actual knowledge that they are collecting personal information from children."[236]

The FTC developed a multi-factorial test to determine whether a given website targets children. The most important factors include the subject matter (visual or audio content), the age of models on the site, the age of the actual or intended audience and "whether a site uses animated characters or other child oriented features."[237] The Commission defines an entity as an "operator" depending on who owns, controls, and pays for the collection of information. If COPPA applies, the operator must link to a notice of its information practices on the homepage of the website or online service. This notice must extend to each area where it collects personal information from children. The FTC requires the link to be clear and prominent.

Personal information is defined to include: (1) an individuals' first and last name, (2) home or other physical address, (3) an e-mail address or other online contact information, (4) a telephone number, (5) a Social Security number, (6) a persistent identifier such as a code, and (7) any other information concerning the child or the parents of that child the operator collects online from the child.

Personal information may be collected directly from a child or passively through devices such as cookies. A cookie is a set of data that a website server gives to a browser the first time the user visits the site. The server updates this data with each return visit. The remote server saves the user information contained within the cookie. The user's browser does the same as a text file stored in the Netscape or Explorer system folder. A New York federal district court found no cause of action in favor of Internet users whose personal information such as names, e-mail addresses, telephone numbers, and searches performed was collected. The court dismissed all federal and state claims, finding it implausible that website visitors did not consent to the use of cookies.[238]

In May 2008, the Texas Attorney General settled the first COPPA action filed by a state attorney general. The government charged DollPalace.com with violating COPPA in unlawfully collecting personal information from children without obtaining parental consent. DollPalace.com, a site for cartoon dolls, conditioned website access on children completing a ten page questionnaires about themselves and their friends. The Texas Attorney General found that COPPA was violated because third parties could easily circumvent the parental consent feature of the sites. The Texas Attorney General found that third parties could easily circumvent the parental consent feature of the sites. Social media sites such as Facebook must comply with COPPA and must not sign up members under the age of 13. Still, children below the age of 13 will inevitably misrepresent their age to evade sign-up restriction. Children were participating in interactive chat rooms

---

[236] 16 C.F.R. § 312.

[237] 15 U.S.C. § 6101.

[238] In re Doubleclick Privacy Litigation, 154 F. Supp. 2d 497 (S.D. N.Y. 2001). (finding no cause of action in favor of Internet users whose personal information such as names, e-mail addresses, telephone numbers, searches performed and other personal information was being systematically collected by the defendant's cookies and dismissing all federal and state claims finding it implausible that website visitors did not consent to the use of cookies). Cookies "are computer programs commonly used by websites to store useful information such as usernames, passwords, and preferences, making it easier for users to access Web pages in an efficient manner. [The DoubleClick] cookies collect . . . [personal] "information such as names, e-mail addresses, home and business addresses, telephone numbers, searches performed on the Internet, Web pages or sites visited on the Internet . . .'" Id. at 502.

and forums without their parents' knowledge. In May of 2011, 7.5 million Facebook users were below the minimum COPPA age 13 threshold.[239] In March of 2012, the Federal Trade Commission have asked members of U.S. House of Representatives to amend COPPA to provide additional protections for children and teens that will enable law enforcement deletion of publicly available information of minors. In March of 2012, the FTC announced that it had settled a COPPA case with RockYou Inc. The FTC's complaint charged the social media site with violating the COPPA rule by:

> not spelling out its collection, use and disclosure policy for children's information;

> not obtaining verifiable parental consent before collecting children's personal information; and

> not maintaining reasonable procedures, such as encryption to protect the confidentiality, security, and integrity of personal information collected from children.[240]

RockYou settled charges that it failed to protect the security of its 32 million users. The FTC charged the social media site with violating COPPA because it collected information from 179,000 children without their parents' consent. "RockYou's knowing collection of and failure to delete children's personal information was also contrary to the representations in its privacy policy, the FTC contended. These false and misleading representations constituted deceptive acts or practices in violation of FTC Act § 5, the agency alleged."[241] RockYou was charged with violating "the COPPA Rule, 16 C.F.R. pt. 312 by failing to: provide adequate notice about how it collects and uses children's information; provide direct notice to parents; obtain parental consent; and establish reasonable procedures to protect children's personal information."[242]

The FTC settlement requires RockYou to implement and maintain a data security program and pay a $250,000 civil penalty to settle the COPPA charges. The FTC also settled a claim against a social media site, Xanga, which registered 1.6 million children under the age of 13, without obtaining their parents' consent and was the first FTC consent order involving mobile applications.[243] The FTC imposed a $50,000 civil penalty on Xanga as part of the settlement agreement. In another COPPA enforcement action, the virtual world of Playdom was assessed $3 million for collecting and disclosing personal information from hundreds of thousands of children under age 13 without their parents' prior consent in *U.S. v. Playdom, Inc.*[244]

In 2012, the FTC filed several enforcement actions against mobile applications for violating COPPA's disclosure requirements.[245] Regulatory agencies are beginning to mount enforcement actions against mobile application providers. In May 2008, the

---

[239] Emil Protalinski, Daughter Posts Sexually Explicit Photos, Dad Sues Facebook, ZDNET (Sept. 7, 2011).

[240] FTC Press Release, FTC Charges That Security Flaws in RockYou Game Site Exposed 32 Million E–Mail Addresses and Passwords (March 27, 2011).

[241] RockYou Settles FTC Data Protection Charges, Agrees to COPPA Rule Penalty, 7 ELEC. COM. & L. REP. (BNA) 643 (April 4, 2012).

[242] Id.

[243] United States v. W3 Innovations d/b/a/Broken Thumbs Apps., No. CV–11–03958–PSG (N.D. Cal. Aug. 15, 2011).

[244] No. SACV11–00724 (C.D. Cal. May 12, 2011).

[245] FEDERAL TRADE COMMISSION, PROTECTING CONSUMER PRIVACY IN AN ERA OF RAPID CHANGE: RECOMMENDATIONS FOR BUSINESSES AND POLICYMAKERS 15 (March 2012).

Texas Attorney General settled the first COPPA action filed by a state attorney general. The government charged DollPalace.com with violating COPPA in unlawfully collecting personal information from children without obtaining parental consent. DollPalace.com, a site for cartoon dolls, conditioned website access on children completing a ten page questionnaires about them and their friends. The Texas Attorney General found the parental consent feature of sites as easily circumvented. Websites that are collecting information from children under the age of thirteen must comply with COPPA.

(C) HIPAA's Online Privacy Rules

Congress enacted the Health Insurance Portability & Accountability Act of 1996 ("HIPAA") to allay the increasing public concern about the threat to privacy posed by interconnected electronic information systems. These concerns include: (1) protecting and enhancing the rights of consumers by providing them access to their health information and controlling the inappropriate use of that information; (2) improving the quality of health care in the U.S. by restoring trust in the health care system among consumers, health care professionals, and the multitude of organizations and persons committed to the delivery of care; and (3) improving the efficiency and effectiveness of health care delivery by creating a national framework for health privacy protection building on efforts by states, health systems, and individual organization and persons.[246] HIPAA applies to information created or maintained by health care providers who engage in certain electronic transactions, health plans, and health care clearinghouses. HIPPA prohibits a person from knowingly using your unique health identifier or wrongfully obtaining "individually identifiable health information relating to individual or disclosing individually identifiable health information to another person."[247]

Online health providers will need to comply with information security requirements to comply with HIPAA. Section 501 of HIPAA requires each institution to protect the security and confidentiality of personal information. Fines for violating HIPAA range from $25,000 for multiple violations of the same standard in a calendar year up to $250,000. The criminal penalty for egregious violations of HIPPA is up to 10 years in prison. The Internet poses a major risk to the continual safety and security of HIPPA information. A 24/7 website must provide adequate disclosures about data. Pharmaceutical manufacturer Eli Lilly and Co. inadvertently released the e-mail addresses of 669 medical patients who had registered at its website to receive messages regarding health related matters, such as reminders to take certain medications.[248] Eli Lilly settled with the states, but no individual plaintiff received a monetary award.

(D) Gramm–Leach–Bliley Act

President Clinton signed the Gramm–Leach–Bliley Act ("GLBA") on November 12, 1999. Subtitle A of Title V of the GLBA on the "Disclosure of Nonpublic Personal Information" applies to many Internet transactions. Congress' intent in enacting the GLBA was to provide consumers with access and control over private financial information maintained by banks and other institutions along with the opportunity to correct any errors. The GLBA gives the Federal Trade Commission the power to enforce

---

[246] Standards for Privacy of Individually Identifiable Health Information, 65 Fed. Reg. 82,462, 82,463 (Dec. 28, 2000) (codified at 45 C.F.R. pts. 160, 164).

[247] 42 U.S.C. § 1320d–6.

[248] Lilly Privacy Violation Charges Are Settled, N.Y. TIMES (Jan. 19, 2002) at C3.

the financial privacy rules. This federal statute defines financial institutions as "any institution the business of which is engaging in financial activities as described in the Bank Holding Company Act of 1956."[249] If a company is "significantly engaged" in providing financial products or services to consumers, it must comply with the privacy provisions of Subtitle A of Title V of GLBA.[250] The GLBA mandates financial institutions to inform their customers of the institution's privacy policies and practices with respect to information shared with both affiliated and non-affiliated third parties. The GLBA prohibits financial institutions from disclosing nonpublic personal information about customers to nonaffiliated third parties without first advising customers of the possibility of disclosure. Financial institutions must give customers an "opt out" procedure if they do not wish their financial information to be shared with third parties.[251]

SEC's Regulation S–P ("S–P") implements the privacy rules of the GLBA. Section 504 requires the SEC and other federal agencies to adopt rules, which implement notice requirements and restrictions on sharing a consumer's information. S–P requires brokers, dealers, investment companies, and investment advisers to provide notice of their privacy policy and to protect the privacy of customer information. Financial institutions must provide individuals with statutorily prescribed disclosures in initial as well as annual privacy notices. The GLBA regulation also specifies the affiliated and nonaffiliated third parties to which they may disclose personal information. Accordingly, financial institutions were required to post privacy notices and institute safeguards by July 1, 2001. S–P dictates that online companies provide customers with a clear and conspicuous notice of their privacy policies and practices. The online company needs to provide annual notices to its customers, post its privacy notice on its website, and offer its customers the option of opting out of disclosures.

§ 7.7   STATE REGULATION OF ONLINE PRIVACY

California's online privacy statute applies to any operator of a website or online service collecting personally identifiable information about individual California residents, even if there has no physical presence in that state. An online company will be in violation of California law unless it "conspicuously posts its privacy policy on its website."[252] Online companies have thirty days after being notified of noncompliance to post their online privacy policies. California mandates every online company's policy must: (1) complete an audit of each category of personally identifiable information collected or shared with third parties or other entities on the Internet about website visitors; (2) give consumers notice if there is a process for reviewing and revising their personally identifiable information; and (3) describe the process by which the operator notifies consumers as to any material change in their privacy policy.

The California statute gives online companies alternative ways of complying with the statutory requirement that conspicuous posting of their online privacy policy must be made: (1) the company may post its privacy page on its homepage; or a website may post an icon that hyperlinks to a web page displaying the actual privacy policy. The icon must be on the homepage or "the first significant page after entering the website, and if the

---

[249] 12 U.S.C. § 1843(K).

[250] 15 U.S.C. §§ 6801, 6809.

[251] The FTC promulgated the GLBA Final Rules governing financial institutions. 488 Subtitle A of Title V of the Gramm–Leach-Bliley Act is entitled "Disclosure of Nonpublic Personal Information" (Title V).

[252] Cal. Bus. & Prof. §§ 22575, 22579.

icon contains the word privacy."[253] A company must also use a color that contrasts with the background color of the web page or is otherwise distinguishable. Finally, a website operator may include a hyperlink to a web page on which the actual privacy policy is posted if the hyperlink is located on the website's homepage. The text link must include the word "privacy" and be written in capital letters equal to or greater in size than the surrounding text.

The California online privacy statute determines conspicuousness by the standard of the reasonable person. Many other states have enacted privacy statutes. Massachusetts' privacy statute, for example, provides, "A person shall have a right against unreasonable, substantial, or serious interference with his privacy."[254] To date, Massachusetts courts have decided no cases that address whether an employer's secret monitoring of employees' social media postings violate that state's privacy statute. Legislatures have been slow to recognize that employees are even entitled to notice of surveillance of their online activities.

§ 7.8   THIRD PARTY DISCLOSURE OF PRIVATE INFORMATION

In *Bartnicki v. Vopper*,[255] the U.S. Supreme Court held a journalist had an absolute First Amendment privilege for broadcasting a private recording that was surreptitiously intercepted by an unknown person. Bartnicki was the teacher's union chief negotiator in a contentious labor dispute with a high school. A third party intercepted his cell phone conversation with the union president. At one point in the cell phone conversation, the Union President thundered: "If they're not going to move for three percent, we're gonna [sic]have to go to their homes . . . To blow off their front porches. . ."[256] A journalist obtained a taped copy of this cell phone statement after an unknown third party left a copy in the defendant's mailbox. The Court held the journalist was not liable for violation of the ECPA for broadcasting the taped conversation. The Court commented, "The normal method of deterring unlawful conduct is to impose an appropriate punishment on the person who engages in it."[257]

The *Bartnicki* Court noted it would be unusual to punish a law-abiding journalist for the criminal act of an anonymous third party interceptor. The U.S. Supreme Court in *Bartnicki* held the First Amendment prohibited imposition of civil liability on defendant for his "repeated intentional disclosure of an illegally intercepted cellular telephone conversation" concerning matter of public concern.[258] The Court recognized the perils of requiring the public disclosure of private conversations and its "chilling effect on private speech."[259] This case "has significant implications for Internet law because of the vast opportunities for republication of information enabled by the Internet."[260]

---

[253] Id.

[254] MGLA ch. 214, § 1B.

[255] 532 U.S. 514 (2001).

[256] Id. at 518.

[257] Id. at 529.

[258] Id. at 517.

[259] Id. at 533.

[260] MARK LEMLEY ET AL., SOFTWARE AND INTERNET LAW 955 (3rd ed. 2006).

§ 7.9   CONSUMER PRIVACY BILL OF RIGHTS

In February of 2012, the Obama Administration presented a Consumer Privacy Bill of Rights as a blueprint for consumer privacy in a networked world. The proposed legislation implements the Consumer Privacy Bill of Rights to commercial sectors that are not subject to other federal data privacy laws. The Consumer Bill of Rights incorporated privacy principles formulated by The Organization for Economic Cooperation and Development ("OECD"). The OECD proposed an action plan for electronic commerce at a 1998 Ottawa Ministerial Conference. The OECD Privacy Guidelines were incorporated into the Directive on Data Protection that went into effect in October 1998 in the European Union.[261] The European Commission's Directive on Data Protection went into effect in October of 1998, and prohibits the transfer of personal data to non-European Union countries that do not meet Article 25, which is the European Union ("EU") 'adequacy' standard for privacy protection.[262]

While the United States and the EU share the goal of enhancing privacy protection for their citizens, the United States takes a different approach to privacy from that taken by the EU. European data protection law is slowly becoming the standard for Internet privacy. Nevertheless, the EU data protection directive has limited applicability to social networks:

> European data protection laws are intended to protect individual citizens from the dangers of data processing by governments and commercial businesses but not to curtail individual communications and information gathering. European data protection laws do not protect you from yourself or your friends.[263]

Online activities are increasingly likely to be subject to European privacy regulations in the interconnected world of the Internet. The Consumer Privacy Bill of Rights, drawn in large part, from OECD principles, states:

> Individual Control: Consumers have a right to exercise control over what personal data companies collect from them and how they use it.

> Transparency: Consumers have a right to easily understandable and accessible information about privacy and security practices.

> Respect for Context: Consumers have a right to expect that companies will collect, use, and disclose personal data in ways that are consistent with the context in which consumers provide the data.

> Security: Consumers have a right to secure and responsible handling of personal data.

---

[261] Michael L. Rustad & Sandra R. Paulsson, Monitoring Employee E-mail and Internet Usage: Avoiding the Omniscient Electronic Sweatshop: Insights from Europe, 7 U. PA. J. LAB. & EMP. L. 829, 866 (2005) ("European countries have formulated an all-encompassing cultural and legal response to privacy-based actions as compared to the United States, which continues to delineate a sharp distinction between private and public workplaces.").

[262] Export Government, Helping U.S. Companies Export, http://export.gov/safeharbor/ (last visited June 28, 2013).

[263] Lothar Determann: Social Media Privacy: A Dozen Myths and Facts, STANFORD TECHNOLOGY LAW. REVIEW. ¶ 4 (2012).

Access and Accuracy: Consumers have a right to access and correct personal data in usable formats, in a manner that is appropriate to the sensitivity of the data and the risk of adverse consequences to consumers if the data is inaccurate.

Focused Collection: Consumers have a right to reasonable limits on the personal data that companies collect and retain.

Accountability: Consumers have a right to have personal data handled by companies with appropriate measures in place to assure they adhere to the Consumer Privacy Bill of Rights.[264]

The Obama Administration seeks to improve global interoperability between the U.S. consumer data privacy framework and other countries' frameworks, through mutual recognition; the development of codes of conduct through multi-stakeholder processes; and enforcement cooperation. If Congress enacts this proposed statute, it will help to harmonize U.S. privacy law with the Eurozone's Data Protection Directive. The U.S. must also consider privacy regulations of individual nations. The Swedish Data Protection Act, for example, prohibits companies from harvesting names, addresses, and other personal information from its website without prior consent. Companies will need to examine the data protection laws and practices of many countries to ensure they will not be sued in a distant forum. American based companies doing business online are subject to EU privacy regulations.

§ 7.10 GLOBAL PRIVACY ISSUES

Global Internet companies will need to comply with the privacy laws of every country where they handle the data of consumers. In 2011, Facebook entered into a settlement agreement with the FTC, which prohibits the social media site from making misrepresentations about the privacy or security of its users' personal information. The Facebook settlement requires that social media sites enact comprehensive privacy programs. The settlement also prohibits social media sites from misrepresenting their compliance with the U.S.–E.U. Safe Harbor Principles. U.S. companies must not only localize their privacy policies for Europe but for every country where they collect personally identifiable data. Mix Telematics is, for example, a leading global provider of fleet and mobile asset management solutions delivered as software-as-a-service, or SaaS. Mix Telematics Inc., for example must comply with The Protection of Personal Information Bill, or "POPI," which is likely to be enacted in South Africa in late 2013. The global Internet lawyer representing e-commerce companies must anticipate being subject to diverse privacy regimes as Mix Telematics acknowledges in a SEC Filing:

If POPI becomes law, we anticipate being subject to a variety of obligations thereunder to take steps to protect personal information. Although we are continuing to evaluate the potential impact of POPI, taking into account our existing privacy and data security practices and procedures, we do not believe its implementation will have a material impact on our business.[265]

Mix Telematics also notes that it must comply with the EU"s data protection directive:

---

[264] THE WHITE HOUSE, CONSUMER DATA PRIVACY IN A NETWORKED WORLD (2012).
[265] Mix Telematics Inc., SEC F-1 Filing (July 3, 2013).

We are subject to regulation under the laws of the European Union. Of particular relevance with regard to the regulation of our solutions are matters of data protection and privacy. More broadly, any processing of personal data in the course of the provision of services is governed by the European Union data protection regime. The framework legislation at a European Union level in respect of data protection is Directive 95/46/EC, which we refer to as the Data Protection Directive. The Data Protection Directive protects the individual's right to privacy with respect to the processing of personal data. Each European Union member state is obligated to implement the principles contained in the Data Protection Directive.[266]

Mix Telematics must also comply with the Australian Regulatory Environment:

The National Privacy Principles contained in the Privacy Act 1988 regulate the collection, use, retention, disclosure and security of personal information. Personal information is defined as 'information or an opinion (including information or an opinion forming part of a database), whether true or not, and whether recorded in a material form or not, about an individual whose identity is apparent, or can reasonably be ascertained, from the information or opinion.' Personal information includes location-based information where the information enables the location of an individual to be ascertained. Australian privacy laws in general prohibit the transfer of personal information outside Australia unless the individual to whom the information relates has consented to the transfer or there is a data transfer agreement in place between the transferor and the transferee under which the transferee agrees to offer the same protections as are provided under Australian privacy laws. Amendments to these laws imposing stricter regulation will become effective in March 2014. These amendments include a provision making an organization, which transfers data outside Australia responsible for any breaches of Australian privacy laws when personal information is transferred outside Australia, regardless of whether there is consent or a data transfer agreement in place. There are also proposals to introduce privacy breach reporting which have not yet been enacted.[267]

An online company like Mix Telematics needs to complete a comprehensive legal audit in every country where it generates or processes data to determine whether they are subject to regulations or exempt.[268]

(A) Data Protection

The most dramatic differences are between U.S. and European paradigms governing Internet privacy. Lothar Determan punctures a hole in the widespread view among academics and policymakers that European privacy protection is greater than in the United States with its sectorial approach:

Fact is that the U.S. approach to privacy legislation is different from the European approach: Congress reviewed and consciously rejected a proposal for European-style, omnibus privacy legislation in 1974. Since then the U.S. has been addressing data processing activities only with respect to specific, compelling

---

[266] Id.

[267] Id.

[268] Id.

threats, via general consumer protection laws and narrowly crafted statutes. U.S. laws have been enforced effectively in practice and also have been continuously supplemented and updated to address specific threats; for example, data security breach notification laws were passed in California in 2002. European legislatures, on the other hand, have tried since 1970 to regulate the processing of personal data through broad, omnibus legislation based on a general prohibition of automated data processing with limited exceptions, requiring companies to obtain prior government approvals for many data-related activities. European data protection laws have not historically differentiated much with respect to particular threats, industries, or types of data. They have remained relatively static over the years.[269]

European privacy law is unified but is aspirational without strong mechanisms for enforcement. Europe does not have a tradition of enforcement by private attorneys general or class actions and critics claim its privacy regime is:

> overbroad, under-enforced, outdated and awaiting reality checks in courts. Take data security breaches, for example: the broad, omnibus information requirements under existing European data protection laws have arguably always required companies to inform data subjects of security breaches,28 however, in practice European companies have rarely disclosed breaches. Now, ten years after California passed the first law specifically requiring data security breach notifications, the European Union is working on similar legislation to address the serious threats to data security that have become acute in the last two decades.30 In general, the European Union considers its own privacy law regime so deficient and outdated that it has recently proposed a complete overhaul, specifically referencing a need to update the rules on personal data in social media.31 Thus, it seems a myth that the European Union is somehow ahead of the U.S. in terms of social media privacy protections.[270]

Nevertheless, EU authorities are mounting challenges to privacy policies that target European consumers. Enforcement actions have compelled a number of social media sites' to revise their privacy policies. Badoo, a U.K. based social network site, which is popular in Europe and Latin America, instructs users that their "Terms apply whenever you visit Badoo, whether or not you have chosen to register with us, so please read them carefully. By accessing, using, registering for or receiving services offered on Badoo, you are accepting and agreeing to be bound by the Terms."[271] In reality, the great majority of users do not read, much less analyze these terms.

A reasonable user, for example, is unlikely to know that he or she was consenting to Badoo's privacy policy without carefully reading the lengthy, often difficult to follow, set of provisions. In August of 2012, the German Federation of Consumer Groups charged Facebook "with giving away customer data via its new app centre without notifying users."[272] Hamburg Germany's Commissioner for Data Protection and Freedom of Information reopened an investigation of Facebook's privacy policies

---

[269] Lothar Determann: Social Media Privacy: A Dozen Myths and Facts, STANFORD TECHNOLOGY LAW. REVIEW. ¶ 8 (2012).

[270] Id. at ¶ 9.

[271] Badoo, Terms and Conditions of Use (2012).

[272] Reuters, German Consumer Group Sets Facebook Privacy Ultimatum, REUTERS NEWS SERVICE (Aug. 27, 2012).

relevant to "tagging photos, retaining and deleting data" and whether users have sufficient control over their personally identifiable information.[273]

In 2012, a Berlin court ruled that Facebook violates German data protection laws by transmitting "advertising e-mails to potential new users by gathering details from current users' accounts through the social media giant's Friend Finder feature."[274] The German court "also ruled on terms and conditions set out by Facebook that say any content generated by users can be used by the organization by holding that the conditions were not sufficiently specific and that the intellectual property rights of pictures and other content posted should remain with users."[275] The Council of Europe ("COE") has identified data protection as a priority in Internet Governance for the next few years. The COE endeavors to protect children's privacy with the new media by developing new tools for better management of private data. The COE also seeks tools to delete or remove accessibility to content produced by children.[276] The COE strives to raise awareness of the freedom of expression for all who use social media or other web-based applications.[277] Most U.S. companies have not revised their terms of service for the European market, despite their robust privacy law-in-the-books:

> In the meantime, U.S. social media companies are offering their services very successfully and without significant modifications in Europe. Europeans use such services much like U.S. users. Some European government agencies are taking steps to enforce local laws, but so are U.S. authorities and class action attorneys. Thus, all in all, European data protection laws do not appear to be ahead of U.S. laws or appear to protect privacy interests with respect to social media better than do U.S. privacy laws.[278]

The Federal Trade Commission, the chief privacy constable in the United States, filed legal actions against Facebook and Google over their privacy policies. Companies have new legal obligations to protect data as transborder data flows go global on the Internet. A Northern Ireland man filed suit in a Belfast High Court contending that salacious photographs of his daughter she posted herself on Facebook have placed her in "danger of attracting pedophiles."[279] The twelve-year-old girl received requests from men "to post sexual messages and photos on Facebook."[280]

One of eBay's subsidiaries, IAC (which has merged into Gmarket and is now named eBay Korea), notified its twenty million users of a data breach in January 2008 that compromised personally identifiable information including name, address, resident registration number and some transaction and refund data. Korean eBay users filed a number of representative lawsuits arising out of this data breach: not including credit card information or real time banking information).

---

[273] Id.

[274] Jabeen Bhatti, German Law Applies to Ban Facebook Use of Friend Finder to Solicit New Users, ELEC. COM. & L. REP. (BNA) (March 21, 2012).

[275] Id.

[276] COUNCIL OF EUROPE, INTERNET GOVERNANCE 5–6 (2012–2015) (20 Sept., 2011).

[277] Article 16(1) of Treaty on the Functioning of the European Union (TFEU), as introduced by the Lisbon Treaty, establishes the principle that everyone has the right to the protection of personal data.

[278] Id. at ¶ 11.

[279] Emil Protalinski, Daughter Posts Sexually Explicit Photos, Dad Sues Facebook, ZDNET.COM (Sept. 7, 2011).

[280] Id.

Approximately 149,000 users sued IAC over this breach in several lawsuits in Korean courts and more may do so in the future (including after final determination of liability). Trial for a group of representative suits began in August 2009 in the Seoul Central District Court, and trial for other suits began later in the Seoul Central District Court. There is some precedent in Korea for a court to grant "consolation money" for data breaches without a specific finding of harm from the breach. Such precedents have involved payments of up to approximately $200 per user.

In January 2010, one bench of the Seoul Central District Court ruled that IAC had met its obligations with respect to defending the site from intrusion and, accordingly, had no liability for the breach. This January 2010 ruling was appealed by approximately 34,000 plaintiffs to the Seoul High Court. In September 2012, a bench of the Seoul High Court announced its decision upholding the Seoul Central District Court's January 2010 decision for three cases involving 55 plaintiffs (who did not appeal to the Korea Supreme Court). Between April and June 2013, three benches of the Seoul High Court upheld the Seoul Central District Court's January 2010 ruling in 15 additional cases involving 23,466 plaintiffs. The Seoul High Court's decision in seven of these 15 cases has been appealed by 22,886 plaintiffs to the Korea Supreme Court so far with one case pending appeal. Five additional cases before two other benches of the Seoul High Court are currently being heard de novo, and decisions are expected later in 2013 or 2014. Currently, the Korea Supreme Court is reviewing a total of eight cases with 22,889 plaintiffs, including one case appealed from the Daegu High Court. In January 2013, the Seoul Western District Court ruled in favor of IAC with respect to two cases filed by 2,291 plaintiffs following the January 2010 ruling, and 2,284 plaintiffs proceeded to appeal the January 2013 decision of the Seoul Western District Court to the Seoul High Court.[281]

Canada's Privacy Commissioner launched an investigation of Google's new privacy policy in 2012. The principal issue is Google's retention of personally identifiable information and the linking of various Google applications including its Android mobile telephones. The Commissioner was critical of Google's delisting or de-identifying personal information.[282] The Federal Trade Commission ("FTC") asked Microsoft, Google, Mozilla, and other browser makers to develop a "do not track" option so they could opt out of all tracking.[283] In early 2012, state, federal, and European agencies launched an investigation into Google for alleged privacy violations. The privacy practices of Google and other Internet companies is a hot regulatory issue in the United States and Europe.

(B) Data Protection Directive

The Council of Europe adopted the European Convention on Human Rights ("ECHR") in 1950. Article 8 of the ECHR treats the right to respect for an individual's private and family life, home, and correspondence as a basic right.[284] The Data

---

[281] eBay SEC 10Q Filing (July 19, 2013).

[282] Peter Menyasz, Canada Privacy Chief Raises New Round Of Questions Over New Google Privacy Policy, ELEC. COM. & L. REP. (BNA) (March 21, 2012).

[283] Chloe Albanesius, Google, Mozilla Back White House "Do Not Track" Plan, PC MAG. (Feb. 23, 2012).

[284] Article 8 of the ECHR recognizes the Right to Respect for Private and Family life. Article 8 says: "(1) everyone has the right to respect for his private and family life, his home and his correspondence, and (2) there shall be no interference by a public authority with the exercise of this right except such as is in

Protection Directive of October 1995 commands any EU company to comply with specific rules for processing and transferring European consumer data. Each EU Member State has enacted legislation fulfilling the legal grounds defined in the Directive: consent, contract, legal obligation, vital interest of the data subject, and the balance between the legitimate interests of the people controlling the data versus the people on whom data is held (i.e., data subjects). The European Court of Human Rights has ruled, "Article 8 of the European Convention on Human Rights requires that domestic law must provide appropriate safeguards to prevent any misuse of personal data."[285] Wolf and Maxwell explain how the EU's region-wide Directive works in practice:

> In the EU, by contrast, a region-wide Directive, with national laws in twenty-eight jurisdictions to implement the requirements of the Directive, purports to regulate every piece of personal information and is predicated on the notion that privacy is a fundamental human right. Thus, under the approach of across-the-board regulation, there are strict limits on the collection and use of information, although enforcement of those limits has been episodic. Some of the enforcement actions have been criticized, such as a criminal case against Google executives on the grounds of invasion of privacy for a video posted by a YouTube user that depicted a group of Italian students bullying a disabled classmate—a video that Google took down within hours of being notified about it. After removing the video, Google fully cooperated with Italian police to help identify the individual who uploaded the video, and the video was used to convict that individual. Google stated in its official blog that '[i]n these rare but unpleasant cases, that's where our involvement would normally end,' but four Google executives were subsequently arrested and charged with violating Italian privacy laws for not blocking the video, and three of them were convicted of the charge.[286]

In the United States, ISPs do not have a duty to remove content that invades the privacy of others unlike their European counterpart.[287] One of the dangers of imposing a duty to take down content is that it may result in illegitimate take down of content that is expressive and protectable under the First Amendment. The Data Protection Directive gives data subjects control over the collection, transmission, or use of personal information. The Directive gives data subjects the right to be notified of all uses and disclosures about how their personal data is collected and processed.[288] An Internet business must procure explicit consent for the collection of personal data concerning race, ethnicity, or political opinions. Data handlers are required to protect personal information with adequate security. Data subjects have the right to get copies of information collected as well as the right to correct or delete personal data. Article 7

---

accordance with the law and is necessary in a democratic society in the interests of national security, public safety or the economic well-being of the country, for the prevention of disorder or crime, for the protection of health or morals, or for the protection of the rights and freedoms of others."

[285] Andreja Rihter, Privacy on the Internet—What Standards Do We Want? TOWARDS THE COUNCIL OF EUROPE ON INTERNET GOVERNANCE (2012–2015) (24–25 Nov. 2011) at 1.

[286] Christopher Wolf and Winston Maxwell, So Close, Yet So Far Apart: The EU and U.S. Visions of a New Privacy Framework, 26 ANTITRUST ABA 8, 9 (2012).

[287] Gavra v. Google Inc., No. 5:12–cv-06547–PSG (N.D. Cal., July 17, 2013) (holding that Google was entitled to Section 230 immunity arising out of a claim that Google did not remove defamatory content).

[288] Directive 95/46/EC on the protection of individuals with regard to the processing of personal data and on the free movement of such data.

requires the provider to obtain consent from the data subject before entering in to the contract.

Data handlers may not transfer data to other countries without "adequate level of protection" under Article 25. The Data Protection Directive requirement clashed with free expression in a case originating in the Göta Court of Appeal in Sweden. The court asked the EU Advocate General to give its opinion about a case in which a Swedish church member, Bodil Magret Lindqvist, established a homepage on the Internet that posted information about parishioners. Mrs. Lindqvist wrote in an online church bulletin that a church member suffered a foot injury and was on a part-time medical leave. Even though Mrs. Lindqvist promptly removed the homepage after a church member complained about it, the Swedish Government charged her with processing sensitive data without receiving prior written notification. The government fined Mrs. Lindqvist 4,000 Swedish crowns for violating Sweden's Data Protection Directive by transferring personal data to third countries without authorization. The European Court of Justice agreed with the Swedish government that Mrs. Lindqvist was processing personal data by loading information onto the Church's homepage.[289] The *Lindqvist* case illustrates the importance Europeans place on privacy. Foreign developments in data protection law such as the EU's proposed Data Protection Regulation impact companies outside the Eurozone.

An example of such a foreign development is the Proposal for a Regulation of the European Parliament and of the Council on the Protection of Individuals with Regard to the Processing of Personal Data and on the Free Movement of Such Data.[290] Even though the United States is not a member of the European Union, U.S. companies doing business in the Eurozone must nevertheless comply with the core principles of the EU Data Protection Directive. The Federation of German Consumer Organizations ("VZBV") filed an action against Facebook for violation of German consumer and privacy law in November 2010. "The court has decided that users have to be clearly informed that their entire address book will be imported to Facebook and used for invitations to friends."[291] Still, the fact that Facebook gets access to your entire e-mail list "is still not readily apparent."[292]

A Regional Court of Berlin ruled that Facebook's "Friend Finder" and its terms of use agreement violated the Unfair Commercial Practices Directive as well as that country's data protection directive. The German Data Protection Authority investigated Facebook because they are collecting biometric features of users without informing them or obtaining their consent. The American company's adoption of

---

[289] Case C/101/01 Criminal Proceedings Against Bodil Lindqvist; See generally, Flora J. Garcia, Comment, Bodil Lindqvist: A Swedish Churchgoer's Violation of the European Union's Data Protection Directive Should Be a Warning to U.S. Legislators, 15 FORDHAM INTELL. PROP. MEDIA & ENT. L.J. 1205, 1206 (2005) ("The different approaches to privacy in the United States and the European Union are deeply rooted in traditions much broader than the concept of privacy, such as the role of government in private life, the role of the press, and the freedoms that are afforded to the media generally.").

[290] "The draft proposal follows the principle that data processing is not permitted, unless expressly allowed, under Article 6. . . . Meanwhile, the right to be forgotten, found in Article 17,will mean that any data collected—including that which has been sold to third parties—must be deleted if a data subject withdraws consent." Jabeen Bhatti & Josie Le Blond, Business, Legal Community Fear Competitive Harms from Proposed EU Privacy Regulation, ELEC. COMM. L. REPORT (May 22, 2012).

[291] Emil Protalinski, Facebook Loses Friend Finder Ruling in Germany, ZDNET.COM (March 6, 2012).

[292] Id.

European style privacy disclosures supports Wu and Goldsmith's thesis that cyberspace is highly regulatable.

(C) U.S. Safe Harbor

Cross-border flows of personal data are necessary for the expansion of E–Commerce. With the Internet, there are new dangers when personal data is transferred. Counsel for 24/7 companies must oversee what personally identifiable information is collected and how long such data is kept. If a website business processes information, the European Union Directive on Data Protection will classify it as a service provider. Article 25 of the Data Protection Directive forbids the transfer of personal data to countries not providing "adequate protection."[293] The European Directive on Data Privacy became effective on October 25, 1998. The EC negotiated a safe harbor with the United States' Department of Commerce that obliges companies to certify their compliance with the Data Protection Directive.

In the United States, U.S. companies must comply with privacy rules and regulations promulgated under the authority of the Federal Trade Commission, the Health Insurance Portability and Accountability Act (HIPAA) of 1996 and state breach notification laws. Internationally, U.S. companies must comply with every jurisdiction where it handles personally identifiable data. Splunk, a U.S. software company, contends that virtually every jurisdiction in which they operate has its own data security and privacy legal framework.[294] Spunk, which markets its enterprise software in Europe, must comply, with the Data Protection Directive established in the European Union and the Federal Data Protection Act recently implemented in Germany.[295] The European Community achieved greater harmonization of data protection when the EC approved the Data Protection Directive, which expects each of the twenty-eight Member States to enact national legislation protecting "the fundamental rights and freedoms of natural persons, and in particular their right to privacy with respect to the processing of personal data."[296]

The U.S. Department of Commerce, in consultation with the EC, developed a voluntary safe harbor program for U.S. companies. Companies may join a self-regulatory privacy program by developing their own self-regulatory privacy policies. Companies seeking a safe harbor must adhere to the seven principles first formulated by the OECD and embodied in the Data Protection Directive: (1) notice, (2) choice, (3) onward transfer, (4) security, (5) data integrity, (6) access, and (7) enforcement. Companies joining the safe harbor are subject to Federal Trade Commission enforcement under Section 5 of the Federal Trade Commission Act (which prohibits unfair and deceptive acts) or another law or regulation prohibiting such acts. U.S. companies' participation in the Safe Harbor is voluntary. Companies have two routes to qualify for the U.S.–EU Safe Harbor program: (1) They can "join a self-regulatory privacy program that adheres to the U.S.–EU Safe Harbor Framework's requirements; or (2) [They can] develop its own self-

---

[293] Id. at art. 25.
[294] Spunk Inc., SEC 10–Q Filing (June 6, 2013).
[295] Id.
[296] Directive 95/46, art. 1.

regulatory privacy policy that conforms to the U.S.–EU Safe Harbor Framework.[297] The benefits of joining the safe harbor for U.S. companies are:

- All 28 Member States of the European Union will be bound by the European Commission's finding of "adequacy";

- Participating organizations will be deemed to provide "adequate" privacy protection;

- Member State requirements for prior approval of data transfers either will be waived or approval will be automatically granted;

- Claims brought by EU citizens against U.S. organizations will be heard, subject to limited exceptions, in the U.S.; and

- Compliance requirements are streamlined and cost-effective, which should particularly benefit small and medium enterprises.[298]

The Safe Harbor calls for enforcement by government as well as private enforcement. Private sector enforcement requires that companies:

> have in place a dispute resolution system that will investigate and resolve individual complaints and disputes and procedures for verifying compliance. They are also required to remedy problems arising out of a failure to comply with the principles. Sanctions that dispute resolution bodies can apply must be severe enough to ensure compliance by the organization; they must include publicity for findings of non-compliance and deletion of data in certain circumstances. They may also include suspension from membership in a privacy program (and thus effectively suspension from the U.S.–EU Safe harbor program) and injunctive orders.[299]

(D) General Data Protection Regulation

On January 1, 2012, the EC proposed the *Regulation on the Protection of Individuals with Regard to the Processing of Personal Data and on the Free Movement of Such Data* ("General Data Protection Regulation"). The Proposed General Data Protection Regulation will displace the Data Protection Directives.[300] The proposed Regulation offers the EU countries greater harmonization than directives that require national legislation to implement them. U.S. companies oppose the right to be forgotten in large part because of the potential liability and the practical difficulties of erasing content from the web. Wolf and Maxwell describe the proposed Data Protection Regulation as adopting a regional as opposed to national approach:

---

[297] Export.gov, Helping Companies Export, http://export.gov/safeharbor/eu/eg_main_018476.asp (last visited June 28, 2013).

[298] Id.

[299] "The dispute resolution, verification, and remedy requirements can be satisfied in different ways. An organization could meet the requirements by complying with a private sector developed privacy seal program that incorporates and satisfies the Safe Harbor Privacy Principles. If the seal program, however, only provides for dispute resolution and remedies but not verification, then the organization would have to satisfy the verification requirement in an alternate way. An organization could also meet the requirements by complying with government supervisory authorities or by committing to cooperate with the EU data protection authorities." Id.

[300] See Directive 95/46/EC of the European Parliament and of the Council of 24 October 1995 on the protection of individuals with regard to the processing of personal data and on the free movement of such data. ("Data Protection Directive").

Upon final passage of the Regulation, the current 1995 Data Protection Directive would be repealed. The proposed rules are intended to take into account the pervasive new technologies capable of collecting and sharing information about people, and to give individuals more control over their personal information.

Under the new Regulation, individuals and organizations would only need to deal with one supervisory authority, located in the country of their main establishment or residence, rather than the fragmentary jurisdiction currently provided by the Directive. The Regulation would make organizations outside the EU subject to its provisions if they process personal data to offer goods or services to EU residents, or monitor their behavior. And, if they are subject to its rules, with certain exceptions, they must appoint a representative to whom data protection concerns may be addressed.[301]

Enforcement is also delegated to private entities as well as the Federal Trade Commission:

> Depending on the industry sector, the Federal Trade Commission, comparable U.S. government agencies, and/or the states may provide overarching government enforcement of the Safe Harbor Privacy Principles. Where an organization relies in whole or in part on self-regulation in complying with the Safe Harbor Privacy Principles, its failure to comply with such self-regulation must be actionable under federal or state law prohibiting unfair and deceptive acts or it is not eligible to join the safe harbor. At present, U.S. organizations that are subject to the jurisdiction of either the Federal Trade Commission or the Department of Transportation with respect to air carriers and ticket agents may participate in the U.S.–EU Safe Harbor program. The Federal Trade Commission and the Department of Transportation have both stated in letters to the European Commission that they will take enforcement action against organizations that state that they are in compliance with the U.S.–EU Safe Harbor Framework, but then fail to live up to their statements.[302]

The Federal Trade Commission has initiated enforcement actions against companies that do not live up their safe harbor duties:

> Under the Federal Trade Commission Act, for example, an organization's failure to abide by commitments to implement the Safe Harbor Privacy Principles might be considered deceptive and actionable by the Federal Trade Commission. This is the case even where an organization adhering to the Safe Harbor Privacy Principles relies entirely on self-regulation to provide the enforcement required by the Safe Harbor enforcement principle. The FTC has the power to rectify such misrepresentations by seeking administrative orders and civil penalties of up to $12,000 per day for violations.[303]

(1) Central Provisions

The Data Protection Regulation is directly applicable to all of the Member States and "will reduce legal fragmentation and provide greater legal certainty by introducing

---

[301] Christopher Wolf and Winston Maxwell, So Close, Yet So Far Apart: The EU and U.S. Visions of a New Privacy Framework, 26 ANTITRUST ABA J. 8. 10 (2012).

[302] Id.

[303] Id.

a harmonized set of core rules, improving the protection of fundamental rights."[304] Article 1 of the proposed Regulation sets out the same objectives as Directive 95/46/EC. The proposed Data Protection Regulation consists of 88 articles. The key provisions of the General Data Protection Regulation are: (1) an expanded jurisdictional reach applied to non-European companies that process the data of European consumers; (2) the duty to notify consumers of a data breach within 24 hours; (3) require companies to obtain a "specific, informed and explicit" consent before collecting personal data (opt-in provision); and (4) a company's duty to erase personal data upon demand (right to be forgotten).[305] The chief provisions of the General Data Protection are:

- A single set of rules on data protection, valid across the EU. Unnecessary administrative requirements, such as notification requirements for companies, will be removed. This will save businesses around €2.3 billion a year.

- Instead of the current obligation of all companies to notify all data protection activities to data protection supervisors—a requirement that has led to unnecessary paperwork and costs businesses €130 million per year, the Regulation provides for increased responsibility and accountability for those processing personal data.

- For example, companies and organizations must notify the national supervisory authority of serious data breaches as soon as possible (if feasible within 24 hours).

- Organizations will only have to deal with a single national data protection authority in the EU country where they have their main establishment. Likewise, people can refer to the data protection authority in their country, even when their data is processed by a company based outside the EU. Wherever consent is required for data to be processed, it is clarified that it has to be given explicitly, rather than assumed.

- People will have easier access to their own data and be able to transfer personal data from one service provider to another more easily (right to data portability). This will improve competition among services.

- A "right to be forgotten" will help people better manage data protection risks online: people will be able to delete their data if there are no legitimate grounds for retaining it.

- EU rules must apply if personal data is handled abroad by companies that are active in the EU market and offer their services to EU citizens.

- Independent national data protection authorities will be strengthened so they can better enforce the EU rules at home. They will be empowered to fine companies that violate EU data protection rules. This can lead to penalties of up to €1 million or up to 2% of the global annual turnover of a company.

---

[304] Proposal for a Regulation of the European Parliament and of the Council on the Protection of Individuals with Regard to the Processing of Personal Data and on the Free Movement of Such Data ("General Data Protection Regulation") (Jan. 25, 2012) at 3.2.

[305] Jeffrey M. Goetz, A New World of EU Data Protection, MARTINDALE.COM (Feb. 2, 2012).

- A new Directive will apply general data protection principles and rules for police and judicial cooperation in criminal matters. The rules will apply to both domestic and cross-border transfers of data.[306]

The proposed General Data Protection Regulation imports principles for processing personal data drawn from its predecessor, the Data Protection Directive but also strengthens protections. Article 3 defines key concepts such as data subject, personal data, processing, controller, processor, and sets forth the following principles for processing personal data:

(1) This Regulation applies to the processing of personal data in the context of the activities of an establishment of a controller or a processor in the Union.

(2) This Regulation applies to the processing of personal data of data subjects residing in the Union by a controller not established in the Union, where the processing activities are related to:

(A) the offering of goods or services to such data subjects in the Union; or

(B) the monitoring of their behavior.

(3) This Regulation applies to the processing of personal data by a controller not established in the Union, but in a place where the national law of a Member State applies by virtue of public international law.[307]

(2) Opt-in Rules for Cookies

Article 3(2) asserts that non-Eurozone Internet sellers must comply with the Regulation if they target consumers within the EU or monitor their behavior. This provision would make Internet sellers liable for dropping cookies without the consent of EU consumers. Article 5 sets out the principles relating to personal data processing. Personal data must be:

(a) processed lawfully, fairly and in a transparent manner in relation to the data subject;

(b) collected for specified, explicit and legitimate purposes and not further processed in a way incompatible with those purposes;

(c) adequate, relevant, and limited to the minimum necessary in relation to the purposes for which they are processed; they shall only be processed if, and as long as, the purposes could not be fulfilled by processing information that does not involve personal data;

(d) accurate and kept up to date; every reasonable step must be taken to ensure that personal data that are inaccurate, having regard to the purposes for which they are processed, are erased or rectified without delay;

(e) kept in a form which permits identification of data subjects for no longer than is necessary for the purposes for which the personal data are processed; personal data may be stored for longer periods insofar as the data will be processed solely for historical, statistical or scientific research purposes in accordance with the

---

[306] European Commission, Commission Proposes a Comprehensive Reform of Data Protection Rules to Increase Users' Control of Their Data and to Cut Costs for Business, Brussels, Jan. 25, 2012.

[307] European Parliament and Council, Proposed General Data Protection Regulation (2012).

rules and conditions of Article 83 and if a periodic review is carried out to assess the necessity to continue the storage;

(f) processed under the responsibility and liability of the controller, who shall ensure and demonstrate for each processing operation the compliance with the provisions of this Regulation.

(3) Data Minimization

The Regulation adopts a new transparency principle as well as a principle of data minimization. Comprehensive responsibility and liability of the controller was also established. Article 6 sets out the basic principle that consent is the *sine qua non* of fair data collection. Data processing is limited to specified purposes. Article 7 of the Regulation sets out the importance of valid consent as a legal predicate ground for lawful processing of subject data. Subjects have the right to withdraw consent at any time. Article 8 is a special provision for processing of personal data of children in relation to services offered directly to them. Article 9 prohibits the processing or revealing of data on "race or ethnic origin, political opinions, religion or beliefs, trade-union membership, and the processing of genetic data or data concerning health or sex life or criminal convictions or related security measures."[308] The Regulation recognizes exceptions including the consent of the subject and processing to protect the interests of the subject.

(4) Duties of Controllers

Article 4(5) defines controllers as those natural persons or others who control the processing of data. The new Regulation requires controllers to have transparent and easy to understand policies as well as mechanisms for data subjects to exercise their rights, which are spelled out in Articles 11 and 12. Article 11 introduces the obligation on controllers to provide transparent and easily accessible and understandable information. Article 12 requires the controller to provide procedures and mechanisms for exercising the data subject's rights including means for electronic requests, respond to the data subject's request within a defined deadline, and provide explanations for any refusal to act on a data subject's request. Article 15 provides the data subject with the right of access to their personal data and the right to be informed of their right to rectification and to erasure, with a mechanism for complaint.

(5) The Right to Be Forgotten

Under the proposed Data Protection Regulation, European citizens will have the right to expunge or erase personal data and "abstention from further dissemination" under Article 17. Viviane Reding, the EU Justice Commissioner, stated that rationale for a digital eraser: "At present a citizen can request deletion only if [data is] incomplete or incorrect. We want to extend this right to make it stronger in this internet world. The burden of proof shall be on the companies. They will have to show that data is needed."[309] This right further elaborates and specifies the "right of erasure . . . including the obligation of the controller which has made the personal data public to inform third parties on the data subject's request to erase any links to, or copy or

---

308 Id. at art. 8(1).
309 Owen Bowcott, Britain Seeks Opt–Out of New European Social Media Privacy Laws, THE GUARDIAN (April 4, 2013).

replication of that personal data."[310] The "right to be forgotten" "should also be extended in such a way that a controller who has made the personal data public should be obliged to inform third parties which are processing such data that a data subject requests them to erase any links to, or copies or replications of that personal data."[311]

The Data Protection Regulation establishes a general standard of reasonableness for controllers to employ technical measures, in relation to data for the publication of which the controller is responsible. The Proposed Regulation would require controllers to give notice to third parties that a data subject has revoked consent for data that the subject demands to be forgotten. The fundamental right is that subjects should have the right that their personal data are erased and no longer processed. In other words, "where data subjects have withdrawn their consent for processing or where they object to the processing of personal data concerning them or where the processing of their personal data otherwise does not comply with this Regulation."[312]

The right to be forgotten is "relevant, when the data subject has given their consent as a child, when not being fully aware of the risks involved by the processing, and later wants to remove such personal data especially on the Internet."[313] Article 17(1) of the EC's new privacy regulation states:

> The data subject shall have the right to obtain from the controller the erasure of personal data relating to them and the abstention from further dissemination of such data, especially in relation to personal data, which are made available by the data subject while he or she was a child, where one of the following grounds applies:
>
>> (A) the data are no longer necessary in relation to the purposes for which they were collected or otherwise processed;
>>
>> (b) the data subject withdraws consent on which the processing is based according to point (A) of Article 6(1), or when the storage period consented to has expired, and where there is no other legal ground for the processing of the data;
>>
>> (c) the data subject objects to the processing of personal data pursuant to Article 19;
>>
>> (d) the processing of the data does not comply with this Regulation for other reasons.[314]

In addition, the controller has a duty to inform third parties processing data that it is subject to erasure. Article 2 requires the controller to:

> take all reasonable steps, including technical measures, in relation to data for the publication of which the controller is responsible, to inform third parties which are

---

[310] European Commission, Detailed Explanation of the Proposal (2012).

[311] European Commission, Explanatory Memorandum, Proposal for a Regulation on the European Parliament and of the Council on the protection of individuals with regard to the processing of personal data and on the free movement of such data (General Data Protection Regulation at 54.

[312] Id. at 25 (clause 53).

[313] Id.

[314] Proposal for a Regulation of the European Parliament and of the Council on the protection of individuals with regard to the processing of personal data and on the free movement of such data (General Data Protection Regulation), Id. at art. 17(1).

processing such data, that a data subject requests them to erase any links to, or copy or replication of that personal data. Where the controller has authorized a third party publication of personal data, the controller shall be considered responsible for that publication.[315]

This "right to be forgotten" provision will be difficult to implement because of Internet archiving that captures a past Internet site. The beta version of the Wayback Machine enables browsing through over 150 billion web pages archived from 1996 to within a few months of 2012.[316] The right to be forgotten, as conceptualized by the EC, applies to "every photo, status update, and tweet," which "could precipitate a dramatic clash between European and American conceptions of the proper balance between privacy and free speech."[317] Data providers face "ruinous monetary sanctions for any data controller that does not comply with the right to be forgotten or to erasure'—a fine up to 1,000,000 euros or up to two percent of Facebook's annual worldwide income."[318]

(6) Profiling & Aggregating Data

Article 19 provides for the data subject's rights to object to the use of their data for direct marketing purposes. Article 20 concerns the data subject's right not to be subject to a measure based on profiling. Articles 31 and 32 introduce an obligation to notify the data subject of personal data breaches; building on the personal data breach notification in article 4(3) of the E–Privacy Directive 2002/58/EC. Article 33 introduces the obligation of controllers and processors to carry out a data protection affect assessment prior to risky processing operations. This standard establishes a negligence-like standard in determining the radius of the risk. The EC's reform of the 1995 EU data protection is designed to update and modernize the law to reflect the impact of the Internet. The interrelationship of privacy on the global Internet means that U.S. companies will need to comply with the proposed Directive. The Obama Administration and U.S. companies have been lobbying to weaken the proposed privacy directive.

In the United States, the Fourth Amendment governs workplace surveillance in the public sector, but this protection has no application to the private sector. The entire emphasis of privacy protection in the United States is against governmental intrusion as opposed to corporate surveillance. For Europeans, the fundamental right of privacy extends to workplaces in the private and public sector as individuals have a right to establish and develop relationships with other human beings in workplace. Articles 7 and 8 of the Charter of Fundamental Rights of the European Union protect the privacy of family life and personal data.[319] Privacy in the countries of the European Union is a fundamental right, unlike in the United States.[320] The European Court of Human Rights ("ECHR") in Strasbourg, France, is the principal enforcement agency of the Council of Europe Convention for the Protection of Human Rights and Fundamental

---

[315] Id. at art. 17(2).

[316] Internet Archives, Wayback Machine, Frequently Asked Questions (2012).

[317] Jeffrey Rosen, The Right to be Forgotten, 64 STAN L. REV. ONLINE 88 (2012).

[318] Id.

[319] Chapter II Freedoms: Article 7 and 8 of the Charter of Fundamental Rights of the European Union.

[320] Michael L. Rustad & Sandra R. Paulsson, Monitoring Employee E-mail and Internet Usage: Avoiding the Omniscient Electronic Sweatshop: Insights from Europe, 7 U. PA. J. LAB. & EMP. L. 829, 866 (2005).

Freedoms of 1950. "The European Court of Human Rights has held that the protection of private life extends to the employer monitoring of employees and protects e-mails sent from work and Internet use at work."[321] Article 8 of the European Convention for the Protection of Human Rights and Fundamental Freedoms expressly states: "Everyone has the right to respect for his private and family life, his home, and his correspondence."[322] The ECH has expanded the meaning of "private life and correspondence" in Article 8 to encompass Internet-related communications such as e-mail.[323] In *Niemietz v. Germany*,[324] the ECHR expanded the meaning of "private life" to "inner circle, which also encompasses workplace colleagues. This ECHR decision reflects common sense because professional life and private life are often intertwined. The European view is that "correspondence," which includes e-mail communications is protected by Article 8. The ECH ruled that a company's interception of phone calls at work violated Article 8 of the ECHR in *Halford v. United Kingdom Government*.[325] The ECHR reasoned, "Correspondence is not restricted to private correspondence and Article 8 applies whether a communication is private or professional."[326]

In addition to the ECHR, each member state of the EU follows a dual system of privacy regulation composed of national legislation and European Union regulations. In October of 1995, the EC adopted a directive on the protection of individuals with regard to the processing of personal data and on the free movement of such data between member states.[327] As noted in previous section the Data Protection Directive will be displaced by the proposed Data Protection Regulation. The Data Protection Regulation seeks to resolve the problem that European Member States vary in the extent of their privacy protection. The United Kingdom, for example, has weaker privacy protections than France. With the enactment of the Data Protection Regulation, all member states will have the same privacy standards, which will make compliance more manageable. The Proposed Regulation, like its predecessor Data Protection Directive, applies to all personally identifiable data and there is no exemption for either private or public workplaces. Therefore, all companies must obtain consent before they obtain copies of information collected or correct or delete data.[328] In *X v. European Central Bank ("ECB")*,[329] the European Court of Justice ("ECJ") has held that companies must have written and signed e-mail policies at hand as a precondition to monitoring. The *ECB* case arose out of employee "X"'s suspension after he was found to have distributed pornography and political information on the

---

[321] Ariana R. Levinson, Toward a Cohesive Interpretation of the Electronic Communications Privacy Act, 114 W. VA. L. REV. 461, 477 (2012).

[322] The Council of Europe Convention for the Protection of Human Rights and Fundamental Freedoms of 1950, art. 8.

[323] Niemietz v. Germany European Court of Human Rights (No. 13710/88), December 16, 1992 and Halford v. United Kingdom Government, European Court of Human Rights (No. 2065/92), June 25, 1997.

[324] Id.

[325] European Court of Human Rights (No. 20605/92), June 1997.

[326] Id. p. 12, para 32 (citing Huvig v. France, European Court of Human Rights (No. 11105/84), 24 April 1990 (finding a violation of Article 8 even where correspondence was of a purely professional character).

[327] European Parliament and Council Directive 95/46 EC on the Protection of Personal Data [Official Journal L 281 of 23 11 1995].

[328] Data Protection Directive, Id. at art. 12.

[329] ECJ (No. T-333/99) Judgment of 18/10/2001, X/BCE (Rec. 2001, p. II-3021 JA, II-921) (upholding termination of bank employee that downloaded and transmitted pornography as well as political documents to third parties with the bank's computers because the bank had a clear policy that the Internet was to be used for business purposes only).

bank's computer system. In this case, the employee did not challenge the suspension on privacy, but on the validity of the bank's Internet usage policy. The ECB court upheld the suspension concluding that the bank had a right to establish internal disciplinary rules for breaches of an employment agreement.[330] The lesson of the ECB case is that a U.S. company needs a signed agreement from employees in European subsidiaries if it conducts surveillance of their e-mail or Internet activities.

(E) Directive on Privacy and Electronic Communications

The Cookies Directive, Article 5.3 of Directive 2002/58/EC (as amended by Directive 2009/136/EC), "has reinforced the protection of users of electronic communication networks and services by requiring informed consent before information is stored or accessed in the user's (or subscriber's) terminal device.[331] Article 5.3 recognizes two exemptions from the general rule of consumer informed consent so long as they satisfy one of the following criteria:

CRITERION A: the cookie is used "for the sole purpose of carrying out the transmission of a communication over an electronic communications network."

CRITERION B: the cookie is "strictly necessary in order for the provider of an information society service explicitly requested by the subscriber or user to provide the service."[332]

The EU Directive recognizes two categories of cookies: session cookie and persistent cookies:

A 'session cookie' is a cookie that is automatically deleted when the user closes his browser, while a 'persistent cookie' is a cookie that remains stored in the user's terminal device until it reaches a defined expiration date (which can be minutes, days or several years in the future).[333]

The Commission exempts the following cookies from informed consent under certain conditions if they are not used for additional purposes:

(1) User input cookies (session), for the duration of a session or persistent cookies

(2) limited to a few hours in some cases.

(3) Authentication cookies, used for authenticated services, for the duration of a session.

(4) User centric security cookies, used to detect authentication abuses, for a limited persistent duration.

(5) Multimedia content player session cookies, such as flash player cookies, for the duration of a session.

(6) Load balancing session cookies, for the duration of session.

---

[330] Id. p. 4, para. 5.

[331] European Commission, The Working Party on the Protection of Individuals With Regard to the Processing of Personal Data, set up by Directive 95/46/EC of the European Parliament and of the Council of 24 October1995,having regard to Articles 29 and 30 paragraphs 1(a) and 3 of that Directive,

having regard to its Rules of Procedure, (June 7, 2012) http://ec.europa.eu/justice/data-protection/article-29/documentation/opinion-recommendation/files/2012/wp194_en.pdf (last visited May 25, 2013).

[332] Id.

[333] Id. at 2–3.

(7) UI customization persistent cookies, for the duration of a session (or slightly more).

(8) Third party social plug-in content sharing cookies, for logged in members of a social network.[334]

Europe follows an "opt-in" approach to dropping cookies versus the U.S. approach, which is "opt-out."[335] The 2011 Regulations implement a new provision that require users to give consent before dropping a cookie.[336] "Under Regulation 6 of the 2003 Regulations, users of cookies were allowed to deploy them provided that those whose devices they were being dropped on were given clear and comprehensive information about the cookies and were given the opportunity to refuse their having access to the device or store information on it."[337] In the twenty-eight countries of the European Union, cookies cannot be used without a user's permission except for the current session (session cookies.) For persistent cookies (beyond the current session), companies must seek explicit permission (opt-in).[338]

The e-Privacy Directive, effective May 26, 2012, requires websites disclose that they use cookies to track users and requires user's consent before dropping them. A U.S. company targeting European consumers need to comply with the EU Directive by May 26, 2012, which is the end of the one-year grace period. Recently, the EU data protection paradigm has expanded outside of Europe. "Both Dubai and Israel now have adopted stringent, E.U.-style data protection laws, and U.S. healthcare enterprises should be aware of additional compliance burdens of doing business in these attractive new markets."[339]

(F) Global Internet Security

Internet security is just beginning to evolve as a legal duty worldwide. The EU Commission has proposed a Directive requiring notification of security breaches by service providers. The majority of U.S. states require companies to inform customers if their personal data has been stolen or compromised. The duty to disclose encompasses a trend to impose greater legal duties to safeguard customer data. A growing number of state and federal statutes already require companies to tell customers of data theft. Courts have yet to extend a general duty for companies to secure their websites or computer systems and to safeguard customer data. Private consumers have no private cause of action in the event a company fails to incorporate cost-justified precautions to secure their computer system. Europeans have filed suit against companies that violate the privacy of consumers or have failed to notify them of security breaches.

In 2012, The Tribunal of Milan convicted three Google executives for violating Italy's data protection law. The conviction arose out of a third party's "online posting of

---

[334] Id. at Summary & Guidelines.

[335] The Privacy and Electronic Communications (EC Directive) (Amendment) Regulations (2011).

[336] Osborne Clarke, New ePrivacy Regulations in Force (June 17, 2011).

[337] Stephen Groom, New E-Privacy Regulations in Force, http://www.osborneclarke.co.uk/publications/services/commercial/upstream/upstream-june-2011/new-eprivacy-regulations-in-force.aspx (September, 2012).

[338] EUROPEAN COMMISSION, COOKIES, INTERNET PROVIDERS GUIDE, THE EU INTERNET HANDBOOK (2012).

[339] Vadim Schick, Data Privacy Concerns for U.S. Healthcare Enterprises' Overseas Ventures, 4 J. HEALTH & LIFE SCI. L. 173 (2011) .

a video showing a disabled person being bullied and insulted."[340] The speaker in the video called the child, who suffered from Down's syndrome, a Mongoloid, and an offensive term. The video was posted for a period of two months before Google took it down. Google stated that it was unable to provide documentation of all comments and flaggings. Evidence exists only for a flagging of the video on November 5, 2006 and an e-mail request for removal on the following day. The Milan court charged executives of Google Italy with offenses such as aggravated defamation and invasion of privacy, which are crimes in Italy. The defendants were acquitted of defamation but convicted of violating Italy's Data Protection Act. "This is the crime of "illicit treatment of personal data" (*trattamento illecito dei dati*), contained in Article 167 of the Italian Data Protection Code. It is perpetrated when someone, with a view to obtaining a gain or to causing harm, processes personal data in breach of certain provisions of the same code."[341]

(G) Workplace Privacy

Privacy has been regarded as a fundamental right throughout Europe since the middle of the Eighteenth Century. Americans, in contrast, have little by way of statutory protection for privacy outside a few sectors such as health care and financial services. Europeans find the U.S. approach to privacy to be too amorphous, lacking the focus or saliency of this value in the legal system and in the culture.

(H) Do Not Track Specifications

In June of 2013, the World Wide Web Consortium ("W3C") issued an unofficial draft for Do Not Track ("DNT") specifications. The W3C specifications define the following definitions:

A *user* is an individual human. When user agent software accesses online resources, whether or not the user understands or has specific knowledge of a particular request, that request is "made by the user."

The term *user agent* refers to any of the various client programs capable of initiating HTTP requests, including but not limited to browsers, spiders (web-based robots), command-line tools, native applications, and mobile apps [*HTTP11*].

A *network interaction* is the set of HTTP requests and responses, or any other sequence of logically related network traffic caused by a user visit to a single web page or similar single action. Page re-loads, navigation, and refreshing of content cause a new network interaction to commence.

A *party* is any commercial, nonprofit, or governmental organization, a subsidiary or unit of such an organization, or a person. For unique corporate entities to qualify as a common party with respect to this document, those entities *MUST* be commonly owned and commonly controlled and *MUST* provide easy discoverability of affiliate organizations. A list of affiliates *MUST* be available through a single

---

[340] Giovanni Sartor and Mario Viola de Azevedo Cunha, The Italian Google-Case: Privacy, Freedom of Speech and Responsibility of Providers for User Generated Contents, 18 INT. J. LAW & INFO. TECH. 356 (2012).

[341] Id. (discussing issues in the case).

user interaction from each page, for example, by following a single link, or through a single click.[342]

Under the proposed W3C, the outsourced *service provider* is considered to be the same party as its client if the service provider:

(1) acts only as a data processor on behalf of the client;

(2) ensures that the data can only be accessed and used as directed by that client;

(3) has no independent right to use or share the data except as necessary to ensure the integrity, security, and correct operation of the service being provided; and

(4) has a contract in place that outlines and mandates these requirements.[343]

The W3C proposal will serve as good guidance for courts and legislatures because of its careful definitions such as tracking: *"Tracking* is the retention or use, after a network interaction is complete, of data records that are, or can be, associated with a specific user, user agent, or device."[344]

Collecting, retaining, using, and sharing are also key concepts defined succinctly in the proposed specifications.[345] The W3C proposal employs common sense in defining the first party as "the party with which the user intentionally interacts. In most cases on a traditional web browser, the first party will be the party that owns and operates the domain visible in the address bar."[346] Another reasonable assumption is to treat the person who owns or operates branded widgets, search boxes, or other commercial services as first parties. Nevertheless, the W3C proposal acknowledges that:

> In most network interactions, there will be only one first party with which the user intends to interact. However, in some cases, a resource on the Web will be jointly operated by two or more parties, and a user would reasonably expect to communicate with all of them by accessing that resource. User understanding that multiple parties operate a particular resource can, for example, be accomplished through inclusion of multiple parties' brands in a domain name, or prominent branding on the resource indicating that multiple parties are responsible for content or functionality on the resource with which a user reasonably would expect to interact by accessing the resource. Simple branding of a party, without more, will not be sufficient to make that party a first party in any particular network interaction.[347]

The key standard for user preferences is as follows:

---

[342] World Wide Web Consortium, Tracking Compliance and Scope, Unofficial Draft, (June 14, 2013).

[343] Id.

[344] Id.

[345] The June 14 proposal defines these terms as follows:

A party collects data if it receives the data and shares the data with other parties or stores the data for more than a transient period. A party retains data if data remains within a party's control beyond the scope of the current network interaction. A party uses data if the party processes the data for any purpose other than storage or merely forwarding it to another party.

A party shares data if the party enables another party to receive or access that data.

[346] Id.

[347] Id.

A user agent *MUST* offer users a minimum of two alternative choices for a Do Not Track preference: unset or DNT: 1. A user agent *MAY* offer a third alternative choice: DNT: 0.

If the user's choice is DNT:1 or DNT:0, the tracking preference is *enabled*; otherwise, the tracking preference is *not enabled*.

A user agent *MUST* have a default tracking preference of unset (not enabled).

User agents and websites are responsible for determining the user experience by which a tracking preference is controlled. User agents and websites *MUST* ensure that tracking preference choices are communicated to users clearly and accurately and shown at the time and place the tracking preference choice is made available to a user. User agents and websites *MUST* ensure that the tracking preference choices describe the parties to whom DNT applies and *MUST* make available brief and neutral explanatory text to provide more detailed information about DNT functionality.

That text *MUST* indicate that:

1. if the tracking preference is communicated, it limits collection and use of web viewing data for certain advertising and other purposes;

2. when DNT is enabled, some data may still be collected and used for certain purposes, and a description of such purposes; and

3. if a user affirmatively allows a particular party to collect and use information about web viewing activities, enabling DNT will not limit collection and use from that party.

User agents and websites *MUST* obtain an explicit choice made by a user when setting controls that affect the tracking preference expression.

A user agent *MUST* transmit the tracking preference according to the [*TRACKING–DNT*] specification.

Implementations of HTTP that are not under control of the user *MUST NOT* generate or modify a tracking preference.[348]

The W3C sets the following compliance rule for first parties:

If a first party receives a DNT:1 signal the first party *MAY* engage in its normal collection and use of information. This includes the ability to customize the content, services, and advertising in the context of the first party experience.

The first party *MUST NOT* pass information about this network interaction to third parties who could not collect the data themselves under this standard. Information about the transaction *MAY* be passed on to service providers acting on behalf of the first party.[349]

Third-party compliance rules are also set forth in the proposed W3C specification:

If a third party receives a DNT: 1 signal, then:

---

[348] Id.

[349] Id.

1. the third party *MUST NOT* collect, retain, share, or use information related to the network interaction as part of which it received the DNT: 1 signal outside of the permitted uses as defined within this standard and any explicitly-granted exceptions provided in accordance with the requirements of this standard;

2. the third party *MUST NOT* use information about previous network interactions in which it was a third party, outside of the permitted uses as defined within this standard and any explicitly-granted exceptions, provided in accordance with the requirements of this standard.

The third party *MAY* nevertheless collect, use, and retain such information for the set of permitted uses described below. Further, parties *MAY* collect, use, and retain such information in order to comply with applicable laws, regulations, and judicial processes.

Outside the permitted uses listed below, the third party *MUST NOT* collect, retain, share, or associate with the network interaction identifiers that identify the specific user, user agent, or device. For example, a third party that does not require unique user identifiers for one of the permitted uses must not place a unique identifier in cookies or other browser-based local storage mechanisms.

Third parties that disregard a DNT signal *MUST* signal so to the user agent, using the response mechanism defined in the [*TRACKING–DNT*] specification.[350]

When a third party receives a DNT:1 signal, that third party *MAY* nevertheless collect, retain, share or use data related to that network interaction if the data is de-identified as defined in this specification. It is outside the scope of this specification to control short-term, transient collection and use of data, so long as the information is not transmitted to a third party and is not used to build a profile about a user or otherwise alter an individual user's user experience outside the current network interaction. For example, the contextual customization of ads shown as part of the same network interaction is not restricted by DNT: 1.

Section 5.1.4 requires third parties to implement reasonable security to protect data:

Third parties *MUST* use reasonable technical and organizational safeguards to prevent further processing of data retained for permitted uses. While physical separation of data maintained for permitted uses is not required, best practices *SHOULD* be in place to ensure technical controls ensure access limitations and information security. Third parties *SHOULD* ensure that the access and use of data retained for permitted uses is auditab.[351]

The proposed specification recognizes exceptions such as debugging code. In addition, the specification contemplates user consent to personalization.[352] Section

---

[350] Id.

[351] Id

[352] The W3C proposal addresses user-oriented exceptions as noted below:

When a user sends a DNT: 0 signal, the user is expressing a preference for a personalized experience. This signal indicates explicit consent for data collection, retention, processing, disclosure, and use by the recipient of this signal to provide a personalized experience for the user. This recommendation places no restrictions on data collected from requests received with DNT: 0.

Seven also develops a methodology for dealing with multiple user preferences.[353] Section Eight requires parties that unknowingly collect data to take prompt remedial measures to delete that information.[354]

The operator of a website may engage in practices otherwise proscribed by this standard if the user has given explicit and informed consent. This consent may be obtained through the API defined in the companion [TRACKING–DNT] document, or an operator of a website may also obtain out of band consent to disregard a Do Not Track preference using a different technology. If an operator is relying on out of band consent to disregard a Do Not Track preference, the operator must indicate this consent to the user agent as described in the companion [TRACKING–DNT] document. Id.

[353] Section 7 states:

Multiple systems may be setting, sending, and receiving DNT and/or opt-out signals at the same time. As a result, it will be important to ensure industry and web browser vendors are on the same page with respect to honoring user choices in circumstances where "mixed signals" may be received. As a general principle, more specific settings override less specific settings.

1. No DNT Signal / No Opt–Out: Treat as DNT unset
2. DNT Signal / No Opt–Out: Treat as DNT: 1
3. Opt–Out / No DNT Signal: Treat as DNT: 1
4. Opt–Out / DNT User–Granted Exception: Treat as DNT: 0 for that site; DNT User–Granted Exception is honored. Id. at Section 7.

[354] Section Eight states:

a party learns that it possesses information in violation of this standard, it MUST, where reasonably feasible, delete or de-identify that information at the earliest practical opportunity, even if it was previously unaware of such information practices despite reasonable efforts to understand its information practices. Id. at § 8.

Chapter 8

PROSECUTING CYBERCRIMES

§ 8.1   OVERVIEW OF CYBERCRIMES

In 2012 alone, the Internet Crime Complaint Center reported 289,874 complaints.[1] "The most common complaints received in 2012 included FBI impersonation e-mail scams, various intimidation crimes, and scams that used computer 'scareware' to extort money from Internet users."[2] Cybercrime refers to a class of criminal acts, which are enabled by the Internet such as the phishing attacks that were launched hours after the Boston Marathon bombing.[3] Lawyers who have a website presence are targeted by phishers masquerading as legitimate clients. Here's an example: "I am contacting your firm in regards to a breach of contract matter with a client in your locality. Do let me know if you are currently accepting new clients."

"Computer crimes cost U.S. businesses billions of dollars every year. Many of these foreseeable economic losses would have been prevented if companies had taken even basic security measures."[4] In 2012, the IC3 received 289,874 consumer complaints with an adjusted dollar loss of $525,441,110.[5] Cybercrimes, unlike traditional crimes, do not involve face-to-face criminality. Cybercriminals maintain websites where one can buy names, addresses, and Social Security or credit card numbers. Therefore, the Internet is much like new wine in old bottles; facilitating traditional crimes. For example, the *BBC* reported that an Australian teenager posted a picture of a massive cache of cash that she was helping to count. Within hours, armed masked men appeared at the door and demanded the money.[6] The Internet has lowered the costs of perpetuating street crimes because victims' personal information is posted on websites.[7] International cybercrime flourishes in the cross-border Internet but is also targeted at victims located within the boundaries of the United States.[8] Counterfeit pharmaceutical products sold on websites threaten the public health and cost the industry hundreds of millions of dollars as noted in a Chilling Effects Clearinghouse blog:

---

[1] Internet Crime Complaint Center (IC3), IC3 Crime Report Released, FBI National Office, May 14, 2013) (IC3 is a partnership between the Federal Bureau of Investigation (FBI), the National White Collar Crime Center (NW3C) and the Bureau of Justice Assistance (BJA)).

[2] Id.

[3] Internet Crime Complaint Center (IC3), Beware of Possible Fraud Associated With the Boston Marathon (April 25, 2013), http://www.ic3.gov/media/2013/130425.aspx (last visited July 5, 2013).

[4] Former Justice Department CyberLawyer Peter Toren Authors Guide to Protection Against High–Tech Theft and Intellectual Property Violations, BUSINESS WIRE, Sept. 12, 2003 (quoting Peter Toren).

[5] IC3gov., 2012 Internet Crime Report, http://www.ic3.gov/media/annualreport/2012_IC3Report.pdf (last visited July 13, 2013).

[6] Mike Flacy, Teenage Girl Posts Picture of Cash on Facebook, Family Robbed Within Hours, DIGITAL TRENDS, May 29, 2012,www.digitaltrends.com/social-media/teenage-girl-posts-picture-of-cash-on-facebook-family-robbed-within-hours/.

[7] Neal Kumar Katyal, Criminal Law in Cyberspace, 149 U. PA. L. REV. 1003, 1006 (2001) (explaining that cybercrime consumes less resources than real space crime such as a bank robbery).

[8] SUSAN W. BRENNER, CYBERCRIME: CRIMINAL THREATS FROM CYBERSPACE 170 (2010).

With the Internet as the third largest market for distributing counterfeit goods, the lethal drugs have taken position in the rich world too. The World Health Organization presents numbers stating that 50% of all drugs bought online are imitations. Viagra, the drug for erectile dysfunction, tops the list of knock-offs seen by Pfizer, and has for a long time been available for purchase online for USD $ 1 per pill, while the price at the pharmacy is $15. Would the attitude towards money saving and avoidance of embarrassment be different if we knew that every other blue pill contains lead paint, acid and is potentially lethal? Would it still be worth saving $14, knowing that you may actually pay with your life? Will we think differently about it when the fake trade has now expanded to include even Tamiflu, Plavix, and Casodex, used to treat influenza, blood clots, and prostate cancer, respectively?[9]

This chapter examines the big policy issues about cybercrime and reviews the major federal statutes in addition to the Cybercrime Convention. It was the first large-scale international attempt to begin updating the criminal law to address Internet enabled crimes. The Convention is not a transnational substantive law statute, but rather a pact by signatories to pass domestic cybercrime legislation. What the Convention did was spur some countries to develop new national legislation to address issues such as the spread of computer viruses, online child pornography, or the interception of computer communications. Conduct considered criminal in one society is protected expression in another. For example, Grenada enacted new Internet crime legislation "that makes it a crime to offend people through websites such as Facebook and Twitter."[10]

This also chapter investigates the evolving law of cybercrimes concerning computer hacking, viruses, economic espionage, trade secret misappropriation, intellectual property theft, and cyber terrorism. The focus will be on Internet-related crimes "that use or target computer networks, which we interchangeably refer to as 'computer crime,' 'cybercrime,' and 'network crime.' Examples of computer crime include computer intrusions, denial of service attacks, viruses, and worms."[11] Cybercrime is borderless and by its very nature, and difficult to detect. Online intruders, unlike those at traditional crime scenes, will typically leave few digital footprints. Law enforcement lacks the expertise and the resources to police cybercrime in a meaningful way. The use of false e-mail headers, offshore sites, and anonymous re-mailers are as significant to online intruders as the automobile was to car thieves or bank robbers in the 1920s and 1930s.[12] Just as the automobile created the need to update the criminal law because thieves were simply fleeing the jurisdiction, legislatures must be aware that cybercriminals exploit gaps in the law.[13] In 1990, a court mentioned the word

---

[9] Chilling Effects.org, A Sick Crime (June 17, 2013), http://www. chillingeffects. org/weather.cgi? WeatherID=766 (last visited June 17, 2013).

[10] Associate Press, Grenada Makes It a Crime to Offends Persons on Facebook, Twitter (June 29, 2013).

[11] U.S. DEPT. OF JUSTICE, MANUAL ON PROSECUTING COMPUTER CRIMES v (2012) (discussing scope of computer crime prosecution by the U.S. Department of Justice).

[12] See Michael L. Rustad, Private Enforcement of Cybercrime on the Electronic Frontier, 11 S. CAL. INTERDISC. L.J. 63, 66 (2001) ("Law enforcement resources in cyberspace cannot keep pace with sophisticated cybercrime subcultures in anonymous offshore havens.").

[13] In the first decades of the twentieth century, the automobile shaped the path of the law. One unobtrusive measure of the lasting impact of automobile law is the number of topics covered in Prosser's treatise on tort law. The index for the Fifth Edition lists the following tort doctrines influenced by automobile law: liability for unavoidable accidents, assured clear distance rule, gratuitous liability of bailors, vicarious

"Internet" for the first time in a judicial opinion in *United States v. Morris*.[14] In *Morris*, the Second Circuit upheld a graduate student's conviction under the CFAA for releasing an infamous worm that caused hundreds of educational and military computers on the Internet to crash.[15]

This was the first documented case where a computer virus shut down the then extant Internet.[16] During the early years of the Internet, cybercrime law had not yet evolved to address unique Internet technological dilemmas. In *United States v. LaMacchia*,[17] a Massachusetts federal court dismissed a wire fraud complaint against defendant who distributed pirated software over Internet. The case involved a student-hacker who used Massachusetts Institute of Technology's computer network to set up an electronic bulletin board on the Internet.[18] The defendant encouraged subscribers to upload software, such as Excel 5.0 and computer games but did not charge them for access.[19]

The federal prosecutor indicted LaMacchia for conspiring to violate the wire fraud statute through illegal copying and distribution of software.[20] In *LaMacchia*, the United States District Court for the District of Massachusetts held that a wire fraud statute could not be used to prosecute for criminal copyright infringement against the operator of a computer bulletin board that provided users with free access to copyrighted software.[21] Cybercrime encompasses violations of criminal law perpetrated online or using the Internet as an instrumentality.

"Computer criminals are simply too talented and defensive measures too weak to stop them."[22] For example, "94% of the targeted companies didn't realize they had been breached until someone else told them. The median number of days between the start of an intrusion and its detection was 416, or more than a year."[23] Internet companies are particularly vulnerable to cybercrimes. The interconnected system of computers makes it possible for hackers, ex-employees, and experts in corporate espionage to steal

---

liability for bailors, compensation systems, compulsory liability insurance, consent statutes, liability of gratuitous donors, incapacitated drivers, entrusting to unsuitable driver, family immunity, family purpose doctrine, assumption of risk for guests (passengers), statutes, imputed contributory negligence (bailments, consent statutes, driver and passengers, husband and wife, joint enterprise, parent and child), joint enterprise, impact of liability insurance, no-fault plans, vicarious liability of owners, deficiencies of the law (attorneys, delay, fees, inadequate insurance coverage, liability only for fault, litigation, and uninsured defendants), remedies for deficiencies of law (Columbia plan, compulsory insurance, financial responsibility laws, full aid insurance, Keeton–O'Connell plan, no-fault plans, Saskatchewan plan, security responsibility laws, unsatisfied judgment funds, voluntary schemes), and injury by thief of unlocked car. W. PAGE KEETON KEETON, PROSSER, AND KEETON ON THE LAW OF TORTS (5th ed. 1984) at 1264–65.

[14] 928 F.2d 504, 505 (2d Cir. 1991).

[15] Id.

[16] Id. at 505 ("Morris released into [the] Internet, a national computer network, a computer program known as a 'worm' that spread and multiplied, eventually causing computers at various educational institutions and military sites to 'crash' or cease functioning.").

[17] 871 F. Supp. 535, 545 (D. Mass. 1994).

[18] Id. at 536.

[19] Id.

[20] Id.

[21] Id. at 540–45; see also David J. Loundy, Alleged Software Pirate Thwarts Prosecution, CHICAGO DAILY L. BULL., Jan. 12, 1995, at 6 (describing LaMacchia's wire fraud prosecution).

[22] Devlin Barrett, U.S. Outgunned in Hacker War, WALL ST. J., March 28, 2012, at 2C.

[23] Id.

information, such as trade secrets, and use them in a competitor's business without leaving physical evidence.

Cybercriminals are increasingly conducting economic espionage using sophisticated software operating outside U.S. territorial borders. The U.S. Justice Department indicted a Brazilian cybercriminal, Leni de Abreu Neto, for participating in a conspiracy with a 19–year-old man from the Netherlands, Nordin Nasiri, "to use, maintain, lease and sell an illegal botnet."[24] A botnet is a network of computers infected with malicious software, known as bot code. The malevolent bot code exploits vulnerabilities of computers connected to the Internet and searches for other computers to infect. The criminals' botnet was a network of 100,000 computers infected with malware used to transmit spam e-mail, disable computers, and launch denial of service attacks.

This example underscores many features of cybercrime, the most obvious being the ease of committing crimes across international borders. Despite difficulties, during the 2007 fiscal year alone, the U.S. Justice Department charged 2,470 defendants with identity theft, and successfully prosecuted an online hack/pump/dump scheme perpetrated by an online brokerage house.[25] However, online companies are not typically liable for the cybercrimes of their employees unless it directed or otherwise ratified online postings or e-mail transmissions constituting crimes. This chapter begins with an examination of most important federal computer crime statutes deployed against cybercrimes. The second part of this chapter examines the rapidly evolving duty to implement reasonable security.

(A) Perspectives on Computer Crimes

(1) What Computer Crime Includes?

During the Revolutionary War, America's Founding Fathers routinely employed spies to learn about the techniques and processes of English industry.[26] Thomas Jefferson, John Adams, and other U.S. diplomats in Europe recruited artisans and "were also not averse to promoting industrial espionage."[27] Jefferson, for example, sought to acquire wool carding and spinning machinery built by English artisans in France.[28] Both James Madison and Thomas Jefferson incorporated the "acquisition of European technology into their larger vision of American diplomacy."[29] In Jefferson's first State of the Union address, he noted how he intended to jump-start the U.S. economy by the introduction of "new and useful inventions from abroad."[30]

The first computer crime statutes were enacted in the 1980s at the state and federal level. Orin Kerr divides computer crime into two categories: computer misuse

---

[24] Press Release, United States Department of Justice (Aug. 21, 2008) www.justice.gov/criminal/cybercrime/press-releases/2008/ netoIndict.pdf.

[25] The President's Identity Theft Task Force Report, September 2008, http://www.idtheft.gov/reports/IDTReport2008.pdf (last visited Aug. 1, 2013).

[26] DORON S. BEN–ATAR, TRADE SECRETS: INTELLECTUAL PIRACY AND THE ORIGINS OF AMERICAN INDUSTRIAL POWER 1 (2005).

[27] Id. at 123.

[28] Id. at 130.

[29] Id. at 159.

[30] Id. at 157.

crimes and traditional crimes.[31] Computer misuse is a relatively new category of computer crime involving deliberate interference with the functioning of the computer. In contrast, traditional computer crimes use the computer to facilitate crimes such as child pornography, trade secret misappropriation, and online stalking. Online stalking does not fit neatly into the traditional tort of assault because it lacks the element of imminence except maybe in the case of a live chat. Orin Kerr identifies three major topics of inquiry in computer crime: (1) Fourth Amendment search and seizure (procedural computer crime law); (2) Statutory Privacy Law, which includes the ECPA (federal wiretap act) and the SCA; and (3) Disputes where the victim and the defendant are in different jurisdictions. Questions regarding cross border enforcement of state criminal statutes often arise in the field of cybercrime. This chapter of the Global Internet Hornbook focuses on Kerr's categories of computer crime.

(2) The Nature of Computer Crime

Computer crimes are often more difficult to detect than crime in the streets. Most cybercriminals are not physically present at the crime scene. The Internet enables anonymous communication and such communication is difficult to trace because of false e-mail headers and anonymous re-mailers. Most computer crimes are frequently isolated events making investigation difficult. The U.S. Department of Justice summarizes how the Internet has affected computer crime:

> Criminals use mobile phones, laptop computers, and network servers in the course of committing their crimes. In some cases, computers provide the means of committing crime. The Internet can be used to deliver a death threat via email; to launch hacker attacks against a vulnerable computer network, to disseminate computer viruses, or to transmit images of child pornography. In other cases, computers merely serve as convenient storage devices for evidence of crime. For example, a drug dealer might keep a list of who owes him money in a file stored in his desktop computer at home, or a money laundering operation might retain false financial records in a file on a network server. Indeed, virtually every class of crime can involve some form of digital evidence.[32]

Relational crimes are easier to prosecute because police can often do an investigation focusing on multiple clues. Internet crimes may involve creating small economic losses for many consumers therefore making it unlikely that any one victim will report it or file a claim. For causes of action based upon privacy violations and espionage, there may be little by way of provable damages. Despite the proliferation of cybercrime, prosecutors are more concerned with crime in the streets than crime on computer systems and corporate victims are frequently unwilling to report the crime because of the negative impact on public relations.

A publicly owned company may sufferin the value of its stocks if reports are made public about unauthorized intrusions. Companies face new cybersecurity risks because data and its devices are mobile unlike fixed mainstream computers. A software company's recent 10–K filing with the Securities and Exchange Commission discloses how computer security issues potentially threaten their business objectives:

---

[31] ORIN S. KERR, COMPUTER CRIME LAW 1 (2d ed. 2009).
[32] U.S. DEPT. OF JUSTICE, MANUAL ON PROSECUTING COMPUTER CRIMES x (2012).

Security experts have identified computer worm programs that target handsets running on certain operating systems. Although these worms have not been widely released and do not present an immediate risk to our business, we believe future threats could lead some end users to seek to reduce or delay future purchases of our products, reduce, or delay the use of their handsets. Wireless carriers and handset manufacturers may increase their expenditures on protecting their wireless networks and mobile phone products from attack, which could delay adoption of new handset models. Any of these activities could adversely affect our revenues and this could harm our business, operating results and financial condition.[33]

- Cybercrime is increasingly a global phenomenon. A 2013 United Nations study concluded:

- Cybercrime acts show a broad distribution across financial-driven acts, computer content related acts, as well as acts against the confidentiality, integrity and accessibility of computer systems.

- Perceptions of relative risk and threat vary between Governments and businesses.

- Individual cybercrime victimization is significantly higher than for 'conventional' crime forms. Victimization rates for online credit card fraud, identify theft, responding to a phishing attempt, and experiencing unauthorized access to an email account, vary between 1 and 17 per cent of the online population.

- Individual cybercrime victimization rates are higher in countries with lower levels of development, highlighting a need to strengthen prevention efforts in these countries.

- Private sector enterprises in Europe report victimization rates of between 2 and 16 per cent for acts such as data breach due to intrusion or phishing.

- Criminal tools of choice for these crimes, such as botnets, have global reach. More than one million unique IP addresses globally functioned as command and control servers for botnets in 2011.

- Internet content targeted for removal by governments includes child pornography and hate speech, but also defamation and government criticism, raising human rights law.

- Some estimates place the total global proportion of internet traffic estimated to infringe copyright at almost 24 per cent.[34]

(3) Types of Cybercrimes Reported

The Internet Crime Complaint Center ("IC3"), sponsored by the FBI and the National White Collar Crime Center, created a database of the most common online cybercrimes that were the subject of consumer complaints. The Table below categorizes the most common Internet-related crimes.

---

[33] Mandalay Media, Inc., 10–K Filing to the Securities & Exchange Commission (March 31, 2008).

[34] United Nations on Drug and Crimes, Comprehensive Study on Cybercrime (Feb. 2013) at 25.

Frequently Reported Internet Crimes	Brief Description	Number of Complaints
Auto Fraud	"Fraudulent vehicle sales, criminals attempt to sell vehicles they do not own. An attractive deal is created by advertising vehicles for sale on various online platforms at prices below market value. Often the fraudsters claim they must sell the vehicles quickly because they are relocating for work, being deployed by the military, or have a tragic family circumstance and are in need of money."[35]	17, 159[36]
FBI Impersonation Scam	"Complaints that directly spoof the name of FBI Director Robert Mueller continue to make up a large part of the government impersonation e-mail scams. Those complaints include elements of Nigerian scam letters (also known as 419 scams) incorporating get-rich inheritance scenarios, bogus lottery winning notifications and occasional extortion threats."[37]	14,141[38]
Intimidation/Extortion Schemes	Telephone Calls ("a twist to the pop-up scareware scheme, victims began receiving telephone calls from individuals allegedly claiming" that malware has been detected on their computers; Other subtypes: Payday Loan scams, Process Server and Grandparent Scam; "the scam involves fraudsters calling elderly individuals claiming to be a grandson or granddaughter or other young relatives in a legal or financial crisis." The crises generally are described as a grandchild being arrested or in a car accident in dire financial need. [39]	8,324[40]
Hitman Scheme	"The scam originated as a person sending an e-mail portraying himself as a hit man hired to kill	1,354[42]

---

[35] Internet Crime Complaint Center, 2012 Internet Crime Report (2013) at 8.
[36] Id.
[37] Id. at 9.
[38] Id.
[39] Id. at 10.
[40] Id. at 11.

	the victim. The e-mail instructed the recipient to pay an amount of money to ensure the hit man did not carry out the death contract.[41]	
Scareware/Ransomware	"The pop-ups, known as scareware or fake or rogue anti-virus software, cannot easily be closed by clicking "close" or the "X" button. The scareware baited users into purchasing software that would allegedly remove viruses from their computers. If the users clicked on the pop-ups to purchase the software, forms to collect payment information appeared and the users were charged for the bogus products."[43]	1969[44]

The IC3 also reported real estate frauds, romance swindles, non-delivery of payment, and Nigerian 419 schemes. Romance schemes, for example, are often perpetrated by foreign cybercriminals exploiting vulnerable individuals.[45] Cybercriminals construct new schemes or new variations on schemes to keep ahead of law enforcement. The lesson from each year's IC3 report on Internet crime is the creativity in constructing new ways to defraud vulnerable consumers. Law enforcement officers are overwhelmed by cybercrimes originating in foreign venues and often lack the financial and human resources to investigate, let alone prosecute them.

§ 8.2   COMPUTER FRAUD AND ABUSE ACT

(A) Criminal Law Provisions

The Computer Fraud and Abuse Act ("CFAA") is a criminal anti-hacking statute designed to prohibit the unauthorized access to electronic data. Congress attempted to strike an "appropriate balance between the Federal Government's interest in computer crime and the interests and abilities of the States to proscribe and punish such offenses."[46] Originally, only a criminal statute, the CFAA now recognizes a private cause of action as well by the victims of computer crimes. The CFAA is not only the chief federal statute for prosecuting cybercrimes such as computer intrusions, but also enables "private attorneys general" to file civil actions to file damages for those suffering damages or losses from computer intrusions. As with many U.S. statutes, federal prosecution is supplemented by civil actions. The chart below provides a quick roadmap of the relevant CFAA offenses:

---

[42] Id.

[41] Id. at 12.

[43] Id. at 13.

[44] Id.

[45] "Perpetrators use the promise of love and romance to entice and manipulate online victims. A perpetrator scouts the Internet for victims, often finding them in chat rooms, on dating sites and even within social media networks. These individuals seduce victims with small gifts, poetry, claims of common interest or the promise of constant companionship. Once the scammers gain the trust of their victims, they request money, ask victims to receive packages and reship them overseas or seek other favors." Id. at 16.

[46] See S. Rep. No. 99–432, at 4 (1986).

CFAA Criminal Offenses and Statutory Sections

CFAA Offense	CFAA Statutory Section
Obtaining National Security Information	18 U.S.C. § 1030(a)(1)
Accessing a Computer and Obtaining Information	18 U.S.C. § 1030(a)(2)
Trespassing in a Government Computer	18 U.S.C. § 1030(a)(3)
Accessing to Defraud and Obtain Value	18 U.S.C. § 1030(a)(4)
Damaging a Computer or Information	18 U.S.C. § 1030(a)(5)
Trafficking in Passwords	18 U.S.C. § 1039(a)(6)
Threatening to Damage a Computer	18 U.S.C. § 1030(a)(7)
Attempt and Conspiracy	18 U.S.C. § 1030(b)
Forfeiture	18 U.S.C. § 1030(i) & (j)

The CFAA imposes criminal penalties on any person who, among other prohibitions, "intentionally accesses a computer without authorization or exceeds authorized access, and thereby obtains . . . information from any protected computer," defined as a computer "used in or affecting interstate or foreign commerce or communication."[47] "Any person who suffers damage or loss by reason of a violation of [the CFAA] may maintain a civil action against the violator to obtain compensatory damages and injunctive relief or other equitable relief."[48] The enactment of CFAA illustrates the problem of legal lag.[49] Prior to the CFAA, there was no statute addressing unauthorized access. The CFAA has "been invoked involving a variety of

---

[47] 18 U.S.C. § 1030(a)(2), (e)(2).

[48] Id. at 1030(g).

[49] One of the earliest commentators described how the Internet raised new dilemmas for disparate fields of the law. See LANCE ROSE, NETLAW: YOUR RIGHTS IN THE ONLINE WORLD (1995). (Questions discussed by Rose in this book include: Do we need to devise a new law for copyrights online? Does the online world resemble developing countries more than the Wild West? What legislation do we need for the ever-evolving Internet? Is a website more like a television station or a newspaper? Is an online service like a phone company or a publisher? Should someone who uses the Internet be regarded as a public figure for purposes of libel law? Does borrowing a library book differ legally from downloading material from a library? How should the criminal law be adapted to deal with new forms of social deviance, such as theft, hacking, viruses, invasion of privacy, work place stress, and deskilling? What new ethical standards are necessary to resolve dilemmas online?).

Web-based activities that the drafter did not contemplate at all."[50] The CFAA, for example, could not have foreseen the use of bots or automated software to extract information from websites or other online conduct.[51] In the wake of 9–11, Congress enacted the Patriot Act, which broadened the meaning of a protected computer.[52]

The CFAA creates liability for persons who: (1) intentionally accesses a computer without authorization or exceeds authorized access, and thereby obtains information from any protected computer, in violation of § 1030(a)(2)(C); (2) knowingly and with intent to defraud, accesses a protected computer without authorization, or exceeds authorized access, and by means of such conduct furthers the intended fraud and obtains anything of value, in violation of § 1030(a)(4); or (3) intentionally accesses a protected computer without authorization, and as a result of such conduct, recklessly causes damage, or causes damage and loss, in violation of § 1030(a)(5)(B)–(C).

The 1986 revisions to the CFAA updated the law criminalizing additional computer-related acts.[53] Congress amended the CFAA to penalize the theft of property via computer that occurs as a part of a scheme to defraud.[54] Congress also amended the statute to punish those who intentionally alter, damage, or destroy data belonging to others.[55] This provision "was designed to cover such activities as the distribution of malicious code and denial of service attacks. Finally, Congress also included in the CFAA a provision criminalizing trafficking in passwords and similar items."[56]

The CFAA prohibits anyone from intentionally accessing a computer used in interstate or foreign commerce without authorization (or by exceeding authorized access) and thereby obtains access to information.[57] The CFAA refers to "exceed[ing] authorized access" and accessing a computer "without authorization" but there is some question as to whether these terms are interchangeable or given different meanings.[58] Exceeding authorized access is defined as accessing a computer with authorization and using such access to obtain or alter information in the computer that the computer user is not entitled to obtain or alter.[59] The CFAA refers to "exceed[ing] authorized access" and accessing a computer "without authorization" but there is some question as to whether these terms are interchangeable or given different meanings.[60] While some district courts view the terms as virtually the same, "others have given them different applications and meanings."[61] Congress updated the CFAA again in 1988 and:

---

[50] JULIE E. COHEN, CONFIGURING THE NETWORKED SELF: LAW, CODE, AND THE PLAY OF EVERYDAY PRACTICE 159 (2012).

[51] Id. at 158.

[52] "In the USA PATRIOT Act, Congress amended the definition of "protected computer" to make clear that this term includes computers outside of the United States so long as they affect "interstate or foreign commerce or communication of the United States." 18 U.S.C. § 1030(e)(2)(B) (2001)." U.S. DEPT. OF JUSTICE, MANUAL ON PROSECUTING COMPUTER CRIMES 5 (2012).

[53] U.S. DEPT. OF JUSTICE, MANUAL ON PROSECUTING COMPUTER CRIMES 2 (2012).

[54] Id.

[55] Id.

[56] Id.

[57] 18 U.S.C. § 1030(a)(2)(C).

[58] See e.g., 18 U.S.C. § 1030(a)(1); § 1030(a)(5)(A)(I).

[59] 18 U.S.C. § 1030(e)(6).

[60] See e.g., 18 U.S.C. § 1030(a)(1); § 1030(a)(5)(A)(I).

[61] U.S. DEPT. OF JUSTICE, MANUAL ON PROSECUTING COMPUTER CRIMES 9 (2012).

Eliminated the requirement in 18 U.S.C. § 1030(a)(2)(C) that information must have been stolen through an interstate or foreign communication, thereby expanding jurisdiction for cases involving theft of information from computers;

Eliminated the requirement in 18 U.S.C. § 1030(a)(5) that the defendant's action must result in a loss exceeding $5,000 and created a felony offense where the damage affects ten or more computers, closing a gap in the law;

Expanded 18 U.S.C. § 1030(a)(7) to criminalize not only explicit threats to cause damage to a computer, but also threats to (1) steal data on a victim's computer, (2) publicly disclose stolen data, or (3) not repair damage the offender already caused to the computer;

Created a criminal offense for conspiring to commit a computer hacking offense under section 1030;

Broadened the definition of "protected computer" in 18 U.S.C. § 1030(e)(2) to the full extent of Congress's commerce power by including those computers used in or affecting interstate or foreign commerce or communication; and

Provided a mechanism for civil and criminal forfeiture of property used in or derived from section 1030 violations.[62]

Cybercrime prosecutors use the CFAA to address computer intrusions and hacking. Further, the CFAA is the Swiss Army Knife used in most cybercrime prosecution. U.S. federal prosecutors typically use the CFAA in cases where a cybercriminal has used viruses, worms or malware to penetrate a computer's firewall in order to steal or destroy data.[63] In addition, prosecutors in Economic Espionage Act cases often include a CFAA count. Section 1030(a)(5)(A) prohibits knowingly causing the transmission of a "program, information, code, or command" and because of such conduct, intentionally causing damage to a protected computer. The U.S. Department of Justice Manual for Prosecuting Computer Crimes states that this subsection applies:

> equally to offenders who are authorized to use the victim computer system (an "insider"), to those not authorized to use it (an "outsider"), and to those who have never accessed the system at all. The term "program, information, code, or command" broadly covers all transmissions that are capable of having an effect on a computer's operation. This includes software code (such as a worm), software commands (such as an instruction to delete information), and network packets designed to flood a network connection or exploit system vulnerabilities. In the ordinary case where the attacker releases a worm or initiates a denial of service attack, the government should easily meet this element of the crime.[64]

The CFAA gives prosecutors a wide array of tools to address Internet-related crimes. Section 1030 criminal offenses are summarized in the chart below:

---

[62] Id. at 3.

[63] On January 25, 2003, a virus-like attack on vulnerable computers on the Internet exploited a known flaw in popular database software from Microsoft Corp. called "SQL Server 2000." Within a few hours, the world's digital pipelines were overwhelmed, slowing down Web browsing and e-mail delivery. "Monitors reported detecting at least 39,000 infected computers, which transmitted floods of spurious signals that disrupted the operations of hundreds of thousands of other systems." Ted Bridis, Virus–Like Attack Slows Web Traffic, Associated Press, (Jan. 25, 2003).

[64] U.S. DEPT. OF JUSTICE, MANUAL ON PROSECUTING COMPUTER CRIMES 37 (2012).

Summary of Criminal Penalties for CFAA Offenses

Type of Offense	Section in the CFAA	Initial Prison Sentence
Obtaining National Security Information	18 U.S.C. § 1030(a)(1)	10 years (rarely used)
Accessing a Computer and Obtaining Information	18 U.S.C. § 1030(a)(2)	1 or 5 years
Trespassing in a Government Computer and Obtaining Information	18 U.S.C. § 1030(a)(3)	1 year
Accessing a Computer and Obtaining Information (Without Authorization)	18 U.S.C. § 1030(a)(2)	1 or 5 years
Accessing a Computer to Defraud & Obtain Value	18 U.S.C. § 1030(a)(4)	5 years
Intentionally Damaging by Knowing Transmission	18 U.S.C. § 1030(a)(5)	10 years
Recklessly Damaging by Intentional Access	18 U.S.C. § 1030(a)(5)(B)	1 or 5 years
Negligently Causing Damage & Loss by Intentional Access	18 U.S.C. § 1030(a)(5)(C)[65]	1 year
Trafficking in Passwords	18 U.S.C. § 1030(a)(6)	1 year

---

[65] For section 1030(a)(5)(C) violations only, the statute also requires that the defendant's conduct cause "loss," which the statute defines as "any reasonable cost to any victim, including the cost of responding to an offense, conducting a damage assessment, and restoring data, program, system, or information to its condition prior to the offense, and any revenue lost, cost incurred, or other consequential damages incurred because of interruption of service." 18 U.S.C. § 1030(e)(11). " Id. at 41.

Extortion with Computers[66]	18 U.S.C. § 1030(a)(7)	5 years

The above table summarizes the CFAA offenses and the statutorily prescribed punishment for the first offenses. Section (a)(1) punishes the act of obtaining national security information without or in excess of authorization.[67] The U.S. Department of Justice Manual on Prosecuting Computer Crimes highlights the statutory meaning of protected computer under the CFAA:

> The term "protected computer," 18 U.S.C. § 1030(e)(2), is a statutory term of art that has nothing to do with the security of the computer. Briefly, "protected computer" covers computers used in or affecting interstate or foreign commerce and computers used by the federal government and financial institutions.

> Section 1030(e)(2) defines protected computer as: a computer—

> (A) exclusively for the use of a financial institution or the United States Government, or, in the case of a computer not exclusively for such use, used by or for a financial institution or the United States Government and the conduct constituting the offense affects that use by or for the financial institution or the Government; or (B) which is used in or affecting interstate or foreign commerce or communication . . . . 18 U.S.C. § 1030(e)(2). Note that the computer must be "used in or affecting" not "used by the defendant in"—that is, it is enough that the computer is connected to the Internet; the statute does not require proof that the defendant also used the Internet to access the computer or used the computer to access the Internet.[68]

(1) Obtaining National Security Information

The elements of an (a)(1) offense require that a defendant: (1) had knowingly accessed a computer without or in excess of authorization; (2) obtained national security information; (3) had reason to believe the information could injure the U.S. or benefit a foreign nation; and (4) made a willful communication, delivery, transmission (or attempt) or willfully retained the information. National security cybercrimes are rarely prosecuted; most computer crime enforcement is directed at domestic cybercriminals.[69]

(2) Accessing Computer Without Authorization

The broadest provision of the CFAA[70] "is § 1030(a)(2)(C), which makes it a crime to exceed authorized access of a computer connected to the Internet without any culpable intent."[71] Accessing a computer or information is covered by (a)(2) of the CFAA. The court in *United States v. Drew*[72] rejected the theory that "the latter two

---

[66] U.S. DEPT. OF JUSTICE, MANUAL ON PROSECUTING COMPUTER CRIMES 11 (2012).

[67] Id. at 12.

[68] Id. at 4.

[69] The U.S. Justice Department acknowledges that Section 1030(a)(1) "that punishes the act of obtaining national security information without or in excess of authorization" is "infrequently used." U.S. DEPT. OF JUSTICE, MANUAL ON PROSECUTING COMPUTER CRIMES 11 (2012).

[70] 18 U.S.C. § 1030.

[71] United States v. Nosal, 676 F.3d 854 (9th Cir. 2012).

[72] 259 F.R.D. 449, 457 (C.D. Cal. 2009).

elements of the section 1030(a)(2)(C) crime [obtaining information from a protected computer] will always be met when an individual using a computer contacts or communicates with an Internet website."[73] The CFAA prohibits exceeding authorized access to a computer and obtaining information.[74] However, the Fourth Circuit in *WEC Carolina Energy Solution LLC v. Miller*[75] held that an ex-employee that downloaded trade secrets during the course of his employment and used that information for a presentation for his new employer did not access his employer's computer without authorization.

While still employed by WEC the energy company provided "him with a laptop computer and cell phone, and authorized his access to the company's intranet and computer servers."[76] Miller "had access to numerous confidential and trade secret documents stored on . . . computer servers, including pricing terms, pending projects[,] and the technical capabilities of WEC."[77] WEC instituted a policy to protect its trade secrets "that prohibited using the information without authorization or downloading it to a personal computer. These policies did not restrict Miller's authorization to access the information, however."[78]

The court went so far as to rule that the CFAA does not impose liability for a mere violation of a use policy.[79] Under the *WEC* court's narrow reading of the CFAA, the terms "without authorization" and "exceeds authorized access" only apply when an individual accesses a computer without permission, or obtains or alters information on a computer beyond that which he is authorized to access.[80] The path of CFAA law reflected in *WEC* suggests that employers will find it difficult to pursue civil actions against ex-employees. In *State Analysis, Inc. v. American Financial Services Assoc.*,[81] the court considered a case where one defendant has a password to a website and shares it with a third party who did not have the password. The court found that the password sharer did not act "without authorization" even though the terms of service agreement prohibited sharing passwords. The court acknowledged, however, that the third person would be without authorization if they used the shared password to access the website.[82]

(3) Trespassing in a Government Computer

Trespassing in a government computer and obtaining information is covered by 18 U.S.C. § 1030(a)(3). Under (a)(3), the government must prove that the defendant: (1) intentionally accessed; (2) without authorization; (3) a nonpublic computer that was exclusively for the use of the U.S. Government, or was used by or affected by the use of a U.S. Government computer.

---

[73] Id.

[74] 18 U.S.C. § 1030(a)(2).

[75] WEC Carolina Energy Solutions LLC v. Miller, 2012 U.S. App. LEXIS 15441 *12–*13 (4th Cir., July 26, 2012).

[76] Id. at *4.

[77] Id.

[78] Id.

[79] Id. at *14.

[80] WEC Carolina Energy Solutions LLC v. Miller, 2012 U.S. App. LEXIS 15441 *16–*17 (4th Cir., July 26, 2012).

[81] 621 F. Supp. 2d 309, 317 (E.D. Va. 2009).

[82] Id.; See also, LVRG Holdings LLC v. Brekka, 581 F.3d 1127 (9th Cir. 2009).

(4) Accessing to Defraud

In an unauthorized use case, the CFAA requires a defendant to: (1) knowingly and (2) with intent to defraud (3) access a protected computer (4) without authorization or exceeding authorized access (5) in order to further the intended fraud and (6) the defendant obtained something of value, including use of the computer or data that exceeded $5,000 over a one-year period.[83]   In *Shurgard Storage Centers, Inc. v. Safeguard Self Storage, Inc.*,[84] the court determined that a plaintiff need not prove common law fraud in order to have a CFFA action under 1030(a)(4) In denying the defendant's motion to dismiss, the court held that the word "fraud" as used in section 1030(a)(4) simply means "wrongdoing."[85]

(5) Damaging Computers or Data

Damaging a computer or information is addressed by 18 U.S.C. § 1030(a)(5), which criminalizes multiple offenses.[86] Section 1030(a)(5)(A) makes it a crime to knowingly cause transmission of a program, information, code, or command such as a computer virus that intentionally causes damage. Similarly, Section 1030(a)(5)(B) criminalizes the intentional access of a computer without authorization resulting in damage. Finally, Section 1030(a)(5)(C) makes it a crime to intentionally access a protected computer without authorization causing damage or loss. Section 1030(a)(5)'s offenses will constitute felonies if they result in damage or loss of $5,000 during the year. In addition, this section applies if the defendantmodifies medical care of a person, causes physical injury, threatens public health or safety, or damages computer systems used for justice, national defense or national security and civil liability. Finally, it is a felony to affect ten or more protected computers during a year regardless of damages or loss.[87]

(6) Trafficking in Passwords

Section 1030(a)(6) prohibits a person from knowingly trafficking in computer passwords and similar information with intent to defraud, when the trafficking affects interstate or foreign commerce, or when the password may be used to access a computer used by or for the U.S. Government without authorization. The elements of the CFAA for trafficking in passwords include: (1) trafficking; (2) in computer password or similar information; (3) knowingly and with intent to defraud; and (4) trafficking affects interstate or foreign commerce or a computer used by or for the U.S. Government. The term "trafficking" in section 1030(a)(6) is defined by reference to the

---

[83] 18 U.S.C. § 1030(a)(4).

[84] 119 F. Supp. 2d 1121, 1123 (W.D. Wash. 2000).

[85] Id.

[86] The U.S. Justice Department notes 18 U.S.C. § 1030(a)(5) is a flexible tool for prosecution. "Criminals can cause damage to computers in a wide variety of ways. For example, an intruder who gains unauthorized access to a computer can send commands that delete files or shuts the computer down. Intruders can initiate a "denial of service attack" that floods the victim computer with useless information and prevents legitimate users from accessing it. A virus or worm can use up all of the available communications bandwidth on a corporate network, making it unavailable to employees. When a virus or worm penetrates a computer's security, it can delete files, crash the computer, install malicious software, or do other things that impair the computer's integrity. Prosecutors can use section 1030(a)(5) to charge all of these different kinds of acts." U.S. DEPT. OF JUSTICE, MANUAL ON PROSECUTING COMPUTER CRIMES 35 (2012).

[87] U.S. DEPT. OF JUSTICE, MANUAL ON PROSECUTING COMPUTER CRIMES 35 (2012).

definition of the same term in 18 U.S.C. § 1029, and means "transfer, or otherwise dispose of, to another, or obtain control of with intent to transfer or dispose of."[88]

(7) Threatening to Harm a Computer

Section 1030(a)(7) addresses extortion, which prohibits threats to harm a computer or data. Prosecutors must prove that the defendant has: (1) intent to extort money or any other thing of value; (2) transmitted the threat in interstate or foreign commerce; and (3) made a threat to damage a protected computer, reveal confidential information, or demand money in connection with the extortion. The CFAA, in both criminal and civil actions, applies to computers connected to the Internet, and defines a "protected computer" to mean computers:

> exclusively for the use of a financial institution or the United States Government, or, in the case of a computer not exclusively for such use, used by or for a financial institution or the United States Government and the conduct constituting the offense affects that use by or for the financial institution or the Government or a computer used in interstate or foreign commerce or communication, including a computer located outside the United States used in a manner that affects interstate or foreign commerce or communication of the United States.[89]

Attempts and conspiracy to commit computer crimes are crimes addressed in amendments to the CFAA. Inchoate offenses such as attempt, conspiracy, and aiding and abetting are commonly covered in federal computer statutes. However, to date, federal prosecutors are unable to prosecute inchoate cybercrime in any meaningful way.

(B) CFFA's Civil Liability

The CFAA extends a private cause of action to a victim who suffers "loss" because of a violation of the Act's prohibitions.[90] The CFAA defines the term "loss" as the reasonable cost to any victim, including the cost of responding to an offense, conducting a damage assessment, and restoring the data, system, or information to its condition prior, as well as "any revenue lost, cost incurred, or other consequential damages."[91]

The CFAA allows for private right of action if the violation caused:

(I) loss to one or more persons during any [one]-year period (and, for purposes of an investigation, prosecution, or other proceeding brought by the United States only, loss resulting from conduct affecting one or more other protected computers) aggregating at least $5,000 in value;

(II) the modification or impairment, or potential modification or impairment, of the medical examination, diagnosis, treatment, or care of [one] or more individuals;

(III) physical injury to any person;

(IV) a threat to public health or safety; [or]

---

[88] 18 U.S.C. § 1029(e)(5).

[89] 18 U.S.C. § 1030(e)(2).

[90] To bring a civil action under 18 U.S.C. § 1030(a)(5) the action "must involve one of the five factors in (a)(5)(B) [but] it need not be one of the three offenses in (a)(5)(A)." Shamrock Foods Co. v. Gast, 535 F. Supp. 2d 962, 964 (D. Ariz. 2008).

[91] 18 U.S.C. § 1030(e)(11).

(V) damage affecting a computer used by or for an entity of the United States Government in furtherance of the administration of justice, national defense, or national security. . . [92]

Plaintiffs may file civil actions against cybercriminals, provided the access is either "without authorization" or "exceeds authorized access."[93] The CFAA, 18 U.S.C. § 1030(g), grants a private cause of action against anyone who violates section 1030 if the "conduct involves 1 of the factors set forth in subclauses (I), (II), (III), (IV), or (V) of subsection (c)(4)(A)(i) above. As noted above subclause (I) states: "loss to 1 or more persons during any 1–year period . . . aggregating at least $5,000 in value."[94] To bring an action successfully under § 1030(g) based on a violation of § 1030(a)(4), [the plaintiff] must show that [the defendant]: (1) accessed a "protected computer," (2) without authorization or exceeding such authorization that was granted, (3) "knowingly" and with "intent to defraud," and thereby (4) "further [ed] the intended fraud and obtain[ed] anything of value," causing (5) a loss to one or more persons during any one-year period aggregating at least $5,000 in value.[95]

In most cases, it is not difficult for a plaintiff to prove intrusion of a "protected computer," specifically defined, for these purposes, as a computer "which is used in or affecting interstate or foreign commerce or communication . . ."[96] The CFAA requires the plaintiff to prove "that [the defendant] accessed a protected computer without authorization and, as a result caused an annual loss of at least $5,000."[97]

(1) United States v. Morris

The Internet was mentioned in a court's decision for the first time in a 1990 CFAA case in which a first year Cornell University computer science student released a worm or virus, subsequenty infecting hundreds of educational and military computers. In *United States v. Morris*,[98] the defendant released a computer virus that shut down the nascent Internet. Morris, was convicted of accessing a federal interest computer without authorization since his worm broke into computers and exploited a "hole" or "bug" (an error) in both "SEND MAIL," an e-mail program, and a "finger demon" program, a program providing information about the users of another computer.[99] Morris' computer replicated and reinfected computers exponentially, causing machines to crash or become "catatonic."[100] The Second Circuit Court of Appeals upheld the CFAA conviction, finding Morris to be without authority to transmit his worm to protected computers.

---

[92] 18 U.S.C. § 1030(g).

[93] Id.

[94] 18 U.S.C. § 1030(c)(4)(A)(i)(I).

[95] LVRC Holdings LLC v. Brekka, 581 F.3d 1127, 1132 (9th Cir. 2009).

[96] 18 U.S.C. § 1030(e)(2)(B).

[97] "No action may be brought under this subjection unless such action is begun within 2 years of the date of the acted complained of or the date of the discovery of the damage." Id.

[98] 928 F.2d 504 (2d Cir. 1991).

[99] Id. at 506.

[100] Id.

(2) *United States v. Ivanov*

In order to violate the CFAA, it is necessary for the defendant to do more than merely access computers and view data.[101] In *United States v. Ivanov*,[102] a federal court addressed the issue of whether a defendant in a foreign country could be prosecuted for violating the CFAA when the wrongdoing took place in Russia. Federal prosecutors indicted Aleksey Vladimirovich Ivanov of Chelyabinsk, Russia for CFAA offenses including conspiracy, extortion, and possessing illegal access devices.[103] The indictment alleged that these crimes had been committed against the Online Information Bureau ("OIB") whose business and infrastructure were based in Vernon, Connecticut. Ivanov filed a motion to dismiss since Ivanov's computer crimes were committed in Russia. The district court refused to dismiss the action, ruling that the detrimental effects of Ivanov's actions were felt by OIB in Connecticut. Ivanov was caught in a sting operation created by the FBI, where he was invited to interview for a position in a fake computer company set up as a honey pot by FBI agents in Seattle.

He was arrested during the "job interview." Ivanov was prosecuted for accessing a company's computers without authorization. The Russian hacker was convicted upon proof that he knowingly obtained, altered, or caused the transmission of information with the intent to defraud. Ivanov pleaded guilty and was sentenced to serve 48 months and following his release, an additional period of supervised probation. In 2001, Congress amended the CFAA to encompass computers located outside the United States when it enacted the Patriot Act.

(3) *U.S. v. Drew*

The Internet is a cynosure for high profile crimes, often committed anonymously. In *United States v. Drew*,[104] a federal prosecutor charged Lauri Drew, a homemaker, with violating the CFAA by masquerading as a teenage boy, stalking a 13–year-old girl, and inducing her to commit suicide. Prosecutors charged Drew and unnamed co-conspirators with intentionally accessing a computer used in interstate and foreign commerce without authorization or in excess of authorized access to further the intentional infliction of emotional distress.

Drew contacted the victim, Megan Meier, through the MySpace network (on which she had her own profile) using the Josh Evans pseudonym and "proceeded to make romantic overtures to Meier, only to cut them off suddenly four weeks later with the callous statement, "The world would be a better place without you."[105] Megan Meier killed herself shortly after receiving this message from Lauri Drew masquerading as Josh Evans. To cover up her role in Meier's death, Drew caused the Josh Evans MySpace account to be deleted.[106] After Meier's death, prosecutors charged Lauri Drew and her unnamed co-conspirators with knowingly agreeing with each other to intentionally access a computer used in interstate and foreign commerce without

---

[101] 18 U.S.C. § 1030(a)(4).

[102] 175 F. Supp. 2d 367 (D. Conn. 2001).

[103] Id. at 367.

[104] 259 F.R.D. 449 (C.D. Cal. 2009).

[105] CALVIN ROSS, Policing the Net, NAPA VALLEY REG. (May 20, 2008, 12:00 AM), http://napavalleyregister. com/business/columnists/calvin-ross/article_b9540bc8–a19b-5984–befa-a0a1d1813b1b.html (last visited June 25, 2013).

[106] U.S. v. Drew, 259 F.R.D. at 451. (C.D. Cal. 2009).

authorization. Then, in excess of authorized access, and by means of an interstate communication, theyobtained information from that computer to further a tortious act, namely, intentional infliction of emotional distress.

The prosecutor's theory was that Lauri Drew violated the CFAA when she intentionally breached MySpace's terms of service by creating a fictitious account. The issue in *U.S. v. Drew* was whether the intentional breach MySpace's Terms of Service, without more, constituted a misdemeanor crime for purposes of 18 U.S.C. § 1030(a)(2)(C). Lauri Drew deliberately masqueraded as an adolescent boy; she posted a photograph of a juvenile without his permission and pretended to be that juvenile in order to communicate with Meagan Meier.[107] MySpace's terms of use stated, "All registration information [must be] truthful and accurate."[108] Therefore, Drew's fictitious profile violated MySpace's terms of service agreement. The court held that treating a violation of a website's terms of use agreement as a statutory violation, without more, conflicted with the void-for-vagueness doctrine. "Arising under the Due Process Clauses of the Fifth and Fourteenth Amendments, the vagueness doctrine has two primary goals: to provide fair warning of proscribed criminal conduct, and to provide explicit standards to prevent arbitrary and discriminatory enforcement of the law."[109]

(4) Int'l Airport Centers v. Citrin

On the criminal liability side of CFAA, the statute recognizes criminal offenses where the defendant has accessed a computer "without authorization."[110] It is a straightforward determination whether a defendant had access or not to a protected computer. The more difficult question is how to classify a defendant who has some authorized access to a computer system, but exceeds the scope of permitted access.[111] Courts struggle with the meaning of when a defendant accesses a computer "without authorization" or "exceeds authorized access."[112] Congress failed to define the meaning of "without authorization" when it enacted the CFAA. Nevertheless, Congress did define the meaning of "exceeds authorized access," which was "to access a computer with authorization and to use such access to obtain or alter information in the

---

[107] Id.

[108] Id.

[109] Backpage.com, LLC v. Cooper, 2013 WL 1558785 *23 (M.D. Tenn., Jan. 3, 2013).

[110] See 18 U.S.C. § 1030(a)(3), (a)(5)(B), (a)(5)(C).

[111] "It is relatively easy to define the universe of individuals who lack any authorization to access a computer. When someone from this group of people accesses the computer, the access is necessarily "without authorization" for purposes of the CFAA. See e.g., United States v. Ivanov, 175 F. Supp. 2d 367 (D. Conn. 2001) (Russian hacker accessed victim company's computers without authorization). A more difficult question is whether a person with some authorization to access a computer can ever act "without authorization" with respect to that computer. The case law on this issue is muddy, but, as discussed below, there is growing consensus that such "insiders" cannot act "without authorization" unless and until their authorization to access the computer is rescinded. Prosecutors rarely argue that a defendant accessed a computer "without authorization" when the defendant had some authority to access that computer. However, several civil cases have held that defendants lost their authorization to access computers when they breached a duty of loyalty to the authorizing parties, even if the authorizing parties were unaware of the breach. See e.g., Int'l Airport Ctrs., LLC v. Citrin, 1 440 F.3d 418, 420–21 (7th Cir. 2006)." U.S. DEPT. OF JUSTICE, MANUAL ON PROSECUTING COMPUTER CRIMES 6 (2012).

[112] See 18 U.S.C. § 1030(a)(1), (a)(2), (a)(4).

computer that the accesser is not entitled so to obtain or alter."[113] The U.S. Justice Department reads the legislative history of the CFAA to reflect:

> The legislative history of the CFAA reflects an expectation that persons who "exceed authorized access" will be insiders (e.g., employees using a victim's corporate computer network), while persons who access computers "without authorization" will typically be outsiders (e.g., hackers). *See* S. Rep. No. 99–432, at 10 (1986), *reprinted in* 1986 U.S.C.C.A.N. 2479 (discussing section 1030(a)(5), "insiders, who are authorized to access a computer, face liability only if they intend to cause damage to the computer, not for recklessly or negligently causing damage. By contrast, outside intruders who break into a computer could be punished for any intentional, reckless, or other damage they cause by their trespass.").[114]

Many CFAA cases interpret the threshold requirement to assert a CFAA claim for civil liability, to be proof that the defendant accessed a protected computer "without authorization" or in a manner that "exceeds authorized access" granted by the plaintiff. In *Int'l Airport Centers v. Citrin*,[115] Citrin was employed by International Airport Centers ("IAC"), a company engaged in the real estate business. IAC issued Citrin a computer where he was to compile data on properties. Citrin left IAC; deleted data from his computer before returning it; and wrote over backup files. IAC filed a CFAA lawsuit against Citrin, which did not require proof that the defendant accessed a computer at all; much less, that such access occurred without or in excess of authorization.[116] Judge Richard Posner, writing for the Seventh Circuit panel, found that Citrin violated the CFAA. In dicta, the court observed that an employee could lose authorization to access his employer's computer by breaching a duty of loyalty to the employer. *Citrin* is cited for the proposition that a breach of loyalty alone is enough to render an employee to be "without authorization."[117]

(5) LVRC Holdings v. Brekka

Congress enacted the CFAA to punish computer hackers, however, the guidelines/rules/procedure (?) do (does, if you choose "procedure") not mesh well . . . not mesh well with the fact pattern where an employee has authorization to use a computer system but exceeds the scope of what he or she is permitted to access.[118] Courts have struggled with the application of the CFAA to an ex-employee. Today, most federal courts would not interpret the meaning of "without authorization" too expansively. For example, in *LVRC Holdings LLC v. Brekka*,[119] the Ninth Circuit

---

[113] 18 U.S.C. § 1030(e)(6).

[114] U.S. DEPT. OF JUSTICE, MANUAL ON PROSECUTING COMPUTER CRIMES 6 (2012).

[115] 440 F.3d 418 (7th Cir. 2006).

[116] 18 U.S.C. § 1030(a)(5)(A).

[117] U.S. DEPT. OF JUSTICE, MANUAL ON PROSECUTING COMPUTER CRIMES at 6 (2012).

[118] "The Citrin/Shurgard line of cases has been criticized by courts adopting the view that, under the CFAA, an authorized user of a computer cannot access the computer "without authorization" unless and until the authorization is revoked. Most significantly, the Ninth Circuit recently rejected Citrin's interpretation of "without authorization" and found that, under the plain language of the CFAA, a user's authorization to access a computer depends on the actions of the authorizing party and not on the user's duty of loyalty. See LVRC Holdings LLC v. Brekka, 581 F.3d 1127, 1133–34 (9th Cir. 2009) ("It is the employer's decision to allow or to terminate an employee's authorization to access a computer that determines whether the employee is with or 'without authorization.'"). Id. at 7.

[119] 581 F.3d 1127 (9th Cir. 2009).

determined that an employee does not exceed authorized access to a computer by accessing information unless the employee has no authority to access the information under *any* circumstances. Brekka was an employee at an addiction treatment center who was negotiating with his employer, LVRC Holdings, for an ownership stake in the business.

During negotiations, Brekka e-mailed several business documents to his and his wife's personal e-mail accounts. The negotiations broke down, and Brekka left his employment with LVRC. LVRC later discovered the e-mails Brekka had sent to himself and sued him under § 1030(g), which provides for a private right of action under the CFAA. "The Ninth Circuit held in *Brekka* that it is the *employer's* actions that determine whether an employee acts without authorization to access a computer in violation of § 1030."[120]

The court stated that there was "no dispute that if Brekka accessed LVRC's information on the Load website after he left the company in September 2003, [he] would have accessed a protected computer "without authorization" for purposes of the CFAA."[121]   The U.S. Justice Department describes Brekka as a bellwether case reflecting the path of the law:

> Based on this recent case law, courts appear increasingly likely to reject the idea that a defendant accessed a computer "without authorization" in insider cases— cases where the defendant had some current authorization to access the computer. Accordingly, prosecutors should think carefully before charging such defendants with violations that require the defendants to access a computer "without authorization" and instead consider bringing charges under those subsections that require proof that the defendant exceeded authorized access.[122]

(6) United States v. Nosal

In *United States v. Nosal,*[123] the Ninth Circuit, in an *en banc* opinion, rejected *Brekka*'s expansive interpretation of the CFAA. The Ninth Circuit held that employees who have permission to access information on their company's computer, but use that permission for purposes violating a company's computer use policy, is not subject to prosecution under the CFAA. Judge Kozinski wrote:

> Computers have become an indispensable part of our daily lives. We use them for work; we use them for play. Sometimes we use them for play at work. Many employers have adopted policies prohibiting the use of work computers for non-business purposes. Does an employee who violates such a policy commit a federal crime? How about someone who violates the terms of service of a social networking website? [124]

The Ninth Circuit answered this question in the negative in a case where a former employee violated a company's terms of service agreement. In Nosal, the government brought criminal charges under the CFAA against David Nosal for encouraging

---

[120] Id.

[121] Id. at 1136.

[122] U.S. DEPT. OF JUSTICE, MANUAL ON PROSECUTING COMPUTER CRIMES 8 (2012) (interpreting recent CFAA case law on insiders charged with CFAA on the civil side of the ledger).

[123] 676 F.3d 854 (9th Cir. 2012) (en banc).

[124] Id. at 856.

corporate employees to access confidential information on their employer's computer system and to transfer the information to Nosal, a former employee of Korn–Ferry, an executive recruiting firm.[125] Although he no longer had access to Korn–Ferry's computer system, Nosal convinced current employees to access Korn–Ferry's computer system and download data from the firm's computer system, which he would then use to form a competing executive recruiting firm.[126] He no longer had access to the Korn–Ferry's computer system but convinced current employees to access Korn–Ferry's computer system and download data from the firm's computer system, which he would use to form a competing executive recruiting firm.[127] The prosecutor's case rested on the theory that Nosal induced current company employees to use their legitimate credentials to access the company's proprietary database and provide him with information that violated their terms of use.[128] The employees were authorized to access the information but violated a corporate policy by disclosing it to Nosal.

The Ninth Circuit held that the phrase "'exceeds authorized access' in the CFAA is limited to violations of restrictions on *access* to information, and not restrictions on its use."[129] The court reasoned that the plain language of the CFFA "targets unauthorized procurement or alteration of information, not its misuse or misappropriation" but does not address unauthorized access.[130] Because Nosal's accomplices had permission to access the company database and obtain the information contained within, the court held thatthe government's charges fail to meet the element of "without authorization, or exceeds authorized access."[131]

The court rejected the government's argument that "the language could refer to someone who has unrestricted physical access to a computer, but is limited in the use to which he can put the information."[132] The CFAA does not explicitly address the situation where someone exceeds authorized access to a protected computer. This thorny issue requires courts to determine whether exceeding authorized access constitutes a crime under CFAA. A court applying *Nosal* will not find a CFAA violation if an employee or ex-employee simply exceeds authorization. In contrast, a court applying *Brekka* will stretch the CFAA to treat any violations of use restrictions as a federal offense. Courts are beginning to adopt *Nosal* court's narrow reading of the meaning of "exceeding authorized access."[133]

---

[125] Id.

[126] Id.

[127] Id.

[128] Id. at 857. ("[A]ssume an employee is permitted to access only product information on the company's computer but accesses customer data: He would "exceed [ ] authorized access" [as defined in § 1030(e)(6)] if he looks at the customer lists.").

[129] Id. at 863–6.

[130] Id.

[131] 18 U.S.C. § 1030(a)(4).

[132] United States v. Nosal, 676 F.3d at 857.

[133] See e.g., Serbite Agency Inc. v. Platt, No. 11–3526 (D. Minn., Aug. 7, 2012) (following the narrower reading of the CFAA adopted by Nosal finding no offense even though a former insurance company Vice President exceeded his authorized access forwarding e-mails containing confidential information for at least 74 clients to his personal e-mail account).

(7) Weingand v. Harland Financial Solutions

In *Weingand v. Harland Financial Solutions*,[134] Michael Weingand filed suit against his ex-employer, Harland Financial, contending that he was wrongfully terminated and retaliated against. Harland Financial counterclaimed that Weingand violated the CFAA, the California penal code, and committed business torts such as conversion, unfair competition, and the negligent interference with prospective advantage.[135] Harland Financial's CFAA counterclaim was that its former employee violated the CFAA by accessing their business files without permission. The company claimed that Weingand "received permission to access Harland's computer system based on his representations that he sought to get his "personal files" after his termination, but that he had no authority with respect to the additional files he accessed."[136] The court granted Harland Financial's motion to amend its counterclaim adding a CFAA count because it made at "least a reasonable inference that his authorization extended only to accessing and copying said personal files and that he exceeded that authorization."[137] The court reasoned that an employee not authorized to access business information, even though he had access to the company's network for his own records, could nevertheless violate the CFAA.[138] The court also ruled that Harland's business tort claims would survive a Rule 12(b)(6) motion.[139] The civil cases confirm the difficulty of determining the meaning of exceeding authorization based upon breaching a terms of service agreement as opposed to computer code.[140]

§ 8.3 ELECTRONIC COMMUNICATIONS PRIVACY ACT (ECPA)

(A) Overview of the ECPA

Congress created a federal privacy right when it enacted the Electronic Communications Privacy Act of 1986 ("ECPA"). The U.S. Senate Judiciary Committee

---

[134] 2012 WL 2327660 (N.D.Cal., June 19, 2012).

[135] This economic tort requires a showing that: (1) the existence of an economic relationship between the plaintiff and a third party; (2) that the defendant was aware of the relationship and acted wrongfully with the purpose of disrupting the relationship; (3) that the relationship was disrupted; and (4) that the plaintiff suffered damages that flow proximately from the disruption. The wrongful act must be conduct that was wrongful by some legal measure other than the fact of interference itself.

[136] Id. at *2.

[137] Id. (citing United States v. Nosal, 676 F.3d 854, 857 (9th Cir.2012).

[138] Id. at *3. (Thus, "although Nosal clearly precluded applying the CFAA to violating restrictions on use, it did not preclude applying the CFAA to rules regarding access. Nor did it speak to the situation presented here, where Plaintiff was no longer employed by Defendant and allegedly no longer had generalized authorization or permission to access files, including the files in question. Moreover, the exact nature and scope of Plaintiff's authorization as a factual matter (verbal, physical, or otherwise), is not properly before the Court based on the pleadings alone, and thus a precise delineation of whether the events in question may or may not be covered under the statute is premature on this Rule 15 motion" to amend Harland Financials counterclaim).

[139] Id. at *5–*8.

[140] The Justice Department acknowledges the inherent difficulties of finding exceeding authorization The Manual for Prosecutors states: "Note that one author argues that the law would be better off if all "unauthorized access" cases were based only on code-based restrictions, arguing that "contract-based" restrictions are harder to define. Orin S. Kerr, "Cybercrime's Scope: Interpreting 'Access' and 'Authorization'

in Computer Misuse Statutes," 78 N.Y.U. L. Rev. 1596 (2003). U.S. DEPT. OF JUSTICE, MANUAL ON PROSECUTING COMPUTER CRIMES 9 (2012) (noting that the author was essentially reading "exceeding authorized access" out of the CFAA.

approved a bill to update the ECPA in light of technological advancements, such as the growth of "cloud computing," that have occurred since the law was originally passed in 1986.[141] The ECPA prohibits the interception of "any wire, oral, or electronic communication."[142] Title I of the ECPA amended the Wiretap Act to address the interception of electronic communications. The statute defines "intercept" as "the aural or other acquisition of the contents of any wire, electronic, or oral communication through the use of any electronic, mechanical, or other device."[143] In addition, interception must occur contemporaneously with the communication.[144] The term "electronic communication" is intended to cover e-mail as well as a broad range of communication activities.[145] The ECPA is divided into three titles:

> Title I is the former Wiretap Act. The ECPA amended the Wiretap Act by, inter alia, adding the word 'electronic' to the types of communications protected from interception, as well as by amending the definition of interception to include more than just aural forms of interception. Title II of the ECPA, generally referred to as the Stored Communications Act, is an entirely new title that prohibits anyone but an authorized user from accessing stored electronic communications, including e-mail and voice mail. The Stored Communications Act ("SCA") prohibits intentionally accessing without authorization a facility through which an electronic communication service is provided, and thereby obtaining access to an electronic communication while it is in electronic storage.[146]

The SCA also provides for the recovery of civil damages by a person aggrieved by a violation of the statute.[147] Thus, the ECPA Amendments now divide the former Wiretap Act into Title I, II, and III. The former Title III of the Omnibus Crime Control and Safe Streets Act is now Title I of the ECPA. Title I of the ECPA now regulates the interception of any conversation, including electronic conversations. Title II of the ECPA regulates access to stored e-mail, fax communications, and voicemail.[148]

The ECPA, like the CFAA, recognizes a private attorneys general role or a civil action in addition to criminal sanctions. The U.S. Department of Justice Manual states:

> Section 2511(1)(a)'s text describes only three elements: (1) intentionally, (2) intercepts, and (3) communication. However, embedded in the definitions are additional requirements that indictments and jury instructions frequently include: specifically, the requirements that an interception be done with a 'device,' and that it be done contemporaneously with transmission.[149]

---

[141] Alexei Alexis, Senate Judiciary Committee Approves Leahy Bill to Protect Privacy of 'Cloud' Data, BNA BLOOMBERG: ELECTRONIC COMMERCE AND LAW REPORT (April 24, 2013).

[142] 18 U.S.C. § 2511(1)(a).

[143] 18 U.S.C. § 2510(4).

[144] United States v. Szymuszkiewicz, 622 F.3d 701, 705–06 (7th Cir. 2010).

[145] An "electronic communication," is defined as "any transfer of signs, signals, writings, images, sounds, data, or intelligence of any nature transmitted in whole or in part by a . . . system that affects interstate or foreign commerce." 18 U.S.C. § 2510(12).

[146] 18 U.S.C. § 2701(a).

[147] 18 U.S.C. § 2707(a).

[148] Laura W. Morgan, Marital Cybertorts: The Limits of Privacy in the Family Computer, 20 J. AM. ACAD. MATRIM. LAW. 231, 234 (2007).

[149] U.S. DEPT. OF JUSTICE, MANUAL ON PROSECUTING COMPUTER CRIMES 61 (2012).

Title I of the Wiretap Act sanctions three types of activities: (1) intercepting or endeavoring to intercept electronic communications, (2) disclosing or endeavoring to disclose unlawfully intercepted information, and (3) using the content of unlawfully intercepted information.[150] The ECPA extended the Wiretap Act to include new technologies, such as electronic communication.[151] The ECPA states in relevant part:

> It shall not be unlawful . . . to intercept or access an electronic communication made through an electronic communication system that is configured so that such electronic communication is readily accessible to the general public.[152]

The ECPA requires proof the government intentionally intercepted electronic communications, which means the person committing the interception has to know or have reason to know the information has been illegally intercepted. Electronic communications include "any transfer of signs, signals, writing, images, sounds, data, or intelligence of any nature transmitted in whole or in part by a wire, radio, electromagnetic, photoelectric, or photo-optical system that affects interstate or foreign commerce, with certain exceptions."[153] Section 2511 of the ECPA provides a private right of action for "any person whose wire, oral, or electronic communication is intercepted, disclosed, or intentionally used in violation of this chapter."[154] Section 2511(1) prohibits any person from making an illegal interception or disclosing or using illegally intercepted material.[155] The ECPA definition appears to be straightforward, but is deceptively complex:

> The Wiretap Act defines an "intercept" as "the aural or other acquisition of the contents of any wire, electronic, or oral communication through the use of any electronic, mechanical, or other device." 18 U.S.C. § 2510(4). Although only twenty-five words long, this definition is surprisingly complex. It uses no fewer than five terms that are each themselves separately defined in section 2510— "contents," "wire communication," "electronic communication," "oral communication," and "electronic, mechanical, or other device."[156]

A prosecutor must prove that the interception of an electronic communication is contemporaneous.[157] To establish a *prima facie* case for a violation of § 2511(1)(A), a plaintiff must prove five elements: "that a defendant (1) intentionally (2) intercepted, endeavored to intercept or procured another person to intercept or endeavor to intercept (3) the contents of (4) an electronic communication or (5) using a device."[158] Congress enacted the ECPA in 1986 to "clarify federal privacy protections and standards in light of dramatic changes in new computer and telecommunication

---

[150] 18 U.S.C. § 2511.

[151] 18 U.S.C. §§ 2701–2711.

[152] 18 U.S.C. § 2511(2)(g)(I).

[153] 18 U.S.C. § 2510(12).

[154] 18 U.S.C. § 2520.

[155] 18 U.S.C. § 2511(1).

[156] See 18 U.S.C. § 2510(1), (5), (8) & (12).

[157] "Most courts have held that both wire and electronic communications are "intercepted" within the meaning of Title III only when such communications are acquired contemporaneously with their transmission. An individual who obtains access to a stored copy of the communication left behind after the communication reached its destination does not "intercept" the communication. U.S. DEPT. OF JUSTICE, MANUAL ON PROSECUTING COMPUTER CRIMES 63 (2012).

[158] In re Pharmatrak Inc., Privacy Litig., 329 F.3d 9, 18 (1st Cir. 2003).

technologies."[159] Many states have enacted statutes with functionally equivalent provisions to punish illegal wiretaps.

The ECPA may order service providers to disclose stored communications and transaction records including the name, telephone, or instrument number and other subscriber confirming information including temporary network addresses.[160] The ECPA requires the government to show facts, capable of articulation, illustrating reasonable grounds relevant to a criminal investigation to support orders for service providers to turn over customer information. The subscriber whose information is turned over to the government has no reasonable expectation of privacy and is thus not protected under the Fourth Amendment of the U.S. Constitution.[161]

ECPA Provisions

Intercepting a Communication	18 U.S.C. § 2511(1)(a)
Disclosing an Intercepted Communications	18 U.S.C. § 2511(1)(c)
Using an Intercepted Communications	18 U.S.C. § 2511(1)(d)

Within the ECPA, Congress also created a private action which authorizes plaintiffs to seek monetary damages against a person who "intentionally intercepts, endeavors to intercept, or procures any other person to intercept or endeavor to intercept, any wire, oral, or electronic communication."[162] The First Circuit in *United States v. Councilman*,[163] held e-mail messages no longer in electronic storage could not be intercepted as defined by the ECPA.[164] In *Councilman*, the defendant, both a book dealer and an e-mail service provider, created software redirecting incoming e-mails from Amazon.com to customers of the defendant's company. The indictment charged the book dealer and provider with making copies of e-mail messages before they were delivered to their intended recipients. The Justice Department summarized the complex history of the *Councilman* case:

> The indictment charged this as a Wiretap Act violation. Two of the three judges held that email messages acquired from a computer's random access memory or hard disk were not intercepted 'contemporaneously' with transmission. On rehearing en banc, the First Circuit reversed the panel decision, holding that email in "electronic storage"—a statutory term meaning "temporary, intermediate storage," *see* 18 U.S.C. § 2510(17)—can be intercepted under the Wiretap Act . . . Federal prosecutors charged the defendant with conspiring to intercept electronic communications. The First Circuit dismissed the indictment against Councilman,

---

[159] 132 Cong. Rec. S. 14441 (1986).

[160] 18 U.S.C. § 2703.

[161] United States v. Perrine, 518 F.3d 1196, 1204 (10th Cir. 2008).

[162] 18 U.S.C. § 2511(1)(a).

[163] 418 F.3d 67, 79 (1st Cir. 2005).

[164] See generally, Katherine A. Oyama, E–Mail Privacy After United States v. Councilman: Legislative Options for Amending ECPA, 21 BERKELEY TECH. L.J. 499, 501 (2006) ("[I]t is imperative that Congress amend ECPA and close the gap in privacy safeguards for e-mail highlighted in Councilman").

reasoning he copied incoming e-mails from Amazon already in storage. By definition, a message in storage cannot be intercepted. The court ruled e-mails already in storage (opened or unopened) could not be intercepted but were subject to the SCA.[165]

After *Councilman*, the U.S. Justice Department advises its prosecutors to assume that the "contemporaneous" element must be proven.[166]

(B) ECPA Defenses

The ECPA includes two statutory exceptions: the "ordinary course of business"[167] exception and an "activity which is a necessary incident to the rendition of service."[168] Regarding the former, ECPA defines "intercept" as "acquisition of . . . electronic . . . communication through . . . any . . . device," but "provides an ordinary course of business exception . . . within its definition of "electronic . . . or other device" under § 2510(5)(a)[169]

(1) Ordinary Course of Business Exception

The ECPA "ordinary course of business" exception may support employers monitoring their employees' email.[170] To satisfy the ordinary course of business exception, the employer has to demonstrate that (i) the device used to intercept the electronic communication is "a telephone or telegraphic instrument, equipment or facility, or a . . . component thereof," either provided or installed by the employer, and (ii) that the device is used by the employer within the ordinary course of the business. However, the employer is only allowed to intercept long enough to determine the nature of the communication. If the communication is personal, the employer must cease and desist from intercepting the communications further.

In *Arias v. Mutual Center Alarm Service*,[171] more than a hundred former employees of an alarm services firm sought monetary damages against their employer for intercepting telephone conversations under the federal wiretap statute. The ex-employees claimed that their former employer unlawfully intercepted private and privileged telephone conversations by recording such conversations with a Dictaphone 9102 machine beginning in 1995. The federal circuit court of appeals affirmed a summary judgment for the employer holding that the consent of one of the parties to a telephone conversation was not necessary to apply the ordinary course of business exception to the federal wiretapping provisions. The *Arias* court also found the alarm company's covert interception of employee telephone calls fell within the "ordinary course of business" exception.

---

[165] U.S. DEPT. OF JUSTICE, MANUAL ON PROSECUTING COMPUTER CRIMES 64 (2012).

[166] In practice, prosecutors should assume that the "contemporaneous" element applies. When a defendant has interfered with the way that a computer system processes incoming or outgoing messages, causing copies to be stored or forwarded to him at approximately the same time that the computer handled them, then it is safe to argue that the contemporaneity element has been satisfied. Id. at 65.

[167] 18 U.S.C. § 2510(5)(a)(ii).

[168] 18 U.S.C. § 2511(2)(a)(I).

[169] Hall v. EarthLink Network, Inc., 396 F.3d 500, 503–04 (2d Cir. 2005).

[170] 18 U.S.C. § 2510(5)(a)(i).

[171] 1998 W.L. 612865 (S.D. N.Y., Sept. 11, 1998).

Nevertheless, the Sixth Circuit U.S. Court of Appeals refused to apply the "ordinary course" exception of the ECPA in *Adams v. City of Battle Creek*.[172] In *Adams*, a city police department secretly monitored or tapped a department-supplied pager of one of its officers. The court held that the Department did not qualify for the "ordinary course of business" exception given that the officer had no notice of the monitoring. In *City of Battle Creek*, the Police Department had the erroneous belief that its officer was assisting drug dealers. The court reasoned that the ordinary course exception required that the use be (1) for a legitimate business purpose, (2) routine, and (3) with notice. The court rejected the department's argument that it had a reason to monitor the pager because of the department's general prohibition against the personal use of these devices. The court reasoned that this was an after-the-fact justification or pretext for intercepting the plaintiff's pager, especially where the policy had not been enforced and the department was aware that many officers had used pagers for personal use.

(2) Business Exception

The business exception to ECPA provides that a provider may intercept electronic communications within its network "as may be necessarily incident to the rendition of the service or to the protection of the rights or property of the provider of that service."[173] The ECPA contains an ordinary course of business exception that applies to "any electronic, mechanical, or other device."[174] If an ISP acquires the contents of information in the ordinary course of business, it is not classifiable as an interception under the ECPA.

(3) Consent of Users

"An interception is lawful if the interceptor is a party to the communication, or if one of the parties to the communication consents to the interception."[175] The ECPA allows service providers or anyone else to intercept and disclose an electronic communication where either the sender or recipient of the message has effectively consented to disclosure, explicitly or implicitly. Section 2511(2)(d) of the ECPA prohibits employers from intercepting e-mail messages, but the Act does not apply if an employee consents to e-mail monitoring. Consent, as defined by the ECPA, also encompasses implied consent, which in the context of e-mail monitoring, is an employer's prior notice that it will monitor Internet usage and e-mail.[176]

(4) The Patriot Act Exceptions

Section 2709 of the ECPA was originally enacted as part of Title II of the SCA, in 1986, and amended in 1993 and 1996.[177] "Shortly after the terrorist attacks of September 11, 2001, however, Congress again amended § 2709 by means of Title V, Section 505 of the Uniting and Strengthening America by Providing Appropriate Tools Required to Intercept and Obstruct Terrorism Act of 2001 ("USA Patriot Act")."[178] The

---

[172] 250 F.3d 980 (6th Cir. 2001).

[173] 18 U.S.C. § 2702(c)(3).

[174] 18 U.S.C. § 2510(5).

[175] U.S. DEPT. OF JUSTICE, MANUAL ON PROSECUTING COMPUTER CRIMES 79 (2012).

[176] 18 U.S.C. § 2511(2)(c)–(d).

[177] See John Doe, Inc. v. Mukasey, 549 F.3d 861 (2d Cir. 2009) (partially invalidating § 2709(c) to the extent that the provisions fail to provide for government initiated judicial review).

[178] Doe v. Gonzales, 449 F.3d 415, 418 (2d. Cir. 2006).

USA Patriot Act amended the ECPA to list crimes for which investigators may get a wiretap order for wire communications.[179] The USA Patriot Act permits federal government agents to intercept e-mail and monitor other Internet activities. Congress authorized the Federal Bureau of Investigation ("FBI") to issue National Security Letters ("NSLs") to wire or electronic communication service providers, which allowed the FBI to gain access to subscriber information relevant to authorized terrorism investigations. A NSL is defined as an administrative subpoena that allows the FBI to gain access to, among other things, subscriber information, or electronic communication transactional records held by Internet service providers when this information is relevant to international terrorism or clandestine intelligence activities.[180]

(5) ECPA Case Law

The ECPA criminalizes the interception of electronic communications,[181] and also provides for the recovery of civil damages for an interception.[182] In *United States v. Riggs*,[183] one of the first convictions under the federal Wire Act, the court held that defendants were in violation of the ECPA when they gained unauthorized access to Bell South computers. The violation arose when hackers, known as "Prophet" and "Knight Lightning," gained unauthorized access to Bell South's 911 computer files and published them in a hacker's newsletter.[184] The defendants also sent "communications to each other via electronic mail" and published an issue of PHRACK, which contained a series of tutorials about breaking into computer systems.

Similarly, many of the U.S. Justice Department's prosecutions under the Economic Espionage Act also include counts for the ECPA as well as the CFAA. One of the greatest dangers for companies is that malicious hackers, disaffected employees, or unknown third parties will maliciously divulge trade secrets online. Malicious ex-employees can make customer lists or business records disappear and with the push of a button distribute them to millions around the world. Once an intruder distributes a trade secret to millions on the Internet, it is reasonably certain that it can no longer be classified as a trade secret.[185]

§ 8.4   STORED COMMUNICATIONS ACT

(A) SCA *Prima Facie* Case

The Stored Communications Act ("SCA") prohibits "intentionally accessing without authorization a facility through which an electronic communication service is provided," and thereby obtaining access to an "electronic communication while it is in electronic storage."[186] It also provides for the recovery of civil damages by a person

---

[179] 18 U.S.C. § 2516(1)(c) (explaining procedures for government interception of electronic communications to combat terrorism and outlining offenses that warrant such wiretapping).

[180] 18 U.S.C. § 2709(b)(1).

[181] 18 U.S.C. § 2511(1)(a).

[182] 18 U.S.C. § 2520(a).

[183] 739 F. Supp. 414 (N.D. Ill. 1990).

[184] United States v. Riggs, 743 F. Supp. 556, 556–57 (N.D. Ill. 1990).

[185] Anacomp, Inc. v. Shell Knob Servs., 1994 U.S. Dist. LEXIS 223 (S.D.N.Y. 1994) (entering preliminary injunction to protect computer manuals in diagnostic software).

[186] 18 U.S.C. § 2701(a).

aggrieved by a violation of the statute.[187] The federal court in *United States v. Weaver* stated:

> Under the Stored Communications Act, the terms "storage" and "electronic storage" are not the same. The Stored Communications Act refers back to the Wiretap Act for definitions. 18 U.S.C. § 2711. The Wiretap Act does not define "storage," but it defines "electronic storage" as: (A) any temporary, intermediate storage of a wire or electronic communication incidental to the electronic transmission thereof, and (B) any storage of such communication by an electronic communication service for purposes of backup protection of such communication. 18 U.S.C. § 2510(17).[188]

Once an e-mail is received and stored in a computer system it falls under the Stored Communications Act (SCA) or Title II, regardless of how temporary the storage.[189] For purposes of the SCA, "electronic storage" is defined as any temporary, intermediate storage of an electronic communication incidental to the electronic transmission thereof,[190] and any storage of such communication by an electronic communication service for purposes of backup protection of such communication,[191] Congress enacted the SCA "to protect privacy interests in personal and proprietary information from the mounting threat of computer hackers 'deliberately gaining access to, and sometimes tampering with, electronic or wire communications' by means of electronic trespass."[192]

Title II protects stored communications from unauthorized or exceeded authorized access, but it does not apply to a person or entities providing the wire or electronic communications service.[193] Further, it does not apply to the user of that service or in a situation where the service was intended for that user.[194] This would in many cases authorize employers to monitor emails, since employers often provide the electronic communication for their employees and the service is intended to be used within the scope of employment.

The SCA punishes those who do not have authority to access an electronic communications service facility but who obtain access to a wire or electronic

---

[187] 18 U.S.C. § 2707(a).

[188] United States v. Weaver, 636 F. Supp. 2d 769, 772 (C.D. 2009).

[189] The Electronic Communications Storage Act, 18 U.S.C. §§ 2701–2711 states that it is a violation for anyone who intentionally accesses without authorization a facility through which an electronic communication service is provided and thereby obtains, alters, or prevents authorized access to a wire or electronic communication while it is in electronic storage in such system violates the act. 18 U.S.C. § 2701(a) "Electronic storage" is defined as (A) any temporary, intermediate storage of a wire or electronic communication incidental to the electronic transmission thereof; and (B) any storage of such communication by an electronic communication service for purposes of backup protection of such communication. 18 U.S.C. §§ 2510(17) and 2711(1) (definitions of the Electronic Communications Privacy Act, 18 U.S.C. §§ 2510–2521, also known as the Wiretap Act, applicable to the Electronic Communications Storage Act). Title II creates civil liability for one who: (1) intentionally accesses without authorization a facility through which an electronic communication service is provided; or (2) intentionally exceeds an authorization to access that facility; and thereby obtains, alters, or prevents authorized access to a wire or electronic communication while it is in electronic storage in such system. 18 U.S.C. §§ 2510 et seq.

[190] 18 U.S.C. § 2510(17)(A).

[191] 18 U.S.C. § 2510(17)(B).

[192] Devine v. Kapasi, 729 F.Supp.2d 1024, 1026 (N.D.Ill.2010) (citing S. Rep. No. 99–541, at 3 (1986)).

[193] 18 U.S.C. § 2701(a).

[194] 18 U.S.C. § 2701(a) and (c)(1).

communication in electronic storage.[195] An SCA violation requires that a person: (1) intentionally access without authorization a facility through which an electronic communication service is provided or intentionally exceed authorization to access that facility, and (2) thereby obtain, alter, or prevent authorized access to an electronic communication while it is in electronic storage.[196] Section 2701(c)(1) exempts from subsection (A) "conduct authorized by the person or entity providing a wire or electronic communications service."[197] Many states have enacted "little SCA" that are state wiretap statutes that parallel the provisions of the ECPA.

The SCA creates rights held by "customers" and "subscribers" of network service providers in both content and non-content information held by two particular types of providers. The SCA bars electronic communications service providers from divulging to any person or entity the contents of a communication while held in their electronic storage.[198] The SCA created a service provider exception, permitting a provider to divulge an electronic communication to a person employed or authorized or whose facilities are used to forward such communication to its destination, or as may be necessarily incident to the rendition of the service or to the protection of the rights or property of the provider of that service.[199]

The SCA defines an electronic communication service ("ECS") as "any service which provides to users thereof the ability to send or receive wire or electronic communications."[200] The SCA creates a civil right of action to protect against persons who gain unauthorized access to an electronic communication storage facility. A person violates § 2701 if he or she "intentionally accesses without authorization a facility through which an electronic communication service is provided; or intentionally exceeds an authorization to access that facility; and thereby obtains, alters, or prevents authorized access to a wire or electronic communication while it is in electronic storage in such system."[201]

The ECPA defines an "electronic communications service" as "any service which provides to users thereof the ability to send or receive wire or electronic communications."[202] An Internet actor such as employer will violate the SCA by intentionally accessing an e-mail server through which they provide an electronic communication service. The SCA prohibits an ECS from knowingly divulging to any person or entity the contents of a communication while in electronic storage by that service, unless, among other exceptions not relevant to this appeal, that person or entity is an addressee or intended recipient of such communication.[203]

---

[195] 18 U.S.C. § 2701(a).
[196] Id.
[197] 18 U.S.C. § 2701(c)(1).
[198] 18 U.S.C. § 2702.
[199] 18 U.S.C. § 2702(b)(5).
[200] 18 U.S.C. § 2510(15).
[201] 18 U.S.C. § 2701.
[202] 18 U.S.C. § 2510(15).
[203] 18 U.S.C. § 2702(a)(1), (b)(1), & (b)(3).

(B) SCA Defenses

The SCA posits a statutory exception for conduct that is authorized by the person or entity providing the electronic communications service.[204] This means a company providing e-mail service to its employees may access the service without violating the SCA. Non-providers do not violate the SCA by accessing computer communications in electronic storage if it acts with the knowledge and consent of the person or entity that provides the electronic communication service. The SCA explicitly provides that good faith reliance on a warrant is a complete defense to a civil action. Defendants in ECPA cases will have a functionally equivalent defense for good faith reliance on a warrant.[205]

§ 8.5 ECPA & SCA CASE LAW

(A) Private Attorneys General

The ECPA's civil action provisions illustrate the role of the "private attorney general" enabling private litigants to file lawsuits for private damages that also benefit the public.[206] Congress has enacted scores of private attorney general statutes in diverse fields. In *In re Facebook Privacy Litigation,*[207] Facebook users filed a class action contending that the social media site divulged private information about users to advertisers without users' consent and were liable under SCA.[208] The federal court found that the Facebook users did not allege that the communications at issue were sent to Facebook or to its advertisers and thus could not state a claim under the SCA. The court denied Facebook's motion to dismiss on the ground that the plaintiffs lacked standing under Article III of the Wiretap Act; but granted defendant's motion to dismiss on all other counts.

(1) Konop v. Hawaiian Airlines

In *Konop v. Hawaiian Airlines, Inc.,*[209] a Hawaiian Airlines pilot sued his employer for violation of the SCA after a manager viewed his website without his consent. The plaintiff was a Hawaiian Airlines pilot who "created and maintained a website where he posted bulletins critical of his employer, its officers, and the incumbent union, Air Line Pilots Association ("ALPA")."[210] "Konop controlled access to his website by requiring visitors to log in with a user name and password . . . Pilots Gene Wong and James Gardner were included on this list. . . . In December 1995, Hawaiian vice

---

[204] 18 U.S.C. § 2701(c)(1) (the SCA "does not apply with respect to conduct authorized by the person or entity providing a wire or electronic/ communications service.").

[205] 18 U.S.C. § 2707(e).

[206] Michael L. Rustad, Commentary, Smoke Signals from Private Attorneys General in Mega Social Policy Cases, 51 DePaul L. Rev. 511, 517 (2001) (describing those acting as private attorneys general as advancing the public interest).

[207] 791 F. Supp. 2d 705 (N.D. Cal. 2011).

[208] Id. at 708 ("Plaintiffs allege that Defendant intentionally and knowingly transmitted personal information about Plaintiffs to third-party advertisers without Plaintiffs' consent.").

[209] 302 F.3d 868 (9th Cir. 2002).

[210] Id. at 872.

president James Davis asked Wong for permission to use Wong's name to access Konop's website. Wong agreed."[211]

Afterwards, the Hawaiian Airline's manager accessed the pilot's website.[212] The SCA exempts from liability, "conduct authorized by a user of [the electronic communication service] with respect to a communication of or intended for that user."[213] While the manager had the consent of the two non-management employees to use their passwords, there was no evidence either of those employees had ever been "users" of the pilot's website. Later that day, the pilot received word that the Hawaiian Airlines Vice President was upset by the contents of the website. [214] The pilot then became aware that the Airline's President had unauthorized access to his site[215] and learned that the President of the Hawaiian Airlines "had obtained the contents of his website and was threatening to sue [him] for defamation based on statements contained on the website."[216]

The plaintiff filed an ECPA claim believing the company official secretly obtained the contents of his website and was not authorized to access his website. The district court entered judgment against the pilot on his ECPA Wiretap Act claim but entered judgment in favor of the plaintiff on his SCA claim. The federal appeals court ruled that the airline violated the SCA because the two pilots were not "users" of the website at the time they authorized the airline officer to use their names.[217]

The *Konop* Court's *en banc* opinion reasoned that they were following precedent in construing the definition of intercept narrowly when it comes to electronic communications.[218] Nevertheless, the court held that the airline violated the SCA because the two pilots who shared their log-in information with the manager were not "users" of the website and therefore could authorize the manager, a third party, access to any of Konop's electronic communications.[219] With respect to the plaintiff's Wiretap claim, the court had to decide if the manager intercepted an "electronic communication."

A transfer of information from a website owner to an Internet user involves a web server sending a copy of a document to the Internet user's computer for viewing; this constitutes an "electronic communication" within the meaning of the Wiretap Act.[220] The seizure of unread e-mail residing on a host computer did not match the narrow meaning of "intercept" as required by Title I of the Wiretap Act, which contemplates

---

[211] Id. at 872–73. To protect access, Konop programmed the website to allow access when a person entered the name of an eligible person, created a password, and accepted the terms and conditions of use. These terms and conditions prohibited any member of Hawaiian's management from viewing the website and prohibited users from disclosing the website's content. Id.

[212] Id.

[213] 18 U.S.C. § 2701(c)(2).

[214] Konop, Id. at 872.

[215] Id. at 872.

[216] Id. at 873.

[217] Id. at 875.

[218] Id. (agreeing with precedent that supported reading the term "intercept" narrowly).

[219] Id. at 880 (defining use in the ordinary way as, "to put into action or service, avail oneself of, employ"). The SCA does not define user and therefore the court took it upon itself to apply this ordinary meaning. Id.

[220] 18 U.S.C. § 2510(12); see also 302 F.3d at 876 (explaining that Konop's website engaged in electronic communication). Konop transmitted documents to a server where they were stored, when users visit the website the server transmits a copy of Konop's document to the user, when the server sends the copy to the user's computer a "transfer of information has occurred." Id.

"intercept" as occurring during or contemporaneously with transmission.[221] The court did not find liability under the Wiretap Act for accessing a private website without authorization. Employing the password and user name of an authorized user, the defendant viewed the pages published at the website. The Ninth Circuit held that the defendant's actions did not violate the Wiretap Act because "for a website such as Konop's to be intercepted . . ., it must be acquired during transmission, not while it is in electronic storage."[222]

Since the *Konop* case, Congress has amended the ECPA to eliminate storage from the definition of wire communication. The court acknowledged that the airline's manager would have avoided SCA liability if he gained access to Konop's website by using information obtained from real users. However, as previously discussed, the individuals from whom the executive obtained the access information had never actually used Konop's website; therefore, they were never "users" under the language of the SCA. The *Konop* court relied on this simple and perhaps overly literal interpretation of the statute to reverse the district court's grant of summary judgment to Hawaiian, on Konop's SCA claim.[223]

(2) *Bohach v. City of Reno*

The court rejected an ECPA claim in *Bohach v. City of Reno*,[224] by two police officers. While under internal investigation, the police officers sought an injunction pursuant to the ECPA, to prevent disclosure of the contents of electronic messages sent between them. The court held that the police officers had no right to restrain disclosure of electronic messages and that the police department had a right to retrieve pager text messages saved on the department's computer system. The police department did not violate Title II of the ECPA or the privacy rights of the officers. The *Bohach* court reasoned the department was a provider of electronic communications services.[225] The *Bohach* court classified stored transmissions of a paging system as storage, irrespective of whether the storage of paging messages was classifiable as temporary, intermediate, or incidental "to its impending 'electronic transmission,' or more permanent storage for backup purposes."[226]

The issue in *Bohach* was whether a government employee has a reasonable expectation of privacy in messages sent through government-issued communications equipment when his employer has notified him that his use of the equipment is subject to monitoring without notice. The court found that the employee had no expectation of privacy in police pagers because of the department order that messages would be logged onto the system, and banned certain types of messages. In *Bohach*, all messages were "recorded and stored not because anyone is "tapping" the system, but simply because that's how the system works. It is an integral part of the technology."[227] The

---

[221] 302 F.3d at 878.

[222] Id. at 879.

[223] Lothar Determann and Robert Sprague, Intrusive Monitoring: Employee Privacy Expectations Are Reasonable in Europe, Destroyed in the United States, 26 BERKELEY TECH. L.J. 979, 1000 (2011).

[224] 932 F. Supp. 1232 (D. Nev. 1996).

[225] Id. at 1237 (ruling that "The City is the 'provider' of the 'electronic communications service' to Police Department's terminals, computer and software" enabled communications).

[226] Id. at 1236.

[227] Id. at 1234.

court held that the retrieval of alphanumeric pager messages stored in computer files did not constitute an interception for purposes of the ECPA.[228]

(3) In re Pharmatrak

In *In re Pharmatrak, Inc.,*[229] the First Circuit reversed a lower court ruling that Pharmatrak violated the ECPA with its website monitoring software. In this case, one of the defendants, Pharmatrak, sold its "NETcompare" service to pharmaceutical companies wanting information about consumers' visits to their websites.[230] NETcompare captured personally identifiable information-name, address, telephone number, and e-mail address-entered by consumers on the pharmaceutical companies' web pages. The court found these details to be "contents" of "electronic communications."[231] The court also found the defendant's NETcompare software to be a "device" under ECPA.[232] NETcompare's capture of consumer's personally identifiable information was classified as an "interception."[233] The software's capture of personally identifiable information of a small percentage of website visitors was not by design.[234] The affected plaintiffs filed a class action against Pharmatrak and the pharmaceutical companies asserting they violated the ECPA.

The First Circuit reversed a Massachusetts federal district court's granting of summary judgment in favor of Pharmatrak. The First Circuit held that the lower court incorrectly interpreted the "consent" exception to the ECPA and remanded the case for further proceedings. The court ruled Pharmatrak had the burden to prove it had the consent of users. Pharmatrak assured the companies that data collection on individual users would not occur. Nevertheless, Pharmatrak collected user identifying information primarily because one of its clients had employed the "get" method to transmit information entered by users.

When the "get" method was used, information entered by users into the online form was appended to the next URL. Thus, NETcompare, which routinely recorded the full URLs of the web pages accessed by a user before and after visiting a client pharmaceutical company's website, also recorded personal information appended to the next URL. The court concluded that it did not need to address the "real-time requirement" of the ECPA since Pharmatrak acquired the information contemporaneous with transmission by the Internet users. The court held that

---

[228] Id.

[229] 329 F.3d 9 (1st Cir. 2003).

[230] Id. at 12.

[231] Id. at 18.

[232] Id.

[233] Id. at 22.

[234] "NETcompare operated as follows. A pharmaceutical client installed NETcompare by adding five to ten lines of HTML code to each web page it wished to track and configuring the pages to interface with Pharmatrak's technology. When a user visited the website of a Pharmatrak client, Pharmatrak's HTML code instructed the user's computer to contact Pharmatrak's web server and retrieve from it a tiny, invisible graphic image known as a "clear GIF" (or a "web bug"). The purpose of the clear GIF was to cause the user's computer to communicate directly with Pharmatrak's web server. When the user's computer requested the clear GIF, Pharmatrak's web servers responded by either placing or accessing a "persistent cookie" on the user's computer. On a user's first visit to a web page monitored by NETcompare, Pharmatrak's servers would plant a cookie on the user's computer. If the user had already visited a NETcompare web page, then Pharmatrak's servers would access the information on the existing cookie." Id. at 13. A "web bug" is typically a text file or graphic embedded in a web page or in an e-mail's HTML code. Web bugs are also known as "invisible GIFs." Id.

Pharmatrak intercepted electronic communications without their consent. "The Pharmatrak defendant's java/Javascript programs recorded the URLs that the users visited, which means that they copied the users' web commands before those commands were sent out over the Internet. The web commands were in the same type of temporary, intermediate, and incidental storage that the e-mails at issue in this case."[235]

This was enough for the court to conclude that the contemporaneity test of the ECPA was satisfied. Pharmatrak invoked a statutory exception under the ECPA claiming, among other things, they had received the consent of those companies. The First Circuit recognized consent was one of the statutory exceptions to ECPA liability. The *Pharmatrak* court noted that some courts had distinguished between communications acquired in transit and those acquired from storage after transmission for the purposes of deciding whether there had been an "interception" under the Wiretap Act. The court observed, "Traveling the Internet, electronic communications are often—perhaps constantly—both "in transit" and "in storage" simultaneously, a linguistic but not a technological paradox."[236] Pharmatrak "collected certain information meant to permit the pharmaceutical companies to do intra-industry comparisons of website traffic and usage."[237]

(4) McVeigh v. Cohen

In *McVeigh v. Cohen*,[238] a federal court ruled that the U.S. Navy violated plaintiff's rights under ECPA, Navy policy, and the Fourth and Fifth Amendments by intercepting America Online e-mails in which plaintiff referred to his homosexuality. McVeigh, a U.S. Navy officer, demonstrated that he was likely success to prevail on the merits of his claim that the Navy violated "Don't Ask, Don't Tell, Don't Pursue" policy, when they investigated his sexual orientation. In *McVeigh*, the Navy commenced investigation to determine whether officer was e-mail user who had indicated homosexual interests and marital status as "gay" in anonymous e-mail user profile. The ECPA violation occurred when the Navy sought "information from an online service provider without a warrant.

(B) Social Media & the ECPA

Facebook and other social media sites provide electronic communications services subject to ECPA.[239] The ECPA may come into play in a family court proceeding if a spouse intercepts messages from the other spouse's lover. Such an action could violate the wiretapping laws, and the spouse could incur penalties or be subject to a civil lawsuit for the violation.[240] A poster on Facebook will not likely have a good cause of action against Facebook absent a showing of injury or violation of its privacy policy.[241]

---

[235] United States v. Councilman, 373 F.3d at 214 (1st Cir. 2004).

[236] In re Pharmatrak, Inc., 329 F.3d 9, 21–22 (1st Cir. 2003).

[237] Id. at 12.

[238] 983 F. Supp. 215 (D.D.C. 1996).

[239] Crispin v. Christian Audigier, 717 F. Supp. 2d 965, 980–82 (C.D. Cal. 2010).

[240] Shawn L. Reeves, Social Media Discovery in Family Court, THE SCITECHLAWYER (Spring 2012) at 12.

[241] In re Am. Airlines, Inc. Privacy Litig., 370 F. Supp. 2d 552, 560–61 (N.D. Tex. 2005) (holding that American Airlines was not liable under the ECPA for disclosure of personal information provided to them by plaintiffs under the addressee or intended recipient exception, even if the disclosure was contrary to American's privacy policy).

A U.S. Judicial Panel on Multidistrict Litigation ordered consolidation of scores of complaints against Facebook for improperly tracking users' Internet activities after they had logged out of their Facebook accounts. Many of these claims are asserted under the CFAA and the SCA.[242]

In *Hubbard v. MySpace*,[243] MySpace users filed a class action against the social media site contending that it violated the SCA because the site disclosed members' account information in response to law enforcement's warrant. The court granted a motion to dismiss ruling that the warrant was sufficient and not invalidated by the SCA. In *In re Facebook Privacy Litigation*,[244] Facebook users filed an ECPA claim against the social networking site. The plaintiffs alleged that their privacy was invaded when they clicked on an advertisement banner displayed on the site sending personally identifiable information to the advertiser. The court found as a matter of law that the Facebook users had no ECPA or SCA causes of action.

In *Low v. LinkedIn Corp.*,[245] the district court dismissed a class action suit against LinkedIn under the SCA. The class action complaint alleged the social networking site for dropping cookies that tracked class members' browsing history in violation of the SCA. The court reasoned that the plaintiffs did not demonstrate proof of how they were injured and that the bare assertion of embarrassment and humiliation was not enough. The court reasoned that emotional, economic harm from online disclosure of personal information or browsing histories must be concrete and particularized to individual plaintiffs to permit recovery under the SCA.

The class representative contended that the personal information of the class members, including "personally identifiable browsing histor[ies]," were allegedly disclosed by Defendant to third party advertising and marketing companies through the use of "cookies" or "beacons." The plaintiff's class action included counts for the SCA; the California Constitution; the California Unfair Competition Law; the California False Advertising Law; the California Consumer Legal Remedies Act; common law breach of contract; breach of implied covenant of good faith and fair dealing; common law invasion of privacy; conversion; and unjust enrichment.[246] The court granted LinkedIn's motion to dismiss with leave to amend.

(C) Child Pornography Crimes & Sexting

In the United States, it is a violation of social norms in every state to create, use, or distribute child pornography. The relevant elements prohibit the transmission of child pornography as stated in section 2252(a) and include: (1) an active intention to give or transfer a specific depiction [of a minor] to another person and (2) active participation in the actual delivery. "Sexting is "the practice of sending or posting sexually suggestive text messages and images, including nude or semi-nude photographs via cellular telephones or over the Internet."[247] Overzealous prosecutors

---

[242] In re Facebook Internet Tracking Litig. (N. D. Cal., Feb. 8, 2012) (consolidating cases arising out of Facebook's practice of using tracking cookies to collect information on users when they were logged out—without the users' knowledge).

[243] 788 F. Supp.2d 319 (S.D. N.Y. 2011).

[244] 791 F. Supp.2d 705 (N.D. Cal. 2011).

[245] No. 11–1468 (N.D. Cal., Nov. 11, 2011).

[246] Id.

[247] Terri Day, The New Digital Dating Behavior—Sexting: Teens' Explicit Love Letters: Criminal Justice or Civil Liability, 33 HASTINGS COMM. & ENT. L.J. 69, 71 (2001); Sanches v. Carrollton–Farmers

have prosecuted under aged girls for sending nude pictures of themselves to peers. "Two highly publicized stories of sexting involve Jessica ("Jessie") Logan and Philip Alpert. Jessie became a victim of sexting. Unable to deal with the emotional distress she suffered when her nude picture digitally circulated throughout her school, Jessie committed suicide."[248]

Philip Alpert faced criminal charges for violating child pornography laws for the unauthorized e-mailing of his ex-girlfriend's nude picture. As a registered sex offender, he will suffer the consequences of his sexting well into his adult life. Although certainly culpable of causing harm, it could be argued that Alpert, too, is a victim of sexting. "In Pennsylvania, three teenage girls between the ages of fourteen and seventeen were charged with disseminating child pornography when they sexted their boyfriends. The boys who received the photos were charged with possession of child pornography."[249] Treating sexting as child pornography is disproportionately harsh much like using a machine gun to kill a fly.

Louisiana enacted the "Unlawful Use or Access of Social Media," that prohibits registered sex offenders who were previously convicted of crimes involving minors or juveniles from "using or accessing of social networking websites, chat rooms, and peer-to-peer networks."[250] This Louisiana state statute does not define "using" or "accessing," but does defines social networking website, chat room, and peer-to-peer network broadly. Under our current laws, with the advent and prevalence of sexing and virtual sexual behavior, many, many citizens are engaging in behavior that could make them felons.[251] While "[a]ny social problem that exists at the intersection of adolescence, sex, technology, and criminal law compels strong reactions from all sides . . . it often results in sensationalism and oversimplification of complex and multifaceted issues making it more difficult to discuss the problem rationally and productively."[252]

A federal court ruled in *Backpage.com v. McKenna*[253] that the Communications Decency Act likely preempts a Washington state statute, which seeks to criminalize "the offense of advertising commercial sexual abuse of a minor."[254] The constitutionality of the Washington statute was challenged by Backpage.com, a website that operates an online-classified advertising service located at www.backpage.com, which "hosts millions of advertisements per month throughout the country."[255] Backpage.com charges users "$5–$10 to post ads in the adult category, $1 to post ads in

---

Branch Indep. Sch. Dist., No. 10–10325, 2011 U.S. App. LEXIS 14313 (5th Cir. July 13, 2011) (regarding a high school student was suspended from the cheerleading team for posting inappropriate Facebook pictures; the student then allegedly harassed another student that she believed turned her in to school authorities).

[248] Day, The New Digital Dating, Id. at 71.

[249] Id.

[250] LSA–R.S.14:91.5.

[251] See Jordan J. Szymialis, Sexting: A Response To Prosecuting Those Growing Up with a Growing Trend, 44 IND. L. REV. 301 (2010).

[252] Mary G. Leary, Sexting or Self-Produced Child Pornography? The Dialogue Continues—Structured Prosecutorial Discretion within a Multidisciplinary Response, 17 VA. J. SOC. POL'Y & L. 486, 487–88 (2010).

[253] 2012 U.S. Dist. LEXIS 105189 (W.D. Wash. July 27, 2012).

[254] Id. at *3.

[255] Id. at *4.

the dating category, or otherwise post ads for free."[256] A Washington state law, SB 6251, made it a felony:

> to knowingly publish, disseminate, or display or to "directly or indirectly" cause content to be published, disseminated or displayed if it contains a "depiction of a minor" and any "explicit or implicit offer" of sex for "something of value." Under the proposed law, it is not a defense that the defendant did not know the age of the person depicted and the defendant may not rely on representation by or the apparent age of the person depicted. The only defense allowed under the law is that a defendant obtained and retained government or school identification for the person depicted.[257]

The *Backpage.com* court ruled that SB 6251 is inconsistent with Section 230 of the Communications Decency Act (CDA) and therefore expressly preempted. The court reasoned that online service providers such as Backpage.com were neither publishers nor speakers of information because third party advertisers provided the information.[258] Backpage.com therefore cannot be criminally liable for advertisements created by third parties "namely ads for commercial sex acts depicting minors.[259] Countless courts have given service providers a broad immunity for websites that display third-party content, so long as they are not too involved in the creation of the content.[260] Nevertheless, the federal court therefore granted the plaintiffs' motion for a preliminary injunction barring enforcement of the law.[261] State attorneys general drafted a letter urging Congress to amend Section 230 to address particularly egregious website conduct. A Tennessee federal court also struck down a Tennessee statute's attempt to criminalize sex ads on Backpage.com on preemption grounds.[262]

Civil actions have also been filed against the distributors or producers of child pornography. In a Alabama state court case, the plaintiff claimed that, beginning in "January of 2003, defendant Anita Pierson began photographing her minor child T.B. at the studio of BSM Publication, Inc., while representing that her and defendant Jeff Pierson were operating a Christian modeling agency."[263] Plaintiff further claimed that, without her knowledge, the Piersons and BSM created, marketed, and distributed photographs depicting T.B. and other child models in a sexually explicit manner. Defendants Marc Evan Greenberg, Jeffrey Robert Libman, and Webe Web Corporation were the alleged recipients and distributors of the photographs, placing them on websites that catered to adult males with sexual orientations toward underage girls.

---

[256] Id.

[257] Id. at *11.

[258] Id. at *24.

[259] Id.

[260] Chapter 6 discusses the broad immunity provisions of the CDA as construed by the courts.

[261] Id. at *65.

[262] Backpage.com, LLC v. Cooper, 2013 WL 1558785 (M.D. Tenn., Jan. 3, 2013).

[263] T.B., a Minor by and through her Mother and Next Friend, Kim Butler v. Jeff Pierson, 2012 WL 6931716 (Ala.Cir.Ct. Sept. 11, 2012) ("Child sexual exploitation is an evil that states have an undisputed interest in dispelling. However despicable this evil, though, the Constitution stands as a shield against broad assaults by states on the rights of their citizens. The Constitution tells us that—when freedom of speech hangs in the balance—the state may not use a butcher knife on a problem that requires a scalpel to fix. Nor may a state enforce a law that flatly conflicts with federal law. Yet, this appears to be what the Tennessee legislature has done in passing the law at issue.").

The jury awarded the plaintiff $250,000 to compensate them for embarrassment and for defamation per se.

The State of Washington entered in a $2,400,000 settlement with the innocent victims of a negligent investigation of alleged purchasing and trafficking in internet child pornography.[264] The Washington State Patrol investigated, arrested, and searched the home of an innocent couple who were victims of credit card and identity theft.[265] One of the plaintiffs, "a fire Lieutenant, was wrongfully arrested and charged with possession of, trafficking in, and financing child pornography."[266] A search of the plaintiffs' home revealed no child pornography and ultimately local officers found the plaintiffs were victimized by identity theft and credit card fraud. Their credit cards were "used to pay reoccurring hosting fees for a website to which an unknown individual had, at an undetermined date and time, uploaded several images of child pornography."[267]

The Ninth Circuit ruled that plaintiffs had "made a substantial showing of the officers' reckless or intentional disregard for the truth," had made out "a judicial deception claim for" one of the plaintiff's arrest, and held Washington State Patrol officers were "not entitled to qualified immunity."[268] The State Police Officers "utilized false information and omitted material facts to obtain both the arrest warrant and search warrants at issue. In the application for the search warrant,"[269] the plaintiffs "claimed that the investigators used "Gestapo" type tactics in how they handled the case by not verifying the evidence they had prior to arresting one of the defendants.[270]

§ 8.6   OTHER INTERNET–RELATED CRIMINAL STATUTES

(A) Identity Theft

The Identity Theft Penalty Enhancement Act ("ITPEA"), which took effect July 15, 2004, established a new offense of aggravated identity theft.[271] Section 1028A applies when a defendant "knowingly transfers, possesses, or uses, without lawful authority, a means of identification of another person" during and in relation to any felony violation of certain enumerated federal offenses. Prosecutors can deploy this statutory provision against hackers that misappropriate credit card information or other personally identifiable information obtained through fraudulent e-mails.[272] In general, those who violate section 1028A are subject to a mandatory two-year term of imprisonment.[273] In cases of terrorism related aggravated identity theft, including that related to section 1030(a)(1) Section 1028A imposes an additional five-year term of imprisonment.[274] Congress broadened the definition of protected computers to include computers that

---

[264] Chism v. Washington State Patrol, 2012 WL 4803759 (Wash.Super. June 2, 2012).

[265] Id.

[266] Id.

[267] Id.

[268] Id.

[269] Id.

[270] Id.

[271] 18 U.S.C. § 1028(a).

[272] U.S. DEPARTMENT OF JUSTICE, MANUAL FOR PROSECUTING COMPUTER CRIMES, Id. at 100.

[273] 18 U.S.C. § 1028A(a)(1).

[274] 18 U.S.C. § 1028A(a)(2).

"affect foreign commerce or communications when it enacted the Identity Theft Enforcement and Restitution Act of 2008."[275]

(B) Access Device Fraud

Access device fraud is a relatively new cybercrime to address theft using payment devices.[276] Congress defined "access" broadly to avoid the problem of legal lag as new technologies evolve. "Unauthorized" access devices include lost, stolen, or revoked devices, whereas "counterfeit" ones include fictitious, altered, or forged devices.[277] Conviction for access device fraud may result in a 10–year prison sentence.[278]

(C) Civil RICO in Cyberspace

When Congress enacted the Racketeer Influenced and Corrupt Organizations Act ("RICO"), it provided for a civil cause of action in addition to the federal criminal statute. Plaintiffs asserted causes of action under civil RICO in a number of early cybertort cases because Section 230 of the Communications Decency Act would not shield the statutory cause of action. To claim enterprise liability in the racketeering context, a plaintiff must allege: (1) an ongoing organization with a decision-making framework or mechanism for controlling the group, (2) that various associates function as a continuing unit, and (3) that the enterprise exists separate and apart from the pattern of racketeering activity.[279]

RICO defines an enterprise as a group of persons associated together for a common purpose of engaging in a course of conduct and requires evidence of an ongoing organization, formal or informal, and by evidence that the various associates function as a continuing unit. The federal RICO statute[280] requires the plaintiff to prove four elements: (1) conduct by a person, (2) of an enterprise (3) through a pattern (4) of racketeering activity.[281] Section 1962(d) creates liability for conspiring to violate another section of RICO. The Civil RICO identifies numerous federal violations that can serve as predicate acts of racketeering, including mail fraud, wire fraud, and criminal copyright infringement.[282]

In a civil RICO claim, a plaintiff may use various federal statutes including the CFAA, ECPA, or SCA as predicate acts of racketeering, including mail and wire fraud. A claim for wire fraud requires: (1) the existence of a scheme or artifice to defraud or obtain money or property by false pretenses, representations or promises, and (2) that the defendant use interstate wire, radio or television communications in furtherance of the scheme to defraud. The predicate act for a civil RICO is as essential as a hole in the donut. Civil RICO is actionable for a conspiracy to sell defective products over the

---

[275] 18 U.S.C. § 1030(e)(2)(B).

[276] 18 U.S.C. § 1029.

[277] 18 U.S.C. § 1029(e)(2) & (3).

[278] 18 U.S.C. § 1029(a)(3) & (c)(1)(A)(I).

[279] The federal RICO statute make it unlawful to use income from a pattern of racketeering activity: (1) to acquire an interest in, establish or operate an enterprise involved in interstate commerce; (2) to acquire or maintain an interest in such enterprise through a pattern of racketeering activity; (3) to conduct or participate in the conducting of such enterprise through racketeering activity; and (4) to conspire to do any of the foregoing acts. Simpson Electric Corp. v. Leucadia, Inc., 72 N.Y.2d 450 (1988).

[280] 18 U.S.C. § 1961.

[281] 18 U.S.C. § 1962.

[282] 18 U.S.C. § 1961(1)(B).

Internet without any intent of issuing refunds. The jury awarded punitive damages in *Planned Parenthood, Inc. v. Am. Coalition of Life Activists*,[283] a case where anti-abortion activists posted Old West-style "wanted dead or alive" posters portraying doctors that performed abortions. Each time a doctor was murdered, the website displayed the victim's name with a line through it. The physicians depicted on the virtual posters won a $109 million verdict including punitive damages under the civil Rico statute. The Planned Parenthood case is one of the largest Internet-related verdicts in history.

Planned Parenthood filed an action against the anti-abortion activists who developed the website, contending that the wanted posters constituted a true threat of imminent harm. The trial court also granted a permanent injunction prohibiting the defendants from publishing the posters or contributing materials to the pro-life website because such publication was made with intent to harm.[284] The *Planned Parenthood* court awarded a multi-million dollar punitive damages award in favor of the physicians. This 98 to 1 high ratio verdict was remanded to the district court for a review for constitutional excessiveness. A three-judge panel of the Ninth Circuit reversed the entire judgment, but the decision was in turn reversed when an en banc panel ruled that the online "wanted-type poster" could be actionable. The Ninth Circuit panel reinstated the compensatory damages but reversed the punitive damages award.

In *Vo Group, LLC v. Opinion Corp.*,[285] a trial court refused to dismiss a Civil RICO claim against the PissedConsumer website. The court noted that a moving party must show three things in a civil RICO case: (1) a violation of the RICO statute; (2) an injury to business or property and (3) the injury was caused by the violation of Section 1962.[286] In *Vo Group*, the plaintiff sued the PissedConsumer gripe website that allowed anonymous individuals to post allegedly defamatory statements associated with services such as reselling and financing vacation properties.[287]

Vo Group contended that PissedConsumer was engaging in racketeering activities including commercial bribery and the federal Hobbes Act.[288] "PissedConsumer demanded $5,000 to remove defamatory posts, that such a demand constituted extortion."[289] The court refused to dismiss the RICO conspiracy claim as well as the substantive RICO claims based upon the Hobbs Act and commercial bribery.[290] The court's reasoning was that it could not determine at such an early stage in the trial whether PissedConsumer engaged in these illegal practices.[291]

---

[283] 290 F.3d 1058 (9th Cir. 2002).

[284] Planned Parenthood, Inc. v. Am. Coalition of Life Activists, Inc., 41 F. Supp. 2d 1130, 1155 (D. Or. 1999) (finding that the "actions of the defendants in preparing, publishing and disseminating these true threats objectively and subjectively were not protected speech under the First Amendment" and issuing a permanent injunction).

[285] No. 11–8758 (N.Y. Sup. Ct., May 22, 2012).

[286] Id. at *6 (citing 18 U.S.C. § 1962).

[287] Id. at *2.

[288] Id. at *7.

[289] Id. at *9.

[290] Id. at *10.

[291] Id. at *13.

Offshore websites may easily evade civil law enforcement by disappearing. In *John Does v. Franco Productions*,[292] young college athletes were awarded $ 506 million against Internet distributors for compensatory and punitive damages based upon invasion of privacy, unlawful use of the plaintiffs' images for monetary gain, and mail and wire fraud under civil RICO laws.[293] In *Franco Productions*, the defendants used hidden cameras to film college athletes in locker rooms, restrooms, and wrestling meets.[294] The secret videotapes were advertised as "hot young dudes" and sold on the Internet. The tapes carried names like "Straight Off the Mat" and "Voyeur Time" and depicted hundreds of young athletes in various degrees of nudity. The federal district court had previously held that the ISP was not liable for any tort action because of the broad immunity granted to providers by Section 230 of the Communications Decency Act ("CDA").[295] A federal court also refused to recognize aider and abettor liability on the part of the web host for the illicit videos.[296] The federal court's default judgment against the primary defendants was uncollectible because they fled to an offshore haven.[297] The enforcement of cybertort judgments is often unlikely because the defendant may have only a virtual presence and no traceable assets to seize.[298] Defendants can disappear across national borders to a jurisdiction beyond the reach of due?process at the click of a mouse.

(D) Anti–Stalking

Since 2000, scores of states have enacted anti-stalking criminal law statutes. Nevertheless, litigants have been more likely to use the federal anti-stalking statute. To prove stalking the government must establish defendants: (1) employed a facility of interstate commerce; (2) to engage in a course of conduct with the intent to place a person in reasonable fear of death or serious bodily injury either to that person or to a partner or immediate family member; and (3) the course of conduct actually put that person in reasonable fear of death or serious bodily injury to himself or his partner or immediate family member.[299] Anti-stalking statutes are notoriously difficult to draft.

To prove a conspiracy to commit interstate stalking, the government must also prove that the charged defendants agreed to participate in a conspiracy to commit interstate stalking. Finally, with regard to aiding and abetting, a defendant is punishable as the principal if the government establishes, beyond a reasonable doubt, that the defendant

---

[292] 2000 U.S. Dist. LEXIS 8645 (N.D. Ill. June 21, 2000).

[293] Id.

[294] Id.

[295] See John Doe v. GTE Corp., 2003 U.S. App. LEXIS 21345 (7th Cir. Oct. 21, 2003); Does 1 Through 30 Inclusive v. Franco Prods., 99 C 7885, 2000 U.S. Dist. LEXIS 8645, at *10–16 (N.D. Ill. June 22, 2000), aff'd sub nom. Doe v. GTE Corp., 347 F.3d 655 (7th Cir. 2003).

[296] Doe v. GTE Corp., 347 F.3d 655, 659, 663 (7th Cir. 2003) (affirming dismissal of tort claim that web host aided and abetted sale of secretly obtained video tapes showing undressed athletes).

[297] College Athletes Sue over Videos Made by Hidden Cameras, LEGAL INTELLIGENCER, July 28, 1999, at 4.

[298] The Seventh Circuit, in John Doe v. GTE Corp., 2003 U.S. App. LEXIS 21345 (7th Cir. Oct. 21, 2003), affirmed the district court's dismissal of the liability claims of GTE, web host and ISP, for hosting the illicit distribution of the tapes of college athletes. The Seventh Circuit agreed with the lower court that Section 230 of the Communication Decency Act immunized the web host, even though it enabled the pornographer to post illicit content invading the privacy of the college athletes.

[299] United States v. Fullmer, 584 F.3d 132, 163 (3d Cir. 2009) (discussing 18 U.S.C. § 2261A).

committed the stalking or aided, abetted, counseled, commanded, induced or procured the substantive act of stalking by another person.[300]

§ 8.7 INTERNATIONAL CYBERCRIME ENFORCEMENT

At present, there is no Internet wide treaty addressing cybercrimes or even the procedural aspects of policing Internet-reality crime. Not all countries connected to the Internet regard computer attacks as crimes. Many countries connected to the global Internet do not embrace U.S. style free expression and have no equivalent to U.S. constitutionally based legal norms and values. China, for example, ordered ISPs to monitor private e-mails and impose legal sanctions for illegal postings appearing on websites they host. China is a leading home for the producers of badware, such as spyware, that tracks computer users' key strokes and mouse clicks. A Stopbadware.org report studying 200,000 websites uncovered "ten network blocks that contain the largest number of badware sites and six of the ten originated in China."[301]

The United States is responsible for about one in five badware sites. In August of 2008, a federal grand jury indicted eleven defendants located in Eastern Europe, China, and the United States for exploiting vulnerabilities in many U.S. retail companies, including TJX. The cybercriminals were located in a global network and stole more than 40 million credit card numbers. The U.S. grand jury charged the defendants with an international conspiracy to commit unlawful access to TJX and many computer systems, in violation of the CFAA.[302] The codefendants were also charged with federal wire fraud,[303] credit and debit card fraud,[304] identity theft,[305] and money laundering in violation.[306]

(A) Personal Jurisdiction in Cross–Border Cases

Physical presence in the United States usually supplies the only prerequisite for personal jurisdiction in a federal criminal prosecution. The Internet casts doubt on the legitimacy of sovereignty due to its extraterritorial nature. In criminal jurisdiction cases, U.S. courts stretch the detrimental effects test developed under *Strassheim v. Milton Daily*,[307] to the Internet. The detrimental effects test should not be confused with the *Calder* effects test used in personal jurisdiction cases discussed in Chapter 3. In *Strassheim*, the U.S. Supreme Court held acts done outside a jurisdiction, but intended to produce and producing detrimental effects within it, warranted the exercise of criminal personal jurisdiction.

The *Strassheim* court's three-part test asks: (1) was the defendant's act outside the state? (2) Was the act intended to produce detrimental effects within the state? and (3) Was the defendant's act the actual cause of detrimental effects within the state? Historically, minimum contacts have had no place in determining whether a state may assert criminal personal jurisdiction over a foreign defendant. It is clear that U.S.

---

[300] 18 U.S.C. § 2.

[301] Center for Internet & Society, China Hosts Majority of Badware Sites (June 24, 2008).

[302] 18 U.S.C. § 1030.

[303] 18 U.S.C. § 1343.

[304] 18 U.S.C. § 1029.

[305] 18 U.S.C. § 1028(a).

[306] 18 U.S.C. § 1956.

[307] 221 U.S. 280 (1911).

courts will not extend the minimum contacts framework to Internet-related criminal cases.

(B) Cybercrime Convention

The Convention on Cybercrime, sponsored by the Council of Europe ("COE"),[308] is the first international treaty addressing computer crime and Internet-related crime. The Cybercrime Convention concluded in Budapest in 2001 with an international treaty to improve cooperation between nation states in the fight against cybercrime, harmonizing the law, and improving investigative techniques.[309] The United States became a signatory country in 2006. Articles 2–4 compel signatory states to enact national legislation addressing computer crimes such as illegal access, illegal interception, and data interference. Article 5 criminalizes the creation or transmission of computer viruses or malware and expects states to enact legislation adopting the doctrine of corporate liability for cybercrimes. Articles 7 and 8 of the Convention criminalizes computer related forgery and fraud. Article 9 constitutes an agreement to criminalize the production and distribution of child pornography.

In Articles 10 and 11, the signatories agreed to criminalize copyright infringement, as well as aiding and abetting computer crimes. Article 17 of the Cybercrime Convention also treats computer crime as an extraditable offense and calls for mutual assistance in the investigation and prosecution of computer crimes. Article 24 provides mechanisms for obtaining an "expeditious preservation of data" on a computer system or server in another territory. Parties must promptly disclose traffic data and may refuse a request only if compliance would threaten sovereign immunity security, the public order, or other essential interests. Article 23 of the Convention obliges signatories to cooperate in criminal investigations "to the widest extent possible."[310]

The Cybercrime Convention recognizes the need for a mechanism allowing law enforcement to investigate offenses and obtain evidence quickly and efficiently, while remaining aware of each nation's sovereignty and constitutional and human rights. The Cybercrime Convention does not demand "dual criminality" as a condition for mutual assistance consistently throughout the treaty. Dual criminality is the reciprocal criminalization of a specific crime by both countries. In September 2011, the COE made the control of cybercrime one of its Internet governance priorities,[311] seeking greater trans-border law enforcement access to data and choice of jurisdiction. Another priority includes tackling illegal Internet content hosted outside the territorial jurisdiction of a single country. The COE seeks to develop new cyber security measures to protect data on cloud computing. Additional priorities for the COE's cybercrime initiative include:

---

[308] The Council of Europe, based in Strasbourg France, is a transnational political institution

created in 1949 to promote greater unity among its member states. Today the Council seeks to protect human rights and democracy, to foster peace among the forty-six Member States, and to develop a common response to political, social, cultural, and legal challenges.

[309] Council of Europe, Convention on Cybercrime: CETS No.: 185, Budapest, 23 XI 2001; http://conventions.coe.int/Treaty/Commun/QueVoulezVous.asp?NT=185&CL=ENG.

[310] Id. at art. 23.

[311] COUNCIL OF EUROPE, INTERNET GOVERNANCE 6 (2012–2015).

(1) Expanding technical assistance to countries worldwide with focus on high-tech crime and other specialized units, training of law enforcement officials, prosecutors and judges, enhancing law enforcement/Internet service provider co-operation, financial investigations and confiscation of crime proceeds, protection of children against sexual exploitation and abuse, prevention of the criminal misuse of domains and protection of critical Internet resources, efficient international co-operation, and safeguards and conditions for investigative powers;

(2) Combating criminal money flows through the Internet including money laundering and Internet gaming;

(3) Preventing terrorist use of the Internet by supporting the implementation of the Convention on the Prevention of Terrorism (CETS No. 196) in combination with the Budapest Convention on Cybercrime;

(4) Developing measures to combat the distribution of counterfeit medical products and other illicit products via the Internet, in particular with a view to the adoption and implementation of the Convention on the counterfeiting of medical products and similar crimes involving threats to public health. [312]

The Cybercrime Convention is not what it is cracked up to be because it is aspirational and has no mechanism for enforcing cybercrimes nor does it enact specific statutes. There is no Internet-related treaty defining computer crimes and setting international standards for transborder search and seizure. At present, there is no centralized transnational Internet crime constable. A difficulty facing the international community is to detecting and punishing cybercrimes while preserving radically different rights, freedoms, and mores. Law enforcement around the world is better suited to solve crime in the streets than Internet crimes hatched in the suites in a foreign venue. In the United States, relatively few state attorneys general even have a computer crime unit. Each state has enacted a state computer crime statute[313] but few states make computer crime a priority.

(C) Economic Espionage Act

The Economic Espionage Act ("EEA") was enacted to punish and deter state sponsored espionage to protect our nation's competitiveness.[314] The EEA criminalizes the misappropriation or theft of trade secrets and confidential information. The federal statute provides criminal and civil penalties for the theft of trade secrets.[315] Congress has yet to amend the EEA to give private attorneys general standing to file a statutory tort action against those who misappropriate business information and information products. Federal prosecutors are the only parties who can bring EEA lawsuits. To qualify for trade secret protection, the owner must have taken reasonable measures to

---

[312] Id.

[313] The elements of a violation of the Virginia Computer Crimes Act ("VCCA") are that the defendant (1) uses a computer or computer network; (2) without authority; and (3) either obtains property or services by false pretenses, embezzles or commits larceny, or converts the property of another. Va. Code § 18.2–152.3.

[314] See Economic Espionage Act of 1996, Pub. L. No. 104–294, 110 Stat. 3488 (codified at 18 U.S.C. §§ 1831–1839 (2000)); see also J. Michael Chamblee, Validity, Construction, and Application of Title I of Economic Espionage Act of 1996, 177 A.L.R. Fed. 609, 617–18 (2005) (The EEA was enacted to fill a gap in the law. "Other federal statutes, such as the National Stolen Property Act, 18 U.S.C. § 2314, and the Mail and Wire Fraud Statutes, 18 U.S.C. § 1341 and 18 U.S.C. § 1343, were also of limited use in combating the problem of economic espionage.").

[315] 18 U.S.C. §§ 1831, 1832.

keep such information secret; and the information derives independent economic value, actual or potential from not being generally known to, and not being readily ascertainable through proper means by the public. The EEA criminalizes stealing or appropriating trade secrets whether by "fraud, artifice, or deception."[316]

Section 1831 of the EEA covers misappropriation by foreign governments or their agents, which is punishable by fines up to $500,000 or imprisonment of up to fifteen years. Offending organizations may be subject to fines of up to $10,000,000.[317] Section 1832 covers misappropriation intended to benefit persons and corporations. Persons are subject to fines and up to 10 years of imprisonment, while organizations are subject to fines of up to $5,000,000.[318] The EEA imposes criminal penalties for a person who "copies, duplicates, sketches, draws, photographs, downloads, uploads, alters, destroys, photocopies, replicates, transmits, delivers, sends, mails, communicates or conveys a trade secret."[319] Since 1996, there have been relatively few EEA prosecutions in contrast to the CFAA and ECPA.

(D) Who the Cybercriminals Are

The Internet Crime Complaint Center reported that many "Grandparent" schemes originated in South American countries such as the Dominican Republic, Haiti, Guatemala and Peru.[320] To conceal their identity, the cybercriminals used bogus telephone companies that appeared on their caller ID. A United Nations study noted that 60% of all Internet users are in developing countries, with 45 percent under the age of 25.[321] Mobile phones and Internet access open up criminal careers for those willing to use illegitimate means to attain financial ends. The UN study concluded that in the future hyper-connected society all crime will have some nexus to internet protocol (IP) connectivity.[322] The UN study concluded that cybercrime perpetrators had the following characteristics:

- Upwards of 80 per cent of cybercrime acts are estimated to originate in some form of organized activity, with cybercrime black markets established on a cycle of malware creation, computer infection, botnet management, harvesting of personal and financial data, data sale, and 'cashing out' of financial information.

- Cybercrime often requires a high degree of organization to implement, and may lend itself to small criminal groups, loose *ad hoc* networks, or organized crime on a larger scale. The typology of offenders and active criminal groups mostly reflect patterns in the conventional world.

- In the developing country context in particular, sub-cultures of young men engaged in computer-related financial fraud have emerged, many of whom begin involvement in cybercrime in their late teenage years.

---

[316] 18 U.S.C. § 1831(a)(1).

[317] Id.

[318] 18 U.S.C. § 1832.

[319] 18 U.S.C. § 1831(a)(2).

[320] Internet Crime Complaint Center, 2012 Internet Crime Report, Id. at 10.

[321] UNODC, UNITED NATIONS OFFICE ON DRUGS AND CRIME, COMPREHENSIVE STUDY OF CYBERCRIME (2013) at 1.

[322] Id.

- The demographic nature of offenders mirrors conventional crime in that young males are the majority, although the age profile is increasingly showing older (male) individuals, particularly concerning child pornography offences.

- While some perpetrators may have completed advanced education, especially in the computer science field, many known offenders do not have specialized education.

- There is a lack of systematic research about the nature of criminal organizations active in cyberspace; and more research is needed regarding the links between online and offline child pornography offenders.[323]

The Economist reports a burgeoning digital arms trade in software to penetrate computer systems.[324] Internet hackers are now often state-sponsored that purchase cybertools to exploit Internet Explorer, Windows 8 and 7, the iPhones, Android, Chrome or Windows Vista.[325] The U.S. or Israel are suspected in a 2010 computer worm attack "called Stuxnet [that] was revealed to have attacked Iran's nuclear kit."[326] The exploits, developed in-house, "plant sabotage charges" and then "erase their tracks."[327]

---

[323] Id. at 39.

[324] Cyber-Security: The Digital Arms Trade: The Market for Software That Helps Hackers Penetrate Computer Systems, THE ECONOMIST (March 9, 2013) at 65.

[325] Id.

[326] Id.

[327] Id.

Chapter 9

CONTENT REGULATION ON THE INTERNET

§ 9.1   OVERVIEW OF INTERNET REGULATIONS

Content on the Internet is accessible around the world to billions of Internet users with radically different religious beliefs, political ideologies, social mores, and legal cultures. Given the diversity in legal cultures, it is not surprising that countries will have different views as to what content can be regulated in cyberspace. Google reported that Thailand asked it to "remove 149 YouTube videos for allegedly insulting the monarchy in violation of Thailand's *lèse-majesté* law."[1] Google reported blocking "70% of these videos from view in Thailand in accordance with local law."[2] Counsel representing companies such as Google will need to make difficult decision about whether to comply with takedown requests from countries with radically different legal systems and cultural sensitivities. Google, for example, refused to remove a "YouTube video that satirized Italian Prime Minister Silvio Berlusconi's lifestyle."[3] In July of 2013, the United Kingdom adopted an on-by-default online pornography filter. "While Web users today can opt into activating such a family-friendly filter through their Internet service provider (ISP), in the future they will have to opt out."[4]

Google made a strategic decision to block access to a 14–minute trailer entitled "Innocence of Muslims." The maker of the amateurish film portrayed Mohammed, the founder of Islam, as a child molester, sexual deviant, and as an uncouth barbarian. Islamic fundamentalist clerics called for the killing of the director and other participants in the film. Immediately after the translation of the film trailer into Arabic, its posting on YouTube incited violence throughout the Middle East. The film inspired protest and even insurrection in many countries including Afghanistan, Somalia, Syria, Turkey and the United Kingdom. The cascading after effects of posting this amateurish, low budget film trailer on YouTube illustrates how the Internet can be used to incite violence on a scale far greater than with the use of traditional media. Social media sites are now an integral part of national security around the world. An Electronic Freedom Foundation's amicus brief explained that:

> Today, platforms such as YouTube, Facebook, Twitter, Flickr, BlogSpot, and others enable people around the world to reach out to a global audience, sharing information, ideas, and commentary. Moreover, as recent events in the Middle East underscore, that ability has led to the development of new and potent forms of political expression and organizing.[5]

---

[1] Google Transparency Report, http://www.google.com/trans parencyreport/removals/government/.

[2] Id.

[3] Id.

[4] David Myer, Why Opt-in Porn is a Terrible Idea, Bloomberg Business Week Technology (July 22, 2013).

[5] Viacom v. YouTube, 2010 U.S. 2nd Cir. Briefs 840674; 2011 U.S. 2nd Cir. Briefs LEXIS (April 7 2011) (brief of Electronic Freedom Foundation).

In the past two decades, members of Congress have introduced hundreds of U.S. statutes proposed to regulate illegal or harmful content on the Internet. These initiatives have largely failed as the Internet transcends national borders. While the U.S. government first developed the Internet, the U.S. Government is no longer in a controlling position and cannot legitimately impose its common law principles to govern the Internet. Internet businesses targeting China's 1.4 billion consumers will need to comply with that country's Internet regulations. U.S. companies, for example, must comply with the EU's regulations for data protection, distance sales, jurisdiction, choice of law, and mandatory consumer rules. E-businesses must continually respond and adapt to diverse legal systems. Google, for example, received over 1,000 requests to remove content in the second half of 2011. Google's *2012 Transparency Report* acknowledges that foreign governments make routine demands for them to censor or remove content they find objectionable. Google's *2012 Report* states, "Governments ask companies to remove content for many different reasons. For example, some content removals are requested due to allegations of defamation, while others are due to allegations that the content violates local laws prohibiting hate speech or pornography."[6]

China's proposed amendments to its Internet Information Service Management Rules makes it a crime to post "information damaging the honor or interests of the State and spreading rumors, pornography or other content prohibited by laws and administrative regulations."[7] China's proposed Internet rules create a "filtering regime, real identity system, and policies" that are the functional equivalent of the Great Firewall.[8] John Gilmore of the Electronic Freedom Foundation stated: "The Net interprets censorship as damage and routes around it."[9] The decentralized architecture of the Internet makes it difficult for any one country to remove objectionable content; the best they can do is to shut the Internet down in their country.[10] From a U.S. perspective, it is somewhat problematic that corporations controlling the Internet like Google are cooperating with governments to seek to suppress expression.

A large number of countries connected to the Internet do not have a strong tradition of the right of expression. A traditional Islamic jurist would likely find an unveiled female face on a social media site to be shameful. Not only Islamic republics have blasphemy laws; the Republic of Ireland introduced a blasphemy law that created crimes for incitement including "blasphemous Internet statements in defiance of the law."[11] Counsels need to ensure that designers consider language, culture, and legal requirements prior to launching a website. Lawyers of the twenty-first century need to be less U.S. centric as cyberspace is a cross-border legal environment. The shrinking of national boundaries by the Internet creates new problems in compliance for any

---

[6] Google, Transparency Report (2012).

[7] Sarah Haack, Software, Foreign Trade Groups Criticize Draft Amendments to Chinese Internet Rules, ELEC. COM. & L. REP. (BNA) (July 6, 2012).

[8] Id.

[9] "This was quoted in Time Magazine's December 6, 1993 article "First Nation in Cyberspace", by Philip Elmer–DeWitt. It's been reprinted hundreds or thousands of times since then, including the NY Times on January 15, 1996, Scientific American of October 2000, and CACM 39(7):13." John Gilmore, Homepage, http://www.toad.com/gnu/ (last visited Oct. 6, 2013).

[10] Mark A. Lemley & Lawrence Lessig, The End of End-to-End: Preserving the Architecture of the Internet in the Broadband Era, 48 U.C.L.A. L. REV. 925, 940 (2001) (explaining how the architecture of the Internet is software-driven).

[11] David Nash, Blasphemy in the Christian World: A History (2010) at Preface.

company engaging in electronic commerce in radically different cultures and legal systems.

The difference between illegal and harmful conduct is that the former is criminalized. Politicians justify content regulation by expressing "concerns about the proliferation of pornographic and illegal material on the Internet."[12] The U.S. approach has favored a self-regulatory approach by industry. Nevertheless, U.S. companies conducting e-commerce face the inevitable task of complying with content regulations throughout the world. "No single organization controls any membership in the Web, nor is there any single centralized point from which individual Websites or services can be blocked."[13] Nevertheless, a large number of repressive regimes are blocking their citizens' access to certain content. The Open Net Initiative discovered Armenia, Bahrain, China, Ethiopia, Gaza and the West Bank, Indonesia, Iran, Kuwait, Burma/Myanmar, Oman, Pakistan, Qatar, Saudi Arabia, South Korea, Sudan, Syria, Turkmenistan, United Arab Emirates, Uzbekistan, Vietnam, and Yemen to be engaged in substantial or pervasive content filtering.[14] The borderless Internet is constrained by many conflicting domestic regulations restricting speech.

Carnegie–Mellon researchers found widespread evidence that the Chinese government was deleting messages from popular microblogs. The researchers "conducted a statistical analysis of 56 million messages (212,583 of which have been deleted out of 1.3 million checked, more than 16 percent) from the domestic Chinese microblog site Sina Weibo, and 11 million Chinese–language messages from Twitter."[15] The researchers found that the Chinese Government was deleting postings with politically sensitive terms.[16] This empirical evidence illustrates the danger of government regulation as noted by John Perry Barlow in his *A Declaration of Independence of Cyberspace* discussed in Chapter 2.[17]

Additionally, this chapter examines the controversial issue of Internet content regulation and discusses leading developments around the world.[18] Countries differ in their use of code to filter content depending upon their speech tradition and culture. Recall David Johnson and David Post's argument for the Internet as a new sovereignty in Chapter 2.[19] Fifteen years later, we are no closer to a specialized Internet

---

[12] CHRISTOPHER D. MARSDEN, REGULATING THE GLOBAL INFORMATION SOCIETY 69 (2000).

[13] Reno v. ACLU, 521 U.S. 844, 853 (1997).

[14] Open Net Initiative, Global Internet Filtering in 2012 at a Glance (April 3, 2012).

[15] David Bamman, Brendan O'Connor, and Noah A. Smith, Censorship and Deletion Practices in Chinese Social Media, 17 FIRST MONDAY 3 (March 5, 2012).

[16] Id.

[17] Barlow, who was a lyricist for The Grateful Dead, co-founded the Electronic Freedom Foundation ("EFF") with Mitch Kapor of Lotus. The EFF is opposed to excessive restraints on Internet and overly aggressive assertion of intellectual property rights.

[18] "Code is law; the architecture of the Internet and the software that runs on it will determine to a large extent how the Net is regulated in a way that goes far deeper than legal means could ever achieve (or at least ever achieve alone). Technological advances have also produced many tempting options for regulation and surveillance that may severely alter the balance of privacy, access to information and sharing of intellectual property. By regulating behavior, technological architectures or codes embed different values and political choices. Yet code is often treated as a technocratic affair, or something best left to private economic actors pursuing their own interests. If code is law, then control of code is power." Berkman Center for Internet & Society (2012), http://cyber.law.harvard.edu/is2012/Control_and_Code:_Privacy_Online.EFOR3).

[19] David R. Johnson & David Post, Law and Borders—The Rise of Law in Cyberspace, 48 STAN. L. REV. 1367 (1996).

jurisdiction. The cliché that the Internet is not governable is so ingrained that it is nearly void of meaning altogether Today the leading questions are: Who should regulate the Internet? How extensive should content regulations be and by what authority?

§ 9.2   INDECENT SPEECH & CENSORSHIP ON THE INTERNET

The Supreme Court struck down a number of statutes aimed at regulating Internet decency on First Amendment grounds. Downloading content takes the form of a file, which can be copied from the Internet to the user's own computer.[20] "Content can range from simple text files, graphics, and video to computer programs, updates, and patches."[21] Without overstatement, the Internet has revolutionized free speech in the United States. The study of Internet regulation encompasses content regulation and is relevant to E–Commerce activities.[22] Content regulation is more easily regulated at the source for child pornography and illegal content.[23]

The First Amendment generally prohibits the regulation of speech based on content, and even "indecent" speech has inherent First Amendment protection.[24] The First Amendment of the U.S Constitution states, "Congress shall make no law . . . abridging the freedom of speech."[25] The United States, as well as many other countries throughout the world, has policies in favor of, and protecting, their citizens' right to express their opinions on the Internet. The U.S. Supreme Court has repeatedly reinforced this value of expression through many diverse decisions regarding what constitutes acceptable sources of information. Justice Potter Stewart in *Ginzburg v. United States*[26] stated:

> Censorship reflects a society's lack of confidence in itself. It is a hallmark of an authoritarian regime. Long ago, those who wrote our First Amendment charted a different course. They believed a society can be truly strong only when it is truly free. In the realm of expression, they put their faith, for better or for worse, in the enlightened choice of the people, free from interference of a policeman's intrusive thumb or a judge's heavy hand. So it is that the Constitution protects coarse expression as well as refined, and vulgarity no less than elegance. A book worthless to me may convey some value to my neighbor. In the free society to which our Constitution has committed us, it is for each to choose for himself.[27]

(A) Communications Decency Act of 1996

Chapter 6 examined how courts have stretched Section 230 of the Communications Decency Act of 1996 ("CDA") into a broad shieldC from immunity for service providers for cybertorts, pornography, and ongoing crimes. This chapter

---

[20] GRAHAM J.H. SMITH, INTERNET LAW & REGULATION 1 (4th ed. 2007).

[21] Id. at 7.

[22] MADELEINE SCHACHTER & JOEL KURTZBERG, LAW OF INTERNET SPEECH (2008).

[23] DALE WELDEAU JORGENSON, MEASURING AND SUSTAINING THE NEW ECONOMY: REPORT OF A WORKSHOP (2002) (quoting Vinton Cerf).

[24] Sable Communications Inc. v. FCC, 492 U.S. 115 (1989).

[25] U.S. Const. 1st Amend.

[26] 383 U.S. 463 (1966).

[27] Id. at 498.

examines the CDA as a means of controlling obscene or indecent information on the Internet. In 1996, Congress enacted the CDA through Title V of the Telecommunications Act.[28] The CDA criminalized the transmission of materials deemed to be either "obscene or indecent" for Internet users under the age of eighteen.[29] Shortly after Congress enacted the CDA, plaintiffs filed a declaratory judgment in the U.S. district court, asking the court to declare the statute unconstitutional. A three-judge panel of the federal appeals court enjoined enforcement of the CDA's framework for controlling obscenity on the Internet. In *Reno v. ACLU*,[30] the U.S. Supreme Court upheld a lower court's judgment that the CDA violated the First Amendment because it was overly vague. The *Reno* Court found that the CDA's vague provisions chilled free speech since speakers could not be certain if the statute restricted their speech.[31] In particular, the Court found the CDA's "contemporaneous community standard" for obscene materials to be overly broad.[32]

The Court noted that such criminal sanctions "may well cause speakers to remain silent rather than communicate even arguably unlawful words, ideas, and images."[33] The Court reasoned that applying the community standards test to the Internet would mean that any communication available to a "nationwide audience will be judged by the standards of the community most likely to be offended by the message."[34] To satisfy strict scrutiny, the government must not only prove it had a compelling interest, but also show that the CDA was necessary to further that interest. The Court found that the CDA was unconstitutional because of its facial over breadth in attempting to impose the "community standards" test to the Internet.

The only part of the CDA that survived is the immunity given providers for third parties' postings, Section 230. Section 230(c)(2) of the CDA "allows [an interactive service provider] to establish standards of decency without risking liability for doing so."[35] Information content provider is defined to mean "any person or entity that is responsible, in whole or in part, for the creation or development of information

---

[28] "The Telecommunications Act of 1996, Pub. L. 104–104, 110 Stat. 56, was an unusually important legislative enactment. As stated on the first of its 103 pages, its primary purpose was to reduce regulation and encourage "the rapid deployment of new telecommunications technologies." The major components of the statute have nothing to do with the Internet; they were designed to promote competition in the local telephone service market, the multichannel video market, and the market for over-the-air broadcasting." Reno v. ACLU, 521 U.S. 844, 860 (1997).

[29] The CDA "criminalizes the "knowing" transmission of "obscene or indecent" messages to any recipient less than 18 years of age. Section 223(d) prohibits the "knowing" sending or displaying to a person under 18 of any message "that, in context, depicts or describes, in terms patently offensive as measured by contemporary community standards, sexual or excretory activities or organs." Affirmative defenses are provided for those who take "good faith, ... effective ... actions" to restrict access by minors to the prohibited communications, § 223(e)(5)(A), and those who restrict such access by requiring certain designated forms of age proof, such as a verified credit card or an adult identification number, § 223(e)(5)(B). A number of plaintiffs filed suit challenging the constitutionality of §§ 223(a)(1) and 223(d)" Id. at 860.

[30] 521 U.S. 844 (1997).

[31] Id. at 871–72 (1997) (construing the term "patently offensive," noting that vagueness of content-based regulation raises special First Amendment concerns because of its obvious chilling effect on free speech).

[32] The Court noted that "the "community standards" criterion as applied to the Internet means that any communication available to a nationwide audience will be judged by the standards of the community most likely to be offended by the message." Reno, 521 U.S. at 877–878.

[33] Id. at 872.

[34] Id. at 901.

[35] Goddard v. Google, 2008 U.S. Dist. LEXIS 101890 at *22 (N.D. Cal. 2008).

provided through the Internet or any other interactive computer service."[36] The CDA states in relevant part that service providers are not liable for "Good Samaritan" block and screening of offensive material. Section 230(c) states:

(c) Protection for "Good Samaritan" blocking and screening of offensive material

(1) Treatment of publisher or speaker

No provider or user of an interactive computer service shall be treated as the publisher or speaker of any information provided by another information content provider.

(2) Civil Liability

No provider or user of an interactive computer service shall be held liable on account of (A) any action voluntarily taken in good faith to restrict access to or availability of material that the provider or user considers to be obscene, lewd, lascivious, filthy, excessively violent, harassing, or otherwise objectionable, whether or not such material is constitutionally protected; or

(B) any action taken to enable or make available to information content providers or others the technical means to restrict access to material described in paragraph (1).[37]

Section 230(e)(3) further provides that: "No cause of action may be brought and no liability may be imposed under any State or local law that is inconsistent with this section."[38] Courts have stretched the term "interactive computer service" in CDA Section 230 to mean nearly any website or online service. Section 230(c)(1) has afforded Internet service providers ("ISPs") protection for secondary liability (torts committed by third parties). In addition, Section 230(c)(2) shields ISPs from all civil liability arising out of claims for filtering and monitoring content.[39]

In a decade and a half of litigation, courts have almost never ruled that a given online service was outside of the CDA's sphere of application. The statute defines "interactive computer service" to mean "any information service, system, or access software provider that provides or enables computer access by multiple users to a computer server, including specifically a service or system that provides access to the Internet and such systems operated or services offered by libraries or educational institutions."[40] Chapter 6 examined how courts have stretched Section 230 into an immunity for service providers for cybertorts, pornography, and ongoing crimes. In fact, Section 230 has spawned pornography and cybertorts because they are profitable without the possibility of legal liability.

(B) Child Online Protection Act

The United States Supreme Court called the Internet "the most participatory form of mass speech yet developed."[41] After the Court struck down the CDA in *Reno* v.

---

[36] 47 U.S.C. § 230(f)(3).

[37] 47 U.S.C. § 230(c)(2).

[38] 47 U.S.C. § 230(e)(3).

[39] 47 U.S.C. § 230(c)(2).

[40] Id.

[41] Reno v. ACLU, 521 U.S. 844, 863 (1997) (citing ACLU v. Reno, 929 F. Supp. 824, 883 (E.D. Pa. 1996)).

American Civil Liberties Union, Congress enacted the Child Online Protection Act ("COPA").[42] COPA prohibits any person from "knowingly and with knowledge of the character of the material, in interstate or foreign commerce by means of the World Wide Web, making any communication for commercial purposes that is available to any minor and that includes any material that is harmful to minors."[43] COPA imposed criminal penalties of six months in prison and a $50,000 fine.[44] COPA's scope was restricted to obscene materials on the World Wide Web, whereas the earlier statute applied to all electronically disseminated information. COPA's provisions only apply to commercial publishers of content on the World Wide Web.

Under COPA, whether material published on the World Wide Web is "harmful to minors" is governed by a three-part test: (A) Would the average person, applying contemporary community standards, find taking the material as a whole and with respect to minors, to pander to the prurient interest?; (B) Does the material depict, describe, or represent, in a manner patently offensive with respect to minors, an actual or simulated sexual act or sexual contact, an actual or simulated normal or perverted sexual act, or a lewd exhibition of the genitals or post-pubescent female breast?; and (C) Taken as a whole, does the material lack serious literary, artistic, political, or scientific value for minors?[45] The dictionary definition of prurient interest is that it is evidenced "by or arousing an immoderate or unwholesome interest or desire; especially marked by, arousing, or appealing to sexual desire."[46]

COPA sought to use digital certificates to verify users were old enough to view online pornography.[47] Defendants could assert, as a complete defense, that they restrict access to minors by requiring a credit card, debit card, or access card.[48] COPA immunized services providers from liability.[49] Nevertheless, after a decade of litigation and a remand from the U.S. Supreme Court, COPA was struck down after a complicated series of opinions. In *ACLU v. Reno,* the federal court granted a preliminary injunction enjoining enforcement of COPA.[50] The United States Supreme Court vacated and remanded for consideration, narrowly questioning whether COPA's use of "community standards" to identify material that was harmful to minors violated the First Amendment.

The U.S. Supreme Court vacated the Third Circuit's judgment in *Ashcroft v. ACLU.*[51] Content-based prohibitions, enforced by severe criminal penalties, have the constant potential to be a repressive force in the lives and thoughts of a free people.[52]

---

[42] 47 U.S.C. § 231.

[43] 47 U.S.C. § 231(a)(1).

[44] Id.

[45] 47 U.S.C. § 231(e)(6).

[46] Merriam–Webster, Prurient, http://www.merriam-webster. com/dictionary/prurient.

[47] "If an individual or entity has restricted access by minors to material that is harmful to minors through the use of a credit card, debit account, adult access code, or adult personal identification number, a digital certificate that verifies age or by any other reasonable measures that are feasible under available technology, the individual will not be liable if a minor should access this restricted material." 47 U.S.C. § 231(c)(1).

[48] 47 U.S.C. § 231(c)(1).

[49] 47 U.S.C. § 231(b).

[50] 31 F. Supp.2d 473 (E.D. Pa. 1999).

[51] 535 U.S. 564 (2002).

[52] Id.

The *Ashcroft* Court found that COPA's reliance on "community standards" to identify what material is harmful to minors did not by itself make COPA substantially overbroad. The Court did not decide whether COPA was unconstitutionally vague or could withstand strict scrutiny.

In *ACLU v. Mukasey*,[53] the Third Circuit considered these issues on remand and again struck down COPA on grounds of vagueness and over breadth; finding the statute violated the First Amendment in failing to tailor its restrictions to survive strict scrutiny. The Third Circuit held that the government failed to demonstrate that COPA was a more effective and less restrictive alternative to the use of filters. The federal appeals court observed, "Filters are more flexible than COPA because parents can tailor them to their own values and needs and to the age and maturity of their children and thus use an appropriate flexible approach differing from COPA's "one size fits all" approach."[54]

(C) Children's Internet Protection Act ("CIPA")

In 2000, Congress enacted the Children's Internet Protection Act ("CIPA"),[55] which requires public libraries and schools to install software filters to block obscene or pornographic images. The anti-obscenity federal statute addresses the issue of public access to offensive content over the Internet on school and library computers. CIPA provides that a public library may not receive federal assistance to provide Internet access unless it installs software to block images that constitute obscenity or child pornography, and to prevent minors from obtaining access to material that is harmful to them. Schools and libraries subject to CIPA are required to adopt and implement an Internet safety policy addressing: (A) access by minors to inappropriate matter on the Internet; (B) the safety and security of minors when using electronic mail, chat rooms and other forms of direct electronic communications; (C) unauthorized access, including so-called "hacking," and other unlawful activities by minors online; (D) unauthorized disclosure, use, and dissemination of personal information regarding minors; and (E) measures restricting minors' access to materials harmful to them.

In *United States v. American Library Ass'n*,[56] the Court upheld CIPA and reasoned that the statute did not violate the First Amendment because the purpose of the software was to block obscene or pornographic images and to prevent minors from obtaining access to harmful material. Congress did not impose an impermissible condition on federal subsidies to public libraries by requiring them to install Internet filters to block obscenity. The plurality opinion stated that the federal assistance programs for helping libraries secure Internet access was a valid statutory purpose. "Under the Spending Clause of the Constitution, Congress has "wide latitude" to appropriate public funds, and to place conditions on the appropriation of public funds, in furtherance of the

---

[53] 534 F.3d 181 (3dCir. 2008) (affirming district court decision that the Child Online Protection Act (COPA) facially violated First Amendment because, although government had compelling interest to protect minors from exposure to harmful material on Web, government failed to meet its burden of showing that COPA was narrowly tailored so as to survive strict scrutiny analysis, and that COPA was more effective and less restrictive alternative to use of filters and government's promotion of them in effectuating COPA's purposes).

[54] Id. at 203.

[55] 47 U.S.C. § 231(1)(B).

[56] 539 U.S. 194 (2003).

general welfare."[57] Justice Rehnquist's plurality opinion reasoned that Internet access in public libraries is neither a "traditional" nor a "designated" public forum.

"The public forum principles . . . are out of place in the context of this case."[58] The plurality's conclusion that forum analysis and judicial scrutiny did not apply was key to its decision to uphold the statute. The plurality stated that any concerns over filtering software's alleged tendency to erroneously "overblock" access to constitutionally protected speech was dispelled by the ease with which library patrons could have the filtering software disabled. The Court also observed that because public libraries had traditionally excluded pornographic material from their collections, they could impose a parallel limitation on its Internet assistance programs.

(D) The Child Pornography Prevention Act of 1996

The Child Pornography Prevention Act of 1996 ("CPPA")[59] made it a crime to create sexually explicit images that appear to depict minors but were produced without using any real children. The statute prohibits, in specific circumstances, possessing or distributing these images, which may be created by using adults who look like minors or by using computer imaging.[60] In *Ashcroft v. Free Speech Coalition*,[61] the U.S. Supreme Court held that the ban on virtual child pornography unconstitutionally overbroad since it proscribed speech which was neither child pornography nor obscene and thus abridged the freedom to engage in a substantial amount of lawful speech.[62] Justice Kennedy, writing for the Court, noted, "The Government offers in support of limiting the freedom of speech have no justification in our precedents or in the law of the First Amendment."[63] The provision abridges the freedom to engage in a substantial amount of lawful speech; for this reason, it is overbroad and unconstitutional The Court also held that the government was not permitted to bar protected virtual child pornography as a means to enforce its proper ban of actual child pornography.

(E) The Protect Act of 2003

After the Court's decision in *Free Speech Coalition*, "Congress went back to the drawing board and produced legislation with the unlikely title of the Prosecutorial Remedies and Other Tools to end the Exploitation of Children Today (Protect Act of 2003)."[64] The Protect Act criminally sanctions the advertising, promotion, presentation, distribution, and solicitation of child pornography. This federal criminal statute also

---

[57] U.S. Const. art. I, § 8, cl. 1.

[58] United States v. American Library Assn., Id. at 205.

[59] 18 U.S.C. §§ 2251 et seq.

[60] CPPA "prohibits any visual depiction, including any photograph, film, video, picture, or computer or computer-generated image or picture that is, or appears to be, of a minor engaging in sexually explicit conduct. The prohibition on any visual depiction does not depend at all on how the image is produced. The section captures a range of depictions, sometimes called virtual child pornography, which include computer-generated images, as well as images produced by more traditional means. For instance, the literal terms of the statute embrace a Renaissance painting depicting a scene from classical mythology, a picture that appears to be of a minor engaging in sexually explicit conduct. The statute also prohibits Hollywood movies, filmed without any child actors, if a jury believes an actor appears to be a minor engaging in actual or simulated sexual intercourse." 18 U.S.C. § 2256(2).

[61] 535 U.S. 234, 255 (2002).

[62] Id. at 258.

[63] Id. at 256.

[64] United States v. Williams, 128 S. Ct. 1830, 1836 (2008).

penalizes speech accompanying, or seeking the transfer of, child pornography via reproduction or physical delivery, from one person to another.[65] The Protect Act classifies primary producers as including "all those who actually create a visual representation of actual sexually explicit conduct, through videotaping, photographing, or computer manipulation."[66] Secondary producers upload such images to a website or otherwise manage the content of the website.[67] The statute requires the producer to inspect the depicted individual's government issued picture identification and determine her or his name and date of birth.[68]

In *United States v. Williams,*[69] the U.S. Supreme Court upheld the pandering provision of the Protect Act of 2003. The Protect Act makes it illegal to send material, or purported material, in a way that "reflects the belief, or is intended to cause another to believe," that the material contains illegal child pornography.[70] In *Williams*, the defendant used a sexually explicit screen name, signed in to a public Internet chat room and conversed with a Secret Service agent masquerading as a mother of a young child. The defendant offered to trade the agent sexually explicit pictures of his four-year-old daughter in exchange for similar photos. His chat room message said "Dad of toddler has "good" pics of her an [sic] me for swap of your toddler pics, or live cam."[71] The defendant was charged with one count of promoting, or "pandering," material intended to cause another to believe the material contained illegal child pornography and carried a sixty-month mandatory minimum sentence.

The defendant challenged the constitutionality of the Protect Act's pandering provision and the Eleventh Circuit found this part of the statute both substantially overbroad and vague, and therefore facially unconstitutional. In a 7–2 opinion, the U.S. Supreme Court reversed the Eleventh Circuit. Justice Scalia's majority opinion concluded that the federal anti-child pornography statute did not, on its face, violate the First Amendment right to free speech. The *Williams* Court found that offers to provide or obtain child pornography to be categorically excluded from the First Amendment.

(F) School Censorship of Internet Content

School districts have been a hothouse of Internet-related First Amendment lawsuits due to social media postings, which blight the reputations of administrators and undermine school discipline. When do unflattering postings about school administrators or the cyberbullying of fellow students justify school discipline? School districts around the United States face difficult policy decisions about social media postings that "threaten academic environments when they are used to bully, defame or engage in hate speech against students, administrators, and faculty."[72] In *Layshock v. Hermitage Sch. Dist.*,[73] the school district suspended Justin Layshock for ten days and

---

[65] 18 U.S.C. § 2252A(a)(3)(B).

[66] 28 C.F.R. § 75.1(c)(1).

[67] 28 C.F.R. § 75.1(c)(2).

[68] 18 U.S.C. § 2257(b)(1) (2006); 28 C.F.R. § 75.9(b)–(c).

[69] 553 U.S 285 (2008).

[70] 18 U.S.C. § 2252A(a)(3)(B).

[71] United States v. Williams, Id. at 1837.

[72] Karen M. Bradshaw and Souvik Saha, Academic Administrators and the Challenge of Social–Networking Websites, in SAUL LEVMORE & MARTHA C., NUSSBAUM, THE OFFENSIVE INTERNET: PRIVACY, SPEECH, AND REPUTATION (2010) at 140, 144.

[73] No. 07–4465, 2011 U.S. App. LEXIS 11994 (3d Cir. June 13, 2011) (Jordan, J., concurring).

demoted him to an academically inferior educational program because of his Internet posting mocking his high school principal. The issue in *Layshock* was whether the school district violated a student's First Amendment free-speech rights. In *Layshock,*[74] the court addressed how the new technologies were raising difficult issues for school administrators:

> For better or worse, wireless [I]nternet access, smart phones, tablet computers, social networking services like Facebook, and stream-of-consciousness communications via Twitter give an omnipresence to speech that makes any effort to trace First Amendment boundaries along the physical boundaries a recipe for serious problems in our public schools.[75]

The federal court granted Layshock summary judgment as to his expression claim, but ruled in favor of the district as to the due process claim. The Third Circuit in *Layshock v. Hermitage Sch. Dist.*[76] affirmed the lower court decision. An *en banc* opinion of the Third Circuit vacated this district court decision.[77] In *PFLAG v. Camdenton R–III School Dist.,*[78] a court entered an injunction against a school district's use of filters to block websites directed at lesbian, gay, bisexual, and transgender ("LGBT") youth. Nevertheless, Congress has repeatedly attempted to constrain obscene and pornographic materials on the Internet. The Internet creates new dilemmas for school administrators as students often create incendiary websites about school administrators or classmates outside of their territorial jurisdiction.[79] The question then becomes whether the school district has any authority to punish students for postings that defame administrators, teachers, or fellow students.[80]

§ 9.3   APPLYING THE FIRST AMENDMENT IN CYBERSPACE

The Federal Communications Commission ("FCC") controls decency in broadcast media but has no jurisdiction to control decency on the Internet.[81] In *Sable Communications Inc. v. FCC,*[82] the U.S. Supreme Court struck down a Communications Act provision that would have prohibited all indecent "dial-a-porn" telephone messages. The Court's reasoning was that the First Amendment protects sexual expression, which is indecent but not obscene. The *Sable* Court required the prosecution to demonstrate it was promoting a compelling interest only if it chooses the least restrictive means to further the interest articulated. As a content based restriction

---

[74] Id.

[75] Id. at *42.

[76] Layshock v. Hermitage Sch. Dist., 593 F.3d 249 (3dCir. 2010).

[77] Id.

[78] 2012 WL 510877 (W. D. Mo. Feb. 16, 2012).

[79] Layshock v. Hermitage Sch. Dist., No. 07–4465, 2011 U.S. App. LEXIS 11994, at *42 (3d Cir. June 13, 2011) (Jordan, J., concurring) ("For better or worse, wireless [I]nternet access, smart phones, tablet computers, social networking services like Facebook, and stream-of-consciousness communications via Twitter give an omnipresence to speech that makes any effort to trace First Amendment boundaries along the physical boundaries a recipe for serious problems in our public schools.").

[80] See e.g., Sanches v. Carrollton–Farmers Branch Indep. Sch. Dist., No. 10–10325, 2011 U.S. App. LEXIS 14313 (5th Cir. July 13, 2011) (regarding a high school student was suspended from the cheerleading team for posting inappropriate Facebook pictures; the student then allegedly harassed another student that she believed turned her in to school authorities).

[81] Sable Communications Inc. v. FCC, 492 U.S. 115 (1989).

[82] 492 U.S. 115 (1989).

on expression, the statute may only be upheld if it survives strict scrutiny. A court will strike down government regulations unless the legislature has narrowly tailored it to serve that interest.

(A) Dormant Commerce Clause

The Commerce Clause of the U.S. Constitution provides: "The Congress shall have Power . . . To regulate Commerce . . . among the several States. . . ."[83] The Supreme Court has long recognized that this affirmative grant of authority to Congress also encompasses an implicit or "dormant" limitation on the authority of the States to enact legislation affecting interstate commerce.[84] The Internet is likely a unique aspect of commerce that demands national treatment. "The Internet is wholly insensitive to geographic distinctions" and itself "represents an instrument of interstate commerce."[85] Online services are in some respects like the classified pages of newspapers, but in others, they operate like common carriers such as telephone services.[86] The Internet raises difficult issues in determining the power of a state to prescribe conduct outside its borders. The federal court in *Am. Library Ass'n v. Pataki*[87] stated:

> The unique nature of the Internet highlights the likelihood that a single actor might be subject to haphazard, uncoordinated, and even outright inconsistent regulation by states that the actor never intended to reach and possibly was unaware were being accessed. Typically, states' jurisdictional limits are related to geography; geography, however, is a virtually meaningless construct on the Internet.[88]

In *Am. Library Ass'n v. Pataki*,[89] libraries challenged the constitutionality of a New York state statute, which attempted to keep people from transmitting material harmful to minors via the Internet. The plaintiffs filed a lawsuit seeking declaratory and injunctive relief contending that the state statute violated the First Amendment and also burdened interstate commerce in violation of the Commerce Clause. The court granted the preliminary injunction, holding that the plaintiffs showed a likelihood of success on the merits. The *Pataki* court analogized the Internet to highways and railroads in reaching its decision. Thus, "[t]he Internet, like . . . rail and highway traffic . . ., requires a cohesive national scheme of regulation so that users are reasonably able to determine their obligations."[90] The district court in *Am. Library Ass'n v. Pataki*,[91] traced the Dormant Commerce Clause back to Justice Johnson's 1824 concurring opinion in *Gibbons v. Ogden*,[92] discussing whether New York could restrain the navigation of out-of-state steamboats in its waters.

---

[83] U.S. Const., art. I, § 8, cl. 3.

[84] Healy v. Beer Institute, et al., 491 U.S. 324, 326 & n. 2 (1989).

[85] Amer. Libraries Assoc. v. Pataki, 969 F.Supp. 160, 173 (S.D.N.Y. 1997).

[86] See also Chicago Lawyers' Comm. for Civ. Rights Under Law, Inc. v. Craigslist, Inc., 519 F.3d 666 (7th Cir. 2008).

[87] 969 F. Supp. 160 (S.D.N.Y. 1997).

[88] Id. at 168–169.

[89] Id.

[90] Id. at 182

[91] Id. at 168–69.

[92] 22 U.S. 1 (1824).

The *Pataki* court noted how the Commerce Clause prohibits state regulations that discriminate or unduly burden interstate commerce, even if they are facially nondiscriminatory. A "dormant" or "negative" aspect of this grant of power is that a state's power to impinge on interstate commerce may be limited in some situations.[93] Courts evaluate state regulations under a balancing test, which requires them to uphold a state regulation serving an important public interest, unless the benefits of the regulation outweigh the burden placed on interstate commerce. In this case, the burden on interstate commerce exceeded the benefits of preventing indecent materials from being available to minors.

(B) Content–Specific Regulations

"Permitting government officials' unbridled discretion in determining whether to allow protected speech presents an unacceptable risk of both indefinitely suppressing and chilling protected speech."[94] In order to survive constitutional scrutiny, there must be a very compelling government interest. An injunction enjoining Internet speech is a prior restraint, which will be upheld only in the most exceptional circumstances.[95] In *Federal Communications Commission v. Pacifica Foundation*,[96] the U.S. Supreme Court upheld the Federal Communications Commission's ability to restrict the use of "indecent" material in broadcasting.

(C) Content–Neutral Regulations

In the context of the First Amendment, "a content neutral regulation with an incidental effect on speech component must serve a substantial governmental interest, the interest must be unrelated to the suppression of free expression, and the incidental restriction on speech must not burden substantially more speech than is necessary to further that interest."[97] A content neutral regulation need not employ the least restrictive means but it must avoid burdening "substantially more speech than is necessary to further the government's legitimate interests."[98] Courts uphold content neutral restrictions on time, place, or manner of protected speech so long as the government narrowly tailors the regulation to serve a significant governmental interest.[99]

In *A.B. v. State*,[100] a lower court held that a middle school student inciting postings about her school principal's disciplinary policies, were protected political speech, dismissing a state criminal harassment claim. The Indiana Court of Appeals, however, affirmed on different grounds; they reasoned the state failed to prove the requisite elements of criminal harassment. The First Amendment protects seditious speech by middle school students unless the school district proves that the postings will seriously corrode school discipline.

---

[93] Quill Corp. v. North Dakota, 504 U.S. 298 (1992).

[94] 11126 Baltimore Boulevard, Inc. v. Prince George's County, 58 F.3d 988, 994 (4th Cir. 1995).

[95] See generally, Geoffrey R. Stone, Content Regulation and the First Amendment, 25 WM. & MARY L. REV. 189 (1983).

[96] 438 U.S. 726 (1978).

[97] Universal City Studios, Inc. v. Corley, 273 F.3d 429, 454 (2d Cir. 2001).

[98] Id.

[99] City of Renton v. Playtime Theatres, Inc., 475 U.S. 41 (1986) (upholding municipal zoning of X-rated theatres. Content neutral rules are unrelated to specific topics or subjects).

[100] 863 N.E.2d 1212 (Ind. Ct. App. 2007).

(D) Facial Attacks on Internet Speech

A court considering a facial challenge on either over breadth or vagueness must first determine "whether and to what extent the statute reaches protected conduct or speech. The second [step] is determining the "plainly legitimate sweep" of the statute, that is, the sweep justified by the government's interest. The third [step] is determining . . . the statute's burden on speech."[101]

(1) Vagueness

Plaintiffs may challenge content-based restrictions of speech on vagueness grounds. "Content-based prohibitions, enforced by severe criminal penalties, have the constant potential to be a repressive force in the lives and thoughts of a free people. To guard against that threat the United States Constitution demands that content-based restrictions on speech be presumed invalid and that the government bear the burden of showing their constitutionality. A content-based limitation on speech will be upheld only where the state demonstrates that the limitation is necessary to serve a compelling state interest and that it is narrowly drawn to achieve that end."[102]

The vagueness doctrine is an outgrowth of the Due Process Clause of the Fifth Amendment. In *Reno v. American Civil Liberties Union*,[103] the Court struck down a part of the Communications Decency Act ("CDA") on grounds of vagueness and overbreadth. The Court reasoned the CDA's use of the undefined terms "indecent" and "patently offensive" would have a chilling effect on speakers and therefore, raised special First Amendment concerns. The CDA's vagueness undermined the likelihood it had been carefully tailored to the congressional goal of protecting minors from potentially harmful materials.

(2) Overbreadth

Overbreadth is the constitutional infirmity where a regulation prohibits more conduct or protected speech than is necessary. The First Amendment's "overbreadth doctrine" is a tool for striking down Internet-related content regulations as facially invalid if they prohibit a substantial amount of protected speech. Courts will strike down content regulations on overbreadth "grounds if less restrictive alternatives would be at least as effective in achieving the legitimate purposes the statute was enacted to serve."[104] The Court in *Reno v. American Civil Liberties Union*,[105] found the CDA's expansive coverage of content unprecedented, and acknowledged that the breadth of the content-based restriction placed a heavy burden on the government to explain why they could not enact a less restrictive provision. Void for vagueness, in contrast, is when a regulation is so ambiguous or indeterminate that a person is unable to determine with certainty what acts are proscribed.

---

[101] Connection Distributing Co. v. Keisler, 505 F.3d 545, 555 (6th Cir. 2007).

[102] Backpage.com, LLC v. McKenna, 881 F. Supp. 2d 1262, 1283 (W.D. Wash. 2012).

[103] 521 U.S. 844 (1997).

[104] Ashcroft v. ACLU, 542 U.S. 656, 666 (2004).

[105] 521 U.S. 844 (1997).

(E) Categories of Unprotected Speech

The Virginia Supreme Court struck down a notorious spammer's criminal conviction on the First Amendment's overbreadth grounds. In *Jaynes v. Commonwealth of Virginia*,[106] the court upheld the conviction of a defendant who violated Virginia's Computer Crime Act by sending over 10,000 commercial e-mails within a 24–hour period to subscribers of America Online, Inc. ("AOL") on each of three separate occasions. The spammer used routing and transmission information, bypassing AOL's security controls, which trespassed on AOL's proprietary network. He sent tens of thousands of e-mails to AOL subscribers intentionally falsifying the header information and sender domain names before transmitting the e-mails to the recipients.

The *Jaynes* court found Virginia's statute criminalizing the falsification of IP addresses as overly broad and burdening the right to engage in anonymous speech. The court explained that the state statute criminalized otherwise unprotected speech, such as pornography or defamation. The court applied a strict scrutiny standard and therefore required the statute to be narrowly drawn. The *Jaynes* court found the computer crime statute was overbroad in prohibiting communications because it contained political, religious, or other speech.

In *United States v. Kilbride*,[107] an e-mail spammer was indicted under an eight-count complaint including the CAN–SPAM Act for distributing pornographic e-mail spam messages. The spammers were convicted of transmitting e-mails with materially false header information because they used fictitious e-mail addresses and registered domain names using a false contact name and phone number. The court also found that Kilbride materially falsified information within the meaning of Section 1037, when he had a third party alter e-mail headings. The federal appeals court affirmed the defendants' convictions and sentences for CAN–SPAM, fraud and conspiracy to commit fraud in connection with electronic mail, interstate transportation and interstate transportation for sale of obscene materials, and conspiracy to commit money laundering.

§ 9.4   CYBERBULLYING

(A) Federal Legislative Proposals

In 2008, the U.S. House of Representatives introduced the Cyberbullying Prevention Act in response to a middle-aged woman whose cyberbullying caused a thirteen-year-old girl to commit suicide. This federal statute states: "Whoever transmits in interstate or foreign commerce any communication, with intent to coerce, intimidate, harass, or cause substantial emotional distress to a person, using electronic means to support severe, repeated, and hostile behavior, shall be fined under this title or imprisoned."[108] The proposed statute would make cyberbullying a federal crime, but it is likely overbroad or too vague.[109] Nevertheless, it will be difficult to enact such a federal statute to withstand

---

[106] 666 S.E.2d 303 (Va. 2008).

[107] 584 F.3d 1240 (2009).

[108] Cyberbullying Prevention Act, H.R. 6123, 110th Cong. (2d Sess. 2008).

[109] BNA ELECTRONIC LAW & COMMERCE, Federal Anti-Bullying Bill Raises First Amendment Questions (June 11, 2008).

constitutional scrutiny. In 2011, Representative Sheila Jackson Lee introduced H.R. 83, the Bullying Prevention and Intervention Act of 2011.[110]

(B) State Anti–Bullying Legislation

New Jersey enacted the Anti–Bullying Bill of Rights in the wake of the suicide of Tyler Clementi. Clementi, a Rutgers University undergraduate, committed suicide after a roommate used a webcam to record him kissing a male. The roommate streamed the secret video on the Internet and tweeted about it. A *New York Law Journal* article describes the factual setting that led a court to impose sentence on the cyberbullies:

> Tyler Clementi and Dharun Ravi were freshmen roommates at Rutgers University. On Sept. 19, 2010, Mr. Clementi asked his roommate if he could have their room to himself until midnight. During that time, Mr. Ravi went to his classmate, Molly Wei's room and tweeted that he turned on his surreptitiously planted webcam and watched Mr. Clementi "making out with a dude." Numerous media sources have alleged that Mr. Ravi, with Ms. Wei at his side, streamed this encounter live on the Internet. It is also believed that Mr. Clementi learned of his roommate's tweet and webcam. The episode quickly became the subject of dormitory gossip. On Sept. 21, 2010, Mr. Ravi tweeted about a second attempt to secretly broadcast Mr. Clementi that evening on iChat . . . Ravi and Ms. Wei have since been charged with various counts of invasion of privacy under New Jersey criminal law, making it a crime to observe (fourth degree), or record or disclose images of (third degree) another person's sexual contact without the consent of the participant.[111]

In March of 2012, a New Jersey court found Ravi guilty of bias intimidation charges, invasion of privacy, and spoliation of evidence. The court sentenced Ravi to serve a 30–day prison sentence for bias intimidation. A growing number of states have enacted criminal statutes punishing cyberbullying and online harassment. The Berkman Center found forty-eight states to have enacted statutes addressing school bullying. These statutes raise First Amendment and due process issues because they "place significant limits on the public schools' ability to punish certain speech, to reach speech acts that occur off-campus, to search student property such as computers and cell phones, to engage in investigations, and to discipline students."[112]

§ 9.5   COUNTERING HATE ON THE NET

The Internet is a haven for hate groups and stalkers who target women and racial or cultural minorities. The Anne Frank Foundation estimates the number of hate websites advocating racist violence to be at least 8,000.[113] Thousands of websites are dedicated to advancing the cause of white supremacy. Germany alone has three hundred registered hate websites. In *Planned Parenthood of the Columbia/Willamette, Inc. v.*

---

[110] DENA T. SACCO, ET AL., AN OVERVIEW OF STATE ANTI-BULLYING LEGISLATION AND OTHER RELATED LAWS (Berkman Center, Harvard University) (Feb. 23, 2012).

[111] Andrew S. Kaufman & Betsy D. Baydala, Cyberbullying and Intentional Infliction of Emotional Distress 245 N.Y. LAW J. 1 (Feb. 9, 2011).

[112] See generally, Naomi Harlin Goodno, How Public Schools Can Constitutionally Halt Cyberbullying: A Model Cyberbullying Policy That Considers First Amendment, Due Process, and Fourth Amendment Challenges, 46 WAKE FOREST L. REV. 641, 655–74 (2011) (discussing constitutional issues of cyberbullying statutes).

[113] EU Observer, EU Report Shows Increase in Racist Crimes, http://euobserver.com/news/919.

American Coalition of Life Activists,[114] pro-life activists posted "GUILTY" posters identifying the names, addresses, and photographs of physicians that provided abortions.

The website, developed by the American Coalition of Life Activists ("ACLA"), personally identified the plaintiffs on "Deadly Dozen "GUILTY" posters." ACLA compiled the "Nuremberg Files" to collect evidence against abortion doctors in the hopes a court would convict them for crimes against humanity. Even after some of the "guilty" doctors who performed abortions were murdered, the defendants continued to post more doctors to their website. The plaintiffs argued that the distribution of the abortion providers on Old West-style Deadly Dozen "WANTED" posters constituted a threat of force against the doctors singled out, which violated the federal Freedom of Access to Clinics Entrances Act. Pro-life radicals later murdered three physicians featured in the "WANTED" posters.[115]

The jury returned a verdict in the physicians' favor, and awarded $108.5 million in punitive damages. The district court also "enjoined ACLA from publishing the posters or providing other materials with the specific intent to threaten [the physicians]."[116] On appeal, the Ninth Circuit held the website constituted a true threat as defined under the Freedom of Access to Clinics Entrances Act and affirmed the ACLA's liability, but vacated the $108.5 million punitive damages award for the district court to determine whether it comported with due process. The Ninth Circuit's decision sent a signal to ISPs, which unplugged the "Nuremberg Files" site.

§ 9.6   ADULT ENTERTAINMENT & PORNOGRAPHY

The Internet is a massive purveyor of pornography but distributors or transmitters of non-child pornography are rarely prosecuted. Federal criminal statutes proscribe the production and transportation of obscene matters:

> Whoever knowingly produces with the intent to transport, distribute, or transmit in interstate or foreign commerce, or whoever knowingly transports or travels in, or uses a facility or means of, interstate or foreign commerce or an interactive computer service (as defined in section 230(e)(2) of the Communications Act of 1934) in or affecting such commerce, for the purpose of sale or distribution of any obscene, lewd, lascivious, or filthy book, pamphlet, picture, film, paper, letter, writing, print, silhouette, drawing, figure, image, cast, phonograph recording, electrical transcription or other article capable of producing sound or any other matter of indecent or immoral character, shall be fined under this title or imprisoned not more than five years, or both.

---

[114] 290 F.3d 1058 (9th Cir. 2002).

[115] "On March 10, 1993, Michael Griffin shot and killed Dr. David Gunn as he entered an abortion clinic in Pensacola, Florida. Before this, a "WANTED" and an "WANTED" poster with Gunn's name, photograph, address and other personal information were published. The "WANTED" poster describes Gunn as an abortionist and invites participation by prayer and fasting, by writing. . . . On August 21, 1993, Dr. George Patterson, who operated the clinic where Gunn worked, was shot to death. A "WANTED" poster had been circulated prior to his murder, indicating where he performed abortions and that he had Gunn perform abortions for his Pensacola clinic. In July 1994, Paul Hill murdered Dr. John Bayard Britton after being named on an "unWANTED" poster that Hill helped to prepare. One gives Britton's physical description together with his home and office addresses and phone numbers, and charges "crimes against humanity"; another also displays his picture." Id. at 1064.

[116] Id. at 1063.

The transportation as aforesaid of two or more copies of any publication or two or more of any article of the character described above, or a combined total of five such publications and articles, shall create a presumption that such publications or articles are intended for sale or distribution, but such presumption shall be rebuttable.[117]

It is unclear how federal courts are to determine what community applies to Internet-relate pornography.[118] Many federal courts apply the standard of *Miller v. California*,[119] in determining whether an Internet-related work is subject to regulation as obscenity. The *Miller* test has three prongs: (1) whether the average person, applying contemporary community standards would find that the work, taken as a whole, appeals to the prurient interest; (2) whether the work depicts or describes, in a patently offensive way, sexual conduct specifically defined and (3) whether the work, taken as a whole, lacks serious literary, artistic, political, or scientific value.[120] Federal criminal statutes also address Internet pornography. Section 2252(a)(A)(2) prohibits any person from knowingly receiving or distributing child pornography that has traveled in interstate or foreign commerce. This scienter requirement extends both to the sexually explicit nature of the material and to the age of the performer.[121] The statute requires proof that the defendants knowingly possessed and distributed photographs of minors. Section 2257 requires publishers of pornographic material to verify the age of models and this provision applies equally well to cyberspace.

In *Breitfeller v. Playboy*,[122] the plaintiffs filed suit against several defendants for distributing a video of the plaintiffs, 17–year-old girls at the time who were participating in a wet t-shirt contest in Florida. The court rejected the plaintiffs' argument that because the defendants failed to obtain identification or age records as required by § 2257, Playboy knew or should have known there was a risk the images contained minors, and that its decision to remain ignorant as to the plaintiffs' ages therefore satisfied the statute's *knowingly* requirement. Overzealous prosecutors charged teenagers who took sexually explicit photos of themselves and sexted boyfriends or other peer group members, with violating 18 U.S.C. § 2252(a). In *Clark v. Roccanova*,[123] the court ruled that sexting by a 14 year old girl to minors could constitute a violation by the girl of child pornography laws. Criminal prosecutions for online pornography often turn on whether a community standard has been violated. Courts differ as to whether there should be a national versus a local community standard in Internet-related obscenity cases.[124]

---

[117] 18 U.S.C. § 1465.

[118] See generally, Dawn L. Johnson, It's 1996: Do You Know Where Your Cyberkids Are? Captive Audiences and Content Regulation on the Internet, 15 J. MARSHALL J. COMPUTER & INFO. L. 51 (1996) (describing risks involving children and Internet access); see also generally Patrick T. Egan, Note, Virtual Community Standards: Should Obscenity Law Recognize the Contemporary Community Standard of Cyberspace, 30 SUFFOLK L. REV. 117 (1996) (discussing legal challenges presented by cyberporn).

[119] 413 U.S. 15, 24 (1973).

[120] United States v. Miller, 413 U.S. 15, 24 (1973).

[121] United States v. X-Citement Video, Inc., 513 U.S. 64, 78 (1994).

[122] No. 8:05CV405 T30TGW, 2007 WL 294233, at *4–5 (M.D. Fla. Jan. 29, 2007).

[123] 2011 WL 665621 (E.D. Ky. February 14, 2011).

[124] United States v. Little, 365 Fed. Appx. 159 (11th Cir. 2010); United States v. Kilbride, 584 F.3d 1240, 1252–54 (9th Cir. 2009).

§ 9.7　CROSS–BORDER CONTENT REGULATION

(A)　EU Data Retention

The European Commission ("EC") is charged with developing a legal framework to advance free competition in the Single Market. The Commission has powers of initiative, implementation, management, and control; which allows it to formulate harmonized regulations. "The European Union, as a community, has issued a "Green Paper" on the protection of minors and human dignity on audiovisual and information services and its companion "*Illegal and Harmful Content* on the *Internet*."[125] In the United States' Internet service providers ("ISPs") have no duty to take down content that is harmful or illegal except if it infringes copyright law. The European Union's Electronic Commerce Directive's "notice, *take-down* and *put-back*" regime compels ISPs to remove tortious or other objectionable material. In Europe, ISPs have a duty to take down harmful and illegal content once they have notice of its character.[126] The duty to take down illegal or harmful conduct is another difference between New Europe and Old U.S. The European Commission announced in 2012 that ISPs that hosts websites have a duty to take down harmful or illegal content such as racist content, child abuse content or spam. The Commission noted that Article 14 of the E-Commerce Directive is the basis for developing better procedures for taking down illegal content.[127]

(B)　Foreign Filtering of Content

Born in the United States, the Internet has evolved to include hundreds of countries throughout the globe. The Internet's global drift raises the question of how content can be controlled when content crosses countless international borders. Foreign filtering and censorship is unfortunately becoming a norm in China, the Middle East, and many other countries. Governments throughout the world impose content regulations on Internet activities. During the 2008 Olympics, China blocked Internet content that challenged its repressive political regime. Hardly a day goes by without a country imposing new access controls. In July of 2012, China continued to block Bloomberg's website after it published a story about the wealth of Xi Jinping, who is the heir apparent to succeed as President.[128]

China also controls hubs to effect temporary blackouts of the Internet in key areas to stifle the political opposition. An oppressive regime can literally take down the Internet in their country by controlling hubs. In the United States, Congress is debating having a kill switch for the Internet in the event of a national emergency. An Internet kill switch would activate single shut off mechanism for all Internet traffic. "The Internet itself has a generally distributed and redundant architecture seemingly making it difficult to disrupt."[129] Companies such as SPRINT and MCI constructed their own interrelated computer networks connected to the NSFNET.

---

[125] BERT J. DEMPSEY & PAUL JONES, INTERNET ISSUES AND APPLICATIONS 49 (1998).

[126] CHRISTOPHER T. MARSDEN, INTERNET CO-REGULATION: EUROPEAN LAW, REGULATORY GOVERNANCE AND LEGITIMACY 164 (2011) (discussing notice and take down regime of the Electronic Commerce Directive).

[127] European Commission, The EU Single Market, Notice-and-Action Procedures (2012), http://ec.europa.eu/internal_market/e-commerce/notice-and-action/index_en.htm.

[128] Jamil Anderlini, China Censors Block Xi Web Searches, INVESTORS CHRONICLE (June 29, 2012).

[129] LAURA DiNARDIS, PROTOCOL POLITICS: THE GLOBALIZATION OF INTERNET GOVERNANCE 194 (2009).

The BBC cited a University of Washington study reporting, "Since 2003, 64 people have been arrested for publishing their views."[130] Bloggers were arrested for such acts exposing human rights abuses, government corruption, and the suppression of protest. Since 2003, half of the arrests relating to content regulations arose in three countries: China, Egypt, and Iran.[131] The number of Chinese Internet users is estimated to range between 165 million to 210 million, and that number is growing by the tens of millions each year.[132] This skyrocketing number of Chinese Internet users is emblematic of increased struggles for human rights in many less developed countries. Information will be more accessible to the public, yet this may exacerbate struggles over human rights. In Hong Kong, under the Control of Obscene and Indecent Articles Ordinance, it is illegal to distribute any material "not suitable to be published to any person" or "not suitable to be published to any juvenile."[133]

A Malaysian deputy minister warned bloggers "that there were laws pertaining to sedition, defamation, and libel."[134] Gopalan Nair, a former Singaporean living in the U.S., became the first foreign blogger to be arrested and charged with "threatening, abusing, or insulting a public servant."[135] The French Government mounted a number of challenges to liquor advertisements on the Internet, which were noncompliant with French law. A court ruled Heineken must shut down its French website because the Internet was not on a 1991 list of approved media for alcohol publicity.[136] These examples are emblematic of the radically different cultural and political systems of countries connected to the Internet. It is difficult to conceive of transnational content controls, which will not result in a race to the bottom to enact the most restrictive restrictions.

---

[130] BBC, Blogger Arrest Hit Record High, http://news.bbc.co.uk/2/hi/technology/7456357.stm (last visited June 28, 2013).

[131] Id.

[132] Pew Institute, China's Online Population Explosion (July 12, 2007).

[133] Hong Kong Ordinances, Ch. 390 § 2 (1998).

[134] BBC (May 8, 2008).

[135] Cyberspace, ASIA MEDIA FORUM (2008).

[136] French Legal Tangle, AFP (June 6, 2008).

Chapter 10

COPYRIGHTED WORKS IN CYBERSPACE

What would have been different about copyright law if the Internet had never been invented? The list would begin with the 1976 Copyright Act's amendments protecting digital technologies. Internet-related copyright litigation over the ownership of user-generated content, deep linking, liability for remote links, framing, peer-to-peer file sharing, and the Digital Millennium Copyright Act's immunities and anti-circumvention rules were enacted to accommodate copyright law to the digital world.[1] The Internet has spawned a copyright infringement ecosystem with "one-click hosters or "cyberlockers" such as Rapidshare, Megaupload, Mediafire, and Hotfile.[2] Courts have stretched copyright law in a "series of cases and statutes that enshrine the idea of property interests in cyberspace."[3] In 1996, more than one hundred countries entered into two treaties that were explicitly enacted to renovate copyright law for the Internet: the World Intellectual Property Organization ("WIPO") Copyright Treaty ("WCT") and the WIPO Performances and Phonograms Treaty ("WPPT").

These Internet-related treaties require signatories to provide meaningful remedies for copyright owners against those who circumvented or bypassed technical measures protecting copyrighted works. The Internet has reshaped the contours of copyright law along with all branches of Intellectual Property Rights ("IPRs"). The large-tail trend is for copyright owners to seek "broader rights and increased commoditization."[4] Copyright law was once a sleepy backwater but today Internet copyright disputes are the subject of weekly front-page stories in the *Wall Street Journal* and *The Economist*. Even though The World Wide Web is less than two decades old, it is difficult to envision copyright law before peer-to-peer file sharing, the licensing of content, the Digital Millennium Copyright Act, and social media content. It is now difficult to imagine the contours of copyright law without bandwidth, browsers, and digital data. A large number of Internet-related copyright issues are in flux. With the rise of the Internet, copyright law needs to be refocused from copying to a greater emphasis on transmission and access. How do service providers obtain immunity from claims of secondary copyright infringement for materials posted by third parties? How does the

---

[1] Congress enacted the Digital Millennium Copyright Act (DMCA), 17 U.S.C. §§ 1201 et seq. (2006) to fulfill its obligations under the 1996 WIPO Copyright treaties. See Universal City Studios v. Corley, 273 F.3d 429, 440 (2d Cir. 2001) ("The DMCA was enacted in 1998 to implement the World Intellectual Property Organization Copyright Treaty ('WIPO Treaty')."). The DMCA created both civil remedies, see 17 U.S.C. § 1203 (2006), and criminal sanctions against circumventing copyright protection or marketing anti-circumvention devices. See 17 U.S.C. § 1204 (2006). The DMCA specifically authorizes a court to grant temporary and permanent injunctions on such terms, as it deems reasonable to prevent or restrain a violation. See 17 U.S.C. § 1203(b)(1) .

[2] Tobias Lauinger, Martin Szydlowski, Kaan Onarlioglu, Gilbert Wondracek,Engin Kirda, and Christopher Kruegelz, Clickonomics: Determining the Effect of Anti-Piracy Measures for One-Click Hosting, NORTHEASTERN UNIVERSITY REPORT (2013) at 1.

[3] Dan Hunter, Cyberspace as Place and the Tragedy of the Digital Anticommons, 91 CAL. L. REV. 9191 CAL. L. REV. 439, 443 (2003).

[4] JULIE E. COHEN, CONFIGURING THE NETWORKED SELF: LAW, CODE, AND THE PLAY OF EVERYDAY PRACTICE 9 (2012).

Internet change the concept of fair use? How does the Internet change the contours of copyright law? How can copyright owners exercise their right to take down infringing content and whether they must consider fair use prior to making a request? What rights and remedies do copyright owners have if they prove infringement? This chapter answers these and other questions about the path of Internet-related copyright law.

§ 10.1 OVERVIEW OF COPYRIGHT LAW

In 1469, the city-state of Venice granted John of Speyer the exclusive privilege for all printing for a five-year period. The protection of literary works by copyright coincided with the invention of the printing press.[5] Copyright law was prefigured in England when Queen Mary chartered the stationers—the book publishers and sellers—by letters patent on May 4, 1557. The earliest copyright statute to grant rights to authors, as opposed to stationers—the book publishers and sellers—was the Statute of Anne, enacted on April 10, 1710. The Statute of Anne set the term of copyrights for authors at twenty-one years.[6] The sole rights of copyright owners were to print and reprint works.

The Patent and Copyright Clause of the U.S. Constitution grants Congress the power to "promote the Progress of Science and useful Arts, by securing for limited times to authors and inventors the exclusive right to their respective writings and discoveries."[7] The federal law of copyright recognizes property interests in expression that is the product of the human intellect. Ideas, such as the quantum theory of physics, are not protectable, but a book explaining this theory would be copyrightable. Ideas are not copyrighted; only expression of the ideas is. The power to determine the duration of copyright terms rests with Congress. Congress enacted the first federal copyright statute in 1790 under its authority granted in the Copyright Clause of the U.S. Constitution. Congress has amended the U.S. Copyright Act many times over the last two centuries.

Paul Goldstein coined the "The Celestial Jukebox," to describe the new technologies and the internationalization of copyright.[8] The digital world "promises both new strains and new opportunities for copyright law, domestically and worldwide."[9] The attributes of digital information are: "fidelity, compression, and malleability."[10] Goldstein describes the metaphorical celestial jukebox as:

> A technology-packed satellite orbiting thousands of miles above Earth, awaiting a subscriber's order—like a nickel in the old jukebox, and the punch of a button—to connect him to any number of selections from a vast storehouse via a home or office receiver that combines the power of a television set, radio, CD player, VCR, telephone, fax, and personal computer. Today the celestial jukebox is only a metaphor; its infrastructure—much of which will certainly be earthbound—is far from complete. Nevertheless, the pace of technological development is so fast and

---

[5] ROBERT P. MERGES & JANE C. GINSBURG, FOUNDATIONS OF INTELLECTUAL PROPERTY 271 (2006).

[6] Benjamin Kaplan, AN UNHURRIED VIEW OF COPYRIGHT LAW (1967).

[7] U.S. Const. art. I, § 8, cl. 8.

[8] PAUL GOLDSTEIN, COPYRIGHT'S HIGHWAY: THE LAW AND LORE OF COPYRIGHT FROM GUTENBERG TO THE CELESTIAL JUKEBOX 3 (1994).

[9] Id.

[10] Id. at 197.

the forces of market demand so strong that the celestial jukebox, however configured, will be in place sometime early in the twenty-first century.[11]

In *Eldred v. Ashcroft*,[12] the U.S. Supreme Court upheld the Copyright Term Extension Act ("CTEA"), which increased existing and future copyrights by twenty years. The history of copyright law is a history of legal lag. Today's copyright law is not up to the task of stemming widespread online copyright infringement. Copyright is a form of protection provided by federal law to the authors of works and this includes software programs, digital content, and materials on websites.[13] Courts have extended copyright law through cases and statutes that preserve the idea of property interests in cyberspace. While the World Wide Web did not become part of mainstream American culture until the mid-1990s, the widespread use of the Internet dramatically changed the course of copyright law. The requirements for copyright protection are the same in cyberspace as they are in the brick-and-mortar world. Copyright grants federal rights for "original words of authorship fixed in any tangible medium of expression."[14] Copyright law is purely a federal law branch of intellectual property law, as is patent law. Copyright comprises the brick-and-mortar of the knowledge economy. Courts have had little difficulty in applying well-worn groves of intellectual property law to cyberspace and "This has led to a series of cases and statutes that enshrine the idea of property interests in cyberspace."[15]

The U. S. Supreme Court stated, "The sole interest of the United States and primary object in conferring the monopoly [of copyright protection] lie in the general benefits derived by the public from the labors of authors."[16] Since the mid-1990s, the U.S. Congress and courts have stretched the law of copyright to accommodate electronic rights. Copyright law, too, limps along, attempting to adjust to the Internet, through which peer-to-peer users can make perfect copies of copyrighted materials and distribute them with the click of a mouse. Peer-to-peer file sharing programs, such as Gnutella, LimeWire, KaZaa Lite, GigaTribe and Emule, allow its members to share all types of digital media.[17] MicrosTorrent and TorrentReactor are important peer sharing networks in Europe. In many countries, people buy legal software and distribute it on these peer-to-peer networks for free. In the Czech Republic, for example, hardly anyone buys software except companies. In Sweden, users of Pirate Bay established a political party, the Pirate Party, which won 7.1% of the votes in a 2012 election

(A) The Scope of Copyright Law Protection

Courts have had little difficulty extending copyright protection to software, websites, and other Internet-related intellectual property. Copyright is secured automatically when the work is created, and a work is "created" when it is fixed in a copy or phonorecord for the first time. Section 102 of the U.S. Copyright Act extends copyright protection to original works of authorship fixed in any tangible medium of

---

[11] Id. at 199.

[12] 537 U.S. 186 (2003).

[13] 17 U.S.C. §§ 101–103.

[14] 17 U.S.C. § 102(A).

[15] Dan Hunter, Cyberspace as Place and the Tragedy of the Digital Anticommons, 91 CAL. L. REV. 439, 443 (2003).

[16] Sony Corporation v. Universal City Studios, Inc., 464 U.S. 417, 429 (1984).

[17] United States v. C.R., 792 F. Supp. 2d 343, 352 (S.D. N.Y. 2011).

expression. This includes: (1) literary works, (2) musical works, including any accompanying words, (3) dramatic works, including any accompanying music, (4) pantomimes and choreographic works, (5) pictorial, graphic, and sculptural works, (6) motion pictures and other audiovisual works, (7) sound recordings, and (8) architectural works.[18] Literary works, other than audiovisual works, must be expressed in words, numbers or other verbal or numerical symbols.[19] To be classified as a literary work, the U.S. Copyright Act requires no showing of "literary merit." Software, for example, has no literary merit but it is a copyrightable literary work.[20]

A "derivative work" is a work based upon one or more pre-existing works. Section 103 of the U.S. Copyright Act provides that compilations and derivative works fall within the subject matter of copyright.[21] Software programs may qualify as derivative works if they recast, transform, or adapt extant software. Websites, too, may be protectable. Copyright law applies equally well to cyberspace. The U.S. Copyright Act gives the copyright owner the right to make derivative works.[22] In the past two decades, courts have had little difficulty extending copyright protection to software, websites, and other Internet-related IPRs. "Whether in the virtual or real world, the legal standards are the same regarding: (1) the definition of a copyright and the purpose underlying copyright protection; (2) the requirements for a work to be protected by copyright; and (3) what constitutes infringement of a copyright."[23]

Federal copyright law defines a modification as copying from or adapting "all or part of the work in a fashion requiring copyright permission, other than the making of an exact copy."[24] A modification to computer software is broadly defined as any change made to the computer software that impact functionality. Software license agreements need to address whether the licensee receives modification and at what price. Another significant issue is to determine who owns modifications created by customers. Proprietary software licensing agreements generally restrict the right of customers to make modifications whereas open source licenses encourage them.[25]

---

[18] 17 U.S.C. § 102(a).

[19] 17 U.S.C. § 101.

[20] KINNEY & LANGE, P.A. INTELLECTUAL PROPERTY LAW FOR BUSINESS LAWYERS (2008-2009 Edition) at §5.3 (citing NEC Corp. v. Intel Corp., 645 F. Supp. 590, 595 (N.D. Cal. 1986).

[21] 17 U.S.C. § 103.

[22] Copyright in a work vests initially in the author or authors of the work but it can be assigned or transferred, if memorialized by a writing. (i.e. I have assigned ownership of this Global Internet Law Hornbook to my publisher, West Publishing Co. In the case of employees, the works made for hire doctrine vests ownership in the employer, so long as the works were created in the employee's scope of duties).

[23] G. Peter Albert, Jr. & Rita Abbati, Using and Protecting Copyrighted Works on the Internet, Chapter 4 in G. PETER ALBERT, JR. AND AMERICAN INTELLECTUAL PROPERTY LAW ASSOCIATION, INTELLECTUAL PROPERTY LAW IN CYBERSPACE (2011) at 127.

[24] Gnu.org, General Public License, GNU Operating System, http://www.gnu.org/copyleft/gpl.html(last visited March 7, 2010) (defining modification).

[25] "Free software and open source software incorporates a copyleft licensing regime. "Open source software authors want the widest dissemination possible of their information products. For these authors and developers, the traditional view that copyright holder must have access to the greatest economic gain possible in exchange for producing a copyright-protected work is not only outdated, but unfounded." ROD DIXON, OPEN SOURCE SOFTWARE LAW 2 (2004). Open source proponents use copyright law to give users access to source code. The goal is for users to use the source code to improve the software. Id. "On a larger scale, the argument that freedom requires openness better describes the essential features of the software distribution model used by the community. Id. at 3.

(B) Exclusive Rights of Copyright Owners

Authors receive a bundle of rights under Section 106 that include the right: (1) to reproduce the copyrighted work in copies or phonorecords, (2) to prepare derivative works based upon the copyrighted work, (3) to distribute copies or phonorecords of the copyrighted work to the public by sale or other transfer or ownership, or by rental, lease, or lending, (4) in the case of literary, musical, dramatic, and choreographic works, pantomimes, motion pictures, and other audiovisual works, to perform the copyrighted work publicly, (5) in the case of literary, musical, dramatic, and choreographic works, pantomimes and pictorial, graphic, or sculptural works— including the individual images of a motion picture or other audiovisual work—to display the copyrighted work publicly, and (6) in the case of sound recordings, to perform the copyrighted work publicly by means of a digital audio transmission.[26]

The U.S. Copyright Act grants owners the exclusive right to "perform the copyrighted work publicly."[27] The U.S. Copyright Act's Transmission Clause defines that right to include the right "to transmit or otherwise communicate a performance . . . of the work . . . *to the public*, . . . whether the members of the public are capable of receiving the performance . . . receive it in the same place or in separate places and at the same time or at different times."[28] Cable operators, for example, pay licensing and retransmission consent fees to retransmit copyrighted programming. A "derivative work" is a work based upon one or more preexisting works such as a translation or film version of a novel, or any other recasting of an original copyrighted work.[29]

The authors of joint works are co-owners of the copyrights.[30] A "joint work" is a work prepared by two or more authors with the intention that their contributions be merged into inseparable or interdependent parts of a unitary whole. With "works made for hire," however, it is the employer not the employee who is classified as the author of the works. The employer owns all the rights comprised in the copyright unless the parties otherwise agree. "Works made for hire" only apply to software or other works "prepared by an employee within the scope of his or her employment.[31] One of the risky aspects of overly relying on the work for hire doctrine is that a court may disagree with an employer's labeling. It is possible that a court will classify a programmer working on a software development project to be an independent contractor rather than an employee. The developer needs to be sure that any independent contractors assign their copyrights to them. In the absence of a work for hire agreement, the copyright vests in the programmer not the software maker.

(C) Copyright Term Extension

The CTEA of 1998 extended U.S. copyright terms by an additional 20 years. The U.S. Copyright Act of 1976 extended the term for the life of the author plus 50 years, or 75 years for a work made for hire. The CTEA extended these terms to life of the author plus 70 years and for works of corporate authorship to 120 years after creation or 95

---

26 17 U.S.C. § 116.

27 17 U.S.C. § 106(4).

28 Id.

29 17 U.S.C. § 101.

30 17 U.S.C. § 201(b).

31 See 17 U.S.C. § 101.

years after publication, whichever endpoint is earlier. "For joint authors, the copyright term is the life of the last surviving author plus 70 years."[32]

§ 10.2   ELEMENTS OF COPYRIGHT LAW

Copyright protection, whether on a website, social media, or any other Internet-related medium, applies only if a work satisfies two criteria: originality, and fixation. The U.S. Copyright Act of 1976 governs U.S. copyrights.[33] Copyright can persist in a website or other creation even if it incorporates non-original contributions. Section 102(A) of the U.S. Copyright Act describes copyright subject matter: "Copyright protection subsists in original works of authorship fixed in any tangible medium of expression, now known or later developed, from which they can be perceived, reproduced, or otherwise communicated, either directly or with the aid of a machine or a device."[34] The copyright owner is generally the author, but a major exception to this rule is the U.S. Copyright Act's conclusive presumption that works created by employees in the scope of employment vest with the employer.[35]

The U.S. Copyright Act defines software as a literary work. In 1974, Congress created the Commission on New Technological Uses of Copyright ("CONTU"), which released a 1978 report urging Congress to expand copyright protection to protect software. In 1980, Congress updated the U.S. Copyright Act of 1976 to include "computer programs" within the sphere of application as "literary works."[36] Section 101, Title 17, of the U.S. Code defines "computer program," and software, to mean "a set of statements or instructions to be used directly or indirectly in a computer in order to bring about a certain result."[37] As a result, software makers may protect their copyrighted software from infringement.[38] Computer software is protectable whether in "object code (the binary code—a series of zeros and ones—that computers can read) [or in] source code (the spelled-out program commands that humans can read)."[39] For software program creators, copyright is automatically vested "in a program at the moment it is created without regard to whether it is ever registered."[40] Copyright is vested in owners now of independent creation—so long as there is a minimum spark of originality, and the fixation requirements are met.

(A) Originality

The originality hurdle in U.S. copyright law is very low when compared to copyright law in many other countries. *Feist Publications, Inc. v. Rural Telephone Service Co.*[41] illustrates a core example of the minimal originality requirement, where the U.S.

---

[32] Albert and Abbati, Using and Protecting Copyrighted Works on the Internet, Id. at 128.

[33] 17 U.S.C. §§ 101–102.

[34] 17 U.S.C. § 102.

[35] 17 U.S.C. § 201(b).

[36] 17 U.S.C. § 101.

[37] Id.

[38] 17 U.S.C. § 106.

[39] 17 U.S.C. § 101; Control4 Corporation, SEC S-1–A Filing (July 18, 2013) (defining source code in licensing agreements to mean "the instructions for computer programs and applications that are designed to be readable by the human eye, which when compiled or otherwise altered become usable by a computer. Source Code includes all related diagrams, flow charts, and programmers notes.").

[40] Montgomery v. Noga, 168 F.3d 1282, 1288 (11th Cir. 1991).

[41] Feist Publications, Inc. v. Rural Telephone Service Co., 499 U.S. 340 (1991).

Supreme Court held the plaintiff's database composed of "white pages" telephone number listings was not entitled to copyright protection because it did not clear the minimum threshold of originality required under the U.S. Copyright Act. The alphabetic listing of names did not satisfy the originality element.[42] "Original," as the term is used in copyright, means "the work was independently created by the author, and that it possesses at least some minimal degree of creativity."[43]

A telephone directory could satisfy the originality requirement where the compiler, in an original way, "chooses which facts to include, in what order to place them, and how to arrange the collected data so that they may be used effectively by readers."[44] The *Feist* Court explained that the requirement of originality is satisfied when shown that the work has some slight degree of creativity; an original work need not be novel, and may be crude or obvious. "To be sure, the requisite level of creativity is extremely low; even a slight amount will suffice."[45]

However, the Court found that compilations of telephone numbers lacked this slight amount of originality. The Court conceded that a compilation of facts could possess the requisite originality if the author made choices as to what facts to include, their ordering, and arrangement. However, even under these circumstances copyright protection extends only to those components of the work that are original to the author—not to telephone numbers themselves. This fact/expression dichotomy severely limits the scope of protection in fact-based works such as databases. The *Feist* Court rejected a "sweat of the brow" theory that was adopted by the European Union countries and extends a compilation's copyright protection beyond selection and arrangement to the facts themselves.[46] The U.S.-Eurozone divide is great when it comes to database protection as Europeans have *sui generis* protection for a fifteen-year period for databases not qualifying for copyright protection because they lack originality.[47] The U.S. does not recognize *sui generis* protection for databases lacking originality. In the United States, if a database lacks originality, the creator will use licensing or trade secrets to protect its creation.

(B) Fixation

An author must fix a work of authorship in a tangible medium of expression to satisfy the fixation requirement. A work is "fixed" in a tangible medium of expression when it is "sufficiently permanent or stable to permit it to be perceived, reproduced, or otherwise communicated for a period of more than transitory duration."[48] For fixation to occur, the work must be fixed for a period of more than transitory duration and be fixed

---

[42] Id. at 348.

[43] Id.

[44] Id.

[45] Id. at 345.

[46] Telephone directories are not protectable because simply alphabetizing names, numbers, and addresses is not original for purposes of the U.S. Copyright Act. Id. at 348.

[47] "The Directive on the legal protection of Databases was adopted in February 1996. The Directive created a new exclusive "sui generis" right for database producers, valid for 15 years, to protect their investment of time, money and effort, irrespective of whether the database is in itself innovative ("non-original" databases). The Directive harmonised also copyright law applicable to the structure and arrangement of the contents of databases ("original" databases). The Directive's provisions apply to both analogue and digital databases." Europa, The EU Single Market, Protection of Databases (2013), http://ec.europa.eu/internal_market/copyright/prot-databases/index_en.htm (last visited Oct. 5, 2013).

[48] 17 U.S.C. § 101.

in a tangible medium of creation. The creator may communicate the fixation with the help of a machine or device, and need not be directly perceptible. Merely loading a computer operating system into a computer's Random Access Memory ("RAM") creates a copy under the U.S. Copyright Act.[49] However, it is unclear whether something in dynamic RAM is fixed for establishing a copyright. The acts of transmitting an e-mail or viewing a web page—both of which store copies in the user's computer RAM—qualify as copies for purposes of the U.S. Copyright Act. The Ninth Circuit, in *MAI Systems Corp. v. Peak Computer*,[50] held that simply loading a computer operating system into RAM, which is accomplished by turning the computer on, created a fixed copy for purposes of the U.S. Copyright Act. Internet copying, such as caching temporary copies of websites, would qualify as a fixed copy under the reasoning of the *MAI* court. Generally, a "cache" is "a computer memory with very short access time used for storage of frequently or recently used instructions or data."[51]

(C) Exclusions from Copyright

Copyright protects expression, not ideas.[52] The U.S. Supreme Court in *Baker v. Selden* forged the "idea/expression" dichotomy.[53] Selden copyrighted a book in which he described a method of bookkeeping and sued Baker when the latter published a book on bookkeeping with functionally equivalent methods, but with different columns and headings. The Court ruled that Selden could not copyright his method of accounting, but could copyright the forms used to implement a system of bookkeeping. The Court held that a copyright in a practical method of accounting did not prevent others from using that method.[54] The takeaway point for Internet law is that copyright cannot protect ideas, concepts, methods, or systems.

Governmental works are similarly not protectable by copyright. Government works are defined as "work of the United States Government" or of an employee of the United States Government as part of that person's official duties.[55]

The functionality of a website, protocol, or programming language does not qualify for copyright or trademark protection. Patent law is the branch of intellectual property that protects functionality. In practice, it is difficult to separate functionality from expression.[56]

---

[49] MAI Systems Corp. v. Peak Computer, 991 F.2d 511, 517 (9th Cir. 1993).

[50] 991 F.2d 511, 517 (9th Cir. 1993).

[51] United States v. Ziegler, 474 F.3d 1184, 1186 (9th Cir. 2007).

[52] In no case does copyright protection for an original work of authorship extend to any idea, procedure, process, system, method of operation, concept, or discovery, regardless of the form in which it is described, explained, illustrated or embodied in. 17 U.S.C. § 102(B).

[53] 101 U.S. 99 (1880).

[54] Id. at §§ 101–102.

[55] 17 U.S.C. § 101.

[56] See generally, MARTIN P. MICHAEL, U.S. COPYRIGHT LAW-SEPARABILITY/FUNCTIONALITY: A BIG HURDLE FOR MOST INDUSTRIAL DESIGNS (2012) at 3 (Courts hold that utilitarian works such as mannequins and Halloween costumes are entitled to copyright protection, even though the aesthetic aspects of those works could not possibly be physically separated from their utilitarian aspects. See Chosun Int'l, Inc. v. Chrisha Creations, Ltd., 413 F.3d 324 (2d Cir. 2005) (plush animal Halloween costumes may be entitled to protection if aesthetic features separable from function of work as a costume. . . . Works that would otherwise be considered sculptural will not be denied protection simply because they are put to a utilitarian function.).

(D) Derivative Works

A "derivative work" is a work based upon one or more preexisting works such as "a translation, musical arrangement, dramatization, fictionalization, motion picture version, sound recording, art reproduction, abridgment, condensation, or any other form in which a work may be recast, transformed, or adapted."[57] Films based upon books are classifiable as derivative works. Dr. Seuss's 1971 environmentalist tale, *The Lorax*, was made into a movie in 2012. *The Devil in the White City*, by Erik Larson, chronicling the true story of a serial killer operating at the same time as the Chicago World's Fair of 1893, is in film pre-production.

Editorial revisions, annotations, elaborations, or other modifications such as an altered or updated website, may qualify as a derivative work. A translation, musical arrangement, or abridgment of a work may be "recast, transformed, or adapted" into a derivative work.[58] Courts have not provided clear guidance on what constitutes a derivative work for computer programs. A derivative work of a program may consist of revisions, elaborations, or enhancements of the original software code. To constitute a derivative work, these revisions must represent an "original work of authorship."[59] A proprietary software company prohibits customers from developing derivative works.[60]

(E) Automatic Creation & Notice

Copyright arises automatically during creation of a work of authorship—even if the author does not include a copyright notice or fails to register the work with the U.S. Copyright Office. It is advisable, however, to include a copyright notice—i.e. the letter c in a circle: ©, or the word "Copyright" and the first year of publication of a work (e.g. Copyright 2013 Michael L. Rustad)—because registration and notice confer benefits on the copyright owner. A copyright registration certificate is evidence of the validity of the copyright so the holder of the registration certificate need not put on evidence of ownership or originality in the copyrighted work.[61]

A Certificate of Registration constitutes *prima facie* evidence of the validity of a copyright, but only if it was obtained within five years of the first publication of the work.[62] Registration is a requirement for filing a copyright infringement case. Copyright infringement occurs when an individual violates an exclusive right of the copyright owner. The copyright owner's exclusive rights include the reproduction, the preparation of derivative forms, the distribution, and the display of copyrighted works.[63] Posting a copyrighted photograph on a blog without the owner's permission violates the owner's exclusive rights. A defendant in a copyright infringement suit cannot use an "innocent infringer" defense to mitigate actual or statutory damages if there is a proper copyright notice affixed to a work.[64]

---

[57] 17 U.S.C. § 101.

[58] Id. at 17 U.S.C. § 101.

[59] Id.

[60] Id.

[61] 17 U.S.C. § 410(c).

[62] Id.

[63] See 17 U.S.C. § 106.

[64] 17 U.S.C. § 401(d).

(F) Work Made for Hire

In general, the creator of a copyrightable work is the rights holder. The "work for hire" doctrine is an exception to this general rule; it applies where a person creates, but is not the owner of a copyrightable work. The "Work for Hire" doctrine makes an employer the copyright owner for works prepared by their employee within the scope of employment—even if the employer does nothing more than hire the employee who creates the work.

(G) Software Copyrights

Since the passage of the Computer Software Copyright Act in 1980, computer programs have been protected by copyright as "literary work."[65] Computer software is entitled to the same copyright protection as all other original works of authorship. Nevertheless, numerous issues were left open to the courts, such as whether certain portions of computer programs are protectable as "expression" or unprotectable as "ideas." These issues include whether infringement may result from: copying not just the actual computer code, but the "structure, sequence, and organization" of a program;[66] copying the "look and feel" of a computer program's interface;[67] and decompilation, a form of reverse engineering necessitating the making of a copy of the original program in order to effectuate.

Copyright law has a continuing vitality with the new information technologies because computer software is copyrightable whether in object or source code form. In the 1970s, software was largely protected by trade secrets because of uncertainty whether code was copyrightable. Nevertheless, the U.S. Copyright Act of 1976 classified computer software as a "literary work" subject to copyright so long as it met the criteria of qualifying as an original work of authorship fixed in any tangible medium of expression. "For original computer programs. . . copyright automatically inheres in the work at the moment it is created without regard to whether it is registered."[68]

§ 10.3 OVERVIEW OF COPYRIGHT INFRINGEMENT

Copyright issues are a significant part of Internet-related IPRs. Copyright law potentially protects all facets of a website: materials; documents; computer programs;

---

[65] 17 U.S.C. §§ 101, 117.

[66] See Whelan Assocs., Inc. v. Jaslow Dental Lab., Inc., 797 F.2d 1222, 1237–38 (3d Cir. 1986) (finding infringement because of similarity in structure between programs despite lack of literal copying); SAS Inst., Inc. v. S & H Computer Sys., Inc., 605 F.Supp. 816, 829–31 (M.D. Tenn. 1985) (concluding infringement exists because program used detailed organizational structure of plaintiff's program).

[67] See Johnson Controls, Inc. v. Phoenix Control Sys., Inc., 886 F.2d 1173, 1176 (9th Cir. 1989) See Johnson Controls, Inc. v. Phoenix Control Sys., Inc., 886 F.2d 1173, 1176 (9th Cir. 1989) (holding reasonable person would conclude program captured "total concept and feel" of plaintiff's program). On the other hand, one court, despite noting that the "look and feel" concept is not helpful in distinguishing between copyrightable and noncopyrightable elements of a computer program, found the "Lotus 1–2–3" spreadsheet copyrightable and defendant liable for infringement because the "menu structure, taken as a whole—including the choice of command terms, the structure and order of those terms, their presentation on the screen, and the long prompts," met the requirements for copyrightability. Lotus Dev. Corp. v. Paperback Software Int'l, 740 F. Supp. 37, 68 (D. Mass 1990).

[68] Montgomery v. Noga, 168 F.2d 282, 286 (11th Cir. 1999).

pictures; artwork; photographs; sounds; video text; designs; HTML code; as well as the content of many other works posted on the Internet. The U.S. Copyright Office call for legislative action is to find new ways to deter rogue websites that enable widespread copyright infringement of copyrighted works, particularly motion pictures, television programs, books, and software.[69] It is unclear to what extent U.S. copyright law protects rights of owners against infringing acts that originate in other countries connected to the Internet. Copyright law is territorial while the Internet is cross-border by its very nature.

In the past two decades, courts have generated a distinct body of law for copyright law to accommodate cyberspace. In the past ten years, the cutting edge of online copyright law is peer-to-peer ("P2P") software litigation. Social-media related copyright cases and P2P sharing lawsuits continue to dominate the legal landscape. The discussion of direct and secondary infringement cases demonstrates how the Internet shapes and will continue to shape copyright law for the near future. Federal copyright law recognizes four kinds of copyright infringement: (1) direct copyright infringement, (2) contributory copyright infringement, (3) vicarious copyright infringement and (4) inducement to commit infringement. The U.S. Supreme Court explained the distinction between direct and secondary copyright infringement in *Metro–Goldwyn–Mayer Studios, Inc. v. Grokster, Ltd.*[70] In *Metro–Goldwin–Mayer Studios, Inc. v. Grokster, Ltd.*,[71] the U.S. Supreme Court unanimously held that "one who distributes a device with the object of promoting its use to infringe copyright, as shown by clear expression or other affirmative steps taken to foster infringement is liable for the resulting acts of infringement by third parties."[72] The *Grokster* Court unanimously held the P2P defendants distributed their software in order to promote copyright infringement.[73]

The "mere knowledge of infringing potential or actual infringing uses would not be enough here to subject [a defendant] to liability."[74] "Vicarious copyright liability is an "outgrowth" of *respondeat superior*, imposing liability on those with a sufficiently supervisory relationship to the direct infringer."[75] As noted by the Supreme Court, one "infringes vicariously by profiting from direct infringement while declining to exercise a right to stop or limit it."[76] To prevail on a contributory or vicarious copyright claim, a plaintiff must show direct infringement by a third party.[77] To establish infringement, a copyright owner must demonstrate that: (1) the defendant has actually copied the plaintiff's work; and (2) the copying is illegal because a substantial similarity exists between the defendant's work and the protectable elements of the plaintiff's.

---

[69] Maria A. Pallante, Crackdown on Rogue Websites by U.S. Copyright Office, 16 BLOOMBERG BNA, COMM. & LAW REPORT 1809, 1809 (2011).

[70] Metro–Goldwyn–Mayer Studios Inc. v. Grokster, Ltd., 545 U.S. 913, 919 (2005).

[71] 545 U.S. 913 (2005).

[72] Id. at 936–37.

[73] See id. at 936–37 (adopting the reasoning of Sony Corp. v. Universal City Studios, and providing reasons why this type of behavior constitutes infringement).

[74] Id. at 937.

[75] A&M Records v. Napster, 239 F.3d 1004, 1022 (9th Cir. 2001).

[76] Metro–Goldwyn–Mayer Studios, Inc. v. Grokster, Ltd., 545 U.S. 913, 930 (2005).

[77] UMG Records, Inc. v. MP3.Com Inc., 2000 U.S. Dist. LEXIS 13293 (S.D.N.Y. Sept. 6, 2000) (ruling that MP3.com was a willful infringer imposing statutory damages of $25,000 for each copyrighted compact disc in the defendant's online database).

A copyright owner proves unauthorized copying by proffering direct or indirect evidence. A plaintiff relying on indirect evidence must show that the defendant had access to the work in question, and that there exists substantial similarity between the works such that the ordinary observer, unless he set out to detect the disparities, would be inclined to overlook them and regard their aesthetic appeal as the same. Though "registration is not a condition of copyright protection,"[78] "no civil action for infringement of the copyright in any United States work shall be instituted until preregistration or registration of the copyright claim has been made in accordance with this title."[79]

The first Internet copyright infringement cases were against the operators of computer bulletin boards. "The elements of a copyright-infringement claim are (1) ownership of the copyright by the plaintiff and (2) copying by the defendant."[80] In 1993, a Florida federal court became the first to find a computer bulletin board liable for copyright and trademark infringement when it displayed Playboy's copyrighted photographs.[81] That same year, a court ruled that a software program was copied—for purposes of the U.S. Copyright Act—each time when it was installed into the computer's random access memory ("RAM").[82] In *MAI Systems*, the court found the operator of an electronic bulletin board liable where subscribers downloaded copyrighted Sega computer games without permission of the copyright owner. A court ordered an injunction ordering the operator of the bulletin board to stop enabling subscribers to copy Sega games. This decision created a swirl of uncertainty as to whether Internet activities such as caching, or viewing content, constituted copyright infringement because technically these activities also met the *MAI Systems* test for copying.

The ten-year war against P2P file sharing networks has resulted in a number of high profile victories for copyright owners, but has done little to stem the tide of P2P sharing.[83] ReDigi, a web-based storage locker, was found liable for infringing copyright owners' exclusive rights because it allowed users to resell their legally acquired digital music files. ReDigi allowed its users to upload tracks that have been purchased on iTunes. The user can choose either to stream the file for his personal use or to sell the file to another ReDigi user. Once a user chooses to sell the file, his access to it is immediately terminated. The court found that ReDigi infringed two of the exclusive rights of record companies, the reproduction and distribution rights. The court found that neither the fair use defense nor the first sale doctrine excused that infringement. ReDigi satisfied the volitional conduct requirement to render them liable for direct infringement. ReDigi was also liable for secondary infringement: liability for contributory infringement because they knew or should have known that the service would encourage infringement and they materially contributed to their users' infringement.[84]

---

[78] 17 U.S.C. § 408(a).

[79] 17 U.S.C. § 411(a).

[80] Zomba Enters. v. Panorama Records, Inc., 491 F.3d 574 (6th Cir. 2007).

[81] Playboy Enterprises Inc. v. Frena, 839 F. 1552 (M.D. Fla. 1993).

[82] MAI Systems Corp. v. Peak Computer, Inc., 991 F.2d 518 (9th Cir. 1993).

[83] REBECCA GIBLIN, CODE WARS: 10 YEARS OF P2P SOFTWARE LITIGATION vi (2011) (foreward by Jane Ginsburg).

[84] Capitol Records, LLC v. ReDigi, Inc., 2013 WL 1286134 (S.D. N.Y. March 30, 2013).

(A) Direct Infringement

(1) Prima Facie Case

To prevail in a direct infringement case, a plaintiff must satisfy two requirements: (1) it must show ownership of the allegedly infringed material, and (2) it must demonstrate that defendants committed an act of "copying" this material.[85] Under the Copyright Act, 'copying' means that a defendant has infringed one or more of the copyright owner's five exclusive rights under 17 U.S.C. § 106. These exclusive rights include the right to reproduce, distribute, publicly display, perform, or create derivative works of the copyrighted work.[86] "When anyone other than the copyright owner or the lawful transferee of a copyright exercises any of the exclusive rights afforded by the U.S. Copyright Act, there is an infringement of the copyright."[87] In an Internet-related case, the plaintiff must have proof that defendants have copied, reproduced, distributed, adapted, and/or publicly displayed copyrighted works. In the past decade, the U.S. music industry has begun to file and win direct infringement lawsuits against the individuals who share copyrighted files on P2P services.[88]

Liability for direct copyright infringement arises from the violation of any one of the exclusive rights of a copyright owner, including the exclusive right to authorize others to reproduce, distribute, perform, display, and prepare derivative works from the copyrighted work. Sharing music or video files with other Internet users is an infringement of the copyright owner's distribution right.[89] Virtual stores like iTunes have sold more than $1 billion of digital works through their Internet downloadable software program, allowing users to purchase songs, electronic books, movies, and television shows. In order to install the iTunes software program, the consumer must agree to the license agreement terms that appear on the computer screen, by clicking the button that reads: "I accept the terms of the licence agreement."[90] Free P2P sharing programs permit users to swap music, software, video, and other copyrighted materials with others. In 1998, Shawn Fanning, a Northeastern University student, invented Napster, which enabled users to exchange music over the Internet. Napster was the pioneering P2P sharing program permitting users to exchange "Moving Pictures Experts Group, Audio Layer III" ("MP3") music files stored on individual computer hard drives with other Napster users. An MP3 is a compression system that has the feature of reducing bytes at no cost to maintain a good sound quality.

Rebecca Giblin notes how Shawn Fanning's Napster was the first skirmish in a ten-year war between rights holders and P2P software providers.[91] The lesson learned from the P2P litigation is that "despite being ultimately successful in holding

---

[85] Perfect 10, Inc., v. Amazon.com, Inc., 508 F.3d 1146, 1159 (9th Cir. 2007).

[86] 17 U.S.C. § 106.

[87] KURT M. SAUNDERS, PRACTICAL INTERNET LAW FOR BUSINESS (2001) at 81.

[88] Id. at 2.

[89] See e.g., Atlantic Recording Corp. v. Howell, 554 F. Supp. 2d 976 (D. Ariz. 2008) (holding that making content available is not the equivalent of distribution).

[90] MICHAEL L. RUSTAD, UNDERSTANDING, SALES, LEASES, AND LICENSES IN A GLOBAL PERSPECTIVE (2008) at 436.

[91] REBECCA GIBLIN, CODE WARS: 10 YEARS OF P2P LITIGATION 1 (2011).

individual P2P providers liable for their users' infringement, their litigation strategy has failed to bring about any [reduction] in P2P development and infringement."[92]

In computer science terms, the personal computer used by the consumer is the "client," and the computer that hosts the web page is the "server." The "client" obtains information from a centralized source—namely the server. In a P2P distribution network, the information available for access does not reside on a central server. In a P2P network, each computer is playing the role of both server and client. The central server of most P2P networks will index the information made available by end-users on the network and allow individual users to connect to each other. While courts generally enforce clickwrap agreements—such as those used by iTunes—they may refuse enforcement where the licensor violates fundamental norms of fairness.[93] At a minimum, a user must have reasonable notice of the terms of a license, and the opportunity to manifest their assent. P2P computer programs include WinMX, BitTorrent, Torrent, Shareaza, eDonkey/Overnet, and eMule.

One who reproduces or distributes a copyrighted work during the term of the copyright has infringed the copyright, unless licensed by the copyright owner. A plaintiff in a direct infringement suit must prove the defendant copied the constituent elements of work that are original. If a plaintiff cannot show that the defendant directly copied a work, he or she must submit "fact-based showings that the defendant had access to the plaintiff's work and that the two works are substantially similar."[94]Assuming that a plaintiff establishes a *prima facie* direct infringement case, the defendant may avoid liability if he or she can demonstrate fair use, or another copyright defense.[95] "Fair use" is a statutory exception that allows the use of a copyrighted work for certain purposes without requiring permission. Section 107 of the U.S. Copyright Act states that "the fair use of a copyrighted work, including such use by reproduction in copies for purposes such as criticism, comment, news reporting, teaching, scholarship, or research, is not an infringement of copyright."[96]

(2) Copyright Damages

Under 17 U.S.C. § 504(c), the copyright owner must choose as to whether they recover statutory damages in lieu of actual damages for infringement. Many copyright owners chose to pursue statutory rather than actual damages because of the difficulty of proving the causal connection between infringement and lost sales or other revenues. Nevertheless, when a copyright owner establishes that a defendant's infringement was "willful, the court in its discretion may increase the amount of statutory damages to a sum not more than $150,000."[97] "As a general rule, a determination as to willfulness requires assessment of a party's state of mind, a factual issue that is not usually susceptible to summary judgment, although exceptions may be

---

[92] Id. at 2.

[93] Clickwrap is a commonly used term for agreements requiring a computer user to "consent to any terms or conditions by clicking on a dialog box on the screen in order to proceed with [a] . . . transaction." Feldman v. Google, Inc., 513 F. Supp. 2d 229, 236 (E.D. Pa. 2007).

[94] Funky Films, Inc. v. Time Warner Entm't Co., 462 F.3d 1072, 1076 (9th Cir. 2006).

[95] Playboy Enterprises Inc. v. Frena, 839 F. Supp. 1552 (M.D. Fla. 1993).

[96] 17 U.S.C. § 107.

[97] 17 U.S.C. § 504(c)(2).

made where the evidence of willfulness is unassailable."[98] "To prove that infringement was "willful" under the Copyright Act, the plaintiff must show (1) that the defendant knew its conduct was infringing or (2) that the defendant's actions were the result of reckless disregard or willful blindness to the prospect that its conduct was infringing."[99] "In evaluating the infringer's state of mind, courts have looked to factors including 'whether the infringer was on notice that the copyrighted work was protected; whether the infringer had received warnings of the infringements; [and] whether the infringer had experience with previous copyright ownership, prior lawsuits regarding similar practices, or work in an industry where copyright is prevalent."[100]

In July of 2010, Judge Nancy Gertner applied the U.S. Supreme Court's punitive damages jurisprudence in *BMW v. Gore* to statutory copyright damages in *Sony BMG Music Entertainment v. Tenenbaum*.[101] The federal district court jury awarded the music industry plaintiffs $ 675,000 in statutory damages after finding that Joel Tenenbaum willfully infringed Viacom's copyrights when he downloaded thirty songs using P2P technology.[102] The jury concluded that Tenenbaum's conduct was willful and imposed "damages of $ 22,500 per song, yielding a total award of $ 675,000."[103] The U.S. Copyright Act entitles plaintiffs to choose between recovery of actual and statutory damages any time before the court renders its final judgment.[104] The First Circuit affirmed in part and vacated the district court opinion finding the award against Tenenbaum to be constitutionally excessive.[105] In 2013, the First Circuit upheld the statutory damages against charges that it was constitutionally excessive.[106]

---

[98] United States Media Corp. v. Edde Enm't, Inc., 1996 WL 520901, at *7, 1996 U.S. Dist. LEXIS 13389, at *21 (S.D.N.Y. Sept. 10, 1996).

[99] Agence France v. Morel, 2013 WL 146035 (S.D. N.Y., Jan. 14, 2013) (quoting United States Media Corp. v. Edde Enm't, Inc., 1996 WL 520901, at *7, 1996 U.S. Dist. LEXIS 13389, at *21 (S.D.N.Y. Sept. 10, 1996)).

[100] Id. at *17 (Marshall v. Marshall, 2012 WL 1079550, at *25, 2012 U.S. Dist. LEXIS 45700, at *91 (E.D.N.Y. March 30, 2012) (citations omitted). Infringement is generally not willful if a party reasonably and in good faith believes that its conduct is innocent, despite warnings to the contrary. N.A.S. Import, Corp. v. Chenson Enterprises, Inc., 968 F.2d 250, 252 (2d Cir.1992); see also Marshall, 2012 WL 1079550, at *25–26, 2012 U.S. Dist. LEXIS 45700, at *92–93. The burden of proving willfulness is on the copyright holder.").

[101] 721 F. Supp. 2d 85, 103 (D. Mass. 2010).

[102] Id. at 87.

[103] Id.

[104] See 17 U.S.C. § 504(c)(1) (2006) (highlighting options for copyright owner proving infringement).

[105] Sony BMG Music Entm't v. Tenenbaum, 660 F.3d 487 (1st Cir. 2011) (affirming the finding of copyright infringement against Tenenbaum but reversing the reduction in damages, reinstating the original award, and remanding for consideration of whether to reduce the award by a common law remittitur).

[106] Sony BMG Music Entertainment v. Tenenbaum, 2013 WL 3185436 (1st Cir., June 25, 2013) (ruling that $675,000 statutory damages award did not violate constitutional due process and was below the statutory maximum).

(B) Three Types of Secondary Copyright Infringement

Secondary Copyright Liability

Contributory	Vicarious	Inducement
"One who, with knowledge of the infringing activity, induces, causes or materially contributes to the infringing conduct of another."[107]	One who "has the right and ability to supervise the infringing activity and also has a direct financial interest in such activities."[108]	"One, who distributes a device with the object of promoting its use to infringe copyright, as shown by clear expression or other affirmative steps taken to foster infringement, is liable for the resulting acts of infringement by third parties."[109]

To prevail on a claim of trademark infringement under the Lanham Act, holder of registered trademark must show that another person is using: (1) reproduction, counterfeit, copy or colorable imitation of mark; (2) without registrant's consent; (3) in commerce; (4) in connection with sale, offering for sale, distribution, or advertising of any goods or services; (5) where such use is likely to cause confusion, or to cause mistake or to deceive.[110] "All theories of secondary liability for copyright and trademark infringement require some underlying direct infringement by a third party."[111] Secondary copyright infringement encompasses three theories: contributory, vicarious, and inducement liability.[112] All three theories require a showing of underlying direct infringement. The concept of secondary copyright infringement is akin to aiding and abetting on the criminal side of the law. P2P sharing of video and music files is an Internet-related development that has reshaped the law of secondary copyright infringement. Evidence of active steps to induce direct copyright infringement includes activities such as advertising an infringing use or instructing users how to access infringing content.

The U.S. legal system is reticent to premise liability when a defendant sells a commercial product with an infringing use as well as a lawful use. Many of the emblematic secondary infringement cases have come in the context of P2P sharing that permits users to swap music, software, video, and other copyrighted materials with others. In the digital era, computer companies prefer to distribute their software directly to the Internet. The DMCA shields Internet service providers from secondary copyright liability—assuming that they have a registered copyright agent and enforce a

---

[107] Gershwin Publishing Co. v. Columbia Artists Management Inc., 443 F.2d 1159, 1162 (2d Cir. 1971).

[108] Id. at 1162–63.

[109] MGM Studios Inc. v. Grokster, Ltd., 545 U.S. 913, 934 (2005).

[110] Lanham Act, § 32(1)(a), 15 U.S.C. § 1114(1)(a).

[111] LouisVuitton Malletier, S.A. v. Akanoc Solutions, Inc., 591 F. Supp. 2d 1098, 1104 (N.D. Cal. 2008).

[112] Viacom Int'l, Inc. v. YouTube, Inc., 2012 U.S. App. LEXIS 6909 *20 (2d Cir. 2012).

policy of removing infringing materials.[113] Amazon.com, for example, posts its "Notice and Procedure for Making Claims of Copyright Infringement" prominently in its user agreement.

Beginning in 2004, the Motion Picture Association of America ("MPAA") filed many actions against websites linking to illegal content. Plaintiffs have filed suit against Twitter for advertising or linking to websites, which copied photographs and other infringing content. In addition, the MPAA and RIAA are pursuing thousands of lawsuits against college students and other recidivist infringers around the country who download copyrighted content by using BitTorrent. BitTorrent represents the next generation of file-sharing applications displacing one-to-one FTP including BitComment, BitLord, and other many-to-many distributed systems. The advantage of BitTorrent is that it accelerates downloading time by separating files into many segments and then transmits them over a network; at any given moment, a client may be receiving, and sending, different pieces of the same file from different users. File sharers that use P2P software to exchange movies and music are direct infringers and statutory awards can amount to hundreds of thousands of dollars.

Nevertheless, the direct infringers using these P2P services often do not make for deep-pocketed defendants. During the first wave of P2P infringement cases, large copyright owners seldom targeted direct infringers—such as college students—illegally downloading of music and videos. Until the last few years, nearly all P2P copyright infringement enforcement actions targeted the secondary infringers rather than the primary users.

(1) Contributory Infringement

A defendant who has not directly infringed on a copyright may still be liable for contributory infringement if the defendant (1) has knowledge of another's infringing conduct and (2) induces, causes, or materially contributes to that conduct.[114] Contributory infringement was a doctrine imported from tort law.[115] To prevail in a contributory copyright infringement lawsuit, the plaintiff must prove: (1) direct copyright infringement by a third party, (2) knowledge by the defendant the third party was directly infringing, and (3) defendant's material contribution to the infringement. The idea underlying contributory infringement is to prove that the defendant actively encourages infringement.[116]

Thus, to state a claim of contributory infringement, a plaintiff must show knowledge, as well as material contribution, to the infringing conduct.[117] Contributory infringers must either know or have reason to know of the direct infringement. A defendant is contributorily liable for copyright infringement if the defendant knowingly induces, causes, or materially contributes to the infringing conduct of another.[118] In an

---

[113] 17 U.S.C. § 512(d).

[114] Perfect 10, Inc. v. Amazon.com, Inc., 508 F.3d 1146, 1171 (9th Cir. 2007).

[115] "Direct or indirect intellectual property infringement constitutes a tort, and joint tortfeasor liability provides that one who knowingly participates in or furthers a tort is jointly and severally liable with the primary tortfeasor. In contrast to vicarious liability, which is concerned with relationships, the emphasis of contributory liability is on fault." REBECCA GIBLIN, CODE WARS: 10 YEARS OF P2P SOFTWARE LITIGATION 26 (2011).

[116] Gershwin Publ'g Corp. v. Columbia Artists Mgmt., Inc., 443 F.2d 1159, 1162 (2d Cir. 1971).

[117] Perfect 10, Inc. v. Visa Int'l Serv. Ass'n, 494 F.3d 788 (9th Cir. 2007).

[118] Ellison v. Robertson, 357 F.3d 1072, 1076 (9th Cir. 2004).

Internet case, plaintiffs will have a claim for contributory copyright infringement if a third party website hosts and distributes infringing content while contributing to this infringing conduct. The issue in contributory infringement cases in P2P litigation is "what knowledge is necessary to support liability" and "what does it mean to "materially contribute" to infringement?"[119]

(2) Vicarious Infringement

A defendant is liable for vicarious copyright infringement if the defendant "profit[s] from direct infringement while declining to exercise a right to stop or limit it."[120] Vicarious infringement evolved out of the common law principle of *respondeat superior* and is entrenched in copyright law. To state a claim for vicarious copyright infringement, a plaintiff must allege the defendant has: (1) the right and ability to supervise the infringing conduct and (2) a direct financial interest in the infringing activity. Where credit card companies did not induce or materially contribute to the infringement of a publisher's copyrighted material, the court found that the companies were neither contributorily, nor vicariously liable for copyright or trademark infringement; rather, they processed credit card payments to access allegedly infringing websites.[121]

In *Perfect 10,* the plaintiff, a publisher of an adult magazine, "Perfect 10," and the operator of that magazine's subscription website—both of which featured copyrighted images of models owned by the plaintiff—asserted that the defendants were contributorily and vicariously liable because they processed credit card payments to allegedly infringing websites. The appellate court found defendants did not induce or materially contribute to the infringing activity. The infringement stemmed from the failure to get a license to distribute the copyrighted images, not from processing payments. The court held the defendants were not vicariously liable because they had no right or ability to control the infringing activity.

(3) Inducement or Encouraging Infringement

Inducement is a theory that the *Grokster* Court (discussed below) imported from patent law.[122] When a single actor commits all the elements of patent infringement, that actor is liable for direct infringement under 35 U.S.C. § 271(a). It is unclear whether inducement is a separate secondary copyright cause of action or *merely* a type of contributory copyright infringement. The U.S. Supreme Court explained that, "[o]ne infringes contributorily by intentionally inducing or encouraging direct infringement."[123] In *Grokster*, the Court adopted an "inducement rule," finding that, "[o]ne who distributes a device with the object of promoting its use to infringe copyright, as shown by clear expression or other affirmative steps taken to foster infringement, is liable for the resulting acts of infringement by third parties."[124] The Court adopted the inducement rule for copyright:

---

[119] REBECCA GIBLIN, CODE WARS, Id. at 27.

[120] Metro–Goldwyn–Mayer Studios, Inc. v. Grokster, Ltd., 545 U.S. 913, 930 (2005).

[121] Perfect 10, Inc. v. Visa Int'l Serv. Ass'n., 494 F.3d 788 (9th Cir. 2007).

[122] See 35 U.S.C. § 271(b) ("Whoever actively induces infringement of a patent shall be liable as an infringer.").

[123] Metro–Goldwyn–Mayer Studios Inc. v. Grokster, Ltd., 545 U.S. 913, 930 (2005).

[124] Id. at 936.

For the same reasons that Sony took the staple-article doctrine of patent law as a model for its copyright safe-harbor rule, the inducement rule, too, is a sensible one for copyright. We adopt it here, holding that one who distributes a device with the object of promoting its use to infringe copyright, as shown by clear expression or other affirmative steps taken to foster infringement, is liable for the resulting acts of infringement by third parties.[125]

The Court made it clear that "mere knowledge of infringing potential or actual infringing uses would not be enough here to subject [a defendant] to liability."[126] The Court described how Grokster induced direct infringement in its advertising and business model; targeting millions of consumers. The Court noted that the "probable scope of copyright infringement [on the defendants' file-sharing networks] is staggering."[127] The Court further stated:

> Inducement liability goes beyond that, and the distribution of a product can itself give rise to liability where evidence shows that the distributor intended and encouraged the product to be used to infringe. In such a case, the culpable act is not merely the encouragement of infringement but also the distribution of the tool intended for infringing use.[128]

The guidepost of *Grokster* is the greater willingness of the Court to approve imposing secondary liability on third parties that facilitate intellectual property crimes and infringement. "Several courts have expressed doubt that inducement of infringement states a separate claim for relief."[129] A lower court held that the *YouTube* defendants were entitled to safe harbor protection under the Digital Millennium Copyright Act ("DMCA") primarily because they had insufficient notice of the particular infringements in suit in *Viacom Int'l, Inc. v. YouTube, Inc.*[130] The DMCA's safe harbor protects service providers against secondary copyright infringement from third party postings if they have posted their registered copyright agent and have implemented policy to deal with repeat infringers.[131] In *Viacom Int'l, Inc. v. YouTube, Inc.*,[132] the Second Circuit affirmed in part, vacated in part, reverse in part and remanded the case back to the lower court affirming the lower court's holding that the § 512(C) safe harbor requires knowledge or awareness of specific infringing activity.

The appeals court stated that the "first and most important question on appeal is whether the DMCA safe harbor at issue requires "actual knowledge" or "aware[ness]" of facts or circumstances indicating "specific and identifiable infringements."[133] The DMCA safe harbor requires the website have no knowledge of, or financial benefit from, infringing activity on its network, have a copyright policy, provide proper notification of that policy to its subscribers, and list an agent on its website to respond to copyright infringement complaints.

---

[125] Id.

[126] Id. at 937.

[127] Id. at 940.

[128] Id.

[129] DSB Kollective Co., Ltd. v. Tran, 2011 U.S. Dist. LEXIS 147538 (N.D. Ca., Dec. 21, 2011).

[130] 718 F. Supp. 2d 514, 529 (S.D.N.Y. 2010).

[131] 17 U.S.C. § 512 (1998).

[132] 676 F.3d 19 (2d Cir. 2012).

[133] Id. at 24.

The Second Circuit instructed the lower court to consider first the scope of the statutory provision and then its application to the record in this case. Nevertheless, the court vacated the lower court's entry of summary judgment ruling, "[a] reasonable jury could find that YouTube had actual knowledge or awareness of specific infringing activity on its website."[134] The court also held that the lower court erred by interpreting the "right and ability to control" infringing activity to require "item-specific" knowledge.[135] Finally, the court affirmed the district court's holding that three of the challenged YouTube software functions fell within the safe harbor for infringement that occurs "by reason of" storage at the direction of the user, and remanded for further fact-finding with respect to a fourth software function. In April 2012, a Hamburg, Germany court "ruled that online video platform YouTube must install filters to prevent users from uploading some music videos whose rights are held by Germany's Gema, a music-royalties collecting body."[136]

A defendant's intent to foster infringement is established by evidence of the defendant's clear expression of such an intent, or of affirmative steps taken by the defendant to foster infringement. An advertisement or solicitation that broadcasts a message designed to stimulate others to commit violations is direct evidence of inducement. Such evidence, however, is not the exclusive way of proving inducement liability. The court explained that there was a difference between inducement and contributory infringement. "A defendant may be held liable for contributory copyright infringement if, with knowledge of the infringing activity, it materially contributes to the infringing conduct of another."[137]

In *Arista Records v. Lime Group,*[138] the federal court granted summary judgment on the plaintiffs' claim of inducement of copyright infringement against the distributor of LimeWire, a P2P file-sharing program. Evidence in the record showed that 93% of the content on LimeWire infringed on copyrights held by the plaintiffs. To establish a claim for inducement, a plaintiff must show that the defendant: (1) engaged in purposeful conduct that encouraged copyright infringement; with (2) the intent to encourage such infringement. Unlike an inducement claim, a claim for contributory infringement does not require a showing that the defendant intended to foster infringement. Rather, to establish a material contribution claim, a plaintiff must show that the defendant: (1) had actual or constructive knowledge of the infringing activity; and (2) encouraged or assisted others infringement, or provided machinery or goods that facilitated infringement. A defendant's contribution to a third party's infringing activities must be "material" to give rise to a claim for contributory infringement. The court found that LimeWire had the "right and ability to limit the use of its product for infringing purposes, including by (1) implementing filtering; (2) denying access; and (3) supervising and regulating users."[139]

Nevertheless, LimeWire "has not exercised any meaningful supervisory control over LimeWire users' infringing activity, or provided a legitimate reason for its failure

---

[134] Id. at 26.

[135] Id.

[136] Juergen Baetz, German Rules Against YouTube in Rights Case, SEATTLE POST–INTELLIGENCER (April 20, 2012) at B1.

[137] Id. at 432.

[138] 784 F. Supp. 2d 398 (S.D. N.Y. 2011).

[139] Id. at 436.

to do so."[140] The court found that the record was insufficient "to permit the Court to assess the "technological feasibility or commercial viability" of LimeWire's potential non-infringing uses."[141] The court denied LimeWire's motion for summary judgment based on the evidence that LimeWire (1) had the right and ability to supervise and control LimeWire users' infringing activities; and (2) possessed a direct financial interest in the infringing activity. Courts do not agree whether inducement is a separate theory or merely a subtype of contributory infringement.[142]

§ 10.4　PEER–TO–PEER FILE SHARING

(A) Napster

Napster.com ("Napster") was the pioneering P2P sharing service; permitting the exchange of MP3 music files stored on individual computer hard drives with other Napster users. Many record companies and music publishers filed copyright infringement lawsuits against Napster for facilitating P2P transmissions of copyrighted content resulting in the landmark case: *A & M Records v. Napster, Inc.* Napster defended its actions by asserting fair use.[143] The *Napster* court found Napster had diminished the copyright owners' commercial sales because users were downloading content without paying royalties or fees. The court rejected Napster's fair use argument finding that commercial use of the copyrighted material occurred through Napster's users' "repeated and exploitative unauthorized copies of copyrighted works . . . made to save the expense [of] purchasing authorized copies."[144]

The federal appeals court rejected Napster's argument that it was not liable for direct or contributory copyright infringement. The Ninth Circuit in the *Napster* case ruled that DMCA § 512(A) did not protect Napster's referencing and indexing activities. The court upheld the lower court's decision, finding that visitors to the Napster site engaged in direct copyright infringement. In addition, the court held Napster liable for contributory infringement because Napster not only had knowledge of the infringing activity, it also contributed to the infringing conduct. Napster was also found to be vicariously liable because it had a direct financial interest in the visitor's infringing activities.

(B) Grokster

In *Metro–Goldwyn–Mayer Studios, Inc. v. Grokster, Ltd.,*[145] the United States Supreme Court found that "[o]ne infringes contributorily by intentionally inducing or encouraging direct infringement."[146] The *Grokster* Court based its inducement theory upon evidence that P2P networks intended and encouraged their products for file sharing. The Court unanimously held that because the P2P defendants intentionally distributed their software, they knowingly promoted copyright infringement. The

---

[140] Id. at 435.

[141] Id. at 434.

[142] See, e.g., Arista Records LLC v. Usenet.com, Inc., 633 F.Supp.2d 124, 150 n. 17 (S.D.N.Y.2009) ("it is worth noting that several courts recently have expressed doubt as to whether inducement of infringement states a separate claim for relief, or rather whether it is a species of contributory infringement.").

[143] A & M Records, Inc. v. Napster, Inc., 239 F.3d 1004 (9th Cir. 2001).

[144] Id. at 1015.

[145] 545 U.S. 913 (2005).

[146] Id. at 930.

Court stated that, "[m]ere knowledge of infringing potential or actual infringing uses would not be enough here to subject [a defendant] to liability."[147] The Court then described how Grokster induced direct infringement in its advertising and business model targeting millions of consumers. "The probable scope of copyright infringement," just with respect to the two networks at issue there, was "staggering."[148] The Court imported the Doctrine of Inducement from Section 271(b) of the Patent Code, stating "[w]hoever actively induces infringement of a patent shall be liable as an infringer."[149]

A patent infringement action based upon inducement requires the plaintiff to prove the defendant encouraged another's infringement, and mere knowledge of the direct infringer's activities is not enough. Inducement in copyright law, as well as patent law, is the active aiding and abetting theory of infringement. Viacom International, Inc. filed a $1 billon copyright infringement claim against YouTube for enabling users to upload 150,000 unauthorized copyrighted videos on its service. A federal court later ruled that Viacom must produce its logging database and data fields for all YouTube videos.[150]

(C) Cyberlocker Services

"Cyberlockers" are third party file sharing services that provide password-protected hard drive space online. A user has the option of sharing the cyberlocker password information with friends, who can then privately download any content a user has placed online. This easily leads to the sharing of copyrighted works. In *Perfect 10, Inc. v. Megaupload Ltd.*,[151] Perfect 10 contended that Megaupload, an online storage company, stored billions of dollars of pirated media on their servers, uploaded by users, including its copyrighted images and videos. When a visitor to Megaupload's website attempted to download this content, they were "offered the opportunity to purchase a membership" to Perfect 10's subscription-only website.[152] The court dismissed the vicarious liability claim but denied Megaupload's motion to dismiss the claim of contributory infringement. The FBI seized Megaupload's servers and arrested Kim Dotcom, also known as Dr. Evil, Megaupload's founder, director, and sole shareholder of Vestor Ltd.

The FBI and the U.S. Justice Department charged Megaupload with generating $175 million in illicit copyright proceeds.[153] "The Megaupload episode also led the hacking collective, Anonymous, to launch a wave of retaliatory attacks that temporarily took down the websites of the FBI and the U.S. Justice Department."[154] The Motion Picture Association of America ("MPAA") filed suit against Hotfile.com, another cyberlocker. Many cyberlocker services are shutting down in the wake of the FBI takeover of Megaupload. Many academics and privacy groups view this

---

[147] Id. at 937.

[148] Id. at 923.

[149] 35 U.S.C. § 271(b).

[150] Viacom Intern., Inc. v. YouTube, Inc., 2008 WL 2260018 (S.D. N.Y. 2008).

[151] 2011 No. 11CV0191–IEG (S.D. Cal. July 27, 2011).

[152] Id.

[153] Alex Vorro, Megaupload.com Accused of Massive Copyright Infringement, INSIDE COUNSEL (Jan. 2012).

[154] Jeff Roberts, Court Filings Suggest Google Fighting Feds Over Megaupload E-mails, PAIDCONTENT.ORG (March 2, 2012).

prosecution as overreaching by zealous prosecutors. Copyright owners have won nearly every P2P case, but these victories have not had any impacts on file sharing practices.

§ 10.5   LINKS, FRAMING, BOOKMARKS, & THUMBNAILS

(A) Hyperlinks

Hyperlinks are an essential component of the Internet, which enables the creation of a "single body of knowledge."[155] Website visitors make use of links to surf from one website to another simply by clicking on hypertext as opposed to typing in Internet addresses. "Typically the linked text is blue or underlined when displayed, and when selected by the user, the referenced document is automatically displayed, wherever in the world it actually is stored."[156] A mere link is a reference to content, not the publication of content. "The power of the Web stems from the ability of a link to point to any document, regardless of its status or physical location."[157]

> Links may also take the user from the original Website to another Website on another computer connected to the Internet. These links from one computer to another, from one document to another across the Internet are what unify the Web into a single body of knowledge, and what makes the Web unique.[158]

Typically, there is no copyright infringement when linking to a third party's website when that website contains infringing materials. In *Bernstein v. J.C. Penney*, a federal court in California dismissed a copyright infringement claim against J.C. Penney for linking to a Swedish website with infringing content.[159] In that case, the site with the infringing material was several links distant from J.C. Penney's website.[160] "Deep linking" occurs when a defendant's link bypasses the principal web page containing the trademark owner's logo and third party advertising.[161] "Deep Linking" also deprives the trademark owner of revenues from online advertising.[162] Ticketmaster.com claimed a deep link from Microsoft's web page exploiting its trademark. Microsoft removed the deep link and settled the case before a court ruling. A Canadian Supreme Court in *Crookes v. Newton*,[163] held that a mere hyperlink could not be considered a publication.[164]

---

[155] ACLU v. Reno, 929 F. Supp. 824, 836–37 (E.D. Pa. 1996).

[156] Id. at 836.

[157] Id. at 837.

[158] Id.

[159] Bernstein v. J.C. Penney, Inc., 1998 WL 906644 (C.D. Calif. 1998).

[160] Id.

[161] "Deep linking refers to links on a website to the interior of another website bypassing the home page of the second one. For example, a deep link is created where website "X" links to a document or web age belonging to "Z" and the link bypasses the intended route to the site, and it is not made evident that the shortcut has taken place." SLA, Does Deep Linking Infringe Copyright? http://www.sla. org/content/Shop/ Information/infoonline/ 2000/sep00/copyright.cfm.

[162] The copyright issues occur when the defendant copies URLs and engages in "deep hyper-linking to . . . interior web pages." Ticketmaster Corp. v. Tickets.com, 2003 U.S. Dist. LEXIS 648 *19 (C.D. Cal., March 7, 2003); see Brian D. Wassom, Copyright Implications of "Unconventional Linking" on the World Wide Web: Framing, Deep Linking and Inlining, 49 CASE W. RES. L. REV. 181, 208 (1998).

[163] 2011 SCC 47.

[164] Gregory Bordan, Canada: Developments In Internet Law: Defamation and Hyperlinks, MONDAQ (Nov. 28, 2011).

Nevertheless, in *Universal Music Australia Pty. Ltd. v. Cooper*, the Australian federal court ruled that a website was liable for copyright infringement because it had well-organized h hyperlinks to other website with infringing contents to many other pages, the evidence is that the website was user friendly and attractive and that visitors could readily select from a variety of catalogues of popular sound recordings for download. The digital copies of the sound recordings were downloaded by way of hyperlinks on the website, most of which appear to have been associated with MP3 digital music files stored on remote websites that would automatically download to the visitor's computer upon activation of the link on the website by a mouse click. As a consequence of clicking on the hyperlink trigger on the website, music files were downloaded directly from the remote website on which they were stored to the computer of the internet user who had accessed the Cooper website.

(B) Framing

"Framing" is displaying content from another website while still maintaining advertisements from the original site. "Framing refers to the process whereby one website can be visited while remaining in a previous website." "Framing allows the user to visit one website "while remaining in a previous website."[165] This method of online advertising causes a second website to appear on a part of another site.[166]

> The framed page moves simultaneously with the outer window. If the outer window is closed or minimized, the framed page also closes or minimizes. The purpose of framing is to create a single seamless presentation that integrates the content of the two web pages into what appears to be single web page.[167]

The practice of framing causes the plaintiffs' website to appear in a form not envisioned by the website developer. Framing allows a party to superimpose its advertising on all linked websites. To date, no appellate court has weighed in on framing. In *Washington Post v. Total News, Inc.*,[168] the Washington Post along with other publishers- the *Los Angeles News, Dow Jones, CNN,* and USA Today- charged that TotalNews infringed its copyrights and trademarks, and misappropriated their news material.

> TotalNews' advertising was framed across the screen bottom, and the "news frame," the largest frame, appeared in the center and right. Clicking on a specific news organization's link allowed the reader to view the content of that particular organization's website, including any related advertising, within the context of the "news frame." In some instances, the framing distorted or modified the appearance of the linked website, including the advertisements.[169]

In-line links incorporate a link into a picture on the first web page that directs a user to a second web page. The second page is thus said to have an in-line link. TotalNews encased the linked sites with the Total News frame along with affiliated

---

[165] Id. at 46.

[166] Digital Equipment Corp. v. AltaVista Technology, Inc. 960 F. Supp. 456, 461 (D. Mass. 1997).

[167] Wells Fargo & Co. v. WhenU.com, Inc. 293 F. Supp. 2d 734, 748–49 (E.D. Mich. 2003).

[168] No. 97 Civ. 1190 (S.D. N.Y. Feb. 20, 1997).

[169] The Washington Post, et al. v. TotalNews, Inc., et al., Southern District of New York, Civil Action Number 97–1190, summarized in, Netlitigation, http://www.netlitigation.com/http://www.netlitigation.com/netlitigation/cases/post.htm.

banner ads. The district court did not decide the case because the parties reached an out of court settlement.

(C) Bookmarks

The Seventh Circuit in *Flava Works v. Gunter*[170] determined that myVidster was not a contributory infringer merely because a website visitor bookmarks video and later clicks on the bookmark and views the video. The federal district court issued a preliminary injunction against the social media site, which was vacated by the U.S. Court of Appeals. Flava Works produced and distributed videos "of black men engaged in homosexual acts."[171] Patrons of myVidster, a social media site, "find videos on the Internet and if they want to make them available to other patrons of myVidster," bookmark them.[172] Judge Richard Posner, writing of the court, found that myVidster was not liable for contributory infringement for inline linking. Judge Posner analogized myVidster to a "telephone exchange connecting two telephones . . . providing a connection between the server that hosts the video and the computer of myVidster's visitor."[173]

The court acknowledged that myVidster "may have done a bad thing by bypassing "Flava's pay wall" by enabling viewing the uploaded copy, but it does not constitute copyright infringement."[174] The direct infringers are Flava's customers who copied his copyrighted videos and posted them to the Internet.[175] The court reasoned that myVidster could be liable for contributory infringement under an inducement theory but there was no evidence in the record supporting that claim.[176] Flava was also not entitled to an injunction since it did not produce evidence that myVidster induced social media users to infringe copyrights.[177]

(D) Thumbnails of Copyrighted Images

"The more transformative the new work, the less important the other factors, including commercialism, become."[178] In *Kelly v. Arriba Soft Corp.*,[179] Ditto.com, a search engine retrieved images by matching the keyword searched with the description of image files sorted in Ditto's database.[180] Leslie Kelly, a Western art photographer filed suit against Ditto.com for reproducing and displaying images on its search engine.[181] Ditto would index the images and "display them in "thumbnail" form on the

---

[170] 2012 U.S. App. LEXIS 15977 (7th Cir. Aug. 2, 2012).

[171] Id. at *2.

[172] Id. at *6.

[173] Id. at *8.

[174] Id. at *9.

[175] Id.

[176] Id. at *10–*11.

[177] Id. at *26.

[178] Kelly v. Arriba Soft Corp., 336 F.3d 811, 818 (9th Cir. 2003).

[179] 77 F. Supp.2d 1116 (C.D. Cal. 1999).

[180] G. Peter Albert, Jr. & Rita Abbati, *Using and Protecting Copyrighted Works on the Internet*, Chapter 4 in G. PETER ALBERT, JR. AND AMERICAN INTELLECTUAL PROPERTY LAW ASSOCIATION, INTELLECTUAL PROPERTY LAW IN CYBERSPACE (2011) at 191.

[181] The Electronic Freedom Foundation described the factual setting for this thumbnail and framing case: "Ditto was sued by Les Kelly a photographer after Kelly discovered that Ditto had indexed his own website and the images found there. Ditto.com prevailed before the trial court but suffered a defeat on appeal before the Ninth Circuit in San Francisco. Although the Ninth Circuit found that Ditto.com's use of

search results page."[182] The Ninth Circuit found Arriba Soft's use of thumbnails was transformative because the greatly reduced copies of copyrighted images used in the thumbnails were for a different purpose. In 2002, the Ninth Circuit affirmed the district court's holding that thumbnails infringed Kelly's copyrighted photographs, but fair use permitted the use of the thumbnails in Ditto.com's image index.[183] In a 2003 decision,[184] the Ninth Circuit upheld the panel's ruling that search engines could use thumbnails of images, but withdrew the portion of the opinion dealing with inline linking or framing.

In *Perfect 10, Inc. v. Google, Inc.*,[185] the plaintiff created photographs of nude models for commercial distribution. After publishing a magazine, Perfect 10, began offering access to these pictures on its password protected paid subscription website. Google's search engine used a web crawler to copy thumbnail images of Perfect 10's copyrighted photographs for use in its search engine. In *Perfect 10*, the Ninth Circuit held Google's thumbnail-sized reproduction of entire copyrighted images in its search engine results page to be "highly transformative."[186] Google's use of the copyrighted images was to find content, which was a radically different purpose than the original copyright owner's use. The Ninth Circuit held that Perfect 10 was not likely to prevail its copyright infringement arising out of Google's "in-line links" that allowed Internet users to view infringing copyrighted images on third party's websites. In addition, the court found no vicarious or contributory infringement in its use of thumbnails or in-line links.

§ 10.6 DATABASE PROTECTION

In 1991, the U.S. Supreme Court held in *Feist Publications, Inc., v. Rural Telephone Service Co.*[187] that compiling information alone without a minimum of original creativity does not satisfy the originality element of the U.S. Copyright Act. Nevertheless, if a data compilation has a "minimal degree of creativity," to satisfy originality, copyright protection may be available.[188] Feist had copied information from Rural's white page telephone listings, and Rural sued for copyright infringement. The Court rejected Rural's "sweat of the brow" argument finding that there was no infringement since Rural had no copyright in the telephone white databases. The European Union, on the other hand, follows a "sweat of the brow" approach and protects databases that are otherwise unprotectable by U.S. copyright law.

The U.S. approach diverges sharply with the EU's approach. Prior to the Database Directive, European countries differed in their approaches to database protection. The United Kingdom, for example, endorsed the "sweat of the brow" approach and granted

---

thumbnail images was allowed under the copyright law doctrine of "fair use" it held Ditto.com liable for infringement of the public display right for opening a new window to display the image. This technique is known as "in-line linking" or "framing" and is commonly used by numerous other Web search engines including Lycos Google and AltaVista." Electronic Freedom Foundation, Kelly v. Arriba Soft, https://www.eff.org/cases/kelly-v-arriba-soft.

[182] Id.

[183] 280 F.3d 934 (9th Cir. 2002).

[184] 336 F.3d 811 (9th Cir. 2003).

[185] 508 F.3d 1146 (9th Cir. 2007).

[186] Id. at 1165.

[187] 499 U.S. 340 (1991).

[188] Id. at 345.

protection to database works considering "skill, labour and judgment," even though the databases might not be either creative or original.[189] The European Union enacted the Database Directive in 1996, granting legal protection of databases in any form.[190] Article 6 of the Directive provides for copyright protection for databases, while Article 9 provides for a *sui generis* right of protection.[191] Article 7 notes that the object of "protection" is to protect database developers who have made "qualitatively and/or quantitatively a substantial investment in either the obtaining, verification or presentation of the contents to prevent extraction."[192] Under EU's dual system for protecting databases, copyright law protects compilations meeting the requirements of fixation, and origination, for a 70–year term. The *sui generis* term of protection for databases, not satisfying the requirement for copyright protection, is "fifteen years from the first of January of the year following the date of completion."[193]

The purpose of the *sui generis* right is to protect the authors of databases from wholesale extraction, or appropriation of substantial portions of the database. This right covers substantial copying from databases, but not unsubstantial copying. The 1996 Directive requires member states to provide a *sui generis* right for the maker of a database which provides remedies for the "substantial investment in either obtaining, verification or presentation of the contents to prevent *extraction* and/or re-utilization of the whole, or a substantial part" of a database.[194] "Extraction" is a form of misappropriation of a database defined by the Directive as meaning "the permanent or temporary transfer of all or a substantial part of the content of a database."[195] The Database Directive recognizes an exception to the *sui generis* protection for data used in either teaching, or scientific research.[196] *Sui generis* database protection was prefigured by the Nordic countries "catalogue rule"; providing "short-term protection for catalogues, tables and similar fact-based compilations."[197]

The Database Directive requires the twenty-eight member states of the European Union to adopt legislation preventing "the extraction and/or reutilization of the whole or a substantial part, evaluated qualitatively and/or quantitatively, of the contents of [a] database."[198] The U.S. publishing industry has lobbied Congress to adopt similar *sui generis* legislation to protect U.S.-based databases. "In an attempt to get around the *Feist* opinion, database compilers in the United States attempted for many years to convince Congress to grant *sui generis* rights, but eventually gave up."[199] Academics

---

[189] John Cross, Amy Landers, Michael Mireles, & Peter Yu, Global Issues in Intellectual Property Law 108 (2010).

[190] Council Directive 96/9/EC of 11 March 1996 on the Legal Protection of Databases, Id. at art. 1.

[191] Sui generis statutes are narrow generally addressing a specific subject matter versus broader statutes such as The U.S. Copyright Act, the Patent Act, and the Lanham Act. The Semiconductor Chip Act, 17 U.S.C. § 901 is an example of a sui generis statute.

[192] Id. at art. 7.

[193] Id. at art. 10(1).

[194] Id.

[195] Id. at art. 7(2)(B).

[196] Id. at art. 9.

[197] John Cross, Amy Landers, Michael Mireles, & Peter Yu, Global Issues in Intellectual Property Law 116 (2010).

[198] Council Directive 96/9/EC of 11 March 1996 on the Legal Protection of Databases.

[199] WILLIAM PATRY, HOW TO FIX COPYRIGHT 72 (2012).

have criticized *sui generis* statutory protection for databases on both constitutional, and public policy grounds.[200]

§ 10.7 LIMITATIONS ON EXCLUSIVE RIGHTS

(A) First Sale Doctrine

Chapter Four introduced the First Sale doctrine, which is a copyright law doctrine broadly applicable to the distribution of software.[201] Section 109 of the U.S. Copyright Act permits the owner of a particular copy, or phonorecord, lawfully made under the copyright law to sell, or otherwise dispose of possession of that copy or phonorecord without the authority of the copyright owner.[202] Under the "first sale" doctrine, once the copyright holder has sold a copy of the copyrighted work, the owner of the copy could "sell or otherwise dispose of the possession of that copy" without the copyright holder's consent.[203] Because of this, the owners of software sell licenses to sidestep the first sale doctrine.[204] If a software vendor sold software rather than licensed it, the purchaser of a copy of the software could copy the software and distribute it with impunity.[205]

To prevail under the first sale doctrine as a defense to copyright infringement, a defendant must establish that title to the copy passed through a first sale by the copyright holder to a purchaser.[206] In *UMG Recordings, Inc. v. Augusto,*[207] the federal court held that the boilerplate language used on a promotional CD did not create a license, and therefore the resale of these already-distributed copies was protected by the first sale doctrine. Courts determine whether there has been a sale or licensing using an economic realities test, as opposed to the labels parties to the sale use. Calling an agreement a license does not make it so.[208]

In *Microsoft Corp. v. Harmony Computers & Electronic, Inc.,*[209] Microsoft sought declaratory relief, injunctive relief, and treble damages because Harmony Computers sold Microsoft's Windows without a license. Microsoft contended that Harmony

---

[200] See e.g., Yochai Benkler, Constitutional Bounds of Database Protection: The Role of Judicial Review in the Creation and Definition of Private Rights in Information, 15 BERKELEY TECH. L.J. 535 (2000) & Malla Pollack, The Right to Know?: Delimiting Database Protection at the Juncture of the Commerce Clause, the Intellectual Property Clause, and the First Amendment, 17 CARDOZO ARTS & ENT. L. J. 47 (1999).

[201] Conceptually, the [first sale] doctrine springs from the common law right to control the disposition of chattels in one's lawful possession." JULIE E. COHEN ET AL., COPYRIGHT IN A GLOBAL INFORMATION ECONOMY 369 (2d ed. 2006).

[202] 17 U.S.C. § 109 (2008).

[203] Bobbs–Merrill Co. v. Straus, 210 U.S. 339, 350 (1908).

[204] Software publishers rarely sell software, but rather license it to avoid the first sale doctrine. See Adobe Systems Inc. v. One Stop Micro, Inc., 84 F. Supp. 2d 1086, 1091 (N.D. Cal. 2000) ("[V]irtually all end users do not buy—but receive a license for—software. The industry uses terms such as "purchase," "sell," "buy," . . . because they are convenient and familiar, but the industry is aware that all software . . . is distributed under license."); S.O.S., Inc. v. Payday, Inc., 886 F.2d 1081, 1088–89 & n.9 (9th Cir. 1989) (software license provided that series of programs "is the property of S.O.S." therefore, licensee "would be entitled to possess a copy of the software to enable it to exercise its limited right of use, but would not own that copy").

[205] 17 U.S.C. § 109(a).

[206] Id.

[207] 558 F. Supp.2d 1055 (C.D. Cal 2009).

[208] Microsoft Corp. v. DAK Industries, 66 F.3d 1091, 1095 (9th Cir. 1995) (discussing the economic realities test).

[209] 846 F. Supp. 208 (E.D. N.Y. 1994).

exceeded the scope of its license agreement, thus constituting copyright infringement. Harmony Computers bought Microsoft software bundled with personal computers. Harmony contended it had the power to resell Microsoft software under the first sale doctrine of the U.S. Copyright Act. However, the court found Microsoft Products were not subject to the first sale doctrine of the U.S. Copyright Act because they were licensed not sold. Microsoft's chain of distribution gives users or possessors of Microsoft Products a bare license to use rather than ownership of the software. The court found Harmony Computers infringed Microsoft's copyrighted software when it exceeded the scope of the license agreement.

(B) Public Domain Information

Copyright law does not encompass public domain information. The Fifth Circuit held that a code writing organization could not prevent a website operator from posting the text of a city's model building code. The court concluded that the model building code was in the public domain and not protected by copyright, notwithstanding a software licensing agreement and a copyright notice prohibiting copying and distribution. The federal appeals court held that when the operator copied only "the law" which he obtained from the organization's publication, and when he reprinted only "the law" of those municipalities, he did not infringe the organization's copyrights in its model building codes. The court reasoned the operator was posting laws on his website with precisely the form adopted by the municipalities.[210]

(C) Defense of Fair Use

"Fair use" is a statutory exception to the copyright owner's exclusive right "to reproduce the copyrighted work in copies."[211] A defendant has the burden of proof and production in demonstrating its copying is shielded by copyright law's doctrine of fair use. The fair use doctrine evolved from a common law doctrine and is now codified as Section 107 of the U.S. Copyright Act. The U.S. Copyright Act's four statutory factors determine whether a given copyrighted work constitutes fair use. These factors are:

> (1) The purpose and character of the use including whether such use is of a commercial nature or is for nonprofit educational purposes; (2) the nature of the copyrighted work; (3) the amount and substantiality of the portion used in relation to the copyrighted work as a whole; and (4) the effect of the use upon the potential market for or value of the copyrighted work.[212]

Perfect 10, an adult entertainment site, sued Google for direct and indirect copyright infringement because the search engine failed to monitor access to copyrighted photographs of nude models.[213] The *Perfect 10* court held Google's use of thumbnails of copyrighted images owned by the adult entertainment company qualified as a transformative use. Google's software does not recognize and index the images, but provides search results with greatly reduced lower resolution images called thumbnails. Google's use of the copyrighted images was to help a user find content; something which was a radically different purpose than the original copyright owner's

---

[210] Veeck v. Southern Bldg. Code Cong. Int'l Inc., 293 F.3d 791 (5th Cir. 2002).

[211] 17 U.S.C. § 106(1).

[212] 17 U.S.C. § 107.

[213] Perfect 10, Inc. v. Amazon.com, Inc., 487 F.3d 701, 719 (9th Cir. 2007).

use. It is unclear how fair use applies to social media sites such as Pinterest, where users routinely post copyrighted images and content. To date, no court has addressed how fair use applies to Twitter and hundreds of other social networking sites.

(D) Reverse Engineering

The U.S. Supreme Court defined reverse engineering broadly, as "starting with the known product and working backwards to divine the process which aided in its development or manufacture."[214] Software reverse engineering is a social good because it enables programmers to develop software that is interoperable with established platforms—such as the Microsoft Office products. With software licensing, the licensor grants the licensee the right to use software for a term, but there is seldom any physical asset to return. The license grant is the most important term of a license agreement because it determines the scope of rights transferred to the licensee. The licensor never passes title or assigns intellectual property rights under a software license. In fact, software licensors will often include an anti-reverse engineering clause stating that the licensee may not "unlock," reverse engineer, decompile, disassemble, or otherwise translate the object-code versions of the software included.

Microsoft's standard software agreement for Windows states: "Limitations on reverse engineering, decompilation, and disassembly: You may not reverse engineer, decompile, or disassemble the Software, except and only to the extent that such activity is permitted by applicable law notwithstanding this limitation."[215] Nevertheless, a customer may reverse engineer software to extract non-copyrightable elements in the software. Reverse engineering is taking apart the underlying code of software. The Fifth Circuit in *Vault Corp. v. Quaid Software, Ltd.*,[216] affirmed a district court's finding that a shrinkwrap license was an unenforceable contract of adhesion and the U.S. Copyright Act of 1976 preempted the Louisiana Software License Enforcement Act. The Fifth Circuit held that the U.S. Copyright Act preempted the Louisiana Software License Enforcement Act's provisions prohibiting decompilation or disassembly of computer programs. The court specifically ruled that clauses based upon this act were unenforceable and preempted.

Reverse engineering, as a fair use, is firmly established in U.S. law. In *Bowers v. Baystate Tech, Inc.*, the First Circuit held, "private parties are free to contractually forego the limited ability to reverse engineer a software product under the exemptions of the U.S. Copyright Act."[217] The Federal Circuit held, in a 2–1 decision, that the U.S. Copyright Act does not preempt a so-called "shrinkwrap" license prohibiting reverse engineering of computer software.[218] The appeals court also stated that the court recognized the contractual waiver of affirmative defenses and statutory rights,

---

[214] Kewanee Oil Co. v. Bicron Corp., 416 U.S. 470, 476 (1974).

[215] Microsoft HTML End User License Agreement, http://msdn.microsoft.com/en-us/http://www.netlitigation.com/library/windows/http://msdn.microsoft.com/en-us/library/windows/desktop/ms669979%28v=vs.85%29.aspx (April 14, 2012).

[216] 847 F.2d 255 (5th Cir. 1988).

[217] See Bowers v. Baystate Techs., Inc., 320 F.3d 1317, 1325 (Fed. Cir. 2003) (reverse engineering is a fair use under 17 U.S.C. § 107).

[218] Id. at 1323–26.

therefore, the defendants could contractually waive their fair use right to reverse engineer.[219]

(E) Transformative Use

The first factor in a fair use inquiry is determining the "purpose and character of the use."[220] Courts determine whether the new work "supersedes" the original work, or is transformative in the sense that it "adds something new, with a *further purpose* or different character."[221] Transformative use is a fundamental change in a plaintiff's copyrighted work, or use of the copyrighted work in a radically different context; the plaintiff's copyrighted work is "transformed" into a new creation.[222] However, in *Campbell v. Acuff–Rose Music, Inc.*,[223] the Court reasoned: "If we allow any weak transformation to qualify as parody we weaken the protection of copyright."[224] "The more transformative the new work, the less important the other factors, including commercialism, become."[225]

(F) Independent Creation

Proof of access and substantial similarity raises a presumption of copying: a claim, which a defendant may rebut with evidence of independent creation.[226] The issue is whether the disputed material is a copy, or an independent creation. Whether the evidence of independent creation is sufficient to rebut the *prima facie* case of copyright infringement is a question for the fact finder, whatever the contours of the burden of establishing the defense. If a content creator created material without access to copyrighted material, it can defend successfully against a claim of copyright infringement. Copyright owners must prove that an infringer had access to their copyrighted materials to sustain an infringement action. The defendant in an infringement case may interpose the affirmative defense that she independently created a work of authorship. However, subconscious copying is no defense to infringement.

§ 10.8 DIGITAL MILLENNIUM COPYRIGHT ACT

(A) Overview of the DMCA

The Digital Millennium Copyright Act ("DMCA") was the first time that Congress revised copyright law to accommodate Internet technologies. The DMCA was enacted in 1998 to implement two World Intellectual Property Organization ("WIPO") treaties: the WIPO Copyright Treaty ("WCT"), and the WIPO Performances and Phonograms Treaty ("WPPT").[227] The DMCA also addresses other significant copyright-related

---

[219] Sony Computer Entm't, Inc. v. Connectix Corp., 203 F.3d 596, 602 (9th Cir. 2000) (reverse engineering was fair use for the purpose of gaining access to the unprotected elements of software).

[220] 17 U.S.C. § 107 (2002).

[221] Harper & Row, Publishers, Inc. v. Nation Enterprises, 471 U.S. 539, 562 (1985).

[222] Campbell v. Acuff–Rose Music, Inc., 510 U.S. 569, 579 (1994).

[223] 510 U.S. at 599.

[224] Id.

[225] Id. at 579.

[226] Taylor Corp. v. Four Seasons Greetings, LLC, 403 F.3d 958, 967 (8th Cir. 2005).

[227] The Stockholm Agreement of July 14, 1967, created WIPO as a world organization for copyrights and for revision of related treaties.

issues and is part of the frequently amended U.S. Copyright Act. Title I, the "WIPO Copyright and Performances and Phonograms Treaties Implementation Act of 1998," implements the WIPO Copyright and Performances and Phonographs Treaty Implementation Act by criminalizing the circumvention or removal of Digital Rights Management ("DRM")—digital locks on copyrighted materials—and by prohibiting trafficking in tools that are primarily designed, valued or marketed for such circumvention. Title II, the "Online Copyright Infringement Liability Limitation Act" ("OCILLA") creates four "safe harbors" that enable qualifying service providers to limit their liability for claims of copyright infringement when engaging in certain types of activities.[228] A federal court described OCILLA's statutory purpose:

> Title II of the DMCA (the Online Copyright Infringement Liability Limitation Act) was enacted because service providers perform a useful function, but the great volume of works placed by outsiders on their platforms, of whose contents the service providers were generally unaware, might well contain copyright-infringing material which the service provider would mechanically "publish," thus ignorantly incurring liability under the copyright law. The problem is clearly illustrated on the record in this case, which establishes that " site traffic on YouTube had soared to more than 1 billion daily video views, with more than 24 hours of new video uploaded to the site every minute," and the natural consequence that no service provider could possibly be aware of the contents of each such video. To encourage qualified service providers, Congress in the DMCA established a 'safe harbor' protecting the service provider from monetary, injunctive or other equitable relief for infringement of copyright in the course of service such as YouTube's. The Act places the burden of notifying such service providers of infringements upon the copyright owner or his agent. It requires such notifications of claimed infringements to be in writing and with specified contents and directs that deficient notifications shall not be considered in determining whether a service provider has actual or constructive knowledge.[229]

Titles III, IV, and V contain miscellaneous provisions addressing other copyright issues. The Internet has created an entirely new set of copyright rules for intermediaries such as service providers. The DMCA adapted copyright law to the Internet and followed Judge Easterbrook's advice by developing new property rights where there were none. The DMCA prohibits any person from circumventing a technological measure that controls access to a work protected under Title 17 Copyrights.[230] To circumvent a technological measure" means "to descramble a scrambled work, to decrypt an encrypted work, or otherwise to avoid, bypass, remove, deactivate, or impair a technological measure, without the authority of the copyright owner . . ."[231] Under the DMCA "a technological measure "effectively controls access to a work" if the measure, in the ordinary course of its operation, requires the application of information, or a process or a treatment, with the authority of the copyright owner, to gain access to the work."[232]

---

[228] 17 U.S.C. 512(c).

[229] Viacom Intern. Inc. v. YouTube, Inc., 2013 WL 1689071 *2 (S.D. N.Y. April 18, 2013).

[230] 17 U.S.C. § 1201(a)(1)(A).

[231] 17 U.S.C. § 1201(a)(3).

[232] 17 U.S.C. § 1201(a)(3)(B).

The anti-circumvention provisions of the DMCA prohibit circumvention of "technological protection measures" that "effectively control access" to copyrighted works.[233] The DMCA provides that a party may use a technological protection measure ("TPM") to prevent unauthorized access to and copying of copyrighted software. The DMCA provided a "safe harbor" for Internet Service Providers (ISPs) for intermediate and temporary storage of digital copies and other housekeeping tasks during Internet transmissions of copyrighted data.

(B) Title I's Provisions

Title I of the DMCA added Chapter 12, entitled "Copyright Protection and Management Systems," to the U.S. Copyright Act. The DMCA distinguishes between circumvention and trafficking. Trafficking in qualified technology that circumvents technological measures that controls either *access* to a copyrighted work, or protects the author's *rights*, are both prohibited, while the actual act of circumvention is only prohibited when it circumvents a technological measure that controls *access*; not protecting the author's rights. The WCT requires signatory powers to provide remedies against defendants circumventing digital rights management ("DRM") tools or tampering with copyright management information. DRM tools restrict the use and copying of digital information such as music or movies. Congress had the statutory purpose of facilitating "the robust development and world-wide expansion of electronic commerce, communications, research, development, and education in the digital age."[234]

(1) Anti–Circumvention Provisions

The DMCA makes it a crime to "circumvent a technological protection measure that effectively controls access" to copyrighted works.[235] "A technological measure "effectively controls access to a work" if the measure, in the ordinary course of its operation, requires the application of information, or a process, or a treatment, with the authority of the copyright owner, to gain access to the work."[236] "To "circumvent a technological measure" means to descramble a scrambled work, to decrypt an encrypted work, or otherwise to avoid, bypass, remove, deactivate, or impair a technological measure, without the authority of the copyright owner."[237] Decryption, by means of computer software of encrypted movies on digital versatile disks (DVDs), constitutes "circumvention" for purposes of this provision.[238]

The encoding schemes used by DVD producers are technological measures because they control access to works protecting the rights of copyright owners. Apple's FairPlay and Microsoft Windows Digital Rights Managers, for example, provide controls on the

---

[233] See 17 U.S.C. § 1201(a)(2)(A)–(C) (highlighting conduct which DMCA's anti-circumvention provisions seek to prevent). The anti-circumvention provision of the Digital Millennium Copyright Act states: "No person shall circumvent a technological measure that effectively controls access to a work protected under this title. id. [T]o 'circumvent a technological measure' means to descramble a scrambled work, to decrypt an encrypted work, or otherwise to avoid, bypass, remove, deactivate, or impair a technological measure, without the authority of the copyright owner." Id. § 1201(a)(3)(A).

[234] S. Rep. No. 105–190, at 1–2 (1998).

[235] 17 U.S.C. § 1201(a)(1)(A).

[236] 17 U.S.C. § 1201(a)(3)(B).

[237] 17 U.S.C. § 1201(a)(3)(A).

[238] 17 U.S.C. § 1201(a)(2).

viewing or playing of copyright materials. The latest DRM systems use forensics watermarking to augment traditional controls. Software "that circumvents "digital walls" in violation of the DMCA . . . is like a skeleton key that can open a locked door, a combination that can open a safe, or a device that can neutralize the security device attached to a store's products" or "a digital crowbar."[239] The DMCA's anti-circumvention prohibitions criminalize picking digital locks protecting access to copyrighted materials.

(2) Anti–Trafficking Provisions

The DMCA's anti-trafficking provisions cover those who traffic in, or manufacture, import, offer to the public, or provide, any technology, product, service, device, component, or part thereof, that can circumvent "a technological measure" controlling *access* to a copyrighted work.[240] The DMCA protects the *rights* of an author—such as copying, distribution, or any of the other exclusive rights embodied in Section 106 of the U.S. Copyright Act.[241] A "Prohibited Device" is one that (1) is primarily designed for circumvention; (2) has limited uses for legitimate commercial purposes (other than circumvention); or (3) is marketed for use in circumventing copyright protection.[242] Congress provides for a penalty of up to five years imprisonment for a defendant's first offense in manufacturing, importing, offering to the public, or trafficking in such a device, technology, product, or service.

(C) Title II's Safe Harbors

The Online Copyright Infringement Liability Limitation Act ("OCILLA") created limitations on liability for network service providers who fulfill specific safe-harbor exemptions. OCILLA developed a mechanism of takedown notices for infringing content on websites. In response, the service provider must remove the infringing material from the provider's website. Upon receipt of the counter-notice, the service provider must replace the subscriber's material on the website. The OCILLA seeks to limit the liability of ISPs for copyright infringement by their subscribers. The notice, takedown, put back, and immunity sections of the DMCA are prime examples of how the Internet has reshaped copyright law.

Title II of the DMCA, OCILLA, protects online service providers ("OSPs") who meet certain safe harbor requirements from liability for all monetary relief for direct, vicarious, and contributory infringement.[243] To qualify for protection under any of the DMCA § 512 safe harbors, a party must meet a set of threshold criteria. First, the party must in fact be a service provider, defined, in part, as an OSP, network access administrator, or the operator of facilities.[244] A party that qualifies as an OSP must also satisfy certain conditions of eligibility; including adopting, reasonably implementing, and informing subscribers of a policy that provides for the termination of accounts of recidivist copyright infringers.[245]

---

[239] Universal City Studios v. Corley, 273 F.3d 429, 453 n. 27 (2d Cir. 2001).

[240] 17 U.S.C. § 1201(a)(2).

[241] 17 U.S.C. § 1201(b)(1).

[242] 17 U.S.C. § 1201(a)(2).

[243] Hendrickson v. eBay, Inc., 165 F. Supp. 2d 1082 (C.D. Cal. 2001).

[244] 17 U.S.C. § 512(k)(1)(B).

[245] 17 U.S.C. § 512(i)(1)(A).

Under 17 U.S.C. § 512(c)(1)(A), "a service provider can receive safe harbor protection only if it (i) does not have actual knowledge that the material or an activity using the material on the system or network is infringing; (ii) in the absence of such actual knowledge, is not aware of facts or circumstances from which infringing activity is apparent; or (iii) upon obtaining such knowledge or awareness, acts expeditiously to remove, or disable access to, the material."[246] A service provider is eligible for the § 512(c) safe harbor only if it "does not receive a financial benefit directly attributable to the infringing activity, in a case in which the service provider has the right and ability to control such activity."[247] *when Safe harbor applies*

"Congress imported the 'red flag' test of § 512(c)(1)(A)(ii) which divests service providers of their immunity if they fail "to take action with regard to infringing material when it is 'aware of facts or circumstances from which infringing activity is apparent.'"[248] Service providers can lose the protection of the DMCA safe harbors if they have actual or apparent (also called "red flag") knowledge of infringing content.[249] It is unclear what red flags would constitute an OSP's actual notice, assuming that they received no notice from the copyright owner.[250] The unsettled issue is whether "red flags" of knowing copyright infringement should make social media and other websites liable for secondary infringement.[251] The Second Circuit in *Viacom International Inc. v. YouTube Inc.*[252] concluded that a service provider's specific knowledge of infringing material, even absent a takedown notice, may possibly demonstrate red flag knowledge only as to those specific infringing materials. In *UMG Recordings, Inc. v. Veoh Networks, Inc.*,[253] the Ninth Circuit upheld a website's safe harbor for secondary copyright infringement from Veoh, which was a video-sharing site. The court reaffirmed that the "red flag test" applied that the burden remains with the copyright holder rather than the service provider. Under this test, the video-sharing website's "general knowledge that it hosted copyrightable material and that its services could be used for infringement was insufficient to constitute a red flag."[254] Nevertheless, a "service provider cannot willfully bury its head in the sand to avoid obtaining such specific knowledge."[255]

Even viewing the evidence in the light most favorable to UMG as we must here, however, we agree with the district court that there is no evidence that Veoh acted in

---

[246] UMG Recordings, Inc. v. Veoh Networks, Inc., 106 U.S.P.Q.2D (BNA) 1253 (9th Cir. 2013).

[247] 17 U.S.C. § 512(c)(1)(B).

[248] Perfect 10, Inc. v. CCBill LLC, 481 F.3d 751, 763 (9th Cir. 2007).

[249] 17 U.S.C. §§ 512(c)(1)(A) and (d)(1).

[250] See UMG Recordings, Inc. v. Veoh Networks, Inc., 665 F.Supp.2d 1099, 1108 (C.D.Cal.2009) ("[I]f investigation of facts and circumstances is required to identify material as infringing, then those facts and circumstances are not red flags.") (internal citations omitted); Perfect 10, Inc. v. CCBill LLC, 488 F.3d 1102, 1114 (9th Cir.2007) ("We do not place the burden of determining whether [materials] are actually illegal on a service provider.").

[251] Mark Fischer, The Next Great Copyright Act, DuaneMorris Copyright Blog, http://blogs.duanemorris.com/duanemorrisnewmedialawblog/entry/the_next_great_copyright_acthttp://blogs.duanemorris.com/duanemorrisnewmedialawblog/entry/the_next_great_copyright_act (last visited July 12, 2013).

[252] 676 F.3d 19 (2d Cir. 2012).

[253] UMG Recordings Inv. v. Veoh Networks, Id.

[254] Id.

[255] Id. (citing Viacom Int'l v. YouTube, Inc., 676 F.3d 19, 31 (2d Cir. 2012).

such a manner.[256] Rather, the evidence demonstrates that Veoh promptly removed infringing material when it became aware of specific instances of infringement. Although the parties agree, in retrospect, that at times there was infringing material available on Veoh's services, the DMCA recognizes that service providers who do not locate and remove infringing materials they do not specifically know of should not suffer the loss of safe harbor protection.[257] A DMCA notice of infringement is not the same thing as 'red flag' knowledge.[258]

To qualify for the DMCA safe harbor, service providers must also accommodate, and not interfere with, standard technical measures that are used by copyright owners to identify or protect copyrighted works, or they are divested of the safe harbors of § 512(a)–(d) Additionally, the OSP must remove or block access to the copyrighted material upon receiving notice of alleged infringement from the copyright owner or assignee.[259] The notice must give sufficient information to identify the various infringing or pirated items. The next section is a guide to the four OSP safe harbors, which vary significantly in their preconditions.

(1) Transitory Digital Network Communications

The DMCA immunizes service providers for all copyright infringement "by reason of the provider's transmitting, routing, or providing connections for, material through a system or network controlled or operated by or for the service provider, or by reason of the intermediate and transient storage of that material."[260] The definition of an OSP is narrower for transitory digital network communications than the other safe harbors in § 512(b)–(d) This safe harbor applies only to OSPs qualifying under OCILLA's narrow definition, which means those "entities that transmit, route, or provide connections for digital online communications, between or among points specified by user."[261] To qualify for the transitory digital network communications safe harbor, OSPs may not modify content transmitted, routed, or connected. Someone other than the OSP must initiate the transmission of the material.[262]

(2) System Caching

Caching is a desirable practice because it eliminates the delay of successive searches for the same material and thus decreases the demands on their Internet connection.[263] The DMCA immunizes service providers for caching and the other two safe harbors if they fall within the broad definition of "a provider of online services or

---

[256] Id.

[257] Id. at 42.

[258] UMG Recordings Inc. v. Shelter Capital Partners L.L.C., 106 U.S.P.Q.2d 1253 (9th Cir. 2013).

[259] 17 U.S.C. § 512(c).

[260] 17 U.S.C. § 512(a).

[261] See 17 U.S.C. § 512(k)(1)(A).

[262] 17 U.S.C. § 512(k)(1)(A) (providing as in Section 512(a) "the term 'service provider' means an entity offering the transmission, routing, or providing of connections for digital online communications, between or among points specified by a user, of material of the user's choosing, without modification to the content of the material as sent or received. By contrast, § 512(k)(1)(B) provides that, as used in this section, other than § 512(a). By contrast, § 512(k)(1)(B) provides that, as used in this section, other than § 512(a), the term "service provider" means a provider of online services or network access, or the operator of facilities therefor, and includes an entity described in § 512(k)(1)(A). "§ 512(k)(1)(A)." UMG Recordings, Inc. v. Veoh Networks, Inc., 106 U.S.P.Q.2D (BNA) 1253 (9th Cir. 2013).

[263] ACLU v. Reno, 929 F. Supp. 824, 848–39 (E.D. Pa. 1996).

network access" and those that operate such services.[264] OSPs routinely cache or replicate identifiable web pages to improve the speed of accessing information from a source server, and then store the cached copies of the stored web pages on a separate server called a "proxy server." Before the DMCA's system caching safe harbor, there was uncertainty as to the liability of OSPs for the desirable practice of caching, which is technically making a copy under the U.S. Copyright Act. OSPs also create "mirror caches", or identical websites, on different servers.

Think of caching and other safe harbors as the OSP serving as a pipeline for transmitting, routing, or storing information "without selection of the material by the service provider."[265] Service providers are protected by these "pipeline safe harbors" if they have neither a direct financial interest, nor the right to control content.[266] If the OSP is creating or modifying the content rather than serving as a pipeline, it will not have the benefit of the safe harbors. A service provider may not select the recipients of the material except as an automatic response to the request of another person, nor may service providers keep copies or modify materials transmitted except for temporary storage. OSPs claiming the caching safe harbor must expeditiously respond to takedown notices and remove, or disable, objectionable content. Assuming these preconditions are satisfied, § 512(b) shields service providers from injunctive, or monetary remedies for caching copyrighted materials.

(3) Storage Exemption

This section examines how service providers can qualify for the storage exemption. This DMCA safe harbor protects a service provider from infringement liability "by reason of the storage at the direction of a user" of copyrighted material if the service provider meets certain conditions, including a lack of knowledge of the infringement. The storage exemption safe harbor provision of DMCA limits the liability of online service providers for copyright infringement that occurs, "by reason of the storage at the direction of a user of material" residing on a system or network, controlled, or operated by or for the service provider.[267] To qualify for this safe harbor, OSPs cannot have actual knowledge the material or activity is infringing or be aware infringing activities are apparent.

In addition, they must: (1) perform a qualified storage or search function for Internet users; (2) lack actual or imputed knowledge of the infringing activity; (3) receive no financial benefit directly from such activity in a case where the provider has the right and ability to control it; (4) act promptly to remove or disable access to the material when the designated agent is notified that it is infringing; (5) adopt, reasonably implement, and publicize a policy of terminating repeat infringers; and (6) accommodate and not interfere with standard technical measures used by copyright owners to identify or protect copyrighted works.[268]

Service providers can claim the storage exemption only if they satisfy certain qualifying preconditions, including having a registered agent for responding to

---

[264] 17 U.S.C. § 512(k)(1)(B).

[265] 17 U.S.C. § 512(a)(2) (2010).

[266] Ellison v. Robertson, Inc., 189 F. Supp. 2d 1051 (C.D. Cal. 2002) (holding AOL qualified for a DMCA safe harbor).

[267] 17 U.S.C. § 512(c)(1) (2010).

[268] Verizon Intern. Inc. v. YouTube Inc., 253 F.R.D. 256 (S.D. N.Y. 2008).

complaints, and adhering to the notice, takedown, and put back procedures discussed later. In *Obodai v. Media*,[269] A New York federal district court ruled that Demand Media Inc. was eligible for the user storage safe harbor under the Digital Millennium Copyright Act. The court found that Demand did not have either actual or imputed knowledge of third party infringement on its humorous website, Cracked.[270] The Second Circuit affirmed this finding that Demand was not liable for third party postings on its website.[271]

(4) OSP's Registered Agent

To qualify for the storage exemption safe harbor for information residing on systems or networks, the OSP must designate an agent to receive notice from copyright owners when there is a complaint of infringement. The OSP must also post the agent's name on its website and register the agent with the Library of Congress' Copyright Office and provide the following required information:

> (A) the name, address, phone number, and electronic mail address of the agent. (B) other contact information, which the Register of Copyrights may deem appropriate. The Register of Copyrights shall maintain a current directory of agents available to the public for inspection, including through the Internet, and may require payment of a fee by providers to cover the costs of maintaining the directory.[272]

OSPs are required to maintain a DMCA agent to receive takedown notices and respond expeditiously to takedown notices. Suffolk University Law School, for example, must appoint an agent designated to receive notification of a claimed copyright infringement under the DMCA. If the Law School did not maintain an agent, or fulfill the other requirements of § 512, they would be subject to secondary copyright liability arising out of third party postings, even when they are not the content creator. A service provider must act "expeditiously to remove, or disable access to, the material" when it (1) has actual knowledge; (2) is aware of facts or circumstances from which infringing activity is apparent; or (3) has received notification of claimed infringement meeting the requirements of § 512(c)(3).

(5) Takedown & Put–Back Rules

"If a computer system operator learns of specific infringing material available on his system and fails to purge such material from the system, the operator knows of and contributes to direct infringement. But absent any specific information which identifies infringing activity, a computer system operator cannot be liable for contributory infringement merely because the structure of the system allows for the exchange of copyrighted material."[273] The DMCA's notice, takedown, and put-back procedures are triggered when a copyright owner, or an assignee, gives written notice to the

---

[269] 2012 WL 2189740 (S.D.N.Y., June 13, 2012).

[270] Plaintiff asserts that a registered user with the screenname 'socialway' published 32 items on his Cracked profile, and that the plaintiff owns the copyrights for these items. The items have titles like 'How to Pick a Credit Card Now,' 'How to Bank With Good Institutions,' and 'How to Become Awful at Math,' and satirize traditional self-improvement advice." Id. at *1.

[271] Obodai v. Demand Media, No. 12–2450 (Second Circuit, May 29, 2013).

[272] 17 U.S.C. § 512(c)(2).

[273] UMG Recordings, Inc. v. Veoh Networks, Inc., 106 U.S.P.Q.2D (BNA) 1253 (9th Cir. 2013).

designated agent of the service provider under § 512(c)(3)(A). The DMCA takedown rules are inapplicable to trademark, patent infringement, or other non-copyright infringing postings. The copyright owner is able to find the contact information for the service provider's agent because, as mentioned above, that information is posted on the website of the U.S. Copyright Office.

The copyright owner must give the provider's designated agent a written takedown notice which includes: (1) a physical or electronic signature of a person authorized to act on behalf of the copyright owner of the right allegedly infringed; (2) identification of the copyrighted works allegedly infringing; (3) identification of the parts of the copyrighted work that are infringing and thus should be removed; (4) sufficient information to contact copyright owner or complaining party; (5) a statement by the complainant in the good faith belief that the material is infringing; and (6) a statement that the information in the notice is accurate.

The copyright owner's complaint must declare, under penalty of perjury, that he, or she, is authorized to represent the copyright holder, and that he, or she, has a good-faith belief the use is infringing; thus, a notification must do more than identify the infringing item. Section 512(f)(1)–(2) of the DMCA provides remedies if a person "knowingly materially misrepresents" information "(1) that material or activity is infringing, or (2) that material or activity was removed or disabled by mistake or misidentification."[274] Those persons who knowingly misrepresent the facts in take-down notices:

> [S]hall be liable for any damages, including costs and attorneys' fees, incurred by the alleged infringer, by any copyright owner or copyright owner's authorized licensee, or by a service provider, who is injured by such misrepresentation, as the result of the service provider relying upon such misrepresentation in removing or disabling access to the material or activity claimed to be infringing, or in replacing the removed material or ceasing to disable access to it.[275]

Once the OSP's designated agent receives a notice that substantially complies with the DMCA's requirements, it must expeditiously remove the identified material. However, the service provider's duty to remove, or block access to infringing materials is not triggered by mere constructive notice. Under the DMCA, copyright owners need not identify all infringing works when multiple copyrights are infringed. The DMCA requires only substantial compliance with the notification; as long as the copyright owner provides a representative list if there are multiple infringements.[276] Upon removal, the next step is for the service provider to give notice to the user or subscriber that posted the allegedly infringing copyright content that it has removed or disabled it. By July of 2013, the Recording Industry Association of America issued its twenty fifth million URL to Google to take down URLs tied to infringing materials.[277]

The DMCA provides that a user whose material has been removed or disabled may have a right to a put back of the disputed content. After the user who posted the objectionable material receives notice, he or she, has a statutory right to send a written

---

[274] 17 U.S.C. § 512(f)(1)–(2).

[275] 17 U.S.C. § 512(f)(2).

[276] ALS Scan v. RemarQ, 239 F.3d 619, 625 (4th Cir. 2001).

[277] David Murphy, RIAA Records 25th Million URL Takedown on Google, PC MAGAZINE (July 7, 2013), http://www.pcmag.com/article2/0,2817,2421429,00.asp?google_editors_picks=true.

counter-notification to the OSP's designated agent. The counter notice must minimally contain the subscriber's signature—physical or digital—identify the material removed, and give a statement that the user has a good-faith belief that the material was mistakenly removed or disabled.[278] After receiving a counter-notification, the agent then must promptly (1) provide the person who filed the original takedown notice with a copy of the counter notification, and (2) advise that it will replace the removed material or cease disabling access to it in ten business days.[279] Unless the person who provided the takedown notice—the copyright owner or their assignee—gives notice that he or she has filed a copyright infringement lawsuit or other judicial action, the OSP must replace or reactivate the removed material no sooner than 10, and no later than 14 business days.[280] The takedown procedures of the DMCA only apply to copyright materials because a website has no duty to takedown material that constitutes an ongoing tort or other wrongdoing.

(6) Information Location Tools

Section 512(d) is the OSP safe harbor used by search engines such as Google, or Yahoo! The OSP safe harbor limits an Internet Service Provider's liability for monetary relief, as well as injunctive relief, for secondary copyright infringement for activities such as "linking users to an online location containing infringing material or infringing activity, by using information location tools" such as "a directory, index, reference, pointer, or hypertext link."[281]

(D) DMCA Anti–Circumvention Rules

Congress faced an insurmountable policy decision in its anti-circumvention and trafficking provisions, which had the effect of constraining fair use as well as infringing uses. The DMCA that prohibits "offering to the public, providing, or otherwise trafficking in" any technology designed to circumvent a technological measure controlling access to a copyrighted work is implicated when one presents, holds out, or makes available a circumvention technology or device, knowing its nature, for the purpose of allowing others to acquire it.[282] The DMCA's anti-circumvention provision states: "[n]o person shall circumvent a technological measure that effectively controls access to a work protected under this title."[283] The DMCA defines circumvention as descrambling or decrypting encrypted works or bypassing, removing or avoiding technological measures protecting copyrighted works.[284] The DMCA prohibits trafficking in tools primarily designed for circumvention.[285]

In *Craigslist, Inc. v. Naturemarket, Inc.*,[286] the federal magistrate explained the plaintiff's burden in 17 U.S.C. § 1201(a)(2) cases as proof of: (1) ownership of a valid copyright on a work, (2) effectively controlled by a technological measure, which has

---

[278] 17 U.S.C. § 512(g)(3)(C).

[279] 17 U.S.C. § 512(g)(2)(B).

[280] 17 U.S.C. § 512(g)(2)(C).

[281] 17 U.S.C. § 512(d).

[282] 17 U.S.C. § 1201(a)(2).

[283] Id. § 1201(a)(1)(A).

[284] See § 1201(a)(3)(A) (defining circumvention).

[285] See § 1201(b)(1) (defining action constituting an additional violation).

[286] 694 F. Supp. 2d 1039 (N.D. Cal. 2010). 694 F. Supp. 2d 1039 (N.D. Cal. 2010).

been circumvented, (3) that third parties can now access (4) without authorization, in a manner that (5) infringes or facilitates infringing a right protected by the U.S. Copyright Act, because of a product that (6) the defendant either (i) designed or produced primarily for circumvention; (ii) made available despite only limited commercial significance other than circumvention; or (iii) marketed for use in circumvention of the controlling technological measure.[287] Congress's intent in enacting the DMCA's circumvention rules was to preserve the traditional defenses to copyright infringement, such as fair use. In addition, the DMCA was not intended to enlarge or diminish vicarious or contributory liability for copyright infringement.

However, the courts have determined the proper balance between the DMCA's copyright protection measures and fair use. In *Universal City Studios, Inc. v. Reimerdes*,[288] several motion picture studios brought action under the DMCA to enjoin Internet website owners from posting, or downloading, computer software decrypting digitally encrypted movies on digital versatile disks ("DVDs"), and from including hyperlinks to other websites making decryption software available. The federal court ruled the Internet posting of decryption software violated DMCA provisions prohibiting trafficking in technology circumventing measures controlling access to copyrighted works.

The *Reimerdes* court also ruled that posting hyperlinks to other websites offering decryption software violated DMCA. The court rejected the defendant's First Amendment challenge finding the DMCA's anti-trafficking provision to be content-neutral as applied to a decryption computer program. The court ruled that the DMCA's anti-trafficking provision was not overly broad, and that the plaintiffs were entitled to an injunction enjoining the defendants from posting decryption software, or hyperlinking to other websites making such software available. The Second Circuit upheld the *Reimerdes* decision in *Universal City Studios, Inc. v. Corley*.[289]

The Second Circuit held the decryption software qualified as "speech" for First Amendment purposes because the computer code combined non-speech and speech elements. The *Corley* court found the DMCA anti-circumvention regulation to have an incidental effect on a speech component and found the government's interest in preventing unauthorized access to encrypted copyrighted material to be substantial as the governmental interest was unrelated to the suppression of free expression. The federal appeals court upheld the injunction finding it to be a content neutral restriction on owners' speech. The court also found the injunction did not burden substantially more speech than necessary to further the government's interest. Finally, the injunction did not eliminate owners' "fair use" of copyrighted materials and was therefore constitutional.

(E) Exemptions & First Amendment Challenges

The DMCA exempts nonprofit libraries, archives, and educational institutions so long as these organizations make a good faith determination when acquiring a copy of a protected work. The Congressional ban on anti-circumvention devices was a response to both Hollywood and the music industry's goal of using protective technologies to

---

[287] Id. at 1055–56. Id. at 1055–56.
[288] 111 F. Supp. 2d 294 (S.D. N.Y. 2000).
[289] 273 F.3d 429 (2d Cir. 2001).

protect their products that could otherwise be easily copied and distributed widely on the Internet.

(1) Reverse Engineering

The DMCA recognizes the right to circumvent the technological measure for purposes of reverse engineering. The DMCA recognizes a reverse engineering exception to the ban on circumvention.[290] "The exception allows reverse engineering of computer programs if the reverse engineer lawfully obtains the program, seeks permission from the copyright owner, only uses the results of their efforts to create an interoperable computer program and does not publish the results. The resulting program must only interoperate with the reverse engineered software, however, and cannot interoperate with the technologically protected content (movie, book, video game, etc.) itself."[291] Section 1201(f) of the DMCA states that:

> [A] person who has lawfully obtained the right to use a copy of a computer program may circumvent a technological measure for the sole purpose of identifying and analyzing those elements of the program that are necessary to achieve interoperability of an independently created computer program with other programs, and that have not previously been readily available to the person engaging in the circumvention, to the extent any such acts of identification and analysis do not constitute infringement under this title.[292]

(2) DMCA & Fair Use

The Digital Millennium Copyright Act's anti-circumvention provisions prohibit circumvention of "technological protection measures" that "effectively control access" to copyrighted works.[293] In *Lenz v. Universal Music Corp.*,[294] a California district court ruled that a copyright owner had to consider the fair use doctrine in formulating good faith belief in connection with takedown notice under the DMCA. The court further concluded the "use of the material in the manner complained of is not authorized by the copyright owner, its agent, or the law."[295] A California court held Universal to be acting in bad faith by issuing a takedown notice for a 29–second video of her 18–month-old child dancing to Prince's song, Let's Go Crazy that had been uploaded to YouTube. YouTube removed the video and Lenz sent a counter-notification pursuant to 17 U.S.C. § 512(g) asserting that her family video constituted fair use of the song and thus did not infringe Universal's copyrights. Universal sent her a removal notice asserting Prince's wishes not to have his songs posted on YouTube. The court found Universal's failure to consider fair use as sufficient to state a misrepresentation claim

---

[290] 17 U.S.C. § 1201(f).

[291] Boalt Hall, Reverse Engineering, Chilling Effects.org, http://chillingeffects.org/reverse/ (last visited May 27, 2013).

[292] Id.

[293] 17 U.S.C. § 1201 17 U.S.C. § 1201(a)(2)(A)–(C) (highlighting conduct which DMCA's anti-circumvention provisions seek to prevent). The anti-circumvention provision of the Digital Millennium Copyright Act states: "No person shall circumvent a technological measure that effectively controls access to a work protected under this title. Id. [T]o 'circumvent a technological measure' means to descramble a scrambled work, to decrypt an encrypted work, or otherwise to avoid, bypass, remove, deactivate, or impair a technological measure, without the authority of the copyright owner." Id. § 1201(a)(3)(A).

[294] 2008 WL 3884333 (N.D. Cal. 2008).

[295] Lenz v. Universal Music Corp., 572 F. Supp. 2d 1150, 1154 (N.D. Cal. 2008) (stating that copyright owners must evaluate fair use before submitting a takedown notice).

pursuant to the DMCA.[296] The *Lenz* court also ruled the plaintiff alleged a cognizable injury in responding to a bad faith takedown notice. The court sent a deterrent message to copyright owners that mechanically filing DMCA takedown notices without taking fair use into account. In the *post-Lenz* period, copyright owners risk being penalized for filing takedown notices of material protected by fair use.

(F) Chilling Effects of the DMCA

Congressional failure to provide direction to copyright owners in considering fair use when they request takedowns is just one example of problems with implementing DMCA's takedown and put-back rules. An empirical study of almost 900 takedown notices revealed that many were questionable because they targeted materials protected by fair use. The authors concluded that the DMCA notice, takedown, and put-back procedures have a chilling effect on expression.[297] The DMCA's takedown policy presents the empirical reality that non-infringing material will be removed. A study of DMCA takedowns documented the removal of content protected by "fair use or other substantive defenses, very thin copyright or non-copyrightable subject matter."[298] In 2007, Michelle Malkin, a prominent conservative columnist, blogged about Hip–Hop performer Akon's misogynist lyrics. Universal Music Group ("UMG"), Akon's record company, sent YouTube a takedown notice even though Malkin's commentary constituted fair use.

YouTube restored Malkin's podcast after she filed a counter notice. The Electronic Freedom Foundation maintains a Hall of Shame publicizing the most egregious requests to take down protected material from copyright owners who assert material is infringing—even though it is protected by fair use. The Hall of Shame lists homemade "literal video" mashups of music videos, as well as a teenager singing the holiday classic, "Winter Wonderland," for her friends. The Hall of Shame recounts the case of Perez Hilton recording a video in which he called then—Miss California, Carrie Prejean, a "dumb bitch" in response to her public opposition to same-sex marriage. In response, The National Organization for Marriage ("NOM") incorporated a clip of his tirade into an advertisement called "No Offense," depicting same-sex marriage opponents as under attack. The advertisement also included a brief clip of the Miss USA pageant where Prejean made her statement opposing same-sex marriage.[299]

Lawyers for the Miss Universe Organization issued a DMCA takedown notice claiming that the NOM advertisement violated its copyright "by including a portion of the TV broadcast of the pageant."[300] YouTube restored the video after NOM sent them a *counter notice* contending that the short clip of the pageant was protected by fair use. Generally, a DMCA counter notice will assert the First Amendment, or claim fair use, under the U.S. Copyright Act as compelling reasons why content should be restored. Congressional failure to provide direction to copyright owners in considering fair use

---

[296] 17 U.S.C. § 512(c)(3)(A)(v).

[297] Jennifer M. Urban & Laura Quilter, Efficient Process or "Chilling Effects"? Takedown Notices Under Section 512 of the Digital Millennium Copyright Act, 22 Santa Clara Computer & High Tech. L.J. 621, 683 (2006).

[298] Id. at 666.

[299] Blogger and Pageant Operators Try to Block Advocacy Non-Profit Aid, Electronic Frontier Foundation, https://www.eff.org/takedowns/blogger-and-pageant-operators-try-https:// www. eff.org/ takedowns/blogger-and-pageant-operators-try-block-advocacy-non-profit-ad.

[300] Id.

when they request takedowns contributes to the problem of improvident takedown requests. The concern is that large media moguls and corporations will use takedown requests to chill or discourage free speech and expression for ordinary citizens who do not have knowledge of the fair use doctrine, or their rights to legal representation.

§ 10.9 CRIMINAL COPYRIGHT LAW

A person or entity commits criminal copyright infringement if the person or entity infringes a copyright: (A) for purposes of commercial advantage or private financial gain; (B) by the reproduction or distribution, including by electronic means, during any 180–day period, of 1 or more copies or phonorecords of one or more copyrighted works, which have a total retail value of more than $1,000; or (C) by the distribution of a work being prepared for commercial distribution, by making it available on a computer network accessible to members of the public, if such person knew or should have known that the work was intended for commercial distribution.[301]

§ 10.10 COPYRIGHT ISSUES IN THE CLOUDS

Cloud computing raises new concerns for copyright owners seeking to protect content from being illegally shared by mobile users. Cloud computing enables copyrighted works to be illegally transmitted and distributed as never before. Myxer.com, for example, is a cloud service allowing users to upload sound files and create ringtones, which they can then download and send to their phones. Cloud computing raises new copyright issues. In *Capitol Records Inc v. MP3tunes LLC*,[302] MP3tunes, a cloud music provider, ran a music locker service where users could upload their music library onto MP3tunes servers and access their music over the Internet. The *MP3tunes* court ruled that the music locker business did not infringe on copyright by observing that the cloud provider stored only one copy of a particular song, no matter how many users added it to their music library, as a space saving technique. The court held that the DMCA does not require vigilant copyright monitoring by a company having users that upload infringing content. A DMCA takedown notice for a song in the locker of one user does not require removal of that song from all users' accounts.

In *Disney Enterprises Inc. v. Hotfile Corp.*,[303] a cloud storage company offered "cyberlockers" to users to store their digital content. Users wishing to download content from the Cyberlockers paid Hotfile Corp. a fee for the service. Copyrighted content was then shared between users while Hotfile collected fees. The *Disney Enterprises* court ruled that this activity did not make Hotfile directly liable for copyright infringement solely because they provide the service, which others used to infringe copyright. The court would not predicate liability because Hotfile took no direct action to violate copyrights.

§ 10.11 COPYRIGHT ISSUES IN SOCIAL NETWORKS

Increasingly, the intersection between contract law and copyright law is the nexus for Internet disputes. Fan fiction on social media sites raises new issues as to who

---

[301] 17 U.S.C. § 506(a)(1).

[302] No. 1:07–CV–09931–WHP–FM (S.D.N.Y. 2011).

[303] No. 11–20427–CIV–(S.D. Fla. July 8, 2011).

owns derivative works. "For example, if fans contribute in the "cloud" to a collaborative novel, the work could be jointly owned by all of the contributors, if that's what the terms of service say. There are many possible variations, for example the website terms of service might provide that the website—and not the authors—own the copyright."[304] Social media sites, such as Pinterest and YouTube, address user-generated content in their terms of use.[305] YouTube, for example, states in its terms of use, that users submitting content grant a non-exclusive, worldwide, royalty free license to the social media site.[306] LinkedIn's terms of use requires users to grant to LinkedIn a non-exclusive, non-transferable license to user-generated content:

> You own the information you provide LinkedIn under this Agreement, and may request its deletion at any time, unless you have shared information or content with others and they have not deleted it, or it was copied or stored by other users. Additionally, you grant LinkedIn a nonexclusive, irrevocable, worldwide, perpetual, unlimited, assignable, sublicenseable, fully paid up and royalty-free right to us to copy, prepare derivative works of, improve, distribute, publish, remove, retain, add, process, analyze, use and commercialize, in any way now known or in the future discovered, any information you provide, directly or indirectly to LinkedIn, including, but not limited to, any user generated content, ideas, concepts, techniques and/or data to the services, you submit to LinkedIn, without any further consent, notice and/or compensation to you or to any third parties. Any information you submit to us is at your own risk of loss. By providing information to us, you represent and warrant that you are entitled to submit the information and that the information is accurate, not confidential, and not in violation of any contractual restrictions or other third party rights.[307]

Twitter is a real-life communications platform that enables users to communicate with short messages.[308] Creators of these frequent, short messages, or "tweets," post them to their profiles, blogs or send them to followers.[309] Courts have yet to address whether "tweets" are copyrightable, but downloaded photographs on this service are protectable. In *Agence Fr. Presse v. Morel,*[310] FP sought a declaratory judgment that it did not infringe Daniel Morel's exclusive rights in his copyrighted photographs of the earthquake in Haiti.[311] Daniel Morel, the copyright owner of these photographs, counterclaimed that AFP violated the Copyright Act of 1976, the DMCA, and the Lanham Act.[312] In the aftermath of the devastating earthquake, Morel was able to access the Internet and open an account on Twitter that has a Twitpic feature enabling

---

[304] Mark Fischer, Fifty Shades of Grey and Fan Fiction: Do You Own Your User–Generated Content, DUANE MORRIS COPYRIGHT BLOG (March 12, 2013).

[305] Id.

[306] Id.

[307] LinkedIn, Terms of Service, http://www.linkedin.com/static?key=user_agreement (last visited July 12, 2013).

[308] See Twitter Help Center, Getting to Know Twitter, What Is It?, Twitter, Oct. 6, 2011, archived at http://www.webcitation.org/62ErvH9TN (describing Twitter's networking platform).

[309] Id. (stating that tweets are limited to 140 characters and are updated on a profile page or blog).

[310] 769 F. Supp. 2d 295 (S.D. N.Y. 2011).

[311] Id. at 298.

[312] Id. (noting Morel's counterclaims against third parties Getty Images, CBS Broadcasting, ABC, and Turner Broadcasting).

users to upload pictures and share them with Internet users.[313] Twitter and Twitpic are separately incorporated and have different terms of service agreement. "Twitpic's terms of service provide[s], '[b]y uploading your photos to Twitpic, you give Twitpic permission to use or distribute your photos on Twitpic.com or affiliated sites.'" [314]

Twitpic's terms of service also acknowledged: "'[a]ll images uploaded are copyright (c) their respective owners.'"[315] Morel uploaded the photographs from the earthquake in Haiti on Twitpic and tweeted on Twitter that he had "'exclusive earthquake photos,' and linked his Twitter page to his Twitpic page."[316] He did not include a copyright notice, but his "Twitpic page included the attributions 'Morel'" and 'by photomorel' next to the images."[317] "A few minutes after Morel posted his photographs, "Lisandro Suero . . ., a resident of the Dominican Republic, copied the photographs, posted them on his Twitpic page, and tweeted that he had 'exclusive photographs of the catastrophe for credit and copyright.'"[318] "Suero is not a photographer and was not in Haiti during the earthquake . . . [and he] did not attribute the [earthquake] photographs to Morel [on his Twitpic page.]"[319]

AFP placed Morel's photograph on its online photo database called Image Forum, "and transmitted them to Getty, an image licensing company."[320] "Morel's photographs were labeled with the credit line 'AFP/Getty/Lisandro Suero,' designating AFP and Getty as licensing agents and Suero as photographer."[321] Getty, who has exclusive rights to license AFP's images in North America, licensed "Morel's photos to numerous third-party news agencies, including CBS and CNN" without the proper attribution.[322] Approximately eight hours after CNN uploaded these pictures and broadcast them, AFP learned that the photographs were improperly attributed to Suero rather than Morel.[323] Several hours later, AFP "issued a wire instruction to change the photographer credit from Suero to Morel."[324] "However, Getty continued to sell licenses to charities, relief organizations, and news outlets that variously credited AFP, Suero, or Morel as the photographer," and all images identified AFP/Getty as the source.[325] Morel is represented exclusively by Corbis, Inc., a photography-licensing agency that competes directly with Getty and serves as Morel's "worldwide licensing agent for

---

[313] Id. (mentioning that Morel worked as a photojournalist in Haiti for over twenty-five years, was present at the time of the January 2010 earthquake, and took photos that he later uploaded to Twitpic via his Twitter account).

[314] Id. at 298–99.

[315] See Morel, 769 F. Supp. 2d at 299 (establishing clear copyright ownership of photographs uploaded to Twitpic).

[316] See id. (referencing the manner in which Morel uploaded his photos to Twitpic, and commenting that he included clear marks of ownership).

[317] See id. (describing what identifications were placed on the images).

[318] See id. (illustrating that someone else was taking credit for Morel's images).

[319] Id.

[320] Id. (accounting for AFP's conduct in furtherance of the alleged infringement).

[321] Morel, 769 F. Supp.2d at 300.

[322] Id. at 299–300 (characterizing the incorrect licensing by Getty upon which the basis of this claim is founded).

[323] Id. at 300 (noting when AFP realized its improper attribution occurred and tried to contact Morel).

[324] Id. (detailing the corrective actions taken by AFP).

[325] Id. (observing that the mistaken attribution was perpetuated subsequent to AFP's discovery that Morel was the actual photographer).

images he submits to Corbis."[326] After AFP received notice of Corbis's contract with Morel, it "transmitted Morel's photographs to Corbis."[327]

In Morel's counterclaim to AFP's declaratory judgment action, he argued that "AFP and Getty failed to observe or enforce the credit change instruction or the 'kill,' continued to license, sell Morel's photographs, and 'derived a direct financial benefit' as a result."[328] He also contended that "AFP and Getty 'refused to exercise [their] ability to supervise' their customers or 'inform them of their infringing activities.'"[329] Morel argued that despite many requests to cease and desist, AFP continued to publish his photos, "many of which credit Suero as photographer."[330] The court ruled AFP and another defendant did not have a license to use Morel's photographs and were therefore infringers.[331] The court found that AFP was liable for infringement in disregarding Morel's rights by licensing his images of the Haitian earthquake to third parties without permission.[332] The federal court reasoned that while Twitter's terms of service granted Twitter and Twitpic a license to use and reproduce Morel's photographs, it did not confer such rights on other users.[333] The court refused to dismiss Morel's claim of contributory infringement because AFP licensed his images to third parties without permission.[334] The court dismissed Morel's claim of vicarious infringement because Morel did not demonstrate that AFP had a direct financial interest in their affiliate's exploitation of the images.[335] The *Morel* case signifies how the Internet is playing havoc with the principles of copyright law.[336]

In *Agence France Presse v. Morel*[337] the French news service sought a declaratory judgment that it had not infringed Morel's copyrights in the earthquake photographs. Morel counterclaimed against news service, international distributor of photographs, and newspaper company, contending that they willfully infringed his copyrights. The claim against the news service was predicated upon secondary copyright infringement and the DMCA. The court ruled that Agence France did not have license to use photographs in website's news feed under website's terms of service. The court ruled that there were issues of fact that precluded summary judgment on whether distributor was entitled to benefit of safe harbor under DMCA as well as contributory

---

[326] Id. (indicating that the licensing agency that represents Morel directly competes with Getty).

[327] See Morel, 769 F. Supp. 2d at 301 (indicating that the licensing agency that represents Morel directly competes with Getty).

[328] Id.

[329] Id. (mentioning the lack of supervision regarding infringement).

[330] Id. (illustrating the continued publication of incorrectly accredited photographs).

[331] Id. at 303 (concluding that AFP failed to establish it had properly licensed Morel's photographs).

[332] Id. at 304 (stating that AFP was liable for inducing infringement).

[333] See Morel, 769 F. Supp.2d at 303 (clarifying that the Twitter and Twitpic licensing agreement could not be construed to include a right of use and reproduction for third parties).

[334] Id. at 304 (noting that permission to use the photos could not be granted when AFP was unable to prove that a license existed in the first place).

[335] Id. (explaining the standard required for claiming vicarious infringement).

[336] See James Joyner, Twitter Law: Are Tweets Copyrighted?, OUTSIDE THE BELTWAY BLOG, March 30, 2009, archived at http://www.webcitation.org/62LFTmTpS (introducing the topic of whether tweets are copyrightable). Mark Cuban, owner of the Dallas Mavericks of the NBA, asks whether ESPN is violating copyright when it reprints or rebroadcasts tweets. See id. Cuban asks, "[i]s a tweet copyrighted by default when it[']s published? Can there possibly be a fair use exception for something that is only 140 characters or less?" Id.

[337] 2013 WL 146035 (S.D. N.Y. Jan. 14, 2013).

infringement. The court rejected Agency France's contention that it was a third party beneficiary to the Twitter TOS and derives a license from those terms of service.[338] The court found an issue of fact whether the distributor was a service provider under OCILLA.[339]

§ 10.12 INTERNATIONAL ISSUES

Internet companies need to determine whether they can protect their intellectual property rights in their software products before they do business in a foreign country. In general, copyright laws are not extraterritorial and each country administers and enforces intellectual property rights. Different countries connected to the Internet have different intellectual property regimes, despite international treaties attempting to harmonize IP laws. The United States is also a signatory to the Berne Convention for the Protection of Literary and Artistic Works. Article 2 of the Berne Convention protects artistic and literary works. Computer software, whether in source or object code, are classified as literary works. For example, a creator of a computer program from any country that is a signatory of the Berne Convention has the same rights in all other countries that are signatories to the Convention as they allow their own nationals. The Berne Convention signatories agree to protect works of authors who are nationals of one of the countries of the Convention, or in the country where the copyright owner publishes the work. Before the Berne Convention, copyright protection was purely national and an author had no rights outside the country where they registered their copyright. The Berne Convention and the Paris Convention signatories created International bureaus, which merged in 1893 to create the United International Bureaus for the Protection of Intellectual Property (BIRPI). In 1967, BIRPI became the World Intellectual Property Organization ("WIPO"), and in 1974, it became an organization within the United Nations. WIPO has 184 Member States and administers twenty-four international treaties, including two Internet-related copyright treaties signed in December 1996: the WIPO Copyright Treaty and the WIPO Performance and Phonograms Treaty. As a global provider of software, many Internet companies will enter into a distribution agreement with a European company to deliver its comprehensive computer security products to the twenty-eight countries of the European Union.

A U.S. company will give a distributor the exclusive right to distribute digital content in Europe, the Middle East, and Africa or it may directly license its global information technology solutions worldwide through its own distribution network. If a distributor licensed software in countries outside the boundaries of the agreed upon geographic area, it will be liable for breach of the distribution agreement as well as copyright infringement. International intellectual property protection is challenging especially because of different intellectual property regimes and different traditions of enforcement. Software licensors market products in a global marketplace and therefore must protect their own intellectual property rights, while avoid infringing the rights of others. Before launching a new software product globally, a software maker needs to conduct an audit to inventory the intellectual property assets and determine how to comply with U.S. copyright law as well as the copyright law of countries where they do business. The rest of this section examines some other global Internet copyright issues.

---

[338] Id. at *10.

[339] Id. at *16.

(A) Personalty Not Commodification

Takedown disputes will increasingly involve parties in different countries, which raise an issue of the extraterritoriality. The problem with copyright protection is that it does not necessarily transcend national borders. The Internet is cross-border by definition and copyright law continues to evolve in order to find the correct balance between the rights of copyright owners and users of social media and other Internet-related technologies. There are great differences between how the U.S. and European civil code countries approach copyright law that must be taken into account protecting rights and avoiding infringing the rights of others on the global Internet.[340] In the U.S., moral rights are undeveloped because U.S. copyright law "is work-centered, as compared to author- or producer-centered."[341]

Victor Hugo's descendants filed an action based on moral rights against a French journalist who wrote and published a sequel to Hugo's *Les Miserables*.[342] Likewise, the great-grandson of Victor Hugo also argued that Disney's cartoon film *The Hunchback of Notre Dame* violated the integrity of the author's work; a moral right not followed in U.S. copyright law, but recognized in the Berne Convention for the Protection of Literary and Artistic Works protecting the moral rights of authors (*droit moral*).[343] Article 6(b) of the Berne Convention provides that "the means of redress for safeguarding the [right of integrity] shall be governed by the legislation of the country where protection is claimed."[344] The right of integrity, for example, is "inalienable and perpetual" thereby protecting the artist against "any distortion or alteration of his or her creation once the completed work has been transferred or made the subject of publication performance."[345] Moral rights include the right of attribution, integrity, spirit, and personality. VARA exclusively grants authors of works that fall under the protection of the Act the following rights: (1) to claim authorship; (2) to prevent the use of one's name on any work the author did not create; (3) to prevent use of one's name on any work that has been distorted, mutilated, or modified in a way that would be prejudicial to the author's honor or reputation; and (4) to prevent distortion, mutilation, or modification that would prejudice the author's honor or reputation.

The United States enacted the Visual Artists Rights Act of 1990 ("VARA") to implement the Berne Convention. Regardless of assignment or ownership of rights, VARA protects the expectation that a visual work will not be revised, altered, or distorted. VARA has little application to the Internet since it only protects works of visual art that have attained the status of "recognized stature." "The Internet raises the potential for infringement of an author's *moral rights*. Issues raised specifically by

---

[340] Peter K. Yu, Moral Rights 2.0, in LANDMARK INTELLECTUAL PROPERTY CASES AND THEIR LEGACY, 13, 13-15 (CHRISOPHER HEATH & ANSELM KAMPERMAN SANDERS Ed. 2011) (describing differences the treatment of moral rights between the United States and Europe).

[341] JOHN CROSS, AMY LANDERS, MICHAEL MIRELES, & PETER YU, GLOBAL ISSUES IN INTELLECTUAL PROPERTY LAW 118 (2010).

[342] Stuart Jeffires, Hugo's Heirs Hate "Miserable" Sequel: Publisher Who Dared to Produce a Follow–Up to a Great Man's Classic Work Is Sued for £410,000, THE OBSERVER (London) (June 3, 2001) at 26.

[343] Id.

[344] Patrick W. Begos, The Berne Convention (1997) <http://www.molton.com/artlaw/berne.html>.

[345] Id.

the Internet include the circumstances"—where their creations are presented when a website links to another site.[346]

While moral rights have been applied primarily to works of art created in a tangible medium, they can apply to online modifications as well. "Two moral rights are of primary importance in respect of works placed on the Internet: the right of attribution and the right of integrity."[347] Moral rights may be infringed when "a digitized copy of the Work [is made] available for browsing on a server over the Internet" and the author is not identified; thereby violating the author's right of attribution.[348] The right to false attribution could be extended to computer programs or website creations. Similarly, manipulating an electronic or digitalized photograph could violate the right not to have an artist's work distorted, mutilated, or modified. Any "assignment of economic rights is not accompanied by assignment of moral rights . . . French rights, may provide a remedy where infringement relating to a digital work is disseminated over the Internet."[349]

In *Gilliam v. American Broadcasting Co.*,[350] the British creators of the television series, *Monty Python's Flying Circus*, argued that the rebroadcast series that shortened the programs and edited them greatly violated their moral rights.[351] The *Gilliam* court held that the Lanham Act protected the creators from the excessive mutilation or altered versions of their comedic television series.[352] The court defined the concept of *droit moral*, or moral right, as, "including the right of the artist to have his work attributed to him in the form in which he created it."[353] The Second Circuit stated that: "American Copyright Law, as presently written does not recognize moral rights or provide a cause of action for their violation, since the law seeks to vindicate the economic rather than the personal rights of authors."[354]

French authors, for example, have patrimonial or moral rights to works that they create not found in the United States.[355] An E–Business hiring a French designer needs to consider moral rights when drafting their website development contracts. A U.S. business needs to acquire moral rights or seek permission to alter materials on a website. Content license agreements, for example need to include terms covering moral right not recognized under U.S. copyright law. Similarly, U.S. copyright law centers on economic rights whereas Europeans stress "personality or moral rights."[356] Similarly, the EU's Database Protection Directive gives database developers *sui generis*

---

[346] MAREE SAINSBURY, MORAL RIGHTS AND THEIR APPLICATION IN AUSTRALIA 147 (2003).

[347] PETER N. GRABOSKY, RUSSELL G. SMITH, CRIME IN THE DIGITAL AGE: CONTROLLING TELECOMMUNICATIONS AND CYBERSPACE 116 (1998).

[348] SIMON STOKES, ART AND COPYRIGHT 95 (2001).

[349] CATHERINE COLSTON & JONATHAN GALLOWAY, MODERN INTELLECTUAL PROPERTY 450 (2010).

[350] 538 F.2d 14 (2d Cir. 1976).

[351] Id. at 25.

[352] Id. at 26.

[353] Id. at 24.

[354] Id. at 25–26.

[355] See e.g., Turner Entertainment Co. v. Huston, Court d' appel [CA] [regional court of appeal] Versailles, civ. Ch., ch., Dec. 19, 1994 (Fr.) (holding that Turner Entertainments violated film director's moral rights when it colorized a black and white cinematographic work entitled 'Asphalt Jungle').

[356] Id. at 118 (noting how author's rights are reflected in droit d'auteur in France, Urheberrecht in Germany, diritto d'autore in Italy," by way of example).

protection for nonoriginal, noncreative databases.[357] Doctrines such as transformative use, nominative use or fair use are less well developed in other legal systems that do not recognize the First Amendment. The rest of this section examines some other global Internet copyright issues.

(B) Copyright Protection for Dress Design

The U.S. does not extend copyright protection to dress design unlike France, which includes it within the scope of copyright protection. In *Sarl Louis Feraud Intern. v. Viewfinder, Inc.*[358] Feraud and Balmain, two French high-fashion designers filed a copyright infringement case against Viewfinder, who operated a website called "firstView.com." Viewfinder posted "photographs of fashion shows held by designers around the world, including photographs of plaintiffs' fashion shows."[359] "The firstView website contains both photographs of the current season's fashions, which may be viewed only upon subscription and payment of a fee, and photographs of past collections, which are available for free."[360] Feraud and Balmain, along with several other design houses, each filed an infringement suit against Viewfinder in the Tribunal de Grande Instance de Paris seeking money damages from Viewfinder for alleged unauthorized use of their dress designs and unfair competition.[361] The fashion designers' causes of action were predicated upon "Viewfinder displaying photographs of the designers' fashion shows, which revealed designs from their upcoming collection, on the firstView.com website."[362] "Viewfinder was served in New York in accordance with the terms of the Hague Convention on the Service of Judicial and Extrajudicial Documents in Civil or Commercial Matters."[363]

The French court issued default judgment against Viewfinder. "The French court ordered Viewfinder to remove the offending photographs, and awarded damages of 500,000 francs for each plaintiff, costs of the action, and a fine ("*astreinte* ") of 50,000 francs a day for each day Viewfinder failed to comply with the judgment."[364] The plaintiffs sought enforcement of the French judgment in a New York district court, which held "that enforcing the French Judgments would be repugnant to the public policy of New York because it would violate Viewfinder's First Amendment rights."[365] The court vacated an order of judgment and dismissed the French plaintiff's action on grounds that the First Amendment and the copyright doctrine of fair use protected Viewfinder's actions.[366] The Second Circuit found the record to be too undeveloped to make this conclusion and remanded the case for further development of the facts.[367] The court stated: "Whether such protections are sufficiently comparable to that required by the public policy of New York is a question best addressed in the first

---

[357] Id. at 108 (discussing European Parliament and Council Directive 96/9 on the Legal Protection of Databases).

[358] 489 F.3d 474 (2d Cir. 2007).

[359] Id. at 476.

[360] Id.

[361] Id. at 477.

[362] Id.

[363] Id.

[364] Id.

[365] Id. at 477–78.

[366] Id. at 478.

[367] Id. at 483.

instance by the district court on a fully-developed record."[368] This case illustrates how the rise of the Internet leads to different copyright regimes clashing. While the Berne Convention and the DMCA have resulted in much harmonization, national differences in copyright law are italicized by the Internet.[369]

(C) Extraterritoriality

In general, intellectual property rights are left to each nation to enforce. A copyright infringement claim may not be brought in U.S. courts for conduct committed entirely outside the territorial boundaries of the United States.[370] With the growth of the Internet, it is "increasingly common for parties outside the United States to copy a protected invention, work, mark, or trade secret."[371] Copyright law, like the other branches of intellectual property, is limited by the principle of territoriality; meaning that the copyright protection applies only within the territorial jurisdiction of the United States.[372] Protecting IP on the Internet presents a challenge to the principle of territoriality because "intellectual property rights in a single object can simultaneously exist, and be exploited, in dozens of countries."[373]

(D) National Treatment

The Berne Convention for the Protection of Literary and Artistic Works that took effect in 1886 is the principal treaty governing international copyright protection. "Berne's 164 member states agree to provide a minimum level of copyright protection and to treat authors from other member countries as well as they treat their own."[374] Article 18 of the Berne Convention requires countries to protect the works of other member states unless the works' copyright term has expired in either the country where protection is claimed or the country of origin. Under the Berne Convention, copyrighted works that fall into the public domain after the expiration of a full copyright term in the United States, or the country of origin, is not protected under § 514 of the Uruguay Round Agreements Act. The Berne Convention grants worldwide copyright protection in member states that now includes the United States.

The concept of national treatment is embodied in Article 5(1) that provides authors with "the rights which their respective laws do now or may hereafter grant to their nationals, as well as the rights specifically granted by the Convention."[375]

---

[368] Id. at 484.

[369] Marketa Trimble, The Potential Worldwide Application of the U.S. Fair Use Doctrine—Sarl Louis Ferard and SA Pierre Balman v. Viewfinder, Inc., 30 EUR. INTELL. PROP. L. REV. 38 (2008).

[370] The leading case is Subafilms, Ltd. v. MGM-Pathe Communications Co., 24 F.3d 1088 (9th Cir. 1994) (copyright infringement action brought by rights owner of the Beatles' song, Yellow Submarine). The Subafilm court held that "a primary activity outside the boundaries of the United States, not constituting an infringement cognizable under the Copyright Act, cannot serve as the basis for holding liable under the Copyright Act one who is merely related to that activity within the United States." Id. at 1093 quoting 3 DAVID NIMMER & MELVILLE B. NIMMER, NIMMER ON COPYRIGHT § 12.04[A][3][b], at 12–86. Nevertheless, "contributory liability can exist regardless of the location of the defendant's servers as long as the underlying direct infringements occurred in the United States." Perfect 10, Inc. v. Yandex N.V., 2013 WL 3668818 (N.D. Cal. July 12, 2013).

[371] JOHN CROSS ET AL., GLOBAL ISSUES IN INTELLECTUAL PROPERTY LAW 1, 1 (2009).

[372] Subafilms, Ltd. v. MGM-Pathe Communications Co., 24 F.3d 1088 (9th Cir. 1994) (stating that it was indisputable that the United States' Copyright Laws do not apply outside the country's territorial borders).

[373] PAUL GOLDSTEIN, CASES AND MATERIAL ON INTERNATIONAL INTELLECTUAL PROPERTY 18 (2000).

[374] Golan v. Holder, 132 S.Ct. 873, 874 (2012).

[375] Id. at 20.

National treatment is also a bedrock principle of multilateral and regional trade agreements addressing intellectual property such as the GATT–Uruguay Round. National treatment is also embodied in Article 3 of the Agreement on Trade–Related Aspects of Intellectual Property Rights ("TRIPS").[376]

(E) Global Copyright Treaties

Citizens of the United States enjoy copyright protection in any member country of TRIPS so long as they register their works of authorship in the U.S. Copyright Office. Copyright protection is accorded to original works fixed in a tangible medium of expression. The United States is a member of a number of multilateral treaties administered by the World Intellectual Property Organization ("WIPO"). WIPO was formed by a Convention signed at Stockholm on July 14, 1967. WIPO's International Bureau of Intellectual Property administers intellectual-property treaties. WIPO spearheaded two Internet-related copyright treaties approved on December 20, 1996.

(F) SOPA

In the fall of 2011, Congress considered several controversial bills spearheaded by the copyright industries that would allow blocking orders against ISPs and the removal of pirate websites. The Stop Online Piracy Act ("SOPA") was a proposed U.S. House of Representatives statute to expand the ability of U.S. law enforcement to fight online trafficking in copyrighted works. The companion statute in the U.S. Senate was the Protection Intellectual Property Act ("PIPA"). "SOPA and PIPA allow not only site blocking orders against ISPs, but also the removal of pirate websites from search engine search results and the prevention of advertising networks and credit card processors from dealing with infringing websites."[377] SOPA requires the providers of Internet search engines to:

> take technically feasible and reasonable measures, as expeditiously as possible, but in any case within 5 days after being served with a copy of the order, or within such time as the court may order, designed to prevent the foreign infringing site that is subject to the order, or a portion of such site specified in the order, from being served as a direct hypertext link.[378]

Wikipedia.org ("Wikipedia") is an online free-content encyclopedia that is multilingual and worked on by users/contributors around the world. Wikipedia's collaborative format has morphed into a diverse, multi-user, recursive encyclopedia that is tailored for different substantive topics or areas of interest. "Wiki[pedia] users create general categories and then classify their contributions. Singular category names refer to specific objects of discussion, while plural ones refer to broader discussions or topics."[379] As of September 2012, Wikipedia posted 4,045,430 articles in total in the English version alone.[380] On January 18, 2012, Wikipedia, Reddit, TwitPic,

---

[376] MICHAEL L. RUSTAD & CYRUS DAFTARY, E-BUSINESS LEGAL HANDBOOK § 8.02[B] (3rd ed. 2003).

[377] Peter Dalton & Jeremy Harris, Online Service Provider Liability—Key Developments in A New Sphere of Copyright Enforcement, Mondaq.com (March 14, 2012) http://www.mondaq.comhttp://www.mondaq.com/x/168240/IT+Internet/Online+Service+Provider+Liability+Key+Developments+In+A+New+Sphere+Of+Copyright+Enforcement.

[378] Stop Online Piracy Act of 2011–2012, H.R. 3261, 112th Cong. § 102 (2012).

[379] A. Michael Froomkin, Habermas@Discourse.Net: Toward a Critical Theory of Cyberspace, 116 HARV. L. REV. 749, 761 (2003).

[380] Wikipedia: Size of Wikipedia (September 5, 2012) http://en.wikipedia.org/wiki/Wikipedia:Size_of_Wikipedia.

and 7,000 other websites went "black" to express their opposition to SOPA and PIPA.[381] SOPA and PIPA stalled in committee in part because of the worldwide backlash against the proposed statutes. A Northeastern University Report noted that the controversial aspect of SOPA was that it would enable investigators to take down entire website as opposite to individual files:

> One of the main proposals included in SOPA was a takedown notice system similar to the DMCA, but targeting entire foreign sites instead of single hosted files. While some argued that this notice-based regime would make it possible to prevent copyright infringement in a timely manner, others were concerned that this system would be ripe for abuse of all sorts and they saw it as a threat to freedom of speech.[382]

The SOPA proposal had two principal provisions:

> Interrupting the flow of money to infringing sites, and blocking user access to such sites. In detail, upon receipt of a notice from a copyright holder, payment processors and advertising services would have been required to end their business relationship with the infringing site, and ISPs would have been required to block their customers from accessing the site.[383]

(G) ACTA

The Anti–Counterfeiting Trade Agreement ("ACTA") was a proposed multinational treaty of which the goal was to establish uniform standards for enforcing intellectual property rights. ACTA fortified the enforcement provisions of the TRIPS agreement by targeting counterfeit goods, generic goods, and widespread copyright infringement. The Electronic Freedom Foundation is concerned that ACTA is a special interest legislation that will have a chilling impact on Internet expression. One controversial feature is that ISPs "adopt three strikes Internet disconnection policies, and a global expansion of DMCA-style [Digital Millennium Copyright Act]."[384] ACTA negotiations did not include stakeholders from civil society, and the U.S. Trade Representative required that information industry stakeholders sign nondisclosure agreements ("NDAs"). NDA signatories include information industry moguls including Google, Dell, Intel, Business Software Alliance, Rupert Murdoch's News Corporation, Sony Pictures, Time Warner, the Motion Picture Association of America, and Verizon. In March of 2012, the European Parliament voted to refer ACTA to the European Court of Justice, which stalled ratification for Eurozone countries.[385] A minister of Slovenia publicly apologized to her family for formerly supporting ACTA.

(H) European ISPs & No Duty to Monitor Content

The issue of whether Internet service providers should monitor illegal content remains a contentious issue. The European Court of Justice ("ECJ") in *Belgische*

---

[381] SOPA and PIPA Outline (September 5, 2012) http://sopastrike.com.

[382] Tobias Lauinger, Martin Szydlowski, Kaan Onarlioglu, Gilbert Wondracek,Engin Kirda, and Christopher Kruegelz, Clickonomics: Determining the Effect of Anti-Piracy Measures for One-Click Hosting, Northeastern University Report (2013) at 1.

[383] Id. at 11.

[384] ACTA Talks Focus on Three Strikes, No Appeal Deal for Software Pirates, COMPUTER WEEKLY (Nov. 4, 2009).

[385] BLOOMBERG BNA ELECT. COMM. L. REV. (March 27, 2012).

Vereniging van Auteurs, Componisten en Uitgevers CVBA[386] ruled that an Internet Service Provider ("ISP") had no obligation to monitor illegal content. SABAM, the petitioner, is a management company representing authors, composers and publishers of musical works. Netlog was an ISP that ran an online social networking platform. Netlog's service enabled users to register and acquire a personal space known as a "profile," which was completed by the user and became available globally. SABAM contended that Netlog enabled users to, "make use, by means of their profile, of the musical and audio-visual works in SABAM's repertoire, making those works available to the public in such a way that other users of that network can have access to them without SABAM's consent and without Netlog paying it any fee."[387]

SABAM sought an injunction requiring Netlog to install a filtering system that would monitor information stored by the hosting service provider with no limitation in time, would be directed at all future infringements, and is intended to protect not only existing works, but also works that have not yet been created at the time when the system is introduced. The court ruled that Netlog need not install a system for filtering content to prevent infringing files being made available to users. The court reasoned that imposing an injunction would be the functional equivalent of requiring ISPs to monitor content, contrary to European Directives.

(I) Website Blocking & *In Rem* injunctions

Website blocking is injunctions against intermediaries, who have no direct or indirect copyright liability for their own actions. U.S. courts seldom issue *in rem* injunctions blocking websites in large part because of the First Amendment of the U.S. Constitution. A growing number of European courts engage in injunctions that block websites.[388] "The UK High Court created the precedent in 2011 when it ruled that BT provider had to block access to the Newzbin2 website after the Motion Picture Association (MPA) had claimed the site infringed the copyright of six major film studios. Since then, MPA has also obtained a court order forcing other UK ISPs, including Sky and Talk Talk, to block their customers' access to Newzbin2."[389] In 2013, the UK's High Court "ordered Britain's six biggest internet service providers to block access to three websites that provide links to pirated music, films and television shows."[390]

In 2012, Denmark ordered "an ISP to block access to the US-based streaming music service Grooveshark as well in a case brought to court in 2011 by a group of more than 30 rightholders collectively known as Rettigheds Alliancen. The Danish Bailiff Court ruled that both Grooveshark and its users infringed recording label copyrights and granted an injunction forcing an ISP to initiate the service blocking."[391] Finland, too, ordered an Elisa, an ISP, to begin blocking TPB. "In Finland, in May 2011, local rightholders groups filed a lawsuit at the District Court of Helsinki asking

---

[386] SABAM v. Netlog NV (3rd Chamber, 16 February 2012).

[387] Id.

[388] Martin Husovec, In Rem Jurisdictions: Case of Website Blocking, International Max Planck Research School for Competition and Innovation (April 27, 2013), http://papers.ssrn.com/sol3/papers.cfm? abstract_id=2257232.

[389] More ISP Blocking in Different European Countries European Digital Rights (Feb. 29, 2012), http://www.edri.org/edrigram/number10.4/isp-blocking-europe.

[390] Robert Cookson, ISPs Ordered to Block Pirate Websites, DIGITAL MEDIA (Feb. 28, 2013).

[391] Martin Husovec, In Rem Jurisdiction, Id. at 1.

that local ISP Elisa should start blocking TPB. Although Elisa refused, it was eventually forced to comply by subsequent court order in October 2011."[392]

Courts of United Kingdom (3), Netherlands (1), Belgium (1), Finland (1), Denmark (2), Greece (1), Austria (1) and Italy (2) were reported to issue such injunctions.[393] Most European "website blocking cases are usually civil proceedings of private plaintiffs holding copyright or trade mark rights against the Internet access providers, who as defendants are asked to employ certain technical means to make the access to disputed websites more difficult for its subscribers (an uncircumventable website block is technically impossible)."[394] Member States require courts to issue injunctions to block websites Art. 8(3) of the InfoSoc Directive (for copyright and related rights) and third sentence of Art. 11 of the Enforcement Directive (for other intellectual property rights).[395]

The relevant provision of the Enforcement Directive states: "Member States shall also ensure that rightholders are in a position to apply for an injunction against intermediaries whose services are used by a third party to infringe an intellectual property right."[396] The InfoSoc Directive applying to copyright law has functionally equivalent language.[397] Website blocking is typically against blameless intermediaries such as website. Intermediary liability is often the last resort for intellectual property claimants "where it is impossible or impracticable to identify or sue any of the tort liable persons due to cross border context, anonymity of tortfeasors or merely due to enforcement inefficiency (e.g. massive scale).[398] "Although at first sight injunctions against innocent parties might seem to be an effective enforcement tool supplementing deficiencies of the tort law in the on-line environment, these injunctions are considerably vulnerable to abuse and have a similarly great potential to negatively influence innovation."[399]

(J) Ancillary Copyright

Ancillary copyright or what is sometimes known, as "neighboring rights" of authors would assess intermediaries for unpaid Internet use of transmitting copyrighted works. The German Bundestag is considering enacting provisions making Google, Twitter and other websites liable for ancillary copyrights fees for providing brief summaries of copyrighted news stories. The German Parliament is considering enacting a '*Leistungsschutzrecht*' law for news publishers.[400] The law, known as

---

[392] Id.

[393] Id.

[394] Id.

[395] Id.

[396] Id.

[397] Id.

[398] Id. at 8.

[399] Id. at 19.

[400] "Urheberrecht (the right of an author, which under German law cannot be assigned): copyright Leistungsschutzrecht (the right protecting commercial activity in connection with copyright, for example publishing): ancillary copyright. Leistungsschutzrecht, literally 'right protecting performance', is not easy to translate into English. It's sometimes called a neighbouring right, which is OK if you realize it's neighbouring copyright. Ancillary copyright is commonly used, but perhaps misleading, in that the right is not actually copyright. Uexküll's dictionary has wettbewerbsrechtlicher Leistungsschutz: accomplishment-related protection under German law. It's a form of industrial property right, not really a form of intellectual

"ancillary copyright" in English, would require search engines and others—perhaps even Facebook, Twitter and individual bloggers—to pay news publishers if they link to or even briefly summarize news content."[401] Ancillary copyright, under the proposed statute, would work in the following way:

> If this bill is enacted as-is, search engines would no longer be allowed to display snippets unless they had received permission first. This is very crucial aspect of this *Leistungsschutzrecht*. It is not meant as an opt-out tool that allows you to operate a search engine unless the publisher objects and has his websites removed. Quite the opposite, it is up to the search engine operator to ask for permission first.

> LSR would grant news publishers an exclusive right to "make public" news content for one year, though what exactly "news content" would be is unclear. Part of the proposed law defines this as essentially doing what the press "usually does," explicitly mentioning informing, offering opinions and entertaining.[402]

It is unclear whether the Bundestag will enact ancillary copyright and whether it will exempt bloggers. *Der Spiegel* reported: "Google will still be permitted to use "snippets" of content from publishers' websites in its search results.[403] The proposed ancillary statute illustrates Goldsmith and Wu's argument that individual countries do not hesitate to impose rules over the Internet.

> If this bill is enacted as-is, search engines would no longer be allowed to display snippets unless they had received permission first. This is very crucial aspect of this *Leistungsschutzrecht*. It is not meant as an opt-out tool that allows you to operate a search engine unless the publisher objects and has his websites removed. Quite the opposite, it is up to the search engine operator to ask for permission first.

> LSR would grant news publishers an exclusive right to "make public" news content for one year, though what exactly "news content" would be is unclear. Part of the proposed law defines this as essentially doing what the press "usually does," explicitly mentioning informing, offering opinions and entertaining.[404]

It is unclear whether the Bundestag will enact ancillary copyright and whether it will exempt bloggers. *Der Spiegel* reported: "Google will still be permitted to use "snippets" of content from publishers' websites in its search results.[405] The proposed ancillary statute illustrates Goldsmith and Wu's argument that individual countries do not hesitate to impose rules over the Internet.

(K) DMCA Takedown & Extraterritoriality

DMCA takedown disputes will increasingly involve parties in different countries, which raise an issue of the extraterritoriality. The problem with copyright protection is

---

property right." Ancillary copyright/Leistungsschutzrecht, http://www.transblawg.eu/index.php?/archives/4048–Ancillary-copyrightLeistungsschutzrecht.html (last visited July 2, 2013).

[401] Matthias Schindler, German Parliament Hears Experts on Proposed Law to Limit Search Engines From Using News Content, SEARCHENGINE LAND (Jan. 31, 2013).

[402] Id.

[403] Id.

[404] Id.

[405] Id.

that it does not necessarily transcend national borders. In *Shropshire v. Canning*,[406] a California district court reviewed a DMCA takedown dispute concerning that great holiday song, "Grandma Got Run Over By a Reindeer."[407] Elmo Shropshire, the co-owner of the musical composition of the holiday song, filed suit against Canning, a resident of eastern Ontario.[408] The plaintiff charged that Canning uploaded and failed to remove an infringing video on YouTube that combined synchronized pictures of reindeers with audio of "The Irish Rovers," singing Shropshire's song about the unfortunate "Grandma."[409] The court entered a motion to dismiss Shropshire's action because the court could not discern any "act of infringement that occurred entirely within the United States."[410] The Canning court found "[t]he creation of the video, however, occurred entirely in Canada, and thus cannot constitute copyright infringement under well-settled law."[411] The Internet is cross-border by definition and copyright law lags behind in protecting content crossing national borders.

(L) Linking

In *Universal Music Australia Pty. Ltd. v. Cooper*,[412] the Australian federal court ruled that a website was liable for copyright infringement because it had well-organized hyperlinks to other website with infringing contents to many other pages, the evidence is that the website was user friendly and attractive and that visitors could readily select from a variety of catalogues of popular sound recordings for download. The digital copies of the sound recordings were downloaded by way of hyperlinks on the website, most of which appear to have been associated with MP3 digital music files stored on remote websites that would automatically download to the visitor's computer upon activation of the link on the website by a mouse click. Because of clicking on the hyperlink trigger on the website, music files were downloaded directly from the remote website on which they were stored to the computer of the internet user who had accessed the Cooper website.

(M) International Copyright Protection

Software publishers need to determine whether they can protect their intellectual property rights in their software products before they do business in a foreign country. In general, software licensing laws are not extraterritorial and each country administers and enforces intellectual property rights. The United States is also a signatory to the Berne Convention for the Protection of Literary and Artistic Works. Article 2 of the Berne Convention protests artistic and literary works. Computer software, whether in source or object code, are classified as literary works. A creator of a computer program from any country that is a signatory of the Berne Convention has the same rights in all other countries that are signatories to the Convention as they allow their own nationals. The Berne signatories agree to protect works of authors who are nationals of one of the countries of the Convention, or in the

---

[406] No. 10–CV–01941–LHK, 2011 WL 90136 (N.D. Cal. Jan. 11, 2011).

[407] Id. at *1 (reviewing the issue that arose between YouTube, the plaintiff, and the defendant).

[408] Id. (providing the personal backgrounds of the different parties).

[409] Id. (summarizing Canning's alleged actions).

[410] Id. at *4 (confirming that United States copyright laws do not extend outside of U.S. borders, and therefore the court was unable to find accompanying acts of infringement).

[411] Id. at *3.

[412] [2005] FCA 972 (14 July 2005).

country where the copyright owner publishes the work. Before the Berne Convention, copyright protection was purely national and an author had no rights outside the country where they registered their copyright. The Berne Convention and the Paris Convention signatories created International bureaus, which merged in 1893 to create the United International Bureaus for the Protection of Intellectual Property (BIRPI). In 1967, BIRPI became the World Intellectual Property Organization ("WIPO"), and in 1974, it became an organization within the United Nations. WIPO has 184 Member States and administers twenty-four international treaties, including two Internet-related copyright treaties signed in December 1996: the WIPO Copyright Treaty and the WIPO Performance and Phonograms Treaty. As a global provider of software, many Internet companies will enter into a distribution agreement with a European company to deliver its comprehensive computer security products to the twenty-eight countries of the European Union.

Chapter 11

TRADEMARKS ON THE GLOBAL INTERNET

It is now difficult to imagine the contours of trademark law without considering new methods of infringement enabled by bandwidth, browsers, and digital data. "New legal theories will be developed and old laws will in turn be modified, manipulated and in some cases mothballed. It is an exciting time to gird oneself for battle on this new galactic front."[1] Domain name cyberpirates attempting to sell a domain name containing a corporation's famous trademark did not exist prior to the mid-1990s. Beginning in the mid-1990s, entrepreneurs registered thousands of domain names containing the trademarks of famous companies in the hopes of selling them back for a ransom price. In the past two decades, trademark law has been reworked to accommodate to the challenges posed by domain names and cybersquatting.[2] Without Internet websites, no court would need to decide issues such as whether a pop-up ad infringed a company's trademark or constituted an unfair business practice in cyberspace.[3] Congress enacted the Anticybersquatting Consumer Protection Act of 1999 ("ACPA") to prohibit the bad-faith and abusive registration of distinctive marks as Internet domain names. The ACPA was intended to prevent "cybersquatting," which refers to the bad faith, abusive registration, and use of the distinctive trademarks of others as Internet domain names, with the intent to profit from the goodwill associated with those trademarks. Congress amended the Lanham Act to deter the practice of selling (or ransoming) domain names. Congress gave trademark owners an *in rem* remedy to file infringement claims where the domain name owner cannot be located. The Internet marketplace is built upon bedrock of trademarks.

Trademark law must continue to evolve to address new societal and technological developments. Trademark law was transformed in the United States by the "growth of machine-made merchandise" during the late nineteenth century and early twentieth century.[4] Today E–Commerce creates a "state of siege" in trademark practices because "goods and services are being injected into the market place at warp speed while the justice system strains to keep pace with new types of trademark conflicts concerning the identification of the new commodities."[5] This chapter examines Internet-related trademark and domain name issues. A trademark is "a word, phrase, symbol or design, or a combination thereof, that identifies and distinguishes the source of the goods of

---

[1] Darryl C. Wilson, Battle Galactical: Recent Advances and Retreats in the Struggle for the Preservation of Trademark Rights on the Internet, 12 J. HIGH TECH. L. 1, 1 (2011).

[2] See e.g., Mattel, Inc. v. Adventure Apparel, No. 00 Civ. 4085 (RWS), 2001 U.S. Dist LEXIS 13885, at *13 (S.D.N.Y. Sept. 6, 2001) (finding cybersquatting in case where defendant registered domain names "barbiesbeachwear.com" and "barbiesclothing.com" and "parked" them at Adventure Apparel website).

[3] See e.g., U–Haul International v. WhenU.com, 279 F. Supp.2d 723 (E.D. Va. 2003) (granting defendant's motion for summary judgment dismissing, trademark infringement, copyright infringement, and unfair competition claims brought by website owner against pop-up advertiser because pop-ups did not constitute "use" nor display copyrighted works or constitute a derivative work; observing that pop-up appeared in a separate window thus not altering website content).

[4] NORMAN F. HESSELTINE, A DIGEST OF THE LAW OF TRADE–MARKS AND UNFAIR TRADE 1 (1906).

[5] Id.

one party from those of others."[6] Amazon.com, for example, has a trademark clause listing its trade name as well as trademarks including Amazon, Amazon.com, Amazon.com & Design, Amazon.com Anywhere, Amazon.com Auctions, Amazon.com Books, Amazon.com Outlet, and scores of other marks.[7] The U.S. Congress created a federal system for the registration, protection, and regulation of trademarks when it enacted the Lanham Act of 1946. The term 'trademark' also extends to 'trade dress,' which has come to include not only a product's packaging, but also the product's "total image and overall appearance."[8] Further protection extends to websites if they serve to identify the producer.

The Internet's disregard of geographic borders creates conflicts between concurrent users, which would never have arisen in the purely brick-and-mortar world. If trademarks of competitors are used in metatags, there is a potential risk of being exposed to infringement lawsuits in foreign countries. In the United States, trademark fair use may protect the use of metatags, but this doctrine may be applied differently in other legal cultures. In order to assert a successful fair use defense to a trademark infringement claim, the defendant must prove three elements: that the use was made (1) other than as a mark, (2) in a descriptive sense, and (3) in good faith.[9]

The concept of trademark fair use may not be recognized in other IP regimes. The terms of trademark registration vary significantly from one country to another. Special attention must also be made to Internet-related issues. In response, courts have come to recognize an "Internet trio" of confusion factors: (1) similarity of the marks, (2) relatedness of the goods and services, and (3) simultaneous use of the Internet for marketing.[10] While trademark law traditionally works well in product counterfeiting cases, it is increasingly ill-fitted to the Internet. While trademark law's core principles remain, "legal decisions directed toward the resolution of these conflicts commonly known as domain name disputes continually chip away at the viability of the historic application of trademark law."[11] In the 1990s, "cybersquatters" registered thousands of domain names containing the trademarks of companies in the hopes of selling them back for a ransom price.

> Cybersquatting involves the registration as domain names of well-known trademarks by non-trademark holders who then try to sell the names back to the trademark owners. Since domain name registrars do not check to see whether a domain name request is related to existing trademarks, it has been simple and inexpensive for any person to register as domain names the marks of established companies. This prevents use of the domain name by the mark owners, who not infrequently have been willing to pay "ransom" in order to get "their names" back.[12]

---

[6] United States Patent & Trademark Office, Trademark FAQs, What is a Trademark? (2012).

[7] Amazon.com, Inc., Conditions of Use.

[8] 15 U.S.C. § 1125(a) (2006).

[9] 15 U.S.C. § 1115(b)(4).

[10] See e.g., Perfumebay.com Inc. v. eBay Inc., 506 F.3d 1165 (9th Cir. 2007).

[11] Darryl C. Wilson, Battle Galactica: Recent Advances and Retreats in the Struggle for the Preservation of Trademark Rights on the Internet, 12 J. HIGH TECH. L. 1, 1 (2011).

[12] David A. Gauntlet, Strategies for Funding IP Litigation: Insurance and Its Implications, ALI/ABA (2002).

Like Swiss Army Knives, domain names can perform a variety of functions and can have nearly infinite uses.[13] Domain names can be used for various technical services such as e-mail, a website, file transfers, and can support subdomains. In addition, it can support all kinds of practical uses or purposes—speech and expression, E–Commerce, social networking, education, entertainment, and so on. Some uses of domain names are generally agreed to be abusive or even criminal—such as phishing and malware distribution, which perpetrate theft and fraud. Other uses—such as adult pornography or political criticism—are considered abusive or illegal in some jurisdictions. Domain names in sponsored TLDs ("Top–Level Domains") may by design be restricted to certain uses or users.[14]

The hottest new area is the nexus between trademark law and torts—such as trade secret misappropriation, defamation, privacy/publicity and e-personation. Chapters 6 and 12 examine these IP-related Internet torts. New trademark issues such as using a competitor's name in metatags and/or domain names are also evolving at a faster pace. The latest trademark-related abuse is "username squatting": where entrepreneurs register usernames containing another's mark with the intent to sell the username to the trademark owner for a profit. For example, Coca Cola and Nike were allegedly "victims of squatters of their Twitter identities."[15] Name space disputes do not have a goodness of fit with traditional trademark law, which will be explained in the first section of this chapter.

§ 11.1   OVERVIEW OF INTERNET–RELATED TRADEMARK LAW

The U.S. Trademark Office uses the terms "trademark" and "mark" to "refer to both trademarks and service marks whether they are word marks or other types of marks. A service mark is the same as a trademark. It differs only in that it identifies and distinguishes the source of a service rather than a product."[16] In the United States, trademark law is found in the common law, state statutes and the Lanham Act of 1946 ("Lanham Act"). The term "trademark" includes "any word, name, symbol, or device, or any combination thereof . . . used by a person . . . to identify and distinguish his or her goods . . . from those manufactured or sold by others and to indicate the source of the goods, even if that source is unknown."[17] A service mark is defined by the USPTO as, "A word, phrase, symbol or design, or a combination thereof, that identifies and distinguishes the source of a service rather than goods."

The Lanham Act provides a civil action against any person who shall, without consent of the registrant, use in commerce any reproduction, counterfeit copy, or

---

[13] Each time an Internet user seeks access to a website, they use domain names. "Every end-user's computer that is connected to the Internet is assigned a unique Internet Protocol number ('IP address'), such as 123.456.78.90, that identifies its location (i.e., a particular computer-to-network connection) and serves as the routing address for email, pictures, requests to view a web page, and other data sent across the Internet from other end-users." Coalition. for ICANN Transparency, Inc. v. VeriSign, Inc., 611 F.3d 495, 500 (9th Cir. 2010).Coal. for ICANN Transparency, Inc. v. VeriSign, Inc., 611 F.3d 495, 500 (9th Cir. 2010). Id. at 409. The domain name is analogous to a telephone number or a mailing address. Id. at 410.

[14] ICANN.org, Registration Abuse Policies Working Group: Final Report (RAPWG), (Submitted 29 May 2010) at 21.

[15] Lisa P. Ramsey, Brandjacking on Social Networks: Trademark Infringement by Impersonation of Markholders, 58 BUFF. L. REV. 851, 852 (2010) (describing misuses of brand names on the Internet).

[16] United States Patent & Trademark Office, Basic Facts About Registering a Trademark (2009).

[17] 15 U.S.C. § 1127.

colorable imitation of a registered mark in connection with the sale, offering for sale, distribution, or advertising of any goods with which such use is likely to cause confusion, or to cause mistake, or to deceive.[18] The Lanham Act was enacted to protect consumers and manufacturers from deceptive representations of affiliation and origin. Paul Goldberg compares the role of trademark to other branches of intellectual property law:

> If copyright is the law of authorship and patent is the law of invention, trademark is the law of consumer marketing. Courts protect the terms Coca Cola, McDonald's, and Kodak against imitation or unauthorized use, not because they represent creative or inventive leaps of the mind, but because they signify a single source of a product and a certain consistent level of quality to consumers. Trademark law aims to ensure that, whether in Portland, Maine, or Oregon, a traveler coming upon a fast-food restaurant with the familiar golden arches will get the same food offered in all other McDonald's restaurants. Just as copyright overlaps patents, it also overlaps trademarks. When the Walt Disney Company gets a court order stopping the publication of unauthorized cartoons featuring Mickey Mouse, it is not only because Mickey Mouse is a trademark, indicating Disney as its source, but also because Disney owns the copyright in the Mickey Mouse image.[19]

To qualify as a trademark, the mark must be distinctive; the stronger a mark the more the public remembers it and associates it with the trademark owner's goods and services.[20] In fact, this association is the *sine qua non* of a trademark as the symbol signifying the source.[21] Fanciful, or coined marks, have the highest level of protection, followed by arbitrary and suggestive marks.[22] Fanciful that either "words [were] invented solely for their use as trademarks,"—or arbitrary—common words "applied in an unfamiliar way."[23] These marks are inherently strong and do not require proof of secondary meaning.

Suggestive, arbitrary, and fanciful marks are deemed inherently distinctive; descriptive marks receive protection only upon a showing that they have acquired secondary meaning; and generic marks are not protectable.[24] A California district court concluded that the term "sex.com" was generic.[25] Descriptive and generic marks reside at the bottom of the distinctiveness hierarchy because protection is provided only to marks used to identify and distinguish goods or services in commerce, subject to common law rights of another that used the mark before the registrant's filing date.[26]

---

[18] 15 U.S.C. § 1114(a).

[19] PAUL GOLDSTEIN, COPYRIGHT'S HIGHWAY: THE LAW AND LORE OF COPYRIGHT FROM GUTENBERG TO THE CELESTIAL JUKEBOX 10 (1994).

[20] 2 MCCARTHY ON TRADEMARKS AND UNFAIR COMPETITION § 11:2 (4th ed. 2012).

[21] Id.

[22] Id.

[23] Genesee Brewing Co., Inc v. Stroh Brewing Co., 124 F.3d 137, 143 (2d Cir. 1997).

[24] See Northern Light Technology, Inc. v. Northern Lights Club, 97 F. Supp.2d 96 (D. Mass. 2000).

[25] Kremen v. Cohen, No. C 98–20718 JW, 2000 WL 1811403, at *5 n.11 (N.D. Cal. Nov. 27, 2000).

[26] 15 U.S.C. § 1051.

(A) Path of Trademark Law

Trademarks were prefigured by the use of marks made on Minoan pottery from 3500 B.C. The earliest English law reflecting a form of trademark was a Thirteenth Century law addressing bakers stamping mark on the bread they baked.[27] The guild houses of Brussels, Belgium incorporated marks as early as the Sixteenth Century.[28] Stetson® for hats and caps was first used in commerce in 1866.[29] Pillsbury® for flour was first used in commerce in 1873. In the twentieth century, courts began to expand what could be trademarked. Coca Cola®'s bottle was registered as a three dimensional mark in 1977.[30] In 1987, Owens–Corning was granted a trademark for the color pink in insulation.[31] Clarke's Osewez® was granted a trademark on a fragrance for use on their sewing thread and embroidery yarn in 1991.[32] The USPTO considered the registration of Internet Domain Names at trademarks in 1997.[33]

A trademark composed of a domain name is registrable in USPTO as a trademark or service mark only if it distinctive and thus functions as a source identifier. Trademarks not only identify the origin of goods and services, which is the traditional function of trademarks, but they also fulfill a consumer protection role in being a mark of quality, and finally, companies use trademarks as a way of advertising and publicizing their goods or services.

Traditional or conventional trademarks are unique identifiers that employ words, logos, pictures, symbols, or combinations of these elements. American Express for example trademarked the phrase, "Don't Leave Home Without it." Microsoft's Window's icon is an example of a picture or symbol. IBM is an example of using letters. Beginning in the late twentieth century, the Trademark Office recognizes more nonconventional trademarks as represented in the chart below.

Type	Company	Trademark
Color Marks	Owens–Corning	Pink Color for Insulation
Trade Dress	Coca Cola	Shape of the Coke Bottle
Sound Marks	MGM	MGM's lion's roar
Motion Marks	Sony Ericsson	Flipbook of twenty images
Lacquered Sole	Christian	Lacquered red

---

[27] University of Texas, Trademark Timeline (2012).

[28] "The fat makers occupy "La Brouette" (the Wheelbarrow), the cabinetmakers and the barrel makers "Le Sac" (the Bag), the boatmen "Le Cornet" (the Horn), the haberdashers "Le Renard" (the Fox), the Four Crowned (sculptors, stone cutters, masons and slaters) "La Colline" (the Hill) and the carpenters "Le Pot d'Etain" (the Pot of Tin)." Grand Place, History of the Guildhouses, http://www.ilotsacre.be/site/en/curiosities/grand_place-brussels.htm.

[29] University of Texas, Trademark Timeline, Id.

[30] Id.

[31] Id.

[32] Id.

[33] Id.

on Shoes	Louboutin	sole on footwear.
Fragrance Marks	Kalin Manchev	Rose oil scent

The nonconventional use of trademark has expanded to include single color trademarks, sound trademarks, three dimensional trademarks, shape trademarks and even scent trademarks. In the twenty first century, trademark law is beginning to evolve further to address websites and domain names. Mobile application names and icons constitute a new frontier for trademark protection.

While the Lanham Act is flexible, one of the controversies is whether trademark should continually be expanded to address Internet activities. Just as in the brick-and-mortar world, trademarks used on websites influence consumers' purchasing decisions. Strong trademarks help E–Commerce companies create an online identity, build consumer trust, and distinguish them from the competition. "Trademark law serves the important functions of protecting product identification, providing consumer information, and encouraging the production of quality goods and services."[34] Trademark protection "is the law's recognition of the psychological function of symbols."[35]

Thus, a consumer purchasing an Apple iPhone5 knows that they can expect the degree of quality consistent with the Apple brand.[36] Trademarks on the Internet also enable sellers and service providers to build goodwill and a following among consumers. A trademark can have more than one owner and the Lanham Act permits concurrent use of the same mark in different geographic areas provided there is no likelihood of confusion, mistake, or deception. Nevertheless, the Internet creates legal dilemmas for courts because it is unclear how this doctrine should operate on the borderless Internet.

(B) Federal Trademark Registration

Congress enacted the Lanham Act in 1946 to provide national protection for trademarks used in interstate and foreign commerce in order to promote competition and the maintenance of product quality.[37] A company will claim rights in its trademarks or service marks by labeling its product with the "TM," "SM," and "®" symbols. Under the Lanham Act, the user of a mark can register it with the USPTO, and if the registrant then satisfies further conditions including continuous use for five consecutive years, the right to use the registered mark in commerce to designate the origin of the goods specified in the registration becomes "incontestable," outside certain enumerated exceptions.[38] Even if a registered trademark has not yet achieved incontestable status, a certificate of registration of the mark on the USPTO's principal

---

[34] Lamparello v. Falwell, 420 F.3d 309, 313 (4th Cir. 2005). See also, Qualitex Co. v. Jacobson Prods. Co., 514 U.S. 159, 164 (1995).

[35] Avery Dennison Corp. v. Sumpton, 189 F.3d 868, 873 (9th Cir. 1999) (quoting Mishawaka Rubber & Woolen Mfg. Co. v. S.S. Kresge Co., 316 U.S. 203, 205 (1942)).

[36] Apple.com, iPhone (2008).

[37] Park 'N Fly, Inc. v. Dollar Park and Fly, Inc., 469 U.S. 189, 193 (1985).

[38] After five (5) years of continuous use, the Lanham Act allows the owner of a registered trademark to obtain "incontestable" status. Once a registration has achieved incontestable status, that status is treated as conclusive evidence of the registrant's right to use the trademark, subject to enumerated defenses. 15 U.S.C. §§ 1065, 1115(b).

register constitutes *prima facie* evidence of its validity.[39] Under the Lanham Act, registration of a mark serves as prima facie evidence of both the mark's validity and the registrant's exclusive right to use it in commerce.[40]

Most trademark infringement cases turn on whether the defendant's use of the plaintiff's mark is likely to cause consumer confusion. The Lanham Act provides a civil action for the holder of a registered mark, whether or not incontestable, "against anyone employing an imitation of it in commerce when 'such use is likely to cause confusion, or to cause mistake, or to deceive.'"[41] The Trademark Act of 1946, as amended,[42] governs the federal registration of trademarks. A company will claim rights in its trademarks or service marks by labeling its product with the "TM," "SM," and "®" symbols. A *service mark* is the same as a trademark, except that it identifies and distinguishes the source of a service rather than a product and is defined by the USPTO as, "A word, phrase, symbol or design, or a combination thereof, that identifies and distinguishes the source of a service rather than goods."[43]

The federal trademark statute establishes a system for the registration and protection of trademarks used in commerce. Trademark applicants need to consider (1) the mark they want to register; (2) the goods and/or services in connection with which you wish to register the mark; and (3) whether they will be filing the application based on actual existing use of the mark or a bona fide intention to use the mark in the future.[44] A trademark application "must specify the proper "basis" for filing, whether current use of the mark in commerce or on an intent to use the mark in commerce in the future."[45] The U.S. Trademark Office publishes approved trademarks on the Principal Register of the United States Patent and Trademark Office ("USPTO"). The Lanham Act describes a trademark as being a limited property right in a particular word, phrase, or symbol, and federal trademark protection is only available for marks "used in commerce."[46]

The USPTO refers to the term, "trademark" to include both trademarks and service marks. The term of a federal trademark registration is 10 years and can be renewed indefinitely with 10–year renewal terms. Trademark owners must file an affidavit, or a declaration of continued use, with the USPTO to keep the registration alive between the fifth and sixth year after the date of initial registration. Failure of the registrant to provide the affidavit results in cancellation of the trademark registration. Trademarks may be established by using a mark in commerce, without a federal registration. However, the USPTO explains the advantages of owning a federal trademark registration on the Principal Register:

---

[39] 15 U.S.C. § 1057(b).

[40] Lanham Act, § 33(a), 15 U.S.C. § 1115(a).

[41] 15 U.S.C. § 1114(a).

[42] 15 U.S.C. § 1051.

[43] United States Patent & Trademark Office, Trademark FAQs, "What is a Service Mark?" (2012).

[44] USPTO.gov, Trademark Basics (2012), http://www.uspto. gov/trademarks/basics/index.jsp.

[45] Id.

[46] 15 U.S.C. § 1127.

- Public notice of your claim of ownership of the mark;

- A legal presumption of your ownership of the mark and your exclusive right to use the mark nationwide on or in connection with the goods/services listed in the registration;

- The ability to bring an action concerning the mark in federal court;

- The use of the U.S. registration as a basis to obtain registration in foreign countries;

- The ability to record the U.S. registration with the U.S. Customs and Border Protection (CBP) Service to prevent importation of infringing foreign goods;

- The right to use the federal registration symbol ®; and

- Listing in the United States Patent and Trademark Office's online databases.[47]

Trademark applicants register marks in the USPTO. The two principal rights in a trademark are a federal trademark registration, and the right to use the mark. In general, the first party who *either* uses a mark in commerce or files an application in the trademark office has the ultimate right to register that mark. The date of first use anywhere is the date when the goods were first sold or transported, or, the services were first rendered under the mark, if such use is bona fide and in the ordinary course of trade.[48] Trademark priority is determined by the first to use a mark in interstate commerce. Under U.S. Trademark Law, it is the first person to use a mark rather than the first to register it who has priority. Factors determining first use include which party first affixed the mark to a product, or which party's name appeared with the trademark. Other factors considered are which party maintained the quality and uniformity of the product, or created the good will associated with a product.

Registration with the Trademark Office gives the owner exclusive rights only in the United States. However, marks may be registered in different countries; a practice that is recommended for companies selling goods and rendering services outside of the U.S. extraterritorial protection requires the trademark owner to register in each country where protection is sought. The registration of trademarks signals constructive notice of mark ownership, and creates a legal presumption in favor of ownership. Trademark registrants have the right to bring infringement or dilution actions in federal court. Finally, registration is a predicate to the U.S. Customs Department preventing the importation of infringing goods.

(C) State Trademark Law

Trademark registration procedures vary widely from state to state. Under the California state trademark law, online companies need to register their trademarks to receive protection. However, under the Massachusetts commonwealth trademark law, online companies need not register with the Commonwealth to receive protection, but they may if they want to. In 2006, Massachusetts adopted the International Trademark Association's Revised Model State Trademark Bill ("INTA–MSTB"); an online company, or an individual, may register a trademark or service with the Corporation Division, so long as the mark is used in the Commonwealth. The use must be *bona fide*, and not to

---

[47] USPTO, Trademark FAQS, "What are the Benefits of Trademark Registration?" (2012).
[48] 15 U.S.C. § 1127.

reserve a right in the mark. A trademark is considered in use when it is affixed on the goods or containers, and on the tags, labels, displays or documents associated with the goods, and those goods are sold or transported within the Commonwealth. Similarly, service marks are used or displayed in the sale or advertising of services. The Internet marginalized the value of state trademark registration because, by definition, cyberspace disputes are rarely between citizens of the same state.

(D) Trademark Applications

(1) Territorial Extent of Trademarks

U.S. trademarks are filed in the United States Patent and Trademark Office and only give the successful applicant protection in the territory of the United States. Trademarks are territorially bounded; they only afford protection in the country granted, however, trademark owners may obtain protection in the Eurozone by a single trademark filing in the Trademarks and Designs Registration Office of the European Union in Alicante, Spain. Trademark applications must include: (1) the name of the applicant, (2) a name and address for correspondence, (3) a clear drawing of the mark, (4) a listing of the goods or services, and (5) the filing fee for at least one class of goods or services. "An application for registration under § 1(A) of the Trademark Act must include one specimen for each class, showing use of the mark on or in connection with the goods, or in the sale or advertising of the services, in commerce."[49]

The Madrid system for the international registration of marks functions under the Madrid Agreement (1891), and the Madrid Protocol (1989). The Madrid system is administered by the International Bureau of WIPO located in Geneva, Switzerland. One of the advantages of the Madrid system is that a trademark owner may obtain protection in several countries by filing a single application within their own national or regional trademark office provided they are members of the Madrid Union.[50] WIPO describes the international mark:

> so registered is equivalent to an application or a registration of the same mark effected directly in each of the countries designated by the applicant. If the trademark office of a designated country does not refuse protection within a specified period, the protection of the mark is the same as if that Office had registered it. The Madrid system also simplifies greatly the subsequent management of the mark, since it is possible to record subsequent changes or to renew the registration through a single procedural step. Further countries may be designated subsequently.[51]

(2) Actual & Intent to Use Applications

The Lanham Act, as amended by the 1988 Trademark Law Revision Act, states, "[t]he term 'use in commerce' means the bona fide use of a mark in the ordinary course of trade, and not made merely to reserve a right in a mark."[52] The Lanham Act provides that:

---

[49] 15 U.S.C. § 1051(a)(1).

[50] World Intellectual Property Organization, Madrid System for the International Registration of Trademarks, http://www.wipo.int/madrid/en/.

[51] Id.

[52] 15 U.S.C. § 1127.

For purposes of this chapter, a mark shall be deemed to be in use in commerce—

(1) on goods when—

(A) it is placed in any manner on the goods or their containers or the displays associated therewith or on the tags or labels affixed thereto, or if the nature of the goods makes such placement impracticable, then on documents associated with the goods or their sale, and

(B) the goods are sold or transported in commerce, and

(2) on services when it is used or displayed in the sale or advertising of services and the services are rendered in commerce, or the services are rendered in more than one State or in the United States and a foreign country and the person rendering the services is engaged in commerce in connection with the services.[53]

The Lanham Act allows two types of use applications: (1) actual use, and (2) intent to use ("ITU"). ITU applications require intent to use the trademark in commerce in the future. The Lanham Act requires proof of "use in commerce" meaning there is a *bona fide* use of a mark in the ordinary course of trade—the mark cannot only be used to reserve a right to a particular mark. In the brick-and-mortar world, the term "use in commerce" originated where trademarks were affixed on goods or containers. On the Internet, such use of trademarks "in commerce" occurs in website sales. In general, the first party who either uses a mark in commerce or files an ITU application in the Trademark Office holds the first right to register that mark.

The U.S. Trademark Office may accept evidence an applicant has used a mark "in commerce" for five years as *prima facie* evidence of distinctiveness.[54] A trademark owner will typically use trademarks on the product and its packaging, while service marks advertise services. The purpose of the Lanham Act is to "regulate commerce within the control of Congress by making actionable the deceptive and misleading use of marks in such commerce" and "to protect persons engaged in such commerce against unfair competition."[55]

(E) The Distinctiveness Spectrum

A trademark must be distinctive to be protectable reflecting the source and quality of the goods or services as opposed to mere descriptive. Trademarks in cyberspace must meet the same standard of distinctiveness as must be met in the bricks-and-mortar world. Trademarks are classified by courts on a continuum of distinctiveness: (1) generic (not protectable), (2) descriptive (protectable only if the mark acquires secondary meaning), (3) suggestive, (4) arbitrary, or (5) fanciful (strong marks).[56] The Federal Circuit, for example, drew upon "extensive precedent" in ruling that merely combining ".com" and "advertising" does not result in a descriptive mark, but is generic.

---

[53] Id.

[54] 15 U.S.C. § 1054(f).

[55] 15 U.S.C. § 1127.

[56] See also Burke-Parsons-Bowlby Corp. v. Appalachian Log Homes, Inc., 871 F.2d 590, 593–94 (6th Cir. 1989) ("Validity of a registered trademark is contingent on determining first whether the mark is (1) arbitrary and fanciful; (2) suggestive; (3) descriptive; or (4) generic.").

Courts considering whether a mark is sufficiently distinctive to warrant trademark protection evaluate the mark based on a hierarchy of classifications. Proceeding from the least eligible for protection to the most, the hierarchy is as follows: generic, descriptive, suggestive, arbitrary, and fanciful.[57] "Courts classify the distinctiveness or conceptual strength of a mark as: (1) generic, like "Diet Chocolate Fudge Soda"; (2) descriptive, like "Security Center"; (3) suggestive, like "Coppertone"; or (4) arbitrary like Apple or (5) fanciful, like "Kodak or Xerox.[58] Trademark strength is assessed along to separate dimensions: "(1) 'conceptual strength,' or 'placement of the mark on the spectrum of marks,' which encapsulates the question of inherent distinctiveness; and (2) 'commercial strength' or 'the marketplace recognition value of the mark.'"[59]

(1) Generic Trademarks

Generic trademarks are marks that lack the distinctive qualities to be protectable. A generic mark is the antithesis of a distinctive mark "Generic terms are those that refer to the genus of which a particular product or service is a species, i.e., the name of the product or service itself."[60] To determine whether a term is generic, the court looks to whether consumers understand the word as one that only refers to a particular producer's goods, or whether the consumer understands the word to refer specifically to the goods themselves. Generic terms cannot be valid marks subject to trademark protection, whereas a descriptive mark can be valid and protectable if it has acquired secondary meaning. "Whether a mark is generic is a question of fact."[61] Unlike descriptive marks, generic marks are never entitled to trademark protection. A generic mark is the antithesis of a distinctive mark.

(2) Descriptive Trademarks

Descriptive marks "define a particular characteristic of the product in a way that does not require any exercise of the imagination."[62] "Examples of descriptive marks include "After Tan post-tanning lotion" and "5 Minute glue."[63] In the context of the Internet, "secure software" is descriptive. "Descriptive marks are not inherently distinctive; rather, they require a showing of secondary meaning before they receive trademark protection."[64] "Secondary meaning" exists when, "in the minds of the public, the primary significance of a product feature or term is to identify the source of the product rather than the product itself."[65] A comment to the Restatement (Third) of Competition describes how trademarks can evolve into secondary meaning states:

> Secondary meaning exists only if a significant number of prospective purchasers understand the term, when used in connection with a particular kind of good, service, or business, not merely in its lexicographic sense, but also as an indication

---

[57] 2 McCarthy on Trademarks and Unfair Competition § 11:1 (4th ed. 2012).

[58] Sabinsa Corp. v. Creative Compounds, LLC, 609 F.3d 175, 185 (3d Cir. 2010).

[59] 2 J. Thomas McCarthy, McCarthy on Trademarks and Unfair Competition § 11.83 (4th ed. 1999).

[60] Id. at § 12.23.

[61] Advertise.com, Inc. v. AOL Adver., Inc., 616 F.3d 974, 977 (9th Cir. 2010).

[62] Id.

[63] George & Co., LLC v. Imagination Entm't Ltd., 575 F.3d 383, 394 (4th Cir. 2009).

[64] Id.

[65] Id.

of association with a particular, even if anonymous, entity. The concept of secondary meaning is also applicable to designations such as graphic designs, symbols, packaging features, and product designs. In these contexts, secondary meaning denotes that the feature, although not inherently distinctive, has come through use to be uniquely associated with a particular source. A designation that has acquired secondary meaning thus distinguishes the goods, services, or business of one person from those of others.[66]

Courts use multiple factors to determine whether a specific mark has attained secondary meaning determination: (1) advertising expenditures, (2) consumer studies linking the mark to a source, (3) unsolicited media coverage of the product, (4) sales success, (5) attempts to plagiarize the mark, and (6) length and exclusivity of the mark's use.[67] Secondary meaning is based upon the totality of the facts. In *Labrador Software, Inc., v. Lycos, Inc.*, Labrador Software filed a lawsuit against Lycos, an Internet search service, which used a black Labrador retriever image in its Internet search product. The court denied the injunction, holding that Labrador Software's trademark was only descriptive and not entitled to protection, absent a showing of secondary meaning.[68] Microsoft's Windows is a trademark that is descriptive, but has acquired secondary meaning, as is International Business Machines for computers.

(3) Suggestive Trademarks

Suggestive trademarks "suggest, but do not describe, the nature or characteristics of the product."[69] "Suggestive marks require consumer "imagination, thought, or perception" to determine what the product is," whereas descriptive marks conveys "an immediate idea of the ingredients, qualities or characteristics of the goods"[70] and include "JAGUAR for fast, luxurious cars and EXPLORER for an Internet search engine."[71] Examples of suggestive marks are Coppertone®, Orange Crush®, and Playboy. "The primary criteria for distinguishing between a suggestive mark and a descriptive mark are the imaginativeness involved in the suggestion, that is, how immediate and direct is the thought process from the mark to the particular product."[72] "Microsoft" is a trademark that is suggestive as "Netscape" when referencing the Internet landscape.

(4) Arbitrary Trademarks

Arbitrary marks, which are also inherently distinctive, typically involve common words that have no connection with the actual product because "they do not suggest or describe any quality, ingredient, or characteristic," so the mark can be viewed as "arbitrarily assigned." Arbitrary marks "are common words used in a manner which do not suggest or describe any quality, ingredient, or characteristic of the goods they serve." "Camel® cigarettes" and "Apple® computers" are examples of arbitrary marks.

---

[66] RESTATEMENT (THIRD) OF UNFAIR COMPETITION, § 13 cmt. e (1995).

[67] J.T. Colby & Co. v. Apple Inc., 2013 U.S. Dist. LEXIS 65959 (S.D. N.Y., May 8, 2013) at *21 (discussing secondary meaning factors).

[68] Labrador Software, Inc. v. Lycos, 32 F. Supp. 31 (D. Mass. 1999).

[69] STEPHEN M. MCJOHN, INTELLECTUAL PROPERTY: EXAMPLES AND EXPLANATIONS 384 (2012).

[70] Id. at 221.

[71] American Bar Association, What is a Trademark? (2009).

[72] City of Carlsbad v. Shah, 08CV1211 AJB WMC, 2012 WL 424418 (S.D. Cal. Feb. 9, 2012) (quoting Self–Realization Fellowship Church v. Ananda Church of Self–Realization, 59 F.3d 902, 911 (9th Cir.1995)).

In *Mango's Tropical Cafe, Inc. v. Mango Martini Rest. & Lounge, Inc.,* the plaintiff argued the mark "Mango's" was arbitrary when used to identify a restaurant because it has no connection to restaurant services. The court opined that the term "Mango's" could reasonably be classified as *suggestive* since it could imply a food and drinking establishment in South Florida where mangoes are used in any number of recipes. "Apple Computer Corp. is a good *example* of an arbitrary mark because most computers are not made of apples." Lotus software is also arbitrary, as is SUN for computers.

(5) Fanciful Trademarks

Federal trademark law places arbitrary and fanciful trademarks at the highest level of protection. "Fanciful marks, which are inherently distinctive, typically involve made-up words created for the sole purpose of serving as a trademark." Clorox®, Kodak®, Polaroid®, and Exxon® are examples of fanciful marks. Fanciful marks are not words in the dictionary, and there is no logical connection to the goods or services. Fanciful marks are coined, or made up, by the trademark owner and therefore not found in the dictionary. Exxon, Kodak, Rolex, Xerox, and Electrolux are fanciful marks because they had no predefined meaning until they were used as trademarks. "Terms which are originally descriptive or *fanciful* may become generic if, in the minds of the consuming public, they no longer signify. For example, aspirin, cellophane, and thermos began as trademarks but are now generic terms."

(6) Summary of Trademark Continuum

The *sine qua non* of a trademark is it identifies the source of particular goods. To qualify as a trademark, the mark must be distinctive. Marks are classified on a continuum of increasing distinctiveness: (1) generic, (2) descriptive, (3) suggestive, (4) arbitrary, or (5) fanciful. Fanciful or "coined" marks are the strongest marks, followed by arbitrary, suggestive, and descriptive marks. A "fanciful" mark is a combination of letters or other symbols signifying nothing other than the product or service to which the mark has been assigned. Suggestive, arbitrary, or fanciful trademarks, due to their intrinsic nature, serve to identify a particular source of product.

Suggestive marks require imagination and creativity. For example, Microsoft's mark is suggestive as it connotes software for microcomputers. Descriptive marks describe the goods or services being sold, and receive protection only upon a showing they have acquired secondary meaning.[73] Secondary meaning arises when consumers have come to identify a trademark with a company over time. In that case, a descriptive mark that a trademark owner could not register initially may achieve trademark status and be subject to registration, at some time in the future. Because the strength of a trademark for purposes of the likelihood-of-confusion analysis depends on the interplay between conceptual and commercial strength, the existence of inherent distinctiveness is not the end of the inquiry. "Context is critical to a distinctiveness analysis, and the level of distinctiveness of a mark can be determined only by reference to the goods or services that the mark identifies."[74] This is the factor often described as commercial recognition. The *sine-qua-non* of commercial recognition is secondary meaning through advertising. For example, the mark "Super-encrypted software" connotes computer security. Notably,

---

[73] Northern Light Technology, Inc. v. Northern Lights Club, 97 F. Supp. 2d 96 (D. Mass. 2000).

[74] Advertise.com, Inc. v. AOL Adver., Inc., 616 F.3d 974, 977 (9th Cir. 2010).

a weak descriptive mark may gain secondary meaning through online advertising or publishing.

"Descriptive" marks are not inherently distinctive, but may acquire the distinctiveness, which will allow them to be protected.[75] This acquired distinctiveness is generally called "secondary meaning."[76] "Secondary meaning" is acquired when "in the minds of the public, the primary significance of a product feature . . . is to identify the source of the product rather than the product itself."[77] While survey evidence is the most direct and persuasive evidence of whether a mark has acquired secondary meaning, consumer surveys are not a prerequisite to establishing secondary meaning.

Nor is such evidence indispensable to the broader question of commercial recognition."[78] The secondary meaning inquiry is a fact-sensitive one, involving "evidence showing duration, extent and nature of use in commerce, and advertising expenditures in connection therewith (identifying types of media and attaching typical advertisements)," as well as "statements from the trade or public, or both, or other appropriate evidence tending to show that the mark distinguishes such goods."[79] Although a trademark may be found distinctive, the Lanham Act may not protect it if the mark "comprises immoral, deceptive, or scandalous matter; or matter which may disparage or falsely suggest a connection with persons, living or dead, institutions, beliefs, or national symbols, or bring them into contempt, or disrepute."[80]

(7) Incontestability

For a trademark to be enforceable it must be valid; one way to show a mark's validity is through its "incontestability." A trademark registered for five or more years becomes "incontestable."[81] Incontestability is conclusive evidence of the validity of the registered mark, 15 U.S.C. § 1115(b), except as to certain statutorily enumerated challenges, including the functionality of the mark.[82]

(F) Trade Name

Apple is a "trade name," meaning that it is a name used by a person to identify his or her business or vocation.[83] Amazon.com, eBay, YouTube, and Facebook, are examples of Internet-related trade names. Trade names, like trademarks, must be distinctive to be protectable. A domain name may qualify as a trade name if the domain name is used to distinguish the company, for instance, to give information on that company and its activities.[84] Domain names may also "be perceived as a trade mark when the website itself is a product or service."[85]

---

[75] Qualitex v. Jacobsen Prods. Co., 514 U.S. 159, 163 (1995).

[76] Id.

[77] Id.

[78] Maker's Mark Distillery, Inc. v. Diageo N. Am., 679 F.3d 410, 421 (6th Cir. 2012).

[79] 37 C.F.R. § 2.41.

[80] 15 U.S.C. § 1052(a).

[81] 15 U.S.C. § 1065.

[82] 15 U.S.C. § 1115(b)(8).

[83] 15 U.S.C. § 1127.

[84] GRAHAM J. H. SMITH, INTERNET LAW AND REGULATION 209 (2007).

[85] Id.

(G) Service Marks

A service mark, as its name suggests, identifies the source of services as opposed to a source of goods. E*Trade, for example, is a service mark for online investing. The U.S. Patent and Trademark Office uses the terms "trademark" and "mark" to refer to both trademarks and service marks whether they are word marks or other types of marks. A service mark is the same as a trademark. Those claiming rights in a mark will label their products with the symbols "TM", "SM", or "®". The Trademark Office allows a company to use the "ᵀᴹ" (trademark) or "ˢᴹ" (service mark) designation, which signals rights even if it has not registered its marks. However, a company may not use the federal registration symbol "®" until the Trademark Office of the USPTO actually registers a mark—not while an examination is pending.

(H) Functional Limits of Trademarks

Congress adopted the functionality doctrine by explicitly prohibiting trademark registration or protection under the Lanham Act for a functional product. § 1052(e)(5) prohibits the registration of a mark, which comprises any matter that, as a whole, is functional. Even a registered mark may be invalidated if it is deemed functional.[86] A trademark is functional "if it is essential to the use or purpose of the article or if it affects the cost or quality of the article. A trademark may be determined to be functional under traditional functionality doctrine."[87] Something is functional if it is essential to the use or purpose of the article or if it affects the cost or quality of the article.[88] The functionality doctrine developed as a common law rule prohibiting trade dress or trademark rights in the functional features of a product or its packaging.[89]

> The purpose of the doctrine is to preserve the distinction between the realms of trademark law and patent law. The functionality doctrine prevents trademark law, which seeks to promote competition by protecting a firm's reputation, from instead inhibiting legitimate competition by allowing a producer to control a useful product feature.[90]

> The functionality doctrine ensures that the proper boundaries are kept between patent law and trademark law. "If a product's functional features could be used as trademarks," the trademark owner would have a perpetual monopoly because trademark registrations may be "extended forever."[91]

---

[86] 15 U.S.C. § 1052(e)(5).

[87] Qualitex Co. v. Jacobson Prods. Co., 514 U.S. 159, 165 (1995).

[88] See Playboy Enters. v. Netscape Commc'ns Corp., 354 F.3d 1020, 1030–31 (9th Cir. 2004), ("Nothing about the marks used to identify PEI's products is a functional part of the design of those products" since "PEI could easily have called its magazine and its models entirely different things without losing any of their intended function.").

[89] Trade dress is the total image or overall design or appearance of a product or its packaging. Two Pesos, Inc. v. Taco Cabana, Inc., 505 U.S. 763, 765 (1992).

[90] Rosetta Stone Ltd. v. Google, 2012 U.S. App. LEXIS 7082 (4th Cir. April 9, 2012).

[91] Stephen W. Feingold & Howard S. Hogan, Unique Online Trademark Issues, in G. Peter Albert, Jr. and Intellectual Property Law Association, Intellectual Property in Cyberspace (2d ed. 2011) at 309.

(I) What a Domain Name Is

A domain name is part of a Uniform Resource Locator ("URL"), which is the address of a site or document on the Internet. If the domain name is "SPC.COM," the term "SPC" is a second-level domain ("SLD") and the term "COM" is a top-level domain ("TLD"). The SLD is before the dot (".") and is usually the company's trade name or trademark. Thus, in the URL: "http" is the protocol; "www" indicates that the site is on the Web, "SEB.com" is the SLD. SEB is the SLD whereas the .com is the first-level domain. The "com" TLD means commercial signifying for profit organizations. The SLD part of the domain name is what creates trademark law disputes. The first trademark/domain disputes occurred when domain name registrants incorporated another party's trademark as the SLD.

The manifest function of a domain name—or Web address—is to identify and locate computers on the Internet. The Internet Corporation for Assigned Names and Numbers ("ICANN") is seeking ways to minimize the abuses and misuses of domain name registrations that include deceptive and fraudulent practices such as: "cybersquatting, front-running, gripe sites, deceptive and/or offensive domain names, fake renewal notices, name spinning, pay-per-click, traffic diversion, false affiliation, cross-TLD registration scam, and domain kiting/tasting."[92] A Working Group for ICANN identified "cybersquatting" as an example of registration abuse. The ICANN study found certain other abuses, listed below, not classified as cybersquatting, but as forms of registration abuse:

> Gripe/Complaint Sites a.k.a. "Sucks Sites": Websites that complain about a company's or entity's products or services and uses a company's trademark in the domain name (e.g. companysucks.com).

> Pornographic/Offensive Sites: Websites that contain adult or pornographic content and uses a brand holder's trademark in the domain name (e.g. brandporn.com).

> Offensive strings: Registration of stand-alone dirty words within a domain name (with or without brand names).

> Registration of deceptive domain names: Registration of domain names that direct unsuspecting consumers to obscenity or direct minors to harmful content— sometimes referred to as a form of "mousetrapping."[93]

§ 11.2 WEBSITE TRADE DRESS

It is an unsettled issue whether trade dress can be protected for websites, but there is no doubt that trade dress applies to products sold on websites.[94] The design or packaging of a product may acquire a distinctiveness; serving to identify the product

---

[92] Amy E. Bivins, ICANN Staff Seeks Comments on Uniformity of Contracts to Address Registration Abuse, BLOOMBERG BNA ELECTRONIC COMMERCE & LAW REPORT (July 28, 2012).

[93] INTERNET CORPORATION FOR ASSIGNED NAMES & NUMBERS (ICANN) REGISTRATION ABUSE POLICIES WORKING GROUP FINAL REPORT (Submitted 29 May 2010) at 36.

[94] Xuan–Thao N. Nguyen, Should It Be a Free For All? The Challenge of Extending Trade Dress Protection to the Look and Feel of Websites in the Evolving Internet, 49 AM. U.L. REV. 1233, 1276–77 (2000) ("The purpose of Section 43(a) of the Lanham Act is to protect consumers from being deceived as to the source of a product or service. To fulfill that purpose, it is logical to extend trade dress protection to the overall look and feel of websites that are inherently distinctive or have acquired secondary meaning and are non-functional.").

with its manufacturer or source. Marks classified as suggestive, arbitrary or fanciful are considered inherently distinctive, whereas descriptive marks are tentatively considered non-distinctive and can only attain distinctive status upon an affirmative showing of secondary meaning. A design or package, which acquires this secondary meaning, assuming other requisites are met, is a "trade dress" which may not be used in a manner likely to cause confusion as to the origin, sponsorship, or approval of the goods. In these respects, protection for trade dress exists to promote competition.

Trade dress generally refers to characteristics of the visual appearance of a product or its packaging that signify the source of the product to consumers.[95] The Bubble Calculator, for example, employs bubbly trade dress to call Internet consumer's attention to the name of trademarked product, "Bubble Calculator." In *Two Pesos, Inc. v. Taco Cabana, Inc.*, the U.S. Supreme Court decided that the term "trademark" extends to "trade dress," which means a product's "total image and overall appearance" if it is a source identifier.[96] The Court also found trade dress to be protectable under Section 43(a) of the Lanham Act prohibiting the use of false designations of origin, false descriptions, and false representations in the advertising and sale of goods and services.

Section 43(a) of the Lanham Act recognizes two distinct protectable interests: (1) protection against unfair competition in the form of an action for false advertising; and (2) protection against false association in the form of a lawsuit for false endorsement. The Court explained that trade dress, which is inherently distinctive, is protectable under Section 43(a) even if the plaintiff cannot demonstrate secondary meaning since the trade dress itself identified products or services as coming from a specific source. The Court noted the shape and general appearance of the restaurant as well as "the identifying sign, the interior kitchen floor plan, the decor, the menu, the equipment used to serve food, the servers' uniforms, and other features [all reflected] on the total image of the restaurant."[97]

Trade dress is entitled to protection under the Lanham Act if: (1) it is inherently distinctive or has acquired distinctiveness through secondary meaning; (2) it is primarily nonfunctional; and (3) its imitation would result in a likelihood of confusion in consumers' minds as to the source of the product.[98] In order for a party to succeed on a claim of trademark infringement, it must demonstrate that (1) its mark merits protection and (2) the allegedly infringing use is likely to result in consumer confusion.

Trade dress represents the total image of a product—i.e. the overall impression created—and not the individual features. The greater the similarity of marks in terms of appearance, sound, and meaning, the greater the likelihood of confusion. However, showing that both the trademark owner and the domain name, market products or services on the Internet "does not shed light on the likelihood of consumer confusion."[99] A showing of actual confusion among significant number of consumers provides strong support for a finding of likelihood of confusion.[100]

---

[95] 1 McCarthy on Trademarks and Unfair Competition § 8:1 (4th ed. 2012).

[96] Two Pesos, Inc. v. Taco Cabana, Inc., 505 U.S. 763, 764 n. 1 (1992).

[97] Id. at 764.

[98] Faegre & Benson, LLP v. Purdy, 367 F. Supp. 2d 1238, 1244 (D. Minn. 2005).

[99] Network Automation, Inc. v. Advanced Sys. Concepts, Inc., 638 F.3d 1137, 1151 (9th Cir. 2011).

[100] Id. at 1150.

Under federal trademark law, an Internet website's "look and feel" is protectable trade dress. "The ultimate inquiry in trade dress infringement is whether considering all the circumstances, likelihood exists that consumers will be confused about the source of the allegedly infringing product."[101] Section 43(a) protects unregistered trade dress, as well as registered trade dress.[102] In trade dress cases, the *prima facie* case first asks whether trade dress is functional, and then proceeds to examine whether there is a likelihood of confusion.[103] A trademark owner, for example, filed suit against a competitor that offered for sale a product bearing imitations of Living Essentials' 5 HOUR ENERGY® Trademark and Packaging Trade Dress over the Internet.

§ 11.3 ROAD MAP OF INTERNET–RELATED TRADEMARK CLAIMS

Domain names represent valuable commercial commodities for companies because they offer 24–hour-a-day exposure on the Internet. Beginning in the dotcom boom years of the late 1990s, popular domain names began to be valued in millions of dollars. Greater than 20,000 disputes between trademark owners and domain names were decided during the period 2000–2011.[104] Many domain name disputes involve multiple causes of action. To state a trademark infringement claim under the Lanham Act, a plaintiff must allege facts showing that (1) its mark is protectable, and (2) the defendant's use of an identical or similar mark in commerce is likely to cause confusion among consumers.[105] To prove trademark infringement, a plaintiff must show that the defendant's use of the mark would likely cause an appreciable number of the purchasing public to be misled, or to become confused as to the source, sponsorship, or affiliation of the defendant's goods or services.[106]

If another company palms off on a company's trade names, service marks, or trademarks, the plaintiff will have a cause of action for false designation of origin. The standard that a company must prove is that another company's use of its mark is likely to create a "likelihood of confusion." The likelihood of confusion is "the touchstone of trademark infringement as well as unfair competition."[107] In a trademark infringement suit under the Lanham Act, the trademark owner will need to demonstrate a likelihood of confusion. In a trademark infringement action, the key factors include the "similarity of the defendant's mark with the trademark owners, the strength of the mark" and whether the "parties sold the same product through the same channels of trade."[108]

---

[101] Xuan–Thao Nguyen, Should It Be a Free for All? The Challenge of Extending Trade Dress Protection to the Look and Feel of Websites in the Evolving Internet, 49 AM. U.L. REV. 122 (2000).

[102] Two Pesos, Inc., Id. at 768.

[103] Faegre & Benson, Id. at 1246.

[104] See Christopher Gibson, The UDRP and Compagnie Gervais Danone v Sequential Inc. Podcast, http://www.law.suffolk.edu/about/news/pods.cfm.

[105] See Donchez v. Coors Brewing Co., 392 F.3d 1211, 1215 (10th Cir. 2004).

[106] Section 1114 of the Lanham Act prohibits the "use in commerce any reproduction, counterfeit, copy, or colorable imitation of a registered mark in connection with the sale, offering for sale, distribution, or advertising of any goods . . . with which such good is likely to cause confusion, or to cause mistake, or to deceive." 15 U.S.C. § 1114.

[107] 3 J. THOMAS MCCARTHY, MCCARTHY ON TRADEMARKS & UNFAIR COMPETITION § 23:1 (4th ed. 2012).

[108] Sabinsa Corp. v. Creative Compounds, LLC, 609 F.3d 175 (3d Cir. 2010).

U.S. trademark owners have a choice of either (a) filing a complaint in a U.S. federal court of proper jurisdiction against the domain-name holder (or under the ACAP, an in-rem action concerning the domain name) or (b) in cases of abusive registration submit a complaint to an approved UDRP dispute-resolution service provider (see Section 11.18–11.20). A domain name's registration agreement with all accredited registrars incorporates the UDRP provisions. One of the UDRP provisions states that the Internet domain name registrar "will cancel, transfer, or otherwise make changes to domain name registrations" upon "receipt of an order from a court . . . of competent jurisdiction, requiring such action."[109] Sections 11.18 through 11.20 of this chapter cover UDRP causes of action. Trademark owners that choose UDRP proceedings have advantages of speedy and inexpensive resolution, but arbitral providers have no authority to award damages. Four approved arbitral entities: World Intellectual Property Organization (WIPO), National Arbitration Forum (NAF), Asian Domain Dispute Resolution Centre, and the Czech Arbitration Court Arbitration Center for Internet Disputes conduct UDRP proceedings. UDRP panels have decided the vast majority of domain name disputes over the past decade (50,000). In contrast, there have been less than 100 cases filed under the Anticybersquatting Protection Act. Filing UDRP actions are less expensive and quicker than federal court filings.

Lanham Act Causes of Action

Cause of Action	Type of Claim	How Liability is Determined
Trademark Infringement Act, 15 U.S.C. § 1114(1)	Trademark infringement by incorporating owner's trademark in defendant's mark.	Likelihood of Confusion Test: with the sale of a good constitutes infringement if it is likely to cause consumer confusion as to the source of those goods or as to the sponsorship or approval of such goods.
Federal Trademark Dilution Act (FDTA): 15 U.S.C. § 1125(c)	Owners of a famous mark that is distinctive are entitled to an injunction against other persons that cause dilution by blurring or dilution by tarnishment of a famous mark.	Impairs the mark's distinctiveness, whether or not the mark is used on a competing product or in a way that is likely to cause customer confusion. Federal dilution claims consider all relevant factors including advertising, sales, actual recognition, and whether the mark is registered. In blurring cases, courts consider the degree of similarity, inherent or

---

[109] Uniform Doman Name Dispute Resolution Policy http://www.icann.org/en/help/dndr/udrp/policy (September 7, 2012).

		acquired distinctiveness, extent owner is exclusively using the mark, degree of recognition of famous mark, and whether user of mark intended to create an association with the famous mark. Finally, the actual association between the defendant's mark and the famous mark are compared. See 15 U.S.C. § 1125(c).
False designation of origin and unfair competition, 15 U.S.C. § 1125(a)(1)(A)	False designation of origin by incorporating an owner's trademark in domain name.	Does the defendant's use of its mark used in commerce cause a likelihood of confusion, mistake, or deception?
False or misleading description or representation: § 43(a) (1)(B) of the Lanham Act, 15 U.S.C. § 1125(a)(1)(B)	False or misleading description of fact, or false or misleading representations.	False or misleading representations in commercial advertising. Section 43(a) of the Lanham Act prohibits the defendant from engaging in commercial activities that mislead the public.
Anticybersquatting Consumer Protection Act: 15 U.S.C. § 1125(d)	Domain names registered in bad faith identical or confusingly similar to a trademark.	Bad faith intent to profit from the mark and registers, traffics in, or uses a domain name that is identical or confusingly similar to a distinctive mark, or dilutes a famous mark.

§ 11.4 LIKELIHOOD OF CONFUSION AND RELATED CAUSES OF ACTION

(A) Direct Infringement

The Lanham Act of 1946 provides a federal cause of action for trademark infringement or false designation of origin claims. The Lanham Act recognizes trademark infringement claims under Section 32(1) of the Lanham Act.[110] To succeed in an infringement or counterfeiting claim, a plaintiff must establish the following:

---

[110] 15 U.S.C. § 1114(1).

(1) that it possesses a valid mark; (2) that the defendants used the mark; (3) that the defendants' use of the mark occurred in commerce; (4) that the defendants used the mark in connection with the sale or advertising of any goods; and (5) that the defendants used the mark in a manner likely to confuse consumers.[111]

A plaintiff must prove sufficient evidence for two elements to survive a Fed. R. Civ. P. 12(b)(1) motion to dismiss for lack of subject matter jurisdiction: (1) the trademark violation was in connection with any goods or services, and (2) the defendant used the trademark in commerce.[112] Under Section 32 of the Lanham Act, the owner of a mark registered with the Patent and Trademark Office can bring a civil action against a person alleged to have used the mark without the owner's consent.[113] The Lanham Act specifically prohibits person from reproducing, counterfeiting, copying, or colorably indicating a registered mark . . . "which such use is likely to cause confusion."[114]

Courts consider the following factors in determining whether there is a likelihood of confusion or unfair competition: (1) strength or weakness of plaintiff's mark, (2) the degree of similarity with defendant's mark, (3) class of goods, (4) marketing channels used, (5) evidence of actual confusion, and (6) intent of the defendant. No one factor is determinative as the likelihood of confusion test considers the totality of facts under the circumstances.[115] Under Section 35 of the Lanham Act, a plaintiff seeking damages for counterfeiting and infringement has the option of seeking either actual, or statutory damages—but not both.[116] For example, Louis Vuitton, a French high-end retailer and subsidiary of the Louis Vuitton Moet–Hennessey holding company ("LVMH"), will have an action against an Internet website that advertises colorable imitations or counterfeits of its handbags, wallets, luggage, shoes, belts, scarves, sunglasses, charms, watches, and jewelry and other branded merchandise. The French luxury goods manufacturer will contend that consumers will be misled, confused, and disappointed by the quality of these imposter products, and that the brand will suffer loss of sales for their genuine products.

---

[111] 15 U.S.C. § 1114(a).

[112] "The Lanham Act provides: any person who, in connection with any goods or services, or any container for goods, uses in commerce any word, term, symbol, or device, or any combination thereof, or any false designation of origin, false or misleading description of fact, or false or misleading representation of fact which (A) is likely to cause confusion, or to cause mistake, or to deceive as to the affiliation, connection, or association of such person with another person, or as to the origin, sponsorship, or approval of his or her goods, services, or commercial activities by another person, or (B) in commercial advertising or promotion, misrepresents the nature, characteristics, qualities, or geographic origin of his or her or another person's goods, services, or commercial activities, shall be liable in a civil action by any person who believes that he or she is likely to be damaged by such act." 15 U.S.C. § 1125(a)(1).

[113] 15 U.S.C. § 1114.

[114] 15 U.S.C. § 1114(1)(B).

[115] See e.g., E. & J. Gallo Winery v. Gallo Cattle Co., 967 F.2d 1280, 1290 (9th Cir. 1992). Courts consider the following factors in determining whether there is a likelihood of confusion or unfair competition: (1) strength or weakness of plaintiff's mark, (2) the degree of similarity with defendant's mark, (3) class of goods, (4) marketing channels used; (5) evidence of actual confusion, and (6) intent of the defendant. No one factor is determinative as the likelihood of the confusion test considers the totality of facts under the circumstances. See e.g., Americana Trading Inc. v. Russ Berrie & Co., 966 F.2d 1284, 1287 (9th Cir. 1992).

[116] "Section 43(a) of the Lanham Act is virtually identical to Section 32 except is applies only to registered marks but to marks recognized under the common law." Feingold & Hogan, Issues Unique Online Trademark Issues, Id. at 308–309.

Trademark owners can seek remedies for infringement including (1) injunctive relief, (2) accounting for profits made while misusing the owner's trademarks, (3) damages including treble damages for willful infringement, (4) attorney's fees in the 'exceptional case' and (5). costs of filing the action. A high-end designer, retailer, and brand holder, like Louis Vuitton, may recover actual damages equal to (1) defendant's profits, (2) any damages sustained by the plaintiff, and (3) the costs of the action.[117] The brand holder may elect instead to recover statutory damages for the use of a counterfeit mark that courts compute per counterfeit mark per type of goods or services sold, offered for sale, or distributed.[118] "In 2006, statutory awards ranged from not less than $500 to not more than $100,000 per counterfeit mark per type of goods sold if the use of the mark was not willful, or up to $1,000,000 per mark if the use was willful. These amounts were doubled beginning in October 13, 2008."[119]

(B) Likelihood of Confusion

To prevail on a claim of trademark infringement under the Lanham Act,[120] a plaintiff must prove that they have a protectable ownership interest in a trademark and that a defendant's use of the mark is likely to cause consumer confusion. More precisely, a plaintiff must show: (1) it owns a valid, protectable, and nonfunctional mark, (2) the mark is inherently distinctive or acquired secondary meaning, (3) the defendant uses, produces, counterfeits, copies, or imitates that mark in commerce without the plaintiff's consent, and (4) the consuming public is likely to be confused with the defendant's goods or services.[121] Trademark owners can seek remedies for infringement including: (1) injunctive relief, (2) accounting for profits made while misusing the owner's trademarks, (3) damages including treble damages for willful infringement, (4) attorneys' fees in the "exceptional case," and (5) costs.

The usual test used to measure a likelihood of confusion is whether the similarity of the marks is "likely to confuse consumers about the source of the products."[122] Likelihood of confusion case law instructs courts to examine nine factors: (1) the strength or distinctiveness of the plaintiff's mark as actually used in the marketplace; (2) the similarity of the two marks to consumers; (3) the similarity of the goods or services that the marks identify; (4) the similarity of the facilities used by the mark holders; (5) the similarity of advertising used by the mark holders; (6) the defendant's intent; (7) actual confusion; (8) the quality of the defendant's product; and (9) the sophistication of the consuming public.[123]

---

[117] 15 U.S.C. § 1117(a).

[118] 15 U.S.C. § 1117(c).

[119] Louis Vuitton Malletier S.A. v. LY USA, Inc., 2012 U.S. App. LEXIS 6391, *62 (2d Cir. 2012) (enjoining defendants from continuing the use of the Louis Vuitton Marks or confusingly similar trademarks within domain name extensions, metatags or other markers within website source code, from use on any web page (including as the title of any web page), any advertising links to other websites from search engines' databases or cache memory, and any other form of use of such terms which is visible to a computer user or serves to direct computer searches to websites registered by, owned, or operated by the defendants including the Internet websites operating under their domain names).

[120] 15 U.S.C. § 1114.

[121] 15 U.S.C. § 1114(a).

[122] North Am. Med. Corp. v. Axiom Worldwide, Inc., 522 F.3d 1211, 1218–20 (11th Cir. 2008).

[123] George & Co., LLC v. Imagination Entm't Ltd., 575 F.3d 383, 393 (4th Cir. 2009); 15 U.S.C. § 1125(d)(1)(B)(i)(I)–(IX).

However, in order to assess the likelihood of confusion caused by the opposing party's marks, many courts apply the eight factors articulated in *Polaroid v. Polaroid Electronics Corp.*[124] So-called *Polaroid* factors are (1) the strength of the plaintiffs' mark; (2) the similarity of the marks; (3) the proximity of the parties' products; (4) the likelihood that the plaintiff will bridge the gap; (5) actual consumer confusion; (6) bad faith of the defendant in adopting the similar mark; (7) the quality of the defendant's products; and (8) sophistication of the consumer.

In addition, courts in several jurisdictions often apply the *Sleekcraft* factors to determine the likelihood of confusion in trademark infringement lawsuits. The factors are as follows: (1) the similarity of the marks, (2) the relatedness or proximity of the two companies' products or services, (3) the strength of the registered mark, (4) the marketing channels used, (5) the degree of care likely to be exercised by the purchaser in selecting goods, (6) the accused infringer intent in selecting its mark, (7) evidence of actual confusion and (8) the likelihood of expansion in product lines.[125]

Courts assess the totality of facts under the circumstances in determining whether there is a likelihood of confusion.[126] To evaluate the strength factor, courts "focus on the distinctiveness of a mark and its recognition among the public."[127] The three most important factors in conflicts between domain names and trademarks are: (1) the similarity of the marks, (2) relatedness of the goods and services offered, and (3) simultaneous use of the Internet as a marketing channel.[128] In trademark infringement cases based upon initial interest confusion, the owner of the mark must demonstrate the likelihood of confusion, not just diversion of Internet traffic.[129] Under the Lanham Act, the trademark owner can recover up to three times actual damages and obtain injunctive relief. In cybersquatting cases, a trademark owner may claim actual damages include the profits the domain name registrant made from his use of the mark, as well as losses sustained by the mark holder as a result of the domain name registrant's actions, such as lost sales or harm to the mark's reputation.[130] Under the Anticybersquatting Consumer Protection Act of 1999, the trademark owner has the option of pursuing either actual damages or statutory damages, which range between $1,000 and $100,000 per domain.[131] The court uses its discretion to fix the actual amount awarded.[132] In "exceptional cases," a trademark owner can recover attorney's

---

[124] 287 F.2d 492 (2d Cir. 1961).

[125] AMF Inc. v. Sleekcraft Boats, 599 F.2d 341, 348–49 (9th Cir. 1979).

[126] Hotmail Corp v. Van$ Money Pie, Inc., 1998 WL 388389 *5 (N.D. Cal. 1998).

[127] Therma-Scan, Inc. v. Thermoscan, Inc., 295 F.3d 623, 631 (6th Cir. 2002).

[128] Brookfield Commc'ns, Inc. v. W. Coast Enm't Corp., 174 F.3d 1036, 1054 n. 16 (9th Cir. 1999).

[129] Id. at 1149.

[130] "The cybersquatting section of the Lanham Act, 15 U.S.C. § 1125(d), makes a person liable for the "bad faith intent to profit" from a protected mark by using a domain name that is identical or confusingly similar." PetMed Express, Inc. v. MedPets.com, Inc., 336 F.Supp.2d 1213, 1218 (S.D.Fla.2004). "Liability for federal cyberpiracy occurs when a plaintiff proves that (1) its mark is a distinctive or famous mark entitled to protection, (2) the defendant's domain names are identical or confusingly similar to the plaintiff's marks, and (3) the defendant registered the domain names with the bad faith intent to profit from them." Id.

[131] "In a case involving a violation of section 1125(d)(1) of this title, the plaintiff may elect, at any time before final judgment is rendered by the trial court, to recover, instead of actual damages and profits, an award of statutory damages in the amount of not less than $1,000 and not more than $100,000 per domain name, as the court considers just." 15 U.S.C. § 1117(d).

[132] Id.

fees against the domain name registrant found to have registered the domain name in bad faith.[133]

In *Network Automation, Inc. v. Advanced Systems Concepts, Inc.*,[134] the Ninth Circuit ruled that Network Automation Incorporated's ("Network") use of keywords incorporating Advanced System Concepts ("Systems") trademarks did not violate the Lanham Act. Network and Systems were competitors selling job scheduling and management software. Both advertised their products on the Internet. Network purchased the keyword "ActiveBatch" from Google—ActiveBatch being the name of the product produced by Systems. When Internet users typed "ActiveBatch" into various search engines, a results page was produced showing Network's website as a sponsored link.

The Ninth Circuit Court of Appeals determined that the lower court was correct in finding Network's use of keywords to constitute the prerequisite "use in commerce." Commercial use was found in Network's use of System's mark to purchase keywords to advertise its products for sale on the Internet. Nevertheless, the Ninth Circuit reversed the district court ruling that System was not entitled to an injunction. The appellate court held that the district court did not apply the *Sleekcraft* factors correctly and further that the lower court did not determine whether there was a likelihood of confusion. The failure of the plaintiff to prove likelihood of confusion was also key to the holding in *General Steel Domestic Sales v. Chumley*.[135] In *Chumley,* the court found that Armstrong's statements about General Steel's warranties supported a finding of false advertising. *In Chumley,* General Steel filed trademark, unfair advertising, and false advertising claims against Chumley, who owns and runs Armstrong, a steel buildings competitor.

General Steel requested an injunction and disgorgement of profits contending that Armstrong's use of the phrase "General Steel Buildings" (or the lowercase "general steel") in its Google AdWords advertisement copy, as a paid keyword through the AdWords program, and in the text of several websites created by Armstrong. General Steel argued that Armstrong infringed General Steel's registered federal trademark in violation of the Lanham Act, 15 U.S.C. §§ 1114(1), 1125(A), and constitutes unfair competition under Colorado law. To succeed on its trademark claim, General Steel's burden was: (1) that it has a valid and protectable mark in the term "General Steel"; (2) that Armstrong used "General Steel" in commerce without General Steel's consent; and (3) that there is a likelihood of confusion between "General Steel" and Armstrong's use of "General Steel Buildings."

The court found no dispute that General Steel did not consent to Armstrong's use of the words, "General Steel." There was also no dispute that the phrase "General Steel" was protectable by trade and used in commerce. Because the "General Steel" mark was incontestable, there was no issue of the mark's distinctiveness. General Steel was unable to prove likelihood of confusion based upon the following factors: (1) the degree of similarity between the marks, (2) the strength of the plaintiff's mark, (3) the defendant's intent in using the mark, (4) differences between the parties' products and strategies, (5) the degree of care purchasers are likely to exercise for the product or

---

[133] 15 U.S.C. § 1117.

[134] 638 F.3d 1137 (9th Cir. 2011).

[135] 2013 U.S. Dist. LEXIS 64932 (D. Colo. May 17, 2013).

service, and (6) evidence of actual confusion. The Colorado federal court found that General Steel produced no evidence of actual confusion. The court acknowledged that several of the factors weighed in favor of actual confusion and that initial interest confusion might occur. However, the court concluded that the fifth factor was determinative. The purchasers of steel buildings were likely to take care in purchasing that product. The court concluded:

> While Armstrong was using the term to refer to plaintiff's company, the Court does not find the record supports the finding that such use was likely to cause confusion among consumers in light of all of the surrounding information that identified Armstrong Steel as the source of the website and distinguished Armstrong Steel from General Steel.[136]

The court also observed that "the actual uses of the keywords "general steel" in website text occurred either in the context of a clear comparison or in a context that, while puzzling, was unlikely to confuse consumers as to source."[137] The court also

(C) False Advertising

The Lanham Act imposes liability on those who "in commercial advertising or promotion, misrepresents the nature, characteristics, qualities, or geographic origin of his or her or another person's goods, services, or commercial activities."[138] Under the Lanham Act, this cause of action imposes liability on those who "in commercial advertising or promotion, misrepresents the nature, characteristics, qualities, or geographic origin of his or her or another person's goods, services, or commercial activities."[139] In order to prevail on a false advertising claim, the plaintiff must prove four elements: "(1) that defendant made material false or misleading representations of fact in connection with the commercial advertising or promotion of its product; (2) in commerce, (3) that are either likely to cause confusion or mistake as to (a) the origin, association or approval of the product with or by another, or (b) the characteristics of the goods or services; and (4) injure the plaintiff."[140]

(D) Reverse Confusion

Reverse confusion, as the result of trademark infringement in violation of the Lanham Act, typically occurs when the defendant's advertising and promotion swamps the plaintiff's reputation in the market that customers purchase the plaintiff's goods under the mistaken impression that they are getting the goods of the defendant.[141] Confusion of sponsorship "occurs where the goods do not directly compete. In this situation, the goods are unrelated enough that no inference arises that they originated from the same source, but the similarity of the trademarks erroneously suggests a connection between the sources."[142] With reverse confusion, customers purchase the

---

[136] Id. at *30.

[137] Id. at *34.

[138] 15 U.S.C. § 1125(a)(1)(B).

[139] Id.

[140] Id. at *35–*36.

[141] Lanham Act, §§ 32(1)(a), 43(a), 15 U.S.C. §§ 1114(a), 1125.

[142] Ameritech, Inc. v. Am. Info. Techs. Corp., 811 F.2d 960, 964–65 (6th Cir. 1987); See also Malletier v. Burlington Coat Factory Warehouse Corp., 426 F.3d 532, 539 n.4 (2d Cir. 2005). Banff, Ltd. v. Federated Dep't Stores, Inc., 841 F.2d 486, 490 (2d Cir. 1988) ("Reverse confusion is the misimpression that the] junior user is the source of the senior user's goods."). See also Lang v. Retirement Living Pub. Co., Inc., 949 F.2d

senior user's goods under the misimpression that the junior user is the source of the senior user's goods and that harm may occur if the junior user saturates the market and overwhelms the senior user.[143] Reverse confusion diminishes the value of the trademark and the senior user's business. "Harm from the reverse confusion may occur because the junior user "saturates the market" and overwhelms the senior user, causing harm to the value of the trademark and the senior user's business."[144]

The First Circuit notes "[a] reverse confusion case is proven only if the evidence shows that the junior user was able to swamp the reputation of the senior user with a relatively much larger advertising campaign."[145] "There is no actionable reverse confusion in the absence of a showing of likely confusion as to source or sponsorship. A trademark holder must show a *likelihood* of confusion; it need not show actual confusion, but actual confusion will strengthen the holder's infringement claim."[146]

In *J.T. Colby v. Apple Inc.*,[147] a group of publishing companies contended that Apple infringed their trademark and created a likelihood of reverse confusion, "in that consumers will likely believe that its books are in fact published by or affiliated with Apple."[148] The plaintiffs employed the unregistered trademark iBook's and brought a trademark infringement action against the defendant. The Southern District of New York granted Apple a summary judgment ruling that the publishers "failed to present sufficient evidence that their iBook's mark is entitled to trademark protection or that their mark is likely to suffer from reverse confusion with Apple's iBooks mark."[149] The plaintiffs had failed to establish that it had any enforceable trademark rights or that Apple's use of "iBooks" for its e-reader software would create a likelihood of reverse confusion. In reverse confusion cases, too, *the Polaroid* factors apply equally well.[150]

(E) Secondary Trademark Infringement

(1) Contributory Trademark Infringement

Contributory trademark infringement occurs under the Lanham Act when the defendant either: (1) intentionally induces a third party to infringe on the plaintiff's mark; or (2) enables a third party to infringe on the mark while knowing or having reason to know that the third party is infringing, yet failing to take reasonable remedial measures.[151]   To be liable for contributory trademark infringement,[152] a

---

576, 583 (2d Cir. 1991)("Reverse confusion exists when a subsequent user selects a trademark that is likely to cause consumers to believe, erroneously, that the goods marketed by the prior user are produced by the subsequent user.").

[143] 15 U.S.C. § 1125(a).

[144] Visible Sys. Corp. v. Unisys Corp., 551 F.3d 65, 72 (1st Cir. 2008).

[145] Id. (citing McCarthy on Trademarks and Unfair Competition).

[146] Id. (citations omitted).

[147] 2013 U.S. Dist. LEXIS 65959 (S.D. N.Y., May 8, 2013).

[148] Id at *1.

[149] Id. at *2.

[150] "Taking all of the Polaroid factors into account, and drawing all inferences in the plaintiffs' favor, the plaintiffs have failed to raise a genuine issue of material fact with respect to likelihood of confusion. On balance, the Polaroid factors weigh heavily against a finding that an appreciable number of ordinary prudent consumers are likely to be confused. Indeed, apart from the fact that both parties use marks presenting a variation of the word IBOOKS, there is little in the record to suggest that consumers will mistakenly believe plaintiffs' books originate with, are sponsored by, or are affiliated with Apple." Id at *82–*83.

[151] Lanham Act, §§ 32(1)(a), 43(a), 15 U.S.C. §§ 1114(1)(a), 1125(a).

defendant must have: (1) intentionally induced the primary infringer to infringe; or (2) continued to supply an infringing product to an infringer with knowledge that the infringer is mislabeling the particular product supplied.[153] When the primary infringer supplies a service rather than a product, a court must consider the extent of control exercised by the defendant over the third party's means of infringement. The knowledge requirement is objective and is satisfied where the defendant knows or has reason to know of the infringing activity.[154] Any liability for contributory infringement will depend upon whether or not the contributing party intended to participate in the infringement, or actually knew about the infringing activities. Secondary liability for infringement arises when "a manufacturer or distributor intentionally induces another to infringe a trademark, or . . . continues to supply its product to one whom it knows or has reason to know is engaging in trademark infringement."[155]

When the alleged direct infringer supplies a service rather than a product, under the second prong of this test, the court must consider the extent of control exercised by the defendant over the third party's means of infringement. For liability to attach there must be direct control and monitoring of the instrumentality used by a third party to infringe the plaintiff's mark.[156] In *Sony Corps. v. Universal City Studios*, the U.S. Supreme Court determined the manufacturers of Betamax video tape recorders were not secondarily liable because these machines had a substantial legitimate use.[157] In *Perfect 10 v. Visa Int'l Service Ass'n*,[158] the court noted the necessity of demonstrating a nexus between the payment processing services provided by Visa and the alleged infringing activities. Contributory infringement cannot be based upon the operation of a website that processes credit cards without proof of the other elements. The court dismissed the claim against Visa with leave to amend contributory and vicarious infringement claims against the credit card company.

The first Internet-related case to address contributory trademark infringement was *Lockheed Martin Corp. v. Network Solutions, Inc.*,[159] where the Ninth Circuit held that Network Solutions was not contributorily liable for the trademark infringement of a domain name.[160] In *Gucci America, Inc. v. Hall & Assocs.*,[161] the court refused to dismiss Gucci's claim against an ISP for contributory trademark infringement

---

[152] This form of secondary liability was first recognized by the Supreme Court in Inwood Laboratories, Inc. v. Ives Laboratories, Inc., 456 U.S. 844 (1982). In Inwood, the U.S. Supreme Court recognized for the first time that liability under the Lanham Act may be imposed on those who facilitate trademark infringement, stating that where a "distributor intentionally induces another to infringe a trademark, or if it continues to supply its product to one whom it knows or has reason to know is engaging in trademark infringement, [it] is contributorily responsible for any harm done as a result of the deceit." Id. at 854. With contributory infringement in cyberspace, liability is imposable upon instigators and facilitators of direct infringement.

[153] 4 MCCARTHY ON TRADEMARKS AND UNFAIR COMPETITION § 25:19 (4th ed. 2012).

[154] See e.g., Sega Enters. Ltd. v. MAPHIA, 948 F. Supp. 923, 933 (N.D. Cal. 1996).

[155] Inwood Labs., Inc. v. Ives Labs., Inc., 456 U.S. 844, 854 (1982).

[156] Sony Corp. v. Universal City Studios, 464 U.S. 417 (1984).

[157] The Sony test determines "whether a company's product is capable of substantial or commercially significant non-infringing uses." Id. at 952 (citing Sony Corp. of Am. v. Universal City Studios, Inc., 464 U.S. 417, 442 (1984)). The Court reasoned that inducement requires an "unlawful purpose" that encourages infringement. Grokster, 545 U.S. at 938. The Court predicated active inducement upon proof that the defendant's "statements and actions" promoted direct infringement. Id. at 935.

[158] 2004 WL 1773349, at *4 (N. D. Cal. Aug. 5, 2004).

[159] 194 F.3d 980, 983–85 (9th Cir. 1999).

[160] Id. at 987.

[161] 135 F. Supp. 2d 409, 416 (S.D.N.Y. 2001).

predicated upon the claim it hosted a direct trademark infringer.[162] Mere knowledge of third party infringement is an insufficient basis for contributory trademark infringement.[163] Secondary infringement also requires proof of direct infringement. A party proves trademark infringement under the Lanham Act by showing (1) that it owns a trademark, (2) that the infringer used the mark in commerce without authorization, and (3) that the use of the alleged infringing trademark is likely to cause confusion among consumers regarding the origin of the goods offered by the parties.[164]

(2) Vicarious Trademark Infringement

Vicarious liability in trademark law draws in large part upon the concepts of *respondeat superior* or vicarious liability in tort law. Vicarious liability for trademark infringement under the Lanham Act arises when common-law principles of agency impose liability on the defendant for the infringing acts of its agent.[165] "Thus, liability for vicarious trademark infringement requires a finding that the defendant and the infringer have an apparent or actual partnership, have authority to bind one another in transactions with third parties or exercise joint ownership or control over the infringing product."[166] Vicarious liability for trademark infringement requires "a finding that the defendant and the infringer have an apparent or actual partnership, authority to bind one another in transactions with third parties, or exercise joint ownership or control over the infringing product."[167] Courts typically apply a four-part test to determine partnership: (1) parties' sharing of profits and losses; (2) parties' joint control and management of business; (3) contribution by each party of property, financial resources, effort, skill, or knowledge to business; and (4) parties' intention to be partners.[168]

In *Perfect 10 v. Visa International*,[169] the Ninth Circuit refused to find Visa vicariously liable for its role in enabling payment of website access to content violating the copyrights and trademarks of a third party magazine publisher. The appeals court uncovered no affirmative acts by the defendants suggesting third parties should infringe the publisher's trademarks.[170] The Ninth Circuit said even if defendants allowed the infringing merchants to use their logos, trade name, or trademarks, they would not be liable for false advertising because they had no duty to investigate the truth of the statements made by others.[171] "Vicarious liability for trademark infringement requires a finding that the defendant and the infringer have an apparent or actual partnership, have authority to bind one another in transactions with third

---

[162] Id. at 412.

[163] Id. at 421 ("Trademark plaintiffs bear a high burden in establishing "knowledge" of contributory infringement. A trademark owner's mere assertion that its domain name is infringed is insufficient to impute knowledge of infringement. Moreover, while uncertainty of infringement is relevant to the question of an alleged contributory infringer's knowledge, a trademark owner's demand letter is insufficient to resolve this inherent uncertainty.").

[164] 15 U.S.C. § 1114(1)(a).

[165] Lanham Act, §§ 32(1)(a), 43(a), 15 U.S.C. §§ 1114(1)(a), 1125(a).

[166] Rosetta Stone Ltd. v. Google, Inc., 2012 U.S. App. LEXIS 7082 *50 (April 9, 2012).

[167] Hard Rock Café Licensing Corp. v. Concession Servs. Inc., 955 F.2d 1143, 1150 (7th Cir. 1992).

[168] Id.

[169] 494 F.3d 788 (9th Cir. 2007).

[170] Id.

[171] Id.

parties or exercise joint ownership or control over the infringing product."[172] Moreover, "the tests for secondary trademark infringement are even more difficult to satisfy than those required to find secondary copyright infringement."[173]

The court found Visa did not encourage the improper conduct at issue; they merely processed credit card payments.[174] The court also found payment processing for infringing Internet websites by credit card companies did not constitute intentional inducement of infringement even though it did provide "critical support" to infringing websites.[175] The court found no inducement because it did not "affirmative acts by Defendants suggesting that third parties infringe Perfect 10's mark, much less induce them to do so."[176]

§ 11.5   TRADEMARK DILUTION REVISION ACT OF 2006

To state a *prima facie* dilution claim under the Federal Trademark Dilution Act ("FTDA"), 15 U.S.C. § 1125(c), a trademark owner must show the following: (1) it owns a famous mark that is distinctive; (2) Defendant has commenced using a mark in commerce that allegedly is diluting the famous mark; (3) that a similarity between Defendant's mark and the famous mark gives rise to an association between the marks; and (4) that the association is likely to impair the distinctiveness of the famous mark or likely to harm the reputation of the famous mark. Until 1996, trademark dilution was based entirely upon state law because federal law did not recognize the dilution doctrine. The FTDA was passed in 1996[177] and was amended substantially in 2006 with the passage of the Trademark Dilution Revision Act of 2006 ("TDRA"). [178] The TDRA provides:

[T]he owner of a famous mark . . . shall be entitled to an injunction against another person who . . . commences use of a mark or trade name in commerce that is likely to cause dilution by blurring or dilution by tarnishment of the famous mark, regardless of the presence or absence of actual or likely confusion, of competition, or of actual economic injury.[179]

Under the TDRA, "a mark is famous if it is widely recognized by the general consuming public of the United States as a designation of source of the goods or services of the marks owner."[180] To determine the requisite degree of fame, the court may consider all relevant factors including: (i) the duration, extent, and geographic reach of advertising and publicity of the mark, whether advertised or publicized by the owner or third parties; (ii) the amount, volume and geographic extent of sales or goods;

---

[172] Id. at 807.

[173] Perfect 10, Inc. v. Visa Int'l Serv. Ass'n, 494 F.3d 788, 806 (9th Cir.2007).

[174] Id.

[175] Id. at 807.

[176] Id.

[177] The Federal Trademark Dilution Act (FTDA) recognized new remedies for the dilution of famous trademarks. The court determines whether a trademark is famous by balancing eight statutory factors. Federal Trademark Dilution Act of 1995, Pub. L. 104–98, sec. 3, § 43, 109 Stat. 985, 985–986 (codified as amended at 15 U.S.C. § 1125(c)(1). The FTDA factors include the duration and extent of use of the mark, the nature of the advertising, and the acquired distinctiveness of the mark. 15 U.S.C. § 1125(c)(1). These factors favor the marks of the largest and most powerful companies. Pub. L. No. 104–98, 109 Stat. 985 (1996).

[178] Rosetta Stone Ltd. v. Google, Inc., 2012 U.S. App. LEXIS 7082 *56 (April 9, 2012).

[179] 15 U.S.C. § 1125(c)(1).

[180] 15 U.S.C. § 1125(c)(2)(A).

(iii) the extent of the mark's actual recognition; (iv) whether the mark is registered. The TDRA statute defines "dilution by blurring" as the "association arising from the similarity between a mark or trade name and a famous mark that impairs the distinctiveness of the famous mark."[181] "[D]ilution by tarnishment" is defined as the "association arising from the similarity between a mark or trade name and a famous mark that harms the reputation of the famous mark."[182]

Blurring is "whittling away" of the trademark while tarnishment links trademarks to shoddy or unwholesome products. The TDRA amended the Lanham Act to render one liable to the owner of a trademark who, with "a bad faith intent to profit from that mark," "registers, traffics in or uses a domain name" that is either identical or confusingly similar to a "distinctive" mark or is identical, confusingly similar or dilutive of a "famous mark."[183]

(A) Federal Dilution Claim

The Federal Trademark Dilution Act's ("FTDA") purpose, as shown in its legislative history, was to "protect famous trademarks from subsequent uses that blur the distinctiveness of the mark or tarnish or disparage it, even in the absence of likelihood of confusion."[184] Dilution, under the FTDA, is the "lessening of the capacity of a famous mark to identify and distinguish goods or services regardless of the presence or absence of: (1) competition between the owner of the famous mark and other parties, or (2) likelihood of confusion, mistake, or deception."[185] Approximately half of the states recognize dilution but vary as to whether a plaintiff must prove damages from tarnishment or blurring.

In determining whether a mark or trade name is likely to cause dilution violative of the Lanham Act by blurring, the court may consider all relevant factors, including (i) the degree of similarity between the mark or trade name and the famous mark, (ii) the degree of inherent or acquired distinctiveness of the famous mark, (iii) the extent to which the owner of the famous mark is engaging in substantially exclusive use of the mark, (iv) the degree of recognition of the famous mark, (v) whether the user of the mark or trade name intended to create an association with the famous mark, and (vi) any actual association between the mark or trade name and the famous mark.[186] In 1995, U.S. President Bill Clinton signed the FTDA, amending the Lanham Act to protect the owners of famous trademarks from dilution.[187] The FTDA provides:

> that the owner of a famous mark shall be entitled, subject to the principles of equity and upon such terms as the court deems reasonable, to an injunction against another person's commercial use in commerce of a mark trade name, if such use begins after the mark has become famous and causes dilution of the distinctive quality of the mark.[188]

---

[181] 15 U.S.C. § 1125(c)(2)(B).

[182] 15 U.S.C. § 1125(c)(2)(C).

[183] 15 U.S.C. § 1125(c).

[184] H.R. Rep. No. 104–374, at 2 (1995).

[185] 15 U.S.C. § 1127.

[186] Lanham Act, § 43(c), 15 U.S.C. § 1125(c).

[187] 15 U.S.C. § 1125(c).

[188] Id.

The Trademark Dilution Revision Act of 2006 ("TDRA") amended Section 43(c) of the Lanham Act[189] to enable trademark owners of famous trademarks to file a federal anti-dilution action. The TDRA prohibits use of a trademark that is "likely to cause dilution by tarnishment [of a famous mark]."[190] The TDRA gives the owner of a *famous* and *distinctive* mark the right to an injunction against a person who uses the mark in commerce, in a manner that is likely to cause dilution by *blurring* or *tarnishing* the famous mark. Under the TDRA, there is still a cause of action "regardless of the presence or absence of actual or likely confusion, of competition, or of actual economic injury."[191] To get relief under the TDRA, a trademark owner must first show that their mark is both famous and distinct. The TDRA extends to those marks that are inherently distinctive, and to those deriving distinctiveness from secondary meaning.[192] Second, the owner must show one of two forms of dilution: blurring and tarnishment as first developed under the common law. "Dilution by tarnishing occurs when a junior mark's similarity to a famous mark causes consumers mistakenly to associate the famous mark with the defendant's inferior or offensive product."[193]

(B) The Nuts & Bolts of the TDRA

The plain language of the TDRA now makes it clear that a claim for dilution is actionable when use of a famous mark in commerce "is *likely* to cause dilution regardless of the presence or absence of actual or likely confusion, of competition, or of actual economic injury."[194] The TDRA applies only to trademarks that are "famous" within the meaning of the statute. Under the statute, a famous mark is one, which is "widely recognized by the general consuming public of the United States as a designation of source of the goods or services of the marks' owner."[195] Thus, the plaintiff must establish that its mark is famous as a condition precedent before any dilution of its mark can be found. As a threshold matter in all trademark cases, the plaintiffs must now establish their ownership of the mark in question. o prevail under the TDRA of 2006, the plaintiff must show: (1) ownership of a famous mark that is distinctive, (2) a defendant used a mark in commerce that allegedly is diluting the famous mark, (3) a similarity between the defendant's mark and the famous mark giving rise to an association between marks, and (4) the association is likely to impair the distinctiveness of the famous mark or likely to harm the reputation of the famous mark.

Dilution is not concerned with confusion in the marketplace. Rather, dilution theory provides that if customers or prospective customers see the plaintiff's famous

---

[189] Id.

[190] Gilliam v. American Broadcasting Co., Inc., 538 F.2d 14, 24–25 (2d Cir. 1976).

[191] 15 U.S.C. § 1125(c)(1).

[192] "A trademark acquires a secondary meaning if the words have been used so long and so exclusively by one producer with reference to his goods or articles that, in that trade and to that branch of the purchasing public, the word or phrase has come to mean that the article is his product. The number of search engine hits, standing alone, is inadequate to demonstrate that consumers associate the mark with a particular product or producer." Utah Lighthouse Ministry v. Found. for Apologetic Info. & Research, 527 F.3d 1045, 1052 (10th Cir. 2008).

[193] Hasbro, Inc. v. Internet Entm't Group, Ltd., 1996 U.S. Dist. LEXIS 11626, 1996 WL 84858 (W.D. Wash. 1996) (holding that sexually explicit "candyland.com" diluted Hasbro's trademark "Candy Land" children's board game).

[194] 15 U.S.C. § 1125(c)(1).

[195] Id. at § 1125(c)(2)(A).

mark used by other persons in a non-confusing way to identify other sources for many different goods and services, then the ability of the famous mark to clearly identify and distinguish only one source might be "diluted" or weakened.[196] Trademark owners first need to establish their trademarks are famous under a multi-factorial analysis:

(1) the degree of inherent or acquired distinctiveness of the mark;

(2) the duration and extent of use of the mark in connection with the goods or services with which the mark is used;

(3) the duration and extent of advertising and publicity of the mark;

(4) the geographical extent of the trading area in which the mark is used;

(5) the channels of trade for the goods or services with which the mark is used;

(6) the degree of recognition of the mark in the trading areas and channels of trade used by the marks' owner and the person against whom the injunction is sought;

(7) the nature and extent of use of the same or similar marks by third parties.[197]

Under the FTDA, "a mark is famous if it is widely recognized by the general consuming public of the United States as a designation of source of the goods or services."[198] The TDRA expressly states that one of the factors that can be considered is"[w]hether the mark was registered . . . on the principal register."[199] The Trademark Dilution Revision Act of 2006 amended the Federal Trademark Dilution Act to provide that the owner of a famous, distinctive mark is entitled to an injunction against the use of a mark that is "likely" to cause dilution of the famous mark.[200] Under federal law, an owner of a "famous, distinctive mark" is entitled to an injunction against the user of a mark that is likely to cause dilution of the famous mark.[201] The requirement that the mark be "famous" and "distinctive" significantly limits the pool of marks that may receive dilution protection. Federal dilution is actionable in two situations under the TDRA: (1) dilution by "blurring" and (2) dilution by "tarnishment."[202]

The TDRA will likely draw from the well of the common law in conceptualizing blurring as the whittling away of the distinctiveness of a trademark. In contrast, dilution by "tarnishment" occurs when association arising from the similarity between a mark or trade name and a competing mark harms the reputation of the mark. Similarly, a domain name can tarnish a trademark, as in *Mattel, Inc. v. Jcom, Inc.,*[203] where the Barbie trademark was used on an adult entertainment web site.[204] The court held that the use of the Barbie trademark combined with particular fonts and color schemes tarnished the mark.[205]

---

[196] Rosetta Stone Ltd. v. Google, Inc., 2012 U.S. App. LEXIS 7082 *56 (April 9, 2012).

[197] 15 U.S.C. § 1125(c)(1).

[198] 15 U.S.C. § 1125(c)(2)(A).

[199] 15 U.S.C. § 1125(c)(2)(A)(iv).

[200] 15 U.S.C. § 1125(c)(1).

[201] Id.

[202] Id.

[203] 48 U.S.P.Q.2d (BNA) 1467, (S.D.N.Y. 1996).

[204] Id. at 1470.

[205] See also, Hasbro, Inc. v. Internet Entm't Group, Ltd., No. C96–130WD, 1996 U.S. Dist. LEXIS 11626, at *2–3 (W.D. Wash. Feb. 9, 1996) (finding adult entertainment website tarnished distinctive mark of famous board game).

"[D]ilution by tarnishment" is defined as the "association arising from the similarity between a mark or trade name and a famous mark that harms the reputation of the famous mark."[206] For purposes of TDRA cases,[207] the creation of an association between a famous mark and activity that disparages and defiles the famous mark constitutes tarnishment. Tarnishment creates consumer aversion to the famous brand—*e.g.,* when the plaintiff's famous trademark is "linked to products of shoddy quality, or is portrayed in an unwholesome or unsavory context" such that "the public will associate the lack of quality or lack of prestige in the defendant's goods with the plaintiff's unrelated goods."[208] Ben and Jerry's Homemade Inc., a maker of ice cream, filed a trademark suit based upon tarnishment against Cabellero Video "barring it from selling its "Ben & Cherry's" series of 10 DVDs with titles including "Peanut Butter D–Cups" and "Boston Cream Thigh."[209] In contrast, blurring is a whittling away of the distinctive features of a trademark.

(C) TDRA Blurring

The TDRA defines "dilution by blurring" as the "association arising from the similarity between a mark or trade name and a famous mark that impairs the distinctiveness of the famous mark."[210] Thus, blurring under the federal statute involves the classic "whittling away" of the selling power and strength of the famous mark. "Blurring" is when a trademark loses its ability to trigger an association in a consumer's mind between the trademark and a particular producer of goods or services. Some customers, upon seeing the mark in a domain name would no longer instantly associate the owner with the mark. "Dilution by blurring" may "be found "regardless of the presence or absence of actual or likely confusion, of competition, or of actual economic injury," 15 U.S.C. § 1125(c)(1)."[211] To establish dilution, "there must be some mental association between plaintiff's and defendant's marks." The TDRA law specifies six non-exhaustive factors for the courts to consider in determining whether there is dilution by blurring:

(i) The degree of similarity between the mark or trade name and the famous mark.

(ii) The degree of inherent or acquired distinctiveness of the famous mark.

(iii) The extent to which the owner of the famous mark is engaging in substantially exclusive use of the mark.

(iv) The degree of recognition of the famous mark.

(v) Whether the user of the mark or trade name intended to create an association with the famous mark.

(vi) Any actual association between the mark or trade name and the famous mark.[212]

---

[206] 15 U.S.C. § 1125(c)(2)(C).

[207] 15 U.S.C. § 1125.

[208] Scott Fetzer Co. v. House of Vacuums Inc., 381 F.3d 477, 489 (5th Cir.2004).

[209] Bob Van Voris, BLOOMBERG LAW (Sept. 12, 2012).

[210] 15 U.S.C. § 1125(c)(2)(B).

[211] Starbucks Corp. v. Wolfe's Borough Coffee, Inc., 588 F.3d 97, 105 (2d Cir. 2009).

[212] 15 U.S.C. § 1125(c)(2)(B)(i)–(vi).

The 2006 TDRA overrules the Supreme Court's ruling in *Moseley v. V Secret Catalogue, Inc.*,[213] which interpreted the prior federal Anti–Dilution Act to require prevailing plaintiffs to prove actual dilution.[214] Before *Moseley,* courts were deeply divided on the issue of whether the plaintiff must demonstrate actual damages in a federal dilution case. Some courts reasoned that dilution, in contrast to infringement, does not require a showing of consumer confusion because it protects only the distinctiveness of the mark and not against consumer harm. However, other courts required a TDRA plaintiff to prove actual dilution. After the TDRA of 2006, dilution by blurring may be found "regardless of the presence or absence of actual or likely confusion, of competition, or of actual economic injury."[215]

In *Starbucks Corp. v. Wolfe's Borough Coffee, Inc.*,[216] the famous trademark owner sold coffee products in retail locations and supplied coffees to restaurants, supermarkets, and other businesses. The competitor was a relatively small company that began selling a coffee with Charbucks, a name similar to Starbuck's mark. The Second Circuit found that the lower court erred in that the "Charbucks Marks were minimally similar to the Starbucks Marks. Although "Ch" arbucks is similar to "St" arbucks in sound and spelling, it is evident from the record that the Charbucks Marks—as they are presented to consumers—are minimally similar to the Starbucks Marks."[217]

In addition to demonstrating that the plaintiff's mark is protected, the plaintiff must prove that the defendant's use of the allegedly infringing mark would likely cause confusion as to the origin or sponsorship of the defendant's goods with plaintiff's goods."[218] "The Charbucks line of products are presented as either "Mister Charbucks" or "Charbucks Blend" in packaging that displays the "Black Bear" name in no subtle manner, and the packaging also makes clear that Black Bear is a "Micro Roastery" located in New Hampshire."[219]

The Second Circuit determined that remand was warranted as to plaintiffs' claim of trademark dilution by blurring under 15 U.S.C. § 1125(c)(2)(B) because (1) the district court erred to the extent it required "substantial" similarity between the marks, and (2) the determination of an "intent to associate" did not require the additional consideration of whether bad faith corresponded with that intent. However, the claim for dilution by tarnishment failed because the competitor's line of coffee was marketed as a product of "very high quality," which was inconsistent with the concept of "tarnishment." The trademark infringement and unfair competition claims failed under the Polaroid test because, (1) the "bridging the gap" factor was irrelevant and thus did not favor plaintiffs where the two products were in direct competition with

---

[213] 537 U.S. 418, 433 (2003).

[214] Congress displaced the FTDA with the TDRA in the wake of the Supreme Court's ruling in Moseley v. Victoria's Secret Catalogue, Inc., 537 U.S. 418 (2003), in which the Court had held that a plaintiff must show actual dilution—as opposed to likelihood of dilution—in order to prevail under the then-current Federal Trademark Dilution Act.

[215] 15 U.S.C. § 1125(c)(1).

[216] 588 F.3d 97 (2d Cir. 2009).

[217] Id. at 108.

[218] Id. at 114.

[219] Id. at 108.

each other, and (2) there was no likelihood that consumers would confuse the marks.[220] In November of 2013, the Second Circuit ruled that Starbucks did not prove that consumers would be confused by the blurring of their brand and that Charbucks could continue using the Charbucks marks.[221]

Prior to the TDRA of 2006, U.S. federal courts weighed in as to what constituted famousness. In early federal dilution cases, well-known companies often had difficulty to demonstrate that their marks were "famous." In *Avery Dennison Corp. v. Sumpton*,[222] the trademark owner of the "AVERY" and "DENNISON" brands of office products filed suit against Jerry Sumpton, an entrepreneur who sold vanity domain names and registered domain names with these trademarks. The Ninth Circuit held that Avery Dennison did not establish the "famousness" element and therefore had no TDRA cause of action. The court also found that the plaintiff failed to demonstrate commercial use by the defendant as Mr. Sumpton was selling the domain names for use for surname domain names—not for commercial use. The court did not find the words "AVERY" and "DENNISON" to constitute famous marks although they had been used for over seventy years and had generated sales of $3 billion. The lesson from this case is that the FTDA's delimiters of famousness and commercial use prevent many trademark owners from pursuing a federal dilution claim.[223] The Lanham Act protects the owner of a famous trademark against another's use of a nearly identical mark that dilutes the distinctiveness of, or tarnishes, the famous trademark.[224]

In *Visa Int'l Service Ass'n v. JSL Corp.*,[225] the Nevada district court held that use of "evisa.com" by a business to promote its language service diluted the Visa International trademark. The court stated that the defendant's use of the trademark "evisa.com" created "actual dilution" because it was substantially similar to the plaintiff's famous "Visa" mark. Moreover, the court explained that businesses commonly place an "e" before their trademark to denote the online version of their business. Specifically, the *Visa* court held that dilution occurred because of Visa being unable to use "evisa.com" to market its product. More significantly, the court did not rely on direct evidence of actual dilution or that consumers actually associated defendant's evisa.com mark with the plaintiff. The court found the FTDA of 1996 only required the holder of a famous mark to show a likelihood of dilution arising out of defendant's use of a mark.

Notably, the district court was obligated to interpret the FTDA as directed by the U.S. Supreme Court in *Moseley*, because the case was filed before the 2006 amendment of the FTDA. Accordingly, the Visa court held that the plaintiff did not need to prove actual confusion given the near identity of the parties' respective marks. The district

---

[220] Under the Polaroid test, the court weighs eight factors: (1) strength of the trademark; (2) similarity of the marks; (3) proximity of the products and their competitiveness with one another; (4) evidence that the senior user may "bridge the gap" by developing a product for sale in the market of the alleged infringer's product; (5) evidence of actual consumer confusion; (6) evidence that the imitative mark was adopted in bad faith; (7) respective quality of the products; and (8) sophistication of consumers in the relevant market.

[221] Jonathan Stempel, Starbucks Loses 'Charbucks Appeal.' REUTERS (Nov. 15, 2013).

[222] 189 F.3d 868 (9th Cir. 1999).

[223] Cf. Archdiocese of St. Louis v. Internet Entertainment Group, Inc., 1999 WL 66022, at *1 (E.D. Mo. Feb. 12, 1999) (holding that "Papal Visit 1999" was a famous trademark for purposes of the FTDA and enjoining pornographic website using a domain name incorporating that mark).

[224] 15 U.S.C. § 1125(c).

[225] 533 F. Supp. 2d 1089 (D. Nev. 2007).

court further found the FTDA protected Visa because the "evisa" mark weakened the ability of the Visa to identify its respective goods and services. The "evisa" mark diverted Internet searchers because consumers were not brought to Visa's website when entering "evisa.com." Following the appropriate standard, the *Visa* court found that the plaintiff's "Visa" mark was famous and distinctive, thus entitling it to protection under the FTDA. The court ruled the defendant was making a commercial use of the mark "to promote a language service business," that began after the plaintiff's mark became famous. As a result, the court granted Visa International's motion for summary judgment, finding that JSL Corp. violated the FTDA.

(D) Defenses to Federal Dilution Actions

The older FTDA definition of fair use was limited to "use of a famous mark by another person in comparative commercial advertising or promotion to identify the competing goods or services of the owner of the famous mark."[226] Section 15 U.S.C. § 1125(c)(3), which amends the Lanham Act pursuant to the Trademark Dilution Revision Act, expressly excludes from its reach any fair use, including a nominative or descriptive fair use, or facilitation of such fair use, of a famous mark by another person other than as a designation of source for the person's own goods or services.[227] The statute specifically provides comparative advertising and parody as examples of non-dilutive fair uses.[228] A federal claim for dilution is not actionable if it involves "[a]ny fair use . . . of a famous mark by another person other than as a designation of source for the person's own goods or services, including in connection with . . . advertising or promotion that permits consumers to compare goods or services."[229]

In response to First Amendment, or associational policy concerns, the FTDA exempts certain uses of a famous mark. FTDA defenses include the following: (1) the mark is not famous; (2) the use is classified as a parody; (3) noncommercial use of the mark; (4) fair use of a famous mark is permitted in comparative advertisements and (5) dilution is not likely. Just as with any trademark action, a defendant may assert a right to use a trademark in a news commentary, a comparative advertisement. Fair use is a statutory defense under the current FTDA.[230] Fair use, while not expressly labeled as such in the FTDA, is also a defense against federal dilution.[231]

§ 11.6 STATE ANTI–DILUTION ACTIONS

Companies that cannot seek federal anti-dilution protection may be able to file state anti-dilution claims that do not require proof that the company is famous. About half of the states have enacted anti-dilution statutes. Traditionally, dilution was conceptualized as the gradual whittling away of a trademark's selling power and value through its use by others on dissimilar products. Prior to passage of the FTDA, a trademark owner's only recourse for dilution was to seek relief in the state courts for

---

[226] 15 U.S.C. § 1125(c)(4)(A).

[227] 15 U.S.C. § 1125(c)(3)(A).

[228] 15 U.S.C. § 1125(c)(3)(A)(i)–(ii).

[229] 15 U.S.C. § 1125(c)(3)(A).

[230] See 15 U.S.C. § 1125(c)(3)(A) (2006) ("Any fair use, including a nominative or descriptive fair use, or facilitation of such fair use, of a famous mark by another person other than as a designation of source for the person's own goods or services" is not "actionable as dilution by blurring or dilution by tarnishment.").

[231] Rosetta Stone Ltd. v. Google, Inc., 2012 U.S. App. LEXIS 7082 (4th Cir. April 9, 2012).

blurring or tarnishment. Massachusetts enacted the first trademark dilution statute in 1947. "By the time the FTDA was enacted in 1996, only twenty-six states had *anti-dilution* statutes on the books."[232] Dilution occurs when a mark is unable to clearly serve as a source of goods or services. Dilution gives trademark owners a cause of action for whittling away of the mark in situations where there is no proof of likelihood of confusion. The concept of trademark dilution was originally a business tort and a form of unfair competition. Dilution evolved as a state law remedy to protect trademarks from blurring or tarnishment.[233] State anti-dilution actions survive the FTDA and vary widely, depending upon the jurisdiction.

Trademark dilution occurs when a use of a trademark by someone other than the owner impairs the mark's distinctiveness; whether or not the mark is used on a competing product or in a way that is likely to cause customer confusion. A distinction is made between *trademark dilution* and *trademark infringement*. For a trademark dilution claim, the harm is not based on the potential for consumer confusion; a dilution claim can still arise where consumers have not been and are not likely to be confused about the source of goods or services offered under the same or similar trademarks. Even if customers are not confused, the registration of the domain name arguably harms a trademark owner, because it would lessen the strong association, which the company has spent millions of dollars developing.

(A) State Antidilution: Blurring

Blurring occurs when a defendant "creates noise around a mark so that it cannot function as a mark."[234] Blurring occurs ". . . where the defendant uses or modifies the plaintiff's trademark to identify the defendant's goods and services, raising the possibility that the mark will lose its ability to serve as a unique identifier of the plaintiff's product."[235] Courts determine that blurring exists based on a multi-factorial study of six factors: (1) the similarity of the marks, (2) the similarity of the products covered, (3) the sophistication of the consumers, (4) the existence of predatory intent, (5) the renown of the senior mark, and (6) the renown of the junior mark.

(B) State Anti–Dilution: Tarnishment

Tarnishment creates to the reputation of a trademark. Tarnishment is generally associated with goods or services that are disreputable, poor quality, or sexual content such as when an adult entertainment site uses the mark, Papal Visit.[236] Plaintiffs bring claims of dilution by tarnishment when the defendant is "using the same mark or a confusingly similar mark in connection with pornography."[237] Tarnishment occurs when a trademark is connected to shoddy, unwholesome, or other less than desirable context so the public will associate the trademark with low prestige products or

---

[232] BNA, 63 U.S.P.Q. 2d 170 (2002).

[233] Mead Data Cent., Inc. v. Toyota Motor Sales, U.S.A., Inc., 875 F.2d 1026 (2d Cir. 1989) (New York state anti-dilution action).

[234] JACQUELINE LIPTON, INTERNET DOMAIN NAMES, TRADEMARKS AND FREE SPEECH 246 (2010).

[235] Merck & Co., Inc. v. Mediplan Health Consulting, Inc., 425 F. Supp. 2d 402, 417 (S.D. N.Y. 2006).

[236] See Archdiocese of St. Louis v. Internet Entertainment Group, Inc., 34 F. Supp. 2d 1145, 1146 (E.D. Mo. 1999) (enjoining adult entertainment site from using plaintiffs' trademarks as its Internet domain name).

[237] GERALD R. FERRERA, ROBERT BIRD, JONATHAN J. DARROW, CYBERLAW: TEXT AND CASES 112 (2011).

services. In *Mattel Inc. v. Internet Dimensions, Inc.,*[238] the federal court in the Southern District of New York enjoined an online pornographer's use of the phrase "Barbie's Play Pen" on its adult entertainment website because it diluted Mattel's trademark "Barbie" for dolls.

§ 11.7 FALSE DESIGNATION OF ORIGIN

The most important issue in an action for trademark infringement of false designation of origin under the Lanham Act is whether the unauthorized use of the mark is "likely to cause confusion."[239] Confusion exists where there is a likelihood that an appreciable number of ordinary prudent purchasers will be misled or confused as to the source or origin of the goods in question or where consumers are likely to believe that the mark's owner sponsored, endorsed, or otherwise approved of the defendant's use of the mark.[240] To prevail in a *false designation of origin*, or in an infringement case, the plaintiff needs to prove that defendant's use of the trademark would likely cause an appreciable number of the purchasing public to be misled or confused as to the source, sponsorship, or affiliation of defendant's goods or services.[241] The unfair competition or, "consumer confusion" provision, of Section 43 of the Lanham Act,[242] is intended to prevent confusion, mistake, or deception regarding the source of goods or services. Section 43 of the Lanham Act provides:

(1) Any person who, on or in connection with any goods or services, or any container for goods, uses in commerce any word, term, name, symbol, or device, or any combination thereof, or any false designation of origin, false or misleading description of fact, or false or misleading representation of fact, which—

(A) is likely to cause confusion, or to cause mistake, or to deceive as to the affiliation, connection, or association of such person with another person, or as to the origin, sponsorship, or approval of his or her goods, services, or commercial activities by another person, or

(B) in commercial advertising or promotion, misrepresents the nature, characteristics, qualities, or geographic origin of his or her or another person's goods, services, or commercial activities.[243]

The core element of any trademark infringement cause of action, or false designation of origin, is whether there is a "likelihood of confusion."[244]

A plaintiff is required to show that its marks are valid and that a defendant's use of those marks is likely to cause consumer confusion whether the cause of action arises out of trademark infringement, unfair competition, or false designation of origin.

To state a claim under the Lanham Act, a plaintiff must allege: (1) the defendant uses a false designation of origin; (2) such false designation of origin occurs in interstate commerce in connection with goods or services; (3) is likely to cause

---

[238] 55 U.S.P.Q. 2d 1620 (S.D. N.Y. 2000).
[239] 15 U.S.C. §§ 1114(1), 1125(a)(1)(A).
[240] Dallas Cowboys Cheerleaders, Inc. v. Pussycat Cinema, Ltd., 604 F.2d 200, 204–05 (2d Cir. 1979).
[241] McGregor–Doniger, Inc. v. Drizzle Inc., 599 F.2d 1126 (2d Cir. 1979).
[242] 15 U.S.C. § 1125(a)(1)(A).
[243] 15 U.S.C. § 1125(a).
[244] Id.

confusion, mistake or deception as to the origin, sponsorship or approval of the plaintiff's goods and services by another person; and (4) the plaintiff has been or is likely to be damaged.[245] In *Ron Paul 2012 Presidential Campaign Comm., Inc. v. Does*,[246] the defendants owned a YouTube and Twitter account named "NHLiberty4Paul." Under this pseudonymous website, the defendants uploaded a video on YouTube entitled "Jon Huntsman's Values" that attacked the former Republican primary nominee before concluding with the text: "American Values and Liberty—Vote Ron Paul." Shortly after the video's release, the Ron Paul Campaign filed a complaint asserting a claim for: (1) false designation of origin in violation of the Lanham Act,[247] (2) false description and representation in violation of the Lanham Act,[248] and (3) common law libel and defamation. The federal court denied the Ron Paul Campaign's request for expedited discovery ruling it had grave doubts about whether the plaintiff satisfied the commercial use requirement for false designation of origin.

A plaintiff must demonstrate that the statement in the challenged advertisement is false. A plaintiff may prove falsity because the advertisement is literally false on its face or, while not literally false, is nevertheless likely to mislead or confuse customers. Either theory requires that the plaintiff show that "the false or misleading representation involved an inherent or material quality of the product."[249] "The false advertising provision of Section 43 of the Lanham Act is intended to prevent confusion, mistake, or deception regarding the characteristics or qualities of goods or services."[250] Section 43(a) covers false or misleading misrepresentations of fact "which is likely to cause confusion, or to cause mistake, or to deceive as to the affiliation, connection or association of such person with another person, or as to the origin, sponsorship, or approval of his or her goods, services, or commercial activities by another person."[251]

§ 11.8   FALSE ENDORSEMENT

False endorsement under Section 43(a) of the Lanham Act is when a plaintiff's identity is associated with a product in a way that misleads the consumer about that person's sponsorship. To state a false endorsement claim, the plaintiff must allege facts that, if true, would establish that his or her name was: (1) used in commerce, (2) is distinctive and (3) a likelihood of confusion exists.[252] The elements of a false endorsement claim are akin to the tort of the right of publicity. Section 43(a) covers a false or misleading misrepresentation of fact, which ". . . is likely to cause confusion, or to cause mistake, or to deceive as to the affiliation, connection, or association of such person with another person, or as to the origin, sponsorship, or approval of his or her goods, services, or commercial activities by another person."[253] A false endorsement claim requires allegations of an "unauthorized use of [a] celebrity's identity," such as the "misuse" of "visual likeness, vocal imitation, or other uniquely distinguishing

---

[245] 15 U.S.C. § 1125(a).

[246] 2012 U.S. Dist. LEXIS 30911 (N.D. Ca., March 8, 2012).

[247] 15 U.S.C. § 1125(a).

[248] Id.

[249] CJ Prods. LLC v. Snuggly Plushez LLC, 809 F. Supp. 2d 127 (E.D. N.Y. 2011).

[250] 15 U.S.C. § 1125(a)(1)(B); see also, MCW, Inc. v. Badbusinessbureau.com, L.L.C., 2004 U.S. Dist. LEXIS 6678 (N.D. Tex., April 19, 2004).

[251] 15 U.S.C. § 1125(a)(1)(A).

[252] 15 U.S.C. § 1125(a)(1).

[253] 15 U.S.C. § 1125(a)(1)(A).

characteristic."[254] Courts apply a "likelihood of confusion" test to false endorsement claims similar to the multi-factorial test applied in infringement cases. In false endorsement cases, the defendants may interpose First Amendment, trademark fair use, parody, and other trademark defenses as was the case in *Diller v. Barry Driller Inc.*,[255] In *Diller*, Hollywood mogul Barry Diller sued the operators of BarryDriller.com, a copycat digital service that streamed television signals over the Internet. Diller, whose name was connected with Aereo's Internet-broadcasting service filed suit for false endorsement under the Lanham Act as well as California's right of publicity. The federal district court granted Diller a preliminary injunction, rejecting Driller's defenses of parody since Diller's mark was being used for purely a commercial use. The court applied a likelihood of confusion test to the false endorsement claim ruling that Diller would likely succeed since the sound and appearance of the names were so familiar. The parties settled the lawsuit in May of 2012. The defendant agreed to stop "using the phrases 'Barry Diller,' 'Barry Driller,' 'BarryDriller.com.' 'Barry Driller Inc.' and/or 'BarryDriller Content Systems PLC' in connection 'with any commercial or business-related activity.'"[256]

§ 11.9 ANTICYBERSQUATTING ACT OF 1999

The Anticybersquatting Consumer Protection Act ("ACPA")[257] is the principal tool used by trademark owners to reclaim domain names containing their trademarks and trade names from cybersquatters.[258] Cybersquatting "occurs when a person other than the trademark holder registers the domain name of a well-known trademark and then attempts to profit from this by either ransoming the domain name back to the trademark holder or by using the domain name to divert business from the trademark holder to the domain name holder."[259] Plaintiff must prove the following to prevail in a ACPA claim: (1) it has a valid trademark entitled to protection; (2) its marks are distinctive or famous; (3) the defendant's domain name is identical or confusingly similar to the owner's mark; and (4) the defendant used, registered, or trafficked in the domain name (5) with a bad faith intent to profit.[260] The ACPA sets forth nine factors to determine the defendant's bad faith, which is often a centerpiece for domain name/trademark disputes:

(I) the trademark or other intellectual property rights of the person, if any, in the domain name;

(II) the extent to which the domain name consists of the legal name of the person or a name that is otherwise commonly used to identify that person;

(III) the person's prior use, if any, of the domain name in connection with the bona fide offering of goods or services;

---

[254] Pesina v. Midway Mfg. Co., 948 F. Supp. 40, 43 (N.D. Ill. 1996).

[255] Diller v. Barry Driller Inc., 104 U.S.P.Q.2d 1676 (N.D. Cal., Sept. 10, 2012).

[256] Tim Kenneally, Barry Diller, Alki David Settle Leegal Spat Over BarryDriller.com, The Wrap Covering Hollywoopd (May 21, 2013).

[257] 15 U.S.C. § 1125(d) (2006).

[258] The ACPA is part of the federal Lanham Act. 15 U.S.C. § 1125(d).

[259] WFTV, Inc. v. Maverik Production Ltd. Liability Co., Slip Copy, 2013 WL 3119461 *8 (M.D.Fla. June 18, 2013) (quoting DaimlerChrysler v. The Net Inc., 388 F.3d 201, 205 (6th Cir.2004)).

[260] Id.

(IV) the person's bona fide noncommercial or fair use of the mark in a site accessible under the domain name;

(V) the person's intent to divert consumers from the mark owner's online location to a site accessible under the domain name that could harm the goodwill represented by the mark, either for commercial gain or with the intent to tarnish or disparage the mark, by creating a likelihood of confusion as to the source, sponsorship, affiliation, or endorsement of the site;

(VI) the person's offer to transfer, sell, or otherwise assign the domain name to the mark owner for financial gain without having used, or having an intent to use, the domain name in the bona fide offering of any goods or services, or the person's prior conduct indicating a pattern of such conduct;

(VII) the person's provision of material and misleading false contact information when applying for the registration of the domain name, the person's intentional failure to maintain accurate contact information, or the person's prior conduct indicating a pattern of such conduct;

(VIII) the person's registration or acquisition of multiple domain names which the person knows are identical or confusingly similar to marks of others that are distinctive at the time of registration of such domain names, or dilutive of famous marks of others that are famous at the time of registration of such domain names, without regard to the goods or services of the parties; and

(IX) the extent to which the mark incorporated in the person's domain name registration is or is not distinctive and famous within the meaning of subsection (c) of 15 U.S.C. § 1125.[261]

Courts weigh the factors in 15 U.S.C. § 1125(d)(1)(B)(i) to determine whether a domain name registrant had a bad faith intent to profit from its domain name registration. "The paradigmatic case of bad-faith intent to profit involves a registrant who essentially holds hostage a domain name that resembles a mark with the intention of selling it back to the mark's owner. Other examples include registering well-known marks to prey on consumer confusion by misusing the domain name to divert customers from the mark owner's site to the cybersquatter's own site, and targeting distinctive marks to defraud consumers, including to engage in counterfeiting activities."[262] The ACPA addresses: (1) registration, use, or trafficking in, a domain name; (2) that is identical or confusingly similar to a distinctive or famous trademark; (3) with a bad-faith intent to profit from the mark.[263] Before Congress enacted the ACPA, plaintiffs deployed the Lanham Act and charged dilution against cybersquatters.[264] To evaluate whether a plaintiff's registration or use of a domain name is unlawful, ACPA instructs courts to look for evidence of bad-faith intent to profit from the domain name.[265]

---

[261] 15 U.S.C. § 1125(d)(1)(B)(i).

[262] Isystems v. Spark Networks, 102 U.S.P.Q.2D (BNA) 1055, 1056 (5th Cir. 2012).

[263] Id.

[264] See e.g., Panavision Int'l. LP v. Toeppen, 141 F.3d 1316 (9th Cir. 1998) (employing the Lanham Act to reclaim domain name).

[265] Generally, a defendant is directly liable under the ACPA if he (1) registers, traffics in, or uses a domain name that is (2) identical or confusingly similar to a famous or distinctive mark owned by the plaintiff with (3) a bad-faith intent to profit from the mark. See e.g., DSPT Int'l, Inc. v. Nahum, 624 F.3d

Cybersquatters typically register well-known brand names as Internet domain names in order to force the rightful owners of the marks to pay a ransom for the right to engage in electronic commerce under their own name. A company may have a federal trademark action if a competitor registers a domain name identical or confusingly similar to their trademark under the ACPA if it can prove bad faith and that the defendant has no fair use or other defense.[266]

(A) ACPA Overview

Congress enacted the ACPA on November 29, 1999 to protect consumers and American businesses, as well as to nurture electronic commerce by prohibiting the bad faith and abusive registration of distinctive marks as Internet domain names. Congress passed the ACPA in 1999 "in response to concerns over the proliferation of cybersquatting—the Internet version of a land grab."[267] The ACPA's legislative history, the statute's Senate Report, cites as examples of people who act with "bad faith intent to profit" are those who:

> (1) register well-known brand names as Internet domain names in order *to extract payment* from the rightful owners of the marks;" (2) "register well-known marks as domain names and warehouse those marks *with the hope of selling them* to the highest bidder;" (3) "register well-known marks to *prey on* consumer confusion by misusing the domain name to divert customers from the mark owner's site to the cybersquatter's own site;" (4) "target distinctive marks *to defraud consumers,* including to engage in counterfeiting activities."[268]

The ACPA amends the federal Lanham Act creating a cause of action for trademark owners against those who incorporate their mark or one confusingly similar into a domain name. In order to state a claim for cybersquatting under the ACPA, a trademark owner must show the defendant (1) registered, trafficked in, or used a domain name, (2) that is confusingly similar to the plaintiff's trademark, and (3) had a bad faith intent to profit from that domain name.[269] The ACPA, which amended the Lanham (Trademark) Act, 15 U.S.C. §§ 1501 et seq., states:

> A person shall be liable in a civil action by the owner of a mark, including a personal name which is protected as a mark under this section, if, without regard to the goods or services of the parties, that person—
>
> (i) has a bad faith intent to profit from that mark, including a personal name which is protected as a mark under this section; and
>
> (ii) registers, traffics in, or uses a domain name that—

1213, 1218–19 (9th Cir.2010). In determining bad faith, courts evaluate the unique circumstances of the case; survey the nine bad-faith factors set forth in the ACPA; and consider the availability of the ACPA's statutory safe-harbor defense, which protects any defendant who " 'believed and had reasonable grounds to believe that the use of the domain name was a fair use or otherwise lawful.'" Rearden LLC v. Rearden Commerce, Inc., 683 F.3d 1190, 1220 (9th Cir.2012) (quoting 15 U.S.C. § 1125(d)(1)(B)(ii)).

[266] 15 U.S.C. § 1125(d)(1).

[267] Virtual Works, Inc. v. Volkswagen of Am., Inc., 238 F.3d 264, 267 (4th Cir.2001).

[268] S. Rep. No. 106–140 (1999).

[269] 15 U.S.C. § 1125(d)(1)(A); Verizon Cal. Inc. v. Navigation Catalyst Sys., Inc., 568 F. Supp. 2d 1088, 1094 (C.D. Cal. 2008).

(I) in the case of a mark that is distinctive at the time of registration of the domain name, is identical or confusingly similar to that mark.[270]

Cybersquatters have the intent to profit from registering domain names containing the marks of others. The ACPA addresses "a new form of piracy on the Internet caused by acts of "cybersquatting," which refers to the deliberate, bad faith, and abusive registration of Internet domain names in violation of the rights of trademark owners."[271] The ACPA applies retroactively to domain names registered before Congress enacted the statute. In order to prevail in an ACPA action, the owner must first prove that they have a valid and protectable trademark, which must be either distinctive or famous. Owners of generic trademarks, like "videotape" or "aspirin," may not seek protection under the ACPA.

Second, the trademark owner must prove that a disputed domain name is identical or confusingly similar to a protectable mark. For famous marks, like Louis Vuitton or Victoria's Secret, the trademark owner must prove that the disputed domain name dilutes their mark though there is no requirement that they prove actual damages. Third, the trademark owner must demonstrate that the defendant registered, used, or trafficked in domain names with bad faith intent to benefit. The ACPA lists nine factors a court may consider in determining whether a domain name registrant was in bad faith, though these factors are not exhaustive:

(1) the registrant's trademark or other intellectual property rights in the domain name; (2) whether the domain name contains the registrant's legal or common name; (3) the registrant's prior use of the domain name in connection with the bona fide offering of goods or services; (4) the registrant's bona fide noncommercial or fair use of the mark in a site accessible by the domain name; (5) the registrant's intent to divert customers from the mark owner's online location that could harm the goodwill represented by the mark, for commercial gain or with the intent to tarnish or disparage the mark; (6) the registrant's offer to transfer, sell, or otherwise assign the domain name to the mark owner or a third party for financial gain, without having used the mark in a legitimate site; (7) the registrant's providing misleading false contact information when applying for registration of the domain name; (8) the registrant's registration or acquisition of multiple domain names that are identical or confusingly similar to marks of others; and (9) the extent to which the mark in the domain is distinctive or famous.[272]

A plaintiff pursuing a cybersquatting claim under the ACPA must show that: "(1) the defendant registered, trafficked in, or used a domain name; (2) the domain name is identical or confusingly similar to a protected mark owned by the plaintiff; and (3) the defendant acted 'with bad faith intent to profit from that mark.'"[273] Bad faith is a wider inquiry than merely examining the nine statutory factors that are to guide courts.[274]

---

[270] 15 U.S.C. 1125(d)(1)(A).

[271] S. Rep. No. 106–140 (1999) at 4.

[272] 15 U.S.C. § 1125(d)(1)(B).

[273] DSPT Int'l, Inc. v. Nahum, 624 F.3d 1213, 1218–19 (9th Cir. 2010).

[274] Pensacola Motor Sales, Inc. v. Eastern Shore Toyota, LLC, 684 F.3d 1211, 1221 (11th Cir. 2012) ("The Anticybersquatting Consumer Protection Act lists nine factors that a court may consider when determining whether a domain name infringer had a bad faith intent to profit from the trademark. 15 U.S.C. § 1125(d)(1)(B). It also specifies that the factors that may be considered are not limited to the nine that are listed. § 1125(d)(1)(B). And regardless of which direction the bad faith factors point, the act states: Bad faith

The ACPA is a part of the Lanham Act and provides prevailing plaintiffs with remedies "including injunctive relief, forfeiture or cancellation of the disputed domain name or transfer of the name to the plaintiff, the plaintiff's actual damages, the defendant's profits, costs, statutory damages of $1,000 to $100,000 per domain name in lieu of actual damages, and attorney's fees in "exceptional cases."[275] Trademark owners may recover attorneys' fees in ACPA actions.[276]

(B) Elements of ACPA Claims

The ACPA provides that a person is liable to a trademark owner if: "[T]hat person (i) has a bad faith intent to profit from that mark . . . and (ii) registers, traffics in, or uses a domain name that [is] identical or confusingly similar to" a distinctive or famous mark.[277] The core element in a cybersquatting case is proof of a bad faith intent to profit from a distinctive or famous mark. A trademark is famous only if the owner can prove that the mark "is widely recognized by the general consuming public of the United States as a designation of source of the goods or services of the mark's owner."[278] The ACPA lists nine factors to assist courts in determining whether there has been a bad faith registration.[279]

(C) ACPA Safe Harbor

The ACPA recognizes a safe harbor provision for a defendant who acted in good faith. If "the court determines that the person believed and had reasonable grounds to believe that the use of the domain name was a fair use or otherwise lawful," then the defendant will not be held liable under the ACPA.[280] In *Panavision Int'l, L.P. v.*

---

intent shall not be found in any case in which the court determines that the person believed and had reasonable grounds to believe that the use of the domain name was a fair use or otherwise lawful. § 1125(d)(1)(B)(ii). That statutory defense is often referred to as the safe harbor defense."). Rearden LLC v. Rearden Commerce, Inc., 683 F.3d 1190, 1220 (9th Cir. 2012) ("As to bad faith, the notion implicates three analyses: (1) surveying the nine non-exclusive and permissive statutory factors that "may" be considered in "determining whether a person has a bad faith intent," 15 U.S.C. § 1125(d)(1)(B)(i); (2) taking into account the unique circumstances of each case, which represent "'the most important grounds for finding bad faith,'" and which affect the examination (and weight) of the nine permissive factors as well as any other relevant considerations, Lahoti v. VeriCheck, Inc., 586 F.3d 1190, 1202 (9th Cir. 2009) (quoting Interstellar Starship Servs., Ltd. v. Epix, Inc., 304 F.3d 936, 946 (9th Cir. 2002)); and (3) considering the availability of the safe harbor for any defendant who "believed and had reasonable grounds to believe that the use of the domain name was a fair use or otherwise lawful," 15 U.S.C. § 1125(d)(1)(B)(ii)).

[275] David M. Kelly, Statutory Damages Under the Anticybersquatting Protection Act, BNA PATENT, TRADEMARK & COPYRIGHT JOURNAL (June 13, 2008).

[276] 15 U.S.C. § 1117(a).

[277] Id.

[278] 15 U.S.C. § 1125(c)(2)(A).

[279] (1) The registrant's trademark or other intellectual property rights in the domain name; (2) whether the domain name contains the registrant's legal or common name; (3) the registrant's prior use of the domain name in connection with the bona fide offering of goods or services; (4) the registrant's bona fide noncommercial or fair use of the mark in a site accessible by the domain name; (5) the registrant's intent to divert customers from the mark owner's online location that could harm the goodwill represented by the mark, for commercial gain or with the intent to tarnish or disparage the mark; (6) the registrant's offer to transfer, sell, or otherwise assign the domain name to the mark owner or a third party for financial gain, without having used the mark in a legitimate site; (7) the registrant's providing misleading false contact information when applying for registration of the domain name; (8) the registrant's registration or acquisition of multiple domain names that are identical or confusingly similar to marks of others; and (9) the extent to which the mark in the domain is distinctive or famous. 15 U.S.C. § 1125(d)(1)(B).

[280] 15 U.S.C. § 1125(d)(1)(B)(ii).

Toeppen,[281] Dennis Toeppen registered scores of domain names containing the trademarks of famous companies, and then sought to sell them to the owners of the marks for a profit. Toeppen posted an aerial vision of Pana, Illinois, on the website Panavision.com and the word, "hello," as a transparently pre-textual gesture to try to prove legitimate use.[282] The federal court rejected this ploy finding Toeppen liable for misappropriating the trademark of Panavision through his practice of registering trademarks as domain names and then selling them to the trademark owners. The court found that Dennis Toeppen registered the domain name "panavision.com" in order to get a ransom from Panavision.

Toeppen was using the domain panavision.com to display photographs of Pana, Illinois and, when asked to cease using the domain name, he offered to sell it for $13,000. After Panavision refused to buy the domain name from Toeppen, he registered their other trademark, Panaflex, as a domain name. Because Toeppen registered the "PANAVISION" mark as a domain name to palm off on the recognition of the "PANAVISION" name and mark, the Ninth Circuit determined that this misuse or exploitation of the value of the mark rose to the level of commercial use under the Lanham Act, even though Toeppen never used it to sell goods or services. [283]

(D) ACPA Remedies

(1) Actual or Statutory Damages

Under the ACPA, "the plaintiff may elect, at any time before final judgment is rendered by the trial court, to recover, instead of actual damages and profits, an award of statutory damages in the amount of not less than $1,000 and not more than $100,000 per domain name, as the court considers just."[284] Courts have great discretion in determining the size of an ACPA award. In general, when a plaintiff requests statutory damages, the Court has "wide discretion in determining the amount of statutory damages to be awarded, constrained only by the specified maxima and minima."[285] "The statutory damages provision serves to sanction or punish defendants in order to deter future wrongful conduct."[286]

(2) Injunctive Relief

The Lanham Act provides, in relevant part, "The several courts vested with jurisdiction of civil actions arising under this chapter shall have the power to grant

---

[281] 141 F.3d 1316 (9th Cir. 1998).

[282] Id. at 1319.

[283] In Panavision International v. Toeppen, 938 F. Supp. 616 (C.D. Cal. 1996), a domain name cyberpirate was found liable in a lawsuit in California because his attempt to sell a domain name containing a corporation's famous trademark was deemed sufficient for jurisdiction. Id. at 622. The defendant appealed this decision, and the Ninth Circuit affirmed personal jurisdiction in the trademark case filed by owners of the marks PANAVISION and Panaflex. Panavision Int'l, L.P. v. Toeppen, 141 F.3d 1316, 1322 (9th Cir. 1998). The defendant cybersquatter had registered the domain names panavision.com and panaflex.com, and posted pictures of Pana, Illinois, on one website and the word "hello" on the other. Id. at 1319. He then attempted to sell the domain names to Panavision. Id. The court premised jurisdiction on the defendant's intention of doing business in California and his tortious attempt to extort money from a California trademark owner. Id. at 1321–22. The court upheld jurisdiction, employing the "effects test." Id. at 1321.

[284] 15 U.S.C. § 1117 (d).

[285] WFTV, Inc. v. Maverik Production Ltd. Liability Co., Slip Copy, 2013 WL 3119461 at *13 (M.D.Fla. June 18, 2013) (citations omitted).

[286] Id.

injunctions, according to the principles of equity and upon such terms as the court may deem reasonable, to prevent the violation of any right of the registrant of a mark registered in the [USPTO] or to prevent a violation under subsection (a), (c), or (d) of section 1125 of this title."[287] After the Supreme Court's 2006 decision in *eBay Inc. v. MercExchange*,[288] a plaintiff in IP cases should assume that they must prove the traditional equitable elements in seeking an injunction. An ACPA plaintiff seeking a permanent injunction must therefore demonstrate that: (1) it suffered an irreparable injury; (2) remedies at law, such as monetary damages, are inadequate to compensate for the injury; (3) considering the balance of the hardships between plaintiff and defendants, a remedy in equity is warranted; and (4) the public interest would not be disserved by a permanent injunction.

(3) Transfer of Domain Names

In many instances, the plaintiff's sole goal in an ACPA case is to gain control of a domain name and thus the Lanham Act provides the following regarding cybersquatting cases: "In any civil action involving the registration, trafficking, or use of a domain name under this paragraph, a court may order the forfeiture or cancellation of the domain name or the transfer of the domain name to the owner of the mark."[289] The plaintiff will seek a court order to transfer the disputed domain name to them. Plaintiff sill typically attach a copy of a "WHOIS" search confirms who the domain name registrant is, their administrative contact and technical contact as well as the current registrar. A court order will typically order both the registrant and the registrar to transfer a domain name that is proven to be the instrumentality for cybersquatting.[290]

(4) In Rem Actions Against Domain Names

In cybersquatting cases, the domain name registrant would be difficult to locate. The ACPA authorizes trademark owners to proceed in an *in rem* action, where the *in personam* action is non-availing. A trademark owner may proceed *in rem* against the domain name only if they have exhausted reasonable efforts to locate the bad faith registrant.[291] The cybersquatting section of the Lanham Act provides that service of process in an *in rem* action may be accomplished by sending notice of the alleged violation and intent to proceed under the ACPA to the registrant of the domain name at the postal and e-mail addresses provided by the registrant to the registrar, and by publishing notice of the action as the court may direct promptly after filing the action.[292] The ACPA gives trademark owners the right to file *in rem* action against the domain name in the judicial district where the domain name registrar, domain name registry, or other domain name authority registered or assigned the domain name is located. *In rem* jurisdiction means something is directed at *res*, or real, property, rather than a person—*in personam*.

---

[287] 15 U.S.C. § 1116(a).

[288] 547 U.S. 388 (2006).

[289] 15 U.S.C. § 1125(d)(1)(C).

[290] This was the nature of the order in WFTV, Inc. v. Maverik Production Ltd. Liability Co., Slip Copy, 2013 WL 3119461 at *17 (M.D. Fla. June 18, 2013) (citations omitted).

[291] The ACPA requires the trademark owner to demonstrate that there is no personal jurisdiction or the plaintiff cannot locate the defendants after exercising due diligence. 15 U.S.C. § 1125(d)(2)(A)(ii).

[292] 15 U.S.C. § 1125(d)(2)(A)–(B).

The ACPA enacted an *in rem* provision that allows trademark owners to file suit against the domain name, where personal jurisdiction is not available against the individual or entity that registered the domain name in bad faith. *In rem* jurisdiction, in contrast, is jurisdiction over a thing or a *res*. Early *in rem* cases were against ships that violated the law of nations or public international law.[293] *In rem* jurisdiction in admiralty actions are heard in the U.S. federal district courts. Similarly, *in rem* jurisdiction over domain names is also a remedy only found in federal courts. Trademark owners may assert *in rem* jurisdiction where the domain name is confusingly similar or identical to its mark and the abusive registrant is not locatable.

However, the trademark owner has the burden of demonstrating the domain name infringes their trademark and they have been unable to obtain in personam jurisdiction over the defendant or been unable to locate the defendant through diligent efforts.[294] In Internet-related cases, the plaintiff has the burden of demonstrating personal jurisdiction is unavailing in order to pursue an *in rem* action.[295] Harrods, the famous retail giant, filed an ACPA *in rem* action against sixty domain names after it was unable to locate the registrant.[296] The Fourth Circuit held that *in rem* jurisdiction over domain names was constitutional concluding that courts in Virginia ". . . could constitutionally exercise *in rem* jurisdiction over them."[297] The court also ruled that under the ACPA, damages in an *in rem* action are, ". . . limited to a court order for the forfeiture or cancellation of the domain name or the transfer of the domain name to the owner of the mark."[298] The concept of *in rem* jurisdiction is seeking jurisdiction over property rather than persons. The ACPA allows the "owner of a mark" to bring an *in rem* action where a domain name allegedly violates the owner's right in a trademark.

Trademark owners may seek an *in rem* remedy if the abusive domain name registrant is not locatable despite a diligent effort to find him or her.[299] An illustrative case occurred in July of 2012 when a Virginia federal court ordered VeriSign, an accredited domain name registrar, to transfer 265 "infringing domain names" from VeriSign to Go Daddy in *Montblanc–Simplo GmbH v. Cheapmontblancpens.com.*[300] The disputed domain names were registered in the name of Richemont International, Ltd, but in fact, the registrants were based in China using the domain names to sell fake Mont Blanc pens violating the pen company's famous trademarks.[301]

The trademark owner must file his or her claim for *in rem* jurisdiction in the federal district court in which the domain name registry, registrar, or other domain names authority is located. The ACPA provides for *in rem* jurisdiction both where the registrar and registry are located, and also states that the site of a domain in an *in rem* action lies in the judicial district where the domain name registrar and/or registry is

---

[293] See e.g., The Malek Adhel, 43 U.S. (2 How.) 210, 233–34 (1844).

[294] 15 U.S.C. § 1125(d)(1).

[295] America Online, Inc. v. Aol.org, 259 F. Supp. 2d 449, 451 (E.D. Va. 2003) (holding in rem jurisdiction is proper over domain name registered in jurisdiction but personal jurisdiction is improper where registrant has no other contacts with forum); See also, Starcom Mediavest Group v. Mediavestw.com, No. 10–4025, 2010 WL 3564845 (September 13, 2010) (ordering transfer of the domain name, mediavestw.com).

[296] Harrod's Ltd. v. Sixty Internet Domain Names, 302 F.3d 214, 225 n. 7 (4th Cir. 2002).

[297] Id.

[298] 15 U.S.C. § 1125.

[299] 15 U.S.C. § 1125(d)(2)(A).

[300] Amy E. Bivins, Mont Blanc Obtains 265 Domain Names by Default Under ACPA in Rem Provision, BLOOMBERG BNA ELECTRONIC COMMERCE & LAW REPORT (July 28, 2012).

[301] Id.

located.[302] In *Porsche Cars N. Am., Inc. v. Porsche.net*,[303] the Fourth Circuit affirmed the lower court's dismissal of the automobile manufacturer's *in rem* action. On February 23, 2001, the district court found it had jurisdiction over British domain names under the ACPA. Just three days before the scheduled trial in Virginia, the owner of the British domain names notified the court that their registrant had decided to submit to personal jurisdiction in California.

The district court ruled that an *in rem* remedy was not properly invoked. The circuit court disagreed ruling Porsche.net waited too long to object to *in rem* jurisdiction. The Fourth Circuit vacated the district court's order dismissing the case and remanded without reaching the question of whether there was a basis for *in rem* jurisdiction premised on Porsche's trademark dilution claims. Trademark owners rarely file *in rem* actions under the ACPA because they can file UDRP proceedings, which are cheaper and faster to attain the same result of extinguishing or transferring a domain name that infringes their mark.

§ 11.10 KEYWORD TRADEMARK LITIGATION

Google has created the AdWords program; which, in effect, is a full-employment act for trademark litigators. However, in recent years plaintiffs rarely prevail in competitive keyword cases. Trademark owners have filed multiple trademark infringement lawsuits against Google and its customers arising out of the use of the AdWords context-advertising program. AdWords allows an advertiser to bid on keywords or terms that an Internet user might enter into a Google search thereby triggering the display of a sponsor's advertisement. When a user enters a keyword, Google displays the links generated by its own algorithm in the main part of the page, along with the advertisements in a separate "sponsored links" section next to or above the objective results. Google will link advertisements and sponsored hyperlinks to given keywords it sells. "Another program the defendant offers is the "Keyword Suggestion Tool," which it uses to recommend keywords to advertisers."[304] A leading trademark scholar, views the issue as whether keyword placement is unfairly "drawing [the] power and goodwill of these famous marks. The question is whether this activity is fair competition or whether it is a form of unfair free riding on the fame of well-known marks."[305]

"Keyword advertising is now a staple for search engine sites, generating a considerable portion of their revenue and allowing them to continue providing their services for free."[306] In keyword advertising cases such as *Hearts on Fire Co. v. Blue Nile, Inc.*, the ". . . likelihood of confusion will ultimately turn on what the consumer saw on the screen and reasonably believed, given the context."[307] In *Hearts on Fire*, a diamond wholesaler alleged that an Internet diamond retailer infringed its trademark when it used the wholesaler's trademark as a keyword to trigger search engine advertisements known as "sponsored links." The Massachusetts federal court

---

[302] Fleetboston Financial Corp. v. Fleetbostonfinancial.com, 138 F. Supp. 2d 121 (D. Mass. 2001).

[303] 302 F.3d 248 (4th Cir. 2002).

[304] Rescuecom Corp. v. Google, Inc., 456 F. Supp. 2d 393, 397 (N.D. N.Y. 2006).

[305] 4 MCCARTHY ON TRADEMARKS AND UNFAIR COMPETITION § 25:70.1 at p. 25–171 (4th ed. 2012).

[306] Stuart M. Saunders, Confusion Is the Key: A Trademark Law Analysis of Keyword Banner Advertising, 71 FORDHAM L. REV. 543, 545 (2002).

[307] Hearts on Fire Co. v. Blue Nile, Inc., 603 F. Supp. 2d 274, 289 (D. Mass. 2009).

determined that dismissal of the trademark owner's lawsuit was not warranted and found the purchase of trademarks to trigger pop-up or banner advertisements to be use in commerce. The purchase of the trademarked keyword to trigger sponsored links constituted a "use" within the meaning of the Lanham Act because, on the facts of the case, a computer user's search for the trademarked phrase necessarily involved a display of that trademark as part of the search-results list.

The court found the diamond wholesaler to have stated a claim for trademark infringement, even where the Internet retailer's sponsored links did not display the protected mark, because, (1) initial interest confusion could support a claim under the Lanham Act where the wholesaler plausibly alleged that consumers were confused, and not simply diverted, and (2) the wholesaler offered sufficient allegations to support its claim that consumers were likely confused, and potentially misled, by the retailer's use of the trademark as a trigger for its sponsored links. Another theory that is frequently asserted is the keyword advertisements result in blurring to trademarks. A federal court rejected that claim in *Scooter Store, Inc. v. SpinLife.com, LLC*.[308] The *Scooter Store* court ruled that there could be no blurring because the keyword metatags were not visible to consumers. In *Playboy Enterprises, Inc. v. Welles*,[309] the Ninth Circuit reversed a federal district court's grant of a preliminary injunction that restrained Welles from using the registered trademarks "Playboy" and "Playmate" as metatags in her websites. Terri Welles graced the cover of Playboy in 1981 as the *Playboy* Playmate of the Year for 1981. Playboy Enterprises International ("PEI") challenged her use of the title "*Playboy* Playmate of the Year 1981," and her use of other trademarked terms on her website. PEI contended Welles infringed the following trademarked terms on her website: (1) the terms "Playboy" and "Playmate" in the metatags of the website, (2) the phrase "Playmate of the Year 1981" on the masthead of the website, (3) the phrases "*Playboy* Playmate of the Year 1981" and "Playmate of the Year 1981" on various banner ads, and (4) her repeated use of the abbreviation "PMOY '81" as the watermark on the pages of the website.

The Ninth Circuit decided in Welles' favor, holding her use of the *Playboy* mark constituted fair use. The court also rejected Playboy's dilution claim, ruling the defendant was selling Terri Welles products only. The court found Welles was not trying to divert traffic from *Playboy* and recognized a nominative use defense to Ms. Welles's use of the "Playboy" and "Playmate" trademarks in her website advertisements.

(A) Use in Commerce & the Net

Many Internet-related cases turn on the element of "Use in Commerce," which is like the hole in a donut in a trademark infringement claim.[310] Many of the early Internet-related "Use in Commerce" cases arose out of domain name cases involving the defendant, Dennis Toeppen. Toeppen was an early domain name entrepreneur that registered famous trademarks as domain names through Network Solutions, Inc.

---

[308] 2012 WL 4498904 (S.D. Ohio Sept. 27, 2012).

[309] 279 F.3d 796 (9th Cir. 2002).

[310] "Use in commerce" is defined in 15 U.S.C. § 1127 as follows:

The term "use in commerce" means the bona fide use of a mark in the ordinary course of trade, and not made merely to reserve a right in a mark.

15 U.S.C. § 1127.

("NSI") for $100, and then offered them for sale to the "rightful trademark owners, preventing the trademark owners from doing business on the Internet unless they pay Toeppen's fee, which ranged between $10,000 and $15,000."[311] In *Intermatic Inc. v. Toeppen*,[312] the federal court held that the defendant's use of the Internet satisfied the "In Commerce" requirement when the defendant registered a domain name identical to the plaintiff's trademark name and used it on the Internet. The Illinois federal court found Toeppen guilty of cybersquatting because he registered the domain name with the intention of reselling it to the plaintiff or some other party.

The issue in *Intermatic* is whether "commercial use" was satisfied even though the defendant did not intend to sell goods or services similar to the plaintiff's, which would constitute infringement. The court held that "there is little question that the "in commerce" requirement would be met in a typical Internet message, be it trademark infringement or false advertising."[313] Mr. Toeppen found himself embroiled in a similar situation a few years later when the Ninth Circuit applied similar reasoning finding that his action of registering a domain name and attempting to resell the domain name to the trademark owner with the same name satisfied the commercial use requirement imposed by the Lanham Act.[314] In *Panavision International v. Toeppen*, the court acknowledged that the mere registration of a trademark as a domain name without more did not constitute a commercial use of the trademark.

(B) Commercial Use in Keywords

In more recent cases, the issue of commercial use often turns on whether "use" of a trademark under the Lanham Act requires that the trademark is displayed or visible to consumers. Commercial use, the third requirement of any trademark infringement lawsuit, is a major obstacle especially because the use of the plaintiff's trademark in metatags is invisible. Section 45 of the Lanham Act,[315] provides: "[T]he word "commerce" means all commerce which may lawfully be regulated by Congress." "The term "Use in Commerce" means the *bona fide* use of a mark in the ordinary course of trade, and not made merely to reserve a right in a mark."[316] In the brick-and-mortar world, marks were used in commerce when placed or displayed on containers, "or on the tags or labels affixed thereto, or if the nature of the goods makes such placement impracticable, then on documents associated with the goods or their sale."[317] Commercial use is also a requirement for goods sold, or services rendered, in E–Commerce. Many of the Internet-related commercial use issues involve the question of whether covert use of trademarks by advertisers constitutes "use in commerce under the Lanham Act."[318] In many of the "covert use" cases, plaintiffs are unable to clear the use in commerce hurdle.

Keywords "keyed" to famous trademarks trigger pop-ups, which is an example of the covert use of trademarks by online advertisers. The problem is that keywords use a

---

[311] Panavision Int'l v. Toeppen, 141 F.3d 1316, 1319 (9th Cir. 1998).

[312] 947 F.Supp. 1227, 1239 (N.D. Ill. 1996).

[313] Id. (citing 1 GILSON, TRADEMARK PROTECTION AND PRACTICE § 5.11[2], p. 5–234 (1996)).

[314] Panavision Int'l, L.P. v. Toeppen, 141 F.3d 1316, 1325 (9th Cir. 1998).

[315] 15 U.S.C. § 1127.

[316] Id.

[317] Id.

[318] 10 U.S.C. § 1051.

competitor's trademark to tout the products and services of the competitor of the keyworded trademark owner. Adware companies deliver pop-up ads for a competitor's products or service when an Internet user keys in a keyword of a trademark. "Adware" is software that generates advertisements while a consumer browses the Internet. Trademark owners argue that this covert use of a competitor's trademarks in adware essentially misappropriates their goodwill, diverting sales; thus constituting infringement.

In order to prevail in a keyword case, a trademark owner must demonstrate that the defendant's use of their mark is likely to cause confusion as to the affiliation, connection, or association of defendant with plaintiff, or as to the origin, sponsorship, or approval of the defendant's goods, services, or commercial activities by plaintiff.[319] Commercial use is the Achilles Heel in keyword litigation. During the past decade, a large number of courts have grappled with how commercial use should be interpreted in cyberspace.[320] The major issue in many keyword cases is whether the defendant has made "Use in Commerce" of the plaintiff's trademark. To prevail in a trademark infringement claim, a plaintiff must not only establish that it has a valid mark entitled to protection and that they used the mark in commerce, but the defendant used the mark in commerce.

(1) 1–800 Contacts, Inc. v. WhenU.Com, Inc.

In *1–800 Contacts, Inc. v. WhenU.com, Inc.*,[321] the Second Circuit reversed the district court's issuance of a preliminary injunction that enjoined WhenU.com from causing "pop up" advertisements to appear on Internet user's computer screens when they went to the 1–800 Contacts website or each time a trademark is entered into a search engine. The federal appeals court reasoned that WhenU.com's use of 1–800 Contacts' trademarks did not constitute "use in commerce"; a predicate for a finding of trademark infringement under the Lanham Act. However, the plaintiff's trademark claim failed because WhenU.com's pop-up ads did not actually display the 1–800 Contacts' trademark. The court found the defendant's use of the plaintiffs' trademarks as "analogous to an individual's private thoughts about a trademark. Such conduct simply does not violate the Lanham Act."[322] The *1–800 Contacts* case ended when the U.S. Supreme Court refused to accept the contact maker's writ of certiorari. Still, keyword litigation continues to drone on and on even though few courts believe that the plaintiff can satisfy the commercial use requirement.

(2) Rescuecom Corp. v. Google

In *Rescuecom Corp. v. Google*,[323] the Second Circuit held that Google's recommendation and sale to its customers of the plaintiff's trademark as a keyword, coupled with the fact that Google "displays, offers, and sells [the plaintiff's] mark to Google's advertising customers when selling its advertising services," is tantamount to

---

[319] 15 U.S.C. § 1125(a)(1)(A).

[320] See generally, Margreth Barrett, Internet Trademark Suits and the Demise of 'Trademark Use,' 39 U.C. DAVIS L. REV. 371, 376–87 (2006).

[321] 414 F.3d 400 (2d Cir. 2005).

[322] Id. at 409.

[323] 562 F.3d 123 (2d Cir. 2009).

use in commerce.[324] Google used the trademark in its Keyword Suggestion Tool, where it was recommended to potential advertisers that the keyword was available for a fee. Rescuecom filed suit against Google for selling its trademark as a keyword to its competitors. Thus, whenever an Internet user typed "Rescuecom" as a search term, the competitor's hyperlink appeared linked to the competitors' websites among the search results. The court found Google's use of Rescuecom's trademark in a keyword did not satisfy the "trademark use" requirement as it applies to 15 U.S.C. § 1051 whereby it is necessary for establishing infringement and false origin actions.

Rescuecom was unable to establish "trademark use" because they could not prove that: (1) any of the search results, except the links belonging to plaintiff, displayed plaintiff's trademark, that (2) defendant's activities affected the appearance or functionality of plaintiff's website, or that (3) defendant placed plaintiff's trademark on any goods, containers, displays, or advertisements. In *Google, Inc. v. American Blind & Wallpaper Factory, Inc.,*[325] the court found Google's sale of trademarked terms in its advertising program did constitute "Use in Commerce" for purposes of the Lanham Act, and denied summary judgment to Google.

Rosetta Stone filed a trademark infringement, dilution, and unfair competition lawsuit against Rocket Languages, a competitor, for "piggybacking," the practice of using "trademarked words of big brands in the text of search ads to divert traffic from the sites of bigger advertisers to their own sites."[326] Rosetta Stone charged Rocket Languages, a competitor, with misusing its trademark and variations in sponsored link advertisements. Rocket Language bought keywords so when potential Rosetta customers clicked the links in advertisements, seeking "ROSETTA STONE" products; they were instead taken to websites operated by Rocket Languages. Rosetta also contends Rocket Language advertisements diluted and tarnished the "ROSETTA STONE" mark and the reputation of its products. One Rocket Language advertisement asked: "Is Rosetta Spanish a Scam?" in the header of the advertisement and "Don't Buy Rosetta Spanish Before You Read This" in the text of the advertisement.

Rosetta contends these "comparison reviews" gave the consumer the false impression they were unbiased statements. Rosetta Stone sued Google in 2010 for trademark infringement and the federal court held Google's practice of auctioning marks, as keyword triggers for links sponsored by third party advertisers did not constitute direct trademark infringement.[327] In *Rosetta Stone Ltd. v. Google, Inc.,*[328] the Fourth Circuit affirmed the district court's order with respect to the vicarious infringement and unjust enrichment claims,[329] but vacated the court's order with respect to the direct infringement, contributory infringement and dilution claims and

---

[324] Id. at 129.

[325] 2007 WL 1848665 (N.D. Cal. 2007).

[326] Dan Slater, Unhappy With its Google Search Results, Rosetta Stone Sues Competitor, THE WALL STREET JOURNAL (July 7, 2008).

[327] Rosetta Stone Ltd. v. Google, Inc., 730 F.Supp.2d 531 (E.D. Va. 2010).

[328] 2012 U.S. App. LEXIS 7082 (4th Cir., April 9, 2012).

[329] The plaintiffs' claim of unjust enrichment must also fail. To prevail on a claim for unjust enrichment under New York law the plaintiff must demonstrate that (1) defendant was enriched; (2) at the plaintiff's expense, and (3) equity and good conscience militate against permitting defendant to retain what plaintiff is seeking to recover.

remanded these claims for further proceeding. Keyword advertising lawsuits are seldom successful in recent years.[330]

§ 11.11 SPONSORED BANNERS & POP–UPS

In the first decade of the twenty-first century pop-up cases were one of the hottest trademark-related issues. The plaintiff in these cases was a trademark owner who claimed that pop-up advertisers caused ads to appear on a user's computer screen that confused consumers. Gator's software, for example, tracked the user's Internet usage, and delivered ads to consumer's computer based upon their prior Internet usage. The more objectionable pop-ups appeared on the user's screen and concealed or partially covered up website content that the user was viewing. Trademark infringement claims may be predicated upon the defendant's use of unidentified banner ads on the Internet user's search page. Playboy, for example, objected to a competitor's ad appearing as a pop-up banner ad along the margin of the search result when the searcher entered "Playboy" and/or "Playmate"—both trademark terms owned by Playboy.[331] The search engine incorporated calibration keywords in its software application. The *Playboy* court found the banner advertisements objectionable because they did not clearly identify the sponsor of the ad, thereby creating a likelihood of confusion.

In *Washingtonpost.newsweek Interactive Company, LLC, et al. v. The Gator Corporation*,[332] a Virginia federal court issued a preliminary injunction, enjoining defendant Gator Corporation from causing pop-up ads to appear on a user's computer screen at the same time the user is viewing sixteen different news organizations. The court held that plaintiffs were likely to prevail on their trademark infringement claim given that the pop-ups concealed part of the websites. Pop-up and banner advertisement cases began to be filed less frequently in the second decade of the new millennium.

§ 11.12 METATAGS

(A) Invisible Trademark Violations

Some search engines index each discernible word on every web page, while others index by invisible metatags. A "metatag" is an invisible code in Hypertext Markup Language ("HTML") that describes the contents of a Web page. Search engines in the 1990s used metatags to determine page rank; although, currently Google and other search engines have other methods for determining page rank. Meta elements are HTML or XHTML, which provide metadata about a Web page, which are invisible.[333] "Web publishers can include trademarks in their "keyword metatags," which are index terms readable by a search engine."[334] Metatags are hypertext markup language tags

---

[330] "Trademark owners rarely win keyword advertising lawsuits in court. Reinforcing this conclusion, another trademark owner lost a trial over competitive keyword advertising despite a number of key facts in its favor. Given how often trademark owners lose keyword advertising lawsuits, why do they keep wasting their time and money?" Eric Goldman, Suing Over Trademark Advertising Is a Bad Business Decision for Trademark Owners, FORBES.COM (May 14, 2013) (reviewing cases).

[331] Playboy Enterprises Inc. v. Netscape Communications Corp., 354 F.3d 1020, 1023 (9th Cir. 2004).

[332] No. 02–909–A (E.D. Va., July 12, 2002).

[333] The following is an example of metatags: This is the Web Page Title. This will appear on your SearchSight.com Listing. Searchsight.com, Meta Tag Example (2012).

[334] GRAEME B. DINWOODIE & MARK D. JANIS, TRADEMARK LAW AND THEORY: A HANDBOOK OF CONTEMPORARY RESEARCH at 427 (2008).

that provide information describing the content of the web pages that are read by search engines. Companies will sometimes use well-known trademarks of rivals as metatags for their own webpages to attract users who type in the well-known mark into a search engine. Defendants incorporating another company's trademarks in their metatags may be liable for trademark causes of action because their intent is to benefit from the goodwill associated with the mark.[335]

Search engines allow website owners and administrators to control their positioning and description in search engine results. Litigants have not been successful in pursuing tort-based interference with contract or First Amendment based causes of action, against search engines for manipulating results or search engine bias.[336] Chapter 11, Trademarks on the Global Internet, explores the issue of whether incorporating another company's trademarks in metatags or keywords constitute "commercial use" in an infringement action. White hat technique "such as redesigning content on a website to attract search engines are permissible under search engines' term of service and a legitimate way to raise website's ranking in search engine results."[337] The reason why a website wants more hits is to increase its "per click," or other online advertising revenue.[338]

Trademark owners file suit against individuals or companies that incorporated the metatags of popular companies in their website to jump-start their page rank. The recent trend is for courts to find that merely incorporating the plaintiff's trademark in invisible code does not demonstrate "Use in Commerce."[339] Nevertheless, if a website uses metatags deceptively to misrepresent its sites, courts will find liability for trademark infringement. A few courts continue to find that use of a plaintiff's trademark in metatags constitutes infringement. In *North American Medical Corp. v. Axiom Worldwide, Inc.,*[340] Axiom incorporated North American Medical's ("NAM") trademarked terms within its metatags to influence Internet search engines.[341] Adagen was an authorized distributor of NAM's traction devices.

Axiom, a competitor of NAM, manufactured a physiotherapeutic device. NAM and Adagen allege Axiom engaged in unfair competition by infringing NAM's trademarks when it included their trademarks in metatags on its website. Axiom used two of NAM's registered trademarks in its metatags on its website: the terms "Accu–Spina" and "IDD Therapy." Even though no mention was made of the trademarks, the trademarks in the metatags influenced Internet search engines to the degree that when a computer user entered NAM's trademarked terms in Google's search engine, the search engine returned Axiom's website as the second most relevant search result.

---

[335] Brookfield Communs., Inc. v. West Coast Entertainment Corp., 174 F.3d 1036, 1062 (9th Cir. 1999) (holding use of trademark "moviebuff.com" in metatags of a competitor's website constituted initial interest confusion).

[336] Oren Bracha & Frank Pasquale, Federal Search Commission? Access, Fairness and Accountability in the Law of Search, 93 CORNELL L. REV. 1149, 1207 (2008).

[337] James Grimmelman, The Structure of Search Engine Law, 93 IOWA L. REV. 1 (2007).

[338] 4 MCCARTHY ON TRADEMARKS AND UNFAIR COMPETITION § 25:70.25 (4th ed. 2012) (stating that "[R]etailer placement of goods and retail promotions like coupons are traditional forms of legitimate advertising and that in cyberspace shopping, on-line intermediaries like GOOGLE and YAHOO! have stepped into the role of the brick and mortar retailer.").

[339] S&L Vitamins v. Australian Gold, Inc., 521 F.Supp.2d 188 (E.D.N.Y. 2007).

[340] 522 F.3d 1211 (11th Cir. 2008).

[341] North Am. Med. Corp. v. Axiom Worldwide, Inc., 522 F.3d 1211 (11th Cir. 2008).

The Eleventh Circuit affirmed the lower court's finding that the misuse of metatags constitutes trademark infringement and false advertising. The court found a likelihood of success on the merits of the infringement claims. The appeals court held there was a likelihood of confusion when the defendant included trademarks of competitors in metatags. Such a misuse of the metatags suggested the competitor's products and those of the manufacturer had the same source, or that the competitor sold both lines. The *Axiom Worldwide* court also found a likelihood of success on the merits of the false advertising claims.[342]

In *Brookfield Communications, Inc. v. West Coast Entertainment Corp.*, the Ninth Circuit determined that West Coast Entertainment Corp. ("West Coast"), a video specialty store that had used the term "movie buff" in certain slogans since the late 1980s, could not also use that term in its domain name or in metatags on its website.[343] Brookfield Communicaions ("Brookfield") was an informaion conen provider for he enerainmen indusry ha developed a daabase abou movies and regisered he rademark "Moviebuff." West Coast utilized terms similar to Brookfield's trademark in its metatags and invisible code.[344] When an Internet user would input "MovieBuff" into an Internet search engine, the list produced by the search engine would yield both West Coast's and Brookfield's websites.

West Coast planned to launch a website with the domain name moviebuff.com, but the court determined that the use of Brookfield's trademark as a metatag would divert traffic from Brookfield to West Coast's website. West Coast had registered the domain name in February of 1996, but it did not use the name until it launched its website. West Coast also obtained a federal registration of the term "The Movie Buff's Movie Store," and used the words "movie buff" in advertising. Brookfield claimed "priority use" in commerce of the phrase having used the mark first in 1993; although it did not get federal registration until September of 1998.

The *Brookfield* court compared the misuse of metatags and the diversion of web traffic from the rightful trademark owner's site to placing a sign employing another's trademark in front of one's store. The court ruled in favor of Brookfield under the Lanham Act and California Code § 17200—the unfair competition law. The *Brookfield* court based its ruling on initial interest confusion, even though there was "no proof [that] consumers ever thought that they were patronizing West Coast rather than Brookfield."[345]The court found the domain name moviebuff.com was functionally equivalent to the trademark, "Moviebuff."[346] "West Coast's trademarked slogan included the words: "movie buff," a generic term for a movie enthusiast. Thus, there is nothing deceptive or confusing about describing its site with a metatag using the word "Moviebuff."[347] Professor Yu distinguishes between merely incorporating a plaintiff's

---

[342] 15 U.S.C. § 1125(A).

[343] Brookfield Communications, Inc. v. West Coast Entertainment Corp., 174 F.3d 1036 (9th Cir. 1999).

[344] LEE B. BURGUNDER, LEGAL ASPECTS OF MANAGING TECHNOLOGY 409 (2010).

[345] TERESA SCASSA AND MICHAEL EUGENE DETURBIDE, ELECTRONIC COMMERCE AND INTERNET LAW IN CANADA 225 (2004).

[346] Brookfield Communications, Id. at 1055.

[347] PETER K. YU, Intellectual Property and Information Wealth: Trademark and unfair Competition 106 (2007).

trademark and misrepresenting a website causing consumer confusion in order to divert a competitor's customers.[348]

(B) Initial Interest Confusion

Initial Interest Confusion ("IIC") occurs on the Internet when a company creates confusion "from the unauthorized use of trademarks to divert Internet traffic, thereby capitalizing on a trademark holder's goodwill."[349] IIC ". . . occurs when a customer is lured to a product by the similarity of the mark, even if the customer realizes the true source of the goods before the sale is consummated."[350] Initial interest confusion is, in effect, a misappropriation of good will.[351] "What is important is not the duration of the confusion; it is the misappropriation of goodwill."[352] A growing number of courts are skeptical about the continuing vitality of IIC.[353] The leading initial interest case is *Brookfield Communications, Inc. v. West Coast Entertainment Corp.*[354] described above. The first to use a mark in commerce is the senior user, and others are junior users. The *Brookfield* court reasoned that Web surfers typing in *Brookfield's* "MovieBuff" products would be sent to "westcoastvideo.com and this is the emblem of an IIC.

The court acknowledged that Internet users would not be confused by thinking they were at Brookfield's website. Rather, the confusion was only IIC that was fleeting confusion at best.[355] The court compared IIC to setting up a false billboard sign on the highway for a fast food restaurant. When the interstate traveler exits the highway, they find they have been diverted to a competitor's restaurant. A consumer would not be confused by a Taco Bell sign and leaving the highway to find a Chipotle. This comparison lacks a goodness of fit to Internet searches:

> First, in the billboard analogy, the searcher is not actively conducting a search. Rather, the driver is passively exposed to content (the billboard). The court's hypothetical assumes that the content is impactful enough to cause the driver to instantly develop a search objective and start implementing the search. The court further presumes that the search objective is to find West Coast Video, an assumption that may be reasonable in context.[356]

In *Hearts on Fire Co. v. Blue Nile, Inc.*, the Massachusetts district court stated: "In the trademark infringement context, many cases will fall somewhere between the incarnations of so-called initial interest confusion—the misleading billboard or the choice-enhancing menu. The court's task is to distinguish between them. The deceptive billboard analogy often is inapt in the Internet context."[357] The court describing IIC as

---

[348] See Niton Corp. v. Radiation Monitoring Devices, Inc., 27 F. Supp. 2d 102 (D. Mass. 1998) (entering a preliminary injunction predicated upon the finding of initial interest confusion).

[349] Austl. Gold, Inc. v. Hatfield, 436 F.3d 1228, 1239 (10th Cir. 2006).

[350] Id.

[351] Promatek Indus., Ltd. v. Equitrac Corp., 300 F.3d 808, 812 (7th Cir. 2002).

[352] Id.

[353] Playboy Enterprises, Inc. v. Netscape Communications Corp., 354 F.3d 1020 (9th Cir. 2001).

[354] 174 F.3d 1036 (9th Cir. 1999).

[355] "The purpose of a trademark is to help consumers identify the source, but a mark cannot serve a source-identifying function if the public has never seen the mark and thus is not meritorious of trademark protection until it is used in public in a manner that creates an association among consumers between the mark and the mark's owner." Id. at 1051.

[356] Eric Goldman, Deregulating Relevancy in Internet Trademark Law, 54 EMORY L. J. 507, 570 (2005).

[357] Hearts on Fire Co. v. Blue Nile, Inc. 603 F.Supp. 2d 274, 287 (D. Mass. 2003).

involving "one specific type of pre-sale confusion: It involves confusion at the very earliest stage—not with respect to the source of specific goods or services under consideration, but during the process of searching and canvassing for a particular product."[358] The court noted that ultimately the consumer ". . . is never confused as to the source or origin of the product he eventually purchases, but he may have arrived there through either misdirection or mere redirection."[359]

The ICC doctrine recognized by the *Brookfield* court is closely akin to the concept of rapid cognition.[360] A quick glance at a trademark gives a consumer a split second profile of the quality of goods and services. The Tenth Circuit refused to recognize the ICC in *1–800 Contacts, Inc. v. Lens.com, Inc.*,[361] In *1–800 Contacts*, the retailer of replacement contact lenses brought Lanham Act trademark-infringement action against competitor that used Internet advertising in which search engine displayed competitor's advertisement when customers performed search using keywords that resembled retailer's registered "1800CONTACTS" service mark. The dispute was one of hundreds that has arisen out of Google's AdWords program "An advertiser using AdWords pays Google to feature one of its ads onscreen whenever a designated term, known as a keyword, is used in a Google search."[362] The court stated that initial interest confusion could occur in the following scenario:

> Applying that description to this case, initial-interest confusion would arise as follows: a consumer enters a query for "1–800 Contacts" on Google; sees a screen with an ad for Lens.com that is generated because of Lens.com's purchase of one of the nine Challenged Keywords; becomes confused about whether Lens.com is the same source as, or is affiliated with, 1–800; and therefore clicks on the Lens.com ad to view the site. Lens.com has exploited its use of 1–800's mark to lure the confused consumer to its website.[363]

The court found neither initial interest confusion or direct confusion and thus no violation by the AdWords advertiser's use of keywords that resembled 1–800's service mark.

§ 11.13 DEFENSES TO TRADEMARK INFRINGEMENT ACTIONS

Trademarks may be used on the Internet without the trademark owners' consent and not trigger an infringement action. This happens when the use of the mark is protected by fair use, nominative use, or is entitled to a First Amendment-related defense. Just as copyright law has built-in speech safeguards in the fair use doctrine and the idea/expression distinction, trademark law also addresses First Amendment concerns in part because "The Federal Dilution Act exempts from its coverage fair use in comparative advertising, noncommercial use, and all forms of news reporting and news commentary."[364]

---

[358] Id.

[359] Id.

[360] MALCOLM GLADWELL, BLINK: THE POWER OF THINKING WITHOUT THINKING (2005).

[361] 2013 WL 3665627 (10th Cir. July 16, 2013).

[362] Id. at *1.

[363] Id. at *10.

[364] BEVERLY W. PATTISHALL, DAVID CRAIG HILLIARD, JOSEPH NYE WELCH, TRADEMARKS AND UNFAIR COMPETITION 160 (5th ed. 2002). Rebecca Tushnet, Trademark Law as Commercial Speech Regulation, 58 S.

(A) Trademark Fair Use

(1) Traditional Fair Use

Kent Stuckey, author of the text *Internet and Online Law*, states: "The fair use defense protects use of another's trademark when it is used not in a trademark sense."[365] Just as the fair use defense permits copying of an author's expression purposes, trademark law permits "fair uses" of a trademark owner's marks. The "fair use" defense permits a party's use, "otherwise than as a mark," of a term "which is descriptive of and used fairly and in good faith only to describe the goods or services of such party."[366] "The 'fair use' defense protects use of another's trademark when it is used not in a trademark sense . . . or services or their geographic origin."[367] "The classic fair use analysis is appropriate where a defendant has used the plaintiff's mark only to describe his own product, and not at all to describe the plaintiff's product."[368] "Classic fair use cases typically turn on whether the defendant was making a trademark use or simply using the common terms for their everyday meaning."[369]

(2) Nominative Fair Use

Nominative fair use is not infringement so long as the use is: (1) not as a trademark, but (2) fairly and in good faith (3) to describe the goods and services.[370] Nominative fair use is when the defendant uses the trademarked term to describe the plaintiff's product, "even if the defendant's ultimate goal is to describe his own product."[371] A federal court ruled that use of a trademark in a site's metatags constitutes nominative fair use because searchers would have a much more difficult time locating relevant websites if the law outlawed such truthful, non-misleading use of a mark. The same logic applies to nominative use of a mark in a domain name.[372] In *Designer Skin LLC v. S & L Vitamins, Inc., et al.,*[373] the federal court dismissed a trademark dilution claim arising out of the defendant's use of plaintiff's marks in both metatags and search engine key words. The court reasoned that such use of the marks was protected by nominative fair use unless there was a suggestion of sponsorship by the trademark owner. Notably, the court reached this result because plaintiff failed to submit adequate evidence as to the impact this use of its marks had on the listing of defendant's site in search results for plaintiff's mark.

The court left open the possibility that such a use of plaintiff's mark may not qualify as a nominative fair use if in fact it caused defendant's site to appear at or near the top of search engine results for plaintiff's mark, and thereby suggested that

---

CAR. L. REV. 737 (2007) (contending there is a clash between commercial speech under the First Amendment and the federal trademark statute).

[365] KENT STUCKEY, INTERNET AND ONLINE LAW 7–36 (1996).

[366] 15 U.S.C. § 1115(b)(4).

[367] Stuckey, Internet and Online Law, Id. at 7–36.

[368] PACCAR Inc. v. TeleScan Techs., 319 F.3d 243, 256 n. 21 (6th Cir. 2003).

[369] Stephen W. Feingold & Howard S. Hogan, Unique Online Trademark Issues in G. Peter Albert Jr. and American Intellectual Property Law Association, Intellectual Property in Cyberspace (2d ed. 2012) at 397.

[370] Cairns v. Franklin Mint Co., 292 F.3d 1139, 1151 (9th Cir. 2002).

[371] Mattel Inc. v. Walking Mountain Prods., 353 F.3d 792, 809 (9th Cir. 2003).

[372] Toyota Motor Sales, U.S.A., Inc. v. Tabari, 610 F.3d 1171, 1179 (9th Cir. 2010).

[373] Designer Skin, LLC v. S & L Vitamins, Inc., 560 F. Supp. 2d 811 (D. Ariz. 2008).

plaintiff sponsored or endorsed defendant's site. Regarding a trademark infringement claim on an Internet website, the nominative fair use defense might be unavailable where the use of marks in metatags causes the user's site to regularly appear above the mark holder's in searches for one of the trademarked terms.[374] The nominative fair use doctrine allows a company to mention a competitor's trademark or service mark in a comparative Internet advertisement.[375]

The nominative fair use analysis allows a defendant to use the plaintiff's mark to describe the plaintiff's product; so long as the goal is for the defendant to describe her own product.[376] The difference between nominative fair use and classic fair use is due to the modern recognition that a descriptive term that acquired distinctiveness was protectable. The concern was that everyday, descriptive terms would be protectable.[377] A computer repair shop, for example, can advertise that it fixes Dell laptops even though "Dell" is a registered trademark. To qualify under fair use, there are three requirements. In *New Kids On The Block v. News America Publishing, Inc.*,[378] the Ninth Circuit adopted a three part test for nominative fair use test:

> first, the product or service in question must be one not readily identifiable without use of the trademark; second, only so much of the mark or marks may be used as is reasonably necessary to identify the product or service; and third, the user must do nothing that would, in conjunction with the mark, suggest sponsorship or endorsement by the trademark holder.[379]

Fair use also allows comparative advertising and employing another's trademark in a manner such as the Pepsi Challenge that featured taste tests between Coca Cola and Pepsi in malls around the country in the 1980s. To prevail on the fair use defense, the defendant must establish that it has used the plaintiff's mark, in good faith. This was the case in Playboy v. Welles, where Terri Welles used Playboy's marks, Playmate and Playboy in metatags for her website. The *Playboy* court found Ms. Welles's use of metatags was protected by the "*nominative fair use*" defense of another's trademark as she was Playboy's Playmate of the Year for 1981.[380] The trial court refused to enter an injunction in favor of Playboy enjoining Welles' use of trademarked terms such as '*Playmate*' and '*Playboy*' on her website. The Ninth Circuit affirmed lower court ruling that the use of Playboy's trademarks in metatags in the wallpaper was not within the nominative fair use shield as it was not necessary to describe Welles.

(B) First Amendment in Cyberspace

Fan Sites, rogue sites, or grip sites that mention trademarks in the course of criticizing companies are generally protected by the First Amendment unless a court

---

[374] Id.

[375] J.K. Harris & Co., LLC v. Kassel, 253 F. Supp.2d 1120, 1125–26 (N.D. Cal. 2003).

[376] The FTDA also expressly includes "nominative" fair use as a defense. 15 U.S.C. § 1125(c)(3)(A). Nominative fair use is often asserted in comparative advertising cases.

[377] Stephen W. Feingold & Howard S. Hogan, Unique Online Trademark Issues in G. Peter Albert Jr. and American Intellectual Property Law Association, Intellectual Property in Cyberspace (2d ed. 2012) at 397.

[378] 971 F.2d 302 (9th Cir. 1992).

[379] Id. at 308.

[380] Playboy Enterprises, Inc. v. Welles, 7 F. Supp.2d 1098, 1104 (S.D. Cal. 2001), aff'd by Playboy Enterprises, Inc. v. Welles, 279 F3d 796 (9th Cir. 2002).

finds that those sites are deceptive, and create consumer confusion. "Gripe Sites," such as PissedConsumer.com, makes clear that it is not affiliated with trademarks as the domain name incorporates, and indeed is critical, of the companies that own the marks and therefore does not present a likelihood of confusion.[381] In *Bihari v. Gross*,[382] the court found that a "Gripe Site" critical of the plaintiff's interior design work did not violate Marianne Bihari's trademark because no reasonable consumer would believe that the plaintiff or her company, Bihari Interiors, sponsored the site. The court also found that the "Gripe Site" was not diverting users from the Bihari Interior site.[383] Companies will find it difficult to enjoin websites critical of their goods and services, which have become ubiquitous on the Internet.

In the early years of the Internet, trademark owners often won lawsuits against domain name registrants who incorporated their trade names or marks. An early example of such a complaint occurs in, *Bally Total Fitness Holding Corp. v. Faber*,[384] where a critic of the chain of health clubs set up an anti-Bally website entitled, "Bally's sucks"—a "sucks" site. Bally Total Fitness ("Bally's") filed suit for trademark dilution because the defendant was using its trademarks in an unauthorized manner.

The federal court in California granted summary judgment in favor of Faber, reasoning no reasonable person would think Bally's is affiliated with or endorses the anti-Bally site.[385] The court also found "fair use" in the website's use of Bally's intellectual property.[386] The "Gripe Site", www.compupix.com/ballysucks, dedicated to complaints, creates no likelihood of confusion, "because no reasonable visitor to gripe site would assume it to come from same source or think it to be affiliated with, connected with, or sponsored by Bally's."[387] In addition, courts have upheld the right to gripe sites where trade secrets where asserted by the trademark owner.[388]

(C) Trademark Parodies

A parody is a "simple form of entertainment conveyed by juxtaposing the irreverent representation of the trademark with the idealized image created by the mark's owners."[389] In *Lyons Partnership v. Giannoulas*,[390] the Fifth Circuit ruled that the Ted Giannoulas's creation of the sports mascot The Famous Chicken stepping on a Barney lookalike constituted a parody protectable by the First Amendment of the U.S. Constitution. A parody makes a trademark the brunt of its joke, or satirical message, and therefore does not infringe upon the trademark. In *L.L. Bean v. Drake Publishers*, the First Circuit held that a sexually oriented parody of L.L. Bean's catalog, called the

---

[381] Ascentive, LLC v. Opinion Corp., 2011 U.S. Dist. LEXIS 143081 (E.D. N.Y., Dec. 13, 2011).

[382] 119 F. Supp. 2d 309 (S.D.N.Y. 2000).

[383] See also, Taubman Co. v. Webfeats, 319 F.3d 770, 777–78 (6th Cir. 2003) (no Lanham Act violation where gripe site with domain name taubmansucks.com that provided editorial on conflict between website creator and plaintiff corporation did not create any possibility of confusion).

[384] 29 F. Supp. 2d 1161 (C.D. Cal. 1998).

[385] Id. at 1163.

[386] Id. at 1167.

[387] Id.

[388] Ford Motor Co. v. 2600 Enters., 177 F. Supp. 2d 661, 662, 666 (E.D. Mich. 2001) (denying injunctive relief to Ford Motor Co., which sought to enjoin defendants from maintaining domain name, "FuckGeneralMotors.com," that takes user directly to Ford Motor Co.'s official website at "ford.com").

[389] L.L. Bean, Inc. v. Drake Publishers, Inc., 811 F.2d 26, 34 (1st Cir. 1987).

[390] 179 F.3d 384 (5th Cir. 1999).

"L. L. Beam Sex Catalog," in a commercial adult-oriented magazine, constituted non-commercial use of the trademark.[391] Parody of trademarks is permitted as long as it is not closely connected with commercial use.[392] In *Louis Vuitton Mallettier S.A. v. Haute Diggity Dog,* the Fourth Circuit ruled that a "Chewy Vuiton" dog chew toy was a successful parody of the French manufacturer's luxury handbags and the "LOUIS VUITTON" marks and trade dress used in marketing and selling those handbags.

The *Louis Vuitton* court reasoned the "Chewy Vuiton" toy was obviously an irreverent and intentional representation of the famous designer's handbag.[393] The *Louis Vuitton* court found no doubt that the dog toy was not an "idealized image" of a mark created by the manufacturer. Moreover, the toy's name immediately conveyed a joking and amusing parody by using something a dog would chew on to poke fun at the elegance and expense of the famous French designer's rather pricey handbags. The parody doctrine is not well developed outside the United States. The strength and recognizability of the mark may make it easier for the audience to realize that the use is a parody and a joke on the qualities embodied in the trademarked word or image.[394] In *Hormel Foods Corp. v. Jim Henson Prods.,*[395] the Second Circuit observed that a successful parody "tends to increase public identification" of the famous mark with its source. The court found "the similarity between the name "Spa'am" and Hormel's mark is not accidental. In Henson's film, Spa'am is the high priest of a tribe of wild boars that worships Miss Piggy as its Queen Sha Ka La Ka La. Although the name "Spa'am" is mentioned only once in the entire movie, Henson hopes to poke a little fun at Hormel's famous luncheon meat by associating its processed, gelatinous block with a humorously wild beast."[396] Hormel contended "that even comic association with an unclean "grotesque" boar will call into question the purity and high quality of its meat product."[397] The Second Circuit noted that the district court:

> found no evidence that Spa'am was unhygienic. At worst, he might be described as "untidy." Moreover, by now Hormel should be inured to any such ridicule. Although SPAM is in fact made from pork shoulder and ham meat, and the name itself supposedly is a portmanteau word for spiced ham, countless jokes have played off the public's unfounded suspicion that SPAM is a product of less than savory ingredients.[398]

A parody must convey two simultaneous—and contradictory—messages: that it is the original, but also that it is *not* the original and is instead a parody. The Fourth Circuit found the FTDA applies only to a "Commercial use in commerce of a mark," leaving no doubt "that it did not intend for trademark laws to impinge the First Amendment rights of critics and commentators."[399] In short, "a mark shall be deemed to be in use in commerce . . . on services when it used or displayed in the sale or

---

[391] RAYMOND S.R. KU & JACQUELINE D. LIPTON, CYBERSPACE LAW: CASES AND MATERIALS (2006) at 234.

[392] RICHARD A. SPINELO, CYBERETHICS: MORALITY AND LAW IN CYBERSPACE (2010) at 105.

[393] Louis Vuitton Malletier S.A. v. Haute Diggity Dog, 507 F.3d 252 (4th Cir. 2007).

[394] MCCARTHY ON TRADEMARKS AND UNFAIR COMPETITION § 31:153 (4th ed. 1999).

[395] 73 F.3d 497, 503 (2d Cir. 1996).

[396] Id. at 501.

[397] Id.

[398] Id.

[399] Lamparello v. Falwell, 420 F.3d 309, 313 (4th Cir. 2005).

advertising of services and the services are rendered in commerce."[400] In *Lamparello*, the Fourth Circuit determined that Christopher Lamparello's domain name, www.fallwell.com, a website critical of Reverend Jerry Falwell and his views on homosexuality, did not constitute cybersquatting. The appellate court reasoned Reverend Falwell was unable to show that Lamparello had a bad faith intent to profit from his use of the fallwell.com domain name. The court also noted Lamparello had not engaged in the type of conduct described in the statutory factors as typifying the bad faith intent to profit essential to a successful cybersquatting claim.

In *People for the Ethical Treatment of Animals v. Doughney*,[401] the organization People for the Ethical Treatment of Animals ("PETA") brought action against Michael Doughney citing trademark infringement, dilution, and cybersquatting for Doughney's use of the domain name, peta.org. Doughney argued that his website, People Eating Tasty Animals, was a parody of People for the Ethical Treatment of Animals, thus protected by the First Amendment. A Virginia district court granted summary judgment to PETA. The court, using the *Bantam* test, held that Doughney's site did not constitute a parody because there was no "simultaneous conveyance," that the site was at once a PETA site and a parody. Similarly, for the infringement and unfair competition claims, the court found that Doughney used PETA's trademark "in commerce" based on a two-part rationale; first, because his website offered links to other websites offering "goods and services" thereby providing the needed "connection with goods and services" required by the Lanham Act, and second, because Doughney recommended that PETA "settle" or "make him an offer" in order to purchase the domain name from him thereby making Doughney a cybersquatter.

(D) Trademark Laches

Laches is an equitable defense consisting of three elements: (1) delay in asserting one's trademark rights; (2) lack of excuse for the delay; and (3) undue prejudice to the alleged infringer caused by the delay.[402] The federal Lanham Act remedies are subject to the "principles of equity, which include the "doctrine of laches" and using that doctrine to bar an infringement claim (because plaintiff took no action)."[403] To avoid the equitable defense of laches, or "sleeping on your rights," trademark owners should conduct public searches of social media and other websites. Non-generic, non-misleading, genuine and continuous use of trademarks is necessary for continuous protection. In cybersquatting cases, the trademark owner should not wait too many years to file a complaint either in federal court or in a UDRP dispute-resolution proceeding.

Notably, a UDRP panel rejected the laches defense in a dispute over the domain name Charterbusiness.com, even though the trademark owner delayed filing a complaint for seven years.[404] Laches is an equitable defense that can be asserted to

---

[400] 15 U.S.C. § 1127.

[401] 263 F.3d 359 (4th Cir. 2001).

[402] INTERNATIONAL TRADEMARK ASSOCIATION, 2 TRADEMARK LAW HANDBOOK 280 (2008).

[403] Hot Wax, Inc. v. Turtle Wax, Inc., 191 F.3d 813, 822, 824 (7th Cir. 1999).

[404] Charter Communications, Inc. v. CK Ventures Inc./Charterbusiness.com, Case No. D2010–0228 ("WIPO") (June 20, 2010).

rebut a claim of irreparable harm or in defense of a claim "that a defendant used h. her mark in a manner that caused confusion."[405]

(E) Disclaimers

It is unclear whether disclaimers are effective in shielding or limiting liability for trademark infringement or dilution. Some courts have found that disclaimers are effective in preventing trademark confusion.[406] Other courts found disclaimers effective in counter claims of willful trademark infringement.[407] In still other cases, it was the "effective disclaimer together with the presence of other factors that tend to reduce the likelihood of confusion, combine to support a finding of no trademark liability."[408]

§ 11.14 FALSE ADVERTISING

For standing pursuant to the 'false advertising' prong of § 43(a) of the Lanham Act, 15 U.S.C. § 1125(a)(1)(B), "a plaintiff must show: (1) a commercial injury based upon a misrepresentation about a product; and (2) that the injury is 'competitive,' or harmful to the plaintiff's ability to compete with the defendant."[409] "[W]hen plaintiff competes directly with defendant, a misrepresentation will give rise to a presumed commercial injury that is sufficient to establish standing."[410] Website false advertising claims are cognizable under both the Lanham Act and state law. Plaintiffs will have a false advertising claim if they can prove that the defendant used their trademarks to lure customers to its website and then sell competing products. To prevail in a Lanham Act false advertising case, the plaintiff must prove: (1) the online advertisements of the defendant were false or misleading; (2) the online ads deceived, or had the capacity to deceive website visitors; (3) the deception had a material effect on purchasing decisions; (4) the misrepresented product or service affects interstate commerce; and (5) the plaintiff has been, or is likely to be, injured as a result of the false advertising.[411]

In *Johnson & Johnson Vision Care, Inc. v. 1–800 Contacts, Inc.*, the Eleventh Circuit found that the defendant's use of the manufacturer's trademarks within its website's metatags was a "use in commerce" within the meaning of the Lanham Act. The appeals court found that the district court's finding of a "likelihood of confusion" was not clearly erroneous for purposes of plaintiffs' Lanham Act trademark infringement claims. The court also upheld the Eleventh Circuit's finding that the defendant made false statements in its advertising and the statements were material to a consumer's purchasing decisions.

---

[405] LISA E. CRISTAL & NEAL S. GREENFIELD, TRADEMARK LAW & THE INTERNET: ISSUES, CASE LAW, AND PRACTICE TIPS 146 (2001).

[406] Stephen W. Feingold & Howard S. Hogan, Unique Online Trademark Issues, in G. Peter Albert, Jr. and Intellectual Property Law Association, Intellectual Property in Cyberspace (2d ed. 2011) at 425.

[407] Id.

[408] Id.

[409] TrafficSchool.com, Inc. v. Edriver Inc., 653 F.3d 820, 826 (9th Cir. 2011).

[410] Id. at 827.

[411] Johnson & Johnson Vision Care, Inc. v. 1–800 Contacts, Inc., 299 F.3d 1242 (11th Cir. 2002).

§ 11.15 TRADEMARK ISSUES IN SOCIAL MEDIA

Trademark rights and remedies are undeveloped in social networks. Misusing or abusing another company's trademarks on Twitter, Facebook, or other social networks is not covered by the UDRP, as these sites are not classifiable as domain name registrars. Similarly, the ACPA rules for cybersquatting do not apply to misuses of trademarks on social networks. Trademark squatting in social media occurs when a user masquerades as a well-known company or celebrity. In the first trademark masquerading case, Tony LaRussa, a former Major League baseball manager, filed a complaint against Twitter for trademark infringement, false designation of origin, trademark dilution, cybersquatting, misappropriation of name, misappropriation of likeness, invasion of privacy, and intentional misrepresentation.[412] LaRussa's complaint alleged that an unknown Twitter user opened an account under the name, "Tony La Russa."[413] "The Twitter page consisted of unauthorized photo and written statements which included, "lost 2 out of 3, but we made it out of Chicago without one drunk driving incident or dead pitcher." Upon La Russa's filing, Twitter removed the account in question."[414]   Shortly after, Twitter removed the account, La Russa withdrew his complaint.[415]

§ 11.16 TYPOSQUATTERS, HIJACKERS, & REVERSE HIJACKERS

(A) Typosquatters

A "domain name" is any alphanumeric designation that is registered with or assigned by any domain name registrar, domain name registry, or other domain name registration authority as part of an electronic address on the Internet.[416] "Typosquatting" is the practice of registering a domain name to benefit from users who mistype a domain name and land on the mistyped domain. A classic example is the "typosquatter" who registered domain names that employed misspellings of popular child oriented websites, such as Teletubbies.com (telletubbies.com) and Disneyland.go.com (disnyland.com), to attract children to adult entertainment sites, and to enhance clickstream revenue. The typosquatter took advantage of children's foreseeable misspellings to receive a fee for each child's clickstream.

Typosquatters rely upon adult Internet users mistyping domain names as well. Dotster, a domain name registrar, registered the domain name "wwwVulcanGolf.com," which is a period away from the domain name www.VulcanGolf.com.[417] Vulcan filed suit against Dotster claiming the defendant "intentionally registered this domain name without the period after the "www" expecting that a certain number of Internet users will mistype the name and will land on the webpage."[418] Dotster was liable because it benefited from their blatantly deceptive domain. "When a user clicks on the

---

[412] Trademark Law Developments, 25 BERKELEY TECH. L.J. 4 (2010) (Complaint, No. 02487393 (Cal. Super. Ct. May 6, 2009)).

[413] Id.

[414] Id.

[415] Id.

[416] 15 U.S.C. § 1127.

[417] Vulcan Golf, LLC v. Google Inc., 552 F. Supp. 2d 752, 760 (N.D. Ill. 2008).

[418] Id. at 760.

advertising, Google and the parking companies and/or the domain owners receive revenue from that advertiser."[419]

(B) Trademark Hijackers

In the mid-1990s, trademark owners were uncertain as to whether a cybersquatter's incorporation of their trademarks domain names fell under "commercial use" for purposes of the Lanham Act. In 1996, the Ninth Circuit became the first federal appellate court to treat cybersquatting as "commercial use" in *Panavision International, L.P. v. Toeppen.*[420] Panavision charged Dennis Toeppen with cyberpiracy by registering domain names containing valuable trademarks.[421] When Panavision's attorney sent a letter to Toeppen ordering him to stop using the domain name, Toeppen offered to "'settle the matter' if Panavision would pay him $ 13,000 in exchange for the domain name."[422] Panavision filed an action for dilution under federal and state law, and the district court granted summary judgment in its favor on all claims.[423] In his appeal, Toeppen argued his registration of the domain name containing Panavision's trademark did not constitute commercial use.[424] The Ninth Circuit held Toeppen made commercial use of Panavision's mark in "his attempt to sell the trademarks themselves."[425] The court affirmed the lower court, concluding Toeppen diluted Panavision's trademarks within the meaning of the Federal Trademark Dilution Act, as well as under California state law.[426] Trademark hijacking is the practice of cybersquatter registering a domain name that is identical or confusingly similar to a plaintiff's trade name or trademark.

In contrast, a "reverse domain name hijacking" occurs when a cybersquatters or person with no legitimate interest in a mark files a complaint against the domain name registrant who does have a legitimate interest in the mark. Reverse cybersquatting lawsuits are filed in order to extract a nuisance settlement or a ransom. Under the Lanham Act, "a domain name registrant who is aggrieved by an overreaching trademark owner may commence an action to declare that the domain name registration or use by the registrant is not unlawful under the Lanham Act."[427] The Lanham Act's reverse domain name provision was enacted as part of the Anticybersquatting Protection Act:

> A domain name registrant whose domain name has been suspended, disabled, or transferred under a policy described under clause (ii) (II) may, upon notice to the mark owner, file a civil action to establish that the registration or use of the domain name by such registrant is not unlawful under this chapter. The court may grant injunctive relief to the domain name registrant, including the

---

[419] 552 F. Supp. 2d 752, 760 (N.D. Ill. 2008).
[420] 141 F.3d 1316 (9th Cir. 1998).
[421] Id.
[422] Id. at 1318.
[423] Id. at 1319.
[424] Id. at 1324
[425] Id. at 1325.
[426] Id.
[427] 15 U.S.C. § 1114(2)(D)(v).

reactivation of the domain name or transfer of the domain name to the domain name registrant.[428]

Domain names violate the right of trademark owners when they interfere or infringe with trademarks. The first domain name dispute occurred when MTV VJ Adam Curry filed a domain name registration for MTV.com.[429] "Although MTV originally showed little interest in the domain name or the Internet, when Adam Curry left MTV the company wanted to control the domain name. After a federal court action was brought, the dispute settled . . . ."[430] The parties entered into a settlement in which Curry agreed to transfer ownership of the domain name to MTV. In *Telemedia Network Inc. v. Sunshine Films, Inc.*, an adult entertainment company modified a domain name to redirect traffic of a rival to its own website; a practice known as "domain name hijacking."[431] The California Court of Appeals described how Sunshine Films "surreptitiously re-direct[ed] [web] traffic," for www.sexnet.com to Sunshine Film's web address thereby in effect "hijacking" the sexnet.com domain name using the Sexnet mark. The diversion of traffic occurred when customers trying to access Sexnet found a website operated by Sunshine with no content. Sunshine's purpose was to raise revenue through deceptive means. Congress enacted, the Truth in Domain Names Act of 2003, which states:

> (A) Whoever knowingly uses a misleading domain name with the intent to deceive a person into viewing obscenity on the Internet shall be fined under this title or imprisoned not more than 2 years or both.

> (b) Whoever knowingly uses a misleading domain name with the intent to deceive a minor into viewing material that is harmful to minors on the Internet shall be fined under this title or imprisoned not more than 4 years or both.[432]

(C) Reverse Domain Name Hijacking

Reverse domain name hijacking is when a trademark owner attempts to take a domain name by making a false cybersquatting claim against the rightful owner of the domain name. Paragraph 1 of the UDRP Rules defined Reverse Domain Name Hijacking:

> Reverse Domain Name Hijacking means using the Policy in bad faith to attempt to deprive a registered domain-name holder of a domain name. Reverse domain name hijacking is the overreaching use of the mechanisms established to remedy cybersquatting against a registrant with a legitimate interest in his domain name.[433]

---

[428] Id.

[429] See generally, MTV Networks v. Curry, 867 F. Supp. 202 (S.D.N.Y. 1994).

[430] Daniel A. Tysver, Domain Name Disputes, Welcome to Bitlaw, http://www.bitlaw. com/internet/ domain. html#disputes (last visited Sept. 12, 2011); Joan Meadows, Trademark Protection for Trademarks Used as Internet Domain Names, 65 U CIN. L. REV. 1323, 1337 (1997) (noting the "parties settled out of court in March 1995, with MTV receiving ownership of the domain name as part of the settlement").

[431] Telemedia Network Inc. v. Sunshine Films, Inc., 2002 WL 31518870 (Cal. Ct. App. 2d Dist. 2002).

[432] 18 U.S.C. § 2252(b).

[433] See Barcelona.com, Inc. v. Excelentisimo Ayuntamiento de Barcelona, 330 F.3d 617, 625 (4th Cir. 2003) ("To balance the rights given to trademark owners against cybersquatters, the ACPA also provides some protection to domain name registrants against "overreaching trademark owners.").

Thus, Section 1114(2)(D)(v) authorizes a domain name registrant to sue trademark owners for "reverse domain name hijacking."

§ 11.17 LANHAM ACT DAMAGES

Section 43 of the Lanham Act allows "any person who believes that he or she is likely to be damaged" by the proscribed conduct to bring a civil action.[434] In any Section 1125(d) case, "the plaintiff may elect, at any time before final judgment is rendered by the trial court, to recover, instead of actual damages and profits, an award of statutory damages in the amount of not less than $1,000 and not more than $100,000 per domain name, as the court considers just."[435] Under the Lanham Act, when "a violation under section 43(a) . . . ha[s] been established in any civil action . . . , the plaintiff shall be entitled . . . to recover (1) defendant's profits, (2) any damages sustained by the plaintiff, and (3) the costs of the action."[436]

§ 11.18 ICANN'S GOVERNANCE

(A) Overview of ICANN

The Internet Corporation for Assigned Names and Numbers ("ICANN"), created in 1998 to work in conjunction with the U.S. Department of Commerce, is responsible for the technical functions of the Internet. ICANN is a non-profit organization that oversees domain name disputes and controls domain name issues. ICANN coordinates the assignment of IP address numbers, protocol parameter and port numbers, and the stable operation of the Internet's root server systems. ICANN is a quasi-governmental forum for developing policies governing the Internet's core technical elements, including the domain name system ("DNS"). ICANN operates based on a civil society consensus, with affected stakeholders meeting to coordinate policies. Network Solutions, LLC was in a monopoly position from 1979 until the 1990s as the only registrar for domain names and had the exclusive right to allocate .com; .org; and .net addresses.

Today it is one of many domain name registrars accredited by ICANN. Network Solutions, like many registrars, offers web related services in addition to the registration of domain names. Currently, Network Solutions registers 7.8 million domain names. To register its domain name, an eBusiness may choose from hundreds of registrars and it is both an inexpensive and quick process. No single entity—academic, corporate, governmental, or non-profit—administers the Internet. It exists and functions because of the fact that hundreds of thousands of separate operators of computers and computer networks independently decided to use common data transfer protocols to exchange communications and information with other computers, which in turn exchange communications and information with still other computers.[437] ICANN is the closest thing to a single entity responsible for key infrastructure of the Internet.

---

[434] 15 U.S.C. § 1125(a).

[435] 15 U.S.C. § 1117(d).

[436] 15 U.S.C. § 1117(a).

[437] ACLU v. Reno, 929 F. Supp. 824, 832 (E.D. Pa. 1996).

Each time an Internet user seeks access to a website, they ". . . enter the domain-name combination that corresponds to the IP Address and is routed to the host computer."[438]

A domain name represents a company's gateway on the Internet. Memorable domain names are valuable intangible assets, as well as the subject disputes, to trademark owners. The NSF awarded Network Solutions an exclusive contract to register domain names and allocate "dot com" names. In the early years of the Internet, registration of domain names was free but beginning in 1995, the NSF charged a $50 annual fee for registrations. ICANN has certified hundreds of domain name registries and administrates the Uniform Domain Name Resolution Policy ("UDRP"). Today, there are over 900 domain name registrars and the price of domain names has dropped as low as $6. Many domain name registries charge $8 to $10 per domain name. The Internet gold rush commercialized the web in a short period and domain names were purchased on a first-come-first-served basis.[439]

A domain name is an alphanumeric designation that allows an Internet user to access a particular website. Every domain name consists of the top-level domain (such as .com, .net, or .org), which is preceded by the second level domain. Each domain name is a chain of character strings, called "labels", separated by dots. A domain name consists of two parts: a Top–Level Domain ("TLD") and a Second–Level Domain ("SLD"). TLDs are the right-hand part of a web address. For example, in the domain "IBM.com," the ".com" part is the TLD. The SLD is the rest of the address, in this example, the "IBM" part of the address. In general, the SLD may consist of combinations of letters, numbers, and some typographic symbols. SLDs commonly refer to the organization that registered the domain name while the TLD refers to the final segment of a domain name (e.g., the ".gov" in "www.uscourts.gov"); while a Second Level Domain ("SLD") refers to the second to last segment in a name (e.g., "uscourts").

Each number sequence of SLDs and TLDs constitutes a unique Internet address. Because the Internet is a global network of computers, each computer connected to the Internet must have a unique address. Internet addresses are in the form nnn.nnn. nnn.nnn where nnn must be a number from 0–255. This address is known as an IP address.[440] ICANN approves the Top–Level generic domains representing the domain name's suffix, operates the Internet Assigned Numbers Authority ("IANA"), and maintains the DNS root zone.

ICANN approved only six TLDs: (1) ".edu" for educational institutions, (2) ".org" for non-governmental and non-commercial organizations, (3) ".gov" for governmental entities, (4) ".net" for networks, (5) ".com" for commercial users, and (6) nation specific domains, such as ".us" in the United States.[441] Currently, there are more than 250 country codes TLDs ("ccTLD"). A ccTLD is composed of two letters such as .se for Sweden; .af for Afghanistan; .rs for Serbia; and .ca for Canada. The ccTLDs registration procedures vary significantly depending on the country's policy

---

[438] Lockheed Martin Corp. v. Network Solutions, Inc., 194 F.3d 980 (9th Cir. 1999) (describing how domain names work).

[439] As late as 1994, a commentator wrote that "advertisements on the current Internet computer network are not common because of that network's not-for-profit origins." Trotter Hardy, The Proper Legal Regime for "Cyberspace", 55 U. PITT. L. REV. 993, 1027 (1994).

[440] Rohan Chakraborty, How Does the Internet Work, ROHANGRR (May 6, 2012) http://rohanrgr.blogspot.com/2012/05/how-does-Internet-work.html#!/2012/05/how-does-Internet-work.html.

[441] Sporty's Farm L.L.C. v. Sportsman's Market, Inc. 202 F.3d 489, 492 (2d Cir. 2000).

preferences. Sweden, for example, followed a "prior assessment" domain name system that required companies to have a corporate presence in their country before they could register a domain name.

Although in 2000, Sweden changed its domain name registration rules to one based on a race to the registry. Most country level registries register domain names on a first-come-first-served basis, rather than prior assessment. However, countries have enormous freedom in managing country level domains. In 2005, the European Commission enacted legislation permitting European companies to register .eu names. Europe's TLD is available to companies and organizations: established in the European Union and to every resident's citizen, it does not replace the existing national country code TLDs (such as .fr, .de, .pl or .uk), but complements them and gives users the option of having a pan-European Internet identity on their websites and e-mail addresses.[442]

Examples of generic top-level domains consist of the .com; .info; .net; and .org domains. On June 20, 2011, ICANN approved a plan to increase the number of generic top-level domains ("gTLDs") companies to register their trademarks as gTLDs. A gTLD is a category of TLDs maintained by the Internet Assigned Numbers Authority ("IANA"). In 2012, ICANN launched a generic gTLD program introducing new gTLD namespaces. Registrants are now beginning to apply to ICANN to register gTLDs such as .travel or .computer, as well as suffixes for cities, e.g. .Miami, .Boston, .London, .Cairo, and .Munich.

Companies and individuals filed 2,000 applications as of May 2012, and, by the time you read this, there will likely be a gold rush for gTLDS. In July of 2008, ICANN first approved plans for new gTLDs that could greatly expand the number and possibilities of suffixes; the exact number will depend on how many applications it receives. ICANN is undecided on how to allocate these gTLDs in order to monetize them for their full market value. Domain registrants may soon be able to register in non-English languages such as Chinese and Arabic. Coca Cola, for example, will be able to register .coke, and IBM.com can register .IBM as a gTLD. Understanding how domain names works will be useful in Chapter 11 where the conflict between domain names and trademarks will be examined in detail. Domain names, like the real estate market, are all about "location, location, location."

Beginning in the mid-1990s, registrants began to register domain names that were either identical, or confusingly similar, to famous or distinctive trademarks. Domain name disputes continued to be litigated under diverse causes of action including: (1) trademark infringement; (2) trademark dilution; and (3) Unfair competition. All of these remedies are deployed against cybersquatters that register domain names for reselling them for a profit because, as mentioned previously, cybersquatters do not intend to use the domain name themselves, but only wish to resell it back to the famous company.

(B) Internet Assigned Numbers Authority

The Internet Assigned Numbers Authority ("IANA") is the ICANN operated entity that controls numbers for protocols, Country Code Top–Level Domains, and maintains the IP Address allotments. IANA delegates or re-delegates Top–Level domains and

---

[442] Europa, The .eu Top Level Domain (2009).

manages the domain name system root. The registration of domain names within two letter Country Code Top–Level Domains ("CCTLDs") such as UK (United Kingdom), SE (Sweden) or AU (Australia) are administered by country code managers. The DNS is a "directory, organized hierarchically, of all the domain names and their corresponding computers registered to particular companies and persons using the Internet."[443] On November 25, 1998, ICANN and the Commerce Department entered into a Memorandum of Understanding, in which they agreed jointly to develop and test the mechanisms and procedures that should be in place in the new, privatized DNS. Specifically, ICANN and the Commerce Department agreed to collaborate on "written technical procedures for operation of the primary root server including procedures that permit modifications, additions, or deletions to the root zone file."[444]

The Internet Protocol Addressing system uses "IPv4 addresses, which are 32 bit numbers often expressed as 4 octets in "dotted decimal" notation (for example, 192.0.2.53)."[445] The term "Internet Protocol address" means a numerical label that is assigned to each device that participates in a computer network that uses the Internet Protocol for communication. An Internet Protocol address ("IP address") is a unique 32–bit numeric address, written as numerals separated by periods, identifying each sender or receiver of information traveling across the Internet. The first part of the IP Address identifies the particular network on the Internet and the second identifies the particular device within the network. IPv6 is a new IP address standard designed to succeed IP version 4 that will expand the number of devices that may be connected to the Internet. This address space will be greatly expanded by IPv6 to space for an estimated trillion addresses. The differences between IPv4 and IPv6 are like comparing the circumference of a tennis ball to the sun.[446]

"IPv6 addresses are 128 bit numbers and are conventionally expressed using hexadecimal strings (for example, 2001:0db8:582:ae33: 29)."[447] VeriSign explains how IPv6 solves the scarcity problem of IP addresses:

> IPv6 solves this address scarcity problem by using 128–bit addressing, creating a massively larger number of addresses (the actual number is typically described as 2 to the 128th power—or "340 trillion trillion trillion"—widely believed to be more than the Internet will need for decades). While the technical foundations of IPv6 are well-established in the Internet standards development community, significant work remains to deploy and begin using IPv6 capabilities, continually refining interworking and transitional co-existence with IPv4, and providing a platform for continued growth and innovation on the Internet.[448]

IANA manages the DNSRoot Zone (assignments of ccTLDs and gTLDs), as well as the .int registry, and the .arpa zone. IANA also works with the Internet Engineering Task Force ("IETF") as Internet architects in formulating new protocols necessary for the functioning of the Internet. The IETF is a large international body of "network

---

[443] ICANN, What is the Domain Name System? (2008).

[444] Name Space, Inc. v. Network Solutions, Inc., 202 F.3d 573, 579 (2d Cir. 2000).

[445] IANA, Number Resources (2008).

[446] Veni Markovski, Remarks, The Geopolitics of Internet Governance, Center for Strategic & International Studies (May 23, 2013).

[447] Id.

[448] Verisign, What is IPv6 (2012), http://www.verisigninc.com/en_US/why-verisign/innovation-initiatives/ipv6/index.xhtml?cmp=SEMG09:04 (last visited June 25, 2013).

designers, vendors and researchers concerned with the evolution of the Internet architecture and the smooth operation of the Internet."[449]

§ 11.19 UNIFORM DOMAIN NAME RESOLUTION POLICY

The Internet Corporation for Assigned Names and Numbers (ICANN) oversees the administration of domain names and the primary arbitral process known as the Uniform Domain Name Dispute Resolution Policy (UDRP). In a UDRP proceeding, the trademark owner must prove that a registrant registered a domain name identical or confusingly similar to a trademark in bad faith.[450] Since the first UDRP arbitrated case in 1999, more than 35,000 arbitration cases have been decided with growth surging in lockstep with the expansion of the Internet. While the very first domain name was registered for commercial purposes in 1985, the exponential growth of the Internet has included every conceivable purpose and brought us to our current state where more than 200 million domain names are active.[451]

The World Intellectual Property Organization ("WIPO") developed the UDRP as an efficient alternative dispute resolution system to efficiently resolve disputes between trademark owners and domain name registrants. WIPO is an agency of the United Nations that administers many international treaties. WIPO, for example, entered into a cooperative agreement with the World Trade Organization ("WTO") in 1996. It is also the sponsoring agency behind the Madrid Agreement concerning the international registration of marks and its protocols. WIPO's UDRP policy and rules also plays a role in harmonizing IP law by providing uniform remedies for trademark owners against cybersquatters and other abusive domain name practices.

UDRP panels have the power to cancel or transfer domain name registration. ICANN can also order such relief upon receipt of an order from a court or arbitral tribunal.[452] UDRP panels have no authority to award monetary damages, statutory damages, or any other remedies typically awarded for Lanham Act infringement or dilution claims.[453] UDRP proceedings or, panels, tend to favor trademark owners, who are the most frequent complainants because they can forum-shop and find panelists, or "arbitrators more likely to rule in the complainant's favor."[454] UDRP formed a Registration Abuse Policies Working Group and uncovered abuses of the domain name registration policy such as:

> Occasional non-uniformity and non-predictability of decisions, and what if any responsibility or procedures the dispute resolution providers have to ensure general uniformity and quality. Inconsistency between decisions in cases that present similar situations, notably gripe sites that contain trademarks within domain names.

---

[449] IETF, Overview of the IETF (2008).

[450] ICANN Dispute Resolution Policy.

[451] Darryl C. Wilson, Battle Galactica: Recent Advances and Retreats in the Struggle for the Preservation of Trademark Rights on the Internet, 12 J. HIGH TECH. L. 1, 42 (2011).

[452] UDRP Policy, § 3.

[453] The Uniform Domain Name Dispute Resolution Policy ("UDRP"), the Rules for Uniform Domain Name Dispute Resolution Policy ("UDRP Rules"), and the Supplemental Rules for providers are posted at http://icann.org.

[454] UDRP.ORG, REGISTRATION ABUSE POLICIES WORKING GROUP: FINAL REPORT (Submitted 29, May 2010).

Complainants have the ability to re-file a complaint for the same name against the same respondent—in effect re-trying the same case in hopes of achieving a different outcome. The UDRP requires the complainant prove that the domain name ". . . has been registered and is being used in bad faith." However, many UDRP cases have been decided without the domain names having ever been used. Observers have noted that the usage requirement has sometimes been ignored in the UDRP "case law" that has developed over the years. This suggests study of the body of UDRP precedent and "case law" that has accumulated over the years, including whether it is consistent, and whether it is in keeping with the Policy itself. The UDRP is too expensive and too time-consuming for some brand owners, who wish to pursue large numbers of potentially infringing domain names. The UDRP procedures lack some safeguards that are generally available in conventional legal proceedings, such as appeals. Such are unavailable even when a panelist orders an action that is clearly inconsistent with his or her finding in a case.

As an unintended consequence of the UDRP policy, there are instances where third parties seek to abuse the UDRP. One example of such abuse is Reverse Domain Name Hijacking ("RDNH"). RDNH can occur when a trademark owner attempts to secure a domain name by making false cybersquatting claims against a domain name's rightful owner using a trademark registration as leverage. These registrants believe that the lack of meaningful penalties against abusive complainants provides inadequate incentive for a panel to render such a finding of RDNH, and provides no effective deterrent to bad faith complainant abuse of the UDRP. In part due to lack of uniform criteria for finding the existence of RDNH and other bad faith complaints, disagreement exists regarding their actual rate of occurrence. This issue of criteria could receive further consideration, and whether penalties for intentional bad faith complaints should be available.[455]

§ 11.20 UNIFORM DISPUTE RESOLUTION SERVICE PROVIDERS

Currently, UDRP panels are organized by four providers: (1) Asian Domain Name Dispute Resolution Centre, (2) National Arbitration Forum, (3) World Intellectual Property Organization, and (4). The Czech Arbitration Center. The websites and supplemental rules for these providers are provided in the chart below.

FOUR UDRP PROVIDERS

Asian Domain Name Dispute Resolution Centre
Dispute Proceedings/Decisions: https://www.adndrc.org/hk/case_decision.php
Supplemental Rules: https://www.adndrc.org/hk_supplemental_rules.html
National Arbitration Forum

---

[455] Id. at 27–30.

Dispute Proceedings/Decisions: http://domains.adrforum.com/decision.aspx
Supplemental Rules: http://domains.adrforum.com/users/icann/resources/UDRP%20Supple mental%20Rules%20eff%20March%201%202010.pdf [PDF, 53 KB]
WIPO (World Intellectual Property Organization)
Dispute Proceedings/Decisions: http://www.wipo.int/amc/en/domains/search/index.html
Supplemental Rules: http://www.wipo.int/amc/en/domains/rules/
The Czech Arbitration Court Arbitration Center for Internet Disputes
Dispute Proceedings/Decisions: http://www.adr.eu/adr/decisions/index.php
Supplemental Rules: http://www.adr.eu/arbitration_platform/udrp_supplemental_rules.php

ICANN-accredited registrars in all gTLDs (.aero, .asia, .biz, .cat, .com, .coop, .info, .jobs, .mobi, .museum, .name, .net, .org, .pro, .tel and .travel) have adopted the Uniform Domain–Name Dispute Resolution Policy (UDRP).[456] A holder of trademark rights may initiate dispute proceedings arising from alleged abusive registrations of domain names (for example, cybersquatting). The UDRP is a policy between a registrar and its customer and is included in registration agreements for all ICANN-accredited registrars. All domain name registrars must follow the UDRP policy. Under the UDRP, most types of trademark-based domain-name disputes are resolvable by agreement, court action, or arbitration before a registrar will cancel, suspend, or transfer a domain name. The UDRP arbitration panel decides cases arising out of abusive registrations of domain names such as cybersquatting.

Under the UDRP's expedited proceedings, the owner of trademark rights files a complaint with an approved dispute-resolution service provider. UDRP panels are limited in what remedies they may impose. Panels may order that a registrar cancel, transfer, or change a domain name registration and have no authority to award monetary damages or attorney's fees. The UDRP has been adopted by ICANN and is incorporated by reference in every domain name registration. Jurisdiction is not an issue because the domain name registrant has agreed in advance to submit to UDRP should a trademark dispute arise.

---

[456] "All registrars must follow the Uniform Domain–Name Dispute–Resolution Policy (often referred to as the "UDRP"). Under the policy, most types of trademark-based domain-name disputes must be resolved by agreement, court action, or arbitration before a registrar will cancel, suspend, or transfer a domain name. Disputes alleged to arise from abusive registrations of domain names (for example, cybersquatting) may be addressed by expedited administrative proceedings that the holder of trademark rights initiates by filing a complaint with an approved dispute-resolution service provider." ICANN, Uniform Dispute Resolution Policy, http://www.icann.org/en/help/dndr/udrp (last visited May 18, 2013).

The RES (Rapid Evaluation Service) is the first domain name dispute policy of its kind. The ICM Registry adopted it with an effective date of September 1, 2011. The RES applies to second-level domain names ending in .xxx. The RES is a new procedure to provide "a prompt remedy to address a limited class of situations in which there is objectively clear abuse of well-known, distinctive registered trademarks or service marks of significant commercial value, or of personal or professional names of individuals."[457] A RES complainant must show:

> (i) the domain name in the .XXX TLD is identical or confusingly similar to a registered, textual trademark or service mark of national effect that the complainant owns and uses in the relevant jurisdiction(s) where it is registered; and

> (ii) the respondent has no rights or legitimate interests in respect of the domain name in the .XXXTLD; and

> (iii) the domain name in the .XXX TLD has been registered and is being used in bad faith or, if unused, is not conceivably susceptible to use in good faith.[458]

Res complaints filed for impersonation require the following:

> (i) that the complainant is a natural person or the authorized representative or agent of a natural person; and (ii) that a registered domain name in the .XXX TLD substantially corresponds to the personal, professional or "stage name" of such person, or name by which such person is commonly known; and (iii) that the domain name in the .XXX TLD has been registered with an unlawful intent or for the apparent and demonstrated purpose of harassment or embarrassment in relation to the complainant absent any conceivable fair use defense or any defense that the registration of the domain name in the .XXX TLD is coincidental, or that the domain name was otherwise legitimately registered for purposes relating to a fictional character or personal, professional or other name in bona fide use by the registrant thereof.[459]

(A) Hypothetical Case: Lady Gidget

You are a new associate in a law firm specializing in intellectual property litigation. Let us assume that Lady Gidget, a prominent entertainer, seeks your advice on the following case. She is the owner of U.S. Trademark Registrations for the mark LADY GIDGET for entertainment services and related goods. Lady Gidget has used her name and mark professionally for entertainment services since 1999. Lady Gidget's music and other entertainment endeavors have often been controversial for featuring explicit sexual content. In addition, nude photographs of Lady Gidget have appeared in Penthouse magazine, and she has published a coffee-table book entitled Lady Gidget's Sexting book featuring sexually explicit photographs and text. Parisia Enterprises is in the business of developing websites.

On or about May 29, 2010, Parisia purchased the registration for the disputed domain name LadyGidget.com from Pro Domains for $20,000. On June 4, 2010, Parisia

---

[457] .XXX Rapid Evaluation Service Policy Version 1.0, http://domains.adrforum.com/users/icann/resources/RES-Policy.pdf (last visited May 18, 2013).

[458] Id.

[459] Id. at 3.

registered LaddyGidget as a trademark in Tunisia. On or about June 8, 2010, Parisia began operating an "adult entertainment portal website." The website featured sexually explicit photographs and text, and contained a notice stating: "LadyGidget.com is not affiliated or endorsed by the Catholic Church or Lady Gidget or her various enterprises." In our hypothetical, Lady Gidget would file a complaint against Parisia with a dispute-resolution service provider. Lady Gidget has her choice of the following UDRP providers: Asian Domain Name Resolution Centre, National Arbitration Forum, WIPO, and the Czech Arbitration Court Arbitration Center for Internet Disputes. Plaintiffs have the option of a choosing a one person or three person UDRP panel. In order to prevail, Lady Gidget will need to prove three things: (1) She has trademark rights in a mark that is similar to Parisia's Domain, (2) that Parisia does not have a legitimate use for the domain, and (3) that Parisia registered and used the domain in bad faith.

(B) Madonna v. Parisi

(1) Madonna's Argument

This extended explanation is based upon the facts in *Madonna Ciccone, p/k/a Madonna v. Dan Parisi and "Madonna.com,"*[460] a 2000 case decided by the WIPO Arbitration and Mediation Center. In accordance with the ICANN Uniform Domain Name Dispute Resolution Policy, dated October 24, 1999, and the ICANN Rules, Madonna filed the true-life action for UDRP. She filed her complaint with the WIPO Arbitration and Mediation Center on July 21, 2000 (e-mail) and on July 24, 2000 (hardcopy). In the Madonna domain case, the complainant charged that Parisi's domain name was identical to her registered and common law trademark MADONNA in which she owns rights. She further contended that Parisi had no legitimate interest or rights in the domain name. Finally, she charged Parisi with obtaining and using the disputed domain name with the intent to attract Internet users to a pornographic website for commercial gain based on confusion with her name and mark.

(2) Parisi's Defense

Parisi, who was represented by counsel, did not dispute that the domain name was identical or confusingly similar to Madonna's trademark. His argument was that Madonna could not demonstrate a lack of his legitimate interest in the domain name because he, (1) made demonstrable preparation to use the domain name for a bona fide business purpose, (2) holds a *bona fide* trademark in the word MADONNA, and (3) has attempted to make *bona fide* noncommercial use of the name by donating it to the Madonna Rehabilitation Hospital. He also contended that he did not register and use the domain name in bad faith. He claimed that his primary motivation was not to sell the dispute name. He also stated that he did not register the domain name with intent to prevent Madonna from using her mark as a domain name.

Further, he claimed he was "not engaged in a pattern of registering domain names to prevent others from doing so."[461] He pointed to a disclaimer on the website that disclaims any association with Madonna. He argues that this disclaimer precludes a

---

[460] Madonna Ciccone, p/k/a Madonna v. Dan Parisi, Case No. D2000–0847 ("WIPO") (Oct. 12, 2000), http://www.wipo.int/amc/en/domains/decisions/html/2000/d2000–0847.html.
[461] Id.

finding of commercial use based on confusion with her mark. He also claimed that Madonna could not claim trademark dilution based upon tarnishment because she already had associated herself with sexually explicit creative work.

(3) WIPO Panel's Decision

UDRP dispute-resolution providers are strictly circumscribed in what they must consider in deciding a domain name dispute. UDRP panels resemble the formalistic methods of mechanical jurisprudence critiqued by the legal realists of the 1930s and 1940s. The UDRP policy dictates what a plaintiff must prove to prevail. Paragraph 4(a) of the Policy directs that the complainant must prove each of the following that:

(i) [the domain name registered by the respondent] is identical or confusingly similar to a trademark or service mark in which the complainant has rights; and

(ii) [the respondent has] no legitimate interests in respect of the domain name; and

(iii) [the] domain name has been registered and used in bad faith.[462]

Paragraph 15 of the Rules states that the "Panel shall decide a complaint on the basis of the statements and documents submitted and in accordance with the Policy. . ."[463] Paragraph 10 of the Rules provides that the "Panel shall determine the admissibility, relevance, materiality and weight of the evidence."[464] In the *Madonna* case, the panels found that there were material issues of fact and could not decide the case on a summary-judgment like standard. Parisi acknowledged that the Madonna.com domain name was identical or confusingly similar to Madonna's trademark. The panel found 4(a)(i) of the UDRP policy to be satisfied by Parisi's admission. The panel found sufficient evidence from Madonna's attorney tending to show that Parisi lacks any rights or legitimate interest in the domain name, Madonna.com. The UDRP panel found Parisi's claim of rights or legitimate interests not persuasive. The panel acknowledged that Parisi used Madonna.com to offer goods or services for an adult entertainment website, which constituted prior use of the domain name. The panel found that Parisi had not explained why he chose Madonna as a domain name. The panel found that he selected and used the name to trade on Madonna's fame.

The UDRP panel found no other explanation for Parisi's choice of the Madonna mark. Parisi contended that he had rights in the domain name because he registered MADONNA as a trademark in Tunisia prior to notice of this dispute. The panel stated that a mere registration of a trademark does not equate with a legitimate interest under UDRP's Policy observing: "If an American-based Respondent could establish "rights" vis-à-vis an American Complainant through the expedient of securing a trademark registration in Tunisia, then the ICANN procedure would be rendered virtually useless."[465] The panel found Parisi's registration of the Madonna mark in Tunisia to be done solely to protect his interest in the domain name.

---

[462] ICANN, Uniform Domain Name Dispute Resolution Policy.

[463] Id. at para. 15.

[464] Id. at para. 10.

[465] Madonna Ciccone, p/k/a Madonna v. Dan Parisi, Case No. D2000–0847 ("WIPO") (Oct. 12, 2000).

The panel observed that Tunisia does not have an examination procedure in granting trademarks. The panel also did not place any weight on Parisi's alleged offer to transfer the domain name to the Madonna Hospital in Lincoln, Nebraska. They found that Madonna satisfied the requirements of Paragraph 4(a)(ii) of the UDRP Policy. The panel also found Madonna satisfied Paragraph 4(b)(iv) of the UDRP Policy proving Parisi's bad faith registration and use of the domain name. Proving the respondent's bad faith:

> (iv) by using the domain name, you have intentionally attempted to attract, for commercial gain, Internet users to your website or other on-line location, by creating a likelihood of confusion with the complainant's mark as to the source, sponsorship, affiliation, or endorsement of your website or location or of a product or service on your website or location.

In addition, the panel found evidence that Parisi adopted "madonna.com" for the specific purposes of trading off the name and reputation of Madonna. The panel further found that Parisi offered no alternative explanation for his adoption of the name.[466] The panel found that Parisi did not explain why "madonna.com" was worth $20,000 to him, or why that name was thought to be valuable as an attraction for a sexually explicit website. The WIPO panel concluded, "The only plausible explanation for Respondent's actions appears to be an intentional effort to trade upon the fame of Complainant's name and mark for commercial gain. That purpose is a violation of the Policy, as well as U.S. Trademark Law." The panel gave short shrift to Parisi's use of a disclaimer on his adult entertainment website and found it insufficient to avoid a finding of bad faith. The panel noted that Parisi's disclaimer did nothing to dispel initial interest confusion that is inevitable from Respondent's actions. Such confusion is a basis for finding a violation of Complainant's rights.[467] The WIPO panel had little difficulty in finding evidence of Parisi's bad faith registration and use of the disputed domain name, Madonna.com. The panel distinguished Madonna's case from an earlier ICANN decision involving the musician Gordon Sumner, a.k.a. Sting.[468]

The panel found evidence in the record supporting Madonna's claim that Parisi's "registration of the domain name prevents Complainant from reflecting her mark in the corresponding .com domain name and that Respondent has engaged in a pattern of such conduct." The panel found this factor of bad faith as well as the tarnishment claims to be inconclusive. The panel concluded that there was evidence showing Parisi's deliberate attempt to trade on Madonna's fame for commercial purposes, which satisfied the requirements of Paragraph 4(a)(iii) of the Policy. The panel concluded that Parisi lacked rights or a legitimate interest in the domain name Madonna.com and

---

[466] Id.

[467] See Brookfield Communications Inc. v. West Coast Entertainment Corp., 174 F.3d 1036 (9th Cir. 1999).

[468] See Gordon Sumner p/k/a/ Sting v. Michael Urvan, Case No. 2000–0596 ("WIPO") (July 24, 2000). "In the Sting decision there was evidence that the Respondent had made bona fide use of the name Sting prior to obtaining the domain name registration and there was no indication that he was seeking to trade on the good will of the well-known singer. Here, there is no similar evidence of prior use by Respondent and the evidence demonstrates a deliberate intent to trade on the good will of complainant. Where no plausible explanation has been provided for adopting a domain name that corresponds to the name of a famous entertainer, other Panels have found a violation of the Policy. See Julia Fiona Roberts v. Russell Boyd, Case No. D2000–0210 ("WIPO") May 29, 2000; Helen Folsade Adu p/k/a Sade v. Quantum Computer Services Inc., Case No. D2000–0794 ("WIPO") (September 26, 2000)."

found that Parisi registered and used the mark in bad faith. The panel ruled that the domain name should be transferred from Parisi to Madonna.

(C) The Nuts & Bolts of the Uniform Dispute Resolution Policy

(1) Domain Name Registration

The year 1999 marked the release of the World Intellectual Property Organization (WIPO)'s Uniform Dispute Resolution Policy ("UDRP"), a truly transnational quasi-legal institution. The UDRP "has been adopted by all ICANN-accredited registrars. It has also been adopted by certain managers of country-code top-level domains (e.g., .nu, .tv, .ws)."[469] The UDRP policy provides trademark owners with an expedited administrative procedure to resolve disputes over abusive practices such as "cybersquatting," "reverse cybersquatting", and other abusive domain name registration abuses. A federal court described the three principal actors key to understanding the domain name system:

> First, companies called "registries" operate a database (or "registry") for all domain names within the scope of their authority. Second, companies called "registrars" register domain names with registries on behalf of those who own the names. Registrars maintain an ownership record for each domain name they have registered with a registry. Action by a registrar is needed to transfer ownership of a domain name from one registrant to another. Third, individuals and companies called "registrants" own the domain names. Registrants interact with the registrars, who in turn interact with the registries.[470]

Individuals or legal entities register domain names with ICANN-accredited registrars. The first step in registering a domain name is to choose an accredited registry from the ICANN list of hundreds of approved and accredited domain name registries. The U.S., the United Kingdom, and Canada have the largest number of registries. Australia, France, Germany, India, and Korea also have many registries. Under the DNS, the registrant is the company or individual to whom the domain name actually belongs. A website operator must signify an administrative contact at the point of registration. The administrative contact is a person authorized by the registrant to make changes in the domain name; for example, the administrative contact may transfer, cancel, or assign rights to the domain name. Charges for domain name registration are competitive, although some charge as little as $10.

The UDRP is a policy between a registrar and its customer and is included in registration agreements for all ICANN-accredited registrars. Each ICANN-approved Registrar requires domain name registrants to agree to submit to the UDRP dispute resolution. The UDRP Policy is incorporated into all Registration Agreements and is followed by all registrars. Registrars are companies that register domain names and accredited by ICANN. During the accreditation process, registrars agree to adhere to the Uniform Domain Name Dispute Resolution Policy. ICANN posts a list of Approved Dispute–Resolution Service Providers. In addition, to the Policy there are Rules for Uniform Domain Name Dispute Resolution Policy. Dispute–Resolution service

---

[469] Internet Corporation for Assigned Names & Numbers, Uniform Domain Name Resolution Policy, http://www.icann.org/en/help/dndr/udrp/policy.

[470] Office Depot, Inc. v. Zuccarini, 2010 U.S. App. LEXIS 4052 (9th Cir., Feb. 26, 2010).

providers do the administrative work of processing complaints, vetting arbitrators, and overseeing cases.

Domain name registrants agree in advance to settle disputes with trademark owners under the UDRP policy. "The Uniform Domain–Name Dispute Resolution Policy ("UDRP") has been adopted by ICANN-accredited registrars in all gTLDs (.aero, .asia, .biz, .cat, .com, .coop, .info, .jobs, .mobi, .museum, .name, .net, .org, .pro, .tel and .travel)."[471] This means that domain name registrants agree to UDRP proceedings arising from alleged abusive registrations of domain names—for example, cybersquatting—may be initiated by a holder of trademark rights. Trademark owners like Madonna will generally prevail under the UDRP if they can prove a domain name is either identical or confusingly similar to their trademark or service mark.

Domain name registrants with no right or legitimate interest in a domain name may have their registration cancelled. Bad faith registrations may have their registration cancelled or transferred to the true owner. The emblem of bad faith is when a registrant obtains a domain name for the sole purpose of selling, renting, or transferring the registration to the true owner for a profit, which is the classic test for cybersquatting. Another test for bad faith is whether the registrant registers the domain name to prevent the true owners from using it.

(2) Liability of the Domain Name Registrars

A federal court in 1999 became the first to rule that a domain name registrar was not liable for direct infringement or liable for dilution because it had not made commercial use of the mark in its capacity as the sole and exclusive domain name registrar.[472] Domain name registrars have no liability for direct, contributory, or vicarious trademark infringement for accepting the registration of an Internet domain name that is confusingly similar to a plaintiff's service mark or trademark. Domain name registries may not face liability for intellectual property infringement, but may be liable for negligence, conversion, or other torts, where they do not act reasonably. In *Solid Host, NL v. Namecheap, Inc.*,[473] a California court held that a domain name registrar is immune from trademark infringement claims for failing to prevent the registration of domain names infringing a trademark owner's registered marks.

In *Kremen v. Cohen*,[474] the Ninth Circuit reversed a lower court ruling and held that Network Solutions converted a registrant's domain name when it transferred it to an ex-convict because of a forged letter. Network Solutions, the domain name registry, did not attempt to contact the plaintiff nor did it take any steps to determine the authenticity of the fake letter requesting the transfer of the domain name. This is the first case to hold that a domain name registrar could convert a domain name despite its intangible nature.

The *Baidu* court applied the contributory trademark infringement test articulated in its 2010 decision in *Tiffany (NJ) Inc. v. eBay, Inc.*[475] Tiffany, Inc. ("Tiffany") a renowned jewelry seller, instituted a trademark lawsuit against eBay, asserting

---

[471] ICANN, Domain Name Dispute Resolution Policy, http://www.icann.org/en/help/dndr#udrp.

[472] Lockheed Martin Corp. v. Network Solutions, Inc., 194 F.3d 980 (9th Cir. 1999).

[473] 652 F. Supp.2d 1091, 1104 (C.D. Cal. 2009).

[474] 337 F.3d 1024 (9th Cir. 2003).

[475] 600 F.3d 93 (2d Cir. 2010).

diverse causes of action including trademark infringement, trademark dilution and false advertising, arising from eBay's advertising and listing practices. Tiffany alleged that eBay had contributorially infringed on the Tiffany trademark by allowing third parties to list counterfeit Tiffany goods for sale on its website. The circuit court noted the significant efforts made by eBay to prevent sales of counterfeit Tiffany goods, pointing out that when "complaints gave eBay reason to know that certain sellers had been selling counterfeits, those sellers' listings were removed and repeat offenders were suspended from the eBay site."[476] Nevertheless, Tiffany argued that eBay was a contributory infringer because it "continued to supply its services to the sellers of counterfeit Tiffany goods while knowing or having reason to know that such sellers were infringing Tiffany's mark."[477] The court rejected the argument articulating a contributory infringement test: "For contributory trademark infringement liability to lie, a service provider must have more than a general knowledge or reason to know that its service is being used to sell counterfeit goods.

Some contemporary knowledge of which particular listings are infringing or will infringe in the future is necessary."[478] The *Tiffany* court found that eBay was not liable for trademark infringement for counterfeit merchandise sold on eBay's website because eBay promptly removed all listings that Tiffany challenged as counterfeit and spent millions of dollars taking affirmative steps toward the removal and monitoring of counterfeit Tiffany merchandise.[479] Additionally, the court in *Tiffany* found that eBay was not liable for contributory trademark infringement because eBay only had general knowledge of counterfeit sales through its website, holding that contemporary knowledge of particular listings would have been necessary to support contributory liability.[480]

In *Baidu Inc. v. Beijing Baidu Netcom Science & Technology Co.*,[481] a domain name registrar was liable under a theory of negligent enablement. Baidu filed a lawsuit for trademark infringement, breach of contract, and gross negligence against Register.com, a domain name registry, for negligent security in enabling a cyberattack on its website. "Baidu, Inc. provides Chinese and Japanese language Internet search services," that enables Internet users to locate online information such as, "Web pages, news, images, multimedia files, and blogs through the links provided on its websites."[482] On January 11, 2010, a hacker who gained "unauthorized access to Baidu's account at Register," hijacked Baidu's website.

The cybercriminal, masquerading as Baidu's agent, requested a change of its e-mail address in an online chat with Register.com's service representative. The Baidu service representative asked the intruder to provide security information and the intruder gave the incorrect answer. Nevertheless, the Register.com representative gave the intruder information that enabled him to gain unauthorized access to Baidu's account. The hacker rerouted Internet traffic intended for Baidu to a web page displaying an Iranian flag and a broken Star of David proclaiming: "This site has been

---

[476] Id. at 109.

[477] Id. at 106.

[478] Id. at 107.

[479] Id. at 103.

[480] Id. at 107–08

[481] 2010 WL 2900313 (S.D.N.Y., July 22, 2010).

[482] Bloomberg Business Week, Baidu Inc.-Spon ADR (BIDU:NASDAQ GS) (Jan. 14, 2010).

hacked by the Iranian Cyber Army." The hijacking of the Baidu website diverted Internet traffic for approximately five hours.

Baidu filed suit in a New York federal court bringing claims for breach of the terms of service agreement, gross negligence, and secondary trademark infringement. Register.com's terms of service agreement limits its liability for interrupted service and other errors or omissions. The federal court held that Baidu's complaint for negligence could go forward because Register.com's gross negligence was outside the sphere of the terms of service. The court ruled that Register.com was not entitled to immunity because it was acting as a registrar. The *Baidu* court found that Register.com was neither registering a domain name or maintaining it when it gave the intruder unauthorized information enabled it to control Baidu's website. Nevertheless, the court held that Register.com was not secondarily liable for trademark infringement.

Under the *Tiffany* test, a provider like Register.com must have knowledge of infringement in order to have secondary liability. The court found that Register.com did not induce infringement given that the intruder had tricked the registrar and that it had no knowledge of direct infringement. A court will typically find contributory infringement if it knew or had reason to know identified vendors were engaging in infringing activity. While this case stands for the proposition that a domain name's registrar does not preclude the possibility of its liability for falling for a social engineering scheme, Professor Eric Goldman contends that it is difficult to find trademark infringement by the intruder, let alone contributory infringement by Register.com on these facts.[483]

Trademark owners sometimes assert the right to a DMCA takedown, but the takedown procedures do not cover trademark infringement on a website. In a 2011 case, Free Press posted a video on YouTube critical of "covert media consolidation." Free Press was critical of how TV stations outsourced their local news. Newport Television sent Free Press, a cease-and-desist letter, alleging that they infringed their copyright by depicted "a brief image of affiliated news logos during a campaign video." YouTube removed the video but it was restored after a counter-notice.[484] The Electronic Frontier Foundation ("EFF") charged Warner Music Group with using Content Id or audio fingerprinting tools to "remove lots of videos that were clearly fair uses, sight unseen."

§ 11.21 TYPES OF UDRP CASES

Five paradigmatic categories of cases are typically decided by WIPO arbitral panels in deciding whether a given domain name is "confusingly similar" to a trademark: (1) cases where the domain name and trademark are wholly identical, or, in cases where the trademark owner has a registered domain name, the generic Top–Level Domain ("gTLD") might be different; (2) cases where a registrant's domain name incorporates the surname of a celebrity; (3) cases where a generic or descriptive word has been added to the trademark (such as "my", "direct", "e-"); (4) cases where anti-corporate websites append the word "sucks" at the end of trade names; and (5)

---

[483] Eric Goldman, Baidu Can Maintain Negligence Claims Against Register.com for Lax Security Practices, Which Allegedly Facilitated Cyber–Attack-Baidu v. Register.com, TECHNOLOGY & MARKETING LAW BLOG (Posted Aug. 3, 2010).

[484] Electronic Freedom Foundation, Hall of Shame (2012).

typosquatting cases where the domain name registrant relies on Internet users mistyping famous trademark names.

(A) Incorporating Another's Trademark

The classic illustration of incorporating another's trademark in a domain name was *Playboy Enterprises International, Inc. v. Good Samaritan Program.*[485] In this WIPO case, *Playboy* magazine founder and complainant in the case, Hugh M. Hefner, objected to Good Samaritan's registration of the domain name "hughhefner.com" with BulkRegister, a domain name registry. Playboy Enterprises, which holds the trademark "Hugh M. Hefner," met the three elements of UDRP Policy 4(a) because: (1) Good Samaritan's domain name was identical to Playboy's trademarks, (2) Good Samaritan had no rights or legitimate interests in the domain name, and (3) Good Samaritan's domain name was registered and was used in bad faith. The UDRP panel decided the case on the complaint given compelling evidence Good Samaritan was a cybersquatter. The panel found it appeared from Good Samaritan's own statements it sought substantial consideration in the form of celebrity endorsement or linkage to successful commercial websites in return for its services. The UDRP panel concluded, "Good Samaritan registered "hughhefner.com" for the purpose of transferring it to Playboy in return for valuable consideration in excess of its costs directly related to the domain name."[486]

(B) Common Law TM Rights of Celebrities

The USPTO maintains a database of trademarks. The complainant must prove common law rights if the trademark or service mark is not registered. A celebrity's name alone is not protected under the UDRP, or the common law. The *sine qua non* of common law rights is the personal name meaning a source of goods or services.[487] The purpose of trademark law is to protect consumers by providing accurate product identification.[488] Kevin Spacey, for example, has common law rights in his name because he uses his name as a trademark as a way of identifying his performances. A single cybersquatter took advantage of the goodwill in the names of well-known personalities by registering domain names that contained the names of those celebrities. UDRP panels ruled against the cybersquatter who registered Kevin Spacey's name, as well as domain names containing the name of other well-known celebrities including Larry King, Pierce Brosnan, Celine Dion, Pamela Anderson, Carmen Electra, Michael Crichton, and Julie Brown.[489] UDRP panels typically refuse to transfer or cancel domain name registrations of surnames unless the plaintiff proves he or she has common law rights or that their name has a secondary meaning in the marketplace.

Many celebrities and public figures have filed UDRP complaints to transfer or cancel domain names based upon common law rights, including "Madonna, Julia

---

[485] WIPO Case No. D2001–0241 (2001).

[486] Id.

[487] Nicole Kidman v. John Zuccarini, WIPO Case No. D2000–1415 (2001) (ruling nicholekidmannude.com was confusingly similar to Nicole Kidman's common law mark in her name).

[488] Qualitex Co. v. Jacobson Prods. Co., 514 U.S. 159 (1995).

[489] Jeffrey Archer v. Alberta Hotrods tda CELEBRITY 1000, WIPO Case No. D2006–0431 (2006); Kevin Spacey v. Alberta Hot Rods, NAF Case No. FA114437 (1992).

Roberts, Eminem, Pamela Anderson, JK Rowling, Michael Crichton and Ronaldo."[490] The cybersquatter registered a domain name with famous actress Julia Robert's name and launched the website http://www.juliaroberts.com, which featured a photograph of a woman named "Sari Locker." The cybersquatter then placed the domain name up for auction on eBay. Asserting common law trademark rights, the famous actress contended the domain name "juliaroberts.com" is identical and confusingly similar to the name "Julia Roberts."

The WIPO panel agreed the name "Julia Roberts" has sufficient secondary association with the famous actress, and that she had common law trademark rights under U.S. Trademark Law. The panel transferred the domain name to Ms. Roberts, finding bad faith registration on the part of the registrant because he had registered more than fifty other domain names, including movie stars' names within "madeleinestowe.com" and "alpacino.com" and a famous Russian gymnast's name, "Elena produnova.com." Many UDRP panels have recognized common law rights in a trademark sufficient to enable a celebrity to succeed in a UDRP proceeding. The famous person must show their surname serves as a source for goods or other common law trademark usage. "It has now become well-established jurisprudence that the Policy does not discriminate between those marks in the U.S. that are based on common law usage (unregistered marks) or grounded in federal registration."[491] In many of the famous surname cases, the respondent owns hundreds or even thousands of names. Searching a celebrity's name creates initial interest confusion when the individual is taken to the cybersquatter's website rather than to the celebrity's site. In *Jason Giambi and Jeremy Giambi v. Tom Meagher,*[492] a UDRP panel rejected a request to transfer giambi.com to the baseball playing brothers as the Giambi surname had not yet attained a secondary meaning in the marketplace.

(C) Appending Descriptive or Generic Words

Cybersquatting registrants with no rights to famous trademarks palm off on their goodwill by simply adding one or more generic or descriptive words to the celebrity or company's name. A UDRP panel is likely to find a domain name confusingly similar when it is used in the same industry as a well-known trademark, as with "statefarm-claimshelp.com."[493] However, in *Safeguard Operations LLC v. Safeguard Storage,*[494] the NAF panel ruled the respondent had a legitimate interest in the domain name "safeguard-storage.com" because of the preparations it undertook to operate a self-storage business under the name "Safeguard Storage" before receiving notice of the instant domain name dispute. As a result, the UDRP panel refused to direct the respondent to transfer the disputed domain to Complainant Safeguard Operations LLC, owner of several federally registered trademarks containing the word "Safeguard," which marks its uses in connection with its operation of self-storage facilities.

---

[490] IPFrontline, WIPO Continues Efforts to Curb Cybersquatting (2005). In re Julia Roberts v. Russell Boyd, WIPO Case No. D2000–0210 (May 29, 2000).

[491] Office of Personnel Management v. MS Technology, Inc., 2003 WL 23472306 (2003).

[492] NAF Case No. FA114745 (2002).

[493] State Farm Mutual Automobile Insurance Co. v. LaFaive, NAF Case No FA0008000095407 (2000).

[494] NAF Case No. FA0604000672431 (2006).

(D) Anti–Corporate Websites

Companies seeking to shut down gripe sites are far more likely to find success under the UDRP panels than in the U.S. federal courts, which often refuse to enjoin gripe sites because of the First Amendment. The fourth category of UDRP cases deal with complaint sites, a.k.a. "sucks" domain names (i.e., names with the complainant's trademark and a negative term such as "sucks"). In a UDRP proceeding, the domain name, AirFranceSucks.com, was transferred to Airline but "the airline's victory at arbitration was not without controversy: panelists disagreed about what the word "sucks" really means to Internet users."[495] The UDRP panel acknowledged that there is a split of UDRP panels on whether the word "sucks" added to a trademark is confusingly similar.[496] Most UDRP panels facing the issue have found such domain names are confusingly similar to the complainants' marks. Defendants will be more likely to be successful in mounting First Amendment or expression challenges to cybersquatting causes of action in U.S. federal courts.

A UDRP found that the domain name Radioshacksucks.com was not redirected to a "gripe" Website, but was pointing to a Website with various pay-per-click links mainly aimed at directing visitors to competing third party commercial websites. The Panel ruled in favor of Radio Shack and transferred the name.[497] In one case, the "sucks" site was found to be confusingly similar to the complainant's mark because a search engine would bring up the "sucks" site when the mark itself was entered as a search term.[498] UDRP panels distinguish between complaint websites expressing feelings about products and services, and those constructed for the sole purpose of extorting money from the trademark owners.

Rather than asking whether the domain name causes confusion as to source, the panel should compare the domain name and the mark for similarity.[499] In *Wal–Mart Stores, Inc. v. McLeod*, the panel acknowledged the importance of protecting protest sites as trademarks to identify the object of their criticism. However, the panel found the "Wall–Mart sucks" site was not being used for protest, but rather was offered for sale for far more than the costs of registration. The court then found the defendant's site to be in bad faith, constituting trademark piracy. Other panels have noted many Internet users do not speak English or do not know the word "sucks." Ultimately, these panels have held domain names adding the word "sucks" to a trademark of another company was confusingly similar to the mark incorporated. In *Koninklijke Philips Electronics N.V. v. In Seo Kim*,[500] a minority of panels have ruled "sucks" sites are not confusingly similar. In *Homer TLC, Inc. v. Green People*,[501] a panel refused to transfer "Home Depot Sucks.com" to Home Depot. The website "Home Depot Sucks.com" was operating as a "protest site" and the panel found no basis for transferring the protest site's domain

---

[495] Societé Air France v. Virtual Dates, Inc., Case No. D2005–0168 (May 24, 2005).

[496] "The Panel is fully aware that there is a split among the UDRP decisions regarding whether a "-sucks" domain name is confusingly similar to the trademark to which it is appended. The majority of the decisions have found confusing similarity. In a minority of decisions, and in some dissenting opinions, Panelists have deemed a "-sucks" addition to a well-known trademark to be an obvious indication that the domain name is not affiliated with that trademark owner." Id.

[497] TRS Quality, Inc. v. Gu Bei, Case No. D2009–1077 (Sept. 25, 2009).

[498] Cabela's Inc. v. Cupcake Patrol, NAF Case No. FA0006000095080 (2000).

[499] Wal–Mart Stores, Inc. v. MacLeod, WIPO Case No. D2000–0662 (2000).

[500] WIPO Case No. D2001–1195 (2001).

[501] NAF Case No. FA0508000550345 (2005).

name. The pejorative terms "sucks" added to the trademark did not create a likelihood of confusion. The Panel further found the protest site had a legitimate interest in this domain because respondent had used the domain as the home of a website critical of Home Depot for seven years; hence, it was not registered in bad faith.

(E) UDRP Typosquatting

The fifth paradigmatic UDRP case is the "typosquatting" case, i.e., where one letter in a well-known brand is replaced with another letter in order to direct traffic to the typosquatter's website. UDRP panels generally disfavor such strategies, especially when evidenced by bad faith. In *Toronto–Dominion Bank v. Karpachev*,[502] the WIPO panel concluded the domain name "tdwatergouse.com" was confusingly similar to the TD WATERHOUSE mark. John Zuccarini, a recidivist typosquatter, was the respondent in *Six Continents Hotels, Inc. v. John Zuccarini*.[503] The WIPO panel found that Zuccaarini acted in bad faith, and transferred the domain name "hoildayinn.com" to the owner of the Holiday Inn hotel chain. In *TIPI Holdings v. Zuccarini*,[504] the Delaware corporation charged Zuccarini with registering the domain names "autotader.com" and "autotradr.com." Zuccarini omitted in one case the letter "r" in "trader," and in another case, the letter "e" in "trader" in order to divert website users who mistakenly mistyped or misspelled "autotrader" in trying to reach the "autotrader.com" website.

The court observed Zuccarini had been on the respondent side in cases filed by Encyclopedia Britannica, Dow Jones & Company, Yahoo! Inc., Abercrombie & Fitch Stores, Inc., Saks & Company, America Online, United Feature Syndicate, Disney Enterprises, and scores of other well-known trademark owners. In *IMDb, Inc. v. Seventh Summit Ventures*,[505] the panel refused a request from the world's largest online movie database to transfer the domain name "indb.com" because in "the Internet context, consumers are aware that domain names for different Websites are quite often similar, because of the need for language economy, and that very small differences matter."[506] The panel even considered the scarcity of useful and recognizable domain names.

(F) Comparative Advantages: UDRP vs. Court Actions

U.S. trademark owners have a choice as to whether to file federal trademark lawsuits under the ACPA or pursue UDRP remedies. The advantage of the UDRP is speed and low expense. Trademark litigation may cost hundreds of thousands of dollars and take years to complete the appellate process. In contrast, UDRP proceedings may cost only a few thousand if conducted *pro se* and decisions are rendered in a few weeks.[507]

---

[502] WIPO Case No. D2000–1571 (2001).

[503] WIPO Case No. D2003–0161 (2003).

[504] WIPO Case No. D2001–0791 (2001).

[505] NAF Case No. 050300436735 (2005).

[506] Id.

[507] "The UDRP offers many benefits to trademark owners. UDRP proceedings are inexpensive, fast, efficient and readily accessible. There are no jurisdictional issues since domain registrants agree contractually to be bound by the UDRP, and issues are generally non-existent as proceedings are conducted via email. UDRP filing requirements are relatively straightforward, and there are no evidentiary

requirements, discovery, testimony, hearings or motion practice of the type common in federal court proceedings, thereby significantly decreasing costs compared to federal lawsuits. In addition, successful claimants in a UDRP action may have the disputed domain transferred to them, rather than simply cancelled or put on hold as under the previous dispute policy." CONNIE L. ELLERBACH, UDRP VERSUS ACPA: CHOOSING THE RIGHT TOOL TO CHALLENGE CYBERSQUATTING, Fenwick & West (2003).

However, UDRP panels have no power to award damages, attorneys' fees, or costs. Another advantage of the UDRP is that every domain name registrant is subject to its jurisdiction, whereas a plaintiff will need to demonstrate minimum contacts to hale a defendant into federal court. In many instances, a trademark owner is only seeking transfer or termination of the domain name, which can be accomplished more efficiently under the UDRP. The UDRP proceeding has resulted in tens of thousands of domain names transferred to their rightful trademark owner over the past decade. Professor Darryl C. Wilson of Stetson Law School writes about a single case, which resulted in the transfer of 1,542 domains to the Intercontinental Hotels Group.[508]

§ 11.22 ICANN'S NEW TLDS AND GTLDS

The Internet's DNS enables users to locate websites by domain names that are easy to remember rather than "all-numeric IP addresses (such as "192.0.34.65") assigned to each computer on the Internet. Each domain name is made up of a series of character strings (called "labels") separated by dots. The right-most label in a domain name is referred to as its "Top–Level domain" ("TLD")."[509] The Internet Corporation for Assigned Names and Numbers ("ICANN") initially created seven Top Level Domains (.com, .edu, .gov, .int, .mil, .net, and .org) in the 1980s. In early 2012, ICANN opened up the registration of new TLD's to include cities such as .nyc and .nola. ICANN also "launched the .XXX sponsored Top–Level domain (the ".XXX sTLD")."[510]

Wealthy elites can purchase their own global Top–Level domain (gTLD) for a dotFamilyName for $185,000 or greater.[511] ICANN expanded "the number of possible Internet domain name endings from the current 22—such as .com, .org and .net (which are separate of the country-specific domain endings such as .uk)—to allow domains . . . in any language or script."[512] ICANN will likely introduce over 400 new gTLDs beginning in 2012. It is likely that the new TLDs and gTLDS will produce a new wave of trademark-related lawsuits.

---

[508] "Inter-Continental Hotels v. Kirchhof was a noteworthy UDRP case because it resulted in a record number of domain names being transferred. The case was filed by two Complainants, which is not expressly addressed in procedural terms under the rules of the UDRP, although complaints may include multiple domain names. As the arbitrator noted, the rules do not expressly include nor preclude multiple complainants. he Complainants were both members of the same corporate structure, InterContinental Hotels Group, and thus were deemed to have a common interest. The 1,542 domain names in dispute were also very similar in structure and format. For example, they included "crown-plaza-with a city name.com," "holiday-express-city name.com," "holiday-inn-city name.com," "candle-wood-suites-city name.com," and so on. The domains also resolved to similar websites thus the cases by the Complainants were basically identical. The Respondent failed to submit any written response to the complaints making it fairly easy for the arbitrator to order a transfer of the disputed domains." Darryl C. Wilson, Battle Galactica: Recent Advances and Retreats in the Struggle for the Preservation of Trademark Rights on the Internet, 12 J. HIGH TECH. L. 1, 42 (2011) (citations omitted).

[509] ICANN, Top–Level Domains (gTLDs), http://archive. icann.org/en/tlds/.

[510] Launch of .XXX Top–Level Domain Requires Consideration and Planning for Brand Owners, JD SUPRA (Aug. 12, 2011).

[511] The Importance of Being Your Own gTLD, NEWSTEX WEB BLOG (Oct. 11, 2011).

[512] Charles Arthur, ICANN Announces Huge Expansion of Web Domain Names from 2012, GUARDIAN UNLIMITED (June 20, 2011).

§ 11.23 GLOBAL TRADEMARK ISSUES

(A) Global E–Business Concerns

Global e-businesses, such as Overstock.com or Amazon.com, have a number of difficult barriers to establish their trademarks worldwide. Amazon.com, for example, must ensure that another company is not using its mark in a foreign jurisdiction. Lawyers representing emergent e-businesses must make difficult decisions to determine where to seek protection. An Oracle Executive states that his company translates its products into ". . . twenty-three different languages, including Spanish and Latin American Spanish, Portugal Portuguese and Brazilian Portuguese."[513] Trademarks, by their very nature, are symbols and often language-based signifiers. Lawyers seeking trademark protection in foreign countries must consider translation challenges "particularly where multiple language may be spoken within a particular nation."[514] Trademark law has been harmonized but there are still differences in how a company obtains trademark rights ". . . for the same subject matter from one jurisdiction to another."[515] U.S. trademark protection tends to be broader than in Europe giving protection to "nontraditional marks such as colors, smells, sounds, and taste."[516] In June 2008, the Paris Court of Commerce ruled that eBay and eBay International AG were liable for failing to prevent the sale of counterfeit items on its websites awarding French companies:

> approximately EUR 38.6 million in damages and issued an injunction (enforceable by daily fines of up to EUR 100,000) prohibiting all sales of perfumes and cosmetics bearing the Dior, Guerlain, Givenchy and Kenzo brands over all worldwide eBay sites to the extent that they are accessible from France. We appealed this decision, and in September 2010, the Paris Court of Appeal reduced the damages award to EUR 5.7 million and modified the injunction.[517]

EBay appealed this decision to the French Supreme Court, and in May 2012, the court reduced the damages award and remanded the case to an appeals court. EBay prevailed in a United Kingdom case based upon a similar claim:

> In May 2009, the U.K. High Court of Justice ruled in the case filed by L'Oreal SA, Lancome Parfums et Beaute & Cie, Laboratoire Garnier & Cie and L'Oreal (UK) Ltd against eBay International AG, other eBay companies, and several eBay sellers (No. HC07CO1978) that eBay was not jointly liable with the seller co-defendants as a joint tortfeasor, and indicated that it would certify to the European Court of Justice (ECJ) questions of liability for the use of L'Oreal trademarks, hosting liability, and the scope of a possible injunction against intermediaries. In July 2011, the ECJ ruled on the questions certified by the U.K. High Court of Justice. It held that (a) brand names could be used by marketplaces as keywords for paid search advertising without violating a trademark owner's rights if it were clear to consumers that the goods reached via the key word link

---

[513] Oracle Corp. Secs. Litig., 2009 U.S. Dist. LEXIS 50995 *14 (N.D. Ca., June 16, 2009).

[514] JOHN CROSS, AMY LANDERS, MICHAEL MIRELES & PETER YU, GLOBAL ISSUES IN INTELLECTUAL PROPERTY LAW 162 (2010).

[515] Id.

[516] Id.

[517] EBay, SEC 10Q Filing (July 19, 2013).

were not being offered by the trademark owner or its designees but instead by third parties, (b) that marketplaces could invoke the limitation from liability provided by Article 14 of the ecommerce directive if they did not take such an active role with respect to the listings in question that the limitation would not be available, but that even where the limitation was available, the marketplace could be liable if it had awareness (through notice or its own investigation) of the illegality of the listings, (c) that a marketplace would be liable in a specific jurisdiction only if the offers on the site at issue were targeting that jurisdiction, a question of fact, (d) that injunctions may be issued to a marketplace in connection with infringing third party content, but that such injunctions must be proportionate and not block legitimate trade and (e) that trademark rights can only be evoked by a rights owner as a result of a seller's commercial activity as opposed to private activity. The matter will now return to the U.K. High Court of Justice for further action in light of the ECJ opinion.[518]

Trademark disputes arising out of the Internet activities are creating a patchwork of conflicting views of secondary infringement.

(B) European Community Trademarks

The Community Trademark ("CTM") is a trademark valid across the countries in the European Union registered in OHIM in Alicante, Spain, in accordance with CTM Regulations.[519] The EU trademark regulation has been amended and the European Commission has adopted implementing rules for the CTMR, the fees payable to OHIM ("Office of Harmonization for the Internal Market"), and the rules of procedure of the Boards of Appeal of OHIM. A CTM is a trademark valid across the European Union ("EU") assuming it is registered with OHIM in accordance with the provisions of the CTM Regulations. The advantage of the CMT is that it accords protection for the EU as a whole. A CTM is valid for 10 years and can be renewed indefinitely for periods of ten years. The CTM gives the owner "the exclusive right to use the trademark and to prevent third parties to use, without consent, the same or a similar mark for identical or similar goods and/or services as those protected by the CTM."[520] The EU's CTM system provides for one single registration procedure for European-wide protection. The principal attributes of the CTM system are:

- a single application
- a single language of procedure
- a single administrative centre and
- a single file to be managed.[521]

The OHIM depicts the stages in obtaining and defending the CMT, which share much common ground with U.S. trademark procedures.

---

[518] Id.

[519] Council Regulation (EC) No 40/94 of 20 December 1993 on the Community trademark.

[520] OHIM, What is a Community trademark (CTM)? http://oami.europa.eu/ows/rw/pages/CTM/communityTradeMark/communityTradeMark.en.do.

[521] Id.

<Chart: Stage of a CMT Trademark>[522]

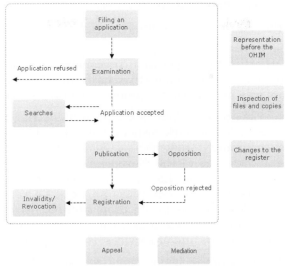

Many of the stages in the life a CMT trademark have functional equivalents in U.S. trademark procedures. Trademark examiners determine whether a trademark is protectable under the procedures of the U.S. Trademark Office. Trademark owners or those challenging validity will seek recourse in both the Trademark Trial and Appeals Board, and the federal courts. For the CMT, the Decisions of the European Court of Justice, the European General Court, and the Boards of Appeal of OHIM, will determine the contours of CMT trademark protection; including challenges to validity, and whether a trademark should be revoked.

The CTM grants its owner an exclusive right in the 28 member states of the European Union in an efficient manner for a reasonable cost when compared to filing for protection in each individual European country. "After any future enlargement of the European Union, any CTM registered or applied for will be automatically extended to the new member states without formality or fee."[523] As under U.S. law, CTM owners must maintain their marks: "Use it or lose it."[524] In the chart above, this is represented by the box for invalidity/revocation. As in the United States, there is a prohibition against seeking protection for functionality for European trademarks. The OHIM explains the difference between trademarks, and industrial property rights called "patents" in the United States:

All industrial property rights are intended to protect the creativity of businesses and individuals. However, they do not cover the same aspects.

---

[522] OHIM, The Registration Process, http://oami.europa.eu/ows/rw/pages/CTM/regProcess/regProcess. en.do.

[523] Id.

[524] "TMs shall be put to genuine use in the Community within a period of five years following registration (Article 15 CTMR). Genuine use may be found when the mark has been used in only one part of the Community, such as in a single Member State or in a part thereof. Any person (legal or natural) can protect their registered CTM against revocation on the grounds of lack of use—provided it is put to genuine use in the Community after the initial five-year post-registration grace period or if there are proper reasons for such non-use." Id. "Thus, the best defence against revocation action is pre-emptive: non-generic, non-misleading, genuine and continuous use of the Community trademark at all times. Use it or lose it!" Id.

A trademark identifies the origin of goods and services of one undertaking so as to differentiate them from those of its competitors.

A design covers the appearance of a product. A design cannot protect the function of a product.

A patent covers the function, operation or construction of an invention. To be patentable, a function must be innovative, have an industrial application and be described in such a way as to permit reproduction of the process.[525]

In Europe, trademarks are classified as a type of industrial property, protected by intellectual property rights. Trademark owners can get Eurozone protection for their marks by receiving a community trademark ("CTM"). A CTM is a trademark valid across the twenty-eight countries of the European Union for an initial term of ten years, which is harmonized with the Lanham Act term for U.S. trademarks. Like a U.S. trademark, a CTM is valid for ten years and can be renewed indefinitely for periods of ten years. "A CTM confers on its proprietor an exclusive right to use the trademark and to prevent third parties to use, without consent, the same or a similar mark for identical or similar goods and/or services as those protected by the CTM."[526]

"A designation of the European Union (country code EM) covers all the countries that are Member States of the European Union, namely Austria (AT), Benelux (consisting of Belgium, Luxembourg and the Netherlands) (BX), Bulgaria (BG), Cyprus (CY), Czech Republic (CZ), Germany (DE), Denmark (DK), Estonia (EE), Spain (ES), Finland (FI), France (FR), United Kingdom (GB), Greece (GR), Hungary (HU), Ireland (IE), Italy (IT), Lithuania (LT), Latvia (LV), Malta (MT), Poland (PL), Portugal (PT), Romania (RO), Sweden (SE), Slovenia (SI), Slovakia (SK)."[527]

(C) Madrid Protocol for International Registration of Marks

"The Madrid system for the international registration of marks (the Madrid system) established in 1891 functions under the Madrid Agreement (1891), and the Madrid Protocol (1989). It is administered by the International Bureau of WIPO."[528] International registration is governed by the Madrid Protocol system and allows one-stop registration in multiple countries. Under the Madrid Agreement, an international application must be based on a mark that has already been registered ("basic registration") in the Office of origin. "An international mark so registered is equivalent to an application or a registration of the same mark effected directly in each of the countries designated by the applicant. If the trademark office of a designated country does not refuse protection within a specified period, the protection of the mark is the same as if it had been registered by that Office."[529] The OHIM describes the Madrid Protocol as enabling international registration of trademarks with a system administered by the WIPO.

CTM application or a registered CTM can be used as the basis to extend protection internationally via an International Registration (IR). This is governed by the Madrid

---

[525] OHIM, What is a Trademark? http://oami.europa.eu/ows/rw/pages/CTM/trademark.en.do.

[526] Office for the Harmonization in the Internal Market (Trademark and Designs) ("OHIM") What is a Community Trademark (CMT)? (2012).

[527] WIPO, International Application and Registration (2012).

[528] WIPO, Madrid System for International System of Marks (2012).

[529] Id.

Protocol system, which offers CTM owners/applicants the possibility to have their trademarks [sic] protected in several countries besides the EU member states by simply filing one application directly with their own national or regional trademark office. The Madrid Protocol is an essential instrument in trademark protection around the world. It is an international registration system administered by the World Intellectual Property Organization ("WIPO") in Geneva. It has been in operation since April 1996 and has been ratified by many countries around the world, including most European countries individually, as well as the US, Japan, Australia, China, Russia, and, in October 2004, by the European Community.

> If the basic mark chosen is a CTM application or registration, the international application must be filed directly at OHIM. In order to use OHIM as the "Office of Origin," the CTM owner/applicant must be a national of a country of the European Union. Alternatively, the CTM owner/applicant must have a real and effective industrial or commercial establishment or domicile within the European Union, i.e. not all CTM owners/applicants can file IR applications based on a CTM.[530]

The Madrid Protocol, ratified by the European Community in 2004, "offers CTM owners/applicants the possibility to have their trademarks protected in several countries besides the EU member states by simply filing one application directly with their own national or regional trademark office."[531] The Madrid System can only be used by a person from a member of the Madrid Union, which includes the United States and many of its major trading partners. "If your mark is not put to use, its registration is liable to be cancelled on the application of a third party that can show that it has not been used,"—i.e. the U.S. law idea of "Use it, or lose it." "In most countries, a mark will not be so cancelled unless it can be established that there has been at least three years of non-use. In this context, it would be advisable to check the legal position in the country or countries for which your mark has been registered."[532] A registered Community Trademark is valid for ten years from the date of filing of the application. It can be renewed indefinitely for further periods of ten years.

(D) Internet–Related Foreign Trademark Litigation

In *Voyageurs du Monde, Terres d'Aventure v. Google*, the Tribunal De Grande Instance (T.G.I.) held that Google's Adwords program violated the trademarks of two French travel agencies.[533] "In 2004, Voyageurs du Monde and Terres d'Aventure learned that Google had suggested the trademarks 'Voyageurs du Monde', 'Terres d'Aventure,' and 'Terdav' to competitors as keywords to be purchased on its AdWords service. Consequently, when the terms 'voyageurs du monde' and 'terres d'Aventure' were entered into Google's search engine, the user would see ads of, and links to, the websites of plaintiffs' direct competitors on the Google search results page.[534] The T.G.I. held that Google was liable for deceptive and misleading advertising and "the French duty of loyalty and good faith under Article 1382 of the Civil Code by failing to monitor whether the competitors had obtained authorization from Voyageurs du

---

[530] OHIM, Extending a CMT Mark Outside the EU (2012).

[531] Id.

[532] WIPO, International Protection and Registration (2012).

[533] Voyageurs du Monde, Terres d'Aventure v. Google, Tribunal De Grande Instance [T.G.I.] Paris, Jan. 7, 2009, cited in Trademark Law Developments, 25 BERKELEY TECH. L.J. 493, 496 (2010).

[534] Id. at 496–497.

Monde or Terres d'Aventure for use of the companies' trademarks as keywords."[535] "The court awarded 200,000 to Voyageurs du Monde and 150,000 to Terres d'Aventure in damages and interest. Google filed an appeal to the Court of Appeals of Paris on February 2, 2009."

---

[535] Id.

Chapter 12

TRADE SECRETS IN CYBERSPACE

The power of computer technology has increased exponentially, resulting in more powerful means for the theft and transfer of proprietary information. The rapid growth of the Internet is a reflection of this boom. In fact, the corollary is also true: the Internet is now a tool for the destruction of trade secret assets.[1] This chapter examines Internet-related trade secret issues. Trade secret misappropriation, whether direct or contributory, is essentially a tort and implies the invasion of some legally protected right of the owner. Trade secrets protection and the remedy of misappropriation give the trade secret owner a competitive advantage. The common law of trade secrets was first conceptualized as a business tort in the 19th century. Today, trade secrets are classified as a branch of IP rooted in tort law and the law of contracts. The emblem of a trade secret is that "some element must be unknown to the public."[2] For Internet companies, confidential information such as customer lists, business methods, and source code are extremely valuable. Such information is especially vulnerable because the interconnected system of computers makes it easy for hackers, ex-employees, and corporate spies to steal information without leaving physical evidence.

Trade secret protection is particularly hazardous in a networked world where intangible assets may be lost at the click of a mouse.[3] Calling something a trade secret is not enough in a world of mobile technology, mobile phones, and instant messaging. "Employees must protect trade secrets—on social media as much as elsewhere. With respect to social media, companies find a greater risk that through connections with company-internal and external persons and informal communications modes, employees tend to disclose information more lightly."[4] "Social media poses new risks for trade secrets that may be revealed to the public through inadvertent status updates."[5] Theft of trade secrets is now occurring on portable devices, such as mobile phones. "Hackers' preferred modus operandi, security experts say, is to break into employees' portable devices and leapfrog into employers' networks—stealing secrets while leaving nary a trace."[6] Estimates of stolen trade secrets and other confidential information is $300 billion to $1 trillion.[7] Flash drives, mobile phones, and e-mail are the chief

---

[1] Mark Halligan, Protection of U.S. Trade Secret Assets: Amendments to the Economic Espionage Act of 1996, 7 J. MARSHALL REV. INTELL. PROP. L. 656, 657 (2008).

[2] See Kewanee Oil Co. v. Bicron Corp., 416 U.S. 470, 476 (1974).

[3] See generally, Andrew Beckerman–Rodau, Trade Secrets—The New Risks to Trade Secrets Posed by Computerization, 28 RUTGERS COMPUTER & TECH. L.J. 227, 233 n.34 (2002) (describing the difficulties of protecting trade secrets in the networked world of computers).

[4] Lothar Determann, Social Media @ Work—A Checklist for Global Businesses, 17 ELEC. COM. & L. REP. (BNA) 556 (March 21, 2012).

[5] Id.

[6] Nicole Perlroth, Traveling Light in Time of Digital Thievery, N.Y. TIMES (Feb. 12, 2012).

[7] Intellectual Property: Can You Keep a Secret, THE ECONOMIST (March 16, 2013) at 67.

instrumentalities for stealing digital asset.[8] Companies are turning away from patent protection to trade secrets to protect their company's assets.[9]

Misappropriation means "the disclosure or use of a trade secret of another without express or implied consent by a person who, at the time of disclosure, knew or should have known that knowledge of the trade secret was acquired under circumstances giving rise to a duty to maintain its secrecy."[10] The trade secret owner must prove that the defendant "under circumstances giving rise to a duty" to maintain confidentiality.[11] "Thus, the hallmark of a trade secret is not its novelty but its secrecy."[12] Proprietary software licensors continue to use trade secrets to protect the secrecy of their source code.

Consequently, during the development of an Internet-related business, trade secret protection is critically important to prevent competitors and third parties from misappropriating the fruits of their investment. Trade secret law is difficult to export to the Internet because the law has traditionally been state law. Courts conceptualized trade secret misappropriation as a business tort in the nineteenth century and through much of the twentieth century.[13] Trade secret law was traditionally conceptualized as a common law tort. Today trade secrets are classified as the fourth branch of intellectual property ("IP") law, whether based upon on a contract or torts theory and covered by state rather than federal law. A vast majority of U.S. states have adopted some version of the Uniform Trade Secrets Act. Global Internet law has been slow to adopt cross-border remedies for the misappropriation of trade secrets. Internet businesses must be concerned with the international protection of intellectual property.

§ 12.1 WHAT IS A TRADE SECRET?

Does information derive value from not being generally known? If so, it is classifiable as a trade secret? The three most important factors in determining whether something is a trade secret are: 1) the extent to which the information is known outside of the business; 2) extent to which employees know it and those involved in the business; and the 3) extent of measures taken to guard the secrecy of the information. Today, the formula for Coca Cola is perhaps the best-known example of a trade secret, having been a closely guarded secret since the company's founding in 1892.[14] Once a secret is revealed, whether generally or on the Internet, it cannot be retrieved. Just as you cannot un-ring a bill or squeeze the toothpaste back into the tube, a trade secret cannot be reclaimed. Unlike patents, copyrights, or trademarks, state tort law is the only protection for trade secrets. Trade secret misappropriation evolved as a business tort action at common law. Trade secrets are neither patentable nor subject to copyright

---

[8] Id.

[9] Id.

[10] Cal. Civ. Code § 3426.1(b).

[11] Avtec Systems, Inc. v. Peiffer, 21 F.3d 568, 575 (4th Cir. 1994).

[12] Id.

[13] Robert G. Bone, A New Look at Trade Secret Law: Doctrine in Search of Justification, 86 CALIF. L. REV. 241, 245 (1998) (contending that Roman law prefiguring trade secret protection is not comparable to modern trade secret law).

[14] Coca-Cola Bottling Co. v. Coca-Cola Co., 269 F. 796 (3d Cir. 1920). See generally, Rockwell Graphic Sys., Inc. v. DEV Indus., Inc., 925 F.2d 174, 180 (7th Cir. 1991) (noting, "trade secret protection is an important part of intellectual property, a form of property that is of growing importance to the competitiveness of American industry" and that "[t]he future of the nation depends in no small part on the efficiency of industry, and the efficiency of industry depends in no small part on the protection of intellectual property.").

because these forms of intellectual property mandate disclosure. Disclosure is the death knell for a trade secret, destroying its emblematic feature of secrecy.

§ 12.2　TRADE SECRETS GOVERNED BY STATE LAW

(A)　Restatement (First) of Torts, §§757, 758 (1939).

Trade secrets were originally a tort of misappropriation governed by the Restatement (First) of Torts, § 757. Trade secret misappropriation is the only branch of intellectual property law largely governed by state law. The common law of trade secrets evolved as a tort action like trademark infringement prior to the federal Lanham Act. In Section 757 of the First Restatement of Torts (1939), the American Law Institute acknowledged that no exact definition of trade secrets was possible. One of the basic attributes of property is the right of possession. The states adopted the Restatement (First) of Torts, §§757, 758 (1939) in misappropriation cases.[15] In particular, § 757, comment b, listed six factors to be considered in determining whether information constitutes a trade secret: (1) The extent to which the information is known outside the claimant's business; (2) The extent to which it is known by employees and others involved in the business; (3) The extent of measures taken by the claimant to guard the secrecy of the information; (4) The value of the information to the business and its competitors; (5) The amount of effort or money expended by the business in developing the information; and (6) The ease or difficulty with which the information could be properly acquired or duplicated by others.[16]

(B)　Uniform Trade Secrets Act

The Uniform Trade Secrets Act ("UTSA") is a Model Statute drafted by the National Conference of Commissioners on Uniform State Law ("NCCUSL") to update and harmonize the law concerning the misappropriation of trade secrets. UTSA displaced the First Restatement of Torts' approach to trade secrets in the 1980s and 1990s.

At common law, trade secret misappropriation was classified as a business tort. Today, nearly every state has enacted The Uniform Trade Secrets Act ("UTSA"). UTSA is a model statute approved by the National Conference of Commissioners of Uniform State Law ("NUCCUSL"), now the Uniform Law Commission ("ULC"). NCCUSL approved UTSA and its 1985 Amendments in August of 1985.[17] NCCUSL approved the UTSA "to protect against the wrongful disclosure or wrongful appropriation of trade secrets, know-how or other information maintained in confidence by another."[18] Numerous state legislatures enacted UTSA through out the country as all but Massachusetts, New York, and North Carolina have enacted it by July 1, 2013. NCCUSL provides the following summary of UTSA:

---

[15]　Id.

[16]　RESTATEMENT (FIRST) TORTS, §757, CMT. (B).

[17]　National Conference of Commissioners of Uniform State Law (Approved Aug. 9, 1985 for introduction into the states), http://www.uniformlaws.org/shared/docs/trade%20secrets/utsa_final_85.pdf (last visited July 25, 2013).

[18]　NCCUSL, History of the Uniform Trade Secrets Act, http://www.uniformlaws.org/shared/docs/trade%20secrets/utsa_final_85.pdf (last visited July 26, 2013).

At common law, misappropriation of a trade secret could give rise to a remedy. However, the existing law contains many uncertainties and ambiguities. The Uniform Trade Secrets Act is an effort to codify the common law with proper clarification of rights and remedies. A trade secret is, basically, information of commercial value. The form of that information can be exceedingly variable. Key to the need for protection is the fact that others do not generally know the information and it is not readily ascertainable by proper means. A trade secret, generally, would be exclusive knowledge, of economic value, which has been generated by the labors of a specific person or persons who have an interest in protecting its value. Such information may be patentable or subject to copyright. This makes no difference. Patents and copyrights provide only a limited monopoly. It may be in the best interests of those who have patentable ideas or information subject to copyright to keep their secrets, rather than to take the limited monopoly. The essence of trade secrets protection is that a person with a trade secret may have a remedy in equity and law, if the secret has been misappropriated.[19]

The sphere of trade secret protection appears broader with UTSA than under § 757 of the Restatement (First). The few states that have yet to adopt UTSA follow either the Restatement (First) or the Restatement of the Law (Third) Unfair Competition.

(C) UTSA's Definition of Trade Secrets

UTSA defines trade secrets broadly as information that has either potential or actual economic value.[20] SPSS, Inc., for example, classifies its analytical algorithms as trade secrets and protects them with security measures. A company like SPSS will not find it onerous to prove that its analytical algorithms have potential or actual value. UTSA further requires that the person or entity claiming protection to prove it:

> derives independent economic value, actual or potential, from not being generally known to, and not being readily ascertainable by proper means by, other persons who can obtain economic value from its disclosure or use, and 2. Is the subject of efforts that are reasonable under the circumstances to maintain its secrecy.[21]

In order to qualify as a trade secret, the information must be secret, and must not be of public knowledge or of a general knowledge in the appropriate trade or business. Secrecy is the principal issue in most trade secret litigation. Coca Cola company officials have kept the recipe for Coca Cola syrup locked in a vault for more than a century. A comment to UTSA § 1 notes that the definition of a trade secret in UTSA includes information that has not yet been used, but has potential value:

---

[19] Testimony of Stephen Chow, Massachusetts H.R. 23 (July 2013).

[20] UTSA defines a trade secret to mean" information, including [but not limited to] [technical or non-technical data]a formula, pattern, compilation, program device, method, technique, [drawing]or process,[financial data, or list of actual or potential customers] that: (i) [is sufficiently secret to]derive[s] [independent–strike out] economic value, actual or potential, from not being generally known to, [and not being readily ascertainable by proper means–strike out], other persons who can obtain economic value from its disclosure or use, and (ii) is the subject of efforts that are reasonable under the circumstances to maintain its secrecy." UTSA § 1(4).

[21] Id.

The broader definition in the proposed Act extends protection to a plaintiff who has not yet had an opportunity or acquired the means to put a trade secret to use. The definition includes information that has commercial value from a negative viewpoint, for example the results of lengthy and expensive research, which proves that a certain process will not work, could be of great value to a competitor.[22]

(D) UTSA Misappropriation Action

Today, most trade secret misappropriation is governed by the UTSA, which is a state statute. Misappropriation means acquiring a trade secret by "improper means" or from someone who has acquired it through "improper means."[23] Improper means encompassing theft, bribery, misrepresentation, espionage, or inducing a breach of a nondisclosure or confidentiality agreement. UTSA § 1(2) defines misappropriation as an:

acquisition of a trade secret of another by a person who knows or has reason to know that the trade secret was acquired by improper means; or (ii) disclosure or use of a trade secret of another without express or implied consent by a person who (A) used improper means to acquire knowledge of the trade secret; or (B) at the time of disclosure or use knew or had reason to know that his knowledge of the trade secret was (I) derived from or through a person who has utilized improper means to acquire it; (II) acquired under circumstances giving rise to a duty to maintain its secrecy or limit its use; or (III) derived from or through a person who owed a duty to the person seeking relief to maintain its secrecy or limit its use; or (C) before a material change of his position, knew or had reason to know that it was a trade secret and that knowledge of it had been acquired by accident or mistake.[24]

To state a claim for misappropriation of trade secrets under the Uniform Trade Secrets Act, a plaintiff must allege that: (1) the plaintiff owned a trade secret; (2) the defendant misappropriated the trade secret; and (3) the defendant's actions damaged the plaintiff.[25] The essence of misappropriation is that the defendant acquired the trade secret using improper means. The NCCUSL drafters describe what is meant by "proper means" in a Reporter's comment:

(1). Discovery by independent invention;

(2). Discovery by "reverse engineering", that is, by starting with the known product and working backward to find the method by which it was developed. The acquisition of the known product must, of course, also be by a fair and honest means, such as purchase of the item on the open market for reverse engineering to be lawful;

(3). Discovery under a license from the owner of the trade secret;

(4). Observation of the item in public use or on public display;

(5). Obtaining the trade secret from published literature.[26]

---

[22] UTSA § 1, cmt.

[23] UTSA § 1.

[24] UTSA § 1(2).

[25] .Nexsales Corp. v. Salebuild, Inc, 11–CV–3195, 2012 U.S. Dist. LEXIS 7890, 2012 WL 216260 at *2 (N.D. Cal. Jan. 24, 2012).

[26] UTSA § 1, cmt.

Software licensors frequently include anti-reverse engineering clauses in their software license agreements even though discovery by "reverse engineering" does not constitute an improper method to acquire a trade secret.

(E) Reasonable Means to Protect Secrets

Trade secret misappropriation actions are predicated upon the owner's having taken reasonable precautions to prevent the public disclosure of information. Accidental or other public disclosure of a trade secret destroys its status as a trade secret. Roger Milgrim, the leading authority on trade secrets, describes computer software as the "single most important "product" eligible for trade secret protection."[27] Trade secrets in software derive their economic values from their secrecy. For example, trade secret protection lasts indefinitely so long as the software vendor is able to keep its source code secret. "A trade secret once lost, is, of course, lost forever."[28] A company needs to prove that its efforts in protecting its trade secrets are reasonable under the circumstances. At a minimum, an Internet company must label source code, plans, and other documents with a legend that these materials are confidential and proprietary.

(1) Nondisclosure Agreements

The legend marking these materials is evidence that the company employs reasonable measures to keep trade secrets confidential. Licensors will typically enter into nondisclosure agreements ("NDAs") with their employees, consultants, and joint ventures as a reasonable means of protecting software code.[29] An NDA is a contractual arrangement that requires a recipient of confidential information to keep that information secret. A NDA determines the scope of the confidential relationship between the parties and supplants any implied covenants or duties of confidence.[30]

A typical NDA states that, to trigger either party's obligations, the disclosed information must be: "(1) marked as confidential at the time of disclosure; or (2) unmarked, but treated as confidential at the time of disclosure, and later designated confidential in a written memorandum summarizing and identifying the confidential information."[31] It is common for NDA's to calibrate their sphere of application as parties seek to know the extent of their obligation. An NDA, for example, may "explicitly excludes from its scope any information that: (1) the recipient possessed prior to disclosure; (2) was a matter of public knowledge; (3) was received from a third party without a duty of confidentiality attached; (4) was independently developed by the recipient; (5) was disclosed under operation of law; or (6) was disclosed by the recipient with the discloser's prior written approval."[32] Another recommended practice

---

[27] ROGER MILGRIM, MILGRIM ON TRADE SECRETS, 1.05[5][b] (2005).

[28] Anacomp, Inc. v. Shell Knob Servs., 1994 U.S. Dist. LEXIS 223 (S.D.N.Y. 1994).

[29] "A joint venture claim requires a plaintiff to demonstrate (1) a community of interest in the performance of a common purpose; (2) joint control or right of control; (3) a joint proprietary interest in the subject matter of the venture; (4) a right to share in profits; and (5) a duty to share in any losses which may be sustained. When analyzing these factors, a court is to consider them as signposts, likely indicia, but not prerequisites." Gibson v. NCL (Bah.) Ltd., 2012 U.S. Dist. LEXIS 74653 at *24 (S.D. Fla., May 30, 2013) (applying Florida law).

[30] See Faigan v. Signature Grp. Holdings, Inc., 211 Cal.App.4th 726, 150 Cal.Rptr.3d 123, 134 (Cal. Ct. App. 2012) ("There cannot be a valid express contract and an implied contract, each embracing the same subject, but requiring different results.").

[31] Convolve, Inc. v. Compaq Computer Corp., 2013 WL 3285331 *3 (2d Cir., July 1, 2013).

[32] Id.

is to be clear about what period is covered by the NDA. For example: "This NDA covers any confidential disclosures between January 1, 2013 and January 1, 2016."

NDAs are generally considered a reasonable means of protecting software code especially in a development contract. NDAs are unsuitable for a mass-market product where there may be millions of potential users. If a software maker is developing customized software or building a specialized company website, counsel will typically draft nondisclosure agreements or NDAs that bind its employees, consultants, customers, and other third parties. If a recipient of confidential information violates an NDA, the trade secret owner will not only have a breach of contract action, but often a misappropriation of trade secret cause of action. Information is not classifiable as a trade secret unless the owner takes reasonable measures under the circumstances to maintain its secrecy.[33] An E–Commerce company will need to implement reasonable computer security to protect the confidentiality of online trade secrets. E–Commerce companies will typically require employees to sign non-compete agreements.

The idea of a nondisclosure agreement is that the software vendor will be able to disclose trade secrets such as models, computer programs, customer lists, and other confidential matters without losing trade secret protection. Typically, the nondisclosure agreement will stipulate that the customers, without the developer's prior written consent, are not permitted to disclose trade secrets. Therefore, software developers and their customers will enter into mutual nondisclosure agreements because the developer will typically have access to its customer's intellectual property when configuring or customizing software. A company's nondisclosure agreements should limit the parties' duty of confidentiality to data or information which is not generally available. A Virginia company required third party/licensees to enter into the following nondisclosure agreement to protect its software-related trade secrets:

> The Consultant/Representative acknowledges that he will, as a result of an association with Decision Insights, Inc., have access to and be in a position to receive information of a confidential or proprietary nature including trade secrets. The Consultant/Representative agrees that he will not, during the association with Decision Insights or thereafter, disclose to anyone whomsoever or use in any manner whatsoever any confidential or proprietary information, whether patentable or unpatentable, concerning any inventions, discoveries, improvements, processes, methods, trade secrets, research or secret data (including but not limited to, models, formulas, computer programs and software developments), or other confidential matters possessed, owned, or used by Decision Insights that may be obtained or learned by the Consultant/in the course of, or as a result of his association with Decision Insights, except as such disclosure or use may be required in the normal course of doing business with Decision Insights and pursuant to Decision Insights Inc.['s] prior written consent.[34] Courts determine the enforceability of nondisclosure agreements by a multi-factorial test:

> (1) Is the restraint, from the standpoint of the employer, reasonable in the sense that it is no greater than is necessary to protect the employer in some legitimate business interest? (2) From the standpoint of the employee, is the restraint reasonable in the sense that it is not unduly harsh and oppressive in curtailing his

---

[33] UTSA § 1(4).

[34] Decision Insights, Inc. v. Sentia Group, Inc., 311 Fed. Appx. 586, 594 (4th Cir. 2009).

legitimate efforts to earn a livelihood? (3) Is the restraint reasonable from the standpoint of a sound public policy?[35]

Ex-employees or consultants who develop a software program for one company, leave the company, and begin marketing and selling a substantially similar program for another company are common in the software industry. For example, in the late 1980s, Par Microsystems, Inc. developed a computer software accounting program with the help of Robert S. Johnson, a computer design employee. Johnson accepted employment with Pinnacle Development Corporation and shortly after, Pinnacle began the marketing and sales of a similar computer software accounting program. Upon Par's discovery of this program, they took legal action against Johnson and Pinnacle for copyright infringement, and the jury awarded them $100,000.[36] The remedies for the misappropriation of trade secrets include damages (UTSA § 3), injunctive relief (UTSA § 2), and attorneys' fees (UTSA § 4) if the plaintiff proves bad faith.

NDAs can also function as a means to protect patented software. In April of 2009, a Rhode Island jury ruled that Microsoft should pay Uniloc USA and Singapore $388 million in damages for patent infringement arising out of a breach of a NDA. In April of 2009, a Rhode Island jury ruled that Microsoft should pay Uniloc USA and Singapore $388 million in damages for patent infringement arising out of a breach of a NDA. This case arose out of Microsoft's study of Uniloc's product activation software to address its piracy problem. Uniloc had a § 216 patent for a registration system that permitted a software user to run the program only if the registered user submitted a code to use the software. The patented software required the user to enter an identification code on the client that matched the server side for the software to be activated. The court ruled that Microsoft breached the NDA and violated Uniloc's patent in producing software relying upon the 216 patent. This case illustrates the multiple functions of NDAs, which can be drafted to protect patents.

(2) Idea Submission Policies

Information-based businesses will often adopt idea submission policies to avoid conflicts concerning ownership or interests in intellectual property rights. Idea submission policies are terms of service when customers, employees, or third parties submit ideas to the company. One of the chief purposes of an idea submission policy is to avoid disputes over whether the company misappropriated or disclosed a trade secret. The typical idea submission terms of service will grant the company "an unrestricted, irrevocable license to use, reproduce, perform, modify, transmit and distribute those materials or information and [the submitter] also agree[s] that [the company] is free to use all concepts, know-how or techniques that [the submitter] send [the company] for any purpose."[37] Such policies may also require the submitter to agree that: "[the company] will consider the submission to be non-confidential and non-proprietary, [the company] shall have no obligations concerning the submission, contractual or otherwise (including but not limited to an obligation to keep the submission confidential), and shall not be liable for any use of disclosure of any submission. [the

---

[35] Id.

[36] Par Microsystems, Inc. v. Pinnacle Development Corp & Johnson, Case No. 93–2114–D (D. Texas 1997).

[37] LG Electronics, Unsolicited Idea Submission Policy (2012).

company] shall be entitled to unrestricted use of the submission for any purpose whatsoever, commercial or otherwise, without compensation to the [submitter]."[38]

(F) Uniform Trade Secret Act Remedies

The types of information protected by trade secrets include source code, compilations, programs, devices, methods, techniques, and processes. The UTSA provides a broad range of remedies, including: preliminary injunctive relief, monetary damages, lost profits, consequential damages, lost royalties, attorney's fees, and punitive damages.[39] A plaintiff will often seek injunctive relief if they suspect that former employees are violating or about to violate NDAs. Courts may enjoin actual or threatened misappropriation of trade secrets.[40] UTSA § 2 states:

> a) Actual or threatened misappropriation may be enjoined. Upon application to the court, an injunction shall be terminated when the trade secret has ceased to exist, but the injunction may be continued for an additional reasonable period of time in order to eliminate commercial advantage that otherwise would be derived from the misappropriation.[41]

In determining whether to grant a preliminary injunction in trade secret litigation, courts weigh four factors: (1) the probability that the movant will succeed on the merits, (2) the threat of irreparable harm to the movant, (3) the balance between the harm to the movant and any harm that granting the injunction will cause to other parties to the litigation, and (4) the public interest. UTSA permits the owner of a trade secret to recover damages (actual), profits, and punitive damages up to two times the actual amount of damages if the misappropriation is willful and malicious.

Trade secret owner may claim a reasonable royalty for the loss of revenue attributable to the misappropriation of a trade secret. UTSA § 4 states that attorney's fees may be recoverable where a claim of misappropriation is made in bad faith, a motion to terminate an injunction is made or resisted in bad faith, or willful and malicious misappropriation exists. Section 3 of UTSA also gives the court the power to award "exemplary damages in an amount not exceeding twice any award," upon a finding of "willful and malicious misappropriation." Section 6 of the UTSA statute of limitations states that aggrieved parties may seek relief within three years after the owner discovers the misappropriation or should have discovered it.

(G) Defenses in UTSA Litigation

(1) Reverse Engineering

Reverse engineering is a process by which a computer or software engineer works backward to determine how the software works. In the anti-reverse engineering clause, a customer will be in breach of the license agreement if it discloses, decompiles, disassembles, or reverse engineers licensed software. A software engineer and lawyer gives the following benefits of reverse engineering: (1) personal education; (2) to fix defects in tools; (3) to understand and work around (or fix) defects in third-party

---

[38] eBay Inc., Unsolicited Idea Submissions (2012).

[39] UTSA § 3.

[40] UTSA § 2.

[41] UTSA § 2(a).

products; (4) to make my product compatible with (able to work with) another product; (5) to make my product compatible with (able to share data with) another product; (6) to learn the principles that guided a competitor's design; (7) to determine whether another company had stolen and reused some of my company's source code and (8) to determine whether a product is capable of living up to its advertised claims.[42] The public good of reverse engineering is to enable "interoperability."

Users of European software have a right to reverse engineer software under the 1991 Software Directive.[43] Software makers cannot require consumer to waive mandatory consumer rules. The European Software Directive also permits "the making of a back-up copy by a person having a right to use the computer program may not be prevented by contract insofar as it is necessary for that use."[44] In the context of software, a customer may reverse engineer software to extract non-copyrightable elements in the software. Reverse engineering includes taking apart the underlying code of software. Under the Uniform Trade Secrets Act and the common law, defendants misappropriate trade secrets only when they acquire confidential information by "improper means" such as theft, bribery, economic espionage, or misrepresentation. Reverse engineering is not an "improper means" to discover trade secrets.[45] In *Mid–Michigan Computer Sys. v. Marc Glassman, Inc.*,[46] the Sixth Circuit upheld a $2 million compensatory damages award and a $5 million punitive damages award against a licensee that secretly copied source code from its licensor. The licensor entered into a license agreement with the defendant to maintain prescription and billing records for customers.

(2) First Amendment Defenses

In recent years, courts have ruled that the tort of misappropriation must give way to the First Amendment. For example, the First Amendment of the U.S. Constitution protected a website operator's posting of DeCSS that enables users to evade the "content scramble system" which both encrypts DVDs and is designed to prevent their unauthorized use and duplication.[47] The California appellate court ruled since the DeCSS that the website operator posted was already public knowledge, the defendant could not be liable for misappropriation since there was no trade secret.[48] In *Ford Motor Co. v. Lane*[49] the federal court denied a motion for a preliminary injunction to prevent Lane from disclosing alleged trade secrets on the Internet because the proposed

---

[42] Cem Kaner, Article 2B and Reverse Engineering (1998) http://www.badsoftware.com/reversea.htm (last visited June 19, 2013).

[43] Council Directive of March 14, 1991, on Legal Protection of Computer Programs, 91/250/EEC, OJ No. L 122/42 (1991).

[44] Id. at art. 5(2).

[45] UTSA § 1, cmt. 2 (noting that reverse engineering is a proper means of acquiring a trade secret).

[46] 416 F.3d 505 (6th Cir. 2005).

[47] DeCSS is computer software capable of decrypting content on a commercially produced DVD video disc. CSS stands for content scramble system. DeCSS decrypts or unscrambles DVS content.

[48] DVD Copy Control Assn. Inc. v. Andrew Bunner, 116 Cal.App.4th 241 (2004) (holding dissemination of DeCSS software on the Internet destroyed trade secret status).

[49] 67 F. Supp. 2d 745, 746 (E.D. Mich. 1999).

injunction would "constitute an invalid prior restraint of free speech in violation of the First Amendment."[50]

§ 12.3   RESTATEMENT (FIRST) OF TORTS

The tort of misappropriation is the improper acquisition or disclosure of a trade secret by one who "knew or had reason to know" that acquisition occurred "under circumstances giving rise to a duty" to maintain confidentiality.[51] Massachusetts, New York, and the District of Columbia continue to follow the Restatement of Torts' approach to trade secrets and have yet to adopt UTSA. Trade secret misappropriation evolved as a tort and the Restatement (First) of Torts, 757–758 (1939) was followed by most states until the UTSA swept the country. The First Restatement of Torts defines a trade secret as "any formula, pattern, device, or compilation of information which is used in one's business, and which gives him an opportunity to get an advantage over competitors who do not know or use it."[52]

The definition of a trade secret under Section 757 is based in part "upon the ease or difficult with which the information could be properly acquired or duplicated by others."[53] The Restatement of Torts, Section 757 requires trade secrets to contain "a substantial element of secrecy so that, except by the use of improper means, there would be difficulty in acquiring the information." A key factor of secrecy is the ease or difficulty with which others can acquire information properly. The Restatement has similar factors to UTSA in determining whether information qualifies as a trade secret:

> (1) the extent to which the information is known outside of [the] business; (2) the extent to which it is known by employees and others involved in [the] business; (3) the extent of measures taken by [the business] to guard the secrecy of the information; (4) the value of the information to [the business] and [its] competitors; (5) the amount of effort or money expended by [the business] in developing the information; and (6) the ease or difficulty with which the information could be properly acquired or duplicated by others.[54]

Courts have yet to trace the contours of cyberspace trade secret protection. Companies failing to implement reasonable Internet security measures will likely endanger the status of their trade secrets under both the UTSA and the Restatement (First) of Torts. Common security problems include buffer overflows, format string problems, SQL injection, command injection, failure to handle errors, cross-site scripting, failing to protect network traffic, and unauthenticated key exchange, and the customer's failure to use cryptographically strong random numbers.[55]   Software

---

[50] Cf. Andrew Beckerman–Rodau, Prior Restraints and Intellectual Property: The Clash Between Intellectual Property and the First Amendment from an Economic Perspective, 12 FORDHAM INTELL. PROP. MEDIA & ENT. L.J. 1, 5 (2001) ("Trade secrets, despite any expressive component, should be treated as property that falls outside the domain of the First Amendment. The very existence of a trade secret depends on maintaining its secrecy."). See also, Richard A. Epstein, Privacy, Publication, and the First Amendment: The Dangers of First Amendment Exceptionalism, 52 STAN. L. REV. 1003, 1006, 1035–46 (2000) (expressing skepticism about the First Amendment defense against the misappropriation of trade secrets).

[51] Avtec Systems, Inc. v. Peiffer, 21 F.3d 568, 575 (4th Cir. 1994).

[52] RESTATEMENT (SECOND) OF TORTS, § 757, cmt. b.

[53] RESTATEMENT (SECOND) OF TORTS, § 757.

[54] RESTATEMENT (FIRST) OF TORTS, § 757, CMT. B.

[55] Michael Howard's Web Log, The 19 Deadly Sins of Software Security, http://blogs.msdn.com/michael_howard/archive/2005/07/11/437875.aspx. (last visited July 10, 2013).

security was featured in the *Wall Street Journal* with a headline reporting that fundamentalist insurgents were using software to intercept video feeds of U.S. military operations in Iraq. The U.S. Department of Defense and intelligence authorities learned that Shiite militants used a $26 off-the-shelf software application to intercept hours and hours of video feeds from Predator, an unmanned aircraft, in Iraq.[56] Shiite fighters used this intercepted intelligence to eliminate the element of surprise from certain U.S. military missions.[57]

In late 2009, Citibank was victimized by a Russian cyber gang suspected of hacking into its computer and purloining tens of millions of dollars.[58] Most enterprises have "software security on their radar." Companies are using diverse computer security tools such as "code analysis, application scanning, penetration testing," and firewalls.[59] An empirical study of the first decade of Economic Espionage Act ("EEA") prosecutions (1996 to 2006) found that many information-based companies were victimized by trade secret misappropriation including: C & D Semiconductor Services, Cisco, IBM, Intel, Jasmine Networks, Lucent Technologies, Sun Microsystems, Varian, and Smart software.[60]

In a real-life incident, the American public learned about the catastrophic software failure that paralyzed the New York Mercantile Exchange and interrupted telephone service in several East Coast cities in February 1998.[61] Common security problems include buffer overflows, format string problems, SQL injection, command injection, failure to handle errors, cross-site scripting, failing to protect network traffic, and unauthenticated key exchange, and the customer's failure to use cryptographically strong random numbers.[62] Software security was featured in a *Wall Street Journal* page one headline reporting that fundamentalist insurgents were using software to intercept video feeds of U.S. military operations in Iraq. The U.S. Department of Defense and intelligence authorities learned that Shiite militants used a $26 off-the-shelf software application to intercept hours and hours of video feeds from Predator unmanned aircraft in Iraq.[63]

Shiite fighters used this intercepted intelligence to eliminate the element of surprise from certain U.S. military missions.[64] In late 2009, Citibank was victimized by a Russian cyber gang suspected of hacking into its computer and purloining tens of

---

[56] Siobhan Gorman, Yochi J. Dreazen & August Cole, Insurgents Hack U.S. Drones: $26 Software Is Used to Breach Weapons in Iraq; Iranian Backing Suspected, WALL ST. J. (Dec. 17, 2009) at 1.

[57] Id.

[58] Siobhan Gorman & Evan Perez, FBI Probes Hack at Citibank: Russian Cyber Gang Suspected of Stealing Tens of Millions; Bank Denies Breach, WALL ST. J (Dec. 22, 2009) at 1.

[59] PR Newswire, Poll Finds Software Security Programs in Place (March 9, 2010) http://www.your-story.org/poll-finds-software-security-top-priority-for-enterprises-137022/ (reporting survey of RSA Conference 2010).

[60] See generally, Michael L. Rustad, The Negligent Enablement of Trade Secret Misappropriation, 22 Santa Clara Computer & High Tech. L.J. 455 (2006).

[61] Id.

[62] Michael Howard's Web Log, The 19 Deadly Sins of Software Security, http://blogs.msdn.com/michael_howard/archive/2005/07/11/437875.aspx. (last visited July 10, 2013).

[63] Siobhan Gorman, Yochi J. Dreazen & August Cole, Insurgents Hack U.S. Drones: $26 Software Is Used to Breach Weapons in Iraq; Iranian Backing Suspected, WALL ST. J. (Dec. 17, 2009) at 1.

[64] Id.

millions of dollars.[65] Most enterprises have "software security on their radar." Companies are using diverse computer security tools such as "code analysis, application scanning, penetration testing," and firewalls.[66] An empirical study of the first decade of Economic Espionage Act ("EEA") prosecutions (1996 to 2006) found that many information-based companies were victimized by trade secret misappropriation including: C & D Semiconductor Services, Cisco, IBM, Intel, Jasmine Networks, Lucent Technologies, Sun Microsystems, Varian, and Smart software.[67]

§ 12.4 TRADE SECRET MISAPPROPRIATION IN CYBERSPACE

Trade secret misappropriation actions by software companies are increasingly common. Roger Milgrim, the leading authority on trade secrets, describes computer software as the "single most important 'product' eligible for trade secret protection."[68]

Some of the initial cyberlaw cases involved litigation to vindicate the misappropriation of the Church of Scientology's secret religious doctrine. The first online trade secrets cases arose out Church of Scientology's lawsuit to enjoin further electronic distribution of secret church doctrine. A California federal court said, "posting works to the Internet makes them "generally known," at least to the relevant people interested in the news group.[69] In the Internet economy, employees are highly mobile. Courts often balance the employees' right to work against the employer's right to protect trade secrets. The Religious Technology Center of the Church of Scientology was the plaintiff in a number of path-breaking Internet-related cases. In *Religious Tech. Center v. Lerma*,[70] an ex-Scientologist published Church documents on the Internet. The Religious Technology Center ("RTC") sought a temporary restraining order prohibiting Lerma from further distribution of documents the church protected as trade secrets. The *Lerma* court stated:

> As other courts who have dealt with similar issues have observed, posting works to the Internet makes them "generally known". . . Once a trade secret is posted on the Internet, it is effectively part of the public domain, impossible to retrieve. Although the person who originally posted a trade secret on the Internet may be liable for trade secret misappropriation, the party who merely downloads Internet information cannot be liable for misappropriation because there is no misconduct involved in interacting with the Internet.[71]

In *DoubleClick v. Henderson*,[72] DoubleClick, the developer of proprietary online banner advertisements, sought an injunction to enjoin two ex-employees from working for a competitor for at least one year. DoubleClick required its employees to sign NDA to

---

[65] Siobhan Gorman & Evan Perez, FBI Probes Hack at Citibank: Russian Cyber Gang Suspected of Stealing Tens of Millions; Bank Denies Breach, WALL ST. J (Dec. 22, 2009) at 1.

[66] PR Newswire, Poll Finds Software Security Programs in Place (March 9, 2010) http://www.your-story.org/poll-finds-software-security-top-priority-for-enterprises-137022/ (reporting survey of RSA Conference 2010).

[67] See generally, Michael L. Rustad, The Negligent Enablement of Trade Secret Misappropriation, 22 Santa Clara Computer & High Tech. L.J. 455 (2006).

[68] ROGER MILGRIM, MILGRIM ON TRADE SECRETS, 1.05[5][b] (2005).

[69] Religious Technology Center v. Netcom, 907 F. Supp. 1361 (N.D. Cal. 1995).

[70] 908 F. Supp. 1362 (E.D. Va. 1995).

[71] Id.

[72] 1997 WL 731413 (N.Y. Sup. Ct. 1997).

maintain the confidentiality of information provided by its clients, and a covenant not to compete. Even in the absence of a NDA, employees owed their employer a fiduciary duty not to divulge confidential information. In a Church of Scientology case, *Religious Technology Center v. F.A.C.T.Net, Inc.*,[73] a Colorado court held the online publication of a confidential document belonging to the Church of Scientology made the information "generally known," therefore destroying the trade secret. The federal court in *Religious Technology Center v. Netcom On–Line.com*,[74] suggested that trade secrets might not be irretrievable after being posted on the Internet. The Netcom court stated it was "not persuaded that trade secret status should be deemed destroyed at this stage merely by the posting of the trade secret to the Internet."[75]

In *Religious Technology Center v. Netcom*,[76] the court dealt further with the scope of intellectual property rights on the Internet. Two organizations sued a former minister, who had been a vocal critic of the Church of Scientology, for posting writings of the founder, L. Ron Hubbard, on the Internet. The Scientologists had undertaken a variety of methods to keep the information secret, such as locked cabinets, electronic sensors attached to documents, locked briefcases for transporting works, alarms, photo identifications, security personnel, and confidentiality agreements. The *Netcom* court found the Church had made more than an adequate showing of reasonable efforts to maintain secrecy. With respect to the Internet posting of church doctrine, the court found even though posting information on a site might not be akin to publishing it in a newspaper or on television, it would no longer be classified as a trade secret. The lesson learned from Netcom is that trade secrets can be lost at a click of the mouse and a company needs to implement reasonable computer security to protect digital data it wishes to keep secret. In summary, the Church of Scientology trade secret cases stand for the proposition that the posting of information onto the Internet results in a trade secret being generally known.

The Internet economy is known for a rapid turnover in employees, and online companies face the constant danger an ex-employee will misappropriate trade secrets for use in a competitor's business. A covenant restraining an employee from competing with her former employer upon termination of employment is reasonable if the restraint is no greater than is required for the protection of the employer. Courts will also consider whether the non-compete agreement imposes an undue hardship on the employee and whether it is injurious to the public. In *DoubleClick, Inc. v. Henderson*,[77] several employees planned to leave the Internet advertising mogul in order to start a dot-com startup. DoubleClick confiscated one of the employee's laptops and found information on the hard drive, including e-mails and future business plans suggested that he was engaged in economic espionage. The information found on the hard drive, included e-mails, and future business plans, which provided evidence of misappropriation of trade secrets. DoubleClick discovered an e-mail from his employee stating that he "cut and pasted" DoubleClick's 1996 Business Plan to create Alliance's draft business plan.

---

[73] 901 F. Supp. 1519 (D. Colo. 1995).

[74] LEXIS 23572 (N.D. Cal., Jan. 3, 1997).

[75] DVD Copy Control Assn., Inc. v. McLaughlin, No. CV 786804, 2000 WL 488512, at *3 (Super. Ct. Santa Clara County, Cal. Jan. 21, 2000) (referring to Religious Technology Center v. Netcomon.Line.com supra).

[76] 907 F. Supp. 1361 (N.D. Cal. 1995).

[77] No. 116914/97, 1997 WL 731413 (N.Y. Sup. Ct. Nov. 7, 1997).

DoubleClick summarily fired the employees and sought an injunction to enjoin them from sharing trade secrets with competitors.

The ex-employees argued that much of the information DoubleClick classified as trade secrets was already made public because it was displayed on the online company's website. The court found there was evidence the ex-employees intended to use trade secrets to advise Alta Vista, DoubleClick's largest client. The court, however, refused to enjoin the ex-employees for a one-year period sought by DoubleClick, noting it was too long given the ever-evolving Internet advertising industry. The court limited the injunction to six months. The DoubleClick case illustrates many novel issues in trade secret cases.

In *PhoneDog v. Kravitz*,[78] the court refused to dismiss a claim that an ex-employee misappropriated the password/login information for a Twitter account. Kravitz, PhoneDog's ex-employee, continued to use a Twitter account used to publicize PhoneDog's website after his employment. Kravitz also argued that passwords to Twitter accounts do not derive any actual or potential independent economic value under the UTSA because they do not provide any substantial business advantage. He also contended that PhoneDog did not make any reasonable efforts to maintain the secrecy of the Twitter password. The court ruled that PhoneDog sufficiently pleaded a misappropriation claim. The company requested that its ex-employee relinquish use of the account and he merely changed the Twitter handle on the account, while continuing to misappropriate confidential information. The extent of Internet security measures taken by the owner of the trade secret need not be absolute but must be reasonable under the circumstances. In PhoneDog, the company password protected its Twitter account. Trade secret owners must protect the confidentiality of software and documentation.

§ 12.5   TRADE SECRETS IN A GLOBAL INTERNET

(A) Economic Espionage Act

Congress enacted the Economic Espionage Act ("EEA") in 1996 to criminalize the misappropriation of trade secrets.[79] An empirical study of all EEA prosecutions from the federal criminal statute's enactment in 1996 to August 1, 2005 uncovered fewer than fifty economic or espionage prosecutions filed in federal courts.[80] In the first decade of EEA prosecutions, the U.S. Department of Justice did not file a single case against a hacker stealing trade secrets by "exploiting known software defects" during an Internet transmission.

Prior to the EEA, prosecutors pursued the theft of trade secrets by using existing law such as the 1934 National Stolen Property Act, which was intended to punish thieves who also fled across state borders in automobiles. While the National Stolen Property Act applied to tangible goods, it was not clearly applicable to the unauthorized transfer of intangibles such as intellectual property. Congress enacted the EEA to bridge that gap in

---

[78] 2011 WL 5415612 (N. D. Cal., Nov. 8, 2011).

[79] See Economic Espionage Act of 1996, Pub. L. No. 104–294, 110 Stat. 3488 (codified as amended at 18 U.S.C. §§ 1831–39 (2000).

[80] Michael L. Rustad, The Negligent Enablement of Trade Secret Misappropriation, 22 SANTA CLARA COMPUTER & HIGH TECH. L.J. 455, 458 (2006) (presenting empirical findings from study of the first decade of Economic Espionage Act prosecutions).

trade secret law by creating two new federal crimes for trade secret misappropriation.[81] The causes of action for EEA causes of action are highlighted in the table below.

Economic Espionage Act

Section 1831(A)(3)	The defendant intended or knew his actions would benefit a foreign government, foreign instrumentality, or foreign agent	The defendant knowingly received, bought, or possessed a trade secret, knowing the same to have been stolen or appropriated, obtained, or converted without authorization
Section 1832(A)(3)	The defendant intended to convert a trade secret to the economic benefit of anyone other than the owner	The defendant knowingly received, bought, or possessed a trade secret, knowing the same to have been stolen or appropriated, obtained, or converted without authorization; must satisfy interstate commerce

The EEA criminalizes two types of offenses: (1) economic espionage that benefits foreign governments or entities (§ 1831); and (2) the theft of trade secrets benefits any person but the true owner (§ 1832). Both Sections 1831 and 1831 require proof of a trade secret. The government may not charge a defendant with violating the EEA unless "the owner thereof has taken reasonable measures to keep such information secret." Section 1831 of the EEA addresses the problem of misappropriation by foreign governments or their agents and criminalizes data theft with fines of up to $500,000 and imprisonment of up to fifteen years.[82] Offending organizations may be subject to fines of up to $10,000,000.

In contrast, § 1832 applies to domestic trade secret theft. Section 1832 covers misappropriation intended to benefit individuals and corporations other than the true owner. It is a broader provision, applying "to anyone who knowingly engages in the theft of trade secrets, or an attempt or conspiracy to do so." Under § 1832, individuals are subject to fines and up to ten years of imprisonment, while organizations are subject to fines of up to $5,000,000. Section 1839(3)(b) of the EEA requires that information must derive "independent economic value, actual or potential, from not being generally known to, and not being readily ascertainable through proper means by the public."[83] Although the EEA provides criminal sanctions and civil damages for the misappropriation of trade secrets, it does not permit civil action filed by private attorneys general.

---

[81] Id.

[82] 17 U.S.C. § 1832.

[83] 18 U.S.C. § 1839(3)(B).

China and the former Russian Republics are active in economic espionage hiding "behind the anonymity of proxy computers and dispersed routers in third world countries to pilfer proprietary corporate information to accelerate their own economic development."[84] According to the study, "most computer-network espionage against American economic targets has focused on the following areas: information and communications technology; assessments of supplies of scarce natural resources; technologies for clean energy and health care systems or pharmaceuticals; and military data, especially maritime systems, and air and space technologies."[85] Foreign collectors of sensitive economic information are able to operate in cyberspace with relatively little risk of detection by their private sector targets.

All but a few of the EEA prosecutions have been under Section 1832, not 1831. The U.S. Justice Department has been reticent to initiate prosecutions against foreign governments and foreign agents under the EEA. In 2012, the Justice Department launched a high profile EEA prosecution to include a Chinese company that was, in fact, an operation of the Chinese Government.[86] In many EEA prosecutions, the defendant is also charged with violation of the Computer Fraud and Abuse Act ("CFAA"). The theft of trade secrets may also be a crime under the federal CFAA or violate state computer crime statutes.[87] This federal statute applies if a computer was used to further a fraud scheme, such as obtaining trade secrets and related materials by misrepresentations.[88] The internationalization of trade secret theft requires cooperation between law enforcement to supplement private enforcement, which is the first line of defense against misappropriation.

(B) International Trade Secret Protection

Trade secret protection in the United States is generally protected by the Uniform Trade Secrets Act, a state statute. "Trade secret protection is not recognized in many countries, and no international agreement exists with respect to the subject matter."[89] Foreign countries that do recognize trade secrets may have limitations on the duration of protection.[90] U.S. e-businesses can restrain the importation of products imported into the United States using a misappropriated trade secret process.[91] World Trade Organization member states are required to provide adequate protection for undisclosed information. Article 39(2) of the Agreement on Trade Related Aspects of

---

[84] Thom Shanker, U.S. Report Accuses China and Russia of Internet Spying, N.Y. TIMES (Nov. 3, 2011).

[85] Id.

[86] The Economist reports that a third of all Economic Espionage Act prosecutions since 1996 "involved people born in China or seeking to help its government or businesses." Intellectual Property: Can You Keep a Secret, The Economist (March 16, 2013) at 67.

[87] Michael L. Rustad, The Negligent Enablement of Trade Secret Misappropriation, 22 SANTA CLARA COMPUTER & HIGH TECH. L.J. 455, 494 (2006) (presenting empirical findings from study of the first decade of Economic Espionage Act cases demonstrating that the greatest threat was employees or ex-employees as opposed to hackers hacking into computer systems).

[88] 18 U.S.C. § 1030(a)(2)(C).

[89] ALLAN S. GUTTERMAN, TECHNOLOGY–DRIVEN CORPORATE ALLIANCES: A LEGAL GUIDE FOR EXECUTIVES 39 (1994).

[90] Id.

[91] Marcia Swihart Orgill, Protecting Against the Overseas Theft of Trade Secrets, Beyond the Fine Print, dannamckitrick.com (Jan. 31, 2012) (discussing TianRui Group Co., et al. v. ITC, 661 F.3d 1322 (Fed Cir. Oct. 11, 2011), where the Federal Circuit held that the U.S. International Trade Commission can exclude imports manufacturing enabled by a process protected by trade secrets, even when the product was manufactured outside the United States.

Intellectual Property Rights ("TRIPS") also establishes an obligation to protect trade secrets.

(C) Trade Secret Misappropriation & Foreign Defendants

Two North Carolina -based data mining companies claimed a defendant violated the Racketeer Influenced and Corrupt Organization Act ("RICO") when it raided the plaintiffs' staff and stole proprietary software processes. A federal jury in Charlotte returned a $4,178,292 verdict for the plaintiffs. The jury also awarded $7,500 to the defendant company on its counterclaim for slander. Plaintiff Two Bit Dog, LLC was an affiliated website-based marketer of pet products. Plaintiffs claimed Defendant Red F Marketing and the other defendants, some of whom were former employees of the plaintiffs, violated federal racketeering laws by conspiring to take Bridgetree-owned software.

"After Li's departure from Bridgetree, Red F, with Li as an employee, opened an office near Bridgetree's office in Xian, China. Li also allegedly convinced about 20 other Bridgetree employees to leave the company for Red F's China office." The North Carolina data mining companies also contended, "Defendant Mali Xu, a former employee, told Bridgetree employees and Chinese government officials that Bridgetree was closing its Xian office. Xu also allegedly took Bridgetree's books and computers and refused to return them." Plaintiffs argued that Xu violated state computer fraud laws, along with federal copyright protection laws. Defendant Elton Scripter, a local IBM Corporate employee, was alleged to have conspired with Li to win an important contract with IBM, using technology allegedly stolen from Bridgetree.

Scripter had previously worked for plaintiff. The plaintiffs contended that the defendants violated civil RICO, misappropriated its trade secrets, committed unfair trade practices, and violated the Computer Fraud and Abuse Act. The Chinese defendants were dismissed from the lawsuit because of the difficulties of serving process. The jury awarded the plaintiffs $4,178,292, less $7,500 awarded to defendants on a counterclaim for slander. The award included $653,292 for misappropriation of information and damages; $25,000 in punitive damages; and $3,500,000 for conversion of plaintiff's computer files.

Chapter 13

PATENT LAW AND THE INTERNET

§ 13.1 OVERVIEW OF INTERNET–RELATED PATENT LAW

(A) Internet–Related Patent Wars

Internet patents are predominately about methods of doing online business. For example, 1–800–Flowers.com, eBay, Amazon.com, Buy.com, Drugstore.com, E-loan, Freemarkets, MP3.com, and Priceline.com are high profile businesses that have built upon business method patents. No single development has spurred the growth of Internet-related patents more than *State Street Bank & Trust Co. v. Signature Financial Group, Inc.*[1] The Federal Circuit validated the use of computer-related patents for doing business, which has had a profound impact on the Internet economy. In the immediate aftermath of the July 1998 decision, there was a 45% increase in the number of computer-related patents issued during the patent office's fiscal year ending on September 30, 1998.[2] Since *State Street Bank*, the filing of so-called Internet business method patents has skyrocketed.[3] The public policy underlying patent law is to "confer on its holder a legal monopoly, for a limited period to commercially exploit an invention."[4] Today America's information-based economy is increasingly built on a foundation of patents defined as limited duration property rights "relating to an invention, granted by the United States Patent and Trademark Office in exchange for public disclosure of the invention."

This chapter introduces the Internet-related foundations of patent protection, patentability, and the patenting process. In every technological era, the patent system supports innovation. Internet business methods, software, and computer software are critical to e-commerce. "The innovations of the "knowledge economy"—of "digital prosperity"—have been dominant contributors to today's economic growth and societal change." The demand for patent lawyers has increased, due in large part to the Internet, cloud computing, software, and E–Commerce patents. Internet patents protect software and other computer-related technologies to perform various business methods. Patents protect innovations including the hardware and software that comprises the Internet's infrastructure. Business methods have been controversial since their inception.

An estimated 11,000 patents cover Internet-related business methods. Patent law vests the patentee with a limited monopoly interest to make, use, and sell the invention or discovery. A patent is a "right to exclude others from making, using and

---

[1] 149 F.3d 1368, 1373 (Fed. Cir. 1998) (holding that a business method based upon mathematical algorithms was patentable).

[2] John T. Aquino, Patently Permissive: USPTO Filings Up After Ruling Expands Protection for Business and Net Software, A.B.A. J., May 1999, at 30.

[3] MICHAEL L. RUSTAD & CYRUS DAFTARY, E-BUSINESS LEGAL HANDBOOK § 4.05[F] at 4–187 (2003).

[4] United Kingdom Patent Office, Should E-Patents Be Granted for Computer Software or Ways of Doing Business? (May 1, 2001).

selling his invention during the term of the patent." A patent applicant must demonstrate its invention, as a whole is useful and accomplish a practical application. That is, it must produce a "useful, concrete and tangible result." Patent owners will license or assign their exclusive rights to others. Patent law protection is territorial, while the Internet is borderless.

Nevertheless, hardly a day goes by without an Internet-related patent infringement lawsuit being filed. Apple's patent lawsuit alleging that Samsung copied software in its smartphone gained momentum in June of 2012 when a federal judge issued an injunction enjoining "sales of Samsung's Galaxy Tab 10.1 tablet computer pending the outcome of the trial." Apple contends that "Samsung copied "rubber banding," the term used to describe the way smartphone images pull away from the edge and bounce back when a user over scrolls with a finger." In August of 2012, a California federal jury held Samsung violated several of Apple's patents awarding a billion dollar verdict for patent infringement damages.

The federal jury found that Samsung willfully infringed Apple's patents for "tap to zoom" and "finger sliding" commands. This Internet-related patent lawsuit promises to be the largest patent verdict in world history and Samsung will appeal the verdict to the U.S. Court of Appeals for the Federal Circuit. Shortly after this verdict was announced, a Seoul South Korean court ruled, "Apple infringed two Samsung technology patents, while Samsung violated one of Apple's patents. The South Korean court awarded small damages to both companies and said they must halt sales of the infringing products in South Korea." The smartphone wars feature litigants such as "Apple Inc., Samsung Electronics Co., and Microsoft Corp." who are engaged in scorched earth patent litigation over patents and licensing.

In June of 2013, the U.S. International Trade Commission "ruled that Apple violated a Samsung patent covering technology used to send information over wireless networks." The ruling does not impact iPhone 5 or fourth generation iPads, but does mean that older Apple inc. products cannot be imported because they allegedly use infringing patents allowing "certain iPhones and iPads made to work on AT & T Inc.'s network."[5] The patent at issue is a "method for encoding/decoding a transport format combination indicator ("TFCI") in a CDMA mobile communication system."[6] This battle of the mobile phone titans promises to be a scorched earth battle with no settlement in sight.

In March of 2012, Yahoo! filed a patent infringement lawsuit against Facebook just as the social media market leader was making its Initial Public Offering ("IPO"). Yahoo!'s patent lawsuit alleges that Facebook had infringed ten different Yahoo! patents that are fundamental to social media, such as "personalized advertising, customized portal pages and news feeds, recommendations to connect with other suggested users (and screen out spammers), social music and messaging applications, and authorizing some users (but not others) to see different sections of your content."[7] Facebook filed a counterclaim charging that Yahoo! infringed ten of its patents "through its home page

---

[5] Id.

[6] Id. at A6.

[7] Tim Carmody, *Yahoo! Sues Facebook in a Web Patent Showdown*, EPICENTER (March 13, 2012).

and Flickr photo-sharing service and in ads displayed throughout its site."[8] In July of 2012, Yahoo! filed another patent lawsuit against Facebook in a California federal district court contending that the social media giant's methods for creating profiles drew in large part from Yahoo!'s patented social networking technology.

In August of 2009, Microsoft sought an injunction to delay enforcement of a $290 million patent infringement lawsuit assessed in favor of i4i, a Toronto company that owned the XML patent. The court's injunction requires Microsoft to stop licensing its "Word program within 60 days until the issue can be fully resolved."[9] The federal court ruled that Microsoft's new Word program violated the Canadian company's software patent. Back in November of 2007, Microsoft also lost a patent infringement case where the jury found that Microsoft's operating systems infringed three claims of the two patents. The patents in contention shared a common specification aimed at resolving the problem of illicit copying and unauthorized use of computer software.[10] The Sixth Circuit upheld a jury verdict of willful infringement by the manufacturer on all three claims and awarded damages of $115 million.[11]

The American Intellectual Property Law Association's survey confirms the high cost of defending patent infringement lawsuits; in high stake cases, the median total cost in 2011 was $5 million.[12]An example of patent litigation can be found in the August of 2012 case, where a federal court vacated a patent infringement award against Research in Motion ("RIM"). Mformation filed suit against RIM, alleging violation of a patent describing a "system and method for remote control and management of wireless devices," winning a unanimous jury verdict in San Francisco that RIM was liable for infringement.[13] The $147 million figure was based on royalties of past sales to nongovernment customers in the U.S.[14] Nevertheless, the federal court "determined that Mformation failed to establish that RIM infringes its patent."[15]

"Patents have become a top priority for technology companies as many of them, including Google Inc. and Apple Inc., become embroiled in patent-related lawsuits."[16] Facebook agreed to pay Microsoft Corporation $550 million for hundreds of patents that it originally purchased from America Online. Companies like Facebook need a robust portfolio of software patents to stave off lawsuits by patent trolls and to protect their intellectual property. Software patents are twice as likely as any other type of patent to be challenged in court.

---

[8] Victoria Slind–Flor, Yahoo, Orion, Under Armor, Fuku: Intellectual Property, BLOOMBERG NEWS (April 30, 2012).

[9] Will Microsoft Stop Selling Office Over Word Woes? DEVICE.COM (Aug. 21, 2009) at 1.

[10] Specifications" means the physical, technical, functional and/or performance requirements for software or other products.

[11] z4 Techs., Inc. v. Microsoft Corp., 507 F.3d 1340 (6th Cir. 2007).

[12] American Intellectual Property Law Association, AIPLA 2011 Economic Survey (reporting survey of patent litigation costs from sample of AIPLA members).

[13] Mformation Techs., Inc. v. Research in Motion Ltd., 2010 U.S. Dist. LEXIS 23258 at *3.

[14] Jim Brodkin, RIM's $147 Million Patent Penalty Wiped Out by Judge, Arstechnica.com (Aug. 9, 2012), http://arstechnica.com/tech-policy/2012/08/rims-147–million-patent-penalty-wiped-out-by-judge.

[15] Id.

[16] Alexei Oreskovic and Diane Bartz, Facebook Pays Microsoft $550 Million for AOL Patents, REUTERS (April 24, 2012).

Business method patents are seven times as likely to be the subject of litigation.[17] The principal investigators of a major patent litigation study conclude that software patents are more vulnerable to challenges in the courts because of their abstract nature and their lack of clear boundaries.[18] Most of the high profile cases against software moguls are for patent infringement rather than breaches of license agreements.

Microsoft settled a case filed by PalTalk for $90 million in 2009 because their Xbox videogame system allegedly violated the New York company's patents. The term "patent troll" or non-practicing entity obtains a software patent without the intention to make a product but to collect licensing fees. To date, patent trolls have largely targeted proprietary software companies such as Microsoft, Adobe, and other members of the Business Software Alliance. In July of 2008, a patent troll filed suit against IBM, Oracle, SAP, and Adobe for infringement for faster server software.[19] The same company filed suit versus "Intel, AMD, Sun, Nvidia, Real Networks and Raza Microelectronics on a different patent charge."[20]

Mark Lemley contends that the technology companies are expending huge sums to defend themselves against patent trolls that should go to research and development.[21] "For example, Google bought Motorola Mobility for $12.5 billion— mostly for its patents."[22] A White House Report states:

> Patent Assertion Entities ("PAEs"), also known as "patent trolls," do not play such roles. Instead, they focus on aggressive litigation, pursuing such practices as: threatening to sue thousands of companies at once, without specific evidence of infringement against any of them; creating shell companies that make it difficult for defendants to know who is suing them; and asserting that their patents cover inventions not imagined at the time they were granted.[23]

In May of 2012, a California jury found that Oracle America Inc. "failed to prove Google Inc.'s infringement of patents on the Java operating system by Android-based cell phones."[24] In April of 2009, a Rhode Island jury ruled that Microsoft should pay Uniloc USA and Singapore $388 million in damages for patent infringement arising out of a breach of a nondisclosure agreement ("NDA"). This case arose out of Microsoft's study of Uniloc's product activation software to address its piracy problem. Uniloc had a § 216 patent for a registration system that permitted a software user to run the program only if the registered user submitted a code to use the software. The patented

---

[17] JAMES BESSEN & MICHAEL J. MEURER, PATENT FAILURE: HOW JUDGES, BUREAUCRATS, AND LAWYERS PUT INNOVATORS AT RISK (Princeton, New Jersey: Princeton University Press, 2008) at 143 (presenting data from the late 1990s finding that the annual cost of software patent litigation was $3.88 billion versus only .10 billion in profits realized from software claims).

[18] Id. at 22, 27.

[19] Editors, IBM, Oracle, SAP & Adobe Sued, CLIENT SERVER NEWS (USA) (July 28, 2008), available at 2008 WLNR 24338760.

[20] Id.

[21] Vivek Wadhwa, Where Are the Jobs? Ask the Patent Trolls, N.Y. TIMES (May 7, 2012) (quoting Mark Lemley).

[22] Id.

[23] WHITE HOUSE, PATENT ASSERTION AND U.S. INNOVATION, Executive Office of the President (Report was prepared by the President's Council of Economic Advisers, the National Economic Council, and the Office of Science & Technology Policy) (June 2013) at Executive Summary.

[24] BNA, BNA'S PATENT, TRADEMARK AND COPYRIGHT JOURNAL (May 24, 2012).

software required the user to enter an identification code on the client side that matched the server side for the software to be activated. The court ruled that Microsoft breached the NDA and violated Uniloc's patent in producing software relying upon the § 216 patent.[25]

Patent portfolios are increasingly valuable assets. An Apple–Microsoft–Oracle–Nokia consortium bought Nortel's patent portfolio for $4.5 billion. Microsoft bought Novell's patent portfolio for $450 million and some of AOL's patents for $1 billion.[26] Critics of Internet-related patents contend that these innovations would develop without the type of patent protection that dampens competition. All patents balance antitrust concerns against market dominance.[27] To establish antitrust injury under Sherman Act, plaintiff must plead specific facts showing that challenged action has had actual adverse effect on competition as a whole in relevant market, not just on plaintiff as competitor.[28] Internet-related business method patents give the holder the right to control the use of the technology. The level and extent of the control depends upon the business method. Patent holders that obtain a patent to discourage competitors will have a chilling impact on E–Commerce.[29] Too much patent protection for Internet-related business method patents may not be desirable because it undermines competitiveness. The trend towards propertization of software and eBusiness methods has led to a more complex online business environment. Many E–Commerce related patent disputes center on the issue of whether a business method is patentable. As such, the Internet is increasingly the cauldron for patent disputes. This chapter will describe how patent law is attempting to keep up with the Internet.

(B) Constitutional and Statutory Basis

The path of patent law was prefigured "in England in 1624, and in this country with the adoption of our Constitution." The U.S. Constitution grants Congress the power "to promote the progress of science and useful arts, by securing for limited times to . . . inventors the exclusive right to their respective . . . discoveries." Abraham Lincoln told the story of how any man might "instantly use what another man had invented, so that the inventor had no special advantage from his invention." President Lincoln noted how the U.S. "patent system changed this, secured to the inventor for a limited time exclusive use of his inventions, and thereby added the fuel of interest to the fire of genius in the discovery and production of new and useful things." Congress passed the Patent Act of 1793, which today is embodied in the Patent Act of 1952. The U.S. federal patent statute was significantly revised in 2011 when President Obama signed the America Invents Act ("AIA") into law.

---

[25] Joe Mullin, Patent Litigation Weekly: Uniloc Keeps Filing Software Suits, and NPE Patents Fare Poorly At Trial, CORP. COUNSEL (Sept. 27, 2010).

[26] Id.

[27] "The presence of strong network effects in some technology markets can be a differentiating factor, as can the pace of change. But I think people often underestimate the level of innovation and the pace of change in non-technology markets. These days few companies can afford to stand still. A lot of purely technological innovation happens in non-technology companies now, so technological factors might come into play more often." Interview with Edward Felten, FTC Chief Technologist, 25 ANTITRUST ABA 47, 47 (2011).

[28] Sherman Act, §§ 1, 2, 15 U.S.C. §§ 1, 2.

[29] Michael A. Carrier, Unraveling the Patent–Antitrust Paradox, 150 U. PA. L. REV. 761, 826 (2002).

§ 13.2 U.S. PATENT ACT

Congress has from time to time revised the federal patent statute. The first patent law was enacted in 1790. Patent laws underwent a general revision which was enacted on July 19, 1952, and which came into effect on January 1, 1953. On November 29, 1999, Congress enacted the American Inventors Protection Act of 1999 ("AIPA"), which further revised the patent laws. In 2011, Congress again amended the U.S. Patent Act when it enacted the America Invents Act. The U.S. Patent Act declares, "Patents shall have the attributes of personal property," including "the right to exclude others from making, using, offering for sale, or selling the invention." Patent law is a negative monopoly or property right since the patentee has the right to exclude others from making, using, or selling his or her invention. As a result, patent owners often license their patents for use by others.

The Leahy–Smith America Invents Act ("AIA") represents a sea change in U.S. patent law as the United States aligns its law with the rest of the world in recognizing patents rights by adopting the First Inventor to File ("FITF") system. FITF displaces the previously followed rule of awarding patents to the first-to-invent ("FI") system where the creation of the invention marked the determinative point for patent protection. Under this system, applicants got a patent "after disclosing the invention as long as a patent is filed within one year of the disclosure." The FI patent system created problems for multinational companies filing "patents around the world . . . governed by different legal standards that affect whether an invention is patentable." AIA's newly aligned FITF system is equivalent to U.C.C. Article 9's chief rule that the first to file or perfect obtains protection under the law. Under the AIA, the FITF is determined by the race to the registry, in this case to the USPTO.

Patent examiners in the USPTO determine whether the boundaries of the claim sought by the applicant qualify for patent protection. Under the AIA reforms, the USPTO now offers applicants an opportunity to have patent applications reviewed on an expedited basis, for a substantial fee. Small entities and independent inventors receive a 50 percent discount on the $4800 fee to use this new fast track option. This reform was made in response to criticism for long and drawn-out patent prosecutions.

Post-grant reviews apply to first to file patents (granted after March 16, 2013). Under this AIA procedure, broad validity charges may be asserted against an issued patent nine months from the grant. Post-grant reviews, within the first nine months after a patent has issued, enable the opponent to challenge the claim on variegated grounds.The AIA's inter-partes review applies to issued patents after the first nine months after the grant.

Post-grant reviews apply to first to file patents (granted after March 16, 2013). Under this AIA procedure, broad validity charges may be asserted against an issued patent nine months from the grant. The AIA's inter-partes review applies to issued patents after the first nine months after the grant. Post-grant reviews, within the first nine months after a patent has issued, enable the opponent to challenge the claim on variegated grounds.

The AIA initiated new methods for challenging patents, developed several new third-party challenges, including post grant review, inter partes review and devised a transitional program for covered business method patents. An *inter partes* review may be instituted upon a showing that there is a reasonable likelihood that the petitioner would prevail with respect to at least one claim challenged. *Inter partes* review is a new trial proceeding conducted at the Board to review the patentability of one or more claims in a patent. The grounds for review are limited to those grounds that could be raised under Sections 102 or 103, and only because of prior art consisting of patents or printed publications. The *inter partes* review process can only be initiated by a third party or someone who does not own the patent. The petition is filed after the later of either: (1) 9 months after the grant of the patent or issuance of a reissue patent; or (2) if a post grant review is instituted, the termination of the post grant review. The patent owner may file a preliminary response to the petition. The AIA eliminated the possibility of false patent marking complaints by *qui tam* plaintiffs. The AIA's broadening of prior art will extend to disclosures on social media.[30]

§ 13.3   PATENT TYPES

Patent protection is available for the invention of "any new and useful process, machine, manufacture, or composition of matter, or any new and useful improvement thereof."[31] Laws of nature, abstract ideas, and physical phenomena are not patentable based upon judicial limitations on patentability under Section 101. Oliver Wendell Holmes Jr. notes that patents are "property carried to the highest degree of abstraction—a right *in rem* to exclude, without a physical object or content."[32]

Patent examiners "identify the boundaries of the protection sought by the applicant and to understand how the claims relate to and define what the applicant has indicated is the invention."[33] Federal patent law recognizes three types of patent protection: (1) utility patents, (2) design patents, and (3) plant patents. Utility patents, as the name connotes, are any new or useful process. Utility patents may be granted to anyone who invents or discovers any new and useful process, machine, article of manufacture, or composition of matter, or any new and useful improvement of an extant patent. Design Patents may be granted to anyone who invents a new, original, and ornamental design for an article of manufacture. Design patents protect the ornament design of products. Plant patents are awarded to anyone who invents or discovers and asexually reproduces distinct and new varieties of plants.[34]

(A)   Utility Patents

Utility patents account for 95% or more of Internet-related patent. Justice William O. Douglas explains, "The Constitution never sanctioned the patenting of gadgets. Patents serve a higher end—the advance of science."[35] Utility patents are issued for four general types of inventions/discoveries: machines, human made products, compositions of

---

[30] "The definition of prior art has been broadened such that certain disclosures made via social media may serve as prior art against you if you plan on filing for patent rights. Additionally, with the change from a first-to-invent rule to a first-inventor-to-file rule, a detailed disclosure may result in another entity filing for a patent on your invention before you are able to do so." Peter Brody & Mariel Goetz, Ten Things You Need to Know About Social Media and Intellectual Property, BLOOMBERG BNA: ELECTRONIC COMMERCE AND LAW (Feb. 12, 2013).

[31] 35 U.S.C. § 101 (Whoever invents or discovers any new and useful process, machine, manufacture, or composition of matter, or any new and useful improvement thereof, may obtain a patent therefor, subject to the conditions and requirements of this title).

[32] OLIVER WENDELL HOLMES JR.,1 HOLMES-POLLOCK LETTERS 53 (1946, ed. by Mark DeWolfe Howe).

[33] MPEP, 2106 Patent Subject Matter Eligibility [R-6]–2100 Patentability (2012).

[34] Gregory J. Battersby & Charles W. Grimes, Drafting Internet Agreements 2.08 (2000).

[35] Great A. & P. Tea Co. v. Supermarket Equip. Corp., 340 U.S. 147, 155 (1950)(J. Douglas concurring).

matter, and processes.[36] Utility patents include DVD players, air conditioners, plasma televisions, or genetically engineered bacteria. Internet-related patents are typically utility patents subcategorized as process patents if they qualify as new and useful.

(B) Design Patents

A design patent protects the exterior appearance of an object and that appearance must be non-functional.[37] "A design patent covers an object's non-functional visual and tactile characteristics (e.g., the shape and decoration of a table lamp, but not the way its wiring or bulb works)."[38] The ornamental design of a Coca Cola bottle or another beverage container is an example of a design patent. Design patents are relevant to Internet inventions because the USPTO considers computer-generated icons, including full screen images and type fonts, to constitute surface ornamentation.[39] Design patents are granted to those who invent a new, original, and ornamental design for an article of manufacture, though the design must be purely aesthetic and have no functional benefit. Design patents have a fourteen-year term.[40]

(C) Plant Patents

Plant patents are granted to those who invent or discover, and asexually reproduce any distinct and new variety of plant.[41] Plant patents apply to new varieties of plants, other than a tuber propagated plant or a plant found in an uncultivated state. The grant, which lasts for 20 years from the date of filing the application, protects the inventor's right to exclude others from asexually reproducing, selling, or using the plant so reproduced. Plant patents have no obvious connection to Internet law.

§ 13.4 PATENT LAW TERMS

Generally, the term of a new utility patent, which accounts for most Internet-related patents, is 20 years from the date on which the application for the patent was filed in the United States. In special cases, this can reach farther back to the date on which an earlier application for the same invention was filed. Plant patents also have a 20–year term, while design patents only have a term of 14 years from the issue date.

Utility or plant patents issued on applications filed before June 8, 1995 have a term of 17 years from the issuance of the patent or 20 years from the filing, whichever is greater. This rule was modified by the Uruguay Round Agreements Act, which gave rise to the uniform 20–year rule in effect today.[42] In the United States, the patent term begins to run at the time of filing but patent rights in most cases are not available to the patent applicant until the patent issues. U.S. patent grants are effective only within the U.S., U.S. territories, and U.S. possessions.

---

[36] 35 U.S.C. § 101.

[37] 35 U.S.C. §§ 171–173.

[38] Tony Dutra, Internet Advertising Claims Still Held Patent Eligible on High Court Mayo Related Remand, BLOOMBERG BNA ELECTRONIC COMMERCE AND LAW (June 24, 2013).

[39] USPTO, Manual of Patent Examining Procedure, 1504.01(A) (2012).

[40] 35 U.S.C. § 171.

[41] USPTO, What Are Patents? (2012).

[42] 108 Stat. 4809 (1994).

§ 13.5 SECTION 101 PATENTABLE SUBJECT MATTER

Section 101 of the Patent Act states that "any new and useful process, machine, manufacture, or composition of matter, or any new and useful improvement thereof" is patent-eligible, "subject to the conditions and requirements of this title."[43] Congress used "expansive terms" in defining the four categories of inventions eligible for patent protection under § 101: processes, machines, manufactures, and compositions of matter.[44] If a claim, under the broadest reasonable interpretation, covers an invention that does not fall within the four statutory categories, patent examiners are to make a Section 101 rejection. The table below depicts the statutory categories.

Statutory Examples	Brief Description
Process	*Gottschalk v. Benson*, 409 U.S. 63, 70 (1972) ("A process is a mode of treatment of certain materials to produce a given result. It is *an act, or a series of acts,* performed upon the subject-matter to be transformed and reduced to a different state or thing").
Machine (Product)	*Burr v. Duryee*, 68 U.S. (1 Wall.) 531, 570, (1863) (a concrete thing, consisting of parts, or of certain devices and combination of devices); includes mechanical powers or devices to perform some function or achieve a certain result).
Manufacture (Product)	*Diamond v. Chakrabarty*, 447 U.S. 303, 308 (1980) (an article produced from raw or prepared materials by giving to these materials new forms, qualities, properties, or combinations, whether by hand labor or by machinery).
Composition of Matter (Product)	*Diamond v. Chakrabarty*, 447 U.S. 303, 308 (1980) ("all compositions of two or more substances and . . . all composite articles, whether they be the results of chemical union, or of mechanical mixture, or whether they be gases, fluids, powders or solids.").

(A) Subject Matter

Patent examiners determine first whether a given claim qualifies as a process, machine, manufacture or composition of matter. If the claim is not classified as any of these four categories, the claim is ineligible. A claimed invention must be classifiable as a process, machine, manufacture, or composition of matter. Products include (1) machines, (2) articles of manufacture, and compositions of matter. A product can be both a manufacture and a composition of matter. Computer related inventions are often classifiable as machines in patent applications. If not, the claim is ineligible under § 101.

---

[43] Id.

[44] Bilski v. Kappos, 130 S. Ct. 3218, 3225 (2010).

(B) Judicial Exceptions to Patentability

If the claim falls within one of the statutory categories, the examiner is to determine whether any of the three judicial exceptions nonetheless bars such a claim. Laws of nature, natural phenomenon and abstract ideas constitute the judicial exceptions. Patent examiners therefore must ask: "Is the claim as a whole directed to a practical application of the abstract idea, law of nature or natural phenomenon?" If the answer is yes, the claim is not eligible for patent protection; it is ineligible per se.

Algorithms and formulas are not patentable because they do not fit within any of the aforementioned four categories. Abstract ideas are not patentable because they serve as the tools for scientific inquiry and technology.[45] You cannot patent formulas. The physics formula, $a = F/m$, represents Newton's second law. The equation provides the response of a body of mass m to a force F. Newton's second law of nature or other laws of nature are not patentable, but the expression of an idea is within the scope of patentable subject matter.[46] The USPTO MPEP for patent examiners gives the following examples:

(a) A claim that is directed to a machine comprising a plurality of structural elements that work together in a defined combination based on a mathematical relationship, such as a series of gears, pulleys and belts, possesses structural limitations that show that it is a tangible embodiment, providing evidence that the mathematical relationship has been applied (a practical application). Additionally, that tangible embodiment is limited by the claimed structure and would not cover all substantial practical uses of the mathematical relationship. The claim would be eligible for patent protection:

(b) On the other hand, a claim that is directed to a machine ("What is claimed is a machine that operates in accordance with F=ma.") and includes no tangible structural elements under the broadest reasonable interpretation, covers the operating principle based on a mathematical relationship with no limits on the claim scope. Thus, as no tangible embodiment is claimed, there would be no evidence of a practical application. The claim would wholly embrace the mathematical concept of F=ma and would not be eligible subject matter.

(c) As another example, a claim to a non-transitory, tangible computer readable storage medium per se that possesses structural limitations under the broadest reasonable interpretation standard to qualify as a manufacture would be patent-eligible subject matter. Adding additional claim limitations to the medium, such as executable instructions or stored data, to such a statutory eligible claim would not render the medium non-statutory, so long as the claim as a whole has a real world use and the medium does not cover substantially all practical uses of a judicial exception. The claim as a whole remains a tangible embodiment and

---

[45] Gottschalk v. Benson, Id. at 67.

[46] Descriptions of the natural operations of the world cannot be patented. "[N]o one can appropriate this power exclusively to himself, under the patent laws. The same may be said of electricity, and of any other power in nature, which is alike open to all. . . ." Le Roy v. Tatham, 14 How. (55 U.S.) 156, 175 (1852). Nor can mathematical formulas and algorithms, the concise expressions of natural laws, be patented. Gottschalk v. Benson, 409 U.S. 63, 71–72 (1972).

qualifies as a manufacture. Additional claim limitations would be evaluated in terms of whether they distinguish over the prior art.[47]

The idea/expression dichotomy is found in copyright law as well as patent law. Laws of nature are neither patentable nor protectable by copyright.

§ 13.6   ELEMENTS OF PATENTABILITY

In *Diamond v. Chakrabary*, the U.S. Supreme Court interpreted the subject matter of patents "to include anything under the sun that is made by man." The Court found that the live, human-made microorganism useful in breaking up crude oil is patentable subject matter under 35 U.S.C. § 101. Justice Burger, writing for the Court found that Chakrabary's microorganism constitutes a "manufacture" or "composition of matter" within the meaning of the patent statute. Patents are not granted for all new and useful inventions and discoveries.

Patentability requires first patent subject matter and novelty, non-obviousness, and utility. The federal patent statute requires, a claim to have some utility (§ 101) be novel (§ 102) and be non-obvious (§ 103) to be patentable. Section 101 states that patents must have novelty and utility.

(A)   Novelty

The invention must be new and demonstrably different from the prior art. Section 102 spells out what it means to be novel. The requirement for novelty in 35 U.S.C. § 102 means that a patent claim cannot already be published or used in the prior art. Section 102 states:

(A) Novelty; Prior Art—A person shall be entitled to a patent unless—

(1) the claimed invention was patented, described in a printed publication, or in public use, on sale, or otherwise available to the public before the effective filing date of the claimed invention; or

(2) the claimed invention was described in a patent issued under section 151, or in an application for patent published or deemed published under section 122(b), in which the patent or application, as the case may be, names another inventor and was effectively filed before the effective filing date of the claimed invention.

(B)   Patentability: Non–Obviousness

Section 103 requires that the claim to be nonobvious when measured against prior art. Subject matter as a whole would not have been obvious at the time to person of ordinary skill in the art. Thus, non-obviousness is measured by prior art and what would not be obvious to a person skilled in the prior art. An invention must also not be the functional equivalent of an invention covered by a previously issued patent. An invention is not patentable if the claimed subject matter was disclosed before the date of filing or before the date of priority, if a priority is claimed, of the patent application. The obviousness requirement is the most difficult obstacle to be overcome.

---

[47] USPTO.gov, MPEP Manual, Patent Subject Matter Elgibility, http://www.uspto.gov/web/offices/pac/mpep/s2106.html (last visited May 22, 2013).

(C) Patentability: Utility

The invention must be useful to satisfy the utility requirement. A claimed invention must be useful or have a utility that is specific, substantial and credible. This means that the invention must satisfy some practical use, not against public policy. The utility requirement is seldom a significant for patent prosecutors. To comply with the utility requirement of U.S. patent law, an invention must be capable of achieving some minimal useful purpose.

(D) Statutory Bar

A patent application must be filed within a year of public disclosure or use or thus be statutorily barred. The one-year statutory bar states: "A person shall be entitled to a patent unless-(a) the invention was known or used by others in this country, or patented or described in a printed publication in this or a foreign country, before the invention thereof by the applicant." Under 35 U.S.C. § 102(b), a patent was invalid if "the invention was in public use or on sale in this country" more than one year prior to the date the patent application was filed. "Whether a patent is invalid for a public use or sale is a question of law, reviewed *de novo*, based on underlying facts, reviewed for substantial evidence following a jury verdict." The party challenging the validity of a patent must prove by clear and convincing evidence that the product used or on sale prior to the critical date was embodied by the claimed invention.

§ 13.7 USPTO APPLICATIONS

(A) Overview of Patent Application Process

The United States Patent and Trademark Office ("USPTO"), located in Crystal City, Virginia, is the federal agency that issues U.S. patents. Inventors file applications with the USPTO, a federal agency of the U.S. Department of Commerce responsible for issuing patents. There are two kinds of patent applications, provisional (12–month grace period) and regular (20 year period measured from filing date of regular patent). Provisional applications are placeholders that give companies time to file a regular provision. Provisional applications are governed by 35 U.S.C. § 111(b). The purpose of a provisional patent is to serve as a placeholder for priority assuming that the provisional application is converted to a regular application. Most countries have their own patent office. Parties seeking patent rights across borders will need to file claims in each country's patent office. Alternately, an application can be filed under the Patent Cooperation Treaty ("PCT"), which equates to an application in every country that is a signatory to the treaty.

Under U.S. patent law, utility patent applications consist of a brief abstract of the invention, background about the invention, descriptions of drawings, a detailed explanation of how to make/use the invention, and one or more claims. Patents can be "conceptualized as having two parts: the specification and the claims." The patent applicant must fulfill the disclosure requirements, thus they must provide a written description to allow enablement, and disclose the best mode. The *quid pro quo* for a patent is the exclusive use of the claim in return for disclosing the best way of carrying out the invention (best mode). A patent application is required to contain drawings, if drawings are necessary to understand the subject matter to be patented. Most patent applications contain drawings. The drawings must show every feature of the invention as specified in the claims. Omission of drawings may cause an application to be considered incomplete and no application filing date will be granted by the USPTO.

Anatomy of Section 112 Disclosures

Written Description	Explains with specificity what is claimed or what the invention is
Enablement	How to make/use invention, Test: Person of ordinary skill in relevant subject area of invention (subject area called an "art") without further experimentation.
Best Mode	Best way of making or using the invention.

(B) Anatomy of a Patent Application

The first page of every patent gives general information such as the inventor's name, the attorney's name, and priority date. A patent application will typically include (1) a specification, (2) a drawing, and (3) an oath by the applicant. Every patent begins with a short title of the invention. The specifications are "a written description of the invention, and of the manner and process of making it and using it, in such full, clear, concise, and exact terms . . . to make and use the same." The specification concludes with "one or more claims particularly pointing out and distinctly claiming the subject matter, which the applicant regards as his invention." Claims may be drafted as independent claims, dependent claims and multiple dependent claims.

With the dependent form, reference is made to a claim previously described. "A claim in dependent form shall be construed to incorporate by reference all the limitations of the claim to which it refers." Multiple dependent claims "shall be construed to incorporate by reference all the limitations of the particular claim in relation to which it is being considered." The USPTO Commissioner may require a patent applicant to "furnish a model of convenient size to exhibit advantageously the several parts of his invention."

(C) Examination of Patent Application

Section 111 sets forth the elements of a U.S. patent application that shall include: "(A) a specification as prescribed by Section 112 of this title; (B) a drawing as prescribed by Section 113 of this title; and (C) an oath by the applicant as prescribed by Section 115 of this title.[48] Section 111 sets forth two kinds of patent applications, regular and provisional.[49]

---

[48] 35 U.S.C. § 111.

[49] Section 35 U.S.C. § 111(b) spells out the ground rules for provisional applications: "(1) AUTHORIZATION.—A provisional application for patent shall be made or authorized to be made by the inventor, except as otherwise provided in this title, in writing to the Director. Such application shall include—(A) a specification as prescribed by the first paragraph of section 112 of this title; and (B) a drawing as prescribed by section 113 of this title. (2) CLAIM.—A claim, as required by the second through fifth paragraphs of section 112, shall not be required in a provisional application. 35 U.S.C. § 111(b)(1)(A)–(B). In addition, the provisional application "must be accompanied by the fee required by law." 35 U.S.C. § 111(b)(3).

(B) The fee may be submitted after the specification and any required drawing are submitted, within such period and under such conditions, including the payment of a surcharge, as may be prescribed by the

Examiners investigate complete applications (but not provisional ones) to determine whether the "five primary requirements of patentability are satisfied: (1) Patentable subject matter, (2) novelty, (3) utility, (4) non-obviousness, and (5) enablement." Most generally, patent claim consists of the elements comprising the invention. A patent examiner may reject a claim because it is non-statutory subject matter or is obvious or anticipated in prior art. Every case involving a § 101 issue must begin with this question: "What, if anything, did the applicant invented or discovered?" Stated generally, examiners determine whether the applicant adequately describes how to make and use the invention.

The original patent law system in the United States did not require patent examination. Until 1836, no administrative body examined the validity of patents. The federal Patent Act, enacted in 1952, is codified in Title 35 of U.S. Code. The USPTO patent examiners are "persons of legal knowledge and scientific ability" who determine the patentability of inventions. Patent prosecution is conducted by registered members of the patent bar. Patent examiners examine the claims of an applicant to determine whether it is patentable. The patent claims define the matter and scope of the invention.

One of the principal tasks of the patent examiner is to compare the claims with prior art to determine novelty and non-obviousness. An examiner must also evaluate whether the combination of claimed elements exists in prior art. Examiners also decide if the statutory requirements of enablement, written description, and best mode are satisfied.[50]

(D) Specifications

The specifications include the description and the claims. The specifications will generally summarize or describe the invention as a whole. "When a patentee thus describes the features of the "present invention" as a whole, this description limits the scope of the invention."[51] "The specification is a written description of the invention and of the manner and process of making and using the same."[52] The specifications of the patent application includes the drawings, the written description of the invention, and the description of how to make and use the invention concluding with the claims, which begin on a new page. Claims must "particularly point out and distinctly claim the subject matter which the application regards as his invention."[53] The specification must be in clear, full, concise, and exact terms to enable any person skilled in the art or science to which the invention pertains to make and use the same. Specifications are the part of the patent application showing the examiner how a claim is distinguished from other inventions. "It must describe completely a specific embodiment of the process; machine, manufacture, composition of matter or improvement invented, and must explain the mode of operation or principle whenever applicable."[54] "The best mode

---

Director. (C) Upon failure to submit the fee within such prescribed period, the application shall be regarded as abandoned, unless it is shown to the satisfaction of the Director that the delay in submitting the fee was unavoidable or unintentional. (4) FILING DATE.—The filing date of a provisional application shall be the date on which the specification and any required drawing are received in the Patent and Trademark Office.

[50] 35 U.S.C. § 101.

[51] Verizon Services Corp. v. Vonage Holdings Corp., 503 F.3d 1295, 1308 (Fed. Cir. 2007).

[52] USPTO, Manual of Patent Examining Procedure, 608.01 (2006).

[53] 35 U.S.C. § 112.

[54] 37 C.F.R. § 1.71.

contemplated by the inventor of carrying out his invention must be set forth."[55] The best mode can be conceptualized as involving two prongs:

> First, it must be determined whether, at the time the application was filed, the inventor possessed a best mode for practicing the invention. This subjective inquiry focuses on the inventor's state of mind at the time of filing. Second, if the inventor did possess a best mode, it must be determined whether the written description disclosed the best mode such that a person skilled in the art could practice it. This is an objective inquiry, focusing on the scope of the claimed invention and the level of skill in the art.[56]

Technically claims are also part of the specifications, but practitioners treat specifications and claims as distinctively different concepts. The specification shall conclude with one or more claims particularly pointing out and distinctly claiming the subject matter, which the applicant regards as his invention.

(E) Patent Claiming

Claims are the metes and bounds of an invention and describe what is being protected by a patent. In a patent infringement case, the trial judge construes the claim in what is called a Markman Hearing. A patent owner's monopoly is delineated by the claims so the applicant "must particularly point out and distinctly claim the subject matter which the applicant regards as his invention." "To prove literal infringement, a plaintiff must show that the accused device contains each and every limitation of the asserted claims." In patent infringement cases, the court must first construe the disputed claims and then compare the claims to the allegedly infringing devices.

(F) Enablement

Specifications must not only describe in full and exact terms the claim but also satisfy enablement. Enablement as the term suggests means the claim must "enable" a person of ordinary skill in the relevant art or science to make and use the invention. Enablement is a separate requirement from the written description. An invention could be adequately described without being enabling, such as a chemical formula with no disclosed or apparent method of making; or be enabled without adequate description, such as a method of making a material without any specific formulation. The public policy underlying enablement is to prevent overly broad patent grants. The patent examiner will ultimately grant the patent or reject it. Once there is a final rejection or issuance, the correspondence between the examiner and the applicant is made public in a file known as the "file history" or the "prosecution history." With the age of the Internet, the file wrapper is virtual.

(G) Patent Invalidity

The Patent Act provides that "[a] patent shall be presumed valid" and that "[t]he burden of establishing invalidity of a patent or any claim thereof shall rest on the party asserting such invalidity." Patent invalidity must be established by clear and

---

[55] Id.

[56]Gene Quinn, Best Mode Requirement, IPWATCHDOG.COM (Feb. 15, 2008), http://www.ipwatchdog.com/patent/advanced-patent/best-mode/.

convincing evidence. Clear and convincing evidence produces an abiding conviction that the truth of the factual contentions are highly probable.

To anticipate a patent claim, a prior art reference must describe each and every claim limitation and enable one of skill in the art to practice an embodiment of the claimed invention without undue experimentation. Obviousness is a question of law based on factual underpinnings. "To invalidate a patent claim based on obviousness, a challenger must demonstrate by clear and convincing evidence that a skilled artisan would have been motivated to combine the teachings of the prior art references to achieve the claimed invention, and that the skilled artisan would have had a reasonable expectation of success in doing so."

Grounds for Invalidity

No Subject Matter	Non-statutory subject matter
Double Patenting	Another patent or pending application with the same claim
Section 112, No Enablement	Claim is not adequately described so that a person skilled in the art can use or make the invention. The disclosures must be so a person in the arts can practice it (enablement).
Section 102, Novelty, Non-obviousness	Claim was anticipated in prior art

"Internet and business method/E–Commerce patents are also particularly subject to invalidity findings based on lack of enablement and/or utility."[57] Problems arise for E–Commerce patents in meeting the describing "the claimed invention sufficiently to enable one skilled in the art to make and use the invention. 35 U.S.C. § 101 requires that the invention have a useful purpose, or Utility."[58]

(H) Patent Terms

The term of a utility patent "filed prior to June 8, 1995 is the later of (1) 17 years from the date of issuance of the patent, or (2) 20 years from the first U.S. filing date for the patent." On April 1, 2013, the USPTO "published an Interim Final Rule implementing several changes made to the patent term adjustment statute by the AIA Technical Corrections Act of January 14, 2013."[59] The Interim Rule provides:

Effective immediately, PTA no longer needs to be reviewed and challenged at allowance. For any patent granted on or after January 14, 2013, a patentee should file a post-issuance Application for PTA to request correction of any PTA errors that occurred at any time during application pendency. There will be a transition period for the new rules, in which the patentee of a patent granted on or after

---

[57] Bay Area Intellectual Property Group, LLC, Business Method/Internet/E–CommercePatents, http://www.bayareaip.com/Internet_eCommerce_Business_Method_Patent/Internet_eCommerce_Business_Method_Patent.htm.

[58] Id.

[59] Fish and Richardson, Patent Alert—Revisions to Patent Term Adjustment: Interim Final Rule (April 5, 2013).

January 14, 2013, who previously filed (or could have filed) an Application for PTA under the old rules to challenge PTA at allowance may file again under the new rules to request correction of any PTA error that occurred at any time during application pendency. Such a further post-issuance Application for PTA is a prerequisite for later filing a civil action (see section (2) below), since without it there would be no USPTO decision under the new rules to set the 180-day period for filing a civil action.[60]

(I) Assignment, and Sale of Patents

Patent law provides for the transfer or sale of a patent by a written agreement called an "assignment" that can transfer the entire interest in the patent. With an assignment, the owner of the patent is the assignor and assignee is the recipient of the patent rights. Once an assignment is made, the assignee has the same rights as the original patentee. Patent licensing is the chief way a company commodifies its patent portfolio and comes in different types: broadly classified as exclusive, semi-exclusive or non-exclusive.

§ 13.8 INTERNET RELATED PATENTS

Dan Burk was the first scholar to address the dilemmas of dissolving "geographic, political, and temporal barriers made possible by global computer networks may pose a new challenge to the operation of U.S. patent law—a challenge not yet fully realized and likely impossible for the framers of the present patent code to anticipate, but a challenge whose parameters can already be seen. Differences between the laws of jurisdictions mean that network users run the risk of violating the law in one country or another."[61]

(A) Software Patents

Internet-related patents are relatively recent and as recently as the 1980s, it was unclear whether software could be patented. In recent years, there has been a large number of Internet business method patents issued. Today software patents are primarily utility patents including compilers, application programs, and protection for "process or method performed by a computer game."[62] Disputes over software patents are emblematic of a litigation crisis since the development of the Internet.[63] Many practitioners and policymakers contend that the USPTO needs to reduce the scope of software patents or eliminate them altogether. [64]

During the 1980s, the patentability of software-related inventions was an unsettled question. In the early software industry, lawyers used trade secrets or the

---

[60] Id.

[61] Dan L. Burk, Patents in Cyberspace: Territoriality and Infringement on Global Computer Networks, 68 TUL. L. REV. 1, 38-39 (1993).

[62] See e.g., Altari Games Corp. v. Suffolk Software Company of America, Inc., 975 F.2d 832 (Fed. Cir. 1992).

[63] JAMES BESSEN & MICHAEL J. MEURER, PATENT FAILURE: HOW JUDGES, BUREAUCRATS, AND LAWYERS PUT INNOVATORS AT RISK 2008) at 143. (presenting data from the late 1990s finding that the annual cost of software patent litigation was $3.88 billion versus only .10 billion in profits realized from software claims).

64 Andrew T. Spence, The Patent, Trial and Appeal Board Construes 'Processor' as Means-Plus-Function in the Latest Salvo Against Computer-Implemented Inventions, BNA Bloomberg: Electronic commerce & law report (May 17, 2013).

law of copyright assuming that software was not patentable. The electronic commerce infrastructure is built on bedrock of software patents owned by International Business Machines Corporation ("IBM"), Oracle Corporation, Novell, Inc., and Microsoft. IBM was one of the first software makers to seek protection for patents. IBM is the world's leading owner of software patents and earned $650 million in royalties from its patent portfolio in 1996. [65]

Amazon.com is the owner of one of the best-known Internet patents. Amazon.com's "1–click method" online ordering patent.[66] U.S. Patent 5960411 (1990), is entitled "Method and system for placing a purchase order via a communications network." The patentability of software was well established in the U.S. by the late 1990s. Software patents have been granted for such diverse Internet related activities as hyperlinking, audio software, file formats, and search engines. A software patent application must clearly describe what the computer does when it performs the steps dictated by software code.

Software patents are on the rise because of the increased competence of the USPTO and the formulation of Examination Guidelines for Computer–Related Inventions.[67] Software was conceptualized as unpatentable subject matter until the 1980s because it incorporated algorithms. In *Gottschalk v. Benson,*[68] the U.S. Supreme Court ruled a discovery of a novel and useful mathematical formula may not be patented. In *Benson*, the Supreme Court considered claims to computer-implemented methods "for converting binary-coded decimal (BCD) numerals into pure binary numerals." [69] Justice William O. Douglas, writing for the majority, said a process must transform and reduce material to a different state and the formula was not patentable without Congressional authorization.[70]

In *Parker v. Flook,* [71] the Court considered whether a "Method For Updating Alarm Limits" was protectable where the only novel feature of the method was a mathematical formula claim for a method of calculation.[72] In *Parker*, the Court did not automatically disqualify claim merely because it contained an algorithm, but without a tangible output, one cannot patent "a novel and useful mathematical formula."[73] In *Diamond v. Diehr,*[74] the U.S. Supreme Court recognized for the first time a process controlled by computer software as being patentable.[75] In *Diamond*, the invention at issue was a computer

---

[65] Big Blue is Out to Collar Software Scofflaws, BUS. WK. (Mar. 17, 1997) at 29.

[66] U.S. Patent No. 5,960,411 (issued September 28, 1999).

[67] United States Patent & Trademark Office, Examination Guidelines for Computer–Related Invention, 1184 U.S. PAT. & TRADEMARK OFFICE OFFICIAL GAZETTE 87 (1996).

[68] 409 U.S. 63 (1972).

[69] Id. at 64.

[70] Id.

[71] 437 U.S. 584 (1978).

[72] The rules defining the pre-existing constraints and operations of the human environment are laws of nature and abstract realities, not patent-eligible inventions. "The underlying notion is that a scientific principle, such as that expressed in respondent's algorithm, reveals a relationship that has always existed." Parker v. Flook, 437 U.S. 584, 593 n.15 (1978). "'[A]n original cause; a motive; these cannot be patented, as no one can claim in either of them an exclusive right.'" Flook, 437 U.S. at 589 (quoting Le Roy, 14 How. (55 U.S.) at 175).

[73] Id.

[74] 450 U.S. 175 (1981).

[75] Diamond v. Chakrabarty, 447 U.S. 303, 308-09 (1980) ("In choosing such expansive terms as 'manufacture' and 'composition of matter,' modified by the comprehensive 'any,' Congress plainly contemplated that the patent laws would be given wide scope.")

program that determined how rubber should be heated in order to be best "cured." The U.S. Supreme Court reasoned that the invention was not merely a mathematical algorithm, but a useful and nonobvious process for molding rubber that was patentable.[76]

In *Akamai Technologies, Inc. v. Limelight Networks, Inc.*,[77] a jury found Limelight infringed an Internet content delivery patent asserted by Akamai Technologies, and handed down a verdict of $45.5 million. In *Akamai*, the patent claim covered software for delivering the embedded objects of a web page. Limelight argues a reasonable jury could conclude the company believed it did not infringe or cause others to infringe Akamai's patents because of Akamai's prior history of suing infringers.[78] Software patents are controversial in large part because of computer professionals' distrust of them. [79]

Suits brought by Patent Assertion Entities ("PAEs") "jumped by nearly 250 percent in just the last two years, rising from 29 percent of all infringement suits to 62 percent of all infringement suits. Estimates suggest that PAEs may have threatened over 100,000 companies with patent infringement last year alone."[80] PAEs focus on the software industry "tak[ing] advantage of uncertainty about the scope or validity of patent claims, especially in software-related patents because of the relative novelty of the technology and because it has been difficult to separate the "function" of the software (e.g. to produce a medical image) from the "means" by which that function is accomplished."[81]

(B) E–Business Methods

Prior to the mid-1990s, business methods were considered to be too abstract to be patentable. Business methods qualify as "patentable eligible subject matter" if they are a new and useful process. At a bare minimum, the process must produce a useful, concrete, and tangible result to qualify as a business method.[82] Conventional wisdom states that business methods were not patentable and were exceptions to the general rule that processes are patentable. In 1908, the Second Circuit held a bookkeeping system, whose purpose was to prevent embezzlement by wait staff, was an unpatentable algorithm,

---

[76] Id. at 308-09 ("In choosing such expansive terms as 'manufacture' and 'composition of matter,' modified by the comprehensive 'any,' Congress plainly contemplated that the patent laws would be given wide scope.").

[77] 2008 WL 364401 (D. Mass. 2008).

[78] JAMES BESSEN & MICHAEL J. MEURER, PATENT FAILURE: HOW JUDGES, BUREAUCRATS, AND LAWYERS PUT INNOVATORS AT RISK 143 (2008) (presenting data from the late 1990s finding that the annual cost of software patent litigation was $3.88 billion in contrast to a total of $10 billion in profits realized from software claims).

[79] "Software patents have been controversial in part because the software-publishing industry grew up largely without patents and most computer professionals oppose patenting software. But judicial decisions during the 1990s eliminated certain obstacles to software patents, and now close to 200,000 software patents have been granted. . . . [D]espite being a relatively new area for patenting, software patents accounted for 38 percent of the total cost of patent litigation to public firms during the late 1990s. This does not appear to be a temporary problem that is dissipating as the Patent Office adapts—the probability that a software patent will be litigated has been increasing substantially rather than decreasing." JAMES BESSEN AND MICHAEL MEURER, PATENT FAILURE: HOW JUDGES, BUREAUCRATS, AND LAWYERS PUT INNOVATORS AT RISK 23 (2008).

[80] WHITE HOUSE, PATENT ASSERTION AND U.S. INNOVATION, Executive Office of the President (Report was prepared by the President's Council of Economic Advisers, the National Economic Council, and the Office of Science & Technology Policy (June 2013) at Executive Summary.

[81] Id.

[82] State Street Bank & Trust Co. v. Signature Fin. Group, Inc., 149 F.3d 1368 (Fed. Cir. 1998) (holding business methods are patentable). Technically, business method patents are utility patents for any process synthesizing software or code with business techniques or methodologies.

thereby carving out the business method exception in *Hotel Security Checking Co. v. Lorraine Co.*[83] Courts accepted this business method exception for ninety years until the Federal Circuit reversed course in *State Street Bank & Trust Co. v. Signature Fin. Group, Inc.*[84] No single development has spurred the growth of Internet-related patents more than the *State Street* case that legitimated business method patents previously thought to be unpatentable.

In *State Street*, Judge Giles Rich, writing for the panel, accepted a patent held by Signature Financial Group for a "hub and spoke" method of computing interest in mutual funds. The business method made it possible for mutual fund managers to pool their assets into a partnership, allowing tax advantages and administrative savings. The mere presence of a mathematical algorithm does not preordain that the USPTO will reject a patent claim. The Federal Circuit held a programmed computer using this mathematical algorithm was patentable so long as it produced a useful, concrete, and tangible result. In *State Street*, the court found the algorithm or formula produced a "concrete and tangible result," namely a final share price for each mutual fund within the partnership as determined by their contributions to the pool, was a practical application and thus patentable. Since *State Street*, the number of business method patents has skyrocketed.

The validation of business methods patents was extended in *AT&T Corp. v. Excel Communications, Inc.* when the Federal Circuit approved a patent incorporating Boolean algebra to determine the long-distance carriers involved in a telephone call creating a switching signal for billing purposes. The court reasoned because this was not an attempt to patent the Boolean principle, but rather a patent on the process to create the discrete switching signal, it was patentable subject matter. The patent created a concrete and tangible result, and was therefore patentable. In the wake of *State Street* and *AT&T*, the USPTO required business method patents to press forward the technological arts. Only four years later in *Ex Parte Lundgren*, the Board of Patent Appeals and Interferences found no statutory or legal requirement for a technological arts test.

In *Ex parte Langemyr*, the Patent Trademark Office ("PTO") Board said an algorithm for modeling a physical system "executed in a computer apparatus" was not tied to a particular machine, but could be performed on any general purpose computer, and was therefore a process, rather than a machine. Because Langemyr's invention did not physically transform matter or energy from one form to another, it was not classifiable as a patentable process. The majority of software programs can be executed on any general purpose machine, and manipulate data and numbers, rather than matter or energy. Today, the USPTO uses a specifically devised classification system for business process patents. Most E–Commerce, Internet, or data processing business methods are classified as Class 705. The number of Class 705 patents issuing skyrocketed from 120 to 1,191 from 1996 to 2006. Most E–Commerce methods, but not all, are related to financial and business data processing.

Priceline, for example, holds a patent on an auction method for selling tickets. Netcraft filed suit against eBay and PayPal for infringing upon two related business method patents with variations on Internet Billing Methods. The USPTO has approved scores of business method patents for Internet purchasing, online advertising, and

---

[83] 160 F. 467 (2d Cir. 1908).
[84] 149 F.3d 1368 (Fed. Cir. 1998).

marketing. The USPTO was criticized for granting too many e-business patents whose only novelty was that they were Internet-related.

(C) Post–State Street Developments

Tens of thousands of business method patent applications have been filed since *State Street* opened the floodgates. In 2000, "Amazon.com was granted a patent on its affiliates program, which allows owners of other Websites to refer customers to Amazon.com in exchange for a fee." Amazon.com's "one-click" technology for online shopping was issued a patent. Another example is Amazon.com's 1–Click, a "method, and system for placing a purchase order via a communications network" sparked one of the most famous Internet patent debates. The patent permitted customers to make online purchases with a single click, using a pre-defined address and credit card number. A federal court granted Amazon.com an injunction enjoining Barnes & Noble for using a single-click Express Checkout on their online store. The parties settled before a trial to determine the validity of the one-click method. Richard Stallman, President of the Free Software Foundation, published a letter calling for a boycott of Amazon.com, saying the Barnes & Noble suit was "an attack against the World Wide Web and against E–Commerce in general."

Jeff Bezos, Chairman and CEO of Amazon.com, published an open letter in response calling for patent law reforms. Bezos proposed to abbreviate the life of the patent term to three to five years for software and business method patents. The rationale for an abbreviated patent term is that most software or business methods will have a short shelf life. Amazon.com and Barnes & Noble settled their patent infringement dispute in 2000, with Barnes & Noble licensing the 1–Click patent. In 2006, in response to a request by blogger and patent enthusiast Peter Calveley, the USPTO opened the 1–Click patent for re-examination. Amazon's patent underwent reexamination by the USPTO in October 2007. After four-years of reexamination, Amazon's much-maligned 1–click patent is emerging from reexamination largely unscathed. In a recent notice of intent to issue a reexamination certificate, the USPTO confirmed the patentability of original claims 6–10 and amended claims 1–5 and 11–26. The approved-of amendment adds the seeming trivial limitation that the one-click system operates as part of a "shopping cart model." Thus, for infringement to occur, an E–Commerce retailer must use a shopping cart model (presumably non-1–click) alongside of the 1–click version.

(D) Limits on Business Methods

Congress amended the U.S. Patent Act to create a prior commercial use defense limiting the reach of business methods.

> It shall be a defense to an action for infringement under section 271 of this title with respect to any subject matter that would otherwise infringe one or more claims for a method in the patent being asserted against a person, if such person had, acting in good faith, actually reduced the subject matter to practice at least 1 year before the effective filing date of such patent, and commercially used the subject matter before the effective filing date of such patent.

(E) Blocking Patents

Patents have multiple functions. If "the exclusionary power provided by patents is aimed at keeping competitors off a particular market or technology field rather than at protecting an invention, patents become a strategic blocking" device. Patents may be used as a sword (positively) or as a shield (negatively). Blocking patents negative role is to prevent others from using their invention without licensing their technology. Blocking patents, for example, delayed the development of Internet standards in the late 1990s and first decade of the twentieth century. Competitors will enter into cross-licensing agreements to allow the mutual developments of their inventions.

§ 13.9 INTERNET–RELATED PATENT LITIGATION

(A) Direct Infringement

The Patent Act provides that: "[e]xcept as otherwise provided in [the Act], whoever without authority makes . . . any patented invention, within the United States * * * during the term of the patent therefore, infringes the patent." Direct infringement is predicated on a theory of strict liability, whereas induced and contributory infringement require showing both the presence of an underlying act of direct infringement and that the accused had a specific intent to aid and abet the direct infringement. In *Florida Prepaid Postsecondary Educ. Expense Bd. v. Coll. Sav. Bank,*[85] the U.S. Supreme Court observed that "[a]ctions predicated on direct patent infringement . . . do not require any showing of intent to infringe; instead, knowledge and intent are considered only with respect to damages."[86] The new patent litigation explosion is happening in the field of Internet-related infringement lawsuits. In *Summit 6 Inc. v. Research in Motion,*[87] Summit 6 Inc., was the holder of a patent covering software that automatically processes digital photos before they are transmitted over a network by client devices, such as cell phones. Summit 6 filed suits against multiple Internet companies including "Research in Motion, Samsung, Multiply, Facebook, and Photobucket for infringing their patent by operating websites where digital content is compressed or otherwise processed on users' personal computers or mobile devices before being uploaded to and received by a remote server."[88] "The plaintiff filed suit in the United States District Court for the Northern District of Texas, accusing the defendants Samsung Electronics Co. Ltd. and Samsung Telecommunications America, Inc., Research in Motion, Multiply, Facebook, and Photobucket of patent infringement."[89] All defendants except for Samsung Electronics and Samsung Telecommunications settled pre-trial. The jury found that the defendants infringed Summit 6's patent and awarded $15 million in damages.[90]

(B) Contributory Infringement

Patent law holds liable not only those who infringe a patent, but also those who assist others in doing so. A party can assist in an act of infringement either by directing another to infringe (induced infringement), or by supplying parts or services that are specially suited to infringe (contributory infringement). Contributory infringement is defined:

---

[85] 527 U.S. 627, 645 (1999).

[86] 5 DONALD CHISUM, PATENTS § 16.02[2], 16–31 (rev. ed. 1998) ("It is, of course, elementary, that an infringement may be entirely inadvertent and unintentional and without knowledge of the patent.").

[87] 2013 WL 3214329 (N.D. Tex., April 15, 2013).

[88] Id.

[89] Id.

[90] Id.

Whoever offers to sell or sells within the United States or imports into the United States a component of a patented machine, manufacture, combination or composition, or a material or apparatus for use in practicing a patented process, constituting a material part of the invention, knowing the same to be especially adapted for use in an infringement of such patent, and not a staple article or commodity of commerce suitable for substantial non-infringing use, shall be liable as a contributory infringement. [91]

(C) Inducement

Section 271(b) recognizes liability for actively inducing infringement.[92] "Unlike direct infringement of a patent, induced infringement is not a strict liability tort. Inducement requires that the alleged infringer knowingly induced infringement and possessed specific intent to encourage another's infringement."[93] Patent inducement, however, "does not require that the induced party be an agent of the inducer or be acting under the inducer's direction or control to such an extent that the act of the induced party can be attributed to the inducer as a direct infringer. It is enough that the inducer causes, urges, encourages, or aids the infringing conduct and that the induced conduct is carried out." [94]

"When a single actor commits all the elements of patent infringement, that actor is liable for direct infringement under 35 U.S.C. § 271(a). When a single actor induces another actor to commit all the elements of infringement, the first actor is liable for induced infringement under § 271(b)."[95] The federal circuit explains that patent inducement, unlike direct infringement, is not a strict liability cause of action:

> Induced infringement is in some ways narrower than direct infringement and in some ways broader. Unlike direct infringement, induced infringement is not a strict liability tort; it requires that the accused inducer act with knowledge that the induced acts constitute patent infringement. In fact, this court has described the required intent as follows: "[I]nducement requires that the alleged infringer knowingly induced infringement and possessed specific intent to encourage another's infringement." On the other hand, inducement does not require that the induced party be an agent of the inducer or be acting under the inducer's direction or control to such an extent that the act of the induced party can be attributed to the inducer as a direct infringer. It is enough that the inducer "cause[s], urge[s], encourage[s], or aid[s]" the infringing conduct and that the induced conduct is carried out. [96]

The takeaway point is that patent inducement is more difficult to prove than direct inducement. First, the patent owner must be prepared to demonstrate that actions by the induced party are attributable to the inducer. Second, the patent owner must demonstrate that the inducer had knowledge of its inducement. Finally, the elements of direct infringement by the induced party must be proven.

---

[91] 35 U.S.C. § 271(b).

[92] Id.

[93] Akamai Techs., Inc. v. Limelight Networks, Inc., 692 F.3d 1301, 1308 (Fed. Cir. 2012).

[94] Id.

[95] Id. at 1305.

[96] Id. at 1308.

(D) Emblematic Lawsuits

In *DDR Holdings v. Hotels.com,*[97] a jury found two companies infringed on patents allowing websites to offer products from a centralized location to consumers referred from other websites without the consumers becoming aware they had left the referring website. DDR, the plaintiffs, contended they were co-owners of the patents, and said they founded an Internet business in the late 1990s based on their invention.[98] The patent allegedly related to computerized methods and equipment that permit better electronic commerce through the Internet.[99] The plaintiffs claimed that a large number of well-known Internet companies infringed their patent through which they offered "products from a centralized location to consumers who are referred from a website, without the consumers easily perceiving that they have left the referring website."[100] The patent in dispute enabled owners of referring websites to profit each time a consumer purchased goods or services, "without the need to manage the offsite product delivery system or losing the customers to a competing website."[101] DDR contended: "A number of companies were infringing on the patents by making, causing to be made, using, selling, offering for sale and/or importing systems, devices and/or services that practice or embody the patented invention as part of their normal operation and intended operation."[102]

The case was decided against only two defendants, Digital River, Inc., and National Leisure Group. However, DDR's action was against a host of Internet companies. And their complaint contended that "Expedia Inc. infringed on the patents with its TravelNow/EAN and WWTC platforms for United.com and Market E websites. DDR claimed Travelocity.com LP infringed on the patents with its Travelpn and WCT platforms for American Express, AAA, AAA Washington, Bestfares, Cheapfares.com, Cheapseats, Continental.com Hotels, and Yahoo! websites. DDR said International Cruise & Excursion Gallery Inc. and OurVacationStore.com infringed on the patents with their OVS/IC templating platforms for American Express and RCI websites."[103] DDR filed suits "against Hotels.com LP, Expedia Inc., Travelocity.com LP, Site59.com LLC, Internetwork Publishing Corporation d/b/a/ Lodging.com, Neat Group Corporation, Orbitz Worldwide LLC, International Cruise & Excursion Gallery Inc., Ourvacationstore.com Inc., National Leisure Group Inc., World Travel Holdings Inc. and Digital River Inc." in federal court in Texas.[104] DDR contended that the defendants committed direct infringement literally and through the doctrine of equivalents "or by inducing   or   contributing   to   their   nfringement   by   others."[105] DDR sought monetary damages under the Patent Act, an injunction and a declaratory judgment.[106] Moreover, the defendants argued that they did not infringe DDR's patent, either   directly   or   under   the   doctrine   of   equivalents.

---

[97] 2012 WL 7996942 (E. D. Tex., Oct. 12, 2012).

[98] Id.

[99] Id.

[100] Id.

[101] Id.

[102] Id.

[103] Id.

[104] Id.

[105] Id.

[106] Id.

The two defendants going to trial contended that DDR's patent was invalid because it was obvious and that they did not infringe a valid and/or enforceable claim of the patents directly, literally, or under the doctrine of equivalents.[107] The jury found that the plaintiff had proved both defendants directly infringed their patents awarding $750,000 in damages.[108] The final judgment imposed "$750,000 against e-commerce website builder Digital River Inc. and another $750,000 against travel company National Leisure Group Inc., and also said that DDR is entitled to prejudgment interest in the litigation,"[109]

(E) E–Business Patent Trolls

The Business Software Alliance declares the patent troll's business, as litigation abuse because these patent owners have no economic purpose in obtaining patent protection other than holding up companies who build software products. On June 4, 2013, the White House rolled out legislative proposals to control the rising tide of patent trolls. "President Barack Obama spoke about the problem of patent litigation at a recent Google+ hangout, saying that patent trolls "don't actually produce anything themselves" and instead develop a business model "to essentially leverage and hijack somebody else's idea and see if they can extort some money out of them." Patent trolls or non-practicing entities (NPEs) do not serve a beneficial role and havea chilling effect on innovation by blocking Internet-related claims. Critics fear outsized Internet-related business methods will result in companies paying higher licensing fees in its online activities to NPEs. Patent law reformers call for Congress to act to thwart a litigation crisis created by abusive patent trolls. One of the problems with the concept of the patent troll is the over inclusive descprition, which includes many universities and research institutes that have patent portfolios but do not themselves use them in inventions. Section 19(d) of the America Invents Act is aimed at patent trolls by eliminating "the practice of joining unrelated defendants in the same suit."[110] This provision will allow unrelated defendants to be joined in a single action only if they are jointly or severally liable or there are common questions of fact.[111]

(F) The Supreme Court's Patent Jurisprudence

(1) Importance of Injunctive Relief to Protect Internet Patents

Courts have traditionally been inclined to grant injunctions against patent infringement. The injunctive remedy is often more important than monetary damages in intellectual property cases. The injunction is classified as an equitable remedy and used to order defendants to refrain from infringing intellectual property rights. Vuitton et Fils S.A. ("Vuitton"), for example, seeks injunctions against counterfeiters that infringe the Vuitton trademark by selling goods on online auction sites. The standards for the issuance of injunctive relief require a showing of the inadequacy of legal remedies. In Internet cases injunctions are often critical, because these cases are about market share and primacy and not just about the money. Under Rule 65 of the Fed. R.

---

[107] Id.

[108] Id.

[109] Ana Sarfo, Judge Upholds a $1.5M Verdict for NPE in Eastern Texas, Law360 (June 24, 2013).

[110] Tracie L. Bryant, The American Invents Act: Slaying Trolls, Limiting Joinder, 25 HARV. J. LAW & TECH. 674, 675 (2012).

[111] Id.

Civ. P., a plaintiff must demonstrate irreparable harm and hardship that outweighs that of the defendant, and that they are likely to succeed on the merits. Judges are also to consider whether an order of injunctive relief will harm the public. In Internet cases, the patent owner will seek to enjoin another from using its patent.

In *eBay Inc. v. MercExchange L.L.C.*,[112] the Supreme Court unanimously determined that a federal court should not automatically issue an injunction simply because they have found patent infringement. The case arose out of dispute between eBay, the Internet's largest auction site and MercExchange, which owned U.S. Patent 5,845,265, which covers eBay's "Buy It Now" function. In 2000, eBay initiated negotiations with MercExchange to purchase its online auction patent portfolio. When eBay abandoned the negotiations to purchase the patent, MercExchange filed suit against eBay for patent infringement. MercExchange prevailed in a 2003 Virginia jury trial that found eBay had willfully infringed the patent incorporated in its "Buy It Now" function. MercExchange sought an injunction to prevent eBay's continual use of the patent, but the federal trial court denied its request. The Federal Circuit Court of Appeals reversed the trial court reasoning that its decision was consistent with its long-standing practice of issuing permanent injunctions against patent infringement absent exceptional circumstances.

The long-standing rule in the Federal Circuit was to issue injunctions liberally in patent infringement cases so long as the plaintiff could prove an ongoing infringement. To put it bluntly, the federal court of appeals did not require patent owners to demonstrate irreparable harm. In eBay, the lower court refused to enjoin the online auction house finding that damages were adequate. The Federal Circuit Court of Appeals reversed, ruling that in patent infringement cases an injunction issues absent exceptional circumstances. The *MercExchange* Court ruled that the Federal Circuit improperly applied a presumed irreparable injury test as opposed to the traditional four-factor test for the issuance of a permanent injunction. The Supreme Court reversed the Federal Circuit's traditional practice of liberally issuing injunctions in patent infringement cases.

The *MercExchange* Court ruled that federal courts must now weigh four factors before issuing an injunction: (1) that the plaintiff has suffered an irreparable injury; (2) that remedies available at law are inadequate to compensate for that injury; (3) that considering the balance of hardships between the plaintiff and defendant, a remedy in equity is warranted; and (4) that the public interest would not be disserved by a permanent injunction. The Courts finding that permanent injunctions are subject to the ordinary rules governing equitable relief means that relief is discretionary, as opposed to issued routinely. The upshot of the *MercExchange* decisions is that the owners of Internet patents will not be able to rely upon a presumption that an injunction would issue to enjoin infringing activities, which was the Federal Court's long-standing practice. Injunctive relief is critically imperative in Internet-related patent litigation because of the rapidity with which online businesses can attain market share. In the Internet based economy, the earliest mover has enormous advantages and patent law is a method for excluding others.

---

[112] 547 U.S. 388 (2006).

(2) Bilski v. Kappos

In *Bilski v. Kappos*,[113] the U.S. Supreme Court unanimously upheld the Federal Circuit's decision that the application for a method of hedging risk was "an unpatentable abstract idea" that was outside the scope of the U.S. Patent Act, § 101. The patent application in *Bilski* was a procedure for helping buyers and sellers how to protect against price fluctuations in the volatile energy market. The purpose was to develop a process that would hedge against price changes. The patent examiner rejected the application, explaining that it was a mere manipulation of an abstract idea and solves a mathematical problem without limits to practical application. The Board of Patent Appeals and Interferences affirmed, concluding that the application only involved mental steps that transformed physical matter and was directed to an abstract idea. The Federal Circuit heard the case *en banc* and affirmed, reasoning that the machine-or-transformation test was the sole test for determining the patentability of a process under Section 101.[114]

The Federal Circuit's view was that an invention is a "process" only if (1) tied to a particular machine or apparatus, or (2) it transforms a particular article into a different state or thing. The Court granted certiorari to determine whether the process patent was excluded from patentable subject matter. The Court held that Federal Circuit incorrectly endorsed the machine-or-transformation test for a process. The Court reasoned that this test was not the sole test in deciding whether an invention is a patent-eligible process. The Court decided that the process patent for hedging could be rejected on precedents concerning the unpatentability of abstract ideas. *Bilski* is expected to incite change on Internet-related claims. In *Bilski*, the court was concerned that to allow "petitioners to patent risk hedging would pre-empt use of this approach in all fields."[115] The Court upheld the Federal Circuit's denial of patent but disagreed with the appeals court in its assessment of process patents. The Court explained that "[i]f a high enough bar is not set" for process patents—which "raise special problems in terms of vagueness and suspect validity"—"patent examiners and courts could be flooded with claims that would put a chill on creative endeavor and dynamic change."[116]

The Court explained that Bilski's application essentially disclosed "the basic concept of hedging or protecting against risk" and that allowing him "to patent risk hedging would preempt use of this approach in all fields, and would effectively grant a monopoly over an abstract idea."[117] "Under *Bilski*, generally tying a claim to a digital computer, without more, is not sufficient to confer patent eligibility."[118] The *Bilski* decision limits the availability of process patents. However, the court did not reach the issue of how patent law applies where there is "ubiquitous access to the Internet."[119]

---

[113] 130 S.Ct. 3218 (2010).

[114] The Federal Circuit, in its en banc opinion, declared that the "machine-or-transformation" test is the only test for determining patent-eligible subject matter for process patents under 35 U.S.C. § 101. In re Bilski, 545 F.3d 943, 956-61 (Fed. Cir. 2008).

[115] In re Bilski, Id. at 3231.

[116] Id. at 3229.

[117] Id. at 3231.

[118] M.J. Edwards & Donald Steinberg, The Implications of Bilski: Patentable Subject Matter in the United States, 49 IDEA 411, 425 (2009).

[119] GEORGE B. DELTA & JEFFREY MATSUURA, 2 LAW OF THE INTERNET (2008) at 7–19.

While the Court does not outright exclude methods of doing business, it demonstrates that it is predisposed to strictly scrutinizing them.[120] *Bilski* calls for a rigorous review of software and Internet-related process claims. [121]

In *Cybersource Corp. v. Retail Decisions, Inc.*,[122] the Federal Circuit affirmed a district court's ruling that a patent claim for detecting fraud in a credit card transaction between a consumer and a merchant over the Internet was invalid. The patentee brought an infringement suit against a competitor and the competitor defended based on invalidity under 35 U.S.C. § 101. The lower court found that the Internet-related process for determining fraud merely recited an unpatentable mental process for collecting data. In *MySpace, Inc. v. Graphon Corp.*,[123] the Federal Circuit ruled that a patent relating to the ability to create, modify, and store database records over a computer network was invalid as anticipated and obvious based on prior art. A dissenting judge would have applied *In Re Bilski* reasoning that Graphon's patents fell outside the ambit of section 101 "because they are *too* useful and *too* widely applied to possibly form the basis of any patentable invention."[124]

(3) *Mayo Collaborative Services*

In *Mayo Collaborative Services v. Prometheus Laboratories*,[125] the U.S. Supreme Court determined the contours of what constituted patentable subject matter under Section 101 of the Patent Act. The Court in *Prometheus* considered patent claims covering processes that help physicians who use thiopurine drugs to treat patients with autoimmune diseases. The process involved measuring patient metabolite levels to determine the dosage that will minimize the likelihood that the drug dosage will be ineffective or harmful. The Court held the patent claims not eligible for patent protection because they failed to transform unpatentable natural laws into patentable applications of those laws.[126]

"To put the matter more succinctly, the claims inform a relevant audience about certain laws of nature; any additional steps consist of well understood, routine, conventional activity already engaged in by the scientific community; and those steps, when viewed as a whole, add nothing significant beyond the sum of their parts taken separately."[127] To be patent eligible, an application of a natural law "must do more than simply state the law of nature while adding the words "apply it."[128] The Court found that the process claims in *Prometheus* involved "well-understood, routine, conventional activity previously engaged in by researchers in the field."[129] The Court's decision in Prometheus demonstrates its willingness to scrutinize patent process

---

[120] Bilski v. Kappos, 130 S. Ct. 3218, 3225 (2010 ("Congress took this permissive approach to patent eligibility to ensure that 'ingenuity should receive a liberal encouragement.'").

[121] Id. (stating "The Court's precedents provide three specific exceptions to § 101's broad patent-eligibility principles: 'laws of nature, physical phenomena, and abstract ideas.'")

[122] 654 F.3d 1366 (Fed. Cir. 2011).

[123] 672 F.3d 1250 (Fed. Cir. 2012).

[124] Id. at 1264 (J. Mayer, dissenting).

[125] 132 S.Ct. 1289 (2012).

[126] The Court distinguished between, on the one hand, claims that would tie up laws of nature, natural phenomena, or abstract ideas, and, on the other, claims that merely "embody, use, reflect, rest upon, or apply" those fundamental tools. Id. at 1293.

[127] Id. at 1298.

[128] Id. at 1294 (quoting Gottschalk v. Benson, 409 U. S. 71, 72 (1972).

[129] Id.

claims in other contexts such as the e-business patents or Internet-related patents. After *Prometheus*, patented process that focuses upon use of natural law must also contain other elements or combination of elements, sometimes referred to as "inventive concept," sufficient to ensure that the patent in practice amounts to significantly more than a patent upon the natural law itself. These cases and statutory developments discussed in this chapter reflect the empirical reality that patent law is evolving to address new technologies including the Internet.

(G) Cross-Border Patent Issues

Patent protection applies only to the country where protection is sought. Thus, an e-business that seeks patent protection in Sweden or Denmark must apply for patent protection in these countries. A company will incur substantial costs in seeking patent protection in foreign countries. The U.S. is a signatory to the Paris Convention of 1883, which is a treaty administered by the World Intellectual Property Organization. The Paris Convention gives patent applicants the same treatment as if they were a national of the foreign country granting rights. This is the principle of national treatment that entitles patent owners with the same legal remedies as national owners of a patent. Internet-related patent disputes are beginning to heat up in the Eurozone. The Mannheim Regional Court (Landgericht Mannheim) "dismissed two separate lawsuits brought by technology giants Apple Inc. and Samsung Electronics Co. against each other, the first relating to a patent dealing with the slide-to-unlock feature on mobile devices and the other the 3G/UMTS essential patent."[130] The EC is launching a formal investigation into the possibility that "South Korea's Samsung Electronics Co. Ltd. is using standards-essential patents to sue Apple Inc. and other rivals."[131] Cross-border Internet disputes are the footprints of an increasingly globalized Internet law.

---

[130] 17 ELEC. COMM. & L. REP. (BNA) 480 (Mar. 14, 2012).
[131] 17 ELEC. COM. & L. REP. (BNA) 263 (Feb. 8, 2012).

Table of Cases

Table of Statutes

825

Index

References are to Pages